JEE MAIN & ADVANCED TEST SERIES

40+ Tests

MATHEMATICS

JEE MAIN & ADVANCED TEST SERIES

40+ Tests

MATHEMATICS

Author
Rizwan Ahmed Ansari

ARIHANT PRAKASHAN (SERIES), MEERUT

ARIHANT PRAKASHAN (SERIES), MEERUT

卐 **ADMINISTRATIVE & PRODUCTION OFFICES**

Regd. Office
'Ramchhaya' 4577/15, Agarwal Road, Darya Ganj, New Delhi -110002
Tele: 011- 47630600, 43518550

Head Office
Kalindi, TP Nagar, Meerut (UP) - 250002, Tel: 0121-7156203, 7156204

卐 **SALES & SUPPORT OFFICES**

Agra, Ahmedabad, Bengaluru, Bareilly, Chennai, Delhi, Guwahati, Hyderabad, Jaipur, Jhansi, Kolkata, Lucknow, Nagpur & Pune.

卐 **ISBN** 978-93-27194-16-6

卐 **PRICE** ₹ 375.00

PO No. : TXT-59-T051819-2-23

Published By Arihant Publications (India) Ltd.

For further information about the books published by Arihant, log on to www.arihantbooks.com or e-mail at info@arihantbooks.com

Follow us on   

Contents

THE QUALIFIERS (Unit Tests Based on JEE Main & Advanced Syllabus) **1-39**

- Qualifier 1 3-4
- Qualifier 2 5-6
- Qualifier 3 7-9
- Qualifier 4 10-11
- Qualifier 5 12-13
- Qualifier 6 14-15
- Qualifier 7 16-18
- Qualifier 8 19-20
- Qualifier 9 21-23
- Qualifier 10 24-25
- Qualifier 11 26-27
- Qualifier 12 28-30
- Qualifier 13 31-33
- Qualifier 14 34-35
- Qualifier 15 36-37
- Qualifier 16 38-39

PART TESTS (Based on Class 11th & 12th Syllabus) **41-55**

- Part Test 1 JEE Main (Class 11 Syllabus) 43-45
- Part Test 2 JEE Advanced (Class 11 Syllabus) 46-49
- Part Test 3 JEE Main (Class 12 Syllabus) 50-51
- Part Test 4 JEE Advanced (Class 12 Syllabus) 52-55

THE KNOCKOUTS (JEE Main) **57-84**

- Knockout 1 59-60
- Knockout 2 61-62
- Knockout 3 63-65
- Knockout 4 66-67
- Knockout 5 68-70
- Knockout 6 71-72
- Knockout 7 73-75
- Knockout 8 76-78
- Knockout 9 79-81
- Knockout 10 82-84

THE KNOCKOUTS (JEE Advanced) **83-114**

- Knockout 11 85-90
- Knockout 12 91-96
- Knockout 13 97-102
- Knockout 14 103-108
- Knockout 15 109-114

THE REAL NUTS [Latest JEE (Main & Advanced) Solved Papers] **115-137**

- Real Nut 1 *(24 June 2022) Shift I* 117-119
- Real Nut 2 *(26 June 2022) Shift II* 120-122
- Real Nut 3 *(29 June 2022) Shift I* 123-125
- Real Nut 4 *(25 July 2022) Shift I* 126-128
- Real Nut 5 *(27 July 2022) Shift II* 129-131
- Real Nut 6 *(JEE Advanced 2022)* 132-137

Solutions **139-354**

(The Qualifiers, Part Tests, Knockouts and Real Nuts)

Syllabus

JEE MAIN

UNIT I Sets, Relations and Functions

Sets and their representation, Union, intersection and complement of sets and their algebraic properties, Power set, Relation, Types of relations, equivalence relations, functions, one-one, into and onto functions, composition of functions.

UNIT II Complex Numbers and Quadratic Equations

Complex numbers as ordered pairs of reals, Representation of complex numbers in the form $a+ib$ and their representation in a plane, Argand diagram, algebra of complex numbers, modulus and argument (or amplitude) of a complex number, square root of a complex number, triangle inequality, Quadratic equations in real and complex number system and their solutions. Relation between roots and co-efficients, nature of roots, formation of quadratic equations with given roots.

UNIT III Matrices and Determinants

Matrices, algebra of matrices, types of matrices, determinants and matrices of order two and three. Properties of determinants, evaluation of deter-minants, area of triangles using determinants. Adjoint and evaluation of inverse of a square matrix using determinants and elementary transformations, Test of consistency and solution of simultaneous linear equations in two or three variables using determinants and matrices.

UNIT IV Permutations and Combinations

Fundamental principle of counting, permutation as an arrangement and combination as selection, Meaning of P(n,r) and C (n,r), simple applications.

UNIT V Mathematical Induction

Principle of Mathematical Induction and its simple applications.

UNIT VI Binomial Theorem and its Simple Applications

Binomial theorem for a positive integral index, general term and middle term, properties of Binomial coefficients and simple applications.

UNIT VII Sequences and Series

Arithmetic and Geometric progressions, insertion of arithmetic, geometric means between two given numbers. Relation between AM and GM Sum upto n terms of special series: $\sum n, \sum n^2, \sum n^3$. Arithmetico - Geometric progression.

UNIT VIII Limit, Continuity and Differentiability

Real valued functions, algebra of functions, polynomials, rational, trigonometric, logarithmic and exponential functions, inverse functions. Graphs of simple functions. Limits, continuity and differenti-ability. Differentiation of the sum, difference, product and quotient of two functions. Differentiation of trigonometric, inverse trigonometric, logarithmic, exponential, composite and implicit functions; derivatives of order upto two. Rolle's and Lagrange's Mean Value Theorems. Applications of derivatives: Rate of change of quantities, monotonic - increasing and decreasing functions, Maxima and minima of functions of one variable, tangents and normals.

UNIT IX Integral Calculus

Integral as an anti - derivative. Fundamental integrals involving algebraic, trigonometric, exponential and logarithmic functions. Integration by substitution, by parts and by partial fractions. Integration using trigonometric identities. Evaluation of simple integrals of the type

$$\int \frac{dx}{x^2 \pm a^2}, \int \frac{dx}{\sqrt{x^2 \pm a^2}}, \int \frac{dx}{a^2 - x^2}, \int \frac{dx}{\sqrt{a^2 - x^2}},$$

$$\int \frac{dx}{ax^2 + bx + c}, \int \frac{dx}{\sqrt{ax^2 + bx + c}}, \int \frac{(px + q)\,dx}{ax^2 + bx + c},$$

$$\int \frac{(px + q)\,dx}{\sqrt{ax^2 + bx + c}}, \int \sqrt{a^2 \pm x^2}\,dx \quad \text{and} \quad \int \sqrt{x^2 - a^2}\,dx$$

Integral as limit of a sum. Fundamental Theorem of Calculus. Properties of definite integrals. Evaluation of definite integrals, determining areas of the regions bounded by simple curves in standard form.

UNIT X Differential Equations

Ordinary differential equations, their order and degree. Formation of differential equations. Solution of differential equations by the method of separation of variables, solution of homogeneous and linear differential equations of the type $\frac{dy}{dx} + p(x)y = q(x)$

UNIT XI Coordinate Geometry

Cartesian system of rectangular coordinates in a plane, distance formula, section formula, locus and its equation, translation of axes, slope of a line, parallel and perpendicular lines, intercepts of a line on the coordinate axes.

Straight lines

Various forms of equations of a line, intersection of lines, angles between two lines, conditions for concurrence of three lines, distance of a point from a line, equations of internal and external bisectors of angles between two lines, coordinates of centroid, orthocentre and circumcentre of a triangle, equation of family of lines passing through the point of intersection of two lines.

Circles, Conic sections

Standard form of equation of a circle, general form of the equation of a circle, its radius and centre, equation of a circle when the end points of a diameter are given, points of intersection of a line and a circle with the centre at the origin and condition for a line to be tangent to a circle, equation of the tangent. Sections of cones, equations of conic sections (parabola, ellipse and hyperbola) in standard forms, condition for $y=mx + c$ to be a tangent and point (s) of tangency.

UNIT XII Three Dimensional Geometry

Coordinates of a point in space, distance between two points, section formula, direction ratios and direction cosines, angle between two intersecting lines. Skew lines, the shortest distance between them and its equation. Equations of a line and a plane in different forms, intersection of a line and a plane, coplanar lines.

UNIT XIII Vector Algebra

Vectors and scalars, addition of vectors, components of a vector in two dimensions and three dimensional space, scalar and vector products, scalar and vector triple product.

UNIT XIV Statistics and Probability

Measures of Dispersion Calculation of mean, median, mode of grouped and ungrouped data. Calculation of standard deviation, variance and mean deviation for grouped and ungrouped data.

Probability Probability of an event, addition and multiplication theorems of probability, Baye's theorem, probability distribution of a random variate, Bernoulli trials and Binomial distribution.

UNIT XV Trigonometry

Trigonometrical identities and equations. Trigonometrical functions. Inverse trigonometrical functions and their properties. Heights and Distances.

UNIT XVI Mathematical Reasoning

Statements, logical operations And, or, implies, implied by, if and only if. Understanding of tautology, contradiction, converse and contra positive.

JEE ADVANCED

Sets, Relations and Functions

Sets and their representations, different kinds of sets (empty, finite and infinite), algebra of sets, intersection, complement, difference and symmetric difference of sets and their algebraic properties, De-Morgan's laws on union, intersection, difference (for finite number of sets) and practical problems based on them.

Cartesian product of finite sets, ordered pair, relations, domain and codomain of relations, equivalence relation Function as a special case of relation, functions as mappings, domain, codomain, range of functions, invertible functions, even and odd functions, into, onto and one-to-one functions, special functions (polynomial, trigonometric, exponential, logarithmic, power, absolute value, greatest integer etc.), sum, difference, product and composition of functions.

Algebra

Algebra of complex numbers, addition, multiplication, conjugation, polar representation, properties of modulus and principal argument, triangle inequality, cube roots of unity, geometric interpretations.

Statement of fundamental theorem of algebra, Quadratic equations with real coefficients, relations between roots and coefficients, formation of quadratic equations with given roots, symmetric functions of roots.

Arithmetic and geometric progressions, arithmetic and geometric means, sums of finite arithmetic and geometric progressions, infinite geometric series, sum of the first n natural numbers, sums of squares and cubes of the first n natural numbers.

Logarithms and their properties, permutations and combinations, binomial theorem for a positive integral index, properties of binomial coefficients.

Matrices

Matrices as a rectangular array of real numbers, equality of matrices, addition, multiplication by a scalar and product of matrices, transpose of a matrix, elementary row and column transformations, determinant of a square matrix of order up to three, adjoint of a matrix, inverse of a square matrix of order up to three, properties of these matrix operations, diagonal, symmetric and skew-symmetric matrices and their properties, solutions of simultaneous linear equations in two or three variables.

Probability and Statistics

Random experiment, sample space, different types of events (impossible, simple, compound), addition and multiplication rules of probability, conditional probability, independence of events, total probability, Bayes Theorem, computation of probability of events using permutations and combinations.

Measure of central tendency and dispersion, mean, median, mode, mean deviation, standard deviation and variance of grouped and ungrouped data, analysis of the frequency distribution with same mean but different variance, random variable, mean and variance of the random variable.

Trigonometry

Trigonometric functions, their periodicity and graphs, addition and subtraction formulae, formulae involving multiple and sub-multiple angles, general solution of trigonometric equations.

Inverse trigonometric functions (principal value only) and their elementary properties.

Analytical Geometry

Two dimensions: Cartesian coordinates, distance between two points, section formulae, shift of origin.

Equation of a straight line in various forms, angle between two lines, distance of a point from a line; Lines through the point of intersection of two given lines, equation of the bisector of the angle between two lines, concurrency of lines; Centroid, orthocentre, incentre and circumcentre of a triangle.

Equation of a circle in various forms, equations of tangent, normal and chord. Parametric equations of a circle, intersection of a circle with a straight line or a circle, equation of a circle through the points of intersection of two circles and those of a circle and a straight line. Equations of a parabola, ellipse and hyperbola in standard form, their foci, directrices and eccentricity, parametric equations, equations of tangent and normal.

Locus problems.

Three dimensions: Distance between two points, direction cosines and direction ratios, equation of a straight line in space, skew lines, shortest distance between two lines, equation of a plane, distance of a point from a plane, angle between two lines, angle between two planes, angle between a line and the plane, coplanar lines.

Differential Calculus

Limit of a function at a real number, continuity of a function, limit and continuity of the sum, difference, product and quotient of two functions, L'Hospital rule of evaluation of limits of functions.

Continuity of composite functions, intermediate value property of continuous functions.

Derivative of a function, derivative of the sum, difference, product and quotient of two functions, chain rule, derivatives of polynomial, rational, trigonometric, inverse trigonometric, exponential and logarithmic functions.

Tangents and normals, increasing and decreasing functions, derivatives of order two, maximum and minimum values of a function, Rolle's theorem and Lagrange's mean value theorem, geometric interpretation of the two theorems, derivatives up to order two of implicit functions, geometric interpretation of derivatives.

Integral Calculus

Integration as the inverse process of differentiation, indefinite integrals of standard functions, definite integrals as the limit of sums, definite integral and their properties, fundamental theorem of integral calculus.

Integration by parts, integration by the methods of substitution and partial fractions, application of definite integrals to the determination of areas bounded by simple curves. Formation of ordinary differential equations, solution of homogeneous differential equations of first order and first degree, separation of variables method, linear first order differential equations.

Vectors

Addition of vectors, scalar multiplication, dot and cross products, scalar and vector triple products, and their geometrical interpretations.

JEE MAIN & ADVANCED

The Qualifiers

One Test For each Unit of JEE Mathematics

To ensure good score in JEE, You must be sure of the good understanding of each unit of JEE Syllabus. You must complete these tests with atleast 75% score, then only move to the next section.

QUALIFIER 01

Sets, Relations and Functions

Section I Objective Type Questions

1. If set R has 8 elements and set T has 28 elements, then

(a) $28 \le n(R \cup T) \le 36$ (b) $0 \le n(R \cap T) \le 28$
(c) $28 \le n(R \cap T) \le 36$ (d) $0 \le n(R \cup T) \le 28$

2. The set $S = \{1, 2, 3, 4, 5, \ldots, 12\}$ is to be partitioned into three sets P, Q, R of equal size. Thus, $P \cup Q \cup R = S$, $P \cap Q = Q \cap R = P \cap Q = \phi$. The number of ways to partition S is

(a) $\frac{12!}{3!(3!)^4}$ (b) $\frac{12!}{(4!)^3}$ (c) $\frac{12!}{(3!)^4}$ (d) $\frac{12!}{3!(4!)^3}$

3. If $A = \{(x, y) : x^2 + y^2 = 16\}$ and $B = \{(x, y) : 36x^2 + 9y^2 = 144\}$, then $A \cap B$ contains

(a) one point (b) three points
(c) two points (d) four points

4. Let $f(x) = (x+1)^2 - 1, x \ge 1$, then the set $\{x : f(x) = f^{-1}(x)\}$ is

(a) $\left\{0, -1, \frac{-3 + i\sqrt{3}}{2}, \frac{-3 - i\sqrt{3}}{2}\right\}$
(b) $\{0, 1, -1\}$
(c) $\{0, -1\}$
(d) Empty set

5. A relation $R = \{(x, y) : |x - y|$ is divisible by $3\}$, where $x, y \in R$ (set of real numbers), then R is

(a) symmetric (b) reflexive
(c) transitive (d) All of these

6. A relation R defined on the set of natural numbers (N) by aRb, iff the greatest common divisor of a and b is 2, then the relation R is

(a) reflexive but not symmetric
(b) reflexive and transitive
(c) symmetric only
(d) equivalence

7. Let X be the set of all graduate engineers (B.Tech. degree holder) in India. Elements x and y in the set X are said to be related, if they passed engineering from Jai Prakash University (JPU). Which one of the following statement is correct?

(a) Relation is reflexive and symmetric only.
(b) Relation is symmetric and transitive only.
(c) Relation is reflexive and transitive only.
(d) Relation is reflexive, symmetric and transitive.

8. Let R be the set of real numbers.

Statement I $A = \{(x, y) \in R \times R : y - x$ is an integer$\}$ is an equivalence relation of R.

Statement II $B = \{(x, y) \in R \times R : x = \alpha y$ for some rational number $\alpha\}$ is an equivalence relation of R.

(a) Statement I is false and Statement II is true.
(b) Both Statements I and II are true but Statement II is a correct explanation for Statement II.
(c) Both Statements I and II are true but Statement II is not a correct explanation for Statement I.
(d) Statement I is true and Statement II is false.

9. Consider the following relation R on the set of real square matrices of order 3. $\{(A, B) | A = P^{-1} BP$ for some invertible matrix $P\}$

Assertion R is an equivalence relation

Reason For any two invertible matrices of order 3×3. M and N, $(MN)^{-1} = N^{-1} M^{-1}$.

(a) If both assertion and reason are correct and reason is the correct explanation of the assertion.
(b) If both assertion and reason are correct but reason is not correct explanation of the assertion.
(c) If assertion is correct but reason is incorrect.
(d) If assertion is incorrect but reason is correct.

10. The domain of definition of the function

$$f(x) = \frac{\sqrt{\sin x - \frac{1}{\sqrt{2}}}}{\sqrt{\frac{3x}{2} - x^2 - \frac{1}{2}}} \text{ is}$$

(a) $\left[-1, \frac{\pi}{4}\right]$ (b) $\left(\frac{\pi}{4}, 1\right)$ (c) $\left[\frac{\pi}{4}, 1\right)$ (d) $\left(\frac{1}{2}, \frac{\pi}{4}\right]$

11. The range of the function $y = f(x)$ given by the equation $(28)^x + (8)^y = 8$ is $R - A$, then A equals (where R is the set of real numbers)

(a) $[1, \infty)$ (b) $(-\infty, 1)$ (c) $(1, \infty)$ (d) $(-\infty, 1]$

12. The domain and range of the function

$$f(x) = \frac{\log_e([x] + [-x] + 1)}{\sqrt{x(3 - x)}} \text{ respectively, are}$$

(where [·] denotes greatest integer function)

(a) singleton set and pair set (b) pair set and null set
(c) pair set and singleton set (d) pair set and pair set

13. If $f: R \to S$ defined by $f(x) = \sin x - \sqrt{3} \cos x + 1$ is onto, then the interval of S is

(a) $[-1, 3]$ (b) $[0, -1]$ (c) $[1, 1]$ (d) $[0, 1]$

14. If $\phi(h(x)) = |\sin x|$ and $h(\phi(x)) = (\sin\sqrt{x})^2$, then

(a) $h(x)$ is even and $\phi(x)$ is odd.
(b) $h(x)$ is even and $\phi(x)$ is neither even nor odd.
(c) $h(x)$ is odd and $\phi(x)$ is neither even nor odd
(d) $h(x)$ is odd and $\phi(x)$ is even.

15. What should be the minimum value of x so that

$$\left[\frac{x+8}{2}\right]+\left[\frac{x+6}{2}\right]+\left[\frac{x+4}{2}\right]+\left[\frac{x+2}{2}\right]+\left[\frac{x+7}{2}\right]+\left[\frac{x+5}{2}\right]+\left[\frac{x+3}{2}\right]+\left[\frac{x+1}{2}\right]+[x]=21,$$ where [.] denotes the greatest integer function.

(a) 1 (b) 2 (c) 3 (d) 4

16. Let $f(x) = x + 2|x+1| + 2|x-1|$. If $f(x) = \lambda$ has atleast one real solution, then the range of λ is

(a) $(3, \infty)$ (b) $[3, \infty)$ (c) $(-\infty, 3]$ (d) $(-\infty, \infty)$

17. The sum of integral values of 'a' for which the equation $4\cos^{-1}(-|x|) = a$ has exactly two solutions is

(a) 49 (b) 60 (c) 20 (d) 57

18. The number of solutions of the equation $y = \frac{1}{3}[\sin x + [\sin x + [\sin x]]]$ and $[y + [y]] = 2\cos x$, where [.] represents greatest integer less than or equal to x.

(a) no solution (b) one solution
(c) two solution (d) three solution

19. Let f be a real valued function such that $f(x) + 2f\left(\frac{2020}{x}\right) = 3x,\ x \neq 0$, then $xf(x)$ equals

(a) $\frac{4040 - x^2}{x}$ (b) $4004 - x^2$ (c) $\frac{4040 - x}{x}$ (d) $4040 - x^2$

20. If 'f' is a polynomial such that $f\left(\frac{1-x}{1+x}\right) \cdot f\left(\frac{1+x}{1-x}\right) = f\left(\frac{1-x}{1+x}\right) + f\left(\frac{1+x}{1-x}\right)$, where $f(1) \neq 0$ and $x \neq \pm 1$ and $f(3) = 28$, then the value of $\frac{1}{605}\left(\sum_{n=1}^{10}(f(n) - 1)\right)$ is

(a) 5 (b) 55 (c) 50 (d) 3025

Section II *Numerical Value Questions*

21. If $n(A) = 31$ and $n(A \cap B) = 3$, then $n[(A \cap B)' \cap A]$ is equal to

22. If $A \equiv \{x \in R : |x| < 3\}$ and $B = \{x \in R, |x - 2| \geq 3\}$, then $B - A = R - (P, Q)$ the value of $P + Q$ is

23. Let Z be the set of integer, if $A = \{x \in Z : 2^{(x+2)(x^2 - 5x + 6)} = 1\}$ and $B = \{x \in Z : -3 < 2x - 1 < 9\}$, then the number of subsets of the set $A \times B$ is 2^K, then the value of K is

24. If the function $f: R \to A$ given by $f(x) = \frac{x^2}{x^2 + 1}$ is surjection, then $A \in [k, m)$. Then, the value of $k + m$ is

25. Given $x + \sin y = 2021$ and $x + 2021 \cos y = 2020$, where $0 \leq y \leq \frac{\pi}{2}$. The value of $[x + y]$, where $[\cdot]$ represents greatest integer function, is

26. If $f(x) = \{x\} + \{x+1\} + \{x+2\} + \{x+3\} + \ldots + \{x+99\}$, where {} denotes fractional part function and $[\cdot]$ denotes greatest integer function, then $[f(\sqrt{2})]$ is equal to

27. If $f(x)$ is an odd function with period 2, then value of $f(4)$ is

28. If $f(x)$ is a periodic function having period 7 and $g(x)$ is a periodic function having period 11, then the period of

$$\Delta(x) = \begin{vmatrix} f(x) & f\left(\frac{x}{3}\right) \\ g(x) & g\left(\frac{x}{5}\right) \end{vmatrix}$$ is

29. Let $f: R - \left\{\frac{\alpha}{6}\right\} \to R$ be defined by $f(x) = \frac{5x+3}{6x - \alpha}$, then the value of α for which $(fof)(x) = x$ for all $x \in R - \left\{\frac{\alpha}{6}\right\}$ is

30. Let $f: (0, \infty) \to (1, \infty)$ be a function such that $g(x) = \int_0^x f(t)\, dt$. If $g(x^2) = x^2(1 + x)$ and $h(x) = f^{-1}(x)$, then $h(10)$ equals

Answers

1 (a)	2 (b)	3 (c)	4 (c)	5 (d)	6 (c)	7 (d)	8 (d)	9 (a)	10 (c)
11 (a)	12 (c)	13 (a)	14 (b)	15 (a)	16 (b)	17 (d)	18 (a)	19 (d)	20 (a)
21 (28)	22 (2)	23 (15)	24 (1)	25 (2021)	26 (41)	27 (0)	28 (1155)	29 (5)	30 (36)

See detailed solutions on page no. 141

QUALIFIER 02

Complex Numbers, Quadratic Equations, Inequations and Logarithms

Section I *Objective Type Questions*

1. If $z = x + iy$ and $z^{1/3} = a - ib$, where $a, b \in R$ and $b \neq 0, \pm 1$, then $\frac{x}{a} - \frac{y}{b} = \lambda(a^2 - b^2)$, where λ is equal to

(a) -4 (b) -3
(c) 4 (d) 10

2. Let $f(z)$ is a complex polynomial in variable z, when $f(z)$ is divided by $(z - i)$ and $(z + i)$, the remainder is $\frac{1+i}{2}$ and $\frac{3i+1}{2}$, respectively. Then, the remainder when $f(z)$ is divided by $(z^2 + 1)$ is

(a) $iz + 1$ (b) $iz + i + 1$
(c) $\frac{1}{2}(1 + 2i - z)$ (d) $1 + 2i - z$

3. If z_1 and z_2 are two complex numbers such that $|z_1| = |z_2| + |z_1 - z_2|$, then which one is correct?

(a) $\text{Re}\left(\frac{z_1}{z_2}\right) = 0$ (b) $\text{Re}\left(\frac{z_1}{z_2}\right) = \text{Im}\left(\frac{z_1}{z_2}\right)$
(c) $\text{Im}\left(\frac{z_1}{z_2}\right) = 0$ (d) None of these

4. If $|z_1| = |z_2| = 1$ and $\text{Re}(z_1 \cdot \bar{z}_2) = 0$, where $z_1 = a + ib$ and $z_2 = c + id$, then the pair of complex numbers $\omega_1 = a + ic$ and $\omega_2 = b + id$, satisfy

(a) $|\omega_1| = |\omega_2| = 1$
(b) $|\omega_1| = 1, |\omega_2| = 0$
(c) $|\omega_1| = 1, \text{Re}(\omega_1 \bar{\omega}_2) = 1$
(d) $|\omega_2| = 0, \text{Re}(\omega_1 \bar{\omega}_2) = 0$

5. Least positive argument of the 4th root of the complex number $2 - \sqrt{12}i$ is

(a) $5\pi/12$ (b) $9\pi/12$
(c) $\pi/3$ (d) $\pi/12$

6. If $\text{Im}\left(\frac{2z+1}{iz+1}\right) = -4$, then the locus of z in the complex plane is

(a) a hyperbola (b) a circle
(c) a straight line (d) an ellipse

7. If $1, \omega, \omega^2, \omega^3, \ldots, \omega^{n-1}$ are the nth roots of unity, then $(2-\omega)(2-\omega^2)(2-\omega^3)\ldots(2-\omega^{n-1})$ equals

(a) $2^{n-1}[{}^{2n+1}C_1 + {}^{2n+1}C_2 + {}^{2n+1}C_3 + \ldots + {}^{2n+1}C_n] - 1$
(b) $2^{n-1}, {}^nC_1 + {}^nC_2 + {}^nC_3 + \ldots + {}^nC_n$
(c) $2^{n+1}, {}^nC_1 + {}^nC_2 + {}^nC_3 + \ldots + {}^nC_n$
(d) $2^{n-1}, {}^nC_1 - {}^nC_2 + {}^nC_3 - \ldots + (-1)^{n-1}C_n$

8. If $\lambda \in [-1, 1]$, then the value of x for which $4x^3 - 3x - \lambda = 0$ has a root lies in

(a) $\left[\frac{1}{2}, 1\right]$ (b) $\left(\frac{1}{2}, 1\right)$
(c) $[-1, 1]$ (d) $\left[0, \frac{1}{2}\right]$

9. If $0 \le a \le \pi$, then the quadratic equation $(\cos a - 1)x^2 + \sin a + (\cos a)x = 0$ has

(a) imaginary roots with positive y-intercept.
(b) real roots with non-negative y-intercept.
(c) real roots with negative y-intercept.
(d) imaginary roots with negative y-intercept.

10. If the sum of roots of the equation
$$x^2 - (2t^{4\log_t a} - 1)x + 7a = 0 \text{ is } 511, \text{ where } t > 1.$$
Then, the product of the roots is

(a) an irrational number (b) a palindrome number
(c) a prime number (d) a perfect number

11. If the quadratic equations $(1 - 2a)x^2 - 6ax - 1 = 0$ and $ax^2 - x + 1 = 0$ have atleast one real root is common, then the value of parameter 'a' is

(a) 3/4 (b) 4/3 (c) 2/9 (d) 9/2

12. Let α and β are roots of $x^2 - 3x + 5 = 0$, then the value $\frac{5\alpha \cdot \beta^{2016} + 3\alpha^{2017} \cdot \beta + \alpha \cdot \beta^{2018}}{\alpha^{2016} + \beta^{2016}}$ is

(a) 5 (b) 15 (c) 40 (d) 25

13. Solution set of the equation
$$\sqrt{4^x - 2^{x+1} + 1} + \sqrt{4^x - 2^{x+3} + 16} = 3 \text{ is}$$

(a) $x \in [1, 2]$ (b) $x \in (0, 2]$
(c) $x \in (0, 2)$ (d) $x \in [0, 2]$

14. If $\alpha, \beta \in C$ and $\gamma, \delta \in R^+$ are the four roots of the equation $(x-1)^4 + (x-5)^4 = 82$, where $\gamma < 4$ and $\delta > 3$, then $\dfrac{|\text{Re}(\alpha)| + \delta}{|\text{Im}(\beta)| + \gamma}$ is equal to

(a) 1 (b) 2 (c) 3 (d) 4

15. The number of real solution of the equation $\left(\dfrac{9}{10}\right)^x = -3 + x - x^2$ is

(a) 1 (b) 2 (c) 0 (d) 3

16. If $x, y \in [0, 10]$, then the number of solutions (x, y) of the inequation $3^{\sec^2 x - 1} \cdot \sqrt{9y^2 - 6y + 2} \le 1$ is

(a) Infinite (b) 0 (c) 10 (d) 4

17. Solution set of the inequality $2^x + 2^{|x|} \ge 2\sqrt{2}$ is

(a) $(-\infty, \log_2(\sqrt{2}-1)] \cup \left[\dfrac{1}{2}, \infty\right)$

(b) $\left[\dfrac{1}{2}, \infty\right)$

(c) $\left(\dfrac{1}{2}, \log_2(\sqrt{2}-1)\right)$

(d) $(-\infty, \infty)$

18. Solution of inequality $\log_{\sin(\pi/3)}(x^2 - 3x + 2) \ge 2$ is

(a) $\left[\dfrac{1}{2}, \dfrac{5}{2}\right]$

(b) $\left[\dfrac{1}{2}, 1\right) \cup \left(2, \dfrac{5}{2}\right]$

(c) $\left[\dfrac{1}{2}, 1\right] \cup \left[2, \dfrac{5}{2}\right]$

(d) $\left(\dfrac{1}{2}, \dfrac{5}{2}\right)$

19. If $\log_{0.3}(x-1) < \log_{0.09}(x-1)$, then x lies in the interval.

(a) $(2, \infty)$ (b) $(1, 2)$
(c) $(-2, -1)$ (d) None of these

20. If $\log_3(\log_2 x) + \log_{\frac{1}{3}}\left(\log_{\frac{1}{2}} y\right) = 1$ and $xy^2 = 9$, then

(a) number of possible ordered pairs (x, y) is 1.
(b) $xy = 9$
(c) number of possible ordered pairs (x, y) is 3.
(d) $x + y = \dfrac{6561}{9}$

Section II *Numerical Value Questions*

21. In a geometrical progression, first term and common ratio are both $\frac{1}{2}(\sqrt{3} + i)$. Then, the absolute value of the nth term of the progression is ......

22. Let $a = \cos\left(\dfrac{8\pi}{11}\right) + i\sin\left(\dfrac{8\pi}{11}\right)$ and $b = \text{Re}(a + a^2 + a^3 + a^4 + a^5)$, then $\left|b + \dfrac{\sqrt{3}i}{2}\right|$ is ......

23. For all complex number z_1 and z_2 satisfying $|z_1| = 12$ and $|z_2 - 3 - 4i| = 5$, then minimum value of $|z_1 - z_2|$ is ....

24. If ω is complex cube root of unity and a, b, c are such that $\dfrac{1}{a+\omega} + \dfrac{1}{b+\omega} + \dfrac{1}{c+\omega} = 2\omega^2$ and $\dfrac{1}{a+\omega^2} + \dfrac{1}{b+\omega^2} + \dfrac{1}{c+\omega^2} = 2\omega$, then the value of $\dfrac{1}{a+1} + \dfrac{1}{b+1} + \dfrac{1}{c+1}$ is equal to

25. If α and β are positive real roots of $x^2 - (1 - 2\lambda)x + \lambda^2 = 0$, where λ is an integer, then the value of $|\sqrt{\alpha} - \sqrt{\beta}|$ is ....

26. If α and β be the roots of the equation $x^2 + 3x + 1 = 0$, then the value of $\left(\dfrac{\alpha}{1+\beta}\right)^2 + \left(\dfrac{\beta}{\alpha+1}\right)^2$ is equal to ....

27. If $(2+\sqrt{3})^{x^2 - 2x + 1} + (2-\sqrt{3})^{x^2 - 2x - 1} = \dfrac{2}{2-\sqrt{3}}$, then $x = \alpha, \beta$, then $2000\alpha + 2000\beta$ equals ......

28. If $\cos x + \cos^2 x = 1$. Let $A = \sin^{12} x + 3\sin^{10} x + 3\sin^8 x + \sin^6 x + 2$, then the value of $\log_{\tan\frac{\pi}{3}} A$ is ......

29. If the least integral value satisfying the equation $\log_3 \sqrt{x^2 - 4x + 4} = 2^{\log_2(\log_3(|x| - 2))}$ is α, then $(\alpha)^{(\alpha)}$ is ....

30. If area of region represented by inequality $\log_{\sqrt{2}}\left(\dfrac{|z|^2 - |z| + 8}{|z| + 1}\right) < 4$ is $k\pi$, then the value of $\sqrt{k+1}$ is ....

Answers

1 *(c)*	2 *(c)*	3 *(c)*	4 *(a)*	5 *(a)*	6 *(b)*	7 *(b)*	8 *(a)*	9 *(b)*	10 *(d)*
11 *(c)*	12 *(b)*	13 *(d)*	14 *(a)*	15 *(c)*	16 *(d)*	17 *(a)*	18 *(b)*	19 *(a)*	20 *(a)*
21 *(1)*	22 *(1)*	23 *(2)*	24 *(2)*	25 *(1)*	26 *(18)*	27 *(4000)*	28 *(2)*	29 *(256)*	30 *(4)*

See detailed solutions on page no. 145

QUALIFIER 03

Matrices and Determinants

Section I Objective Type Questions

1. If A is a skew symmetric matrix of order 2 and B, C are matrices $\begin{bmatrix}1 & 4\\2 & 9\end{bmatrix}, \begin{bmatrix}9 & -4\\-2 & 1\end{bmatrix}$ respectively, then $A^3BC + A^5(B^2C^2) + A^7(B^3C^3) + \ldots + A^{2019}(B^{1008}C^{1008})$ is

(a) a symmetric matrix
(b) an identity matrix
(c) a skew symmetric matrix
(d) None of the above

2. If the matrix $\begin{bmatrix}0 & 2\beta & \gamma\\ \alpha & \beta & -\gamma\\ \alpha & -\beta & \gamma\end{bmatrix}$ is orthogonal, then

(a) $\alpha = \pm\frac{1}{\sqrt{2}}$ (b) $\beta = \pm\frac{1}{\sqrt{6}}$ (c) $\gamma = \pm\frac{1}{\sqrt{3}}$ (d) All of these

3. If A is nilpotent matrix of index 2, then $\forall\ n \in N$, $A(I \pm A)^n$ equals

(a) I (b) $I + A$
(c) A (d) $I - A$

4. Let $a_1 = \lim\limits_{x \to 1}\left(\frac{x}{\ln x} - \frac{1}{x \ln x}\right)$, $a_2 = \lim\limits_{x \to 0}\frac{x^3 - 16x}{4x + x^2}$,

$a_3 = \lim\limits_{x \to 0}\frac{\ln(1 + \sin x)}{x}$ and $a_4 = \lim\limits_{x \to -1}\frac{(x+1)^3}{3[\sin(x+1) - (x+1)]}$,

then the matrix $M = \begin{bmatrix}a_1 & a_2\\a_3 & a_4\end{bmatrix}$ is

(a) involutory (b) orthogonal
(c) nilpotent (d) None of these

5. Let $A = \begin{bmatrix}3 & -1\\0 & 2\end{bmatrix}$, suppose A satisfies the equation $x^2 + ax + b = 0$ for some real numbers a and b. Let α, β be the roots of $at + b + t^2 = 0$, then $\frac{1}{\alpha^2 - 3\alpha + 4} + \frac{1}{\beta^2 - 3\beta + 4}$ is equal to

(a) $\frac{4}{3}$ (b) $\frac{3}{4}$ (c) $\frac{1}{4}$ (d) $\frac{1}{2}$

6. If $A = \begin{bmatrix}-4 & -1\\3 & 1\end{bmatrix}$, then determinant of the matrix $(A^{100} - 2A^{99} - A^{98})$ is

(a) 100 (b) 99 (c) -25 (d) -100

7. Let $A = \begin{bmatrix}0 & 1\\1 & 0\end{bmatrix}$ and $B = \sum\limits_{r=1}^{2017} A^r$, then $|B|$ is equal to

(a) 2020 (b) 2021
(c) -2017 (d) -2021

8. If $A = \text{diag}(d_1, d_2\ d_3, d_4)$ where, $d_1, d_2, d_3, d_4 > 0$ is a diagonal matrix of order 4 such that $d_1 + 2d_2 + 4d_3 + 8d_4 = 16$, then the maximum value of $f(x) = \log_{(\tan x + \cot x)}(\det\cdot(A))$, where $x \in \left(0, \frac{\pi}{2}\right)$ is

(a) 1 (b) 2
(c) 1/3 (d) 1/4

9. If a, b, c are different, then the value of x satisfying $\begin{vmatrix}0 & x^2 - a & x^3 - b\\x^2 + a & 0 & x^2 + c\\x^4 + b & x - c & 0\end{vmatrix} = 0$ is

(a) a (b) 0
(c) b (d) 2

10. If $\begin{vmatrix}x & a & a & a\\a & x & a & a\\a & a & x & a\\a & a & a & x\end{vmatrix} = (x + 3a)\cdot f(x)$, then $f(3a) - f(a)$ is equal to

(a) $8a^3$ (b) 0
(c) $8a$ (d) a^3

11. If $f(x) = \begin{vmatrix}x + a^2 & x^4 + 1 & 3\\x + b^2 & 2x^4 + 2 & 3\\x + c^2 & 3x^4 + 7 & 3\end{vmatrix}$, where $x \neq 0$ and $f'(x) = 0$, then a^2, b^2, c^2 are in

(a) GP (b) AP
(c) HP (d) None of these

12. Let $f: N \to N$ be defined by $f(x) = (x+1)^2 + x - [\sqrt{(x+1)^2 + (x+1)}]^2$, where $[\cdot]$ denotes greatest integer function. Suppose a, b, c are three distinct natural numbers. Let $\Delta = \begin{vmatrix}f(a) & a^2 & a\\f(b) & b^2 & b\\f(c) & c^2 & c\end{vmatrix}$, then Δ is equal to

(a) $-(a + b - c)$ (b) $a + b + c$
(c) 1 (d) 0

13. Let $\Delta(x)=\begin{vmatrix} x-1 & 2x^2-5 & x^3-1 \\ 2x^2+5 & 2x+2 & x^3+3 \\ x^3-1 & x+1 & 3x^2-2 \end{vmatrix}$ and $(ax+b)$ be the remainder, when $\Delta(x)$ is divided by x^2-1, then $4a+2b$ is divisible by

(a) 2 and 7 (b) 1 and 9
(c) 8 and 4 (d) 3 and 5

14. If $f(x)=\begin{vmatrix} 2\cos^2 x & \sin 2x & \sin x \\ \sin 2x & 2\sin^2 x & -\cos x \\ \sin x & -\cos x & 0 \end{vmatrix}$, then $\int_0^{\pi/2}\{f'(x)+f(x)\}dx$ is equals

(a) $-\pi$ (b) π
(c) 2π (d) -2π

15. If A and B are two non-singular matrices of order 3 such that $AA'=2I$ and $A^{-1}=A'-A\cdot(2B^{-1})$, then det($B$) equals

(a) $8\sqrt{2}$ (b) $16\sqrt{2}$
(c) $\sqrt{2}$ (d) 28

16. If $bx^2+ax+c=0, ax^2+bx+c=0$ and $ax^2+cx+b=0$, each equation has equal roots, then $\begin{vmatrix} 3 & a & bc \\ 3 & b & ac \\ 3 & c & ab \end{vmatrix}$ is equal to

(a) $3abc$ (b) abc
(c) $3(a-b)(b-c)(c-a)$ (d) $\frac{3}{4}(a-b)(b-c)(c-a)$

17. If $a+b+c\neq 0$ and the system of equations $ax+by+cz=0, bx+cy+az=0$ and $cx+ay+bz=0$ has a non-trivial solution, then the roots of the equation $at^2+bt+c=0$ are

(a) real
(b) imaginary
(c) real positive
(d) None of the above

18. The solution of the equations $x+y+z=6, x+2y+3z=14$ and $x+4y+7z=30$ is

(a) $x=k-2, y=8+2k, z=k$, where $k\in R$
(b) $x=k, y=2k, z=k$, where $k\in R$
(c) $x=2k, y=3k-1, z=k$, where $k\in R$
(d) $x=k-2, y=8-2k, z=k$, where $k\in R$

19. The system of equations $\alpha x+y+z=\alpha-1$, $x+\alpha y+z=\alpha-1$ and $x+y+\alpha z=\alpha-1$ has no solution, if α equals

(a) 2 (b) 1
(c) -2 (d) either -2 or 1.

20. Let α_1,α_2 and β_1,β_2 be the roots of $ax^2+bx+c=0$ and $px^2+qx+r=0$, respectively. If the system of equations $\alpha_1 y+\alpha_2 z=0$ and $\beta_1 y+\beta_2 z=0$ has a non-trivial solution, then

(a) $\frac{b^2}{q^2}=\frac{ac}{pr}$ (b) $\frac{c^2}{r^2}=\frac{ab}{pq}$ (c) $\frac{a^2}{q^2}=\frac{bc}{pr}$ (d) None of these

Section II *Numerical Value Questions*

21. Let three matrices $A=\begin{bmatrix} 2 & 1 \\ 4 & 1 \end{bmatrix}, B=\begin{bmatrix} 3 & 4 \\ 2 & 3 \end{bmatrix}$ and $C=\begin{bmatrix} 3 & -4 \\ -2 & 3 \end{bmatrix}$, then $tr(A)+tr\left(\frac{ABC}{2}\right)+tr\left(\frac{A(BC)^2}{4}\right)+tr\left(\frac{A(BC)^3}{8}\right)+\ldots\infty$ equals

22. If $A=\begin{bmatrix} 2 & 3 & 0 \\ 1 & \sin^2 x & -\cos^2 x \\ \cos^2 x & \cos^4 x & \sin^4 x \end{bmatrix}$ and $A(\text{adj}A)=k\begin{bmatrix} 1 & 0 & 0 \\ 0 & 1 & 0 \\ 0 & 0 & 1 \end{bmatrix}$, then the value of $k+9$ is

23. If for a matrix $A, |A|=6$ and adj $A=\begin{bmatrix} 1 & -2 & 4 \\ 4 & 1 & 1 \\ -1 & P & 0 \end{bmatrix}$, then the value of P is

24. If $x\in R$ and $n\in I$, then the value of determinant
$$\Delta=\begin{vmatrix} \sin(n\pi) & \sin x-\cos x & \log(\tan x) \\ \cos x-\sin x & \cos\left[(2n+1)\frac{\pi}{2}\right] & \log(\cot x) \\ \log(\cot x) & \log(\tan x) & \tan(n\pi) \end{vmatrix}$$ is

25. If $U_n=\begin{vmatrix} 1 & k & k \\ 2n & k^2+k+1 & k^2+k \\ 2n-1 & k^2 & k^2+k+1 \end{vmatrix}$ and $\sum_{n=1}^{k} U_n=72$, then k equals to

26. If $\begin{vmatrix} 3^2+k & 4^2 & 3^2+3+k \\ 4^2+k & 5^2 & 4^2+4+k \\ 5^2+k & 6^2 & 5^2+5+k \end{vmatrix}=0$, then the value of $\sqrt{2^k\cdot\sqrt{2^k\cdot\sqrt{2^k}}\ldots\infty}$ is

27. Suppose A, B and C are angles of a triangle and let $\Delta=\begin{vmatrix} e^{2iA} & e^{-iC} & e^{-iB} \\ e^{-iC} & e^{2iB} & e^{-iA} \\ e^{-iB} & e^{-iA} & e^{2iC} \end{vmatrix}$, then the value of $(4-\Delta)$ is

28. Let λ and α be real. The set of all values of λ for which the system of linear equations

$\lambda x + (\sin\alpha)y + (\cos\alpha)z = 0$

$x + (\cos\alpha)y + (\sin\alpha)z = 0$

$-x + (\sin\alpha)y - (\cos\alpha)z = 0$

has a non-trivial solution is $[-u, v]$, then $2021\left(\frac{u^2}{v^2}\right)$ is

29. If the system of linear equations $(\cos\theta)x + (\sin\theta)y + \cos\theta = 0$, $(\sin\theta)x + (\cos\theta)y + \sin\theta = 0$ and $(\cos\theta)x + (\sin\theta)y - \cos\theta = 0$ is consistent, then the number of possible values of $\theta \in [0, 2\pi]$ is

30. The number of values of k (where $k \in N$) for which the system of equations $(k-1)x + (3k+1)y + 2kz = 0$, $(k-1)x + (4k-2)y + (k+3)z = 0$ and $2x + (3k+1)y + 3(k-1)z = 0$ has a common non-zero solution is

Answers

1 (c)	2 (d)	3 (c)	4 (c)	5 (b)	6 (c)	7 (c)	8 (b)	9 (b)	10 (a)
11 (b)	12 (d)	13 (d)	14 (a)	15 (b)	16 (d)	17 (b)	18 (d)	19 (c)	20 (a)
21 (6)	22 (8)	23 (2)	24 (0)	25 (8)	26 (2)	27 (8)	28 (2021)	29 (2)	30 (1)

See detailed solutions on page no. 149

QUALIFIER 04

Permutation-Combination and Probability

Section I Objective Type Questions

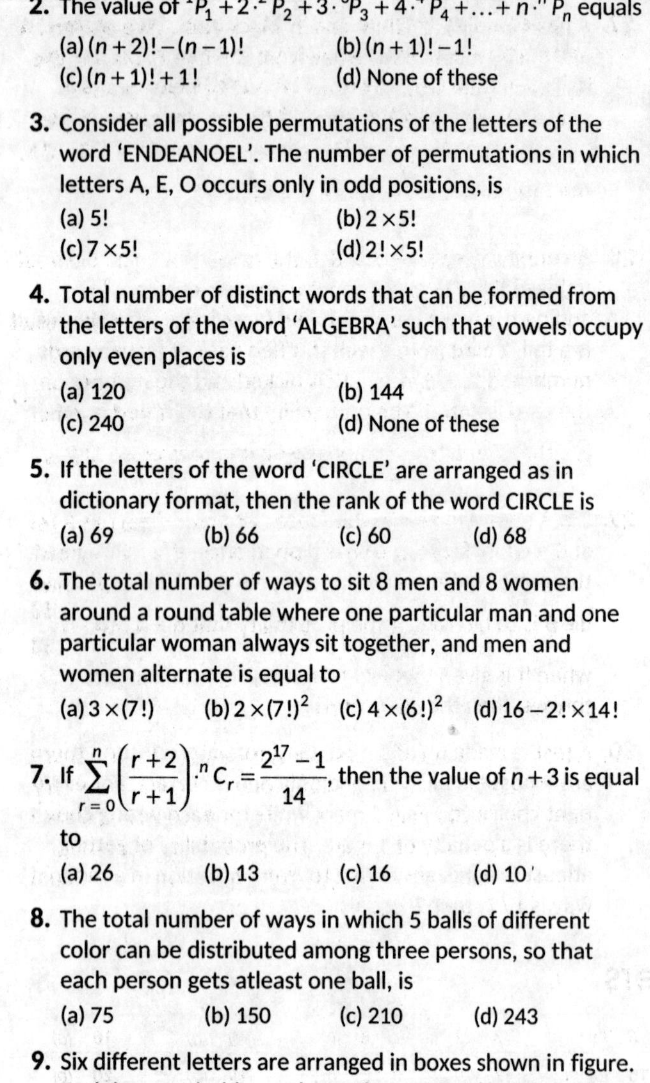

1. Highest power of 6 in 200! is

(a) 90 (b) 197
(c) 96 (d) 97

2. The value of ${}^1P_1 + 2\cdot{}^2P_2 + 3\cdot{}^3P_3 + 4\cdot{}^4P_4 + \ldots + n\cdot{}^nP_n$ equals

(a) $(n+2)! - (n-1)!$ (b) $(n+1)! - 1!$
(c) $(n+1)! + 1!$ (d) None of these

3. Consider all possible permutations of the letters of the word 'ENDEANOEL'. The number of permutations in which letters A, E, O occurs only in odd positions, is

(a) 5! (b) $2\times 5!$
(c) $7\times 5!$ (d) $2!\times 5!$

4. Total number of distinct words that can be formed from the letters of the word 'ALGEBRA' such that vowels occupy only even places is

(a) 120 (b) 144
(c) 240 (d) None of these

5. If the letters of the word 'CIRCLE' are arranged as in dictionary format, then the rank of the word CIRCLE is

(a) 69 (b) 66 (c) 60 (d) 68

6. The total number of ways to sit 8 men and 8 women around a round table where one particular man and one particular woman always sit together, and men and women alternate is equal to

(a) $3\times(7!)$ (b) $2\times(7!)^2$ (c) $4\times(6!)^2$ (d) $16 - 2!\times 14!$

7. If $\sum_{r=0}^{n}\left(\frac{r+2}{r+1}\right)\cdot{}^nC_r = \frac{2^{17}-1}{14}$, then the value of $n+3$ is equal to

(a) 26 (b) 13 (c) 16 (d) 10

8. The total number of ways in which 5 balls of different color can be distributed among three persons, so that each person gets atleast one ball, is

(a) 75 (b) 150 (c) 210 (d) 243

9. Six different letters are arranged in boxes shown in figure. Each box can hold exactly one letter. Number of ways in which letters can be arranged so that none of the rows remain empty, is

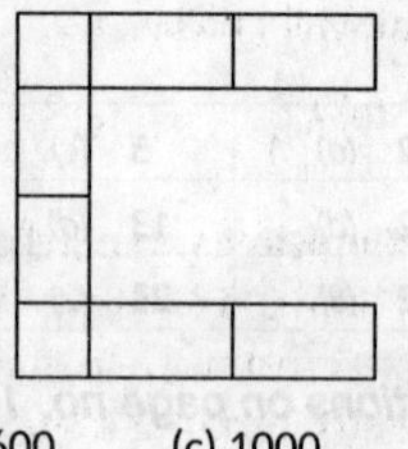

(a) 7206 (b) 9600 (c) 1000 (d) 10800

10. Total number of ways in which 7 green caps and 8 blue caps can be arranged in a row, if exactly one pair of green caps is side by side, is (assume all caps to be like except for the colour)

(a) 504 (b) 405 (c) 276 (d) 104

11. A bag contains 30 balls of which 11 are white, 7 are yellow, 7 are black and 5 are green. The probability that a ball drawn at random is either white or black or green is

(a) 1/30 (b) 15/28 (c) 7/10 (d) 23/30

12. Consider two independent events A and B such that $P(A) = 3\cdot P(B)$, $P(A\cup B) = 13/16$, then the value of $P(A)$ is

(a) 1/3 (b) 2/3 (c) 3/4 (d) 1/4

13. If A, B, C are events such that $P(A) = 0.3$, $P(B) = 0.4$, $P(C) = 0.8$, $P(A\cap B) = 0.08$, $P(A\cap C) = 0.28$, $P(A\cap B\cap C) = 0.09$. If $P(A\cup B\cup C) \geq 0.75$, then the range of $x = P(B\cap C)$ lies in the interval.

(a) $0.23 \leq x \leq 0.48$ (b) $0.23 \leq x \leq 0.46$
(c) $0.20 \leq x \leq 0.48$ (d) $0.15 \leq x \leq 0.39$

14. If A and B are events such that $P(\bar{A}\cup\bar{B}) = \frac{3}{4}$, $P(\bar{A}\cap\bar{B}) = \frac{1}{4}$ and $P(A) = \frac{1}{3}$, then $P(\bar{A}\cap B)$ is

(a) $\frac{12}{14}$ (b) $\frac{5}{12}$ (c) $\frac{1}{12}$ (d) $\frac{6}{12}$

15. Two brothers Razi (R) and Tauseef (T) appeared in IIT-JEE exam. The probability that Razi will crack the exam is 2/5 and probability that Tauseef will crack the exam is 3/4. The probability that only one from these two brothers cracked the exam is

(a) 2/20 (b) 11/20
(c) 17/20 (d) None of these

16. Let p denote the probability that a man aged x years will die in a year. The probability that out of n men $A_1, A_2, A_3, \ldots, A_n$, each aged x, A_1 will die in a year and will be the first to die is

(a) $\frac{1}{n}[1-(1-p)^n]$ (b) $\frac{1}{n}[1-(1-p)^{2n}]$

(c) $[1-(1-p)^n]$ (d) $\frac{1}{n}[1+(1-p)^n]$

17. There are two bags, bag 1 contains 3 white and 2 red balls and bag 2 contains 4 white and 5 red balls. A ball is drawn randomly from bag 1 and put in bag 2. Now, 2 balls are drawn from bag 2 and found to be red. Then, the probability that white ball was drawn from bag 1 to bag 2 is

(a) $>\frac{1}{4}$ (b) $<\frac{1}{4}$ (c) $>\frac{3}{4}$ (d) $<\frac{1}{2}$

18. A batch of 50 transistors was purchased from three different companies A, B and C. 18 of them were manufactured by A, 20 by B and the rest were manufactured by C. The companies A and C produce excellent quality transistors with probability equal to 0.9, B produces the same with the probability equal to 0.6. Then, the probability of the event that an excellent quality transistor chosen at random is manufactured by the company B is

(a) 4/13 (b) 7/11 (c) 15/17 (d) 3/11

19. If the mean and variance of a binomial variate X are 2 and 1 respectively, then the probability that X takes a value atleast one is

(a) 2/3 (b) 15/16 (c) 7/8 (d) 4/5

20. In a binomial distribution, difference of mean and variance is 1 and difference of their squares is 11. Then, the probability to get success exactly 3 times is

(a) ${}^{36}C_3\left(\frac{1}{6}\right)^2\left(\frac{5}{6}\right)^3$ (b) ${}^{36}C_3\left(\frac{1}{6}\right)^3\left(\frac{5}{6}\right)^3$

(c) ${}^{36}C_2\left(\frac{1}{6}\right)^3\left(\frac{5}{6}\right)^3$ (d) None of these

Section II *Numerical Value Questions*

21. The number of seven digit integers, with sum of the digits equal to 10 and formed by using the digits 1, 2 and 3 only is

22. Number of arrangements of a, b, c and d in which neither a, b nor c, d come together is

23. A work can completed by 3 men or 5 women in 5 days. The total number of ways workforce can be selected if work has to be finished in 5 days and available workforce is 10 men and 8 women is, (If workforce has either only men or only women)

24. There are 15 points in a plane out of which 6 of them are collinear. Then, the number of quadrilaterals formed by joining these points as vertices is

25. In an election the number of contestants is one more than the number of seats. If a particular voter can vote in 126 different ways, then the number of candidates if a voter can give minimum 1 and maximum equal to the number of seats is

26. If 'a' is an integer lying in $[-5, 30]$, then the probability that the graph of $y = x^2 + 2(a+4)x - 5a + 64$ is strictly above the X-axis is $\frac{2}{k}$, then k is

27. A bag contains 'a' white and 'b' black balls. Two players, A and B alternately draw a ball from the bag, replacing the ball each time after the draw till one of them draws a white ball and wins the game. A begins the game, if the probability of A winning the game is three times that of B, the ratio of $a:b$ is $\frac{\lambda}{k}$, then $\lambda + k$ equals

28. An unbiased coin is tossed. If the result is a head, a pair of unbiased dice is rolled and the number obtained by adding the numbers on the two faces is noted. If the result is a tail, a card from a well shuffled pack of eleven cards numbered 2, 3, 3, 4, ... , 12 is picked and the number on the card is noted. The probability that the noted number is either 7 or 8 is $\frac{P}{792}$, then the digit in tens place of P is

29. Die A has 4 red and 2 white faces whereas die B has 2 red and 4 white faces. A coin is flipped once. If it falls a head, the game continues by throwing die A, if it falls tail, then die B is to be used. If the probability that die A used is $\frac{32}{33}$ when it is given that red turns up every time in first n throws, then the value of n is

30. A test is made up of 5 questions, for each question there are 4 possible answers and only one is correct. For every right choice you gain 1 mark while for each wrong choice there is a penalty of 1 mark. The probability of getting atleast 3 marks answering to every question in a random way is $1/k$, then k equals

Answers

1 (d)	2 (b)	3 (b)	4 (d)	5 (d)	6 (b)	7 (c)	8 (b)	9 (d)	10 (a)
11 (d)	12 (d)	13 (a)	14 (b)	15 (b)	16 (a)	17 (a)	18 (a)	19 (b)	20 (b)
21 (77)	22 (8)	23 (176)	24 (1170)	25 (7)	26 (9)	27 (3)	28 (9)	29 (5)	30 (64)

See detailed solutions on page no. 153

QUALIFIER 05

Binomial Theorem and Mathematical Induction

Section I Objective Type Questions

1. If ${}^{n-1}C_r = (\lambda^2 - 3)\, {}^nC_{r+1}$ then λ belongs to

(a) $[3, \infty)$ (b) $[-2, 3)$
(c) $(\sqrt{3}, 2]$ (d) $[-\sqrt{3}, \sqrt{3}]$

2. If $n \in N$ and $(1 - 2x + 5x^2 + 10x^3)(1+x)^n = a_0 + a_1x + a_2x^2 + \dots$ and $a_1^2 = 2a_2$, then value of $a_0 + n$ is

(a) 3 (b) 4
(c) 5 (d) 7

3. If in the expansion of $\left(\frac{1}{x} + x\tan x\right)^5$ the ratio of 4th term to the 2nd term is $\frac{2}{27}\pi^4$, then the value of x is

(a) $\frac{\pi}{4}$ (b) 1 (c) $\frac{\pi}{2}$ (d) $\frac{\pi}{3}$

4. The greatest value of the term independent of x in the expansion of $\left(x\sin\theta + \frac{\cos\theta}{x}\right)^{10}$ is

(a) 3^5 (b) ${}^{10}C_5$
(c) $\frac{{}^{10}C_5}{2^5}$ (d) $2^5\, {}^{10}C_5$

5. The total number of terms that are dependent of x in the expansion $\left(x^2 - 2 + \frac{1}{x^2}\right)^{53}$ is equal to

(a) 105 (b) 10
(c) 106 (d) None of these

6. If $(1 + x + x^2)^n = \sum_{r=0}^{2n} a_r x^r$, then the value of $\sum_{k=0}^{3r} (-1)^k \cdot a_k\, {}^nC_{3r-k}$ (where $3r \le n$) equals

(a) $(-1)^{3r} \cdot {}^nC_{3r}$ (b) ${}^nC_r$
(c) ${}^nC_{3r}$ (d) $(-1)^r \cdot {}^nC_r$

7. The coefficient of x^{32} in the expansion of $[(1+x)(2+x)(3+x)]^{10} \cdot (2+x)(3+x)^2$ is

(a) 86 (b) 68
(c) 64 (d) 46

8. If C_r stands for ${}^nC_r$, then the coefficient of $\lambda^n\mu^n$ in the expansion of $[(1+\lambda)(1+\mu)(\lambda+\mu)]^n$ is

(a) $\sum_{r=0}^{n} C_{r+2}^2$ (b) $\sum_{r=0}^{n} C_r^2$ (c) $\sum_{r=0}^{n} C_{r+3}^2$ (d) $\sum_{r=0}^{n} C_r^3$

9. The coefficient of middle term in the binomial expansion in powers of x, of $(1+\alpha x)^4$ and $(1-\alpha x)^6$ is same, if α equals

(a) $\frac{3}{5}$ (b) $\frac{10}{3}$ (c) $\frac{3}{10}$ (d) $-\frac{5}{3}$

10. If 'a' is the sum of the coefficients of the two middle terms in the expansion of $(1+x)^{2n-1}$ and b is the coefficient of the middle term in the expansion of $(1+x)^{2n}$, $n \in N$, then

(a) $a = b$ (b) $a > b$ (c) $a < b$ (d) $a = 3b$

11. $2({}^2C_2 + {}^3C_2 + {}^4C_2 + \dots + {}^{n-1}C_2 + {}^nC_2) + {}^{n+1}C_2$, $n \in N$ is equal to

(a) $\sum_{r=1}^{n} r(r-1)$ (b) $\sum_{r=1}^{n} r^2$
(c) $\sum_{r=1}^{n} r^3$ (d) $\sum_{r=1}^{n} r$

12. If ${}^{31}C_5 - {}^{30}C_4 - {}^{29}C_4 - {}^{28}C_4 - \dots - {}^nC_4 = 1$, $(n \in N, n \ge 4)$, then n is equal to

(a) 5 (b) 10
(c) 15 (d) 20

13. The value of ${}^{505}C_5 - 5 \cdot {}^{404}C_5 + 10 \cdot {}^{303}C_5 - 10 \cdot {}^{202}C_5 + 5 \cdot {}^{101}C_5$ is equal to

(a) $(101)^5$ (b) $(101)^3$
(c) 201 (d) $(301)^5$

14. $\frac{{}^nC_0}{1} - \frac{{}^nC_1}{4} + \frac{{}^nC_2}{9} - \frac{{}^nC_3}{16} + \dots + (-1)^n \cdot \frac{{}^nC_n}{(n+1)^2}$ is equal to

(a) 0

(b) $\frac{1}{(n+1)}\left[1 + \frac{1}{2} + \frac{1}{3} + \dots + \frac{1}{n+1}\right]$

(c) $\frac{1}{n}\left[1 + \frac{1}{2} + \frac{1}{3} + \dots + \frac{1}{n}\right]$

(d) None of the above

15. If $a = ({}^{100}C_0 + {}^{100}C_3 + {}^{100}C_6 + \ldots + {}^{100}C_{99})$, $b = ({}^{100}C_1 + {}^{100}C_2 + {}^{100}C_3 + \ldots)$ and $c = ({}^{100}C_1 - {}^{100}C_2 + {}^{100}C_4 - {}^{100}C_5 + \ldots)$, then value of $\left(a - \frac{b}{2}\right)^2 + \frac{3}{4}c^2$ is equal to

(a) 1 (b) 4 (c) 5 (d) 10

16. If $a_n = \sqrt{7 + \sqrt{7 + \sqrt{7 + \ldots}}}$ having n radical signs. Then, by mathematical induction, which one is true?

(a) $a_n > 4, \forall n \ge 1$ (b) $a_n < 4, \forall n \ge 1$
(c) $a_n < 3, \forall n \ge 1$ (d) None of these

17. Let $P(n) = 2^{3n} - 7n - 1$, then $P(n)$ is divisible by

(a) 63 (b) 49 (c) 94 (d) 36

18. For all $n \in N$, $3(5^{2n+1}) + 2^{3n+1}$ is divisible by

(a) 18 (b) 16 (c) 25 (d) 17

19. For all $n \in N$, $10^n + 3(4^{n+2}) + 5$ is divisible by

(a) 3 (b) 4 (c) 5 (d) 11

20. If p is a natural number, then $\forall n \in N$, $p^{n+1} + (p+1)^{2n-1}$ is divisible by

(a) $p^2 - p - 1$ (b) $p^2 + p - 1$
(c) $p^2 - p + 1$ (d) $p^2 + p + 1$

Section II *Numerical Value Questions*

21. In the expansion of $\left(2x + \frac{1}{2x}\right)^6$, if the coefficient of x^2 is λ times the coefficient of x^{-2}, then λ equals

22. The natural number λ, for which the coefficient of x^{60} in the binomial expansion of $\left(x^\lambda + \frac{1}{x^2}\right)^{25}$ is 2300, is

23. The term independent of x in the expansion of $\left(1 - \frac{1}{x} + 3x^5\right)\left(2x^2 - \frac{1}{x}\right)^8$ is

24. If the term independent of x in the expansion of $\left(\frac{x^2}{2} - \frac{1}{x}\right)^9$ is k, then $2k$ is equal to

25. The number of rational terms in the binomial expansion of $(\sqrt{2} + \sqrt[3]{3})^{18}$ is

26. The sum of all rational terms in the expansion of $(\sqrt{2} + 3^{\frac{1}{5}})^{10}$ is equal to

27. The total number of integral values of x for which only the fourth term in the expansion of $\left(2 + \frac{3x}{8}\right)^{10}$ has the maximum numerical value is

28. If the middle term of $\left(\frac{1}{x} + x \cdot \sin x\right)^{10}$ is equal to $\frac{63}{8}$, then the number of values of x in $[0, 2\pi]$ is

29. For every natural number n, $(2 \cdot 7^n + 3 \cdot 5^n - 5)$ is divisible by

30. If 'n' is any odd positive integer, then $n(n^2 - 1)$ is divisible by

Answers

1 (c)	2 (d)	3 (d)	4 (c)	5 (c)	6 (b)	7 (b)	8 (d)	9 (c)	10 (a)
11 (b)	12 (a)	13 (a)	14 (b)	15 (a)	16 (b)	17 (b)	18 (d)	19 (a)	20 (d)
21 (16)	22 (3)	23 (400)	24 (21)	25 (4)	26 (41)	27 (2)	28 (2)	29 (24)	30 (24)

See detailed solutions on page no. 156

QUALIFIER 06

Sequence and Series

Section I Objective Type Questions

1. The sum of the first and fifth terms of an AP is 26 and the product of the second and fourth terms is 160. Then, the sum of the first six terms of the progression is

(a) 69 or 87 (b) 87 or 109
(c) 59 or 69 (d) -69 or 87

2. The numbers $3^{2\sin 2\alpha - 1}$, 14 and $3^{4 - 2\sin 2\alpha}$ form first three terms of an AP, its fifth term is

(a) -25 (b) -12
(c) 40 (d) 53

3. If $\log_2(5\times 2^x + 1), \log_4(2^{1-x} + 1)$ and 1 are in AP, then x equal

(a) $1 - \log_2 5$ (b) $\log_5 2$
(c) $\log_2 2 - \log_5 2$ (d) None of these

4. If the ratio between the sums of n terms of two AP's is $3n + 8 : 7n + 15$, then the ratio between their 12th terms is

(a) 16 : 7 (b) 7 : 16
(c) 74 : 169 (d) None of these

5. Let S_n denote the sum to n terms of an AP. If the common difference is equal to $S_n - \lambda S_{n-1} + S_{n-2}$, then $\lambda =$

(a) 3 (b) 2 (c) -2 (d) 1

6. If $\alpha, \beta, \gamma, \delta$ are in AP and $\int_0^2 f(x)\,dx = -4$, where

$$f(x) = \begin{vmatrix} x+\alpha & x+\beta & x+\alpha-\gamma \\ x+\beta & x+\gamma & x-1 \\ x+\gamma & x+\delta & x-\beta+\delta \end{vmatrix}$$

then the common difference d is given by

(a) ± 2 (b) ± 1
(c) ± 3 (d) None of these

7. Let p_r denote the sum of first r terms of AP whose first term is $r + 1$ and common difference is $2r + 2$, then $p_1 + p_2 + p_3 + \ldots + p_n$ is

(a) $\dfrac{n(n+1)(n+2)(3n+1)}{12}$ (b) $\dfrac{n(n+1)(n+2)^3}{6}$

(c) $\dfrac{n(n+1)(n+3)(3n-1)}{12}$ (d) None of these

8. Let t_n be the nth term of GP with common ratio (CR) 'r'. If $r < 0$, $\dfrac{t_6}{t_8} = \dfrac{1}{4}$ and $t_3 + t_7 = 100$ and $t_1 = \dfrac{a}{b}$, then the value of $a + b$ is (a and b are coprime numbers)

(a) 24 (b) 50 (c) $\dfrac{25}{17}$ (d) 42

9. Let a, b and c are in GP with common ratio r, where $a \neq 0$ and $0 < r \leq \dfrac{1}{2}$. If $3a$, $7b$ and $15c$ are the first three terms of an AP, then the 4th term of this AP is

(a) a (b) $\dfrac{3a}{2}$

(c) $\dfrac{2a}{3}$ (d) $\dfrac{7}{3}a$

10. A person drops a ball from an 80 m tall building and each time the ball bounces, it rebounds to x% of its previous height. If the ball travels a total distance of 320 m, then the value of x is

(a) 50 (b) 30 (c) 60 (d) 70

11. If $5^x + 5^{x-1} + 5^{x-2} + \ldots + 5^{x-2000} = 7^x + 7^{x-1} + 7^{x-2} + \ldots + 7^{x-2000}$, then $x - 2000 =$

(a) $\dfrac{\ln[3(5^{2001} - 1)] - \ln[2(7^{2001} - 1)]}{\ln(7/5)}$

(b) $2000\ln(7/5)$

(c) $\dfrac{\ln[5^{2001} - 1] - \ln[2(7^{2000} - 1)]}{\ln(5/7)}$

(d) None of the above

12. If a, b, c are in GP and $\log a - \log 2b$, $\log 2b - \log 3c$ and $\log 3c - \log a$ are in AP, then a, b, c are the length of the sides of a triangle which is

(a) right angle (b) acute angle
(c) equilateral angle (d) obtuse angle

13. If x, y, z are in GP and $\tan^{-1} x, \tan^{-1} y, \tan^{-1} z$ are in AP, then

(a) $x = y = z$ or $y \neq 1$
(b) $x = 1/z$
(c) $x = y = z$, but their common value is not necessarily zero
(d) $x = y = z = 0$

14. Minimum value of $n\sin\alpha + \frac{1}{n}\cos\alpha$, where $n > 0$ and α is fixed in (0, 1), is

(a) $\sqrt{2}\cdot\sin 2\alpha$ (b) $\sqrt{\sin 2\alpha}$
(c) 0 (d) $\sqrt{n^2 + n^{-2}}$

15. If m is the AM of two distinct real numbers l and n, l $(l, n > 1)$ and G_1, G_2 and G_3 are geometric mean between l and n, then $G_1^4 + 2G_2^4 + G_3^4$ equals

(a) $4lmn^2$ (b) $4l^2m^2n^2$
(c) $4l^2mn$ (d) $4lm^2n$

16. The sum of series $1 + \frac{4}{3} + \frac{10}{9} + \frac{28}{27}$ upto n terms is

(a) $n - \frac{1}{3} + \frac{1}{3\cdot 2^{n-1}}$ (b) $\frac{7}{6}n + \frac{1}{6} - \frac{1}{3\cdot 2^{n-1}}$
(c) $\frac{5}{3}n - \frac{7}{6} + \frac{1}{2\cdot 3^{n-1}}$ (d) $n + \frac{1}{2} - \frac{1}{2\cdot 3^{n-1}}$

17. The sum of infinity of the series
$1 + \frac{2}{3} + \frac{6}{3^2} + \frac{10}{3^3} + \frac{14}{3^4} + \dots$, is

(a) 2 (b) 3 (c) 4 (d) 6

18. Let $S = \frac{8}{5} + \frac{16}{65} + \frac{24}{325} + \dots + \frac{128}{2^{18}+1}$, then $S =$

(a) $\frac{1000}{544}$ (b) $\frac{1088}{545}$ (c) $\frac{545}{1088}$ (d) $\frac{1054}{954}$

19. The sum $\sum_{k=1}^{20} k\cdot\frac{1}{2^k}$ is equal to

(a) $2 - \frac{11}{2^9}$ (b) $1 - \frac{11}{2^9}$ (c) $2 - \frac{21}{2^{20}}$ (d) $2 - \frac{3}{2^{17}}$

20. For any complex number $\lambda = p + iq$ where $p, q \in R$.
If $\lambda = \cos\left(\frac{2\pi}{9}\right) + i\sin\left(\frac{2\pi}{9}\right)$, then
$|\lambda + 2\lambda^2 + 3\lambda^3 + \dots + 9\lambda^9|^{-1} =$

(a) $\frac{9}{2}\sin 20°$ (b) $\frac{9}{2}$ 20°
(c) $\frac{2}{9}\sin 20°$ (d) $\frac{9}{2}\cos 20°$

Section II *Numerical Value Questions*

21. An AP whose first term is unity and in which the sum of the first half of any even number of terms to that of the second half of the same number of terms is in constant ratio, the common difference d is given by ______

22. Concentric circles of radii 1, 2, 3, 4, ..., 100 cm are drawn. The interior of the smallest circle is coloured red and the angular regions are coloured alternately green and red, so that no two adjacent regions are of the same colour. If the total area of the green regions (in sq cm) is $k\pi$, then the value of k is ____

23. If the terms $\sqrt{a-x}, \sqrt{x}, \sqrt{a+x}$ are in AP and all are integers where $a, x > 0$, then the least composite value of a is ____

24. If $(1+x^2)^2(1+x)^n = a_0 + a_1x + a_2x^2 + \dots$ and if a_0, a_1, a_2 are in AP, then $n = \alpha, \beta$. So, $\alpha + \beta =$ ______

25. Between 1 and 31, k arithmetic means are inserted such that the ratio of 7th and $(k-1)$th means is 5 : 9, then the value of k is ____

26. a, b, c, d are in GP are in ascending order such that $a + d = 112$ and $b + c = 48$. If the GP is continued with 'a' as the first term, then the sum of the first six term is ____.

27. Let $S \subseteq (0, \pi)$ denote the set of values of x satisfying the equation $8^{(1 + |\cos x| + |\cos^2 x| + \dots \text{ to } \infty)} = 4^3$, then total number of values of S is equal to ____

28. If S_n denotes sum of first n terms of a series and if $S_{n+2} - S_n = (n+2)^2$, then S_{10} is (given that $T_1 + T_2 = 4$) ___

29. If $10^9 + 2(11)(10)^8 + 3(11)^2(10)^7 + \dots + 10\cdot(11)^9 = k(10)^9$, then k is equal to

30. The value of $1 + \frac{1^3+2^3}{1+2} + \frac{1^3+2^3+3^3}{1+2+3} + \dots + \frac{1^3+2^3+3^3+\dots+15^3}{1+2+3+\dots+15} - \frac{1}{2}(1+2+3+\dots+15)$ is ____

Answers

1 (a)	2 (d)	3 (a)	4 (b)	5 (b)	6 (b)	7 (a)	8 (d)	9 (a)	10 (c)
11 (a)	12 (d)	13 (c)	14 (a)	15 (d)	16 (d)	17 (b)	18 (b)	19 (a)	20 (c)
21 (2)	22 (5050)	23 (20)	24 (5)	25 (14)	26 (1456)	27 (2)	28 (220)	29 (100)	30 (620)

See detailed solutions on page no. 159

QUALIFIER 07

Limits, Continuity and Differentiability

Section I Objective Type Questions

1. $\lim_{x\to 0} \dfrac{\tan(\pi \sin^2 x)+(|x|-\sin(x[x]))^2}{x^2}$ is equal to (where $[\cdot]$ denotes greatest integer function)

(a) 10 (b) $\pi+1$
(c) $\pi-1$ (d) does not exist

2. The value of $\lim_{x\to \frac{\pi}{2}} \left[\dfrac{\sin x-(\sin x)^{\sin x}}{1-\sin x+\ln(\sin x)}\right]$ is

(a) 3 (b) 4
(c) 1 (d) 2

3. $\lim_{x\to a}\left[\left\{\left(\dfrac{a^{1/2}+x^{1/2}}{a^{1/4}-x^{1/4}}\right)^{-1} - \dfrac{2(ax)^{1/4}}{x^{3/4}-a^{1/4}x^{1/2}+a^{1/2}x^{1/4}-a^{3/4}}\right\}^{-1} - \sqrt{2}^{\log_4 a}\right]^8$ is

(a) $a^{3/4}$ (b) a
(c) a^2 (d) None of these

4. If $g(x)$ is a polynomial satisfying $g(x)\cdot g(y)=g(x)+g(y)+g(xy)-2$ for all real x and y and $g(2)=5$, then $\lim_{x\to 3} g(x)$ is

(a) 3 (b) 2
(c) 50 (d) 10

5. $\lim_{n\to\infty} \dfrac{n}{(n!)^{1/n}}$ is equal to

(a) 1 (b) e
(c) $\dfrac{1}{e}$ (d) $\int_0^1 \ln x\, dx$

6. If $\lim_{n\to\infty} \dfrac{\sqrt[n]{n!}}{n}=e^{2k}$, then the value of $\sin^{-1}\left(k+\dfrac{1}{2}\right)$ equals

(a) 1 (b) -1 (c) 0 (d) None of these

7. Let $f(x)=\begin{cases} -2\sin x & \text{if } x\le -\pi/2 \\ A\sin x+B & \text{if } -\dfrac{\pi}{2}<x<\pi/2 \\ \cos x & \text{if } x\ge \pi/2 \end{cases}$

The values of A and B so that $f(x)$ is continuous everywhere are

(a) $A=-1, B=1$ (b) $A=0, B=1$
(c) $A=-1, B=-1$ (d) $A=1, B=-1$

8. The value of $f(1)$ for which the function $f(x)=\dfrac{x^{m+1}-(m+1)x+m}{(x-1)^2}$ is continuous at $x=1$ is

(a) $\dfrac{m(m+1)}{4}$ (b) $\dfrac{m(m-1)}{2}$
(c) $\dfrac{m(m+1)}{2}$ (d) $\dfrac{m(m-1)}{4}$

9. Discuss the continuity of the function

$$f(x)=\begin{cases} \dfrac{a^{2[x]+\{x\}}-1}{2[x]+\{x\}} & , \quad x\ne 0 \\ \log_e a & , \quad x=0 \end{cases} \quad (a\ne 1)$$

at $x=0$, where $[\cdot]$ and $\{\cdot\}$ are the greatest integer and fractional part function respectively.

(a) $f(x)$ is continuous at $x=0$
(b) $f(x)$ is differentiable at $x=0$
(c) $f(x)$ is discontinuous at $x=0$
(d) None of the above

10. The value of $a+b$ for which the function $f(x)=\begin{cases} \dfrac{x(1+a\cos x)-b\sin x}{x^3} & , \quad x\ne 0 \\ 1 & , \quad x=0 \end{cases}$ is continuous at $x=0$ is

(a) -4 (b) -3 (c) -2 (d) -1

11. Let $f(x)=\begin{cases} \dfrac{a(1-x\sin x)+b\cos x+5}{x^2} & , \quad x<0 \\ 3 & , \quad x=0 \\ \left\{1+\left(\dfrac{cx+dx^3}{x^2}\right)\right\}^{1/x} & , \quad x>0 \end{cases}$

If $f(x)$ is continuous at $x=0$, then the value of $a+b+c+d+5$ is equal to

(a) ln3 (b) ln2 (c) 0 (d) 5

12. If $\lim_{x \to 0} f(x) = \begin{cases} \dfrac{(4^x - 1)^3}{\sin\left(\dfrac{x}{4}\right)\log\left(1 + \dfrac{x^2}{3}\right)}, & x \neq 0 \\ K, & x = 0 \end{cases}$ is continuous at $x = 0$, then K is equal to

(a) $12(\log 4)^2$ (b) $96(\log 2)^3$
(c) $(\log 4)^3$ (d) None of these

13. Let f be a function defined by $y = f(x)$ where $x = 2t - |t|$ and $y = t^2 + t|t|$ for $t \in R$, then

(a) $f(x)$ is discontinuous at $x = 0$
(b) $f(x)$ is non-differentiable at $x = 0$
(c) $f(x)$ is both continuous and differentiable at $x = 0$
(d) $f(x)$ is neither continuous function nor differentiable at $x = 0$

14. Let $x + 4|y| = 6y$, after expressing y as a function of x i.e., $y = f(x)$, $f(x)$ is

(a) Continuous and differentiable at $x = 0$
(b) Continuous but non-differentiable at $x = 0$
(c) Discontinuous at $x = 0$ and differentiable at $x = 1$
(d) Continuous at $x = 1$ and differentiable at $x = 0$

15. If $f(x) = \max.\{\sin x, \sin^{-1}(\cos x)\}$, then

(a) f is differentiable everywhere
(b) f is discontinuous at $x = \dfrac{n\pi}{2}, n \in I$
(c) f is continuous everywhere but not differentiable
(d) f is non-differentiable at $x = \dfrac{n\pi}{2}, n \in I$

16. Consider the function

$f(x) = \begin{cases} \min(|x|, \sqrt{1 - x^2}) & , -1 \le x < 1 \\ [|x|] & , 1 < |x| < 2 \end{cases}$ then

(a) $f(x)$ is continuous on $x \in (-2, 2) - \{\pm 1\}$ and derivable on $x \in (-2, 2) - \left\{\pm 1, \dfrac{\pm 1}{\sqrt{2}}, 0\right\}$
(b) $f(x)$ is continuous and differentiable on $x \in (-2, 2) - \{-1, 1\}$
(c) $f(x)$ is continuous on $x \in (-1, 2) - \{0, 1\}$ and differentiable on $x \in (-1, 2) - \left\{1, \dfrac{-1}{\sqrt{2}}, \dfrac{1}{\sqrt{2}}, 0\right\}$
(d) None of the above

17. Let $f(x) = \begin{cases} -2 & , \text{for } -3 \le x \le 0 \\ x - 2 & , \text{for } 0 < x \le 3 \end{cases}$ and $g(x) = f(|x|) + |f(x)|$, then in the interval $(-3, 3)$, $g(x)$ is non-differentiable at $x =$

(a) 0, 2 (b) 1, 2 (c) $-2, 1$ (d) ± 2

18. The set of all points where the function $f(x) = \sqrt{1 - e^{-x^2}}$ is differentiable is

(a) $(-\infty, \infty) - \{0\}$ (b) $(0, \infty)$
(c) $(-\infty, \infty)$ (d) $(-1, \infty)$

19. If $f(x)$ is a differentiable function such that $f'(1) = 4$ and $f'(4) = \dfrac{1}{2}$, then the value of $\lim_{x \to 0} \dfrac{f(x^2 + x + 1) - f(1)}{f(x^4 - x^2 + 2x + 4) - f(4)}$ is

(a) 4 (b) 16 (c) -4 (d) Does not exist

20. Let $f(x + y) = f(x) + f(y) + 2xy - 1 \, \forall x, y \in R$. If $f(x)$ is differentiable and $f'(0) = \sin\phi$, then

(a) $f(x) < 0, \forall x \in R$ (b) $f(x) > 0, \forall x \in R$
(c) $f(x) \le -3/4, \forall x \in R$ (d) $-1 \le f(x) \le 1, \forall x \in R$

Section II *Numerical Value Questions*

21. If $\lim_{x \to \infty} \left(\dfrac{x^2 + x + 1}{x + 1} - ax - b\right) = 4$ then $a - b$ equals

22. Let $L = \lim_{x \to -\infty} \left(\dfrac{x^4 \cdot \sin\left(\dfrac{1}{x}\right) + x^2}{1 + |x|^3}\right)$ then $2L + 10 =$

23. The value of the limit
$\lim_{n \to \infty} \left[\dfrac{e^{1/n}}{n^2} + 2 \cdot \dfrac{(e^{1/n})^2}{n^2} + 3 \cdot \dfrac{(e^{1/n})^3}{n^2} + \ldots + \dfrac{(e^{1/n})^n}{n}\right]$ is

24. A function $f(x)$ is defined as $f(x) = \dfrac{k \sin x + \sin 2x}{x^3} (x \neq 0)$. If the function is continuous at $x = 0$, then $k - 5f(0) =$

25. Let $F(x) = \begin{cases} \left(1 + x + \dfrac{f(x)}{x}\right)^{\frac{1}{x}} & , x \neq 0 \\ e^3 & , x = 0 \end{cases}$ and

$G(x) = \begin{cases} \left(1 + \dfrac{f(x)}{x}\right)^{\frac{1}{x}} & , x \neq 0 \\ k & , x = 0 \end{cases}$ where $f(x)$ is some function of x. If $F(x)$ is continuous at $x = 0$, then the value of $\ln k$ so that $G(x)$ is also continuous at $x = 0$ is ______

26. Let $f(x)$ be a continuous function $\forall x \in R$ such that
$\lim_{x \to \pi/4} \dfrac{\int_2^{\sec^2 x} f(t)\, dt}{x^2 - \dfrac{\pi^2}{16}} = \dfrac{k}{\pi} f(a)$, where $a, k \in N$, then the value of k^a is equal to ____

27. Let $f(x) = \begin{cases} \cos^{-1}\{\cot x\} & , x < \dfrac{\pi}{2} \\ \pi[x] - 1 & , x \ge \dfrac{\pi}{2} \end{cases}$

If the jump of discontinuity at $x = \dfrac{\pi}{2}$ is $A + B$, then the value of $\left(\dfrac{4A}{\pi} - B\right)$ is equal to _____

28. If $f(a)=2, f'(a)=1, g(a)=-1$ and $g'(a)=2$, then the value of $\lim_{x\to a}\left[\frac{g(x)\cdot f(a)-g(a)f(x)}{x-a}\right]$ is

29. Let $f(x)$ and $g(x)$ be two functions such that $f(x)=x^2\cdot g(x)$ and $\lim_{x\to 0} g(x)\cdot \operatorname{cosec} x=\frac{f'''(0)}{\lambda}$. The value of λ is

30. If $f(x)$ is a differentiable function defined for all positive real numbers such that $xf(x)=x+\int_1^x f(t)\,dt$, then the value of $\sum_{k=1}^{10} f(e^k)$ is

Answers

1 *(d)*	2 *(d)*	3 *(c)*	4 *(d)*	5 *(b)*	6 *(c)*	7 *(a)*	8 *(c)*	9 *(c)*	10 *(a)*
11 *(a)*	12 *(b)*	13 *(d)*	14 *(b)*	15 *(c)*	16 *(a)*	17 *(a)*	18 *(a)*	19 *(a)*	20 *(b)*
21 *(5)*	22 *(8)*	23 *(1)*	24 *(3)*	25 *(2)*	26 *(64)*	27 *(3)*	28 *(5)*	29 *(6)*	30 *(65)*

See detailed solutions on page no. 163

QUALIFIER 08

Differentiation and Application of Derivatives

Section I Objective Type Questions

1. Suppose ϕ is a twice differentiable function satisfying $\phi''(x) = -\phi(x)$. Define function $f(x)$ and $g(x)$ such that $f(x) = \phi'(x)$ and $g(x) = [\phi(x)]^2 + [f(x)]^2$. If $g(1) = 1$, then $g(100)$ is equal to

(a) 100 (b) 10 (c) 1 (d) 0

2. If $\sin y = x \cdot \sin(a + y)$ and $\frac{dy}{dx} = \frac{k}{1 + x^2 - 2x \cos a}$, then the value of $(2k \cos a)$ is

(a) $\sin a$ (b) $2 \sin a$ (c) $\sin 2a$ (d) $\cos 2a$

3. If $y = \left(1 + \frac{1}{x}\right)^x$, then $y_2(2)$ is equal to (where $y_2 = \frac{d^2y}{dx^2}$)

(a) $\left(\frac{-1}{3} + \ln 3/2\right)^2 - \frac{1}{8}$ (b) $\frac{9}{4}\left(\frac{-1}{3} + \log_e 3/2\right)^2 - \frac{1}{8}$

(c) $\frac{9}{4}\left(\frac{1}{3} - \log_e 3/2\right)^2 - \frac{1}{8}$ (d) None of these

4. In terms of a parameter 't' and a constant 'k' a curve is specified as follows $x = t + \frac{1}{t}, y = t^k + \frac{1}{t^k}$

If $\left(\frac{dy}{dx}\right)^2 = \lambda \left(\frac{y^2 - 4}{x^2 - 4}\right)$, then the value of λ in terms of k is

(a) $2k^2$ (b) $k^2/2$ (c) k^2 (d) None of these

5. If $y^2 = a^2 \cos^2 x + b^2 \sin^2 x$, then $\frac{d^2y}{dx^2} + y =$

(a) 0 (b) $\frac{ab}{y}$ (c) $\frac{a^2b^2}{y^2}$ (d) $\frac{a^2b^2}{y^3}$

6. If f is a continuous function on [0, 1], differentiable in (0, 1) such that $f(1) = 0$, then their exists some $c \in (0, 1)$ such that

(a) $f'(c) + cf(c) = 0$ (b) $cf'(c) + f'(c) = 0$

(c) $f'(c) - cf(c) = 0$ (d) $cf'(c) - f(c) = 0$

7. If the function $f(x) = ax^3 + bx^2 + 11x - 6$ satisfies the Rolle's theorem in [1, 3] and $f'\left(2 + \frac{1}{\sqrt{3}}\right) = 0$, then the value of a and b are respectively.

(a) $-6, 1$ (b) $1, -6$ (c) $-2, 1$ (d) $1, -2$

8. Suppose, ϕ and ψ are differentiable functions on [0, 1] and $\phi(0) = 4, \phi(1) = 16$ and $\psi(0) = 0, \psi(1) = 3$. Then, these exists $a \in (0, 1)$ such that $\frac{\phi'(a)}{\psi'(a)} = \lambda$. Then, λ is equal to

(a) 1 (b) 2 (c) 4 (d) 8

9. The ends P and Q of a rod of length $\sqrt{5}$ are sliding along the curve $y = 2x^2$. Let α and β be the x-coordinate of the ends. At the moment when P is at (0, 0) and Q is at (1, 2), the value of the derivative $\frac{d\beta}{d\alpha}$ is

(a) $\frac{1}{3}$ (b) 3 (c) $\frac{1}{9}$ (d) 9

10. A man walks along a straight path at the speed of 4ft/sec. A search light is located on the ground 20 ft. from the path and is kept focused on the man. The rate at which the searchlight rotating when the man is 15ft. from the point on the closest to the searchlight is

(a) $\frac{16}{125}$ rad/sec (b) 0.128 m/s

(c) $\frac{125}{16}$ rad/sec (d) 1.28 m/s

11. Let $g(x) = 2 \cdot f\left(\frac{x}{2}\right) + f(2 - x)$ and $f''(x) < 0$ for all $x \in (0, 2)$. Then, $g(x)$ is

(a) decreasing on (0, 4/3) and increasing on (4/3, 2)

(b) increasing on (0, 4/3) and decreasing on (4/3, 2)

(c) increasing on (4/3, 2) and increasing on (0, 4/3)

(d) None of the above

12. Let $f: R \to R$ be a function defined by $f(x) = 2x^3 - 21x^2 + 78x + 24$. Number of integers in the solutions set of x satisfying the inequality $f(f(f(x) - 2x^3)) \geq f(f(2x^3 - f(x)))$ is

(a) 5 (b) 6 (c) 4 (d) None of these

13. Let ϕ is twice differentiable in [0, 1] and $\phi''(x) > 0$. Let $f(x) = \phi(1 - x) + \phi(x)$ for $x \in [0, 1]$. Then,

(a) f is increasing on [0,1] (b) f is decreasing on [0, 1]

(c) f is decreasing on $\left[\frac{1}{2}, 1\right]$ (d) f is increasing on $\left[\frac{1}{2}, 1\right]$

14. Sum of the x and y coordinate of a point on the curve $3x^2 - 4y^2 = 72$ which is nearest to the line $3x + 2y + 1 = 0$ is

(a) -3 (b) 3 (c) 0 (d) 9

15. The equation of the tangent to the curve $x = t^2 + 3t - 8$ and $y = 2t^2 - 2t - 5$ at the point $P(2, -1)$ is

(a) $y = \frac{6}{7}(x-1)$ (b) $6x + 7y - 17 = 0$

(c) $x + 7y - 13 = 0$ (d) $6x - 7y - 19 = 0$

16. If the tangent at $A(2, 8)$ on the curve $y = x^3$ meets the curve again at B, then the coordinate of B is

(a) (4, 64) (b) $(-4, -64)$ (c) $(-2, -8)$ (d) None of these

17. The radius of a sphere was measured and found to be 21 cm with a possible error in measurement of atmost 0.05 cm. The maximum error in using this value of the radius to compute the volume of the sphere is

(a) 200 cm^3 (b) 300 cm^3 (c) 177 cm^3 (d) 277 cm^3

18. The curve $y = \frac{2x}{1+x^2}$ has

(a) exactly three points of inflection separated by a point of maximum and a point of minimum.

(b) exactly two points of inflection with a point of minimum lying between them.

(c) exactly three points of inflection separated by two points of maximum.

(d) exactly two points of inflection with a point of maximum lying between them.

19. If $a > b > 0$, then maximum value of $\frac{ab(a^2 - b^2)\sin x \cdot \cos x}{a^2 \sin^2 x + b^2 \cos^2 x}$ where $x \in (0, \pi/2)$ is

(a) ab (b) $a^2 - b^2$ (c) $\frac{a^2 + b^2}{2}$ (d) $\frac{a^2 - b^2}{2}$

20. The global maximum value of $f(x) = \cot x - \sqrt{2}\operatorname{cosec} x$ in interval $(0, \pi)$ is equal to

(a) 1 (b) 0 (c) -1 (d) non-existent

Section II *Numerical Value Questions*

21. If $f(x) = \sin^2 x + \sin^2\left(x + \frac{\pi}{3}\right) + \cos x \cdot \cos\left(x + \frac{\pi}{3}\right)$ and $g\left(\frac{5}{4}\right) = 1$, then $gof(x) =$ ______

22. If $f(x) = \cot^{-1}\left(\frac{x^x - x^{-x}}{2}\right)$, then the value of $2 + f'(1) =$

23. If $f(x) = \prod_{n=1}^{100} (x-n)^{n(101-n)}$ then $\frac{f(101)}{f'(101)} = \frac{1}{\lambda}$. The value of $5050 \log_{2525}(\lambda/2)$ is equal to

24. If the function $f(x) = x^3 - 6ax^2 + 5x$ satisfies the conditions of Lagrange's mean value theorem (LMVT) for the interval [1, 2] and the tangent to the curve $y = f(x)$ at $x = 7/4$ is parallel to the chord that joins the points of intersection of the curve with the ordinates $x = 1$ and $x = 2$. Then, the value of $12a$ is ______

25. Two friends Asif (A) and Sohrab (S) start with velocities V at the same time from the junction of two roads inclined at 45° to each other. If Asif and Sohrab travel by different roads, then the rate at which they are being separated is $\sqrt{\alpha - \sqrt{\beta}}\, V$. Hence, $\alpha + \beta$ is equal to

26. The tangent to $y = ax^2 + bx + \frac{7}{2}$ at (1, 2) is parallel to the normal at the point $(-2, 2)$ on the curve $y = x^2 + 6x + 10$. Then, the value of $\left(\frac{7}{2}a + b\right)$ is ______

27. Let $f(x) = \begin{cases} 2 - x + a^2 - 9a - 9 &, \ x < 2 \\ 2x - 3 &, \ x \geq 2 \end{cases}$ where 'a' is a positive constant. If $f(x)$ has local minimum at $x = 2$, then the least integral value of 'a' is ______

28. If the function $f(x) = 2x^3 - 9ax^2 + 12a^2x + 1$ attains its maximum and minimum at p and q respectively such that $p^2 = q$, then 'a' equals ______

29. Let P be a point on the curve $C_1 : y = \sqrt{2 - x^2}$ and Q be a point on the curve $C_2 : xy = 9$, both P and Q lie in the first quadrant. If 'd' denotes the minimum value between P and Q then the value of d^2 is

30. The range of 'λ' for which the function $f(x) = (4\lambda - 3)(x + \log 5) + 2(x - 7)\cot\frac{x}{2} \cdot \sin^2\frac{x}{2}$ does not possess critical points is $(-\infty, A) \cup (B, \infty)$, then $|3A + B| =$

Answers

1 (c)	2 (c)	3 (b)	4 (c)	5 (d)	6 (b)	7 (b)	8 (c)	9 (c)	10 (a)
11 (b)	12 (a)	13 (d)	14 (a)	15 (d)	16 (b)	17 (d)	18 (a)	19 (d)	20 (c)
21 (1)	22 (1)	23 (5050)	24 (105)	25 (4)	26 (1)	27 (10)	28 (2)	29 (8)	30 (2)

See detailed solutions on page no. 168

QUALIFIER 09

Indefinite and Definite Integrations

Section I *Objective Type Questions*

1. The value of $\int \frac{x+\sqrt[3]{x^2}+\sqrt[6]{x}}{x(1+\sqrt[3]{x})}dx$ is

(a) $\frac{1}{2}x^{\frac{4}{3}}+3\tan^{-1}\sqrt[6]{x}+c$ (b) $\frac{3}{2}x^{\frac{4}{3}}+4\tan^{-1}\sqrt[6]{x}+c$

(c) $\frac{1}{2}x^{\frac{2}{3}}+3\tan^{-1}\sqrt[6]{x}+c$ (d) $\frac{3}{2}x^{\frac{2}{3}}+6\tan^{-1}\sqrt[6]{x}+c$

2. The value of the integral $\int \frac{dx}{(x-1)^{\frac{3}{4}}(x+2)^{\frac{5}{4}}}$ is

(a) $\frac{2}{3}\left(\frac{x+2}{x-1}\right)^{\frac{1}{4}}+c$ (b) $\frac{4}{3}\left(\frac{x-1}{x+2}\right)^{\frac{1}{4}}+c$

(c) $\frac{4}{3}\left(\frac{x+2}{x-1}\right)^{\frac{1}{4}}+c$ (d) $\frac{2}{3}\left(\frac{x-1}{x+2}\right)^{\frac{1}{4}}+c$

3. If $\int \frac{2+3\cos x}{\sin x+2\cos x+3}dx=\frac{m}{n}x+\frac{p}{q}\log|\sin x+2\cos x+3|$ $+\frac{r}{s}\tan^{-1}(\phi(x))+k$ where GCD $(m,n)=$ GCD $(p,q)=$ GCD $(r,s)=1$, then $\left(\frac{m}{n}+\frac{p}{q}+\frac{r}{s}\right).\ \phi(0)$ equals

(a) $\frac{2}{7}$ (b) $\frac{1}{10}$ (c) $\frac{1}{5}$ (d) $\frac{17}{10}$

4. If $\int \frac{2x+7}{\sqrt{8x+4-5x^2}}dx=-\frac{2}{5}f(x)+\frac{43}{5\sqrt{5}}g(x)+c$, then the domain of function $[f(x)+g(x)]$ is

(a) $\left[-\frac{2}{75},2\right)$ (b) $\left(-\frac{2}{5},2\right]$

(c) $(-\infty,2)$ (d) $\left(-\frac{2}{5},2\right)$

5. If $\int \frac{x-1}{(x+1)\sqrt{x^3+x^2+x}}dx=\psi(x)+c$, then $\psi(1)$ equals

(a) $\frac{\pi}{6}$ (b) $\frac{\pi}{4}$ (c) $\frac{2\pi}{3}$ (d) $\frac{2\pi}{6}$

6. Let $I=\int \frac{1}{(5+4\cos x)^2}dx$ and $A=m\tan^{-1}\left(n\tan\frac{x}{2}\right)+p\cdot\left(\frac{\sin x}{5+4\cos x}\right)+c$, where $m,n,p\in R$, $A=I$ and $c=$ constant of integration, then $2n^2-m-\frac{p}{3}$ equals

(a) 1 (b) -1

(c) $-\frac{3}{2}$ (d) 0

7. $\int \frac{x^2-1}{x^3\sqrt{2x^4-2x^2+1}}dx$ equals

(a) $2\sqrt{2+\frac{2}{x^2}-\frac{1}{x^4}}+c$ (b) $\frac{1}{2}\sqrt{2-\frac{2}{x^2}-\frac{1}{x^4}}+c$

(c) $\frac{1}{2}\sqrt{2-\frac{2}{x^2}+\frac{1}{x^4}}+c$ (d) None of these

8. If $\int \sin^4 x\cdot\cos^2 x\,dx=\frac{1}{32}\left[\frac{\sin 6x}{m}+\frac{\sin 4x}{n}+\frac{\sin 2x}{p}+qx\right]$ $+c$, then $m+n+p+q$ is

(a) 4 (b) 3

(c) $\frac{1}{10}$ (d) -4

9. If $f\left(\frac{3x-4}{3x+4}\right)=x+2$, $x\neq-\frac{4}{3}$ and $\int f(x)dx=A\log_e|1-x|$ $+Bx+C$, then the ordered pair (A,B) is equal to

(a) $\left(\frac{8}{3},-\frac{2}{3}\right)$ (b) $\left(-\frac{8}{3},\frac{2}{3}\right)$

(c) $\left(-\frac{8}{3},-\frac{2}{3}\right)$ (d) None of these

10. $\int e^x\left[\frac{2\tan x}{1+\tan x}+\cot^2\left(x+\frac{\pi}{4}\right)\right]dx$ is equal to

(a) $e^x\tan\left(x-\frac{\pi}{4}\right)+c$ (b) $e^x\tan\left(\frac{\pi}{4}-x\right)+c$

(c) $e^x\tan\left(\frac{3\pi}{4}-x\right)+c$ (d) None of these

11. If $f(t)=\int_{2t}^{t^2}\tan^{-1}\left|\frac{(1+t)^2-x}{1+x}\right|dx$, then minimum value of $f(x)$ is

(a) $\frac{\pi}{4}$ (b) $\frac{3\pi}{2}$ (c) $-\frac{\pi}{4}$ (d) π

12. Let $I(n)=\int_0^1 x^n\cdot e^{-\sqrt{x}}\,dx$. Then, $I\left(n+\frac{1}{2}\right)-2(n+1)\cdot I(n)$ equals

(a) $-\frac{2}{e}$ (b) $\frac{e}{2}$ (c) $\frac{2}{e}$ (d) $-\frac{e}{2}$

13. $\int_3^7\sqrt{(x-3)(7-x)}\,dx$ is equal to

(a) 10π (b) 8π
(c) 17π (d) 2π

14. $\int_{-1}^{1}\frac{x^4}{1+e^{x^7}}dx=\frac{\ln k}{e^{\lambda}}$, then $(k+\lambda)$ is

(a) a prime number (b) a perfect number
(c) an irrational number (d) a number divisible by 5

15. The value of $\int_0^{10}\frac{3^x}{3^{[x]}}dx$, where $[\cdot]$ denotes GIF, is

(a) $\frac{20}{\log_e 3}$ (b) $\frac{1}{\log_e 3}$
(c) $20\log_2 3$ (d) None of these

16. Let $I=\dfrac{(5050)\int_0^1(1-x^{50})^{100}}{\int_0^1(1-x^{50})^{101}}dx$ then I is

(a) an even number (b) an odd number
(c) a negative integer (d) an irrational number

17. Let $f(x)$ be a function defined on R such that $f'(x)=f'(1-x)$ for all $x\in[0,1]$, $f(0)=1$ and $f(1)=41$. Then, $\int_0^1 f(x)\,dx$ equals

(a) 21 (b) $\sqrt{41}$ (c) -41 (d) -24

18. The least value of the function $g(x)$ given by $g(x)=\int_{\frac{7\pi}{6}}^{x}(4\sin t+3\cos t)dt$ on the interval $\left[\frac{7\pi}{6},\frac{4\pi}{3}\right]$ is

(a) $\frac{1+\sqrt{3}}{3}$ (b) $\frac{\sqrt{3}-1}{3}$

(c) $\frac{7(1-\sqrt{3})}{2}$ (d) $-\left(\frac{\sqrt{3}+1}{2}\right)$

19. If λ is positive integer, then the number of values of 'λ' satisfying $\int_0^{\frac{\pi}{2}}\left[\lambda^2\left(\frac{\cos 3t}{4}+\frac{3}{4}\cos t\right)+\lambda\sin t-20\cos t\right]dt\le-\frac{\lambda^2}{3}$ are

(a) 1 (b) 4
(c) 3 (d) 2

20. Let $I(n)=\int_1^e(1+\log x)^n dx$, $n\in N$, then $I(n+1)+(n+1)I(n)$ equals

(a) $2^n\cdot e-1$ (b) $2^{n+1}e+1$
(c) $2^n e+1$ (d) $2^{n+1}e-1$

Section II Numerical Value Questions

21. Let $f(x)=\int\frac{x^2+1}{\sqrt[3]{x^3+3x+6}}dx$ and $f(-1)=\frac{1}{\sqrt[3]{2}}$, then the value of $f(-2)$ is

22. If $\int\frac{dx}{\sin(x-3)\sin(x-7)}=\frac{1}{\sin\alpha}\ln\left|\frac{\sin(x+\beta)}{\sin(x-\gamma)}\right|+c$, then $\{\alpha+\beta+\gamma\}$ is equal to (where $\{\cdot\}$ fractional part function).

23. $\int\sqrt{\frac{x+1}{x+2}}\times\frac{1}{x+3}dx=m\log\left|\frac{\sqrt{p}+z}{\sqrt{p}-z}\right|+n\log\left|\frac{1+z}{1-z}\right|+c$, where $m,n\in R$ and $p\in R^+$, $Z=\sqrt{\frac{x+1}{x+2}}$, then m^2+n^2-p equals

24. If $\int\frac{\sqrt{\sin^3\theta}+\sqrt{\cos^3\theta}}{\sqrt{\sin^3\theta\cdot\cos^3\theta}\sqrt{\sin(\theta+\alpha)}}d\theta=f(\theta,\alpha)+c$, then $f\left(\frac{\pi}{4},\frac{\pi}{4}\right)$ equals

25. $\int\frac{\sqrt{x}}{\sqrt{x}+\sqrt[3]{x}}dx=\phi(x)+c$. If $\phi(1)=\frac{a+b\log_e 2}{10}$, then $|a-b|$ is equal to

26. Let $f(x)$ be a non-negative continuous function defined on R, such that $f(x)+f\left(x+\frac{1}{2}\right)=3$, $\forall\, x\in R$. Then, the value of $\int_0^{100}f(x)dx$ is

27. If $\int_3^4\frac{1}{\sqrt{(x-3)(4-x)}}dx=k$, then the value of $\sin k+\tan k=$

28. The value of $\int_0^{100}[\sqrt{x}]dx$, where [.] denotes the greatest integer function, is

29. If $f(x)+f(8-x)=0$ and $\int_0^8 \frac{1}{1+2^{f(x)}}dx=\lambda$, then (product of divisors of λ) – (sum of divisors of λ) =

30. If $\int_0^{\frac{\pi}{2016}} \frac{1}{(\cot 1008x)^{1008}+1}dx=\frac{\pi}{4\lambda}$, then λ equals

Answers

1 *(d)*	2 *(b)*	3 *(b)*	4 *(d)*	5 *(c)*	6 *(d)*	7 *(c)*	8 *(a)*	9 *(b)*	10 *(a)*
11 *(c)*	12 *(a)*	13 *(d)*	14 *(c)*	15 *(a)*	16 *(b)*	17 *(a)*	18 *(c)*	19 *(b)*	20 *(d)*
21 *(2)*	22 *(0)*	23 *(1)*	24 *(0)*	25 *(97)*	26 *(150)*	27 *(0)*	28 *(615)*	29 *(1)*	30 *(1008)*

See detailed solutions on page no. 173

QUALIFIER 10

Area Bounded by Curves and Differential Equations

Section I Objective Type Questions

1. Area bounded by the curve $x = \begin{cases} -2-y, & y<-1 \\ y^3, & -1\le y\le 1 \text{ and} \\ 2-y, & y>1 \end{cases}$

$x=0$ is,

(a) $\frac{3}{2}$ (b) $\frac{4}{7}$ (c) $\frac{3}{8}$ (d) None of these

2. Area bounded by the curve $f(x)=\sin^{-1}(\sin x)$, $x\in\left[-\frac{\pi}{2}, 2\pi\right]$ is

(a) $\frac{\pi^2}{3}$ (b) $-\frac{\pi^2}{4}$

(c) $-\frac{\pi^2}{8}$ (d) $\frac{5\pi^2}{8}$

3. Let $f: R\to R$ be a function defined as $f(x)=x+\sin x$. If $g(x)=f^{-1}(x)$, then $\int_0^{\pi} g(x)dx$ is

(a) $\frac{\pi^2+4}{2}$ (b) $\frac{\pi^2-4}{3}$

(c) $\frac{\pi^2-4}{2}$ (d) None of these

4. Area lying between the curves $y^2=2x$ and $y=x$ is

(a) $\frac{1}{3}$ (b) $\frac{3}{4}$ (c) $\frac{2}{3}$ (d) $\frac{5}{4}$

5. Let $y=f(x)=\max\left\{\sin x, \cos x, \frac{1}{2}\right\}$, then the area of the region bounded by the curves $y=f\{x\}$, X-axis, Y-axis and $x=\pi$ is

(a) $\left(\sqrt{2}+\sqrt{3}+\frac{\pi}{2}\right)$ sq units (b) $\left(\sqrt{2}+\frac{\sqrt{3}}{2}+\frac{\pi}{2}\right)$ sq units

(c) $\left(\sqrt{2}+\sqrt{3}-\frac{5\pi}{12}\right)$ sq units (d) $\left(\sqrt{2}+\frac{\sqrt{3}}{2}+\frac{\pi}{12}\right)$ sq units

6. Let $g(x)=x+1$ and $h(x)=x^2+2x+2$ such that $h(x)=fog(x)$, then the area enclosed by the curve $y=f(x)$ and the pair of tangents drawn to it from the origin is

(a) $\frac{3}{2}$ (b) 2 (c) $\frac{2}{3}$ (d) $\frac{1}{3}$

7. The curve $y=ax^2+bx+c$ passes through the point $(2,6)$ and its tangent at origin is the line $y=x$. The area bounded by the curve, the tangent line and $x+1=0$ is

(a) $\frac{1}{3}$ sq unit (b) $\frac{2}{3}$ sq unit (c) $\frac{1}{6}$ sq unit (d) 3 sq units

8. Let $f(x)=x^2$, $g(x)=\sin x$ and $\alpha, \beta(\alpha<\beta)$ be the root of the equation $6x^2-11\pi x+3\pi^2=0$. Then, the area (in sq. units) bounded by the curve $y=fog(x)$, the ordinates $x=\alpha$, $x=\beta$ and the X-axis is

(a) $\frac{5\pi}{6}+\frac{\sqrt{3}}{8}$ (b) $\frac{7\pi}{12}-\frac{\sqrt{3}}{8}$ (c) $\frac{5\pi}{3}-\frac{\sqrt{7}}{8}$ (d) $\frac{7\pi}{12}+\frac{\sqrt{3}}{8}$

9. Let a function satisfies the condition $f(0)=0$, $f'(0)=1$ and $f''(x)=2f'(x)$. Then, the area (in sq. units) bounded by the curve $y=f(x)$, $y=0$ and $x-1=0$ is equal to

(a) $\frac{e^2-3}{4}$ (b) $e-1$ (c) 4 (d) $\frac{e^2}{4}-3$

10. Consider the area bounded by $f(x)=e^{-x}+3$, $g(x)=\log_e(x+2)$, $x=-1$ and Y-axis. The areas divided by the line passing through the points of intersection of these curves with the coordinate axes are in the ratio

(a) $(3.14\ln 2):e$ (b) $(3+2\ln 2):e$
(c) $e:(3-2\ln 2)$ (d) $e:(3+2\ln 2)$

11. Solution of the differential equation $(2x+y+1)dy-(4x+2y-1)dx=0$, is

(a) $\frac{1}{4}[2x+y+\ln(2x+y)]=x+c$

(b) $2x+y-\ln(2x+y)=c$

(c) $\frac{3}{4}[2x-y+\ln(2x-y)]=x+c$

(d) None of the above

12. Solution of the differential equation $x\cos\left(\frac{y}{x}\right)(ydx+xdy)=y\sin\left(\frac{y}{x}\right)(xdy-ydx)$, is

(a) $y\cos\left(\frac{y}{x}\right)=$ constant (b) $xy\sin\left(\frac{y}{x}\right)=$ constant

(c) $yx\cos\left(\frac{x}{y}\right)=$ constant (d) $xy\cos\left(\frac{y}{x}\right)=$ constant

13. The solution of the differential equation $\frac{dy}{dx}=-\left(\frac{y+\sin x}{x}\right)$ satisfying condition $y(0)=1$ does not passes through the point

(a) $\left(\pi,-\frac{2}{\pi}\right)$ (b) $\left(\frac{\pi}{2},-\frac{2}{\pi}\right)$ (c) $\left(-\frac{\pi}{2},\frac{2}{\pi}\right)$ (d) None of these

14. If $y=\frac{x}{\ln|cx|}$, where c is an arbitrary constant, is the general solution of the differential equation $\frac{dy}{dx}=\frac{y}{x}+\phi\left(\frac{x}{y}\right)$, then the function $\phi\left(\frac{x}{y}\right)$ is

(a) $\frac{x^2}{y^2}$ (b) $-\frac{y^2}{x^2}$ (c) $\frac{y^2}{x^2}$ (d) $-\frac{y}{x}$

15. A function $y=f(x)$ satisfies the differential equation $f(x)=\sin 2x-\cos x+(1+\sin^2 x)f'(x)=0$ with initial condition $y(0)=0$. The value of $f\left(\frac{\pi}{6}\right)$ is equal to

(a) $\frac{2}{5}$ (b) $\frac{4}{5}$ (c) 2 (d) $\frac{5}{2}$

16. The curve with the property that the projection of the ordinate on the normal is constant and has a length equal to a is

(a) $x+\sqrt{a^2-y^2}=c$ (b) $(y-a)^2=cx$

(c) $ay=\tan^{-1}(x+c)$ (d) $a\cdot\ln\left|\sqrt{y^2-a^2}+y\right|=x+c$

17. A mothball evaporates at a rate proportional to the instantaneous surface area. Its radius reduces to half in value in one day. The time required for the ball to disappear completely is

(a) $\frac{3}{2}$ days (b) 2 days (c) $\frac{7}{4}$ day (d) 4 ln 2 days

18. Solution of the differential equation $(e^{x^2}+e^{y^2})y\frac{dy}{dx}+e^{x^2}(xy^2-x)=0$, is

(a) $e^{y^2}(y^2-1)+e^{x^2}=C$ (b) $e^{x^2}(y+1)+e^{y^2}=(y^2-1)+C$

(c) $e^{x^2}(y^2-1)+e^{y^2}=C$ (d) None of these

19. A normal is drawn at a point $P(x,y)$ of a curve. It meets the X-axis at Q. If PQ is of constant length k, then the equation of such a curve passing through $(0,k)$ is

(a) $x^2-y^2=k^2$ (b) $x^2+y^2=k^2$

(c) $x^2+y^2=k$ (d) None of these

20. A curve satisfies the differential equation $\sqrt{x^4-x^2}\,dy-\sqrt{y^4-y^2}\,dx=0$

If $y(0)=0$, then curve also passes through the point

(a) (2, 2) (b) (2, 3) (c) (2, –2) (d) (3, 2)

Section II *Numerical Value Questions*

21. The area (in sq. units) bounded by the curve $y=f(x)=|x-1|+|x|+|x+1|$, for all $x\in R$, X-axis and the lines $x=-1$ and $x=2$ is A, then the value of $2A$ equals

22. The area of the region enclosed by the curve $y=\left|x-\frac{1}{x}\right|$, $(x>0)$ and the line $y=2$ is equal to

23. The area enclosed by $[|x|]+[|y|]=2$ is m. Then, the number of positive integral divisors of m is

24. If the ratio of the area into which the circle $x^2+y^2=64a^2$ is divided by the curve $y^2=12ax$ is $\alpha\pi+\sqrt{\beta}:\gamma\pi-\sqrt{\beta}$, then $[(\alpha+\gamma)-2\beta]$ is equal to

25. Let f be a real valued differentiable function on R (the set of all real numbers) such that $f(1)=1$. If the y-intercept of the tangent at any point $P(x,y)$ on the curve $y=f(x)$ is equal to the cube of the abscissa of P, then the value of $f(-3)$ is equal to

26. Let $x\frac{dy}{dx}-y=x^2(xe^x+e^x-1)$ for all $x\in R-\{0\}$ such that $y(1)=e-1$. If $y(2)=\lambda y(1)(y(1)+2)$, then the value of λ is

27. The value of $\int_{-2}^{2}\max(x+|x|,x-[x])dx$, where [·] denotes the greatest integer function, is

28. If $y(x)$ satisfies the differential equation $\frac{dy}{dx}=\sin 2x+3y\cot x$ and $y\left(\frac{\pi}{2}\right)=2$, then the value of $\left[\frac{y\left(\frac{\pi}{6}\right)+4}{9-2\sqrt{3}}\right]\cdot y'\left(\frac{\pi}{3}\right)$ is equal to

29. Solution of $\frac{dy}{dx}+\sin\left(\frac{x+y}{2}\right)=\sin\left(\frac{x-y}{2}\right)$ is $\log_e\left(\tan\frac{y}{\alpha}\right)+\beta\sin\left(\frac{x}{\gamma}\right)=c$, then $\alpha+\beta+\gamma$ equals

30. If $x\,dy=y(dx+y\,dy)$, $y(1)=1$ and $y(x)>0$, then $y(-3)$ is equal to

Answers

1 (a)	2 (d)	3 (c)	4 (c)	5 (d)	6 (c)	7 (a)	8 (d)	9 (a)	10 (c)
11 (a)	12 (d)	13 (d)	14 (b)	15 (a)	16 (d)	17 (b)	18 (c)	19 (b)	20 (a)
21 (19)	22 (2)	23 (6)	24 (6)	25 (9)	26 (4)	27 (5)	28 (2)	29 (8)	30 (3)

See detailed solutions on page no. 178

QUALIFIER 11

Point and Coordinates, Straight Line, Pair of Straight Lines and Circle

Section I Objective Type Questions

1. If $P(x_1, y_1)$, $Q(x_2, y_2)$ and $R(x_3, y_3)$ are three points such that x_1, x_2 and x_3 are in AP and y_1, y_2 and y_3 are in AP, then the points P, Q and R

(a) form an equilateral triangle
(b) form an isosceles triangle
(c) are collinear
(d) form a right angled triangle

2. $OABC$ is a square and P, Q are the middle points of the sides AB and BC respectively, the ratio of the areas of the square and the ΔOPQ is

(a) 8:3 (b) 3:8 (c) 4:1 (d) 4:3

3. Let $A(3, 4)$ be a given point and $B(x, y)$ be a variable point such that $|x| = 6$. The total number of positions of B with integral coordinates, so that $AB \le 4$ is

(a) 5 (b) 6 (c) 4 (d) 8

4. Two equal sides of an isosceles triangle are given by the equations $7x - y + 3 = 0$ and $x + y - 3 = 0$ and its third side passes through the point $(1, -10)$. Then, equation of the third side can be

(a) $x - 3y = 31$ or $3x + y = 0$
(b) $x + 3y - 31 = 0$ or $3x + y + 7 = 0$
(c) $3x + y + 7 = 0$ or $x - 3y = -31$
(d) $3x + y + 7 = 0$ or $x - 3y - 31 = 0$

5. Let $A(p, 0)$, $B(4, 0)$, $C(5, 6)$ and $D(1, 4)$ are the vertices of a quadrilateral $ABCD$. If $\angle ADC$ is obtuse, then the maximum integral value of p is

(a) 1 (b) 3 (c) 2 (d) 0

6. Let $A(0, 0)$, $B(2, 0)$, $C(2, 2)$ and $D(0, 2)$ are the vertices of a square $ABCD$. The square is rotated through an angle of 30° in the anticlockwise direction so that AB makes an angle of 30° with positive direction of X-axis in its new position. Equation of the diagonal BD in the new position is

(a) $(2 - \sqrt{3})x + y = 2(\sqrt{3} - 1)$
(b) $(2 - \sqrt{3})x + y = (2\sqrt{3} - 1)$
(c) $(\sqrt{3} + 1)x + (\sqrt{2} - 1)y = 3$
(d) $(\sqrt{3} - 1)x + y = (2 - \sqrt{3})$

7. P_n is the foot of the perpendicular from the origin O, on the line $3x + 4y = n$, where n is a positive integer. If $OP_1 + OP_2 + OP_3 + \dots + OP_n = 9$, then n is equal to

(a) 8 (b) 9 (c) 90 (d) None of these

8. $A(2, 8)$, $B(1, 1)$ and $C(3, 3)$ are three given points. M is the mid-point of BC. AM is produced to meet X-axis at D and O is the origin. Then, the coordinates of the circumcentre and orthocentre of ΔOMD as well as centroid of the ΔCMD are, respectively,

(a) $(2, 0), (1, 1), \left(\frac{7}{3}, \frac{5}{3}\right)$
(b) $(-1, -1), (-2, 0), \left(\frac{7}{3}, \frac{5}{3}\right)$
(c) $(-1, 1), \left(\frac{7}{3}, \frac{5}{3}\right), (2, 2)$
(d) $(1, 1), (2, 0), \left(\frac{7}{3}, \frac{5}{3}\right)$

9. A line with positive rational slope, passes through the point $M(6, 0)$ and is at a distance of 5 units from $N(1, 3)$. The slope of line equals

(a) $\frac{15}{8}$ (b) $\frac{8}{15}$
(c) $\frac{8}{5}$ (d) $\frac{5}{8}$

10. A line through $A(-5, -4)$ meets the lines $x + 3y + 2 = 0$, $2x + y + 4 = 0$ and $x - y - 5 = 0$ at the points B, C and D, respectively. If $\left(\frac{15}{AB}\right)^2 + \left(\frac{10}{AC}\right)^2 = \left(\frac{6}{AD}\right)^2$, then the equation of the line is

(a) $2x - 3y - 11 = 0$ (b) $2x + 3y + 11 = 0$
(c) $x + y + 22 = 0$ (d) $2x + 3y + 22 = 0$

11. If θ is an angle between the lines given by the equation $6x^2 + 5xy - 4y^2 + 7x + 13y - 3 = 0$, equation of the line passing through the point of intersection of the lines and making an angle θ with the positive X-axis is

(a) $2x + 11y + 13 = 0$ (b) $11x + 2y - 11 = 0$
(c) $11x - 2y + 13 = 0$ (d) $2x - 11y + 2 = 0$

12. If $x-3y=a, px+2y=b$ and $px+y=c$ form a right angled triangle, then

(a) $p^2-6p-12=0$ (b) $p^2-9p+12=0$
(c) $p^2-9p+18=0$ (d) $p^2-6p-18=0$

13. If combined equation of two sides AB and AC of a triangle is $x^2-xy-2y^2+x+y=0$ and $(1,1)$ is orthocentre, then circumradius of ΔABC is

(a) $\frac{10\sqrt{2}}{3}$ (b) $\frac{5\sqrt{2}}{3}$ (c) $\frac{3\sqrt{2}}{5}$ (d) $\frac{3}{10\sqrt{2}}$

14. If $8x^2+8xy+\lambda y^2+26x+13y+15=0$ represents a pair of parallel straight lines, the distance between them is equal to

(a) $\frac{7}{2\sqrt{5}}$ (b) $\frac{7\sqrt{5}}{2}$ (c) $\frac{2\sqrt{7}}{5}$ (d) $\frac{2}{5\sqrt{2}}$

15. Two variable chords AB and BC of a circle $x^2+y^2=a^2$ are such that $AB=BC=a$, then locus of point of intersection of tangents at A and C is a circle of radius.

(a) $4a$ (b) $2a$ (c) $a\sqrt{2}$ (d) None of these

16. If the line $2x+3y=3$ intersects the circle $x^2+y^2-4=0$ at A and B and $M(\alpha,\beta)$ is point of intersection of the tangents A and B, then $\frac{\alpha}{\beta}$ is equal to

(a) $\frac{3}{2}$ (b) $\frac{32}{3}$ (c) $\frac{7}{3}$ (d) $\frac{2}{3}$

17. Chord of the curve $4x^2+y^2-x+4y=0$ which subtend a right angle at the origin pass through a fixed point, whose coordinate are

(a) $\left(\frac{1}{5},-\frac{4}{5}\right)$ (b) $\left(-\frac{1}{5},\frac{4}{5}\right)$ (c) $\left(-\frac{1}{5},\frac{4}{5}\right)$ (d) None of these

18. The length of the greatest common tangent to the circles $x^2+y^2=4$ and $x^2+y^2-12x+27=0$ is

(a) $\sqrt{31}$ (b) $\sqrt{35}$ (c) $\sqrt{11}$ (d) $\sqrt{27}$

19. If two distinct chords, drawn from the point (p,q) on the circle $x^2+y^2=px+qy$ (where $pq\neq 0$) are bisected by the X-axis, then

(a) $p^2<8q^2$ (b) $p^2=8q^2$ (c) $p^2=q^2$ (d) $p^2>8q^2$

20. A circle $S=0$ passes through the points of intersection of circles $x^2+y^2-2x+4y=1$ and $x^2+y^2+4x-2y-5=0$ and cuts the circle $x^2+y^2-4=0$ orthogonally. Then, the length of tangent from origin on circle $S=0$ is

(a) 3 (b) 0 (c) 4 (d) 2

Section II *Numerical Value Questions*

21. The locus of image of the point $(\lambda^2,2\lambda)$ in the line mirror $x-y+1=0$, where λ parameter is $(x-a)^2=b(y-c)$ where a, b and $c\in 1$, then the value of $(a+b+c)$ is

22. If the pairs of lines $x^2+2xy+ay^2=0$ and $ax^2+2xy+y^2=0$ have exactly one line in common and the joint equation of the other two lines $\alpha x^2+\beta xy+\gamma y^2=0$, where α, β and $\gamma\in N$, then lowest value of $\alpha+\beta+\gamma=$.......

23. If the lines $(-\sin\theta)x+y=0$, $x+\sin\theta=0$ and $(\sin\theta)x+y+1=0$ are concurrent, then the number of values of θ in $(0,2\pi)$ is

24. Number of points on X-axis at a distance $p(p<5)$ from the point $(3,5)$ is

25. If the length of the common chord of circle $x^2+y^2+8y+1=0$ and $x^2+y^2+2kx-1=0$ is $2\sqrt{6}$, then the value of $|k|$ is

26. Let C be a circle, whose centre lies on the X-axis. Suppose C touches the line $3x+4y=5$ at $(1,1)$. If (α,β) lies on the circle C, then $\left|\frac{6}{5}\alpha+\frac{8}{5}\beta-2\right|$ can not exceed

27. If the point (α,α^4) lies on or inside the triangle formed by the lines $x^2y+xy^2-2xy=0$, then the largest possible value of $\alpha^2+\alpha+1$ is

28. If the circles $C_1: x^2+y^2+(3+\sin\alpha)x+(2\cos\beta)y=0$ and $C_2: x^2+y^2+(2\cos\beta)x+ky=0$ touch each other, then maximum possible value of k is

29. Reflection of the point $A(5,12)$ in the line $y=x\tan\theta$ is $P(\alpha,\beta)$. The locus of P as θ varies is the curve $x^2+y^2=(k+10)^2$, then the value of k is

30. Line $x+y=2$ is common tangent of two circles C_1 and C_2 with radii 1 and 2 and its points of contact are $A(1,1)$ and $B(\alpha,\beta)$, respectively. Line $2x-y=4$ is the radical axis of C_1 and C_2, then $\left(\frac{5-\beta}{\alpha}\right)+\cos[\log_{(\alpha+2\beta)}(\beta+2\alpha)]$ is equal to

Answers

1 (c)	2 (a)	3 (a)	4 (d)	5 (c)	6 (a)	7 (b)	8 (d)	9 (b)	10 (d)
11 (c)	12 (c)	13 (b)	14 (a)	15 (b)	16 (d)	17 (a)	18 (b)	19 (d)	20 (d)
21 (4)	22 (16)	23 (4)	24 (0)	25 (3)	26 (5)	27 (3)	28 (2)	29 (3)	30 (3)

See detailed solutions on page no. 184

QUALIFIER 12

Conic Sections (Parabola, Ellipse and Hyperbola)

Section I *Objective Type Questions*

1. The equation of latusrectum of a parabola is $x+y=8$ and equation of the tangent at the vertex is $x+y=12$, then the length of latusrectum is

(a) $8\sqrt{2}$ (b) 8 (c) $2\sqrt{2}$ (d) $4\sqrt{2}$

2. Suppose, the normals at three different points on the parabola $y^2=x$ pass through the point $(a,0)$, then parabola $y^2=x$ pass through the point $(a,0)$, then

(a) $a>1$ (b) $a>\frac{1}{2}$ (c) $a<1$ (d) $a<\frac{1}{2}$

3. A circle touches the parabola $y^2=4x$ at $M(1,2)$ and also touches its directrix. The y-coordinate of the point of contact of the circle and the directrix is

(a) $2\sqrt{2}$ (b) $\sqrt{2}$
(c) 5 (d) None of these

4. If $x+y=6$ is a normal to the parabola $y^2=8x$ at point (a,b) with $b<0$, then $|b|-7$ is equal to

(a) 4 (b) 3 (c) 1 (d) 5

5. Let $ABCD$ be a square such that the side AB is on the line $2x-y=17$ and two vertices C and D are on the parabola $y=x^2$. If length of side of $ABCD$ is less than 10 and its area is A, then $\frac{1}{65}A$ is equal to

(a) $\frac{6}{65}$ (b) 10 (c) 4 (d) None of these

6. Let S be the focus of the parabola $y^2=8x$ and let PQ be the common chord of the circle $x^2+y^2-2x-4y=0$ and the given parabola. The area of the ΔPQS is

(a) 8 (b) 6 (c) 4 (d) None of these

7. Let the equations of two ellipse of $E_1:\frac{x^2}{3}+\frac{y^2}{2}=1$ and $E_2:\frac{x^2}{16}+\frac{y^2}{b^2}=1$. If the product of their eccentricities is $\frac{1}{2}$, then the length of the minor axis of ellipse E_2, is

(a) 2 (b) 4
(c) 9 (d) 16

8. The latusrectum of a conic is 6 and its eccentricity is $\frac{1}{2}$. Then the length of focal chord making an angle 45° with the major axis is

(a) less than 6 (b) greater than 6
(c) less than 7 (d) greater than 8

9. An ellipse is rotated through a right angle in its own plane about its centre, which is fixed; the locus of the point of intersection of a tangent of the ellipse in its original with its tangent at the same point in the new position is

(a) $(x^2+y^2)(x^2+y^2-a^2-b^2)=2(a^2-b^2)xy$
(b) $(x^2+y^2)(a^2+b^2)=2(a^2-b^2)xy$
(c) $(x^2+y^2)(a^2-b^2)=2(a^2+b^2)xy$
(d) $(x^2+y^2)(x^2+y^2-a^2-b^2)=2(a^2+b^2)xy$

10. Let $f(x)$ be a decreasing function and positive for all x and an ellipse be $\frac{x^2}{f(k^2+2k+5)}+\frac{y^2}{f(k+11)}=1$. Then,

(a) When $k\in(-3,2)$ then major axis will be X-axis and when $k\in(-\infty,-3)\cup(2,\infty)$ then major axis will be Y-axis
(b) When $k\in(-3,2)$ then major axis will be X-axis and when $k\in(-\infty,2)\cup(3,\infty)$ then major axis will be Y-axis
(c) When $k\in(-\infty,-3)\cup(2,\infty)$ then major axis will be X-axis and when $k\in(-3,2)$ then major axis will be Y-axis
(d) When $k\in(-3,2)$ then major axis will be X-axis and when $k\in(2,3)$ then major axis will be Y-axis

11. The line passing through the extremity A of the major axis and extremity B of the minor axis of the ellipse $x^2+9y^2=9$ meets its auxiliary circle at the point M. Then, the area of the triangle with vertices at A, M and origin O is

(a) $\frac{31}{10}$ (b) $\frac{29}{10}$ (c) $\frac{21}{10}$ (d) $\frac{27}{10}$

12. The distance between a tangent to the parabola $y^2=4x$ and a parallel normal which is inclined at an angle of 60° with the axis is

(a) $\frac{1}{\sqrt{3}}$ (b) $\sqrt{3}$
(c) $4\sqrt{3}$ (d) $\frac{4}{\sqrt{3}}$

13. Equation of one of the common tangent of $y^2 = 4x$ and $\frac{x^2}{4}+\frac{y^2}{3}=1$ is

(a) $x-2y-4=0$ (b) $x-2y+4=0$
(c) $2x+y-4=0$ (d) $x+2y+4=0$

14. A normal to the hyperbola $\frac{x^2}{4}-\frac{y^2}{1}=1$, has equal intercepts on positive X and Y-axes. If this normal touches the ellipse $\frac{x^2}{a^2}+\frac{y^2}{b^2}=1$, then the value of $\frac{9}{25}(a^2+b^2)$ is

(a) 1 (b) 2
(c) 3 (d) 4

15. If the tangent at (h, k) of $\frac{x^2}{a^2}-\frac{y^2}{b^2}=1$ meets the auxiliary circle at (α_1, β_1) and (α_2, β_2), then

(a) k is Arithmetic mean of β_1 and β_2
(b) k is Geometric mean of β_1 and β_2
(c) k is Harmonic mean of β_1 and β_2
(d) None of the above

16. The equation of the transverse and conjugate axes of a hyperbola are respectively $x+2y-3=0$, $2x-y+4=0$ and their respective lengths are $\sqrt{2}$ and $\frac{2}{\sqrt{3}}$. The equation of the hyperbola is

(a) $\frac{2}{5}(x+2y-3)^2-\frac{3}{5}(2x-y+4)^2=1$
(b) $\frac{2}{5}(2x-y+4)^2-\frac{3}{5}(x+2y-3)^2=1$
(c) $2(x+2y-3)^2-3(2x-y+4)^2=1$
(d) $2(2x-y+4)^2-3(x+2y-3)^2=1$

17. Let C be the curve $x=\frac{5y-7}{2y-1}$, we can write C as $\left(x-\frac{5}{2}\right)\left(y-\frac{1}{2}\right)=-\frac{9}{4}$. This represents a hyperbola.

The total number of lattice points (x, y) is

(**Note** lattice points means, the points where x and y both are integers)

(a) 6 (b) 4
(c) 8 (d) 12

18. Normal at point $(5, 3)$ to the rectangular hyperbola $xy-y-2x-2=0$ meets the curve again at

(a) $(0, -2)$ (b) $(-1, 0)$
(c) $\left(\frac{1}{4}, \frac{-10}{3}\right)$ (d) $\left(\frac{3}{4}, -14\right)$

19. The equation of common tangent to the parabola $y^2=8x$ and the hyperbola $3x^2-y^2=3$ is

(a) $x \pm y+1=0$ (b) $x \pm y-2=0$
(c) $2x \pm y+1=0$ (d) $x \pm 2y+1=0$

20. A hyperbola passes through the foci of the ellipse $\frac{x^2}{25}+\frac{y^2}{16}=1$. The transverse and conjugate axes of the hyperbola coincide with major and minor axes of the given ellipse. If the product of eccentricities of the given ellipse and the hyperbola is 1 and a focus of hyperbola is $(k, 0)$ then $|k|$ equals

(a) $\frac{10}{7}$ (b) 5
(c) 10 (d) None of these

Section II *Numerical Value Questions*

21. If the line $y=mx+c$ is normal to the parabola $y^2=16x$, then $c+dm+em^3=0$ where $d+e=$ ....

22. In a square matrix $A=[a_{ij}]$ of order 3; $a_{ii}=m_i+i$, where $i=$ 1, 2, 3, m_i's are slopes $(|m_1|<|m_2|<|m_3|)$ of the 3 normals concurrent at the point $(9, -6)$ to the parabola $y^2=4x$. Rest of all other entries are one the value of $t_r(A)$ is equal to

23. Consider the parabola $y^2=8x$. Let Δ_1 be the area of the triangle formed by the end points of its latusrectum and the point $P\left(\frac{1}{2}, 2\right)$ on the parabola and Δ_2 be the area of the triangle formed by drawing tangents at P and at the end points of the latusrectum. Then, $\frac{\Delta_1}{\Delta_2}$ is

24. Consider the curve $f(x, y)=0$ which satisfies the differential equation $\frac{dy}{dx}+\frac{1}{x-y^2+4}=0$ such that $y(1)=-1$. If $f(x, y)$ represents a conic then the length of its latusrectum is

25. If the straight line $4ax+3by=24$ is a normal to the ellipse $\frac{x^2}{a^2}+\frac{y^2}{b^2}=1$ $(a>b)$, then (a^2-b^2) is equal to

26. Let C be the centre of the ellipse E whose equation is $3x^2+4y^2-12x+8y+k=0$ where $k<28$. Let A and B be two points on the ellipse such that $\angle ACB=\frac{\pi}{2}$, then $(28-k)((CA)^{-2}+(CB)^{-2})=C$

27. The ellipse $E_1: \frac{x^2}{9}+\frac{y^2}{4}=1$ is inscribed in a rectangle R whose sides are parallel to the coordinate axes. Another ellipse E_2 passing through the point $(0, 4)$ circumscribes the rectangle R. The eccentricity of the ellipse E_2 is e then $2e=$

Let C be a conic which is reflection of hyperbola $\frac{(x-2)^2}{3}-\frac{(y-1)^2}{4}=-1$ in the line $x+y-1=0$.

28. Let $e(\lambda)$ be eccentricity of the hyperbola $\frac{x^2}{a^2+\lambda}-\frac{y^2}{b^2+\lambda}=1$ where $a^2>b^2$ and $\lambda \geq 1$. If $e(\lambda)$ is least when $\lambda=\lambda_0$. Then, $3\lambda_0$ is equal to

29. Tangents are drawn from any point on the hyperbola $4x^2-9y^2=36$ to the circle $x^2+y^2-9=0$. If the locus of the mid-point of the chord of contact is $\left(\frac{x^2}{9}-\frac{y^2}{4}\right)=\lambda\left(\frac{x^2+y^2}{9}\right)^2$, then λ is equal to

30. Let locus of point of intersection of perpendicular, tangents to conic C be S, from a point $P(4,2)$ pair of tangents PA and PB are drawn to S. Diameter of circumcircle of ΔPAB will be

Answers

1 *(a)*	2 *(b)*	3 *(a)*	4 *(d)*	5 *(c)*	6 *(c)*	7 *(b)*	8 *(b)*	9 *(a)*	10 *(a)*
11 *(d)*	12 *(d)*	13 *(d)*	14 *(c)*	15 *(c)*	16 *(b)*	17 *(a)*	18 *(d)*	19 *(c)*	20 *(b)*
21 *(12)*	22 *(6)*	23 *(2)*	24 *(1)*	25 *(10)*	26 *(7)*	27 *(1)*	28 *(3)*	29 *(1)*	30 *(5)*

See detailed solutions on page no. 188

QUALIFIER 13

Trigonometry

Section I Objective Type Questions

1. Consider a triangle with sides 2, 5 and 9 cm. If a man runs around the triangle in such a way that he is always at a distance of 1 cm from the sides of a triangle, then the total distance travelled by the man is

(a) $2(7+\pi)$ (b) $8+\pi$
(c) $2(8+\pi)$ (d) None of these

2. Let n be a positive integer such that $\sin\frac{\pi}{2^n}+\cos\frac{\pi}{2^n}=\frac{\sqrt{n}}{2}$ then,

(a) $6\le n\le 8$ (b) $4<n\le 8$ (c) $4\le n<8$ (d) $4<n<8$

3. The value of $\sin\left(\frac{\pi}{14}\right)\sin\left(\frac{3\pi}{14}\right)\sin\left(\frac{5\pi}{14}\right)\sin\left(\frac{7\pi}{14}\right)\sin\left(\frac{9\pi}{14}\right)\cdot\sin\left(\frac{11\pi}{14}\right)\sin\left(\frac{13\pi}{14}\right)$ is

(a) $\frac{1}{64}$ (b) 64 (c) $\frac{1}{32}$ (d) 32

4. The general solution for the inequality $\sin x\cdot\cos x+\frac{1}{2}(\tan x)\ge 1$ is

(a) $x\in\left[n\pi-\frac{\pi}{4}, n\pi-\frac{\pi}{2}\right)$ (b) $x\in\left[n\pi+\frac{\pi}{4},\frac{\pi}{2}-n\pi\right)$
(c) $x\in\left[n\pi+\frac{\pi}{4},\frac{\pi}{2}+n\pi\right)$ (d) None of these

5. The following system of equations $5^{(\text{cosec}^2 x-3\sec^2 y)}=1$ and $2^{(2\,\text{cosec}\, x+\sqrt{3}|\sec y|)}=64$ has solution for x and y then x and y will be (respectively)

(a) $n\pi+(-1)^n\frac{\pi}{6}, m\pi+(-1)^{\frac{m\pi}{4}}, n,m\in I$

(b) $n\pi\pm\frac{\pi}{6}, m\pi\pm\frac{\pi}{6}, n,m\in I$

(c) $n\pi+(-1)^n\frac{\pi}{6}, m\pi\pm\frac{\pi}{6}, n,m\in I$

(d) $n\pi\pm\frac{\pi}{6}, m\pi+(-1)^n\frac{\pi}{6}, n,m\in I$

6. Let $\theta\in\left(0,\frac{\pi}{2}\right)$ and $t_1=(\sin\theta)^{\text{cosec}\,\theta}$, $t_2=(\text{cosec}\,\theta)^{\sin\theta}$, $t_3=(\sin\theta)^{\sin\theta}$ and $t_4=(\text{cosec}\,\theta)^{\text{cosec}\,\theta}$, then

(a) $t_4>t_2>t_3>t_1$ (b) $t_4>t_2>t_1>t_3$
(c) $t_1>t_2>t_3>t_4$ (d) $t_2>t_1>t_3>t_4$

7. If $\exp[(\sin^2 x+\sin^4 x+\sin^6 x+\ldots\infty)\cdot\ln 2]$ satisfies the equation $y^2-9y+8=0$, then the value of $\frac{\cos x}{\cos x+\sin x}$, $0<x<\frac{\pi}{2}$ is

(a) $\frac{\sqrt{3}+1}{2}$ (b) $\frac{\sqrt{3}-1}{2}$ (c) $\sqrt{3}-1$ (d) $\sqrt{3}+1$

8. The minimum value of the expression $\frac{1}{\left[\cos^2\left(\frac{\pi}{4}+x\right)+\sin^2\left(\frac{\pi}{4}-x\right)\right]}$ is

(a) $\frac{1}{2}$ (b) $\frac{1}{\sqrt{2}}$ (c) $\sqrt{2}$ (d) 2

9. The roots of $x^2-4x+1=0$ represent two sides of a triangle. If the angle between them is $\frac{\pi}{3}$, then the perimeter of the triangle is

(a) $14+\sqrt{13}$ (b) $\sqrt{13}$
(c) $2+2\sqrt{3}+\sqrt{4}$ (d) $4+\sqrt{13}$

10. If p_1, p_2 and p_3 are the altitudes of a triangle from vertices A, B and C respectively and Δ is the area of the triangle then $\frac{1}{p_1}+\frac{1}{p_2}-\frac{1}{p_3}=$

(a) 0 (b) 1
(c) $\frac{2}{(a+b+c)\Delta}\cos^2\frac{C}{2}$ (d) $\frac{2ab}{(a+b+c)\Delta}\cos^2\frac{C}{2}$

11. In ΔABC, if $(c-a)(s-b)=(a-b)(s-c)$, then

(a) $2r_1=r_2+r_3$ (b) $r_3=2r_1r_2$ (c) $r_2=2r_3r_1$ (d) $r_2^2=r_1r_3$

12. In ΔABC, if $a\tan A+b\tan B=(a+b)\tan\left(\frac{A+B}{2}\right)$, then which of the following is correct?

(a) ΔABC is a right angled triangle
(b) ΔABC is isosceles
(c) ΔABC is isosceles and right angled
(d) ΔABC is equilateral

13. If the sides of a triangle are three consecutive natural numbers and its largest angle is twice the smallest one, then the sides of the triangle are

(a) 1, 2, 3 (b) 3, 4, 5 (c) 1, 4, 5 (d) 4, 5, 6

14. Reyan standing on a horizontal plane, observes the angle of elevation of the top of a tower to be α. After walking a distance equal to double the height of the tower, the angle of elevation becomes 2α, then α is

(a) $\frac{\pi}{12}$ (b) $\frac{\pi}{18}$

(c) $\frac{\pi}{2}$ (d) $\frac{\pi}{6}$

15. The angle of depression of the top and bottom of a house observed from top of a multistorey building which is at a distance of 40 feet from the house are 45° and 60° respectively. The height of the house is

(a) 40 feet (b) $40\sqrt{3}$ feet

(c) $40(\sqrt{3}+1)$ feet (d) $40(\sqrt{3}-1)$ feet

16. A person in a baloon, which has ascended vertically from flat land at the sea level, observes that the angle of depression of a ship at anchor to be 30°. After descending vertically for 800 m, he finds the angle of depression to be 15°. The horizontal distance of the ship from the point of ascent is

(a) $300(2\sqrt{3}+3)$ (b) $400(2-\sqrt{3})$

(c) $200(\sqrt{3}-2)$ (d) $400(2\sqrt{3}+3)$

17. Total number of real solutions for the equation $\frac{(\sec^{-1}x)^3+(\quad{}^{-1}x)^3}{(\tan^{-1}x+\cot^{-1}x)^3}=7$ is

(a) 2 (b) 1 (c) 4 (d) 0

18. If λ is a total number of solutions for the equation $[\tan^{-1}x]+[\cot^{-1}x]=2$, where [.] represents greatest integer function then the value of $\left[\frac{\sin 2\lambda+\log_{\left(\frac{1}{2}+\lambda\right)}(\lambda+1)}{\cos\lambda+\sqrt{\frac{1}{2}\lambda^2-3\lambda+4}}\right]$ is

(a) 1 (b) $\frac{10}{3}$

(c) 0 (d) None of these

19. The sum of values of x for which $\sin^{-1}\left(x^2-\frac{x^4}{3}+\frac{x^6}{9}+...\right)+\cos^{-1}\left(x^4-\frac{x^8}{3}+\frac{x^{12}}{9}...\right)=\frac{\pi}{2}$, where $0\le|x|<\sqrt{3}$, is

(a) 3 (b) 1 (c) 0 (d) 2

20. Which of the following statement is correct?

(a) If x, y, z are in GP and $\tan^{-1}x$, $\tan^{-1}y$ and $\tan^{-1}z$ are in AP, then $x=y=z=0$

(b) $\sec^2\left(\cot^{-1}\frac{1}{4}\right)+\text{cosec}^2\left(\tan^{-1}\frac{1}{2}\right)=20$

(c) The number of solutions of the equation. $\tan^{-1}\left(\frac{x}{1-x^2}\right)+\tan^{-1}\left(\frac{1}{x^3}\right)=\frac{3\pi}{4}$ in the interval (0, 1) is four.

(d) If $\cot^{-1}\left(\frac{1}{x}\right)+\cot^{-1}\left(\frac{1}{y}\right)+\cot^{-1}\left(\frac{1}{z}\right)=\frac{\pi}{2}$, then $xy+yz+zx=1$

Section II *Numerical Value Questions*

21. If $a\sec\theta=1-b\tan\theta$ and $a^2\sec^2\theta=5+b^2\tan^2\theta$, then $a^2b^2+4a^2=kb^2$ where value of k is

22. If $\cos 2x+a\sin x=2a-7$ possesses a solution then the absolute difference between maximum and minimum value of a is

23. If A, B, C are angles of a triangle and

$$E=\frac{\cos\left(\frac{B-C}{2}\right)}{\cos\left(\frac{B+C}{2}\right)}+\frac{\cos\left(\frac{C-A}{2}\right)}{\cos\left(\frac{C+A}{2}\right)}+\frac{\cos\left(\frac{A-B}{2}\right)}{\cos\left(\frac{A+B}{2}\right)}$$

then the value of E never be less than

24. If $\sin^2x-2\sin x-1=0$ has exactly four different solutions in $x\in[0, n\pi]$, then the minimum value of n can be, $(n\in N)$

25. The ratio of the circumradius to the inradius of ΔABC whose sides are in the ratio $6:7:8$ is

26. In ΔABC, the median to side BC is of length $\frac{1}{\sqrt{11-6\sqrt{3}}}$ and it divides angle A into angles of 45° and 30°. Then length of side BC is

27. At a certain point the angle of elevation of a tower is found to be such that its cotangent is $\frac{3}{5}$, on walking 32 m directly towards the tower its angle of elevation is an angle whose cotangent is $\frac{2}{5}$. Then, the height of tower is

28. An aeroplane flying horizontally 1 km above the ground is observed at an elevation of 60° and after 10 seconds the elevation is observed to be 30°. The uniform speed of the aeroplane in km/h is k, then $\frac{k}{\sqrt{3}}$ is equal to

29. The number of solutions of $2\tan^{-1}(\tan x)=6-x$ is

30. If the roots of the equation $x^3-10x+11=0$ are u, v and w. Then the value of $3\quad{}^{2}(\tan^{-1}u+\tan^{-1}v+\tan^{-1}w)$ is

Answers

1 (c)	2 (b)	3 (a)	4 (c)	5 (c)	6 (a)	7 (b)	8 (a)	9 (d)	10 (d)
11 (a)	12 (b)	13 (d)	14 (a)	15 (d)	16 (d)	17 (b)	18 (c)	19 (c)	20 (d)
21 (9)	22 (4)	23 (6)	24 (4)	25 (2.1333)	26 (2)	27 (160)	28 (240)	29 (3)	30 (6)

See detailed solutions on page no. 193

QUALIFIER **14**

Statistics and Mathematical Reasoning

Section I Objective Type Questions

1. Suppose, mean of the observations 4, 7, a, b, 10, 12 and 13 is 9 and mean deviation from mean is $\frac{16}{7}$. If a and b are integers, then $|b-a|$ is equal to

(a) 2 (b) 1
(c) 0 (d) None of these

2. If the mean deviation of the numbers $1, 1+d, 1+2d, \ldots\ldots, 1+100d$ from their mean is 255, then d is equal to

(a) 20.0 (b) 10.1
(c) 20.3 (d) 10.0

3. Consider, any set of observations $x_1, x_2, x_3, \ldots, x_{101}$, it being given that $x_1 < x_2 < x_3 < \ldots < x_{101}$, then the mean deviation of this set of observations about a point k is minimum, when k equals

(a) x_{50} (b) x_{51}
(c) x_1 (d) $\frac{x_1 + x_2 + x_3 + \ldots + x_{101}}{101}$

4. The standard deviation of a variable x is σ. The standard deviation of the variable $\frac{ax+b}{c}$; a, b and c are constants, is

(a) $\left(\frac{b}{c}\right)\sigma$ (b) $\left|\frac{a}{c}\right|\sigma$
(c) $\left(\frac{a^2}{c^2}\right)\sigma$ (d) None of these

5. If the mean of the numbers a, b, 8, 5 and 10 is 6 and the variance is 6.80, then which one of the following gives possible values of a and b?

(a) $a=1, b=4$ (b) $a=3, b=4$
(c) $a=4, b=5$ (d) None of these

6. The mean and SD of 63 children on an arithmetic test are respectively, (27.6) and (7.1). To them are added a new group of 26, who had less training and whose mean is 19.2 and SD 6.2. The value of the combined group differ from the original as to (i) the mean and (ii) the S.D. is

(a) 25.1 and 7.8 (b) 2.3 and 0.8
(c) 1.5 and 0.9 (d) None of these

7. Let $x_1, x_2, x_3, \ldots, x_n$ be n observations and let x be their arithmetic mean and σ^2 be their variance, then variance of the data with observations $5x_1 - 4, 5x_2 - 4, \ldots\ldots, 5x_n - 4$ is

(a) $25\sigma^2$ (b) $5\sigma^2 - 4$
(c) $25\sigma^2 + 4$ (d) $25\sigma^2 - 16$

8. If $n=5$, mean $=6$, sum of squares of observations $=765$, then approximate value of coefficient of variation.

(a) 150% (b) 160%
(c) 170% (d) 180%

9. Which of the following is the inverse of the proposition? "If a number is prime, then it is odd".

(a) If a number is not odd, then it is a prime.
(b) If a number is not odd, then it is not a prime
(c) If a number is not a prime, then it is not odd
(d) If a number is not a prime, then it is odd

10. The contrapositive of statement "If Siwan is district of Bihar, then Siwan is in India", is

(a) If Siwan is in India, then Siwan is district of Bihar
(b) If Siwan is not in India, then Siwan is not the district of Bihar
(c) If Siwan is in India, then Siwan is not district of Bihar.
(d) If Siwan is district of Bihar, then Siwan is not in India.

11. The negation of statement $(\sim p \vee q) \wedge (\sim p \wedge \sim q)$ is

(a) $(p \vee \sim q) \wedge (p \vee q)$ (b) $(p \wedge \sim q) \vee (p \vee q)$
(c) $(\sim p \vee q) \vee (\sim p \wedge \sim q)$ (d) $(p \wedge \sim q) \wedge (p \vee q)$

12. The true statement among the following is

(a) $p \rightarrow q \equiv \sim q \rightarrow \sim p$ (b) $p \vee \sim p \equiv f$
(c) $p \rightarrow q \equiv q \rightarrow p$ (d) $p \wedge \sim p \equiv t$

13. $(p \wedge \sim q) \wedge (\sim p \vee q)$ is

(a) a contradiction (b) a tautology
(c) Either (a) or (b) (d) Neither (a) nor (b)

14. The compound statement $p \rightarrow (\sim p \vee q)$ is false, then the truth values of p and q are respectively,

(a) F and T (b) F and F
(c) T and F (d) T and T

15. In the truth table for the statement $(p \rightarrow q) \leftrightarrow (\sim p \vee q)$, the last column has the truth value in the following order, is

(a) FFFF (b) FFTT
(c) TTTT (d) TTFF

16. Which of the following statement is a contradiction?

(a) $(\sim p \vee \sim q) \vee (p \vee \sim q)$
(b) $(p \rightarrow q) \vee (p \wedge \sim q)$
(c) $(p \wedge q) \wedge [\sim (P \vee q)]$
(d) $(\sim p \wedge q) \vee (\sim q)$

17. Which of the following is false?

(a) $p \vee \sim p$ is a tautology
(b) $\sim (\sim p) \leftrightarrow p$ is a tautology
(c) $p \wedge \sim p$ is contradiction
(d) $[(p \wedge q) \rightarrow q] \rightarrow p$ is a tautology

18. Which of the following is a contradiction?

(a) $p \rightarrow (q \rightarrow p)$
(b) $p \rightarrow (p \vee q)$
(c) $(p \vee q) \rightarrow (\sim p \wedge \sim q)$
(d) $(p \vee \sim p) \rightarrow (q \wedge \sim q)$

19. The proposition $p \rightarrow \sim (p \wedge \sim q)$ is

(a) a contradiction
(b) a tautology
(c) Either (a) or (b)
(d) Neither (a) nor (b)

20. The Boolean expression $[(p \wedge \sim q) \vee q] \vee (\sim p \wedge q)$ is equivalent to

(a) $p \vee \sim q$ (b) $\sim p \wedge q$
(c) $p \vee q$ (d) $p \wedge q$

Section II *Numerical Value Questions*

21. Let $x_1, x_2, x_3 ...., x_n$ be n observations. Let $w_i = lx_i + k$ for $i = 1, 2, 3, 4, ..., n$, where l and k are constants. If the mean of x_i's is 48 and their standard deviation is 12, the mean of w_i's 55 and standard deviation of w_i's is 15, then the value of $|l - k|$ is ....

22. If the median and the range of four numbers $a, b, 2a + b$ and $a - b$, where $0 < b < a < 2b$, are 15 and 42. The standard deviation (SD) of a and b is

23. The mean and standard deviation (SD) of the marks of 200 candidates were found to be 40 and 15, respectively. Later, it was discovered that a score of 40 was wrongly read as so. The sum of correct mean and correct SD is

24. The standard deviation of the wages of 85 employees is ₹ 28.80. After one year, each of them is given an increment of ₹ 25. The standard deviation of new wages (in ₹) is

25. If $x_1, x_2, x_3, ..., x_{18}$ are observations such that $\sum_{j=1}^{18} (x_j - 8) = 9$ and $\sum_{j=1}^{18} (x_j - 8)^2 = 45$, then standard deviation of these observation is

26. In an examination, there are 30 multiple choice questions. For each correct answer a student gets 4 marks and for each incorrect answer the student gets zero marks. If a student attempts all the questions, then maximum possible standard deviation (SD) of the marks scored by the student is

27. The mean and variance of 7 observations are 8 and 16, respectively. If 5 of the observations are 2, 4, 10, 12 and 14, then the sum of remaining two observations are

28. Suppose, a population A has 100 observations 101, 102, ..., 200 and another population B has 100 observations 151, 152, ..., 250. If V_A and V_B represents the variances of the two populations, respectively, then $\frac{V_A}{V_B}$ is

29. Consider, the first 10 positive integers.If we multiply each number by (− 1) and then add 1 to each number, the variance of the numbers, so obtained is

30. Let $x_1, x_2, x_3, ..., x_n$ be n observations such that $\Sigma x_i^2 = 400$ and $\Sigma x_i = 80$. Then, the minimum possible value of n is

Answers

1 (b)	2 (b)	3 (b)	4 (b)	5 (b)	6 (a)	7 (a)	8 (d)	9 (c)	10 (b)
11 (d)	12 (a)	13 (a)	14 (c)	15 (c)	16 (c)	17 (b)	18 (d)	19 (d)	20 (c)
21 (6.25)	22 (3)	23 (54.93)	24 (28.80)	25 (1.5)	26 (2)	27 (14)	28 (1)	29 (8.25)	30 (16)

See detailed solutions on page no. 199

QUALIFIER 15

Vector Algebra

Section I Objective Type Questions

1. The vector $\hat{i}+\lambda\hat{j}+3\hat{k}$ is rotated through an angle θ and doubled in magnitude, then it becomes $4\hat{i}+(4\lambda-2)\hat{j}+2\hat{k}$. Then, the value of λ equals

(a) $2, -2$ (b) $-\frac{2}{3}, \frac{3}{2}$ (c) $2, -\frac{1}{2}$ (d) $2, -\frac{2}{3}$

2. The position vectors of the points P and Q with respect to the origin O are $\mathbf{a}=\hat{i}+3\hat{j}-2\hat{k}$ and $\mathbf{b}=3\hat{i}-\hat{j}-2\hat{k}$, respectively. If M is a point of PQ, such that OM is the bisector of POQ, then **OM** is

(a) $2(\hat{i}-\hat{j}+\hat{k})$ (b) $\hat{i}+\hat{j}-2\hat{k}$
(c) $2\hat{i}+\hat{j}-2\hat{k}$ (d) None of these

3. If **b** is a vector whose initial point divides the joint of $5\hat{i}$ and $5\hat{j}$ in the ratio $k:1$ and terminal point is origin and $|\mathbf{b}| \le \sqrt{37}$, then k lies in the interval

(a) $(-\infty, -6] \cup \left(-\frac{1}{6}, 6\right)$ (b) $(-\infty, -6] \cup \left[-\frac{1}{6}, \infty\right)$
(c) $[-6, -1/6]$ (d) $[0, 6]$

4. If $\alpha+\beta+\gamma=a\delta$ and $\beta+\gamma+\delta=b\alpha$ and α, β, γ are non-coplanar and α is not parallel to δ, then $\alpha+\beta+\gamma+\delta$ equals

(a) 0 (b) $b\delta$ (c) $a\alpha$ (d) $(a+b)\gamma$

5. If $\mathbf{a}=\hat{i}+\hat{j}+\hat{k}$, $\mathbf{b}=4\hat{i}+3\hat{j}+4\hat{k}$ and $\mathbf{c}=\hat{i}+\alpha\hat{j}+\beta\hat{k}$ are linear dependent vectors and $|\mathbf{c}|=\sqrt{3}$, then

(a) $\alpha=1, \beta=-1$ (b) $\alpha=1, \beta=\pm 1$
(c) $\alpha=-1, \beta=\pm 1$ (d) $\alpha=\pm 1, \beta=1$

6. Let $A=(-4, 0, 3)$ and $B=(14, 2, -5)$, then which of the following point lies on the bisector of the angle between **OA** and **OB** (where 'O' is the origin of reference) is

(a) (2, 1, −1) (b) (1, 1, 2)
(c) (2, 11, 5) (d) (10, 2, −2)

7. Let an incident ray is along the unit vector $\hat{\mathbf{v}}$ and the reflected ray is along the unit vector $\hat{\mathbf{w}}$. The normal is along unit vector $\hat{\mathbf{a}}$ outwards, then the expression for $\hat{\mathbf{w}}$ in terms of $\hat{\mathbf{a}}$ and $\hat{\mathbf{v}}$ is

(a) $\hat{\mathbf{w}}=\hat{\mathbf{v}}+(\hat{\mathbf{a}}\cdot\hat{\mathbf{v}})$ (b) $\hat{\mathbf{w}}=\hat{\mathbf{v}}+(\hat{\mathbf{a}}\cdot\hat{\mathbf{v}})\hat{\mathbf{a}}$
(c) $\hat{\mathbf{w}}=\hat{\mathbf{v}}-2(\hat{\mathbf{a}}\cdot\hat{\mathbf{v}})\hat{\mathbf{a}}$ (d) None of these

8. The vector , directed along the internal bisector of the angle between the vectors $\mathbf{a}=7\hat{i}-4\hat{j}-4\hat{k}$ and $\mathbf{b}=-2\hat{i}-\hat{j}+2\hat{k}$, with $|\mathbf{c}|=5\sqrt{6}$, is

(a) $\frac{5}{3}(-5\hat{i}+5\hat{j}+2\hat{k})$ (b) $\frac{5}{3}(\hat{i}-7\hat{j}+2\hat{k})$
(c) $\frac{5}{3}(\hat{i}+7\hat{j}+2\hat{k})$ (d) $\frac{5}{3}(5\hat{i}+5\hat{j}+2\hat{k})$

9. Let **a**,**b** and **c** be three vectors such that $|\mathbf{a}|=2|\mathbf{b}|=4|\mathbf{c}|$ and $2\mathbf{a}-3\mathbf{b}+6\mathbf{c}=\mathbf{0}$. If θ is the angle between **a** and **b**, then $\cos\theta$ equals

(a) 2/3 (b) 1/3
(c) 3/5 (d) 4/5

10. If the vector $6\hat{i}-3\hat{j}+6\hat{k}$ is decomposed into vectors parallel and perpendicular to the vector $(\hat{i}+\hat{j}+\hat{k})$, then the vectors are

(a) $2(\hat{i}+\hat{j}+\hat{k})$ and $(4\hat{i}-5\hat{j}-8\hat{k})$
(b) $-(\hat{i}+\hat{j}+\hat{k})$ and $(7\hat{i}-2\hat{j}-5\hat{k})$
(c) $-2(\hat{i}+\hat{j}+\hat{k})$ and $(8\hat{i}-\hat{j}-4\hat{k})$
(d) $(\hat{i}+\hat{j}+\hat{k})$ and $(\hat{i}-2\hat{j}-5\hat{k})$

11. The vectors **a**,**b** and **c** are of the same length and, taken pairwise, they form equal angles. If $\mathbf{a}=\hat{i}+\hat{j}$ and $\mathbf{b}=\hat{j}+\hat{k}$, the coordinates of c are

(a) (1, 0, 1), (1, 2, 3) (b) (−1, 1, 2), (1, 0, 1)
(c) $\left(-\frac{1}{3}, \frac{4}{3}, \frac{1}{3}\right), (-1, 1, -3)$ (d) $(1, 0, 1), \left(-\frac{1}{3}, \frac{4}{3}, -\frac{1}{3}\right)$

12. Let $\mathbf{a}=a_1\hat{i}+a_2\hat{j}+a_3\hat{k}$, $\mathbf{b}=b_1\hat{i}+b_2\hat{j}+b_3\hat{k}$ and $\mathbf{c}=c_1\hat{i}+c_2\hat{j}+c_3\hat{k}$ be three non-zero vectors such that is a unit vector perpendicular to both **a** and **b**. If the angle between **a** and **b** is $\pi/6$, then $\begin{vmatrix} a_1 & a_2 & a_3 \\ b_1 & b_2 & b_3 \\ c_1 & c_2 & c_3 \end{vmatrix}^2$ is equal to

(a) 0
(b) 1
(c) $\frac{1}{4}(a_1^2+a_2^2+a_3^2)(b_1^2+b_2^2+b_3^2)$
(d) $\frac{3}{4}(a_1^2+a_2^2+a_3^2)(b_1^2+b_2^2+b_3^2)(c_1^2+c_2^2+c_3^2)$

13. Let **a**, **b**, **c** be three vectors such that $\mathbf{a} \neq 0$ and $\mathbf{a} \times \mathbf{b} = 2\mathbf{a} \times \mathbf{c}$, $|\mathbf{a}| = |\mathbf{c}| = 1$, $|\mathbf{b}| = 4$ and $|\mathbf{b} \times \mathbf{c}| = \sqrt{15}$, if $\mathbf{b} - 2\mathbf{c} = \lambda \mathbf{a}$. Then, λ equals

(a) -1 (b) 1 (c) -4 (d) 2

14. Let $\mathbf{a} = 2\hat{i} + \hat{k}$, $\mathbf{b} = \hat{i} + \hat{j} + \hat{k}$ and $\mathbf{c} = 4\hat{i} - 3\hat{j} + 7\hat{k}$. Let $\mathbf{r} = x\hat{i} + y\hat{j} + z\hat{k}$ be a vector such that $\mathbf{r} \times \mathbf{b} = \mathbf{c} \times \mathbf{b}$ and $\mathbf{r} \cdot \mathbf{a} = 0$. The magnitude of $x + y + z$ is

(a) 7 (b) 5 (c) 9 (d) 3

15. **a** and **c** are unit vectors and $|\mathbf{b}| = 4$. If angle between **b** and **c** is $\cos^{-1}\left(\frac{1}{4}\right)$ and $\mathbf{a} \times \mathbf{b} = 2\mathbf{a} \times \mathbf{c}$, then $\mathbf{b} = \lambda \mathbf{a} + 2\mathbf{c}$, where λ is equal to

(a) $\pm \frac{1}{4}$ (b) $\pm \frac{1}{2}$ (c) ± 1 (d) ± 4

16. If **a**,**b** and **c** are three mutually orthogonal unit vectors, then the triple product $[\mathbf{a} + \mathbf{b} + \mathbf{c} \;\; \mathbf{a} + \mathbf{b} \;\; \mathbf{b} + \mathbf{c}]$ equal

(a) 3 (b) 0 (c) 1 (d) 1 or -1

17. Let **a**,**b** and **c** be three non-zero and non-coplanar vectors and **p**,**q** and **r** be three vectors given by $\mathbf{p} = \mathbf{a} + \mathbf{b} - 2\mathbf{c}$, $\mathbf{q} = 3\mathbf{a} - 2\mathbf{b} + \mathbf{c}$ and $\mathbf{r} = \mathbf{a} - 4\mathbf{b} + 2\mathbf{c}$. If the volume of the parallelopiped determined by **a**,**b** and **c** is V_1 and that of parallelopiped determined by **p**,**q** and **r** is V_2, then $V_2 : V_1$ is equal to

(a) 15 : 1 (b) 3 : 1 (c) 7 : 1 (d) 11 : 1

18. If **u**, **v**, **w** are three vectors of magnitude $\sqrt{3}$, 1, 2 such that $\mathbf{u} \times (\mathbf{u} \times \mathbf{w}) + 3\mathbf{v} = 0$ and θ is the angle between **u** and **w**, then $\cos^2\theta$ is equal to

(a) $\frac{1}{4}$ (b) $\frac{9}{16}$ (c) $\frac{1}{2}$ (d) $\frac{3}{4}$

19. Let **a**,**b** and **c** be the three vectors having magnitudes 1, 5 and 3, respectively, such that the angel between **a** and **b** is θ and $\mathbf{a} \times (\mathbf{a} \times \mathbf{b}) = \mathbf{c}$, then $\tan\theta$ is equal to

(a) 2/3 (b) 3/4 (c) 3/5 (d) 0

20. The line joining the points $6\mathbf{a} - 4\mathbf{b} - 5\mathbf{c}$, $-4\mathbf{c}$ and the line joining the points $-\mathbf{a} - 2\mathbf{b} - 3\mathbf{c}$, $\mathbf{a} + 2\mathbf{b} - 5\mathbf{c}$ intersect at

(a) $-4\mathbf{c}$ (b) $2\mathbf{c}$ (c) $4\mathbf{c}$ (d) $8\mathbf{c}$

Section II *Numerical Value Questions*

21. Let **a**,**b** and **c** be three non-zero vectors, no two of which are collinear. If the vector $\mathbf{a} + 2\mathbf{b}$ is collinear with **c** and $\mathbf{b} + 3\mathbf{c}$ is collinear with **a**, then $|\mathbf{a} + 2\mathbf{b} + 6\mathbf{c}|$ is equal to

22. Let $\mathbf{a} = \hat{i} + \lambda\hat{j} + \hat{k}$ and $\mathbf{b} = \hat{i} + \hat{j} + \hat{k}$. If $|\mathbf{a} + \mathbf{b}| = |\mathbf{a}| + |\mathbf{b}|$ and $f(x) = \int_0^{x^2} \log_2(1 + t^2)\,dt$, then the value of $f'(\lambda)$ is

23. The sum of all possible real values of 'a' for which vectors $\mathbf{r}_1 = \ln|a|\,\hat{i} + a\hat{j} - \hat{k}$ and $\mathbf{r}_2 = (1 + a^2)\hat{i} - \hat{j} - (a - 1)\hat{k}$ are orthogonal is

24. Two adjacent sides of a parallelogram *ABCD* are given by $\mathbf{AB} = 2\hat{i} + 10\hat{j} + 11\hat{k}$ and $\mathbf{AD} = -\hat{i} + 2\hat{j} + 2\hat{k}$. The side *AD* is rotated about *A* by an acute angle α in the plane of the parallelogram, so that *AD* becomes *AD′*. If *AD′* makes a right angle with the side *AB*, cosine of angle α is given by $\frac{\sqrt{\lambda}}{\lambda - 8}$. Then, value of λ is

25. Vectors **a** and **b** are inclined at an angle $\theta = 120$. If $|\mathbf{a}| = 1$, $|\mathbf{b}| = 2$, then $[(\mathbf{a} + 3\mathbf{b}) \times (3\mathbf{a} - \mathbf{b})]^2$ is equal to

26. Let $\mathbf{a}_1, \mathbf{a}_2, \mathbf{a}_3, \ldots, \mathbf{a}_n$ be the sides of a regular polygon inscribed in a circle of unit radius. If $|\mathbf{a}_1 \times \mathbf{a}_2 + \mathbf{a}_2 \times \mathbf{a}_3 + \mathbf{a}_3 \times \mathbf{a}_4 + \ldots + \mathbf{a}_n \times \mathbf{a}_1| = |\mathbf{a}_1 \cdot \mathbf{a}_2 + \mathbf{a}_2 \cdot \mathbf{a}_3 + \mathbf{a}_3 \cdot \mathbf{a}_4 + \ldots + \mathbf{a}_n \cdot \mathbf{a}_1|$, then the smallest possible value of *n* is

27. If $|\mathbf{a}| = |\mathbf{b}| = |\mathbf{c}| = 2$ and $\mathbf{a} \cdot \mathbf{b} = \mathbf{b} \cdot \mathbf{c} = \mathbf{c} \cdot \mathbf{a} = 2$, then $[\mathbf{a}\;\mathbf{b}\;\mathbf{c}]\cos 45°$ is equal to

28. The three unit vectors **a**,**b**,**c** are satisfying $\mathbf{a} \times \mathbf{b} + \mathbf{c} = \mathbf{b} \times \mathbf{c} + \mathbf{a}$, where $\mathbf{a} \cdot \mathbf{c} = 0$. Then, the volume of parallelopiped formed by **a**,**b**,**c** is

29. If **a**,**b** and **c** are unit coplanar vectors, then the scalar triple product $[2\mathbf{a} - \mathbf{b} \;\; 2\mathbf{b} - \mathbf{c} \;\; 2\mathbf{c} - \mathbf{a}]$ is equal to

30. Let $\mathbf{a} = 2\hat{i} + \hat{j} - 2\hat{k}$ and $\mathbf{b} = \hat{i} + \hat{j}$. If **c** is a vector such that $\mathbf{a} \cdot \mathbf{c} = |\mathbf{c}|$, $|\mathbf{c} - \mathbf{a}| = 2\sqrt{2}$ and the angle between $\mathbf{a} \times \mathbf{b}$ and **c** is 30°, then $|(\mathbf{a} \times \mathbf{b}) \times \mathbf{c}|$ is equal to

Answers

1 (d)	2 (c)	3 (b)	4 (a)	5 (d)	6 (b)	7 (c)	8 (b)	9 (a)	10 (b)
11 (d)	12 (c)	13 (c)	14 (a)	15 (d)	16 (d)	17 (a)	18 (d)	19 (b)	20 (a)
21 (0)	22 (2)	23 (0)	24 (17)	25 (300)	26 (8)	27 (4)	28 (1)	29 (0)	30 (1.5)

See detailed solutions on page no. 202

QUALIFIER **16**

Three Dimensional Geometry

Section I Objective Type Questions

1. If RST is a triangle in a plane with vertices $R(1,\alpha,\beta)$, $S(0,1,-1)$ and $T(2,1,0)$. If the median through R is equally inclined to the coordinate axes, then the value of $[(3312\beta^2+626\beta)+271\alpha^7]$ is equal to

(a) 786 (b) 678 (c) 1192 (d) 288

2. Angle between the two straight lines whose direction cosines l, m, n are given by $2l+2m-n=0$ and $mn+nl+lm=0$ is

(a) $\frac{\pi}{6}$ (b) $\frac{\pi}{2}$ (c) $\frac{\pi}{3}$ (d) π

3. The line $\frac{x-2}{1}=\frac{y-3}{1}=\frac{z-4}{-k}$ and $\frac{x-1}{k}=\frac{y-4}{2}=\frac{z-5}{1}$ are coplanar, if

(a) $k=0$ or -1 (b) $k=0$ or 1 (c) $k=0$ or -3 (d) $k=3$ or -3

4. If a line with direction ratios 2, 1, 1 intersects the lines $\frac{x-1}{2}=\frac{y-2}{3}=\frac{z-3}{4}$ and $\frac{x-2}{1}=\frac{y+1}{2}=\frac{z+2}{3}$ at P and Q, then $|\mathbf{PQ}|$ is

(a) $2\sqrt{6}$ (b) $2\sqrt{5}$ (c) $7\sqrt{2}$ (d) None of these

5. The coordinates of a point on the line $\frac{x-1}{2}=\frac{y+1}{-3}=z$ at a distance of $4\sqrt{14}$ from the point $(1,-1,0)$ nearer to the origin is

(a) $(-7,-11,-4)$ (b) $(9,-13,4)$
(c) $(-7,11,-4)$ (d) $(-9,13,-4)$

6. Let the shortest distance between the lines $\frac{x-5}{3}=\frac{y-7}{-1}=\frac{z+2}{1}$ and $\frac{x+3}{-3}=\frac{y-3}{2}=\frac{z-6}{4}$ be d. Then, d lies in the interval

(a) (4, 5) (b) (9, 10) (c) (6, 7) (d) (8, 9)

7. Image of the point P with position vector $7\hat{\mathbf{i}}-\hat{\mathbf{j}}+2\hat{\mathbf{k}}$ in the line whose vector equation is $\mathbf{r}=9\hat{\mathbf{i}}+5\hat{\mathbf{j}}+5\hat{\mathbf{k}}+\lambda(\hat{\mathbf{i}}+3\hat{\mathbf{j}}+5\hat{\mathbf{k}})$ has the position vector

(a) $9\hat{\mathbf{i}}+5\hat{\mathbf{j}}+2\hat{\mathbf{k}}$ (b) $9\hat{\mathbf{i}}-5\hat{\mathbf{j}}-2\hat{\mathbf{k}}$ (c) $9\hat{\mathbf{i}}+5\hat{\mathbf{j}}-2\hat{\mathbf{k}}$ (d) $-9\hat{\mathbf{i}}+5\hat{\mathbf{j}}+2\hat{\mathbf{k}}$

8. The line $\frac{x-2}{3}=\frac{y+1}{2}=\frac{z-1}{-1}$ intersects the curve $xy=c^2$, $z=0$ if c is equal to

(a) ± 1 (b) ± 3 (c) $\pm\sqrt{5}$ (d) $\pm\sqrt{3}$

9. Equation of the plane which bisects the obtuse angle between the planes $4x-3y+12z+13=0$ and $x+2y+2z=9$ is

(a) $x+35y+10z=156$ (b) $3x+y-35z=56$
(c) $x+35y-10z=156$ (d) $x-35y+10z=-136$

10. Let there be two planes A and B such that $A: 2x-3y+4z-3=0$; $B: x-y+z-3=0$, then the reflection of A in B is given by

(a) $4x+3y+2z+1=0$ (b) $4x-3y-3z-4=0$
(c) $4x-3y+2z-15=0$ (d) $x-3y+z=15$

11. Perpendiculars are drawn from points on the line $\frac{x+2}{2}=\frac{y+1}{-1}=\frac{z}{3}$ to the plane $x+y+z=3$. The feet of perpendiculars lie on the line

(a) $\frac{x}{5}=\frac{y-1}{8}=\frac{z-2}{-13}$ (b) $\frac{x}{2}=\frac{y-1}{-7}=\frac{z-2}{5}$
(c) $\frac{x}{2}=\frac{y-1}{3}=\frac{z-2}{-5}$ (d) $\frac{x}{4}=\frac{y-1}{3}=\frac{z-2}{-7}$

12. The distance between the planes $\frac{x}{2}+y-2z+7=0$ and the plane that passes through the points $(1,0,2)$, $(-1,1,2)$, $(5,0,3)$ is equal to

(a) $\sqrt{\frac{7}{3}}$ (b) $\sqrt{\frac{3}{7}}$ (c) 5 (d) 7

13. The equation of the line passing through (1, 2, 3) and parallel to the planes $x-y+2z=5$ and $3x+y+z=6$ is

(a) $\frac{x-1}{-3}=\frac{y-2}{-5}=\frac{z-1}{4}$ (b) $\frac{x-1}{-3}=\frac{y-2}{-5}=\frac{z-1}{4}$
(c) $\frac{x-1}{3}=\frac{y+2}{5}=\frac{z+1}{4}$ (d) $\frac{x-1}{-3}=\frac{y-2}{5}=\frac{z-3}{4}$

14. The distance of the point $(2,1,-2)$ from the line $\frac{x-1}{2}=\frac{y+1}{1}=\frac{z-3}{-3}$ measured parallel to the plane $x+2y+z=4$ is

(a) $\sqrt{20}$ (b) $\sqrt{30}$ (c) 30 (d) $\sqrt{10}$

15. The plane denoted by $\pi_1: 4x+7y+4z+81=0$ is rotated through a right angle about its line of intersection with the plane $\pi_2: 5x+3y+10z=25$. If the plane in its new position be denoted by π and the distance of this plane from the origin is $\sqrt{k}$. Where $k\in N$, then k equals

(a) 106 (b) 108 (c) 122 (d) 212

16. A ray of light comes along a line L and strikes the plane mirror kept along the plane $P=0$ at point B. $A(2, 1, 6)$ is a point on the line L whose image about plane P is A'. It is given that $L: \frac{x-2}{3}=\frac{y-1}{4}=\frac{z-6}{5}$ and the equation of plane is $x+y-2z-3=0$ then the equation of reflected ray (L_1) is

(a) $\frac{x+10}{4}=\frac{y+15}{5}=\frac{z+14}{3}$ (b) $\frac{x+10}{3}=\frac{y+15}{5}=\frac{z+14}{5}$

(c) $\frac{x+10}{4}=\frac{y-5}{15}=\frac{z+2}{-3}$ (d) $\frac{x-10}{4}=\frac{y+\frac{1}{2}}{2}=\frac{z-14}{3}$

17. The length of projection of the line segment joining the points $(1,-1,0)$ and $(-1,0,1)$ in the plane $2x+3y+6z=7$, is equal to

(a) $\frac{13}{7}$ (b) $\frac{\sqrt{329}}{7}$ (c) $\frac{17}{7}$ (d) $\frac{\sqrt{269}}{7}$

18. Given that, $P(1,-1,1)$, $Q(3,2,2)$, $R(1,2,3)$ and $S(3,0,1)$ are four points. Consider the equation of a plane which is parallel to the plane $3x-2y+4z=7$ and passing through $(2,-1,1)$. Which of the following line segment is intersected by plane?

(a) QS (b) QR (c) PR (d) None of these

19. Let the equation of the two planes P_1 and P_2 are
$P_1: \mathbf{r}\cdot(3\hat{\mathbf{i}}-\hat{\mathbf{j}}+2\hat{\mathbf{k}})=4$ and $P_2: \mathbf{r}\cdot(\hat{\mathbf{i}}+\hat{\mathbf{j}}+\hat{\mathbf{k}})=2$
If the equation of the plane containing the line of intersection of the planes P_1 and P_2 and also containing the point with position vector (PV) $(2\hat{\mathbf{i}}+2\hat{\mathbf{j}}+\hat{\mathbf{k}})$ is $ax+by+2z=c$, then the value of $(a+b+c)$ is

(a) 7 (b) 9 (c) 13 (d) 5

20. The point of intersection of line of intersection of two planes $w_1: x-2y+z=1$ and $w_2: x+2y-2z=5$ and of the plane $w: x+y-2z=7$ is (α,β,γ). Then, which of the following is incorrect?

(a) $\alpha+\beta=0$ (b) $\alpha-3\beta+\gamma=3$
(c) $2\beta=\gamma$ (d) $4\alpha+4\gamma=0$

Section II *Numerical Value Questions*

21. A line segment has length 63 and direction ratios are $(3,-2,6)$. If the line makes an obtuse angle with X-axis, then y-component of line vector is

22. If the area of the triangle whose vertices are $A(1,2,3)$, $B(2,-1,1)$ and $C(1,2,-4)$ is λ sq unit, then $\frac{2\lambda}{\sqrt{10}}$ must be

23. If the lines $\frac{x-1}{2}=\frac{y-k}{3}=\frac{z-3}{4}$ and $\frac{x-4}{5}=\frac{y-1}{k}=z$ intersect, then the value of k is

24. Let θ be the angle between the lines $L_1: \begin{cases} x=2t+1 \\ y=-t+1 \\ z=3t+1 \end{cases}$ and $L_2=\begin{cases} x=3s+2 \\ y=6s-1, \text{ where } s,t\in R. \\ z=4 \end{cases}$ If the value of $\int_0^\theta \frac{1}{1+\tan x}dx$ is k, then $\frac{596k}{\pi}$ is equal to

25. The sum of direction ratios of normal to the plane which is equidistant from the line $\frac{x-1}{1}=\frac{y-2}{2}=\frac{z-3}{3}$ and $\frac{x-2}{3}=\frac{y-3}{1}=\frac{z-1}{2}$ is

26. If the lines $\frac{x+1}{-3}=\frac{y-p}{2}=\frac{z+2}{1}$ and $\frac{x}{1}=\frac{y-7}{-3}=\frac{z+7}{2}$ lies in the same plane, then the sum of x, y, z coordinates of their point of intersection is

27. A square $ABCD$ of diagonal $2a$ is folded along the diagonal AC so that the planes DAC and BAC are at right angle. The shortest distance between DC and AB is $\frac{\alpha\cdot a}{\sqrt{\beta}}$, then $\alpha+2\beta$ is equal to

28. If the angle between the plane $x-3y+2z=1$ and the line $\frac{x-1}{2}=\frac{y-1}{1}=\frac{z-1}{-3}$ is θ, then the value of $\operatorname{cosec}\theta$ is

29. If the equation of the plane passing through the point $(-1,2,0)$ and parallel to the lines $\frac{x}{3}=\frac{y+1}{0}=\frac{z-2}{-1}$ and $\frac{x-1}{1}=\frac{y+1}{2}=\frac{z+1}{-1}$ is $ax+by+cz=1$, then the value of $(a+b+c)$ is

30. If the plane $\frac{x}{2}+\frac{y}{3}+\frac{z}{4}=\frac{1}{2}$ intersects X, Y and Z-axis at A, B and C respectively, then volume of the tetrahedron $OABC$, where O is the origin, is

Answers

1 (a)	2 (b)	3 (c)	4 (a)	5 (c)	6 (d)	7 (c)	8 (c)	9 (c)	10 (c)
11 (b)	12 (a)	13 (d)	14 (b)	15 (d)	16 (a)	17 (d)	18 (b)	19 (d)	20 (a)
21 (18)	22 (7)	23 (2)	24 (149)	25 (3)	26 (0)	27 (8)	28 (2)	29 (5)	30 (0.5)

See detailed solutions on page no. 205

JEE MAIN & ADVANCED

Part Tests

Based on Complete Class 11th & 12th Syllabus

This section will check your overall understanding of complete syllabus of class 11 & 12, respectively.

PART TEST 01

(Based on Complete Class 11 Syllabus)

JEE Main Test Paper

Mathematics

*Instructions

- This question paper contains of 30 Questions of Mathematics, divided into two sections : **Section I** Objective Type Questions and **Section II** Numerical Type Questions.
- Section I contains 20 Objective questions and all Questions are cumpulsory (Marking Scheme : Correct + 4, Incorrect – 1).
- Section II contains 10 Numerical value questions out of which only 5 questions are to be attempted (Marking Scheme : Correct + 4, Incorrect 0).

Section I *Multiple Choice Questions*

1. If $A=\{\theta: 2\cos^2\theta+\sin\theta \le 2\}$ and $B=\left\{\theta:\frac{\pi}{2}\le\theta\le\frac{3\pi}{2}\right\}$, then $A\cap B$ is equal to

(a) $\left\{\theta:\frac{\pi}{2}\le\theta\le\frac{5\pi}{6}\right\}$

(b) $\left\{\theta:\pi\le\theta\le\frac{3\pi}{2}\right\}$

(c) $\left\{\theta:\frac{\pi}{2}\le\theta\le\frac{5\pi}{6}\right\}\cup\left\{\theta:\pi\le\theta\le\frac{3\pi}{2}\right\}$

(d) None of the above

2. If $f(x)=\log_2\left(\frac{\sin x-\cos x+3\sqrt{2}}{\sqrt{2}}\right)$, then the range of f is

(a) [1, 4] (b) [1, 2] (c) [−2, 2] (d) None of these

3. Numbers 1, 2, 3, 4, ... , $2n\,(n\in N)$ are printed on $2n$ cards. The probability of drawing a number n is proportional to r. Then, the probability of drawing an even number in one draw is

(a) $\frac{n+2}{n+3}$ (b) $\frac{n+1}{n+3}$

(c) $\frac{1}{2}$ (d) $\frac{n+1}{2n+1}$

4. If α and β are solutions of $\sin^2 x+a\sin x+b=0$ and $\cos^2 x+c\cos x+d=0$, then $\sin(\alpha+\beta)$ equals

(a) $\frac{b^2+d^2}{2bd}$ (b) $\frac{a^2+c^2}{2ac}$

(c) $\frac{2ac}{a^2+c^2}$ (d) $\frac{2bd}{b^2+d^2}$

5. In the expansion of $\left(x^{\frac{2}{3}}+4x^{\frac{1}{3}}+4\right)^5\left(\frac{1}{x^{\frac{1}{3}}-1}+\frac{1}{x^{\frac{2}{3}}+x^{\frac{1}{3}}+1}\right)^{-9}$, the constant term is

(a) 168 (b) 186

(c) 618 (d) 816

6. Let in a triangle, any two sides and included angle are respectively $\sqrt{3}-1$, $\sqrt{3}+1$, 60°, then which of the following is true?

(a) Thirds side $=\sqrt{6}$ units (b) $\angle C=15°$

(c) Triangle is obtuse (d) All the above

7. If $\log_{1/10}(x^2+x)>\log_{1/2}(x^3-x)+\log_2(x-1)$, then x lies in the interval.

(a) $x\in\left(-\infty,\frac{-\sqrt{5}-1}{2}\right)$

(b) $x\in\left(\frac{\sqrt{5}-1}{2},1\right)$

(c) $x\in(1,\infty)$

(d) $x\in\left(\frac{-\sqrt{5}-1}{2},\frac{\sqrt{5}-1}{2}\right)$

8. If $\phi(x)=x^2+x+\frac{3}{4}$ and $\psi(x)=x^2+kx+1$ be two real functions, then the range of 'k' for which $\psi(\phi(x))$ has no real solution, is

(a) $(2,\infty)$ (b) $(-2,\infty)$

(c) $(-2,2)$ (d) $(-\infty,-2)$

9. Let r be the range of $n(\forall\ n\geq 1)$ observations $x_1, x_2, x_3, \ldots, x_n$, if $E=\sqrt{\dfrac{\sum_{i=1}^{n}(x_i-\bar{x})^2}{n-1}}$, then

(a) $E<r\sqrt{\dfrac{n}{n-1}}$ (b) $E=r\sqrt{\dfrac{n}{n-1}}$

(c) $E\geq r\sqrt{\dfrac{n}{n-1}}$ (d) $E<r\sqrt{\dfrac{n^2+1}{n-1}}$

10. The number of points inside or on the circle $x^2+y^2=4$ satisfying $\tan^4 x+\cot^4 x+1=3\sin^2 y$ is

(a) infinity (b) four

(c) one (d) three

11. $\lim\limits_{n\to\infty}\dfrac{n^2+2(n-1)^2+3(n-2)^2+\ldots n\cdot 1^2}{1^3+2^3+\ldots+n^3}$ equals

(a) $\dfrac{8}{3}$ (b) $\dfrac{1}{3}$ (c) $\dfrac{4}{3}$ (d) $\dfrac{2}{3}$

12. Sides of a ΔABC; a, b, c are in GP. If r is the common ratio of this GP, then

(a) $r\in\left(\dfrac{\sqrt{5}+1}{2},\infty\right)$ (b) $r\in\left(\dfrac{\sqrt{5}-1}{2},\dfrac{\sqrt{5}+1}{2}\right)$

(c) $r\in\left(\dfrac{\sqrt{5}+1}{2},\dfrac{\sqrt{5}+3}{2}\right)$ (d) $r\in\left(\dfrac{\sqrt{5}-1}{2},\infty\right)$

13. The statement $(p\Rightarrow q)\Leftrightarrow(\sim p\wedge q)$ is a

(a) tautology (b) contradiction

(c) contigency (d) None of these

14. If pens of a particular brand are all identical, then the number of ways in which we can choose 6 pens out of 8 different brands available in the market, is

(a) ${}^{13}C_8$ (b) ${}^{13}C_5$

(c) ${}^{13}C_6$ (d) 8^6

15. The area (in sq units) of the quadrilaterals formed by the two pairs of straight lines $l^2x^2-m^2y^2-n(lx+my)=0$ and $l^2x^2-m^2y^2+n(lx-my)=0$ is

(a) $\dfrac{n^2}{|l\cdot m|}$ (b) $\dfrac{n^2}{2|l\cdot m|}$

(c) $\dfrac{n^2}{4|l\cdot m|}$ (d) $\dfrac{2n^2}{|l\cdot m|}$

16. If for $0<x<\dfrac{\pi}{2}$, $y=\exp[(\sin^2 x+\sin^4 x+\sin^6 x+\ldots+\infty)\ln 2]$ is a root of the quadratic equation $x^2-9x+8=0$, then the value of $\dfrac{\sin x+\cos x}{\sin x-\cos x}$ is

(a) 0 (b) $2-\sqrt{3}$

(c) $2+\sqrt{3}$ (d) $\sqrt{3}$

17. If $P(2,8)$ is an interior point of a circle $x^2+y^2-2x+4y-\lambda=0$, which neither touches nor intersects the axes, then the set for λ is

(a) $\lambda<-2$ (b) $\lambda<-1$

(c) $\lambda<92$ (d) 0

18. If $f(x)=\log_e\left(\dfrac{1+x}{1-x}\right)$ and $g(x)=\dfrac{3x+x^3}{1+3x^2}$, then $\dfrac{d}{dx}f(g(x))$ is equal to

(a) $3f'(x)$ (b) $-3f'(x)$

(c) $-f'(x)$ (d) $3(f(x))^2\cdot f'(x)$

19. If the curve $y=|x-3|$ touches the parabola $y^2=k(x-4)$, $k>0$, then the latusrectum of the parabola is

(a) 2 (b) 8

(c) 4 (d) 6

20. Tangents are drawn through a point P to the ellipse $4x^2+5y^2=20$ having inclinations α and β such that $\cot\alpha+\cot\beta=2$, the locus of P is

(a) $x^2-4=x^2y^2$

(b) $y^2+4=x^2y^2$

(c) $y^2-4=x^2$

(d) $y^2-4=xy$

Section II *Numerical Value Questions*

21. A line $x=\lambda$, intersects the graph of $y=\log_{16}x$ and $y=\log_{16}(x+7)$. The distance between the points of intersection is 0.25, then the value of λ is ....

22. The square of the minimum distance between the curves $y^2=4x$ and $x^2+y^2-8x+15=0$ is ....

23. If $f_k(\alpha)=\left(\cos\dfrac{\alpha}{k^2}+i\sin\dfrac{\alpha}{k^2}\right)\left(\cos\dfrac{2\alpha}{k^2}+i\sin\dfrac{2\alpha}{k^2}\right)\ldots\left(\cos\dfrac{\alpha}{k}+i\sin\dfrac{\alpha}{k}\right)$, then the value of $\left[\lim\limits_{n\to\infty}f_n(\pi)\right]^4$ is ....

24. If three positive real numbers a, b, c are in AP such that $abc=4$, then the minimum possible value of b is of the form $(\alpha)^{\left(\frac{\beta}{\gamma}\right)}$, where α,β,γ are prime numbers. So, the value of $\alpha+\beta+\gamma$ is ....

25. Let β be the imaginary part of $(z-1)(\cos\alpha+i\sin\alpha)^{-1}+(z-1)^{-1}(\cos\alpha+i\sin\alpha)$, where $z(\neq 1)$ is complex and α is real. If $\beta=0$, then z lies on a circle whose radius is equal to ....

26. If curves $y=x^2+3kx+12$, $k\in R$ and $4y^2-9=0$ meet each other at exactly three distinct points, then the sum of all possible values of k is ....

27. The equation of a line passing through the centre of a rectangular hyperbola is $x - y - 1 = 0$. If one of the asymptotes is $3x - 4y - 6 = 0$ and the equation of other asymptote is $Ax + By + C = 0$, then $2A + B + C$ is equal to …………

28. If 1 lies between the roots of the equation $y^2 - my + 1 = 0$, then the value of $\left[\left(\frac{4|x|}{|x|^2+16}\right)^m\right]$, where $|\cdot|$ and $[\cdot]$ represents absolute value of x and greatest integer less than or equal to x respectively, is …………

29. P is a point on either of the two lines $y - \sqrt{3}|x| = 2$ at a distance of 5 units from their point of intersection. The coordinates of the foot of the perpendicular from P on the bisector of the angle between them are $\left(\alpha, \frac{\beta + \gamma\sqrt{\delta}}{\lambda}\right)$, then $\lambda\alpha + \beta\delta - \gamma$ is equal to …………

30. In a triangular plot ABC with $BC = 7$ m, $CA = 8$ m and $AB = 9$m, a lamp post is situated at the middle point E of the side AC and subtends an angle $\tan^{-1}(3)$ at the point B, then the height of the lamp post is …………

Answers

1	(c)	2	(b)	3	(d)	4	(c)	5	(a)	6	(d)	7	(c)	8	(b)	9	(a)	10	(b)
11	(b)	12	(b)	13	(c)	14	(c)	15	(b)	16	(c)	17	(d)	18	(a)	19	(c)	20	(d)
21	(7)	22	(13)	23	(1)	24	(7)	25	(1)	26	(0)	27	(28)	28	(0)	29	(7)	30	(21)

See detailed solutions on page no. 212

PART TEST 02

(Based on Complete Class 11 Syllabus)

JEE Advanced Test Paper

Mathematics

Section 1

- This section contains **FOUR (04)** questions.
- Each question has **FOUR** options (a), (b), (c) and (d). **ONLY ONE** of these four options is the correct answer.
- For each question, choose the option corresponding to the correct answer.
- Answer to each question will be evaluated according to the following marking scheme:

Full Marks : +3 If ONLY the correct option is chosen;
Zero Marks : 0 If none of the options is chosen (i.e. the question is unanswered);
Negative Marks : –1 In all other cases.

1. Let S_1 be a square of side k. Another square is formed by joining the mid-points of the sides of S_1. The same process is applied to S_2 to form yet another square S_3, and so on. If $A_1, A_2, A_3, \dots$ be the areas and $P_1, P_2, P_3, \dots$ be the perimeters of $S_1, S_2, S_3, \dots$ respectively, then $\lim_{n \to \infty} \frac{A_1 + A_2 + A_3 + \dots + A_n}{P_1 + P_2 + P_3 + \dots + P_n}$ is equal to

(a) $\frac{K}{2(2+\sqrt{2})}$ (b) $\frac{K}{2(2-\sqrt{2})}$ (c) $\frac{2}{K(2+\sqrt{2})}$ (d) $\frac{2}{K}(2+\sqrt{2})$

2. The value of λ for which the roots of the equation $4x^2 - 20\lambda x + 25\lambda^2 + 15\lambda - 66 = 0$ are greater than 2 lies in the interval

(a) $\left(-\infty, \frac{22}{5}\right)$ (b) $(2, \infty)$
(c) $\left(2, \frac{22}{5}\right)$ (d) None of these

3. The number of integral values of K for which the equation $\sqrt{3}\sin x + \sqrt{2\sqrt{3}}\cos x = -K^2 + 4K + 14 + \sin x$ has infinite solution, is

(a) 3 (b) 5 (c) 4 (d) 2

4. Let $C_1 : x^2 + y^2 = 1$, $C_2 : (x-10)^2 + y^2 = 1$ and $C_3 : x^2 + y^2 - 10x - 42y + 457 = 0$ be three circles. A circle C has been drawn to touch the circles C_1 and C_2 externally and C_3 internally. Now, if the circles C_1, C_2 and C_3 start rolling on the circumference of circle C in anticlockwise direction with constant speed, then the locus of centroid of the triangle formed by joining the centres of rolling circles C_1, C_2 and C_3 is

(a) $(x-5)^2 + (y+12)^2 = 25$
(b) $(x+5)^2 + (y-12)^2 = (5)^2$
(c) $(x-5)^2 + (y-12)^2 = 25$
(d) $(x-5)^2 + (y-12)^2 = 5$

Section 2

- This section contains **SIX (06)** questions.
- Each question has **FOUR** options (a), (b), (c) and (d). **ONE OR MORE THAN ONE** of these four option(s) is (are) correct answer(s).
- For each question, choose the option(s) corresponding to (all) the correct answer(s).
- Answer to each question will be evaluated according to the following marking scheme:

Full Marks : +4 If ONLY (all) the correct option(s) is(are) chosen;
Partial Marks : +3 If all the four options are correct but ONLY three options are chosen;
Partial Marks : +2 If three or more options are correct but ONLY two options are chosen, both of which are correct;
Partial Marks : +1 If two or more options are correct but ONLY one option is chosen and it is a correct option;
Zero Marks : 0 If unanswered;
Negative Marks : – 2 In all other cases.

- For example, in a question, if (a), (b) and (d) are the ONLY three options corresponding to correct answers, then choosing ONLY (a), (b) and (d) will get +4 marks; ONLY (a) and (b) will get +2 marks; choosing ONLY (a) and (d) will get +2 marks; choosing ONLY (b) and (d) will get +2 marks; choosing ONLY (a) will get +1 mark; choosing ONLY (b) will get +1 mark; choosing ONLY (d) will get +1 mark; choosing no option(s) (i.e. the question is unanswered) will get 0 marks and choosing any other option(s) will get – 2 marks.

5. If $(x-a)\cos\theta + y\sin\theta = (x-a)\cos\phi + y\sin\phi = a$ and $\tan(\theta/2) - \tan(\phi/2) = 2b$, then

(a) $y^2 = 2bx - (1-a^2)x^2$ (b) $y^2 = 2ax - (1-b^2)x^2$

(c) $\tan\frac{\phi}{2} = \frac{1}{x}(y+bx)$ (d) $\tan\frac{\theta}{2} = \frac{1}{x}(y-bx)$

6. If z is the complex number satisfying $|z-3-4i| \le 10$ and

$\alpha = \sin^{-1}(\sin|z|_{max}), \beta = \cos^{-1}\left[\cos\left(-\frac{|z|_{max}+|z|_{min}}{3}\right)\right]$,

then

(a) $\sin^2\alpha + \cos^2 3\beta = 1$ (b) $\sin^2\alpha + \cos^2 3\beta = -1$

(c) $\alpha - 3\beta = \pi$ (d) $\alpha - 3\beta = -\pi$

7. Let $f: N \to R$ and $g: N \to R$ be two functions and $f(1) = 0.8$, $g(1) = 0.6$, $f(n+1) = f(n)\cos g(n) - g(n)\sin g(n)$ and $g(n+1) = f(n)\sin g(n) + g(n)\cos g(n)$ for $n \ge 1$ and also let $h(n) = g(1) + g(2) + g(3) + \ldots + g(n)$, then

(a) $\lim_{n\to\infty} [f(n) + g(n)] = 0$

(b) $h(n)$ is monotonically decreasing

(c) $\lim_{n\to\infty} [f(n) + g(n)] = -1$

(d) $h(n)$ is monotonically increasing.

8. Let X, Y, Z be three events. If the probability of occuring exactly one event out of X and Y is $(1-K)$, out of Y and Z is $(1-2K)$, out of Z and X is $(1-K)$ and that of occuring three events simultaneously is K^2, then the probability that atleast one out of X, Y and Z will occur, is

(a) less than $\frac{1}{2}$ (b) greater than $\frac{1}{2}$

(c) less than 2/3 (d) None of these

9. The system of equations $\log_{10}(2000ab) - \log_{10} a \cdot \log_{10} b = 4$, $\log_{10}(2bc) - \log_{10} b \cdot \log_{10} c = 1$ and $\log_{10}(ca) - \log_{10} c \cdot \log_{10} a = 0$, has two solutions (a_1, b_1, c_1) and (a_2, b_2, c_2), then

(a) $a_1 + a_2 = 101$ (b) $c_1 c_2 = 100$

(c) $b_1 + b_2 = 25$ (d) $a_1 a_2 = 100$

10. In the given figure vertices of ΔABC lie on $y = f(x) = ax^2 + bx + c$. The ΔABC is right angled isosceles triangle whose hyptotenuse $AC = 4\sqrt{2}$ units, then choose the correct option (s) :

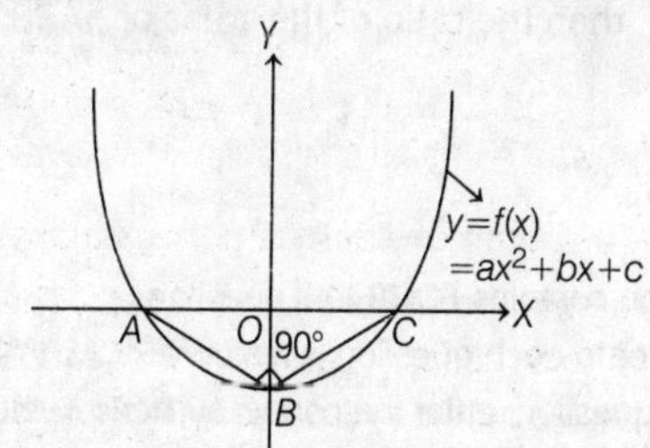

(a) $f(x) = \frac{x^2}{2\sqrt{2}} - 2\sqrt{2}$ (b) Minimum value of $f(x)$ is $-2\sqrt{2}$

(c) $f(x) = \frac{x^2}{2} - \sqrt{2}$ (d) Minimum value of $f(x)$ is $2\sqrt{2}$

Section 3

- This section contains **SEVEN (07)** questions.
- The answer to each question is a **SINGLE-DIGIT INTEGER** ranging from 0 to 9, both inclusive.
- For each question, enter the correct integer corresponding to the answer using the mouse and the on-screen virtual numeric keypad in the place designated to enter the answer.
- Answer to each question will be evaluated according to the following marking scheme:

Full Marks : + 3 If ONLY the correct integer is entered;

Zero Marks : 0 If the question is unanswered.

Negative Marks : – 1 In all other cases.

11. The line $x + y = a$ intersects the X-axis and the Y-axis at A and B respectively. Let R be any point on OB and RS be the perpendicular on the line AB. If area of ΔRSA is $\frac{3}{8}$th of the area of ΔAOB and the ratio $AS : SB = k$, then k is equal to _____

12. The sum of the terms of an infinitely decreasing GP is equal to the greatest value of the function on $f(x) = x^3 + 3x - 9$ on the interval $[-5, 3]$ and the difference between the first and second terms is $f'(0)$. If the common ratio of the progression is r, then $9\left[7r\sin^{-1}\left(\frac{1}{\sqrt{3r}}\right)\right]^{2\log_{\frac{7\pi}{6}} r}$ is equal to _____

13. A variable parabola is drawn through (– 5, 0) and (5, 0) such that its directrix always touches the circle $x^2 + y^2 = 36$. If the locus of the focus of the parabola is $\frac{x^2}{k^2} + \frac{y^2}{11} = 1$, then the value of k is ____

14. The value of λ (where, $\lambda \in N$) for which $\sum_{\mu=1}^{n} f(\lambda + \mu) = 16(2^n - 1)$, where the function '$f$' satisfies $f(x + y) = f(x) \cdot f(y)$ for all $x, y \in N$ and further $f(1) = 2$, is ____

15. If $R_n = \sum_{r=0}^{n-3} {}^nC_r \cdot {}^nC_{r+3}$ and n_1, n_2 are two values of n satisfying $5R_n = 3R_{n+1}$, then the value of $[(1 - n_1)(1 - n_2)]$, where [·] represent greatest integer function, is ____

16. A straight line cuts the X-axis at point $A(1, 0)$ and Y-axis at point B, such that $\angle OAB = \alpha$ (where, $\alpha > \pi/4$). Point C is middle point of AB, if B' is a mirror image of point B w.r.t. the line OC and C' is a mirror image of point C w.r.t. the line BB', then the ratio of the areas of $\Delta ABB'$ and $\Delta BB'C'$ is ____.

17. Consider a function f whose domain is $[-3, 4]$ and range is $[-2, 2]$ with following graph (see figure). Also consider domain and range of $\phi(x) = f(|x|)$ are $[\alpha, \beta]$ and $[\gamma, \delta]$ respectively, such that $(\beta - \alpha + \gamma + \delta) = \lambda$ as well as $\psi(x) = \left| f(x) - \frac{3}{2} \right|$ has range $[p, q]$ and n is the number of real solutions of $\psi(x) = \frac{1}{4}$ such that $(n + p + 2q) = \mu$. If

$$k = \frac{\text{(Difference of unit's and ten's place digits in the value of } \lambda)}{\text{(Sum of digits in the value of } \mu)},$$ then

$[2 \sin k + \tan(2k)]$ is equal to ____

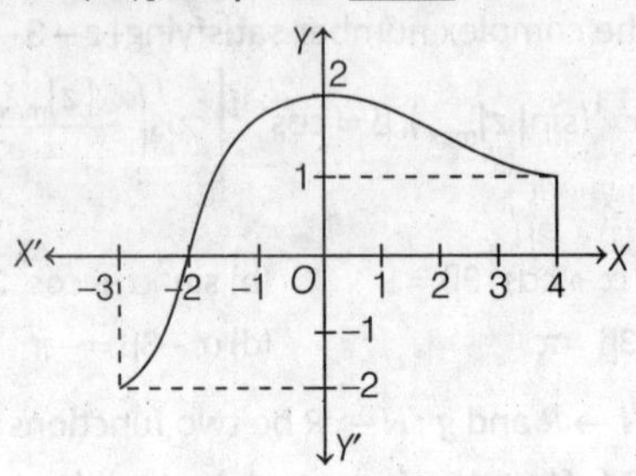

Section 4

- This section contains **FOUR (04)** questions.
- The answer to each question is a **NUMERICAL VALUE**.
- For each question, enter the correct numerical value of the answer using the mouse and the on-screen virtual numeric keypad in the place designated to enter the answer. If the numerical value has more than two decimal places, **truncate/round-off** the value to **TWO** decimal places.
- Answer to each question will be evaluated according to the following marking scheme:
  Full Marks : +3 if ONLY the correct numerical value is entered;
  Zero Marks : 0 In all other cases.

18. If $\sum_{n=0}^{\infty} \frac{\sin(nx)}{3^n} = \frac{a + b\sqrt{b}}{c}$ and $\sin x = \frac{1}{3}$, where $0 < x < \frac{\pi}{2}$, then the value of $a + b + c$, where a, b, c are positive integers, is ____

19. Consider the word P = TERRORIST, then the number of four letter words that can be made using only the letters from the word P, if each word must contains atleast one vowel, is ____

20. The normal at any point (x_1, y_1) of curve is a line perpendicular to tangent at (x_1, y_1). In case of parabola $y^2 = 4ax$, the equation of normal is $y = mx - 2am - am^3$ (where, m is the slope of normal). In case of rectangular hyperbola $xy = c^2$, the equation of normal at $\left(ct, \frac{c}{t}\right)$ is $xt^3 - yt - ct^4 + c = 0$ and the shortest distance between any two curve always exist along the common normal. If normal at (5, 3) of hyperbola $xy - y - 2x - 2 = 0$ intersects the curve again at $(\alpha, \beta - 29)$, then $\frac{\beta}{4\alpha}$ is ____

21. Let $A = 3^{\alpha} 2^{\beta} 5^{\gamma}$ where α, β and γ are natural numbers and $\{\sqrt{A}\} = 0$, where {} denotes fractional part function. Also $f\{x\} = x^3 - k_1 x^2 + k_2 x - 8$ and $f(x) = 0$ has the roots. The number of divisors of A is ____

Section 5

- This section contains **TWO (02)** Matching List Sets.
- Each set has **ONE** Multiple Choice Question.
- Each set has **TWO** lists: **List-I** and **List-II**.
- **List-I** has **Four** entries (I), (II), (III) and (IV) and **List-II** has **Five** entries (P), (Q), (R), (S) and (T).
- **FOUR** options are given in each Multiple Choice Question based on **List-I** and **List-II** and **ONLY ONE** of these four options satisfies the condition asked in the Multiple Choice Question.
- Answer to each question will be evaluated according to the following marking scheme:

Full Marks : +3 ONLY if the option corresponding to the correct combination is chosen;
Zero Marks : 0 If none of the options is chosen (i.e. the question is unanswered);
Negative Marks : –1 In all other cases.

22.

	List-I		List-II
I.	Let f be a function from the set of positive integers to the set of real number i.e. $f: N \to R$, such that $f(1) = 1$, $f(1) + 2f(2) \quad + 3f(3) + ... \quad nf(n) = n(n+1) f(n)$ for $n \geq 2$, then the value of $\frac{1}{f(6)}$ must be	P.	$\frac{2}{3}$
II.	An ellipse of eccentricity $\frac{2\sqrt{2}}{3}$ is inscribed in a circle and a point within the circle is chosen at random. The probability that this point lies outside the ellipse is	Q.	10
III.	If maximum and minimum value of $\phi(x) = {}^{16-x}C_{2x-1} + {}^{20-3x}C_{4x-5}$ are 'M' and 'm', respectively.	R.	12
IV.	Let $f(x, y)$ be a periodic function satisfying $f(x, y) = f(2x + 2y, 2y - 2x)\ \forall$ x, y and $g(x) = f(2^x, 0)$, then the period of $g(x)$ must be	S.	$\frac{3}{2}$
		T.	1

The correct option is
(a) (I) $\to$ (R); (II) $\to$ (P); (III) $\to$ (T); (IV) $\to$ (R)
(b) (I) $\to$ (R); (II) $\to$ (T); (III) $\to$ (Q); (IV) $\to$ (Q)
(c) (I) $\to$ (Q); (II) $\to$ (S); (III) $\to$ (P); (IV) $\to$ (T)
(d) (I) $\to$ (Q); (II) $\to$ (Q); (III) $\to$ (S); (IV) $\to$ (P)

23.

	List-I		List-II
I.	If α and β are the roots of the equation $x^2 + \lambda x \quad + \mu = 0$ and $x^{14244} + \lambda^{7122}$ $x^{7122} + \mu^{7122} = 0$ and if $\frac{\alpha}{\beta}, \frac{\beta}{\alpha}$ are the roots of $x^m + 1 + (x+1)^m = 0$, then the value of $\frac{m}{7122}$ must be qual to	P.	3
II.	The number of values of θ in the interval $\left(-\frac{\pi}{2}, \frac{\pi}{2}\right)$ satisfying the equation $(\sqrt{3})^{\sec^2\theta} = \tan^4\theta + 2\tan^2\theta$ is	Q.	4
III.	The number of real roots of the equation, $e^{4x} + e^{3x} - 4e^{2x} + e^x + 1 = 0$ is	R.	2
IV.	Let $A_0A_1A_2A_3A_4A_5$ be a regular hexagon inscribed in a unit circle with centre at the origin. Then, the product of the lengths of the line segments A_0A_1, A_0A_2 and A_0A_4 is	S.	0
		T.	1

The correct option is
(a) (I) $\to$ (S); (II) $\to$ (Q); (III) $\to$ (P); (IV) $\to$ (R)
(b) (I) $\to$ (R); (II) $\to$ (T); (III) $\to$ (P); (IV) $\to$ (S)
(c) (I) $\to$ (P); (II) $\to$ (Q); (III) $\to$ (T); (IV) $\to$ (Q)
(d) (I) $\to$ (T); (II) $\to$ (R); (III) $\to$ (T); (IV) $\to$ (P)

Answers

1 (a)	2 (c)	3 (d)	4 (c)	5 (b,c,d)	6 (a,d)	7 (c,d)	8 (b)	9 (a,b,c,d)	10 (a,b)
11 (3)	12 (4)	13 (6)	14 (3)	15 (8)	16 (2)	17 (0)	18 (22)	19 (588)	20 (5)
21 (27)	22 (a)	23 (d)							

See detailed solutions on page no. 217

PART TEST 03

(Based on Complete Class 12 Syllabus)

JEE Main Test Paper

Mathematics

*Instructions

- This question paper contains of 30 Questions of Mathematics, divided into two sections : **Section I** Objective Type Questions and **Section II** Numerical Type Questions.
- Section I contains 20 Objective questions and all Questions are cumpulsory (Marking Scheme : Correct + 4, Incorrect − 1).
- Section II contains 10 Numerical value questions out of which only 5 questions are to be attempted (Marking Scheme : Correct + 4, Incorrect 0).

Section I *Multiple Choice Questions*

1. If $\phi(x) = \int_{x^2}^{x^3} \frac{1}{\ln t} dt$, where $x > 0$, then

(a) $\phi(x)$ is minimum at $x = 1$ (b) $\phi(x)$ is maximum at $x = 1$
(c) $\phi(x)$ is neither maximum nor minimum at $x = 1$ but an in increasing function, $\forall x \in R$
(d) $\phi(x)$ is an increasing function, $\forall x \in R^+$ only

2. If $D(x) = \begin{vmatrix} x-2 & (x-1)^2 & x^3 \\ x-1 & x^2 & (x+1)^3 \\ x & (x+1)^2 & (x+2)^3 \end{vmatrix}$, then the coefficient of x in $D(x)$ is

(a) −2 (b) 2 (c) 10 (d) None of these

3. Let $f(x) = \begin{cases} ae^{ax}, & -\infty < x \le 0 \\ x^2 + 4x + 2b, & 0 < x < \infty \end{cases}$ and $g(x) = \sin|bx + a - 2|, x \in R$. If both $f(x)$ and $g(x)$ are differentiable at $x = 0$, then $g(x)$ is non-differentiable at

(a) $x = -\frac{\pi}{4}$ (b) $x = -4$ (c) $x = 4$ (d) $x = \frac{\pi}{4}$

4. The value of $\int_{e}^{e^{7122}} \frac{1}{x}\left(1 + \frac{1 - \ln x}{\ln x \cdot \ln\left(\frac{x}{\ln x}\right)}\right) dx$ is

(a) $2009 - \ln[2010 - \ln 2010]$ (b) $7122 - [\ln(7121 - \ln 7122)]$
(c) $7121 - \ln[7122 + \ln 7122]$ (d) $7121 - [\ln(7122 - \ln(7122))]$

5. The area bounded by $y = x^2$, $y = [x + 1]$, $0 \le x \le 2$ and the Y-axis, where $[\cdot]$ denotes GIF, is

(a) $\frac{4\sqrt{2}}{3} - 1$ (b) $\frac{4\sqrt{2}}{3} + 1$ (c) $\frac{8}{3}$ (d) None of these

6. Let $a_k = k({}^7C_k)$, $b_k = (7-k)({}^7C_k)$ and $A_k = \begin{bmatrix} a_k & 0 \\ 0 & b_k \end{bmatrix}$. If $\sum_{k=0}^{7} A_k = \begin{bmatrix} a & 0 \\ 0 & b \end{bmatrix}$, then the value of $\frac{a+b}{7}$ is equal to

(a) 7 (b) 128 (c) 896 (d) None of these

7. If $\sin^{-1}\lambda + \sin^{-1}\mu + \sin^{-1}\delta = \frac{3\pi}{2}$ and $\phi(2) = 2$, $\phi(x+y) = \phi(x)\cdot\phi(y)\ \forall\ x, y \in R$, then $\lambda^{\phi(2)} + \mu^{\phi(4)} + \delta^{\phi(6)} - \frac{3[\lambda^{\phi(2)}\cdot\mu^{\phi(4)}\cdot\delta^{\phi(6)}]}{\lambda^{\phi(2)} + \mu^{\phi(4)} + \delta^{\phi(6)}}$ equals

(a) 4 (b) 10 (c) 2 (d) Not defined

8. If the system of equations $x + y - 1 = 0$, $2x - y - c = 0$ and $-bx + 3by - c = 0$, where $c < 1$, is consistent, then the possible real values of b are given by

(a) $b \in \left(-\frac{3}{4}, 3\right)$ (b) $b \in \left(-\frac{3}{2}, 4\right)$ (c) $b \in \left(-3, \frac{3}{4}\right)$ (d) None of these

9. If f is a differentiable function for all real x and $f'(x) \le 5$, $\forall x \in R$. If $f(2) = 0$ and $f(5) = 15$, then $f(3)$ is equal to

(a) 0 (b) 2 (c) 15 (d) 5

10. A relation R in the set of non-zero complex numbers is defined by $z_1 R z_2 \Leftrightarrow \frac{z_1 - z_2}{z_1 + z_2}$ is real, then R is

(a) reflexive (b) symmetric (c) transitive (d) equivalence

11. The equation of the line passing through (2, 3, −1) and lying in the plane $2x + y - 5z - 12 = 0$ and perpendicular to this line $2x + y - 5z - 12 = 0 = 4x - 3y + 7z$ is

(a) $\frac{x-2}{3} = \frac{y-3}{1} = \frac{z+1}{-1}$ (b) $\frac{x-2}{3} = \frac{y-3}{-1} = \frac{z+1}{1}$

(c) $\frac{x-2}{8} = \frac{y-3}{3} = \frac{z+1}{7}$ (d) None of these

12. Let P be a point on $x^2 = 4y$ that is nearest to the point $A(0, 4)$, then coordinates of P are

(a) $(1,2)$ (b) $(0, \sqrt{8})$ (c) $(\sqrt{8}, 2)$ (d) $(2, \sqrt{8})$

13. The set of values of λ, so that for all real x, then vectors $\mathbf{u} = \hat{\mathbf{i}} + \lambda\hat{\mathbf{j}} + \lambda x^2\hat{\mathbf{k}}$ and $\mathbf{v} = 5\hat{\mathbf{i}} + 2x\hat{\mathbf{j}} + \lambda\hat{\mathbf{k}}$ include an obtuse angle between them, is

(a) $(-\infty, 0]$ (b) $[0, \infty)$ (c) ϕ (d) $R - \{0\}$

14. If $f(x) = \int \frac{5x^8 + 7x^6}{(x^2 + 1 + 2x^7)^2} dx$ and $f(0) = 0$, then the value of $f(1)$ is

(a) $-\frac{1}{2}$ (b) $\frac{1}{4}$ (c) $\frac{1}{2}$ (d) $-\frac{1}{4}$

15. Let $f : R^+ \to \{-1, 0, 1\}$ defined by $f(x) = \text{sgn}(x - x^4 + x^7 - x^8 - 1)$, where sgn denotes signum function. Then, $f(x)$ is

(a) many-one and onto (b) one-one and onto
(c) many-one and into (d) one-one and into

16. Let $f : R \to R$ defined by $f(x) = x^3 + 3x + 1$ and g is the inverse of f, then the value of $g''(5)$ is equal to

(a) $-\frac{1}{6}$ (b) $-\frac{6}{8}$ (c) $-\frac{1}{96}$ (d) $-\frac{1}{36}$

17. A is one of 6 horses entered for a race and is to be ridden by one of two jockeys B and C. It is 2 to 1 that B rides A, in which case all the horses are equally likely to win. If C rides A, his chances of winning is tripled. What are the odds against winning of A?

(a) 13 : 5 (b) 5 : 18 (c) 5 : 13 (d) None of these

18. The solution of the differential equation

$$f(x)\frac{dy}{dx} = (f(x))^2 + f(x)\cdot y + f'(x)\cdot y \text{ is}$$

(a) $y = f(x) + Ce^x$ (b) $y = -f(x) + Ce^x f(x)$
(c) $y = -C f(x) + e^x$ (d) None of thee

19. Let $f(x) = (pq - q^2 - 2)x + \int_0^x (\sin^4\theta + \cos^4\theta)d\theta$ is a decreasing function of x for all real values, q being any real number independent of x, if

(a) $|p| \le 2$ (b) $p \in (0, 2)$ (c) $p \in (-2, 0)$ (d) None of these

20. Electric current C, measured by a galvanometer, is given by the equation $C = K \cdot \tan\theta$, where K is a constant. Then, the percentage error in the current corresponding to an error 0.7 percent in the measurement of θ when $\theta = 45°$, is

(a) 1.4 (b) 2.2 (c) 2.8 (d) 1.1

Section II *Numerical Value Questions*

21. If the function $f(x)$ defined as $f(x) = \begin{cases} -\frac{x^2}{2}, & x \le 0 \\ x^n \sin\frac{1}{x}, & x > 0 \end{cases}$ is continuous but not derivable at $x = 0$, then the number of integral values of n is ....

22. If the planes $x - cy - bz = 0$, $cx - y + az = 0$ and $bx + ay - z = 0$ pass through a straight line, then the value of $a^2 + b^2 + c^2 + 2abc$ is ....

23. A solid rectangular bricks is to be made from 1 cubic feet of clay. The bricks must be three times as long as it is wide. The width of bricks for which it will have minimum surface area is a. Then, the value of $9a^3$ is ....

24. If $I_n = \int_0^1 (1 + x + x^2 + ... + x^{n-1})$ $(1 + 3x + 5x^2 + ... + (2n-3)x^{n-2} + (2n-1)x^{n-1})dx$, $n \in N$, then the value of $\sqrt{I_{28}}$ is ....

25. Let $\mathbf{a}$, $\mathbf{b}$ and $\mathbf{c}$ be three vectors having magnitude 1, 2 and 3 respectively, satisfy the relation $|[\mathbf{a}\,\mathbf{b}\,\mathbf{c}]| = 6$. Then, the value of $|(\mathbf{a} \times \mathbf{c}) \cdot \mathbf{d}|^2 + |(\mathbf{a} \times \mathbf{c}) \times \mathbf{d}|^2$, where $\mathbf{d}$ is unit vector, is ....

26. The sum of values of p for which the equation $x + y + z = 1$; $x + 2y + 4z = p$ and $x + 4y + 10z = p^2$ have a solution, is ....

27. A number is selected at random from the first twenty-five natural numbers. If it is a composite number, then it is divided by 5. But, if it is not a composite number, it is divided by 2. The probability that there will no remainder on the division, is ....

28. If $g(x) = \lim_{m \to \infty} \frac{x^m f(x) + h(x) + 3}{2x^m + 4x + 1}$ when $x \ne 1$ and $g(1) = e^3$ such that $f(x)$, $g(x)$ and $h(x)$ are continuous function at $x = 1$, then the value of $5f(1) - 2h(1)$ is ....

29. The eccentricity of the ellipse $3x^2 + 4y^2 = 12$ is changed at the rate of 0.1/sec. The time at which it will touch the auxiliary circle, is ....

30. Let $f(x) = \sin^{-1} x_1 + \cos^{-1} x_2 + \sin^{-1} x_3 + \cos^{-1} x_4 + ... + \sin^{-1} x_{2n-1} + \cos^{-} x_{2n}$ and $g(x) = \cos^{-1} x_1 + \sin^{-1} x_2 + \cos^{-1} x_3 + \sin^{-1} x_4 + ... \cos^{-1} x_{2n-1} + \sin^{-1} x_{2n}$, where $n \in N$. If the sum of the least value of $f(x)$ and the greatest value of $g(x)$ be 8π, then the value of n is ....

Answers

1	(c)	2	(a)	3	(b)	4	(d)	5	(a)	6	(b)	7	(c)	8	(a)	9	(d)	10	(d)
11	(b)	12	(c)	13	(a)	14	(b)	15	(c)	16	(d)	17	(a)	18	(b)	19	(a)	20	(d)
21	(1)	22	(1)	23	(2)	24	(28)	25	(9)	26	(3)	27	(0.20)	28	(6)	29	(5)	30	(8)

See detailed solutions on page no. 223

PART TEST 04

(Based on Complete Class 12 Syllabus)

JEE Advanced Test Paper

Mathematics

Section 1

- This section contains **FOUR (04)** questions.
- Each question has **FOUR** options (a), (b), (c) and (d). **ONLY ONE** of these four options is the correct answer.
- For each question, choose the option corresponding to the correct answer.
- Answer to each question will be evaluated according to the following marking scheme:

Full Marks : +3 If ONLY the correct option is chosen;
Zero Marks : 0 If none of the options is chosen (i.e. the question is unanswered);
Negative Marks : – 1 In all other cases.

1. If $\sum_{r=1}^{10} \tan^{-1}\left(\frac{3}{9r^2+3r-1}\right) = \cot^{-1}\left(\frac{x}{\mu}\right)$, where λ and μ are co-prime, then the value of $2\lambda + \mu$ is

(a) 32 (b) 82
(c) 4 (d) None of these

2. Let $f(x)$ be a differentiable function satisfying $f(x) + f\left(x+\frac{1}{2}\right) = 1, \forall x \in R$ and $g(x) = \int_0^x f(t)\,dt$.

If $g(1) = 1$, then the value of $\sum_{n=2}^{\infty}\left(\frac{8}{\sum_{k=1}^{n}(g(x+k^2) - g(x+k))}\right)$ is

(a) 10 (b) $\sqrt{6}$ (c) 6 (d) Does not exist

3. Vectors **a**, **b** and **c** are three unit vectors and **c** is equally inclined to both **a** and **b**.

Let $\mathbf{a} \times (\mathbf{b} \times \mathbf{c}) + \mathbf{b} \times (\mathbf{c} \times \mathbf{a}) = (4 + x^2)\mathbf{b} - (4x\cos^2\theta)\mathbf{a}$.

Then, where **a** and **b** are non-collinear vectors and $x > 0$).

(a) $x = 2, \theta = 0°$ (b) $x = 2, \theta = \frac{\pi}{2}$

(c) $x = 1, \theta = \pi$ (d) $x = 1, \theta = \frac{\pi}{2}$

4. A fair coin is tossed n times, then choose the correct option.

(a) The probability of getting tails an odd number of times is $\frac{1}{2}$ when n is odd

(b) The probability of getting atleast one tail is more than 0.99 for $n = 7$.

(c) Both (a) and (b)

(d) None of the above

Section 2

- This section contains **SIX (06)** questions.
- Each question has **FOUR** options (a), (b), (c) and (d). **ONE OR MORE THAN ONE** of these four option(s) is (are) correct answer(s).
- For each question, choose the option(s) corresponding to (all) the correct answer(s).
- Answer to each question will be evaluated according to the following marking scheme:

Full Marks : +4 If ONLY (all) the correct option(s) is(are) chosen;
Partial Marks : +3 If all the four options are correct but ONLY three options are chosen;
Partial Marks : +2 If three or more options are correct but ONLY two options are chosen, both of which are correct;
Partial Marks : +1 If two or more options are correct but ONLY one option is chosen and it is a correct option;
Zero Marks : 0 If unanswered;
Negative Marks : – 2 In all other cases.

- For example, in a question, if (a), (b) and (d) are the ONLY three options corresponding to correct answers, then choosing ONLY (a), (b) and (d) will get +4 marks; ONLY (a) and (b) will get +2 marks; choosing ONLY (a) and (d) will get +2 marks; choosing ONLY (b) and (d) will get +2 marks; choosing ONLY (a) will get +1 mark; choosing ONLY (b) will get +1 mark; choosing ONLY (d) will get +1 mark; choosing no option(s) (i.e. the question is unanswered) will get 0 marks and choosing any other option(s) will get – 2 marks.

5. Let f be a non-constant differentiable function satisfying $f(xy) = f(x)\cdot f(y)\ \forall\ x, y \in R$ and $f(1+x) = 1 + x(1+g(x))$, where $\lim_{x\to 0} g(x) = 0$ and $f(1) = 1$, then which of the following statement(s) is (are) correct?

(a) Maximum value of $f(x)$ in [0, 1] is 1

(b) The function $\frac{f(x)}{x}$ is continuous function

(c) $\frac{1}{f(x)}$ is unbounded

(d) $\lim_{x\to 0} (1+f(x))^{1/x} = \frac{e}{2}$

6. A ray of light comes along line L and strikes the plane mirror kept along the plane $P = 0$ at B. $A(2, 1, 6)$ is a point on the line L whose image about $P = 0$ is A'. It is given that line L is $\frac{x-2}{3} = \frac{y-1}{4} = \frac{z-6}{5}$ and plane $P = 0$ is $x + y - 2z = 3$, then

(a) the coordinates of A' are $(6, 5, -2)$

(b) equation of the reflected ray is $\frac{x+10}{4} = \frac{y-5}{4} = \frac{z+2}{3}$

(c) the coordinates of A' are (6, 5, 2)

(d) equation of the reflected ray is $\frac{x+10}{4} = \frac{y+15}{5} = \frac{z+14}{3}$

7. Let $\mathbf{r} = \sin x\,(\mathbf{a}\times\mathbf{b}) + \cos y(\mathbf{b}\times\mathbf{c}) + 2(\mathbf{c}\times\mathbf{a})$, where $\mathbf{a}$, $\mathbf{b}$ and $\mathbf{c}$ are three non-coplanar vector. It is given that $\mathbf{r}$ is perpendicular to $\mathbf{a}+\mathbf{b}+\mathbf{c}$. The possible value (s) of $x^2 + y^2$ is/are

(a) $\frac{5\pi^2}{4}$ (b) $\frac{37\pi^2}{4}$ (c) $\frac{73\pi^2}{4}$ (d) $\frac{5\pi^2}{2}$

8. If $g: R \to R$ is one-one onto and differentiable function and graph of $y = g(x)$ is symmetrical about the point (4, 0), then

(a) $g^{-1}(2022) + g^{-1}(-2022) = 8$

(b) $\int_{-2010}^{2018} g(x)\,dx = 0$

(c) If $g'(-100) > 0$, then the roots of $x^2 - g'(10)x - g'(10) = 0$ may be non-real

(d) If $g'(10) = 20$, then $g'(-2) = 20$

9. Let B_1, B_2 and B_3 be three boxes such that initially B_1 contains $2m$ ball (m white ball and m black balls), while B_2 and B_3 are empty. Now from B_1, m balls are transferred to B_2 and remaining m balls are transferred to B_3, number of white and black balls in each being unknown. Then, one ball is drawn from each box B_2 and B_3. Let $P(m)$ denotes the probability that these two drawn balls are of the same colour and it is found that $P(m) > \frac{1000}{2017}$, then possible value(s) of m is (are)

(a) 50 (b) 80

(c) 60 (d) 70

10. Let $f(x) = (x+1)\ln(1+x)$, $g(x) = x + \frac{x^2}{2}$ and $h(x) = x + \frac{x^2}{2} - \frac{x^3}{6}$, then for $x > 0$

(a) $f(x) < g(x)$ (b) $f(x) > h(x)$

(c) $f(x) > g(x)$ (d) $f(x) < h(x)$

Section 3

- This section contains **SEVEN (07)** questions.
- The answer to each question is a **SINGLE-DIGIT INTEGER** ranging from 0 to 9, both inclusive.
- For each question, enter the correct integer corresponding to the answer using the mouse and the on-screen virtual numeric keypad in the place designated to enter the answer.
- Answer to each question will be evaluated according to the following marking scheme:

Full Marks : + 3 If ONLY the correct integer is entered;

Zero Marks : 0 If the question is unanswered.

Negative Marks : – 1 In all other cases.

11. The solution of $x^2 \cdot \frac{dy}{dx} - xy = 1 + \cos\left(\frac{y}{x}\right)$ is $\tan\left(\frac{y}{px}\right) = c - \frac{1}{qx^2}$, where c is constant, then the value of $\frac{p+q}{pq}$ is ____

12. Consider the function $f(x)$, a fourth degree polynomial such that $\lim_{x\to -1}\frac{f(x)}{(x+1)^3} = 1$ and $f'''(0) = 0$, then the sum of the maximum value of $f(x)$ and the subnormal of the curve $y = f(x)$ where it cuts the Y-axis, is ____

13. Let $A=\begin{bmatrix} \sec x & \cos x & \sec^2 x+\cot x\cdot \operatorname{cosec} x \\ \cos^2 x & \cos^2 x & \operatorname{cosec}^2 x \\ 1 & \cos^2 x & \cos^2 x \end{bmatrix}$

where, $x\in\left(0,\frac{\pi}{2}\right)$, then the value of $|AA^T(A^{-1})^2|$ is (where $|B|$ is determinant of matrix B) ______

14. The solution of the differential equation $(x-1)\,dy+y\,dx=x(x-1)\cdot y^{1/3}dx$ is given by $y^{2/3}+k_1(x-1)^{-2/3}+\frac{1}{4}(x-1)^2+\frac{2}{k_2}(x-1)$, then the value of k_2 should be ______

15. Let $\alpha+\beta=1, 2\alpha^2+2\beta^2=1$ and $f(x)$ be a continuous function such that $f(2+x)+f(x)=2$, for all $x\in[0,2]$ and $p=\int_0^4 f(x)\,dx-4$, $q=\frac{\alpha}{\beta}$. Then, the least positive integral values of 'a' for which the equation $ax^2-bx+c=0$ has both roots lies between p and q, where $a,b,c\in N$ is ______

16. Sum of how many terms of the sequence $\cot^{-1}3+\cot^{-1}7+\cot^{-1}13+\cot^{-1}21\ldots$ is $\frac{1}{2}\cos^{-1}\left(\frac{24}{145}\right)$?

17. If $\int\frac{2}{f(x)}dx=\ln(f(x))^2+c$ and $f(2)=2$, then number of solution(s) of the equation $\operatorname{sgn}(\ln(f(|x|)))=1-x^2$ is ______

Section 4

- This section contains **FOUR (04)** questions.
- The answer to each question is a **NUMERICAL VALUE.**
- For each question, enter the correct numerical value of the answer using the mouse and the on-screen virtual numeric keypad in the place designated to enter the answer. If the numerical value has more than two decimal places, **truncate/round-off** the value to **TWO** decimal places.
- Answer to each question will be evaluated according to the following marking scheme:
  Full Marks : +3 ONLY if the correct numerical value is entered;
- Zero Marks : 0 In all other cases.

18. Consider the following three planes

$\pi_1: 2x+y+z=1$

$\pi_2: x-y+z=2$

$\pi_3: kx-y+3z=5$

The three planes intersect each other at point R on XOY plane and at point S on YOZ plane. O is origin. If the coordinates of point P situated at minimum distance from point O on the line RS are (a,b,c), then the value of $\left[\frac{\frac{a}{2}-180b+2c}{100}\right]$ is ______

19. If $\lambda(x)=x+\int_0^1 t(x+t)\cdot\lambda(t)\,dt$, then the value of the definite integral $\int_0^1\lambda(x)\,dx$ can be expressed in the form of rational as $\frac{a}{b}$ (where a and b are coprime), then value of $a+b$ is ______

20. Given, $m,n\in\{0, 1, 2, 3, 4, \ldots, 19, 20\}$. Consider the system of equations

$$x+y+z=4$$
$$2x+y+3z=6$$
$$x+2y+mz=n$$

Let P : denotes the number of ordered pairs (m,n). So that the system of equations has unique solution.

Q: Denotes the number of ordered pairs (m,n). So that the system of equations has no solution.

R: Denotes the number of ordered pairs (m,n). So that the system of equations has infinite solutions.

The value of $\frac{P}{Q\cdot R}$ is ______

21. Let us consider $I_s=\int_0^\infty e^{-t}\cdot t^{s-1}dt, (s>0)$ and $I_m\cdot I_n=\frac{\pi}{\sin(m\pi)}$, where $0<p\le q<1$ and $p+q=1$.

$\prod_{r=1}^{0} I_{\left(\frac{r}{10}\right)}=\lambda\left(\sqrt{\frac{\pi^\mu}{5}}\right)$, where λ and μ are natural numbers, then the value of $(\lambda+\mu)$ is ....

Section 5

- This section contains **TWO (02)** Matching List Sets.
- Each set has **ONE** Multiple Choice Question.
- Each set has **TWO** lists: **List-I** and **List-II**.
- **List-I** has **Four** entries (I), (II), (III) and (IV) and **List-II** has **Five** entries (P), (Q), (R), (S) and (T).
- **FOUR** options are given in each Multiple Choice Question based on **List-I** and **List-II** and **ONLY ONE** of these four options satisfies the condition asked in the Multiple Choice Question.
- Answer to each question will be evaluated according to the following marking scheme:

Full Marks : +3 ONLY if the option corresponding to the correct combination is chosen;
Zero Marks : 0 If none of the options is chosen (i.e. the question is unanswered);
Negative Marks : –1 In all other cases.

22. Consider the following lists

	List-I		List-II
I.	$\int \frac{e^{2x}-1}{e^{2x}+1} dx$ equals	P.	$x-\log[1+\sqrt{1-e^{2x}}]+C$
II.	$\int \frac{1}{(e^x+e^{-x})^2} dx$ equals	Q.	$\log(e^x+1)-x-e^{-x}+C$
III.	$\int \frac{e^{-x}}{1+e^x} dx$ equals	R.	$\log(e^{2x}+1)-x+C$
IV.	$\int \frac{1}{\sqrt{1-e^{2x}}} dx$ equals	S.	$\frac{-1}{2(e^{2x}+1)}+C$
		T.	$\log(e^x-1)+x+C$

The correct option is
(a) (I) → (P); (II) → (Q); (III) → (R); (IV) → (S)
(b) (I) → (R); (II) → (S); (III) → (Q); (IV) → (P)
(c) (I) → (S); (II) → (Q); (III) → (P); (IV) → (R)
(d) (I) → (P); (II) → (R); (III) → (S); (IV) → (T)

23. Match the following lists

	List-I		List-II
I.	$(I-A)^n$ is if A is idempotent	P.	$2^{n-1}(I-A)$
II.	$(I-A)^n$ is if A is involuntary	Q.	$I-nA$
III.	$(I-A)^n$ is if A is nilpotent of 1 and 2	R.	A
IV.	If A is orthogonal, then $(A^T)^{-1}$	S.	$I-A$

The correct option is
(a) (I) → (S); (II) → (P); (III) → (Q); (IV) → (R)
(b) (I) → (R); (II) → (S); (III) → (Q); (IV) → (P)
(c) (I) → (S); (II) → (Q); (III) → (P); (IV) → (R)
(d) (I) → (P); (II) → (R); (III) → (S); (IV) → (S)

Answers

1	(a)	2	(c)	3	(a)	4	(c)	5	(a,c)	6	(a,d)	7	(a,b,c)	8	(a,b,d)	9	(b,c,d)	10	(a,b)
11	(1)	12	(8)	13	(1)	14	(5)	15	(5)	16	(11)	17	(0)	18	(143)	19	(65)	20	(21)
21	(25)	22	(b)	23	(a)														

See detailed solutions on page no. 227

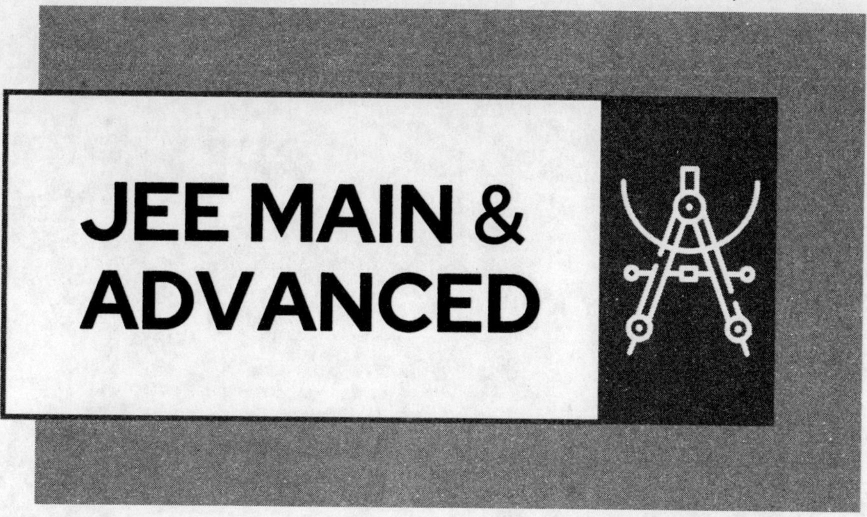

The Knockouts

10 Full Syllabus Mock Tests for JEE Main & 5 for JEE Advanced

Mock Tests given here will help you to be acquainted with Pattern & Level of JEE Main & JEE Advanced. Practicing these tests in systematic manner will ensure your good score in the Exam.

Knockout 01

JEE MAIN LEVEL

Mathematics

*Instructions

- This question paper contains of 30 Questions of Mathematics, divided into two sections : **Section I** Objective Type Questions and **Section II** Numerical Type Questions.
- Section I contains 20 Objective questions and all Questions are cumpulsory (Marking Scheme : Correct + 4, Incorrect – 1).
- Section II contains 10 Numerical value questions out of which only 5 questions are to be attempted (Marking Scheme : Correct + 4, Incorrect 0).

Section I *Multiple Choice Questions*

1. If $f(x) = a|\tan x| + be^{|x|} + c|x|^3$ and if $f(x)$ is differentiable at $x = 0$, then

(a) $a = b = c = 0$ (b) $a = 0, b = 0, c \in R$

(c) $b = c = 0, a \in R$ (d) $c = 0, a = 0, b \in R$

2. Let the curve $y^2 = 4x$ and $(x-4)^2 + y^2 = 16$ have common tangent touching the curves at (a, b) and (c, d) in first quadrant, then $(b + c)$ is

(a) $\frac{8}{3}$ (b) $2\sqrt{2} - 3$

(c) $4\sqrt{2} + \frac{8}{3}$ (d) 0

3. Distance between the parallel tangents having slopes $\left(\frac{-4}{3}\right)$ to the ellipse $\frac{x^2}{18} + \frac{y^2}{32} = 1$, is

(a) $\frac{480}{5}$ (b) $\frac{96}{5}$ (c) $\frac{48}{5}$ (d) $\frac{24}{5}$

4. If $|z - 2 + i| \le 2$, then the greatest and least value of $|z|$ is, respectively

(a) $\sqrt{5} + 1, \sqrt{5} - 1$ (b) $\sqrt{3} + 2, \sqrt{3} - 2$

(c) $2, -2$ (d) $\sqrt{5} + 2, \sqrt{5} - 2$

5. The area bounded by the curves $y = x^2$ and $y = \frac{2}{1 + x^2}$ is

(a) $2\left(\frac{\pi}{4} - \frac{1}{3}\right)$ (b) $\left(\pi - \frac{2}{3}\right)$

(c) $\left(\pi - \frac{1}{3}\right)$ (d) π

6. There are 12 points in a plane of which 5 are collinear. Barring these five points no three are collinear. The number of quadrilaterals one can form using these points, is

(a) ${}^7P_3$ (b) ${}^7C_3$ (c) 420 (d) $10 \cdot {}^7C_3$

7. Let $P(x) = 0$ be a polynomial equation of least possible degree, with rational coefficients, having $\sqrt[3]{7} + \sqrt[3]{49}$ as one of its roots. Then, the product of all the roots of $p(x) = 0$ is

(a) 7 (b) 49 (c) 63 (d) 56

8. Let $D(x) = \begin{vmatrix} g(x+K) & g(x+2K) & g(x+3K) \\ g(K) & g(2K) & g(3K) \\ g'(K) & g'(2K) & g'(3K) \end{vmatrix}$ for some real values differential function 'g' and constant K. Then, $\lim_{x \to 0} \frac{D(x)}{x}$ is

(a) 0 (b) 1 (c) 2 (d) 3

9. For $x, y \in R$, define a relation R by xRy if and only if $x - y + \sqrt{2}$ is an irrational number. Then, R is

(a) reflexive (b) symmetric

(c) transitive (d) equivalence

10. Let $f(x) = \begin{vmatrix} x^3 & \sin x & \tan x \\ \cos x & x^8 & 1 \\ e^{x^2} & \sec x & 2 \end{vmatrix}$, then the value of $\int_{-\pi/2}^{\pi/2} f(x)\,dx$ is given by

(a) 2 (b) 5

(c) π (d) None of these

11. The solution set for this equation

$$\log_3(\sqrt{x} + |\sqrt{x} - 1|) = \log_9(4\sqrt{x} - 3 + 4|\sqrt{x} - 1|) \text{ is}$$

(a) $x \in [0, 1] \cup \{4\}$ (b) $x \in (0, 1) \cup \{4\}$

(c) $x \in [0, 1) \cup \{4\}$ (d) $x \in (-\infty, 1] \cup \{4\}$

12. The Boolean expression $\sim(p \vee q) \vee (\sim p \wedge q)$ is equivalent to

(a) p (b) $\sim p$

(c) q (d) $\sim q$

13. The mean and variance of random variable X having a binomial distribution are 4 and 2 respectively. Then, $P(X=1)$ is

(a) $\frac{1}{16}$ (b) $\frac{1}{8}$ (c) $\frac{1}{4}$ (d) $\frac{1}{32}$

14. If α and β are the coefficient of x^8 and x^{-24} respectively, in the expansion of $\left(x^4+2+\frac{1}{x^4}\right)^{10}$ in powers of x, then $\frac{\alpha}{\beta}$ is equal to

(a) 26 (b) 62 (c) $\frac{13}{2}$ (d) $\frac{32}{3}$

15. Let $f(x)$ is defined as follows

$$f(x)=\begin{cases}(\cos x-\sin x)^{\operatorname{cosec} x}, & -\frac{\pi}{2}<x<0\\ a, & x=0\\ \frac{e^{1/x}+e^{2/x}+e^{3/x}}{a\cdot e^{2/x}+b\cdot e^{3/x}}, & 0<x<\pi/2\end{cases}$$

If $f(x)$ is continuous at $x=0$, then the value of a and b are

(a) $a=e, b=\frac{1}{e}$ (b) $a=\frac{1}{e}, b=e$
(c) $a=0, b=1$ (d) $a=e^2, b=\frac{1}{e^2}$

16. Let A, B, C be pairwise independent events with $P(C)>0$ and $P(A\cap B\cap C)=0$. Then, $P(A'\cap B'|C)$ equals

(a) $P(A')+P(B')$ (b) $P(A')-P(B')$
(c) $P(A')-P(B)$ (d) $P(A)-P(B')$

17. If $S_n=\sum_{k=1}^{n}\tan^{-1}\left(\frac{2K}{2+K^2+K^4}\right)$, then $\lim_{n\to\infty} S_n$ is

(a) $\frac{\pi}{4}$ (b) $\frac{\pi}{2}$ (c) π (d) None of these

18. If for a continuous function f, $f(0)=f(1)=0$, $f'(1)=2$ and $y(x)=f(e^x)e^{f(x)}$, then $y'(0)$ is equal to

(a) 1 (b) 2 (c) 0 (d) None of these

19. The values of x for which the angle between the vectors $\mathbf{a}=x\hat{i}-3\hat{j}-\hat{k}$ and $\mathbf{b}=2x\hat{i}+x\hat{j}-\hat{k}$ is acute and the angle between the vector $\mathbf{b}$ and the axis of ordinates is obtuse, are

(a) 1, 2 (b) 2, –3 (c) all $x<0$ (d) all $x>0$

20. Equation of plane containing lines $\frac{x-1}{1}=\frac{y-1}{2}=\frac{z-1}{3}$ and $\frac{x-1}{1}=\frac{y-1}{3}=\frac{z-1}{5}$

(a) $x-2y+z=2$ (b) $x+2y+3z=3$
(c) $x+2y+z=4$ (d) $x-2y+z=0$

Section II *Numerical Value Questions*

21. The function $f(x)=a\sin x+\frac{1}{4}\sin 4x$ has maximum value at $x=\frac{\pi}{4}$, then the value of a^2 is

22. The mean and variance of n observations $x_1, x_2, x_3, \ldots, x_n$ are 5 and 0 respectively. If $\Sigma x_i^2=400$, then the value of n is equal to

23. If PQ is any focal chord of parabola $y^2=32x$ and length of PQ can never be less than λ units, then the number of divisors of λ is

24. In an examination, the question paper consists of two sections A and B containing 6 and 5 questions respectively. In how many ways a candidate can answer 7 questions, if he is required to select atleast 3 questions from A?

25. Given, $\Delta=\begin{vmatrix}1 & 3\cos\theta & 1\\ \sin\theta & 1 & \cos\theta\\ 1 & \sin\theta & 1\end{vmatrix}$, then the maximum value of Δ is

26. If the orthocentre of the triangle formed by $2x+3y-1=0$, $x+2y-1=0$, $ax+by-1=0$ at the origin, then $\frac{b-a}{4}$ equals

27. If $f(x)=\sqrt{4-x^2}+\sqrt{x^2-1}$, then the maximum value of $(f(x))^2$ is

28. A ball is dropped from the height of 48 m and it bounced $\frac{2}{3}$ of this height. It falls and bounced in same way continuously. The total distance covered by the ball before coming to rest is

29. If $y=y(x)$ is the solution of the differential equation, $x\frac{dy}{dx}=y(\log_e y-\log_e x+1)$, when $y(1)=2$, then $y(2)$ is equal to

30. If the angles of elevation of two towers of heights h_1 and h_2 from the mid-point of the line joining their feet be $\frac{\pi}{3}$ and $\frac{\pi}{6}$, respectively, then $\frac{h_1}{h_2}=$ ....

Answers

1 (b)	2 (c)	3 (c)	4 (d)	5 (b)	6 (c)	7 (d)	8 (a)	9 (a)	10 (d)
11 (a)	12 (b)	13 (d)	14 (a)	15 (b)	16 (c)	17 (a)	18 (b)	19 (c)	20 (d)
21 (2)	22 (16)	23 (6)	24 (315)	25 (10)	26 4	27 6	28 240	29 8	30 3

See detailed solutions on page no. 232

Knockout 02

JEE MAIN LEVEL

Mathematics

*Instructions

1. This question paper contains of 30 Questions of Mathematics, divided into two sections :
   Section I Objective Type Questions and **Section II** Numerical Type Questions.
2. Section I contains 20 Objective questions and all Questions are cumpulsory (Marking Scheme : Correct + 4, Incorrect – 1).
3. Section II contains 10 Numerical value questions out of which only 5 questions are to be attempted (Marking Scheme : Correct + 4, Incorrect 0).

Section I *Multiple Choice Questions*

1. Let A and B two sets containing 2 elements and 4 elements respectively. The number of subsets of $A \times B$ having 3 or more elements is

(a) 256 (b) 220 (c) 219 (d) 211

2. The number of ways of dividing 52 cards amongst four players so that three players have 17 cards each and the fourth player have just one card, is

(a) 52! (b) $\frac{52!}{17!}$ (c) $\frac{52!}{(17!)^3}$ (d) $\frac{52!}{(17!)^2}$

3. If the origin and the roots of the equation $z^2 + pz + q = 0$, $(p^2 < 4q)$ form an equilateral triangle, then p^2 equals

(a) q (b) $3q$
(c) $2q$ (d) None of these

4. If $z = \frac{1 + i\sqrt{3}}{\sqrt{3} + i}$, then $(\bar{z})^{100}$ lies in

(a) I quadrant (b) II quadrant
(c) III quadrant (d) IV quadrant

5. Let $\phi(x) = |x - 2|, \forall x \in R$ and $h(x) = \phi(\phi(\phi(x)))$, then the number of solutions of $h(x) = \frac{3}{2}$ is

(a) 10 (b) 8 (c) 4 (d) 6

6. The values of K for which the points $A(1, 0, 3)$, $B(-1, 3, 4)$, $C(1, 2, 1)$ and $D(K, 2, 5)$ are coplanar, are

(a) 1 (b) 2 (c) –1 (d) 0

7. $\sin 3x < \sin x$ in $[0, 2\pi]$. If the solution set is $(a, b) \cup (c, d) \cup (p, q)$, then $b - a + d - c + q - p$ is

(a) π (b) 3π (c) $\frac{3\pi}{4}$ (d) $\frac{7\pi}{4}$

8. The number of points at which the function $f(x) = \frac{1}{\ln|x - 4|}$ is discontinuous, are

(a) 2 (b) 3 (c) 6 (d) 1

9. If A and B are two events such that $P(A \cup B) = P(A \cap B)$, then the true relation is

(a) $P(A) + P(B) = 0$
(b) $P(A) + P(B) = P(A) \cdot P(B|A)$
(c) $P(A) + P(B) = 2P(A) \cdot P(B|A)$
(d) None of the above

10. In the expansion of $(x + y + z)^{17}$, coefficient of $x^4y^{10}z^3$ is

(a) 17! (b) $\frac{17!}{14!3!}$ (c) $\frac{17!}{4!10!3!}$ (d) None of these

11. Suppose the ellipse $x^2 + \frac{y^2}{a^2} = 1$ intersects the ellipse $\frac{x^2}{4} + y^2 = 1$ in four distinct points. If $a = b^2 - 5b + 7$, then b cannot lie in the set

(a) (2, 3) (b) (–1, 3) (c) (–1, 1) (d) (1, 4)

12. Let p and q be two statements. Then, $(\sim p \vee q) \wedge (\sim p \wedge \sim q)$ is

(a) a tautology
(b) either a tautology or a contradiction
(c) neither a tautology nor a contradiction
(d) a contradiction

13. If $f(x) = \min\{|x|, |x - 2|, 2 - |x - 1|\}$, then the total sum of non-differentiable points are

(a) $\frac{11}{2}$ (b) – 5 (c) 4 (d) 5

14. Suppose a population A has 25 observations 501, 503, ..., 549 and another population B has 25 observation 502, 504, ... , 550. If V_A and V_B represent the variance of two populations respectively, then $\frac{V_A}{V_B}$ is

(a) 2 (b) 1 (c) 5 (d) 4

15. Let L be a normal to the parabola $y^2 = 4x$. If L passes through the point $P(9,6)$. Then L at P is given by

(a) $y = 2x - 3$ (b) $y + 3x - 33 = 0$
(c) $y = 15 + x$ (d) $y - 2x + 12 = 0$

16. Let x be the length of one of the equal sides of an isosceles triangle and let θ be the angle between them. If x is increasing at the rate of $\left(\frac{1}{12}\right)$ m/h and θ is increasing at the rate of $\frac{\pi}{180}$ radian/h, then the rate in m^2/h at which the area of the triangle is increasing when $x = 12$ cm and $\theta = \frac{\pi}{4}$ is

(a) $2^{1/2}\left(1 + \frac{2\pi}{5}\right)$ (b) $\frac{73}{2}\sqrt{2}$
(c) $2^{1/2}\left(\frac{1}{2} + \frac{\pi}{5}\right)$ (d) $\frac{3^{1/2}}{2} + \frac{\pi}{5}$

17. The solution of $\frac{dV}{dt} + \frac{K}{m}V = -g$ is

(a) $V \cdot e^{\frac{K}{m}t} = c - \frac{mg}{K}$
(b) $V = c - \frac{mg}{K}e^{\frac{-K}{m}t}$
(c) $V \cdot e^{\frac{-K}{m}t} = c - \frac{mg}{K}$
(d) $V = c \cdot e^{\frac{-K}{m}t} = \frac{mg}{K}$

18. If $A = \begin{bmatrix} 1 & 0 & 0 \\ 0 & 1 & 1 \\ 0 & -2 & 4 \end{bmatrix}$ and $6A^{-1} = A^2 + cA + dI$, then $(c, d) =$

(a) $(-6, 11)$ (b) $(6, 11)$
(c) $(-6, -11)$ (d) $(6, -11)$

19. Two men are on the opposite side of a tower. They measure the angles of elevation of the top of the tower 45° and 30° respectively. If the height of the tower is 40 m, then the distance between the men is

(a) $40\sqrt{3}$ m (b) 109.28 m
(c) 68.280 m (d) 40 m

20. $A(a+1, a-1)$, $B(a^2+1, a^2-1)$ and $C(a^3+1, a^3-1)$ are given points. $D(11, 9)$ is the mid-point of AB and $E(41, 39)$ is the mid-point of BC. If F is the mid-point of AC, then $(BF)^2$ is equal to $8K^2$, where $K =$

(a) 6 (b) 8 (c) 7 (d) 9

Section II *Numerical Value Questions*

21. Suppose $[x]$ = greatest integer $\le x$. If $x = \alpha, y = \beta$ and $z = \gamma$ Satisfy the system of equations

$$2x + 3|y| + 5[z] = 0$$
$$x + |y| - 2[z] = 4$$
$$x + |y| + [z] = 1$$

then maximum possible value of $\alpha^2 + \beta^2 + \gamma^2 =$.....

22. The volume of the tetrahedron included between the plane $3x + 4y - 5z - 60 = 0$ and the coordinate plane is

23. For a continuous function $f(x)$ such that the area bounded by X-axis, the curve $y = f(x)$ and the ordinates $x = 1$, $x = a$ is equal to $(\sqrt{(1+a^2)} - \sqrt{2})$ for all $a > 1$. Then $f(0) =$

24. The system of equations

$$\alpha x + y + z = \alpha - 1$$
$$x + \alpha y + z = \alpha - 1$$
$$x + y + \alpha z = \alpha - 1$$

has no solution, if $\alpha = 2K$, then $K + 9$ is equal to

25. If $\int \frac{1}{\sin x + \sin 2x} dx = f(x) + C$, then $f\left(\frac{\pi}{2}\right)$ equals

26. Suppose $0 < \theta < \frac{\pi}{2}$, If the eccentricity of the hyperbola $x^2 - y^2 \text{cosec}^2\theta = 5$ is $\sqrt{7}$ times the eccentricity of the ellipse $x^2 \text{cosec}^2\theta + y^2 = 5$, then $\frac{\pi}{\theta}$ is equal to

27. If $\tan^{-1}\left(\frac{x-1}{x-2}\right) + \tan^{-1}\left(\frac{x+1}{x+2}\right) = -\frac{3\pi}{4}$ then number of solutions for x is

28. Let $f(x) = x(x^2 + mx + n) + 2, \forall x \in R$ and $m, n \in R$. If Rolle's theorem holds for $f(x)$ at $x = \frac{4}{3}$ in $x \in [1, 2]$, then $(m + n)$ equals

29. Let C be a circle with centre on the X-axis and touching the line $x + y = 0$ at $(2, -2)$. If (h, k) lies on the circle C, then $h - 2\sqrt{2}$ cannot exceed.

30. If the sum of the first 10 terms of the series $\log_5 x + \log_{5^{1/2}} x + \log_{5^{1/3}} x + \ldots$ is 110. Then, x is equal to

Answers

1	(c)	2	(c)	3	(b)	4	(c)	5	(d)	6	(c)	7	(a)	8	(b)	9	(c)	10	(c)
11	(a)	12	(c)	13	(d)	14	(b)	15	(b)	16	(c)	17	(d)	18	(a)	19	(b)	20	(d)
21	(3)	22	(600)	23	(0)	24	(8)	25	(0)	26	(3)	27	(0)	28	(3)	29	(4)	30	(25)

See detailed solutions on page no. 235

Knockout 03

JEE MAIN LEVEL

Mathematics

***Instructions**

1. This question paper contains of 30 Questions of Mathematics, divided into two sections : **Section I** Objective Type Questions and **Section II** Numerical Type Questions.
2. Section I contains 20 Objective questions and all Questions are cumpulsory (Marking Scheme : Correct + 4, Incorrect – 1).
3. Section II contains 10 Numerical value questions out of which only 5 questions are to be attempted (Marking Scheme : Correct + 4, Incorrect 0).

Section I *Multiple Choice Questions*

1. If $h(x)=\left(\frac{x^3+3x}{3x^2+1}\right)$ and $f(x)=\ln\left(\frac{1+x}{1-x}\right)$. Then, $f(h(x))$ is equal to

(a) $[f(x)]^2$ (b) $-f(x)$
(c) $3f(x)$ (d) $2/3f(x)$

2. If a circle passes through the point (p,q) and cuts the circle $x^2+y^2=r^2$ orthogonally, then the equation of the locus of its centre is

(a) $2px+2qy-(p^2+q^2+r^2)=0$
(b) $2px+2qy-(p^2-q^2+r^2)=0$
(c) $x^2+y^2-3px-4qy+(p^2+q^2-r^2)=0$
(d) $x^2+y^2-2px-3qy+(p^2-q^2-r^2)=0$

3. Solution set of x, if $(x^2+x+1)^x<1$ is given

(a) $x\in(-\infty,-1)$ (b) $x\in(-\infty,1)$
(c) $x\in(-\infty,-1]$ (d) $x\in(-1,\infty)$

4. Let $P=\{z:z\in c, |z-i|=|z+1|\}$ and $Q=\{z:z\in c, |z|=1\}$, then

(a) $P\cap Q=\phi$
(b) $P\cap Q$ consists of atleast two points but is finite
(c) $P\cap Q$ is singleton
(d) $P\cap Q$ is an infinite set

5. The sum of 'n' terms of the series $\frac{1}{1+1^2+1^4}+\frac{2}{1+2^2+2^4}+\frac{3}{1+3^2+3^4}+\ldots$ is

(a) $\frac{n^2+n}{n^2+n+1}$
(b) $\frac{n^2-n}{2(n^2+n+1)}$
(c) $\frac{n^2-n}{2(n^2-n+1)}$
(d) $\frac{n^2+n}{2(n^2+n+1)}$

6. If $\int\frac{(x^2-1)dx}{(x^4+3x^2+1)\tan^{-1}\left(\frac{x^2+1}{x}\right)}=k\cdot\log_e\left|\tan^{-1}\left(\frac{x^2+1}{x}\right)\right|+C$, then k is

(a) 1 (b) 3 (c) $\frac{1}{2}$ (d) $\frac{1}{3}$

7. Mr. A has x children by his first wife and Ms. B has $(x+1)$ children by her first husband. They marry and have children of their own. The whole family has 10 children. Assuming that two children of the same parents do not fight. Then, maximum number of fights that can take place among children

(a) 33 (b) 3 (c) 30 (d) 40

8. The area (in sq units) enclosed by the curves $y=\ln(x+e)$, $x=\ln\left(\frac{1}{y}\right)$ and X-axis is

(a) 4 (b) 2 (c) $\frac{1}{2}$ (d) $\frac{1}{4}$

9. The values of θ and λ in the following equations $\sin\theta x - \cos\theta y + (\lambda+1)z = 0$, $\cos\theta x + \sin\theta y - \lambda z = 0$ and $\lambda x + (\lambda+1)y + \cos\theta z = 0$ have non-trivial solution, are

(a) $\theta = 2n\pi, \lambda$ is any rational number, $n \in I$
(b) $\theta = m\pi, \lambda \in R - \{0\}, m \in I$
(c) $\theta = (2n+1)\frac{\pi}{2}, \lambda \in R, n \in I$
(d) $\theta = (2n+1)\pi, \lambda \in R^+, n \in I$

10. Let p and q be two statements, then $q \leftrightarrow (\sim p \vee \sim q)$ is logically equivalent to

(a) $p \to q$ (b) q
(c) p (d) $\sim p \wedge q$

11. S_1 and S_2 are foci of an ellipse, A be one of the extremities of its minor axes. If ΔS_1S_2A is right angled, then eccentricity of the ellipse is equal to

(a) $\frac{1}{\sqrt{2}}$ (b) $\frac{\sqrt{3}}{2}$
(c) $\sqrt{\frac{3}{2}}$ (d) None of these

12. For complex number z and ω, $|z|^2\omega - |\omega|^2 z = z - \omega$, if and only if

(a) $z = \omega$ or $z\overline{\omega} = 1$ (b) $z = \overline{\omega}$ or $z\overline{\omega} = \frac{1}{2}$
(c) $z = \omega$ or $z\omega = 1$ (d) $z = \overline{\omega}$ or $\overline{z}\omega = 1$

13. If $h(x) = \lim_{n\to\infty}\left(\frac{x^{2n}f(x) + g(x)}{x^{2n}+1}\right)$, then the value of $h(x)$ when $x \in R - [-1,1]$ is

(a) $g(x)$ (b) $f(x)$
(c) $\frac{f(x)+g(x)}{2}$ (d) $\frac{f(x)-g(x)}{2}$

14. The coefficient of variance of numbers 1, 2, 3, ..., n is

(a) $\sqrt{\frac{n-1}{3(n+1)}} \times 100$ (b) $\sqrt{\frac{3(n-1)}{(n+1)}} \times 100$
(c) $\sqrt{\frac{n+1}{3(n-1)}} \times 100$ (d) None of these

15. If the vertices A and B of a ΔABC are given by (2, 5) and (4, −11) respectively and C moves along the line $L \equiv 9x + 7y + 4 = 0$. Then, the locus of the centroid of the ΔABC is parallel to

(a) $7x + 9y - 4 = 0$
(b) $9x - 7y + 4 = 0$
(c) $9x + 7y + 4 = 0$
(d) $4x + 7y - 9 = 0$

16. A coin, weighted so that $P(H) = \frac{2}{3}$ and $P(T) = \frac{1}{3}$ is tossed. If head appears, then a number is selected at random from the numbers 1 through 9; if tails appear, then a number is selected at random from the numbers 1 through 5. The probability p that an even number is selected, is

(a) $\frac{85}{135}$ (b) $\frac{58}{135}$
(c) $\frac{8}{27}$ (d) $\frac{2}{15}$

17. Let a and b be the maximum and minimum values of the function $f(x) = \tan^{-1}(\sin x + \cos x)$ in $\left[0, \frac{\pi}{2}\right]$ respectively, then the value of $\tan(a - b)$ is

(a) $3 + 2\sqrt{2}$ (b) $3 - 2\sqrt{2}$
(c) $2 - \sqrt{3}$ (d) $2 + \sqrt{3}$

18. Tangents are drawn from any points on the hyperbola $\frac{x^2}{9} - \frac{y^2}{4} = 1$ to the circle $x^2 + y^2 = 9$. Then, the locus of mid-point of the chord of contact is given by

(a) $9(x^2 - 9y^2) = 4(x^2 + y^2)^2$
(b) $9(4x^2 - 9y^2) = 4(x^2 + y^2)$
(c) $(x^2 - 9y^2) = (x^2 + y^2)^2$
(d) $9(4x^2 - 9y^2) = 4(x^2 + y^2)^2$

19. Let a function $f : (-1, 3) \to R$ be defined as $f(x) = \min\{x[x], |x[x] - 2| + 2\}$, where $[\cdot]$ denotes the greatest integer function, then $f(x)$ is

(a) neither continuous nor differentiable at exactly three points.
(b) not continuous at only one point and not differentiable at three points.
(c) neither continuous nor differentiable at exactly two points.
(d) not continuous at two points and not differentiable at three points.

20. If $\frac{dy}{dx} = (e^y - x)^{-1}$, where $y(0) = 0$, then y is expressed explicitly as

(a) $\ln(1 + x^2)$
(b) $\frac{1}{2}\ln(1 + x^2)$
(c) $\ln(x + \sqrt{1 - x^2})$
(d) $\ln(x + \sqrt{1 + x^2})$

Section II Numerical Value Questions

21. If parabolas $y^2 = ax$ and $25[(x-3)^2 + (y+2)^2] = (3x - 4y - 2)^2$ are equal, then the value of 'a' is

22. If $2t, t$ and $[t^2 - 14]$, $t \in R - \{0\}$ and $[\cdot]$ denotes the greatest integer function are the first three terms of a GP in order, then the 51th term of the sequence, 1, 3t, 6t, 10t, ... is

23. The coefficient of x^4 in the expansion of $(1 - 3x + 2x^2)^6$ is

24. The minimum value of x for which the inequality $\log_{0.04}(x-1) \geq \log_{0.2}(x-1)$ is true, is

25. Let

$$f(x)=\begin{cases} x|x| & , \quad x\le -1 \\ [1+x]+[1-x] & , \quad -1<x<1 \\ -x|x| & , \quad x\ge 1 \end{cases}$$

where $[\cdot]$ denotes greatest integer function in this question, then the value of $\left[\int_{-2}^{2} f(x)dx\right]+\frac{277}{25}$ is equal to

26. If a flagstaff of 6 m high placed in the top of a tower throws a shadow of $2\sqrt{3}$ m along the ground. Let θ be the angle (in degrees) that the Sun makes with the ground, then $\sqrt{3}\tan\theta$ is equal to

27. If $\mathbf{a}$ is perpendicular to $\mathbf{b}+\mathbf{c}$, $\mathbf{b}$ is perpendicular to $\mathbf{c}+\mathbf{a}$ and $\mathbf{c}$ is perpendicular to $\mathbf{a}+\mathbf{b}$ and $|\mathbf{a}|=|\mathbf{b}|=|2\mathbf{c}|=3$, then $|\mathbf{a}+\mathbf{b}+\mathbf{c}|$ is

28. If A, B, C are the angles of a triangle, then the value of the determinant $\begin{vmatrix} \sin 2A & \sin C & \sin B \\ \sin C & \sin 2B & \sin A \\ \sin B & \sin A & \sin 2C \end{vmatrix}$ is equal to

29. If the straight lines $x=1+S$, $y=-3-\lambda S$, $z=1+\lambda S$, and $x=\frac{t}{2}$, $y=1+t$ and $z=2-t$ with parameters, S and t respectively are coplanar, then $\lambda+4$ equals

30. For the equation of curve $y=a^{1-n}\cdot x^n$, find the value of $(6n)$, so that the subnormal may be of constant length.

Answers

1 *(c)*	2 *(a)*	3 *(a)*	4 *(b)*	5 *(d)*	6 *(a)*	7 *(a)*	8 *(b)*	9 *(c)*	10 *(d)*
11 *(a)*	12 *(a)*	13 *(b)*	14 *(a)*	15 *(c)*	16 *(b)*	17 *(b)*	18 *(d)*	19 *(d)*	20 *(d)*
21 *(6)*	22 *(5304)*	23 *(2355)*	24 *(2)*	25 *(8.08)*	26 *(3)*	27 *(4.5)*	28 *(0)*	29 *(2)*	30 *(3)*

See detailed solutions on page no. 240

Knockout 04

JEE MAIN LEVEL

Mathematics

*Instructions

1. This question paper contains of 30 Questions of Mathematics, divided into two sections : **Section I** Objective Type Questions and **Section II** Numerical Type Questions.
2. Section I contains 20 Objective questions and all Questions are cumpulsory (Marking Scheme : Correct + 4, Incorrect – 1).
3. Section II contains 10 Numerical value questions out of which only 5 questions are to be attempted (Marking Scheme : Correct + 4, Incorrect 0).

Section I *Multiple Choice Questions*

1. If the equation $e^{||x|-2|+b}=2$ has four solutions, then 'b' lies in

(a) $(-2, \ln 2)$ (b) $(0, \ln 2)$ (c) $(\ln 2, -\ln 2)$ (d) $(\ln 2-2, \ln 2)$

2. If $(1+x)^n=C_0+C_1x+C_2x^2+C_3x^3+\ldots+C_nx^n$, then $\sum_{r=0}^{n}\sum_{s=0}^{n}(r+s)C_rC_s$ is equal to

(a) 2^n (b) $n\cdot 2^{2n}$ (c) $n\cdot 2^n$ (d) 2^{2n}

3. For which of the following function on [0, 1] the Lagrange's Mean value Theorem (LMVT) is not applicable to

(a) $f(x)=\begin{cases}\frac{1}{2}-x, & x<\frac{1}{2}\\ \left(\frac{1}{2}-x\right)^2, & x\geq\frac{1}{2}\end{cases}$ (b) $f(x)=\begin{cases}\frac{\sin x}{x}, & x\neq 0\\ 1, & x=0\end{cases}$

(c) $f(x)=x|x|$ (d) $f(x)=|x|$

4. If $y(t)$ is a solution of the differential equation $(1+t)\frac{dy}{dt}-ty=1$ and $y(0)=-1$, then $y(1)$ is equal to

(a) $e+\frac{1}{2}$ (b) $e-\frac{1}{2}$ (c) $-\frac{1}{2}$ (d) $\frac{1}{2}$

5. In a circus, there are ten cages for accommodating ten animals. Out of these, four cages are so small that five out of 10 animals cannot enter into them. In how many ways will it be possible to accommodate 10 animals in these 10 cages?

(a) 86400 (b) 96000
(c) 66400 (d) None of these

6. The sides of a right angled triangle are in AP. Find the length of its smallest side, if the triangle has area 24 cm^2.

(a) 2 cm (b) 6 cm (c) 5 cm (d) 8 cm

7. If $\omega=\alpha+i\beta$, $\beta\neq 0$ and $z\neq 1$ satisfies the conditions $\frac{\omega-\bar{\omega}z}{1-z}$ is purely real, then the set of all values of z is

(a) $\{z:|z|=1\}$ (b) $\{z:z=2\}$
(c) $\{z:z\neq 1\}$ (d) $\{z:|z|=1, z\neq 1\}$

8. If A and B are square matrices of the same order such that $|A|=|B|=1$ and A (adj A + adj B) $=B$, then the value of $|A+B|$ is, (where $|R|=$ determinant of R)

(a) 1 (b) 2 (c) 3 (d) None of these

9. For all values of t and u, orthocentre of the triangle formed by the lines $y=0$, $(1+t)x-ty+t(1+t)=0$ and $(1+u)x-uy+u(1+u)=0$, $(t\neq u)$, lies on the line

(a) $x+y+1=0$ (b) $x-y+1=0$
(c) $x+y=0$ (d) None of these

10. Suppose $p, q\in R$ and let $f(x)=x^2+px+q\ \forall x\in R$. If $f(5+x)=f(5-x)\ \forall\ x\in R$, then

(a) $f(3)<f(4)<f(5)$ (b) $f(5)<f(3)<f(4)$
(c) $f(4)<f(3)<f(5)$ (d) $f(5)<f(4)<f(3)$

11. Let S denote the set of values of r for which $P(-5+r, -3+r)$ is an interior point of the major segment of the circle $x^2+y^2=16$ cut off by the same side of $x+y=2$, then S does not contain

(a) $(4-\sqrt{7}, 0]$ (b) $[0, 5)$
(c) $(4-\sqrt{7}, 4+\sqrt{7})$ (d) $(4-\sqrt{7}, 5)$

12. Bag I contains 5 blue and 4 pink balls. Bag II contains 6 blue and 3 pink balls. One ball is transferred from bag II to bag I and then a ball is drawn from bag II. The ball so drawn is found to be pink. The probability that the transferred ball is blue, is

(a) $\frac{3}{8}$ (b) $\frac{5}{8}$ (c) $\frac{12}{17}$ (d) $\frac{5}{17}$

13. For two data sets each of size 5, the variances are given to be 4 and 5 and the corresponding means are given to be 2 and 4, respectively. The variance of the combined data set is

(a) $\frac{11}{2}$ (b) $\frac{5}{2}$ (c) $\frac{13}{2}$ (d) 6

14. Three circles of radii 1, 2, 3 touch each other externally at A, B and C. The radius of the circle ABC is

(a) $\frac{3}{2}$ units (b) $\frac{1}{2}$ unit (c) 2 units (d) 1 unit

15. If f is differentiable function satisfying $f(x)=\int_0^x \sqrt{1-f^2(t)}\,dt+\frac{1}{2}$, then the value of $\sin^{-1}\{f(\pi)\}$ is equal to

(a) $\frac{-\pi}{3}$ (b) $\frac{-\pi}{6}$ (c) $\frac{\pi}{6}$ (d) $\frac{\pi}{3}$

16. Given that the foci of the ellipse $\frac{x^2}{9}+\frac{y^2}{5}=1$ are $(a_1, 0)$ and $(a_2, 0)$, where $a_1>0$ and $a_2<0$. Let P_1 and P_2 be two parabolas with a common vertex at (0,0) and with foci at $(a_1, 0)$ and $(2a_2, 0)$, respectively. Let T_1 be a tangent to P_1 which passes through $(2a_2, 0)$ and T_2 be a tangent to P_2 which passes through $(a_1, 0)$. The m_1 is the slope of T_1 and m_2 is the slope of T_2, then the value of $\left(\frac{1}{m^2}+m_2^2\right)$ is

(a) 2 (b) 3 (c) 4 (d) 5

17. Let $A=\left\{x\in(-\pi,\pi): x\neq 0, \pm\frac{\pi}{2}\right\}$. The sum of all distinct solutions of the equation $\sqrt{3}\sec x+\operatorname{cosec} x+2(\tan x-\cot x)=0$ in the set A is equal to

(a) $-\frac{2\pi}{9}$ (b) $-\frac{7\pi}{9}$ (c) $\frac{5\pi}{9}$ (d) 0

18. Consider the following two statements.

P : 396 is a multiple of 6. Q : 396 is a multiple of 8.

If V_1 is the truth value of the compound statement P and Q with "and" and V_2 is the truth value of the compound statement connecting P and Q with "or", then the truth value of $V_1 \wedge V_2$ is

(a) True (b) False
(c) either True or False (d) cannot be determined

19. If a, b, c are non-zero complex numbers satisfying $a^2+b^2+c^2=0$ and $\begin{vmatrix} b^2+c^2 & ab & ac \\ ab & c^2+a^2 & bc \\ ac & bc & a^2+b^2 \end{vmatrix}=ka^2b^2c^2$, then k is equal to

(a) 3 (b) 2 (c) 1 (d) 4

20. A random variable X takes the values 0, 1, 2, 3 and its mean is 1.3. If $P(X=3)=2P(X=1)$ and $P(X=2)=0.3$, then $P(X=0)$ is

(a) 0.2 (b) 0.1 (c) 0.3 (d) 0.4

Section II *Numerical Value Questions*

21. Let **a**, **b** and **c** be three non-coplanar vectors and let **p**, **q** and **r** be the vectors defined by the relations

$$\mathbf{p}=\frac{\mathbf{b}\times\mathbf{c}}{[\mathbf{a}\ \mathbf{b}\ \mathbf{c}]}, \mathbf{q}=\frac{\mathbf{c}\times\mathbf{a}}{[\mathbf{a}\ \mathbf{b}\ \mathbf{c}]} \text{ and } \mathbf{r}=\frac{\mathbf{a}\times\mathbf{b}}{[\mathbf{a}\ \mathbf{b}\ \mathbf{c}]}$$

Then, the value of the expression $(\mathbf{a}+\mathbf{b})\cdot\mathbf{p}+(\mathbf{b}+\mathbf{c})\cdot\mathbf{q}+(\mathbf{c}+\mathbf{a})\cdot\mathbf{r}$ is equal to

22. If $\int \sqrt[3]{\tan x}\,dx=\lambda\log\left|\frac{\sqrt{u^2-u+1}}{u+1}\right|+\mu\tan^{-1}\left(\frac{2u-1}{\sqrt{3}}\right)+C$, where $u=(\tan x)^{2/3}$, then $\lambda^2+\mu^2$ is

23. If θ is the acute angle between the tangents drawn from point (1, 4) to the parabola $y^2=4x$, then $4\cos\theta$ is equal to

24. A person standing on the bank of a river observes that the angle subtended by a tree on the opposite bank is 60°. When he retires 40 m from the bank, he finds the angle to be 30°. The breadth of the river is

25. The number of tangents to the curve $x^{3/2}+y^{3/2}=2a^{3/2}$, $a>0$, which are equally inclined to the axes, is

26. Number of solutions of the equation $\sin^{-1}(\sin 6x)=x$ in $x\in[0,\pi]$ is

27. Let $f(1)=-2$ and $f'(x)\geq 4.2$ for $1\leq x\leq 6$. The smallest possible value of $f(6)$ is

28. If a normal to the hyperbola $x^2-4y^2=4$ having equal positive intercepts on the axes is tangent to the ellipse $\frac{x^2}{a^2}+\frac{y^2}{b^2}=1$, then $\frac{3}{5}(a^2+b^2)$ is equal to

29. The plane passing through the point (–2, –2, 2) and containing the line joining the points (1, 1, 1) and (1, –1, 2) makes intercepts on the coordinate axes the sum of whose lengths is .... m

30. If $f(x)=x^2+2bx+2c^2$ and $g(x)=-x^2-2cx+b^2$ are such that $\min f(x)>\max g(x)$, then the relation between b and c is given by $|c|>|b|\cdot k$. So, value of $k^2+\sqrt{2}k+2$ is equal to

Answers

1	(d)	2	(b)	3	(a)	4	(c)	5	(a)	6	(b)	7	(d)	8	(a)	9	(c)	10	(d)
11	(c)	12	(b)	13	(a)	14	(d)	15	(b)	16	(c)	17	(d)	18	(b)	19	(d)	20	(d)
21	(3)	22	(1)	23	(2)	24	(20)	25	(1)	26	(4)	27	(19)	28	(5)	29	(12)	30	(6)

See detailed solutions on page no. 244

Knockout 05

JEE MAIN LEVEL

Mathematics

*Instructions

1. This question paper contains of 30 Questions of Mathematics, divided into two sections : **Section I** Objective Type Questions and **Section II** Numerical Type Questions.
2. Section I contains 20 Objective questions and all Questions are cumpulsory (Marking Scheme : Correct + 4, Incorrect – 1).
3. Section II contains 10 Numerical value questions out of which only 5 questions are to be attempted (Marking Scheme : Correct + 4, Incorrect 0).

Section I *Multiple Choice Questions*

1. If $f:[0,\infty)\to[0,\infty)$ and $f(x)=\dfrac{x}{1+x}$, then the function f is

(a) one-one but not onto
(b) neither one-one nor onto
(c) one-one and onto
(d) onto but not one-one

2. An equation of the line passing through the centre and bisecting the chord $3\sqrt{3}x-5y=14$ of the ellipse $\dfrac{x^2}{5}+\dfrac{y^2}{3}=1$ is

(a) $x-\sqrt{3}y=0$ (b) $x+y=0$
(c) $x+\sqrt{3}y=0$ (d) $x=y$

3. There are 30 balls, out of which 10 are identical and the rest are all different. The number of ways of selecting 10 balls from the group is

(a) $\dfrac{1}{2}\,{}^{20}C_9+2^{19}$ (b) $\dfrac{{}^{20}C_{10}}{2}$
(c) $\dfrac{1}{2}\,{}^{20}C_{10}+2^{21}$ (d) $\dfrac{1}{2}\,{}^{20}C_{10}+2^{19}$

4. Quadratic equations $x^2-6x+a=0$ and $x^2-cx+6=0$ have one root α in common. The other roots of the first and second equations are integers in the ratio 4 : 3. Then, which of the following expressions is negative for $x=\alpha$?

(a) $4x-7$ (b) x^2-6x+9 (c) x^2-3x+1 (d) $2x-3$

5. The relation R defined on the set N of natural numbers by $xRy\Leftrightarrow 2x^2-3xy+y^2=0$ is

(a) equivalence
(b) only symmetric
(c) symmetric but not reflexive
(d) not symmetric but reflexive

6. Solution of the differential equation $\dfrac{dy}{dx}+\dfrac{1}{x}\tan y=\dfrac{1}{x^2}\tan y\cdot\sin y$ is

(a) $2x=\sin y(1+2x)$
(b) $2x=\sin y(1+cx^2)$
(c) $2x+\sin y(1+cx^2)=0$
(d) None of the above

7. If a circle passes through the point of intersection of the coordinate axes with lines $\lambda x-y+1=0$ and $x-2y+3=0$, then value of λ is not equal to

(a) 0 (b) $\dfrac{1}{3}$
(c) $-\dfrac{1}{3}$ (d) 2

8. A signal which can be green or red with probability $\dfrac{4}{5}$ and $\dfrac{1}{5}$ respectively, is received by station A and then transmitted to station B. The probability of each station receiving the signal correctly is $\dfrac{3}{4}$. If the signal received at station B is green, then the probability that the original signal was green is

(a) $\dfrac{20}{23}$ (b) $\dfrac{9}{20}$
(c) $\dfrac{4}{13}$ (d) $\dfrac{6}{7}$

9. The value of $\int_{1/2}^{2} e^{\left|x-\frac{1}{x}\right|}dx$ is equal to

(a) $e\sqrt{e}-2$ (b) $e\sqrt{e}-13$
(c) $e\sqrt{e}+1$ (d) $e\sqrt{e}-1$

10. AB is a vertical tower. The point A is on the ground and C is the middle point of AB. The part CB subtends an angle α at a point P on the ground. If $AP = nAB$, then the correct relation is

(a) $n=(n^2+1)\tan\alpha$ (b) $n=(2n^2+1)\tan\alpha$
(c) $n^2=(2n^2+1)\tan\alpha$ (d) $n=(2n^2-1)\tan\alpha$

11. The least value of the product xyz for which the determinant $\begin{vmatrix} x & 1 & 1 \\ 1 & y & 1 \\ 1 & 1 & z \end{vmatrix}$ is non-negative, is

(a) -1 (b) $-16\sqrt{2}$
(c) -8 (d) $-\sqrt{2}$

12. Coefficient of x^{11} in the expansion of $(1+x^2)^4(1+x^3)^7(1+x^4)^{12}$ is

(a) 1113 (b) 1051
(c) 1120 (d) 1106

13. The SD of a variate x is σ. Then SD of the variate $\frac{ax+b}{c}$, where a, b, c are constants, is

(a) $\left(\frac{a}{c}\right)\sigma$ (b) $\left|\frac{a}{c}\right|\sigma$
(c) $\left(\frac{a^2}{c^2}\right)\sigma$ (d) None of these

14. $\lim_{n\to\infty} [\sqrt{n^2+n+1}-(\sqrt{n^2+n+1})]$, $n \in I$, where $[\cdot]$ denotes greatest integer function, equals

(a) $\frac{1}{2}$ (b) $\frac{1}{4}$ (c) 0 (d) $\frac{2}{3}$

15. Tangents are drawn to the hyperbola $\frac{x^2}{9}-\frac{y^2}{4}=1$, parallel to the straight line $2x-y=1$. If the points of contact of the tangents on the hyperbola are (a,b) and (c,d). Find the value of $|a+d|$, if $a>0$

(a) $\frac{7}{2\sqrt{2}}$ (b) $\frac{9}{2\sqrt{2}}$
(c) $\frac{11}{2\sqrt{2}}$ (d) $\sqrt{2}$

16. If $(p\wedge q)\to r$ has truth value F, then the truth values of p,q,r are respectively

(a) T, F, F (b) F, F, T
(c) T, T, T (d) T, T, F

17. Let $S_n=C_0+3C_1+5C_2+7C_3+\ldots+(2n+1)C_n$, where $C_r={}^nC_r$. If $S_9=2^a\cdot3^b\cdot5^c$, then

(a) $abc=11$ (b) $a+c=10$
(c) $ab+bc+ca=10$ (d) $a+b+c=10$

18. Which of the following statements is true for the function

$$f(x)=\begin{cases} \sqrt{x}, & x\ge1 \\ x^3, & 0\le x\le1 \\ \frac{x^3}{3}-4x, & x<0 \end{cases}$$

(a) $f'(x)$ fails to exist for three distinct real values of x
(b) The function attains its extreme values at x_1 and x_2, such that $x_1\cdot x_2>0$
(c) It is monotonic increasing for all $x\in R$
(d) $f'(x)$ changes its sign twice as x varies from $-\infty$ to ∞

19. If $\omega\ne1$ is a cube root of unity and $(\omega+x)^n=1+12\overline{\omega}+69\omega+\ldots$, then the value of n and x are respectively

(a) 36 and 1 (b) 24 and $\frac{1}{2}$
(c) 18 and $\frac{1}{3}$ (d) 12 and 2

20. Let $f(x)=\frac{x}{(1+x^n)^{1/n}}$ for $n\ge2$ and $g(x)=\underbrace{(fofofo\ldots fof)}_{n-\text{times}}(x)$ then $\int g(x)\cdot x^{n-2}dx$ equals

(a) $\frac{1}{n(n-1)}(1+nx^n)^{1-\frac{1}{n}}+C$
(b) $\frac{1}{n-1}(1+nx^n)^{1-\frac{1}{n}}+C$
(c) $\frac{1}{n(n-1)}(1+nx^n)^{1+\frac{1}{n}}+C$
(d) $\frac{1}{n+1}(1+nx^n)^{1+\frac{1}{n}}+C$

Section II *Numerical Value Questions*

21. If a straight line L intersects the same branch of the rectangular hyperbola H in P,Q and its asymptotes in P' and Q', then $PP'-QQ'$ is equal to

22. Let $f(x)$ be a non-constant twice differentiable function on R such that $f(2+x)=f(2-x)$ and $f'\left(\frac{1}{2}\right)=f'(1)=0$. Then, minimum number of roots of the equation $f'(x)=0$ in $(0, 4)$ is

23. For the given equation, $\sin(\cot^{-1}(1+x))=\cos(\tan^{-1}x)$, find the value of $(-6x)$ such that x satisfies it.

24. Locus of all the points which are at a distance of 3 units from the line $\mathbf{r}=\lambda(\hat{\mathbf{i}}+\hat{\mathbf{j}}+\hat{\mathbf{k}})$ is given by $x^2+y^2+z^2-xy-yz-zx=k$. Then, the value of $(2k)$ is

25. If first row of a matrix A is $[1\ 3\ 2]$. If $\operatorname{adj}A = \begin{bmatrix} -2 & 4 & \alpha \\ -1 & 2 & 1 \\ 3\alpha & -5 & -2 \end{bmatrix}$, then a possible value of det (A), where, $\alpha \in N$, is

26. The number of solution of the equation $1 + \cos x + \cos 2x + \sin x + \sin 2x + \sin 3x = 0$, which satisfy the condition $\frac{\pi}{2} < \left|3x - \frac{\pi}{2}\right| \le \pi$ is

27. Find area (in sq units) of the triangle formed by the X-axis and tangent and normal drawn to the curve $y = x^2$ at (1, 1) is equal to

28. The number of real values of λ for which the system of linear equations

$$2x + 4y + \lambda z = 0,\ 4x + \lambda y + 2z = 0,\ \lambda x + 2y + 2z = 0$$

has infinitely many solutions, is....

29. If the equation of the plane passing through the point $(-1,2,0)$ and parallel to the lines $\frac{x}{3} = \frac{y+1}{0} = \frac{z-2}{-1}$ and $\frac{x-1}{1} = \frac{y+1}{2} = \frac{z+1}{-1}$ is $ax + by + cz = 1$, then the value of $(a + b + c)$ is

30. Let l be the length of the latus rectum of the parabola whose focus is (1, 2) and two tangents are $x - y = 0$ and $x + y = 0$, then $\sqrt{5}l$, is equal to

Answers

1 *(a)*	2 *(c)*	3 *(d)*	4 *(c)*	5 *(d)*	6 *(b)*	7 *(b)*	8 *(a)*	9 *(d)*	10 *(b)*
11 *(c)*	12 *(a)*	13 *(b)*	14 *(a)*	15 *(a)*	16 *(d)*	17 *(c)*	18 *(d)*	19 *(b)*	20 *(a)*
21 *(0)*	22 *(4)*	23 *(3)*	24 *(27)*	25 *(1)*	26 *(2)*	27 *(1.25)*	28 *(1)*	29 *(5)*	30 *(6)*

See detailed solutions on page no. 248

Knockout 06

JEE MAIN LEVEL

Mathematics

*Instructions

1. This question paper contains of 30 Questions of Mathematics, divided into two sections : **Section I** Objective Type Questions and **Section II** Numerical Type Questions.
2. Section I contains 20 Objective questions and all Questions are compulsory (Marking Scheme : Correct + 4, Incorrect – 1).
3. Section II contains 10 Numerical value questions out of which only 5 questions are to be attempted (Marking Scheme : Correct + 4, Incorrect 0).

Section I *Multiple Choice Questions*

1. The domain of the function $f(x)=\sqrt[6]{4^x+8^{(2/3)(x-2)}-52-2^{2(x-1)}}$ is

(a) $[3,\infty)$ (b) $(3,\infty)$ (c) $(-\infty,3]$ (d) $(-\infty,-3)$

2. If $(x-5)^{x^2-5x+6}=1$, then

(a) sum of all integral solutions is 11
(b) sum of all integral solutions is 16
(c) product of all integral solutions is 144
(d) product of all integral solutions is 30

3. If $\int\{x(1-x^2)\}^{1/3}x^{-4}dx=A(x^B-1)^C+K$, then

(a) $A=\dfrac{3}{8}$ (b) $B=2$
(c) $C=-4/3$ (d) $8A+B+3C+1=0$

4. Radius of the circle touching the parabola $y^2=4x$ at the upper end of latus rectum and passing through its focus is

(a) 1 unit (b) $\sqrt{2}$ units (c) $\sqrt{3}$ units (d) 2 units

5. The total number of points of intersection of the curve $y=81^{\sin^2 x}+81^{\cos^2 x}-30$ with the X-axis in the region $-\pi\le x\le\pi$ is

(a) 4 (b) 6 (c) 8 (d) 2

6. For what values of a and b so that

$$f(x)=\begin{cases}\dfrac{a\cdot e^{\frac{1}{|x+2|}}-1}{2-e^{\frac{1}{|x+2|}}}, & -3<x<-2\\ \sin\left(\dfrac{x^4-16}{x^5+32}\right), & -2<x<0\\ b, & x=-2\end{cases}$$

may be continuous at $x=-2$

(a) $a=\sin\left(\dfrac{2}{5}\right)$, $b=\sin\left(\dfrac{-2}{5}\right)$ (b) $a=1, b=0$
(c) $a=0, b=1$ (d) None of these

7. The sum of the terms of the GP $a, ar, ar^2, \dots, \infty$, where '$a$' is the only integral solution for the inequality $\log_{1/2}\left(\dfrac{2a-5}{a-3}\right)\ge 0$ and r is given by the relation $\dfrac{1}{r}=e^{\left(\int_0^{\sqrt{2}-1}\frac{1}{1+x}dx\right)}$ is

(a) $\dfrac{2}{\sqrt{2}-1}$ (b) $\dfrac{\sqrt{2}}{\sqrt{2}-1}$ (c) $\dfrac{2\sqrt{2}}{\sqrt{2}+1}$ (d) $\dfrac{2\sqrt{2}}{\sqrt{2}-1}$

8. The range of 'a' for which the inequality $1+\log_5(x^2+1)\ge\log_5(ax^2+4x+a)$ is valid for all real x is

(a) [2, 3] (b) (2, 3] (c) [2, 3) (d) (2, 3)

9. The statement $(p\Rightarrow q)\Leftrightarrow(\sim p\wedge q)$ is

(a) tautology (b) contradiction
(c) Neither (a) nor (b) (d) None of these

10. The sum of the reciprocals of the intercepts made on the coordinate axes by any line not passing through the origin and through the point of intersection of the lines $2x+3y=6$ and $3x+2y=6$ is

(a) $\dfrac{6}{5}$ (b) $\dfrac{5}{6}$ (c) -1 (d) $\dfrac{-5}{6}$

11. If a is a positive real number, $z=a+2i$ and $z|z|-az+1=0$, then

(a) z is purely imaginary
(b) $a^2=4$
(c) $a^2=2$
(d) no such complex number exists

12. If the standard deviation of the number 2, 3, a and 11 is 3.5, then which of the following is true?

(a) $3a^2-26a+55=0$ (b) $3a^2-23a+44=0$
(c) $3a^2-34a+91=0$ (d) $3a^2-32a+84=0$

13. A vector $\mathbf{x}$ is coplanar with vectors $\mathbf{a}=-\hat{i}+\hat{j}+\hat{k}$ and $\mathbf{b}=2\hat{i}+\hat{k}$ and is orthogonal to the vector $\mathbf{b}$. If $\mathbf{x}\cdot\mathbf{a}=7$, then the vector $\mathbf{x}$ equals

(a) $\frac{-3}{2}\hat{i}+\frac{5}{2}\hat{j}+3\hat{k}$ (b) $\frac{3}{2}\hat{i}+\frac{5}{2}\hat{j}+3\hat{k}$
(c) $3\hat{i}-5\hat{j}+\hat{k}$ (d) None of these

14. The set of natural numbers is divided in groups in the following ways

(1), (2, 3, 4), (5, 6, 7, 8, 9),

then the sum of the numbers in nth group is

(a) $(n+1)^3-n^3$ (b) $(n-1)^3+n^3$
(c) $(n-1)^2+1$ (d) $(n+1)^2+1$

15. If $\frac{dy}{dx}+\sin y+x\cos y+x=0$ and $y(0)=\frac{\pi}{2}$, then $\tan\left[\frac{y(1/4)}{2}\right]$ is equal to

(a) 0.75 (b) 7.5 (c) 75 (d) 0.55

16. Suppose A, B and C are three mutually exclusive and exhaustive events such that $3P(A)=2P(B)$ and $P(B)=2P(C)$, then $\frac{1}{P(A\cup B)}$ is equal to

(a) $\frac{10}{13}$ (b) $\frac{13}{10}$ (c) $\frac{3}{10}$ (d) $\frac{1}{3}$

17. The number of values of k for which the system of equation $(k+1)x+8y=4k$ and $kx+(k+3)y=3k-1$ has no solution is

(a) 1 (b) 2 (c) 3 (d) infinite

18. In the expansion of $(x+y)^m$ has 3 consecutive coefficients in AP, then the smallest possible value of m can be (here $m\in N$) is

(a) 9 (b) 14 (c) 2 (d) 7

19. For $n\in N$ and $\Delta_n=\begin{vmatrix} n! & (n+1)! & (n+2)! \\ (n+1)! & (n+2)! & (n+3)! \\ (n+2)! & (n+3)! & (n+4)! \end{vmatrix}$, then the value of $\lim_{n\to\infty}\frac{(-n^3+2n^2+5n)\cdot\Delta_n}{\Delta_{n+1}}$

(a) -2 (b) 0 (c) 1 (d) -1

20. If A and B are two idempotent matrices of the same order such that $A+B$ is also an idempotent matrix, then $AB+BA$ is a

(a) null matrix (b) unit matrix
(c) non-singular matrix (d) None of these

Section II *Numerical Value Questions*

21. If $|z_1|=1,|z_2|=2,|z_3|=3$ and $|z_1+2z_2+3z_3|=6$, then the value of $|z_2z_3+8z_3z_1+27z_1z_2|$ is

22. Let $L=\lim_{x\to\infty}x^2\cdot\sin\left(\log_e\sqrt{\cos\frac{\pi}{x}}\right)$, then the value of $\frac{-8L}{\pi^2}$ is

23. If the X-axis divides the area of the region bounded by the parabola $y=4x-x^2$ and $y=x^2-x$ in the ratio $a:b$, then ab is equal to

24. If a variable plane forms a tetrahedron of constant volume $64k^3$ with the coordinate planes and the locus of the tetrahedron is $xyz=\lambda k^{\mu}$. Then, $\lambda+\mu$ equals ....

25. The total number of different 9-digit numbers that can be formed from the number 223355888, so that the odd digits occupy even position is, ...

26. $\int_0^{\infty}\left[\frac{x+1}{e^x}\right]dx$, where $[\cdot]$ denotes greatest integer function, is equal to ....

27. A circle touches the line $y=x$ at the point (2,2) and has its centre on Y-axis, then square of its radius is

28. A person standing on the bank of a river observes that the angle subtended by a tree on the opposite bank is 60°. When he retires 40 m from the bank, he finds the angle to be 30°. The breadth of the river is .... m.

29. A function $y=f(x)$ is represented parametrically as follows

$$x=\lambda(t)=t^5-5t^3-20t+7$$

and $$y=\mu(t)=4t^3-3t^2-18t+3,$$

where $t\in[-2,2]$

If $f(x)$ attains minima at $t=\alpha$ and maxima at $t=\beta$, then $\alpha+6\beta$ is equal to ....

30. The tangent to $y=ax^2+bx+\frac{7}{2}$ at (1, 2) is parallel to the normal at the point $(-2, 2)$ on the curve $y=x^2+6x+10$. Then, the value of $(a-2b)$ is ....

Answers

1 (a)	2 (c)	3 (d)	4 (b)	5 (c)	6 (a)	7 (d)	8 (b)	9 (c)	10 (b)
11 (d)	12 (d)	13 (a)	14 (b)	15 (a)	16 (b)	17 (a)	18 (d)	19 (d)	20 (a)
21 (36)	22 (2)	23 (484)	24 (9)	25 (60)	26 (0)	27 (8)	28 (20)	29 (8)	30 (6)

See detailed solutions on page no. 252

Knockout 07

JEE MAIN LEVEL

Mathematics

*Instructions

1. This question paper contains of 30 Questions of Mathematics, divided into two sections : **Section I** Objective Type Questions and **Section II** Numerical Type Questions.
2. Section I contains 20 Objective questions and all Questions are cumpulsory (Marking Scheme : Correct + 4, Incorrect – 1).
3. Section II contains 10 Numerical value questions out of which only 5 questions are to be attempted (Marking Scheme : Correct + 4, Incorrect 0).

Section I *Multiple Choice Questions*

1. Consider the function $f(x)$ satisfying the identity

$f(x)+f\left(\frac{x-1}{x}\right)=1+x, \forall x\in R-\{0,1\}$ and

$g(x)=2f(x)-x+1$. Then, the domain of $y=\sqrt{g(x)}$ is

(a) $\left(-\infty,\frac{1-\sqrt{5}}{2}\right]\cup\left[1,\frac{1+\sqrt{5}}{2}\right]$

(b) $\left[\frac{1-\sqrt{5}}{2},0\right)\cup\left[1,\frac{1+\sqrt{5}}{2}\right]$

(c) $\left(-\infty,\frac{1-\sqrt{5}}{2}\right]\cup(0,1)\cup\left[\frac{1+\sqrt{5}}{2},\infty\right)$

(d) $\left[\frac{-1-\sqrt{5}}{2},0\right]\cup\left[\frac{-1+\sqrt{5}}{2},1\right]$

2. In a ΔABC, $b+c=2a$ and $\angle A=60^\circ$. Let O be an interior point and its distance from three sides are 3, 4, 5 units, then circum radius of ΔABC is

(a) 8 (b) 6

(c) 16 (d) 10

3. Number of solutions of $z\in C$ with $|z|=1$ and $\left|\frac{z}{\bar{z}}+\frac{\bar{z}}{z}\right|=1$ is

(a) 4 (b) 8

(c) 6 (d) 2

4. The angle at which the curve $y=K\cdot e^{Kx}$ intersects the Y-axis is

(a) $\cot^{-1}(K^2)$ (b) $\sin^{-1}\left(\frac{1}{K^2}\right)$

(c) $\tan^{-1}(K^2)$ (d) None of these

5. Infinite number of triangles are formed as shown in figure.

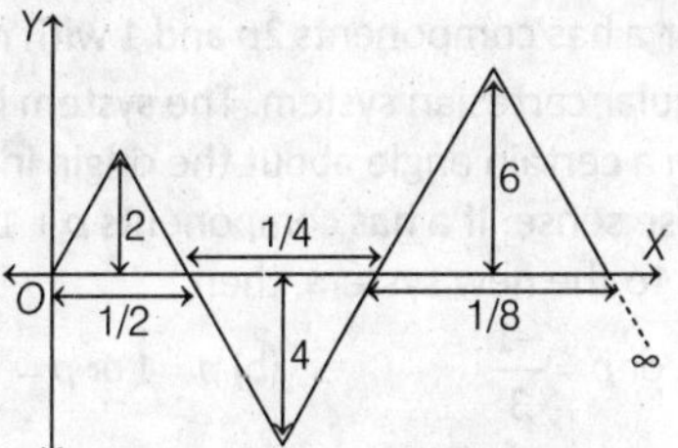

If total area of these triangles is Δ, then $\Delta=$ ....

(a) 1 sq unit (b) 2 sq units

(c) 3 sq units (d) 4 sq units

6. The coefficient of the term independent of x in the expansion of $(1+x+2x^3)\left(\frac{3x^2}{2}-\frac{1}{3x}\right)^9$ is

(a) $\frac{19}{54}$ (b) $\frac{1}{3}$ (c) $\frac{17}{54}$ (d) $\frac{1}{4}$

7. Given a real valued function $f(x)$, defined as

$$f(x)=\begin{cases}\frac{\tan^2\{x\}}{(x^2-[x]^2)}, & x>0\\ 1, & x=0\\ \sqrt{\{x\}\cdot\cot\{x\}}, & x<0\end{cases}$$

where $[x]$ and $\{x\}$ represents greatest integer function and fractional part of x, respectively. Then, mark the incorrect statement.

(a) $\lim_{x\to 0^+} f(x)=1$ (b) $\cot^{-1}\left[\lim_{x\to 0^-} f(x)\right]^{-2}=1$

(c) $\tan^{-1}\left[\lim_{x\to 0^+} f(x)\right]=\frac{\pi}{4}$ (d) $\lim_{x\to 0} f(x)$ does not exists

8. The straight lines l_1, l_2, l_3 are parallel and lie in the same plane. A total number of m points are taken on l_1, n points on l_2, k points on l_3. The maximum number of triangles formed with vertices at these points are

(a) ${}^{m+n+k}C_3$
(b) ${}^{m+n+k}C_3 - {}^mC_3 - {}^nC_3 - {}^kC_3$
(c) ${}^mC_3 + {}^nC_3 + {}^kC_3$
(d) None of the above

9. If A is a square matrix and e^A is defined as $e^A = I + A + \frac{A^2}{2!} + \frac{A^3}{3!} + \ldots = \frac{1}{2}\begin{bmatrix} f(x) & g(x) \\ g(x) & f(x) \end{bmatrix}$, where $A = \begin{bmatrix} x & x \\ x & x \end{bmatrix}$, $0 < x < 1$ and I is a unit matrix. Then, $\int \frac{f(x)}{\sqrt{g(x)}} dx$ is

(a) $\sqrt{e^x - 1} - \operatorname{cosec}^{-1}(e^x) + C$
(b) $\sqrt{e^{2x} - 1} + \sec^{-1}(e^x) + C$
(c) $\frac{2}{\sqrt{e^x - e^{-x}}} + \operatorname{cosec}^{-1}(e^x) + C$
(d) $\frac{2}{\sqrt{e^x - e^{-x}}} - \sec^{-1}(e^x) + C$

10. A vector **a** has components $2p$ and 1 with respect to a rectangular cartesian system. The system is rotated through a certain angle about the origin in the counter clockwise sense. If **a** has components $p+1$ and 1 with respect to the new system, then

(a) $p = 1$ or $p = \frac{-1}{3}$
(b) $p = 1$ or $p = -1$
(c) $p = -1$ or $p = \frac{1}{3}$
(d) $p = 0$

11. The equation of the circle through the vertices of the triangle whose sides are represented by the equation $x + y = 2, 3x - 4y = 6$ and $x - y = 0$ is

(a) $x^2 + y^2 - 4x + 6y - 12 = 0$
(b) $2x^2 + 2y^2 - 8x - 7y + 11 = 0$
(c) $x^2 + y^2 + 4x + 6y - 12 = 0$
(d) $x^2 + y^2 + 4x - 6y - 12 = 0$

12. A bag contains an assortment of blue and red balls. If two balls are drawn at random, the probability of drawing two red balls is five times the probability of drawing two blue balls. Further more, the probability of drawing one ball of each colour is six times the probability of drawing two blue balls. The number of red and blue balls in the bag respectively is

(a) 6, 3
(b) 3, 6
(c) 2, 7
(d) None of these

13. The equation of the line passing through the point (2, 3) and making intercept of length 2 units between the lines $y + 2x = 3$ and $y + 2x = 5$ are

(a) $3x + 4y = 18$
(b) $x - 2 = 0$
(c) Both (a) and (b)
(d) Neither (a) nor (b)

14. If the mean deviation about the median of the numbers $a, 2a, 3a, \ldots\ldots, 50a$ is 50, then $|a|$ equals

(a) 2
(b) 3
(c) 4
(d) 5

15. Given a function $f : [0, 4] \to R$ is differentiable, then for some $a, b \in (0, 4)$, $[f(4)]^2 - [f(0)]^2$ is equal to

(a) $8f'(b)f(a)$
(b) $f'(b)f(a)$
(c) $4f'(b)f(a)$
(d) $2f'(b)f(a)$

16. The determinant $\begin{vmatrix} (1+ax)^2 & (1+ay)^2 & (1+az)^2 \\ (1+bx)^2 & (1+by)^2 & (1+bz)^2 \\ (1+cx)^2 & (1+cy)^2 & (1+cz)^2 \end{vmatrix}$ equals

(a) $[1 + (a+b+c)x][1 + (a+b+c)y][1 + (a+b+c)z]$
(b) $(a+b+c)^2(x+y+z)^2$
(c) $(a+b+c)(x+y+z)$
(d) $2(a-b)(b-c)(c-a)(x-y)(y-z)(z-x)$

17. A piece of wire of length $4L$ is bent at random, to form a rectangle. The probability that its area is at most $\frac{L^2}{4}$ is

(a) $\frac{1}{4}$
(b) $\frac{\sqrt{3}}{2}$
(c) $\frac{2-\sqrt{3}}{2}$
(d) $4 - \sqrt{3}$

18. The distance of the point (1, –2, 3) from the line through (2, –3, 5) which makes equal angle with axes is

(a) $\sqrt{\frac{7}{3}}$ units
(b) $\sqrt{\frac{14}{3}}$ units
(c) 7 units
(d) 3 units

19. $[(p \vee q) \wedge \sim p] \to q$ is a

(a) tautology
(b) contradiction
(c) Neither a tautology nor a contradiction
(d) None of the above

20. Let $f(x) = x^3 - x^2 + x + 1$ and $g(x) = \begin{cases} \max\{f(t); 0 \le t \le x\}, & 0 \le x \le 1 \\ 3 - x, & 1 < x \le 2 \end{cases}$, then $g(x)$ is

(a) continuous in (0, 2) and differentiable in $(0, 1) \cup (1, 2)$
(b) continuous and differentiable in (0, 2) except at $x = 1$
(c) continuous in $(0, 1] \cup [1, 2)$ and differentiable in (0, 2)
(d) Neither continuous in (0, 2) nor differentiable in (0, 2)

Section II *Numerical Value Questions*

21. If $f(x)$ is continuous such that

$f(x) = f(3x - 4y) + f(4y - 2x) - (3x - 4y)(4y - 2x), \forall x, y \in R$ and $\lim_{h \to 0} \frac{f(h)}{h} = 4$, then $f'(2)$ is ....

22. If $x=a, y=b, z=c$ is a solution of the system of linear equations $x+8y+7z=0$, $9x+2y+3z=0$ and $x+y+z=0$ Such that the point (a,b,c) lies on the plane $x+2y+z=6$, then $2a+b+c$ equals ....

23. In ΔABC, the side lengths BC, CA and AB are consecutive positive integers in increasing order. Let **a**, **b**, **c** be the position vector of vertices A, B and C respectively. If $(\mathbf{c}-\mathbf{a})\cdot(\mathbf{b}-\mathbf{c})=0$, then the value of $|\mathbf{a}\times\mathbf{b}+\mathbf{b}\times\mathbf{c}+\mathbf{c}\times\mathbf{a}|$ is equal to ....

24. If normals at points (a, y_1) and $(4-a, y_2)$ to the parabola $y^2=4x$ meet again on the parabola, then $\frac{1}{\sqrt{2}}|y_1+y_2|$ is equal to ....

25. If the differential equation of a curve passing through $\left(0, \frac{-\pi}{4}\right)$ and $(t, 0)$ is $\cos y\left(\frac{dy}{dx}+e^{-x}\right)+\sin y$. $\left(e^{-x}-\frac{dy}{dx}\right)=e^{e^{-x}}$, then the value of $\left|t\cdot e^{e^{-t}}\right|$ is ....

26. Let S be the set which contains all possible values of l, m, n, p, q, r for which

$$A=\begin{bmatrix} l^2-3 & p & 0 \\ 0 & m^2-8 & q \\ r & 0 & n^2-15 \end{bmatrix}$$ be a non-singular idempotent matrix. Then, the sum of all elements of the set S is ....

27. Let f be a continuous function satisfying the equation $\int_0^x f(t)\,dt+\int_0^x t\cdot f(x-t)\,dt=e^{-x}-1$, then the value of $e^{15}\cdot f(15)$ is equal to ....

28. Number of integral values of m for which the equation $\sin x-\sqrt{3}\cos x=\frac{4m-6}{4-m}$ has solution, $x\in[0,2\pi]$, is ....

29. The area between the curves $y=x^2+x-2$ and $y=2x$, for which $|x^2+x-2|+|2x|=|x^2+3x-2|$ is satisfied, is ....

30. Let E be an ellipse such that $x+y=2\sqrt{5}$ is a tangent to E and F passes through $(3,-1)$. If axes of E are along the coordinates axes and e is the eccentricity of E, then $9e^2$ equals ....

Answers

1 (c)	2 (a)	3 (b)	4 (a)	5 (b)	6 (c)	7 (d)	8 (b)	9 (b)	10 (a)
11 (c)	12 (a)	13 (c)	14 (c)	15 (a)	16 (d)	17 (c)	18 (b)	19 (a)	20 (b)
21 (2)	22 (1)	23 (12)	24 (4)	25 (1)	26 (0)	27 (14)	28 (4)	29 (2.33)	30 (8)

See detailed solutions on page no. 256

Knockout 08

JEE MAIN LEVEL

Mathematics

*Instructions

1. This question paper contains of 30 Questions of Mathematics, divided into two sections : **Section I** Objective Type Questions and **Section II** Numerical Type Questions.
2. Section I contains 20 Objective questions and all Questions are cumpulsory (Marking Scheme : Correct + 4, Incorrect – 1).
3. Section II contains 10 Numerical value questions out of which only 5 questions are to be attempted (Marking Scheme : Correct + 4, Incorrect 0).

Section I *Multiple Choice Questions*

1. Let f be differentiable at $x=0$ and $f'(0)=1$, then $\lim_{h\to 0}\frac{f(h)-f(-2h)}{h}$ is equal to

(a) 3 (b) −1 (c) 1 (d) 2

2. In ΔABC, $\tan A$, $\tan B$ and $\tan C$ are in AP and $\tan A = K$, then $\frac{\sin A \sin C}{\sin B}$ equals

(a) $\frac{3}{K^2+2}$ (b) $\frac{3K}{K^2+3}$ (c) $\frac{3K}{K^2+1}$ (d) $\frac{3}{K^2+3}$

3. The ratio in which the area enclosed by the curves $y=\sqrt{4-x^2}$, $y\ge\sqrt{2}\sin\left(\frac{\pi x}{2\sqrt{2}}\right)$ and X-axis is divided by Y-axis is

(a) $\frac{2\pi^2}{\pi+\pi^2-8}$ (b) $\frac{2\pi^2}{2\pi+\pi^2-8}$

(c) $\frac{2\pi^2}{2\pi-\pi^2+8}$ (d) None of these

4. If p, q, r are in AP $(p, q, r \ne 0)$, if p is increased by 1 or r is increased by 2, the numbers become in GP. Then, the value of $q-p$ is

(a) 2 (b) 4 (c) 8 (d) 16

5. For $x, y \in R$, total possible ordered pair (s) (x, y) satisfying the system of equations $\log_{100}|x+y|=\frac{1}{2}$ and $\log_{10} y-\log_{10}|x|=\log_{100} 4$ is/are

(a) $\left(\frac{10}{3},\frac{20}{3}\right)$ (b) $\left(-10,\frac{20}{7}\right)$

(c) $(-10, 20)$ (d) Both (a) and (c)

6. The function $f: R\to R$ defined as $f(x)=\ln\left(\sqrt{\sqrt{x^2+1}+x}+\sqrt{\sqrt{x^2+1}-x}\right)$ is

(a) one-one and onto both
(b) onto but not one-one
(c) one-one but not onto
(d) neither one-one nor onto

7. Consider a ΔABC formed by lines $L_1: x+y=30$, $L_2: y-x=12$ and $L_3: x-3y=30$. If the points (a, a^2) lies in or on the triangle, then the sum of all possible integral values of a is

(a) 4 (b) 3
(c) 6 (d) None of these

8. m and n are chosen from {1, 2, 3, 4 .... , 100} (repetition allowed). The probability that 5 divides 3^m+3^n is

(a) $\frac{1}{16}$ (b) $\frac{1}{4}$ (c) $\frac{5}{12}$ (d) $\frac{3}{8}$

9. Which of the following statement is a tautology?

(a) $[(p\vee q)\wedge\sim p]\wedge(\sim q)$ (b) $(p\wedge q)\wedge(\sim p\vee\sim q)$
(c) $[(p\to q)\wedge\sim q]\to(\sim p)$ (d) None of these

10. A spherical balloon of radius r subtends an angle α at the eye of an observer. If the angle of elevation of the centre of the balloon is β, then the height of the centre of the balloon is

(a) $r\operatorname{cosec}\alpha\cdot\sin\left(\frac{\beta}{2}\right)$ (b) $r\operatorname{cosec}\left(\frac{\alpha}{2}\right)\sin\beta$

(c) $r\sin\alpha\operatorname{cosec}\left(\frac{\beta}{2}\right)$ (d) $r\sin\left(\frac{\alpha}{2}\right)\operatorname{cosec}\beta$

11. Number of different necklace that can be made using 5 beads of one kind, 3 beads of another kind is

(a) 2 (b) 3! (c) 5 (d) 5!

12. Let $x_1, x_2, x_3, x_4, \dots, x_n$ be n observations such that $\Sigma x_i^2 = 400$ and $\Sigma x_i = 80$. Then, a possible value of n among the following is

(a) 9 (b) 15 (c) 18 (d) 12

13. Let $S_n = \cot^{-1}\left(3x + \frac{2}{x}\right) + \cot^{-1}\left(6x + \frac{2}{x}\right) + \cot^{-1}\left(10x + \frac{2}{x}\right) + \dots$ upto n terms, where $x > 0$. If $\lim_{n\to\infty} S_n = 1$, then '$x$' equals

(a) 1 (b) $\tan 1$ (c) $\frac{\pi}{4}$ (d) $\cot 1$

14. The general solution of differential equation $\sin 2x\left(\frac{dy}{dx} - \sqrt{\tan x}\right) - y = 0$, is

(a) $y\sqrt{\cot y} = \tan x + C$ (b) $y = \sqrt{\tan x}(x + C)$

(c) $y = \sqrt{\cot x}(x + C)$ (d) $y\sqrt{\tan x} = \cot x + C$

15. The value of the definite integral $\int_0^{\pi} \frac{x}{1 - \cos\alpha \sin x} dx$ is equal to

(a) $\pi(\pi - \alpha)(\sin\alpha)^{-1}$ (b) $\pi(\pi + \alpha)(\sin\alpha)^{-1}$

(c) $\pi\left(\frac{\pi}{2} + \alpha\right)\sin\alpha$ (d) $\pi(\pi - \alpha)(\sin\alpha)$

16. Let $f(\theta) = \begin{vmatrix} \sin\theta & \cos\theta & \sin\theta \\ \cos\theta & \sin\theta & \cos\theta \\ \cos\theta & \sin\theta & \sin\theta \end{vmatrix}$, then mark the incorrect statement.

(a) $f(\theta) = 0$ has 2 solution in $[0, \pi]$

(b) The minimum value of $\frac{f(\theta)}{\cos\theta + \sin\theta}$ is 0

(c) The maximum value of $\frac{f(\theta)}{\cos\theta + \sin\theta}$ is 1

(d) The range of $\frac{f(\theta)}{1 - \sin 2\theta}$ is $[-\sqrt{2}, \sqrt{2}]$

17. The equation of circle c which touches the line $2x + 3y + 1 = 0$ at the point $(1, -1)$ and is orthogonal to the circle c_1 which has $(0, -1)$ and $(-2, 3)$ as the end points of a diameter is

(a) $2(x^2 + y^2) + 10x + 7y - 1 = 0$

(b) $x^2 + y^2 - 5x - \frac{5}{2}y + \frac{1}{2} = 0$

(c) $2(x^2 + y^2) - 10x - 5y + \frac{1}{2} = 0$

(d) $x^2 + y^2 - 5x - 5y + 1 = 0$

18. For $r = 0, 1, 2, 3, 4, \dots, 10$. Let A, B and C, denote respectively the coefficient of x^r in the expansion of $(1 + x)^{10}, (1 + x)^{20}$ and $(1 + x)^{30}$. Then, $\sum_{r=1}^{10} A_r(B_{10}B_r - C_{10}A_r)$ is equal to

(a) $B_{10} - C_{10}$ (b) 0

(c) $A_{10}(B_{10}^2 - C_{10}A_{10})$ (d) $C_{10} - B_{10}$

19. Given the function $f(x) = \frac{1}{1 - x}$, the points of discontinuity of the composite function $y = f^{3n}(x)$, where $f^n(x) = fofof \dots of$ (n times) are

(a) 0 (b) 1

(c) Both (a) and (b) (d) $3n$

20. If $\mathbf{a} = \hat{\mathbf{i}} + \hat{\mathbf{j}} - \hat{\mathbf{k}}$, $\mathbf{b} = \hat{\mathbf{i}} - \hat{\mathbf{j}} + \hat{\mathbf{k}}$ and $\mathbf{c}$ are unit vectors perpendicular to the vector $\mathbf{a}$ and coplanar with $\mathbf{a}$ and $\mathbf{b}$, then a unit vector $\mathbf{d}$ perpendicular to both $\mathbf{a}$ and $\mathbf{c}$ is

(a) $\frac{1}{\sqrt{6}}(2\hat{\mathbf{i}} - \hat{\mathbf{j}} + \hat{\mathbf{k}})$ (b) $\frac{1}{\sqrt{6}}(\hat{\mathbf{i}} - 2\hat{\mathbf{j}} + \hat{\mathbf{k}})$

(c) $\frac{1}{\sqrt{2}}(\hat{\mathbf{j}} + \hat{\mathbf{k}})$ (d) $\frac{1}{\sqrt{2}}(\hat{\mathbf{j}} - \hat{\mathbf{k}})$

Section II *Numerical Value Questions*

21. Tangents to the parabola $y^2 = 4ax$ drawn at points whose abscissae are in the ratio $\mu^2 : 1$, where $\mu > 1$. If locus of the point of intersection of these tangents is $y^2 = \frac{25}{4}ax$, then μ is equal to

22. If the distance between the plane $Ax - 2y + z = d$ and the plane containing the lines $\frac{x-1}{2} = \frac{y-2}{3} = \frac{z-3}{4}$ and $\frac{x-1}{3} = \frac{y-3}{4} = \frac{z-4}{5}$ is $\sqrt{6}$, then $10A + 3|d|$ is equal to

23. If $\int \frac{1}{x + \sqrt{x^2 - x + 1}} dx = m \cdot \log|t| + n\log|2t - 1| + \frac{p}{2t - 1} + C$, where $t = x + \sqrt{x^2 - x + 1}$, then the value of $2m + n + p$ is

24. The number of distinct real roots of $\begin{vmatrix} \sin x & \cos x & \cos x \\ \cos x & \sin x & \cos x \\ \cos x & \cos x & \sin x \end{vmatrix} = 0$ in the interval $\frac{-\pi}{4} \le x \le \frac{\pi}{4}$ is

25. If the extremities of the latusrectum of the hyperbola $\frac{x^2}{a^2} - \frac{y^2}{b^2} = 1$ with positive ordinates lie on the parabola $x^2 = 3(y + 3)$, then length of the transverse axis is

26. If $\lim_{x\to -2} \frac{\tan \pi x}{x + 2} + \lim_{x\to\infty}\left(1 + \frac{1}{x^2}\right)^x = \lambda$, then $\frac{[\lambda]}{2}$, where $[\cdot]$ denotes greatest integer function, is ....

27. If $a, b \in R$, then the number of complex numbers $a + ib$ for which $(a + ib)^2 = (a - ib)^3$, is ....

28. The slope of the tangent at (x, y) to the curve passing through $\left(1, \frac{\pi}{4}\right)$ is given by $\frac{y}{x} - \cos^2\left(\frac{y}{x}\right)$. If the equation of curve is $y = \phi(x)$, then the value of $\phi(e)$ is ....

29. Let x be the solution set of the equation $A^x = I$, where $A\begin{bmatrix} 0 & 1 & -1 \\ 4 & -3 & 4 \\ 3 & -3 & 4 \end{bmatrix}$ and I is the corresponding unit matrix and $x \subseteq N$, then the minimum value of $\Sigma(\cos^x \theta + \sin^x \theta)$, where $\theta \in R$ is ....

30. Let e be the eccentricity of the ellipse $\frac{x^2}{16} + \frac{y^2}{b^2} = 1$, where $0 < b < 4$. Let p_1, p_2 be the length of perpendicular from $(0, 4e)$ and $(0, -4e)$ to any tangent to the ellipse, then value of $\frac{(p_1^2 + p_2^2)}{8}$ is ....

Answers

1 (a)	2 (b)	3 (b)	4 (b)	5 (d)	6 (d)	7 (a)	8 (b)	9 (c)	10 (b)
11 (c)	12 (c)	13 (d)	14 (b)	15 (a)	16 (c)	17 (b)	18 (d)	19 (c)	20 (c)
21 (4)	22 (28)	23 (1)	24 (1)	25 (6)	26 (2)	27 (6)	28 (0)	29 (2)	30 (4)

See detailed solutions on page no. 260

Knockout 09

JEE MAIN LEVEL

Mathematics

*Instructions

1. This question paper contains of 30 Questions of Mathematics, divided into two sections :
Section I Objective Type Questions and **Section II** Numerical Type Questions.
2. Section I contains 20 Objective questions and all Questions are cumpulsory (Marking Scheme : Correct + 4, Incorrect − 1).
3. Section II contains 10 Numerical value questions out of which only 5 questions are to be attempted (Marking Scheme : Correct + 4, Incorrect 0).

Section I *Multiple Choice Questions*

1. Let $f(x)=x^3-\frac{3x^2}{2}+x+\frac{1}{4}$. Then, the value of $\left[\int_{1/4}^{3/4} f(f(x))\,dx\right]^{-3/2}$ is

(a) 4 (b) $\frac{1}{4}$ (c) 8 (d) $\sqrt{8}$

2. A pair of unbiased dice is rolled together till a sum of either 5 or 7 is obtained. The probability that 5 comes before 7 is

(a) $\frac{3}{5}$ (b) $\frac{2}{5}$

(c) $\frac{4}{5}$ (d) None of these

3. A tetrahedron has vertices $O(0, 0, 0)$, $A(1, 2, 1)$, $B(2, 1, 3)$ and $C(-1,1,2)$, then angle between faces OAB and ABC will be

(a) 60° (b) 90°

(c) $\cos^{-1}\left(\frac{17}{31}\right)$ (d) $\cos^{-1}\left(\frac{19}{35}\right)$

4. If the intercept made on the line $y=mx$ by the lines $x=2$ and $x=5$ is less than 5, then the range of m is

(a) $\left(-\frac{4}{3},\frac{4}{3}\right)$ (b) $\left[-\frac{4}{3},\frac{4}{3}\right)$

(c) $\left(-\infty,-\frac{4}{3}\right)\cup\left(\frac{4}{3},\infty\right)$ (d) None of these

5. Two circles w_1 and w_2 of radii R_1 and R_2 respectively, intersect at a point $A.BC$ is a common tangent. If R is the radius of the circle ABC, then R_1, R, R_2 form

(a) an AP (b) a GP

(c) a HP (d) None of these

6. Two lines draw through the point $P(4,0)$ divide the area bounded by the curves $y=\sqrt{2}\sin\left(\frac{\pi x}{4}\right)$ and X-axis, between the line $x=2$ and $x=4$, into three equal parts. Sum of the slopes of the drawn lines is equal to

(a) $-\frac{\sqrt{2}}{\pi}$ (b) $\frac{-2\sqrt{2}}{\pi}$

(c) $\frac{-2}{\pi}$ (d) $-\frac{4\sqrt{2}}{\pi}$

7. The coefficient of x in $f(x)=\begin{vmatrix} x & (1+\sin x)^3 & \cos x \\ 1 & \ln(1+x) & 2 \\ x^2 & (1+x)^2 & 0 \end{vmatrix}$ is

(a) 0 (b) 4

(c) 1 (d) None of these

8. The intervals of values of 'a' for which the line $y+x=0$ bisects two chords drawn from a point $\left(\frac{1+\sqrt{2}a}{2},\frac{1-\sqrt{2}a}{2}\right)$ to the circle $2x^2+2y^2-(1+\sqrt{2}a)x-(1-\sqrt{2}a)y=0$ is

(a) $(-\infty,\infty)$

(b) $(-\infty,1)\cup(1,\infty)$

(c) $(-2,2)$

(d) $(-\infty,-2)\cup(2,\infty)$

9. Let $f:R\to R$ be a continuous onto function satisfying $f(x)+f(-x)=0$, $\forall\, x\in R$. If $f(-3)=2$ and $f(5)=4$ in $[-5,5]$, then the equation $f(x)=0$ has

(a) exactly three real roots

(b) atleast five real roots

(c) atleast three real roots

(d) exactly two real roots

10. A Scientist is weighing each of 30 fishes. Their mean weight worked out is 30 gm and standard deviation of 2 gm. Later, it was found that the measuring scale was misaligned and always under reported every fish weight by 2 gm. The correct mean and standard deviation (in gm) of fishes are respectively

(a) 32, 4 (b) 28, 2 (c) 28, 4 (d) 34, 4

11. A right circular cone with radius R and height H contains a liquid which evaporates at the rate proportional to its surface area in contact with air proportionality constant $= k > 0$). The time after which the cone is empty

(a) $\frac{H}{k}$ (b) $\frac{k}{H}$

(c) $\frac{2H}{k}$ (d) Hk

12. The angular depressions of the top and foot of a chimney as seen from the top of a second chimney, which is 150 m high and standing on the same level as the first are θ and ϕ respectively, then the distance between their tops when $\tan\theta = \frac{4}{3}$ and $\tan\phi = \frac{5}{2}$, is

(a) $\frac{150}{\sqrt{3}}$ m (b) $100\sqrt{3}$ m (c) 100 m (d) 1150 m

13. If $\int \frac{1}{1+x^4} dx = \frac{1}{m}\tan^{-1}(f(x)) - \frac{1}{n}\log|g(x)| + C$, then

(a) $m = 2n$ (b) $f(2) = \frac{1}{2\sqrt{2}}$

(c) $g(\sqrt{2}) = \frac{1}{5}$ (d) $m + n$ is an integer

14. $\lim_{x \to -1} \frac{1}{\sqrt{|x| - \{-x\}}} =$ ......, where $\{x\}$ = fractional part of x

(a) 1 (b) $\frac{1}{2}$

(c) 2 (d) None of these

15. Which of the following is logically true ?

(a) $p \leftrightarrow q \equiv (p \to q) \wedge (q \to p)$

(b) $p \to q \equiv (\sim p) \vee q$

(c) $(p \leftrightarrow q) \equiv (q \leftrightarrow p)$

(d) All of the above

16. In the two dimensional analytical plane having rectangular Cartesian system, A and B are two points on the curve $y = 2^{x+2}$ such that $\mathbf{OA} \cdot \hat{\mathbf{i}} = -1$ and $\mathbf{OB} \cdot \hat{\mathbf{i}} = 2$, where i is the unit vector in positive direction of X-axis. If $\mathbf{a} = \mathbf{OA}$, $\mathbf{b} = \mathbf{OB}$ and $\mathbf{c} = 2\mathbf{a} + \mathbf{b}$, then the angle θ between $\mathbf{a}$ and $\mathbf{c}$ is, (where O is origin and $\theta \in \left(0, \frac{\pi}{2}\right)$)

(a) $\tan^{-1}(0.5)$ (b) $\cos^{-1}(0.5)$

(c) $\sin^{-1}\left(\frac{1}{3}\right)$ (d) None of these

17. Let S be a square of unit area. Consider any quadrilateral, which has one vertex on each side of s. If a, b, c and d denote the lengths of the sides of the quadrilateral, then the range of $a^2 + b^2 + c^2 + d^2$ is

(a) [0, 4] (b) [1, 2]

(c) [2, 4] (d) [1, 3]

18. Let $P(3\sec\theta, 2\tan\theta)$ and $Q(3\sec\phi, 2\tan\phi)$ where $\theta + \phi = \frac{\pi}{2}$, be two distinct points on the hyperbola $\frac{x^2}{9} - \frac{y^2}{4} = 1$. Then, the ordinate of the point of intersection of the normals at P and Q is

(a) $\frac{11}{3}$ (b) $\frac{-13}{2}$

(c) $\frac{-11}{3}$ (d) $\frac{13}{2}$

19. If the length of projection of the line segment joining (2, 3, 4) and (5, 6, 7) on plane $2x + y + z = 1$ is λ, then the value of λ^8 is

(a) 18 (b) $\sqrt{3}$

(c) 27 (d) 81

20. If the curve $y = x^2 + bx + c$ touches the straight line $y = x$ at the point (1, 1), then b and c are given by

(a) $-1, 1$ (b) $-1, 2$

(c) 2,1 (d) 1,1

Section II *Numerical Value Questions*

21. If the length of focal chord of parabola $y^2 = 36x$ at point $A(t^2, 6t)$ is 100, then the sum of values of t is ....

22. If the pth, qth and rth term of an AP and GP are equal and are a, b, c, then $a^{b-c} b^{c-a} c^{a-b}$ is equal to ....

23. Let λ and α be real. Then, the number of integal values of λ for which the system of linear equations

$$\lambda x + (\sin\alpha) y + (\cos\alpha) z = 0$$
$$x + (\cos\alpha) y + (\sin\alpha) z = 0$$
$$-x + (\sin\alpha) y - (\cos\alpha) z = 0$$

has non- trivial solution is

24. The coefficient of the term independent of x in the expansion of $\left(\frac{x+1}{x^{2/3} - x^{1/3} + 1} - \frac{x-1}{x - x^{1/2}}\right)^{10}$ is ....

25. Number of roots of the equation

$2^{\tan\left(x - \frac{\pi}{4}\right)} - 2(0.25)^{\frac{\sin^2\left(x - \frac{\pi}{4}\right)}{\cos 2x}} + 1 = 0$ is ....

26. In a group of 13 cricket players, 4 are bowlers. Then, the total number of ways so that they form a cricket team of 11 players in which at least 2 bowlers are included, is ....

27. The continued product of the four values of $\left(\cos\frac{\pi}{3}+i\sin\frac{\pi}{3}\right)^{3/4}$ is ....

28. The population of a country increases at a rate proportional to the number of inhabitants. f is the population which doubles in 30 yr, then the population will triple in approximately ...... yr (given $\frac{\ln 3}{\ln 2}=1.5849$)

29. The number of lattice points (i.e. point with both coordinates as integers) on the ellipse $\frac{x^2}{49}+\frac{y^2}{25}=1$ is

30. If $L=\lim_{x\to 0}\frac{(1+x^2)^{1/3}-(1-2x)^{1/4}}{x+x^2}$, then the value of $(16\,L)$ is

Answers

1	(c)	2	(b)	3	(d)	4	(a)	5	(b)	6	(b)	7	(a)	8	(d)	9	(c)	10	(b)
11	(a)	12	(c)	13	(c)	14	(d)	15	(d)	16	(a)	17	(c)	18	(b)	19	(d)	20	(a)
21	(0)	22	(1)	23	(3)	24	(210)	25	(0)	26	(78)	27	(1)	28	(48)	29	(4)	30	(8)

See detailed solutions on page no. 265

Knockout 10

JEE MAIN LEVEL

Mathematics

*Instructions

1. This question paper contains of 30 Questions of Mathematics, divided into two sections : **Section I** Objective Type Questions and **Section II** Numerical Type Questions.
2. Section I contains 20 Objective questions and all Questions are cumpulsory (Marking Scheme : Correct + 4, Incorrect – 1).
3. Section II contains 10 Numerical value questions out of which only 5 questions are to be attempted (Marking Scheme : Correct + 4, Incorrect 0).

Section I *Multiple Choice Questions*

1. If $f(x)$ satisfies the relation $f\left(\frac{5x-3y}{2}\right)=\frac{5f(x)-3f(y)}{2}$, $\forall x, y \in R$ and $f(0)=3$ and $f'(0)=2$, then the period of $\sin(f(x))$ is

(a) π (b) 2π
(c) 3π (d) 4π

2. The statement $[(p \vee \sim q) \vee (\sim p \wedge q)] \wedge r$ is a

(a) tautology
(b) contradiction
(c) contigency
(d) None of the above

3. A circle touches the line $y=x$ at a point P such that $OP=4\sqrt{2}$, where O is origin. The circle contains the point $(-10,2)$ in its interior and the length of its chord on the line $x+y=0$ is $6\sqrt{2}$ units. Then, the equation of the circle is

(a) $x^2+y^2-7x+2y+32=0$
(b) $x^2+y^2+18x+2y+12=0$
(c) $2x^2+2y^2+36x-4y+14=0$
(d) $x^2+y^2+18x-2y+32=0$

4. The product of all values of x satisfying the equation $\sin^{-1}\left[\cos\left(\frac{2x^2+10|x|+4}{x^2+5|x|+3}\right)\right]=\cot\left[\tan^{-1}\left(\frac{9|x|}{2-18|x|}\right)\right]+\frac{\pi}{2}$ is

(a) -3 (b) 9 (c) -1 (d) -9

5. Tangent is drawn to ellipse $\frac{x^2}{27}+y^2=1$ at $(3\sqrt{3}\cos\theta, \sin\theta)$ $\left(\text{where } \theta \in \left(0, \frac{\pi}{2}\right)\right)$. Then, the value of θ such that sum of intercepts on axes made by this tangent is least, is

(a) $\frac{\pi}{6}$ (b) $\frac{\pi}{8}$ (c) $\frac{\pi}{3}$ (d) $\frac{\pi}{4}$

6. If P is the point (2, 1, 6), then the coordinates of the point Q such that PQ is perpendicular to the plane which is passing through the points (2, 1, 0), (5, 0, 1), (4, 1, 1) and the mid-point of PQ lies on it, is

(a) (6, 5, –2) (b) (5, –2, 6)
(c) (–2, 6, 5) (d) None of these

7. Instead of the usual definition of derivative $Df(x)$, if we define a new kind of derivative $D^*F(x)$ by the formula $D^*(x)=\lim_{h\to 0}\frac{f^2(x+h)-f^2(x)}{h}$, where $f^2(x)$ means $[f(x)]^2$ and, if $f(x)=x\log_e x$, then $D^*f(x)\big|_{x=e}$ has the value

(a) $2e$ (b) $4e$
(c) e (d) $\frac{1}{4}e$

8. The length intercepted between the coordinate axes in first quadrant by the common tangent of the circle $x^2+y^2=16$ and the ellipse $\frac{x^2}{25}+\frac{y^2}{4}=1$ is

(a) 14 units (b) $\sqrt{3}$ units
(c) $\frac{14}{3}$ units (d) $\frac{14}{\sqrt{3}}$ units

9. The probability of choosing an integer λ, randomly from the integers 1, 2, 3, ..., $2n$ is proportional to $\log \lambda$. The conditional probability of choosing integer 2, given that an even integer is chosen, is

(a) $\frac{\log 2}{\log 2 + \log(n!)}$ (b) $\frac{\log 2}{n\log 2 + \log(n!)}$

(c) $\frac{\log n}{n\log 2 + \log(n!)}$ (d) $\frac{1}{\log(n!)}$

10. If $f(x) = x^5 + 5x - 1$, then $\int_5^{41} \frac{dx}{[f^{-1}(x)]^5 + 5f^{-1}(x)}$ is equal to

(a) ln6 (b) ln7

(c) 0 (d) $\log_e 42$

11. $e^{|\sin x|} + e^{-|\sin x|} + 4\lambda = 0$ will have exactly four different solutions in $[0, 2\pi]$, if

(a) $\lambda \in R$ (b) $\lambda \in \left[\frac{-e}{4}, \frac{-1}{4}\right]$

(c) $\lambda \in \left[\frac{-1-e^2}{4e}, \frac{-1}{2}\right]$ (d) $\lambda \in \left[\frac{e^2+1}{4e}, \infty\right)$

12. If $\int \frac{(\sqrt{x})^5}{(\sqrt{x})^7 + x^6} dx = a \cdot \ln\left|\frac{x^k}{x^k + 1}\right| + C$, then value of '$a$' and '$k$' respectively

(a) $\frac{5}{2}$ and $\frac{2}{5}$ (b) $\frac{2}{5}$ and $\frac{5}{2}$

(c) $\frac{5}{2}$ and 2 (d) None of these

13. If a variable X takes values 0, 1, 2, 3, ... ,10 with frequencies proportional to the binomial coefficients ${}^{10}C_0, {}^{10}C_1, {}^{10}C_2, \ldots, {}^{10}C_{10}$, then the Var(X) is

(a) $\frac{5}{2}$ (b) $\frac{2}{5}$ (c) 5 (d) 52

14. If the locus of the point$(4t^2 - 1, 8t - 2)$ represents a parabola, then the equation of latusrectum is

(a) $x - 5 = 0$ (b) $2x - 7 = 0$

(c) $x + 5 = 0$ (d) $x - 3 = 0$

15. If α is a root of $x^2 + ax + 1 = 0$, then $\lim_{x \to \frac{1}{\alpha}} \cdot \frac{\sin(x^2 + ax + 1)}{(\alpha x - 1)}$ is equal to

(a) $2a\alpha$ (b) $a\alpha^2$

(c) $\frac{1-\alpha^2}{\alpha^2}$ (d) does not exist

16. The greatest and least value of $|z_1 + z_2|$, if $z_1 = 24 + 7i$ and $|z_2| = 6$ are respectively

(a) 31 and 19 (b) 25 and 19

(c) 31 and 25 (d) 19 and 31

17. If the latusrectum of a hyperbola subtends an angle of 60° at the other focus, then eccentricity of the hyperbola is

(a) 2 (b) $\frac{\sqrt{3}+1}{2}$ (c) $2\sqrt{2}$ (d) $\sqrt{3}$

18. A function $y = f(x)$ satisfies $(x+1)f'(x) - 2(x^2 + x)f(x) = \frac{e^{x^2}}{(x+1)}, \forall x > -1$. If $f(0) = 5$, then $f(x)$ is

(a) $\left(\frac{3x+5}{x+1}\right)e^{x^2}$ (b) $\left(\frac{6x+5}{x+1}\right)e^{x^2}$

(c) $\left(\frac{6x+5}{(x+1)^2}\right)e^{x^2}$ (d) $\left(\frac{5-6x}{x+1}\right)e^{x^2}$

19. If **a** and **b** are not perpendicular to each other and $\mathbf{r} \times \mathbf{a} = \mathbf{b} \times \mathbf{a}$ and $\mathbf{r} \cdot \mathbf{c} = 0$, then **r** is equal to

(a) $\mathbf{a} - \mathbf{c}$ (b) $\mathbf{b} + x\mathbf{a}$ for all scalars x

(c) $\mathbf{b} - \frac{(\mathbf{b} \cdot \mathbf{c})}{(\mathbf{a} \cdot \mathbf{c})}\mathbf{a}$ (d) None of these

20. A man observes that when he moves up a distance c m on a slope, the angle of depression of a point on the horizontal plane from the base of the slope is 30° and when he moves up further a distance c m the angle of depression of that point is 45°. The angle of inclination of the slope with the horizontal is

(a) 60° (b) 45° (c) 30° (d) 75°

Section II *Numerical Value Questions*

21. Let $f(x) = \begin{cases} -2x + \log_{1/2}(\lambda^2 - 6\lambda + 8) &, -2 \le x < -1 \\ x^3 + 3x^2 + 4x + 1 &, -1 \le x \le 3 \end{cases}$, then the sum of all possible positive integer(s) in the range of λ such that $F(x)$ has the smallest value at $x = -1$ is

22. Let $C_n = \int_{1/n+1}^{1/n} \frac{\tan^{-1}(nx)}{\sin^{-1}(nx)} dx$, then $\lim_{n \to \infty} [2n^2 C_n]$ is equal to

23. A box contains 6 balls which may all be of different colours or three each of two colours or two each of three different colours. The number of ways of selecting 3 balls from the box (if a ball of same colour is identical), is

24. Let $f : [1, 3] \to [0, \infty)$ be continuous and differentiable function. If $[f(3) - f(1)] \cdot [f^2(3) + f^2(1) + f(3) \cdot f(1)] = kf^2(c) \cdot f'(c)$, where $c \in (1,3)$, then the value of $2k$ is

25. In the expansion $\left(\sqrt{2}\sqrt[6]{3} + \frac{1}{\sqrt[3]{3}}\right)^n$, if the ratio of 7th term from the beginning to the 7th term from the end is $\frac{1}{6}$, then n is equal to

26. The area bounded by the curves $y = ex\ln x$ and $y = \dfrac{\ln x}{ex}$ is $\left(\dfrac{e^{\alpha}+\beta}{\gamma e}\right)$, then $\alpha - \beta + \gamma$ is equal to

27. The system of equations
$\alpha x - y - z = \alpha - 1,\ x - \alpha y - z = \alpha - 1,\ x - y - \alpha z = \alpha - 1$
has no solution if $\alpha = k$, then the value of $[\pi + k]$, where $[\cdot]$ denotes the greatest integer function, is

28. Roots of the equation $x^2 - 2x - (a^2 - 1) = 0$ lie between the roots of the equation $x^2 - 2(a+1)x + a(a-1) = 0$, if $a \in (\lambda, \mu)$, where λ and $\mu \in R$, then $(7\mu - 4\lambda)$ is equal to

29. Let $f(x) = \begin{vmatrix} \cos x & x & 1 \\ 2\sin x & x^2 & 2x \\ \tan x & x & 1 \end{vmatrix}$, then the absolute value of $\lim_{x \to 0} \dfrac{f'(x)}{x}$ is equal to

30. The number of solutions of the equation $|2\sin x - \sqrt{3}|^{(2\cos^2 x - 3\cos x + 1)} = 1$ in $[0, \pi]$ is

Answers

1	(a)	2	(c)	3	(d)	4	(b)	5	(c)	6	(a)	7	(b)	8	(d)	9	(b)	10	(b)
11	(c)	12	(b)	13	(a)	14	(d)	15	(c)	16	(a)	17	(d)	18	(b)	19	(c)	20	(d)
21	(12)	22	(1)	23	(31)	24	(12)	25	(10)	26	11	27	(1)	28	(8)	29	(2)	30	(3)

See detailed solutions on page no. 269

Knockout 11

JEE ADVANCED

Mathematics

Paper 1

Section 1

- This section contains **EIGHT (08)** question stems.
- The answer to each question is a **NUMERICAL VALUE.**
- For each question, enter the correct numerical value corresponding to the answer in the designated place using the mouse and the on-screen virtual numeric keypad.
- If the numerical value has more than two decimal places, **truncate/round-off** the value to **TWO** decimal places.
- Answer to each question will be evaluated according to the following marking scheme:

Full Marks : +3 If ONLY the correct numerical value is entered at the designated place;

Zero Marks : 0 In all other cases.

1. Consider the circle $x^2+y^2=9$ and the parabola $y^2=8x$. They intersect at P and Q in the first and fourth quadrants, respectively. Tangents to the circle at P and Q intersect the X-axis at R and tangents to the parabola at P and Q intersect the X-axis at S. The value of the ratio of the areas of the ΔPQS and ΔPQR is ______

2. Let $f(n)$ denotes the number of different ways in which the positive integer n can be expressed as the sum of 1's and 2's. e.g. $f(4)=5$, since $4=2+2=2+1+1=1+2+1=1+1+2=1+1+1+1$. Note that order of 1's and 2's are important. The value of $f(6)$ is ______

3. There are n bucket, each of these contain $(n+1)$ balls. The ith bucket contain i red balls and $(n+1-i)$ white balls. Let v_i be the event of selecting ith bucket, $i=1,2,3 \ldots\ldots n$ and w be the event of getting a red ball.

4. Consider two differential function $f(x)$ and $g(x)$ satisfying

$$6\int f(x)\,g(x)\,dx = x^6+3x^4+3x^2+C \text{ and } 2\int \frac{g(x)dx}{f(x)} = x^2+C,$$

where $f(x)>0, \forall\, x\in R$. Then, $\lim\limits_{x\to 0}\frac{\log\{f(x)\}}{g(x)}$ is equal to ______

5. Let α, β and γ are the real numbers such that the system of linear equations

$$x+2y+3z=\alpha;\ 4x+5y+6z=\beta;$$

$$7x+8y+9z=\gamma-1 \text{ is consistent}$$

Let $|M|$ represent the determinant of the matrix

$$M=\begin{bmatrix}\alpha & 2 & \gamma\\ \beta & 1 & 0\\ -1 & 0 & 1\end{bmatrix}$$

Let P be the plane containing are those (α, β, γ) for which above system of linear equations is consistent and D be the square of the distance of the point $(0, 1, 0)$ from the plane P. The value of $|M|$ is ______

6. If $a, b\in$ prime numbers and $a\in \pi$, then free from radical terms or rational terms in the expression of $(a^{1/p}+b^{1/q})^n$ are terms in which indices of a and b are integers. In the expression of $(\sqrt{2}+3^{1/11})^{100}$, the number of irrational terms is ______

7. The number of integer value of 'λ' for which the equation $3\lambda\sin x-(\lambda+\sin x)(\lambda^2-\lambda\sin x+\sin^2 x)=1$ is ______

8. If roots of equation $|x-1|=2[x]-3\{x\}$ is x_i, then the value of $\frac{[\Sigma x_i]}{5}$ (where $[x]$ and $\{x\}$ denotes integral and fractional part of x) is ______

Section 2

- This section contains **SIX (06)** questions.
- Each question has **FOUR** options (a), (b), (c) and (d). **ONE OR MORE THAN ONE** of these four option(s) is (are) correct answer(s).
- For each question, choose the option(s) corresponding to (all) the correct answer(s).
- Answer to each question will be evaluated according to the following marking scheme:

Full Marks : +4 If only (all) the correct option(s) is(are) chosen;
Partial Marks : +3 If all the four options are correct but ONLY three options are chosen;
Partial Marks : +2 If three or more options are correct but ONLY two options are chosen, both of which are correct;
Partial Marks : +1 If two or more options are correct but ONLY one option is chosen and it is a correct option;
Zero Marks : 0 If unanswered;
Negative Marks : – 2 In all other cases.

9. Given two circles intersecting orthogonally having the length of common chord is $\frac{24}{5}$ units. The radius of one of the circle is 3 units, then

(a) the radius of the other circle is 4 units
(b) the length of direct common tangent is $2\sqrt{6}$ units
(c) the angle between the direct common tangent is $\sin^{-1}\left(\frac{4\sqrt{6}}{25}\right)$
(d) Only (b) and (c)

10. In ΔABC, if $AB = AC$ and lengths of the tangents to the incircle from the vertices A and C are 4 and 2, respectively, then identify which of the following statement(s) is (are) correct?
Note Symbols used have usual meaning in ΔABC

(a) $AI : BI : CI = \sqrt{3} : 1 : 1$
(b) $R = \frac{9\sqrt{2}}{4}$
(c) Inradius of ΔABC is $\sqrt{2}$ units
(d) $\Delta R = a^2$

11. If $\int_{-39}^{59} \frac{\sin(2(\{x\} + \{-x\}))}{e^{-\{x\}}}\left(\frac{\tan x - \tan[x]}{1 + \tan x \tan[x]} + \sec^2\{x\}\right)dx$ $= p \cdot e \cdot \sin^2 q$, where $p, q \in N$ and e is Napier's constant and $[\cdot]$ and $\{\cdot\}$ denotes greatest integer and fractional part functions, respectively. Then ,

(a) $(p - q)$ is an odd number
(b) $(p + 6q)$ is a palindrome number
(c) $(p - 168q)$ is a perfect number
(d) $(\sqrt{p} - \sqrt{q})$ is a fibonacci number

12. All possible values of α for which the point (α, α^2) lies inside the triangle formed by the lines $2x + 3y - 1 = 0$, $x + 2y - 3 = 0$ and $5x - 6y - 1 = 0$ is/are

(a) $\alpha \in \left(-\frac{3}{2}, -1\right)$
(b) $\alpha \in \left(-\frac{3}{2}, \frac{1}{3}\right)$
(c) $\alpha \in \left(\frac{1}{2}, 1\right)$
(d) Both (a) and (c)

13. If $R_n = \int_0^{\pi/2} \frac{\sin^2 nx}{\sin^2 x}\,dx$, then

(a) $R_1 = \frac{\pi}{2}$
(b) $R_n = \frac{n\pi}{2}$
(c) $R_n - R_{n-1} = \frac{\pi}{2}$
(d) $R_1, R_2, R_3, \ldots$ are in AP

14. Let $\mathbf{a}, \mathbf{b}$ and $\mathbf{c}$ be non-coplanar unit vectors equally inclined to one another at an acute angle θ, if $\mathbf{a} \times \mathbf{b} + \mathbf{b} \times \mathbf{c} = p\mathbf{a} + q\mathbf{b} + r\mathbf{c}$, then select the correct option(s) among below

(a) $p = \frac{1}{\sqrt{1 + 2\cos\theta}}$
(b) $q = \frac{-2\cos\theta}{\sqrt{1 + 2\cos\theta}}$
(c) $r = \frac{\sqrt{\sec\theta}}{\sqrt{2 + \sec\theta}}$
(d) $p = r = \frac{q}{2}$

Section 3

- This section contains **FOUR (04)** Matching List Sets.
- Each set has **ONE** Multiple Choice Question.
- Each set has **TWO** lists : **List-I** and **List-II**.
- List-I has **FOUR** entries (I), (II), (III) and (IV) and List-II has **FIVE** entries (P), (Q), (R), (S) and (T).
- **FOUR** options are given in each Multiple Choice Question based on **List-I** and **List-II** and **ONLY ONE** of these four options satisfies the condition asked in the Multiple Choice Question.
- Answer to each question will be evaluated according to the following marking scheme:

Full Marks : +3 ONLY if the option corresponding to the correct combination is chose;
Zero Marks : 0 If none of the options is chosen (i.e. the question is unanswered);
Negative Marks : – 1 In all other cases.

15.

	List-I		List-II
I.	If $f(x)=\int_0^{g(x)}\frac{dt}{\sqrt{1+t^3}}$, where $g(x)=\int_0^{\cos x}(1+\sin t^2)dt$, then the value of $f'(\pi/2)$ is equal to	P.	3
II.	If $f(x)$ is a non-zero differentiable function such that $\int_0^x f(t)\,dt=[f(x)]^2\ \forall x$, then $f(6)$ is equal to	Q.	2
III.	If $\int_a^b (2+x-x^2)\,dx$ is maximum, then $(a+b)$ is equal to	R.	1
IV.	Let $a_n=\int_{\frac{1}{n+1}}^{\frac{1}{n}}\tan^{-1}(nx)\,dx$ and $b_n=\int_{\frac{1}{n+1}}^{\frac{1}{n}}\sin^{-1}(nx)\,dx$, then $4\times\left[\lim_{n\to\infty}\frac{a_n}{b_n}\right]$ is equal to	S.	-1
		T.	0

Codes

	I	II	III	IV		I	II	III	IV
(a)	R	S	T	P	(b)	Q	S	T	P
(c)	P	S	R	T	(d)	S	P	R	Q

16.

	List-I		List-II
I.	If a chord of the circle $x^2+y^2=8$ makes equal intercepts of length 'a' on the axes of coordinates, then $\|a\|$ is	P.	$(6,\sqrt{47})$
II.	A point (2, 5) is an interior point of the circle $x^2+y^2-8x-12y+p=0$ and the circle neither cuts nor touches any of the coordinate axes, then the value of $\|\sqrt{p}\|\in$?	Q.	<4
III.	Let $\phi(x,y)=0$ be the equation of a circle. If $\phi(0,t)=0$ has equal roots 2 and $\phi(t,0)$ has roots $\frac{4}{5}$, 5, then the radius of the circle is equal to	R.	4
IV.	A region in XY plane is bounded by the curve $y=\sqrt{25-x^2}$ and the line $y=0$. If the point $P(a,a+1)$ lies in the interior of the region, then the values of $\|a\|\in$?	S.	$\frac{21}{10}$
		T.	$(-1,3)$

Codes

	I	II	III	IV		I	II	III	IV
(a)	Q	P	S	T	(b)	R	S	S	P
(c)	T	R	S	P	(d)	Q	T	R	S

17.

	List-I		List-II
I.	Let $n(s)$ denotes number of solution(s) of the equation $\|x^2-2x-3\|=k$, for $k>4$, then the value of $n(x)$ equals	P.	1
II.	If $f(x)=\frac{1}{1-x}$, then $f(f(f(x)))$ is not defined for x equal to	Q.	2
III.	If 2010 is a root of equation $x^2(1-pq)-x(p^2+q^2)-(1+pq)=0$ and 2010 harmonic means are inserted between p and q, then the value of $\frac{h_1-h_{2010}}{pq(p-q)}$ is	R.	3
IV.	If $f(x)=\min(x^2, x, \text{sgn}(x^2+4x+5))$, then the value of $f(2)$ is equal to	S.	4
		T.	5

Codes

	I	II	III	IV
(a)	P	Q	S	T
(b)	Q	R	S	P
(c)	Q	P	P	P
(d)	T	R	T	P

18.

	List-I		List-II
I.	The locus of the middle point of the line segment joining the points $(0,\sqrt{1-t^2}+t)$ and $(2t,\sqrt{1-t^2}-t)$ cuts an intercept of length 'a' on the line $x+y=1$, then	P.	$a=\sqrt{2}$
II.	Two parallel chords of a circle of radius 2 are at a distance $\sqrt{3}+1$ apart. If the chords subtend at the centre angles $\frac{\pi}{a}$ and $\frac{2\pi}{a}$, where $a>0$, then	Q.	$a=\frac{3}{2}$
III.	If the four point of intersection of the lines $(2x-y+1)(x-2y+3)=0$ with the coordinate axes lie on a circle and 'a' is the positive difference of the coordinates of the centre, then	R.	$a=4$
IV.	The radii of the circles $(x-1)^2+(y-2)^2=1$ and $(x-7)^2+(y-10)^2=4$ are increasing uniformly with respect to time at the rates 0.3 and 0.4 unit/s, respectively. If the circles touch each other after a min, then	S.	$a=3$
		T.	$a=6$

Codes

	I	II	III	IV
(a)	T	Q	R	S
(b)	P	S	S	Q
(c)	P	Q	R	S
(d)	Q	R	T	S

Paper 2

Section 1

- This section contains **EIGHT (08)** questions.
- The answer to each question is a **SINGLE DIGIT INTEGER** ranging from 0 to 9 **BOTH INCLUSIVE**.
- For each question, enter the correct integer corresponding to the answer using the mouse and the on screeen virtual numeric keypad in the place designated to enter the answer.
- Answer to each question will be evaluated according to the following marking scheme:
  Full Marks : +3 If **ONLY** the correct integer is entered;
  Zero Marks : 0 If the question is unanswered;
  Negative Marks : – 1 In all other cases.

1. Let $f(x)=\frac{2x^3}{3}-(x\log_e|x|-x)-kx+10$. If $f(x)$ is strictly increasing for every $x\in R-\{0\}$, then the maximum integral value of k is ______

2. If a curve satisfying $xy_1-4y-x^2\sqrt{y}=0$ passes through $\{1,(\log_e 4)^2\}$, then the value of $\frac{16(\log_e 32)^2}{y(2)}$ is ______

3. Let $E=a^2\cot 9°+b^2\cot 27°+c^2\cot 63°+d^2\cot 81°$ and a,b,c and d be real numbers satisfying $a+b+c+d=5$. If the minimum value of the expression E is equal to $\frac{\sqrt{x}}{y}$ is .... where x and y are coprime positive integers, then the value of $x-30y$ is ______

4. Let A_1,A_2,A_3 and A_4 be the areas of the triangular faces of a tetrahedron and h_1,h_2,h_3 and h_4 be the corresponding altitudes of the tetrahedron. If the volume of tetrahedron is 1/6 cu units, then the minimum value of $(A_1+A_2+A_3+A_4)(h_1+h_2+h_3+h_4)$ (in cu units) is ______

5. a,b and c are all different and non-zero real numbers in AP. If the roots of quadratic equation $ax^2+bx+c=0$ are α and β such that $\frac{1}{\alpha}+\frac{1}{\beta}$, $\alpha+\beta$ and $\alpha^2+\beta^2$ are in GP, then the value of $\left[\left(\frac{a}{c}\right)^4+79\log_3(c/a)\right]$ is equal to ______

6. The total number of solutions of the equation $\sin^2 x-\sin x+\cos x=1$ in the interval $[-4\pi, 4\pi]$ is ______

7. If k is the sum of all value of x such that $\cos^3 3x+\cos^3 5x=8\cos^3 4x\cos^3 x$, where x is measured in degree and $100<x<200$, then $\frac{1}{3}\times$ (sum of digits of k) equal ______

8. Let $F(x)$ be a non-negative continuous function defined on R such that $F(x)+F\left(x+\frac{1}{2}\right)=3$ and the value of $\int_0^{1500}F(x)\,dx$ is $\frac{9000}{\lambda}$. Then, the numerical value of 2λ is ______

Section 2

- This section contains **SIX (06)** questions.
- Each question has **FOUR** options (A), (B), (C) and (D). **ONE OR MORE THAN ONE** of these four option(s) is (are) correct answer(s).
- For each question, choose the option(s) corresponding to (all) the correct answer(s).
- Answer to each question will be evaluated according to the following marking scheme:
  Full Marks : +4 If only (all) the correct option(s) is(are) chosen;
  Partial Marks : +3 If all the four options are correct but ONLY three options are chosen;
  Partial Marks : +2 If three or more options are correct but ONLY two options are chosen, both of which are correct;
  Partial Marks : +1 If two or more options are correct but ONLY one option is chosen and it is a correct option;
  Zero Marks : 0 If unanswered;
  Negative Marks : – 2 In all other cases.

9. Let $a_1, a_2, a_3, \ldots, a_n$ be real constants, x be a real variable and $f(x) = \cos(a_1 + x) + \frac{1}{2}\cos(a_2 + x) + \frac{1}{2^2}\cos(a_3 + x) + \ldots + \frac{1}{2^{n-1}}\cos(a_n + x)$. Given that $f(x_1) = f(x_2) = 0$, then $x_2 - x_1$ is equal to

(a) $k\pi$ (b) $(k+1)\pi$

(c) $(2k+1)\frac{\pi}{2}$ (d) $(2k+1)\pi$

(where, k is integer i.e. $k \in I$)

10. Two different non-parallel lines meet the circle $|z| = r$ in the points a, b and c, d, respectively. If these two lines meet in z, then z will be given by

(a) $z = \frac{a^{-1}+b^{-1}+c^{-1}+d^{-1}}{a^{-1}b^{-1}-c^{-1}d^{-1}}$ (b) $z = \frac{a^{-1}+b^{-1}-c^{-1}-d^{-1}}{a^{-1}b^{-1}-c^{-1}d^{-1}}$

(c) $z = \frac{a^{-1}b^{-1}+c^{-1}d^{-1}}{ab+cd}$ (d) $z = \frac{a^{-1}+b^{-1}+c^{-1}+d^{-1}}{a^{-1}b^{-1}+c^{-1}d^{-1}}$

11. Consider the set of eight vectors $V = [a\hat{i} + b\hat{j} + c\hat{k}$, $a, b, c \in \{-1, 1\}]$. Three non-coplanar vectors can be chosen from V in 2^P way. Then, P is greater than

(a) 5 (b) 4

(c) 3 (d) 2

12. A hyperbola passes through the point $P(\sqrt{2}, \sqrt{3})$ and has foci $(\pm 2, 0)$ and the tangent to the parabola at p also passes through the point $(2\sqrt{p}, q\sqrt{3})$. Then, which of the following is correct?

(a) $p^2 + q^2 = 13$ (b) $(3q + 8p)^{1/2} = 5$

(c) $pq = 6$ (d) $pq = 8$

13. The function $f(x) = x^{1/3}(x-1)$

(a) has two points of inflection

(b) is non-differentiable

(c) has one point of extremum

(d) has range $[-3 \times 2^{-8/3}, \infty)$

14. Any complex number in the polar form can be an expression in Euler's form as $\cos\theta + i\sin\theta = e^{i\theta}$. This form of the complex number is useful in finding the sum of the series $\sum_{r=0}^{n} {}^nC_r(\cos\theta + i\sin\theta)^r = \sum_{r=0}^{n} {}^nC_r(\cos r\theta + i\sin r\theta)$

$= \sum_{r=0}^{n} {}^nC_r e^{ir\theta} = \sum_{r=0}^{n} {}^nC_r (e^{i\theta})^r = (1 + e^{i\theta})^n$.

Also, we know that the sum of binomial series does not change, if r is replaced by $(n-r)$. Using these facts, choose the correct option.

(a) $\sum_{r=0}^{100} {}^{100}C_r(\sin rx) = 2^{100}\cos^{100}\left(\frac{x}{2}\right)\cdot\sin 50x$

(b) In ΔABC, $\sum_{r=0}^{50} {}^{50}C_r a^r b^{n-r}\cos[rB - (50-r)A] = (25 - a - b)^{50}$,

where a, b and c have usual meanings.

(c) $f(\pi/8) = 1$, if $f(x) = \frac{\sum_{r=0}^{50} {}^{50}C_r \cdot \sin^2 rx}{\sum_{r=0}^{50} {}^{50}C_r \cdot \cos^2 rx}$

(d) Only (a) and (c) are true

Section 3

- This section contains **FOUR (04)** questions.
- Each question has **FOUR** options (a), (b), (c) and (d). **ONLY ONE** of these four options is the correct answer.
- Four each question, choose the option corresponding to the correct answer.
- Answer to each question will be evaluated according to the following marking scheme:

Full Marks : +3 If **ONLY** the correct option is chosen;

Zero Marks : 0 If none of the options is chosen (i.e. the question is unanswered);

Negative Marks : –1 In all other cases.

15. The circle $x^2 + y^2 = 1$ cuts the X-axis at P and Q. Another circle with centre at Q and variable radius intersects the first circle at R above the X-axis and the line segment PQ at S. Let r denotes the radius of the variable circle and let A denotes the area of ΔQSR. Let r denotes the value of r for which A is maximum and let A_{max} be the maximum value of A. Which of the following is incorrect?

(a) $A = \frac{1}{2}r^2\sqrt{4 - r^2}$ (b) $\frac{dA}{dr} = \frac{8r - 3r^3}{4\sqrt{4 - r^2}}$

(c) $A_{max} = \frac{4\sqrt{3}}{9}$ (d) $r = \sqrt{\frac{8}{3}}$

16. The value of $\lim_{n\to\infty} \frac{1\cdot2\cdot3 + 2\cdot3\cdot4 + 3\cdot4\cdot5 + \ldots \text{upto } n \text{ terms}}{n(1\cdot2 + 2\cdot3 + 3\cdot4 + 4\cdot5 + \ldots \text{upto } n \text{ terms})}$

(a) $\frac{4}{3}$

(b) $\frac{1}{4}$

(c) $\frac{2}{5}$

(d) $\frac{3}{4}$

17. Through a point $P(\alpha, \beta, \gamma)$ a plane is drawn at right angle to $OP(=p)$ to meet the axes (rectangular) in A, B and C. The area of the ΔABC is

(a) $\frac{p}{2\alpha\beta\gamma}$ (b) $\frac{p^5}{2\alpha\beta\gamma}$

(c) $\frac{p^3}{\alpha\beta\gamma}$ (d) $\frac{p^5}{\alpha\beta\gamma}$

18. Let $\int \frac{5x^9 + 4x^{10}}{(x^5 + x + 1)^3} dx = \frac{x^\alpha}{k(x^\beta + x^\gamma + 1)^\lambda} + C$, where α, β, γ, k and λ are integers and $\int_{\alpha - \beta\lambda}^{\frac{k\pi}{8}} \sqrt[3]{\tan x}\, dx = \frac{1}{k_1}\left(\frac{\pi}{\sqrt{k_2}} - \ln k_3\right)$, where k_1, k_2 and $k_3 \in R$, then choose the incorrect option.

(a) $k = k_1 = k_3 = \lambda =$ the oddest prime

(b) $4\gamma + k_3 = 2k_2 =$ a perfect number

(c) $[(\alpha + \beta + 4\gamma + k + \lambda) - (k_1 + k_2 + k_3)] =$ a perfect square

(d) k_1 and k_2 are two non-consecutive prime numbers

Answers

Paper 1

1 (0.25)	2 (13)	3 (0.67)	4 (0)	5 (1)	6 (105)	7 (4)	8 (0.80)	9 (a,b,c)	10 (a,b,c)
11 (a,b,c, d)	12 (a,c,d)	13 (a,b,c,d)	14 (a,b,c)	15 (d)	16 (a)	17 (c)	18 (b)		

Paper 2

1 (1)	2 (4)	3 (5)	4 (8)	5 (2)	6 (9)	7 (5)	8 (8)	9 (a,b,d)	10 (b)
11 (b,c,d)	12 (a,b,c)	13 (a,b,c,d)	14 (a,b,c)	15 (a)	16 (d)	17 (b)	18 (d)		

See detailed solutions on page no. 275

Knockout 12

JEE ADVANCED

Mathematics

Paper 1

Section 1

- This section contains **EIGHT (08)** questions. The answer to each question is a **NUMERICAL VALUE.**
- For each question, enter the correct numerical value of the answer using the mouse and the on-screen virtual numeric keypad in the place designated to enter the answer. If the numerical value has more than two decimal places, **truncate/round-off** the value to **TWO** decimal places.
- Answer to each question will be evaluated according to the following marking scheme:

Full Marks : +3 If ONLY the correct numerical value is entered.
Zero Marks . 0 In all other cases.

1. Let α,β,γ be the roots of the cubic equation $x^3+ax^2+bx+c=0$, which are in GP (roots are taken in given order). If α and β are such that $\begin{vmatrix} 2 & 1 & 2 \\ 1+\alpha & \alpha & \beta \\ 4-\beta & 3-\beta & \alpha+1 \end{vmatrix}=0$, then the value of $a+b+c$ is ______

2. Consider a differentiable function $f:R\to R$ for which $f'(0)=\ln 2$ and $f(x+y)=2^x f(y)+4^y f(x)$, $\forall x,y\in R$ the minimum value of $f(x)$ is $\frac{-1}{4}$ at which point ______

3. If complex number z satisfies the equation $1+2|z|^2=|z^2+1|^2+2|z+1|^2$, then the value of $|z(z+1)|$ is ______

4. If α, β, γ are positive real numbers such that $\alpha\sqrt{\beta\gamma}+\beta\sqrt{\gamma\alpha}+\gamma\sqrt{\alpha\beta}\geq 1$, then the least value of $\alpha+\beta+\gamma$ is $\sqrt{\lambda}$, then $3\lambda^2+1$ is ______

5. The number of natural numbers which are smaller than $2\cdot 10^8$ and which can be written by means of the digit 1 and 2 is ______

6. The value of $\int_{\sqrt{\ln 2}}^{\sqrt{\ln 3}}\frac{x\sin x^2}{\sin x^2+\sin(\ln 6-x^2)}dx$ is of the from $\frac{\lambda}{\mu}\ln\left(\frac{b}{a}\right)$. Then, $\left|\frac{\sqrt{9\lambda^2+\mu^2}}{b-a}\right|$ is ______

7. If a and b are coprime positive integers and $\sum_{n=0}^{10}\cot^{-1}\left(\frac{1+2^{2n+1}}{2^n}\right)=\cot^{-1}\left(\frac{a}{b}\right)$, then the value of $\log_2\left(\frac{a+b}{a-b}\right)$ is ______

8. On the coordinate plane, ellipse $E:\frac{x^2}{a_1^2}+\frac{y^2}{b_1^2}=1$ where $a_1>b_1>0$ and hyperbola $H:\frac{x^2}{a_2^2}-\frac{y^2}{b_2^2}=1\ (a_2,b_2>0)$ has the same focus points F_1,F_2. $PF_1\perp PF_2$ and point P is one of the intersection points of E and H. If e_1 is the eccentricity of E and e_2 is the eccentricity of H, then the minimum value of $121e_1^2+e_2^2$ is ______

Section 2

- This section contains **SIX (06)** questions.
- Each question has **FOUR** options (A), (B), (C) and (D). **ONE OR MORE THAN ONE** of these four option(s) is (are) correct answer(s).
- For each question, choose the options(s) corresponding to (all) the correct answer(s).
- Answer to each question will be evaluated according to the following marking scheme:

Full Marks : +4 If only (all) the correct option(s) is (are) chosen.
Partial Marks : +3 If all the four options are correct but ONLY three options are chosen.
Partial Marks : +2 If three or more options are correct but ONLY two options are chosen, both of which are correct.
Partial Marks : +1 If two or more options are correct but ONLY one option is chosen and it is a correct option;
Zero Marks : 0 If none of the options is chosen (i.e., the question is unanswered);
Negative Marks : −2 In all other cases.

9. Let $L = \lim\limits_{x \to \infty} x^2 \sin\left(\log_e \sqrt{\cos \frac{\pi}{x}}\right)$, then

$R = \log_{4140\sqrt{-\frac{16L}{\pi^2}}}\left(\sqrt[5]{-\frac{16L}{\pi^2}}\right)$

(a) is not a prime number
(b) has 2, 3, 23 as prime number
(c) is composite number
(d) is palindrome number

10. The line $\frac{x+6}{5} = \frac{y+10}{3} = \frac{z+14}{8}$ is the hypotenuse of an isosceles right angled triangle whose opposite vertex is (7,2,4). Then, the side of the triangle is

(a) $\frac{x+7}{4} = \frac{2-y}{3} = \frac{z+1}{1}$
(b) $\frac{x-7}{2} = \frac{y-2}{-3} = \frac{z-4}{6}$
(c) $\frac{x-7}{3} = \frac{y+2}{-6} = \frac{z+4}{2}$
(d) $\frac{x-7}{3} = \frac{y-2}{6} = \frac{z-4}{2}$

11. If R and Q are two events such that $P(Q) = \frac{1}{2}$ and $P(R) = \frac{2}{3}$, then which of the following is correct?

(a) $P(R' \cap Q) \geq \frac{1}{3}$
(b) $P(Q \cup R) \geq \frac{2}{3}$
(c) $\frac{1}{6} \leq P(Q \cap R) \leq \frac{1}{2}$
(d) $\frac{1}{6} \leq P(Q' \cap R) \leq \frac{1}{2}$

12. If $A = \cos\frac{9\pi}{13} \cdot \cos\frac{3\pi}{13} + \cos\frac{3\pi}{13} \cdot \cos\frac{\pi}{13} + \cos\frac{9\pi}{13} \cdot \cos\frac{\pi}{13}$, then $2A$ is equal to

(a) $\sum_{k=1}^{6} \cos\left(\frac{2k\pi}{13}\right)$
(b) $\frac{1}{2}\sum_{k=1}^{12} \cos\left(\frac{2k\pi}{13}\right)$
(c) $\sum_{k=1}^{12} \cos\left(\frac{2k\pi}{13}\right)$
(d) $-\frac{1}{2}$

13. Let $P = \{1, 2, 3, \ldots, 20\}$ be partitioned into four sets P_1, P_2, P_3 and P_4 of equal size. The number of ways it can be done, is

(a) $\frac{120}{4!5!}$
(b) $\frac{20!}{4^5}$
(c) $\frac{20!}{(5!)^4}$
(d) $\frac{20!}{(4!)^5}$

14. If $\omega = \frac{\sqrt{3}+i}{2}$ and $P = \{\omega^n; n = 1, 2, 3, \ldots\}$. Further

$H_1 = \left\{z \in \not\subset; R \subset z > \frac{1}{2}\right\}$ and $H_2 = \left\{z \in \not\subset; R \subset z < -\frac{1}{2}\right\}$,

where $\not\subset$ is the set of all complex numbers.

If $z_1 \in P \cap H_1, z_2 \in P \cap H_2$ and O represents the origin, then $\angle z_1 O z_2$ is equal to

(a) $\frac{\pi}{2}$
(b) $\frac{\pi}{6}$
(c) $\frac{2\pi}{5}$
(d) $\frac{5\pi}{6}$

Section 3

- This section contains **FOUR (04)** Matching List Sets.
- Each set has **ONE** Multiple Choice Question.
- Each set has **TWO** lists : **List-I** and **List-II**.
- List-I has **FOUR** entries (I), (II), (III) and (IV) and List-II has **FIVE** entries (P), (Q), (R), (S) and (T).
- **FOUR** options are given in each Multiple Choice Question based on **List-I** and **List-II** and **ONLY ONE** of these four options satisfies the condition asked in the Multiple Choice Question.
- Answer to each question will be evaluated according to the following marking scheme:

Full Marks : +3 ONLY if the option corresponding to the correct combination is chose;
Zero Marks : 0 If none of the options is chosen (i.e. the question is unanswered);
Negative Marks : −1 In all other cases.

15.

	List-I		List-II
I.	Tangent drawn to ellipse $\frac{x^2}{27}+\frac{y^2}{1}=1$ at $(3\sqrt{3}\cos\phi, \sin\phi)$ so that the sum of intercepts on the axes made by it is minimum. Then, ϕ equals	P.	$\frac{\pi}{12}$
II.	A tangent drawn to the ellipse $x^2+4y^2=4$ meets the ellipse $x^2+2y^2=6$ at P and Q. The angle between the tangents at P and Q to the second ellipse is	Q.	$\frac{\pi}{6}$
III.	The latusrectum of the ellipse $x^2\tan^2\alpha+y^2\sec^2\alpha=1$ is $\frac{1}{2}$, then α is equal to	R.	$\frac{5\pi}{13}$
IV.	If the tangent to the ellipse $x^2+4y^2=16$ at the point with eccentric angle ϕ is normal to the circle $x^2+y^2-8x-4y=0$, then ϕ equals to	S.	$\frac{7\pi}{6}$
		T.	$\frac{\pi}{2}$

Codes

	I	II	III	IV
(a)	P	Q	S	T
(b)	Q	T	P	T
(c)	Q	R	P	P
(d)	R	S	Q	T

16.

	List-I		List-II
I.	$a_n=\int_0^{\pi/2}\frac{1-\cos 2nx}{1-\cos 2x}dx$	P.	$a_1, a_2, a_3 \dots$ are in AP
II.	$I_n=\int_0^{\pi/4}\tan^n x\,dx$ and $a_n=\frac{1}{I_{n+1}+I_{n+3}}$	Q.	$a_1, a_2, a_3 \dots$ are in GP
III.	$a_n=\int_0^{\pi/4}\frac{\sin^2 nx}{\sin x}dx$ and $a_n=I_n-I_{n-1}\forall n\geq 1$	R.	$a_1, a_2, a_3 \dots$ are in HP $\forall n\geq 0$
IV.	$b_n=\int_0^{\pi/2}\frac{\sin^2 nx}{\sin^2 x}dx$ and $a_n=\frac{b_n}{n}, a_n=b_n-b_{n-1}\ \forall n\geq 1$	S.	$a_1, a_2, a_3 \dots$ is not a constant sequence
		T.	$a_1, a_2, a_3 \dots$ are in AP, GP, HP and is a constant sequence

Codes

	I	II	III	IV
(a)	R	Q	T	P
(b)	P	Q	R	S
(c)	P	P	R	T
(d)	P	S	P	Q

17.

	List-I		List-II
I.	If two distinct chords drawn from the point (a, b) of circle $x^2+y^2-ax-by=0, ab\neq 0$ are bisected at X-axis, then the roots of equation $at^2-8bt+2a=0$ are	P.	real
II.	If the chord $x\cos\theta+y\sin\theta-a=0$ of the circle $x^2+y^2=b^2$ subtends a right angle at centre of circle, then the roots of equation $at^2+\sqrt{2}bt+a=0$ are	Q.	non-real
III.	If the chord of contact of the tangents drawn from any point on the circle $x^2+y^2=a^2$ to the circle $x^2+y^2=b^2$ touches the circle $x^2+y^2=c^2$, then root of equation $bt^2+(a+c)t+b=0$ are $(a>b>c>0)$	R.	equal and real
IV.	If the chord $x+2y-10=0$ of the circle $x^2+y^2=25$ is bisected at point (a, b), then the roots of $t^2+bt+a=0$	S.	distinct and real
		T.	real, distinct and non-rational

Codes

	I	II	III	IV
(a)	Q	R	S	T
(b)	P	Q	S	T
(c)	Q	R	T	S
(d)	Q	T	P	S

18. Let $f(x)=x^2+ax+b, \forall x\in R, f(0)>0$ and $f(x)$ has integral roots. Tangent at $\left(\frac{5}{2}, P\right)$ to $f(x)$ is parallel to X-axis and $g(x)=f(x+1)$

	List-I		List-II
I.	$(a+b)$ can be	P.	-1 or 1
II.	Value of $[P]$ can be (where $[\cdot]$ represents greatest integer function)	Q.	1
III.	Number of points, where $g(\lvert x\rvert)$ is non-differentiable can be	R.	3
IV.	Number of points, where $\lvert g(\lvert x\rvert)\rvert$ is non-differentiable can be	S.	-3 or -1
		T.	5 or 3

Codes

	I	II	III	IV
(a)	P	Q	S	T
(b)	P	S	Q	T
(c)	R	Q	P	S
(d)	T	P	Q	R

Paper 2

Section 1

- This section contains **EIGHT (08)** questions.
- The answer to each question is a **SINGLE DIGIT INTEGER** ranging from 0 TO 9. **BOTH INCLUSIVE**.
- For each question, enter the correct integer corresponding to the answer using the mouse and the on-screen virtual numeric keypad in the place designated to enter the answer.
- Answer to each question will be evaluated according to the following marking scheme:
  Full Marks : + 3 If ONLY the correct integer is entered.
  Zero Marks : 0 If the question is unanswered.
  Negative Marks : –1 In all other cases.

1. If A and B are square matrices of order 2 such that

$$A^2 = I \text{ and } B = \begin{bmatrix} 1 & \sqrt{2} \\ 0 & 1 \end{bmatrix} \text{ and } C = ABA$$

and $(C)^{1989} = A\begin{bmatrix} \alpha & \beta\sqrt{\gamma} \\ 0 & \delta \end{bmatrix} A$ and the absolute value of $(\alpha + \delta) - (\beta + \gamma)$ is $221k$, then the value of k is ______

2. In a triangle, if $(a + b + c)(a + b - c)(c + b - a)$ $(c + a - b) = \dfrac{8a^2b^2c^2}{a^2 + b^2 + c^2}$, then the value of $\dfrac{(\sin^2 A + \sin^2 B + \sin^2 C)^2 + 2(\cos A \cdot \cos B \cdot \cos C)}{2^2 - 2}$ is ______.
(where A, B, C are angles of triangle)

3. If α and β are positive real solution of $x^2 - bx + c = 0$ provided that $\alpha^2 + \sqrt{\beta^2 - 2\beta} = 2\alpha - 1$, then the minimum value of $(b + c)$ is ______

4. If $\mathbf{a} \times (\mathbf{b} \times \mathbf{c}) + (\mathbf{a} \cdot \mathbf{b})\mathbf{b} = (4 - 2\beta - \sin\alpha)\,\mathbf{b} + (\beta^2 - 1)\mathbf{c}$ and $(\mathbf{c} \cdot \mathbf{c})\mathbf{a} = \mathbf{c}$, while $\mathbf{b}$ and $\mathbf{c}$ are non-collinear vectors, then value of β^2 is ______

5. Let (h, k) be a fixed point, where $h > 0, k > 0$. A straight line passing through the point cuts the positive direction of the coordinate axes at the points P and Q. If O is the origin, then the minimum area of the ΔOPQ, if $h = k = 2$, is ______

6. In the following expression of $(x + 3)^{n-1} + (x + 3)^{n-2}(x + 2) + (x + 3)^{n-3}(x + 2)^2 + \ldots + (x + 2)^{n-1}$, then coefficient of x^n is ${}^nC_r\,(p^{n-r} - q^{n-r})$, then the value of $p + q$ is ______

7. The number of real values of x which satisfies the equation $\left|\dfrac{x}{x-1}\right| + |x| = \dfrac{x}{|x-1|}$ is ______

8. The curve that satisfies the differential equation $\dfrac{dy}{dx} = \dfrac{x^2 + y^2}{2xy}$ and passes through (2,1) is a hyperbola with eccentricity $\sqrt{k}$, then $\sin\left(\dfrac{\pi}{k}\right) + 2\cos^2\left(\dfrac{\pi}{2k}\right)$ is equal to ______

Section 2

- This section contains **SIX (06)** questions.
- Each question has **FOUR** options (A), (B), (C) and (D). **ONE OR MORE THAN ONE** of these four option(s) is (are) correct asnswer(s).
- For each question, choose the option(s) corresponding to (all) the correct answer(s).
- Answer to each question will be evaluated according to the following marking scheme:
  Full Marks : +4 If only (all) the correct option(s) is (are) chosen.
  Partial Marks : + 3 If all the four options are correct but ONLY three options are chosen.
  Partial Marks : +2 If three or more options are correct but ONLY two options are chosen, both of which are correct.
  Partial Marks : +1 If two or more options are correct but ONLY one option is chosen and it is a correct option.
  Zero Marks : 0 If none of the options is chosen (i.e. the question is unanswered).
  Negative Marks : –2 In all other cases.

9. If the coordinates of the point where the line $x-2y+z-1=0=x+2y-2z-5$ intersects the plane $x+y-2z=7$ is (α,β,γ), then

(a) $\alpha-\beta+\gamma+1=0$ (b) $\alpha^2+\beta^2+\gamma^2=21$

(c) $\alpha+\beta+\gamma=-7$ (d) $\alpha\beta+\beta\gamma+\gamma\alpha=2$

10. Let a, r, s and t be non-zero real numbers. Let $P(at^2, 2at)$, $Q\left(\frac{a}{t^2}, -\frac{2a}{t}\right)$, $R(ar^2, 2ar)$ and $S(as^2, 2as)$ be distinct points on the parabola $y^2=4ax$. Suppose that PQ is a focal chord and line QR and PK are parallel, where K is the point $(2a, 0)$. Then, the value of r is

(a) $\frac{t^2+1}{t}$ (b) $\frac{t^2-1}{t}$ (c) $\frac{t}{t^2+1}$ (d) t^2+1-t

11. If $\int\left(\frac{\ln a^{a^{x/2}}}{3\cdot a^{5x/2}\cdot b^{3x}}+\frac{\ln b^{b^x}}{2\cdot a^{2x}\cdot b^{4x}}\right)\cdot x dx=$

$\frac{1}{\lambda\cdot\ln(a^\alpha\cdot b^\beta)}\times\frac{1}{a^{2x}\times b^{3x}}\times\ln\left(\frac{1}{\mu\cdot a^{2x}b^{3x}}\right)+K$, then which of the following is/are correct?

(a) $\ln\alpha+\ln\beta=\ln\lambda$ (b) $\ln\lambda-(\ln\alpha+\ln\beta)=\ln\mu-1$

(c) $e^{\alpha\beta}=\mu^\lambda$ (d) $\sin\left[\frac{\pi}{149}\{\ln(e^\lambda)-\beta\cdot\ln(\mu^\alpha)\}\right]=0$

12. If A, B and C are three events, then which of the following is/are correct?

(a) $P(A\cup B\cup C)\le P(A)+P(B)+P(C)$

(b) P (exactly one of A, B and C occur) $\le P(A)+P(B)+P(C)-P(A\cap B)-P(B\cap C)-P(C\cap A)$

(c) P (exactly two of A, B and C occur) $\le P(A\cap B)+P(B\cap C)+P(C\cap A)$

(d) None of the above

13. Define the collections $\{E_1, E_2, E_3, \ldots\}$ of ellipses and $\{R_1, R_2, R_3, \ldots\}$ of rectangles as follows :

$E_1: \frac{x^2}{9}+\frac{y^2}{4}=1$

R_1 : Rectangle of largest area, with sides parallel to the axes, inscribed in E_1;

E_n : Ellipse $\frac{x^2}{a_n^2}+\frac{y^2}{b_n^2}=1$ of the largest area inscribed in R_{n-1}, $n>1$;

R_n : rectangle of largest area, with sides parallel to the axes, inscribed in E_n, $n>1$.

Then, which of the following option(s) is/are correct?

(a) The eccentricities of E_{18} and E_{19} are not equal.

(b) The distance of a focus from the centre in E_9 is $\frac{\sqrt{5}}{32}$ units.

(c) $\sum_{n=1}^{N}(\text{area of } R_n)<24$, for each positive integer N.

(d) The length of latusrectum of E_9 is $\frac{1}{6}$ unit.

14. In a non-right-angled triangle ΔPQR, let p, q, r denote the lengths of the sides opposite to the angles at P, Q, R, respectively. The median from R meets the side PQ at S, the perpendicular from P meets the side QR at E, RS and PE intersect at O. If $p=\sqrt{3}$, $q=1$ and the radius of the circumcircle of the ΔPQR equals 1 unit, then which of the following option(s) is/are correct?

(a) Length of $OE=\frac{1}{6}$ unit

(b) Length of $RS=\frac{\sqrt{7}}{2}$ units

(c) Area of $\Delta SOE=\frac{\sqrt{3}}{12}$ sq units

(d) Radius of incircle of $\Delta PQR=\frac{\sqrt{3}}{2}(2-\sqrt{3})$ units

Section 3

- This section contains **FOUR (04)** questions.
- Each question has **FOUR** options (a), (b), (c) and (d). **ONLY ONE** of these four options is the correct answer.
- Four each question, choose the option corresponding to the correct answer.
- Answer to each question will be evaluated according to the following marking scheme:

Full Marks : +3 If **ONLY** the correct option is chosen;
Zero Marks : 0 If none of the options is chosen (i.e. the question is unanswered);
Negative Marks : –1 In all other cases.

15. Let $4^{\sin x}+3^{\sec y}=11$ and $5(16)^{\sin x}-2(3)^{\sec y}=2$ are two equations. Then, the solution of the given equations is

(a) $x=n\pi+(-1)^n\frac{\pi}{6}$, $y=2m\pi\pm\frac{\pi}{3}$, where $m, n\in I$

(b) $x=n\pi$, $y=2m\pi$, where $m, n\in I$

(c) $x=n\pi+(-1)^n\frac{\pi}{3}$, $y=2m\pi\pm\frac{\pi}{6}$, where $m, n\in I$

(d) No Solution

16. Let f be a function defined by $f(x)=\frac{x-1}{1-x^2+a}$, where $a\in R$. If range of $f(x)$ is $R-\left[-1, \frac{-1}{3}\right]$, then a lies in the interval

(a) $(0, \infty)$ (b) $\left(-\infty, -\frac{1}{2}\right)$

(c) $\left(-\infty, -\frac{1}{4}\right)$ (d) $\left(-\frac{1}{2}, \infty\right)$

17. If $PQ = P$ and $QP = Q$, where P and Q are two square matrices of same order, then $(P^{1192} + Q^{1490})^{2889}$ is equal to

(a) $P + Q$ (b) $2^{2888}(P + Q)$
(c) $2^{2889}(P + Q)$ (d) $2888(P + Q)$

18. If $I = \int_{e^{\pi/6}}^{e^{\pi/2}} \frac{\sin(\log_e(\sin(\log_e x))).\cos(\log_e x)}{x \sin(\log_e x)} dx$, then the value of $\cos^{-1}(I + 1)$ is equal to

(a) $-2\ln 2$ (b) $\log_{10} 2$ (c) $\ln 2$ (d) $\frac{\pi}{6}$

Answers

Paper 1

1 *(−1)*	2 *(−1)*	3 *(1)*	4 *(28)*	5 *(766)*	6 *(5)*	7 *(11)*	8 *(72)*	9 *(a,b,c,d)*	10 *(b,d)*
11 *(b,c,d)*	12 *(a,b,d)*	13 *(c)*	14 *(d)*	15 *(b)*	16 *(c)*	17 *(a)*	18 *(b)*		

Paper 2

1 *(9)*	2 *(2)*	3 *(5)*	4 *(1)*	5 *(8)*	6 *(5)*	7 *(1)*	8 *(2)*	9 *(a,b,d)*	10 *(b)*
11 *(a,b,c,d)*	12 *(a,b,c)*	13 *(c,d)*	14 *(a,b,d)*	15 *(a)*	16 *(c)*	17 *(b)*	18 *(c)*		

See detailed solutions on page no. 285

Knockout 13

JEE ADVANCED

Mathematics

Paper 1

Section 1

- This section contains **EIGHT (08)** questions. The answer to each question is a **NUMERICAL VALUE.**
- For each question, enter the correct numerical value of the answer using the mouse and the on-screen virtual numeric keypad in the place designated to enter the answer. If the numerical value has more than two decimal places, **truncate/round-off** the value to **TWO** decimal places.
- Answer to each question will be evaluated according to the following marking scheme:

Full Marks : + 3 If ONLY the correct numerical value is entered.

Zero Marks : 0 In all other cases.

1. Suppose $f(x)$ is a function satisfying the following conditions.

(i) $f(0)=2$

(ii) f has a minimum value at $x=\frac{5}{2}$

(iii) For all x, $f'(x)=\begin{vmatrix} 2ax & 2ax-1 & 2ax+b+1 \\ b & b+1 & -1 \\ 2(ax+b) & 2ax+2b+1 & 2ax+b \end{vmatrix}$

Thus, the value of $f(2)$ is

2. Let $I=\int_0^{\pi/4}(\pi x-4x^2)\ln(1+\tan x)\,dx$. If the value of $I=\frac{\pi^3\ln 2}{k}$, then k is ______

3. The equation of the curve $y=f(x)$. The tangents at $[1,f(1)],[2,f(2)]$ and $[3,f(3)]$ make angles $\frac{\pi}{6},\frac{\pi}{3}$ and $\frac{\pi}{4}$, respectively with the positive direction of X-axis. Thus, the value of $\int_2^3 f'(x)\cdot f''(x)\,dx+\int_1^3 f''(x)\,dx$ is $\frac{p}{\sqrt{q}}$, then the value of $(p+q)^3$ is equal to ______

4. Let $A(0,1)$, B and C be three points on $\frac{x^2}{4}+\frac{y^2}{1}=1$, be vertices of an equilateral triangle, such that altitude from A on BC is $x=0$. If length of side of this equilateral triangle be K, then $\frac{13K}{\sqrt{12}}$ is ______

5. If $A=\begin{bmatrix} 2 & 0 & 7 \\ 0 & 1 & 0 \\ 1 & -2 & 1 \end{bmatrix}$ and $B=\begin{bmatrix} -x & 14x & 7x \\ 0 & 1 & 0 \\ x & -4x & -2x \end{bmatrix}$ are two matrices such that $(AB)^2=I$ and $AB\neq I$, then the value of $tr\,\{(AB)+(AB)^2+\ldots+(AB)^{50}\}$ is ______

(where $tr\,(A)$ denotes trace of matrix A)

6. Let $P(x)$ be a polynomial of degree 4, with $P(2)=-1$, $P'(2)=0$, $P''(2)=2$, $P'''(2)=-12$ and $P''''(2)=24$, then the sum of digits in the value of $P''(1)$ is ______

7. Let V_n denotes the sum of the first n terms of an arithmetic progression (AP) whose first term is n and the common difference is $(2n-1)$. Then, the sum of $V_1+V_2+\ldots+V_{10}$ is ______

8. If α and β are the roots of the equation $x^2-6x+12=0$ and the value of $(\alpha-2)^{24}-\frac{(\beta-6)^8}{\alpha^8}+1$ is 4^{λ}, then the value of (4λ) is ______

Section 2

- This section contains **SIX (06)** questions.
- Each question has **FOUR** options (A), (B), (C) and (D). **ONE OR MORE THAN ONE** of these four option(s) is (are) correct answer(s).
- For each question, choose the options(s) corresponding to (all) the correct answer(s).
- Answer to each question will be evaluated according to the following marking scheme:

Full Marks : +4 If only (all) the correct option(s) is (are) chosen.
Partial Marks : +3 If all the four options are correct but ONLY three options are chosen.
Partial Marks : +2 If three or more options are correct but ONLY two options are chosen, both of which are correct.
Partial Marks : +1 If two or more options are correct but ONLY one option is chosen and it is a correct option;
Zero Marks : 0 If none of the options is chosen (i.e., the question is unanswered);
Negative Marks : −2 In all other cases.

9. Let *ABC* be a right angled triangle in which hypotenuse is four times the length of perpendicular drawn from the vertex containing right angle, then

(a) $\angle A=75^\circ, \angle B=90^\circ, \angle C=15^\circ$ for $A>C$
(b) $\angle A=30^\circ, \angle B=60^\circ, \angle C=90^\circ$ for $A>C$
(c) $\angle A=15^\circ, \angle B=90^\circ, \angle C=75^\circ$ for $A<C$
(d) $\angle A=60^\circ, \angle B=30^\circ, \angle C=90^\circ$ for $A<C$

10. If $x=a$ satisfied the equation

$$\tan^{-1}(x+2)+\cot^{-1}(\sqrt{4x+20})=\lim_{x\to\frac{\pi}{2}}\frac{\sin(x\cos x)}{\cos(x\sin x)}$$

and $\displaystyle\lim_{x\to 0}\frac{a\sqrt{1+x}-\frac{(1+x)^{1/x}}{e}-bx}{5x+kx^2+x^3}=0$, then

(a) $ab=3$ (b) $a=4$
(c) $a=3$ and $b=1$ (d) $k\in R$

11. If $I_n=\displaystyle\int_{-\pi}^{\pi}\frac{\sin nx}{(1+\pi^x)\cdot\sin x}dx, n=0,1,2,3\ldots\ldots$, then which one of the following is/are true?

(a) $I_n=I_{n+2}$ (b) $\sum_{m=1}^{10} I_{2m}=0$ (c) $I_n=I_{n+1}$ (d) $\sum_{m=1}^{10} I_{2m+1}=10\pi$

12. The 6th term in the expansion of $\left[\sqrt{\{2^{\log(10-3^x)}\}}+\sqrt[5]{\{2^{(x-2)\log 3}\}}\right]^m$ is equal to 21, if it is known that the binomial coefficient of the 2nd, 3rd and 4th terms in the expansion represents respectively, the first, third and fifth terms of an AP (the symbol log stands for decadic (or decimal or standard or briggsian or common) logarithm i.e. logarithm having base 10].

Then, choose the correct option(s) is/are correct.

(a) The value of *m* is 7
(b) The sum of possible values of *x* is 3
(c) Product of all possible values of *x* is 0
(d) The minimum value of expression is 128

13. Let *L* be the line $y=x+k$ and *H* be the hyperbola $xy=9$ and H_1 be the curve obtained by reflecting *H* in *L*. Then,

(a) if $k=3$, then the equation of H_1 is of the form $\lambda xy+\alpha x+\beta y-\gamma=0$, where $\alpha,\beta,\gamma,\lambda\in I$, so that the value of $\alpha\beta+\gamma\lambda$ is 9
(b) if $k=4$, then equation of H_1 is $xy-4x+4y=32$
(c) if $k>0$ and H_1 passes through (5, 5), then the value of *k* is 4
(d) None of the above

14. Consider the system of equations $2x+py+6z=8$, $x+2y+qz=5$ and $x+y+3z=4$, which represents the equation of planes in the space.

Then, choose the correct option(s) is/are correct.

(a) If $p\neq 2, q\neq 3$, then the system has no solution
(b) If $p\neq 2$, $q=3$, then the system has unique solution
(c) If $p=2, q=2$, then the system has infinite number of solution and the equation represent the plane meeting on the line $\frac{x-7}{-4}=y=z+1$.
(d) If $p=2, q=4$, then the system has unique solution and the equation represent the plane meeting on the line $\frac{x-1}{2}=y=1-z$.

Section 3

- This section contains **FOUR (04)** Matching List Sets.
- Each set has **ONE** Multiple Choice Question.
- Each set has **TWO** lists : **List-I** and **List-II**.
- List-I has **FOUR** entries (I), (II), (III) and (IV) and List-II has **FIVE** entries (P), (Q), (R), (S) and (T).
- **FOUR** options are given in each Multiple Choice Question based on **List-I** and **List-II** and **ONLY ONE** of these four options satisfies the condition asked in the Multiple Choice Question.
- Answer to each question will be evaluated according to the following marking scheme:

Full Marks : +3 ONLY if the option corresponding to the correct combination is chose;
Zero Marks : 0 If none of the options is chosen (i.e. the question is unanswered);
Negative Marks : −1 In all other cases.

15.

	List-I		List-II
I.	$\sqrt{2}\int_0^{\infty}\left[\frac{3}{x^2+1}\right]dx$ is equal to	P.	1
II.	$\ln 3\int_{-10}^{10}\frac{3^x}{3^{[x]}}dx$ is equal to	Q.	2
III.	$\int_{-1}^{1}[x[1+\sin\pi x]+1]\,dx$ is equal to	R.	3
IV.	If $\int_0^{\frac{\pi}{2}}\left\{a^2\left(\frac{\cos 3x}{4}+\frac{3}{4}\cos x\right)+a\sin x-20\cos x\,dx \le -\frac{a^2}{3}\right\}$, then '$a$' can be equal to (more than one may be correct)	S.	1, 2, 3, 4
		T.	40

Codes

	I	II	III	IV
(a)	R	T	Q	S
(b)	P	R	S	T
(c)	P	Q	S	R
(d)	T	S	R	P

16.

	List-I		List-II
I.	Area between $y=\lvert\cos^{-1}(\sin x)\rvert - \lvert\sin^{-1}(\cos x)\rvert$ and X-axis, where $x\in\left[\frac{3\pi}{2},2\pi\right]$ is $\frac{k\pi^2}{4}$, then k is equal to	P.	1
II.	The difference between the radii of the smallest and the largest circles which have their centres on the circumference of the circle $x^2+y^2+2x+4y-4=0$ and passes through the point (2, 2) is	Q.	6
III.	If $f(0)=1$, $f(2)=3$ and $f'(2)=5$, then $\int_0^1 xf''(2x)\,dx$ is equal to	R.	2
IV.	If $f(x)=x^3+4x^2+6x$, then $f^{-1}(-4)$ is	S.	−2
		T.	8

Codes

	I	II	III	IV
(a)	Q	S	R	P
(b)	P	Q	R	S
(c)	P	R	Q	S
(d)	P	R	S	Q

17.

	List-I		List-II
I.	Let $abc=8(a,b,c\nless 0)$ and real valued function $f(x)=bc(ax-1)^2-ca(bx-1)^2+ab(cx-1)^2$, has minimum value at $x=\frac{1}{2}$, then the value of $a^{16}+b^{17}+c^{16}$ is	P.	2^{16}
II.	For the equation $\lvert x^2+\sqrt[3]{k}\rvert=16\lvert x\rvert$, $k\in R$ to have a real solution, then value of k can be	Q.	2^{17}
III.	The number of 16 digit number such that the product of any two consecutive digits in the number is a prime is	R.	2^{18}
IV.	The value of ${}^{20}C_1+{}^{20}C_3+{}^{20}C_5+{}^{20}C_7+{}^{20}C_9$ is	S.	$2^{16}, 2^{17}, 2^{18}$
		T.	2^{59}

Codes

	I	II	III	IV
(a)	R	S	Q	R
(b)	P	R	S	T
(c)	P	Q	R	S
(d)	T	S	R	P

18.

	List-I		List-II
I.	If ${}^{(n+1)}C_4+{}^{(n+1)}C_3+{}^{(n+2)}C_3>{}^{(n+3)}C_3$, then possible values of n is/are	P.	2
II.	The remainder when $(3053)^{456}-(2417)^{333}$ is divided by 9 is	Q.	5, 6, 7
III.	The digit in the unit place of the number $183!+3^{183}$ is	R.	6
IV.	If sum of the coefficient of the first, second and third terms of the expansion of $\left(x^2+\frac{1}{x}\right)^m$ is 46, then the index of the term that does not contain x is	S.	7
		T.	0

Codes

	I	II	III	IV
(a)	P	Q	R	S
(b)	P	R	S	T
(c)	T	P	R	Q
(d)	Q	P	S	R

Paper 2

Section 1

- This section contains **EIGHT (08)** questions.
- The answer to each question is a **SINGLE DIGIT INTEGER** ranging from 0 TO 9. **BOTH INCLUSIVE**.
- For each question, enter the correct integer corresponding to the answer using the mouse and the on-screen virtual numeric keypad in the place designated to enter the answer.
- Answer to each question will be evaluated according to the following marking scheme:
  Full Marks : + 3 If ONLY the correct integer is entered.
  Zero Marks : 0 If the question is unanswered.
  Negative Marks : –1 In all other cases.

1. A curve $y = f(x)$ is such that $f(x) \geq 0$ and $f(0) = 0$ and bounds a curvilinear trapezoid with the base $[0, x]$ whose area is proportional to $(n+1)$th power of $f(x)$. If $f(1) = 1$, then $\left[f\left(\frac{5}{2}\right)\right]^n$ is equal to p/q, then $p+q$ is (where, p and q are coprime) ______

2. A piece of wire of length 4 L is bent at random to form a rectangle. The probability that its area is atmost $\frac{L^2}{4}$ is $1 - \frac{\sqrt{p}}{q}$, where p and q are relatively prime, then the value of $\frac{p^2+q^2}{13}$ is ______

3. Let F_1 and F_2 be two foci of the ellipse $\frac{x^2}{p^2+2} + \frac{y^2}{p^2+4} = 1$. Let P be any point on the ellipse, then maximum possible value of $PF_1 \cdot PF_2 - p^2$ is ______

4. Suppose $\frac{3}{(x-1)(x^2+x+1)} = f_1(x) - f_2(x)$, where $f_1(x) = \frac{1}{x-1}$ and $f_2(x) = \frac{x+2}{x^2+x+1}$. If $\frac{x+1}{(x-1)^2(x^2+x+1)} = af_1(x) + \left(b + \frac{c}{x-1}\right) f_2(x) + \frac{d}{(x-1)^2}$, then the value of $\begin{vmatrix} a & b \\ c & d \end{vmatrix} + 9|a+ib|^2$ is ______

5. Consider a parabola $y = \frac{x^2}{4}$ and the point $F(0, 1)$. Let $A_1(x_1, y_1), A_2(x_2, y_2), A_3(x_3, y_3) \ldots A_n(x_n, y_n)$ are n points on the parabola such that $x_k > 0$ and $\angle OFA_k = \frac{k\pi}{2x}$, where $k = 1, 2, 3, 4 \ldots n$. Then, the value of $\lim_{n \to \infty} \frac{1}{n} \sum_{k=1}^{n} FA_k$ is equal to $\frac{\lambda}{\pi}$, then the value of λ is ______

6. Consider three distinct real numbers a, b and c are in GP with $a^2 + b^2 + c^2 = t^2$ and $a + b + c = \alpha t$. The sum of the common ratio and its reciprocal is denoted by S. Thus, the complete set of α^2 belongs to $\left(\frac{1}{p}, q\right) - \{1\}$ and the complete set of S belongs to $(-\infty, r) \cup (s, \infty)$. Thus, $p + q + r + s$ equals ______

7. If $\cos(\alpha - \beta) = 1$ and $\cos(\alpha + \beta) = \frac{1}{e}$, where $\alpha, \beta \in [-\pi, \pi]$, then the number of solution of α and β which satisfy the above two equations, is ______

8. If A and B are two events with $P(A^C) = 0.3$ and $P(B) = 0.4$ and $P(A \cap B^C) = 0.5$. Then, $4 \times [P(B/(A \cup B^C))]$ is equal to ______

Section 2

- This section contains **SIX (06)** questions.
- Each question has **FOUR** options (A), (B), (C) and (D). **ONE OR MORE THAN ONE** of these four option(s) is (are) correct asnswer(s).
- For each question, choose the option(s) corresponding to (all) the correct answer(s).
- Answer to each question will be evaluated according to the following marking scheme:

Full Marks : +4 If only (all) the correct option(s) is (are) chosen.
Partial Marks : + 3 If all the four options are correct but ONLY three options are chosen.
Partial Marks : +2 If three or more options are correct but ONLY two options are chosen, both of which are correct.
Partial Marks : +1 If two or more options are correct but ONLY one option is chosen and it is a correct option.
Zero Marks : 0 If none of the options is chosen (i.e. the question is unanswered).
Negative Marks : –2 In all other cases.

9. Mark the incorrect option(s) for two vectors **a** and **b** such that $\mathbf{a}\times\mathbf{b}=2\hat{i}+2\hat{j}-\hat{k}$ and $\mathbf{a}+\mathbf{b}=\hat{i}-3\hat{j}-4\hat{k}$.

(a) $\mathbf{a}=\frac{(2-\lambda)}{4}\hat{i}+\frac{(3\lambda-2)}{4}\hat{j}+\lambda\hat{k}$ and $\mathbf{b}=\frac{(2+\lambda)}{4}\hat{i}-\frac{(10+3\lambda)}{4}\hat{j}-(4+\lambda)\hat{k}$

(b) $\mathbf{a}=\frac{(2+\lambda)}{4}\hat{i}+\frac{(\lambda-2)}{4}\hat{j}+(\lambda+1)\hat{k}$ and $\mathbf{b}=\frac{(2-\lambda)}{4}\hat{i}-\frac{(10+\lambda)}{4}\hat{j}-4\hat{k}$

(c) $\mathbf{a}=\frac{(2+\lambda)}{4}\hat{i}-\frac{(10+3\lambda)}{4}\hat{j}+(4+\lambda)\hat{k}$ and $\mathbf{b}=\frac{(2-\lambda)}{4}\hat{i}+\frac{(3\lambda-2)}{4}\hat{j}+\lambda\hat{k}$

(d) $\mathbf{a}=\frac{\lambda}{4}\hat{i}+\frac{3\lambda}{4}\hat{j}+\lambda\hat{k}$ and $\mathbf{b}=\frac{(2-\lambda)}{4}\hat{i}+\frac{(10+2\lambda)}{3}\hat{j}-(4-\lambda)\hat{k}$

where, λ being any real numbers.

10. The largest area of a trapezium inscribed in a semi-circle of radius R, if the lower base is on the diameter is

(a) $\frac{3\sqrt{3}}{4}R^2$ (b) $\frac{\sqrt{3}}{4}R^2$ (c) $\frac{3\sqrt{3}}{8}R^2$ (d) None of these

11. Given, $P=(4\cos t, 4\sin t, 3)$, $Q=(8\cos t, 8\sin t, -1)$, $0\le t<2\pi$. Let R be the point of intersection of line PQ and plane $z=0$. Let w be the plane through R and perpendicular to PQ. Let θ be the angle between the normal to w and the line OA, where $A=(10, 10, 40)$ and O is the origin, which of the following is correct?

(a) $R=(7\cos t, 7\sin t, 0)$

(b) Equation of plane w is $x\cos t+y\sin t-z=7$

(c) $\cos\theta=\frac{1}{6}\left(4-\sqrt{2}\sin\left(t+\frac{\pi}{4}\right)\right)$

(d) $\theta=\tan^{-1}\left(\frac{2\sqrt{2}-1}{3\sqrt{2}}\right)$ for which $\cos\theta$ is maximum

12. The area of any cyclic quadrilateral $ABCD$ is given by $A^2=(s-a)(s-b)(s-c)(s-d)$, where $2s=a+b+c+d$; a, b, c and d are the sides of the quadrilateral. Now, consider a cyclic quadrilateral $ABCD$ of area 1 sq unit, then the correct option (s) is/are

(a) the minimum perimeter of the quadrilateral is 4.

(b) the minimum value of the sum of the lengths of diagonals is $2\sqrt{2}$.

(c) when the perimeter is minimum, the quadrilateral is necessarily a square.

(d) None of the above

13. z_1, z_2, z_3 and z_1', z_2', z_3' are non-zero complex numbers such that $z_3=(1-\lambda)z_1+\lambda z_2$ and $z_3'=(1-\mu)z_1'+\mu z_2'$, then which of the following statement(s) is/are true?

(a) If $\lambda, \mu \in R-\{0\}$, then z_1, z_2 and z_3 are collinear and z_1', z_2', z_3' are collinear separately.

(b) If λ, μ are complex number, where $\lambda=\mu$, then triangles formed by points z_1, z_2, z_3 and z_1', z_2', z_3' are similar.

(c) If λ, μ are distinct complex numbers, then points z_1, z_2, z_3 and z_1', z_2', z_3' are not connected by any well defined geometry.

(d) If $0<\lambda<1$, then z_3 divides the line joining z_1 and z_2 internally and, if $\mu>1$, then z_3' divides the line joining of z_1', z_2' (externally).

14. If $P=\lim_{n\to\infty} n^{-n^2}\{(n+2^0)(n+2^{-1})(n+2^{-2})......(n+2^{-n+1})\}^n$, then which of the following is/are true?

(a) P is irrational

(b) P is rational

(c) P equal to $\frac{1}{e^2}$

(d) $P>\lim_{x\to\infty}\left(\frac{1+x}{x}\right)^{\ln x-x}$

Section 3

- This section contains **FOUR (04)** questions.
- Each question has **FOUR** options (a), (b), (c) and (d). **ONLY ONE** of these four options is the correct answer.
- Four each question, choose the option corresponding to the correct answer.
- Answer to each question will be evaluated according to the following marking scheme:

Full Marks : +3 If **ONLY** the correct option is chosen;

Zero Marks : 0 If none of the options is chosen (i.e. the question is unanswered);

Negative Marks : –1 In all other cases.

15. If Δ_1 is the area of the triangle with vertices (0,0), $(a\tan\alpha, b\cot\alpha)$, $(a\sin\alpha, b\cos\alpha)$, Δ_2 is the area of the triangle with vertices (a,b), $(a\sec^2\alpha, b\,\text{cosec}^2\alpha)$, $(a+a\sin^2\alpha, b+b\cos^2\alpha)$ and Δ_3 is the area of the triangle with vertices (0,0), $(a\tan\alpha, -b\cot\alpha)$, $(a\sin\alpha, b\cos\alpha)$, then the total number of values of α for which Δ_1, Δ_2 and Δ_3 are in GP is

(a) 2 (b) 4 (c) infinite (d) 0

16. If a and b are chosen randomly from the set consisting of numbers 1,2,3,4,5 and 6 with replacement. Then, the probability that $\lim_{x\to 0}\left(\frac{a^x+b^x}{2}\right)^{2/x}=6$, is

(a) $\frac{1}{3}$ (b) $\frac{1}{9}$ (c) $\frac{2}{9}$ (d) $\frac{4}{9}$

17. If $f(x)=(x+2)^2-4, x\geq -2$ and $S=\{x: f(x)=f^{-1}(x)\}$, then S is equal to

(a) $\{0,4\}$

(b) $\left\{0, 2, \frac{1}{2}(\sqrt{5}-1)\right\}$

(c) $\{0\}$

(d) $\left\{0, 4, \frac{1}{2}(\sqrt{5}-1), \frac{1}{2}(\sqrt{5}+1)\right\}$

18. The trajectories orthogonal to $(2a-x)y^2=x^3$ is

(a) $(x^2+y^2)^2=C(y^2+2x^2)$

(b) $x^2+y^2=C(y^2+2x^2)$

(c) $(x^2+y^2)=x^3+xy^2$

(d) $(x^2+y^2)^2=Cxy$

Answers

Paper 1

1 *(0.5)*	2 *(192)*	3 *(8)*	4 *(8)*	5 *(50)*	6 *(8)*	7 *(2860)*	8 *(48)*	9 *(a,c)*	10 *(a,b,d)*
11 *(a,b,d)*	12 *(a,c,d)*	13 *(a,b,c)*	14 *(c,d)*	15 *(a)*	16 *(b)*	17 *(a)*	18 *(d)*		

Paper 2

1 *(7)*	2 *(1)*	3 *(4)*	4 *(2)*	5 *(4)*	6 *(6)*	7 *(4)*	8 *(1)*	9 *(b,c,d)*	10 *(a)*
11 *(a,b,c)*	12 *(a,b,c)*	13 *(a,b,c,d)*	14 *(a,d)*	15 *(d)*	16 *(b)*	17 *(c)*	18 *(a)*		

See detailed solutions on page no. 293

Knockout 14

JEE ADVANCED

Mathematics

Paper 1

Section 1

- This section contains **FOUR (04)** questions.
- Each question has **FOUR** options (a), (b), (c) and (d). **ONLY ONE** of these four options is the correct answer.
- For each question, choose the option corresponding to the correct answer.

Answer to each question will be evaluated according to the following marking scheme:

Full Marks : +3 If ONLY the correct option is chosen;
Zero Marks : 0 If none of the options is chosen (i.e. the question is unanswered);
Negative Marks : −1 In all other cases.

1. Let $f(x)=\log_{\left(\frac{25-x^2}{16}\right)}\left(\frac{24-2x-x^2}{14}\right)$, then select the correct option.

(a) The values of x for which $\sqrt{f(x)}\times\log_{\sec^2(8.5)}\left(\frac{25-x^2}{16}\right)>0$ belongs to $(-3,3)$

(b) When $\left(\frac{25-x^2}{16}\right)\in(0,1)$, then $x\in(3,5)$ for which $f(x)>1$

(c) When $\left(\frac{25-x^2}{16}\right)\in(1,\infty)$, then $x\in(-3,-2)$ for which $f(x)>1$

(d) None of the above

2. If a particle in equilibrium is subjected to four forces

$\mathbf{F}_1=-10\hat{\mathbf{k}}, \mathbf{F}_2=u\left(\frac{4}{13}\hat{\mathbf{i}}-\frac{12}{13}\hat{\mathbf{j}}+\frac{3}{13}\hat{\mathbf{k}}\right)$,

$\mathbf{F}_3=v\left(-\frac{4}{13}\hat{\mathbf{i}}-\frac{12}{13}\hat{\mathbf{j}}+\frac{3}{13}\hat{\mathbf{k}}\right)$ and $\mathbf{F}_4=w(\cos\theta\hat{\mathbf{i}}+\sin\theta\hat{\mathbf{j}})$.

Then,

(a) $u=\frac{1}{3}-\cot\theta$

(b) $v=\frac{1}{3}+\cot\theta$

(c) $w=40\cot\theta$

(d) $v=65\left(\frac{1}{3}+\cot\theta\right)$

3. From a point A common tangents are drawn to the circle $x^2+y^2=\frac{a^2}{2}$ and the parabola $y^2=4ax$. Then, the area of the quadrilateral formed (in sq units) by the common tangents drawn from A and the chord of contact of the circle and the parabola is

(a) $\frac{15a}{4}$ (b) $\frac{15}{4}$

(c) $\frac{15a^2}{4}$ (d) None of these

4. $P(u,v,w)$ is a point whose distance from the line $x=y=z$ is twice its distance from the plane $x+y+z=1$ and $uv+vw+uw=0$, then $u^2+v^2+w^2-4(u+v+w)$ equals

(a) -2 (b) 2

(c) 0 (d) 3

Section 2

- This section contains **THREE (03)** question stems.
- There are **TWO (02)** questions corresponding to each question stem.
- The answer to each question is a **NUMERICAL VALUE.**
- For each question, enter the correct numerical value corresponding to the answer in the designated place using the mouse and the on-screen virtual numeric keypad.
- If the numerical value has more than two decimal places, **truncate/round-off** the value to **TWO** decimal places.

Answer to each question will be evaluated according to the following marking scheme:

Full Marks : +2 If ONLY the correct numerical value is entered at the designated place;

Zero Marks : 0 In all other cases.

Question Stem (Q.Nos. 5-6)

Let $A = \begin{bmatrix} 1 & 0 & 0 \\ 1 & 0 & 1 \\ 0 & 1 & 0 \end{bmatrix}$ satisfies $A^n = A^{n-2} + A^2 - I$ for $n \geq 3$ and trace of a square matrix x is equal to the sum of elements in its principal diagonal. Further, consider a matrix $\underset{3\times 3}{U}$ with its column as U_1, U_2 and U_3 such that

$$A^{50}U_1 = \begin{bmatrix} 1 \\ 25 \\ 25 \end{bmatrix}, A^{50}U_2 = \begin{bmatrix} 0 \\ 1 \\ 0 \end{bmatrix} \text{ and } A^{50}U_3 = \begin{bmatrix} 0 \\ 0 \\ 1 \end{bmatrix}$$

5. Trace of A^{50} is ....

6. The value of $|U|$ is ....

Question stem (Q.Nos. 7-8)

For certain curves $y = f(x)$ satisfying $\frac{d^2y}{dx^2} = 6x - 4$, $f(x)$ has local minimum value 5, when $x = 1$.

7. Number of critical point for $y = f(x)$ for $x \in [0,2]$ is ....

8. Global maximum value of $y = f(x)$ for $x \in [0,2]$ is ....

Question stem (Q.Nos. 9-10)

Let $n \geq 2$ be an positive integer. Take 'n' distinct points on a circle and join each pair of points by a line segment. Colour the line segment joining every pair of adjacent points by green and rest by blue. If the number of green and blue line segment are equal. Then,

9. The value of ${}^nC_2$ is ....

10. Then total number of blue line is ....

Section 3

- This section contains **SIX (06)** questions.
- Each question has **FOUR** options (a), (b), (c) and (d). **ONE OR MORE THAN ONE** of these four option(s) is (are) correct answer(s).
- For each question, choose the option(s) corresponding to (all) the correct answer(s).
- Answer to each question will be evaluated according to the following marking scheme:

Full Marks : +4 If only (all) the correct option(s) is(are) chosen;

Partial Marks : +3 If all the four options are correct but ONLY three options are chosen;

Partial Marks : +2 If three or more options are correct but ONLY two options are chosen, both of which are correct;

Partial Marks : +1 If two or more options are correct but ONLY one option is chosen and it is a correct option;

Zero Marks : 0 If unanswered;

Negative Marks : – 2 In all other cases.

For example, in a question, if (a), (b) and (d) are the ONLY three options corresponding to correct answers, then

choosing ONLY (a), (b) and (d) will get +4 marks;

choosing ONLY (a) and (b) will get +2 marks;

choosing ONLY (a) and (d) will get +2 marks;

choosing ONLY (b) and (d) will get +2 marks;

choosing ONLY (a) will get +1 mark;

choosing ONLY (b) will get +1 mark;

choosing ONLY (d) will get +1 mark;

choosing no option(s) (i.e. the question is unanswered) will get 0 marks and choosing any other option(s) will get – 2 marks.

11. A square is inscribed in a circle. If p_1 is the probability that a randomly chosen point of the circle lies within the square and p_2 is the probability that the point lies outside the square, then

(a) $p_1 > p_2$ (b) $p_1 = p_2$

(c) $p_1^2 - p_2^2 < \frac{1}{3}$ (d) $p_1 < p_2$

12. Consider a circle $x^2 + y^2 = a^2$. Let $A(a, 0)$ and $D(\alpha, \beta)$ be the given interior points of the circle. BC be an arbitrary chord of the circle through point D inclined at an angle θ with the positive X-axis. Also, $DB = r_1$ and $DC = r_2$, then which of the following statements is (are) true?

(a) The HM of BD and DC is $\left[-\frac{\alpha^2 + \beta^2 - a^2}{(\alpha\cos\theta + \beta\sin\theta)}\right]$

(b) The locus of the centroid of ΔABC is $\left(x - \frac{a}{3}\right)^2 + (y)^2 = \left(\frac{r_1 + r_2}{3}\right)^2$

(c) The locus of the centroid of ΔABC has radius less than $\frac{2a}{3}$.

(d) The locus of the centroid of ΔABC has radius greater than $\frac{2a}{3}$

13. Let $P_n = \sum_{k=1}^{4n} (-1)^{\frac{k(k+1)}{2}} \cdot \frac{k^2}{2}$. Then, P_n can take values

(a) 136 (b) 1332 (c) 528 (d) 666

14. If α is a variable complex number such that $|\alpha| > 1$ and $z = \alpha + \frac{1}{\alpha}$ lies on a conic, then

(a) eccentricity of the conic is $\frac{2|\alpha|}{1 + |\alpha|^2}$

(b) distance between foci is 4 units

(c) length of latusrectum is $\frac{2(|\alpha|^2 - 1)}{|\alpha|^2 + 1}$

(d) distance between directrices is $\left(|\alpha| + \frac{1}{|\alpha|}\right)^2$

15. Given a ΔABC whose area is unity. If $\angle A = 45°$ and $\angle B = 30°$, then which of the following holds good?

(a) $R^2 = 2(\sqrt{3} - 1)$

(b) The value of R^2 is equal to thrice the altitude from the vertex C

(c) The value of R is equal to the smallest side of the triangle.

(d) Length of angle bisector from the vertex B cannot exceed $\frac{\sqrt{6} + \sqrt{2}}{2}$

16. Which of the following definite integrals reduces to $\frac{\pi}{2}$?

(a) $\int_0^{\pi} \frac{dx}{1 + (\sin x)^{\cos x}}$ (b) $\int_0^{\infty} \frac{x^2 + 1}{x^4 - x^2 + 1} dx$

(c) $\int_0^{\pi/2} \frac{dx}{1 + (\tan x)^5}$ (d) $\int_0^{\pi/2} \{\ln(\sec x)\}(e^{\ln(\ln 2)})^{-1} dx$

Section 4

- This section contains **THREE** (03) questions.
- The answer to each question is a **NON-NEGATIVE INTEGER.**
- For each question, enter the correct integer corresponding to the answer using the mouse and the on-screen virtual numeric keypad in the place designated to enter the answer.
- Answer to each question will be evaluated according to the following marking scheme:

Full Marks : +4 If **ONLY** the correct integer is entered;

Zero Marks : 0 In all other cases.

17. The coefficient of x^{50} in the polynomials after parenthesis have been removed and like terms have been collected in the expansion $(1+x)^{1000} + x(1+x)^{999} + x^2(1+x)^{998} + \dots + x^{1000}$ is $\frac{\lambda!}{\mu!\nu!}$, then the value of $\lambda + 2\mu + 3\nu$ must be $(\nu > \mu)$______

18. Let $f:(0,1) \to (0,1)$ be a differentiable function such that $f'(x) \neq 0 \; \forall \; x \in (0,1)$ and $f\left(\frac{1}{2}\right) = \frac{\sqrt{3}}{2}$, if $f(x) = \lim_{t \to x} \frac{\int_0^x \sqrt{1 - f^2(t)}\, dt}{f(t) - f(x)}$, then the value of $16\left\{f\left(\frac{1}{4}\right)\right\}^2$ is ______

19. The greatest integral value of a such that $\sqrt{9 - a^2 + 2ax - x^2} \geq \sqrt{16 - x^2}$ for atleast one positive value of x, is ______

Paper 2

Section 1

- This section contains **SIX (06)** questions.
- Each question has **FOUR** options (a), (b), (c) and (d). **ONE OR MORE THAN ONE** of these four option(s) is (are) correct answer(s).
- For each question, choose the option(s) corresponding to (all) the correct answer(s).
- Answer to each question will be evaluated according to the following marking scheme:

Full Marks : +4 If only (all) the correct option(s) is(are) chosen;
Partial Marks : +3 If all the four options are correct but ONLY three options are chosen;
Partial Marks : +2 If three or more options are correct but ONLY two options are chosen, both of which are correct;
Partial Marks : +1 If two or more options are correct but ONLY one option is chosen and it is a correct option;
Zero Marks : 0 If unanswered;
Negative Marks : – 2 In all other cases.
For example, in a question, if (a), (b) and (d) are the ONLY three options corresponding to correct answers, then
choosing ONLY (a), (b) and (d) will get +4 marks;
choosing ONLY (a) and (b) will get +2 marks;
choosing ONLY (a) and (d) will get +2marks;
choosing ONLY (b) and (d) will get +2 marks;
choosing ONLY (a) will get +1 mark;
choosing ONLY (b) will get +1 mark;
choosing ONLY (d) will get +1 mark;
choosing no option(s) (i.e. the question is unanswered) will get 0 marks and choosing any other option(s) will get –3 marks.

1. If $f(\theta) = |||3\cos\theta - \sin\theta| + 2\cos\theta| + \cos\theta|$, where $\theta \in \left(\frac{\pi}{2}, \pi\right)$, then

(a) $\int_{\pi/2}^{\pi} f(\theta)\, d\theta = 1$ (b) $f'\left(\frac{5\pi}{6}\right) = -\frac{\sqrt{3}}{2}$

(c) $\int_{\pi/2}^{\pi} f^2(\theta) d\theta = \frac{\pi}{4}$ (d) $f'\left(\frac{2\pi}{3}\right) = -\frac{1}{2}$

2. Let $A = \begin{bmatrix} \sqrt{2} & 1 & 0 \\ 1 & -\sqrt{2} & 0 \\ 0 & 0 & \sqrt{3} \end{bmatrix}$, then the value of $\frac{|A^{-1} + A^T|}{|\text{adj}(\text{adj}A)|}$ is equal to

(a) $-\frac{2^6\sqrt{3}}{3^8}$ (b) $\frac{2^3}{3^6\sqrt{3}}$ (c) $-\frac{2^9\sqrt{3}}{3^6}$ (d) $\frac{2^3}{3^5}$

3. Let P_1 denote the equation of a plane to which the vector $(\hat{\ } + \hat{\ })$ is normal and which contains the line whose equation is $= \hat{\ } + \hat{\ } + \hat{\ } + \lambda(\hat{\ } - \hat{\ } - \hat{\ })$ and P_2 denote the equation of the plane containing the line L and a point with position vector $\hat{\ }$. Which of the following holds good?

(a) The equation of P_1 is $x + y = 2$
(b) The equation of P_2 is $\cdot(\hat{\ } - 2\hat{\ } + \hat{\ }) = 2$
(c) The acute angle between P_1 and P_2s is $\cot^{-1}(\sqrt{3})$.
(d) The angle between P_2 and L is $\tan^{-1}(\sqrt{3})$

4. If $y(x)$ satisfied the differential equation $y' - y\tan x = 2x\sec x$ and $y(0) = 0$, then

(a) $y\left(\frac{\pi}{4}\right) = \frac{\pi^2\sqrt{2}}{16}$

(b) $y\left(\frac{\pi}{3}\right) = \frac{2\pi^2}{3}$

(c) $y'\left(\frac{\pi}{3}\right) = \frac{4\pi}{3} + \frac{2\pi^2}{3\sqrt{3}}$

(d) Solution $y(x)$ is bounded $\forall\, x \in R$

5. The equation $(1 - \tan\theta)(1 + \tan\theta)\sec^2\theta + 2\tan^2\theta = 0$, $\theta \in \left(-\frac{\pi}{2}, \frac{\pi}{2}\right)$ has solutions $\theta_1, \theta_2, \theta_3, \ldots, \theta_n$. Then, which of the following may be correct?

(a) $n = 2$ (b) $n = 4$ (c) $\prod_{i=1}^{n} \theta_i = -\frac{\pi^2}{9}$ (d) $\sum_{i=1}^{n} \theta_i = 0$

6. A boy has a collection of blue and green marbles. The number of blue marbles belong to the set {2, 3, 4, ..., 13}. If two marbles are chosen simultaneously and at random from his collection, then the probability that they have different colours is $\frac{1}{2}$. Possible number of blue marbles is

(a) 12 (b) 6 (c) 3 (d) 10

Section 2

- This section contains **THREE (03)** question stems.
- There are **TWO (02)** questions corresponding to each question stem.
- The answer to each question is a **NUMERICAL VALUE.**
- For each question, enter the correct numerical value corresponding to the answer in the designated place using the mouse and the on-screen virtual numeric keypad.
- If the numerical value has more than two decimal places, **truncate/round-off** the value to **TWO** decimal places.

Answer to each question will be evaluated according to the following marking scheme:

Full Marks : +2 If ONLY the correct numerical value is entered at the designated place;

Zero Marks : 0 In all other cases.

Question Stem (Q.Nos. 7-8)

The function $y=f(x)$ is the solution of differential equation $\sqrt{1-x^2}\dfrac{dy}{dx}-\dfrac{xy}{\sqrt{1-x^2}}=x^4+2x$ in $(-1,1)$ satisfied $y(0)=0$. Then,

7. The value of $y\left(\dfrac{1}{2}\right)$ is of the form $\dfrac{\mu}{\lambda\sqrt{3}}$, then $\dfrac{\lambda}{\mu-1}$ is ______

8. The value of $\int_{-1/2}^{1/2} f(x)\,dx$ is of the from $\left(\dfrac{\pi}{k}-\dfrac{\sqrt{a}}{b}\right)$. Then, $\dfrac{b^2+2(a+1)}{k}$ is ______

Question Stem (Q.Nos. 9-10)

If $f(x)=x^2+ax+3$ and $g(x)=x+b$ and

$$F(x)=\lim_{n\to\infty}\frac{f(x)+x^{2n}\cdot g(x)}{1+x^{2n}}$$

9. If $f(x)$ is continuous at $x=-1$, then $[(a-b)+6]$ is equal to ______

10. If $f(x)$ is continuous at $x=-1$, then $[a+b+\pi]$ (where [.] denotes greatest integer function) is equals ______

Question Stem (Q.Nos. 11-12)

Consider the word "COMMISSIONER"s containing 12 letters of which five are vowels and seven are consonants.

11. Number of 5 lettered word each comprising of 2 vowels and 3 consonants is ______

12. Number of ways in which the letters of word can be arranged, if alike letters are together but separated from the other alike letters is ______

Section 3

- This section contains **TWO (02)** paragraphs. Based on each paragraph, there are TWO (02) questions.
- Each question has **FOUR** options (a), (b), (c) and (d). **ONLY ONE** of these four options is the correct answer.
- For each question, choose the option corresponding to the correct answer.
- Answer to each question will be evaluated according to the following marking scheme:

Full Marks : +3 If ONLY the correct option is chosen;

Zero Marks : 0 If none of the options is chosen (i.e, the question is unanswered);

Negative Marks : −1 In all other cases.

Paragraph (Q.Nos. 13-14)

Evaluating integrals dependents on a parameter : 'Differentiate I w.r.t. the parameter within the sign of integrals taking variables of the integrand as constant. Now, evaluate the integral so obtained as usual as a function of the parameter and then integrate the result to get I. Constant of integration can be computed by giving some arbitrary values to the parameter and the corresponding value of I.

13. The value of $\int_0^1 \dfrac{x^a-1}{\log_e x}dx$ is

(a) $a\log_e(a+1)$ (b) $\log_e(a+1)$

(c) $a\log_e(a-1)$ (d) $\log_e(a-1)$

14. The value of $\dfrac{dI}{da}$, when $I=\int_0^{\pi/2}\log\left(\dfrac{1+a\sin x}{1-a\sin x}\right)\dfrac{dx}{\sin x}$ (where $|a|<1$) is

(a) $\dfrac{\pi}{\sqrt{1-a^2}}$ (b) $-\pi\sqrt{1+a^2}$

(c) $\dfrac{\sqrt{1+a^2}}{\pi}$ (d) None of these

Paragraph (Q.Nos. 15-16)

Let, $\alpha \in R$ such that the point (α, α^2) lies inside the triangle formed by the lines $2x+3y-1=0$, $x+2y-3=0$ and $5x-6y-1=0$.

15. The possible value of α belongs to

(a) $\alpha \in \left(-\frac{3}{2}, \frac{1}{2}\right)$ (b) $\left(-\frac{1}{2}, 1\right)$

(c) $\left(-\frac{3}{2}, -1\right)$ (d) $\alpha \in R$

16. The area of an triangle formed by the three given lines is

(a) $\frac{125}{24}$ sq units (b) 5 sq units

(c) $\frac{120}{24}$ sq units (d) $\frac{121}{24}$ sq units

Section 4

- This section contains **THREE (03)** questions.
- The answer to each question is a **NON-NEGATIVE INTEGER.**
- For each question, enter the correct integer corresponding to the answer using the mouse and the on-screen virtual numeric keypad in the place designated to enter the answer.

Answer to each question will be evaluated according to the following marking scheme:

Full Marks : +4 If ONLY the correct integer is entered;

Zero Marks : 0 In all other cases.

17. Let $\omega = e^{i\frac{\pi}{3}}$ and a, b, c, x, y, z be non-zero complex numbers such that $a+b+c=x$, $a+b\omega+c\omega^2=y$, $a+b\omega^2+c\omega=z$. Then, the value of $\frac{|x|^2+|y|^2+|z|^2}{|a|^2+|b|^2+|c|^2}$ is ....

18. If $(1+x)^n = C_0 + C_1x + C_2x^2 + C_3x^3 + ... + C_nx^n$ and $\sum_{r=0}^{n} (r+1)^2 C_r = 2^{n-2} f(n)$, if roots of the eqūation $f(x)=0$ are α and β, then $\alpha^4+\beta^4$ must be ....

19. If $x, y, z \in R$ are such that they satisfy $x+y+z=1$ and $\tan^{-1} x + \tan^{-1} y + \tan^{-1} z = \frac{\pi}{4}$, then the value of $|x^3+y^3+z^3-3|$ is ....

Answers

Paper 1

1 *(b)*	2 *(d)*	3 *(c)*	4 *(a)*	5 *(3)*	6 *(1)*	7 *(2)*	8 *(7)*	9 *(10)*	10 *(5)*
11 *(a,c)*	12 *(a.b,c)*	13 *(a,c,d)*	14 *(a,b,d)*	15 *(a,c,d)*	16 *(a,d)*	17 *(3954)*	18 *(7)*	19 *(b)*	

Paper 2

1 *(a,b,c,d)*	2 *(a)*	3 *(a,c)*	4 *(a,c)*	5 *(a,d)*	6 *(b,c,d)*	7 *(2)*	8 *(4)*	9 *(3)*	10 *(8)*
11 *(6720)*	12 *(2880)*	13 *(b)*	14 *(a)*	15 *(c)*	16 *(d)*	17 *(3)*	18 *(257)*	19 *(2)*	

See detailed solutions on page no. 302

Knockout 15

JEE ADVANCED

Mathematics

Paper 1

Section 1

- This section contains **FOUR (04)** questions.
- Each question has **FOUR** options (a), (b), (c) and (d). **ONLY ONE** of these four options is the correct answer.
- For each question, choose the option corresponding to the correct answer.
- Answer to each question will be evaluated according to the following marking scheme:

Full Marks : +3 If ONLY the correct option is chosen;
Zero Marks : 0 If none of the options is chosen (i.e. the question is unanswered);
Negative Marks : −1 In all other cases.

1. In the given square, a diagonal is drawn and parallel line segment joining points on the adjacent sides are drawn on both sides of the diagonal. The length of the diagonal is $n\sqrt{2}$ cm. If the distance between consecutive line segments to be $\frac{1}{\sqrt{2}}$ cm, then the sum of the lengths of all possible line segments and the diagonal is

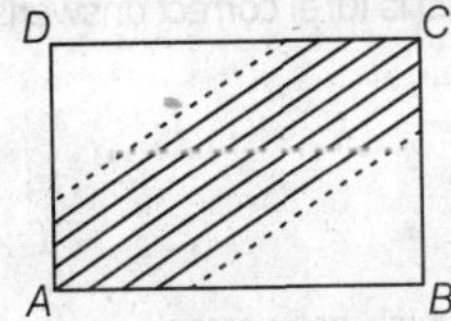

(a) $n(n+1)\sqrt{2}$ m (b) n^2 cm
(c) $n(n+2)$ cm (d) $n^2\sqrt{2}$ cm

2. If $y = \int_0^x f(t)\sin\{k(x-t)\}dt$, then $\frac{d^2y}{dx^2} + k^2y$ equals

(a) 0 (b) y (c) $k \cdot f(x)$ (d) $k^2 \cdot f(x)$

3. Let $\alpha, \beta \in R$ such that $\alpha(x^2 - x) - \beta(x^2+1) + (x^2+x+2) = 0$ $\forall\, x \in R$. The line $\frac{3x}{a} - \frac{4y}{b} + \frac{6}{c} = 0$, where a, b, c are in HP always passes through a fixed point (p, q). If centroid of ΔABC formed by $A(\alpha, \beta)$, $B(p, q)$ and $C(h, k)$ lies on the straight line $3x - 6y + 2 = 0$, then the locus of $C(h, k)$ is

(a) $2x - y = 5$ (b) $2x + y = 5$
(c) $x - 2y = 5$ (d) $x + 2y = 5$

4. Let α, β be the roots of $x^2 - x + p = 0$ and γ, δ be the roots of $x^2 - 4x + q = 0$ such that $\alpha, \beta, \gamma, \delta$ are in GP and $p \geq 2$. If $a, b, c \in \{1, 2, 3, 4, 5\}$, let the number of equation of the form $ax^2 + bx + c = 0$ which have real roots be r, then the minimum value of (pqr) is

(a) 1500 (b) 1536 (c) 34 (d) 1430

Section 2

- This section contains **THREE (03)** question stems.
- There are **TWO (02)** questions corresponding to each question stem.
- The answer to each question is a **NUMERICAL VALUE.**
- For each question, enter the correct numerical value corresponding to the answer in the designated place using the mouse and the on-screen virtual numeric keypad.
- If the numerical value has more than two decimal places, **truncate/round-off** the value to **TWO** decimal places.
- Answer to each question will be evaluated according to the following marking scheme:

Full Marks : +2 If ONLY the correct numerical value is entered at the designated place;
Zero Marks : 0 In all other cases.

Question Stem (Q.Nos. 5-6)

Consider $f(x)=\begin{vmatrix}5 & 7 & 3\\ 2 & 9g^2(x) & 2x^2\\ x & 3g(x)-x^2 & 1\end{vmatrix}-\begin{vmatrix}2 & 4 & 5\\ 2x^2 & 2 & 9g^2(x)\\ 1 & x & 3g(x)-x^2\end{vmatrix}+\begin{vmatrix}2 & x & 0\\ 9g^2(x) & 3g(x)-x^2 & -2\\ 2x^2 & 1 & -1\end{vmatrix}$,

where $g(x)$ is a polynomial function such that $m=\int_0^1 f(x)\,dx$ is minimum.

5. The value of $g(3)$ equals ______

6. The number of points of inflection on the graph of the function $y=\phi(x)$, where $\phi(x)=\int_0^x\left(\int_0^t g(y)dy-(e^t-e^{-t})\right)dt$ is ______

Question stem (Q.Nos. 7-8)

A circular arc of radius 1 subtends an angles of x radians, two tangent lines at P and Q. Let $T(x)$ be the area of triangle $0<x<\frac{\pi}{2}$ as shown in the figure. The point R is the intersection of two tangents drawn at P and Q and let $S(x)$ be the area of the shaded region.

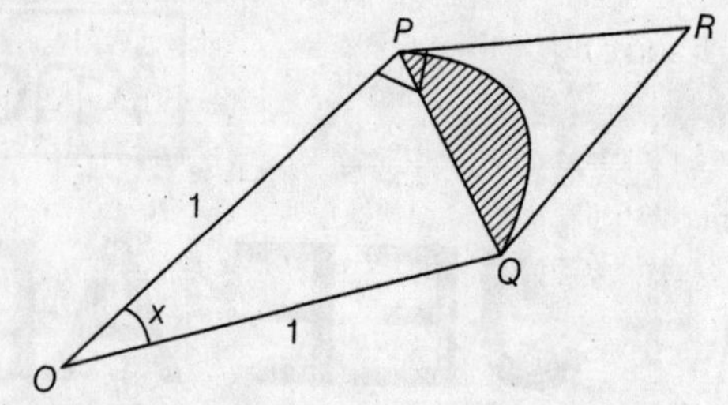

7. The value of $\lim\limits_{x\to 0}\frac{T(x)}{S(x)}$ is ______

8. If α is the root of the equation $\frac{x}{2}-S(x)=T(x), \forall x\in(0,\pi)$, then $[\alpha]+10$ is equal to ...... (where [.] denotes GIF)

Question Stem (Q.Nos. 9-10)

Let a, b, c are be three non-zero real numbers such that the equation $\sqrt{3}a\cos x+2b\sin x=c, x\in\left[-\frac{\pi}{2},\frac{\pi}{2}\right]$ has two distinct real roots α and β such that $\alpha+\beta=\frac{\pi}{3}$.

9. The value of $\frac{b}{a}$ is ______

10. The value of the expression $\left(\frac{a}{2b}\right)^2+\cos^3\left(\frac{\alpha+\beta}{2}\right)$ is $\frac{3\sqrt{p}}{8}+q$, then the value of $\sqrt{p^2+16q^2}$, is ______

Section 3

- This section contains **SIX (06)** questions.
- Each question has **FOUR** options (a), (b), (c) and (d). **ONE OR MORE THAN ONE** of these four option(s) is (are) correct answer(s).
- For each question, choose the option(s) corresponding to (all) the correct answer(s).
- Answer to each question will be evaluated according to the following marking scheme:

Full Marks : +4 If only (all) the correct option(s) is(are) chosen;
Partial Marks : +3 If all the four options are correct but ONLY three options are chosen;
Partial Marks : +2 If three or more options are correct but ONLY two options are chosen, both of which are correct;
Partial Marks : +1 If two or more options are correct but ONLY one option is chosen and it is a correct option;
Zero Marks : 0 If unanswered;
Negative Marks : – 2 In all other cases.
For example, in a question, if (a), (b) and (d) are the ONLY three options corresponding to correct answers, then
choosing ONLY (a), (b) and (d) will get +4 marks;
choosing ONLY (a) and (b) will get +2 marks;
choosing ONLY (a) and (d) will get +2 marks;
choosing ONLY (b) and (d) will get +2 marks;
choosing ONLY (a) will get +1 mark;
choosing ONLY (b) will get +1 mark;
choosing ONLY (d) will get +1 mark;
choosing no option(s) (i.e. the question is unanswered) will get 0 marks and choosing any other option(s) will get – 2 marks.

11. Let a, b and c be distinct complex numbers with $|a|=|b|=|c|=1$ and z_1, z_2 be the roots of the equation $az^2+bz+c=0$ with $|z_1|=1$. Also, let P and Q represents the numbers z_1 and z_2 in the complex plane with $\angle POQ=\theta$, with O being the origin then

(a) $b^2=ac, \theta=\frac{2\pi}{3}$ (b) $\theta=\frac{2\pi}{3}, PQ=\sqrt{3}$

(c) $PQ=2\sqrt{3}, b^2=ac$ (d) $\theta=\frac{\pi}{3}, b^2=ac$

12. The tangent at an extremity (in the first quadrant) of latusrectum of the hyperbola $\frac{x^2}{4}-\frac{y^2}{5}=1$. Meet X-axis and Y-axis at A and B, respectively. Then, $(OA)^2-(OB)^2$, where O is the origin, is equal to

(a) $-\frac{20}{9}$ (b) $\frac{16}{9}$ (c) 4 (d) $-\frac{4}{3}$

13. Assuming the plane $4x-3y+7z=0$ to be horizontal. The equation of the line of greatest slope through the point (2, 1, 1) in the plane $2x+y-5z=0$ is

(a) $\frac{x-2}{3}=\frac{y-1}{1}=\frac{z+1}{-1}$

(b) $\frac{x+2}{3}=\frac{y+1}{3}=\frac{z-1}{2}$

(c) $\frac{x-2}{1}=\frac{y-3}{1}=\frac{z+1}{4}$

(d) $\frac{x-2}{3}=\frac{y-1}{-1}=\frac{z-1}{1}$

14. A cubical die is thrown 9 times and the numbers obtained are written as a 9-digit number. The probability that the number

(a) begins with 246 is $\frac{1}{6^3}$

(b) ends with 135 is $\frac{1}{6^3}$

(c) begins with 246 and ends with 135 is $\frac{1}{6^6}$

(d) begins with 246 or ends with 135 is $\frac{431}{6^6}$.

15. The largest area of a trapezium inscribed in a semi-circle of radius R, if the lower base is on the diameter, is

(a) $\frac{3\sqrt{3}}{4}R^2$ (b) R^2

(c) $\frac{\sqrt{3}}{2}R^2$ (d) $\frac{3\sqrt{3}}{8}R^2$

16. Let **b** and **c** be non-collinear vectors. If $\mathbf{a}\times(\mathbf{b}\times\mathbf{c})+(\mathbf{a}\cdot\mathbf{b})\mathbf{b}=(4-2x-\sin y)\mathbf{b}+(x^2-1)\mathbf{c}$ and $(\mathbf{c}\cdot\mathbf{c})\mathbf{a}=\mathbf{c}$. Then,

(a) $x=1$

(b) $x=-1$

(c) $y=(4n+1)\frac{\pi}{2}, n\in I$

(d) $y=(2n+1)\frac{\pi}{2}, n\in I$

Section 4

- This section contains **THREE** (03) questions.
- The answer to each question is a **NON-NEGATIVE INTEGER.**
- For each question, enter the correct integer corresponding to the answer using the mouse and the on-screen virtual numeric keypad in the place designated to enter the answer.
- Answer to each question will be evaluated according to the following marking scheme:

Full Marks : +4 If **ONLY** the correct integer is entered;

Zero Marks : 0 In all other cases.

17. If the reflection of the ellipse $\frac{(x-4)^2}{16}+\frac{(y-3)^2}{9}=1$ in the mirror line $x-y-2=0$ is $k_1x^2+k_2y^2-160x-36y+292=0$, then $\frac{k_1+k_2}{5}$ is equal to ....

18. If the number of ways of selecting n coupons out of an unlimited number of coupons bearing the letters A, T, C so that they cannot be used to spell the word CAT is 189, then Σn^2 must be ....

19. Let $J=\int_{-5}^{-4}(3-x^2)\tan(3-x^2)dx$ and $K=\int_{-2}^{-1}(6-6x+x^2)\tan(6x-x^2-6)dx$

Then, $(J+K)$ equals ....

Paper 2

Section 1

- This section contains **SIX (06)** questions.
- Each question has **FOUR** options (a), (b), (c) and (d). **ONE OR MORE THAN ONE** of these four option(s) is (are) correct answer(s).
- For each question, choose the option(s) corresponding to (all) the correct answer(s).
- Answer to each question will be evaluated according to the following marking scheme:

Full Marks : +4 If only (all) the correct option(s) is(are) chosen;
Partial Marks : +3 If all the four options are correct but ONLY three options are chosen;
Partial Marks : +2 If three or more options are correct but ONLY two options are chosen, both of which are correct;
Partial Marks : +1 If two or more options are correct but ONLY one option is chosen and it is a correct option;
Zero Marks : 0 If unanswered;
Negative Marks : – 2 In all other cases.
For example, in a question, if (a), (b) and (d) are the ONLY three options corresponding to correct answers, then
choosing ONLY (a), (b) and (d) will get +4 marks;
choosing ONLY (a) and (b) will get +2 marks;
choosing ONLY (a) and (d) will get +2marks;
choosing ONLY (b) and (d) will get +2 marks;
choosing ONLY (a) will get +1 mark;
choosing ONLY (b) will get +1 mark;
choosing ONLY (d) will get +1 mark;
choosing no option(s) (i.e. the question is unanswered) will get 0 marks and choosing any other option(s) will get –3 marks.

1. If p, q, r, s are in AP and

$$f(x)=\begin{vmatrix} p+\sin x & q+\sin x & p-r\sin x \\ q+\sin x & r+\sin x & -1+\sin x \\ r+\sin x & s+\sin x & s-q+\sin x \end{vmatrix}$$ such that

$\int_0^2 F(x)\,dx = -4$, then the common difference of the AP can be

(a) -1 (b) $\frac{1}{4}$

(c) $-\frac{1}{4}$ (d) 1

2. A rod of length of 2 units whose one end is (1, 0, – 1) and other end touches the plane $x-2y+2z+4=0$, then

(a) the rod sweeps the figure whose volume is π cubic units.

(b) the area of the region which the rod traces on the plane is 2π.

(c) the length of projection of the rod on the plane is $\sqrt{3}$ units.

(d) the centre of the region which the rod traces on the plane is $\left(\frac{2}{3}, \frac{2}{3}, -\frac{5}{3}\right)$

3. The perpendicular from the origin to the tangent at any point on a curve is equal to the abscissa of the point of contact. Also curve passes through the point (1, 1). Then,

(a) the length of intercept of the curve on the X-axis is 2

(b) the length of intercept of the curve on the Y-axis is 2

(c) equation of curve is x^2+y^2-2x+0

(d) equation of curve is $x^2+y^2-2y=0$

4. Vectors **A** and **B** satisfying the vector equation $\mathbf{A}+\mathbf{B}=\mathbf{a}$, $\mathbf{A}\times\mathbf{B}=\mathbf{b}$ and $\mathbf{A}\cdot\mathbf{a}=1$, where **a** and **b** are given vectors, are

(a) $\mathbf{A}=\frac{(\mathbf{a}\times\mathbf{b})-\mathbf{a}}{a^2}$ (b) $\mathbf{B}=\frac{(\mathbf{b}\times\mathbf{a})+\mathbf{a}(a^2-1)}{a^2}$

(c) $\mathbf{A}=\frac{(\mathbf{a}\times\mathbf{b})+\mathbf{a}}{a^2}$ (d) $\mathbf{B}=\frac{(\mathbf{b}\times\mathbf{a})-\mathbf{a}(a^2-1)}{a^2}$

5. Given that $x\in[0,1]$ and $y\in[0,1]$. Let A be the event of selecting a point (x, y) satisfying $y^2\le x$ and B be the event selecting a point (x, y) satisfying $x^2\le y$, then

(a) $P(A\cap B)=\frac{1}{3}$ (b) $A\subset B$

(c) $2P(A)=3P(B)$ (d) $P(B)<P(A)$

6. a, b, c are all different and non-zero real numbers in AP. If the roots of the quadratic equation $ax^2+bx+c=0$ are α and β such that $\frac{1}{\alpha}+\frac{1}{\beta}$, $\alpha+\beta$ and $\alpha^2+\beta^2$ are in GP. Then, the value of $\left|\left(\frac{a}{c}\right)^4+79\log_e\left(\frac{c}{a}\right)\right|+5$, is

(a) 7 (b) 2

(c) 1 (d) 6

Section 2

- This section contains **THREE (03)** question stems.
- There are **TWO (02)** questions corresponding to each question stem.
- The answer to each question is a **NUMERICAL VALUE.**
- For each question, enter the correct numerical value corresponding to the answer in the designated place using the mouse and the on-screen virtual numeric keypad.
- If the numerical value has more than two decimal places, **truncate/round-off** the value to **TWO** decimal places.

Answer to each question will be evaluated according to the following marking scheme:

Full Marks : +2 If ONLY the correct numerical value is entered at the designated place;

Zero Marks : 0 In all other cases.

Question Stem (Q.Nos. 7-8)

Let $P=\dfrac{\left(1^4+\frac{1}{4}\right)\left(3^4+\frac{1}{4}\right)\left(5^4+\frac{1}{4}\right)\ldots\left((2n-1)^4+\frac{1}{4}\right)}{\left(2^4+\frac{1}{4}\right)\left(4^4+\frac{1}{4}\right)\left(6^4+\frac{1}{4}\right)\ldots\left((2n)^4+\frac{1}{4}\right)}$ and $\lim_{n\to\infty}(n^{\alpha}p)$ exists.

7. Value of α equals ....

8. Value of $44\left[\lim_{n\to\infty}(n^{\alpha}p)\right]$ equals ....

Question Stem (Q.Nos. 9-10)

There are 18 points in a plane out of which 3 of them fall on a line $L_1=0$, another 4 of them fall on another line $L_2=0$, another five lie on a different line $L_3=0$. No three points other than those stated above are collinear.

9. Number of lines formed by joining the points on the plane is ....

10. If the six points that do not lie on $L_1=0, L_2=0, L_3=0$ are now removed, then the number of n-gon's (polygons with n-sides), where $n>3$ such that not more than two points are selected from each other is ....

Question stem (Q.Nos. 11-12)

A variable line L is drawn through $O(0, 0)$ to meet the lines L_1 and L_2 given by $y-x-10=0$ and $y-x-20=0$ at points A and B, respectively.

11. A point P is taken on L such that $\dfrac{2}{OP}=\dfrac{1}{OA}+\dfrac{1}{OB}$.
Then, the locus of P is of the form $\alpha x+\beta y=\gamma$.
So, $(\alpha+\beta+\gamma)$ is equal to ....

12. Locus of P, if $OP^2=OA\times OB$ is $(y-x)^2$ is equal to ....

Section 3

- This section contains **TWO (02)** paragraphs. Based on each paragraph, there are TWO (02) questions.
- Each question has **FOUR** options (a), (b), (c) and (d). **ONLY ONE** of these four options is the correct answer.
- For each question, choose the option corresponding to the correct answer.
- Answer to each question will be evaluated according to the following marking scheme:

Full Marks : +3 If ONLY the correct option is chosen;
Zero Marks : 0 If none of the options is chosen (i.e, the question is unanswered);
Negative Marks : -1 In all other cases.

Paragraph (Q.Nos. 13-14)

The football teams T_1 and T_2 have to play two games against each other.

It is assumed that the outcomes of two game are independent. The probability of T_1 wining, drawing and loosing a game against T_2 are $\frac{1}{2}, \frac{1}{6}$ and $\frac{1}{3}$ respectively. Each team gets 3 points for a win, 1 point for a draw and '0' point for a loss in a game.

Let, X and Y denote the total points scored by teams T_1 and T_2, respectively after two games.

13. $P(X>Y)$ is $\dfrac{a}{b+1}$, then the value of $(a+b)$ is ....

14. $P(X=Y)$ is $\dfrac{c}{d}$, then the value of $\left(\dfrac{d-c}{23}\right)^2$ is ....

Paragraph (Q.Nos. 15-16)

$$\sum_{r=1}^{n}\tan^{-1}\left(\frac{x_r-x_{r-1}}{1+x_{r-1}x_r}\right)=\sum_{r=1}^{n}(\tan^{-1}x_r-\tan^{-1}x_{r-1})$$
$$=\tan^{-1}x_n-\tan^{-1}x_0, \forall\, n\in N$$

On the basis of above information, answer the following questions.

15. The value of $\operatorname{cosec}^{-1}\sqrt{5}+\operatorname{cosec}^{-1}\sqrt{65}+\operatorname{cosec}^{-1}\sqrt{325}+\ldots$ to ∞ is

(a) π (b) $\frac{3\pi}{4}$ (c) $\frac{\pi}{2}$ (d) $\frac{\pi}{4}$

16. The sum to infinite terms of the series $\cot^{-1}\left(2^2+\frac{1}{2}\right)+\cot^{-1}\left(2^3+\frac{1}{2^2}\right)+\cos^{-1}\left(2^4+\frac{1}{2^3}\right)+\ldots$ is

(a) $\frac{\pi}{4}$ (b) $\frac{\pi}{2}$

(c) $\cot^{-1}2$ (d) $-\cot^{-1}2$

Section 4

- This section contains **THREE (03)** questions.
- The answer to each question is a **NON-NEGATIVE INTEGER.**
- For each question, enter the correct integer corresponding to the answer using the mouse and the on-screen virtual numeric keypad in the place designated to enter the answer.

Answer to each question will be evaluated according to the following marking scheme:

Full Marks : +4 If ONLY the correct integer is entered;

Zero Marks : 0 In all other cases.

17. If $f(x)+f(y)=f\left(\frac{x+y}{1-xy}\right)\forall\, x,y\in R(xy\neq 1)$ and $\lim_{x\to 0}\left(\frac{f(x)}{x}\right)=2$. Then, $[f(1/\sqrt{3})]$ (where [.] represents greatest integer function) is equal to ______

18. If the sum $S={}^{20}C_2+2\cdot{}^{20}C_3+3\cdot{}^{20}C_4+\ldots+19\cdot{}^{20}C_{20}$ can be expressed as $1+p\cdot 2^q$, then the least value of $(p+q)$ is ______

19. A pole l ft long is to be carried horizontally from one corridor to another corridor perpendicular to each other. If the first corridor is d m wide, then the minimum required width of the other corridor is $W_{\min}=[l^{\alpha}-d^{\beta}]^{\gamma}$. So, $(\alpha+\beta)\gamma$ is equal to ______

Answers

Paper 1

1 *(d)*	2 *(c)*	3 *(c)*	4 *(b)*	5 *(3)*	6 *(0)*	7 *(1.5)*	8 *(11)*	9 *(0.5)*	10 *(5)*
11 *(a,b)*	12 *(a)*	13 *(d)*	14 *(a,b,c,d)*	15 *(a)*	16 *(a,c)*	17 *(5)*	18 *(91)*	19 *(0)*	

Paper 2

1 *(a,d)*	2 *(a,c,d)*	3 *(a,c)*	4 *(b,c)*	5 *(a)*	6 *(a)*	7 *(2)*	8 *(5.5)*	9 *(137)*	10 *(48)*
11 *(40)*	12 *(200)*	13 *(16)*	14 *(1)*	15 *(d)*	16 *(c)*	17 *(1)*	18 *(29)*	19 *(2)*	

See detailed solutions on page no. 309

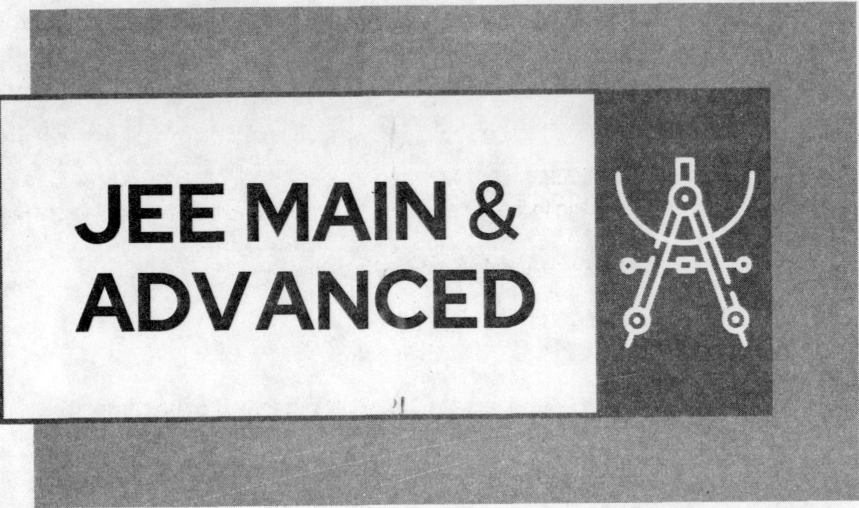

The Real Nuts

Past Year's JEE Main & Advanced Question Papers

Now you are ready for exam, so attempt these Past Exams' Papers and compare your score with the Cut Off Score of that year.

REAL NUT 01

JEE Main 2022

(24 June 2022, Shift-I)

*Instructions

1. This question paper contains of 30 Questions of Mathematics, divided into two sections : **Section A** Objective Type Questions and **Section B** Numerical Type Questions.
2. Section A contains 20 Objective questions and all Questions are cumpulsory (Marking Scheme : Correct + 4, Incorrect – 1).
3. Section B contains 10 Numerical value questions out of which only 5 questions are to be attempted (Marking Scheme : Correct + 4, Incorrect 0).

Section A *Objective Type Questions*

1. Let $A = \{z \in C : 1 \le |z - (1+i)| \le 2\}$ and $B = \{z \in A : |z - (1-i)| = 1\}$. Then, B

(a) is an empty set
(b) contains exactly two elements
(c) contains exactly three elements
(d) is an infinite set

2. The remainder when 3^{2022} is divided by 5 is

(a) 1 (b) 2 (c) 3 (d) 4

3. The surface area of a balloon of spherical shape being inflated, increases at a constant rate. If initially, the radius of balloon is 3 units and after 5 s, it becomes 7 units, then its radius after 9 s is

(a) 9 (b) 10 (c) 11 (d) 12

4. Bag A contains 2 white, 1 black and 3 red balls and bag B contains 3 black, 2 red and n white balls. One bag is chosen at random and 2 balls drawn from it at random, are found to be 1 red and 1 black. If the probability that both balls come from bag A is $\frac{6}{11}$, then n is equal to ....

(a) 13 (b) 6 (c) 4 (d) 3

5. Let $x^2 + y^2 + Ax + By + C = 0$ be a circle passing through (0, 6) and touching the parabola $y = x^2$ at (2, 4). Then, $A + C$ is equal to ....

(a) 16 (b) 88/5 (c) 72 (d) –8

6. The number of values of α for which the system of equations

$$x + y + z = \alpha,$$
$$\alpha x + 2\alpha y + 3z = -1$$
and
$$x + 3\alpha y + 5z = 4$$

is inconsistent, is

(a) 0 (b) 1 (c) 2 (d) 3

7. If the sum of the squares of the reciprocals of the roots α and β of the equation $3x^2 + \lambda x - 1 = 0$ is 15, then $6(\alpha^3 + \beta^3)^2$ is equal to

(a) 18 (b) 24 (c) 36 (d) 96

8. The set of all values of k for which $(\tan^{-1} x)^3 + (\cot^{-1} x)^3 = k\pi^3, x \in R$, is the interval

(a) $\left[\frac{1}{32}, \frac{7}{8}\right)$ (b) $\left(\frac{1}{24}, \frac{13}{16}\right)$ (c) $\left[\frac{1}{48}, \frac{13}{16}\right]$ (d) $\left[\frac{1}{32}, \frac{9}{8}\right)$

9. Let $S = \{\sqrt{n} : 1 \le n \le 50 \text{ and } n \text{ is odd}\}$

Let $a \in S$ and $A = \begin{bmatrix} 1 & 0 & a \\ -1 & 1 & 0 \\ -a & 0 & 1 \end{bmatrix}$.

If $\sum_{a \in S} \det(\text{adj } A) = 100\lambda$, then λ is equal to

(a) 218 (b) 221 (c) 663 (d) 1717

10. For the function $f(x) = 4\log_e(x-1) - 2x^2 + 4x + 5, x > 1$, which one of the following is NOT correct?

(a) f is increasing in (1, 2) and decreasing in $(2, \infty)$
(b) $f(x) = -1$ has exactly two solutions
(c) $f'(e) - f''(2) < 0$
(d) $f(x) = 0$ has a root in the interval $(e, e+1)$

11. If the tangent at the point (x_1, y_1) on the curve $y = x^3 + 3x^2 + 5$ passes through the origin, then (x_1, y_1) does NOT lie on the curve

(a) $x^2 + \frac{y^2}{81} = 2$ (b) $\frac{y^2}{9} - x^2 = 8$

(c) $y = 4x^2 + 5$ (d) $\frac{x}{3} - y^2 = 2$

12. The sum of absolute maximum and absolute minimum values of the function

$f(x) = |2x^2 + 3x - 2| + \sin x \cos x$ in the interval [0, 1] is

(a) $3 + \frac{\sin(1)\cos^2(1/2)}{2}$ (b) $3 + \frac{1}{2}(1 + 2\cos(1)\sin(1))$

(c) $5 + \frac{1}{2}(\sin(1) + \sin(2))$ (d) $2 + \sin\left(\frac{1}{2}\right)\cos\left(\frac{1}{2}\right)$

13. If $\{a_i\}_{i=1}^{n}$ where n is an even integer, is an arithmetic progression with common difference 1, and $\sum_{i=1}^{n} a_i = 192, \sum_{i=1}^{n/2} a_{2i} = 120$, then n is equal to

(a) 48 (b) 96

(c) 92 (d) 104

14. If $x = x(y)$ is the solution of the differential equation $y\frac{dx}{dy} = 2x + y^3(y+1)e^y, x(1) = 0$; then $x(e)$ is equal to

(a) $e^3(e^e - 1)$ (b) $e^e(e^3 - 1)$

(c) $e^2(e^e + 1)$ (d) $e^e(e^2 - 1)$

15. Let $\lambda x - 2y = \mu$ be a tangent to the hyperbola $a^2x^2 - y^2 = b^2$. Then, $\left(\frac{\lambda}{a}\right)^2 - \left(\frac{\mu}{b}\right)^2$ is equal to

(a) −2 (b) −4 (c) 2 (d) 4

16. Let $\hat{\mathbf{a}}$ and $\hat{\mathbf{b}}$ be unit vectors. If **c** is a vector such that the angle between $\hat{\mathbf{a}}$ and **c** is $\frac{\pi}{12}$ and $\hat{\mathbf{b}} = \mathbf{c} + 2(\mathbf{c} \times \hat{\mathbf{a}})$, then $|6\mathbf{c}|^2$ is equal to

(a) $6(3 - \sqrt{3})$ (b) $3 + \sqrt{3}$

(c) $6(3 + \sqrt{3})$ (d) $6(\sqrt{3} + 1)$

17. If a random variable X follows the Binomial distribution $B(33, p)$ such that $3P(X = 0) = P(X = 1)$, then the value of $\frac{P(X=15)}{P(X=18)} - \frac{P(X=16)}{P(X=17)}$ is equal to

(a) 1320 (b) 1088 (c) $\frac{120}{1331}$ (d) $\frac{1088}{1089}$

18. The domain of the function

$$f(x) = \frac{\cos^{-1}\left(\frac{x^2 - 5x + 6}{x^2 - 9}\right)}{\log_e(x^2 - 3x + 2)}$$ is

(a) $(-\infty, 1) \cup (2, \infty)$

(b) $(2, \infty)$

(c) $\left[-\frac{1}{2}, 1\right) \cup (2, \infty)$

(d) $\left[-\frac{1}{2}, 1\right) \cup (2, \infty) - \left\{\frac{3+\sqrt{5}}{2}, \frac{3-\sqrt{5}}{2}\right\}$

19. Let $S = \left\{\theta \in [-\pi, \pi] - \left\{\pm\frac{\pi}{2}\right\} : \sin\theta\tan\theta + \tan\theta = \sin 2\theta\right\}$

If $T = \sum_{\theta \in S} \cos 2\theta$, then $T + n(S)$ is equal to

(a) $7 + \sqrt{3}$ (b) 9 (c) $8 + \sqrt{3}$ (d) 10

20. The number of choices of $\Delta \in \{\wedge, \vee, \Rightarrow, \Leftrightarrow\}$, such that $(p\Delta q) \Rightarrow ((p\Delta \sim q) \vee ((\sim p)\Delta q))$ is a tautology, is

(a) 1 (b) 2 (c) 3 (d) 4

Section B *Numerical Type Questions*

21. The number of one-one functions $f : \{a, b, c, d\} \to \{0, 1, 2, \ldots, 10\}$ such that $2f(a) - f(b) + 3f(c) + f(d) = 0$ is ....

22. In an examination, there are 5 multiple choice questions with 3 choices, out of which exactly one is correct There are 3 marks for each correct answer, −2 marks for each wrong answer and 0 mark if the question is not attempted. Then, the number of ways a student appearing in the examination gets 5 marks is ....

23. Let $A\left(\frac{3}{\sqrt{a}}, \sqrt{a}\right), a > 0$, be a fixed point in the xy-plane. The image of A in Y-axis be B and the image of B in X-axis be C. If $D(3\cos\theta, a\sin\theta)$ is a point in the fourth quadrant such that the maximum area of ΔACD is 12 sq units, then a is equal to ....

24. Let a line having direction ratios 1, −4, 2 intersect the lines $\frac{x-7}{3} = \frac{y-1}{-1} = \frac{z+2}{1}$ and $\frac{x}{2} = \frac{y-7}{3} = \frac{z}{1}$ at the points A and B. Then, $(AB)^2$ is equal to ....

25. The number of points where the function

$$f(x) = \begin{cases} |2x^2 - 3x - 7| & \text{if } x \le -1 \\ [4x^2 - 1] & \text{if } -1 < x < 1 \\ |x+1| + |x-2| & \text{if } x \ge 1 \end{cases}$$

$[t]$ denotes the greatest integer $\le t$, is discontinuous is ....

26. Let $f(\theta) = \sin\theta + \int_{-\pi/2}^{\pi/2} (\sin\theta + t\cos\theta) f(t)\,dt$. Then, the value of $\left|\int_0^{\pi/2} f(\theta)\,d\theta\right|$ is ....

27. Let $\max_{0 \le x \le 2} \left\{\frac{9-x^2}{5-x}\right\} = \alpha$ and $\min_{0 \le x \le 2} \left\{\frac{9-x^2}{5-x}\right\} = \beta$.

If $\int_{\beta-8/3}^{2\alpha-1} \max\left\{\frac{9-x^2}{5-x}, x\right\} dx = \alpha_1 + \alpha_2 \log_e\left(\frac{8}{15}\right)$, then $\alpha_1 + \alpha_2$ is equal to ....

28. If two tangents drawn from a point (α, β) lying on the ellipse $25x^2 + 4y^2 = 1$ to the parabola $y^2 = 4x$ are such that the slope of one tangent is four times the other, then the value of $(10\alpha + 5)^2 + (16\beta^2 + 50)^2$ equals ....

29. Let S be the region bounded by the curves $y = x^3$ and $y^2 = x$. The curve $y = 2|x|$ divides S into two regions of areas R_1 and R_2. If $\max\{R_1, R_2\} = R_2$, then $\frac{R_2}{R_1}$ is equal to ....

30. If the shortest distance between the lines

$$\mathbf{r} = (-\hat{i} + 3\hat{k}) + \lambda(\hat{i} - a\hat{j})$$

and $\mathbf{r} = (-\hat{j} + 2\hat{k}) + \mu(\hat{i} - \hat{j} + \hat{k})$ is $\sqrt{\frac{2}{3}}$, then the integral value of a is equal to ....

Answers

1 *(d)*	2 *(d)*	3 *(a)*	4 *(c)*	5 *(a)*	6 *(b)*	7 *(b)*	8 *(a)*	9 *(b)*	10 *(c)*
11 *(d)*	12 *(*)*	13 *(b)*	14 *(a)*	15 *(d)*	16 *(c)*	17 *(a)*	18 *(d)*	19 *(b)*	20 *(b)*
21 *(31)*	22 *(40)*	23 *(8)*	24 *(84)*	25 *(7)*	26 *(1)*	27 *(34)*	28 *(2929)*	29 *(19)*	30 *(2)*

See detailed solutions on page no. 317

REAL NUT 02

JEE Main 2022

(26 June 2022, Shift-II)

*Instructions

1. This question paper contains of 30 Questions of Mathematics, divided into two sections : **Section A** Objective Type Questions and **Section B** Numerical Type Questions.
2. Section A contains 20 Objective questions and all Questions are cumpulsory (Marking Scheme : Correct + 4, Incorrect – 1).
3. Section B contains 10 Numerical value questions out of which only 5 questions are to be attempted (Marking Scheme : Correct + 4, Incorrect 0).

Section A *Objective Type Questions*

1. Let $f : R \to R$ be defined as $f(x) = x - 1$ and $g : R - \{1, -1\} \to R$ be defined as $g(x) = \dfrac{x^2}{x^2 - 1}$.
Then, the function fog is

(a) one-one but not onto function
(b) onto but not one-one function
(c) both one-one and onto function
(d) neither one-one nor onto function

2. If the system of equations $\alpha x + y + z = 5$, $x + 2y + 3z = 4$, $x + 3y + 5z = \beta$, has infinitely many solutions, then the ordered pair (α, β) is equal to

(a) $(1, -3)$ (b) $(-1, 3)$
(c) $(1, 3)$ (d) $(-1, -3)$

3. If $A = \sum_{n=1}^{\infty} \dfrac{1}{(3 + (-1)^n)^n}$ and $B = \sum_{n=1}^{\infty} \dfrac{(-1)^n}{(3 + (-1)^n)^n}$, then $\dfrac{A}{B}$ is equal to

(a) $\dfrac{11}{9}$ (b) 1
(c) $-\dfrac{11}{9}$ (d) $-\dfrac{11}{3}$

4. $\lim_{x \to 0} \dfrac{\cos(\sin x) - \cos x}{x^4}$ is equal to

(a) $\dfrac{1}{3}$ (b) $\dfrac{1}{4}$
(c) $\dfrac{1}{6}$ (d) $\dfrac{1}{12}$

5. Let $f(x) = \min\{1, 1 + x\sin x\}$, $0 \le x \le 2\pi$. If m is the number of points, where f is not differentiable and n is the number of points, where f is not continuous, then the ordered pair (m, n) is equal to

(a) (2, 0) (b) (1, 0)
(c) (1, 1) (d) (2, 1)

6. Consider a cuboid of sides $2x$, $4x$ and $5x$ and a closed hemisphere of radius r. If the sum of their surface areas is a constant k, then the ratio $x : r$, for which the sum of their volumes is maximum, is

(a) 2 : 5 (b) 19 : 45
(c) 3 : 8 (d) 19 : 15

7. The area of the region bounded by $y^2 = 8x$ and $y^2 = 16(3 - x)$ is equal to

(a) $\dfrac{32}{3}$ (b) $\dfrac{40}{3}$
(c) 16 (d) 19

8. If $\int \dfrac{1}{x}\sqrt{\dfrac{1-x}{1+x}}\, dx = g(x) + c$, $g(1) = 0$, then $g\left(\dfrac{1}{2}\right)$ is equal to

(a) $\log_e\left(\dfrac{\sqrt{3}-1}{\sqrt{3}+1}\right) + \dfrac{\pi}{3}$ (b) $\log_e\left(\dfrac{\sqrt{3}+1}{\sqrt{3}-1}\right) + \dfrac{\pi}{3}$

(c) $\log_e\left(\dfrac{\sqrt{3}+1}{\sqrt{3}-1}\right) - \dfrac{\pi}{3}$ (d) $\dfrac{1}{2}\log_e\left(\dfrac{\sqrt{3}-1}{\sqrt{3}+1}\right) - \dfrac{\pi}{6}$

9. If $y = y(x)$ is the solution of the differential equation $x\dfrac{dy}{dx} + 2y = xe^x, y(1) = 0$, then the local maximum value of the function $z(x) = x^2y(x) - e^x, x \in R$ is

(a) $1 - e$ (b) 0
(c) $\dfrac{1}{2}$ (d) $\dfrac{4}{e} - e$

10. If the solution of the differential equation $\dfrac{dy}{dx} + e^x(x^2 - 2)y = (x^2 - 2x)(x^2 - 2)e^{2x}$ satisfies $y(0) = 0$, then the value of $y(2)$ is ....

(a) -1 (b) 1
(c) 0 (d) e

11. If m is the slope of a common tangent to the curves $\dfrac{x^2}{16} + \dfrac{y^2}{9} = 1$ and $x^2 + y^2 = 12$, then $12m^2$ is equal to

(a) 6 (b) 9
(c) 10 (d) 12

12. The locus of the mid-point of the line segment joining the point (4, 3) and the points on the ellipse $x^2 + 2y^2 = 4$ is an ellipse with eccentricity

(a) $\dfrac{\sqrt{3}}{2}$ (b) $\dfrac{1}{2\sqrt{2}}$
(c) $\dfrac{1}{\sqrt{2}}$ (d) $\dfrac{1}{2}$

13. The normal to the hyperbola $\dfrac{x^2}{a^2} - \dfrac{y^2}{9} = 1$ at the point $(8, 3\sqrt{3})$ on it passes through the point.

(a) $(15, -2\sqrt{3})$ (b) $(9, 2\sqrt{3})$
(c) $(-1, 9\sqrt{3})$ (d) $(-1, 6\sqrt{3})$

14. If the plane $2x + y - 5z = 0$ is rotated about its line of intersection with the plane $3x - y + 4z - 7 = 0$ by an angle of $\dfrac{\pi}{2}$, then the plane after the rotation passes through the point

(a) (2, –2, 0) (b) (–2, 2, 0)
(c) (1, 0, 2) (d) (–1, 0, –2)

15. If the lines $\mathbf{r} = (\hat{i} - \hat{j} + \hat{k}) + \lambda(3\hat{j} - \hat{k})$ and $\mathbf{r} = (\alpha\hat{i} - \hat{j}) + \mu(2\hat{i} - 3\hat{k})$ are coplanar, then distance of the plane containing these two lines from the point $(\alpha, 0, 0)$ is

(a) $\dfrac{2}{9}$ (b) $\dfrac{2}{11}$
(c) $\dfrac{4}{11}$ (d) 2

16. Let $\mathbf{a} = \hat{i} + \hat{j} + 2\hat{k}$, $\mathbf{b} = 2\hat{i} - 3\hat{j} + \hat{k}$ and $\mathbf{c} = \hat{i} - \hat{j} + \hat{k}$ be three given vectors. Let $\mathbf{v}$ be a vector in the plane of $\mathbf{a}$ and $\mathbf{b}$ whose projection on $\mathbf{c}$ is $\dfrac{2}{\sqrt{3}}$. If $\mathbf{v} \cdot \hat{j} = 7$, then $\mathbf{v} \cdot (\hat{i} + \hat{k})$ is equal to

(a) 6 (b) 7
(c) 8 (d) 9

17. The mean and standard deviation of 50 observations are 15 and 2 respectively. It was found that one incorrect observation was taken such that the sum of correct and incorrect observations is 70. If the correct mean is 16, then the correct variance is equal to

(a) 10 (b) 36
(c) 43 (d) 60

18. $16\sin(20°)\sin(40°)\sin(80°)$ is equal to

(a) $\sqrt{3}$ (b) $2\sqrt{3}$
(c) 3 (d) $4\sqrt{3}$

19. If the inverse trigonometric functions take principal values, then $\cos^{-1}\left(\dfrac{3}{10}\cos\left(\tan^{-1}\dfrac{4}{3}\right) + \dfrac{2}{5}\sin\left(\tan^{-1}\left(\dfrac{4}{3}\right)\right)\right)$ is equal to

(a) 0 (b) $\dfrac{\pi}{4}$
(c) $\dfrac{\pi}{3}$ (d) $\dfrac{\pi}{6}$

20. Let $r \in \{p, q, \sim p, \sim q\}$ be such that the logical statement $r \vee (\sim p) \Rightarrow (p \wedge q) \vee r$ is a tautology. Then, r is equal to

(a) p (b) q
(c) $\sim p$ (d) $\sim q$

Section B *Numerical Type Questions*

21. Let $f : R \to R$ satisfy $f(x + y) = 2^x f(y) + 4^y f(x), \forall x, y \in R$. If $f(2) = 3$, then $14 \cdot \dfrac{f'(4)}{f'(2)}$ is equal to ....

22. Let p and q be two real numbers such that $p + q = 3$ and $p^4 + q^4 = 369$. Then, $\left(\dfrac{1}{p} + \dfrac{1}{q}\right)^{-2}$ is equal to ....

23. If $z^2 + z + 1 = 0, z \in C$, then $\left|\sum_{n=1}^{15}\left(z^n + (-1)^n \dfrac{1}{z^n}\right)^2\right|$ is equal to ....

24. Let $X=\begin{bmatrix}0&1&0\\0&0&1\\0&0&0\end{bmatrix}, Y=\alpha I+\beta X+\gamma X^2$ and

$Z=\alpha^2 I-\alpha\beta X+(\beta^2-\alpha\gamma)X^2, \alpha,\beta,\gamma\in R$. If

$Y^{-1}=\begin{bmatrix}1/5&-2/5&1/5\\0&1/5&-2/5\\0&0&1/5\end{bmatrix}$, then $(\alpha-\beta+\gamma)^2$ is equal to ....

25. The total number of 3-digit numbers, whose greatest common divisor with 36 is 2, is ....

26. If $({}^{40}C_0)+({}^{41}C_1)+({}^{42}C_2)+...+({}^{60}C_{20})=\frac{m}{n}\,{}^{60}C_{20}$,

m and n are coprime, then $m+n$ is equal to ....

27. If $a_1(>0), a_2, a_3, a_4, a_5$ are in a GP, $a_2+a_4=2a_3+1$ and $3a_2+a_3=2a_4$, then $a_2+a_4+2a_5$ is equal to ....

28. The integral $\frac{24}{\pi}\int_0^{\sqrt{2}}\frac{(2-x^2)\,dx}{(2+x^2)\sqrt{4+x^4}}$ is equal to ....

29. Let a line L_1 be tangent to the hyperbola $\frac{x^2}{16}-\frac{y^2}{4}=1$ and let L_2 be the line passing through the origin and perpendicular to L_1.

If the locus of the point of intersection of L_1 and L_2 is $(x^2+y^2)^2=\alpha x^2+\beta y^2$, then $\alpha+\beta$ is equal to ....

30. If the probability that a randomly chosen 6-digit number formed by using digits 1 and 8 only is a multiple of 21 is p, then $96\,p$ is equal to ....

Answers

1 *(d)*	2 *(c)*	3 *(c)*	4 *(c)*	5 *(b)*	6 *(b)*	7 *(c)*	8 *(a)*	9 *(d)*	10 *(c)*
11 *(b)*	12 *(c)*	13 *(c)*	14 *(c)*	15 *(b)*	16 *(d)*	17 *(c)*	18 *(b)*	19 *(c)*	20 *(c)*
21 *(248)*	22 *(4)*	23 *(2)*	24 *(100)*	25 *(150)*	26 *(102)*	27 *(40)*	28 *(3)*	29 *(12)*	30 *(33)*

See detailed solutions on page no. 323

REAL NUT 03

JEE Main 2022

(29 June 2022, Shift-I)

*Instructions

1. This question paper contains of 30 Questions of Mathematics, divided into two sections : **Section A** Objective Type Questions and **Section B** Numerical Type Questions.
2. Section A contains 20 Objective questions and all Questions are cumpulsory (Marking Scheme : Correct + 4, Incorrect – 1).
3. Section B contains 10 Numerical value questions out of which only 5 questions are to be attempted (Marking Scheme : Correct + 4, Incorrect 0).

Section A *Objective Type Questions*

1. The probability that a randomly chosen 2×2 matrix with all the entries from the set of first 10 primes, is singular, is equal to

(a) $\frac{133}{10^4}$ (b) $\frac{18}{10^3}$ (c) $\frac{19}{10^3}$ (d) $\frac{271}{10^4}$

2. Let the solution curve of the differential equation $x\frac{dy}{dx} - y = \sqrt{y^2 + 16x^2}$, $y(1) = 3$ be $y = y(x)$. Then, $y(2)$ is equal to

(a) 15 (b) 11 (c) 13 (d) 17

3. In the mirror image of the point (2, 4, 7) in the plane $3x - y + 4z = 2$ is (a, b, c), then $2a + b + 2c$ is equal to

(a) 54 (b) 50 (c) -6 (d) -42

4. Let $f : R \to R$ be a function defined by

$$f(x) = \begin{cases} \max\{t^3 - 3t\}; t \le x & x \le 2 \\ x^2 + 2x - 6; & 2 < x < 3 \\ [x-3] + 9; & 3 \le x \le 5 \\ 2x + 1; & x > 5 \end{cases}$$

where $[t]$ is the greatest integer less than or equal to t. Let m be the number of points where f is not differentiable and $I = \int_{-2}^{2} f(x)dx$. Then, the ordered pair (m, I) is equal to

(a) $\left(3, \frac{27}{4}\right)$ (b) $\left(3, \frac{23}{4}\right)$ (c) $\left(4, \frac{27}{4}\right)$ (d) $\left(4, \frac{23}{4}\right)$

5. Let $\mathbf{a} = \alpha\hat{i} + 3\hat{j} - \hat{k}$, $\mathbf{b} = 3\hat{i} - \beta\hat{j} + 4\hat{k}$ and $\mathbf{c} = \hat{i} + 2\hat{j} - 2\hat{k}$ where $\alpha, \beta \in R$, be three vectors. If the projection of $\mathbf{a}$ on $\mathbf{c}$ is $\frac{10}{3}$ and $\mathbf{b} \times \mathbf{c} = -6\hat{i} + 10\hat{j} + 7\hat{k}$, then the value of $\alpha + \beta$ is equal to

(a) 3 (b) 4 (c) 5 (d) 6

6. The area enclosed by $y^2 = 8x$ and $y = \sqrt{2}x$ that lies outside the triangle formed by $y = \sqrt{2}x$, $x = 1$, $y = 2\sqrt{2}$, is equal to

(a) $\frac{16\sqrt{2}}{6}$ (b) $\frac{11\sqrt{2}}{6}$

(c) $\frac{13\sqrt{2}}{6}$ (d) $\frac{5\sqrt{2}}{6}$

7. If the system of linear equations $2x + y - z = 7$, $x - 3y + 2z = 1$ and $x + 4y + \delta z = k$, where $\delta, k \in R$ has infinitely many solutions, then $\delta + k$ is equal to

(a) -3 (b) 3

(c) 6 (d) 9

8. Let α and β be the roots of the equation $x^2 + (2i - 1) = 0$. Then, the value of $|\alpha^8 + \beta^8|$ is equal to

(a) 50 (b) 250

(c) 1250 (d) 1500

9. Let $\Delta \in \{\wedge, \vee, \Rightarrow, \Leftrightarrow\}$ be such that $(p \wedge q)\,\Delta\,((p \vee q) \Rightarrow q)$ is a tautology. Then, Δ is equal to

(a) $\wedge$ (b) $\vee$

(c) $\Rightarrow$ (d) $\Leftrightarrow$

10. Let $A=[a_{ij}]$ be a square matrix of order 3 such that $a_{ij}=2^{j-i}$, for all $i, j = 1, 2, 3$. Then, the matrix $A^2+A^3+...+A^{10}$ is equal to

(a) $\left(\frac{3^{10}-3}{2}\right)A$ (b) $\left(\frac{3^{10}-1}{2}\right)A$

(c) $\left(\frac{3^{10}+1}{2}\right)A$ (d) $\left(\frac{3^{10}+3}{2}\right)A$

11. Let a set $A=A_1 \cup A_2 \cup ... \cup A_k$, where $A_i \cap A_j = \phi$ for $i \neq j$, $1 \le i, j \le k$. Define the relation R from A to A by $R=\{(x, y): y \in A_i$ if and only if $x \in A_i, 1 \le i \le k\}$. Then, R is

(a) reflexive, symmetric but not transitive

(b) reflexive, transitive but not symmetric

(c) reflexive but not symmetric and transitive

(d) an equivalence relation

12. Let $\{a_n\}_{n=0}^{\infty}$ be a sequence such that $a_0=a_1=0$ and $a_{n+2}=2a_{n+1}-a_n+1$ for all $n \ge 0$. Then, $\sum_{n=2}^{\infty} \frac{a_n}{7^n}$ is equal to

(a) $\frac{6}{343}$ (b) $\frac{7}{216}$ (c) $\frac{8}{343}$ (d) $\frac{49}{216}$

13. The distance between the two points A and A' which lie on $y=2$ such that both the line segments AB and $A'B$ (where B is the point (2, 3)) subtend angle $\frac{\pi}{4}$ at the origin, is equal to

(a) 10 (b) $\frac{48}{5}$ (c) $\frac{52}{5}$ (d) 3

14. A wire of length 22 m is to be cut into two pieces. One of the pieces is to be made into a square and the other into an equilateral triangle. Then, the length of the side of the equilateral triangle, so that the combined area of the square and the equilateral triangle is minimum, is

(a) $\frac{22}{9+4\sqrt{3}}$ (b) $\frac{66}{9+4\sqrt{3}}$ (c) $\frac{22}{4+9\sqrt{3}}$ (d) $\frac{66}{4+9\sqrt{3}}$

15. The domain of the function

$$\cos^{-1}\left(\frac{2\sin^{-1}\left(\frac{1}{4x^2-1}\right)}{\pi}\right) \text{ is}$$

(a) $R-\left\{-\frac{1}{2}, \frac{1}{2}\right\}$

(b) $(-\infty, -1] \cup [1, \infty) \cup \{0\}$

(c) $\left(-\infty, \frac{-1}{2}\right) \cup \left(\frac{1}{2}, \infty\right) \cup \{0\}$

(d) $\left(-\infty, \frac{-1}{\sqrt{2}}\right] \cup \left[\frac{1}{\sqrt{2}}, \infty\right) \cup \{0\}$

16. If the constant term in the expansion of $\left(3x^3-2x^2+\frac{5}{x^5}\right)^{10}$ is $2^k \cdot l$, where l is an odd integer, then the value of k is equal to

(a) 6 (b) 7 (c) 8 (d) 9

17. $\int_0^5 \cos\left(\pi\left(x-\left[\frac{x}{2}\right]\right)\right) dx$, where $[t]$ denotes greatest integer less than or equal to t, is equal to

(a) -3 (b) -2 (c) 2 (d) 0

18. Let PQ be a focal chord of the parabola $y^2=4x$ such that it subtends an angle of $\frac{\pi}{2}$ at the point (3, 0). Let the line segment PQ be also a focal chord of the ellipse $E: \frac{x^2}{a^2}+\frac{y^2}{b^2}=1, a^2>b^2$. If e is the eccentricity of the ellipse E, then the value of $\frac{1}{e^2}$ is equal to

(a) $1+\sqrt{2}$ (b) $3+2\sqrt{2}$ (c) $1+2\sqrt{3}$ (d) $4+5\sqrt{3}$

19. Let the tangent to the circle $C_1: x^2+y^2=2$ at the point $M(-1, 1)$ intersect the circle $C_2: (x-3)^2+(y-2)^2=5$, at two distinct points A and B. If the tangents to C_2 at the points A and B intersect at N, then the area of the ΔANB is equal to

(a) $\frac{1}{2}$ (b) $\frac{2}{3}$ (c) $\frac{1}{6}$ (d) $\frac{5}{3}$

20. Let the mean and the variance of 5 observations x_1, x_2, x_3, x_4, x_5 be $\frac{24}{5}$ and $\frac{194}{25}$ respectively. If the mean and variance of the first 4 observation are $\frac{7}{2}$ and a respectively, then $(4a+x_5)$ is equal to

(a) 13 (b) 15 (c) 17 (d) 18

Section B *Numerical Type Questions*

21. Let $S=\{z \in C: |z-2| \le 1, z(1+i)+\bar{z}(1-i) \le 2\}$. Let $|z-4i|$ attains minimum and maximum values, respectively, at $z_1 \in S$ and $z_2 \in S$. If $5(|z_1|^2+|z_2|^2)=\alpha+\beta\sqrt{5}$, where α and β are integers, then the value of $\alpha+\beta$ is equal to ....

22. Let $y=y(x)$ be the solution of the differential equation

$$\frac{dy}{dx}+\frac{\sqrt{2}y}{2\cos^4 x-\cos 2x}=xe^{\tan^{-1}(\sqrt{2}\cot 2x)},$$

$0<x<\frac{\pi}{2}$ with $y\left(\frac{\pi}{4}\right)=\frac{\pi^2}{32}$. If $y\left(\frac{\pi}{3}\right)=\frac{\pi^2}{18}e^{-\tan^{-1}(\alpha)}$, then the value of $3\alpha^2$ is equal to ....

23. Let d be the distance between the foot of perpendiculars of the points $P(1, 2-1)$ and $Q(2, -1, 3)$ on the plane $-x+y+z=1$. Then, d^2 is equal to ....

24. The number of elements in the set $S=\{\theta \in [-4\pi, 4\pi]: 3\cos^2 2\theta + 6\cos 2\theta - 10\cos^2\theta + 5 = 0\}$ is ....

25. The number of solutions of the equation $2\theta - \cos^2\theta + \sqrt{2} = 0$ in R is equal to ....

26. $50\tan\left(3\tan^{-1}\left(\frac{1}{2}\right)+2\cos^{-1}\left(\frac{1}{\sqrt{5}}\right)\right)+4\sqrt{2}\tan\left(\frac{1}{2}\tan^{-1}(2\sqrt{2})\right)$ is equal to ....

27. Let $c, k \in R$. If $f(x)=(c+1)x^2+(1-c^2)x+2k$ and $f(x+y)=f(x)+f(y)-xy$, for all $x, y \in R$, then the value of $|2(f(1)+f(2)+f(3)+....+f(20))|$ is equal to ....

28. Let $H: \frac{x^2}{a^2}-\frac{y^2}{b^2}=1$, $a>0, b>0$, be a hyperbola such that the sum of lengths of the transverse and the conjugate axes is $4(2\sqrt{2}+\sqrt{14})$. If the eccentricity H is $\frac{\sqrt{11}}{2}$, then value of a^2+b^2 is equal to ....

29. Let $P_1: \mathbf{r}\cdot(2\hat{i}+\hat{j}-3\hat{k})=4$ be a plane. Let P_2 be another plane which passes through the points $(2,-3,2)$ $(2,-2,-3)$ and $(1,-4,2)$. If the direction ratios of the line of intersection of P_1 and P_2 be $16, \alpha, \beta$, then the value of $\alpha+\beta$ is equal to ....

30. Let $b_1b_2b_3b_4$ be a 4-element permutation with $b_i \in \{1, 2, 3, ..., 100\}$ for $1 \le i \le 4$ and $b_i \ne b_j$ for $i \ne j$, such that either b_1, b_2, b_3 are consecutive integers or b_2, b_3, b_4 are consecutive integers.

Then, the number of such permutations $b_1b_2b_3b_4$ is equal to ......

Answers

1 (c)	2 (a)	3 (c)	4 (c)	5 (a)	6 (c)	7 (b)	8 (a)	9 (c)	10 (a)
11 (d)	12 (b)	13 (c)	14 (b)	15 (d)	16 (d)	17 (d)	18 (b)	19 (c)	20 (b)
21 (26)	22 (2)	23 (26)	24 (32)	25 (1)	26 (29)	27 (3395)	28 (88)	29 (28)	30 (18915)

See detailed solutions on page no. 329

REAL NUT 04

JEE Main 2022

(25 July 2022, Shift-I)

*Instructions

1. This question paper contains of 30 Questions of Mathematics, divided into two sections : **Section A** Objective Type Questions and **Section B** Numerical Type Questions.
2. Section A contains 20 Objective questions and all Questions are cumpulsory (Marking Scheme : Correct + 4, Incorrect – 1).
3. Section B contains 10 Numerical value questions out of which only 5 questions are to be attempted (Marking Scheme : Correct + 4, Incorrect 0).

Section A *Objective Type Questions*

1. The total number of functions,

$$f:\{1, 2, 3, 4\} \to \{1, 2, 3, 4, 5, 6\}$$

such that $f(1) + f(2) = f(3)$ is equal to

(a) 60 (b) 90
(c) 108 (d) 126

2. If $\alpha, \beta, \gamma, \delta$ are the roots of the equation $x^4 + x^3 + x^2 + x + 1 = 0$, then $\alpha^{2021} + \beta^{2021} + \gamma^{2021} + \delta^{2021}$ is equal to

(a) –4 (b) –1
(c) 1 (d) 4

3. For $n \in N$, let $S_n = \left\{z \in C : |z - 3 + 2i| = \frac{n}{4}\right\}$ and $T_n = \left\{z \in C : |z - 2 + 3i| = \frac{1}{n}\right\}$. Then, the number of elements in the set $\{n \in N : S_n \cap T_n = \phi\}$ is

(a) 0 (b) 2
(c) 3 (d) 4

4. The number of $q \in (0, 4\pi)$ for which the system of linear equations $3(\sin 3\theta)x - y + z = 2$; $3(\cos 2\theta)x + 4y + 3z = 3$ $6x + 7y + 7z = 9$ has no solution, is

(a) 6 (b) 7
(c) 8 (d) 9

5. If $\lim_{n \to \infty} (\sqrt{n^2 - n - 1} + n\alpha + \beta) = 0$, then $8(\alpha + \beta)$ is equal to

(a) 4 (b) –8
(c) –4 (d) 8

6. If the absolute maximum value of the function $f(x) = (x^2 - 2x + 7)\, e^{(4x^3 - 12x^2 - 180x + 31)}$ in the interval $[-3, 0]$ is $f(\alpha)$, then

(a) $\alpha = 0$ (b) $\alpha = -3$
(c) $\alpha \in (-1, 0)$ (d) $\alpha \in (-3, -1]$

7. The curve $y(x) = ax^3 + bx^2 + cx + 5$ touches the X-axis at the point $P(-2, 0)$ and cuts the Y-axis at the point Q, where y' is equal to 3. Then, the local maximum value of $y(x)$ is

(a) $\frac{27}{4}$ (b) $\frac{29}{4}$
(c) $\frac{37}{4}$ (d) $\frac{9}{2}$

8. The area of the region given by $A = \{(x, y); x^2 \le y \le \min\{x + 2, 4 - 3x\}\}$ is

(a) $\frac{31}{8}$ (b) $\frac{17}{6}$
(c) $\frac{19}{6}$ (d) $\frac{27}{8}$

9. For any real number x, let $[x]$ denote the largest integer less than or equal to x. Let f be a real valued function defined on the interval $[-10, 10]$ by

$$f(x) = \begin{cases} x - [x], & \text{if } [x] \text{ is odd} \\ 1 + [x] - x, & \text{if } [x] \text{ is even} \end{cases}$$

Then, the value of $\frac{\pi^2}{10} \int_{-10}^{10} f(x) \cos \pi x \, dx$

(a) 4 (b) 2 (c) 1 (d) 0

10. The slope of the tangent to a curve $C: y = y(x)$ at any point (x, y) on it is $\frac{2e^{2x} - 6e^{-x} + 9}{2 + 9e^{-2x}}$. If C passes through the points $\left(0, \frac{1}{2} + \frac{\pi}{2\sqrt{2}}\right)$ and $\left(\alpha, \frac{1}{2} e^{2\alpha}\right)$, then e^{α} is equal to

(a) $\frac{3+\sqrt{2}}{3-\sqrt{2}}$ (b) $\frac{3}{\sqrt{2}}\left(\frac{3+\sqrt{2}}{3-\sqrt{2}}\right)$

(c) $\frac{1}{\sqrt{2}}\left(\frac{\sqrt{2}+1}{\sqrt{2}-1}\right)$ (d) $\frac{\sqrt{2}+1}{\sqrt{2}-1}$

11. The general solution of the differential equation $(x - y^2)dx + y(5x + y^2)\,dy = 0$ is

(a) $(y^2 + x)^4 = C\,|(y^2 + 2x)^3|$ (b) $(y^2 + 2x)^4 = C\,|(y^2 + x)^3|$

(c) $|(y^2 + x)^3| = C(2y^2 + x)^4$ (d) $|(y^2 + 2x)^3| = C(2y^2 + x)^4$

12. A line, with the slope greater than one, passes through the point $A(4, 3)$ and intersects the line $x - y - 2 = 0$ at the point B.

If the length of the line segment AB is $\frac{\sqrt{29}}{3}$, then B also lies on the line

(a) $2x + y = 9$ (b) $3x - 2y = 7$

(c) $x + 2y = 6$ (d) $2x - 3y = 3$

13. Let the locus of the centre $(\alpha, \beta), \beta > 0$, of the circle which touches the circle $x^2 + (y-1)^2 = 1$ externally and also touches the X-axis be L. Then, the area bounded by L and the line $y = 4$ is

(a) $\frac{32\sqrt{2}}{3}$ (b) $\frac{40\sqrt{2}}{3}$ (c) $\frac{64}{3}$ (d) $\frac{32}{3}$

14. Let P be the plane containing the straight line $\frac{x-3}{9} = \frac{y+4}{-1} = \frac{z-7}{-5}$ and perpendicular to the plane containing the straight lines $\frac{x}{2} = \frac{y}{3} = \frac{z}{5}$ and $\frac{x}{3} = \frac{y}{7} = \frac{z}{8}$. If d is the distance P from the point $(2, -5, 11)$, then d^2 is equal to

(a) 147/2 (b) 96

(c) 32/3 (d) 54

15. Let ABC be a triangle such that $\mathbf{BC} = \mathbf{a}$, $\mathbf{CA} = \mathbf{b}$, $\mathbf{AB} = \mathbf{c}$, $|\mathbf{a}| = 6\sqrt{2}$, $|\mathbf{b}| = 2\sqrt{3}$ and $\mathbf{b} \cdot \mathbf{c} = 12$. Consider the statements

Statement I $|(\mathbf{a} \times \mathbf{b}) + (\mathbf{c} \times \mathbf{b})| - |\mathbf{c}| = 6(2\sqrt{2} - 1)$

Statement II $\angle ACB = \cos^{-1}\left(\sqrt{\frac{2}{3}}\right)$

Then,

(a) Both statement I and statement II are true

(b) Only statement I is true

(c) Only statement II is true

(d) Both statement I and statement II are false

16. If the sum and the product of mean and variance of a binomial distribution are 24 and 128, respectively, then the probability of one or two successes is

(a) $\frac{33}{2^{32}}$ (b) $\frac{33}{2^{29}}$ (c) $\frac{33}{2^{28}}$ (d) $\frac{33}{2^{27}}$

17. If the numbers appeared on the two throws of a fair six faced die are α and β, then the probability that $x^2 + \alpha x + \beta > 0$, $\forall x \in R$, is

(a) $\frac{17}{36}$ (b) $\frac{4}{9}$ (c) $\frac{1}{2}$ (d) $\frac{19}{36}$

18. The number of solutions of $|\cos x| = \sin x$, such that $-4\pi \le x \le 4\pi$ is

(a) 4 (b) 6 (c) 8 (d) 12

19. A tower PQ stands on a horizontal ground with base Q on the ground. The point R divides the tower in two parts such that $QR = 15$ m. If from a point A on the ground the angle of elevation of R is $60°$ and the part PR of the tower subtends an angle of $15°$ at A, then the height of the tower is

(a) $5(2\sqrt{3} + 3)$ m (b) $5(\sqrt{3} + 3)$ m

(c) $10(\sqrt{3} + 1)$ m (d) $10(2\sqrt{3} + 1)$ m

20. Which of the following statements is a tautology?

(a) $((\sim p) \vee q) \Rightarrow p$ (b) $p \Rightarrow ((\sim p) \vee q)$

(c) $((\sim p) \vee q) \Rightarrow q$ (d) $q \Rightarrow ((\sim p) \vee q)$

Section B *Numerical Type Questions*

21. Let $A = \begin{bmatrix} 2 & -1 & -1 \\ 1 & 0 & -1 \\ 1 & -1 & 0 \end{bmatrix}$ and $B = A - I$. If $\omega = \frac{\sqrt{3}i - 1}{2}$ then the number of elements in the set $\{n \in \{1, 2, \ldots, 100\} : A^n + (\omega B)^n = A + B\}$ is equal to ....

22. The letters of the word 'MANKIND' are written in all possible orders and arranged in serial order as in an English dictionary. Then, the serial number of the word 'MANKIND' is ....

23. If the maximum value of the term independent of t in the expansion of $\left(t^2 x^{\frac{1}{5}} + \frac{(1-x)^{\frac{1}{10}}}{t}\right)^{15}$, $x \ge 0$ is k, then $8k$ is equal to ....

24. Let a and b be two non-zero real numbers. If p and r are the roots of the equation $x^2 - 8ax + 2a = 0$ and q and s are the roots of the equation $x^2 + 12bx + 6b = 0$, such that $\frac{1}{p}, \frac{1}{q}, \frac{1}{r}, \frac{1}{s}$ are is AP, then $a^{-1} - b^{-1}$ is equal to ....

25. Let $a_1 = b_1 = 1$, $a_n = a_{n-1} + 2$ and $b_n = a_n + b_{n-1}$ for every natural number $n \geq 2$. Then, $\sum_{n=1}^{15} a_n \cdot b_n$ is equal to ....

26. Let $f(x) = \begin{cases} |4x^2 - 8x + 5|, \text{if } 8x^2 - 6x + 1 \geq 0 \\ [4x^2 - 8x + 5], \text{if } 8x^2 - 6x + 1 < 0 \end{cases}$

where $[\alpha]$ denotes the greatest integer less than or equal to α. Then, the number of points in R where f is not differentiable is ....

27. If $\lim_{n \to \infty} \frac{(n+1)^{k-1}}{n^{k+1}} [(nk+1) + (nk+2) + \ldots + (nk+n)]$

$= 33 \cdot \lim_{n \to \infty} \frac{1}{n^{k+1}} [1^k + 2^k + 3^k + \ldots + n^k]$,

then the integral value of k is equal to ....

28. Let the equation of two diameters of a circle $x^2 + y^2 - 2x + 2fy + 1 = 0$ be $2px - y = 1$ and $2x + py = 4p$. Then, the slope $m \in (0, \infty)$ of the tangent to the hyperbola $3x^2 - y^2 = 3$ passing through the centre of the circle is equal to ....

29. The sum of diameters of the circles that touch (i) the parabola $75x^2 = 64(5y - 3)$ at the point $\left(\frac{8}{5}, \frac{6}{5}\right)$ and (ii) the Y-axis, is equal to ....

30. The line of shortest distance between the lines $\frac{x-2}{0} = \frac{y-1}{1} = \frac{z}{1}$ and $\frac{x-3}{2} = \frac{y-5}{2} = \frac{z-1}{1}$ makes an angle of $\cos^{-1}\left(\sqrt{\frac{2}{27}}\right)$ with the plane $P: ax - y - z = 0$, $(a > 0)$. If the image of the point $(1, 1, -5)$ in the plane P is (α, β, γ), then $\alpha + \beta - \gamma$ is equal to ....

Answers

1 *(b)*	2 *(b)*	3 *(*)*	4 *(b)*	5 *(c)*	6 *(b)*	7 *(a)*	8 *(b)*	9 *(a)*	10 *(b)*
11 *(a)*	12 *(c)*	13 *(c)*	14 *(c)*	15 *(c)*	16 *(c)*	17 *(a)*	18 *(c)*	19 *(a)*	20 *(d)*
21 *(17)*	22 *(1492)*	23 *(6006)*	24 *(38)*	25 *(27560)*	26 *(3)*	27 *(5)*	28 *(2)*	29 *(10)*	30 *(*)*

See detailed solutions on page no. 334

REAL NUT 05

JEE Main 2022

(27 July 2022, Shift-II)

*Instructions

1. This question paper contains of 30 Questions of Mathematics, divided into two sections : **Section A** Objective Type Questions and **Section B** Numerical Type Questions.
2. Section A contains 20 Objective questions and all Questions are cumpulsory (Marking Scheme : Correct + 4, Incorrect – 1).
3. Section B contains 10 Numerical value questions out of which only 5 questions are to be attempted (Marking Scheme : Correct + 4, Incorrect 0).

Section A *Objective Type Questions*

1. The domain of the function

$f(x) = \sin^{-1}[2x^2 - 3] + \log_2\left(\log_{\frac{1}{2}}(x^2 - 5x + 5)\right)$, where $[t]$ is the greatest integer function, is

(a) $\left(-\sqrt{\frac{5}{2}}, \frac{5-\sqrt{5}}{2}\right)$ (b) $\left(\frac{5-\sqrt{5}}{2}, \frac{5+\sqrt{5}}{2}\right)$

(c) $\left(1, \frac{5-\sqrt{5}}{2}\right)$ (d) $\left(1, \frac{5+\sqrt{5}}{2}\right)$

2. Let S be the set of all $(\alpha, \beta), \pi < \alpha, \beta < 2\pi$, for which the complex number $\frac{1 - i\sin\alpha}{1 + 2i\sin\alpha}$ is purely imaginary and $\frac{1 + i\cos\beta}{1 - 2i\cos\beta}$ is purely real.

Let $Z_{\alpha\beta} = \sin 2\alpha + i\cos 2\beta, (\alpha, \beta) \in S$.

Then, $\sum_{(\alpha, \beta) \in S}\left(iZ_{\alpha\beta} + \frac{1}{i\overline{Z}_{\alpha\beta}}\right)$ is equal to

(a) 3 (b) $3i$ (c) 1 (d) $2 - i$

3. If α and β are the roots of the equation

$x^2 - (5 + 3^{\sqrt{\log_3 5}} - 5^{\sqrt{\log_5 3}})x$
$+3\left(3^{(\log_3 5)^{1/3}} - 5^{(\log_5 3)^{2/3}} - 1\right) = 0$, then the equation, whose roots are $\alpha + \frac{1}{\beta}$ and $\beta + \frac{1}{\alpha}$, is

(a) $3x^2 - 20x - 12 = 0$ (b) $3x^2 - 10x - 4 = 0$

(c) $3x^2 - 10x + 2 = 0$ (d) $3x^2 - 20x + 16 = 0$

4. Let $A = \begin{bmatrix} 4 & -2 \\ \alpha & \beta \end{bmatrix}$

If $A^2 + 4A + 18I = 0$, then $\det(A)$ is equal to ....

(a) –18 (b) 18 (c) –50 (d) 50

5. If for $p \neq q \neq 0$, the function $f(x) = \frac{\sqrt[7]{p(729 + x)} - 3}{\sqrt[3]{729 + qx} - 9}$ is continuous at $x = 0$, then

(a) $7pq\, f(0) - 1 = 0$ (b) $63q\, f(0) - p^2 = 0$

(c) $21q\, f(0) - p^2 = 0$ (d) $7pq\, f(0) - 9 = 0$

6. Let $f(x) = 2 + |x| - |x - 1| + |x + 1|\, x \in R$. Consider

Statement I $f'\left(-\frac{3}{2}\right) + f'\left(-\frac{1}{2}\right) + f'\left(\frac{1}{2}\right) + f'\left(\frac{3}{2}\right) = 2$

Statement II $\int_{-2}^{2} f(x)\, dx = 12$

Then,

(a) Both statement I and statement II are correct
(b) Both statement I and statement II are wrong
(c) Only statement I is correct
(d) Only statement II is correct

7. Let the sum of an infinite GP, whose first term is a and the common ratio is r, be 5. Let the sum of its first five terms be $\frac{98}{25}$. Then, the sum of the first 21 terms of an AP, whose first term is $10ar$, nth term is a_n and the common difference is $10ar^2$ is equal to

(a) $21\, a_{11}$ (b) $22\, a_{11}$ (c) $15\, a_{16}$ (d) $14\, a_{16}$

8. The area of the region enclosed by $y \le 4x^2, x^2 \le 9y$ and $y \le 4$, is equal to

(a) $\frac{40}{3}$ (b) $\frac{56}{3}$ (c) $\frac{112}{3}$ (d) $\frac{80}{3}$

9. $\int_0^2 \left(|2x^2 - 3x| + \left[x - \frac{1}{2}\right]\right) dx$, where $[t]$ is the greatest integer function is equal to

(a) $\frac{7}{6}$ (b) $\frac{19}{12}$ (c) $\frac{31}{12}$ (d) $\frac{3}{2}$

10. Consider a curve $y = y(x)$ in the first quadrant as shown in the figure. Let the area A_1 is twice the area A_2. Then, the normal to the curve perpendicular to the line $2x - 12y = 15$ does **NOT** pass through the point.

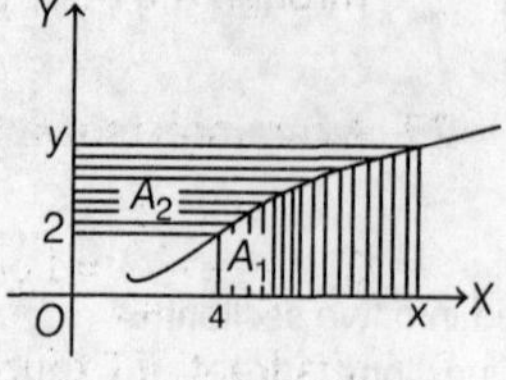

(a) (6, 21) (b) (8, 9)
(c) (10, –4) (d) (12, –15)

11. The equations of the sides AB, BC and CA of a ΔABC are $2x + y = 0, x + py = 39$ and $x - y = 3$ respectively and $P(2,3)$ is its circumcentre. Then, which of the following is **NOT** true?

(a) $(AC)^2 = 9p$ (b) $(AC)^2 + p^2 = 136$
(c) $32 < \text{area}(\Delta ABC) < 36$ (d) $34 < \text{area}(\Delta ABC) < 38$

12. A circle C_1 passes through the origin O and has diameter 4 on the positive X-axis. The line $y = 2x$ gives a chord OA of circle C_1. Let C_2 be the circle with OA as a diameter. If the tangent to C_2 at the point A meets the X-axis at P and Y-axis at Q, then $QA : AP$ is equal to

(a) 1 : 4 (b) 1 : 5 (c) 2 : 5 (d) 1 : 3

13. If the length of the latus rectum of a parabola, whose focus is (a, a) and the tangent at its vertex is $x + y = a$, is 16, then $|a|$ is equal to

(a) $2\sqrt{2}$ (b) $2\sqrt{3}$ (c) $4\sqrt{2}$ (d) 4

14. If the length of the perpendicular drawn from the point $P(a, 4, 2), a > 0$ on the line $\frac{x+1}{2} = \frac{y-3}{3} = \frac{z-1}{-1}$ is $2\sqrt{6}$ units and $Q(\alpha_1, \alpha_2, \alpha_3)$ is the image of the point P in this line, then $a + \sum_{i=1}^{3} \alpha_i$ is equal to

(a) 7 (b) 8
(c) 12 (d) 14

15. If the line of intersection of the planes $ax + by = 3$ and $ax + by + cz = 0, a > 0$ makes an angle $30°$ with the plane $y - z + 2 = 0$, then the direction cosines of the line are

(a) $\frac{1}{\sqrt{2}}, \frac{1}{\sqrt{2}}, 0$ (b) $\frac{1}{\sqrt{2}}, -\frac{1}{\sqrt{2}}, 0$

(c) $\frac{1}{\sqrt{5}}, -\frac{2}{\sqrt{5}}, 0$ (d) $\frac{1}{2}, -\frac{\sqrt{3}}{2}, 0$

16. Let X have a binomial distribution $B(n, p)$ such that the sum and the product of the mean and variance of X are 24 and 128, respectively. If $P(X > n-3) = \frac{k}{2^n}$, then k is equal to

(a) 528 (b) 529 (c) 629 (d) 630

17. A six faced die is biased such that $3 \times P$ (a prime number) $= 6 \times P$ (a composite number) $= 2 \times P(1)$.
Let X be a random variable that counts the number of times one gets a perfect square on some throws of this die. If the die is thrown twice, then the mean of X is

(a) $\frac{3}{11}$ (b) $\frac{5}{11}$ (c) $\frac{7}{11}$ (d) $\frac{8}{11}$

18. The angle of elevation of the top P of a vertical tower PQ of height 10 from a point A on the horizontal ground is $45°$. Let R be a point on AQ and from a point B, vertically above R, the angle of elevation of P is $60°$. If $\angle BAQ = 30°$, $AB = d$ and the area of the trapezium $PQRB$ is α, then the ordered pair (d, α) is

(a) $(10(\sqrt{3}-1), 25)$ (b) $\left(10(\sqrt{3}-1), \frac{25}{2}\right)$

(c) $(10(\sqrt{3}+1), 25)$ (d) $\left(10(\sqrt{3}+1), \frac{25}{2}\right)$

19. Let $S = \left\{\theta \in \left(0, \frac{\pi}{2}\right) : \sum_{m=1}^{9} \sec\left(\theta + (m-1)\frac{\pi}{6}\right) \sec\left(\theta + \frac{m\pi}{6}\right) = -\frac{8}{\sqrt{3}}\right\}$. Then,

(a) $S = \left\{\frac{\pi}{12}\right\}$ (b) $S = \left\{\frac{2\pi}{3}\right\}$

(c) $\sum_{\theta \in S} \theta = \frac{\pi}{2}$ (d) $\sum_{\theta \in S} \theta = \frac{3\pi}{4}$

20. If the truth value of the statement $(P \wedge (\sim R)) \to ((\sim R) \wedge Q)$ is F, then the truth value of which of the following is F?

(a) $P \vee Q \to \sim R$ (b) $R \vee Q \to \sim P$
(c) $\sim (P \vee Q) \to \sim R$ (d) $\sim (R \vee Q) \to \sim P$

Section B *Numerical Type Questions*

21. Consider a matrix $A = \begin{bmatrix} \alpha & \beta & \gamma \\ \alpha^2 & \beta^2 & \gamma^2 \\ \beta+\gamma & \gamma+\alpha & \alpha+\beta \end{bmatrix}$, where α, β, γ are three distinct natural numbers. If $\frac{\det(\text{adj}(\text{adj}(\text{adj}(\text{adj } A))))}{(\alpha-\beta)^{16}(\beta-\gamma)^{16}(\gamma-\alpha)^{16}} = 2^{32} \times 3^{16}$, then the number of such 3-tuples (α, β, γ) is ....

22. The number of functions f, from the set $A = \{x \in N : x^2 - 10x + 9 \le 0\}$ to the set $B = \{n^2 : n \in N\}$ such that $f(x) \le (x-3)^2 + 1$, for every $x \in A$, is ....

23. Let the 9th term in the binomial expansion of $(3+6x)^n$, in the increasing powers of $6x$, to be the greatest for $x=3/2$, the least value of n is n_0. If k is the ratio of the coefficient of x^6 to the coefficient of x^3, then $k+n_0$ is equal to ....

24. $\frac{2^3-1^3}{1\times 7}+\frac{4^3-3^3+2^2-1^3}{2\times 11}+\frac{6^3-5^3+4^3-3^3+2^3-1^3}{3\times 15}+\ldots+\frac{(30)^3-(29)^3+(28)^3-(27)^3+\ldots+2^3-1^3}{15\times 63}$ is equal to ....

25. A water tank has the shape of a right circular cone with axis vertical and vertex downwards. Its semi-vertical angle is $\tan^{-1}\frac{3}{4}$. Water is poured in it at a constant rate of 6 cubic meter per hour. The rate (in square metre per hour), at which the wet curved surface area of the tank is increasing, when the depth of water in the tank is 4 m, is ....

26. For the curve $C:(x^2+y^2-3)+(x^2-y^2-1)^5=0$, the value of $3y'-y^3y''$, at the point $(\alpha,\alpha), \alpha>0$, on C is equal to ....

27. Let $f(x)=\min\{[x-1],[x-2],\ldots,[x-10]\}$ where $[t]$ denotes on greatest integer $\leq t$.

Then, $\int_0^{10} f(x)\,dx+\int_0^{10}(f(x))^2\,dx+\int_0^{10}|f(x)|\,dx$ is equal to ....

28. Let f be a differential function satisfying $f(x)=\frac{2}{\sqrt{3}}\int_0^{\sqrt{3}} f\left(\frac{\lambda^2 x}{3}\right)d\lambda, x>0$ and $f(1)=\sqrt{3}$. If $y=f(x)$ passes through the point $(\alpha, 6)$, then α is equal to ....

29. A common tangent T to the curves $C_1:\frac{x^2}{4}+\frac{y^2}{9}=1$ and $C_2:\frac{x^2}{42}-\frac{y^2}{143}=1$ does not pass through the fourth quadrant. If T touches C_1 at (x_1,y_1) and C_2 at (x_2,y_2), then $|2x_1+x_2|$ is equal to ....

30. Let **a**, **b** and **c** be three non-coplanar vectors such that $\mathbf{a}\times\mathbf{b}=4\mathbf{c}$, $\mathbf{b}\times\mathbf{c}=9\mathbf{a}$ and $\mathbf{c}\times\mathbf{a}=\alpha\mathbf{b}, \alpha>0$. If $|\mathbf{a}|+|\mathbf{b}|+|\mathbf{c}|=\frac{1}{36}$, then α is equal to ....

Answers

1 *(c)*	2 *(c)*	3 *(b)*	4 *(b)*	5 *(b)*	6 *(d)*	7 *(a)*	8 *(d)*	9 *(b)*	10 *(c)*
11 *(d)*	12 *(a)*	13 *(c)*	14 *(b)*	15 *(b)*	16 *(b)*	17 *(d)*	18 *(a)*	19 *(c)*	20 *(d)*
21 *(42)*	22 *(1440)*	23 *(24)*	24 *(120)*	25 *(5)*	26 *(16)*	27 *(385)*	28 *(12)*	29 *(20)*	30 *(*)*

See detailed solutions on page no. 341

REAL NUT 06

JEE Advanced Solved Paper 2022

Paper 1

SECTION 1 (Maximum Marks : 24)

1. This section contains **EIGHT (08)** questions.
2. The answer to each question is a **NUMERICAL VALUE.**
3. For each question, enter the correct numerical value of the answer using the mouse and the on-screen virtual numeric keypad in the place designated to enter the answer. If the numerical value has more than two decimal places, **truncate/round-off** the value to **TWO** decimal places.
4. Answer to each question will be evaluated according to the following marking scheme:
Full Marks : +3if ONLY if the correct numerical value is entered;
Zero Marks : In all other cases.

1. Considering only the principal values of the inverse trigonometric functions, the value of

$$\frac{3}{2}\cos^{-1}\sqrt{\frac{2}{2+\pi^2}}+\frac{1}{4}\sin^{-1}\frac{2\sqrt{2}\pi}{2+\pi^2}+\tan^{-1}\frac{\sqrt{2}}{\pi} \text{ is ......}$$

2. Let α be a positive real number. Let $f: R \to R$ and $g:(\alpha, \infty) \to R$ be the functions defined by $f(x)=\sin\left(\frac{\pi x}{12}\right)$ and $g(x)=\frac{2\log_e(\sqrt{x}-\sqrt{\alpha})}{\log_e(e^{\sqrt{x}}-e^{\sqrt{\alpha}})}$. Then, the value of $\lim_{x\to\alpha^+} f(g(x))$ is ....

3. In a study about a pandemic, data of 900 persons was collected. It was found that
190 persons had symptom of fever,
220 persons had symptom of cough,
220 persons had symptom of breathing problem,
330 persons had symptom of fever or cough or both,
350 persons had symptom of cough or breathing problem or both,
340 persons had symptom of fever or breathing problem or both,
30 persons had all three symptoms (fever, cough and breathing problem).
If a person is chosen randomly from these 900 persons, then the probability that the person has at most one symptom is ....

4. Let z be a complex number with non-zero imaginary part. If $\frac{2+3z+4z^2}{2-3z+4z^2}$ is a real number, then the value of $|z|^2$ is ....

5. Let $\bar{z}$ denote the complex conjugate of a complex number z and let $i=\sqrt{-1}$. In the set of complex numbers, the number of distinct roots of the equation $\bar{z}-z^2=i(\bar{z}+z^2)$ is ....

6. Let $l_1, l_2, \ldots, l_{100}$ be consecutive terms of an arithmetic progression with common difference d_1, and let $w_1, w_2, \ldots, w_{100}$ be consecutive terms of another arithmetic progression with common difference d_2, where $d_1 d_2 = 10$. For each $i = 1, 2, \ldots, 100$, let R_i be a rectangle with length l_i, width w_i and area A_i. If $A_{51}-A_{50}=1000$, then the value of $A_{100}-A_{90}$ is ....

7. The number of 4-digit integers in the closed interval [2022, 4482] formed by using the digits 0, 2, 3, 4, 6, 7 is ....

8. Let ABC be the triangle with $AB = 1$, $AC = 3$ and $\angle BAC = \frac{\pi}{2}$. If a circle of radius $r > 0$ touches the sides AB, AC and also touches internally the circumcircle of the ΔABC, then the value of r is ....

SECTION 2 (Maximum Marks : 24)

1. This section contains **SIX (06)** questions.
2. Each question has **FOUR** options (a), (b), (c) and (d). **ONE OR MORE THAN ONE** of these four option(s) is(are) correct answer(s).
3. For each question, choose the option (s) corresponding to (all) the correct answer (s).
4. Answer to each question will be evaluated according to the following marking scheme:

Full Marks : +4 **ONLY** if (all) the correct option(s) is(are) chosen;
Partial Marks : +3 If all the four options are correct but **ONLY** three options are chosen;
Partial Marks : +2 If three or more options are correct but **ONLY** two options are chosen, both of which are correct;
Partial Marks : +1 If two or more options are correct but **ONLY** one option is chosen and it is a correct option;
Zero Marks : 0 If none of the options is chosen (i.e. the question is unanswered);
Negative Marks : – 2 In all other cases.

9. Consider the equation $\int_1^e \frac{(\log_e x)^{1/2}}{x[a-(\log_e x)^{3/2}]^2}\,dx = 1$, $a \in (-\infty, 0) \cup (1, \infty)$.

Which of the following statements is/are TRUE?

(a) No a satisfies the above equation
(b) An integer a satisfies the above equation
(c) An irrational number a satisfies the above equation
(d) More than one a satisfy the above equation

10. Let $a_1, a_2, a_3, \ldots$ be an arithmetic progression with $a_1 = 7$ and common difference 8. Let $T_1, T_2, T_3, \ldots$ be such that $T_1 = 3$ and $T_{n+1} - T_n = a_n$ for $n \geq 1$. Then, which of the following is/are TRUE ?

(a) $T_{20} = 1604$ (b) $\sum_{k=1}^{20} T_k = 10510$
(c) $T_{30} = 3454$ (d) $\sum_{k=1}^{30} T_k = 35610$

11. Let P_1 and P_2 be two planes given by

$P_1 : 10x + 15y + 12z - 60 = 0$,
$P_2 : -2x + 5y + 4z - 20 = 0$.

Which of the following straight lines can be an edge of some tetrahedron whose two faces lie on P_1 and P_2?

(a) $\frac{x-1}{0} = \frac{y-1}{0} = \frac{z-1}{5}$ (b) $\frac{x-6}{-5} = \frac{y}{2} = \frac{z}{3}$
(c) $\frac{x}{-2} = \frac{y-4}{5} = \frac{z}{4}$ (d) $\frac{x}{1} = \frac{y-4}{-2} = \frac{z}{3}$

12. Let S be the reflection of a point Q with respect to the plane given by $\mathbf{r} = -(t+p)\hat{\mathbf{i}} + t\hat{\mathbf{j}} + (1+p)\hat{\mathbf{k}}$

where t, p are real parameters and $\hat{\mathbf{i}}, \hat{\mathbf{j}}, \hat{\mathbf{k}}$ are the unit vectors along the three positive coordinate axes. If the position vectors of Q and S are $10\hat{\mathbf{i}} + 15\hat{\mathbf{j}} + 20\hat{\mathbf{k}}$ and $\alpha\hat{\mathbf{i}} + \beta\hat{\mathbf{j}} + \gamma\hat{\mathbf{k}}$ respectively, then which of the following is/are TRUE ?

(a) $3(\alpha+\beta) = -101$ (b) $3(\beta+\gamma) = -71$
(c) $3(\gamma+\alpha) = -86$ (d) $3(\alpha+\beta+\gamma) = -121$

13. Consider the parabola $y^2 = 4x$. Let S be the focus of the parabola. A pair of tangents drawn to the parabola from the point $P = (-2, 1)$ meet the parabola at P_1 and P_2. Let Q_1 and Q_2 be points on the lines SP_1 and SP_2 respectively such that PQ_1 is perpendicular to SP_1 and PQ_2 is perpendicular to SP_2. Then, which of the following is/are TRUE ?

(a) $SQ_1 = 2$ (b) $Q_1Q_2 = \frac{3\sqrt{10}}{5}$
(c) $PQ_1 = 3$ (d) $SQ_2 = 1$

14. Let $|M|$ denote the determinant of a square matrix M. Let $g : \left[0, \frac{\pi}{2}\right] \to R$ be the function defined by

$$g(\theta) = \sqrt{f(\theta) - 1} + \sqrt{f\left(\frac{\pi}{2} - \theta\right) - 1}$$

where
$$f(\theta) = \frac{1}{2}\begin{vmatrix} 1 & \sin\theta & 1 \\ -\sin\theta & 1 & \sin\theta \\ -1 & -\sin\theta & 1 \end{vmatrix} + \begin{vmatrix} \sin\pi & \cos\left(\theta + \frac{\pi}{4}\right) & \tan\left(\theta - \frac{\pi}{4}\right) \\ \sin\left(\theta - \frac{\pi}{4}\right) & -\cos\frac{\pi}{2} & \log_e\left(\frac{4}{\pi}\right) \\ \cot\left(\theta + \frac{\pi}{4}\right) & \log_e\left(\frac{\pi}{4}\right) & \tan\pi \end{vmatrix}$$

Let $p(x)$ be a quadratic polynomial whose roots are the maximum and minimum values of the function $g(\theta)$, and $p(2) = 2 - \sqrt{2}$. Then, which of the following is/are TRUE ?

(a) $p\left(\frac{3+\sqrt{2}}{4}\right) < 0$ (b) $p\left(\frac{1+3\sqrt{2}}{4}\right) > 0$
(c) $p\left(\frac{5\sqrt{2}-1}{4}\right) > 0$ (d) $p\left(\frac{5-\sqrt{2}}{4}\right) < 0$

SECTION 3 (Maximum Marks : 12)

1. This section contains **FOUR (04)** Matching List Sets.
2. Each set has **ONE** Multiple Choice Question.
3. Each set has **TWO** lists: **List-I** and **List-II**.
4. **List-I** has **Four** entries (I), (II), (III) and (IV) and **List-II** has **Five** entries (P), (Q), (R), (S) and (T).
5. **FOUR** options are given in each Multiple Choice Question based on **List-I** and **List-II** and **ONLY ONE** of these four options satisfies the condition asked in the Multiple Choice Question.
6. Answer to each question will be evaluated according to the following marking scheme:
   Full Marks : +3 **ONLY** if the option corresponding to the correct combination is chosen;
   Zero Marks : 0 If none of the options is chosen (i.e. the question is unanswered);
   Negative Marks : –1 In all other cases.

15. Consider the following lists:

	List-I		List-II
I.	$\left\{x \in \left[-\frac{2\pi}{3}, \frac{2\pi}{3}\right]: \cos x + \sin x = 1\right\}$	P.	has two elements
II.	$\left\{x \in \left[-\frac{5\pi}{18}, \frac{5\pi}{18}\right]: \sqrt{3}\tan 3x = 1\right\}$	Q.	has three elements
III.	$\left\{x \in \left[-\frac{6\pi}{5}, \frac{6\pi}{5}\right]: 2\cos(2x) = \sqrt{3}\right\}$	R.	has four elements
IV.	$\left\{x \in \left[-\frac{7\pi}{4}, \frac{7\pi}{4}\right]: \sin x - \cos x = 1\right\}$	S.	has five elements
		T.	has six elements

The correct option is

	I	II	III	IV		I	II	III	IV
(a)	P	S	P	S	(b)	P	P	T	R
(c)	Q	P	T	S	(d)	Q	S	P	R

16. Two players P_1 and P_2, play a game against each other. In every round of the game, each player rolls a fair die once, where the six faces of the die have six distinct numbers. Let x and y denote the readings on the die rolled by P_1 and P_2, respectively. If $x > y$, then P_1 scores 5 points and P_2 scores 0 point. If $x = y$, then each player scores 2 points. If $x < y$, then P_1 scores 0 point and P_2 scores 5 points. Let X_i and Y_i be the total scores of P_1 and P_2 respectively, after playing the i th round.

	List-I		List-II
I.	Probability of $(X_2 \geq Y_2)$ is	P.	$\frac{3}{8}$
II.	Probability of $(X_2 > Y_2)$ is	Q.	$\frac{11}{16}$
III.	Probability of $(X_3 = Y_3)$ is	R.	$\frac{5}{16}$
IV.	Probability of $(X_3 > Y_3)$ is	S.	$\frac{355}{864}$
		T.	$\frac{77}{432}$

The correct option is

	I	II	III	IV		I	II	III	IV
(a)	Q	R	T	S	(b)	Q	R	T	T
(c)	P	R	Q	S	(d)	P	R	Q	T

17. Let p, q and r be non-zero real numbers that are, respectively, the 10 th, 100 th and 1000 th terms of an Harmonic progression. Consider the system of linear equations

$$x + y + z = 1$$
$$10x + 100y + 1000z = 0$$
$$qrx + pry + pqz = 0$$

	List-I		List-II
I.	If $\frac{q}{r} = 10$, then the system of linear equations has	P.	$x = 0, y = \frac{10}{9}, z = -\frac{1}{9}$ as a solution
II.	If $\frac{p}{r} \neq 100$, then the system of linear equations has	Q.	$x = \frac{10}{9}, y = -\frac{1}{9}, z = 0$ as a solution
III.	If $\frac{p}{q} \neq 10$, then the system of linear equations has	R.	infinitely many solutions
IV.	If $\frac{p}{q} = 10$, then the system of linear equations has	S.	no solution
		T.	at least one solution

The correct option is

	I	II	III	IV
(a)	T	R	S	T
(b)	Q	S	S	R
(c)	Q	R	P	R
(d)	T	S	P	T

18. Consider the ellipse $\frac{x^2}{4}+\frac{y^2}{3}=1$

Let $H(\alpha, 0)$, $0<\alpha<2$ be a point. A straight line drawn through H parallel to the Y-axis crosses the ellipse and its auxiliary circle at points E and F respectively, in the first quadrant. The tangent to the ellipse at the point E intersects the positive X-axis at a point G. Suppose the straight line joining F and the origin makes an angle ϕ with the positive X-axis.

	List-I		List-II
I.	If $\phi=\frac{\pi}{4}$, then the area of the ΔFGH is	P.	$\frac{(\sqrt{3}-1)^4}{8}$
II.	If $\phi=\frac{\pi}{3}$, then the area of the ΔFGH is	Q.	1
III.	If $\phi=\frac{\pi}{6}$, then the area of the ΔFGH is	R.	$\frac{3}{4}$
IV.	If $\phi=\frac{\pi}{12}$, then the area of the ΔFGH is	S.	$\frac{1}{2\sqrt{3}}$
		T.	$\frac{3\sqrt{3}}{2}$

The correct option is

	I	II	III	IV
(a)	R	S	Q	P
(b)	R	T	S	P
(c)	Q	T	S	P
(d)	Q	S	Q	P

Paper 2

SECTION 1 (Maximum Marks : 24)

1. This section contains **EIGHT (08)** questions.
2. The answer to each question is a **SINGLE DIGIT INTEGER ranging from 0 To 9, BOTH INCLUSIVE.**
3. For each question, enter the correct integer corresponding to the answer using the mouse and the on-screen virtual numeric keypad in the place designated to enter the answer.
4. Answer to each question will be evaluated according to the following marking scheme:

Full Marks : +3 If **ONLY** the correct integer is entered;
Zero Marks : 0 If the question is unanswered;
Negative Marks : –1 In all other cases.

1. Let α and β be real numbers such that $-\frac{\pi}{4}<\beta<0<\alpha<\frac{\pi}{4}$. If $\sin(\alpha+\beta)=\frac{1}{3}$ and $\cos(\alpha-\beta)=\frac{2}{3}$, then the greatest integer less than or equal to $\left(\frac{\sin\alpha}{\cos\beta}+\frac{\cos\beta}{\sin\alpha}+\frac{\cos\alpha}{\sin\beta}+\frac{\sin\beta}{\cos\alpha}\right)^2$ is ....

2. If $y(x)$ is the solution of the differential equation $xdy-(y^2-4y)dx=0$ for $x>0, y(1)=2$, and the slope of the curve $y=y(x)$ is never zero, then the value of $10y(\sqrt{2})$ is ....

3. The greatest integer less than or equal to $\int_1^2 \log_2(x^3+1)dx+\int_1^{\log_2 9}(2^x-1)^{\frac{1}{3}}dx$ is ....

4. The product of all positive real values of x satisfying the equation $x^{[16(\log_5 x)^3-68\log_5 x]}=5^{-16}$ is ....

5. If $\beta=\lim\limits_{x\to 0}\frac{e^{x^3}-(1-x^3)^{\frac{1}{3}}+\{(1-x^2)^{\frac{1}{2}}-1\}\sin x}{x\sin^2 x}$, then the value of 6β is ....

6. Let β be a real number. Consider the matrix $A=\begin{bmatrix}\beta & 0 & 1\\ 2 & 1 & -2\\ 3 & 1 & -2\end{bmatrix}$. If $A^7-(\beta-1)A^6-\beta A^5$ is a singular matrix, then the value of 9β is ....

7. Consider the hyperbola $\frac{x^2}{100}-\frac{y^2}{64}=1$ with focii at S and S_1, where S lies on the positive X-axis. Let P be a point on the hyperbola, in the first quadrant. Let $\angle SPS_1=\alpha$, with $\alpha<\frac{\pi}{2}$. The straight line passing through the point S and having the same slope as that of the tangent at P to the hyperbola, intersects the straight line S_1P at p_1. Let δ be the distance of P from the straight line Sp_1, and $\beta=S_1P$. Then, the greatest integer less than or equal to $\frac{\beta\delta}{9}\sin\frac{\alpha}{2}$ is ....

8. Consider the functions $f, g : R \to R$ defined by $f(x) = x^2 + \frac{5}{12}$ and $g(x) = \begin{cases} 2\left(1 - \frac{4|x|}{3}\right), & |x| \le \frac{3}{4}, \\ 0, & |x| > \frac{3}{4} \end{cases}$

If α is the area of the region $\{(x, y) \in R \times R : |x| \le \frac{3}{4}, 0 \le y \le \min\{f(x), g(x)\}\}$, then the value of 9α is ....

SECTION 2 (Maximum Marks : 24)

1. This section contains **SIX (06)** questions.
2. Each question has **FOUR** options (a), (b), (c) and (d). **ONE OR MORE THAN ONE** of these four option(s) is(are) correct answer(s).
3. For each question, choose the option (s) corresponding to (all) the correct answer (s).
4. Answer to each question will be evaluated according to the following marking scheme:

Full Marks : +4 **ONLY** if (all) the correct option(s) is(are) chosen;
Partial Marks : +3 If all the four options are correct but **ONLY** three options are chosen;
Partial Marks : +2 If three or more options are correct but **ONLY** two options are chosen, both of which are correct;
Partial Marks : +1 If two or more options are correct but **ONLY** one option is chosen and it is a correct option;
Zero Marks : 0 If unanswered;
Negative Marks : – 2 In all other cases.

9. Let $PQRS$ be a quadrilateral in a plane, where $QR = 1$, $\angle PQR = \angle QRS = 70°$, $\angle PQS = 15°$ and $\angle PRS = 40°$. If $\angle RPS = \theta°$, $PQ = \alpha$ and $PS = \beta$, then the interval(s) that contain(s) the value of $4\alpha\beta \sin\theta°$ is/are

(a) $(0, \sqrt{2})$ (b) $(1, 2)$
(c) $(\sqrt{2}, 3)$ (d) $(2\sqrt{2}, 3\sqrt{2})$

10. Let $\alpha = \sum_{k=1}^{\infty} \sin^{2k}\left(\frac{\pi}{6}\right)$.

Let $g : [0, 1] \to R$ be the function defined by $g(x) = 2^{\alpha x} + 2^{\alpha(1-x)}$.

Then, which of the following statements is/are TRUE ?

(a) The minimum value of $g(x)$ is $2^{7/6}$
(b) The maximum value of $g(x)$ is $1 + 2^{1/3}$
(c) The function $g(x)$ attains its maximum at more than one point
(d) The function $g(x)$ attains its minimum at more than one point

11. Let $\bar{z}$ denote the complex conjugate of a complex number z. If z is a non-zero complex number for which both real and imaginary parts of $(\bar{z})^2 + \frac{1}{z^2}$ are integers, then which of the following is/are possible value(s) of $|z|$?

(a) $\left(\frac{43 + 3\sqrt{205}}{2}\right)^{1/4}$ (b) $\left(\frac{7 + \sqrt{33}}{4}\right)^{1/4}$
(c) $\left(\frac{9 + \sqrt{65}}{4}\right)^{1/4}$ (d) $\left(\frac{7 + \sqrt{13}}{6}\right)^{1/4}$

12. Let G be a circle of radius $R > 0$. Let $G_1, G_2, \ldots, G_n$ be n circles of equal radius $r > 0$. Suppose each of the n circles $G_1, G_2, \ldots, G_n$ touches the circle G externally. Also, for $i = 1, 2, \ldots, n-1$, the circle G_i touches G_{i+1} externally, and G_n touches G_1 externally. Then, which of the following statements is/are TRUE ?

(a) If $n = 4$, then $(\sqrt{2} - 1)r < R$
(b) If $n = 5$, then $r < R$
(c) If $n = 8$, then $(\sqrt{2} - 1)r < R$
(d) If $n = 12$, then $\sqrt{2}(\sqrt{3} + 1)r > R$

13. Let $\hat{i}$, $\hat{j}$ and $\hat{k}$ be the unit vectors along the three positive coordinate axes. Let

$\mathbf{a} = 3\hat{i} + \hat{j} - \hat{k}$,
$\mathbf{b} = \hat{i} + b_2\hat{j} + b_3\hat{k}$, $b_2, b_3 \in R$
$\mathbf{c} = c_1\hat{i} + c_2\hat{j} + c_3\hat{k}$, $c_1, c_2, c_3 \in R$

be three vectors such that $b_2 b_3 > 0$, $\mathbf{a} \cdot \mathbf{b} = 0$ and

$$\begin{bmatrix} 0 & -c_3 & c_2 \\ c_3 & 0 & -c_1 \\ -c_2 & c_1 & 0 \end{bmatrix} \begin{bmatrix} 1 \\ b_2 \\ b_3 \end{bmatrix} = \begin{bmatrix} 3 - c_1 \\ 1 - c_2 \\ -1 - c_3 \end{bmatrix}.$$

Then, which of the following is/are TRUE ?

(a) $\mathbf{a} \cdot \mathbf{c} = 0$ (b) $\mathbf{b} \cdot \mathbf{c} = 0$
(c) $|\mathbf{b}| > \sqrt{10}$ (d) $|\mathbf{c}| \le \sqrt{11}$

14. For $x \in R$, let the function $y(x)$ be the solution of the differential equation

$$\frac{dy}{dx} + 12y = \cos\left(\frac{\pi x}{12}\right), \; y(0) = 0$$

Then, which of the following statements is/are TRUE ?

(a) $y(x)$ is an increasing function
(b) $y(x)$ is a decreasing function
(c) There exists a real number β such that the line $y = \beta$ intersects the curve $y = y(x)$ at infinitely many points
(d) $y(x)$ is a periodic function

SECTION 3 (Maximum Marks : 12)

1. This section contains **FOUR (04)** questions.
2. Each question has **FOUR** options (a), (b), (c) and (d). **ONLY ONE** of these four options is the correct answer.
3. Four each question, choose the option corresponding to the correct answer.
4. Answer to each question will be evaluated according to the following marking scheme:

Full Marks : +3 If **ONLY** the correct option is chosen;

Zero Marks : 0 If none of the options is chosen (i.e. the question is unanswered);

Negative Marks : –1 In all other cases.

15. Consider 4 boxes, where each box contains 3 red balls and 2 blue balls. Assume that all 20 balls are distinct. In how many different ways can 10 balls be chosen from these 4 boxes so that from each box at least one red ball and one blue ball are chosen ?

(a) 21816 (b) 85536

(c) 12096 (d) 156816

16. If $M=\begin{bmatrix}\frac{5}{2} & \frac{3}{2}\\ -\frac{3}{2} & -\frac{1}{2}\end{bmatrix}$, then which of the following matrices is equal to M^{2022}?

(a) $\begin{bmatrix}3034 & 3033\\ -3033 & -3032\end{bmatrix}$ (b) $\begin{bmatrix}3034 & -3033\\ 3033 & -3032\end{bmatrix}$

(c) $\begin{bmatrix}3033 & 3032\\ -3032 & -3031\end{bmatrix}$ (d) $\begin{bmatrix}3032 & 3031\\ -3031 & -3030\end{bmatrix}$

17. Suppose that

Box-I contains 8 red, 3 blue and 5 green balls,

Box-II contains 24 red, 9 blue and 15 green balls,

Box-III contains 1 blue, 12 green and 3 yellow balls,

Box-IV contains 10 green, 16 orange and 6 white balls.

A ball is chosen randomly from Box-I; call this ball *b*. If *b* is red, then a ball is chosen randomly from Box-II, if *b* is blue, then a ball is chosen randomly from Box-III, and if *b* is green, then a ball is chosen randomly from Box-IV. The conditional probability of the event 'one of the chosen balls is white' given that the event 'atleast one of the chosen balls is green' has happened, is equal to

(a) $\frac{15}{256}$ (b) $\frac{3}{16}$

(c) $\frac{5}{52}$ (d) $\frac{1}{8}$

18. For positive Integer *n*, define

$$f(n)=n+\frac{16+5n-3n^2}{4n+3n^2}+\frac{32+n-3n^2}{8n+3n^2}+\frac{48-3n-3n^2}{12n+3n^2}+\dots+\frac{25n-7n^2}{7n^2}$$

Then, the value of $\lim_{n\to\infty} f(n)$ is equal to

(a) $3+\frac{4}{3}\log_e 7$ (b) $4-\frac{3}{4}\log_e\left(\frac{7}{3}\right)$

(c) $4-\frac{4}{3}\log_e\left(\frac{7}{3}\right)$ (d) $3+\frac{3}{4}\log_e 7$

Answer Key

Paper 1

1. 2.36	**2.** 0.50	**3.** 0.80	**4.** 0.50	**5.** 4	**6.** 18900	**7.** 569	**8.** 0.84
9. (c, d)	**10.** (b, c)	**11.** (a, b)	**12.** (a, b, c)	**13.** (b, c, d)	**14.** (a, c)	**15.** (b)	**16.** (a)
17. (b)	**18.** (c)						

Paper 2

1. 1	**2.** 8	**3.** 5	**4.** 1	**5.** 5	**6.** 3	**7.** 7	**8.** 6
9. (a, b)	**10.** (a, b, c)	**11.** (a)	**12.** (c, d)	**13.** (b, c, d)	**14.** (c)	**15.** (a)	**16.** (a)
17. (c)	**18.** (b)						

See detailed solutions on page no. 346

Solutions

Qualifiers, Part Tests, Knockouts, Real Nuts

THE QUALIFIERS

Qualifier 1

(Sets, Relations and Functions)

1. (a) Given, $n(R) = 8$ and $n(T) = 28$

We know that

$n(R \cup T) = n(R) + n(T) - n(R \cap T)$

Now, $n(R \cup T)$ will be maximum, if $n(R \cap T) = 0$ i.e., R and T have no any common element.

$\therefore n(R \cup T)_{max} = n(R) + n(T) = 8 + 28 = 36$

Again, $n(R \cup T)$ will be minimum, if $n(R \cap T)$ is maximum i.e., when $R \subset T$.

It means $n(R \cup T)$ will be minimum, if $n(R \cap T) = 8$

$\therefore n(R \cup T) = 8 + 28 - 8 = 28$

Hence, $28 \le n(R \cup T) \le 36$ and $0 \le n(R \cap T) \le 8$

2. (b) Given, $S = \{1, 2, 3, 4, 5, \ldots, 12\}$

Let p = number of elements in set P

q = number of elements in set Q

r = number of elements in set R

$\therefore P, Q, R$ of equal size

$\Rightarrow \quad p = q = r = 4$

Thus, we are to divide 12 elements equally among 3 naming groups.

$\therefore$Total number of ways

$$= \frac{12!}{4!4!4!} = \frac{12!}{(4!)^3}$$

(by permutations concept)

3. (c) **Method (1)** [Equation Solving Approach]

Given, $\quad x^2 + y^2 = 16 \quad$ ...(i)

and $\quad 36x^2 + 9y^2 = 144 \quad$ ...(ii)

From Eq. (i); $y^2 = 16 - x^2$ put in Eq. (ii), we get

$36x^2 + 9(16 - x^2) = 144$

$\Rightarrow 36x^2 + 144 - 9x^2 = 144$

$\Rightarrow \quad 27x^2 = 0$

$\Rightarrow \quad x = 0$

From Eq. (ii);

$36 \times 0 + 9y^2 = 144$

$\Rightarrow \quad y^2 = 16 \Rightarrow y = \pm 4$

Hence, $A \cap B = \{(0, 4), (0, -4)\}$ = set of two points.

Method (2) (Graphical Approach)

Given, $x^2 + y^2 = 16$ represents a circle having centre at (0, 0) and radius 4.

and $36x^2 + 9y^2 = 144$

$\Rightarrow \frac{x^2}{4} + \frac{y^2}{16} = 1$ represents a vertical ellipse having length of semi-major axis = 4 and length of semi-minor axis = 2. Also, centre at (0, 0).

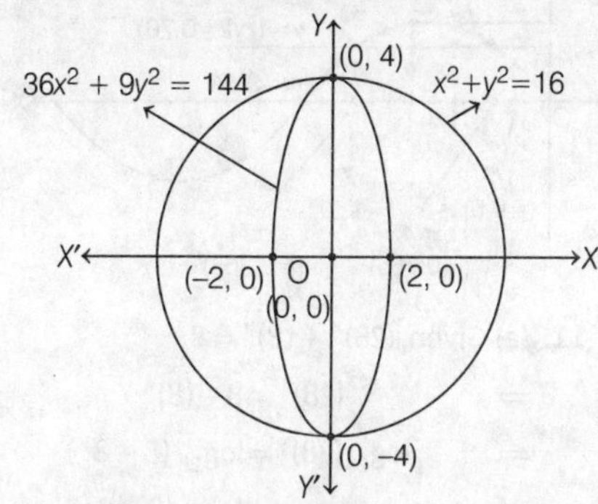

Here, circle and ellipse touch each other at two points. That is, these points (0, 4), (0, – 4) are common to both the curves.

4. (c) We have,

$$f(x) = f^{-1}(x)$$

Then, $\quad f(x) = x$

So, $\quad (x+1)^2 - 1 = x$

$(x+1)^2 = x + 1$

$\Rightarrow \quad x^2 + 1 + 2x = x + 1$

$\Rightarrow \quad x^2 + x = 0$

$\Rightarrow \quad x(x+1) = 0$

$\Rightarrow \quad x = 0, -1$

Hence, required set $\{0, -1\}$.

5. (d) **Reflexivity** Let x be an arbitrary element of R and $x \in R$

$\Rightarrow |x - x| = 0$ which is divisible by 3.

$\Rightarrow x R x$

Hence, R is reflexive.

Symmetric Let $(x, y) \in R$

If $|x - y|$ is divisible by 3, then $|y - x|$ is also divisible by 3.

$\Rightarrow \quad (y, x) \in R$

Hence, R is symmetric.

Transitivity : Let xRy and yRz

$\Rightarrow |x - y| = 3p$ and $|y - z| = 3q$, where p and q are integers

According to the sign of modulus, after adding or subtracting both equations, we can observe that $|x - z|$ is also divisible by 3. $\Rightarrow xRz$

Hence, R is transitive also.

6. (c) Clearly, $GCD(a, a) = a, \forall a \in N$

$\therefore R$ is not reflexive.

If $GCD(a, b) = 2$, then $GCD(b, a)$ is also 2.

Thus, $aRb \Rightarrow bRa$

Hence, R is symmetric.

According to given option, R is symmetric only.

7. (d) **Reflexivity :** xRx iff x and x did engineering from same university (i.e., J.P.U.), which is true.

$\therefore R$ is reflexive.

Symmetricity : $xRy \Rightarrow x$ and y passed engineering from same university.

$\Rightarrow y$ and x also passed engineering from same university. $\Rightarrow yRx$

$\therefore R$ is symmetric.

Transitivity : xRy and yRz

i.e., x and y passed engineering from J.P.U as well as y and z also passed engineering from J.P.U.

$\therefore x, y, z$ all are passed engineering from same university.

$\Rightarrow xRz$.

$\therefore R$ is transitive.

Hence, R is reflexive, symmetric and transitive.

8. (d) **Reflexivity** xRx as $x - x = 0$ is an integer, $\forall x \in A$

$\therefore R$ is reflexive.

Symmetricity Let $(x, y) \in A$

$\Rightarrow y - x$ is an integer.

$\Rightarrow x - y$ is also an integer.

$\therefore R$ is symmetric.

Transitivity Let $(x, y) \in A$ and $(y, z) \in A$

$\Rightarrow y - x$ is an integer and $z - y$ is an integer.

$\Rightarrow y - x + z - y$ is also an integer

$\Rightarrow z - x$ is an integer

$\Rightarrow (x, z) \in A$

$\therefore R$ is transitive.

Hence, R is equivalence relation.

So, statement I is true.

Now, statement II is false because 'B' is not symmetric on R

We observe that

oBx as $0 = 0 \cdot x, \forall x \in R$ but $(x, 0) \notin B$

Statement I is true and statement II is false.

9. (a) **To Check Reflexivity**

As $A = P^{-1}BP$, when $P = I_3$ = Identity matrix of order 3, we get $(A, A) \in R$, $\forall$ real square matrix A of order 3.

$\therefore$ R is reflexive.

To Check Symmetricity

Let us assume $(A, B) \in R$

$\Rightarrow$ There exist a non-singular matrix P such that $A = P^{-1}BP$.

$\Rightarrow B = PAP^{-1} = (P^{-1})^{-1}AP^{-1}$

$\left(\because |P^{-1}| = \frac{1}{|P|} \neq 0 \Rightarrow P^{-1} \text{ is invertible}\right)$

Thus, $(B, A) \in R$

$\therefore$ R is symmetric.

To Check Transitivity

Let us assume $(A, B) \in R$ and $(B, C) \in R$

$\Rightarrow A = P^{-1}BP$ and $B = Q^{-1}CQ$ for some invertible matrices P and Q

$$\therefore \quad A = P^{-1}(Q^{-1}CQ)P = (P^{-1}Q^{-1})\,C(QP) = (QP)^{-1}C(QP)$$

[If M and N be two square matrices of same order, then $(MN)^{-1} = N^{-1}M^{-1}$]

$\Rightarrow \quad (A, C) \in R$

$[\because |QP| = |Q|\cdot|P| \neq 0$ As $|P| \neq 0, |Q| \neq 0]$

$\therefore$ R is transitive.

Hence, R is reflexive, symmetric and transitive.

i.e., R is an equivalence relation.

10. (c) Given, $f(x) = \dfrac{\sqrt{\sin x - \frac{1}{\sqrt{2}}}}{\sqrt{\frac{3x}{2} - x^2 - \frac{1}{2}}}$

For $f(x)$ to be defined :

$\sin x - \frac{1}{\sqrt{2}} \geq 0$

$\sin x \geq \frac{1}{\sqrt{2}} = \frac{1}{1.414} = 0.707$

$\Rightarrow \quad x \in \left[\frac{\pi}{4}, \frac{3\pi}{4}\right]$

i.e., $x \in [0.785, 2.355]$ (see graph) ...(i)

and $\frac{3}{2}x - x^2 - \frac{1}{2} > 0$

$\frac{3}{2}x - x^2 - \frac{1}{2} > 0$

$\Rightarrow -\left(x^2 - \frac{3}{2}x + \frac{1}{2}\right) > 0$

$\Rightarrow \quad x^2 - \frac{3}{2}x + \frac{1}{2} < 0$

$\Rightarrow \quad \left(x - \frac{1}{2}\right)(x - 1) < 0$

$\Rightarrow \quad \frac{1}{2} < x < 1$

$\Rightarrow \quad 0.5 < x < 1$ ...(ii)

From Eqs. (i) $\cap$ (ii) $\Rightarrow x \in [0.785, 1)$ i.e. $x \in \left[\frac{\pi}{4}, 1\right)$

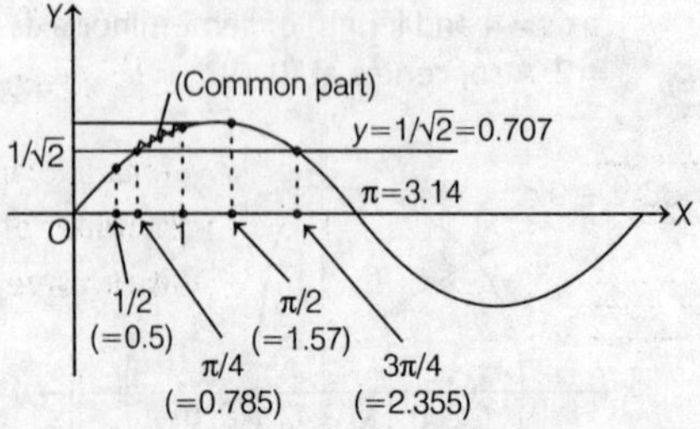

11. (a) Given, $(28)^x + (8)^y = 8$

$\Rightarrow \quad (28)^x = 8 - (8)^y$

$\Rightarrow \quad \log_{28}(28)^x = \log_{28}(8 - 8^y)$

$\Rightarrow \quad x = \log_{28}(8 - 8^y)$

For x to be defined,

$8 - 8^y > 0 \Rightarrow 8^y < 8 \Rightarrow y < 1$

$\Rightarrow \quad y \in (-\infty, 1)$ = Range

If we exclude $[1, \infty)$ from $(-\infty, \infty)$, then we get $(-\infty, 1)$.

$\therefore \quad A = [1, \infty)$

12. (c) Given, $f(x) = \dfrac{\log_e([x] + [-x] + 1)}{\sqrt{x(3 - x)}}$

For $f(x)$ to be defined;

$[x] + [-x] + 1 > 0$

If $x \notin z$ then
$[x] + [-x] = -1$
$\therefore [x] + [-x] + 1 = 0$
becomes zero, and zero never greater than zero.
Hence, reject this case.

If $x \in z$ then,
$[x] + [-x] = 0$
$\therefore [x] + [-x] + 1 = 1$
which is greater than zero.
Hence, the case $x \in z$ will be possible.

and $\quad x(3 - x) > 0$

$\Rightarrow \quad x(x - 3) < 0$

$\Rightarrow \quad 0 < x < 3$

Therefore, domain of f will be $0 < x < 3$ and $x \in z$,

i.e. $x = \{1, 2\}$ = Pair set

and range $= \{f(1), f(2)\} = \{0, 0\} = \{0\}$ = Singleton set.

13. (a) As we know that,

$$-\sqrt{a^2 + b^2} \leq a\sin x + b\cos x \leq \sqrt{a^2 + b^2}$$

So, $-\sqrt{1 + (-\sqrt{3})^2} \leq \sin x - \sqrt{3}\cos x \leq \sqrt{1 + (-\sqrt{3})^2}$

$\Rightarrow -2 \leq \sin x - \sqrt{3}\cos x \leq 2$

$\Rightarrow -2 + 1 \leq \sin x - \sqrt{3}\cos x + 1 \leq 2 + 1$

$\Rightarrow -1 \leq \sin x - \sqrt{3}\cos x + 1 \leq 3$

That is, the range is $[-1, 3]$

Hence, for f to be onto, codomain = Range, i.e. $S = [-1, 3]$

14. (b) Given, $\phi(h(x)) = |\sin x|$

and $\quad h(\phi(x)) = (\sin\sqrt{x})^2$

Clearly, $\phi(x) = \sqrt{x}$ and $h(x) = \sin^2 x$

Domain of $\phi(x)$ is $[0, \infty)$ which is not symmetric about origin.

$\therefore \phi(x)$ is neither even nor odd.

Now, $h(x) = \sin^2 x$

$h(-x) = (\sin(-x))^2 = (-\sin x)^2 = \sin^2 x$

$\because h(x) - h(-x) = 0$

$\therefore h(x)$ is even.

Alternative approach

$\phi(x) = \sqrt{x}, x \in [0, \infty)$

$\phi(-x) = \sqrt{-x}$ = imaginary, $\forall x \in [0, \infty)$

$\therefore \phi(x)$ is neither even nor odd.

15. (a) Given, equation can be rearranged as

$$[x] + \left(\left[\frac{x+1}{2}\right] + \left[\frac{x+2}{2}\right]\right) + \left(\left[\frac{x+3}{2}\right] + \left[\frac{x+4}{2}\right]\right) + \left(\left[\frac{x+5}{2}\right] + \left[\frac{x+6}{2}\right]\right) + \left(\left[\frac{x+7}{2}\right] + \left[\frac{x+8}{2}\right]\right) = 21$$

$\Rightarrow [x] + [x + 1] + [x + 3] + [x + 5] + [x + 7] = 21$

$\left[\because \left[\frac{x}{2}\right] + \left[\frac{x+1}{2}\right] = [x]\right]$

$\Rightarrow [x] + [x] + 1 + [x] + 3 + [x] + 5 + [x] + 7 = 21$

$[\because [x + 1] = [x] + 1]$

$\Rightarrow \quad 5[x] = 5$

$\Rightarrow \quad [x] = 1$

$\Rightarrow \quad 1 \leq x < 2$

$\therefore$ Minimum value of $x = 1$.

16. (b) Given, $f(x)=x+2|x+1|+2|x-1|$

$$\Rightarrow f(x)=\begin{cases} x-2(x+1)-2(x-1), & x<-1 \\ x+2(x+1)-2(x-1), & -1\le x\le 1 \\ x+2(x+1)+2(x-1), & x>1 \end{cases}$$

$$\Rightarrow f(x)=\begin{cases} -3x\ , & x<-1 \\ x+4\ , & -1\le x\le 1 \\ 5x\ , & x>1 \end{cases}$$

Now, draw its graph.

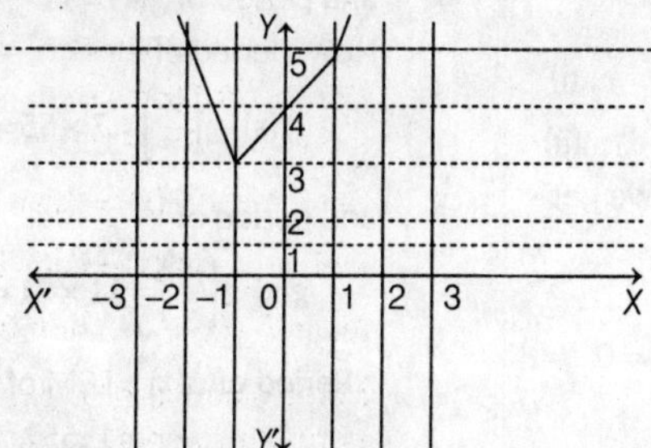

Graph of $f(x)$ is shown in figure above.

Clearly, $y=\lambda$ can intersect $y=f(x)$ at exactly one point only if $\lambda=3$ and at more than one point if $\lambda>3$.

Hence, $\lambda\ge 3$.

17. (d) Given, $4\cos^{-1}(-|x|)=a$

$$\Rightarrow \quad \cos^{-1}(-|x|)=\frac{a}{4} \quad \text{...(i)}$$

For observation, we draw the graph of $y=\cos^{-1}(-|x|)$

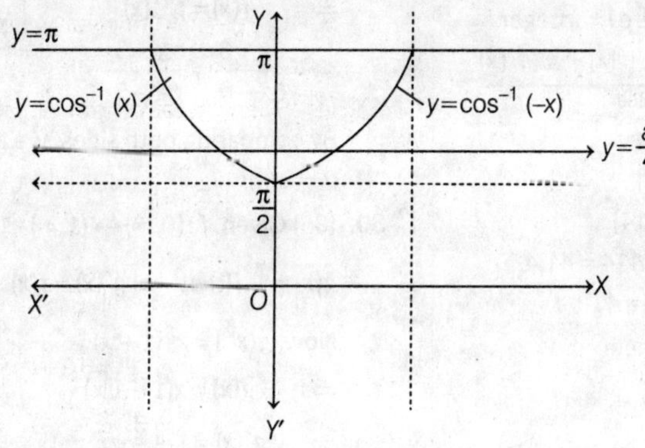

From figure we analyse that, Eq. (i) has two solutions, if line $y=\frac{a}{4}$ intersect the graph between $\frac{\pi}{2}$ and π.

i.e. $\frac{\pi}{2}<\frac{a}{4}\le\pi$

$\Rightarrow 2\pi<a\le 4\pi$

$\therefore$ Integral values of a are 7, 8, 9, 10, 11, 12.

Its sum $=7+8+9+10+11+12=57$

18. (a) Given, $y=\frac{1}{3}[\sin x+[\sin x+[\sin x]]]$

$$=\frac{1}{3}(3\cdot[\sin x]) \quad [\because [x+[y+[z]]]=[x]+[y]+[z]]$$

$$\Rightarrow \quad y=[\sin x] \quad \text{...(i)}$$

and $[y+[y]]=2\cos x$

$\Rightarrow \quad 2[y]=2\cos x$

$\Rightarrow \quad [y]=\cos x$

$\Rightarrow \quad [\sin x]=\cos x$ [from Eq. (i)]

$\because [\sin x]$ gives always integer value(s).

$\therefore \cos x$ has to be integer.

i.e., $\cos x\in\{-1,0,1\}$.

If $\cos x=1$	If $\cos x=0$	If $\cos x=-1$
Then, $x=0$	Then, $x=\pi/2$	Then, $x=\pi$
$\Rightarrow \sin x=0$	$\Rightarrow \sin x=1$	$\Rightarrow \sin x=0$
$\therefore [\sin x]=0(\ne 1)$	$\therefore [\sin x]=1(\ne 0)$	$\therefore [\sin x]=0(\ne -1)$

Hence, no any solution possible.

$\therefore$ Number of solution(s) is zero.

Alternative (Graphically)

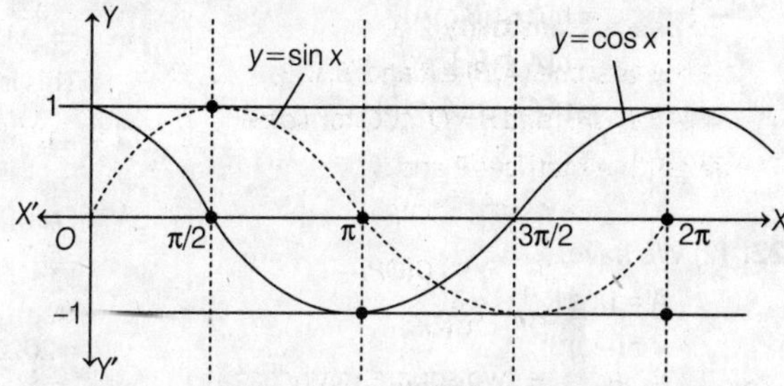

There is no any common point in the graph of $y=\cos x$ and $y=[\sin x]$.

$\therefore$ No solution.

19. (d) Given, $f(x)+2f\left(\frac{2020}{x}\right)=3x$ ...(i)

Replace x by $\frac{2020}{x}$, we get

$$f\left(\frac{2020}{x}\right)+2\cdot f(x)=3\cdot\left(\frac{2020}{x}\right)=\frac{6060}{x} \quad \text{...(ii)}$$

Now, Eq. (i)- 2x Eq. (ii), we get

$$-3f(x)=3x-\frac{12120}{x}=-\left(\frac{12120}{x}-3x\right)$$

$$\Rightarrow \quad f(x)=\frac{12120}{3x}-\frac{3x}{3}$$

$$=\frac{4040}{x}-x=\frac{4040-x^2}{x}$$

$$\Rightarrow x\cdot f(x)=4040-x^2$$

20. (a) Replacing x by $\left(\frac{1-x}{1+x}\right)$, we have

$$f(x)\cdot f\left(\frac{1}{x}\right)=f(x)+f\left(\frac{1}{x}\right)$$

$$\Rightarrow \quad f(x)=1\pm x^n \text{ (Result)}$$

Given, $f(3)=28$

$\therefore$	$1+3^n=28$	$1-3^n=28$
$\Rightarrow$	$3^n=27$	$\Rightarrow -3^n=27$
$\Rightarrow$	$n=3$	$\Rightarrow 3^n=-27$ (Rejected because $3^n>0$ always)

$\therefore \quad f(x)=1+x^3$

Now, $f(n) - 1 = (1 + n^3) - 1 = n^3$

$$\sum_{n=1}^{10}(f(n)-1) = \sum_{n=1}^{10} n^3 = \left(\frac{10 \times 11}{2}\right)^2$$

$$\left(\because \sum_{k=1}^{n} k^3 = \left(\frac{n(n+1)}{2}\right)^2\right)$$

$= (55)^2 = 3025$

$$\therefore \frac{1}{605}\left[\sum_{n=1}^{10}(f(n)-1)\right] = 5$$

21. (28) $n[(A \cap B)' \cap A] = n[(A' \cup B') \cap A]$

$= n[(A' \cap A) \cup (B' \cap A)]$ [Distributive law]

$= n[\phi \cup (B' \cap A)]$

$= n[A \cap B']$

$= n(A) - n(A \cap B)$

$= 31 - 3$

$= 28$

22. (2) We have,

$A = \{x \in R : |x| < 3\}$

$x \in (-3, 3)$

and $B = \{x \in R : |x - 2| \geq 3\}$

$x \in (-\infty, -1] \cup [5, \infty)$

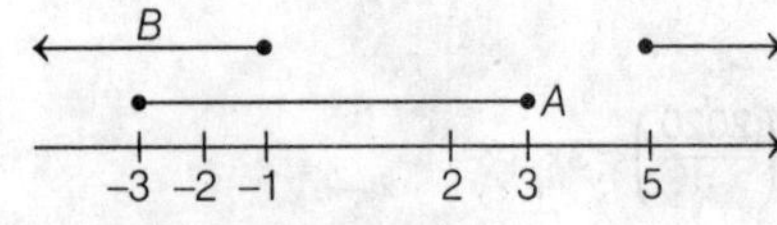

$\Rightarrow B - A = R - (-3, 5)$

Hence, $P + Q = -3 + 5 = 2$

23. (15) We have,

$A = \{x \in Z : 2^{(x+2)(x^2-5x+6)} = 1\}$

So, $2^{(x+2)(x^2-5x+6)} = 2^0$

$\Rightarrow (x+2)(x-2)(x-3) = 0$

$\Rightarrow \quad x = -2, 2, 3$

$A = \{-2, 2, 3\}$

and $\quad B = \{x \in Z : -3 < 2x - 1 < 9\}$

$B = \{0, 1, 2, 3, 4\}$

Hence, $A \times B$ has 15 elements.

So, number of subsets of $A \times B = 2^{15}$

Hence, $K = 15$

24. (1) Given, $f : R \to A$ is defined by

$$f(x) = \frac{x^2}{x^2 + 1}$$

Since, f is surjection.

So, Range (f) = Co-domain (A)

Let $y = \dfrac{x^2}{x^2+1}$

$\Rightarrow \quad x = \sqrt{\dfrac{y}{1-y}}$

$\Rightarrow \quad \dfrac{y}{1-y} \geq 0$

$\Rightarrow \quad y \in [0, 1)$

Hence, Range $(f) = A = [0, 1)$

$\therefore \quad k + m = 0 + 1 = 1$

25. (2021) Given, $x + \sin y = 2021$ ...(i)

$x + 2021 \cos y = 2020$ ...(ii)

Subtracting Eq. (ii) from Eq. (i), we get

$\sin y - 2021 \cos y = 1$

$\Rightarrow \sin y = 1 + 2021 \cos y$

This is possible only when $\cos y = 0$

$\Rightarrow \quad y = \dfrac{\pi}{2}$

From Eq. (i), $x + \sin \pi/2 = 2021$

$\Rightarrow \quad x = 2021 - 1 = 2020$

$\therefore \quad x + y = 2020 + \pi/2$

$= 2020 + 1.57 = 2021.57$

$\Rightarrow \quad [x + y] = [2021.57] = 2021$

26. (41) Given, $f(x) = \{x\} + \{x+1\} + \{x+2\} + \ldots + \{x+99\}$

As we know that,

$\{x + I\} = \{x\}$, where I = integer

$\therefore \quad f(x) = \underbrace{\{x\} + \{x\} + \{x\} + \ldots + \{x\}}_{100}$

$\Rightarrow \quad f(x) = 100\{x\}$

$\therefore \quad f(\sqrt{2}) = 100\{\sqrt{2}\}$

$= 100\{1.414\}$

$= 100 \times 0.414 = 41.4$

Hence, $[f(\sqrt{2})] = [41.4] = 41$

27. (0) As $f(x)$ is an odd function.

$\therefore \quad f(x) = -f(-x)$

Put $x = 0$, $f(0) = -f(0)$

$\Rightarrow \quad 2f(0) = 0$

$\Rightarrow \quad f(0) = 0$ ...(i)

Given $f(x)$ is periodic with period 2.

$\therefore \quad f(x) = f(x+2)$ ...(ii)

Replace x by $x + 2$, we get

$f(x+2) = f(x+4)$ ...(iii)

From Eqs. (ii) and (iii), we have

$f(x) = f(x+4)$ ...(iv)

Put $x = 0$ in Eq. (iv), we get

$f(0) = f(0+4)$

$\Rightarrow \quad f(4) = 0$ [From Eq. (i)]

28. (1155) Given, $\Delta(x) = \begin{vmatrix} f(x) & f\left(\frac{x}{3}\right) \\ g(x) & g\left(\frac{x}{5}\right) \end{vmatrix}$

$\Rightarrow \quad \Delta(x) = f(x) \cdot g\left(\dfrac{x}{5}\right) - g(x) \cdot f\left(\dfrac{x}{3}\right)$

Also, given period of $f(x) = 7$

and period of $g(x) = 11$

Now, period of

$f(x) \cdot g\left(\dfrac{x}{5}\right) = 7 \times 55 = 385$

and period of

$g(x) \cdot f\left(\dfrac{x}{3}\right) = 11 \times 21 = 231.$

$\therefore$ Period of $\Delta(x)$ = LCM of (385, 231)

$= 1155$

29. (5) Let $y = f(x) = \dfrac{5x+3}{6x-\alpha}$

$\Rightarrow 5x + 3 = 6xy - \alpha y$

$\Rightarrow \quad x = \dfrac{\alpha y + 3}{6y - 5}$

So, $f^{-1}(x) = \dfrac{\alpha x + 3}{6x - 5}$

Now, $fof(x) = x$

$\Rightarrow \quad f(x) = f^{-1}(x)$

$\Rightarrow \quad \dfrac{5x+3}{6x-\alpha} = \dfrac{\alpha x + 3}{6x - 5}$

By comparing both sides, we get

$\alpha = 5$

30. (36) Given, $f : (0, \infty) \to (1, \infty)$

$g(x) = \int_0^x f(t)\, dt \Rightarrow g'(x) = f(x)$ ...(i)

Now, $g(x^2) = x^2(1 + x)$

$\Rightarrow \quad g(x) = x(1 + \sqrt{x})$

$\Rightarrow \quad g'(x) = 1 + \dfrac{3}{2}\sqrt{x}$ ...(ii)

From Eqs. (i) and (ii), we get

$f(x) = 1 + \dfrac{3}{2}\sqrt{x} = y$ (say)

$\Rightarrow \quad \sqrt{x} = \dfrac{2}{3}(y-1) \Rightarrow x = \left(\dfrac{2}{3}(y-1)\right)^2$

$\Rightarrow \quad f^{-1}(x) = \dfrac{4}{9}(x-1)^2 = h(x)$ [given]

$\therefore \quad h(10) = \dfrac{4}{9}(10-1)^2 = \dfrac{4}{9} \times 9 \times 9 = 36$

Qualifier 2
(Complex Numbers, Quadratic Equations, Inequations & Logarithms)

1. (c) Given, $z^{1/3} = a - ib$

$\Rightarrow \quad z = (a-ib)^3$

$\Rightarrow x + iy = (a-ib)^3$

$= a^3 + ib^3 - 3a^2 bi - 3ab^2$

$\Rightarrow x + iy = (a^3 - 3ab^2) + i(b^3 - 3a^2 b)$

On equating real and imaginary part, we get

$x = a^3 - 3ab^2$ and $y = b^3 - 3a^2 b$

$\Rightarrow \frac{x}{a} = a^2 - 3b^2$ and $\frac{y}{b} = b^2 - 3a^2$

So, $\frac{x}{a} - \frac{y}{b} = a^2 - 3b^2 - b^2 + 3a^2$

$= 4(a^2 - b^2)$

Hence, $\lambda = 4$.

2. (c) As we know that, if a polynomial $\phi(x)$ is divided by $(x-a)$, then the remainder is $\phi(a)$.

Also, if $\phi(x)$ is divided by a quadratic, then the remainder is a linear expression.

It is given that, $\frac{1+i}{2}$ and $\frac{3i+1}{2}$ are remainders, when $f(z)$ is divided by $(z-i)$ and $(z+i)$, respectively.

$\therefore f(i) = \frac{1+i}{2}$ and $f(-i) = \frac{3i+1}{2}$

Let $(az+b)$ be the remainder, when $f(z)$ is divided by (z^2+1) and let the quotient be $q(z)$ in that case. Then,

$f(z) = (z^2+1)\cdot q(z) + (az+b)$

Now, $\quad f(i) = \frac{1+i}{2}$

$\Rightarrow (i^2+1)\cdot q(i) + (ai+b) = \frac{1+i}{2}$

$\Rightarrow \quad 0 + ai + b = \frac{1+i}{2}$

$\Rightarrow \quad ai + b = \frac{1}{2} + \frac{i}{2}$ ...(i)

and $\quad f(-i) = \frac{1+3i}{2}$

$\Rightarrow -ai + b = \frac{1}{2} + \frac{3i}{2}$ ...(ii)

Eq. (i) + Eq. (ii)

$\Rightarrow \quad 2b = 1 + 2i \Rightarrow b = \frac{1}{2} + i$

From Eq. (i), $ai + \frac{1}{2} + i = \frac{1}{2} + \frac{i}{2}$

$\Rightarrow \quad ai = -\frac{i}{2} \Rightarrow a = \frac{-1}{2}$

Hence, remainder $= az + b$

$= -\frac{1}{2}z + \frac{1}{2} + i = \frac{1}{2}(1 + 2i - z)$

3. (c) Given, $|z_1| = |z_2| + |z_1 - z_2|$

$\Rightarrow (|z_1| - |z_2|)^2 = |z_1 - z_2|^2$

$\Rightarrow |z_1|^2 + |z_2|^2 - 2|z_1|\cdot|z_2|$

$= |z_1|^2 + |z_2|^2 - 2|z_1||z_2|\cos(\theta_1 - \theta_2)$

$\Rightarrow \quad \cos(\theta_1 - \theta_2) = 1$

$\Rightarrow \quad \theta_1 - \theta_2 = 0$

$\Rightarrow \arg(z_1) - \arg(z_2) = 0$

$\Rightarrow \quad \arg\left(\frac{z_1}{z_2}\right) = 0$

$\Rightarrow \frac{z_1}{z_2}$ is purely real.

Hence, $\text{Im}\left(\frac{z_1}{z_2}\right) = 0$

4. (a) Given, $z_1 = a + ib, z_2 = c + id$,

$\omega_1 = a + ic$ and $\omega_2 = b + id$

$|z_1| = |z_2| = 1$

$\Rightarrow \quad a^2 + b^2 = 1$ ...(i)

and $\quad c^2 + d^2 = 1$ ...(ii)

Now, $z_1\bar{z}_2 = (a+ib)(c-id)$

$\Rightarrow \quad z_1\bar{z}_2 = (ac+bd) + i(bc-ad)$

Again, $\text{Re}(z_1\bar{z}_2) = 0$ (given)

$\Rightarrow \quad ac + bd = 0 \Rightarrow ac = -bd$

$\Rightarrow \quad \frac{a}{d} = \frac{b}{-c} = k$ (say) ...(iii)

$\therefore a = kd$ and $b = -kc$

From Eq. (i), $a^2 + b^2 = 1$

$\Rightarrow \quad k^2d^2 + k^2c^2 = 1$

$\Rightarrow \quad k^2(c^2 + d^2) = 1$

$\Rightarrow \quad k = \pm 1 \quad (\because c^2 + d^2 = 1)$

When $k = 1$, $a = d$, $b = -c$ and when $k = -1$, $a = -d$, $b = c$.

$\Rightarrow \quad |a| = |d|$ and $|b| = |c|$

Now, $|\omega_1| = \sqrt{a^2 + c^2} = \sqrt{a^2 + b^2} = 1$

$(\because |c| = |b|)$

and $|\omega_2| = \sqrt{b^2 + d^2} = \sqrt{b^2 + a^2} = 1$

$(\because |d| = |a|)$

Also, $\omega_1\overline{\omega}_2 = (a+ic)(b-id)$

$\Rightarrow \text{Re}(\omega_1\overline{\omega}_2) = ab + cd$

$(\because a = d, b = -c$ or $a = -d, b = c)$

$= -dc + cd = 0$

5. (a) $z^4 = 2 - \sqrt{12}\,i = 2(1 - \sqrt{3}\,i)$

$= 4\left(\frac{1}{2} - \frac{\sqrt{3}}{2}i\right)$

$= 4\left[\cos\left(\frac{-\pi}{3}\right) + i\sin\left(\frac{-\pi}{3}\right)\right]$

$\Rightarrow z = \left[4\left\{\cos\left(\frac{-\pi}{3}\right) + i\sin\left(\frac{-\pi}{3}\right)\right\}\right]^{1/4}$

$\Rightarrow z = \sqrt{2}\left[\cos\left(\frac{2m\pi - (\pi/3)}{4}\right) + i\sin\left(\frac{2m\pi - (\pi/3)}{4}\right)\right]$

For $m = 1$,

$z = \sqrt{2}\left[\cos\left(\frac{5\pi}{12}\right) + i\sin\left(\frac{5\pi}{12}\right)\right]$

$\therefore$ Least positive argument $= \frac{5\pi}{12}$

6. (b) Let $z = x + iy$, then

$\frac{2z+1}{iz+1} = \frac{2(x+iy)+1}{i(x+iy)+1} = \frac{(2x+1)+2iy}{(1-y)+ix}$

$= \frac{[(2x+1)+2iy][(1-y)-ix]}{(1-y)^2 + x^2}$

Given, $\text{Im}\left(\frac{2z+1}{iz+1}\right) = -4$

So, $\frac{2y(1-y) - x(2x+1)}{x^2 + (1-y)^2} = -4$

$\Rightarrow 2x^2 + 2y^2 + x - 2y$

$= 4x^2 + 4(y^2 - 2y + 1)$

$\Rightarrow 2x^2 + 2y^2 - x - 6y + 4 = 0$

$\Rightarrow \quad x^2 + y^2 - \frac{x}{2} - 3y + 2 = 0$ ...(i)

So, Eq. (i) represents a circle.

7. (b) $\because z^n - 1 = (z-1)(z-\omega)(z-\omega^2)$

$(z-\omega^3)\ldots(z-\omega^{n-1})$

$\Rightarrow (z-\omega)(z-\omega^2)(z-\omega^3)\ldots(z-\omega^{n-1})$

$= \frac{z^n - 1}{z - 1}$ ...(i)

Now, putting $z = 2$ in Eq. (i), we get

$(2-\omega)(2-\omega^2)(2-\omega^3)\ldots(2-\omega^{n-1})$

$= \frac{2^n - 1}{2 - 1} = 2^n - 1$

Also, ${}^nC_1 + {}^nC_2 + {}^nC_3 + \ldots + {}^nC_n$

$= 2^n - 1$

But ${}^{2n+1}C_1 + {}^{2n+1}C_2 + {}^{2n+1}C_3 + \ldots$

$+ {}^{2n+1}C_n = 2^{2n} - 1$

8. (a) Given, cubic equation is

$4x^3 - 3x - \lambda = 0$ ...(i)

Let $x = \cos\theta$, then from Eq. (i), we get

$4\cos^3\theta - 3\cos\theta = \lambda$

$\Rightarrow \quad \lambda = \cos(3\theta) \Rightarrow \theta = \frac{1}{3}\cos^{-1}(\lambda)$

$\because \quad x=\cos\theta$

$\Rightarrow \; x=\cos\left(\frac{1}{3}\cos^{-1}(\lambda)\right)$ ...(ii)

Since, $-1\le\lambda\le1$ (given)

Then, $0\le\cos^{-1}(\lambda)\le\pi$

$\Rightarrow \quad 0\le\frac{1}{3}\cos^{-1}(\lambda)\le\frac{\pi}{3}$

($\because \cos x$ is decreasing function)

$\Rightarrow \cos 0\ge\cos\left(\frac{1}{3}\cos^{-1}(\lambda)\right)\ge\cos(\pi/3)$

$\Rightarrow \quad \frac{1}{2}\le x\le 1$ [from Eq. (ii)]

9. (b) Given, quadratic equation can be written as

$(\cos a-1)x^2+(\cos a)x+\sin a=0$ ...(i)

Now, discriminant (D) of Eq. (i) is

$D=\cos^2 a-4(\cos a-1)\cdot\sin a$

$=\cos^2 a-4\cos a\cdot\sin a+4\sin a$

$=(\cos a-2\sin a)^2+4\sin a-4\sin^2 a$

$=(\cos a-2\sin a)^2+4\sin a(1-\sin a)$

Since, $0\le a\le\pi$ (given)

$\therefore \sin a\ge0$ i.e., y-intercept of Eq. (i) is non-negative.

Also, $1-\sin a\ge0,\ \forall\ a\in R$.

So, $D\ge0$ because $(\cos a-2\sin a)^2\ge0$, $\sin a\ge0$ and $(1-\sin a)\ge0$.

Hence, Eq. (i) has real roots with non-negative y-intercept.

10. (d) Given, quadratic equation is

$x^2-(2t^{4\log_t a}-1)x+7a=0$

Sum of roots $=2t^{4\log_t a}-1=511$ (given)

$\Rightarrow \quad 2t^{\log_t a^4}=512$

$\Rightarrow \quad t^{\log_t a^4}=256$

$\Rightarrow \quad a^4=256$

$\Rightarrow \quad (a^2)^2-(16)^2=0$

$\Rightarrow \quad (a^2-16)(a^2+16)=0$

$\Rightarrow \; (a-4)(a+4)(a^2+16)=0$

$\Rightarrow \quad a=-4, 4 \quad (\because a^2\ne-16)$

But, $a>0$ for log to be defined.

$\therefore a=-4$ (Rejected), then $a=4$.

Hence, product of roots

$=7a=7\times4=28$,

which is a perfect number because sum of its divisors equal to two times of itself.

i.e. $1+2+4+7+14+28$

$=56=2\times28$

11. (c) Given, quadratic equations are

$(1-2a)x^2-6ax-1=0$ ...(i)

and $\quad ax^2-x+1=0$ ...(ii)

Here, $(1-2a)\ne0$ and $a\ne0$ (because leading coefficient never be zero).

$\Rightarrow \quad a\ne0,\frac{1}{2}$

If α is a common root of the given equations, then

$(1-2a)\alpha^2-6a\alpha-1=0$ ...(iii)

and $\quad a\alpha^2-\alpha+1=0$ ...(iv)

Eq. (iii) + Eq. (iv)

$\Rightarrow(1-a)\alpha^2-(1+6a)\alpha=0$

$\Rightarrow \quad \alpha=0$ or $\alpha=\frac{1+6a}{1-a}$

But $\alpha\ne0$ as 0 is not a root of any of the given equations.

So, $\alpha=\frac{1+6a}{1-a}$

Hence, $a\left(\frac{1+6a}{1-a}\right)^2-\left(\frac{1+6a}{1-a}\right)+1=0$

[from Eq. (ii)]

$\Rightarrow \; a(1+6a)^2-(1+6a)(1-a)+(1-a)^2=0$

$\Rightarrow a[1+12a+36a^2]-[1+5a-6a^2]+[1-2a+a^2]=0$

$\Rightarrow \; a[1+12a+36a^2-5+6a-2+a]=0$

$\Rightarrow \; a[36a^2+19a-6]=0$

$\Rightarrow \quad a=0$ or $36a^2+19a-6=0$

But $a\ne0$ (from above)

So, $36a^2+19a-6=0$

$\Rightarrow \quad a=\frac{2}{9},-\frac{3}{4}$

From given options,

$a=\frac{2}{9}$

12. (b) Since, α and β are the roots of $x^2-3x+5=0$.

So, $\alpha+\beta=3$ and $\alpha\beta=5$.

Now, $\frac{5\alpha\beta^{2016}+3\alpha^{2017}\beta+\alpha\beta^{2018}}{\alpha^{2016}+\beta^{2016}}$

$=\frac{\alpha^2\beta^{2017}+\alpha^{2018}\cdot\beta+\alpha^{2017}\beta^2+\alpha\beta^{2018}}{\alpha^{2016}+\beta^{2016}}$

$=\frac{\alpha^2\beta(\alpha^{2016}+\beta^{2016})+\beta^2\alpha(\alpha^{2016}+\beta^{2016})}{(\alpha^{2016}+\beta^{2016})}$

$=\alpha^2\beta+\beta^2\alpha=\alpha\beta(\alpha+\beta)$

$=3\times5=15$

13. (d) Given, $\sqrt{4^x-2^{x+1}+1}+\sqrt{4^x-2^{x+3}+16}=3$

$\Rightarrow\sqrt{(2^x)^2-2\cdot2^x\cdot1+(1)^2}+\sqrt{(2^x)^2-2\cdot2^x\cdot4+(4)^2}=3$

$\Rightarrow\sqrt{(2^x-1)^2}+\sqrt{(2^x-4)^2}=3$

$\Rightarrow \quad |2^x-1|+|2^x-4|=3$ ...(i)

(Putting $2^x-1=0,\ 2^x-4=0$

$\Rightarrow \quad 2^x=1, \Rightarrow 2^x=4$

$\Rightarrow \quad x=0, \Rightarrow x=2$)

$-\infty$ ← 0 — 2 → ∞

Case I : When $x\in(-\infty,0)$ i.e. $x<0$

$\Rightarrow-2^x+1-2^x+4=3$ [from Eq. (i)]

$\Rightarrow \quad -2\cdot2^x=-2$

$\Rightarrow \quad 2^x=1\Rightarrow x=0$ but $x<0$

Case II : When $x\in[0,2]$ i.e. $0\le x\le2$

$\Rightarrow2^x-1-2^x+4=3$ [from Eq. (i)]

$\Rightarrow \quad 2^x-2^x=3-3$

$\Rightarrow x\in R$ but $x\in[0,2]$

Hence, $x\in[0,2]$

$-\infty$ ← 0 — 2 → ∞

Case III : When $x\in(2,\infty)$ i.e. $x>2$

$\Rightarrow2^x-1+2^x-4=3$ [from Eq. (i)]

$\Rightarrow \quad 2\cdot2^x=8\Rightarrow2^x=4$

$\Rightarrow \quad x=2$ but $x>2$

Hence, $x\in\phi$

Therefore, $x\in[0,2]$ is the final solution.

14. (a) Given, $(x-1)^4+(x-5)^4=82$ ...(i)

Put $y=\frac{(x-1)+(x-5)}{2}=x-3$

$\Rightarrow x=y+3$, in Eq. (i), we get

$(y+3-1)^4+(y+3-5)^4=82$

$\Rightarrow(y+2)^4+(y-2)^4=82$

$\Rightarrow2[y^4+24y^2+16]=82$

$\Rightarrow y^4+24y^2-25=0$

$\Rightarrow(y^2+25)(y^2-1)=0$

$\Rightarrow y^2=-25$ or $y^2=1$

$\Rightarrow y=\pm5i$ or $y=\pm1$

$\Rightarrow x=3\pm5i$ or $x=4,2\ (\because y=x-3)$

So, $\alpha=3+5i,\beta=3-5i,\gamma=2$ and $\delta=4$ or $\alpha=3-5i,\beta=3+5i,\gamma=2$ and $\delta=4$.

In both cases, $|\text{Re}(\alpha)|=3$ and $|\text{Im}(\beta)|=5$.

Hence, $\frac{|\text{Re}(\alpha)|+\delta}{|\text{Im}(\beta)|+\gamma}=\frac{3+4}{5+2}=\frac{7}{7}=1$

15. (c) We have,

$$\left(\frac{9}{10}\right)^x = -3 + x - x^2$$

$$= -(x^2 - x + 3)$$

$$\left(\frac{9}{10}\right)^x = -\left\{\left(x - \frac{1}{2}\right)^2 + \frac{11}{4}\right\}$$

$\left(\frac{9}{10}\right)^x$ is always positive.

But $-\left\{\left(x - \frac{1}{2}\right)^2 + \frac{11}{4}\right\}$ is negative.

Hence, no real solutions is possible.

16. (d) Given, $3^{\sec^2 x - 1}\sqrt{9y^2 - 6y + 2} \le 1$

$$\Rightarrow 3^{\sec^2 x}\sqrt{\frac{9y^2 - 6y + 2}{9}} \le 1$$

$$\Rightarrow 3^{\sec^2 x}\sqrt{y^2 - \frac{2}{3}y + \frac{2}{9}} \le 1$$

$$\Rightarrow 3^{\sec^2 x}\sqrt{\left(y - \frac{1}{3}\right)^2 + \frac{1}{9}} \le 1 \quad \text{...(i)}$$

$\because \sec^2 x \ge 1 \Rightarrow 3^{\sec^2 x} \ge 3$

and $\sqrt{\left(y - \frac{1}{3}\right)^2 + \frac{1}{9}} \ge \frac{1}{3}$

So, Eq. (i) will be true, if $\sec^2 x = 1$ and $y - \frac{1}{3} = 0$.

$\Rightarrow x = 0, \pi, 2\pi, 3\pi \in [0, 10]$ and $y = \frac{1}{3}$

Hence, total number of solutions are 4.

17. (a) Given, inequation

$$2^x + 2^{|x|} \ge 2\sqrt{2} \quad \text{...(i)}$$

Here, two cases arises.

Case I When $x \ge 0$

$$2^x + 2^x \ge 2\sqrt{2}$$

$$\Rightarrow 2 \cdot 2^x \ge 2\sqrt{2} \Rightarrow 2^x \ge \sqrt{2} \Rightarrow x \ge \frac{1}{2}$$

But, $x \ge 0$

$$\therefore \quad x \in \left[\frac{1}{2}, \infty\right) \text{... } S_1$$

Case II **When $x < 0$**

$$2^x + 2^{-x} \ge 2\sqrt{2} \quad \text{[from Eq. (i)]}$$

$$\Rightarrow \quad z + \frac{1}{z} \ge 2\sqrt{2} \quad (\text{put } 2^x = z)$$

$$\Rightarrow z^2 - 2\sqrt{2}z + 1 \ge 0$$

$$\Rightarrow \quad (z - \sqrt{2})^2 \ge 1$$

$$\Rightarrow \quad |z - \sqrt{2}| \ge 1$$

$$\Rightarrow \quad z - \sqrt{2} \le -1 \text{ or } z - \sqrt{2} \ge 1$$

$$\Rightarrow \quad z \le \sqrt{2} - 1 \text{ or } z \ge \sqrt{2} + 1$$

$$\Rightarrow \quad 2^x \le \sqrt{2} - 1 \text{ or } 2^x \ge \sqrt{2} + 1$$

$$\Rightarrow x \le \log_2(\sqrt{2} - 1) \text{ or } x \ge \log_2(\sqrt{2} + 1)$$

But $x < 0$

$\therefore x \le \log_2(\sqrt{2} - 1)$... S_2

($\because x \ge \log_2(\sqrt{2} + 1)$ is rejected because $x > 0$)

Hence, solution is $S_1 \cup S_2$

$$x \in (-\infty, \log_2(\sqrt{2} - 1)] \cup \left[\frac{1}{2}, \infty\right)$$

18. (b) Given, $\log_{\sin(\pi/3)}(x^2 - 3x + 2) \ge 2$

$$\Rightarrow x^2 - 3x + 2 \le \sin^2 \frac{\pi}{3}$$

$$\left(\because 0 < \sin\frac{\pi}{3} < 1\right)$$

and $\quad x^2 - 3x + 2 > 0$

$\Rightarrow \quad 4x^2 - 12x + 5 \le 0$

and $\quad x^2 - 3x + 2 > 0$

$\Rightarrow (2x - 1)(2x - 5) \le 0$

and $\quad (x - 1)(x - 2) > 0$

$\Rightarrow \frac{1}{2} \le x \le \frac{5}{2}$ and $x < 1$ or $x > 2$.

$-\infty$ ← 1/2 — 1 — 2 — 5/2 → ∞

$$\Rightarrow x \in \left[\frac{1}{2}, 1\right) \cup \left(2, \frac{5}{2}\right]$$

19. (a) We have,

$$\log_{0.3}(x - 1) < \log_{0.09}(x - 1)$$

$$\Rightarrow \log_{0.3}(x - 1) < \frac{1}{2}\log_{0.3}(x - 1)$$

$$\Rightarrow \log_{0.3}(x - 1)^2 < \log_{0.3}(x - 1)$$

$$\Rightarrow \quad (x - 1)^2 > (x - 1)$$

$$\Rightarrow (x - 1)(x - 2) > 0$$

$$\Rightarrow \quad x < 1 \text{ or } x > 2$$

But $\log(x - 1)$ is defined, if $x > 1$.

So, $x \in (2, \infty)$

20. (a) Given,

$$\log_3(\log_2 x) + \log_{1/3}(\log_{1/2} y) = 1 \quad \text{...(i)}$$

and $\quad xy^2 = 9 \quad$ ...(ii)

$$\Rightarrow \log_3(\log_2 x) - \log_3(\log_2(1/y)) = 1$$

$$\left(\text{using, } \log_{a^k}(m) = \frac{1}{k}\log_a m\right)$$

$$\Rightarrow \log_3\left[\frac{\log_2 x}{\log_2 1/y}\right] = 1$$

$$\Rightarrow \quad \log_{1/y} x = 3$$

$$\Rightarrow \quad xy^3 = 1 \quad \text{...(iii)}$$

From Eq. (ii), $xy^2 = 9$

$$\Rightarrow \quad \frac{1}{y^3} \times y^2 = 9 \quad \text{[from Eq. (iii)]}$$

$$\Rightarrow \quad y = \frac{1}{9}$$

$$\therefore \quad x = \frac{1}{y^3}$$

$$\Rightarrow \quad x = \frac{1}{\left(\frac{1}{9}\right)^3}$$

$$\Rightarrow \quad x = 729$$

Here, $xy = 81$ and $x + y = \frac{6562}{9}$

$\therefore (x, y) = \left(729, \frac{1}{9}\right)$ is only one ordered pair.

21. (1) Here, $a = \frac{1}{2}(\sqrt{3} + i)$ and $r = \frac{1}{2}(\sqrt{3} + i)$

$$\therefore \quad t_n = ar^{n-1} = \left[\frac{1}{2}(\sqrt{3} + i)\right]^n \quad (\because a = r)$$

$$= \left[\cos\frac{\pi}{6} + i\sin\frac{\pi}{6}\right]^n$$

$$= \cos\frac{n\pi}{6} + i\sin\frac{n\pi}{6}$$

$$\therefore \quad |t_n| = \sqrt{\cos^2\frac{n\pi}{6} + \sin^2\frac{n\pi}{6}} = 1$$

22. (1) Let $\alpha = \frac{4\pi}{11}$

Now, $b = \text{Re}(a + a^2 + a^3 + a^4 + a^5)$

$$= \cos(2\alpha) + \cos(4\alpha) + \cos(6\alpha) + \cos(8\alpha) + \cos(10\alpha)$$

$$\Rightarrow (2\sin\alpha)b = (\sin 3\alpha - \sin\alpha) + (\sin 5\alpha - \sin 3\alpha) + (\sin 7\alpha - \sin 5\alpha) + (\sin 9\alpha - \sin 7\alpha) + (\sin 11\alpha - \sin 9\alpha)$$

$$= \sin(11\alpha) - \sin(\alpha) = \sin(4\pi) - \sin\alpha$$

$$\Rightarrow \quad b = \frac{-1}{2} \quad (\because \sin 4\pi = 0)$$

Hence, $\left|b + \frac{\sqrt{3}i}{2}\right| = \left|\frac{-1}{2} + \frac{\sqrt{3}i}{2}\right| = 1$

23. (2) Given, $|z_1| = 12 \Rightarrow z_1$ lies on a circle with centre (0, 0) and radius 12 units, and $|z_2 - 3 - 4i| = 5 \Rightarrow z_2$ lies on a circle with centre (3, 4) and radius $= 5$ units.

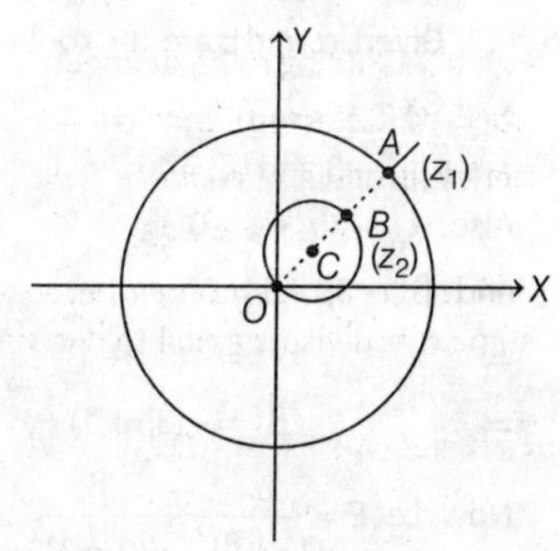

From figure, it is clear that $|z_1 - z_2|$ i.e., distance between z_1 and z_2 will be minimum when they lie at A and B respectively, i.e., $|z_1 - z_2| = AB$
$= OA - OB = 12 - 2(5) = 2$

24. (2) $\because \frac{1}{a+\omega} + \frac{1}{b+\omega} + \frac{1}{c+\omega} = 2\omega^2 = \frac{2}{\omega}$

and $\frac{1}{a+\omega^2} + \frac{1}{b+\omega^2} + \frac{1}{c+\omega^2}$

$$= 2\omega = \frac{2}{\omega^2}$$

It is clear that, ω and ω^2 are the roots of the equation.

$$\frac{1}{a+x} + \frac{1}{b+x} + \frac{1}{c+x} = \frac{2}{x} \quad \text{...(i)}$$

$\Rightarrow \quad x\,\Sigma(b+x)(c+x)$
$= 2(a+x)(b+x)(c+x)$
$\Rightarrow x^3 - (ab+bc+ca)x - 2abc = 0$
$\because$ Coefficient of $x^2 = 0$
Then, sum of roots $= 0$
$\alpha + \omega + \omega^2 = 0$
$\Rightarrow \quad \alpha - 1 = 0$
$\Rightarrow \quad \alpha = 1$
So, third root is 1.
From Eq. (i)

$$\frac{1}{a+1} + \frac{1}{b+1} + \frac{1}{c+1} = \frac{2}{1} = 2$$

25. (1) Given, quadratic equation can be written as

$$x^2 + (2\lambda - 1)x + \lambda^2 = 0 \quad \text{...(i)}$$

Two real roots (α, β) are positive, implies $2\lambda - 1 \le 0$, i.e., $\lambda \le \frac{1}{2}$.
As, λ is an integer, then we get $\lambda \le 0$.
Now, $|\sqrt{\alpha} - \sqrt{\beta}|^2 = (\sqrt{\alpha} - \sqrt{\beta})^2$
$= (\alpha + \beta) - 2\sqrt{\alpha\beta}$
$= (1 - 2\lambda) - 2\sqrt{\lambda^2}$
$= 1 - 2\lambda - 2|\lambda|$
$= 1 - 2(\lambda + |\lambda|) = 1$
$(\because \lambda \le 0 \therefore |\lambda| = -\lambda)$
$\therefore \quad |\sqrt{\alpha} - \sqrt{\beta}| = 1$

26. (18) Given, α and β are the roots of $x^2 + 3x + 1 = 0$
$\therefore \alpha + \beta = -3$ and $\alpha\beta = 1$
Also, $\alpha^2 + 3\alpha + 1 = 0$
and $\beta^2 + 3\beta + 1 = 0$
$\Rightarrow \quad \alpha^2 = -(3\alpha + 1)$
$\Rightarrow \quad \beta^2 = -(3\beta + 1)$
Now, Let $E = \frac{\alpha^2}{(1+\beta)^2} + \frac{\beta^2}{(\alpha+1)^2}$
$= \frac{\alpha^2}{1 + 2\beta + \beta^2} + \frac{\beta^2}{1 + 2\alpha + \alpha^2}$
$= \left(\frac{-(3\alpha+1)}{-\beta}\right) + \left(\frac{-(1+3\beta)}{-\alpha}\right)$
$[\because \alpha^2 + 3\alpha + 1 = 0$
$\Rightarrow \alpha^2 + 2\alpha + 1 = -\alpha$
similarly, $\beta^2 + 2\beta + 1 = -\beta]$
$= 3(\alpha^2 + \beta^2) + (\alpha + \beta)$
$= 3(9 - 2) + (-3) = 18$
$(\because \alpha + \beta = -3$ and $\alpha\beta = 1$
$\Rightarrow (\alpha + \beta)^2 = 9$
$\Rightarrow \alpha^2 + \beta^2 + 2\alpha\beta = 9$
$\Rightarrow \alpha^2 + \beta^2 = 9 - 2)$

27. (4000) $\because 2 - \sqrt{3} = \frac{1}{2 + \sqrt{3}}$ ... (i)

The given equation can be written as,
$(2+\sqrt{3})^{x^2-2x+1}$
$+ \frac{1}{(2+\sqrt{3})^{x^2-2x-1}} = \frac{2}{2-\sqrt{3}}$
$\Rightarrow (2+\sqrt{3})^{x^2-2x+1}$
$+ \frac{1}{(2+\sqrt{3})^{x^2-2x+1} \cdot (2+\sqrt{3})^{-2}}$
$= 2(2+\sqrt{3})$ ... (ii) [from Eq. (i)]
Putting, $(2+\sqrt{3})^{x^2-2x+1} = t$
From Eq. (i),
$t + \frac{(2+\sqrt{3})^2}{t} = 2(2+\sqrt{3})$
$\Rightarrow t^2 - 2(2+\sqrt{3})t + (2+\sqrt{3})^2 = 0$
$\Rightarrow \quad (t - (2+\sqrt{3}))^2 = 0$
$\Rightarrow \quad t = 2 + \sqrt{3}$
$\Rightarrow (2+\sqrt{3})^{x^2-2x+1} = (2+\sqrt{3})$
$\Rightarrow \quad x^2 - 2x + 1 = 1$
$\Rightarrow \quad x(x-2) = 0$
$\Rightarrow \quad x = 0, 2$
i.e., $\alpha = 0, \beta = 2$
So, $2000\alpha + 2000\beta = 4000$

28. (2) Given, $\cos x + \cos^2 x = 1$
$\Rightarrow \quad \cos x = \sin^2 x$ ...(i)
Now, $A = \sin^{12} x + 3 \cdot \sin^{10} x + 3 \cdot \sin^8 x + \sin^6 x + 2$
$\Rightarrow A = \cos^6 x + 3\cos^5 x + 3\cos^4 x + \cos^3 x + 2$ [from Eq. (i)]
$\Rightarrow A = (\cos^2 x + \cos x)^3 + 2$
$= 1 + 2 = 3$
$\therefore \quad \log_{\tan \pi/3} A = \log_{\sqrt{3}} 3 = 2.$

29. (256) Given, equation can be written as
$\log_3|x-2| = 2^{\log_2(\log_3(|x|-2))}$
$\Rightarrow \log_3|x-2| = \log_3(|x|-2)$
$\Rightarrow \quad |x-2| = |x| - 2$
$\Rightarrow |x| - |x-2| = 2$ ...(i)
Putting, $x = 0$ and $x - 2 = 0$
$\Rightarrow \quad x = 0, 2$

$-\infty \longleftrightarrow \infty$ (number line marked 0, 2)

Here, three cases arises.
Case I When $x < 0$ i.e., $x \in (-\infty, 0)$
$\Rightarrow -x + x - 2 = 2$ [from Eq. (i)]
$\Rightarrow \quad -x + x = 2 + 2 \Rightarrow x \in \phi$
Case II When $0 \le x < 2$ i.e., $x \in [0, 2)$
$\Rightarrow \quad x + (x-2) = 2$ [from Eq. (i)]
$\Rightarrow \quad 2x = 4$
$\Rightarrow \quad x = 2$ but $x \in [0, 2)$
So, $x \in \phi$
Case III When $x \ge 2$ i.e., $x \in [2, \infty)$
$\Rightarrow \quad x - (x-2) = 2$ [from Eq. (i)
$\Rightarrow \quad x - x = 2 - 2$
$\Rightarrow \quad x \in R$ but $x \ge 2$
So, $x \in [2, \infty)$
Also, for $\log_2(\log_3(|x|-2))$ to be defined;
$\log_3(|x|-2) > 0 \Rightarrow |x| - 2 > 1$
$\Rightarrow \quad |x| > 3 \Rightarrow x < -3$ or $x > 3$

$-\infty \longleftrightarrow \infty$ (number line marked -3, 2, 3)

Hence, final solution is $x \in (3, \infty)$.
$\therefore$ Least integral value of x is 4 i.e., $\alpha = 4$.
So, $(\alpha)^\alpha = (4)^4 = 256$.

30. (4) Given, $\log_{\sqrt{2}}\left(\frac{|z|^2 - |z| + 8}{|z| + 1}\right) < 4$
$\Rightarrow \quad |z|^2 - |z| + 8 < 4(|z| + 1)$
$\Rightarrow \quad |z|^2 - 5|z| + 4 < 0$
$\Rightarrow (|z| - 4)(|z| - 1) < 0$
$\Rightarrow \quad 1 < |z| < 4$
This gives the area $= 16\pi - \pi = 15\pi$ sq units.
So, $k = 15$

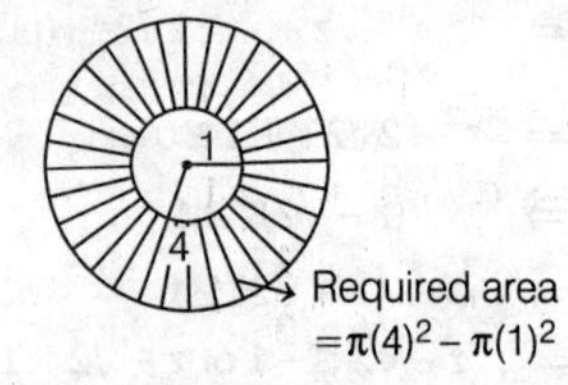

$\therefore \quad \sqrt{k+1} = \sqrt{15+1} = 4$

Qualifier 3
(Matrices and Determinants)

1. (c) Given, A is a skew symmetric matrix.

So, $A' = -A$

Also, $BC = \begin{bmatrix} 1 & 4 \\ 2 & 9 \end{bmatrix}\begin{bmatrix} 9 & -4 \\ -2 & 1 \end{bmatrix} = \begin{bmatrix} 1 & 0 \\ 0 & 1 \end{bmatrix} = I$

So, $B^2C^2 = I, B^3C^3 = I, B^4C^4 = I, \ldots, B^{1008}C^{1008} = I$, then the given matrices reduce to

$A^3 + A^5 + A^7 + A^9 + \ldots + A^{2019}$

which is a skew symmetric matrix because A is skew symmetric matrix.

2. (d) Let $A = \begin{bmatrix} 0 & 2\beta & \gamma \\ \alpha & \beta & -\gamma \\ \alpha & -\beta & \gamma \end{bmatrix}$

$\therefore \quad A' = \begin{bmatrix} 0 & \alpha & \alpha \\ 2\beta & \beta & -\beta \\ \gamma & -\gamma & \gamma \end{bmatrix}$

Since, A is orthogonal, so $AA' = I$

$$\Rightarrow \begin{bmatrix} 0 & 2\beta & \gamma \\ \alpha & \beta & -\gamma \\ \alpha & -\beta & \gamma \end{bmatrix}\begin{bmatrix} 0 & \alpha & \alpha \\ 2\beta & \beta & -\beta \\ \gamma & -\gamma & \gamma \end{bmatrix} = \begin{bmatrix} 1 & 0 & 0 \\ 0 & 1 & 0 \\ 0 & 0 & 1 \end{bmatrix}$$

$$\Rightarrow \begin{bmatrix} 4\beta^2+\gamma^2 & 2\beta^2-\gamma^2 & -2\beta^2+\gamma^2 \\ 2\beta^2-\gamma^2 & \alpha^2+\beta^2+\gamma^2 & \alpha^2-\beta^2-\gamma^2 \\ -2\beta^2+\gamma^2 & \alpha^2-\beta^2-\gamma^2 & \alpha^2+\beta^2+\gamma^2 \end{bmatrix} = \begin{bmatrix} 1 & 0 & 0 \\ 0 & 1 & 0 \\ 0 & 0 & 1 \end{bmatrix}$$

Equating the corresponding elements, we get

$$\left.\begin{matrix} 4\beta^2 + \gamma^2 = 1 \\ 2\beta^2 - \gamma^2 = 0 \end{matrix}\right\}$$

$$\beta = \pm\frac{1}{\sqrt{6}} \text{ and } \gamma = \pm\frac{1}{\sqrt{3}}$$

$\Rightarrow \alpha^2 + \beta^2 + \gamma^2 = 1$

$\Rightarrow \quad \alpha^2 + \frac{1}{6} + \frac{1}{3} = 1$

$\Rightarrow \quad \alpha = \pm\frac{1}{\sqrt{2}}$

3. (c) Since, A is nilpotent matrix of index 2, $A^2 = 0$

For $n = 1$,

$$A(I \pm A) = A \pm A^2 = A \pm 0 = A$$

Now, for $n \geq 2$, $A(I \pm A)^n$

$$= A[I \pm {}^nC_1 A \pm {}^nC_2 A^2 \pm {}^nC_3 A^3 \pm {}^nC_4 A^4 \pm {}^nC_5 A^5 \pm \ldots \pm {}^nC_n A^n]$$

$$= A + A^2[\pm {}^nC_1 \pm {}^nC_2 A \pm {}^nC_3 A^2 \pm \ldots \pm {}^nC_n A^{n-1}]$$

$= A + 0 = A$

Here, $A(I \pm A)^n = A, \forall n \in N$.

4. (c) Given, $a_1 = \lim_{x\to 1}\left(\frac{x}{\ln x} - \frac{1}{x \cdot \ln x}\right)$

$$= \lim_{x\to 1}\left(\frac{x^2-1}{x\ln x}\right) \quad \left[\text{Form}\frac{0}{0}\right]$$

$$= \lim_{x\to 1}\frac{2x}{x\frac{1}{x} + \ln x \cdot 1}$$

[using L-hospital rule]

$$\Rightarrow \quad a_1 = \frac{2\times 1}{1+\ln 1} = 2$$

$$a_2 = \lim_{x\to 0}\left(\frac{x^3-16x}{4x+x^2}\right)$$

$$= \lim_{x\to 0}\left(\frac{3x^2-16}{4+2x}\right) = \frac{-16}{4}$$

$\Rightarrow \quad a_2 = -4$

$$a_3 = \lim_{x\to 0}\frac{\ln(1+\sin x)}{x}$$

$$= \lim_{x\to 0}\left[\frac{\ln(1+\sin x)}{\sin x}\cdot\left(\frac{\sin x}{x}\right)\right]$$

$\Rightarrow \quad a_3 = (1)\cdot(1) = 1$

and $a_4 = \lim_{x\to -1}\frac{(x+1)^3}{3[\sin(x+1)-(x+1)]}$

$$= \lim_{h\to 0}\frac{1}{3\left[\frac{\sin h - h}{h^3}\right]}$$

$[\because$ put $x + 1 = h]$

$$\Rightarrow a_4 = \lim_{h\to 0}\frac{1}{3\left[\frac{\left(h - \frac{h^3}{3!} + \frac{h^5}{5!} - \ldots\right) - h}{h^3}\right]}$$

$$= \frac{1}{3}\times\frac{1}{\left(-\frac{1}{3!} + 0 + 0\ldots\right)}$$

$$= \frac{1}{3}\times\frac{3\times 2\times 1}{(-1)} = -2$$

Now, $M = \begin{bmatrix} a_1 & a_2 \\ a_3 & a_4 \end{bmatrix} = \begin{bmatrix} 2 & -4 \\ 1 & -2 \end{bmatrix}$

As, $M^2 = MM = \begin{bmatrix} 2 & -4 \\ 1 & -2 \end{bmatrix}\begin{bmatrix} 2 & -4 \\ 1 & -2 \end{bmatrix} = \begin{bmatrix} 0 & 0 \\ 0 & 0 \end{bmatrix}$

$\Rightarrow M^2 = 0$ but $M \neq 0$

Hence, M is a nilpotent matrix of order/index 2.

5. (b) Given, A satisfies the equation $x^2 + ax + b = 0$

So, $A^2 + aA + bI_2 = 0$, where

$A = \begin{bmatrix} 3 & -1 \\ 0 & 2 \end{bmatrix}$

$$\Rightarrow \begin{bmatrix} 9 & -5 \\ 0 & 4 \end{bmatrix} + a\begin{bmatrix} 3 & -1 \\ 0 & 2 \end{bmatrix} + b\begin{bmatrix} 1 & 0 \\ 0 & 1 \end{bmatrix} = \begin{bmatrix} 0 & 0 \\ 0 & 0 \end{bmatrix}$$

$$-5 - a = 0$$

$$\Rightarrow \quad a = -5$$

$$4 + 2a + b = 0$$

$\Rightarrow 4 - 10 + b = 0 \Rightarrow b = 6$

So, $t^2 + at + b = 0$ takes the form

$$t^2 - 5t + 6 = 0 \quad \ldots\text{(i)}$$

and α, β are the roots of Eq. (i).

$\therefore \alpha = 2$ and $\beta = 3$

Now, $\frac{1}{\alpha^2 - 3\alpha + 4} + \frac{1}{\beta^2 - 3\beta + 4}$

$$= \frac{1}{2} + \frac{1}{4} = \frac{3}{4}$$

6. (c) Let $B = A^{100} - 2A^{99} - A^{98}$

$$B = A^{98}(A^2 - 2A - I)$$

$$|B| = |A|^{98}|A^2 - 2A - I|$$

Now, $A = \begin{bmatrix} -4 & -1 \\ 3 & 1 \end{bmatrix}$

$$\therefore A^2 - 2A - I = \begin{bmatrix} 13 & 3 \\ -9 & -2 \end{bmatrix} + \begin{bmatrix} 8 & 2 \\ -6 & -2 \end{bmatrix} + \begin{bmatrix} -1 & 0 \\ 0 & -1 \end{bmatrix}$$

$$= \begin{bmatrix} 20 & 5 \\ -15 & -5 \end{bmatrix}$$

$$\Rightarrow |A^2 - 2A - I| = \begin{vmatrix} 20 & 5 \\ -15 & -5 \end{vmatrix} = -25$$

and $\quad |A| = \begin{vmatrix} -4 & -1 \\ 3 & 1 \end{vmatrix} = -1$

Hence, $|B| = (-1)^{98}(-25)$

$$|B| = -25$$

7. (c) Given, $A=\begin{bmatrix}0&1\\1&0\end{bmatrix}$

Then, $A^2=A\cdot A=\begin{bmatrix}0&1\\1&0\end{bmatrix}\begin{bmatrix}0&1\\1&0\end{bmatrix}=\begin{bmatrix}1&0\\0&1\end{bmatrix}=I$

$A^3=A^2\cdot A=\begin{bmatrix}1&0\\0&1\end{bmatrix}\begin{bmatrix}0&1\\1&0\end{bmatrix}=\begin{bmatrix}0&1\\1&0\end{bmatrix}=A$

i.e. $A^3=A$

Similarly, $A^4=I, A^5=A, A^6=I, A^7=A$ and so on.

Now, $\sum_{r=1}^{2017}A^r=(A^1+A^2+A^3+A^4+A^5+A^6+\ldots+A^{2016}+A^{2017})$

$=(A+I+A+I+A+I+\ldots+I+A)$

$=\underbrace{(A+A+A+\ldots+A)}_{1009}+\underbrace{(I+I+I+\ldots+I)}_{1008}$

$=1009A+1008I$

$=\begin{bmatrix}0&1009\\1009&0\end{bmatrix}+\begin{bmatrix}1008&0\\0&1008\end{bmatrix}$

$=\begin{bmatrix}1008&1009\\1009&1008\end{bmatrix}$

$\therefore |B|=(1008)^2-(1009)^2$

$=(1008+1009)(1008-1009)$

$=(2017)(-1)=-2017$

8. (b) Given, $A=\text{diag}(d_1,d_2,d_3,d_4)$

$=\begin{bmatrix}d_1&0&0&0\\0&d_2&0&0\\0&0&d_3&0\\0&0&0&d_4\end{bmatrix}$

$\therefore\ \det\cdot(A)=d_1\cdot d_2\cdot d_3\cdot d_4$

Given, $d_1,d_2,d_3,d_4>0$

Now, using AM $\geq$ GM

$\Rightarrow \dfrac{d_1+2d_2+4d_3+8d_4}{4}\geq(d_1\cdot 2d_2\cdot 4d_3\cdot 8d_4)^{1/4}$

$\Rightarrow \dfrac{16}{4}\geq 2^{3/2}(d_1\cdot d_2\cdot d_3\cdot d_4)^{1/4}$

$\Rightarrow d_1\cdot d_2\cdot d_3\cdot d_4\leq 4$

$\Rightarrow |A|\in(0,4]$

$(\because d_1,d_2,d_3,d_4>0, \therefore d_1d_2d_3d_4>0)$

Now, $f(x)=\log_{(\tan x+\cot x)}|A|$,

$x\in(0,\pi/2)=\dfrac{\ln|A|}{\ln(\tan x+\cot x)}$

Since, we know that

$\tan x+\cot x\geq 2, \forall x\in(0,\pi/2)$

$\therefore f(x)$ will be maximum, when numerator is maximum and denominator is minimum.

Hence, $[f(x)]_{\max}=\dfrac{\log_e 4}{\log_e 2}=\log_2 4=2.$

9. (b) Given,

$$\begin{vmatrix}0&x^2-a&x^3-b\\x^2+a&0&x^2+c\\x^4+b&x-c&0\end{vmatrix}=0 \quad \ldots(i)$$

By substitution method, if we put $x=0$ in LHS of Eq. (i), then the given determinant reduces to the determinant of skew-symmetric matrix of odd order (3×3) which is always zero.

So, $x=0$ is the solution of the given equation.

10. (a) Let $\Delta=\begin{vmatrix}x&a&a&a\\a&x&a&a\\a&a&x&a\\a&a&a&x\end{vmatrix}$

Applying $C_1\to C_1+C_2+C_3+C_4$ and taking $(x+3a)$ common from C_1, we get

$\Delta=(x+3a)\begin{vmatrix}1&a&a&a\\1&x&a&a\\1&a&x&a\\1&a&a&x\end{vmatrix}$

Applying $R_2\to R_2-R_1, R_3\to R_3-R_1$ and $R_4\to R_4-R_1$, we get

$\Delta=(x+3a)\begin{vmatrix}1&a&a&a\\0&x-a&0&0\\0&0&x-a&0\\0&0&0&x-a\end{vmatrix}$

$\Rightarrow \quad \Delta=(x+3a)(x-a)^3 \quad \ldots(i)$

(Expanding along C_1)

Given, $\Delta=(x+3a)\cdot f(x) \quad \ldots(ii)$

From Eqs. (i) and (ii), we get

$f(x)=(x-a)^3$

So, $f(3a)-f(a)=(2a)^3-(0)^3=8a^3$

11. (b) $f'(x)=\begin{vmatrix}1&x^4+1&3\\1&2x^4+2&3\\1&3x^4+7&3\end{vmatrix}+\begin{vmatrix}(x+a^2)&4x^3&3\\(x+b^2)&8x^3&3\\(x+c^2)&12x^3&3\end{vmatrix}+0$

$\Rightarrow f'(x)=0+12x^3\begin{vmatrix}(x+a^2)&1&1\\(x+b^2)&2&1\\(x+c^2)&3&1\end{vmatrix}$

$=12x^3\begin{vmatrix}(x+a^2)&1&1\\(x+b^2)&2&1\\(x+c^2)&3&1\end{vmatrix}$

$=12x^3\begin{vmatrix}(x+a^2)&1&1\\(x+b^2)-(x+a^2)&1&0\\(x+c^2)-(x+b^2)&1&0\end{vmatrix}$

[Applying $R_2\to R_2-R_1, R_3\to R_3-R_2$]

$\Rightarrow f'(x)=12x^3[b^2-a^2+b^2-c^2]=0$

$\because x\neq0\Rightarrow 2b^2=a^2+c^2$

$\therefore a^2,b^2,c^2$ are in AP.

12. (d) If $n\in N$, then $n^2<n^2+n<(n+1)^2$

$\Rightarrow \quad n<\sqrt{n^2+n}<n+1$

$\Rightarrow[\sqrt{n^2+n}]=n$, where $[\cdot]=$ GIF

Similarly, $[\sqrt{(x+1)^2+(x+1)}]$

$=(x+1), \forall x\in N.$

$\therefore \quad f(x)=(x+1)^2+x-(x+1)^2$

$=x, \forall x\in N.$

Thus, $\Delta=\begin{vmatrix}a&a^2&a\\b&b^2&b\\c&c^2&c\end{vmatrix}=0 (\because C_1\equiv C_3)$

13. (d) Let

$$\Delta(x)=\begin{vmatrix}x-1&2x^2-5&x^3-1\\2x^2+5&2x+2&x^3+3\\x^3-1&x+1&3x^2-2\end{vmatrix} \ldots(i)$$

According to problem,

$\Delta(x)=(x^2-1)\cdot p(x)+(ax+b)$

$\therefore \Delta(1)=a+b$ and $\Delta(-1)=-a+b \ldots(ii)$

From Eq. (i), we get

$\Delta(1)=\begin{vmatrix}0&-3&0\\7&4&4\\0&2&1\end{vmatrix}=-(-3)(7-0)=21$

$\Delta(-1)=\begin{vmatrix}-2&-3&2\\7&0&2\\-2&0&1\end{vmatrix}=3(7+4)=33$

So, $a+b=21$ and $-a+b=33$

[from Eq. (ii)]

We get $a=-6$ and $b=27$

$\therefore 4a+2b=-24+54=30$

Hence, 30 is divisible by 3 and 5 both.

14. (a) Given,

$$f(x)=\begin{vmatrix} 2\cos^2 x & \sin 2x & \sin x \\ \sin 2x & 2\sin^2 x & -\cos x \\ \sin x & -\cos x & 0 \end{vmatrix}$$

Applying, $C_1 \to 2\sin x \cdot C_3 + C_1$, we get

$$f(x)=\begin{vmatrix} 2(\cos^2 x+\sin^2 x) & \sin 2x & \sin x \\ 2\sin x\cos x - 2\sin x\cos x & 2\sin^2 x & -\cos x \\ \sin x & -\cos x & 0 \end{vmatrix}$$

$$\Rightarrow f(x)=\begin{vmatrix} 2 & \sin 2x & \sin x \\ 0 & 2\sin^2 x & -\cos x \\ \sin x & -\cos x & 0 \end{vmatrix}$$

Now, applying $C_2 \to C_2 - (2\cos x)C_3$, we get

$$f(x)=\begin{vmatrix} 2 & 0 & \sin x \\ 0 & 2 & \cos x \\ \sin x & -\cos x & 0 \end{vmatrix}$$

$$=-2\cos^2 x - 2\sin^2 x = -2$$

$\therefore f'(x)=0$

Now, $\int_0^{\pi/2} \{f'(x)+f(x)\}\,dx$

$$=\int_0^{\pi/2} -2\,dx = (-2)\frac{\pi}{2} = -\pi$$

15. (b) Given that, $AA'=2I$

$\Rightarrow \quad |AA'|=|2I|=2^3|I|$

$\Rightarrow \quad |A|^2=8\times 1 \ (\because |A|=|A'|)$

$\Rightarrow \quad |A|^2=8$

and $A^{-1}=A'-A\cdot \text{adj}(2B^{-1})$

$\Rightarrow AA^{-1}=AA'-A\cdot A\cdot \text{adj}(2B^{-1})$

$\Rightarrow \quad I=AA'-A^2\cdot \text{adj}(2B^{-1})$

$\Rightarrow \quad I=2I-A^2\cdot \text{adj}(2B^{-1})$

$\Rightarrow \quad A^2\cdot \text{adj}(2B^{-1})=I$

$\Rightarrow |A^2|\cdot|\text{adj}(2B^{-1})|=1$

$\Rightarrow \quad 8|2B^{-1}|^2=1$

$\Rightarrow \quad 8\times\dfrac{64}{|B|^2}=1$

$\Rightarrow \quad |B|^2=64\times 8$

$\therefore \quad |B|=\pm 16\sqrt{2}$

16. (d) $\begin{vmatrix} 3 & a & bc \\ 3 & b & ac \\ 3 & c & ab \end{vmatrix}=\begin{vmatrix} 1 & a & 3bc \\ 1 & b & 3ac \\ 1 & c & 3ab \end{vmatrix}$

Now, according to the question

$a^2-4bc=0$

$\Rightarrow \quad a^2-bc-3bc=0$

$\Rightarrow \quad a^2-bc=3bc$

and $\quad b^2-4ac=0$

$\Rightarrow \quad b^2-ac-3ac=0$

$\Rightarrow \quad b^2-ac=3ac$

and $\quad c^2-4ab=0$

$\Rightarrow \quad c^2-ab-3ab=0$

$\Rightarrow \quad c^2-ab=3ab$

Now, $\begin{vmatrix} 1 & a & a^2-bc \\ 1 & b & b^2-ac \\ 1 & c & c^2-ab \end{vmatrix}$

Also, $\begin{vmatrix} 1 & a & \frac{3}{4}a^2 \\ 1 & b & \frac{3}{4}b^2 \\ 1 & c & \frac{3}{4}c^2 \end{vmatrix}$

$$=\frac{3}{4}(a-b)(b-c)(c-a)$$

$\left[\because a^2-4bc=0 \Rightarrow a^2=4bc \Rightarrow \dfrac{a^2}{4}=bc\right.$

$\Rightarrow \dfrac{3}{4}a^2=3bc$, similarly $\dfrac{3}{4}b^2=3ac$

$\left.\text{and } \dfrac{3}{4}c^2=3ab\right]$

17. (b) For a homogeneous system, we have $\Delta_x=\Delta_y=\Delta_z=0$

Now, for system of equation to have non-zero solution.

Then, $\Delta=\begin{vmatrix} a & b & c \\ b & c & a \\ c & a & b \end{vmatrix}$

$=-(a^3+b^3+c^3-3abc)$

$=0$

$\Rightarrow (a+b+c)[(a-b)^2+(b-c)^2+(c-a)^2]=0$

As, $a+b+c\neq 0$, then $(a-b)^2+(b-c)^2+(c-a)^2=0$.

Then, $a=b=c$

[$\because$ If sum of non-negative term is equal to zero, then each term being equal to zero]

So, $at^2+bt+c=a(t^2+t+1)=0$

Now, discriminant $(D)=1-4=-3<0$.

$\therefore$ Roots of given equation are imaginary.

18. (d) The given system of equations written in matrix form $AX=B$

$$|A|=\begin{vmatrix} 1 & 1 & 1 \\ 1 & 2 & 3 \\ 1 & 4 & 7 \end{vmatrix}$$

$=1(14-12)-1(7-3)+1(4-2)=0$

So, equation has no solution or infinite number of solutions.

Now, decide about this we have to find $(\text{adj}A)B$.

Let C be the matrix of co-factors of elements in $|A|$

such that $C=\begin{bmatrix} C_{11} & C_{12} & C_{13} \\ C_{21} & C_{22} & C_{23} \\ C_{31} & C_{32} & C_{33} \end{bmatrix}$

Now, $C_{11}=2, C_{12}=-4, C_{13}=2,$
$C_{21}=-3, C_{22}=6, C_{23}=-3,$
$C_{31}=1, C_{32}=-2, C_{33}=1,$
where $C_{ij}=(-1)^{i+j}M_{ij}$

$$\text{adj}A=C'=\begin{bmatrix} 2 & -4 & 2 \\ -3 & 6 & -3 \\ 1 & -2 & 1 \end{bmatrix}'$$

$$=\begin{bmatrix} 2 & -3 & 1 \\ -4 & 6 & -2 \\ 2 & -3 & 1 \end{bmatrix}$$

Then, $(\text{adj}A)B=\begin{bmatrix} 2 & -3 & 1 \\ -4 & 6 & -2 \\ 2 & -3 & 1 \end{bmatrix}\begin{bmatrix} 6 \\ 14 \\ 30 \end{bmatrix}$

$$=\begin{bmatrix} 0 \\ 0 \\ 0 \end{bmatrix}=0$$

So, system of equations is consistent and has an infinite number of solutions.

Let us taken any two of the given equations, say (i) and (ii) i.e., $x+y+z=6$ and $x+2y+3z=14$.

Substitute $z=k$, where $k\in R$

$x+y=6-k$

and $\quad x+2y=14-3k$

On solving, we get $x=k-2$, $y=8-2k$ and $z=k$, where $k\in R$.

19. (c) Let $\Delta=\begin{vmatrix} \alpha & 1 & 1 \\ 1 & \alpha & 1 \\ 1 & 1 & \alpha \end{vmatrix}$

Using $C_1 \to C_1+C_2+C_3$, we get

$$\Delta=(\alpha+2)\begin{vmatrix} 1 & 1 & 1 \\ 1 & \alpha & 1 \\ 1 & 1 & \alpha \end{vmatrix}$$

$$=(\alpha+2)\begin{vmatrix} 1 & 1 & 1 \\ 0 & \alpha-1 & 0 \\ 0 & 0 & \alpha-1 \end{vmatrix}$$

(using $R_2 \to R_2 - R_1$ and $R_3 \to R_3 - R_1$)

$\Rightarrow \quad \Delta = (\alpha + 2)(\alpha - 1)^2$

Now, $\Delta = 0 \Rightarrow \alpha = -2, 1$

(For no solution)

For $\alpha = 1$, the system of equation has infinite number of solution.

For $\alpha = -2$, on adding the three equation, we get $0 = -9$

Thus, system of equations has no solution for $\alpha = -2$

20. (a) Since, α_1, α_2 and β_1, β_2 are the roots of $ax^2 + bx + c = 0$ and $px^2 + qx + r = 0$, respectively.

So, $\alpha_1 + \alpha_2 = \frac{-b}{a}, \alpha_1\alpha_2 = \frac{c}{a}$ and

$\beta_1 + \beta_2 = \frac{-q}{p}, \beta_1\beta_2 = \frac{r}{p}$

Since, the given system of equations has a non-trivial solution.

So, $\begin{vmatrix} \alpha_1 & \alpha_2 \\ \beta_1 & \beta_2 \end{vmatrix} = 0$

$\Rightarrow \quad \alpha_1\beta_2 = \alpha_2\beta_1$

$\Rightarrow \quad \frac{\alpha_1}{\beta_1} = \frac{\alpha_2}{\beta_2} = \frac{\alpha_1 + \alpha_2}{\beta_1 + \beta_2} = \sqrt{\frac{\alpha_1\alpha_2}{\beta_1\beta_2}}$

$\Rightarrow \quad \frac{pb}{qa} = \sqrt{\frac{pc}{ra}}$

$\Rightarrow \quad \frac{b^2}{q^2} = \frac{ac}{pr}$

21. (6) As given,

$BC = \begin{bmatrix} 3 & 4 \\ 2 & 3 \end{bmatrix}\begin{bmatrix} 3 & -4 \\ -2 & 3 \end{bmatrix}$

$= \begin{bmatrix} 1 & 0 \\ 0 & 1 \end{bmatrix} = I$

$\therefore tr(A) + tr\left(\frac{ABC}{2}\right) + tr\left(\frac{A(BC)^2}{4}\right) + tr\left(\frac{A(BC)^3}{8}\right) + \dots \infty$

$= tr(A) + tr\left(\frac{A}{2}\right) + tr\left(\frac{A}{2^2}\right) + tr\left(\frac{A}{2^3}\right) + \dots \infty$

$= tr(A) + \frac{1}{2}tr(A) + \frac{1}{2^2}tr(A) + \frac{1}{2^3}tr(A) + \dots \infty$

$= \left(\frac{1}{1 - \frac{1}{2}}\right) tr(A) = 2 \cdot tr(A) = 2 \cdot (2 + 1) = 6$

22. (8) $A(\text{adj} A) = |A| I_3$

$\Rightarrow k = |A| = 2(\sin^6 x + \cos^6 x)$

$\qquad - 3(\sin^4 x + \cos^4 x)$

$= 2(1 - 3\sin^2 x \cdot \cos^2 x)$

$\qquad - 3(1 - 2\sin^2 x \cdot \cos^2 x)$

$\Rightarrow k = -1$

$\therefore \quad k + 9 = -1 + 9 = 8$

23. (2) If A is a square matrix of order $n \times n$, then $|\text{adj} A| = |A|^{n-1}$

Here, $n = 3, |A| = 6$

and $\text{adj} A = \begin{bmatrix} 1 & -2 & 4 \\ 4 & 1 & 1 \\ -1 & P & 0 \end{bmatrix}$

$\therefore \quad |\text{adj} A| = \begin{vmatrix} 1 & -2 & 4 \\ 4 & 1 & 1 \\ -1 & P & 0 \end{vmatrix} = 6^2$

$6 + 15P = 36$

$\Rightarrow \quad P = 2$

24. (0) Given, determinant can be written as

$\Delta = \begin{vmatrix} 0 & \sin x - \cos x & \log(\tan x) \\ -(\sin x - \cos x) & 0 & -\log(\tan x) \\ -\log(\tan x) & \log(\tan x) & 0 \end{vmatrix}$

Above determinant is the determinant of a skew-symmetric matrix of odd order.

Hence, the value of $\Delta = 0$.

25. (8) $\sum_{n=1}^{k} U_n = \begin{vmatrix} \sum_{n=1}^{k} 1 & k & k \\ 2 \cdot \sum_{n=1}^{k} n & k^2 + k + 1 & k^2 + k \\ 2 \cdot \sum_{n=1}^{k} n - \sum_{n=1}^{k} 1 & k^2 & k^2 + k + 1 \end{vmatrix}$

$= \begin{vmatrix} k & k & k \\ k(k+1) & k^2 + k + 1 & k^2 + k \\ k^2 & k^2 & k^2 + k + 1 \end{vmatrix}$

Applying $C_2 \to C_2 - C_1$, we get

$\Rightarrow \sum_{n=1}^{k} U_n = \begin{vmatrix} k & 0 & k \\ k^2 + k & 1 & k^2 + k \\ k^2 & 0 & k^2 + k + 1 \end{vmatrix}$

$\Rightarrow \sum_{n=1}^{k} U_n = k(k^2 + k + 1) - k^3$

$= k(k + 1) = 72 \qquad \text{(given)}$

$\therefore \quad k = 8$

26. (2) Given,

$\begin{vmatrix} 3^2 + k & 4^2 & 3^2 + 3 + k \\ 4^2 + k & 5^2 & 4^2 + 4 + k \\ 5^2 + k & 6^2 & 5^2 + 5 + k \end{vmatrix} = 0$

Applying $C_3 \to C_3 - C_1$, we get

$\begin{vmatrix} 3^2 + k & 4^2 & 3 \\ 4^2 + k & 5^2 & 4 \\ 5^2 + k & 6^2 & 5 \end{vmatrix} = 0$

Applying $R_2 \to R_2 - R_1$ and $R_3 \to R_3 - R_1$, then

$\begin{vmatrix} 9 + k & 16 & 3 \\ 7 & 9 & 1 \\ 16 & 20 & 2 \end{vmatrix} = 0$

$\Rightarrow (9 + k)(18 - 20) - 16(14 - 16) + 3(140 - 144) = 0$

$\Rightarrow -18 - 2k + 32 - 12 = 0$

$\Rightarrow \quad k = 1$

Now, $\sqrt{2^k \cdot \sqrt{2^k \cdot \sqrt{2^k \dots \infty}}}$

$= (2^k)^{\frac{1}{2} + \frac{1}{4} + \frac{1}{8} + \dots \infty} = (2^k)^{\frac{\frac{1}{2}}{1 - \frac{1}{2}}}$

$= (2^k)^1 = 2^1 \qquad (\because k = 1)$

$= 2$

27. (8) Given, $\Delta = \begin{vmatrix} e^{2iA} & e^{-iC} & e^{-iB} \\ e^{-iC} & e^{2iB} & e^{-iA} \\ e^{-iB} & e^{-iA} & e^{2iC} \end{vmatrix}$

Taking e^{iA}, common from R_1, e^{iB} from R_2 and e^{iC} from R_3, we get

$\Delta = e^{i(A+B+C)} \cdot \Delta_1$, where,

$\Delta_1 = \begin{vmatrix} e^{iA} & e^{-i(A+C)} & e^{-i(A+B)} \\ e^{-i(B+C)} & e^{iB} & e^{-i(A+B)} \\ e^{-i(B+C)} & e^{-i(A+C)} & e^{iC} \end{vmatrix}$

But $A + B + C = \pi$, so that $e^{i(A+B+C)}$

$= e^{i\pi} = \cos\pi + i\sin\pi = -1$

Also, $A + C = \pi - B$

$\Rightarrow e^{-i(A+C)} = e^{-\pi i} \cdot e^{iB} = -e^{iB}$

Hence, $\Delta_1 = \begin{vmatrix} e^{iA} & -e^{iB} & -e^{iC} \\ -e^{iA} & e^{iB} & -e^{iC} \\ -e^{iA} & -e^{iB} & e^{iC} \end{vmatrix}$

$= e^{i(A+B+C)} \begin{vmatrix} 1 & -1 & -1 \\ -1 & 1 & -1 \\ -1 & -1 & 1 \end{vmatrix}$

Applying $C_1 \to C_1 + C_2$, we get

$$\Delta_1=(-1)\cdot\begin{vmatrix}0&-1&-1\\0&1&-1\\-2&-1&1\end{vmatrix}$$

$$=(-1)\cdot(-2)\cdot(2)=4$$

So, $\Delta=(-1)\cdot\Delta_1=-4$

Hence, $4-\Delta=4-(-4)=8$

28. (2021) Given, the system has a non-trivial solution.

So, $\begin{vmatrix}\lambda&\sin\alpha&\cos\alpha\\1&\cos\alpha&\sin\alpha\\-1&\sin\alpha&-\cos\alpha\end{vmatrix}=0$

$\Rightarrow \lambda(-\cos^2\alpha-\sin^2\alpha)$

$-(-\sin\alpha\cdot\cos\alpha-\sin\alpha\cdot\cos\alpha)$

$-(\sin^2\alpha-\cos^2\alpha)=0$

$\Rightarrow -\lambda+\sin2\alpha+\cos2\alpha=0$

$\Rightarrow \lambda=\sin2\alpha+\cos2\alpha$

$\Rightarrow \lambda=\sqrt{2}\cos(2\alpha-\pi/4)$

$\because -1\le\cos(2\alpha-\pi/4)\le1, \forall\alpha\in R.$

So, $-\sqrt{2}\le\lambda\le\sqrt{2}$ i.e., $\lambda\in[-\sqrt{2},\sqrt{2}]$

Hence, $2021\left(\frac{u^2}{v^2}\right)=2021\times\frac{2}{2}=2021$

29. (2) Since, given system is consistent, then $\Delta=\Delta_x=\Delta_y=0$.

So, $\Delta_z=0$ (for system to be consistent)

$\Rightarrow \begin{vmatrix}\cos\theta&\sin\theta&\cos\theta\\\sin\theta&\cos\theta&\sin\theta\\\cos\theta&\sin\theta&-\cos\theta\end{vmatrix}=0$

$\Rightarrow -\cos\theta-\sin\theta(-2\sin\theta\cdot\cos\theta)+\cos\theta(-\cos2\theta)=0$

$\Rightarrow -\cos\theta-\cos3\theta=0$

$\Rightarrow 2\cos\theta\cdot\cos2\theta=0$, where $\theta\in[0,2\pi]$

$\Rightarrow \cos\theta=0$ or $\cos2\theta=0$

$\therefore \theta=\frac{\pi}{4},\frac{\pi}{2},\frac{3\pi}{4},\frac{5\pi}{4},\frac{6\pi}{4},\frac{7\pi}{4}$

But at $\theta=\frac{\pi}{4},\frac{3\pi}{4},\frac{5\pi}{4},\frac{7\pi}{4}$

(Rejected), lines are parallel. So, system is inconsistent.

For, $\theta=\frac{\pi}{2},\frac{3\pi}{2}$ system is consistent.

Hence, total number of possible values of $\theta=2$.

30. (1) For non-zero (non-trivial solution)

$|A|=0$

So, $\begin{vmatrix}(k-1)&(3k+1)&2k\\(k-1)&(4k-2)&(k+3)\\2&(3k+1)&3(k-1)\end{vmatrix}=0$

$\Rightarrow\begin{vmatrix}(k-1)&(3k+1)&2k\\0&(k-3)&(-k+3)\\2&(3k+1)&3(k-1)\end{vmatrix}=0$

(using $R_2\to R_2-R_1$)

$\Rightarrow(k-3)\begin{vmatrix}k-1&3k+1&2k\\0&1&-1\\2&3k+1&3k-3\end{vmatrix}=0$

(Taking $(k-3)$ common from R_2)

$\Rightarrow(k-3)\begin{vmatrix}k-1&5k+1&2k\\0&0&-1\\2&6k-2&3k-3\end{vmatrix}=0$

(using $C_2\to C_2+C_3$)

$\Rightarrow 2(k-3)[(k-1)(3k-1)-(5k-1)]=0$

$\Rightarrow \quad 2(k-3)(3k^2-9k)=0$

$\Rightarrow \quad 2(k-3)3(k)(k-3)=0$

$\Rightarrow \quad k=0,3$

But $\quad k\in N$

$\therefore \quad k=3$

Hence, total number of value of $k=1$.

Qualifier 4
(Permutation-combination and Probability)

1. (d) Here, given number 6 is not prime number.

So, first convert that as product of primes.

$6=2\times3$. So, now we will find out the highest powers of 2 and 3.

To find highest power of 2 in 200!.

2	200	
2	100	1st quotient
2	50	2nd quotient
2	25	3rd quotient
2	12	4th quotient
2	6	5th quotient
2	3	6th quotient
	1	last quotient

So, highest power of 2 in 200! is $100+50+25+12+6+3+1=197$.

Similarly, highest power of 3 in 200! is

3	200	
3	66	1st quotient
3	22	2nd quotient
3	7	3rd quotient
	2	last quotient

So, highest power of 3 in 200! is $66+22+7+2=97$.

So, 200! contains $(2)^{197}$ and $(3)^{97}$ or it contains 97 pairs of 2 and 3.

Hence, required power is $(6)^{97}$ as directly. We can say that, smaller in between the two power is the required answer.

2. (b) Since, $n\cdot{}^nP_n=n(n!)=(n+1)!-n!$

Hence, ${}^1P_1=2!-1!$

$2\cdot{}^2P_2=3!-2!$

$3\cdot{}^3P_3=4!-3!$

$\vdots$

$n\cdot{}^nP_n=(n+1)!-n!$

Adding,

${}^1P_1+2\cdot{}^2P_2+3\cdot{}^3P_3+\ldots+n\cdot{}^nP_n=(n+1)!-1!$

3. (b) There are five odd and 4 even positions. Five odd positions can be filled with A, E, E, E, O in $\frac{5!}{3!}$ ways and four even positions can be filled with D, N, N, L in $\frac{4!}{2!}$ ways.

$\therefore$ Required number of permutations

$$=\frac{5!}{3!}\times\frac{4!}{2!}$$

$$=2\times5!$$

4. (d) In 'ALGEBRA' word, 7 letters comprising 3 vowels that includes 2 A's and 4 distinct consonants. Vowels can occupy only even places means only at 2nd, 4th and 8th places. This can be done in (3!)/(2!) $=3$ ways and 4 consonants can be arranged in (4!) ways.

So, total number of ways of such words $=3(4!)=72$

5. (d) In dictionary, the first word will start with *CC* and the number of words that starts with *CC* is $4!=24$, then number of words that starts with *CE* is $4!=24$. Then, we will get CIC and number of words is $3!=6$. Similarly, number of words that starts with *CIE* is $3!=6$. Number of words that starts with CIL is $3!=6$.

Then, next word will be CIRCEL and finally, we will get CIRCLE.

Hence, rank of CIRCLE is 68.

6. (b) Let M_1 and W_1 always sit together.

Number of ways to sit 8 men around the table $=7!$

W_1 can be sit in 2 ways and rows of 7 women can sit in 7! ways.

Hence, rearranged numbers $= 7! \times 2 \times 7! = 2 \times (7!)^2$.

7. (c)

$$\sum_{r=0}^{n}\left(\frac{r+2}{r+1}\right).^{n}C_r = \sum_{r=0}^{n}\left(\frac{r+1+1}{r+1}\right).^{n}C_r$$

$$= \sum_{r=0}^{n} {}^nC_r + \sum_{r=0}^{n} \frac{{}^nC_r}{r+1}$$

$$= 2^n + \sum_{r=0}^{n} \frac{{}^nC_r}{r+1} = 2^n + \frac{2^{n+1}-1}{n+1}$$

$$= \frac{2^n(n+3)-1}{n+1}$$

$\Rightarrow \quad n = 13$

$\therefore n + 3 = 13 + 3 = 16$

8. (b) Clearly, required number of ways.

= Total number of ways in which 5 balls of different colors can be distributed among 3 persons

– Number of ways in which atleast one person gets no ball

$= 3^5 - ({}^3C_1 \times 2^5 - {}^3C_2 \times 1^5)$

$= 243 - (96 - 3) = 150$

9. (d)

[2 | 1 | 1 | 2] $= ({}^3C_2 \cdot 1 \cdot 1\,{}^3C_2)6! = 6480$

[1 | 1 | 1 | 3] $= ({}^3C_1 \cdot 1 \cdot 1 \cdot 1)6! = 2160$

[3 | 1 | 1 | 1] $= (1 \cdot 1 \cdot 1\,{}^3C_1)6! = 2160$

Total = 10800

10. (a) After arranging 8 blue caps, 1 gap for 2 green caps can be selected in ${}^9C_1$ ways.

For the remaining 5 green caps, 5 gaps can be selected from 8 gaps in ${}^8C_5$ ways.

Hence, total number of ways

$= {}^9C_1 \times {}^8C_5$

$$= 9 \times \frac{8 \times 7 \times 6}{1 \times 2 \times 3} = 72 \times 7 = 504$$

11. (d) Total number of balls is 30 and number of balls that are either white or black or green is $11 + 7 + 5 = 23$

So, required probability $= 23/30$

12. (d) We know that

$P(A \cup B) = P(A) + P(B) - P(A \cap B)$

Let $P(A) = x$, then the equation is

$$\frac{13}{16} = x + 3x - 3x^2 = 4x - 3x^2$$

$\Rightarrow \quad 64x - 48x^2 = 13$

$\Rightarrow 48x^2 - 64x + 13 = 0$

$$\Rightarrow x = \frac{64 \pm \sqrt{(64)^2 - 4 \times 48 \times 13}}{2 \times 48}$$

$$= \frac{64 \pm 40}{96}$$

$\Rightarrow x = 24/96 = 1/4$

(ignoring the value more than 1).

13. (a) Since, $P(A \cup B \cup C)$

$= P(A) + P(B) + P(C) - P(A \cap B)$

$- P(B \cap C) - P(C \cap A) + P(A \cap B \cap C)$

$\Rightarrow P(A \cup B \cup C) = 0.3 + 0.4 + 0.8$

$- (0.08 + 0.28 + P(B \cap C)) + 0.09$

$= 1.23 - P(B \cap C)$

$\Rightarrow P(B \cap C) = 1.23 - P(A \cup B \cup C)$

But we know that,

$0 \le P(A \cup B \cup C) \le 1$

and given, $P(A \cup B \cup C) \ge 0.75$

So, $0.75 \le P(A \cup B \cup C) \le 1$

Hence, $0.23 \le P(B \cap C) \le 0.48$.

14. (b) $P(\bar{A} \cup \bar{B}) = \frac{3}{4}$

$\Rightarrow \quad P(\overline{A \cap B}) = \frac{3}{4}$

$\Rightarrow \quad P(A \cap B) = 1 - \frac{3}{4} = \frac{1}{4}$

$P(\bar{A} \cap \bar{B}) = \frac{1}{4}$

$\Rightarrow \quad P(\overline{A \cup B}) = \frac{1}{4}$

$\Rightarrow \quad P(A \cup B) = 1 - \frac{1}{4} = \frac{3}{4}$

$P(A) = \frac{1}{3}$

$\therefore \quad P(\bar{A}) = 1 - \frac{1}{3} = \frac{2}{3}$

Now, $P(\bar{A} \cap B) = P(B) - P(A \cap B)$

Also, $P(A \cup B) = P(A) + P(B) - P(A \cap B)$

$\Rightarrow \quad \frac{3}{4} = \frac{1}{3} + P(B) - \frac{1}{4}$

$\Rightarrow \quad P(B) = \frac{3}{4} - \frac{1}{12} = \frac{2}{3}$

$\therefore P(\bar{A} \cap B) = \frac{2}{3} - \frac{1}{4} = \frac{5}{12}$

15. (b) From the given information

$P(R) = 2/5$ and $P(R') = 1 - 2/5 = 3/5$

and $P(T) = 3/4$ and

$P(T') = 1 - 3/4 = 1/4$

Now, we have two cases:

Case I : Razi (R) cracked the exam and Tauseef (T) failed to crack, then

Probability is

$P(R) \times P(T') = 2/5 \times 1/4 = 1/10$

Case II : Tauseef (T) cracked the exam and Razi (R) failed to crack, then

Probability is $P(R') \times P(T) = 3/5 \times 3/4$

$= 9/20$

Hence, required probability

$= 1/10 + 9/20 = 11/20$

16. (a) Let E_i denote the event that A_i dies in a year.

Then, $P(E_i) = p$ and $P(E'_i) = 1 - p$ for $i = 1, 2, 3, \ldots, n$

Now, P(none of $A_1, A_2, A_3, \ldots, A_n$ dies in a year)

$= P(E'_1 \cap E'_2 \cap E'_3 \cap \ldots \cap E'_n)$

$= P(E'_1) \cdot P(E'_2) \cdot P(E'_3) \ldots P(E'_n)$

$= (1 - p)^n$

Since, $E_1, E_2, \ldots, E_n$ are independent.

Let E denote the event that atleast one of $A_1, A_2, A_3, \ldots A_n$ dies in a year.

Then,

$P(E) = 1 - P(E'_1 \cap E'_2 \cap E'_3 \cap \ldots \cap E'_n)$

$= 1 - (1 - p)^n$

Let F denote the event A_1 is the first to die. Then, $P(F/E) = 1/n$

Also, $P(E \cap F) = P(E) \cdot P(F/E)$

$= \frac{1}{n}[1 - (1 - p)^n]$

17. (a)

A_1 : White ball is drawn from bag 1.

A_2 : Red ball is drawn from bag 1.

B : 2 balls are drawn from bag 2 and found to be red.

$P(B) = P(A_1) \cdot P(B/A_1) + P(A_2) \cdot P(B/A_2)$

$$\Rightarrow P(A_1/B) = \frac{\frac{3}{5} \cdot \frac{{}^5C_2}{{}^{10}C_2}}{\frac{3}{5} \cdot \frac{{}^5C_2}{{}^{10}C_2} + \frac{2}{5} \cdot \frac{{}^6C_2}{{}^{10}C_2}}$$

$= \frac{1}{2} > \frac{1}{4}$

18. (a) Let A, B and C be the events that the transistor chosen is manufactured by the companies A, B and C, respectively.

Let E = event that the transistor is of excellent quality.

Now, $P(A)=\frac{18}{50}, P(B)=\frac{20}{50}, P(C)=\frac{12}{50}$

Also, $P(E/A)=0.9, P(E/B)=0.6, P(E/C)=0.9$

$\therefore P(E)=P(A)\cdot P(E/A)+P(B)\cdot P(E/B)+P(C)\cdot P(E/C)$

$=\frac{18}{50}\times 0.9+\frac{20}{50}\times 0.6+\frac{12}{50}\times 0.9$

$=\frac{39}{50}$

$\therefore$Required probability

$=P(B/E)$

$=\frac{P(B)\cdot P(E/B)}{P(E)}$

$=\frac{\frac{20}{50}\times 0.6}{\frac{39}{50}}=\frac{4}{13}$

19. (b) We have,

$E(x)=np=2$ and $\text{var}(x)=npq=1$

So, $q=\frac{1}{2}$ or $p=\frac{1}{2}$ and $n=4$

Thus, $P(x\geq 1)=1-P(x=0)$

$=1-{}^4C_0\left(\frac{1}{2}\right)^4$

$=1-\frac{1}{16}=\frac{15}{16}$

20. (b) Mean $=np$ and variance $=npq$, where $p+q=1$.

Given, $np-npq=1$ ...(i)

and $(np)^2-(npq)^2=11$

$\Rightarrow (np-npq)(np+npq)=11$

$\Rightarrow 1(np+npq)=11$ [from Eq. (i)]

$\Rightarrow \quad np+npq=11$ ...(ii)

On solving Eqs. (i) and (ii), we get

$np=6$ and $npq=5$.

$\therefore q=5/6, p=1/6$ and $n=36$

Hence, p(success for exactly 3 times)

$={}^nC_3p^3q^3$

$={}^{36}C_3\left(\frac{1}{6}\right)^3\left(\frac{5}{6}\right)^3$

21. (77) We have to form 7 digit number using the digit 1, 2 and 3 only such that sum of the digits 10.

This can be done in 2, 2, 2, 1, 1, 1, 1 or 2, 3, 1, 1, 1, 1, 1 ways

$\therefore$ Total number of ways $=\frac{7!}{3!4!}+\frac{7!}{5!}$

$=35+42=77$

22. (8) Required number of ways

$=(4!)-$ (Number of ways in which a and b are together)

$-$ (Number of ways in which c and d are together)

$+$ (Number of ways in which a and b are together and c and d are together)

$=4!-3!2!-3!2!+2!2!2!=8$

23. (176) Since, work can be completed by 3 men or by 5 women.

Case I : When work is completed by men

Then, the number of ways of selecting work-force (number of ways of selecting 3 men out of 10 men) is ${}^{10}C_3=\frac{10!}{7!3!}=120.$

Case II : When work is completed by women

Then, the number of ways of selecting work-force (number of ways of selecting 5 women out of 8 women) is ${}^8C_5=\frac{8!}{5!3!}=56.$

Now, from fundamental principle of addition, total number of ways is equal to $(120+56)=176$ ways.

24. (1170) Here we have following cases

Cases	Number of points from 6 collinear points	Number of points from other 9 points	Total number of ways
I.	0(in ${}^6C_0=1$ way)	4(in ${}^9C_4=126$ ways)	$1\times 126=126$
II.	1(in ${}^6C_1=6$ ways)	3(in ${}^9C_3=84$ ways)	$6\times 84=504$
III	2(in ${}^6C_2=15$ ways)	2(in ${}^9C_2=36$ ways)	$15\times 36=540$

Total number of ways $=126+504+540$

$=1170$

25. (7) Let the number of contestants is 'n', then a particular voter can give 1 or 2 or 3 or ...... $(n-1)$ votes.

So, number of ways a voter can vote is

${}^nC_1+{}^nC_2+{}^nC_3+\ldots+{}^nC_{n-1}$

Since, ${}^nC_0+{}^nC_1+{}^nC_2+{}^nC_3+\ldots+{}^nC_{n-1}+{}^nC_n=2^n$.

Hence, ${}^nC_1+{}^nC_2+{}^nC_3+\ldots+{}^nC_{n-1}$

$=2^n-{}^nC_0-{}^nC_n=2^n-2=126$ [given]

Thus, $n=7$.

26. (9) Given equation is

$y=x^2+2(a+4)x-5a+64$ ...(i)

As we know that; $y=ax^2+bx+c$ lies completely above X-axis, if leading coefficient (i.e., coefficient of x^2) $a>0$ and discriminant $(D)=b^2-4ac<0$.

So, $4(a+4)^2-4(1)(64-5a)<0$ [from Eq. (i)] (as $1>0$)

$\Rightarrow \quad a^2+16+8a-64+5a<0$

$\Rightarrow \quad a^2+13a-48<0$

$\Rightarrow \quad (a+16)(a-3)<0\Rightarrow -16<a<3$

$\therefore a=-5,-4,-3,-2,-1,0,1,2$ because $a\in[-5,30]$

Here, $n(A)=8$ and $n(S)=36$.

$\therefore \quad P(A)=\frac{n(A)}{n(S)}=\frac{8}{36}=\frac{2}{9}$

$\therefore \quad k=9$

27. (3) Let W denote the event of drawing a white ball at any draw and B that for a black ball. Then,

$P(W)=\frac{a}{a+b}$ and $P(B)=\frac{b}{a+b}$

P(A wins the game) $=P(W$ or BBW or $BBBBW$ or ......)

$=P(W)+P(BBW)+P(BBBBW)+\ldots$

$= P(W) + P(B)\,P(B)\,P(W) + P(B)\,P(B)\,P(B)\,P(B)\cdot P(W) + \ldots$

$= P(W) + P(W)\cdot(P(B))^2 + P(W)(P(B))^4 + \ldots$

$= \dfrac{P(W)}{1-(P(B))^2}$ (using GP series)

$= \dfrac{a(a+b)}{a^2+2ab} = \dfrac{a+b}{a+2b}$

Also, $P(B$ wins the game$)$

$= 1 - \dfrac{a+b}{a+2b} = \dfrac{b}{a+2b}$

According to the given condition,

$\dfrac{a+b}{a+2b} = 3\cdot\dfrac{b}{a+2b}$

$\Rightarrow \quad a = 2b$

$\Rightarrow \quad a : b = 2:1$

So, $\lambda = 2, k = 1$

$\therefore \lambda + k = 2 + 1 = 3$

28. (9) Let $A_1 =$ The toss result in a head.

$A_2 =$ The toss result in a tail.

$E =$ Noted number is 7 or 8.

$P(E) = P(A_1)\cdot P(E/A_1) + P(A_2)\cdot P(E/A_2)$

$= \dfrac{1}{2}\times\dfrac{11}{36} + \dfrac{1}{2}\times\dfrac{2}{11}$

$= \dfrac{193}{792}$

Now, $\dfrac{P}{792} = \dfrac{193}{792}$

$\therefore \quad P = 193$

Hence, tens digit is 9.

29. (5) Let E be the event that a red face appears in each of the first n throws.

A_1 : Die A is used when head has already fallen.

A_2 : Die B is used when tail has already fallen.

Now, $P(E/A_1) = \left(\dfrac{2}{3}\right)^n$ and

$P(E/A_2) = \left(\dfrac{1}{3}\right)^n$.

As per given condition in question,

$\dfrac{P(A_1)\cdot P(E/A_1)}{P(A_1)\cdot P(E/A_1) + P(A_2)\cdot P(E/A_2)} = \dfrac{32}{33}$

$\Rightarrow \dfrac{\frac{1}{2}\times\left(\frac{2}{3}\right)^n}{\frac{1}{2}\times\left(\frac{2}{3}\right)^n + \frac{1}{2}\times\left(\frac{1}{3}\right)^n} = \dfrac{32}{33}$

$\Rightarrow \quad \dfrac{2^n}{2^n+1} = \dfrac{32}{33}$

$\Rightarrow \quad n = 5$

30. (64) To get atleast 3 marks, atleast 4 answers must be right.

Now, $n = 5, p = \dfrac{1}{4}, q = \dfrac{3}{4}$

$[\because p + q = 1]$

$r = 4$ or 5

$P(r \ge 4) = {}^5C_4\left(\dfrac{1}{4}\right)^4\left(\dfrac{3}{4}\right) + {}^5C_5\left(\dfrac{1}{4}\right)^5$

$= 5\times\dfrac{1}{256}\times\dfrac{3}{4} + \dfrac{1}{4^5}$

$= \dfrac{16}{4\times 256} = \dfrac{1}{64}$

$\therefore \quad k = 64$

Qualifier 5 (Binomial Theorem and Mathematical Induction)

1. (c) Given, ${}^{n-1}C_r = (\lambda^2 - 3)\cdot{}^nC_{r+1}$

$\Rightarrow \lambda^2 - 3 = \dfrac{{}^{n-1}C_r}{{}^nC_{r+1}} = \dfrac{r+1}{n}$ ...(i)

But, $0 \le r \le n-1$

$\Rightarrow \quad 1 \le r+1 \le n$

$\Rightarrow \quad \dfrac{1}{n} \le \dfrac{r+1}{n} \le 1$ (as $n > 0$)

$\Rightarrow \quad \dfrac{1}{n} \le \lambda^2 - 3 \le 1$

$\Rightarrow \quad 3 + \dfrac{1}{n} \le \lambda^2 \le 4$

or $\quad 3 < \lambda^2 \le 4$ $(\because n \ge 2)$

$\therefore \quad \lambda \in [-2, \sqrt{3}) \cup (\sqrt{3}, 2]$

According to given option, option (c) is subset of our result.

2. (d) Given, $a_1^2 = 2a_2$ ...(i)

$(1 - 2x + 5x^2 + 10x^3)(1+x)^n$

$= a_0 + a_1x + a_2x^2 + a_3x^3 + \ldots$

On comparing coefficients, we get,

$a_0 = 1$ (constant term) ...(ii)

$n - 2 = a_1$ (coefficient of x) ...(iii)

$5 + {}^nC_2 - 2n = a_2$ ...(iv)

(coefficient of x^2)

From Eq. (i),

$(n-2)^2 = 2a_2$

$\Rightarrow \quad a_2 = \dfrac{(n-2)^2}{2}$ [from Eq. (iii)]

From Eq. (iv),

$5 + \dfrac{n!}{2!\,n-2!} - 2n = \dfrac{(n-2)^2}{2}$

$\Rightarrow 5 + \dfrac{n(n-1)}{2} - 2n = \dfrac{(n-2)^2}{2}$

$\Rightarrow 10 + n^2 - n - 4n = n^2 + 4 - 4n$

$\Rightarrow \quad n = 10 - 4 \Rightarrow n = 6$

$\therefore \quad a_0 + n = 1 + 6 = 7$

3. (d) $T_2 = {}^5C_1\left(\dfrac{1}{x}\right)^4\cdot x\tan x = \dfrac{5\tan x}{x^3}$

$T_4 = {}^5C_3\left(\dfrac{1}{x}\right)^2\cdot x^3\tan^3 x = 10x\tan^3 x$

Now, $\dfrac{T_4}{T_2} = 2x^4\tan^2 x = \dfrac{2\pi^4}{27}$

$\Rightarrow x^4\tan^2 x = \left(\dfrac{\pi}{3}\right)^4\cdot(3)$

$\Rightarrow x^4\tan^2 x = \left(\dfrac{\pi}{3}\right)^4(\sqrt{3})^2$

$\therefore \quad x = \dfrac{\pi}{3}$

4. (c) Given binomial is $\left(x\sin\theta + \dfrac{\cos\theta}{x}\right)^{10}$.

General term

$= T_{r+1} = {}^{10}C_r(x\sin\theta)^{10-r}\cdot\left(\dfrac{\cos\theta}{x}\right)^r$

$= {}^{10}C_r(\sin\theta)^{10-r}(\cos\theta)^r\cdot(x)^{10-2r}$

For term to be independent of x, we put $10 - 2r = 0 \Rightarrow r = 5$

$\therefore T_{5+1} = T_6 =$ Independent term of $x = {}^{10}C_5(\sin\theta)^5\cdot(\cos\theta)^5$

$= \dfrac{{}^{10}C_5\cdot(\sin 2\theta)^5}{2^5}$

Hence, greatest value $= \dfrac{{}^{10}C_5}{2^5}$

[$\because$ maximum value of $\sin 2\theta = 1$]

5. (c) $\dfrac{(1-x^2)^{106}}{x^{106}} = \left(\dfrac{1}{x} - x\right)^{106}$

Now, general term

$= T_{r+1} = {}^{106}C_r\cdot\left(\dfrac{1}{x}\right)^{106-r}\cdot(-x)^r$

$= {}^{106}C_r\cdot(-1)^r\cdot(x)^{106-2r}$

For term to be independent of x put $106 - 2r = 0 \Rightarrow r = 53$

$\therefore \quad T_{r+1} = T_{53+1} = T_{54}$

$=$ Independent term of x.

$\therefore$ Total number of terms dependent of $x = 107 - 1 = 106$

6. (b) $(1-x+x^2)^n = a_0 - a_1x + a_2x^2 - a_3x^3 + \ldots + a_{2n}x^{2n}$ ...(i)

$(1+x)^n = {}^nC_0 + {}^nC_1x + {}^nC_2x^2 + {}^nC_3x^3 + \ldots + {}^nC_nx^n$ ...(ii)

On multiplying Eqs. (i) by (ii) and collecting coefficient of x^{3r}, we get

$$\sum_{k=0}^{3r}(-1)^k \cdot a_k \cdot {}^nC_{3r-k} = {}^nC_r$$

7. (b) $[(1+x)(2+x)(3+x)]^{10}$

$(2+x)(3+x)^2 = (1+x)^{10}(2+x)^{11}(3+x)^{12}$

$= (x^{10} + {}^{10}C_1x^9 + \ldots)(x^{11} + {}^{11}C_1x^{10}(2) + \ldots)(x^{12} + {}^{12}C_1x^{11}(3) + \ldots)$

$\therefore$ Coefficient of $x^{32} = (12)(3) + (11)(2) + (10) = 68$

8. (d) $[(1+\lambda)(\mu+1)(\lambda+\mu)]^n$

$= (1+\lambda)^n(\mu+1)^n(\lambda+\mu)^n$

$$= \sum_{r=0}^{n} C_r\lambda^r \sum_{s=0}^{n} C_s\mu^{n-s}\sum_{t=0}^{n} C_t\lambda^{n-t}\mu^t$$

Since, C_0^3 is the coefficient of $\lambda^0\mu^{n-0}\lambda^{n-0}\mu^0$

i.e. $\lambda^n\mu^n (r=s=t=0)$ etc.

Now, $C_1{}^3$ is the coefficient of $\lambda'\mu^{n-1}\lambda^{n-1}\mu'$ i.e. $\lambda^n\mu^n(r=s=t=1)$ etc.

and C_k^3 is the coefficient of $\lambda^k\mu^{n-k}\lambda^{n-k}\mu^k$

i.e. $\lambda^n\mu^n(r=s=t=k)$

Hence, the coefficient of $\lambda^n\mu^n$ in $(1+\lambda)^n(\mu+1)^n(\lambda+\mu)^n =$

$$C_0^3 + C_1^3 + C_2^3 + C_3^3 + \ldots + C_n^3 = \sum_{r=0}^{n} C_r^3$$

9. (c) We have,

In the expansion of $(1+\alpha x)^4$

Middle term $= {}^4C_2(\alpha x)^2 = 6\alpha^2x^2$

In the expansion of $(1-\alpha x)^6$;

Middle term $= {}^6C_3(-\alpha x)^3 = -20\alpha^3x^3$

$\therefore$ Coefficient of middle term in $(1+\alpha x)^4$ = coefficients of middle term in $(1-\alpha x)^6$

$\Rightarrow \quad 6\alpha^2 = -20\alpha^3$

$\Rightarrow \quad \alpha = 0, -\dfrac{3}{10}$

Hence, option (c) is correct.

10. (a) $a = {}^{2n-1}C_{n-1} + {}^{2n-1}C_n = {}^{2n}C_n$

$b = {}^{2n}C_n$

Hence, $a = b$

11. (b) Given, $2({}^2C_2 + {}^3C_2 + {}^4C_2 + \ldots + {}^nC_2) + {}^{n+1}C_2$

$= 2({}^3C_3 + {}^3C_2 + {}^4C_2 + \ldots + {}^nC_2) + {}^{n+1}C_2$ $\quad [\because {}^2C_2 = {}^3C_3]$

$= 2\cdot({}^{n+1}C_3) + {}^{n+1}C_2$

$$= \frac{(n+1)(n)(n-1)}{3} + \frac{(n+1)(n)}{2}$$

$$= (n)(n+1)\left[\frac{n-1}{3} + \frac{1}{2}\right]$$

$$= \frac{n(n+1)(2n+1)}{6} = \sum_{r=1}^{n} r^2$$

12. (a) Given, ${}^{31}C_5 - {}^{30}C_4 - {}^{29}C_4 - {}^{28}C_4 - \ldots - {}^nC_4 = 1$ ...(i)

As we know that,

${}^nC_r + {}^nC_{r-1} = {}^{n+1}C_r$

$\Rightarrow {}^{n+1}C_r - {}^nC_{r-1} = {}^nC_r$ ...(ii)

So, ${}^{31}C_5 - {}^{30}C_4 = {}^{30}C_5$ [from Eq. (ii)]

$\Rightarrow {}^{30}C_5 - {}^{29}C_4 = {}^{29}C_5$

$\Rightarrow {}^{29}C_5 - {}^{28}C_4 = {}^{28}C_5$

$\Rightarrow {}^{28}C_5 - {}^{27}C_4 = {}^{27}C_5$

and so on

From Eq. (i); ${}^nC_5 = 1$

$\Rightarrow n = 5$ [using above result in Eq. (i)]

13. (a) ${}^{505}C_5 - 5\cdot{}^{404}C_5 + 10\cdot{}^{303}C_5 - 10\cdot{}^{202}C_5 + 5\cdot{}^{101}C_5 - 1 + 1$

= Coefficient of x^5 in $(1+x)^{505} - 5(1+x)^{404} + 10(1+x)^{303} - 10(1+x)^{202} + 5(1+x)^{101} - 1 + 1$

= coefficient of x^5 in $[(1+x)^{101} - 1]^5 + 1$

$= ({}^{101}C_1)^5 = (101)^5$

14. (b) $S = \displaystyle\sum_{r=0}^{n}(-1)^r \cdot \frac{{}^nC_r}{(r+1)^2}$

$$= \frac{1}{n+1}\sum_{r=0}^{n}(-1)^r \cdot \frac{{}^{n+1}C_{r+1}}{r+1}$$

$$= \frac{1}{(n+1)}\left[\sum_{r=0}^{n}\frac{(-1)^r\cdot{}^nC_r}{n+1} + \sum_{r=0}^{n-1}\frac{(-1)^r\cdot{}^nC_{r+1}}{r+1}\right]$$

$$= \frac{1}{(n+1)}\left[\frac{1}{(n+1)} + \sum_{r=0}^{n-1}\frac{(-1)^r\cdot{}^{n-1}C_r}{r+1} + \sum_{r=0}^{n-2}\frac{(-1)^r\cdot{}^{n-1}C_{r+1}}{r+1}\right]$$

$$= \frac{1}{(n+1)}\left[\frac{1}{n+1} + \frac{1}{n} + \sum_{r=0}^{n-2}\frac{(-1)^r\cdot{}^{n-2}C_r}{r+1} + \sum_{r=0}^{n-3}\frac{(-1)^r\cdot{}^{n-2}C_{r+1}}{r+1}\right]$$

$$= \frac{1}{(n+1)}\left[\frac{1}{n+1} + \frac{1}{n} + \frac{1}{n-1} + \ldots + \frac{1}{4} + \frac{1}{3} + \frac{1}{2} + 1\right]$$

$$= \frac{1}{n+1}\left[1 + \frac{1}{2} + \frac{1}{3} + \ldots + \frac{1}{n+1}\right]$$

Alternate method

$$(1-x)^n = \sum_{r=0}^{n}(-1)^r\cdot{}^nC_r\cdot x^r$$

$$\frac{1-(1-x)^{n+1}}{x(n+1)} = \sum_{r=0}^{n}\frac{(-1)^r\cdot{}^nC_r\cdot x^r}{r+1}$$

$$\Rightarrow \frac{1}{n+1}\int_0^1\left[\frac{1-(1-x)^{n+1}}{1-(1-x)}\right]dx = \sum_{r=0}^{n}\frac{(-1)^r\cdot{}^nC_r}{(r+1)^2}$$

$$= \frac{1}{n+1}\int_0^1\frac{1-x^{n+1}}{1-x}\,dx$$

$$= \frac{1}{n+1}\int_0^1(1+x+x^2+\ldots+x^n)\,dx$$

$$= \frac{1}{n+1}\left(1+\frac{1}{2}+\frac{1}{3}+\frac{1}{4}+\ldots+\frac{1}{n}+\frac{1}{n+1}\right)$$

15. (a) Since,

$(1+\omega)^{100} = {}^{100}C_0 + {}^{100}C_1\omega + {}^{100}C_2\omega^2 + {}^{100}C_3\omega^3 + {}^{100}C_4\omega^4 + \ldots$

$\because \; 1+\omega+\omega^2 = 0$

$\Rightarrow \quad 1+\omega = -\omega^2$

Now, $(-\omega^2)^{100} = ({}^{100}C_1 + {}^{100}C_3 + \ldots) - \dfrac{1}{2}({}^{100}C_1 + {}^{100}C_2 + \ldots) + \dfrac{i\sqrt{3}}{2}({}^{100}C_1 - {}^{100}C_2 - \ldots)$

$\Rightarrow (-\omega^2)^{100} = a - \dfrac{1}{2}b + \dfrac{i\sqrt{3}}{2}c$

(as given in question)

So,

$$|(-\omega^2)^{100}| = \sqrt{\left(a - \frac{1}{2}b\right)^2 + \left(\frac{\sqrt{3}}{2}c\right)^2}$$

$$\Rightarrow \quad 1 = \left(a - \frac{b}{2}\right)^2 + \frac{3}{4}c^2$$

16. (b) Let $P(n): a_n = \sqrt{7+\sqrt{7+\sqrt{7+\dots}}}$ (n radical signs)

Step I. : For $n=1$

$P(1): a_1 = \sqrt{7} < 4$

Step II : Assume that,

$a_k < 4 \; \forall \; n \in N, n = k$

Step III : For $n = k+1$

$P(k+1): a_{k+1} = \sqrt{7+\sqrt{7+\sqrt{7+\dots}}}$ [$(k+1)$ radical signs]

$= \sqrt{7+a_k} < \sqrt{7+4}$

$(\because a_k < 4) < 4$ (by assumption)

This is shows that, $a_{k+1} < 4$, i.e. the result is true for $n = k+1$

Hence, by principle of mathematical induction, $a_n < 4, \forall \; n \geq 1$

17. (b) $P(n): 2^{3n} - 7n - 1$

$P(1): 2^3 - 7 - 1 = 8 - 7 - 1 = 0$

$P(2): 2^6 - 7(2) - 1 = 64 - 14 - 1 = 49$

which is divisible by 49.

Let $P(k): 2^{3k} - 7k - 1 = 49\,m$

$\therefore P(k+1) = 2^{3k+3} - 7(k+1) - 1 = 49\lambda$

LHS of $P(k+1) = 2^{3k+3} - 7(k+1) - 1$

$= (2^{3k})(2^3) - 7k - 7 - 1$

$= (49m + 7k + 1)(8) - 7k - 8$ (assuming $P(k)$ to be true)

$= 49(8m) + 56k + 8 - 7k - 8$

$= 49(8m + k) = 49\lambda$

Thus, $P(k+1)$ is divisible by 49 whenever $P(k)$ is divisible by 49.

Hence, $P(n)$ is divisible by 49 for all $n \in N$.

18. (d) Let $P(n): 3(5^{2n+1}) + 2^{3n+1}$

$P(1): 3(5)^3 + 2^4 = 3(125) + 16 = 375 + 16 = 391 = 17(23)$

So, $P(1)$ is divisible by 17.

Let $P(k): 3(5^{2k+1}) + 2^{2k+1} = 17m$

$\therefore P(k+1): 3(5^{2k+3}) + 2^{3k+4} = 17\lambda$

LHS of $P(k+1) = 3(5^{2k+3}) + 2^{3k+4}$

$= 3(5^{2k+1})(5^2) + (2^{3k+1})(2^3)$

$= (17m - 2^{3k+1})(25) + 8(2^{3k+1})$ (assuming $P(k)$ to be true).

$= 17(25m) - 25(2^{3k+1}) + 8(2^{3k+1})$

$= 17(25m) - 17(2^{3k+1}) = 17$

$(25m - 2^{3k+1}) = 17\lambda$

Thus, $P(k+1)$ is divisible by 17 whenever $P(k)$ is divisible by 17.

Hence, $P(n)$ is divisible by 17 for all $n \in N$.

19. (a) Let $P(n): 10^n + 3 \cdot 4^{n+2} + 5$

$P(1): 10 + 192 + 5 = 207$, which is divisible by 3

$P(2): 100 + 3(256) + 5$

$= 105 + 768 = 873$, which is divisible by 3

So, $P(n): 10^n + 3 \cdot 4^{n+2} + 5$ is divisible by 3.

20. (d) Let $f(n) = p^{n+1} + (p+1)^{2n-1}$

For $n = 1$, $f(1) = p^2 + p + 1$, which is divisible by $p^2 + p + 1$.

Assume that the result is true for $n = k$, i.e. $(p^2 + p + 1) \mid f(k)$

Now, we have to prove the result is true for $n = k+1$

$f(k+1) = p^{k+2} + (p+1)^{2k+1} = p^{k+1} \cdot p + (p+1)^{2k-1} \cdot (p+1)^2$

$= p^{k+1} \cdot p + (p+1)^{2k-1} \cdot (p^2 + p + 1)$

$= p[p^{k+1} + (p+1)^{2k-1}] + (p^2 + p + 1) \cdot (p+1)^{2k-1}$

$= pf(k) + (p^2 + p + 1)(p+1)^{2k-1}$

Since, $(p^2 + p + 1) \mid f(k)$

Therefore, $(p^2 + p + 1) \mid f(k+1)$

Hence, by principle of mathematical induction, $(p^2 + p + 1) \mid f(n) \; \forall \; n \in N$.

21. (16) $T_{r+1} = {}^6C_r \cdot (2x)^{6-r} \cdot \dfrac{1}{(2x)^r}$

$= {}^6C_r \cdot (2)^{6-2r} (x)^{6-2r}$

If $6 - 2r = 2$

$\Rightarrow r = 2$ and if $6 - 2r = -2$

$\Rightarrow r = 4$

Coefficient of $x^{-2} = {}^6C_2 \cdot 2^2 = 60$

Coefficient of $x^2 = {}^6C_4 \cdot \dfrac{1}{2^2} = \dfrac{15}{4}$

According to the question,

Coefficient of $x^2 = \lambda$ coefficient of x^{-2}

$\Rightarrow \quad 60 = (\lambda)\left(\dfrac{15}{4}\right)$

$\therefore \quad \lambda = 16$

22. (3) Given binomial $= \left(x^\lambda + \dfrac{1}{x^2}\right)^{25}$

Now, $T_{r+1} = {}^{25}C_r (x^\lambda)^{25-r} \left(\dfrac{1}{x^{2r}}\right)$

Given coefficient $= 2300$

i.e. ${}^{25}C_r = 2300 \Rightarrow r = 3$ or 22

When $r = 3$

Putting $22\lambda - 6 = 60$ = exponent of x

$\Rightarrow \lambda = 3$

When $r = 22$

Putting $3\lambda - 44 = 60$ = index of x

$\Rightarrow \lambda = \dfrac{104}{3}$ (Not possible)

Hence, $\lambda = 3$

23. (400) Given expression

$= \left(1 - \dfrac{1}{x} + 3x^5\right)\left(2x^2 - \dfrac{1}{x}\right)^8$

General term in

$\left(2x^2 - \dfrac{1}{x}\right)^8 = {}^8C_r \cdot (2x^2)^{8-r} \left(\dfrac{1}{x}\right)^r$

$= {}^8C_r \cdot (2)^{8-r} \cdot (x)^{16-3r}$

Put $16 - 3r = 0 \Rightarrow r = \dfrac{16}{3}$ which is not possible.

and $\quad 16 - 3r = 1 \Rightarrow r = 5$

and $\quad 16 - 3r = -5$

$\Rightarrow \quad r = 7$

$\therefore$ Term independent of $x = -{}^8C_5 \cdot 2^3(-1)^5 + 3 \cdot {}^8C_7 \cdot 2(-1)^7$

$= 56 \times 8 - 48 = 448 - 48 = 400$

24. (21) $T_{r+1} = {}^9C_r \left(\dfrac{x^2}{2}\right)^{9-r} \left(-\dfrac{1}{x}\right)^r$

$= {}^9C_r \dfrac{x^{18-3r}}{2^{9-r}} (-1)^r$

$18 - 3r = 0$

$\Rightarrow \quad r = 6$

Hence, the term independent of

$x = \dfrac{{}^9C_6}{2^3} = \dfrac{9 \times 8 \times 7}{6 \times 8} = \dfrac{21}{2} = k$ (given)

$\therefore 2k = 2 \times \dfrac{21}{2} = 21$

25. (4) $T_{r+1} = {}^{18}C_r \cdot 2^{\left(\frac{18-r}{2}\right)} \cdot 3^{\frac{r}{3}}$

For rational term,

$r = 0, 3, 6, 9, 12, 15, 18$ (r should be a multiple of 3)

Also, n should be even because $\dfrac{18-r}{2} \in I$

$\therefore r = 0, 6, 12, 18$

Hence, total number of rational terms $= 4$

26. (41) Given binomial is $(\sqrt{2} + 3^{\frac{1}{5}})^{10}$

$T_{r+1} = {}^{10}C_r \cdot 2^{\frac{10-r}{2}} \cdot 3^{\frac{r}{5}}$

T_{r+1} is rational for $r = 0, 10$

$\therefore$ Sum of rational terms $= {}^{10}C_0 2^5 + {}^{10}C_{10} 3^2 = 41$

27. (2) $|T_{r+1}| > |T_r|$

$$\Rightarrow {}^{10}C_r 2^{10-r}\left(\frac{3}{8}|x|\right)^r > {}^{10}C_{r-1} 2^{11-r}\left(\frac{3}{8}|x|\right)^{r-1}$$

$$\Rightarrow \left(\frac{11-r}{r}\right)\left(\frac{3}{8}|x|\right) > 2$$

$$\Rightarrow \quad |x| > \frac{16r}{3(11-r)} \quad \text{...(i)}$$

Also, $|T_{r+1}| > |T_{r+2}|$

$$\Rightarrow \quad |x| < \frac{16(r+1)}{3(10-r)} \quad \text{...(ii)}$$

[similarly as in Eq. (i)]

From Eqs. (i) and (ii), we get

$2 < |x| < \frac{64}{21}$ (Putting $r = 3$, according to the question)

$$\Rightarrow x \in \left(-\frac{64}{21}, -2\right) \cup \left(2, \frac{64}{21}\right)$$

$$\Rightarrow x \in (-3.0476, -2) \cup (2, 3.0476)$$

$\therefore$ Integral values of $x = -3, 3$

Hence, number of integral values of $x = 2$

28. (2) Given binomial is $\left(\frac{1}{x} + x\sin x\right)^{10}$

$$\text{Middle term} = {}^{10}C_5\left(\frac{1}{x}\right)^5 (x\sin x)^5 = \frac{63}{8}$$

$$\Rightarrow \frac{10 \times 9 \times 8 \times 7 \times 6}{120} \times (\sin x)^5 = \frac{63}{8}$$

$$\Rightarrow \quad (\sin x)^5 = \frac{1}{2^5} \Rightarrow \sin x = \frac{1}{2}$$

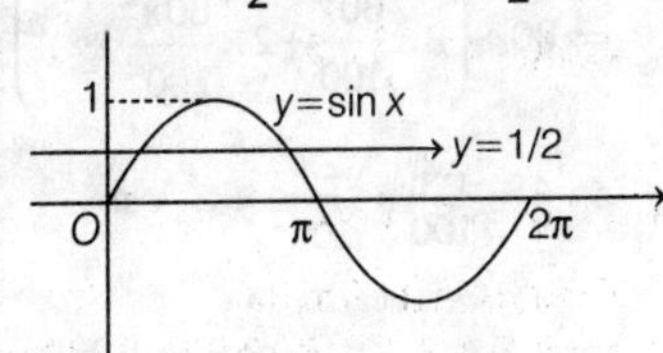

Hence, total number of values of $x = 2$ in $[0, 2\pi]$.

29. (24) Let $f(n) = 2 \cdot 7^n + 3 \cdot 5^n - 5$

For $n = 1$, we have,

$$f(1): 2 \cdot 7^1 + 3 \cdot 5^1 - 5 = 24$$

Therefore, $24 \mid f(1)$

Assume that $24 \mid f(k)$, then

$$f(k+1) = 2 \cdot 7^{k+1} + 3 \cdot 5^{k+1} - 5$$
$$= 2 \cdot 7^k \cdot 7 + 3 \cdot 5^k \cdot 5 - 5$$
$$= 7(2 \cdot 7^k + 3 \cdot 5^k - 5) - 6 \cdot 5^k + 30$$
$$= 7f(k) - 30(5^{k-1} - 1)$$

For $k = 1$, $5^{k-1} - 1 = 0$ and for $k \ge 2$

$$5^{k-1} - 1 = (5-1)(5^{k-2} + 5^{k-3} + \ldots + 5 + 1)$$
$$= 4(5^{k-2} + 5^{k-3} + \ldots + 5 + 1) = 4m$$

(say)

Where, m is some positive integer depending on k.

Thus, $f(k+1) = 7f(k) - 120m$

By induction assumption, $24 \mid f(k)$.

Also, $24 \mid 120\,m$.

Therefore, $24 \mid f(k+1)$

Thus shows that the result is true for $n = k + 1$

Hence by principle of mathematical induction, the result in true for all positive integers n.

30. (24) Let $f(n) = n(n^2 - 1)$

For $n = 1$, $f(1) = 0$, which is clearly divisible by 24.

Assume that, $24 \mid f(2k-1)$ for some $k \in N$, we have

$$f(2k+1) = (2k+1)[(2k+1)^2 - 1]$$
$$= (2k+1)(2k)(2k+2)$$
$$= (2k)(2k - 1 + 2)(2k - 2 + 4)$$
$$= (2k)[(2k-1)(2k-2) + 4k - 4 + 8k - 4 + 8]$$
$$= (2k)[(2k-1)(2k-2) + 12k]$$
$$= (2k-1)(2k)(2k-2) + 24k^2$$
$$= (2k-1)[(2k-1)^2 - 1] + 24k^2 = f(2k-1) + 24k^2$$

Since, $24 \mid f(2k-1)$, it follows that $24 \mid f(2k+1)$

Thus, by principle of mathematical induction.

$24 \mid n(n^2 - 1)$ for all odd positive integers.

Qualifier 6
(Sequence and Series)

1. (a) Let a = first term of AP and d = common difference

According to question,

$$a + (a + 4d) = 26$$
$$\Rightarrow \quad a + 2d = 13$$
$$\Rightarrow \quad a = 13 - 2d \quad \text{...(i)}$$
$$(a+d)(a+3d) = 160$$
$$\Rightarrow (13-d)(13+d) = 160 \quad \text{[from Eq. (i)]}$$
$$\Rightarrow \quad d^2 - 169 = -160$$
$$\Rightarrow \quad d^2 = 9$$
$$\Rightarrow \quad d = \pm 3$$

So, $a = 7$ or 19

$$\therefore \quad S_6 = \frac{6}{2}(14 + 15) \text{ or } \frac{6}{2}(38 - 15)$$
$$\Rightarrow \quad S_6 = 3 \times 29 \text{ or } 3 \times 23$$
$$\Rightarrow \quad S_6 = 87 \text{ or } 69$$

2. (d) Since,

$3^{2\sin 2\alpha - 1}$, 14 and $3^{4 - 2\sin 2\alpha}$ are in AP.

$$\therefore 2 \times 14 = 3^{2\sin 2\alpha - 1} + 3^{4 - 2\sin 2\alpha}$$

$$\Rightarrow \quad 28 = \frac{a}{3} + \frac{3^4}{a}, \text{ where } a = 3^{2\sin 2\alpha}$$

$$\Rightarrow a^2 - 84a + 243 = 0$$
$$\Rightarrow (a - 81)(a - 3) = 10$$
$$\Rightarrow \quad a = 81, a = 3$$
$$\Rightarrow \quad 3^{2\sin 2\alpha} = 3^4 \text{ or } 3^{2\sin 2\alpha} = 3$$
$$\Rightarrow \quad 2\sin 2\alpha = 1 \quad [\because 2\sin 2\alpha \ne 4]$$
$$\Rightarrow \quad \sin 2\alpha = \frac{1}{2} \Rightarrow 2\alpha = \frac{\pi}{6}$$

Thus, the first three terms of the AP are 1, 14, 27.

Hence, its fifth term is 53.

3. (a) The given numbers are AP.

So,

$$2\log_4(2^{1-x} + 1) = \log_2(5 \times 2^x + 1) + 1$$

$$\Rightarrow 2\log_{2^2}\left(\frac{2}{2^x} + 1\right) = \log_2(5 \times 2^x + 1) + \log_2 2$$

$$\Rightarrow \frac{2}{2}\log_2\left(\frac{2}{2^x} + 1\right) = \log_2(5 \times 2^x + 1)2$$

$$\Rightarrow \quad \log_2\left(\frac{2}{2^x} + 1\right) = \log_2(10 \times 2^x + 2)$$

$$\Rightarrow \quad \frac{2}{2^x} + 1 = 10 \times 2^x + 2$$

$$\Rightarrow \quad \frac{2}{y} + 1 = 10y + 2, \text{ where } 2^x = y$$

$$\Rightarrow \quad 10y^2 + y - 2 = 0$$
$$\Rightarrow \quad (5y - 2)(2y + 1) = 0$$
$$\Rightarrow \quad y = \frac{2}{5}, \frac{-1}{2}$$
$$\Rightarrow \quad 2^x = \frac{2}{5} \text{ or } 2^x = \frac{-1}{2}$$

[rejected because $2^x > 0, \forall x \in R$]

$$\Rightarrow \quad x = \log_2(2/5)$$
$$\Rightarrow \quad x = \log_2 2 - \log_2 5$$
$$\Rightarrow \quad x = 1 - \log_2 5$$

4. (b) If the ratio of the sums of n terms two arithmetic progression is given, then the ratio of their nth terms is obtained by replacing n by $(2n - 1)$ in the ratio of the sums of n terms.

Here, we have

Ratio of the sums of n terms

$$=\frac{3n+8}{7n+15}$$

$\therefore$ Ratio of nth terms

$$=\frac{3(2n-1)+8}{7(2n-1)+15}=\frac{6n+5}{14n+8}$$

$\Rightarrow$ Ratio of 12th terms

$$=\frac{6\times12+5}{14\times12+8}$$

$$=\frac{77}{176}=\frac{7}{16}$$

5. (b) We have, $a_n=S_n-S_{n-1}$ ...(i)

and $a_{n-1}=S_{n-1}-S_{n-2}$ ...(ii)

$\therefore\quad d=a_n-a_{n-1}=(S_n-S_{n-1})-(S_{n-1}-S_{n-2})$

[from Eqs. (i) and (ii)]

$\Rightarrow\quad d=S_n-2S_{n-1}+S_{n-2}$

Hence, $\lambda=2$

6. (b) $f(x)=\begin{vmatrix} x+\alpha & x+\beta & x+\alpha-\gamma \\ x+\beta & x+\gamma & x-1 \\ x+\gamma & x+\delta & x-\beta+\delta \end{vmatrix}$

Applying $R_1\to R_1+R_3-2R_2$, we get

$$f(x)=\begin{vmatrix} \alpha+\gamma-2\beta & \beta+\delta-2\gamma & \alpha-\gamma+(-\beta+\delta)+2 \\ x+\beta & x+\gamma & x-1 \\ x+\gamma & x+\delta & x-\beta+\delta \end{vmatrix}$$

$$=\begin{vmatrix} 0 & 0 & 2 \\ x+\beta & x+\gamma & x-1 \\ x+\gamma & x+\delta & x-\beta+\delta \end{vmatrix}$$

(as $\alpha,\beta,\gamma,\delta$ are in AP)

Expanding along R_1, we get

$$f(x)=2\begin{vmatrix} x+\beta & x+\gamma \\ x+\gamma & x+\delta \end{vmatrix}$$

Applying $R_2\to R_2-R_1$, we get

$$f(x)=2\begin{vmatrix} x+\beta & x+\gamma \\ d & d \end{vmatrix}$$

$(\because \beta-\alpha=\gamma-\beta=\delta-\gamma=d)$

$$=2d(x+\beta-x-\gamma)=-2d^2$$

As, $\int_0^2 f(x)\,dx=-4$, we get

$\Rightarrow \int_0^2(-2d^2)\cdot dx=-2d^2[x]_0^2=-4$

$\Rightarrow\ -2d^2[2-0]=-4$

$\Rightarrow\quad d^2=1$

$\Rightarrow\quad d=\pm1$

7. (a) $P_r=\frac{r}{2}[2(r+1)+(r-1)(2r+2)]$

$=r(r+1+(r-1)(r+1))$

$\Rightarrow P_r=r(r+r^2)$

$\Rightarrow P_r=r^2+r^3$

$$\sum_{r=1}^{n}P_r=\sum_{r=1}^{n}r^2+\sum_{r=1}^{n}r^3$$

$$=\frac{n(n+1)}{2}\left[\frac{2n+1}{3}+\frac{n(n+1)}{2}\right]$$

$$=n(n+1)\left[\frac{4n+2+3n^2+3n}{12}\right]$$

$$=\frac{n(n+1)(3n^2+7n+2)}{12}$$

$$=\frac{n(n+1)(n+2)(3n+1)}{12}$$

8. (d) Given, $t_1=$ first term $=\frac{a}{b}$

and $\frac{t_6}{t_8}=\frac{1}{4}$

$$\Rightarrow\quad \frac{\left(\frac{a}{b}\right)r^5}{\left(\frac{a}{b}\right)r^7}=\frac{1}{4}$$

$\Rightarrow\quad r^2=2$

$\Rightarrow\quad r=\pm2$

But, $r<0$

$\therefore\quad r=-2$

Now, $t_3+t_7=100$ (given)

$\Rightarrow\quad \left(\frac{a}{b}\right)r^2+\left(\frac{a}{b}\right)r^6=100$

$\Rightarrow\quad \left(\frac{a}{b}\right)(r^2+r^6)=100$

$\Rightarrow\left(\frac{a}{b}\right)[(-2)^2+(-2)^6]=100$

$\Rightarrow\quad \frac{a}{b}=\frac{100}{68}=\frac{25}{17}$

$\therefore\quad a+b=25+17=42$

9. (a) Since, a,b,c are in GP and $a\neq0$.

So, a, ar, ar^2 be the first three terms of GP. So, $a=a$, $b=ar$, $c=ar^2$

Given, $3a, 7b, 15c$ are in AP,

i.e. $14b=3a+15c$

So, $14ar=3a+15ar^2$

$\Rightarrow\quad 15r^2-14r+3=0$

$\Rightarrow 15r^2-9r-5r+3=0$

$\Rightarrow\quad (3r-1)(5r-3)=0$

$\Rightarrow\quad r=\frac{1}{3},\frac{5}{3}$

But $0<r\le\frac{1}{2}$

$\therefore\quad r=1/3$

So, AP will be $3a, \frac{7a}{3}, \frac{5a}{3}, \frac{3a}{3}$,

i.e. $3a, \frac{7a}{3}, \frac{5a}{3}, a$

Hence, 4th term of this AP $=a$

10. (c) The ball is dropped from the height, $h=80$ m

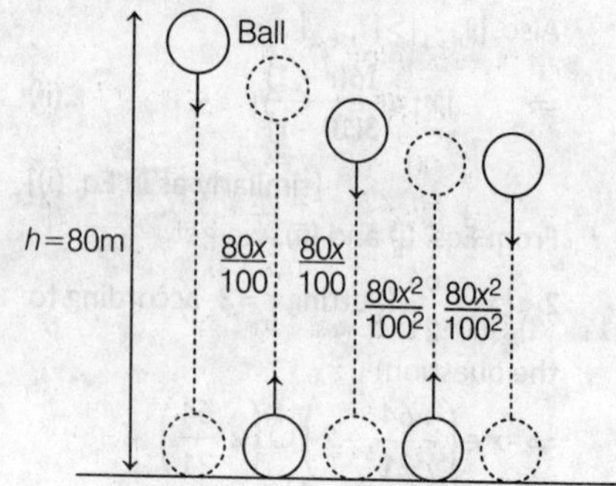

So, initially it travels the distance $=80$ m

Then, it rebounds to x% of its previous height (i.e. 80 m).

So, it rebounds by the distance of $\left(\frac{80x}{100}\right)$ m and from the same height of drops again.

It continues like this till it comes to rest.

So, total distance travelled by the ball $=320$ m (given)

$$\Rightarrow 80+\left(2\times\frac{80x}{100}+2\times\frac{80x^2}{100^2}+\ldots\right)=320$$

$$\Rightarrow 1+\frac{2x}{100}+\frac{2x^2}{100^2}+\ldots=4$$

$$\Rightarrow\quad \frac{\frac{2x}{100}}{1-\frac{x}{100}}=3$$

[using GP series$\left(s_\infty=\frac{a}{1-r}\right)$]

$$\Rightarrow\quad \frac{2x}{100-x}=3$$

$\Rightarrow\quad x=60$

11. (a) $5^x+5^{x-1}+5^{x-2}+\ldots+5^{x-2000}$

$$=5^{x-2000}[1+5+5^2+\ldots+5^{2000}]$$

$$=5^{x-2000}\frac{[5^{2001}-1]}{5-1}$$

$$=\frac{1}{4}(5^{x-2000})(5^{2001}-1)$$

Similarly,

$7^x+7^{x-1}+7^{x-2}+\ldots+7^{x-2000}$

$=\frac{1}{6}(7^{x-2000})(7^{2001}-1)$

Thus, $\frac{1}{4}(5^{x-2000})(5^{2001}-1)$

$=\frac{1}{6}(7^{x-2000})(7^{2001}-1)$

$\Rightarrow \left(\frac{7}{5}\right)^{x-2000}=\frac{3}{2}\left(\frac{5^{2001}-1}{7^{2001}-1}\right)$

$\Rightarrow (x-2000)\log_e(7/5)$

$=\ln[3(5^{2001}-1)]-\ln[2(7^{2001}-1)]$

$\Rightarrow x-2000$

$=\frac{\ln[3(5^{2001}-1)]-\ln[2(7^{2001}-1)]}{\ln(7/5)}$

12. (d) Given, a, b, c are in GP.

So, $b^2=ac$ ...(i)

and $\log a-\log 2b$, $\log 2b-\log 3c$ and $\log 3c-\log a$ are in AP.

Then, $2(\log 2b-\log 3c)$

$=\log a-\log 2b+\log 3c-\log a$

$\Rightarrow \log\left(\frac{2b}{3c}\right)^2=\log\left(\frac{3c}{2b}\right)$

$\Rightarrow \left(\frac{2b}{3c}\right)^2=\frac{3c}{2b}$

$\Rightarrow \frac{\left(\frac{2b}{3c}\right)^2}{\left(\frac{3c}{2b}\right)}=1$

$\Rightarrow 2b=3c$ ...(ii)

$\Rightarrow b=\frac{2a}{3}$ and $c=\frac{4a}{9}$

[from Eqs. (i) and (ii)]

Since, $a+b=\frac{5a}{3}>c$, $b+c=\frac{10a}{9}>a$

and $c+a=\frac{13a}{9}>b$

So, a, b, c are the sides of a triangle. Also, as 'a' is the greatest side, let us find $\angle A$ of ΔABC

$\cos A=\frac{b^2+c^2-a^2}{2bc}=\frac{-29}{48}<0$

Hence, ΔABC is an obtuse angled triangle.

13. (c) It is given that x, y, z are in GP.

$\therefore$ $y^2=xz$ ...(i)

Also,

$\tan^{-1}x, \tan^{-1}y, \tan^{-1}z$ are in AP.

$\therefore$ $2\tan^{-1}y=\tan^{-1}x+\tan^{-1}z$

$\Rightarrow \tan^{-1}\left(\frac{2y}{1-y^2}\right)=\tan^{-1}\left(\frac{x+z}{1-xz}\right)$

$\Rightarrow \frac{2y}{1-y^2}=\frac{x+z}{1-xz}$ [using Eq. (i)]

$\Rightarrow \frac{2y}{1-xz}=\frac{x+z}{1-xz}$

$\Rightarrow 2y=x+z$ ...(ii)

$\Rightarrow x, y, z$ are in AP.

From Eqs. (i) and (ii), we get

$x=y=z$

14. (a) Given, $n>0$ and $\alpha\in(0,1)$

i.e. $\alpha\in$ 1st quadrant because ($1^c\approx 57.3°$)

$\therefore \sin\alpha, \cos\alpha>0$

So, $n\sin\alpha$ and $\frac{1}{n}\cos\alpha$ both are positive

Using AM $\geq$ GM

$\Rightarrow \frac{n\sin\alpha+\frac{1}{n}\cos\alpha}{2}\geq\sqrt{n\sin\alpha\cdot\frac{1}{n}\cos\alpha}$

$\Rightarrow n\sin\alpha+\frac{1}{n}\cos\alpha\geq\sqrt{4\sin\alpha\cdot\cos\alpha}$

$\Rightarrow n\sin\alpha+\frac{1}{n}\cos\alpha\geq\sqrt{2\sin 2\alpha}$

15. (d) m is the AM between l and n,.

So, $m=\frac{l+n}{2}$

and l, G_1, G_2, G_3, m are in GP.

So, $r=\left(\frac{n}{l}\right)^{1/4}$

$\therefore G_1=l^{3/4}n^{1/4}, G_2=l^{1/2}n^{1/2}$

$G_3=l^{1/4}n^{3/4}$

Now, $G_1^4+2G_2^4+G_3^4$

$=l^3n+2l^2n^2+ln^3$

$=ln(l+n)^2$

$=ln(2m)^2$

$=4lm^2n$

16. (d) $1+\frac{4}{3}+\frac{10}{9}+\frac{28}{27}+\ldots$ to n terms

$=1+\sum_{r=1}^{n-1}\frac{3^r+1}{3^r}$

$=1+\sum_{r=1}^{n-1}1+\left(\frac{1}{3}\right)^r$

$=1+(n-1)+\frac{\frac{1}{3}\left(1-\left(\frac{1}{3}\right)^{n-1}\right)}{1-\frac{1}{3}}$

$=n+\frac{1}{2}\left(1-\frac{1}{3^{n-1}}\right)$

$=n+\frac{1}{2}-\frac{1}{2\cdot 3^{n-1}}$

17. (b) Let S be the sum of given series

$S=1+\frac{2}{3}+\frac{6}{3^2}+\frac{10}{3^3}+\frac{14}{3^4}+\ldots$ to ∞

$\Rightarrow S-1=\frac{2}{3}+\frac{6}{3^2}+\frac{10}{3^3}+\frac{14}{3^4}+\ldots$ to ∞ ...(i)

$\Rightarrow (S-1)\frac{1}{3}=\frac{2}{3^2}+\frac{6}{3^3}+\frac{10}{3^4}+\frac{14}{3^5}+\ldots$ to ∞

Subtracting Eq. (ii) from Eq. (i), we get

$\frac{2}{3}(S-1)=\frac{2}{3}+\frac{4}{3^2}+\frac{4}{3^3}+\frac{4}{3^4}+\ldots$ to ∞

$=\frac{2}{3}+\frac{\frac{4}{3^2}}{1-\frac{1}{3}}$

$\frac{2}{3}(S-1)=\frac{2}{3}+\frac{2}{3}$

$S=3$

18. (b) $\because S=\sum_{r=1}^{16}\frac{8r}{(4r^4+1)}$

$\Rightarrow S=\sum_{r=1}^{16}\frac{8r}{(2r^2-2r+1)(2r^2+2r+1)}$

$=2\cdot\sum_{r=1}^{16}\left(\frac{1}{2r^2-2r+1}-\frac{1}{2r^2+2r+1}\right)$

$\Rightarrow S=2\left[\frac{1}{1}-\frac{1}{5}+\frac{1}{5}-\frac{1}{13}+\frac{1}{13}+\ldots+\frac{1}{481}-\frac{1}{545}\right]$

$\Rightarrow S=2\left[1-\frac{1}{545}\right]$

$\Rightarrow S=\frac{1088}{545}$

19. (a) Subtracting both equations

$S=\frac{1}{2^1}+\frac{2}{2^2}+\frac{3}{2^3}+\ldots+\frac{20}{2^{20}}$

$-\ \frac{S}{2}=\frac{1}{2^2}+\frac{2}{2^3}+\ldots+\frac{19}{2^{20}}+\frac{20}{2^{21}}$

$S-\frac{S}{2}=\frac{1}{2}+\frac{1}{2^2}+\frac{1}{2^3}+\ldots+\frac{1}{2^{20}}-\frac{20}{2^{21}}$

$\Rightarrow \frac{S}{2}=\frac{\frac{1}{2}\left[1-\left(\frac{1}{2}\right)^{20}\right]}{\frac{1}{2}}-\frac{20}{2^{21}}$

$\Rightarrow \frac{S}{2}=1-\frac{1}{2^{20}}-\frac{20}{2^{21}}$

$\Rightarrow S = 2 - \frac{2}{2^{20}} - \frac{2 \times 20}{2^{21}}$

$\Rightarrow S = 2 - \frac{1}{2^{19}} - \frac{10}{2^{19}}$

$= 2 - \frac{11}{2^{19}}$

20. (c) Subtracting both equations,

$$s = \lambda + 2\lambda^2 + 3\lambda^3 + \ldots + 9\lambda^9$$
$$-\lambda s = \lambda^2 + 2\lambda^3 + \ldots + 8\lambda^9 + 9\lambda^{10}$$

$s(1-\lambda) = \lambda + \lambda^2 + \lambda^3 + \ldots + \lambda^9 - 9\lambda^{10}$

$\Rightarrow s(1-\lambda) = -9\lambda^{10}$ ($\because \lambda, \lambda^2, \lambda^3, \ldots, \lambda^9$ is sum of 9th root of unity)

$\Rightarrow s = \frac{-9\lambda}{1-\lambda}$

$\therefore |s| = \frac{9}{|1-\lambda|} = \frac{9}{|1-\cos\theta - i\sin\theta|}$

$= \frac{9}{2 \cdot \sin 20^\circ}$

$\Rightarrow |s|^{-1} = \frac{2\sin 20^\circ}{9}$

21. (2) Let S_n denote the sum to n terms of the AP.

According to the given condition,

$\frac{S_n}{S_{2n} - S_n} = k, \forall n \geq 1$

$\Rightarrow \frac{S_1}{S_2 - S_1} = \frac{S_2}{S_4 - S_2}$

$\Rightarrow S_1S_4 - S_1S_2 = S_2^2 - S_1S_2$

$\Rightarrow S_1S_4 = S_2^2$

$\Rightarrow a\left[\frac{4}{2}(2a + (4-1)d\right] = (a + a + d)^2$

$\Rightarrow a(4a + 6d) = (2a + d)^2$

$\Rightarrow 4a^2 + 6ad = 4a^2 + 4ad + d^2$

$\Rightarrow 2ad = d^2$

$\Rightarrow 2a = d \quad (\because d \neq 0)$

As, $a = 1$, we get $d = 2$

22. (5050) Area of green regions

$= \pi[(r_2^2 - r_1^2) + (r_4^2 - r_3^2) + \ldots + (r_{100}^2 - r_{99}^2)]$

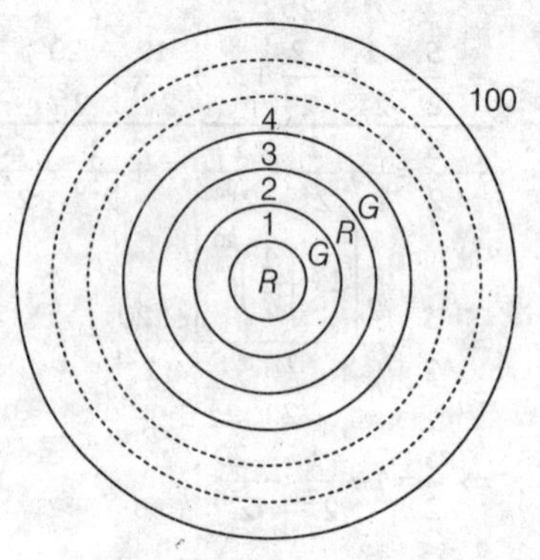

$= \pi[r_1 + r_2 + r_3 + r_4 + \ldots + r_{100}]$

$[\because r_2 - r_1 = r_4 - r_3 = \ldots = r_{100} - r_{99} = 1]$

$= \pi[1 + 2 + 3 + \ldots + 100] = 5050\pi$

$\therefore k = 5050$

23. (20) $\sqrt{a-x}, \sqrt{x}, \sqrt{a+x}$ in AP.

So, $2\sqrt{x} = \sqrt{a-x} + \sqrt{a+x}$

$\Rightarrow 4x = a - x + a + x + 2\sqrt{a^2 - x^2}$ (on squaring)

$\Rightarrow 2x - a = \sqrt{a^2 - x^2}$

$\Rightarrow 4x^2 - 4ax + a^2 = a^2 - x^2$

$\Rightarrow 5x^2 = 4ax$

$\Rightarrow a = \frac{5x}{4}$ (as, $a, x > 0$)

Now, x must be perfect square as $\sqrt{x}$ is an integer.

$\Rightarrow x = 1, 4, 9, 16, \ldots$ etc.

For $x = 1$, $a = \frac{5}{4}$ (rational number)

For $x = 4$, $a = 5$ (prime number)

For $x = 9$, $a = \frac{45}{4}$ (rational number)

For $x = 16$, $a = 20$ (composite number)

Hence, least composite value of $a = 20$

24. (5) We have,

$(1 + x^2)^2 (1 + x)^n = (1 + 2x^2 + x^4)$

$({}^nC_0 + {}^nC_1x + {}^nC_2x^2 + \ldots + {}^nC_nx^n)$

$= {}^nC_0 + {}^nC_1x + ({}^nC_2 + 2 \cdot {}^nC_0)x^2 + \ldots$

$\therefore a_0 = {}^nC_0 = 1, a_1 = {}^nC_1 = n$

and $a_2 = {}^nC_2 + 2 \cdot {}^nC_0 = \frac{1}{2} \cdot n \cdot (n-1) + 2$

As, a_0, a_1, a_2 are in AP.

$\therefore 2a_1 = a_0 + a_2$

$\Rightarrow 2n = 1 + \frac{1}{2}n(n-1) + 2$

$\Rightarrow 4n = 6 + n^2 - n$

$\Rightarrow n^2 - 5n + 6 = 0$

$\Rightarrow (n-2)(n-3) = 0$

$\Rightarrow n = 2, 3$

$\therefore \alpha + \beta = 2 + 3 = 5$

25. (14) Let $A_1, A_2, A_3, \ldots A_k$ be k AM's between 1 and 31.

Then, $1, A_1, A_2, A_3, \ldots, A_k, 31$ is an AP.

Common difference

$(d) = \frac{31-1}{k+1} = \frac{30}{k+1}$

Now, $A_7 = 1 + 7d$

$= 1 + 7\left(\frac{30}{k+1}\right) = \frac{k+211}{k+1}$

and $A_{k-1} = 1 + (k-1)d$

$= 1 + \frac{30}{k+1}(k-1)$

$= \frac{31k - 29}{k+1}$

Given, $\frac{A_7}{A_{k-1}} = \frac{5}{9}$

$\Rightarrow \frac{k+211}{31k-29} = \frac{5}{9}$

$\Rightarrow k = 14$

26. (1456) Given, a, b, c, d are in GP.

So, $a = a, b = ar, c = ar^2, d = ar^3$, where a = first term of GP and r = common ratio.

According to the question,

$a + ar^3 = 112$

$\Rightarrow a(1 + r^3) = 112$ ...(i)

$ar + ar^2 = 48$

$\Rightarrow ar(1 + r) = 48$ ...(ii)

On dividing Eq. (i) by Eq. (ii), we get

$\frac{1 + r^3}{r(1+r)} = \frac{112}{48} = \frac{7}{3}$

$\Rightarrow \frac{1 + r^2 - r}{r} = \frac{7}{3}$

$\Rightarrow 3r^2 - 3r + 3 = 7r$

$\Rightarrow 3r^2 - 10r + 3 = 0$

$\Rightarrow r = 3$

From Eq. (i), $a(28) = 112$

$\Rightarrow a = 4$

$\therefore S_6 = \frac{4(3^6 - 1)}{(3-1)} = 2(728) = 1456$

27. (2) If $x \in S$, then $x \in (0, \pi)$, which implies $|\cos x| < 1$.

So, $S_\infty = 1 + |\cos x| + |\cos^2 x| + |\cos^3 x| + \ldots$ upto ∞

$= 1 + |\cos x| + |\cos x|^2 + |\cos x|^3 + \ldots$ upto ∞

$= \frac{1}{1 - |\cos x|}$

Now, $8^{(1 + |\cos x| + |\cos^2 x| + |\cos^3 x| + \ldots \text{ to } \infty)} = 4^3$ ...(i)

$\Rightarrow (2^3)^{\frac{1}{1-|\cos x|}} = (2^2)^3$

$\Rightarrow 2^{\frac{3}{1-|\cos x|}} = 2^6$

$\Rightarrow \frac{3}{1 - |\cos x|} = 6$

$\Rightarrow \frac{3}{6} = 1 - |\cos x|$

$$\Rightarrow \quad |\cos x| = \frac{1}{2}$$

$$\Rightarrow \quad \cos x = \pm\frac{1}{2}$$

$$\Rightarrow \quad x = \frac{\pi}{3}, \frac{2\pi}{3}$$

$S \subseteq \left\{\frac{\pi}{3}, \frac{2\pi}{3}\right\}$, clearly for $x = \pi/3, 2\pi/3$ the Eq. (i) is satisfied.

Thus, $S = \left\{\frac{\pi}{3}, \frac{2\pi}{3}\right\}$

Hence, total number of values of $S = 2$

28. (220) $S_{n+2} - S_n = (n+2)^2$

$\Rightarrow S_{10} - S_8 = 10^2$

$\Rightarrow S_8 - S_6 = 8^2$

$\Rightarrow S_6 - S_4 = 6^2$

$\Rightarrow S_4 - S_2 = 4^2$

$\therefore S_{10} - S_2 = 4^2 + 6^2 + 8^2 + 10^2$

$\Rightarrow \quad S_{10} = 4(1^2 + 2^2 + 3^2 + 4^2 + 5^2)$

$(S_2 = T_1 + T_2 = 4)$ (given)

$\Rightarrow \quad S_{10} = 4 \times 55 \Rightarrow S_{10} = 220$

29. (100) Let

$$S = 10^9 + 2(11)(10)^8 + 3(11)^2(10)^7 + \ldots + 10(11)^9 \quad \ldots(i)$$

$$\frac{11}{10}S = 11(10)^8 + 2(11)^2(10)^7 + 3(11)^3(10^6) + \ldots + (11)^{10} \quad \ldots(ii)$$

Subtracting Eq. (ii) from Eq. (i), we get

$$S - \frac{11}{10}S = 10^9 + \{11(10)^8 + (11)^2 (10)^7 + \ldots + (11)^9\} - (11)^{10}$$

$$\Rightarrow -\frac{S}{10} = \frac{10^9\left\{1 - \left(\frac{11}{10}\right)^{10}\right\}}{1 - \frac{11}{10}} \ldots (11)^{10}$$

$$\Rightarrow -\frac{S}{10} = -10^{10}\left\{1 - \left(\frac{11}{10}\right)^{10}\right\} - (11)^{10}$$

$$\Rightarrow \quad S = 10^{11} - 10(11)^{10} + 10(11)^{10} = 10^{11} = 100(10)^9$$

Hence, $k = 100$

30. (620) $\frac{1^3}{1} + \frac{1^3 + 2^3}{1+2} + \ldots + \frac{1^3 + 2^3 + \ldots + 15^3}{1 + 2 + 3 + \ldots + 15} - \frac{1}{2}\underbrace{(1 + 2 + 3 + \ldots + 15}_{\left(=\frac{15\times 16}{4}\right)}$

$$T_k = \frac{\frac{k^2(k+1)^2}{4}}{\frac{k(k+1)}{2}} = \frac{k^2(k+1)^2}{4} \times \frac{2}{k(k+1)} = \frac{k(k+1)}{2}$$

$$\therefore S_k = \sum_{k=1}^{15}\left[\left(\frac{k^2}{2} + \frac{k}{2}\right)\right] - \left(\frac{15\times 16}{4}\right)$$

$$= \frac{(15)(16)(31)}{12} + \frac{15\times 16}{4} - \frac{15\times 16}{4}$$

$$S_k = 620$$

Qualifier 7
(Limits, Continuity and Differentiability)

1. (d) Let

$$L = \lim_{x\to 0}\frac{\tan(\pi\sin^2 x) + (|x| - \sin(x[x]))^2}{x^2}$$

$\Rightarrow$ Now, LHL

$$= \lim_{x\to 0^-}\left[\frac{\tan(\pi\sin^2 x)}{x^2} + \left(\frac{-x + \sin x}{x}\right)^2\right]$$

$$\Rightarrow \text{LHL} = \left[\lim_{x\to 0^-}\frac{\tan(\pi\sin^2 x)}{\pi\sin^2 x} \times \frac{\pi\sin^2 x}{x^2}\right] + \left[\lim_{x\to 0^-}\frac{\left(x\left(-1 + \frac{\sin x}{x}\right)\right)^2}{x}\right]$$

$[\because [x] = -1$ when $x \to 0^-$; $\therefore \sin(x[x]) = \sin(-x) = -\sin x]$

$$= \pi + 0 = \pi$$

and

$$\text{RHL} = \lim_{x\to 0^+}\left[\frac{\tan(\pi\sin^2 x)}{x^2} + \left(\frac{x - 0}{x}\right)^2\right]$$

$\left[\because [x] = 0 \text{ when } x \to 0;\ \therefore \sin(x[x]) = \sin 0 = 0\right]$

$$= \pi + 1$$

$\because \quad$ LHL $\neq$ RHL

$\therefore L$ does not exist.

2. (d) Let $L = \lim_{x\to\frac{\pi}{2}}\left[\frac{\sin x - (\sin x)^{\sin x}}{1 - \sin x + \ln(\sin x)}\right]$

Putting $\sin x = z$, as $x \to \pi/2$ then $z \to 1$

$$L = \lim_{z\to 1}\left[\frac{z - z^z}{1 - z + \ln z}\right]$$

$$= \lim_{h\to 0}\left[\frac{(1+h) - (1+h)^{(1+h)}}{1 - (1+h) + \ln(1+h)}\right]$$

(Put $z = 1 + h$ as $z \to 1$ then $h \to 0$)

$$L = \lim_{h\to 0}\left[\frac{(1+h)\{1 - (1+h)^h\}}{-h + \left\{h - \frac{h^2}{2} + \frac{h^3}{3} - \frac{h^4}{4} + \ldots\right\}}\right]$$

$$L = \lim_{h\to 0}\left[\frac{(1+h)\left\{1 - \left(1 + h^2 + h\frac{(h-1)h^2}{2!} + \ldots\right)\right\}}{-\frac{h^2}{2} + \frac{h^3}{3} - \frac{h^4}{4} + \ldots}\right]$$

$$L = \lim_{h\to 0}\left[\frac{-h^2\left\{(1+h)\left(1 - \frac{h(h-1)}{2} + \ldots\right)\right\}}{-h^2\left\{\frac{1}{2} - \frac{h}{3} + \frac{h^2}{4} + \ldots\right\}}\right]$$

$$\Rightarrow L - \frac{(1+0)(1-0-0\ldots)}{\left(\frac{1}{2} - 0 + 0 - \ldots -\right)} \Rightarrow L = 2$$

3. (c) Simplifying the expression in brackets by setting $a^{1/4} = b$ and $x^{1/4} = y$, then function whose limit is required can be written as

$$\left[\left[\left\{\left(\frac{b^2 + y^2}{b - y}\right)^{-1} - \frac{2by}{y^3 - by^2 + b^2y - b^3}\right\}^{-1} - 2^{\frac{1}{2}\log_4 b^4}\right]^8\right.$$

$$= \left[\left\{\frac{b - y}{b^2 + y^2} - \frac{2by}{(y-b)(y^2 + b^2)}\right\}^{-1} - b\right]^8$$

$$= \left[\left\{\frac{(b-y)^2 + 2by}{(b-y)(b^2 + y^2)}\right\}^{-1} - b\right]^8$$

$$= \left[\left\{\frac{1}{b - y}\right\}^{-1} - b\right]^8$$

$$= (b - y - b)^8 = (-y)^8 = y^8 = x^2$$

Hence, the required limit as $x \to a$ is a^2.

4. (d) Given, $g(x)\cdot g(y) = g(x) + g(y) + g(xy) - 2 \quad \ldots(i)$

and $\quad g(2) = 5$

Putting $x = 2$ and $y = 1$ then

$g(2)\cdot g(1) = g(2) + g(1) + g(2) - 2$

$\Rightarrow 5\cdot g(1) = 5 + g(1) + 5 - 2 \Rightarrow g(1) = 2$

Again putting $y=\frac{1}{x}$ in the given equation, we get

$g(x)\cdot g(1/x)=g(x)+g(1/x)+g(1)-2$

$\Rightarrow g(x)\cdot g(1/x)=g(x)+g(1/x)$ ...(ii)

As we know that, if

$f(x)\cdot f(1/x)=f(x)+f(1/x)$,

then $f(x)=1\pm x^n$

From Eq. (ii),

$g(x)=1\pm x^n$

Now, $g(2)=5$ then $g(2)=1+2^n$

or $g(2)=1-2^n$

$\Rightarrow 5=1+2^n$ or $5=1-2^n$

$\Rightarrow 4=2^n$ or $4=-2^n$

(which is not possible)

$\Rightarrow n=2$

Hence, $\lim_{x\to3} g(x)=\lim_{x\to3}(1+x^2)=10$

5. (b) Let $L=\lim_{n\to\infty}\frac{n}{(n!)^{1/n}}$

$$=\lim_{n\to\infty}\frac{n}{(1\cdot2\cdot3\ldots n)^{1/n}}$$

$$=\lim_{n\to\infty}\frac{1}{\left(\frac{1}{n}\cdot\frac{2}{n}\cdot\frac{3}{n}\ldots\frac{n}{n}\right)^{1/n}}$$

Taking $\log_e$ i.e., ln on both sides, we have

$$\ln(L)=\lim_{n\to\infty}-\frac{1}{n}\left[\ln\left(\frac{1}{n}\right)+\ln\left(\frac{2}{n}\right)+\ln\left(\frac{3}{n}\right)+\ldots+\ln\left(\frac{n}{n}\right)\right]$$

$$=\lim_{n\to\infty}\left[\frac{-1}{n}\sum_{r=1}^{n}\ln\left(\frac{r}{n}\right)\right]$$

$$=-\int_0^1 \ln x\,dx$$

(Replace $\frac{1}{n}$ by dx, $\frac{r}{n}$ by x)

$$=-[x\ln x-x]_0^1=-[(0-1)-(0)]=1$$

Hence, $L=e^1=e$

6. (c) Let $L=\lim_{n\to\infty}\frac{\sqrt[n]{n!}}{n}=\lim_{n\to\infty}\left(\frac{n!}{n^n}\right)^{1/n}$

$$\Rightarrow \ln(L)=\lim_{n\to\infty}\frac{1}{n}\ln\left(\frac{1\cdot2\cdot3\cdot4\ldots n}{n\cdot n\cdot n\cdot n\ldots n}\right)$$

$$=\lim_{n\to\infty}\frac{1}{n}\left[\ln\left(\frac{1}{n}\right)+\ln\left(\frac{2}{n}\right)+\ln\left(\frac{3}{n}\right)+\ln\left(\frac{4}{n}\right)+\ldots+\ln\left(\frac{n}{n}\right)\right]$$

$$=\lim_{n\to\infty}\sum_{r=1}^{n}\frac{1}{n}\cdot\ln\left(\frac{r}{n}\right)$$

$$\Rightarrow \ln(L)=\int_0^1 \ln(x)\,dx$$

(Replacing $\frac{r}{n}$ by x and $\frac{1}{n}$ by dx)

$$\Rightarrow \ln(L)=[x\ln x-x]_0^1=-1$$

$\Rightarrow L=e^{-1}=e^{2k}$ (given)

$\therefore k=\frac{-1}{2}$

So, $\sin^{-1}\left(k+\frac{1}{2}\right)=\sin^{-1}(0)=0$

7. (a) Since, $\sin x$ and $\cos x$ are continuous function for all $x\in R$

$f(x)$ is continuous except possibility at $x=-\pi/2$ and $x=\pi/2$

For f to be continuous at $x=-\pi/2$, we must have

$$f(-\pi/2)=\lim_{x\to-\frac{\pi}{2}^+} f(x)$$

$$=\lim_{x\to-\frac{\pi}{2}^+}(A\sin x+B)=-A+B$$

$$\Rightarrow -2\sin\left(\frac{-\pi}{2}\right)=-A+B$$

$\Rightarrow -A+B=2$ ...(i)

Also, for f to be continuous at $x=\pi/2$, we must have

$$f(\pi/2)=\lim_{x\to\frac{\pi}{2}^-} f(x)$$

$$\Rightarrow \cos(\pi/2)=\lim_{x\to\frac{\pi}{2}^-}(A\sin x+B)$$

$\Rightarrow A+B=0$ ...(ii)

On solving Eqs. (i) and (ii), we get $A=-1$ and $B=1$

8. (c) $f(x)$ is continuous at $x=1$ if $\lim_{x\to1} f(x)=f(1)$

So, $f(1)=\lim_{x\to1}\frac{x^{m+1}-(m+1)x+m}{(x-1)^2}$

$$=\lim_{x\to1}\frac{(x^{m+1}-x)-m(x-1)}{(x-1)^2}$$

$$=\lim_{x\to1}\frac{x(x^m-1)-m(x-1)}{(x-1)^2}$$

$$=\lim_{x\to1}\frac{x(x^{m-1}+x^{m-2}+x^{m-3}+\ldots+1)-m}{(x-1)}$$

$$f(1)=\lim_{x\to1}\frac{(x^m+x^{m-1}+x^{m-2}+\ldots+x)-\underbrace{(1+1+1+1+\ldots+1)}_{m\text{-times}}}{(x-1)}$$

$$=\lim_{x\to1}\frac{(x^m-1)+(x^{m-1}-1)+(x^{m-2}-1)+\ldots+(x-1)}{(x-1)}$$

$$=\lim_{x\to1}\frac{x^m-1}{x-1}+\lim_{x\to1}\frac{x^{m-1}-1}{x-1}+\lim_{x\to1}\frac{x^{m-2}-1}{x-1}+\ldots+\lim_{x\to1}\frac{x-1}{x-1}$$

$$=m\times(1)^{m-1}+(m-1)(1)^{m-2}+(m-2)(1)^{m-3}+\ldots+1$$

$$=1+2+3+\ldots+(m-2)+(m-1)+m=\frac{m(m+1)}{2}$$

9. (c) Given,

$$f(x)=\begin{cases}\dfrac{a^{2[x]+\{x\}}-1}{2[x]+\{x\}}, & x\neq0\\ \log_e a, & x=0\end{cases}$$

where $a\neq1$

Now, LHL $=\lim_{x\to0^-} f(x)=\lim_{h\to0} f(0-h)$

$$=\lim_{h\to0}\frac{a^{2[0-h]+\{0-h\}}-1}{2[0-h]+\{0-h\}}$$

$$=\lim_{h\to0}\frac{a^{2[0-h]+\{-1+(1-h)\}}-1}{2[0-h]+\{1-(1-h)\}}$$

$$=\lim_{h\to0}\frac{a^{-2+(1-h)}-1}{-2+(1-h)}$$

$$=\frac{a^{-1}-1}{-1}=1-\frac{1}{a}$$

RHL $=\lim_{x\to0^+} f(x)=\lim_{h\to0} f(0+h)$

$$=\lim_{h\to0}\frac{a^{2[0+h]+\{0+h\}}-1}{2[0+h]+\{0+h\}}$$

$$=\lim_{h\to0}\frac{a^{0+h}-1}{0+h}$$

$$=\lim_{h\to0}\frac{a^h-1}{h}=\log_e a$$

From above, we find that $1-\frac{1}{a}=\log_e a$ (i.e. LHL = RHL) only when $a=1$.

But according to question, $a\neq1$.

So, LHL $\neq$ RHL $=f(0)$

$\therefore f(x)$ is discontinuous at $x=0$.

10. (a) For $f(x)$ to be continuous at $x=0$;

$\lim_{x\to0} f(x)=f(0)$ ...(i)

Now,

$$\lim_{x\to0} f(x)=\lim_{x\to0}\frac{x(1+a\cos x)-b\sin x}{x^3}$$

$$=\lim_{x\to0}\frac{x+ax\left(1-\frac{x^2}{2!}+\frac{x^4}{4!}-\frac{x^6}{6!}+\ldots\right)-b\left(x-\frac{x^3}{3!}+\frac{x^5}{5!}\ldots\right)}{x^3}$$

$$= \lim_{x \to 0} \frac{(1+a-b)x - \left(\frac{a}{2!} - \frac{b}{3!}\right)x^3 + \left(\frac{a}{4!} - \frac{b}{5!}\right)x^5 \ldots}{x^3}$$

For limit to be exist, $1 + a - b = 0$ (necessarily) otherwise

$\lim_{x \to 0} \frac{(1+a-b)x}{x^3}$ will become infinite

Hence, $1 + a - b = 0$ ...(ii)

Also, $\lim_{x \to 0} f(x) = -\left(\frac{a}{2!} - \frac{b}{3!}\right) +$ (higher degree terms will be zero)

From Eq. (i),

$$\frac{-a}{2!} + \frac{b}{3!} = 1$$

$\Rightarrow \quad 6a - 2b + 12 = 0$ ...(iii)

On solving Eqs. (ii) and (iii), we get

$$a = \frac{-5}{2} \text{ and } b = \frac{-3}{2}$$

$\therefore \quad a + b = -4$

11. (a) Given,

$$f(x) = \begin{cases} \frac{a(1 - x\sin x) + b\cos x + 5}{x^2}, & x < 0 \\ 3, & x = 0 \\ \left\{1 + \left(\frac{cx + dx^3}{x^2}\right)\right\}^{1/x}, & x > 0 \end{cases}$$

Here,

Value of function (VF) $= f(0) = 3$

$$\text{RHL} = \lim_{x \to 0^+} f(x) = \lim_{h \to 0} f(0 + h)$$

$$= \lim_{h \to 0} f(h) = \lim_{h \to 0} \left\{1 + \left(\frac{ch + dh^3}{h^2}\right)\right\}^{1/h}$$

Since, $f(x)$ is continuous at $x = 0$, then RHL must be exist.

For existence of RHL, 'c' must be zero.

$\therefore \text{RHL} = \lim_{h \to 0} (1 + dh)^{1/h}$ (Form 1^∞)

$$\Rightarrow \text{RHL} = e^{\lim_{h \to 0} (1 + dh - 1) \times \frac{1}{h}} = e^d$$

Now, LHL

$$= \lim_{x \to 0^-} f(x) = \lim_{h \to 0} f(0 - h) = \lim_{h \to 0} f(-h)$$

$$= \lim_{h \to 0} \frac{a[1 - (-h)\sin(-h)] + b\cos(-h) + 5}{(-h)^2}$$

$$= \lim_{h \to 0} \frac{a(1 - h\sin h) + b\cos h + 5}{h^2}$$

For finite value of LHL, the numerator must tend to zero as $h \to 0$

So, $a + b + 5 = 0$

$\Rightarrow \quad b = -(5 + a)$

$\therefore$ LHL

$$= \lim_{h \to 0} \frac{a - ah\sin h - (5 + a)\cos h + 5}{h^2}$$

$$= \lim_{h \to 0} \frac{(5 + a) - (5 + a)\cos h - ah\sin h}{h^2}$$

$$= \lim_{h \to 0} \left[\frac{(a + 5)(1 - \cos h)(1 + \cos h)}{h^2(1 + \cos h)} - \frac{ah\sin h}{h^2}\right]$$

$$\Rightarrow \text{LHL} = \lim_{h \to 0} \left[\frac{(a + 5)\sin^2 h}{h^2(1 + \cos h)} - \frac{a\sin h}{h}\right]$$

$$= \frac{(a + 5)(1)^2}{1 + 1} - a \times 1$$

$$\Rightarrow \text{LHL} = \frac{a + 5}{2} - a = \frac{5 - a}{2}$$

According to question, $f(x)$ is continuous at $x = 0$

LHL = RHL = VF

$$\Rightarrow \frac{5 - a}{2} = e^d = 3$$

$\Rightarrow a = -1, d = \ln 3, c = 0, b = -4$

$\therefore a + b + c + d + 5$

$= -1 + (-4) + 0 + \ln 3 + 5 = \ln 3$

12. (b) Since, $f(x)$ is continuous at $x = 0$

$$\lim_{x \to 0} f(x) = f(0)$$

$$\Rightarrow \quad \lim_{x \to 0} \frac{(4^x - 1)^3}{\sin\frac{x}{4}\log\left(1 + \frac{x^2}{3}\right)} = K$$

$$\Rightarrow \lim_{x \to 0} \frac{12\left(\frac{4^x - 1}{x}\right)^3}{\left(\frac{\sin\frac{x}{4}}{x/4}\right)\left(\frac{\log\left(1 + \frac{x^2}{3}\right)}{\frac{x^2}{3}}\right)} = K$$

$\Rightarrow \quad 12(\log 4)^3 = K$

$\Rightarrow \quad K = 96(\log 2)^3$

13. (c) For $t \geq 0$ ...(i)

$x = 2t - t = t$ ...(ii)

and $y = t^2 + t^2 = 2t^2$ ...(iii)

From Eqs. (i), (ii) and (iii),

$$y = 2x^2, x \geq 0$$

For $t < 0$ ...(iv)

$x = 2t - (-t) = 3t$

$\Rightarrow \quad t = \frac{x}{3}$ ...(v)

and $y = t^2 - t^2 = 0$ for $t < 0$ ...(vi)

From Eqs. (iv), (v) and (vi),

$$y = 0, \frac{x}{3} < 0$$

i.e. $\quad y = 0, x < 0$

$$\text{Hence, } y = f(x) = \begin{cases} 0, & x < 0 \\ 2x^2, & x \geq 0 \end{cases}$$

Here, LHL = RHL = VF = 0 = unique and finite

$\therefore f(x)$ is continuous at $x = 0$

$$\text{Also, } f'(x) = \begin{cases} 0, & x < 0 \\ 4x, & x > 0 \end{cases}$$

Here, LHD = RHD = 0 = unique and finite

$\therefore f(x)$ is derivable at $x = 0$

Therefore, $f(x)$ is continuous and derivable at $x = 0$

14. (b) Given $x + 4|y| = 6y$ ...(i)

For $\quad y \geq 0$

From Eq. (i), we get

$$x = 6y - 4y$$

$\Rightarrow \quad x = 2y$ when $y \geq 0$

$\Rightarrow \quad y = \frac{x}{2}$ when $\frac{x}{2} \geq 0$

So, $y = \frac{x}{2}$ when $x \geq 0$

For $y < 0$

From Eq. (i), we get

$$x = 6y + 4y$$

$\Rightarrow \quad x = 10y$ when $y < 0$

$\Rightarrow \quad y = \frac{x}{10}$ when $\frac{x}{10} < 0$

$\Rightarrow \quad y = \frac{x}{10}$ when $x < 0$

$$\text{Hence, } y = f(x) = \begin{cases} \frac{x}{2}, & x \geq 0 \\ \frac{x}{10}, & x < 0 \end{cases}$$

To check continuity

Now, $\text{LHL} = \lim_{x \to 0^-} f(x) = \lim_{h \to 0} f(0 - h)$

$$= \lim_{h \to 0} \frac{(0 - h)}{10} = 0$$

$$\text{RHL} = \lim_{x \to 0^+} f(x) = \lim_{h \to 0} f(0 + h)$$

$$= \lim_{h \to 0} \frac{0 + h}{2} = 0$$

Value of function (VF) $= f(0) = \frac{0}{2} = 0$

$\therefore f(x)$ is continuous at $x = 0$ and hence for all $x \in R$

To check differentiability

$$\text{LHD} = f'(0^-) = \lim_{h \to 0} \frac{f(0 - h) - f(0)}{-h}$$

$$= \lim_{h\to 0} \frac{\left(\frac{-h}{10}\right)-0}{-h} = \frac{1}{10}$$

$$\text{RHD} = f'(0^+) = \lim_{h\to 0} \frac{f(0+h)-f(0)}{h} = \lim_{h\to 0} \frac{\left(\frac{h}{2}\right)-0}{h} = \frac{1}{2}$$

$\because$ LHD $\neq$ RHD

$\therefore f(x)$ is not derivable at $x=0$

i.e. $f(x)$ is derivable at all except $x=0$

Hence, $f(x)$ is continuous but not-differentiable at $x=0$

15. (c) Given, $f(x) = \max\{\sin x, \sin^{-1}(\cos x)\}$

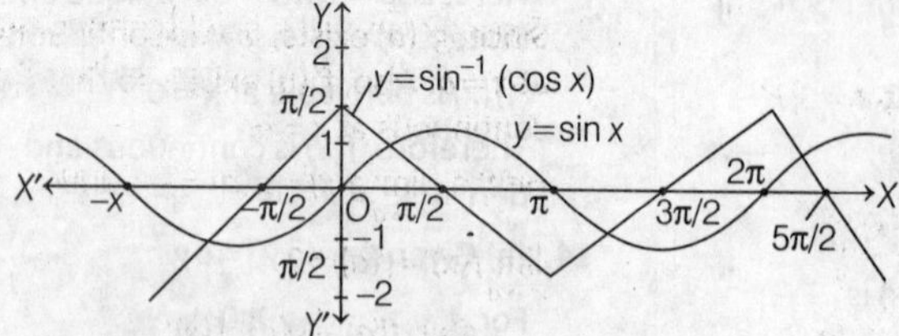

From above figure, it is clear that $f(x)$ is continuous but not differentiable at infinite points.

16. (a) Given,

$$f(x) = \begin{cases} \min(|x|, \sqrt{1-x^2}) & , -1 \le x \le 1 \\ [|x|] & , 1 < |x| < 2 \end{cases}$$

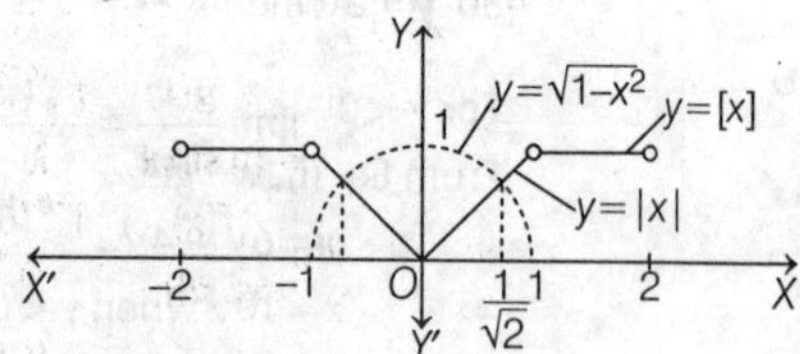

From figure/graph of $f(x)$, this is crystal clear that $f(x)$ is discontinuous at $x = \pm 1$ i.e., continuous on $x \in (-2, 2) - \{\pm 1\}$ and not derivable on

$x \in (-2,2) - \left\{\pm 1, \pm \frac{1}{\sqrt{2}}, 0\right\}$ because at $x = \pm 1, \pm \frac{1}{\sqrt{2}}, 0$ there is hole and sharp edge.

17. (a) From the given function, we have

$$f(|x|) = \begin{cases} -x-2 & , \text{for } -3 \le x \le 0 \\ x-2 & , \text{for } 0 < x \le 3 \end{cases}$$

$$\text{and } |f(x)| = \begin{cases} 2 & , \text{for } -3 \le x \le 0 \\ -x+2 & , \text{for } 0 < x \le 2 \\ x-2 & , \text{for } 2 < x \le 3 \end{cases}$$

$$\therefore g(x) = f(|x|) + |f(x)| = \begin{cases} -x & , \text{for } -3 \le x \le 0 \\ 0 & , \text{for } 0 < x \le 2 \\ 2x-4 & , \text{for } 2 < x \le 3 \end{cases}$$

Since $g(x)$ is expressed in terms of polynomials, it is differentiable, except possibly of $x=0$ and $x=2$

$$g'(0^+) = \lim_{h\to 0} \frac{g(0+h)-g(0)}{h} = \lim_{h\to 0} \frac{0-(-0)}{h} = 0$$

$$g'(0^-) = \lim_{h\to 0} \frac{g(0-h)-g(0)}{-h} = \lim_{h\to 0} \frac{-(0-h)-(-0)}{-h} = \lim_{h\to 0} \frac{h}{-h} = -1$$

$$g'(2^-) = \lim_{h\to 0} \frac{g(2-h)-g(2)}{-h} = \lim_{h\to 0} \frac{0-0}{-h} = 0$$

$$g'(2^+) = \lim_{h\to 0} \frac{g(2+h)-g(2)}{h}$$

$$= \lim_{h\to 0} \frac{(2(2+h)-4)-0}{h} = \lim_{h\to 0} \frac{4+2h-4}{h} = 2$$

$\because g'(0^-) \neq g'(0^+)$ and $g'(2^-) \neq g'(2^+)$

$\therefore g(x)$ is not differentiable at $x = 0, 2$

18. (a) Given, $f(x) = \sqrt{1-e^{-x^2}}$

For $x \neq 0$, we have

$$f'(x) = \frac{1}{2} \cdot \frac{1}{\sqrt{1-e^{-x^2}}} \{-(-2x)\, e^{-x^2}\}$$

$$= \frac{xe^{-x^2}}{\sqrt{1-e^{-x^2}}} = \left[\frac{x}{e^{x^2}\sqrt{1-e^{-x^2}}}\right]$$

$$\text{Now, } f'(0^+) = \lim_{h\to 0} \frac{f(h)-f(0)}{h}$$

$$= \lim_{h\to 0} \frac{\sqrt{1-e^{-h^2}}-0}{h} = \lim_{h\to 0} \left(\frac{e^{-h^2}-1}{-h^2}\right)^{1/2} = 1$$

$$\text{and } f'(0^-) = \lim_{h\to 0} \frac{f(-h)-f(0)}{-h} = \lim_{h\to 0} -\left(\frac{e^{-h^2}-1}{-h^2}\right)^{1/2} = -1$$

Hence, $f(x)$ is not differentiable at $x=0$. Thus, the point of differentiability are $(-\infty, \infty) - \{0\}$.

19. (a) Let $L = \lim_{x\to 0} \frac{f(x^2+x+1)-f(1)}{f(x^4-x^2+2x+4)-f(4)}$ (Form $\frac{0}{0}$)

$$= \lim_{x\to 0} \frac{(2x+1)\, f'(x^2+x+1)}{(4x^3-2x+2) f'(x^4-x^2+2x+4)}$$

(Using L-Hospital rule)

$$= \frac{f'(1)}{2f'(4)} = \frac{4}{2\times\frac{1}{2}} = 4$$

20. (b) Given, $f(x+y) = f(x) + f(y) + 2xy - 1$ ...(i)

and $f'(0) = \sin\phi$

Putting $x = y = 0$ in Eq. (i), we have

$$f(0) = f(0) + f(0) + 0 - 1 \Rightarrow f(0) = 1$$

$$\text{Now, } f'(x) = \lim_{h\to 0} \frac{f(x+h)-f(x)}{h}$$

$$= \lim_{h\to 0} \frac{f(x)+f(h)+2hx-1-f(x)}{h}$$

$$= \lim_{h\to 0} \frac{2hx}{h} + \lim_{h\to 0} \frac{f(h)-1}{h}$$

$$= 2x + \lim_{h\to 0} \frac{f(h)-f(0)}{h} \quad [\because f(0)=1]$$

$$= 2x + f'(0)$$

$\Rightarrow f'(x) = 2x + \sin\phi$ $[\because f'(0) = \sin\phi \text{ given}]$

$\therefore f(x) = x + x\sin\phi + c$

But $f(0) = 1$ then $c = 1$

Hence, $f(x) = x + x\sin\phi + 1$

$$\Rightarrow f(x) = \left(x + \frac{\sin\phi}{2}\right)^2 + \left(1 - \frac{\sin^2\phi}{4}\right) \ge 1 - \frac{\sin^2\phi}{4} \ge \frac{3}{4} > 0$$

$\therefore f(x) > 0, \forall x \in R$

21. (5) We have,

$$\lim_{x\to\infty}\left(\frac{x^2+x+1}{x+1}-ax-b\right)=4$$

$$\Rightarrow \lim_{x\to\infty}\frac{x^2(1-a)+x(1-a-b)+1-b}{x+1}=4$$

For finite and non-zero limit

$$1-a=0 \Rightarrow a=1$$

and $1-a-b=4 \Rightarrow 1-1-b=4$

$$b=-4$$

Then, $a-b=1-(-4)=5$

22. (8) $L=\lim_{x\to-\infty}\left(\frac{x^4\cdot\sin\left(\frac{1}{x}\right)+x^2}{1+|x|^3}\right)$

$$=\lim_{x\to-\infty}\frac{x^3\cdot\left(\frac{\sin(1/x)}{(1/x)}+\frac{1}{x}\right)}{x^3\left(\frac{1}{x^3}+\frac{|x|^3}{x^3}\right)}$$

$$=\frac{1+0}{0-1}=-1$$

So, $2L+10=2\times(-1)+10=8$

23. (1) Let $L=\lim_{n\to\infty}\left[\frac{1\cdot e^{1/n}}{n^2}+2\cdot\frac{(e^{1/n})^2}{n^2}+3\cdot\frac{(e^{1/n})^3}{n^2}+\ldots+n\frac{(e^{1/n})^n}{n^2}\right]$

$$=\lim_{n\to\infty}\sum_{r=1}^{n}\frac{r\cdot(e^{1/n})^r}{n^2}$$

$$=\lim_{n\to\infty}\sum_{r=1}^{n}\frac{1}{n}\cdot\left(\frac{r}{n}\right)(e)^{r/n}$$

Replacing $\left(\frac{r}{n}\right)$ by x and $\left(\frac{1}{n}\right)$ by dx, and change the limit to 0 to 1.

$$L=\int_0^1 x\cdot e^x\cdot dx=[e^x(x-1)]_0^1$$

$$=e^1(1-1)-e^0(0-1)=1$$

24. (3) Let $g(x)=k\sin x+\sin 2x$ and $h(x)=x^3$

Since, $g(0)=0$ and $h(0)=0$

So, $\lim_{x\to0}f(x)=\lim_{x\to0}\frac{k\cos x+2\cos 2x}{3x^2}$

(using L' Hospital rule)

Again, $\lim_{x\to0}x^2=0$ and $\lim_{x\to0}f(x)$ exists,

so $k+2=0 \Rightarrow k=-2$

Hence,

$$\lim_{x\to0}f(x)=\lim_{x\to0}\frac{-2-\sin x-4\sin 2x}{6x}$$

$$=\frac{2}{6}-\frac{4}{3}=-1=f(0)$$

So, $k-5f(0)=-2-5(-1)=3$

25. (2) Since $F(x)$ is continuous at $x=0$ then we must have,

$$\lim_{x\to0}F(x)=F(0)=e^3$$

$$\Rightarrow \lim_{x\to0}\left(1+x+\frac{f(x)}{x}\right)^{1/x}=e^3$$

$$\Rightarrow \lim_{x\to0}e^{\frac{1}{x}\left\{x+\frac{f(x)}{x}\right\}}=e^3$$

$$\Rightarrow \lim_{x\to0}\left(1+\frac{f(x)}{x^2}\right)=3$$

$$\Rightarrow \lim_{x\to0}\frac{f(x)}{x^2}=2 \quad \text{...(i)}$$

For $G(x)$ to be continuous at $x=0$, k should be equal to $\lim_{x\to0}G(x)$.

Now, $\lim_{x\to0}G(x)=\lim_{x\to0}\left(1+\frac{f(x)}{x}\right)^{1/x}$

$$=e^{\lim_{x\to0}\frac{1}{x}\left(\frac{f(x)}{x}\right)}=e^{\lim_{x\to0}\frac{f(x)}{x^2}}=e^2$$

[From Eq. (i)]

$\therefore \quad k=e^2 \Rightarrow \ln k=2$

26. (64) Given, $\lim_{x\to\pi/4}\frac{\int_2^{\sec^2 x}f(t)\,dt}{x^2-\frac{\pi^2}{16}}=\frac{k}{\pi}f(a)$

$$\Rightarrow \lim_{x\to\pi/4}\frac{f(\sec^2 x)\cdot 2\sec^2 x\cdot\tan x}{2x}$$

$$=\frac{k}{\pi}f(a)$$

(using newton Leibnitz Rule)

$$\Rightarrow \frac{f(2)\cdot2\times2\times1}{2\times\frac{\pi}{4}}=\frac{k}{\pi}f(a)$$

$$\Rightarrow \frac{8}{\pi}f(2)=\frac{k}{\pi}f(a)$$

On comparing, $k=8$ and $a=2$

Hence, $k^a=8^2=64$

27. (3) Given, $f(x)=\begin{cases}\cos^{-1}\{\cot x\}, & x<\frac{\pi}{2}\\ \pi[x]-1, & x\geq\frac{\pi}{2}\end{cases}$

$$\lim_{x\to\frac{\pi^-}{2}}f(x)=\lim_{x\to\frac{\pi^-}{2}}\cos^{-1}\cot x$$

$$=\cos^{-1}(0)=\frac{\pi}{2}$$

$$\lim_{x\to\frac{\pi^+}{2}}f(x)=\lim_{x\to\frac{\pi^+}{2}}\pi[x]-1=\pi-1$$

$\therefore$ The jump of discontinuity

$=$ RHL $-$ LHL

$$=(\pi-1)-\frac{\pi}{2}=\frac{\pi}{2}-1=A+B$$

Hence, $A=\frac{\pi}{2}$ and $B=-1$

So,

$$\left(\frac{4A}{\pi}-B\right)=\frac{4}{\pi}\times\frac{\pi}{2}-(-1)=2+1=3$$

28. (5) $\lim_{x\to a}\frac{g(x)\cdot f(a)-g(a)\cdot f(x)}{x-a}$

$$=\lim_{x\to a}\frac{g(x)(f(a)-f(x))+f(x)(g(x)-g(a))}{x-a}$$

$$=-\lim_{x\to a}g(x)\cdot\lim_{x\to a}\frac{f(x)-f(a)}{x-a}$$

$$+\lim_{x\to a}f(x)\cdot\lim_{x\to a}\frac{g(x)-g(a)}{x-a}$$

Since, $g'(a)$ exists, $g(x)$ is continuous at $x=a$. Also, $f'(a)$ exists, so that $f(x)$ is continuous at $x=a$.

Hence, $\lim_{x\to a}g(x)=g(a)=-1$ and

$$\lim_{x\to a}f(x)=f(a)=2$$

$$\lim_{x\to a}\frac{g(x)\cdot f(a)-g(a)\cdot f(x)}{x-a}$$

$$=-g(a)\cdot f'(a)+f(a)\cdot g'(a)$$

$$=-(-1)\cdot1+2\times2=5$$

29. (6) Given, $f(x)=x^2g(x)$ ...(i)

and $\lim_{x\to0}g(x)\cdot \quad x=\frac{f'''(0)}{\lambda}$

$$\Rightarrow \lim_{x\to0}\frac{g(x)}{\sin x}=\frac{f'''(0)}{\lambda}$$

$$\Rightarrow \lim_{x\to0}\frac{f(x)}{x^2\sin x}=\frac{f'''(0)}{\lambda}$$

[using Eq. (i)]

$$\Rightarrow \lim_{x\to0}\frac{f(x)}{x^3}=\frac{f'''(0)}{\lambda}$$

Using L' Hospital rule thrice,

$$\lim_{x\to0}\frac{f(x)}{x^3}=\frac{f'''(0)}{6}$$

Hence, $\lambda=6$

30. (65) Given, $xf(x)=x+\int_1^x f(t)\,dt$ ...(i)

On differentiating, we get

$$\Rightarrow xf'(x)+f(x)\cdot1=1+f(x)$$

$$\Rightarrow f'(x)=\frac{1}{x}$$

$$\Rightarrow f(x)=\ln x+c$$

On putting $x=1$ in Eq. (i), we get $f(1)=1$ and hence $f(1)=\ln(1)+c$

$$\Rightarrow c=1 \Rightarrow f(x)=\ln x+1$$

$$\Rightarrow f(e^k)=k+1$$

$$\therefore \sum_{k=1}^{10}f(e^k)=\sum_{k=1}^{10}(k+1)=\sum_{k=1}^{10}k+\sum_{k=1}^{10}1$$

$$=\frac{10\times11}{2}+10$$

$$=55+10=65$$

Qualifier 8
(Differentiation and Application of Derivatives)

1. (c) Here, $f'(x) = -\phi(x)$

and $\phi''(x) = -\phi(x)$

Then, $g'(x) = 2\phi(x)\phi'(x) + 2f(x)f'(x)$

$= -2\phi''(x)\phi'(x) + 2\phi'(x)\phi''(x)$

$= 0$

$\because g'(x) = 0$

$\Rightarrow g(x) = \text{constant}$

Hence, $g(100) = 1$

2. (c) Given, $\sin y = x\sin(a+y)$ ...(i)

$\Rightarrow \sin y = x(\sin a \cos y + \cos a \sin y)$

$\Rightarrow \tan y = x(\sin a + \cos a \cdot \tan y)$

$\Rightarrow \tan y = x\sin a + x\cos a \tan y$

$\Rightarrow \tan y(1 - x\cos a) = x\sin a$

$\Rightarrow \tan y = \dfrac{x\sin a}{1 - x\cos a}$

$\Rightarrow y = \tan^{-1}\left(\dfrac{x\sin a}{1 - x\cos a}\right)$ ...(ii)

Now differentiating Eq. (ii) w.r.t. x, we get

$$\frac{dy}{dx} = \frac{1}{1 + \dfrac{x^2\sin^2 a}{(1 - x\cos a)^2}} \times \frac{(1 - x\cos a)\sin a - x\sin a(-\cos a)}{(1 - x\cos a)^2}$$

$$\Rightarrow \frac{dy}{dx} = \frac{\sin a}{(1 - x\cos a)^2 + x^2\sin^2 a}$$

$$= \frac{\sin a}{1 + x^2 - 2x\cos a}$$

On comparing, we get $k = \sin a$

Hence, $2k\cos a = 2\sin a\cos a = \sin 2a$

3. (b) Given, $y = \left(1 + \dfrac{1}{x}\right)^x$

$\Rightarrow \ln y = x\ln\left(1 + \dfrac{1}{x}\right)$

$= x[\ln(x+1) - \ln x]$

On differentiating,

$$\frac{1}{y}\cdot y_1 = x\left(\frac{1}{x+1} - \frac{1}{x}\right) + [\ln(x+1) - \ln x],$$

where $y_1 = \dfrac{dy}{dx}$

$$\Rightarrow y_1 = y\left[x\left(\frac{1}{x+1} - \frac{1}{x}\right) + \{\ln(x+1) - \ln x\}\right]$$

Again differentiating

$$y_2 = y_1\left[x\left(\frac{1}{x+1} - \frac{1}{x}\right) + \{\ln(x+1) - \ln(x)\}\right]$$

$$+ y\left[\left(\frac{1}{x+1} - \frac{1}{x}\right) + x\left(-\frac{1}{(x+1)^2} + \frac{1}{x^2}\right) + \left(\frac{1}{x+1} - \frac{1}{x}\right)\right]$$

$$\therefore y_2(2) = y_1(2)\left[2\left(\frac{1}{3} - \frac{1}{2}\right) + \ln 3/2\right]$$

$$+ y(2)\left[\left(\frac{1}{3} - \frac{1}{2}\right) + 2\left(-\frac{1}{9} + \frac{1}{4}\right) + \left(\frac{1}{3} - \frac{1}{2}\right)\right]$$

Since, $y(2) = \left(1 + \dfrac{1}{2}\right)^2 = 9/4$ and

$$y_1(2) = y(2)\left[2\left(\frac{1}{3} - \frac{1}{2}\right) + \ln 3/2\right]$$

$$\Rightarrow y_1(2) = \frac{9}{4}\left(\frac{-1}{3} + \ln 3/2\right)$$

Hence,

$$y_2(2) = \frac{9}{4}\left(\frac{-1}{3} + \ln 3/2\right)^2 + \frac{9}{4}\left(\frac{-1}{18}\right)$$

$$= \frac{9}{4}\left(\frac{-1}{3} + \ln 3/2\right)^2 - \frac{1}{8}$$

4. (c) Given, $x = t + \dfrac{1}{t}$ and $y = t^k + \dfrac{1}{t^k}$

$\therefore \dfrac{dx}{dt} = 1 - t^{-2} = t^{-1}(t - t^{-1})$

$= t^{-1}\sqrt{(t - t^{-1})^2 - 4}$

$= t^{-1}\sqrt{x^2 - 4}$

and $\dfrac{dy}{dt} = kt^{k-1} - kt^{-k-1}$

$= kt^{-1}(t^k - t^{-k}) = kt^{-1}\sqrt{y^2 - 4}$

$\therefore \left(\dfrac{dy}{dx}\right)^2 = k^2\left(\dfrac{y^2 - 4}{x^2 - 4}\right)$

$\therefore \lambda = k^2$

5. (d) Given $y^2 = a^2\cos^2 x + b^2\sin^2 x$ ...(i)

From the given options, we observe that the final answer (or relation) that we need to obtain is independent of $\sin x$ and $\cos x$.

From Eq. (i)

$y^2 = \dfrac{1}{2}[a^2(2\cos^2 x) + b^2(2\sin^2 x)]$

$= \dfrac{1}{2}[a^2(1 + \cos 2x) + b^2(1 - \cos 2x)]$

$= \dfrac{1}{2}[(a^2 + b^2) + (a^2 - b^2)\cos 2x]$

$\Rightarrow 2y^2 - (a^2 + b^2) = (a^2 - b^2)\cos 2x$ ...(ii)

Differentiating Eq. (ii) w.r.t. 'x', we have

$4y\cdot\dfrac{dy}{dx} = -2(a^2 - b^2)\sin 2x$

$\Rightarrow -2y\dfrac{dy}{dx} = (a^2 - b^2)\sin 2x$ ...(iii)

Squaring and adding Eqs. (ii) and (iii),

$$(2y^2 - (a^2 + b^2))^2 + 4y^2\left(\frac{dy}{dx}\right)^2 = (a^2 - b^2)^2$$

$$\Rightarrow \left(\frac{dy}{dx}\right)^2 + y^2 - (a^2 + b^2) = -\frac{a^2b^2}{y^2}$$ ...(iv)

Again differentiating Eq. (iv) w.r.t. x, we get

$$2\cdot\left(\frac{dy}{dx}\right)\left(\frac{d^2y}{dx^2}\right) + 2y\cdot\frac{dy}{dx} = \frac{2a^2b^2}{y^3}\cdot\frac{dy}{dx}$$

$$\Rightarrow \frac{d^2y}{dx^2} + y = \frac{a^2b^2}{y^3}$$

6. (b) Consider a function $g(x) = x\cdot f(x)$

Obviously, $g(x)$ is continuous in $[0,1]$ and differentiable in $(0, 1)$.

As, $f(1) = 0$

$\therefore g(0) = 0 = g(1)$

Hence, Rolle's theorem is applicable for $g(x)$.

So, there exists some $c \in (0,1)$ such that $g'(c) = 0$

$\Rightarrow cf'(c) + f(c) = 0$

$[\because g'(x) = xf'(x) + f(x)]$

7. (b) Given, $f(x) = ax^3 + bx^2 + 11x - 6$

$f(1) = f(3)$ (By Rolle's theorem)

$\Rightarrow a + b + 5 = 27a + 9b + 33 - 6$

$\Rightarrow 13a + 4b + 11 = 0$ ...(i)

Now, $f'(x) = 3ax^2 + 2bx + 11$

So, $f'\left(2 + \dfrac{1}{\sqrt{3}}\right) = 0$

$\Rightarrow 3a\left(2 + \dfrac{1}{\sqrt{3}}\right)^2 + 2b\left(2 + \dfrac{1}{\sqrt{3}}\right) + 11 = 0$

[using Eq. (i)]

$\Rightarrow 6a + b = 0$ ...(ii)

On solving Eqs. (i) and (ii), we get

$a = 1, b = -6$

8. (c) Consider $f(x) = \phi(x) - 4\psi(x)$, $\forall x \in [0,1]$

Clearly, $f(x)$ is differentiable in (0, 1).

Also

$f(0) = \phi(0) - 4\psi(0) = 4 - 4(0) = 4$

and $f(1) = \phi(1) - 4\psi(1) = 16 - 4(3) = 4$

$\therefore f(0) = f(1)$

By Rolle's Theorem, their exist $a \in (0,1)$ such that

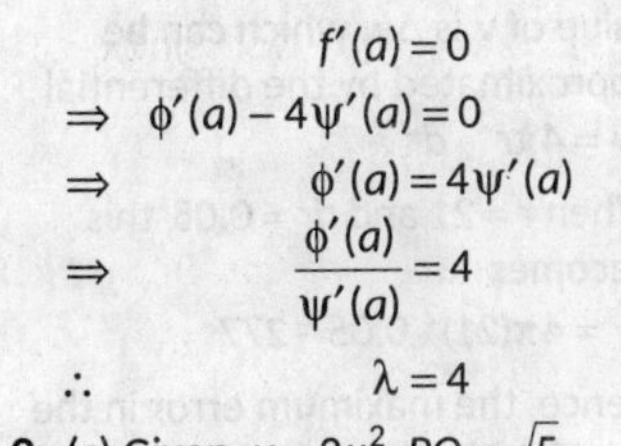

$$f'(a)=0$$
$$\Rightarrow \quad \phi'(a)-4\psi'(a)=0$$
$$\Rightarrow \quad \phi'(a)=4\psi'(a)$$
$$\Rightarrow \quad \frac{\phi'(a)}{\psi'(a)}=4$$
$$\therefore \quad \lambda=4$$

9. (c) Given, $y=2x^2, PQ=\sqrt{5}$

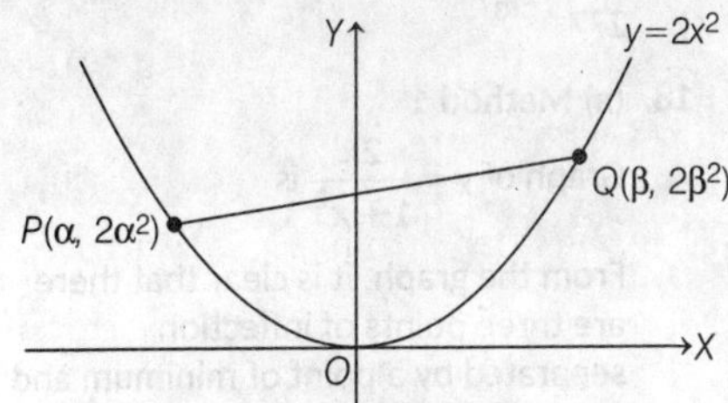

$$(PQ)^2=(\beta-\alpha)^2+(2\beta^2-2\alpha^2)^2$$
$$\Rightarrow (\beta-\alpha)^2+4(\beta^2-\alpha^2)^2=5 \quad \text{...(i)}$$

Differentiating Eq. (i) w.r.t. α, we get

$$2(\beta-\alpha)\left(\frac{d\beta}{d\alpha}-1\right)+8(\beta^2-\alpha^2)$$
$$\left(2\beta\cdot\frac{d\beta}{d\alpha}-2\alpha\right)=0 \quad \text{...(ii)}$$

According to question, $P\equiv(0,0)$ and $Q\equiv(1,2)$

So, $\alpha=0$ and $\beta=1$

From Eq. (ii),

$$2(1-0)\left(\frac{d\beta}{d\alpha}-1\right)+8(1-0)$$
$$\left(2\frac{d\beta}{d\alpha}-0\right)=0$$
$$\Rightarrow 2\frac{d\beta}{d\alpha}-2+16\frac{d\beta}{d\alpha}=0$$
$$\Rightarrow \quad \frac{d\beta}{d\alpha}=\frac{1}{9}$$

10. (a) Draw the diagram (according to question) and let x be the distance from the man to the point on the path closest to the searchlight.

Let θ be the angle from the man to the point on the path closest to the searchlight and the perpendicular to the path.

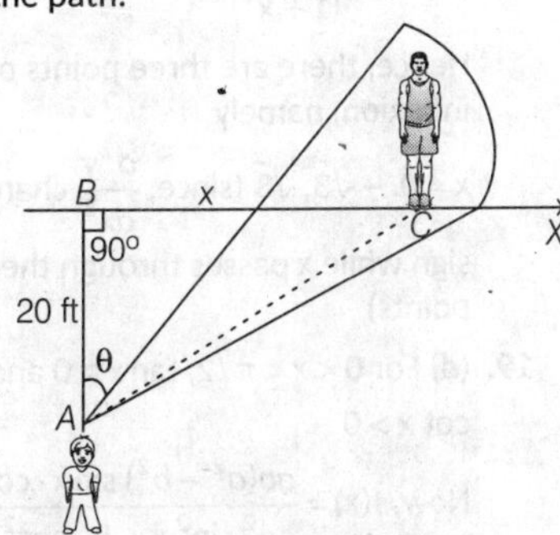

According to question, $\frac{dx}{dt}=4$ ft/sec

and we have to find the value of $\frac{d\theta}{dt}$ when $x=15$ ft

In ΔABC,

$$\tan\theta=\frac{x}{20}$$
$$\Rightarrow \quad x=20\tan\theta \quad \text{...(i)}$$

Differentiating Eq. (i) w.r.t. t, we get

$$\frac{dx}{dt}=20\sec^2\theta\frac{d\theta}{dt}$$
$$\Rightarrow \frac{d\theta}{dt}=\frac{1}{20}\cos^2\theta\cdot\frac{dx}{dt}=\frac{1}{20}\cos^2\theta(4)$$
$$\Rightarrow \frac{d\theta}{dt}=\frac{1}{5}\cos^2\theta$$

When $x=15$ ft, the length of the beam is 25 ft.

So, $\cos\theta=\frac{4}{5}$ and $\frac{d\theta}{dt}=\frac{1}{5}\left(\frac{4}{5}\right)^2$

$$=\frac{16}{125} \text{ rad/sec} = 0.128 \text{ rad/s}$$

Hence, the searchlight is rotating at the rate of $\frac{16}{125}$ rad/sec

11. (b) Given, $g(x)=2\cdot f\left(\frac{x}{2}\right)+f(2-x)$, $\forall\, x\in(0,2)$

$$\Rightarrow g'(x)=f'\left(\frac{x}{2}\right)-f'(2-x), \quad \forall\, x\in(0,2) \quad \text{...(i)}$$

Now, $f''(x)<0, \forall\, x\in(0,2)$ (Given)

So, $f'(x)$ is decreasing function on (0, 2).

For increasing

$g(x)$ is increasing if $g'(x)>0$

From Eq. (i),

$$f'\left(\frac{x}{2}\right)-f'(2-x)>0$$
$$\Rightarrow f'\left(\frac{x}{2}\right)>f'(2-x)$$
$$\Rightarrow \quad \frac{x}{2}<2-x$$

($\because f'$ is decreasing function that why inequality gets reversed)

$$\Rightarrow \quad x<4/3$$

But $0<x<2$

So, $x\in(0,4/3)$ for $g(x)$ to be increasing.

For decreasing

$g(x)$ is decreasing if $g'(x)<0$

From Eq. (i),

$$f'(x/2)-f'(2-x)<0$$
$$\Rightarrow \quad f'(x/2)<f'(2-x)$$
$$\Rightarrow \quad \frac{x}{2}>2-x$$
$$\Rightarrow \quad x>\frac{4}{3} \text{ but } 0<x<2$$

$\therefore x\in(4/3,2)$ for $g(x)$ to be decreasing.

12. (a) Given, $f(x)=2x^3-21x^2+78x+24$

$$\Rightarrow \quad f'(x)=6x^2-42x+78$$
$$=6(x^2-7x+13)$$
$$\Rightarrow \quad f'(x)>0, \forall\, x\in R$$

($\because x^2-7x+13>0\ \forall x\in R$ because $a=1>0$ and $D<0$)

$\Rightarrow f(x)$ is increasing function.

Now, $f(f(f(x-2x^3))\geq f(f(2x^3-f(x))$

$\Rightarrow f(f(x)-2x^3)\geq f(2x^3-f(x))$

($\because f$ is an increasing function $\therefore$ direction of inequality does not change)

$$\Rightarrow \quad f(x)-2x^3\geq 2x^3-f(x)$$
$$\Rightarrow \quad 2f(x)\geq 4x^3$$
$$\Rightarrow \quad f(x)\geq 2x^3$$
$$\Rightarrow 2x^3-21x^2+78x+24\geq 2x^3$$
$$\Rightarrow 7x^2-26x-8\leq 0$$
$$\Rightarrow \left(x+\frac{2}{7}\right)(x-4)\leq 0 \Rightarrow \frac{-2}{7}\leq x\leq 4$$

Hence, integral values of $x=0$, 1, 2, 3, 4.

Therefore, number of integral values of $x=5$

13. (d) $\because f(x)=\phi(1-x)+\phi(x)$

$$\Rightarrow \quad f'(x)=-\phi'(1-x)+\phi'(x)$$

Since, $\phi''(x)>0$ for $x\in[0,1]$

$\Rightarrow \phi'(x)$ is increasing.

$$\therefore \quad x<1-x$$
$$\Rightarrow \quad x<\frac{1}{2}$$

For $x\in\left[0,\frac{1}{2}\right]$

$$x<1-x\Rightarrow\phi'(x)<\phi'(1-x)$$

[ϕ' is increasing]

$$\Rightarrow \quad \phi'(x)-\phi'(1-x)<0$$
$$\Rightarrow \quad f'(x)<0$$

$\Rightarrow f(x)$ is decreasing in $\left[0,\frac{1}{2}\right]$

Again, $x>1-x$

$$\Rightarrow \quad x>\frac{1}{2}$$

For $x\in\left[\frac{1}{2},1\right]$

$$x>1-x\Rightarrow\phi'(x)>\phi'(1-x)$$

[ϕ' is increasing]

$\Rightarrow \phi'(x) - \phi'(1-x) > 10$

$\Rightarrow \quad f'(x) > 0$

$\Rightarrow f(x)$ is increasing in $\left[\frac{1}{2}, 1\right]$

14. (a) Given equation of curve is

$$3x^2 - 4y^2 = 72 \quad \text{...(i)}$$

and equation of line is $3x + 2y + 1 = 0$ ...(ii)

Slope of line (ii) is $(-3/2)$.

Let us locate the point on the curve at which the tangent is parallel to given line.

On differentiating Eq. (i) w.r.t. x, we get $6x - 8y\frac{dy}{dx} = 0$

$$\Rightarrow \left(\frac{dy}{dx}\right)_{(\alpha,\beta)} = \frac{3\alpha}{4\beta} = \frac{-3}{2}$$

$$\frac{\alpha}{\beta} = -2 \quad \text{...(iii)}$$

(Since parallel to $3x + 2y + 1 = 0$)

Also, (α, β) lines on Eq. (i) then

$$3\alpha^2 - 4\beta^2 = 72$$

$$\Rightarrow \frac{3\alpha^2}{\beta^2} - 4 = \frac{72}{\beta^2}$$

$$\Rightarrow 3(4) - 4 = \frac{72}{\beta^2} \text{ [from Eq. (iii)]}$$

$$\Rightarrow \beta^2 = 9 \Rightarrow \beta = \pm 3$$

Thus, the required points are $(-6, 3)$ and $(6, -3)$.

The distance of $(-6, 3)$ from the given line $= \frac{|-18+6+1|}{\sqrt{13}} = \frac{11}{\sqrt{3}}$

and the distance of $(6, -3)$ from the given line $= \frac{|18-6+1|}{\sqrt{13}} = \frac{13}{\sqrt{3}} > \frac{11}{\sqrt{3}}$

So, $(-6, 3)$ is the nearest point.

Hence, required result $= -6 + 3 = -3$

15. (d) Since the given point $P(2, -1)$ lies on the curve

$$\begin{cases} x = t^2 + 3t - 8 \\ y = 2t^2 - 2t - 5 \end{cases}$$

So, $t^2 + 3t - 8 = 2$ ...(i)

and $2t^2 - 2t - 5 = -1$ ...(ii)

From Eq. (i), $(t-2)(t+5) = 0$

$\Rightarrow \quad t = 2, -5$

From Eq. (ii), $(t-2)(t+1) = 0$

$\Rightarrow \quad t = 2, -1$

Hence, to the given point there corresponds the common value $t = 2$

Now, $t = 2$

Now, we determine the value of the derivative at the point P

$$\left.\frac{dy}{dx}\right|_{x=2} = \left(\frac{\frac{dy}{dt}}{\frac{dx}{dt}}\right)_{t=2} = \left(\frac{4t-2}{2t+3}\right)_{t=2} = \frac{6}{7}$$

So, the equation of the tangent to the curve at the point $P(2, -1)$ is

$$y + 1 = \frac{6}{7}(x - 2)$$

$\Rightarrow \quad 7y + 7 = 6x - 12$

$\Rightarrow 6x - 7y - 19 = 0$

16. (b) Given, equation of curve is $y = x^3$ ...(i)

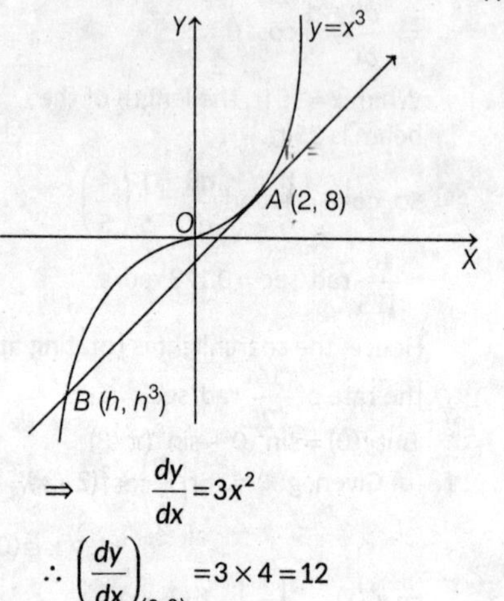

$$\Rightarrow \frac{dy}{dx} = 3x^2$$

$$\therefore \left(\frac{dy}{dx}\right)_{(2,8)} = 3 \times 4 = 12$$

So, equation of tangent at $A(2, 8)$ is $y - 8 = 12(x - 2)$ i.e., $y = 12x - 16$ ...(ii)

On solving Eqs. (i) and (ii), we get

$$x^3 - 12x + 16 = 0 \quad \text{...(iii)}$$

Eq. (iii) must give all points of intersection of line (ii) and curve (i) i.e., points A and B.

But, since line (ii) is tangent at A. So, $x = 2$ will be a repeated root of the equation $x^3 - 12x + 16 = 0$ and another root will be $x = h$ (say).

Now, using the relation between roots and coefficient for Eq. (iii).

Sum of roots $= 2 + 2 + h = \frac{0}{1}$

[$\because$ coefficients of $x^2 = 0$]

$\Rightarrow \quad h = -4$

Hence, the coordinates of B are $(-4, -64)$.

17. (d) If the radius of the sphere is 'r' then its volume is $v = \frac{4}{3}\pi r^3$.

If the error in the measured value of r is denoted by $dr = \Delta r$, then the corresponding error on the calculated value of v is Δv, which can be approximated by the differential $dv = 4\pi r^2 \cdot dr$

When $r = 21$ and $dr = 0.05$, this becomes

$dv = 4\pi(21)^2\, 0.05 \simeq 277$

Hence, the maximum error in the calculated volume is near about $277^{\ 3}$.

18. (a) **Method 1**

Graph of $y = \frac{2x}{1+x^2}$ is

From the graph, it is clear that there are three points of inflection separated by a point of minimum and maximum.

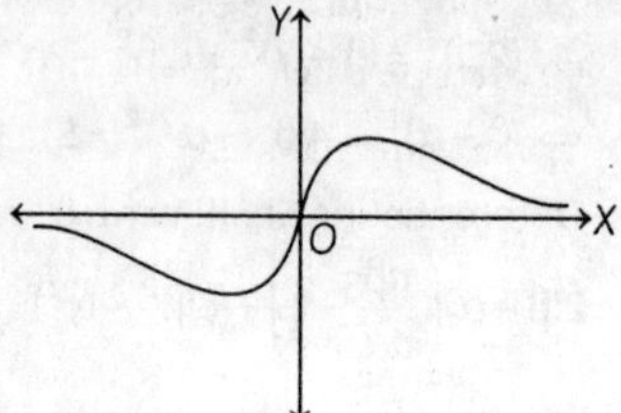

Method 2

Given $y = \frac{2x}{1+x^2}$

$$\Rightarrow \frac{dy}{dx} = \frac{2(1+x^2) - 2x \cdot 2x}{(1+x^2)^2} = \frac{2(1-x^2)}{(1+x^2)^2}$$

$\therefore x = -1$ is a minimum and $x = 1$ is a maximum.

Now,

$$\frac{d^2y}{dx^2} = \frac{(1+x^2)^2 \cdot (-4x) - 2(1-x^2) \cdot 2 \cdot (1+x^2) \cdot 2x}{(1+x^2)^4}$$

$$= \frac{-4x(1+x^2) - 8x(1-x^2)}{(1+x^2)^3}$$

$$= \frac{-4x - 4x^3 - 8x + 8x^3}{(1+x^2)^3}$$

$$= \frac{-12x + 4x^3}{(1+x^2)^3}$$

$$= \frac{4x(x^2 - 3)}{(1+x^2)^3}$$

Hence, there are three points of inflexion, namely

$x = 0, -\sqrt{3}, \sqrt{3}$ (since, $\frac{d^2y}{dx^2}$ changes sign while x passes through these points)

19. (d) For $0 < x < \pi/2$, $\tan x > 0$ and $\cot x > 0$

Now, $f(x) = \frac{ab(a^2 - b^2)\sin x \cdot \cos x}{a^2\sin^2 x + b^2\cos^2 x}$

$$\Rightarrow f(x)=\frac{\frac{ab(a^2-b^2)\sin x\cdot\cos x}{\sin x\cdot\cos x}}{\frac{a^2\sin^2 x+b^2\cos^2 x}{\sin x\cdot \cos x}}$$

$$\Rightarrow f(x)=\frac{ab(a^2-b^2)}{a^2\tan x+b^2\cot x}$$

$$=\frac{ab(a^2-b^2)}{(a\sqrt{\tan x}-b\sqrt{\cot x})^2+2ab}$$

Now, $f(x)$ will be maximum if denominator will be minimum and denominator will be minimum if $(a\sqrt{\tan x}-b\sqrt{\cot x})^2$ will be minimum.

Since, we know that minimum value of any non-negative, term is zero.

So, minimum value of $(a\sqrt{\tan x}-b\sqrt{\cot x})^2=0$

$\therefore$ Maximum value of $f(x)=\frac{ab(a^2-b^2)}{2ab}=\frac{a^2-b^2}{2}$

20. (c) Given,

$$f(x)=\cot x-\sqrt{2}\,\text{cosec} x=\frac{\cos x-\sqrt{2}}{\sin x}$$

$$\Rightarrow f'(x)=\frac{\sin x(-\sin x)-(\cos x-\sqrt{2})\cos x}{\sin^2 x}$$

$$=\frac{-1+\sqrt{2}\cos x}{\sin^2 x}$$

Putting $f'(x)=0$

$$\Rightarrow \quad \cos x=\frac{1}{\sqrt{2}}\Rightarrow x=\frac{\pi}{4}\in(0,\pi)$$

Sign scheme for $f'(x)$

$-\infty$ ← + (0 to $\pi/4$) − ($\pi/4$ to π) → ∞

(Point of local maximum)

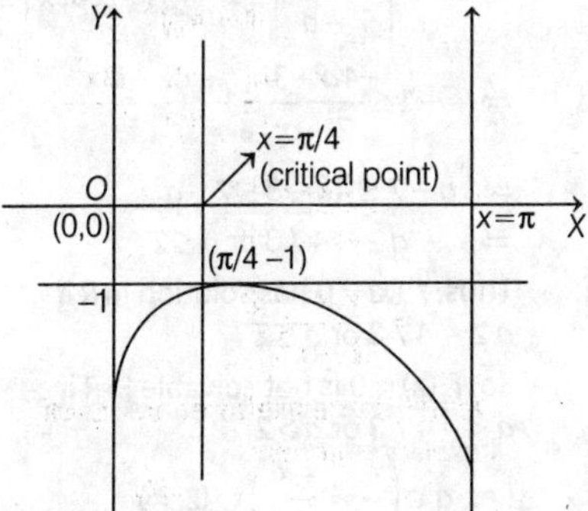

Fig. graph of $(f(x))=\cot x-\sqrt{2}\,\text{cosec}\, x$ in $(0,\pi)$

$\therefore f(x)$ is increasing (point of local maximum) on $(0,\pi/4)$ and $f(x)$ is decreasing on $(\pi/4,\pi)$

Also, $\lim\limits_{x\to0^+}f(x)=\lim\limits_{x\to0^+}\left(\frac{\cos x-\sqrt{2}}{\sin x}\right)$

and

$$\lim_{x\to\pi^-}f(x)=\lim_{x\to\pi^-}\left(\frac{\cos x-\sqrt{2}}{\sin x}\right)\to-\infty$$

Also, $f(x)$ is continuous on $(0,\pi)$.

Clearly, $f(x)<0,\ \forall x\in(0,\pi)$.

$\therefore$ At $x=\pi/4$ (a local maximum point), $f(x)$ takes its absolute maximum value also.

Hence, absolute maximum value of $f(x)|_{x=\pi/4}=1-\sqrt{2}(\sqrt{2})=-1$

21. (1) Given, $f(x)=\sin^2 x+\sin^2(x+\pi/3)+\cos x\cdot\cos(x+\pi/3)$

$$\Rightarrow f'(x)=2\sin x\cdot\cos x+2\sin(x+\pi/3)\cdot\cos(x+\pi/3)-\sin x\cos\left(x+\frac{\pi}{3}\right)-\cos x\cdot\sin(x+\pi/3)$$

$$=\sin 2x+\sin(2x+2\pi/3)-\sin\{(x)+(x+\pi/3)\}$$

$$=2\sin(2x+\pi/3)\cdot\cos\pi/3-\sin(2x+\pi/3)$$

$$=\sin\left(2x+\frac{\pi}{3}\right)-\sin(2x+\pi/3)=0$$

$\Rightarrow f(x)=k$, where k is a constant.

But $f(0)=\sin^2 0+\sin^2(\pi/3)+\cos 0\cdot\cos^2(\pi/3)=5/4$

So, $f(x)=5/4$ for all $x\in R$

Hence, $gof(x)=g(f(x))=g(5/4)=1$

22. (1) Given $f(x)=\cot^{-1}\left(\frac{x^x-x^{-x}}{2}\right)$

Putting $u=x^x$ and using logarithmic differentiation, we get

$$\ln u=x\ln x$$

$$\Rightarrow \quad \frac{1}{u}\cdot\frac{du}{dx}=x\cdot\frac{1}{x}+\ln x$$

$$\Rightarrow \quad \frac{du}{dx}=x^x(1+\ln x)$$

Similarly, if $v=x^{-x}$, we get

$$\frac{dv}{dx}=-x^{-x}(1+\ln x)$$

$$\therefore f'(x)=\frac{-1}{1+\left(\frac{x^x+x^{-x}}{2}\right)^2}\cdot\frac{d}{dx}\left(\frac{x^x-x^{-x}}{2}\right)$$

$$=\frac{-4}{x^{2x}+x^{-2x}+2}\left[\frac{1}{2}\{(x^x+x^{-x})(1+\ln x)\}\right]$$

$$\therefore f'(1)=\frac{-2}{1+1+2}[2(1+\ln 1)]=-1$$

Hence, $2+f'(1)=2+(-1)=1$

23. (5050) Given $f(x)$

$$f(x)=\prod_{n=1}^{100}(x-n)^{n(101-n)}$$

$$\Rightarrow \ln f(x)=\sum_{n=1}^{100}n(101-n)\ln(x-n) \quad \text{...(i)}$$

(note that, after applying log, π changes to Σ)

Differentiating Eq. (i) w.r.t. x, we get

$$\frac{f'(x)}{f(x)}=\sum_{n=1}^{100}\frac{n(101-n)}{(x-n)}$$

$$\Rightarrow \frac{f'(101)}{f(101)}=\sum_{n=1}^{100}\frac{n(101-n)}{(101-n)}$$

$$=\sum_{n=1}^{100}n=5050$$

$$\therefore \quad \frac{f(101)}{f'(101)}=\frac{1}{5050}$$

On comparing, $\lambda=5050$

$$\therefore \quad \frac{\lambda}{2}=\frac{5050}{2}=2525$$

Hence, $5050\log_{2525}(\lambda/2)$

$$=5050\times\log_{(2525)}(2525)$$

$$=5050\times1=5050$$

24. (105) Given, $f(x)=x^3-6ax^2+5x$ ...(i)

$$f(b)=f(2)=8-24a+10=18-24a$$

$$f(a)=f(1)=1-6a+5=6-6a$$

$$f'(x)=3x^2-12ax+5 \quad \text{...(ii)}$$

From Lagrange's Mean Value theorem,

$$f'(x)=\frac{f(b)-f(a)}{b-a}=\frac{18-24a-6+6a}{2-1}$$

$$\therefore f'(x)=12-18a \quad \text{...(iii)}$$

At $x=\frac{7}{4}$,

Put in Eq. (iii)

$$3\times\frac{49}{16}-12a\times\frac{7}{4}+5=12-18a$$

$$\Rightarrow \quad 3a=\frac{147}{16}-7$$

$$\Rightarrow \quad 3a=\frac{35}{16}\Rightarrow a=\frac{35}{48}=8.75$$

The value of $12a=12\times8.75=105$

25. (4) Let L and M be the positions of Asif (A) and Sohrab (S) at any time t

$\because$ velocities are same.

$$OL=OM=x \quad \text{(say)}$$

Let $LM=y$

Then $OM=x$, It is given that $\frac{dx}{dt}=V$

and we need to find $\frac{dy}{dt}$ from ΔMOL

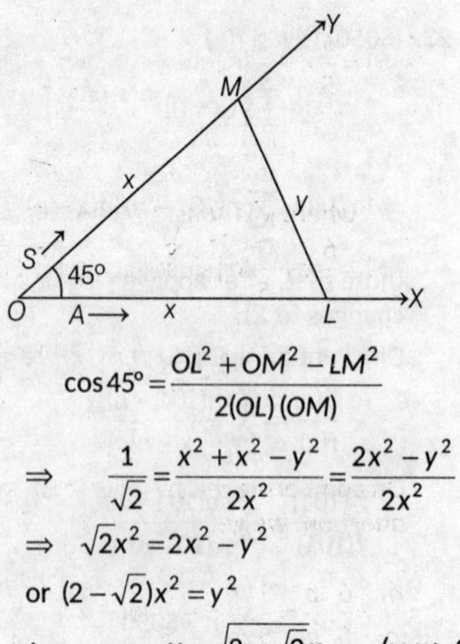

$$\cos 45° = \frac{OL^2 + OM^2 - LM^2}{2(OL)(OM)}$$

$\Rightarrow \quad \frac{1}{\sqrt{2}} = \frac{x^2 + x^2 - y^2}{2x^2} = \frac{2x^2 - y^2}{2x^2}$

$\Rightarrow \quad \sqrt{2}x^2 = 2x^2 - y^2$

or $(2-\sqrt{2})x^2 = y^2$

$\therefore \quad y = \sqrt{2-\sqrt{2}}\,x \qquad (\because x > 0)$

Differentiating it w.r.t. t, we get

$$\frac{dy}{dt} = \sqrt{2-\sqrt{2}}\,\frac{dx}{dt} = \sqrt{2-\sqrt{2}}\,V$$

$$\left(\because \frac{dx}{dt} = V\right)$$

Therefore, Asif and Sohrab being separated from each other at the rate of $\sqrt{2-\sqrt{2}}$ V.

On comparing (by question), we get

$$\alpha = 2, \beta = 2$$

Hence, $\alpha + \beta = 2 + 2 = 4$

26. (1) Given, $y = ax^2 + bx + \frac{7}{2}$

$\Rightarrow \left(\frac{dy}{dx}\right)_{(1,2)} = (2ax + b)_{(1,2)} = 2a + b$

Now, differentiating $y = x^2 + 6x + 10$ w.r.t. x, we get

$$\frac{dy}{dx} = 2x + 6$$

Slope of normal at

$(2, -2) = \left(\frac{-1}{2x+6}\right)_{(-2,2)} = \frac{-1}{2}$

According to question,

$$2a + b = \frac{-1}{2} \qquad \text{...(i)}$$

Since, point (1, 2) satisfies

$$y = ax^2 + bx + 7/2$$

$\Rightarrow \quad 2 = a + b + 7/2$

$\Rightarrow \quad a + b = \frac{-3}{2} \qquad \text{...(i)}$

On solving Eqs. (i) and (ii), we get

$$a = 1, b = \frac{-5}{2}$$

Hence, $\frac{7}{2}a + b = \frac{7}{2} \times 1 - \frac{5}{2} = \frac{2}{2} = 1$

27. (10) $f(x) = \begin{cases} 2 - x + a^2 - 9a - 9, & x < 2 \\ 2x - 3, & x \geq 2 \end{cases}$

$f(x)$ has local minimum of $x = 2$

$\therefore \quad f(2) \leq f(2^-)$

$\Rightarrow \quad 1 \leq a^2 - 9a - 9$

$\Rightarrow a^2 - 9a - 10 \geq 0$

$\Rightarrow (a-10)(a+1) \geq 0$

$\Rightarrow a \in [10, \infty)$ (because a is positive)

Hence, least integral value of $a = 10$

28. (2) Since $f(x) = 2x^3 - 9ax^2 + 12a^2x + 1$ attains maximum and minimum at p and q, respectively.

$\therefore f'(p) = 0, f'(q) = 0$, $f''(p) < 0$ and $f''(q) > 0$

Now, $f'(p) = 0$ and $f'(q) = 0$

$\Rightarrow \quad 6p^2 - 18ap + 12a^2 = 0$

and $6q^2 - 18aq + 12a^2 = 0$

$\Rightarrow \quad p^2 - 3ap + 2a^2 = 0$

and $\quad q^2 - 3aq + 2a^2 = 0$

$\Rightarrow \quad p = a, 2a \qquad \text{...(i)}$

and $\quad q = a, 2a \qquad \text{...(ii)}$

Now, $f''(p) < 0$ and $f''(q) > 0$

$\Rightarrow 12p - 18a < 0$ and $12q - 18q > 0$

$\Rightarrow \quad p < \frac{3}{2}a \qquad \text{...(iii)}$

and $\quad q > \frac{3}{2}a \qquad \text{...(iv)}$

From Eqs. (i), (ii), (iii) and (iv), we get

$$p = a, q = 2a$$

Now, $p^2 = q \Rightarrow a^2 = 2a \Rightarrow a = 0, 2$

But for $a = 0$, $f(x) = 2x^3 + 1$ which does not attain a maximum or minimum for any value of x.

Hence, $a = 2$

29. (8) Given, $C_1 : y = \sqrt{2 - x^2}$ (semicircle)

$C_2 : xy = 9$ (Rectangular hyperbola)

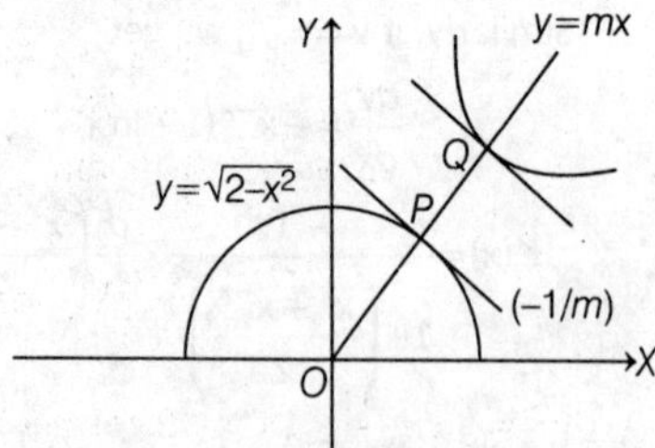

PQ will be minimum if the normal at P on the semicircle is also a normal at Q on $xy = 9$.

Let the normal at P be $y = mx$ $(m > 0)$

Solving it with $xy = 9$, we get

$$mx^2 = 9$$

$\Rightarrow \quad x = \frac{3}{\sqrt{m}}, y = \frac{9\sqrt{m}}{3}$

$(\because x, y > 0$ first quadrant$)$

$\therefore \quad Q \equiv \left(\frac{3}{\sqrt{m}}, 3\sqrt{m}\right)$

Differentiating $xy = 9$, we have

$$x\frac{dy}{dx} + y = 0$$

$\Rightarrow \quad \frac{dy}{dx} = \frac{-y}{x}$

$\therefore \quad \left(\frac{dy}{dx}\right)_Q = -\frac{3\sqrt{m} \cdot \sqrt{m}}{3} = -m$

The tangent at P and Q must be parallel.

$\therefore \quad -m = -\frac{1}{m}$

$\Rightarrow \quad m^2 = 1$

$\Rightarrow \quad m = 1 \qquad (\because m > 0)$

$\therefore$ The normal at P and Q is $y = x$

Solving the normal with the curves, we get

$$P(1, 1) \text{ and } Q(3, 3)$$

$\therefore (PQ)^2 = (d)^2 = 4 + 4 = 8$

30. (2) Given, $f(x) = (4\lambda - 3)(x + \log 5)$

$$+ 2(\lambda - 7)\cot\frac{x}{2} \cdot \sin^2\frac{x}{2}$$

$\Rightarrow f(x) = (4\lambda - 3)(x + \log 5)(\lambda - 7)\sin x$

$\therefore f'(x) = (4\lambda - 3) + (\lambda - 7)\cos x$

If $f(x)$ does not have critical points, then $f'(x) = 0$ does not have any solution in R

Now, $f'(x) = 0$

$\Rightarrow \quad \cos x = \frac{4a - 3}{7 - a}$

$\Rightarrow \quad \left|\frac{4a-3}{7-a}\right| \leq 1 \qquad [\because |\cos x| \leq 1]$

$\Rightarrow \quad -1 \leq \frac{4a-3}{7-a} \leq 1$

$\Rightarrow \quad a - 7 \leq 4a - 3 \leq 7 - a$

$\Rightarrow \quad a \geq -4/3$ or $a \leq 2$

Thus, $f'(x) = 0$ has solution in R if $a \geq -4/3$ or $a \leq 2$

So, $f'(x) = 0$ is not solvable in R if $a < -4/3$ or $a > 2$

i.e., $a \in \left(-\infty, \frac{-4}{3}\right) \cup (2, \infty)$

On comparing, $A = \frac{-4}{3}$ and $B = 2$

Hence, $|3A + B| = \left|3 \times \left(\frac{-4}{3}\right) + 2\right|$

$$= |-4 + 2| = |-2| = 2$$

Qualifier 9
(Indefinite and Definite Integrations)

1. (d) Let $I=\int \frac{x+\sqrt[3]{x^2}+\sqrt[6]{x}}{x(1+\sqrt[3]{x})}dx$ ...(i)

Concept/Approach From above we observe that either cube roots or sixth roots in the integrand. So, we take LCM of (3, 6) which is 6. So that the substitution $x=t^6$ can reduce this expression to an entirely rational form.

Start Putting $x=z^6 \Rightarrow dx=6z^5dz$

From Eq. (i), $I=6\int \frac{z^6+z^4+z}{z^6(1+z^2)}\cdot z^5dz$

$$\Rightarrow I=6\cdot\int \frac{z^5+z^3+1}{1+z^2}dz$$

$$=6\left[\int \frac{z^3(z^2+1)}{(z^2+1)}dz+\int \frac{1}{1+z^2}dz\right]$$

$$\Rightarrow I=6\left[\frac{z^4}{4}+\tan^{-1}(z)\right]+c,$$ where c is constant of integration.

$$\Rightarrow I=\frac{3}{2}x^{\frac{2}{3}}+6\tan^{-1}\sqrt[6]{x}+c$$

$$(\because x=z^6 \Rightarrow z=(x)^{1/6})$$

2. (b) Let $I=\int \frac{dx}{(x-1)^{\frac{3}{4}}(x+2)^{\frac{5}{4}}}$

Concept/Approach From above integrand, we observe the exponents of linear factors (in denominator) carefully; $\left(\frac{3}{4}\right)$ is $\left(\frac{1}{4}\right)$ less than 1 while $\left(\frac{5}{4}\right)$ is $\left(\frac{1}{4}\right)$ more than 1.

Therefore, we can write the denominator as

$$(x-1)^{\frac{3}{4}}(x+2)^{\frac{5}{4}}=(x-1)(x+2)\left(\frac{x+2}{x-1}\right)^{1/4}$$

and then we use the concept of integration by substitution.

Start Putting $\left(\frac{x+2}{x-1}\right)=z^4$

$$\Rightarrow \quad x=\frac{z^4+2}{z^4-1}$$

$$\Rightarrow dx=\frac{-12z^3}{(z^4-1)^2}dz$$

Thus, $I=\int \frac{dx}{(x-1)(x+2)\left(\frac{x+2}{x-1}\right)^{\frac{1}{4}}}$

$$=\int \frac{-12z^3dz}{\left(\frac{3}{z^4-1}\right)\left(\frac{2z^3}{z^4-1}\right)(z^4-1)^2\cdot z}$$

$$=-\frac{4}{3}\int \frac{dz}{z^2}=\frac{4}{3z}+c=\frac{4}{3}\left(\frac{x-1}{x+2}\right)^{\frac{1}{4}}+c,$$

where c is constant of integration.

3. (b) Let $I=\int \frac{2+3\cos x}{\sin x+2\cos x+3}dx$ ...(i)

Let $\frac{2+3\cos x}{\sin x+2\cos x+3}$

$$=\frac{A(D^r)+B(dC \quad D^r)+C}{D^r}$$

$$=\frac{A(\sin x+2\cos x+3)+B(\cos x-2\sin x)+C}{\sin x+2\cos x+3}$$

$$\Rightarrow 2+3\cos x=(A-2B)\sin x+(2A+B)\cos x+3A+C$$

On comparing the coefficients of $\sin x$, $\cos x$ and constant term,

$$\left.\begin{aligned}A-2B&=0\\2A+B&=3\\3A+C&=2\end{aligned}\right\}\text{By solving, we get } A=\frac{6}{5},$$

$B=\frac{3}{5}$ and $C=-\frac{8}{5}$

From Eq. (i),

$$I=\frac{6}{5}\int dx+\frac{3}{5}\int \frac{dz}{z}-\frac{8}{5}\int \frac{1}{\sin x+2\cos x+3}dx,$$

where $z=\sin x+2\cos x+3$

$$\Rightarrow I=\frac{6}{5}x+\frac{3}{5}\ln|\sin x+2\cos x+3|-\frac{8}{5}\int \frac{2+\tan^2\left(\frac{x}{2}\right)\cdot dx}{2\tan\frac{x}{2}+2\left(1-\tan^2\frac{x}{2}\right)+3\left(1+\tan^2\frac{x}{2}\right)}$$

$$\Rightarrow I=\frac{6}{5}x+\frac{3}{5}\ln|\sin x+2\cos x+3|-\frac{8}{5}\int \frac{2\cdot dt}{t^2+2t+5}, \text{ where } t=\tan\frac{x}{2}$$

$$\Rightarrow I=\frac{6}{5}x+\frac{3}{5}\ln|\sin x+2\cos x+3|-\frac{8}{5}\times 2\times\int \frac{1}{(t+1)^2+4}dt$$

$$\Rightarrow I=\frac{6}{5}x+\frac{3}{5}\ln|\sin x+2\cos x+3|-\frac{16}{5}\times\frac{1}{2}\tan^{-1}\left(\frac{t+1}{2}\right)+k,$$

where k is constant of integration.

$$\Rightarrow I=\frac{6}{5}x+\frac{3}{5}\ln|\sin x+2\cos x+3|-\frac{8}{5}\tan^{-1}\left(\frac{1+\tan\frac{x}{2}}{2}\right)+k$$

On comparing this by given data in question, we get

$$\frac{m}{n}=\frac{6}{5}, \frac{p}{q}=\frac{3}{5}, \frac{r}{s}=-\frac{8}{5}, \phi(x)=\frac{1+\tan\frac{x}{2}}{2}$$

Hence, $\left(\frac{m}{n}+\frac{p}{q}+\frac{r}{s}\right)\phi(0)$

$$=\left(\frac{6}{5}+\frac{3}{5}-\frac{8}{5}\right)\cdot\left(\frac{1}{2}\right)=\frac{1}{10}$$

4. (d) Let $I=\int \frac{2x+7}{\sqrt{4+8x-5x^2}}dx=-\frac{1}{5}\int \frac{-10x+8}{\sqrt{4+8x-5x^2}}dx+\frac{43}{5}\times\int \frac{1}{\sqrt{4+8x-5x^2}}dx$

$$\Rightarrow I=-\frac{1}{5}\int \frac{dt}{\sqrt{t}}+\frac{43}{5\sqrt{5}}\int \frac{1}{\sqrt{\frac{4}{5}-\left(x-\frac{4}{3}\right)^2+\frac{16}{25}}}dx,$$

where $t=4+8x-5x^2$

$$\Rightarrow I=-\frac{2}{5}\sqrt{t}+\frac{43}{5\sqrt{5}}\int \frac{1}{\sqrt{\left(\frac{6}{5}\right)^2-\left(x-\frac{4}{5}\right)^2}}dx$$

$$\Rightarrow I=-\frac{2}{5}\sqrt{4+8x-5x^2}+\frac{43}{5\sqrt{5}}\sin^{-1}\left(\frac{x-\frac{4}{5}}{\frac{6}{5}}\right)+c,$$

where c is constant of integration.

$$\Rightarrow I=-\frac{2}{5}\sqrt{4+8x-5x^2}+\frac{43}{5\sqrt{5}}\sin^{-1}\left(\frac{5x-4}{6}\right)+c$$

On comparing, we get

$$f(x)=\sqrt{4+8x-5x^2}$$

and $g(x)=\sin^{-1}\left(\frac{5x-4}{6}\right)$

So, $f(x)+g(x)=\sqrt{4+8x-5x^2}$

$$+\sin^{-1}\left(\frac{5x-4}{6}\right)$$

Domain of $[f(x)+g(x)]$ is

$$\begin{cases}4+8x-5x^2\geq 0\\ -1\leq\frac{5x-4}{6}\leq 1\end{cases}$$

$$\Rightarrow\begin{cases}5x^2-8x-4\leq 0\\ -6+4\leq 5x\leq 6+4\end{cases}$$

$$\Rightarrow\begin{cases}(5x+2)(x-2)=0\\ -2\leq 5x\leq 10\end{cases}\Rightarrow\begin{cases}-\frac{2}{5}\leq x\leq 2\\ -\frac{2}{5}\leq x\leq 2\end{cases}$$

$\Rightarrow x\in\left[-\frac{2}{5},2\right]$ But $x\notin\left\{-\frac{2}{5},2\right\}\Rightarrow$ (at $x=2,-\frac{2}{5}$, I becomes undefined)

Hence, domain of $f(x)+g(x)=\left(-\frac{2}{5},2\right)$

5. (c) Let $I=\int\frac{x-1}{(x+1)\sqrt{x^3+x^2+x}}dx$

$$=\int\frac{x^2-1}{(x+1)^2\sqrt{x^3+x^2+x}}dx$$

$$=\int\frac{x^2-1}{(x+1)^2\cdot x\sqrt{x+1+\frac{1}{x}}}dx$$

Dividing numerator and denominator by x^2, we get

$$I=\int\frac{1-\frac{1}{x^2}}{\left(\frac{x^2+2x+1}{x}\right)\sqrt{x+\frac{1}{x}+1}}dx$$

$$=\int\frac{d\left(x+\frac{1}{x}+1\right)}{\left(x+\frac{1}{x}+2\right)\sqrt{x+\frac{1}{x}+1}}$$

Let $x+\frac{1}{x}+1=u^2$

$$\Rightarrow d\left(x+\frac{1}{x}+1\right)=2u\,du$$

$$I=\int\frac{2u\,du}{(u^2+1)u}=2\tan^{-1}\sqrt{x+\frac{1}{x}+1}+c,$$

where c is constant of integration.

Hence, $\psi(x)=2\tan^{-1}\sqrt{x+\frac{1}{x}+1}$

$$\left[\because\psi(1)=2\tan^{-1}(\sqrt{3})=\frac{2\pi}{3}\right]$$

6. (d) Let $f(x)=\frac{4\sin x}{5+4\cos x}$

Differentiating w.r.t. x, we get

$$f'(x)=\frac{4\cos x(5+4\cos x)-(-4\sin x)\cdot(4\sin x)}{(5+4\cos x)^2}$$

$$\Rightarrow f'(x)=\frac{20\cos x}{(5+4\cos x)^2}+\frac{16}{(5+4\cos x)^2}$$

$$\Rightarrow f'(x)=\frac{5(5+4\cos x)}{(5+4\cos x)^2}-\frac{9}{(5+4\cos x)^2}$$

Integrating w.r.t. x, we get

$$f(x)=5\int\frac{1}{(5+4\cos x)}dx-9\int\frac{1}{(5+4\cos x)^2}dx$$

$$\Rightarrow\int\frac{1}{(5+4\cos x)^2}dx=\frac{5}{9}\int\frac{1}{5+4\cos x}dx-\frac{1}{9}\left(\frac{4\sin x}{5+4\cos x}\right)+c$$

$$=\frac{5}{9}\int\frac{\sec^2\frac{x}{2}}{5\left(1+\tan^2\frac{x}{2}\right)+4\left(1-\tan^2\frac{x}{2}\right)}dx-\frac{1}{9}\left(\frac{4\sin x}{5+4\cos x}\right)+c$$

Let $\tan\left(\frac{x}{2}\right)=z\Rightarrow\sec^2\frac{x}{2}dx=2dz$

$$\int\frac{1}{5+4\cos x}dx=\frac{5}{9}\int\frac{2dz}{9+z^2}-\frac{1}{9}\left(\frac{4\sin x}{5+4\cos x}\right)+c$$

$$=\frac{10}{9}\cdot\frac{1}{3}\tan^{-1}\left(\frac{z}{3}\right)-\frac{4}{9}\left(\frac{\sin x}{5+4\cos x}\right)+c$$

$$=\frac{10}{27}\tan^{-1}\left(\frac{1}{3}\tan\frac{x}{2}\right)-\frac{4}{9}\left(\frac{\sin x}{5+4\cos x}\right)+c$$

$\therefore\ m=\frac{10}{27},n=\frac{1}{3},p=-\frac{4}{9}$

Hence, $2n^2-m-\frac{p}{3}=\frac{2}{9}-\frac{10}{27}+\frac{4}{27}$

$$=\frac{2}{9}-\frac{6}{27}=\frac{2}{9}-\frac{2}{9}=0$$

7. (c) Let $I=\int\frac{x^2-1}{x^3\sqrt{2x^4-2x^2+1}}dx$

Dividing N^r and D^r by x^5, we get

$$I=\int\frac{\frac{1}{x^3}-\frac{1}{x^5}}{\sqrt{2-\frac{2}{x^2}+\frac{1}{x^4}}}dx$$

Let $2-\frac{2}{x^2}+\frac{1}{x^4}=z$

$$\Rightarrow\left(\frac{4}{x^3}-\frac{4}{x^5}\right)dx=dz$$

$$\therefore I=\frac{1}{4}\int\frac{1}{\sqrt{z}}dz=\frac{1}{2}\sqrt{z}+c$$

$$=\frac{1}{2}\sqrt{2-\frac{2}{x^2}+\frac{1}{x^4}}+c$$

8. (a) Let $\cos x+i\sin x=u$ ...(i)

Also, $u^n=\cos nx+i\sin nx$ ...(A)

$\therefore\cos x-i\sin x=\frac{1}{u}$ ...(ii)

$\frac{1}{u^n}=\cos nx-i\sin nx$ ...(B)

On adding Eqs. (i) and (ii), we get

$$2\cos x=u+\frac{1}{u}$$

On subtracting Eq. (i) from Eq. (ii),

$$2i\sin x=u-\frac{1}{u}$$

$\Rightarrow 4\cos^2 x=\left(u+\frac{1}{u}\right)^2$ ...(iii)

$\Rightarrow 16\sin^4 x=\left(u-\frac{1}{u}\right)^4$ ...(iv)

On multiply by Eqs. (iii) and (iv),

$$64\cos^2 x\sin^4 x=\left(u+\frac{1}{u}\right)^2\left(u-\frac{1}{u}\right)^4$$

$$=\left(u^2-\frac{1}{u^2}\right)^2\left(u-\frac{1}{u}\right)^2$$

$$\Rightarrow 64\cos^2 x\cdot\sin^4 x=\left(u^4+\frac{1}{u^4}-2\right)\left(u^2+\frac{1}{u^2}-2\right)$$

$$=\left(u^6+\frac{1}{u^6}\right)-2\left(u^4+\frac{1}{u^4}\right)+(-2+1)\left(u^2+\frac{1}{u^2}\right)+4$$

$$=2\cos 6x-4\cos 4x-2\cos 2x+4$$

[from Eqs. (A) and (B)]

$[\because(\cos\theta+i\sin\theta)^n=\cos n\theta+i\sin n\theta]$

$$\therefore\int\cos^2 x\cdot\sin^4 x\,dx=\frac{1}{32}\left[\int\cos 6x\,dx-2\int\cos 4x\,dx-\int\cos 2x\,dx+2x\right]$$

$$=\frac{1}{32}\left[\frac{\sin 6x}{6}-\frac{\sin 4x}{2}-\frac{\sin 2x}{2}+2x\right]+c$$

Hence, $m=6$, $n=-2$, $p=-2$, $q=2$

$\therefore\ m+n+p+q=4$

9. (b) Given, $f\left(\frac{3x-4}{3x+4}\right)=x+2$ ...(i)

$$x \neq -\frac{4}{3}$$

Let $\frac{3x-4}{3x+4} = u$

$$\Rightarrow \frac{(3x-4)+(3x+4)}{(3x-4)-(3x+4)} = \frac{u+1}{u-1}$$

[Using componendo and dividendo $\left(\frac{N-D}{N+D}\right)$]

$$\Rightarrow \frac{6x}{-8} = \frac{u+1}{u-1} \Rightarrow x = -\frac{4}{3}\left(\frac{u+1}{u-1}\right)$$

$$\Rightarrow x+2 = -\frac{4u+4}{3u-3} + 2$$

$$\Rightarrow x+2 = \frac{2u-10}{3u-3}$$

From Eq. (i),

$$f(u) = \frac{2u-10}{3u-3} = \frac{2}{3}\left(\frac{u-5}{u-1}\right)$$

$$= \frac{2}{3}\left(\frac{u-1-4}{u-1}\right) = \frac{2}{3}\left(1 - \frac{4}{u-1}\right)$$

$$\Rightarrow f(u) = \frac{2}{3} - \frac{8}{3(u-1)}$$

i.e. $f(x) = \frac{2}{3} - \frac{8}{3} \cdot \frac{1}{(x-1)}$

$$\Rightarrow \int f(x)dx = \int \frac{2}{3}dx - \int \frac{8}{3} \times \frac{1}{x-1}dx$$

$$= \frac{2}{3}x - \frac{8}{3}\ln|x-1| + c$$

Hence, $(A, B) - \left(-\frac{8}{3}, \frac{2}{3}\right)$

10. (a) Let

$$I = \int e^x\left[\frac{2\tan x}{1+\tan x} + \cot^2\left(x + \frac{\pi}{4}\right)\right]dx$$

$$\Rightarrow I = \int e^x\left[\frac{2\tan x}{1+\tan x} + \tan^2\left(x - \frac{\pi}{4}\right)\right]dx$$

$\{\because \cot(\theta - 90°) = -\tan\theta,$

$\therefore \left[\cot\left(\theta - \frac{\pi}{2}\right)\right]^2 = \tan^2\theta\}$

$$\Rightarrow I = \int e^x\left[\left\{\frac{2\tan x}{1+\tan x} - 1\right\} + \left\{\tan^2\left(x - \frac{\pi}{4}\right) + 1\right\}\right]dx$$

$$\Rightarrow I = \int e^x\left[\frac{\tan x - 1}{1+\tan x} + \sec^2\left(x - \frac{\pi}{4}\right)\right]dx$$

$$\Rightarrow I = \int e^x\left[\tan\left(x - \frac{\pi}{4}\right) + \sec^2\left(x - \frac{\pi}{4}\right)\right]dx$$

$$\Rightarrow I = e^x \cdot \tan\left(x - \frac{\pi}{4}\right) + c$$

$[\because \int e^x(f(x) + f'(x))dx = e^x f(x) + c]$

11. (c) Given,

$$f(t) = \int_{2t}^{t^2} \tan^{-1}\left|\frac{(1+t)^2 - x}{1+x}\right| dx \quad \text{...(i)}$$

$$= \int_{2t}^{t^2} \tan^{-1}\left|\frac{1+x}{(1+t)^2 - x}\right| dx$$

$\left(\text{using} \int_a^b f(x)dx = \int_a^b f(a+b-x)dx\right)$

$$\Rightarrow f(t) = \int_{2t}^{t^2} \cot^{-1}\left|\frac{(1+t)^2 - x}{1+x}\right| dx \quad \text{...(ii)}$$

On adding Eqs. (i) and (ii), we get

$$2f(t) = \int_{2t}^{t^2} \frac{\pi}{2} \cdot dx$$

$\left(\because \tan^{-1}x + \cot^{-1}x = \frac{\pi}{2}\right)$

$$\Rightarrow \quad 2f(t) = \frac{\pi}{2}(t^2 - 2t)$$

$$\Rightarrow \quad f(t) = \frac{\pi}{4}[(t-1)^2 - 1]$$

$\therefore$ Minimum value of $f(t) = -\frac{\pi}{4}$

12. (a) $I(n) = \int_0^1 x^n \cdot e^{-\sqrt{x}}\, dx$ ...(i)

$$\Rightarrow I\left(n + \frac{1}{2}\right) = \int_0^1 x^{n+\frac{1}{2}} \cdot e^{-\sqrt{x}}dx$$

$$= \int_0^1 \frac{2 \cdot x^{\left[\left(\left(n+\frac{1}{2}\right)+\frac{1}{2}\right)-\frac{1}{2}\right]}}{2} \cdot e^{-\sqrt{x}}dx$$

$$= 2 \cdot \int_0^1 x^{n+1}\left(\frac{1}{2\sqrt{x}} \cdot e^{-\sqrt{x}}\right)dx$$

$$= -2\int_0^1 x^{n+1}\left(-\frac{1}{2\sqrt{x}}e^{-\sqrt{x}}\right)dx$$

$$= -2[x^{n+1}e^{-\sqrt{x}}]_0^1 + 2\int_0^1 (n+1)x^n e^{-\sqrt{x}}dx$$

(using integration by parts)

$$\left(\because \frac{de^{-\sqrt{x}}}{dx} = -\frac{1}{2\sqrt{x}} \cdot e^{-\sqrt{x}}\right)$$

$$= -\frac{2}{e} + 2(n+1)I(n)$$

[from Eq. (i)]

$$\Rightarrow I\left(n + \frac{1}{2}\right) - 2(n+1)I(n) = -\frac{2}{e}$$

13. (d) Concept/Approach

3 —— x —— 7

0 —— t —— 1

Let $\frac{x-3}{7-3} = \frac{t-0}{1-0}$

$\Rightarrow \quad x = 3 + 4t$

$\Rightarrow \quad x - 3 = 4t$ and $7 - x = 4(1-t)$

So, $\quad dx = 4dt$

Start

Let $I = \int_3^7 \sqrt{(x-3)(7-x)}\, dx$

$$= \int_0^1 \sqrt{4t \cdot 4(1-t)}\, 4dt$$

$$\Rightarrow I = 16\int_0^1 \sqrt{t(1-t)}\, dt$$

Let $t = \sin^2 z$

$\Rightarrow dt = 2\sin z \cdot \cos z\, dx$

t	0	1
z	0	π/2

$$\therefore \; I = 16\int_0^{\frac{\pi}{2}} \sin z \cdot \cos z \cdot 2\sin z \cdot \cos z \cdot dz$$

$$= 8\int_0^{\frac{\pi}{2}} \sin^2 2z\, dz$$

$$\Rightarrow I = 4\int_0^{\frac{\pi}{2}} (1 - \cos 4z)dz$$

$$= 4\left[z - \frac{\sin 4z}{4}\right]_0^{\frac{\pi}{2}} = 4\left(\frac{\pi}{2}\right) = 2\pi$$

Alternate Method (2) (Short trick)

$$\int_a^b \sqrt{(x-a)(b-x)}\, dx = \frac{\pi}{8}(b-a)^2$$

Now, $I = \int_3^7 \sqrt{(x-3)(7-x)}\, dx$

$$= \frac{\pi}{8}(7-3)^2 = \frac{\pi}{8} \times 16 = 2\pi$$

14. (c) Let $I = \int_{-1}^1 \frac{x^4}{1+e^{x^7}}dx$ ...(i)

$$\Rightarrow \quad I = \int_{-1}^1 \frac{(-x)^4}{1+e^{(-x)^7}}dx$$

$\left[\text{using} \int_a^b f(x)dx = \int_a^b f(a+b-x)dx\right]$

$$\Rightarrow \quad I = \int_{-1}^1 \frac{x^4 \cdot e^{x^7}}{1+e^{x^7}}dx \quad \text{...(ii)}$$

On adding Eqs. (i) and (ii), we get

$$2I=\int_{-1}^{1}\frac{(1+e^{x^7})x^4}{1+e^{x^7}}dx$$

$\Rightarrow 2I=2\int_0^1 x^4 dx$ (if $f(x)=x^4$, then $f(x)$ is an even function and hence using $\int_{-a}^{a} f(x)dx=2\int_0^a f(x)dx$)

$\Rightarrow \quad I=\frac{1}{5}=\frac{\ln k}{e^{\lambda}}$ (given)

$\therefore \quad \ln k=1\Rightarrow k=e$

and $\quad e^{\lambda}=5\Rightarrow \lambda \ln e=\ln 5\Rightarrow \lambda=\ln 5$

$\therefore (k+\lambda)=e+\ln 5=$ Irrational number

15. (a) Let $I=\int_0^{10}\frac{3^x}{3^{[x]}}dx=\int_0^{10}3^{x-[x]}dx$

$$=10\int_0^1 3^{x-[x]}dx$$

$\Rightarrow \quad I=10\int_0^1 3^{\{x\}}dx=10\int_0^1 3^x dx$

$\Rightarrow \quad I=10\left[\frac{3^x}{\log_e 3}\right]_0^1=\frac{10}{\log_e 3}(3-1)$

$$=\frac{20}{\log_e 3}$$

[$\because$ $\{x\}$ is a periodic function with period 1 where $\{.\}$ denotes fractional part function]

16. (b) Let $I_1=\int_0^1 (1-x^{50})^{100}dx$ and

$I_2=\int_0^1 (1-x^{50})^{101}dx$

Now, $I_2=\int_0^1 (1-x^{50})^{101}1\cdot dx$

$=[(1-x^{50})^{101}\cdot x]_0^1$

$+5050\int_0^1 (1-x^{50})^{100}\cdot x^{49}\cdot x\,dx$

$=-5050\int_0^1 (1-x^{50})^{100}\{(1-x^{50})-1\}dx$

$=-5050\int_0^1 (1-x^{50})^{101}dx$

$+5050\int_0^1 (1-x^{50})^{100}dx$

$\Rightarrow I_2=-5050I_2+5050I_1$

$\Rightarrow \quad \frac{5050I_1}{I_2}=5051=$ an odd number

17. (a) Given, $f'(x)=f'(1-x)$

Integrating on both sides, we get

$f(x)=-f(1-x)+c$ ...(i)

Substituting $x=0$ in Eq. (i), we get

$f(0)=-f(1-0)+c$

$\Rightarrow \quad 1=-41+c\Rightarrow c=42$

From Eq. (i), $f(x)=-f(1-x)+42$

$\Rightarrow f(x)+f(1-x)=42$ ...(ii)

Let $I=\int_0^1 f(x)dx$ ...(iii)

$\Rightarrow I=\int_0^1 f(1-x)dx$ ...(iv)

(Using $\int_a^b f(x)dx=\int_a^b f(a+b-x)dx$)

On adding Eqs. (iii) and (iv), we get

$2I=\int_0^1 (f(x)+f(1-x))\,dx$

$=\int_0^1 42dx=42[x]_0^1$

$\Rightarrow \quad 2I=42\times 1\Rightarrow I=21$

18. (c) Given, $g(x)=\int_{\frac{7\pi}{6}}^{x}(4\sin t+3\cos t)dt$ ...(i)

$\Rightarrow g'(x)=4\sin x+3\cos x$

(Using Netwon-Leibnitz Rule)

If $x\in\left[\frac{7\pi}{6},\frac{4\pi}{3}\right]$ then x is in the third quadrant (Q_3).

In Q_3; $\sin x$ and $\cos x$ both are negative.

$\therefore g'(x)=4\sin x+3\cos x<0$

$\Rightarrow g'(x)$ is decreasing on the interval $\left[\frac{7\pi}{6},\frac{4\pi}{3}\right]$.

$\Rightarrow$ Minimum (least) value of $g(x)$ on $\left[\frac{7\pi}{6},\frac{4\pi}{3}\right]$ is $g\left(\frac{4\pi}{3}\right)$.

Now, $g\left(\frac{4\pi}{3}\right)=\int_{\frac{7\pi}{6}}^{\frac{4\pi}{3}}(4\sin t+3\cos t)dt$

[Putting $x=\frac{4\pi}{3}$ in Eq. (i)]

$\Rightarrow g\left(\frac{4\pi}{3}\right)=[-4\cos t+3\sin t]_{7\pi/6}^{4\pi/3}$

$=-4\left(\cot\frac{4\pi}{3}-\cot\frac{7\pi}{6}\right)$

$+3\left(\sin\frac{4\pi}{3}-\sin\frac{7\pi}{6}\right)$

$=-4\left(-\frac{1}{2}+\frac{\sqrt{3}}{2}\right)+3\left(-\frac{\sqrt{3}}{2}+\frac{1}{2}\right)$

$=\frac{7(1-\sqrt{3})}{2}$

19. (b) $\int_0^{\frac{\pi}{2}}\left[\lambda^2\left(\frac{\cos 3t}{4}+\frac{3}{4}\cos t\right)+\lambda\sin t-20\cos t\right]dt$

$=\left[\frac{\lambda^2}{4}\left(\frac{\sin 3t}{3}+3\sin t\right)+\lambda(-\cos t)-20\sin t\right]_0^{\pi/2}$

$=\frac{\lambda^2}{4}\left[\left(-\frac{1}{3}+3\right)-0\right]-\lambda(0-1)-20(1-0)$

$=\frac{2\lambda^2}{3}+\lambda-20$

According to the given condition,

$$\frac{2\lambda^2}{3}+\lambda-20\le-\frac{\lambda^2}{3}$$

$\Rightarrow \lambda^2+\lambda-20\le 0\Rightarrow(\lambda-5)(\lambda-4)\le 0$

$\Rightarrow -5\le\lambda\le 4$

Since, λ is a positive integer.

$\therefore \lambda=1, 2, 3, 4$ are the positive integers that satisfy the given inequality.

The number of values of $\lambda=4$

20. (d) Given, $I(n)=\int_1^e (1+\log x)^n dx$ ...(i)

Let $1+\log x=z\Rightarrow x=e^{z-1}$

$\Rightarrow \quad dx=e^{z-1}dz$

From Eq. (i), $I(n)=\int_0^2 \underset{\text{I}}{z^n}\cdot \underset{\text{II}}{e^{z-1}}dz$ ...(ii)

Again let $z-1=t\Rightarrow dz=dt$

From Eq. (ii), $I(n)=\int_0^1 \underset{\text{I}}{(1+t)^n}\,\underset{\text{II}}{e^t}\,dt$ ...(iii)

$I(n)=[e^t(1+t)^n]_0^1-\int_0^1 e^t\cdot n(1+t)^{n-1}dt$

(using Integration by parts)

$=2^n\cdot e-1-n\left(\int_0^1 e^t(1+t)^{n-1}dt\right)$

$=2^n e-1-nI(n-1)$ [from Eq. (iii)]

Replacing 'n' by $(n+1)$, we get

$I(n+1)=2^{n+1}\cdot e-1-(n+1)I(n)$

$\Rightarrow I(n+1)+(n+1)I(n)=2^{n+1}e-1$

21. (2) $f(x)=\int \frac{x^2+1}{(x^3+3x+6)^{\frac{1}{3}}}dx$

Put $x^3+3x+6=z^3$

$\Rightarrow (3x^2+3)dx=3z^2\,dz$

$\Rightarrow (x^2+1)dx=z^2dz$

$\therefore f(x)=\int \frac{z^2dz}{z}=\frac{z^2}{2}+c$

$\therefore f(x)=\frac{1}{2}(x^3+3x+6)^{\frac{2}{3}}+c$

$f(-1)=\frac{1}{2}(2)^{\frac{2}{3}}+c=\frac{1}{2^{\frac{1}{3}}}$ [given]

$\Rightarrow c=0$

Hence, $f(x)=\frac{1}{2}(x^3+3x+6)^{\frac{2}{3}}$

$\therefore f(-2)=\frac{1}{2}(-8)^{\frac{2}{3}}$

$=\frac{1}{2}[(-2)^3]^{\frac{2}{3}}=2$

22. (0) $\int \frac{dx}{\sin(x-3)\sin(x-7)}$

$=\frac{1}{\sin(7-3)}\int \frac{\sin\{(x-3)-(x-7)\}}{\sin(x-3)\sin(x-7)}dx$

$=\frac{1}{\sin 4}\int \frac{\sin(x-3)\cos(x-7)-\cos(x-3)\sin(x-7)}{\sin(x-3)\sin(x-7)}dx$

$=\frac{1}{\sin 4}\int [\cot(x-7)-\cot(x-3)]dx$

$=\frac{1}{\sin 4}[\ln|\sin(x-7)|-\ln|\sin(x-3)|]+c$

$=\frac{1}{\sin 4}\ln\left|\frac{\sin(x-7)}{\sin(x-3)}\right|+c$, where c is constant of integration.

Hence, $\alpha=4, \beta=-7, \gamma=3$

So, $\alpha+\beta+\gamma=4-7+3=0$

23. (1) Let $I=\int \sqrt{\frac{x+1}{x+2}}\times\frac{1}{x+3}dx$

$=\int \sqrt{1-\frac{1}{x+2}}\times\frac{1}{x+3}dx$

Let $1-\frac{1}{x+2}=z^2$

$\Rightarrow x+2=\frac{1}{1-z^2}$

$\Rightarrow x+3=\frac{2-z^2}{1-z^2}$

$\Rightarrow dx=\left(\frac{1}{1-z^2}\right)^2(2z\,dz)$

$\therefore I=\int z\cdot\frac{1-z^2}{2-z^2}\cdot\frac{2z}{(1-z^2)}dz$

$=\int \frac{2z^2}{(2-z^2)(1-z^2)}dz$

$=-4\int \frac{1}{2-z^2}dz+2\int \frac{1}{1-z^2}dz$

[using partial fraction]

$=-4\left[\frac{1}{2\sqrt{2}}\ln\left|\frac{\sqrt{2}+z}{\sqrt{2}-z}\right|\right]+2\left[\frac{1}{2}\ln\left|\frac{1+z}{1-z}\right|\right]+c,$

where c is constant of integration

$=-\sqrt{2}\ln\left|\frac{\sqrt{2}+z}{\sqrt{2}-z}\right|+\log_e\left|\frac{1+z}{1-z}\right|+c,$

where $z=\sqrt{\frac{x+1}{x+2}}$

Hence, $m=-\sqrt{2}, n=1, p=2$

So, $m^2+n^2-p=2+1-2=1$

24. (0) Let

$I=\int \frac{\sqrt{\sin^3\theta}+\sqrt{\cos^3\theta}}{\sqrt{\sin^3\theta\cdot\cos^3\theta}\sqrt{\sin(\theta+\alpha)}}d\theta$

$=\int\left(\frac{1}{\sqrt{\cos^3\theta}}+\frac{1}{\sqrt{\sin^3\theta}}\right)\frac{1}{\sqrt{\sin(\theta+\alpha)}}d\theta$

$\Rightarrow I=\int \frac{\sqrt{\cos\theta}\sec^2\theta\,d\theta}{\sqrt{\sin(\theta+\alpha)}}+\int \frac{\sqrt{\sin\theta}}{\sqrt{\sin(\theta+\alpha)}}\text{cosec}^2\theta\cdot d\theta$

(Multiplying in N^r or D^r by $\sqrt{\cos\theta}$ and $\sqrt{\sin\theta}$ in first and second term of integrand respectively. Then applying the basic formula)

$\Rightarrow I=\int \frac{1}{\sqrt{\tan\theta\cdot\cos\alpha+\sin\alpha}}\sec^2\theta\,d\theta-\int\frac{1}{\sqrt{\cos\alpha+\sin\alpha\cdot\cot\theta}}(-\sec^2\theta)\,d\theta$

Let $\tan\theta=z$

$\Rightarrow \sec^2\theta\,d\theta=dz$

and $\cot\theta=1$

$\Rightarrow -\text{cosec}^2\theta\,d\theta=dt$

So, $I=\int\frac{1}{\sqrt{\cos\alpha}}\cdot\frac{1}{\sqrt{z+\tan\alpha}}dz-\int\frac{1}{\sqrt{\sin\alpha}}\cdot\frac{1}{\sqrt{\cot\alpha+t}}dt$

$=\frac{2}{\sqrt{\cos\alpha}}(\sqrt{z+\tan\alpha})-\frac{2}{\sqrt{\sin\alpha}}(\sqrt{t+\cot\alpha})+c$

[where, c is constant of integration]

$=\frac{2}{\sqrt{\cos\alpha}}(\sqrt{\tan\alpha+\tan\alpha})-\frac{2}{\sqrt{\sin\alpha}}(\sqrt{\cot\alpha+\cot\theta})+C$

$=f(\theta,\alpha)$

Hence, $f\left(\frac{\pi}{4},\frac{\pi}{4}\right)=\frac{2\sqrt{2}}{2^{-\frac{1}{4}}}-\frac{2\sqrt{2}}{2^{-\frac{1}{4}}}=0$

25. (97) Let $I=\int\frac{\sqrt{x}}{\sqrt{x}+\sqrt[3]{x}}dx$

Let $x=t^6 \Rightarrow dx=6t^5\,dt$

$\therefore I=\int\frac{t^3}{t^2+t^3}(6t^5)dt=\int\frac{6t^6}{1+t}dt=6\int\frac{(t^6-1)+1}{1+t}dt$

$=6\int\left(\frac{(t+1)(t^5-t^4+t^3-t^2+t-1)}{(t+1)}+\frac{1}{t+1}\right)dt$

$=6\int\left[t^5-t^4+t^3-t^2+t-1+\frac{1}{t+1}\right]dt$

$=6\left[\frac{t^6}{5}-\frac{t^5}{5}+\frac{t^4}{4}-\frac{t^3}{3}+\frac{t^2}{2}-t+\ln|1+1|\right]+c$

where c is constant of integration and $t=x^{\frac{1}{6}}$

$\Rightarrow \phi(1)=6\left[\frac{1}{6}-\frac{1}{5}+\frac{1}{4}-\frac{1}{3}+\frac{1}{2}-1+\ln 2\right]$

$=\frac{-37+60\ln 2}{10}$

Hence, $a=-37, b=60$

$\therefore |a-b|=|-37-60|=97$

26. (150) Given $f(x)+f\left(x+\frac{1}{2}\right)=3$ ...(i)

Replacing x by $\left(x+\frac{1}{2}\right)$, we get

$f\left(x+\frac{1}{2}\right)+f(x+1)=3$ ...(ii)

From Eqs. (i) and (ii), we get

$f(x)=f(x+1)$

Hence, $f(x)$ is periodic with period 1.

Now, $\int_0^{100} f(x)dx = 100\int_0^1 f(x)dx = 100\left[\int_0^{\frac12} f(x)dx + \int_{\frac12}^1 f(x)dx\right]$

$$=100\left[\int_0^{\frac12} f(x)dx + \int_0^{\frac12} f\left(x+\frac12\right)dx\right]$$

$$\left(\int_a^b f(x)dx = \int_{a-m}^{b-m} f(x+m)dx\right)$$

$$=100\int_0^{\frac12} 3dx = 150$$

27. (0) **Method 1**

Concept/Approach

3 —— x —— 4 0 —— t —— 1

Let $\frac{x-3}{4-3}=\frac{t-0}{1-0}$

$\Rightarrow x=3+t \Rightarrow x-3=t$

and $4-x=1-t$

$\Rightarrow \quad dx=dt$

Start Let $I=\int_0^4 \frac{1}{\sqrt{(x-3)(4-x)}}dx$

$=\int_0^1 \frac{1}{\sqrt{t\cdot(1-t)}}dt=\int_0^1 t^{-\frac12}(1-t)^{-\frac12}dt$

Let $t=\sin^2 z \Rightarrow dt=2\sin z\cdot\cos z\cdot dz$

$\therefore\ I=\int_0^{\frac{\pi}{2}}(\sin z)^{-1}(\cos z)^{-1}\cdot 2\sin z\cdot\cos z\cdot dz$

$=2\int_0^{\frac{\pi}{2}} dz=\pi$

So, $k=\pi$

Hence, $\sin k+\tan k=\sin\pi+\tan\pi=0$

Method (2) (Short Cut Method)

Short Trick : $\int_a^b \frac{1}{\sqrt{(x-a)(b-x)}}dx=\pi$,

where $b>a$

So, $\int_3^4 \frac{dx}{\sqrt{(x-3)(4-x)}}=\pi$ (here $4>3$)

Hence,

$\sin k+\tan k=\sin\pi+\tan\pi=0+0=0$

28. (615) $\int_0^{100}[\sqrt{x}]dx=\int_0^1[\sqrt{x}]dx+\int_1^4[\sqrt{x}]dx$

$+\int_4^9[\sqrt{x}]dx+\int_9^{16}[\sqrt{x}]dx+\ldots$

$+\int_{64}^{81}[\sqrt{x}]dx+\int_{81}^{100}[\sqrt{x}]dx$

$=\int_0^1 0\cdot dx+\int_1^4 1\cdot dx+\int_4^9 2\cdot dx$

$+\int_9^{16} 3\cdot dx+\ldots+\int_{64}^{81} 8dx+\int_{81}^{100} 9dx$

$=0+3+2(5)+3(7)+4(9)+5(11)$

$+6(13)+7(15)+8(17)+9(19)=615$

29. (1) Given, $f(x)+f(8-x)=0$

$\Rightarrow \quad f(8-x)=-f(x) \quad \ldots(A)$

and Let $I=\int_0^8 \frac{1}{1+2^{f(x)}}dx \quad \ldots(i)$

$\Rightarrow I=\int_0^8 \frac{1}{1+2^{f(8-x)}}dx=\int_0^8 \frac{1}{1+2^{-f(x)}}dx$

$=\int_0^8 \frac{2^{f(x)}}{1+2^{f(x)}}dx \quad \ldots(ii)$

[using $\int_a^b f(x)dx=\int_a^b f(a+b-x)dx$]

On adding Eqs. (i) and (ii),

$2I=\int_0^8 \frac{1+2^{f(x)}}{1+2^{f(x)}}dx=\int_0^8 dx=8$

$\Rightarrow \quad I=4=\lambda \quad$ (given)

Divisors of λ i.e. divisors of 4 is 1, 2, 4.

Hence, (Divisors product) – (Sum of divisors) $=8-7=1$

30. (1008) Let $I=\int_0^{\frac{\pi}{2016}} \frac{1}{(\cot 1008x)^{1008}+1}dx \quad \ldots(i)$

$I=\int_0^{\frac{\pi}{2016}} \frac{1}{\cot^{1008}\left(1008\left(\frac{\pi}{2016}-x\right)\right)+1}dx$

[using $\int_a^b f(x)dx=\int_a^b f(a+b-x)dx$]

$\Rightarrow I=\int_0^{\frac{\pi}{2016}} \frac{1}{\tan^{1008}(1008x)+1}dx$

$\Rightarrow I=\int_0^{\frac{\pi}{2016}} \frac{(\cot(1008x))^{1008}}{1+(\cot(1008x))^{1008}}dx \quad \ldots(ii)$

On adding Eqs. (i) and (ii),

$2I=\frac{\pi}{2016} \Rightarrow I=\frac{\pi}{4032}$

Hence, $4\lambda=4032 \Rightarrow \lambda=1008$

Qualifier 10
(Area Bounded by Curves and Differential Equations)

1. (a) Given, $x=\begin{cases}-2-y, & y<-1\\ y^3, & -1\le y\le 1\\ 2-y, & y>1\end{cases}$

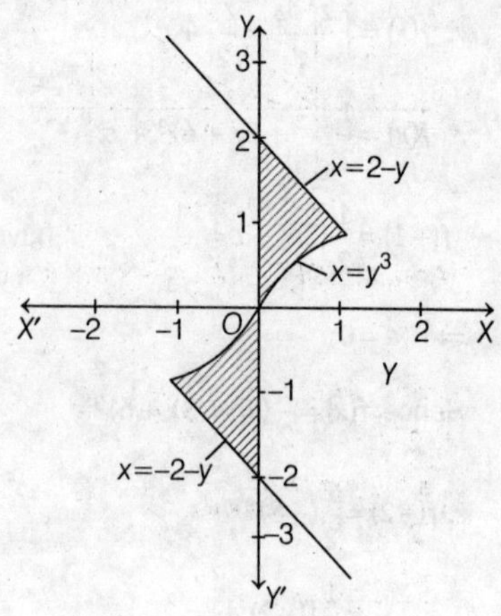

$\therefore$ Required area $=2\int_0^1[(2-x)-x^{1/3}]dx$

$=2\left[2x-\frac{x^2}{2}-\frac{3x^{4/3}}{4}\right]_0^1=2\left[2-\frac12-\frac34\right]=\frac32$

2. (d) Let $f(x)=\sin^{-1}(\sin x)$, $-\frac{\pi}{2}\le x<2\pi$

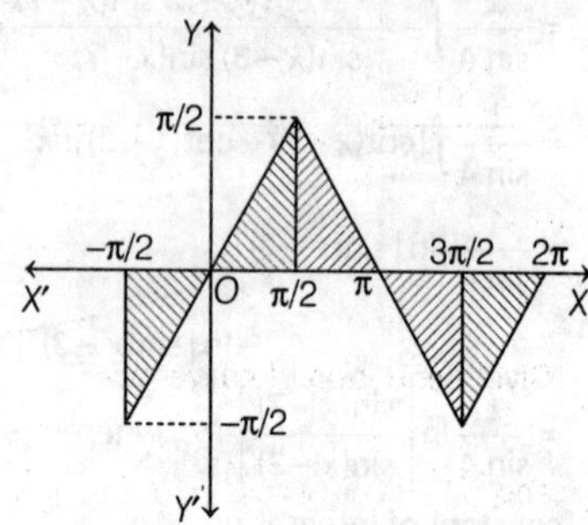

$\Rightarrow f(x)=\begin{cases}x, & -\frac{\pi}{2}\le x<\frac{\pi}{2}\\ \pi-x, & \frac{\pi}{2}\le x<\frac{3\pi}{2}\\ x-2\pi, & \frac{3\pi}{2}\le x<2\pi\end{cases}$

$\therefore$ Required integral = area of the shaded region

$5\int_0^{\pi/2}x\,dx=5\left[\frac{x^2}{2}\right]_0^{\pi/2}$

$=\frac52\left(\frac{\pi^2}{4}\right)-0$

$=\frac{5\pi^2}{8}$

3. (c) Required integral = area of the shaded region

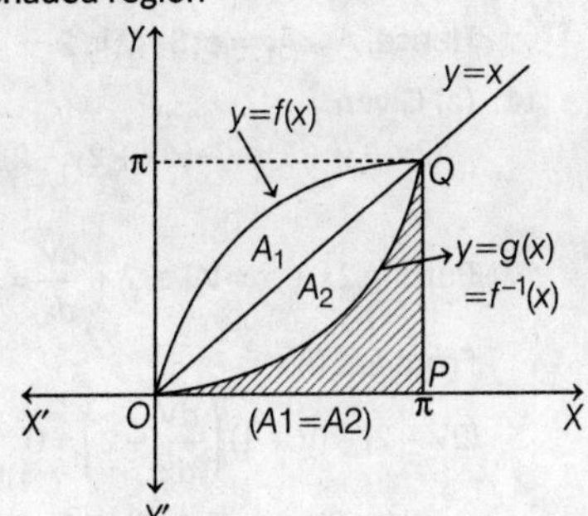

(Area of $\Delta OPQ) - A_2 = \frac{1}{2} \times \pi \times \pi - (A_1)$

$[\because A_1 = A_2]$

$= \frac{\pi^2}{2} - \int_0^{\pi} (x + \sin x - x)\, dx$

$= \frac{\pi^2}{2} - 2\int_0^{\pi/2} \sin x\, dx$

$= \frac{\pi^2}{2} + 2[\cos x]_0^{\pi/2}$

$= \frac{\pi^2}{2} + 2(-1) = \frac{\pi^2 - 4}{2}$

4. (c) **Method (1)** (Proper Method)

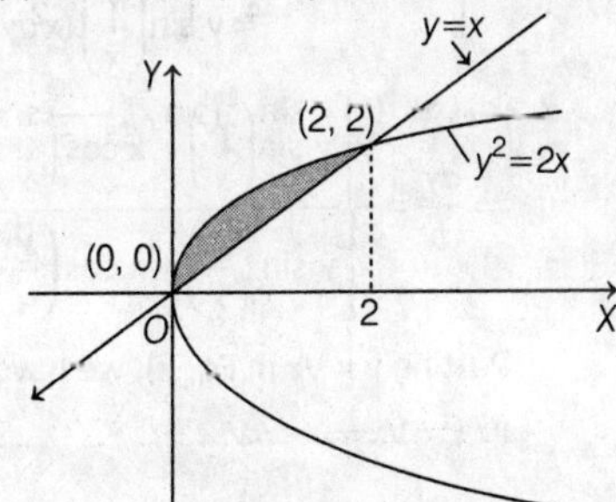

Given, equation of curves are

$y^2 = 2x$ ...(i)

and $y = x$ ...(ii)

Solving Eqs. (i) and (ii), we get

$x^2 = 2x \Rightarrow x(x-2) = 0 \Rightarrow x = 0, 2$

$\therefore$ Points of intersections are (0, 0) and (2, 2).

Hence, required area $= \int_0^2 [\sqrt{2x} - x] dx$

$= \sqrt{2}\int_0^2 \sqrt{x}\, dx - \int_0^2 x\, dx$

$= \sqrt{2} \times \frac{2}{3}\left[x^{\frac{3}{2}}\right]_0^2 - \frac{1}{2}[x^2]_0^2$

$= \sqrt{2} \times \frac{2}{3}\left[2^{\frac{3}{2}} - 0\right] - \frac{1}{2}[4 - 0]$

$= \sqrt{2} \times \frac{2}{3} \times (2^3)^{\frac{1}{2}} - 2$

$= \sqrt{2} \times \frac{2}{3} \times 2\sqrt{2} - 2$

$= \frac{8}{3} - 2 = \frac{2}{3}$ sq units

Method 2 (Short cut Method)

Short Trick The area of the region bounded by the parabola $y^2 = 4ax$ and the line $y = mx$ is $\frac{8a^2}{3m^3}$ sq units.

Start Given, $y^2 = 2x$ comparing with $y^2 = 4ax$, we get $a = \frac{1}{2}$

and $y = x$ comparing with $y = mx$, we get $m = 1$

Hence, required area

$= \frac{8\left(\frac{1}{2}\right)^2}{3 \times (1)^3} = \frac{8 \times \frac{1}{4}}{3} = \frac{2}{3}$ sq unit

5. (d) Given, $f(x) = \max\left\{\sin x, \cos x, \frac{1}{2}\right\}$

$\Rightarrow \quad f(x) = \begin{cases} \cos x, & 0 \le x < \frac{\pi}{4} \\ \sin x, & \frac{\pi}{4} \le x < \frac{5\pi}{6} \\ \frac{1}{2}, & \frac{5\pi}{6} \le x \le \pi \end{cases}$

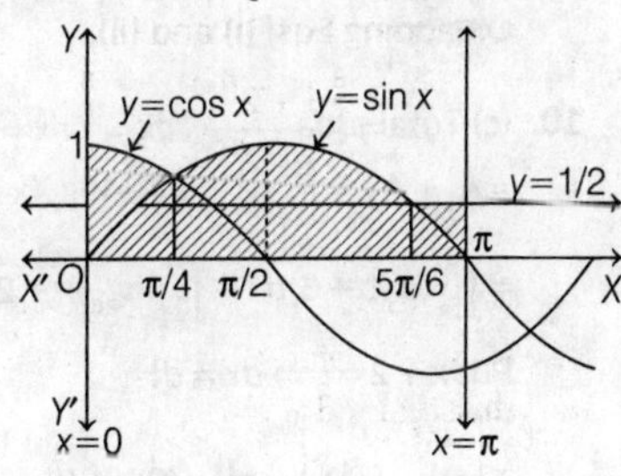

$\therefore$ Required area

$= \int_0^{\pi/4} \cos x\, dx + \int_{\pi/4}^{5\pi/6} \sin x\, dx + \int_{5\pi/6}^{\pi} \frac{1}{2} dx$

$= [\sin x]_0^{\pi/4} + [-\cos x]_{\pi/4}^{5\pi/6} + \frac{1}{2}[x]_{5\pi/6}^{\pi}$

$= \left(\frac{1}{\sqrt{2}} - 0\right) - \left(-\frac{\sqrt{3}}{2} - \frac{1}{\sqrt{2}}\right) + \frac{1}{2}\left(\pi - \frac{5\pi}{6}\right)$

$= \left(\sqrt{2} + \frac{\sqrt{3}}{2} + \frac{\pi}{12}\right)$ sq units

6. (c) We have, $h(x) = fog(x)$

$\Rightarrow \quad x^2 + 2x + 2 = f(g(x))$

$\Rightarrow \quad (x+1)^2 + 1 = f(x+1)$

Let $x + 1 = t$

$\therefore \quad f(t) = t^2 + 1$

Replacing t by x, we get

$f(x) = x^2 + 1$

Let $y = mx$ be tangent to $f(x) = x^2 + 1$.

Then, $mx = x^2 + 1$

$\Rightarrow \quad x^2 - mx + 1 = 0$

For tangency,

Discriminant = 0

$\Rightarrow \quad m^2 - 4 = 0$

$\Rightarrow \quad m \pm 2$

So, $y = 2x$ and $y = -2x$

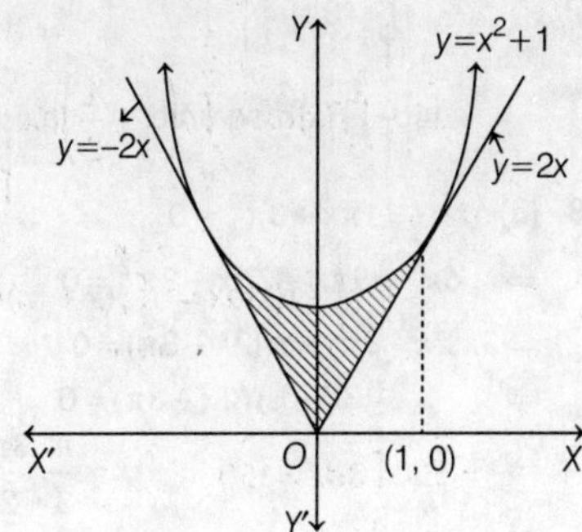

$\therefore$ Required area

$= 2\left[\int_0^1 (x^2 + 1) dx - \int_0^1 2x\, dx\right]$

$= 2\int_0^1 (x^2 - 2x + 1)\, dx$

$= 2\int_0^1 (x-1)^2 dx$

$= \frac{2}{3}[(x-1)^3]_0^1 = \frac{2}{3}$

7. (a) Given that, $y = ax^2 + bx + c$ ...(i)

Also, given the curve passes through (2, 6), then we have,

$6 = 4a + 2b + c$ ...(ii)

On differentiating both sides Eq. (i) w.r.t x, we get

$\frac{dy}{dx} = 2ax + b$

$\therefore \quad \left(\frac{dy}{dx}\right)_{(0,0)} = b \Rightarrow b = 1$

$[\because$ Slope of the line $y = x$ is 1]

Also, the given curve passes through origin.

So, $0 = a \times 0 + b \times 0 + c \Rightarrow c = 0$

From Eq. (ii),

$6 = 4a + 2(1) + 0 \Rightarrow a = 1$

Hence, equation of curve is $y = x^2 + x$.

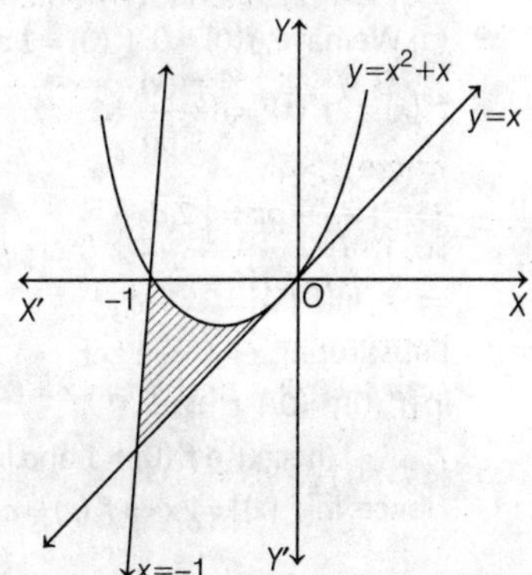

$\therefore$ Required area

$$= \left| \int_{-1}^{0} [x - (x^2 + x)]\, dx \right|$$

$$= \left| \left[-\frac{x^3}{3} \right]_{-1}^{0} \right|$$

$$= \left| -\frac{1}{3} \right| = \frac{1}{3} \text{ sq unit}$$

8. (d) $6x^2 - 11\pi x + 3\pi^2 = 0$

$\Rightarrow \quad 6x^2 - 9\pi x - 2\pi x + 3\pi^2 = 0$

$\Rightarrow 3x(2x - 3\pi) - \pi(2x - 3\pi) = 0$

$\Rightarrow \quad (3x - \pi)(2x - 3\pi) = 0$

$\Rightarrow \quad x = \frac{\pi}{3}, \frac{3\pi}{2}$

Given that,

α, β are the roots of

$6x^2 - 11\pi x + 3\pi^2 = 0$, where $\alpha < \beta$.

So, $\alpha = \frac{\pi}{3}$ and $\beta = \frac{3\pi}{2}$

Also, $y = fog(x) = f(\sin x) = \sin^2 x$

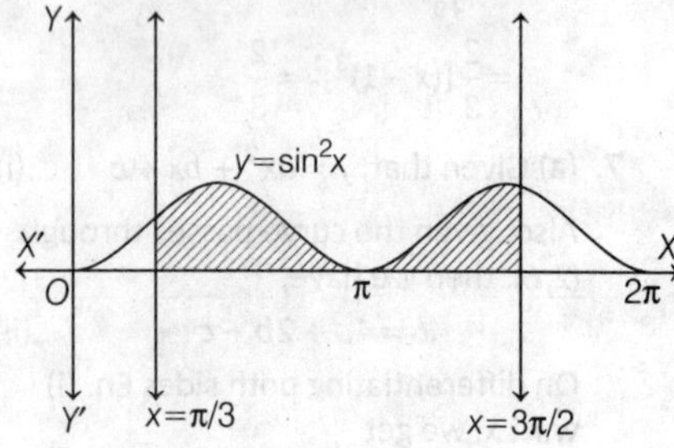

$\therefore$ Required area

$$= \int_{\pi/3}^{\pi} \sin^2 x\, dx + \int_{\pi}^{3\pi/2} \sin^2 x\, dx$$

$$= \frac{1}{2}\int_{\pi/3}^{\pi} (1 - \cos 2x) dx + \frac{1}{2}\int_{\pi}^{3\pi/2} (1 - \cos 2x) dx$$

$$= \frac{1}{2}\left[x - \frac{\sin 2x}{2} \right]_{\pi/3}^{\pi} + \frac{1}{2}\left[x - \frac{\sin 2x}{2} \right]_{\pi}^{3\pi/2}$$

$$= \frac{\pi}{3} + \frac{\sqrt{3}}{8} + \frac{\pi}{4} = \left(\frac{7\pi}{12} + \frac{\sqrt{3}}{8} \right) \text{ sq units}$$

9. (a) We have, $f(0) = 0$, $f'(0) = 1$ and

$f''(x) = 2f'(x) \Rightarrow \frac{f''(x)}{f'(x)} = 2$

$\Rightarrow \quad \int \frac{f''(x)}{f(x)} dx = \int 2\, dx$

$\Rightarrow \quad \ln[f'(x)] = 2x + c$

Substituting $x = 0$, we get

$\ln[f'(0)] = 0 + c \Rightarrow c = 0$

(because $f'(0) = 1$ and $\ln(1) = 0$)

Hence, $\ln[f'(x)] = 2x \Rightarrow f'(x) = e^{2x}$

$\Rightarrow \quad f(x) = \frac{e^{2x}}{2} + k$

Substituting $x = 0$, we have

$f(0) = \frac{1}{2} + k \Rightarrow 0 = \frac{1}{2} + k \Rightarrow k = -\frac{1}{2}$

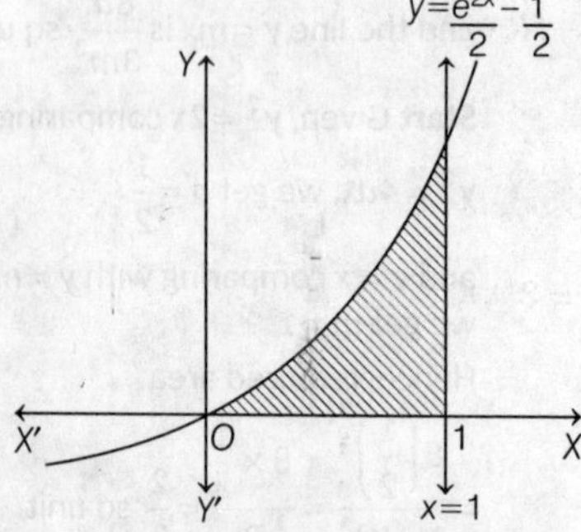

So, $\quad f(x) = \frac{e^{2x}}{2} - \frac{1}{2}$ ...(i)

$$\therefore \text{Required area} = \int_0^1 \left(\frac{e^{2x}}{2} - \frac{1}{2} \right) dx$$

$$= \left[\frac{e^{2x}}{4} - \frac{x}{2} \right]_0^1 = \left(\frac{e^{2x}}{4} - \frac{1}{2} \right) - \left(\frac{1}{4} - 0 \right)$$

$$= \frac{e^2 - 3}{4} \text{ sq units}$$

10. (c) Total area

$$= A_1 + A_2 = \int_{-1}^{0} [e^{-x} + 3 - \log_e(x + 2)] dx$$

$$= \int_{-1}^{0} (e^{-x} + 3) dx - \int_{-1}^{0} \log_e(x + 2) dx$$

Put $x + 2 = t \Rightarrow dx = dt$

$$= \left[\frac{e^{-x}}{-1} + 3x \right]_{-1}^{0} - \int_{1}^{2} \log_e t\, dt$$

$\Rightarrow A_1 + A_2 = -1 - (-e - 3) - [t \log_e t - t]_1^2$

$\Rightarrow A_1 + A_2 = e + 2 - 2[\log_e 2 - 1] + (-1)$

$= e + 3 - 2\ln 2$

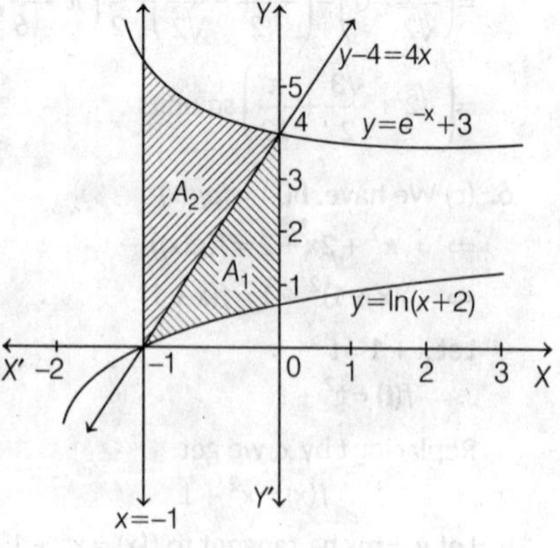

Now, $A_1 = 2 - \int_{-1}^{0} \ln(x + 2) dx$

$= 2 - [2\ln 2 - 1] = 3 - 2\ln 2$

$\therefore A_2 = e + 3 - 2\ln 2 - 3 + 2\ln 2 = e$

Hence, $A_2 : A_1 = e : 3 - 2\ln 2$

11. (a) Given,

$(2x + y + 1)dy - (4x + 2y - 2)dx = 0$ ...(i)

Putting $2x + y = V$ i.e. $2 + \frac{dy}{dx} = \frac{dV}{dx}$

From Eq. (i),

$(2V - 2) - (V + 1)\left(\frac{dV}{dx} - 2 \right) = 0$

$\Rightarrow \frac{dV}{dx} = \frac{2V - 1}{V + 1} + 2 = \frac{2V - 2 + 2V + 2}{V + 1}$

$= \frac{4V}{V + 1} \Rightarrow \frac{V + 1}{4V} dV = dx$

$\Rightarrow \frac{1}{4}\int \left(1 + \frac{1}{V} \right) dV = x + c$

$\Rightarrow \quad \frac{1}{4}(V + \ln V) = x + c$

$\Rightarrow \frac{1}{4}(2x + y + \ln(2x + y)) = x + c$

12. (d) Given, $x \cos\left(\frac{y}{x} \right)(y\, dx + x\, dy)$

$= y \sin\left(\frac{y}{x} \right)(x\, dy - y\, dx)$

$$\Rightarrow \frac{dy}{dx} = \frac{y\left[y \sin\left(\frac{y}{x} \right) + x \cos\left(\frac{y}{x} \right) \right]}{x\left[y \sin\left(\frac{y}{x} \right) - x \cos\left(\frac{y}{x} \right) \right]} \quad \text{...(i)}$$

Putting $y = Vx$ in Eq. (i), we have

$(\because y = Vx \Rightarrow \frac{y}{x} = V$

$\Rightarrow \frac{dy}{dx} = V \times 1 + x\frac{dV}{dx})$

$V + x\frac{dV}{dx} = \frac{V(V \sin V + \cos V)}{V \sin V - \cos V}$

$\Rightarrow \quad x\frac{dV}{dx} = \frac{V(V \sin V + \cos V)}{V \sin V - \cos V} - V$

$= \frac{2V \cos V}{V \sin V - \cos V}$

$\Rightarrow \frac{V \sin V - \cos V}{V \cos V} dv = 2 \cdot \frac{dx}{x}$

$\Rightarrow \quad \left(\tan V - \frac{1}{V} \right) dv = 2 \cdot \frac{dx}{x}$

$\Rightarrow \ln \sec V - \ln V = \ln x^2 + \text{constant}$

$\Rightarrow \frac{\sec V}{Vx^2} = \text{constant}$

$\Rightarrow \frac{1}{xy} \sec\left(\frac{y}{x} \right) = \text{constant}$

$\Rightarrow xy \cos\left(\frac{y}{x} \right) = \text{constant}$

13. (d) Given, $\frac{dy}{dx} = -\left(\frac{y + \sin x}{x}\right)$

$\Rightarrow \quad -xdy = ydx + \sin x\, dx$

$\Rightarrow -\sin x\, dx = xdy + ydx$

$\Rightarrow -\sin x\, dx = d(xy)$

On integrating both sides, we get

$\cos x = xy + c$, where c is constant of integration.

$\because \quad y(0) = 1$ [given]

So, $\cos 0 = 0 \times + c$

$\Rightarrow \quad c = 1$

Hence, $\cos x = xy + 1$ ...(i)

So, Eq. (i) will satisfy the option (a), (b) and (c).

14. (b) Given, $y = \frac{x}{\ln|cx|}$

$\Rightarrow \ln c + \ln|x| = \frac{x}{y}$

On differentiating both sides w.r.t. x, we get

$$\frac{1}{x} = \frac{y - x\frac{dy}{dx}}{y^2} \Rightarrow \frac{y^2}{x} = y - x\frac{dy}{dx}$$

$$\Rightarrow \frac{dy}{dx} = \frac{y}{x} - \frac{y^2}{x^2}$$

Hence, $\phi\left(\frac{x}{y}\right) = -\frac{y^2}{x^2}$

15. (a) Let $f(x) = y$, then $f'(x) = \frac{dy}{dx}$

Given, equation can be written as

$$y \sin 2x - \cos x + (1 + \sin^2 x)\frac{dy}{dx} = 0$$

$$\Rightarrow \frac{dy}{dx} + \left(\frac{\sin 2x}{1 + \sin^2 x}\right)y = \frac{\cos x}{1 + \sin^2 x}$$

(This is linear differential equation)

Integrating factor (IF)

$$= e^{\int \frac{\sin 2x}{1+\sin^2 x}dx} = e^{\int \frac{dz}{z}}$$

[by putting $1 + \sin^2 x = z$

$\Rightarrow \sin 2x\, dx = dz$]

$\Rightarrow \text{IF} = e^{\ln(1+\sin^2 x)} = 1 + \sin^2 x$

Hence, solution is

$$y \times (\text{IF}) = \int \frac{\cos x}{1 + \sin^2 x} \times (\text{IF})\, dx$$

$\Rightarrow y(1 + \sin^2 x) = \int \cos x\, dx + c$

$\Rightarrow y(1 + \sin^2 x) = \sin x + c$ ...(i)

Given, $y(0) = 0$ i.e. When $x = 0$, then $y = 0$

From Eq. (i), $0 = 0 + c \Rightarrow c = 0$

Therefore, $y = \frac{\sin x}{1 + \sin^2 x}$

and hence $y\left(\frac{\pi}{6}\right) = \frac{\sin\left(\frac{\pi}{6}\right)}{1 + \left(\sin\frac{\pi}{6}\right)^2} = \frac{2}{5}$

16. (d) Let $P \equiv (x, y)$ and ordinate $= PM$

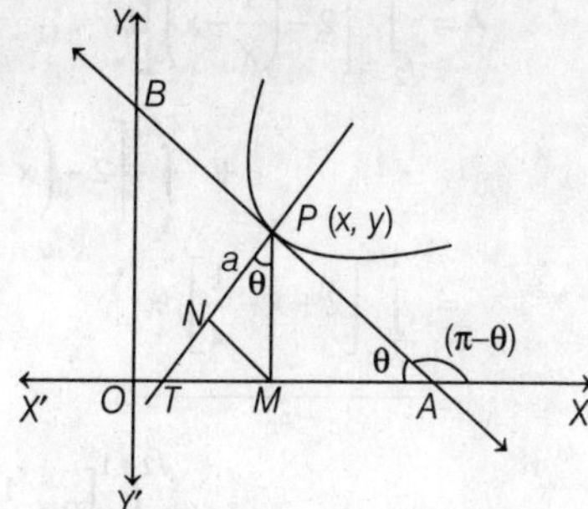

Projection of ordinate on normal $= PN$

$\therefore PN = PM \cos\theta = a$ (given)

$$\therefore \quad \frac{y}{\sqrt{1 + \tan^2\theta}} = a$$

$$\Rightarrow \quad y = a\sqrt{1 + \left(\frac{dy}{dx}\right)^2}$$

$$\Rightarrow \frac{dy}{dx} = \frac{\sqrt{y^2 - a^2}}{a} \text{ (after rearranging)}$$

$$\Rightarrow \int \frac{a dy}{\sqrt{y^2 - a^2}} = \int dx$$

$$\Rightarrow a \ln|y + \sqrt{y^2 - a^2}| = x + c$$

17. (b) Let r be the instantaneous radius of the ball.

Then, $\frac{d\left(\frac{4}{3}\pi r^3\right)}{dt} = k(4\pi r^2)$

[k constant of proportionality]

$\Rightarrow 4\pi r^2 \frac{dr}{dt} = k(4\pi r^2)$

$\Rightarrow \frac{dr}{dt} = k = \text{constant}$

This means the rate at which the radius is decreasing is constant.

$\because$ Half of the ball disappears in one day.

$\therefore$Reamaining half would disappear in one more day.

Hence, total time required in 2 days.

18. (c) Given, $(e^{x^2} + e^{y^2})y\frac{dy}{dx}$

$+ e^{x^2}(xy^2 - x) = 0$ ...(i)

Put $y^2 = t \Rightarrow 2y\frac{dy}{dx} = \frac{dt}{dx}$

From Eq. (i),

$$(e^{x^2} + e^t)\frac{dt}{dx} + 2e^{x^2}(xt - x) = 0$$

$$\Rightarrow e^{x^2} + e^t + 2e^{x^2} \cdot x(t - 1)\frac{dx}{dt} = 0 \text{ ...(ii)}$$

Again, putting $e^{x^2} = z$, then

$$e^{x^2} \cdot 2x\frac{dx}{dt} = \frac{dz}{dt}$$

From Eq. (ii), $z + e^t + \frac{dz}{dt}(t - 1) = 0$

$\Rightarrow \frac{dz}{dt} + \frac{z}{(t - 1)} = -\frac{e^t}{(t - 1)}$ which is linear differential equation

Its $\text{IF} = e^{\int \frac{dt}{t-1}} = e^{\ln(t-1)} = (t - 1)$

Its solution is $z(t - 1) = -\int e^t dt$

$\Rightarrow \quad z(t - 1) = -e^t + c$

$\Rightarrow \quad e^{x^2}(y^2 - 1) = -e^{y^2} + c$

$\Rightarrow e^{x^2}(y^2 - 1) + e^{y^2} = c$

19. (b) The equation of normal at $P(x, y)$ is

$$Y - y = -\frac{dx}{dy}(X - x) \quad \text{...(i)}$$

So, the coordlnates of Q are

$\left(x + y\frac{dy}{dx}, 0\right)$ [Putting $Y = 0$ in Eq. (i)]

Thus, $PQ^2 = (X - x)^2 + (0 - y)^2$

$$= \left(y\frac{dy}{dx}\right)^2 + y^2$$

$$\Rightarrow \quad k^2 = \left(y\frac{dy}{dx}\right)^2 + y^2$$

$$\Rightarrow \quad \left(y\frac{dy}{dx}\right)^2 = k^2 - y^2$$

$$\Rightarrow \quad y\frac{dy}{dx} = \pm\sqrt{k^2 - y^2}$$

$$\Rightarrow \quad \frac{y\,dy}{\sqrt{k^2 - y^2}} = \pm\, dx$$

$$\Rightarrow \int \frac{y\,dy}{\sqrt{k^2 - y^2}} = \pm\int dx$$

$\Rightarrow -\sqrt{k^2 - y^2} = \pm x + c$ ...(ii)

As the curve passes through $(0, k)$, we get

$$-\sqrt{k^2 - k^2} = \pm(0) + c$$

$\Rightarrow \quad c = 0$

From Eq. (i), $-\sqrt{k^2 - y^2} = \pm x + 0$

$\Rightarrow \quad x^2 + y^2 = k^2$

20. (a) We have, $\frac{dy}{dx} = \frac{\sqrt{y^4 - y^2}}{\sqrt{x^4 - x^2}}$

$$= \frac{y\sqrt{y^2 - 1}}{x\sqrt{x^2 - 1}}$$

$\Rightarrow \int \frac{dy}{y\sqrt{y^2-1}} = \int \frac{dx}{x\sqrt{x^2-1}}$

$\Rightarrow \sec^{-1} y = \sec^{-1} x + C$

$\therefore y(0) = 0, \therefore C = 0$

Hence, $\sec^{-1} y = \sec^{-1} x \Rightarrow y = x$ ...(i)

So, Eq. (i) passes through (2, 2).

21. (19) $f(x) = |x-1| + |x| + |x+1|$

$$= \begin{cases} -3x, x \le -1 \\ 2-x, -1 < x \le 0 \\ x+2, 0 < x \le 1 \\ 3x, x \ge 1 \end{cases}$$

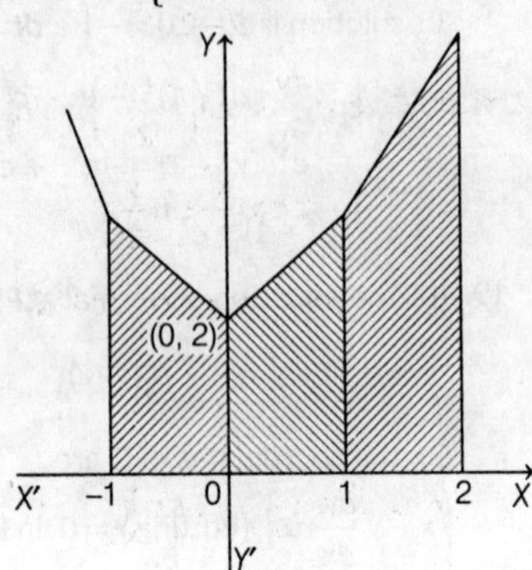

$\therefore$ Required area $= \int_{-1}^{2} f(x)dx$

$= \int_{-1}^{0} (2-x)dx + \int_{0}^{1} (x+2)dx + \int_{1}^{2} 3x\,dx$

$= \left[2x - \frac{x^2}{2}\right]_{-1}^{0} + \left[\frac{x^2}{2} + 2x\right]_{0}^{1} + \frac{3}{2}[x^2]_1^2$

$= \frac{5}{2} + \frac{5}{2} + \frac{9}{2}$

$= \frac{19}{2} = A$

$\therefore 2A = 2 \times \frac{19}{2} = 19$

22. (2)

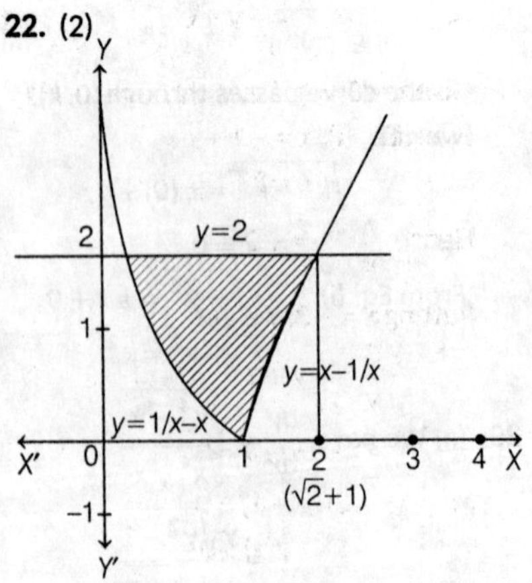

$$y = \begin{cases} \frac{1}{x} - x, 0 < x < 1 \\ x - \frac{1}{x}, x > 1 \end{cases}$$

$\therefore$ Required area

$A = \int_{\sqrt{2}-1}^{1} \left[2 - \left(\frac{1}{x} - x\right)\right] dx + \int_{1}^{\sqrt{2}+1} \left[2 - \left(x - \frac{1}{x}\right)\right] dx$

$= \underbrace{\int_{\sqrt{2}-1}^{1} \left[2 + x - \frac{1}{x}\right] dx}_{A_1} + \underbrace{\int_{1}^{\sqrt{2}+1} \left[2 + \frac{1}{x} - x\right] dx}_{A_2}$

$A_1 = 2x + \frac{x^2}{2} - \ln x \Big|_{\sqrt{2}-1}^{1}$

$= \frac{5}{2} - \left(2\sqrt{2} - 2 + \frac{3 - 2\sqrt{2}}{2} - \ln(\sqrt{2}-1)\right)$

$= \frac{5}{2} - 2\sqrt{2} + 2 - \frac{3 - 2\sqrt{2}}{2} + \ln(\sqrt{2}-1)$

$A_2 = 2x - \frac{x^2}{2} + \ln x \Big|_{1}^{\sqrt{2}+1}$

$= 2\sqrt{2} + 2 - \frac{3 + 2\sqrt{2}}{2} + \ln(\sqrt{2}+1) - \frac{3}{2}$

$\therefore A_1 + A_2 = 5 - 3 + \ln(\sqrt{2}+1) + \ln(\sqrt{2}-1)$

$\therefore A = 2$ sq units

23. (6) **Case I**

Let $[|x|] = 0$ then $[|y|] = 2$

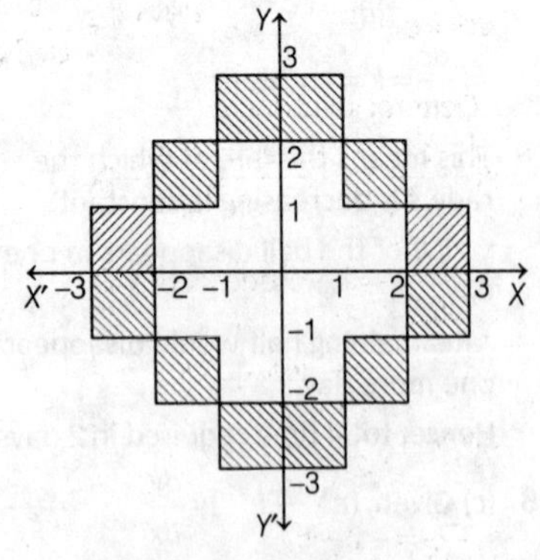

$\Rightarrow 0 \le |x| < 1$, then $2 \le |y| < 3$

$\Rightarrow -1 < x < 1$, then $-3 < y \le -2$ or $2 \le y < 3$

Case II

Let $[|x|] = 1$, then $[|y|] = 1$

$\Rightarrow 1 \le |x| < 2$ then $1 \le y < 2$

$\Rightarrow (-2 < x \le -1$ or $1 \le x < 2)$,

then $(-2 < y \le -1$ or $1 \le y < 2)$

Case III

Let $[|x|] = 2$, then $[|y|] = 0$

$\Rightarrow 2 \le |x| < 3$, then $0 \le y < 1$

$\Rightarrow (-3 < x \le -2$ or $2 \le x < 3)$,

then $-1 < y < 1$

From the cases (I), (II) and (III), we draw the the above graph.

To calculate the required area, we observe from figure, that there are total 12 equal square boxes and area of one square box $= (1)^2 = 1$ sq.units.

Hence, required area

$= 1 + 1 + 1 + 1 + 1 + 1 + 1 + 1 + 1 + 1 + 1 + 1$

$= 12$ sq units

Divisors of 12 are 1, 2, 3, 4, 6, 12.

24. (6) The circle $x^2 + y^2 = 64a^2$ intersects the parabola $y^2 = 12ax$ at the points $A(4a, 4\sqrt{3}a)$ and $B(4a, -4\sqrt{3}a)$.

The smaller area between the curve is shaded in figure and is equal to

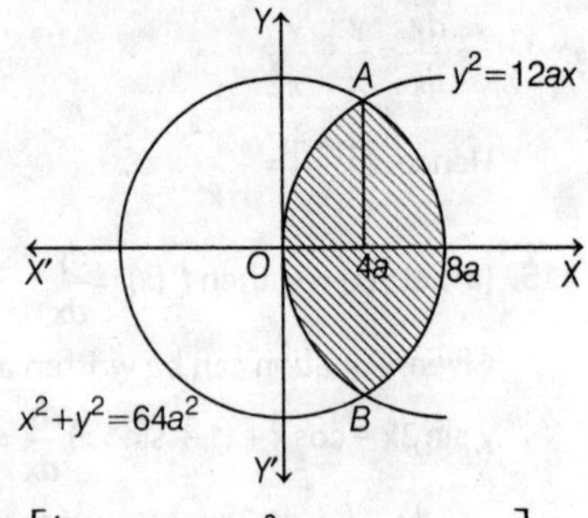

$2\left[\int_{0}^{4a} \sqrt{12ax}\,dx + \int_{4a}^{8a} \sqrt{64a^2 - x^2}\,dx\right]$

$= 4\sqrt{3} \cdot a \cdot \frac{2}{3} x^{\frac{3}{2}} \Big|_0^{4a} + \left(x + \sqrt{64a^2 - x^2} + 64a^2 \sin^{-1} \frac{x}{8a}\right)\Big|_{4a}^{8a}$

$= \frac{16a^2}{3}(4\pi + \sqrt{3})$ sq units

and the larger area is

$64\pi a^2 - \frac{16a^2}{3}(4\pi + \sqrt{3})$

$= \frac{16a^2}{3}(8\pi - \sqrt{3})$ sq units.

Therefore, their ratio is

$4\pi + \sqrt{3} : 8\pi - \sqrt{3}$

On comparing, we get $\alpha = 4, \beta = 3$ and $\gamma = 8$

So, $[(\alpha + \gamma) - 2\beta] = [(4 + 8) - 6] = 6$

25. (9) The equation of the tangent at $P(x, y)$ is $Y - y = \frac{dy}{dx}(X - x)$

This tangent meets the Y-axis at $\left(0, y - x\frac{dy}{dx}\right)$.

Given condition

$$y - x\frac{dy}{dx} = x^3$$

$$\Rightarrow \frac{dy}{dx} + \left(-\frac{1}{x}\right)y = -x^2,$$

which is linear differential equation

$$\text{IF} = e^{\int -\frac{1}{x}dx} = e^{-\ln x} = \frac{1}{x}$$

$\therefore$ General solution of the given equation is

$$y \times \frac{1}{x} = \int -x^2 \times \frac{1}{x} + c$$

$$\Rightarrow \frac{y}{x} = -\frac{x^2}{2} + c$$

$$\Rightarrow y = -\frac{x^3}{2} + cx$$

$$\Rightarrow f(x) = -\frac{x^3}{2} + cx \quad \text{...(i)}$$

$$f(1) = -\frac{1}{2} + c = 1 \quad \text{(given)}$$

$$\therefore \quad c = \frac{3}{2}$$

From Eq. (i), $f(x) = -\frac{x^3}{2} + \frac{3}{2}x$

Hence, $f(-3) = \frac{27}{2} - \frac{9}{2} = 9$

26. (4) Given, $x\frac{dy}{dx} - y = x^2(xe^x + e^x - 1)$

$$\Rightarrow \frac{dy}{dx} + \left(-\frac{1}{x}\right)y = x(xe^x + e^x - 1)$$

which is linear differential equation.

$$\therefore \text{IF} = e^{\int -\frac{1}{x}dx} = e^{-\ln x} = \frac{1}{x}$$

Now, general solution is

$$y \times \frac{1}{x} = \int [e^x(x+1) - 1]dx$$

$$\Rightarrow \frac{y}{x} = xe^x - x + C$$

As, $y(1) = e - 1$

$$\Rightarrow \frac{e-1}{1} = e - 1 + C$$

$$\Rightarrow C = 0$$

So, $\frac{y}{x} = xe^x - x \Rightarrow x + \frac{y}{x} = e^x$

Now, $2 + \frac{y(2)}{2} = 2e^2$

$$\Rightarrow \quad y(2) = 4e^2 - 4$$

and $\quad y(1) = e - 1 \quad$ (given)

Hence, $y(2) = 4(e+1)(e-1)$

$$y(2) = 4(y(1))[y(1) + 2]$$

On comparing with

$y(2) = \lambda y(1)[y(1) + z]$, we get $\lambda = 4$

27. (5) Let $f(x) = \max\{x + |x|, x - [x]\}$, $-2 \le x \le 2$

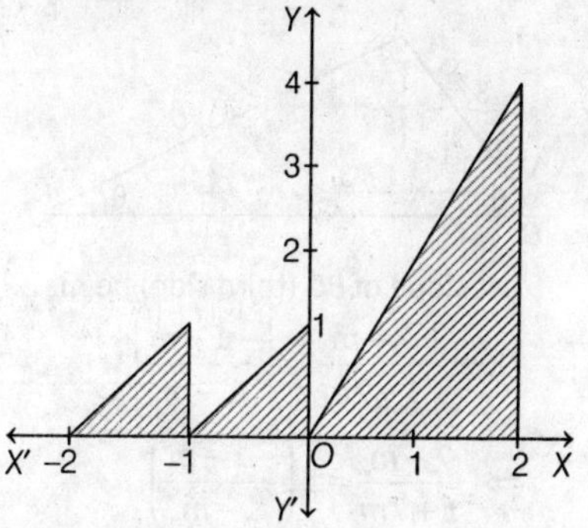

$$\Rightarrow f(x) = \begin{cases} \max\{x - x, x + 2\} \\ \max\{x - x, x + 1\} \\ \max\{x + x, x\} \\ \max\{x + x, x - 1\} \end{cases}$$

$$\Rightarrow f(x) = \begin{cases} x + 2, -2 \le x < -1 \\ x + 1, -1 \le x < 0 \\ 2x, 0 \le x < 2 \end{cases}$$

$\therefore$ Required integral

$$= \text{Area of the shaded region}$$

$$= \frac{1}{2} + \frac{1}{2} + \frac{1}{2} \times (2) \times (4) = 5$$

28. (2) Given, $\frac{dy}{dx} - 3y\cot x = \sin 2x$,

which is linear differential equation.

$$\therefore \text{IF} = e^{-\int 3\cot x\, dx} = e^{-3\ln(\sin x)} = \frac{1}{\sin^3 x}$$

$\therefore$ General solution is

$$y\left(\frac{1}{\sin^3 x}\right) = \int \frac{2\sin x \cdot \cos x}{\sin^3 x}dx$$

$$\Rightarrow \frac{y}{\sin^3 x} = 2\int \operatorname{cosec} x \cot x\, dx$$

$$= -2\operatorname{cosec} x + C$$

Given, $y\left(\frac{\pi}{2}\right) = 2$

$$\therefore \frac{2}{(1)^3} = -2 + c$$

$$\Rightarrow c = 4$$

$\therefore \quad y = (4\sin^3 x - 2\sin^2 x)$ and

$y'(x) = 12\sin^2 x \cdot \cos x - 4\sin x\cos x$

Now, $y\left(\frac{\pi}{6}\right) = 4\left(\frac{1}{2}\right)^3 - 2\left(\frac{1}{2}\right)^2$

$$= \frac{1}{2} - \frac{1}{2} = 0$$

and $y'\left(\frac{\pi}{3}\right) = \left(\frac{12 \times 3}{4} \times \frac{1}{2} - 4 \times \frac{\sqrt{3}}{2} \times \frac{1}{2}\right)$

$$= \frac{9}{2} - \frac{2\sqrt{3}}{2} = \frac{9 - 2\sqrt{3}}{2}$$

Hence, $\left[\frac{y\left(\frac{\pi}{6}\right) + 4}{9 - 2\sqrt{3}}\right] \cdot y'\left(\frac{\pi}{3}\right)$

$$= \frac{(0+4)}{(9 - 2\sqrt{3})} \times \frac{(9 - 2\sqrt{3})}{2} = 2$$

29. (8) Given, $\frac{dy}{dx} + \sin\left(\frac{x+y}{2}\right) = \sin\left(\frac{x-y}{2}\right)$

$$\Rightarrow \frac{dy}{dx} = -2\cos\frac{x}{2} \cdot \sin\frac{y}{2}$$

$$\Rightarrow -\int 2\cos\frac{x}{2}dx = \int \operatorname{cosec}\frac{y}{2}dy$$

$$\Rightarrow c - 2\sin\frac{x}{2} = \ln\left(\tan\frac{y}{4}\right)$$

$$\Rightarrow \log_e\left(\tan\frac{y}{4}\right) + 2\sin\left(\frac{x}{2}\right) = c$$

Hence, $\alpha = 4, \beta = 2$ and $\gamma = 2$

So, $\alpha + \beta + \gamma = 4 + 2 + 2 = 8$

30. (3) Given, $x\,dy = y(dx + y\,dy)$

$$\Rightarrow \quad ydx = (x - y^2)dy$$

$$\Rightarrow \frac{dx}{dy} + \left(-\frac{1}{y}\right)x = -y,$$

which is a linear differential equation.

$$\text{IF} = e^{\int -\frac{1}{y}dy} = e^{-\ln y} = \frac{1}{y}$$

$\therefore$ General solution of the given equation is

$$x \times \frac{1}{y} = \int -y \times \frac{1}{y}dy + c$$

$$\Rightarrow \frac{x}{y} = -y + c \quad \text{...(i)}$$

Given, $y(1) = 1$, i.e. $y = 1$, when $x = 1$

From Eq. (i), $1 = -1 + c$

$$\Rightarrow \quad c = 2$$

Hence, $\frac{x}{y} = -y + 2$

Putting $x = -3$, we get

$$-\frac{3}{y} = -y + 2$$

$$\Rightarrow \quad y^2 - 2y - 3 = 0$$

$$\Rightarrow \quad (y-3)(y+1) = 0$$

$$\because \quad y(x) > 0$$

$$\therefore \quad y = 3$$

Qualifier 11
(Points and Coordinates, Straight Lines, Pair of Straight Lines, Circle)

1. (c) Let x_1, x_2 and x_3 be in AP with common difference d_1 and y_1, y_2 and y_3 be in AP with common difference d_2 so that

$(PQ)^2 = (x_2 - x_1)^2 + (y_2 - y_1)^2 = d_1^2 + d_2^2$

$(QR)^2 = (x_3 - x_2)^2 + (y_3 - y_2)^2 = d_1^2 + d_2^2$

$(PR)^2 = (x_3 - x_1)^2 + (y_3 - y_1)^2$

$= (2d_1)^2 + (2d_2)^2$

and we get, $PQ = QR = \sqrt{d_1^2 + d_2^2}$

$PR = 2\sqrt{d_1^2 + d_2^2}$

$\Rightarrow \quad PR = PQ + QR$

This shows that, P, Q and R are collinear.

2. (a) Taking the coordinates of vertices O, A, B and C as $(0, 0), (a, 0), (a, a)$ and $(0, a)$ respectively, we get the coordinates of P and Q as $\left(a, \frac{a}{2}\right)$ and $\left(\frac{a}{2}, a\right)$ respectively.

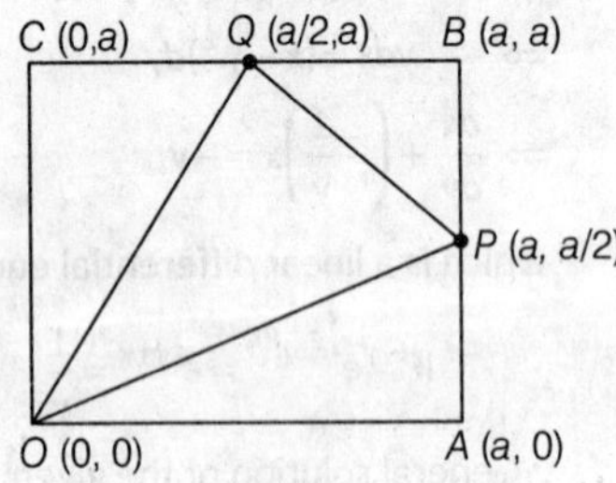

$\therefore$ Area of $\Delta OPQ = \frac{1}{2}\begin{vmatrix} 0 & 0 & 1 \\ a & \frac{a}{2} & 1 \\ \frac{a}{2} & a & 1 \end{vmatrix} = \frac{3a^2}{8}$

and area of the square $= a^2$

$\therefore$ The required ratio is $8:3$

3. (a) Given, $AB \le 4 \Rightarrow (AB)^2 \le 16$

$\Rightarrow (x-3)^2 + (y-4)^2 \le 16$

When $x = -6$, then

$(-6-3)^2 + (y-4)^2 \le 16$

$\Rightarrow \quad 81 + (y-4)^2 \le 16$

$\Rightarrow (y-4)^2 \le -65$, which is not possible for any value of y.

When $x = 6$, then $(6-3)^2 + (y-4)^2 \le 16$

$\Rightarrow 9 + (y-4)^2 \le 16$

$\Rightarrow \quad (y-4)^2 \le 7$

$\Rightarrow |y-4| \le \sqrt{7} \Rightarrow -\sqrt{7} \le y - 4 \le \sqrt{7}$

$\Rightarrow 4 - \sqrt{7} \le y \le 4 + \sqrt{7}$ ($\because \sqrt{7} \simeq 2.65$

$\therefore 4 - \sqrt{7} \simeq 1.35, 4 + \sqrt{7} \simeq 6.65$)

$\Rightarrow y = \{2, 3, 4, 5, 6\}, y \in I$

Hence, total number of positions of B with integral coordinates $= 5$

4. (d) Slope of $AB = m_{AB} = 7$

Slope of $AC = m_{AC} = -1$

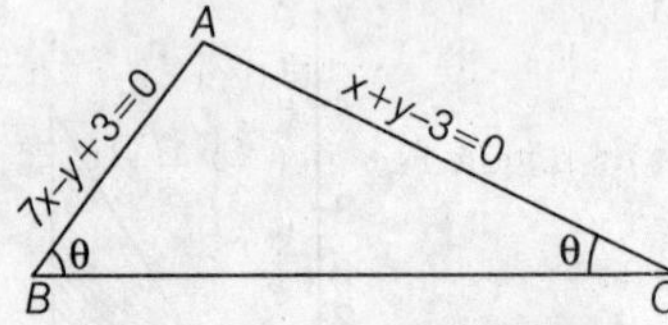

Let slope of BC (third side) be m.

Now, $\left|\frac{7-m}{1+7m}\right| = \left|\frac{-1-m}{1-m}\right|$

$\Rightarrow \quad \frac{7-m}{1+7m} = \pm\left(\frac{-1-m}{1-m}\right)$

$m^2 + 1 = 0$ (no real values of m possible) taking – ve sign, we get

$3m^2 + 8m - 3 = 0$

$\Rightarrow (3m-1)(m+3) = 0$

$\Rightarrow \quad m = \frac{1}{3}, -3$

$\therefore$ Required equation of third side can be $x - 3y - 31 = 0$ or $3x + y + 7 = 0$

5. (c) From given information,

$\cos\angle ADC = \frac{(AD)^2 + (CD)^2 - (AC)^2}{2(AD)\cdot(CD)} < 0$

($\because$ cos(obtuse angle) = – ve)

$\Rightarrow (p-1)^2 + 4^2 + (5-1)^2 + (6-4)^2 < (p-5)^2 + (6)^2$

$\Rightarrow \quad 8p < 24 \Rightarrow p < 3$

$\therefore$ Maximum integral value of $p = 2$.

6. (a) Let $APQR$ be the new position of the square so that $\angle PAB = 30°$ and PR is the new position of the diagonal BD.

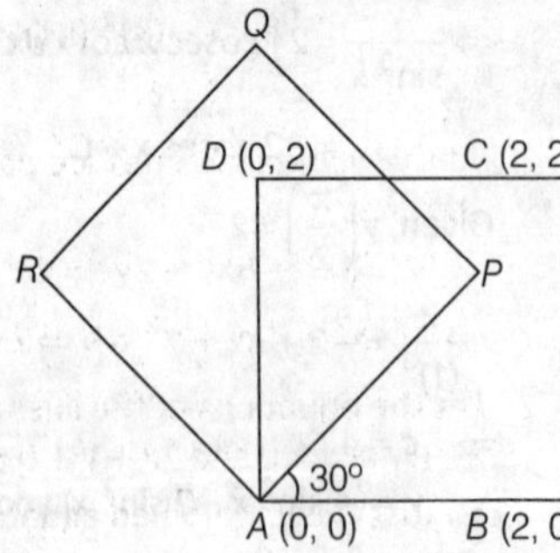

So, coordinates of P are $(2\cos 30°, 2\sin 30°) = (\sqrt{3}, 1)$ and coordinates of R are

$[2\cos(90° + 30°), 2\sin(90° + 30°)] = (-1, \sqrt{3})$

$\therefore$ Equation of PR is

$y - 1 = \frac{\sqrt{3}-1}{-1-\sqrt{3}}(x - \sqrt{3})$

$\Rightarrow \quad (2-\sqrt{3})x + y = 2(\sqrt{3}-1)$

7. (b) $OP_n = \frac{n}{\sqrt{3^2 + 4^2}} = \frac{n}{5}$

So, $OP_1 + OP_2 + OP_3 + \ldots + OP_n$

$= \frac{1}{5}(1 + 2 + 3 + \ldots + n) = 9$ [given]

$\Rightarrow \quad \frac{n(n+1)}{5 \times 2} = 9 \Rightarrow n = 9$

8. (d) Let the coordinates of D be $(x, 0)$.

Then, A, M and D are collinear.

Coordinates of M are

$\left(\frac{3+1}{2}, \frac{3+1}{2}\right) = (2, 2)$

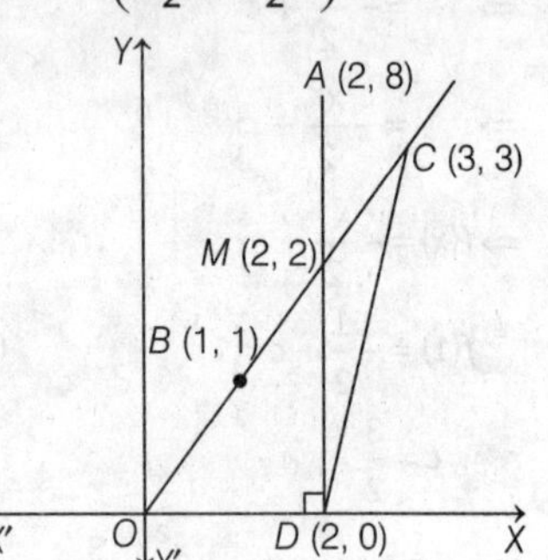

$\because A, M$ and D are collinear.

So, $\begin{vmatrix} x & 0 & 1 \\ 2 & 8 & 1 \\ 2 & 2 & 1 \end{vmatrix} = 0$

$\Rightarrow x(8-2) + (4-16) = 0$

$\Rightarrow \quad x = 2$

So, (this is clear from the figure also) then coordinate of D are $(2, 0)$.

$(OD)^2 = 4, (MD)^2 = 4,$

$(OM)^2 = 4 + 4 = 8 = (OD)^2 + (MD)^2$

Thus, the ΔOMD is right angled triangle, D being the right angle and OM, the hypotenuse.

Circumcentre of ΔOMD is $(1, 1)$ $\rightarrow$ (mid-point of hypotenuse).

Orthocentre of ΔOMD is $D(2, 0)$.

Centroid of the ΔCMD is

$\left(\frac{3+2+2}{3}, \frac{3+2+0}{3}\right) = \left(\frac{7}{3}, \frac{5}{3}\right)$

9. (b) Let the required line be

$(y - 0) = m(x - 6), m > 0$

or $\quad mx - y - 6m = 0 \quad$ ...(i)

As, distance of line (i) from $N(1, 3)$ is 5, we have,

$$\left|\frac{m-3-6m}{\sqrt{1+m^2}}\right|=5$$

$\Rightarrow \quad (3+5m)^2=25(1+m^2)$

$\Rightarrow \quad 9+30m=25$

$\Rightarrow \quad m=\frac{16}{30} \Rightarrow m=\frac{8}{15}$

10. (d) Let equation of the line through $A(-5,-4)$ be $\frac{x+5}{\cos\theta}=\frac{y+4}{\sin\theta}=r$ (say).

If $AB=r$, then coordinates of B which is at a distance r from A are $(r\cos\theta-5, r\sin\theta-4)$.

Since, B lies on the line $x+3y+2=0$

$\therefore r\cos\theta-5+3(r\sin\theta-4)+2=0$

$\Rightarrow r(\cos\theta+3\sin\theta)=15$

$\Rightarrow \quad \frac{15}{r}=\cos\theta+3\sin\theta$

$\Rightarrow \quad \frac{15}{AB}=\cos\theta+3\sin\theta$

Similarly, $\frac{10}{AC}=2\cos\theta+\sin\theta$

and $\frac{6}{AD}=\cos\theta-\sin\theta$

So, from the given relation, we have

$(\cos\theta+3\sin\theta)^2+(2\cos\theta+\sin\theta)^2$

$=(\cos\theta-\sin\theta)^2$

$\Rightarrow 4\cos^2\theta+9\sin^2\theta+12\sin\theta\cos\theta=0$

$\Rightarrow (2\cos\theta+3\sin\theta)^2=0$

$\Rightarrow \quad \frac{\cos\theta}{3}=\frac{\sin\theta}{-2}$

$\therefore$Required equation of the line is

$\frac{x+5}{3}=\frac{y+4}{-2} \Rightarrow 2x+3y+22=0$

11. (c) Let the point of intersection of the given lines be (x_1, y_1), then

$12x_1+5y_1+7=0$

and $\quad 5x_1-8y_1+13=0$

On solving this, we have,

$x_1=-1, y_1=1$

Also, $\quad \tan\theta=\frac{2\sqrt{h^2-ab}}{a+b}$

From the given equation (in question), we have

$a=6, b=-4$ and $h=\frac{5}{2}$,

where $a=$ coefficient of x^2

$b=$ coefficient of y^2

$2h=$ coefficient of xy

$$\therefore \tan\theta=\frac{2\sqrt{\left(\frac{5}{2}\right)^2-6(-4)}}{6-4}$$

$$=\sqrt{\frac{121}{4}}=\frac{11}{2}$$

Hence, equation of the required line is

$y-1=\frac{11}{2}(x+1) \Rightarrow 11x-2y+13=0$

12. (c) If $x-3y=a$ and $px+2y=b$ are perpendicular, then $\frac{1}{3}\left(\frac{-p}{2}\right)=-1$

$\Rightarrow \quad p=6 \quad$ ...(i)

If $x-3y=a$ and $px+y=c$ are perpendicular, then

$\frac{1}{3}(-p)=-1$

$\Rightarrow \quad p=3$

$px+2y=b$ and $px+y=c$ are not perpendicular as

$\left(\frac{-p}{2}\right).(-p)=-1$

$\Rightarrow \quad p^2=-2$

which is not possible.

$\therefore \quad p=6$ and $p=3$

$\Rightarrow \quad (p-6)(p-3)=0$

$\Rightarrow \quad p^2-9p+18=0$

13. (b) Clearly, two sides are $x-2y+1=0$ and $x+y=0$.

As, orthocentre lies on $x-2y+1=0$ is right angled (let at B).

Third side passes through (1, 1) and is perpendicular to $x-2y+1=0$.

Third side is $2x+y-3=0$

$\therefore$Circumradius $=\frac{1}{2}AC=\frac{5\sqrt{2}}{3}$

14. (a) **Method (1)** (Proper Method)

The given equation represents a pair of parallel straight lines, if

$8\times\lambda=(4)^2$ (using $h^2=ab$)

$\Rightarrow \quad \lambda=2$

At this value of λ, lines are parallel to the lines

$8x^2+8xy+2y^2=0$

$\Rightarrow \quad 4x^2+4xy+y^2=0 \Rightarrow 2x+y=0$

Let the equations of the lines be $2x+y+a=0$ and $2x+y+b=0$.

So that their combined equation is

$(2x+y)^2+(a+b)(2x+y)+ab=0$

Comparing with the given equation, we have,

$a+b=\frac{13}{2}, ab=\frac{15}{2} \Rightarrow |a-b|=\frac{7}{2}$

$\therefore$Required distance $=\frac{|a-b|}{\sqrt{2^2+1^2}}=\frac{7}{2\sqrt{5}}$

Method (2) (Short-cut Method)

Short Trick Distance between the pair of parallel lines $=2\sqrt{\frac{g^2-ac}{a(a+b)}}$

So, required distance

$=2\sqrt{\frac{(13)^2-8\times15}{8(8+2)}}=\frac{2\times7}{4\sqrt{5}}=\frac{7}{2\sqrt{5}}$

(where $g=$ coefficient of x

$a=$ coefficient of x^2

$b=$ coefficient of y^2

$c=$ constant term)

15. (b) $AB=AO=BO=a$

$\Rightarrow \quad \angle AOB=60°$

$\Rightarrow \quad \frac{PA}{a}=\sqrt{3} \quad$ (in ΔPAO)

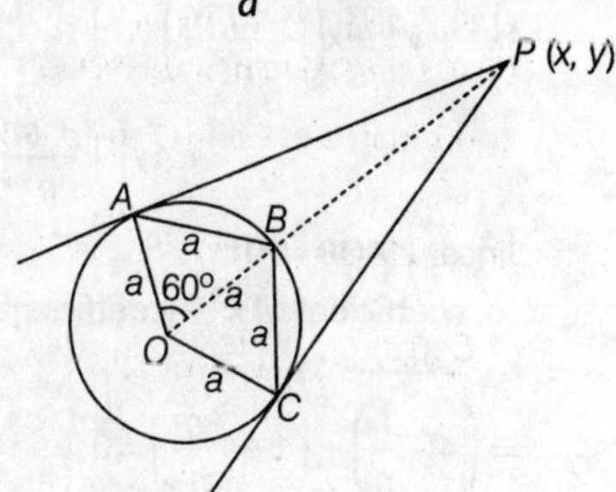

$\Rightarrow \quad x^2+y^2-a^2=3a^2$

$\Rightarrow x^2+y^2=4a^2=(2a)^2$

$\therefore$Radius $=2a$

16. (d) The equation of chord of contact is

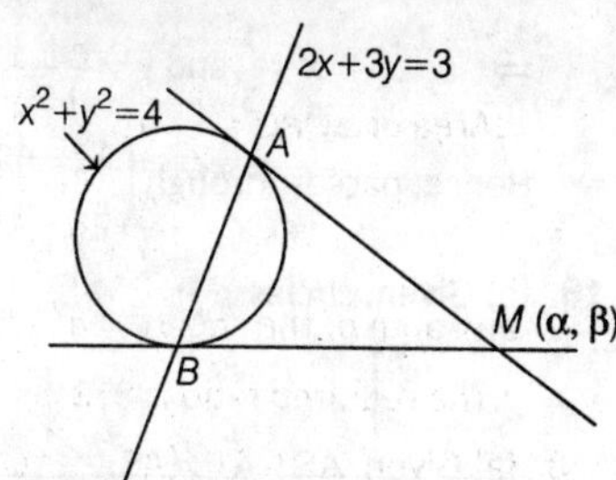

$\alpha x+\beta y=4 \quad$ ...(i)

Also, $\quad 2x+3y=3 \quad$ ...(ii)

Since, Eqs. (i) and (ii) represents same line.

So, $\frac{\alpha}{2}=\frac{\beta}{3}=\frac{4}{3} \Rightarrow \alpha=\frac{8}{3}$ and $\beta=4$

Hence, $\frac{\alpha}{\beta}=\frac{\frac{8}{3}}{4}=\frac{2}{3}$

17. (a) Let equation of chord be

$$lx + my = n \quad ...(i)$$

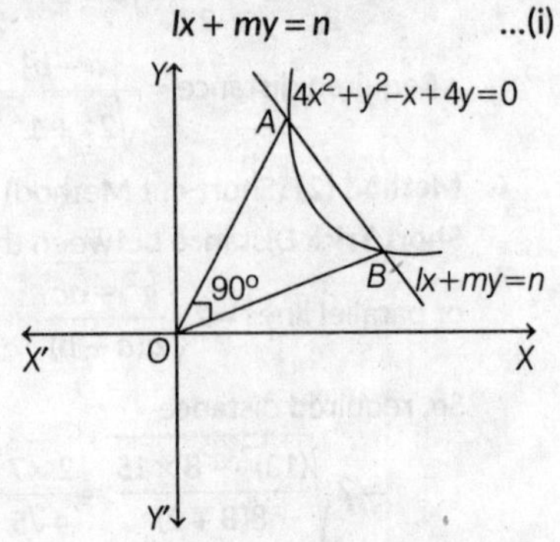

$$\Rightarrow \quad \frac{lx + my}{n} = 1$$

Given, curve C_1:

$$4x^2 + y^2 - x + 4y = 0 \quad ...(ii)$$

Now, the joint equation of a pair of straight lines joining origin to the point of intersection of line (i) and curve (ii) is given by,

$$4x^2 + y^2 - x\left(\frac{lx + my}{n}\right) + 4y\left(\frac{lx + my}{n}\right) = 0$$

Since, $\angle AOB = 90°$

So, coefficient of x^2 + coefficient of $y^2 = 0$

$$\Rightarrow \left(4 - \frac{l}{n}\right) + \left(1 + \frac{4m}{n}\right) = 0$$

$$\Rightarrow \quad 4n - l + n + 4m = 0$$

$$\Rightarrow \quad l - 4m = 5n \quad ...(iii)$$

From Eqs. (i) and (iii), we get,

$$\frac{x}{1} = \frac{y}{-4} = \frac{1}{5}$$

$$\Rightarrow \quad x = \frac{1}{5} \text{ and } y = -\frac{4}{5}$$

Hence, passes through $\left(\frac{1}{5}, -\frac{4}{5}\right)$.

18. (b) Given, circles

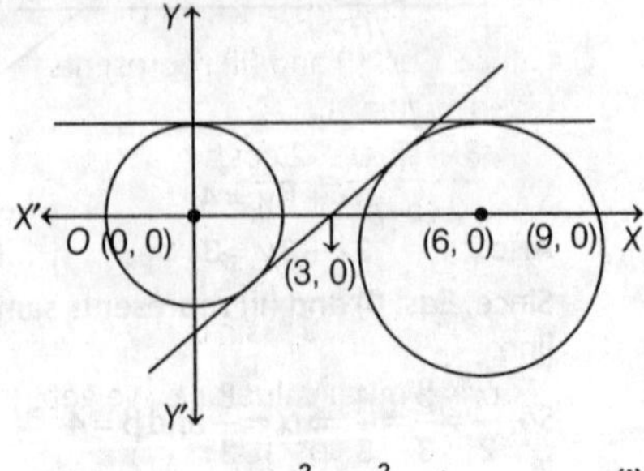

$$x^2 + y^2 = 4 \quad ...(i)$$

and $x^2 + y^2 - 12x + 27 = 0 \quad ...(ii)$

From Eq. (i),

Centre (0, 0) and radius $(r_1) = 2$

From Eq. (ii);

Centre (6, 0) and $r_2 = 3$

$$\therefore L \quad = \sqrt{36 - 1}$$

$[\because L = \sqrt{d^2 - (r_1 - r_2)^2}$ and $L = \sqrt{d^2 - (r_1 + r_2)^2}$, where d = distance between centres of the two circles]

$$= \sqrt{35}$$

and $L = \sqrt{36 - 25} = \sqrt{11}$

Hence, greatest common tangent $= \sqrt{35}$

19. (d) Given, equation of circle is

$$x^2 + y^2 = px + qy$$

$$\Rightarrow \quad x(x - p) + y(y - q) = 0$$

$$\Rightarrow (x - 0)(x - p) + (y - 0)(y - q) = 0 \quad ...(i)$$

Eq. (i) represents the equation of circle in diametric form with (p, q) and $(0, 0)$ as end points of diameter.

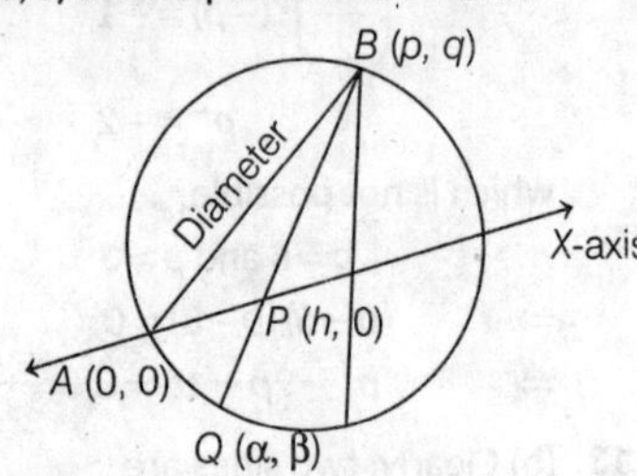

Let $P(h, 0)$ lies on X-axis and $Q \equiv (\alpha, \beta)$ (say).

$\because P$ is the mid-point of BQ.

$$\therefore \frac{\alpha + p}{2} = h, \frac{\beta + q}{2} = 0$$

$$\Rightarrow \quad \alpha = 2h - p, \beta = -q$$

Hence, $Q \equiv (2h - p, -q)$ lies on circle.

So, Q satisfies the equation of circle.

i.e. $(2h - p)(2h - 2p) - q(-2q) = 0$

$$\Rightarrow \quad (2h - p)(h - p) + q^2 = 0$$

$$\Rightarrow \quad 2h^2 - 3ph + p^2 + q^2 = 0 \quad ...(ii)$$

$\because$ X-axis bisect the two distinct chords.

$\therefore h$ will have two values.

Hence, discriminant of (ii) > 0

$$\left[\because h \begin{matrix} \nearrow h_1 \\ \searrow h_2 \end{matrix}\right]$$

$$\Rightarrow 9p^2 - 8(p^2 + q^2) > 0$$

$$\Rightarrow \quad p^2 - 8q^2 > 0$$

$$\Rightarrow \quad p^2 > 8q^2$$

20. (d) Equation of the required circle is $S_1 + \lambda S_2 = 0$

$$\Rightarrow (1 + \lambda)x^2 + (1 + \lambda)y^2 + 2(2\lambda - 1)x + 2(2 - \lambda)y - (1 + 5\lambda) = 0$$

$$\Rightarrow x^2 + y^2 + \frac{2(2\lambda - 1)}{1 + \lambda}x + \frac{2(2 - \lambda)}{1 + \lambda}y - \frac{1 + 5\lambda}{1 + \lambda} = 0$$

Now, using the condition of orthogonality,

$$2g_1g_2 + 2f_1f_2 = c_1 + c_2$$

$$\Rightarrow 2 \times 0 + 2 \times 0 = -4 - \frac{1 + 5\lambda}{1 + \lambda}$$

$$\Rightarrow -4 = \frac{1 + 5\lambda}{1 + \lambda} \Rightarrow \lambda = -\frac{5}{9}$$

So, the equation of the circle is

$$x^2 + y^2 - \frac{19}{2}x + \frac{23}{2}y + 4 = 0 \quad ...(i)$$

Hence, length of the tangent from origin to the circle (i) $= \sqrt{S_1}$

$$= \sqrt{0^2 + 0^2 - \frac{19}{2} \times 0 + \frac{23}{2} \times 0 + 4}$$

$$= \sqrt{4} = 2$$

21. (4) Let $P \equiv (\lambda^2, 2\lambda)$

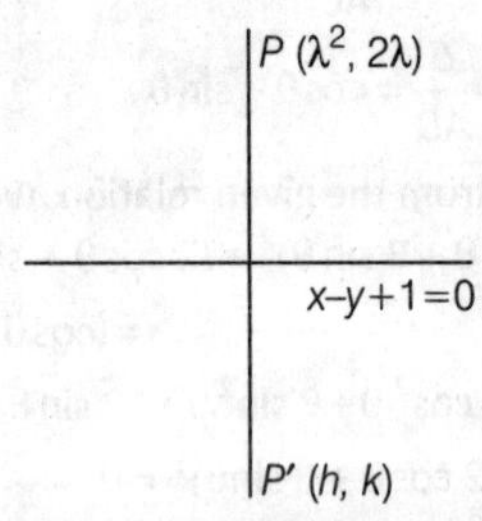

Image of P on $x - y + 1 = 0$ is $P' \equiv (h, k)$ (say)

Now, $\frac{h - \lambda^2}{1} = \frac{k - 2\lambda}{-1} = \frac{-2(\lambda^2 - 2\lambda + 1)}{2}$

$$\Rightarrow \quad h + 1 = 2\lambda \quad ...(i)$$

and $\quad k = \lambda^2 + 1 \quad ...(ii)$

Putting the value of λ from Eq. (i) in Eq. (ii), we get,

$$k - 1 = \left(\frac{h + 1}{2}\right)^2 \Rightarrow 4(y - 1) = (x + 1)^2$$

Hence, $a = -1$, $b = 4$ and $c = 1$

So, $a + b + c = -1 + 4 + 1 = 4$

22. (16) $am^2 + 2m + 1 = 0 \quad ...(i)$

$$m^2 + 2m + a = 0 \quad ...(ii)$$

(let $m = \frac{x}{y}$)

Solving Eqs. (i) and (ii), we get,

$$(a - 1)m^2 + (1 - a) = 0$$

$$\Rightarrow \quad m^2 = 1$$

$$\Rightarrow \quad m = \pm 1$$

If $m=1$ is common root, then $a=-3$

From Eq. (i), $m=1, -\frac{1}{3}$ and from Eq. (ii), $m=1,-3$

If $m=-1$ is common root, then $a=1$

From Eq. (i), $m=-1,-1$ and from Eq. (ii), $m=-1,-1$ (Rejected)

$\therefore$ Other lines are $y=-\frac{x}{3}$ and $y=-3x$.

$\Rightarrow \quad (x+3y)(3x+y)=0$

$\Rightarrow \quad 3x^2+10xy+3y^2=0$

On comparing with

$\alpha x^2+\beta xy+\gamma y^2=0$, we get

$\alpha=3, \beta=10$

and $\gamma=3$

$\therefore \alpha+\beta+\gamma=3+10+3=16$

23. (4) Given equations of lines are

$$(-\sin\theta)x+y=0 \quad \text{...(i)}$$

$$x+\sin\theta=0 \quad \text{...(ii)}$$

$$(\sin\theta)x+y+1=0 \quad \text{...(iii)}$$

On solving Eqs. (i) and (ii), we get

$$(x,y)=(-\sin\theta,-\sin^2\theta) \quad \text{...(iv)}$$

[from Eq. (ii), $x=-\sin\theta$

from Eq. (i), $(-\sin\theta)(-\sin\theta)+y=0$

$\Rightarrow y=-\sin^2\theta$]

Since, Eqs. (i), (ii) and (iii) are concurrent.

So, Eq. (iv) satisfies Eq. (iii).

i.e. $(\sin\theta)(-\sin\theta)-\sin^2\theta+1=0$

$\Rightarrow \quad 1-2\sin^2\theta=0$

$\Rightarrow \quad \cos 2\theta=0$

$\Rightarrow \quad 2\theta=\frac{\pi}{2},\frac{3\pi}{2},\frac{5\pi}{2},\frac{7\pi}{2}$

$\Rightarrow \quad \theta=\frac{\pi}{4},\frac{3\pi}{4},\frac{5\pi}{4},\frac{7\pi}{4}\in(0,2\pi)$

$\therefore$ Number of values of $\theta=4$

24. (0) For any point $P(x, 0)$ on the X-axis, its distance from the given point $A(3,5)$ is $\sqrt{(x-3)^2+(5-0)^2}\geq 5$.

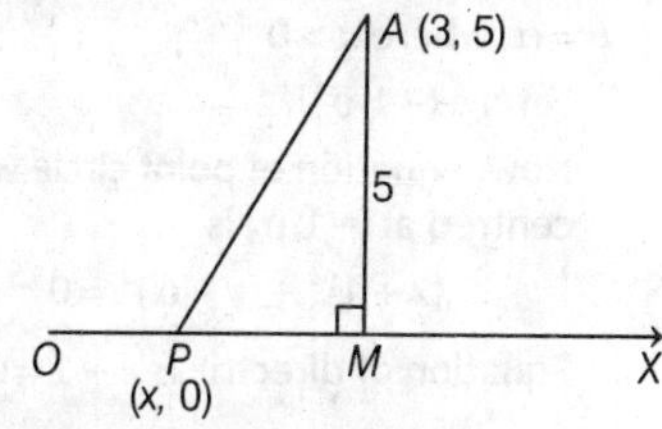

So, there is no point satisfying the given condition inquestion.

Hence, number of points $=0$

Note (a) From the figure, we have, $AP\geq AM$ for all positions of P.

(b) You may think, for this problem, just like.

Given, $p<5 \Rightarrow \sqrt{(x-3)^2+(5-0)^2}<5$

$\Rightarrow (x-3)^2+25<25$

$\Rightarrow (x-3)^2<0$ but there is no value of x for which $(x-3)^2$ becomes negative.

So, $x\in\phi$.

25. (3) Equation of common chord of given circles is

$2kx-8y-2=0 \Rightarrow kx-4y-1=0$

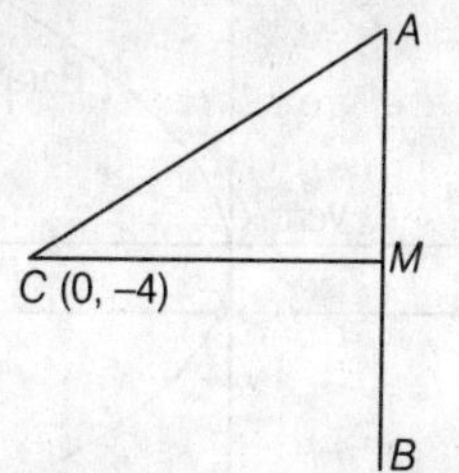

Length of perpendicular from $(0,-4)$ to $kx-4y-1=0$ is

$$CM=\frac{|0+16-1|}{\sqrt{k^2+16}}=\frac{15}{\sqrt{k^2+16}}$$

$CA=$ Radius of circle $=\sqrt{16-1}=\sqrt{15}$

We have,

$AM^2=AC^2-CM^2$

$$=15-\frac{225}{k^2+16}=\frac{15(k^2+1)}{k^2+16}$$

Now, $2\sqrt{6}=AB=2(AM)$

$\Rightarrow \quad 6=AM^2=\frac{15(k^2+1)}{k^2+16}$

$\Rightarrow 2(k^2+16)=5(k^2+1)$

$\Rightarrow \quad |k|=3$

26. (5) Centre of circle lies on the line perpendicular to $3x+4y=5$ and passing through $(1,1)$ i.e. on $4(x-1)-3(y-1)=0$. For its point of intersection with the X-axis, put $y=0$, so that centre of circle is $\left(\frac{1}{4},0\right)$.

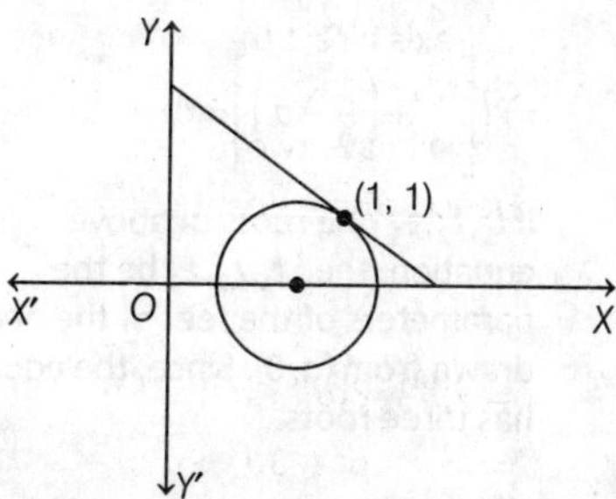

Radius of circle C is

$$\sqrt{\left(1-\frac{1}{4}\right)^2+(1)^2}=\frac{5}{4}$$

As (α,β) lies on the circle, distance of (α,β) from the tangent $3x+4y=5$ can not exceed diameter of circles i.e.

$$\frac{|3\alpha+4\beta-5|}{\sqrt{3^2+4^2}}\leq 2\left(\frac{5}{4}\right)$$

$\Rightarrow |3\alpha+4\beta-5|\leq\frac{25}{2}$

$\Rightarrow \left|\frac{6}{5}\alpha+\frac{8}{5}\beta-2\right|\leq 5$

27. (3) Given, lines are $xy(x+y-2)=0$,

$x=0, y=0$ and $x+y-2=0$.

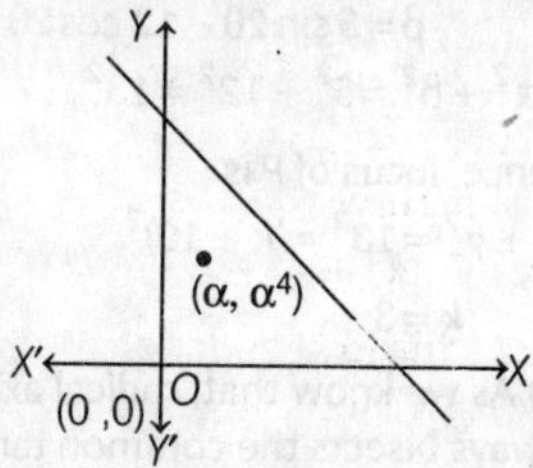

$\because (0,0)$ and (α,α^4) lie on same side of $x+y-2=0$.

$\because \quad (\alpha+\alpha^4-2)(0+0-2)\geq 0$

$\Rightarrow \quad \alpha^4+\alpha-2\leq 0$

$\Rightarrow (\alpha-1)(\alpha^3+\alpha^2+\alpha+2)\leq 0$

$\because \alpha>0$ (because α lies in 1st quadrant (Q_1), $\therefore \alpha^3+\alpha^2+\alpha+2>0, \forall \alpha\in R$)

$\therefore \quad \alpha\leq 1$

$\therefore$ Maximum value of $\alpha=1$

Hence, largest value of $\alpha^2+\alpha+1=3$

28. (2) As, both C_1 and C_2 pass through the origin C_1 and C_2 touch each other at the origin.

Thus, C_1 and C_2 have the same tangent at the origin.

Equation of tangent to C_1 at the origin is

$$(3+\sin\alpha)x+(2\cos\beta)y=0 \quad \text{...(i)}$$

and equation of tangent to C_2 at the origin is

$$(2\cos\beta)x+ky=0 \quad \text{...(ii)}$$

Since, Eqs. (i) and (ii) represents identical lines.

So, $\frac{3+\sin\alpha}{2\cos\beta}=\frac{2\cos\beta}{k}$

$\Rightarrow \quad k=\frac{4\cos^2\beta}{3+\sin\alpha}$

For maximum value of k, we get

$\cos^2\beta=1$

and $\sin\alpha=-1$

Thus, $K_{max}=\frac{4}{3-1}=2$

29. (3) AP is perpendicular to the line $y = x\tan\theta$.

$\Rightarrow \left(\frac{12-\beta}{5-\alpha}\right)\tan\theta = -1$

$\Rightarrow 12-\beta = (\alpha-5)\cot\theta$ ...(i)

Mid-point $\left(\frac{\alpha+5}{2}, \frac{\beta+12}{2}\right)$ of AP lies on $y = x\tan\theta$

$\Rightarrow \beta+12 = (\alpha+5)\tan\theta$ ...(ii)

On solving Eqs. (i) and (ii), we get,

$\alpha = 5\cos 2\theta + 12\sin 2\theta$

$\beta = 5\sin 2\theta - 12\cos 2\theta$

$\therefore \alpha^2 + \beta^2 = 5^2 + 12^2 = 13^2$

Hence, locus of P is

$x^2 + y^2 = 13^2 = (k+10)^2$

$\Rightarrow k = 3$

30. (3) As we know that, radical axis (RA) always bisects the common tangents of two circles.

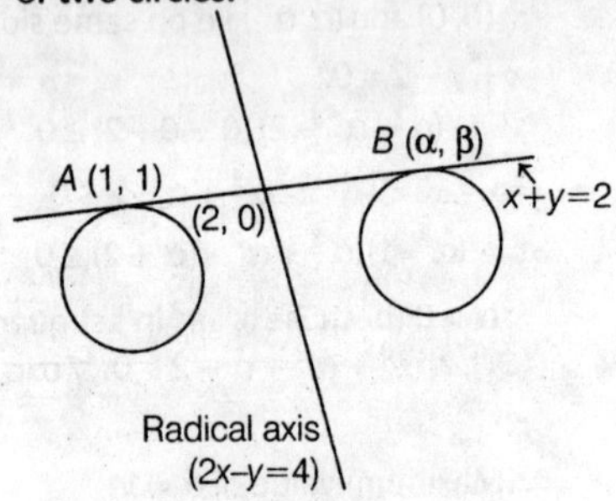

$\therefore$ Point of intersection of common tangent and radical axis

$\left.\begin{array}{l}2x-y=4\\x+y=2\end{array}\right\} \Rightarrow x=2,\ y=0$

$\therefore$ Another point of contact is

$\frac{\alpha+1}{2} = 2, \frac{\beta+1}{2} = 0$

A (1, 1) —— (2, 0) —— B (α, β)

$\Rightarrow \alpha = 3, \beta = -1$

So, $B \equiv (3, -1)$

Hence,

$\left(\frac{5-\beta}{\alpha}\right) + \cos[\log(\alpha+2\beta)(\beta+2\alpha)]$

$= \left(\frac{5+1}{3}\right) + \cos[\log_5 1]$

$= 2 + \cos 0$

$= 2 + 1 = 3$

Qualifier 12
(Conic Sections)

1. (a) Given, equation of tangent at vertex (TAV) is

$$x + y = 12 \quad ...(i)$$

and equation of latusrectum (LR) is

$$x + y = 8 \quad ...(ii)$$

Since, Eqs. (i) and (ii) are parallel.

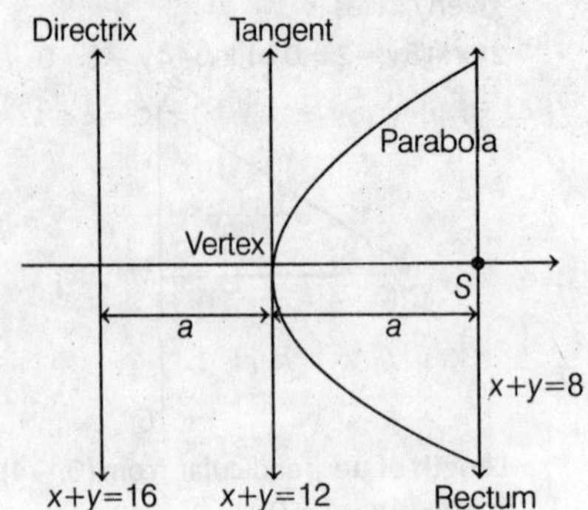

So, distance between Eq.s (i) and (ii)

$$= a = \left|\frac{12-8}{\sqrt{1^2+1^2}}\right| = \frac{4}{\sqrt{2}}$$

Hence, length of latusrectum of a parabola $= 4a = 4 \times \frac{4}{\sqrt{2}} = 8\sqrt{2}$

2. (b) Given, parabola $y^2 = x$

Parametric equation $x = \frac{1}{4}t^2, y = \frac{1}{2}t$

Equation of normal to the parabola at $\left(\frac{t^2}{4}, \frac{t}{2}\right)$ is given by $tx + y = \frac{t}{2} + \frac{t^3}{4}$

This normal passes through $(a, 0)$

$\Rightarrow at = \frac{t}{2} + \frac{t^3}{4}$

$\Rightarrow \frac{t}{2} - at + \frac{t^3}{4} = 0$

$\Rightarrow \frac{t^3}{4} + t\left(\frac{1}{2} - a\right) = 0$

$\Rightarrow t\left[\frac{t^2}{4} + \left(\frac{1}{2} - a\right)\right] = 0$

If t_1, t_2, t_3 one roots of above equation, then t_1, t_2, t_3 be the parameters of the feet of the normals drawn from $(a, 0)$. Since, the equation has three roots.

$\Rightarrow a > \frac{1}{2}$

3. (a) **Concept Involved**

(1) **Point Circle** A circle having radius equal to zero is called point circle. Equation of any point circle having centre at (h, k) is $(x-h)^2 + (y-k)^2 = 0$

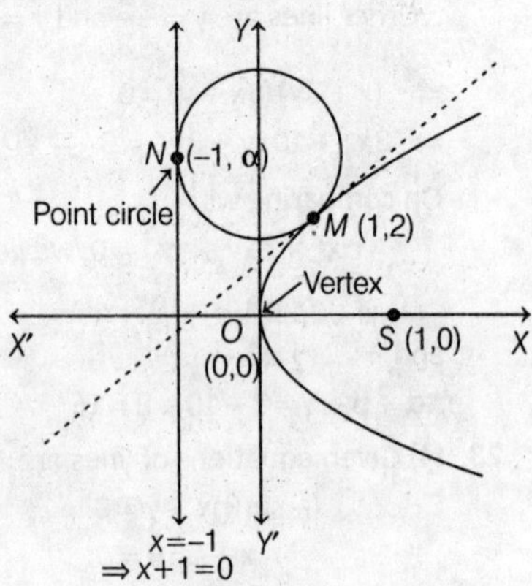

(2) Equation of any circle which is passing through the contact point of circle $S = 0$ and line $L = 0$ is $S + \lambda L = 0$, where λ is a parameter.

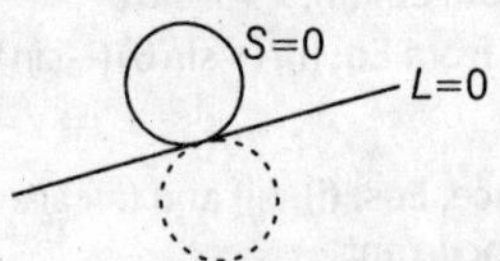

Special Case If given circle $S = 0$ becomes a point circles then required equation remains unchanged i.e. $S + \lambda L = 0$ but figure looks like this

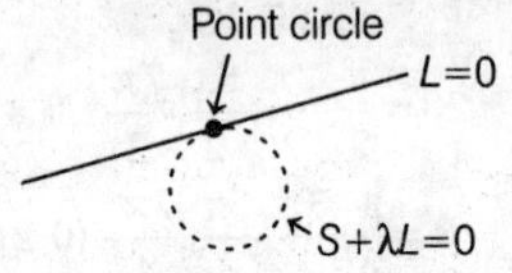

Start

Slope of tangent at $M(1, 2)$ to

$y^2 = 4x$ is $M_T = 1$ ...(i)

Let y-coordinate of the point of contact of the circle and the directrix $= \alpha$, where $\alpha > 0$

Let $N \equiv (-1, \alpha)$

Now, equation of point circle with centred at $(-1, \alpha)$ is

$$(x+1)^2 + (y-\alpha)^2 = 0 \quad ...(ii)$$

Equation of directrix is $x + 1 = 0$ ...(iii)

Hence, equation of any circle passing through Eqs. (ii) and (iii) is

$$S+\lambda L=0$$

$$\Rightarrow (x+1)^2+(y-\alpha)^2+\lambda(x+1)=0 \quad \text{...(iv)}$$

Differentiating Eqs. (iv) w.r.t. x, we get

$$2(x+1)+2(y-\alpha)\frac{dy}{dx}+\lambda=0$$

At $M(1, 2)$

$$2(1+1)+2(2-\alpha)\left(\frac{dy}{dx}\right)_{(1,2)}+\lambda=0$$

$$\Rightarrow 4+(4-2\alpha)m_T+\lambda=0$$

$$\Rightarrow \quad 4+4-2\alpha+\lambda=0$$

$$\Rightarrow \quad \lambda=2\alpha-8 \quad \text{...(v)}$$

Also, $M(1, 2)$ lies on Eq. (iv)

So, $2^2+(2-\alpha)^2+2\lambda=0$

$$\Rightarrow \alpha^2-4\alpha+8+2(2\alpha-8)=0 \quad \text{[from Eq. (v)]}$$

$$\Rightarrow \alpha^2=8 \Rightarrow \alpha=\pm 2\sqrt{2} \text{ but } \alpha>0$$

$$\therefore \quad \alpha=2\sqrt{2}$$

4. (d)

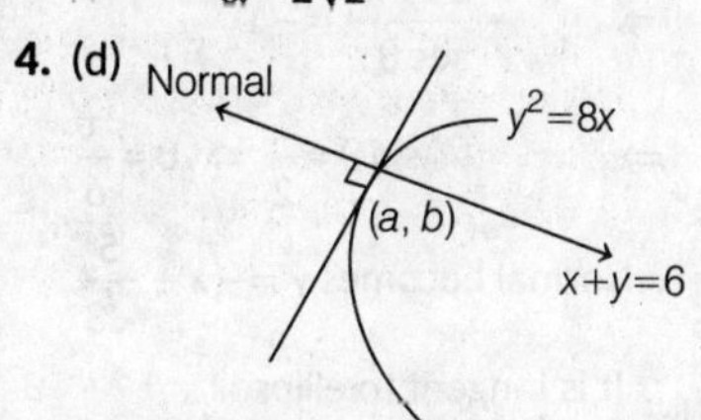

Given, equation of normal is $x+y=6$ ...(i)

and equation of parabola is $y^2=8x$ ...(ii)

since, (a, b) lies on both (i) and (ii), then

$$a+b=6 \quad \text{...(iii)}$$

and $b^2=8a \Rightarrow b^2-8a=0$ ...(iv)

Solving Eqs. (iii) and (iv), we have

$$b^2-8(6-b)=0 \Rightarrow b^2+8b-48=0$$

$$\Rightarrow (b+12)(b-4)=0$$

$$\Rightarrow b=-12 \text{ and } b=4$$

As $b<0$, $b=-12$ (accepted only)

Hence, $|b|-7=|-12|-7=12-7=5$

5. (c) Suppose coordinates of C and D are (x_1, x_1^2) and (x_2, x_2^2) respectively.

Let equation of CD be $y=2x+b$ ($\because$ CD is parallel to AB).

Thus, x_1, x_2 are roots of $x^2=2x+b$

So, sum of roots $(x_1+x_2)=2$ and product of roots $(x_1 \cdot x_2)=-b$

It side of square is S then

$$S^2=(x_2-x_1)^2+(x_2^2-x_1^2)^2$$

$$=(x_2-x_1)^2[1+(x_2+x_1)^2]$$

$$\Rightarrow S^2=[(x_2+x_1)^2-4x_1x_2][1+(2)^2]$$

$$=[(2)^2-4(-b)]\cdot S=5\times 4(1+b)$$

$$=20(1+b)$$

Also, $S^2=CB^2=$ (distance between AB and CD)$^2=\dfrac{|b+17|^2}{5}$

$$\Rightarrow \quad 20(1+b)=\frac{1}{5}(b+17)^2$$

$$(\because |x|^2=(x)^2=|x^2|)$$

$$\Rightarrow 100(1+b)=b^2+34b+289$$

$$\Rightarrow b^2-66b+189=0 \Rightarrow b=3, 63$$

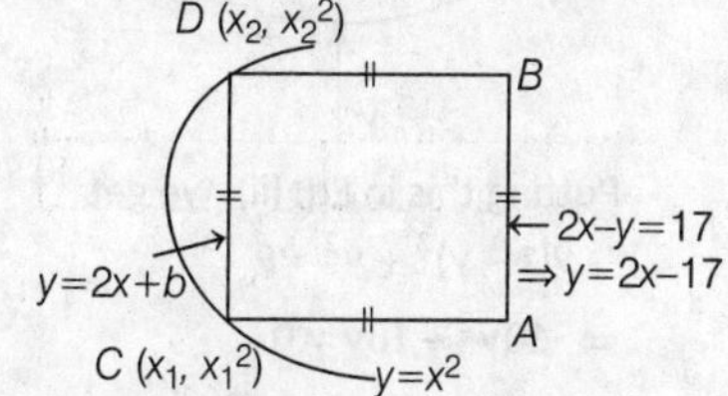

Hence, area

$$(A)=S^2=20(1+4\times 3)=260$$

$$\therefore \frac{1}{65}A=\frac{1}{65}\times 260=4$$

6. (c) Coordinates of S are $(2, 0)$.

Now, we have to find points of intersection of $y^2=8x$ and $x^2+y^2-2x-4y=0$

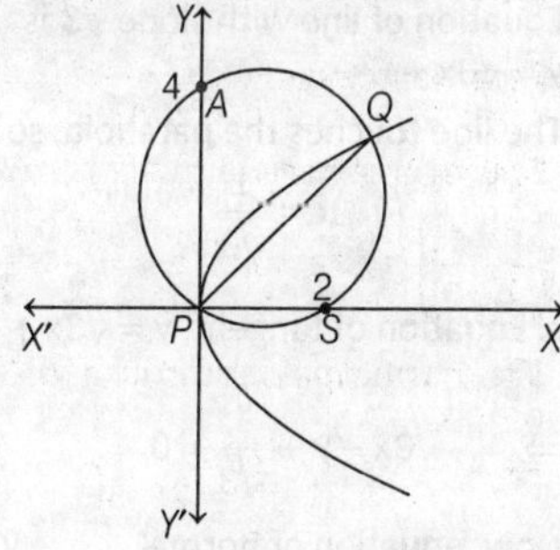

The y coordinates of the point of intersections are given by

$$\frac{y^4}{64}+y^2-\frac{y^2}{4}-4y=0$$

$$\Rightarrow \quad y^4+48y^2-256y=0$$

$$\Rightarrow \quad y(y^3+48y-256)=0$$

$$\Rightarrow y(y-4)(y^2+4y+64)=0$$

$$\Rightarrow \quad y=0, 4$$

Coordinates of P are $(0, 0)$ and that of Q are $(2, 4)$.

$\therefore$ Area of

$$\Delta PQS=\frac{1}{2}\left\|\begin{matrix}0 & 0 & 1\\ 2 & 4 & 1\\ 2 & 0 & 1\end{matrix}\right\|=\frac{1}{2}|1(0-8)|=4$$

7. (b) Given, equation of ellipses

$$E_1: \frac{x^2}{3}+\frac{y^2}{2}=1 \quad \text{...(i)}$$

$$\therefore \quad E_2: \frac{x^2}{16}+\frac{y^2}{b^2}=1 \quad \text{...(ii)}$$

Let e_1 and e_2 be the eccentricities of (i) and (ii) respectively.

$$\therefore \quad e_1=\sqrt{1-\frac{2}{3}}=\frac{1}{\sqrt{3}} \quad \text{...(iii)}$$

Given, product of eccentricities $=\dfrac{1}{2}$

$$\Rightarrow e_1e_2=\frac{1}{2} \Rightarrow e_2=\frac{\sqrt{3}}{2} \quad \text{[from Eq. (iii)]}$$

Now, $e_2=\sqrt{1-\dfrac{b^2}{16}}$ [from Eq. (ii)]

Hence, $\sqrt{1-\dfrac{b^2}{16}}=\dfrac{\sqrt{3}}{2} \Rightarrow 1-\dfrac{b^2}{16}=\dfrac{3}{4}$

$$\Rightarrow \quad b^2=4 \Rightarrow |b|=2$$

$\therefore$ Length of minor axis of $E_2=2|b|=4$

8. (b) Length

$$=\frac{2ab}{a^2m^2+b^2}\sqrt{(1+m^2)(a^2m^2+b^2+c^2)}$$

where, $m=1$ and $c^2=(ae)^2$

$$\Rightarrow \text{Length}=\frac{2\left(\dfrac{2b^2}{a}\right)}{1+\dfrac{b^2}{a^2}}=\frac{2\left(\dfrac{2b^2}{a}\right)}{1+1-e^2} \quad \text{...(i)}$$

$\because$ Latusrectum $=6$ [given]

and $e=\dfrac{1}{2}$

From Eq. (i),

$$\text{Length}=\frac{2\times 6}{2-\left(\dfrac{1}{2}\right)^2}=\frac{12}{2-\dfrac{1}{4}}=\frac{12}{1}\times\frac{4}{7}$$

$$=\frac{48}{7}>6$$

9. (a) Let equation of ellipse

$$\frac{x^2}{a^2}+\frac{y^2}{b^2}=1 \quad \text{...(i)}$$

Let $P(a\cos\theta, b\sin\theta)$ be any point on Eq. (i)

Rotating ellipse (i) anticlockwise by $\dfrac{\pi}{2}$, every point becomes $Q(-b\sin\theta, a\cos\theta)$ and equation becomes

$$\frac{x^2}{b^2}+\frac{y^2}{a^2}=1 \quad \text{...(ii)}$$

Equation of tangent at P is

$$\frac{x}{a}\cos\theta+\frac{y}{b}\sin\theta=1 \quad \text{...(iii)}$$

Equation of tangent at Q is

$$-\frac{x}{b}\sin\theta+\frac{y}{a}\cos\theta=1 \quad \text{...(iv)}$$

Let point of intersection of Eqs. (iii) and (iv) be (α, β). Then, solving Eqs. (iii) and (iv), we have

$$\alpha=\frac{\frac{\cos\theta}{a}-\frac{\sin\theta}{b}}{\frac{\cos^2\theta}{a^2}+\frac{\sin^2\theta}{b^2}}$$

and $\beta=\dfrac{\frac{\cos\theta}{a}+\frac{\sin\theta}{b}}{\frac{\cos^2\theta}{a^2}+\frac{\sin^2\theta}{b^2}}$

Squaring and adding α and β, we get

$$\alpha^2+\beta^2=\frac{1}{\frac{\cos^2\theta}{a^2}+\frac{\sin^2\theta}{b^2}}$$

$$\therefore \frac{\alpha}{\alpha^2+\beta^2}=\frac{\cos\theta}{a}-\frac{\sin\theta}{b}$$

and $\dfrac{\beta}{\alpha^2+\beta^2}=\dfrac{\cos\theta}{a}+\dfrac{\sin\theta}{b}$

Eliminating θ, we get

$$(\alpha^2+\beta^2)(\alpha^2+\beta^2-a^2-b^2)=2(a^2-b^2)\alpha\beta$$

Locus of (α, β)

$$(x^2+y^2)(x^2+y^2-a^2-b^2)=2(a^2-b^2)xy$$

10. (a) **Explanation**

X-axis will be major axis if

$f(k^2+2k+5)>f(k+11)$

$\Rightarrow k^2+2k+5<k+11$

($\because f$ is decreasing function)

$\Rightarrow \quad k^2+k-6<0$

$\Rightarrow \quad (k+3)(k-2)<0$

$\Rightarrow (k-(-3))(k-2)<0$

$\Rightarrow \quad -3<k<2$

$\Rightarrow \quad k\in(-3,2)$

Y-axis will be major axis if

$f(k^2+2k+5)<f(k+11)$

$\Rightarrow k^2+2k+5>k+11$

($\because f$ is decreasing function. So, inequality gets reversed)

$\Rightarrow \quad k^2+k-6>0$

$\Rightarrow (k-(-3))(k-2)>0$

$\Rightarrow k\in(-\infty,-3)\cup(2,\infty)$

11. (d) Equation of given ellipse is

$$\frac{x^2}{9}+\frac{y^2}{1}=1 \quad \text{...(i)}$$

Equation of auxiliary circle is

$$x^2+y^2=9 \quad \text{...(ii)}$$

Equation of line AB is

$$\frac{x}{3}+\frac{y}{1}=1 \Rightarrow x=3(1-y)$$

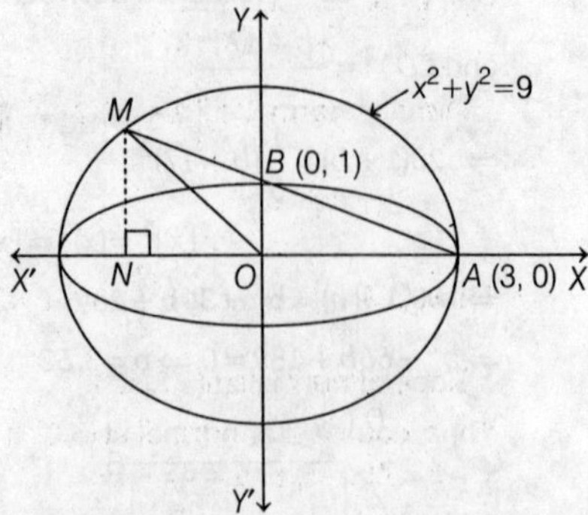

Putting this in Eq. (ii), we get

$9(1-y)^2+y^2=9$

$\Rightarrow 10y^2-18y=0$

$\Rightarrow \quad y=0, \frac{9}{5}$

Thus, y-coordinate of M is $\frac{9}{5}$.

$\therefore$ Area of $\Delta OAM=\left(\frac{1}{2}\right)$

$$(OA)(MN)=\frac{1}{2}(3)\left(\frac{9}{5}\right)=\frac{27}{10}$$

12. (d) Slope of the normal $=\tan 60^\circ=\sqrt{3}$

Equation of line with slope $\sqrt{3}$ is

$y=\sqrt{3}x+C$

The line touches the parabola, so

$$c=\frac{1}{\sqrt{3}}$$

$\therefore$ Equation of tangent, $y=\sqrt{3}x+\frac{1}{\sqrt{3}}$

$\Rightarrow \quad \sqrt{3}x-y+\frac{1}{\sqrt{3}}=0$

Now, equation of normal

$y=\sqrt{3}x-2\sqrt{3}-3\sqrt{3}$

$\Rightarrow \quad \sqrt{3}x-y-5\sqrt{3}=0$

Distance between tangent and

$$\text{normal}=\left|\frac{\frac{1}{\sqrt{3}}+5\sqrt{3}}{\sqrt{3+1}}\right|=\frac{16}{4\sqrt{3}}=\frac{4}{\sqrt{3}}$$

13. (d) Equation of tangent to $y^2=4x$ is

$$y=mx+\frac{1}{m} \quad \text{...(i)}$$

and equation of tangent to $\frac{x^2}{4}+\frac{y^2}{3}=1$ will be

$$y=mx\pm\sqrt{4m^2+3} \quad \text{...(ii)}$$

Now, Eqs. (i) and (ii) represent the same line for common tangents.

$\therefore \quad \frac{1}{m}=\sqrt{(4m^2+3)}$

$\Rightarrow \quad 1=4m^4+3m^2$

$4m^4+3m^2-1=0$

$\Rightarrow (4m^2-1)(m^2+1)=0 \Rightarrow m^2=\frac{1}{4}$

$(\because m^2+1\neq 0)$

$\therefore \quad m=\pm\frac{1}{2}$

$\therefore$ Equation of common tangent will be

$y=\frac{1}{2}x+2$ or $y=-\frac{1}{2}x-2$

i.e. $x-2y+4=0$ or $x+2y+4=0$

14. (c) Equation of normal at $(2\sec\theta, \tan\theta)$ is $\frac{2x}{\sec\theta}+\frac{y}{\tan\theta}=5$

$\because \quad$ Slope $=-1$ [given]

$\Rightarrow \quad \frac{-2\tan\theta}{\sec\theta}=-1$

$\Rightarrow \quad \sin\theta=\frac{1}{2} \Rightarrow \theta=\frac{\pi}{6}$

$\therefore$ Normal becomes $y=-x+\frac{5}{\sqrt{3}}$

$\because$ It is tangent to ellipse.

$\therefore a^2+b^2=\frac{25}{3}\Rightarrow\frac{9}{25}(a^2+b^2)=3$

15. (c) Equation of tangent at (h, k) is

$$\frac{hx}{a^2}-\frac{ky}{b^2}=1 \quad \text{...(i)}$$

Equation of auxiliary circle is

$$x^2+y^2=a^2 \quad \text{...(ii)}$$

From Eq. (i), $x=\frac{a^2}{h}\left(1+\frac{ky}{b^2}\right)$

Putting in Eq. (ii), we get

$$\frac{a^4}{h^2}\left(1+\frac{ky}{b^2}\right)^2+y^2=a^2$$

$$\Rightarrow \frac{a^4}{h^2}\left(\frac{b^4+2b^2ky+k^2y^2}{b^4}\right)+y^2=a^2$$

$$\Rightarrow a^4b^4+2b^2a^4ky+a^4k^2y^2+b^4h^2y^2-h^2b^4a^2=0$$

$$\Rightarrow (a^4k^2+b^4h^2)y^2+2b^2a^4ky+a^4b^4-h^2b^4a^2=0$$

which is quadratic in y. Let y_1 and y_2 be the roots of the equation, then

$$y_1+y_2=\frac{-2b^2a^4k}{a^4k^2+b^4h^2}$$

and $y_1y_2=\dfrac{a^4b^4-h^2b^4a^2}{a^4k^2+b^4h^2}$

$\therefore \frac{1}{y_1}+\frac{1}{y_2}=\frac{y_1+y_2}{y_1y_2}=\frac{-2b^2a^4k}{a^4b^4-h^2b^4a^2}$

$=\frac{-2b^2a^4k}{a^2b^4(a^2-h^2)}$

$=\frac{-2a^2k}{b^2(a^2-h^2)}$

$=\frac{-2k}{(a^2-h^2)}\times\frac{a^2}{b^2}$

[$\because (h,k)$ on the hyperbola;

$\therefore \frac{h^2}{a^2}-\frac{k^2}{b^2}=1 \Rightarrow \frac{a^2}{b^2}=\frac{h^2-a^2}{k^2}$]

$=\frac{-2k}{(a^2-h^2)}\cdot\frac{(h^2-a^2)}{k^2}=\frac{-2k}{-k^2}=\frac{2}{k}$

$\therefore k$ is harmonic between B_1 and B_2.

16. (b) Equation of hyperbola will be

$$\frac{(\text{Perpendicular distance of } P(x,y) \text{ from CA})^2}{(\text{Semi TA})^2} - \frac{(\text{Perpendicular distance of } P(x,y) \text{ from TA})^2}{(\text{Semi CA})^2}$$

where, TA = Transverse Axis

CA = Conjugate Axis

$$\Rightarrow \frac{\left(\frac{2x-y+4}{\sqrt{5}}\right)^2}{\left(\frac{1}{\sqrt{2}}\right)^2}-\frac{\left(\frac{x+2y-3}{\sqrt{5}}\right)^2}{\left(\frac{1}{\sqrt{3}}\right)^2}=1$$

$$\Rightarrow \frac{2}{5}(2x-y+4)^2-\frac{3}{5}(x+2y-3)^2=1$$

17. (a) We can write C as $(2x-5)(2y-1)=-9$

As x, y are integers, we get

If $2x-5=-1$, then $2y-1=9$

$\Rightarrow x=2$ and $y=5 \therefore (x,y)=(2,5)$

If $2x-5=-3$ then $2y-1=3$

$\Rightarrow x=1$ and $y=2 \therefore (x,y)=(1,2)$

If $2x-5=-9$ then $2y-1=1$

$\Rightarrow x=-2$ and $y=1; \therefore (x,y)=(-2,1)$

If $2x-5=1$ then $2y-1=-9$

$\Rightarrow x=3$ and $y=5; \therefore (x,y)=(3,5)$

If $2x-5=3$ then $2y-1=-3$

$\Rightarrow x=4$ and $y=3 \therefore (x,y)=(4,3)$

If $2x-5=9$ then $2y-1=-1$

$\Rightarrow x=7$ and $y=0 \therefore (x,y)=(7,0)$

Thus, there are total 6 lattice points on the hyperbola C.

18. (d) We can write $xy-y-2x-2=0$ as $(x-1)(y-2)=4$

$\Rightarrow \quad y=2+\frac{4}{x-1}$

Any point on this hyperbola is $(1+2t, 2+2/t)$

We have, $\frac{dy}{dx}=-\frac{4}{(x-1)^2}$

$\therefore$ Slope of normal at $\left(1+2t, 2+\frac{2}{t}\right)$ is

$\frac{1}{4}(1+2t-1)^2=t^2$

Now, $(5,3)=\left(1+2t, 2+\frac{2}{t}\right) \Rightarrow t=2$

$\therefore$ Slope of normal at $(5,3)$ is 4.

Thus, equation of normal at $(5,3)$ is $y-3=4(x-5)$ or $y=4x-17$

The point $\left(1+2t, 2+\frac{2}{t}\right)$ will lie on

$y=4x-17$ if $2+\frac{2}{t}=4(1+2t)-17$

$\Rightarrow 8t^2-15t-2=0 \Rightarrow (8t+1)(t-2)=0$

$\Rightarrow \quad t=2, -\frac{1}{8}$

For $t=2$, we get $(5,3)$ and for $t=-\frac{1}{8}$, we get $\left(\frac{3}{4}, -14\right)$

19. (c) **Concept** A straight line $y=mx+c$ will be tangent to the parabola $y^2=4ax$ if $c=\frac{a}{m}$ and also the line $y=mx+c$ will be tangent to hyperbola $\frac{x^2}{a^2}-\frac{y^2}{b^2}=1$ if $c^2=a^2m^2-b^2$.

Start Given equation of parabola is

$$y^2=8x \quad \text{...(i)}$$

and equation of hyperbola is

$$\frac{x^2}{1}-\frac{y^2}{3}=1 \quad \text{...(ii)}$$

So, equation of tangent to (i) will be

$$y=mx+\frac{2}{m} \quad \text{...(iii)}$$

(where m is the slope of tangent line)

Now, Eq. (iii) will be tangent to (ii) if

$\frac{4}{m^2}=1\times m^2-3 \Rightarrow m^4-3m^2-4=0$

$\Rightarrow (m^2-4)(m^2+1)=0$

But $\quad m^2+1 \neq 0$

$\therefore \quad m^2=4$

$\Rightarrow \quad m \pm 2$

So, equation of required tangent is $2x+1=y$ or $2x+1=-y$

i.e. $2x \pm y+1=0$

20. (b) Let equation of the hyperbola be

$$\frac{x^2}{a^2}-\frac{y^2}{b^2}=1 \quad \text{...(i)}$$

Suppose its eccentricity is e.

Eccentricity (e_1) of ellipse $\frac{x^2}{25}+\frac{y^2}{16}=1$ is given by

$16=25(1-e_1^2)$

$\Rightarrow \quad e_1=\frac{3}{5} \quad (\because e_1>0)$

Foci of the ellipse are $(\pm 3, 0)$.

Since, Eq. (i) passes through $(\pm 3, 0)$

So, $\frac{9}{a^2}=1$

$\Rightarrow a^2=9$

Also, $ee_1=1 \Rightarrow e=\frac{5}{3}$

Foci of hyperbola are $(\pm 5, 0)$

[$\because$ foci $=(\pm ae, 0)$]

Hence, $|k|=|\pm 5|=5$

21. (12) Parametric equation of given parabola $x=4t^2, y=8t$

Equation of normal at $(4t^2, 8t)$ is

$$tx+y=8t+4t^3 \quad \text{...(i)}$$

But $y=mx+c$ ...(ii) is normal, then

$\frac{m}{t}=\frac{-1}{1}=\frac{c}{-8t-4t^3}$

$\Rightarrow \quad m=-t$, and $8t+4t^3=c$

$\Rightarrow \quad -8m-4m^3=c$

$\Rightarrow \quad c+8m+4m^3=0$

Here, $d=8, e=4$

$\therefore \quad d+e=12$

22. (6) Equation of normal on $y^2=4x$ will be $y=mx-2m-m^3$.

$\because (9,-6)$ lies on it.

$\therefore \quad -6=9m-2m-m^3$

$\Rightarrow \quad m^3-7m-6=0$

$\Rightarrow (m+1)(m^2-m-6)=0$

$\Rightarrow (m+1)(m-3)(m+2)=0$

$\Rightarrow \quad m=-1,-2,3$

$\therefore \quad A=\begin{bmatrix}0&1&1\\1&0&1\\1&1&6\end{bmatrix}$

[$\because a_{11}=m_i+i$ (given)

$\therefore a_{11}=m_1+1=-1+1=0$

$a_{22}=m_2+2=-2+2=0$

$a_{33}=m_3+3=3+3=6$

and non-diagonal elements are one.

$\therefore$ Trace of $A=tr(A)=0+0+6=6$

23. (2) From figure, $\Delta_1 =$ Area of ΔPAB

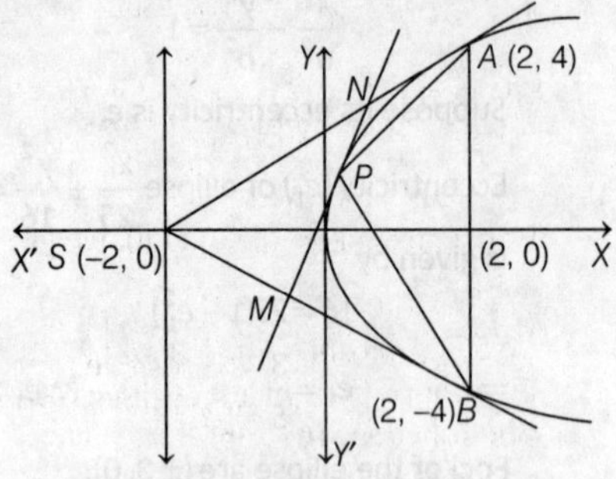

$\Rightarrow \Delta_1 = \frac{1}{2} \times \text{base} \times \text{height}$

$= \frac{1}{2} \times 8 \times \left(2 - \frac{1}{2}\right)$

$\Rightarrow \Delta_1 = 6 \text{ unit}^2$

Equation of tangents at A, B and P are respectively

$y = x + 2,\ y = -x - 2$ and $y = 2x + 1$

These tangents intersect at points $S(-2, 0), N(1, 3)$ and $M(-1, -1)$

$\Delta_2 =$ area of $\Delta SNM = \frac{1}{2}$

$$\left\|\begin{matrix} -2 & 0 & 1 \\ 1 & 3 & 1 \\ -1 & -1 & 1 \end{matrix}\right\| = \frac{1}{2} |-2(3+1) + 1(-1+3)|$$

$= \frac{1}{2} |-8 + 2| = 3 \text{ unit}^2$

Hence, $\frac{\Delta_1}{\Delta_2} = 2$

24. (1) Given, $\frac{dy}{dx} + \frac{1}{x - y^2 + 4} = 0$

$\Rightarrow \frac{dy}{dx} = \frac{1}{y^2 - x - 4}$

$\Rightarrow \frac{dx}{dy} + x = y^2 - 4$ which is linear differential equation

$\text{IF} = e^{\int 1 \cdot dy} = e^y$

General solution is given by

$x \cdot e^y = \int e^y (y^2 - 4) dy + C$

$\Rightarrow x \cdot e^y = e^y (y^2 - 4) - e^y (2y) + e^y \cdot 2 + C$

$\Rightarrow \quad x = (y^2 - 4 - 2y + 2) + c \cdot e^{-y}$

$\Rightarrow \quad x = (y - 1)^2 - 3 + c \cdot e^{-y}$ ...(i)

Since, it passes through $(1, -1)$, then

$1 = 4 - 3 + c \cdot e'$

$\Rightarrow \quad ce = 0$

$\Rightarrow \quad c = 0$

Hence, Eq. (i) will be $(y - 1)^2 = (x + 3)$ which is the equation of shifted parabola with latusrectum $= 4a = 1$

25. (10) Equation of normal is

$4ax + 3by = 24$ (given) ...(i)

and equation of normal to $\frac{x^2}{a^2} + \frac{y^2}{b^2} = 1$ is given by

$\frac{ax}{\cos\theta} - \frac{by}{\sin\theta} = a^2 - b^2$ ...(ii)

Since, Eqs. (i) and (ii) represents same line.

So, $\frac{\frac{a}{\cos\theta}}{4a} = \frac{-\frac{b}{\sin\theta}}{3b} = \frac{a^2 - b^2}{24}$

$\Rightarrow \frac{a}{4a \cos\theta} = \frac{-b}{3b \sin\theta} = \frac{a^2 - b^2}{24}$

I II III

From Eqs. (i) and (ii),

$\tan\theta = -\frac{4}{3} \left(\therefore \sin\theta = -\frac{4}{5}\right)$

From Eqs. (i) and (iii),

$a^2 - b^2 = \frac{-24}{3 \sin\theta}$

$\Rightarrow a^2 - b^2 = \frac{-8}{\left(-\frac{4}{5}\right)}$

$= \frac{8}{1} \times \frac{5}{4} = 10$

26. (7) $3(x - 2)^2 + 4(y + 2)^2 = 28 - k$ ...(i)

Centre of the ellipse is $C(2, -2)$.

Let coordinates of A be

$(2 + r_1 \cos\theta, -2 + r_1 \sin\theta)$

where, $r_1 = CA$

and coordinates of B be

$\left[2 + r_2 \cos\left(\theta + \frac{\pi}{2}\right), -2 + r_2 \sin\left(\theta + \frac{\pi}{2}\right)\right]$

where, $r_2 = CB$

Since, A, B lies on Eq. (i).

$\therefore r_1^2 (3 \cos^2\theta + 4 \sin^2\theta) = 28 - k$ and r_2^2

$(3 \sin^2\theta + 4 \cos^2\theta) = 28 - k$

$\Rightarrow \quad (28 - k)(r_1^{-2} + r_2^{-2}) = 7$

27. (1) Sides of rectangle R are $x = \pm 3$, $y = \pm 2$

Y
(0, 4)
E_2
E_1
X' O X
Y'

Coordinates of vertices of R are $(3, 2)$, $(-3, 2), (-3, -2)$ and $(3, -2)$.

Let equation of E_1 be $\frac{x^2}{a^2} + \frac{y^2}{b^2} = 1$

Since, it passes through $(0, 4)$ and $(3, 2)$, we get

$\frac{4^2}{b^2} = 1$

$\Rightarrow \quad b^2 = 16$

and $\frac{9}{a^2} + \frac{4}{b^2} = 1$

$\Rightarrow \quad a^2 = 12$

Let e be of the eccentricity of the ellipse E_2, then $a^2 = b^2(1 - e^2)$

$\Rightarrow \quad 12 = 16(1 - e^2)$

$\Rightarrow \quad e = \frac{1}{2}$

$\therefore \quad 2e = 2 \times \frac{1}{2} = 1$

28. (3) Given, $e(\lambda)$ be the eccentricity of the hyperbola

$\frac{x^2}{a^2 + \lambda} - \frac{y^2}{b^2 + \lambda} = 1$

So, $[e(\lambda)]^2 = 1 + \frac{b^2 + \lambda}{a^2 + \lambda}$

$= 2 + \frac{b^2 - a^2}{a^2 + \lambda}$ ...(i)

Differentiating Eq. (i) w.r.t. λ, we get

$2 \cdot e(a) \cdot \frac{de}{d\lambda} = -\frac{(b^2 - a^2)}{(a^2 + \lambda)^2}$

$= \frac{a^2 - b^2}{(a^2 + \lambda)^2} > 0$

$(\because a^2 > b^2$ given)

$\therefore e(\lambda)$ is an increasing function on $[1, \infty)$ $(\because \lambda \geq 1$ given)

Hence, least value of $e(\lambda)$ is obtained when $\lambda = 1 (= \lambda_0)$.

Thus, $3\lambda_0 = 3 \times 1 = 3$

29. (1) Given equation can be written as

$\frac{x^2}{9} - \frac{y^2}{4} = 1$ ...(i)

and $x^2 + y^2 = 9$ ...(ii)

Let $P(3 \sec\theta, 2 \tan\theta)$

From P, tangents PA and PB are drawn to circle $x^2 + y^2 = 9$

$\therefore$ Equation of chord of contact AB w.r.t. P is $T = 0$.

$\Rightarrow \quad 3x \sec\theta + 2y \tan\theta = 9$ ...(iii)

Let mid-point of AB is $M(h, k)$.

$\therefore$ Equation of chord w.r.t. M is $T = S_1$

$\Rightarrow hx + ky - 9 = h^2 + k^2 - 9$ ...(iv)

Eqs. (iii) and (iv) represents same line, then

$$\frac{3\sec\theta}{h}=\frac{2\tan\theta}{k}=\frac{9}{h^2+k^2}$$

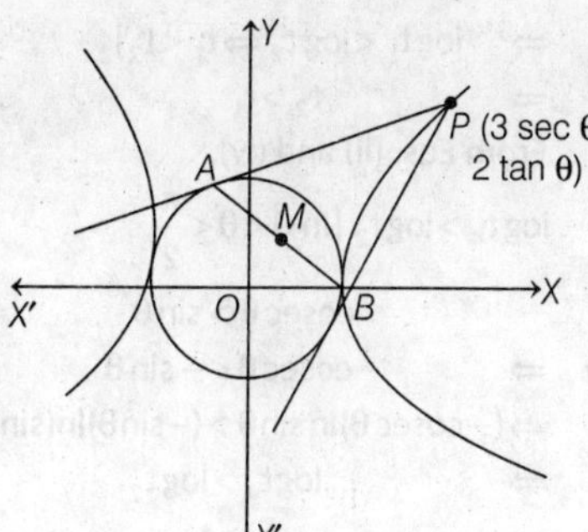

$$\Rightarrow \quad \sec\theta=\frac{h}{3}\left(\frac{9}{h^2+k^2}\right)$$

and $\quad \tan\theta=\frac{k}{2}\left(\frac{9}{h^2+k^2}\right)$

$\because \sec^2\theta-\tan^2\theta=1$

$$\Rightarrow \left(\frac{h^2}{9}-\frac{k^2}{4}\right)=\left(\frac{h^2+k^2}{9}\right)^2$$

On comparing with $\left(\frac{x^2}{9}-\frac{y^2}{4}\right)$

$=\lambda\left(\frac{x^2+y^2}{9}\right)^2$, we get $\lambda=1$

30. (5) A point on $\frac{(x-2)^2}{3}-\frac{(y-1)^2}{4}=-1$ will be $(2+\sqrt{3}\tan\alpha, 1+2\sec\alpha)$

Let its reflection in line $x+y-1=0$ be (h,k)

$$\therefore \frac{h-(2+\sqrt{3}\tan\alpha)}{1}=\frac{k-(1+2\sec\alpha)}{1}$$

$$=\frac{-2(2+\sqrt{3}\tan\alpha+1+2\sec\alpha-1)}{2}$$

$\therefore h=-2\sec\alpha$ and $k=-1-\sqrt{3}\tan\alpha$

$$\Rightarrow \frac{h^2}{4}-\frac{(k+1)^2}{3}=1$$

Locus (i.e. image) will be

$\frac{x^2}{4}-\frac{(y+1)^2}{3}=1$ which is conic C.

Its eccentricity $(e)=\sqrt{1+\frac{3}{4}}=\frac{\sqrt{7}}{2}$

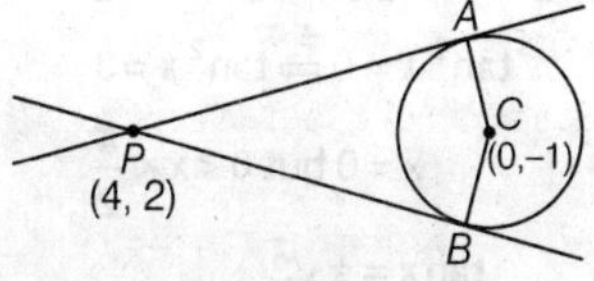

Locus of point of intersection of perpendicular tangents will be director circles.

i.e $x^2+(y+1)^2=4-3$

$(x^2+y^2=a^2-b^2)$

$\Rightarrow x^2+(y+1)^2=1$

Clearly, circumcircle of ΔPAB will be circle with diameter PC.

$=$ Diameter $=PC=5$

Qualifier 13 (Trigonometry)

1. (c) From figure,

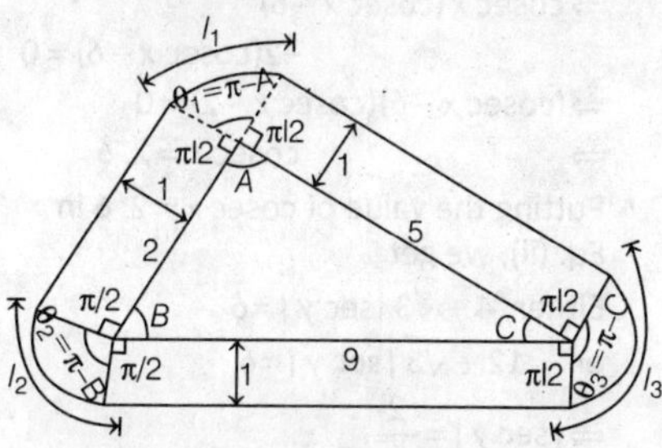

$$\theta_1+A+\frac{\pi}{2}+\frac{\pi}{2}=2\pi$$

$\Rightarrow \theta_1=2\pi-\pi-A=\pi-A$

Similarly, $\theta_2=\pi-B$ and $\theta_3=\pi-c$

i.e. at corners, the man covers three areas, each of central angles

$\theta_1=\pi-A, \theta_2=\pi-B, \theta_3=\pi-c$

As we know that, $\theta-\frac{l}{r}$

But $r=1$ (given)

$\therefore \quad l=\theta$

So, $\quad l_1=\theta_1=\pi-A$

$\quad l_2=\theta_2=\pi-B$

and $\quad l_3=\theta_3=\pi-C$

$\therefore l_1+l_2+l_3=\theta_1+\theta_2+\theta_3$

$=3\pi-(A+B+C)$

$=3\pi-\pi=2\pi$

and total distance covered by the man along three sides $=2+5+9=16$

Hence, required distance (i.e. total distance covered by the man)

$=16+(l_1+l_2+l_3)$

$=16+2\pi=2(8+\pi)$

2. (b) Given, $\sin\frac{\pi}{2^n}+\cos\frac{\pi}{2^n}=\frac{\sqrt{n}}{2}$ ...(i)

$$\sin\left(\frac{\pi}{2^n}\right)+\cos\left(\frac{\pi}{2^n}\right)=\sqrt{2}\sin\left(\frac{\pi}{4}+\frac{\pi}{2^n}\right)$$

which lies in $[-\sqrt{2},\sqrt{2}]$

$\therefore \frac{\sqrt{n}}{2}\in[-\sqrt{2},\sqrt{2}]\Rightarrow\frac{\sqrt{n}}{2}\le\sqrt{2}$

$\Rightarrow \quad \sqrt{n}\le 2\sqrt{2}\Rightarrow n\le 8$ ...(ii)

We observe that, $n=1$ does not satisfy the given equation and for $n>1$, we have

$$\frac{\pi}{2}\ge\frac{\pi}{4}+\frac{\pi}{2^n}>\frac{\pi}{4}\Rightarrow\sin\left(\frac{\pi}{4}+\frac{\pi}{2^n}\right)>\sin\frac{\pi}{4}$$

$$\Rightarrow\sqrt{2}\sin\left(\frac{\pi}{4}+\frac{\pi}{2^n}\right)>1\Rightarrow\frac{\sqrt{n}}{2}>1$$

$\Rightarrow \quad n>4$ ...(iii)

Hence, from Eqs. (ii) and (iii), we get $4<n\le 8$

3. (a) Since, all angles lie in I and II quadrants, they all are positive for sine function. To simplify the given expression, we use

$$\sin\frac{7\pi}{14}=\sin\left(\frac{\pi}{2}\right)=1$$

$$\sin\frac{11\pi}{14}=\sin\frac{3\pi}{14}\Rightarrow\sin\frac{13\pi}{14}$$

$$\sin\left(\pi-\frac{\pi}{14}\right)=\sin\frac{\pi}{14}$$

$$\sin\frac{9\pi}{14}=\sin\frac{5\pi}{14}$$

Now, given expression can be written as $\sin^2\frac{\pi}{14}\sin^2\frac{3\pi}{14}\sin^2\frac{5\pi}{14}$

$$\because \cos\left(\frac{\pi}{2}-\frac{\pi}{14}\right)=\cos\left(\frac{6\pi}{14}\right)=-\cos\left(\frac{8\pi}{14}\right)$$

Similarly, we can write $\cos\left(\frac{\pi}{2}-\frac{3\pi}{14}\right)$

$=\cos\left(\frac{4\pi}{14}\right)$ and $\cos\left(\frac{\pi}{2}-\frac{5\pi}{14}\right)$

$=\cos\left(\frac{2\pi}{14}\right)$

From Eq. (i),

$$\cos^2\left(\frac{8\pi}{14}\right)\cos^2\left(\frac{4\pi}{14}\right)\cos^2\left(\frac{2\pi}{14}\right)$$

$$=\left[\cos\left(\frac{\pi}{7}\right)\cos\left(\frac{2\pi}{7}\right)\cos\left(\frac{4\pi}{7}\right)\right]^2$$

Multiplying and dividing the above expression by $2^3\cdot\sin\left(\frac{\pi}{7}\right)$ we get

$$\left[\left\{\frac{1}{2^3\sin\left(\frac{\pi}{7}\right)}\right\}\cdot 2^3\sin\left(\frac{\pi}{7}\right)\right]^2$$

$$\left[\cos\left(\frac{\pi}{7}\right)\cdot\cos\left(\frac{2\pi}{7}\right)\cdot\cos\left(\frac{4\pi}{7}\right)\right]^2$$

$$=\frac{1}{2^6}\left[\frac{\sin^2\frac{8\pi}{7}}{\sin^2\frac{\pi}{7}}\right]=\frac{1}{2^6}\left[\frac{\sin^2\left(\pi-\frac{8\pi}{7}\right)}{\sin^2\frac{\pi}{7}}\right]$$

$$=\frac{1}{2^6}\left[\frac{-\sin\frac{\pi}{7}}{\sin\frac{\pi}{7}}\right]^2=\frac{1}{2^6}=\frac{1}{64}$$

4. (c) Given, in equation is

$$\sin x \cdot \cos x + \frac{1}{2}(\tan x) \geq 1 \quad \ldots(i)$$

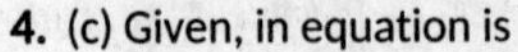

LHS of (i) is defined for all $x \in R$ except $x = n\pi + \frac{\pi}{2}, n \in I$

From Eq. (i), we get

$$2\sin x \cdot \cos x + \tan x \geq 2$$

$$\Rightarrow \sin 2x + \tan x \geq 2$$

$$\Rightarrow \frac{2\tan x}{1+\tan^2 x} + \tan x \geq 2$$

$$\Rightarrow \frac{2y}{1+y^2} + y \geq 2, \text{ where } y = \tan x$$

$$\Rightarrow \frac{2y + y(1+y^2) - 2(1+y^2)}{(1+y^2)} \geq 0$$

$$\Rightarrow 2y + y(1+y^2) - 2(1+y^2) \geq 0 \quad (\because 1+y^2 \geq 1)$$

$$\Rightarrow y^3 - 2y^2 + 3y - 2 \geq 0$$

$$\Rightarrow y^2(y-1) - y(y-1) + 2(y-1) \geq 0$$

$$\Rightarrow (y-1)(y^2 - y + 2) \geq 0$$

$$\Rightarrow y \geq 1 \left(\because y^2 - y + 2 = \left(y - \frac{1}{2}\right)^2 + \frac{7}{4} > 0, \forall y \in R\right)$$

$$\Rightarrow \tan x \geq 1$$

From figure it is clear that $\tan x \geq 1$

$$\Rightarrow x \in \left[\frac{\pi}{4}, \frac{\pi}{2}\right) \text{ in } \left(-\frac{\pi}{2}, \frac{\pi}{2}\right)$$

Hence, general solution is

$$x \in \left[n\pi + \frac{\pi}{4}, n\pi + \frac{\pi}{2}\right), \text{ where } n \in I$$

5. (c) Given, $5^{(\text{cosec}^2 x - 3\sec^2 y)} = 1 = 5^0$ and $2^{(2\,\text{cosec}\, x + \sqrt{3}|\sec y|)} = 64 = 2^6$

$$\Rightarrow \text{cosec}^2 x - 3\sec^2 y = 0 \quad \ldots(i)$$

$$\text{and } 2\,\text{cosec}\, x + \sqrt{3}\,|\sec y| = 6 \quad \ldots(ii)$$

$$\Rightarrow \sqrt{3}\,|\sec y| = 6 - 2\,\text{cosec}\, x$$

$$\Rightarrow 3(\sec y)^2 = (6 - 2\,\text{cosec}\, x)^2 \quad \ldots(iii)$$

Putting the value of $3\sec^2 y$ from Eq. (iii) in Eq. (i), we get

$$\text{cosec}^2 x - (6 - 2\,\text{cosec}\, x)^2 = 0$$

$$\Rightarrow \text{cosec}^2 x - 36 + 24\,\text{cosec}\, x - 4\,\text{cosec}^2 x = 0$$

$$\Rightarrow 3\,\text{cosec}^2 x - 24\,\text{cosec}\, x + 36 = 0$$

$$\Rightarrow \text{cosec}^2 x - 8\,\text{cosec}\, x + 12 = 0$$

$$\Rightarrow \text{cosec}^2 x - 6\,\text{cosec}\, x - 2\,\text{cosec}\, x + 12 = 0$$

$$\Rightarrow \text{cosec}\, x(\text{cosec}\, x - 6) - 2(\text{cosec}\, x - 6) = 0$$

$$\Rightarrow (\text{cosec}\, x - 6)(\text{cosec}\, x - 2) = 0$$

$$\Rightarrow \text{cosec}\, x = 2, 6$$

Putting the value of $\text{cosec}\, x = 2, 6$ in Eq. (ii), we get

Either, $4 + \sqrt{3}\,|\sec y| = 6$

or $\quad 12 + \sqrt{3}\,|\sec y| = 6$

$$\Rightarrow |\sec y| = \frac{2}{\sqrt{3}}$$

or $\quad \sqrt{3}\,|\sec y| = -6$

$$\Rightarrow |\cos y| = \frac{\sqrt{3}}{2} \text{ or } |\sec y| = -2\sqrt{3}$$

(Rejected because modulus always gives us non-negative value)

$$\Rightarrow \cos^2 y = \frac{3}{4} = \cos^2 \frac{\pi}{6}$$

i.e. when $\text{cosec}\, x = 2$, then $\cos^2 y = \frac{3}{4}$

$\sin x = \frac{1}{2}$, then $\cos^2 y = \cos^2 \frac{\pi}{6}$

$$\Rightarrow x = n\pi + (-1)^n \frac{\pi}{6}, \text{ then } y = m\pi \pm \frac{\pi}{6},$$

where m and n both are integers.

6. (a) Given, $t_1 = (\sin\theta)^{\text{cosec}\,\theta}$

$$\Rightarrow \log t_1 = \text{cosec}\,\theta \cdot \log(\sin\theta) \quad \ldots(i)$$

$$t_2 = (\text{cosec}\,\theta)^{\sin\theta}$$

$$\Rightarrow \log t_2 = \sin\theta \log(\text{cosec}\,\theta)$$

$$= \sin\theta \cdot \log\left(\frac{1}{\sin\theta}\right)$$

$$= -\sin\theta \log(\sin\theta) \quad \ldots(ii)$$

$$t_3 = (\sin\theta)^{\sin\theta}$$

$$\Rightarrow \log t_3 = \sin\theta \log(\sin\theta) \quad \ldots(iii)$$

$$t_4 = (\text{cosec}\,\theta)^{\text{cosec}\,\theta}$$

$$\log t_4 = \text{cosec}\,\theta \log(\text{cosec}\,\theta$$

$$= -\text{cosec}\,\theta \log(\sin\theta) \quad \ldots(iv)$$

Now, $\log(\sin\theta) < 0$ (because $0 < \theta < \frac{\pi}{2}$

$\therefore 0 < \sin\theta < 1, \log(\sin\theta) < 0$)

From Eqs. (i) and (ii), $\log t_2 > \log t_1$

$$\Rightarrow [\text{In } 0 < \theta < \frac{\pi}{2}, \text{cosec}\,\theta > -\sin\theta$$

$$\Rightarrow \log(\sin\theta)\,\text{cosec}\,\theta < \log(\sin\theta)(-\sin\theta)$$

$$\left(\because \log(\sin\theta) < 0 \text{ for } 0 < \theta < \frac{\pi}{2}\right)$$

$$\Rightarrow \log t_1 < \log t_2 \Rightarrow t_1 < t_2]$$

$$\Rightarrow t_2 > t_1 \quad \ldots(v)$$

From Eqs. (ii) and (iv),

$\log t_4 > \log t_2$ [In $0 < \theta < \frac{\pi}{2}$,

$$\text{cosec}\,\theta > \sin\theta$$

$$\Rightarrow -\text{cosec}\,\theta < -\sin\theta$$

$$\Rightarrow (-\text{cosec}\,\theta)\ln\sin\theta > (-\sin\theta)\ln(\sin\theta)$$

$$\Rightarrow \log t_4 > \log t_2$$

$$\Rightarrow t_4 > t_2$$

$$\Rightarrow t_4 > t_2 \quad \ldots(vi)$$

From Eqs. (i) and (iii),

$$\log t_3 > \log t_1$$

$$\Rightarrow t_3 > t_1 \quad \ldots(vii)$$

Also, from Eqs. (ii) and (iii),

$$\log t_3 < \log t_2$$

$$[\text{In } 0 < \theta < \frac{\pi}{2}, \sin\theta > -\sin\theta$$

$$\Rightarrow (\sin\theta)\log(\sin\theta) < (-\sin\theta)\log\sin\theta$$

$$\Rightarrow \log t_3 < \log t_2$$

$$\Rightarrow t_3 < t_2]$$

$$\Rightarrow t_3 < t_2 \quad \ldots(viii)$$

Hence, from Eqs. (v), (vi), (vii) and (viii), we have

$$t_4 > t_2 > t_3 > t_1$$

7. (b) Since, $\sin^2 x + \sin^4 x + \sin^6 x + \ldots + \text{up to } \infty$

$$= \frac{\sin^2 x}{1 - \sin^2 x}$$

$$= \frac{\sin^2 x}{\cos^2 x} = \tan^2 x$$

Now, $\exp[(\sin^2 x + \sin^4 x + \sin^6 x + \ldots \text{ up to } \infty)\ln 2]$

$$= e^{\tan^2 x \cdot \ln 2} \; (\because \exp(x) \text{ means } e^x)$$

$$= e^{\ln 2^{\tan^2 x}} = 2^{\tan^2 x}$$

The given equation is $y^2 - 9y + 8 = 0$

$$\Rightarrow (y-1)(y-8) = 0$$

Either $y = 1$ or $y = 8$

$$\Rightarrow 2^{\tan^2 x} = 1 \text{ or } \Rightarrow 2^{\tan^2 x} = 2^3$$

$$\Rightarrow \tan^2 x = 0 \Rightarrow \tan^2 x = 3$$

$$\Rightarrow x = 0 \text{ but } 0 < x < \frac{\pi}{2}$$

$$\Rightarrow \tan x = \pm\sqrt{3}$$

$$\Rightarrow x = \frac{\pi}{3}\left(\text{as } 0 < x < \frac{\pi}{2}\right)$$

Hence,

$$\frac{\cos x}{\cos x+\sin x}=\frac{\cos\left(\frac{\pi}{3}\right)}{\cos\left(\frac{\pi}{3}\right)+\sin\left(\frac{\pi}{3}\right)}$$

$$=\frac{\frac{1}{2}}{\frac{1}{2}+\frac{\sqrt{3}}{2}}=\frac{1}{\sqrt{3}+1}=\frac{\sqrt{3}-1}{2}$$

8. (a) $\dfrac{1}{\left[\cos^2\left(\frac{\pi}{4}+x\right)+\sin^2\left(\frac{\pi}{4}-x\right)\right]}$

$$=\frac{1}{\left(\cos\frac{\pi}{4}\cdot\cos x-\sin\frac{\pi}{4}\cdot\sin x\right)^2+\left(\sin\frac{\pi}{4}\cdot\cos x-\cos\frac{\pi}{4}\sin x\right)^2}$$

$$=\frac{1}{\left(\frac{1}{\sqrt{2}}\cos x-\frac{1}{\sqrt{2}}\sin x\right)^2+\left(\frac{1}{\sqrt{2}}\cos x-\frac{1}{\sqrt{2}}\sin x\right)^2}$$

$$=\frac{1}{(\cos x-\sin x)^2}$$

$$=\frac{1}{\cos^2 x+\sin^2 x-2\sin x\cos x}$$

$$=\frac{1}{1-\sin 2x}$$

Now, to find the minimum value of $\left(\frac{1}{1-\sin 2x}\right)$, we need to find the maximum value of the denominator.

Since, $(\sin 2x)$ is being subtracted (from 1, it means that to maximize the denominator, we need to take the minimum value of $(\sin 2x)$ which is (-1) because $-1\le\sin 2x\le 1$.

So, maximum value of denominator $=2$

Hence, the minimum value of $\left(\frac{1}{1-\sin 2x}\right)=\frac{1}{2}$

9. (d) We have, $x^2-4x+1=0$

$$\Rightarrow\quad x=\frac{4\pm\sqrt{16-4}}{2}=2\pm\sqrt{3}$$

The two sides of the triangle are $(2+\sqrt{3})$ and $(2-\sqrt{3})$ and included angle is $\frac{\pi}{3}$. Let third side be k, then

$$\cos\frac{\pi}{3}=\frac{(2+\sqrt{3})^2+(2-\sqrt{3})^2-k^2}{2(2+\sqrt{3})(2-\sqrt{3})}$$

$$\Rightarrow\quad\frac{1}{2}=\frac{2(4+3)-k^2}{2(4-3)}$$

$$\Rightarrow k^2=13$$

$$\Rightarrow\quad k=\sqrt{13}\qquad(\because k>0)$$

$\therefore$ Perimeter of triangle

$$=(2+\sqrt{3})+(2-\sqrt{3})+\sqrt{13}$$
$$=4+\sqrt{13}$$

10. (d) We have, $\cos^2\frac{C}{2}=\frac{S(S-C)}{ab}$

So that, $\dfrac{2ab}{(a+b+c)\Delta}\cos^2\left(\frac{C}{2}\right)$

$$=\frac{2ab}{2\Delta S}\times\frac{S(S-c)}{ab}=\frac{S-c}{\Delta}\qquad\text{...(i)}$$

Now, the area of ΔABC is

$$\Delta=\frac{1}{2}ap_1\text{ i.e. }p_1=\frac{2\Delta}{a}$$

Similarly, $p_2=\frac{2\Delta}{b}$ and $p_3=\frac{2\Delta}{c}$

So, $\dfrac{1}{p_1}+\dfrac{1}{p_2}-\dfrac{1}{p_3}=\dfrac{a+b-c}{2\Delta}$

$$=\frac{2S-2c}{2\Delta}=\frac{S-c}{\Delta}=\frac{2ab}{(a+b+c)\Delta}\cos^2\frac{C}{2}\text{ [from Eq. (i)]}$$

11. (a) $\because (c-a)(s-b)=(a-b)(s-c)$

$$\Rightarrow\frac{c-a}{s-c}=\frac{a-b}{s-b}$$

$$\Rightarrow\frac{c-a}{(s-a)(s-c)}=\frac{a-b}{(s-a)(s-b)}$$

$$\Rightarrow\frac{\Delta}{s-c}-\frac{\Delta}{s-a}=-\left(\frac{\Delta}{s-b}-\frac{\Delta}{s-a}\right)$$

$$\Rightarrow\frac{\Delta}{s-c}+\frac{\Delta}{s-b}=2\frac{\Delta}{s-a}$$

$$\Rightarrow r_3+r_2=2r_1$$

12. (b) Given,

$$a\tan A+b\tan B=(a+b)\tan\left(\frac{A+B}{2}\right)$$

$$\Rightarrow a\left(\tan A-\tan\frac{A+B}{2}\right)=b\left(\tan\frac{A+B}{2}-\tan B\right)$$

$$\Rightarrow a\left(\frac{\sin A}{\cos A}-\frac{\sin\left(\frac{A+B}{2}\right)}{\cos\left(\frac{A+B}{2}\right)}\right)=b\left(\frac{\sin\left(\frac{A+B}{2}\right)}{\cos\left(\frac{A+B}{2}\right)}-\frac{\sin B}{\cos B}\right)$$

$$\Rightarrow a\left(\frac{\sin A\cos\left(\frac{A+B}{2}\right)-\sin\left(\frac{A+B}{2}\right)\cos A}{\cos A\cos\left(\frac{A+B}{2}\right)}\right)=b\left[\frac{\sin\left(\frac{A+B}{2}\right)\cos B-\sin B\cos\left(\frac{A+B}{2}\right)}{\cos\left(\frac{A+B}{2}\right)\cos B}\right]$$

$$\Rightarrow\quad\frac{a\sin\left(A-\frac{A+B}{2}\right)}{\cos A}=\frac{b\sin\left(\frac{A+B}{2}-B\right)}{\cos B}$$

$$\Rightarrow a\sin\left(\frac{A-B}{2}\right)\cos B=b\sin\left(\frac{A-B}{2}\right)\cos A$$

$$\Rightarrow\quad\sin\left(\frac{A-B}{2}\right)(a\cos B-b\cos A)=0$$

$$\Rightarrow\sin\left(\frac{A-B}{2}\right)(\sin A\cos B-\sin B\cos A)=0$$

$$\Rightarrow\quad\sin\left(\frac{A-B}{2}\right)\sin(A-B)=0$$

$$\Rightarrow\quad 2\sin^2\left(\frac{A-B}{2}\right)\cos\left(\frac{A-B}{2}\right)=0$$

$$\Rightarrow\quad\sin\left(\frac{A-B}{2}\right)=0\Rightarrow A=B$$

$\therefore$ Triangle is isosceles.

13. (d) Let the sides of the triangle be $a-1$, a, $a+1$ where a is a natural number and $a>1$ because $(a-1>0\Rightarrow a>1)$

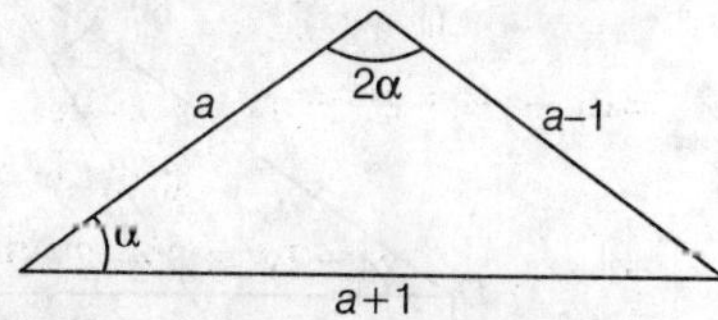

Let α be the smallest angle, then 2α is the greatest angle of the triangle.

Then by the law of sines

$$\frac{\sin\alpha}{a-1}=\frac{\sin 2\alpha}{a+1}$$

$$\Rightarrow\frac{a+1}{a-1}=\frac{2\sin\alpha\cdot\cos\alpha}{\sin\alpha}=2\cos\alpha$$

$$\Rightarrow\cos\alpha=\frac{(a+1)}{2(a-1)}\qquad\text{...(i)}$$

Also, by the law of cosines,

$$\cos\alpha=\frac{(a+1)^2+a^2-(a-1)^2}{2a(a+1)}$$

$$=\frac{a^2+4a}{2a(a+1)}=\frac{a+4}{2(a+1)}\qquad\text{...(ii)}$$

From Eqs. (i) and (ii), we get

$$\frac{a+1}{2(a-1)}=\frac{a+4}{2(a+1)}$$

$\Rightarrow \quad (a+1)^2 = (a+4)(a-1)$

$\Rightarrow a^2 + 2a + 1 = a^2 + 3a - 4$

$\Rightarrow \quad a = 5$

Hence, sides are $(5-1)$, (5) and $(5+1)$ i.e. 4, 5, 6.

14. (a) Let PQ be the tower of height h.

$AB = 2h$

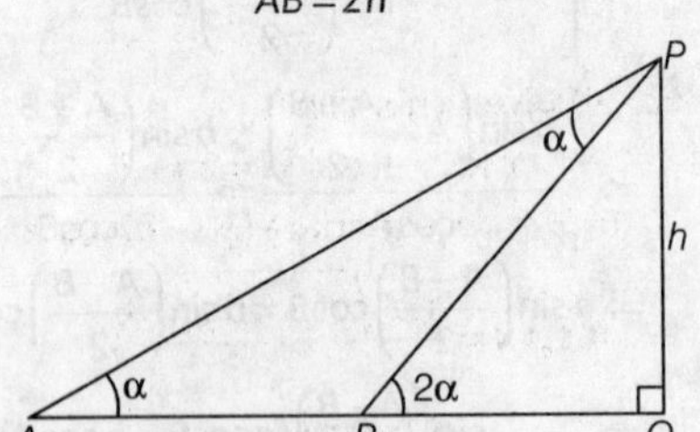

Given, $\angle PAQ = \alpha$ and $\angle PBQ = 2\alpha$

$\therefore \angle APB = \angle PBQ - \angle PAQ$

$= 2\alpha - \alpha = \alpha$

In ΔABP, $\angle BAP = \angle APB = \alpha$

$\therefore \quad PB = AB = 2h$

In ΔPQB, we have

$$\sin 2\alpha = \frac{PQ}{PB} = \frac{h}{2h} = \frac{1}{2}$$

$$\therefore \sin 2\alpha = \sin\frac{\pi}{6} \Rightarrow 2\alpha = \frac{\pi}{6} \Rightarrow \alpha = \frac{\pi}{12}$$

15. (d) Given, distance between house and building = 40 feet

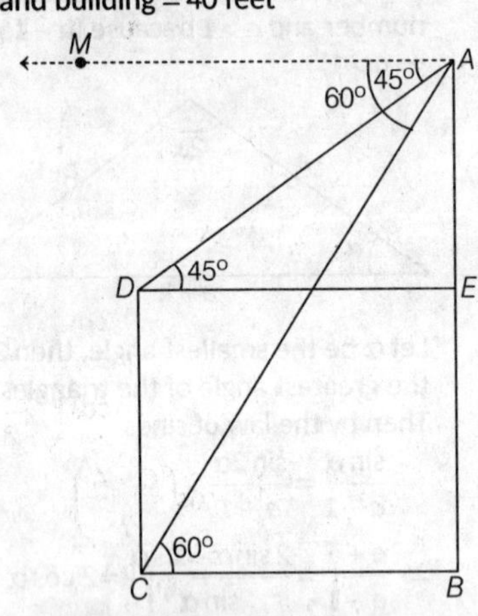

$\Rightarrow BC = DE = 40$ feet

Angles of depression to top and bottom of house from top of building are 45° and 60° respectively.

$\left.\begin{array}{l}\angle MAD = 45° = \angle ADE \\ \angle MAC = 60° = \angle ACB\end{array}\right\}$ (alternate angles)

In ΔADE, $\tan 45° = \dfrac{AE}{40}$

$\Rightarrow \quad AE = 40$ feet

In ΔABC, $\tan 60° = \dfrac{AB}{BC}$

$$\Rightarrow \quad \sqrt{3} = \frac{40 + BE}{40}$$

$\Rightarrow \quad 40 + BE = 40\sqrt{3}$

$\Rightarrow \quad BE = 40(\sqrt{3} - 1)$ feet

Hence, the height of house $= CD = BE = 40(\sqrt{3} - 1)$ feet

16. (d)

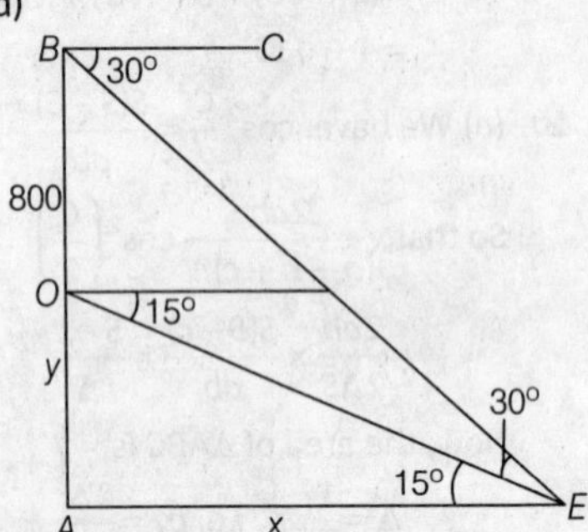

Let B and O be the position of the balloon, respectively, when observed the ship at E, horizontal $EA = x$ m (say), B being the point of ascent of balloon. We have $\angle BEA = 30°$, $\angle OEA = 15°$ and $OA = y$ (say)

In ΔOAE,

$\tan 15° = \dfrac{y}{x}$ ($\because \tan 15° = \tan(45° - 30°)$)

$$= \frac{\tan 45° - \tan 30°}{1 + \tan 45° \tan 30°} = \frac{1 - \frac{1}{\sqrt{3}}}{1 + \frac{1}{\sqrt{3}}}$$

$$\Rightarrow \tan 15° = \frac{\sqrt{3}-1}{\sqrt{3}+1} \times \left(\frac{\sqrt{3}-1}{\sqrt{3}-1}\right)$$

$$= \frac{3 + 1 - 2\sqrt{3}}{3 - 1} = \frac{2(2-\sqrt{3})}{2} = (2 - \sqrt{3})$$

$\Rightarrow y = x(2 - \sqrt{3})$

In ΔABE, $\tan 30° = \dfrac{y + 800}{x}$

$$= \frac{x(2-\sqrt{3}) + 800}{x} = 2 - \sqrt{3} + \frac{800}{x}$$

$$\Rightarrow \frac{1}{\sqrt{3}} - 2 + \sqrt{3} = \frac{800}{x} \Rightarrow x = \frac{800\sqrt{3}}{(4 - 2\sqrt{3})}$$

$= 400(2\sqrt{3} + 3)$

(after taking conjugate)

17. (b) Given, $\dfrac{(\sec^{-1} x)^3 + (\text{cosec}^{-1} x)^3}{(\tan^{-1} x + \cot^{-1} x)^3} = 7$

$$\Rightarrow \frac{(\sec^{-1} x + \text{cosec}^{-1} x)^3 - 3\sec^{-1} x \cdot \text{cosec}^{-1} x(\sec^{-1} x + \text{cosec}^{-1} x)}{\left(\frac{\pi}{2}\right)^3} = 7$$

$[\because a^3 + b^3 = (a+b)^3 - 3ab(a+b)]$

$$\Rightarrow \frac{\pi^3}{8} - 3\sec^{-1} x \cdot \text{cosec}^{-1} x \cdot \frac{\pi}{2} = \frac{7\pi^3}{8}$$

$$\Rightarrow \frac{3\pi}{2}\sec^{-1} x \cdot \text{cosec}^{-1} x = -\frac{3}{4}\pi^3$$

$$\Rightarrow \sec^{-1} x\left(\frac{\pi}{2} - \sec^{-1} x\right) = -\frac{\pi^2}{2}$$

$\Rightarrow t^2 - \dfrac{\pi}{2}t - \dfrac{\pi^2}{2} = 0$, where $t = \sec^{-1} x$

$\Rightarrow \quad 2t^2 - \pi t - \pi^2 = 0$

$\Rightarrow \quad 2t^2 - 2\pi t + \pi t - \pi^2 = 0$

$\Rightarrow \quad 2t(t - \pi) + \pi(t - \pi) = 0$

$\Rightarrow \quad (t - \pi)(2t + \pi) = 0$

$\Rightarrow \quad t = \pi$ or $-\dfrac{\pi}{2}$

$\Rightarrow \sec^{-1} x = \pi$ or $\sec^{-1} x = -\dfrac{\pi}{2}$

But $\sec^{-1} x \in [0, \pi] - \left\{\dfrac{\pi}{2}\right\}$

$\therefore \sec^{-1} x = -\dfrac{\pi}{2}$ (Rejected)

Therefore, $\sec^{-1} x = \pi \Rightarrow x = -1$

Hence, total number of real solution is 1.

18. (c) Given, $[\tan^{-1} x] + [\cot^{-1} x] = 2$ ...(i)

$\because 0 < \cot^{-1} x < \pi$ and

$-\dfrac{\pi}{2} < \tan^{-1} x < \dfrac{\pi}{2}$

$\Rightarrow [\cot^{-1} x] \in \{0, 1, 2, 3\}$

and $[\tan^{-1} x] \in \{-2, -1, 0, 1\}$

For $[\tan^{-1} x] + [\cot^{-1} x] = 2$, following three cases are possible.

Case (I) When $[\tan^{-1} x] = [\cot^{-1} x] = 1$

Then, $1 \le \cot^{-1} x < 2$

and $1 \le \tan^{-1} x < \dfrac{\pi}{2}$

$\Rightarrow x \in (\cot 2, \cot 1]$ and $x \in [\tan 1, \infty)$

($\because \tan^{-1} x$ is an increasing function and $\cot^{-1} x$ is a decreasing function)

$\Rightarrow x \in \phi$ because $\cot 1 < \tan 1$ ...(ii)

Case (II) When $[\cot^{-1} x] = 2$

and $[\tan^{-1} x] = 0$

Then, $2 \le \cot^{-1} x < 3$

and $0 \le \tan^{-1} x < 1$

$\Rightarrow x \in (\cot 3, \cot 2)$ and $x \in [0, \tan 1)$

$\Rightarrow x \in \phi$ because $\cot 2 < 0$ ...(iii)

Case (III) When $[\cot^{-1} x] = 3$

and $[\tan^{-1} x] = -1$

Then, $3 \le \cot^{-1} x < \pi$

and $-1 \le \tan^{-1} x < 0$

$\Rightarrow x \in (-\infty, \cot 3]$ and $x \in [-\tan 1, 0)$

$\Rightarrow x \in \phi$ as $\cot 3 < -\tan 1$ ...(iv)

From Eqs. (ii) $\cup$ (iii) $\cup$ (iv) $\Rightarrow x \in \phi$ i.e. there is no such values of x exist for which Eq. (i) will be true.

Hence, $\lambda = 0$

So, $\left[(\sin(2\lambda) + \log_{\left(\frac{1}{2}+\lambda\right)} (\lambda+1)/(\cos\lambda + \sqrt{\frac{1}{2}\lambda^2 - 3\lambda + 4})\right]$

$= \frac{0+0}{1+2} = \frac{0}{3} = 0$

19. (c) Given $\sin^{-1}\left(x^2 - \frac{x^4}{3} + \frac{x^6}{9} - \dots\right) + \cos^{-1}\left(x^4 - \frac{x^8}{3} + \frac{x^{12}}{9} - \dots\right) = \frac{\pi}{2}$

$\Rightarrow \left(x^2 - \frac{x^4}{3} + \frac{x^6}{9} - \dots\right) = \left(x^4 - \frac{x^8}{3} + \frac{x^{12}}{9} - \dots\right)$

$\Rightarrow$ ($\because \sin^{-1} x + \cos^{-1} y = \frac{\pi}{2}$ is possible only when $x = y$ and $x \in [-1, 1]$)

$\Rightarrow \frac{x^2}{1+\frac{x^2}{3}} = \frac{x^4}{1+\frac{x^4}{3}} \Rightarrow$

($\because$ Sum of GP of infinite terms $= \frac{a}{1-r}$)

$\Rightarrow \frac{3}{3+x^2} = \frac{3x^2}{3+x^4}$ or $x = 0$

$\Rightarrow 9 + 3x^4 = 9x^2 + 3x^4$ or $x = 0$

$\Rightarrow \quad x^2 = 1$ or $x = 0$

$\Rightarrow \quad x = 1, -1$ or $x = 0$

i.e. $\quad x = -1, 1, 0$

Hence, sum of values of

$x = 1 - 1 + 0 = 0$

20. (d)

(a) x, y, z are in GP, then $y^2 = xz$ ...(i)

and $\tan^{-1} x, \tan^{-1} y, \tan^{-1} z$ are in AP.

Then, $2\tan^{-1} y = \tan^{-1} x + \tan^{-1} z$

$\Rightarrow \tan^{-1}\left(\frac{2y}{1-y^2}\right) = \tan^{-1}\left(\frac{x+z}{1-xz}\right)$

$\Rightarrow \tan^{-1}\left(\frac{2y}{1-y^2}\right) = \tan^{-1}\left(\frac{x+z}{1-y^2}\right)$ [from Eq. (i)]

$\Rightarrow 2y = x + z$ or $y = \pm 1$

$\Rightarrow x, y, z$ are in AP as well as GP.

$\Rightarrow x = y = z$ or $y = \pm 1$

option (a) in incorrect.

(b) $\sec^2\left(\cot^{-1}\frac{1}{4}\right) + \text{cosec}^2\left(\tan^{-1}\frac{1}{2}\right)$

$= \sec^2(\tan^{-1} 4) + \text{cosec}^2(\cot^{-1} 2)$

$= 1 + \tan^2(\tan^{-1} 4) + 1 + \cot^2(\cot^{-1} 2)$

$= 1 + 16 + 1 + 4 = 22$

Option (b) is incorrect.

(c) $\because 0 < x < 1$

$\Rightarrow \left(\frac{x}{1-x^2}\right)\left(\frac{1}{x^3}\right) = \frac{1}{x^2(1-x^2)} > 1$

$\therefore \tan^{-1}\left(\frac{x}{1-x^2}\right) + \tan^{-1}\left(\frac{1}{x^3}\right) = \frac{3\pi}{4}$

$\pi + \tan^{-1}\left[\frac{\frac{x}{1-x^2} + \frac{1}{x^3}}{1 - \left(\frac{x}{1-x^2}\right)\left(\frac{1}{x^3}\right)}\right] = \frac{3\pi}{4}$

$\Rightarrow \tan^{-1}\left(-\frac{1}{x}\right) = -\frac{\pi}{4}$

$\Rightarrow \quad x = 1$

$\therefore$ Option (c) is incorrect.

(d) Let $\cot^{-1}\left(\frac{1}{x}\right) = \alpha$, $\cot^{-1}\left(\frac{1}{y}\right) = \beta$, $\cot^{-1}\left(\frac{1}{z}\right) = \gamma$

Then, $\alpha + \beta + \gamma = \frac{\pi}{2}$

$\Rightarrow \quad \alpha + \beta = \frac{\pi}{2} - \gamma$

$\Rightarrow \quad \cot(\alpha + \beta) = \cot\left(\frac{\pi}{2} - \gamma\right) = \tan\gamma$

$\Rightarrow \frac{\cot\alpha \cot\beta - 1}{\cot\beta + \cot\alpha} = \tan\gamma$

$\Rightarrow \frac{\left(\frac{1}{x}\right)\left(\frac{1}{y}\right) - 1}{\frac{1}{y} + \frac{1}{x}} = z$

$\Rightarrow \quad 1 - xy = z(x + y)$

$\Rightarrow \quad xy + yz + zx = 1$

Option (d) is correct.

21. (9) We know that,

$(1 - b\tan\theta)^2 = a^2 \sec^2\theta$

$= 5 + b^2 \tan^2\theta$

$\therefore 1 - 2b\tan\theta + b^2\tan^2\theta = 5 + b^2\tan^2\theta$

$\Rightarrow \quad \tan\theta = -\frac{2}{b}$

Now, $a^2 \sec^2\theta = 5 + b^2\tan^2\theta$

$\Rightarrow a^2(1 + \tan^2\theta) = 5 + b^2\tan^2\theta$

$\Rightarrow \quad a^2\left(1 + \frac{4}{b^2}\right) = 5 + b^2\left(\frac{4}{b^2}\right)$

$\Rightarrow \quad a^2(b^2 + 4) = 9b^2$

$\therefore \quad k = 9$

22. (4) Given equation is

$\cos 2x + a\sin x = 2a - 7$ ...(i)

$\Rightarrow 2\sin^2 x - a\sin x + (2a - 8) = 0$

$\Rightarrow \sin x = \frac{a \pm \sqrt{a^2 - 8(2a-8)}}{4}$

$\Rightarrow \sin x = \frac{a \pm (a-8)}{4}$

$\Rightarrow \sin x = \frac{2a-8}{4}$ or 2

For Eq. (i) to have a solution if

$-1 \le \frac{2a-8}{4} \le 1$

[$\because -1 \le \sin x \le 1, \therefore \sin x = 2$ Rejected]

$\Rightarrow -4 \le 2a - 8 \le 4$

$\Rightarrow \quad 4 \le 2a \le 12$

$\Rightarrow \quad 2 \le a \le 6$

$\therefore a_{\min} = 2$ and $a_{\max} = 6$

Hence, $|a_{\min} - a_{\max}| = |a_{\max} - a_{\min}|$

$= |2 - 6| = |6 - 2| = 4$

23. (6) $\because A + B + C = \pi$ ...(i)

$E = \frac{\cos\left(\frac{B-C}{2}\right)}{\cos\left(\frac{B+C}{2}\right)} + \frac{\cos\left(\frac{C-A}{2}\right)}{\cos\left(\frac{C+A}{2}\right)} + \frac{\cos\left(\frac{A-B}{2}\right)}{\cos\left(\frac{A+B}{2}\right)}$

$= \frac{\cos\left(\frac{B-C}{2}\right)}{\sin\left(\frac{A}{2}\right)} + \frac{\cos\left(\frac{C-A}{2}\right)}{\sin\left(\frac{B}{2}\right)} + \frac{\cos\left(\frac{A-B}{2}\right)}{\sin\left(\frac{C}{2}\right)}$ [from Eq. (i)]

$\left[\frac{B+C}{2} = \frac{\pi}{2} - \frac{A}{2}, \frac{C+A}{2} = \frac{\pi}{2} - \frac{B}{2}, \frac{A+B}{2} = \frac{\pi}{2} - \frac{C}{2}\right]$

$$= \frac{2\cos\left(\frac{A}{2}\right)\cos\left(\frac{B-C}{2}\right)}{\sin A} + \frac{2\cos\left(\frac{B}{2}\right)\cos\left(\frac{C-A}{2}\right)}{\sin B} + \frac{2\cos\left(\frac{C}{2}\right)\cos\left(\frac{A-B}{2}\right)}{\sin C}$$

$$= \frac{\sin B + \sin C}{\sin A} + \frac{\sin A + \sin C}{\sin B} + \frac{\sin B + \sin A}{\sin C}$$ (Using $2\cos A \cdot \cos B = \cos(A+B) + \cos(A-B)$

$$= \left(\frac{\sin B}{\sin A} + \frac{\sin A}{\sin B}\right) + \left(\frac{\sin C}{\sin B} + \frac{\sin B}{\sin C}\right) + \left(\frac{\sin C}{\sin A} + \frac{\sin A}{\sin C}\right)$$

$\Rightarrow$ (after rearranging)

$\because A, B, C$ are angles of a triangle, then $0 < A, B, C < \pi$

$\Rightarrow \quad \sin A, \sin B, \sin C > 0$

Hence, $E \geq 2+2+2$

$\Rightarrow E \geq 6 \left(\text{as } x + \frac{1}{x} \geq 2 \text{ if } x > 0\right)$

Hence, E never be less than 6.

24. (4) $\sin^2 x - 2\sin x - 1 = 0$

$\Rightarrow (\sin x - 1)^2 = 2 \Rightarrow \sin x - 1 = \pm\sqrt{2}$

$\Rightarrow \sin x = 1 - \sqrt{2}$ (because $\sin x \not> 1$)

Hence, there are two solutions in $[0, 2\pi]$ and two more solutions in $[2\pi, 4\pi]$.

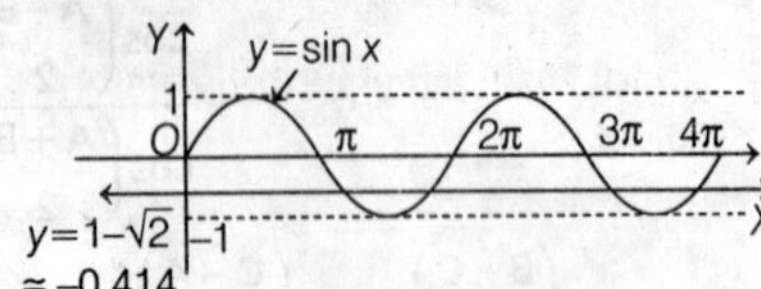

Thus, $(n)_{\min} = 4$

25. (2.133) Since, $\Delta = \frac{1}{2} bc \sin A$

$\Rightarrow \quad \Delta = \frac{1}{2} bc\left(\frac{a}{2R}\right)$

$\left(\because \frac{a}{\sin A} = \frac{b}{\sin B} = \frac{c}{\sin C} = 2R\right)$

$\Rightarrow \quad \Delta = \frac{abc}{4R} \Rightarrow R = \frac{abc}{4\Delta}$

$\Rightarrow \quad R = \frac{1}{4} \times (6k \times 7k \times 8k) \times \frac{1}{\sqrt{s(s-6k)(s-7k)(s-8k)}}$

$\Rightarrow \quad R = \frac{1}{4} \times (6 \times 7 \times 8) \times \frac{k^3}{\sqrt{s(s-6k)(s-7k)(s-8k)}}$

where, $s = \frac{6k + 7k + 8k}{2} = \frac{21k}{2}$

$$\therefore R = \frac{84k^3}{\sqrt{\left(\frac{21k}{2}\right)\left(\frac{9k}{2}\right)\left(\frac{7k}{2}\right)\left(\frac{5k}{2}\right)}}$$

$$= \frac{(84k^3)(4)}{(7\times 3)k^2\sqrt{15}} = \frac{16k}{\sqrt{15}}$$

and $r = \frac{\Delta}{s} = \dfrac{\sqrt{\left(\frac{21k}{2}\right)\left(\frac{9k}{2}\right)\left(\frac{7k}{2}\right)\left(\frac{5k}{2}\right)}}{\frac{21k}{2}}$

$$= \frac{21k^2\sqrt{15}\times 2}{(21k)(4)} = \frac{k\sqrt{15}}{2}$$

Hence, $\frac{R}{r} = \frac{16k}{\sqrt{15}} \times \frac{2}{k\sqrt{15}} = \frac{32}{15}$

$= 2.1333 \ldots$

26. (2) Given, $AD = \frac{1}{\sqrt{11 - 6\sqrt{3}}}$

Let $BD = DC = \frac{a}{2}$

From ΔABD, we get

$$\frac{\frac{a}{2}}{\sin 30^\circ} = \frac{AD}{\sin(105^\circ - C)}$$

$\Rightarrow \quad \sin(105^\circ - C) = \frac{AD}{a} \quad \ldots(\text{i})$

From ΔADC, we have

$$\frac{\frac{a}{2}}{\sin 45^\circ} = \frac{AD}{\sin C}$$

$\Rightarrow \quad \sin C = \sqrt{2}\,\frac{AD}{a} \quad \ldots(\text{ii})$

From Eqs. (i) and (ii), we get

$\sqrt{2}\sin(105^\circ - C) = \sin C$

$\Rightarrow \sqrt{2}(\sin 105^\circ \cdot \cos C - \cos 105^\circ \cdot \sin C) = \sin C$

$\Rightarrow \sqrt{2}\,[\sin(60^\circ + 45^\circ)\cdot\cos C - \cos(60^\circ + 45^\circ)\cdot \sin C] = \sin C$

$\Rightarrow \sqrt{2}\left[\frac{\sqrt{3}+1}{2\sqrt{2}}\cos C + \frac{\sqrt{3}-1}{2\sqrt{2}}\sin C\right] = \sin C$

$\Rightarrow (\sqrt{3}+1)\cos C + (\sqrt{3}-1)\sin C = 2\sin C$

$\Rightarrow (\sqrt{3}+1)\cos C = (3-\sqrt{3})\sin C$

$\Rightarrow (\sqrt{3}+1)^2\cos^2 C = (3-\sqrt{3})^2\sin^2 C$

$\Rightarrow (4+2\sqrt{3})(1-\sin^2 C) = 3(4-2\sqrt{3})\cdot\sin^2 C$

$\Rightarrow \sin^2 C(4+2\sqrt{3}+12-6\sqrt{3}) = 4+2\sqrt{3}$

$\Rightarrow \sin^2 C = \frac{4+2\sqrt{3}}{16-4\sqrt{3}}$

$= \frac{2+\sqrt{3}}{8-2\sqrt{3}} \times \frac{8+2\sqrt{3}}{8+2\sqrt{3}}$

$= \frac{22+12\sqrt{3}}{64-12} = \frac{11+6\sqrt{3}}{26}$

Therefore, from Eq. (ii), we get

$BC = a = \frac{\sqrt{2}\cdot AD}{\sin C}$

$= \sqrt{2}\,\frac{1}{\sqrt{11-6\sqrt{3}}} \times \frac{\sqrt{26}}{\sqrt{11+6\sqrt{3}}}$

$\Rightarrow BC = \frac{\sqrt{2}\cdot\sqrt{26}}{\sqrt{121-108}} \Rightarrow BC = 2$

27. (160) Let the height of tower be AB.

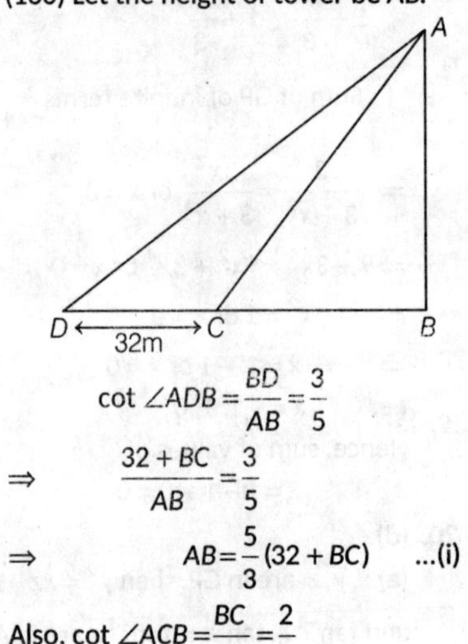

$\cot \angle ADB = \frac{BD}{AB} = \frac{3}{5}$

$\Rightarrow \quad \frac{32 + BC}{AB} = \frac{3}{5}$

$\Rightarrow \quad AB = \frac{5}{3}(32 + BC) \quad \ldots(\text{i})$

Also, $\cot \angle ACB = \frac{BC}{AB} = \frac{2}{5}$

$\Rightarrow \quad \frac{5}{2}BC = AB \quad \ldots(\text{ii})$

From Eqs. (i) and (ii), we get

$\frac{5}{2}BC = \frac{5}{3}(32 + BC)$

$\Rightarrow \quad BC = 64$ m

Hence, the heigth of the tower is

$AB = \frac{5}{2} \times 64 = 160$ m

28. (240) Let P be the initial position of the aeroplane and after 10 seconds its position be Q.

We have, $PL = QM = 1$ km

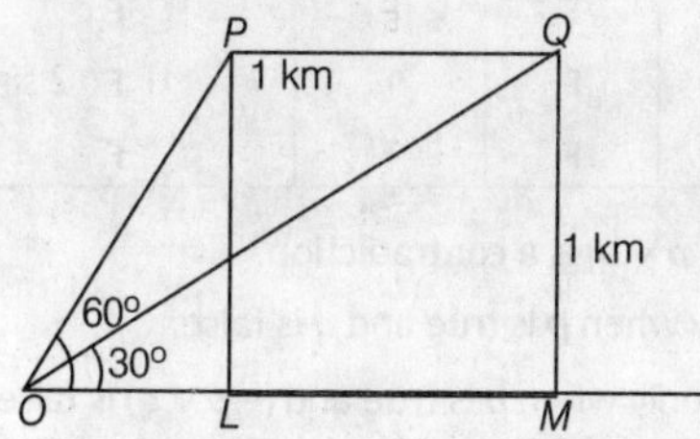

From triangles OPL and OQM, we have

$$\tan 60° = \frac{PL}{OL} \text{ and } \tan 30° = \frac{QM}{OM}$$

$\Rightarrow \quad OL = PL \cot 60°$

and $OM = QM \cot 30°$

$\Rightarrow \quad OL = \frac{1}{\sqrt{3}}$ and $OM = \sqrt{3}$

$[\because PL = QM = 1 \text{ km}]$

$\therefore \quad LM = OM - OL = \left(\sqrt{3} - \frac{1}{\sqrt{3}}\right)$ km

$\therefore \quad PQ = \left(\sqrt{3} - \frac{1}{\sqrt{3}}\right)$ km

In 10 s, the aeroplane travels $\left(\sqrt{3} - \frac{1}{\sqrt{3}}\right)$ km.

Hence, speed of the aeroplane

$$= \left[\frac{\left(\sqrt{3} - \frac{1}{\sqrt{3}}\right)}{10}\right] \text{km/s}$$

$$= \left(\frac{3-1}{10\sqrt{3}} \times 60 \times 60\right) \text{km/h}$$

$$= 240\sqrt{3} \text{ km/h} = k \text{ (given)}$$

$\therefore \quad \frac{k}{\sqrt{3}} = 240\sqrt{3} \times \frac{1}{\sqrt{3}} = 240$

29. (3) We have, $2\tan^{-1}(\tan x) = 6 - x$

$\Rightarrow \quad \tan^{-1}(\tan x) = \frac{6-x}{2}$

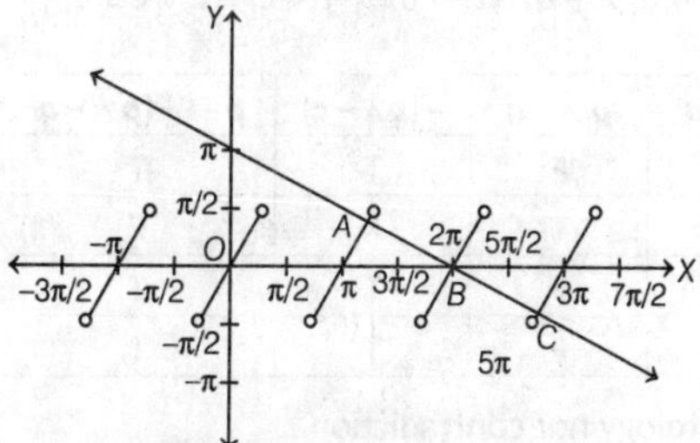

To find the number of solutions, we have to draw the graphs of $y = \tan^{-1}(\tan x)$ and $y = \frac{6-x}{2}$ or $x + 2y - 6 = 0$

From figure, black line intersects the green line atmost 3 points.

Hence, the number of solutions is 3.

30. (6) Given u, v, w are roots of

$$x^3 - 10x + 11 = 0$$

$$\therefore u + v + w + w = -\frac{0}{1} = 0,$$

$$uv + vw + wu = -\frac{10}{1} = -10$$

and $uvw = \frac{-11}{1} = -11$

Let $\tan^{-1} u = \alpha \Rightarrow \tan\alpha = u$

$\tan^{-1} v = \beta \Rightarrow \tan\beta = v$

$\tan^{-1} w = n \Rightarrow \tan\gamma = w$

Now, $\tan(\alpha + \beta + \gamma) = \frac{S_1 - S_3}{1 - S_2}$

[by elementary trigonometry,
$S_1 = \tan\alpha + \tan\beta + \tan\gamma$
$S_2 = \tan\alpha\tan\beta + \tan\beta\tan\gamma + \tan\gamma\tan\alpha$
$S_3 = \tan\alpha\tan\beta\tan\gamma$]

$$-\frac{0-(-11)}{1-(-10)} - \frac{11}{11} = 1$$

$$\therefore \alpha + \beta + \gamma = \tan^{-1}(1) = \frac{\pi}{4}$$

$\Rightarrow 3\operatorname{cosec}^2(\tan^{-1} u + \tan^{-1} v + \tan^{-1} w)$

$$= 3\operatorname{cosec}^2\left(\frac{\pi}{4}\right) = 3 \times 2 = 6$$

Qualifier 14 (Statistics and Mathematical Reasoning)

1. (b) Given, mean of (4, 7, a, b, 10, 12 and 13) = 9

$$9 = \frac{1}{7}(4 + 7 + a + b + 10 + 12 + 13)$$

$\Rightarrow 63 = 46 + a + b \Rightarrow a + b = 17$

Also, mean deviation from mean $= \frac{16}{7}$ (given)

$\therefore \quad \frac{16}{7} = \frac{1}{7}\sum_{i=1}^{7}|x_i - 9|$

$\Rightarrow \quad 16 = 5 + 2 + |a-9| + |b-9| + 1 + 3 + 4$

$\Rightarrow \quad |a-9| + |b-9| = 1$

$\Rightarrow \quad a - 9 = \pm 1$ and $b - 9 = 0$

or $\quad a - 9 = 0$ and $b - 9 = \pm 1$

$\Rightarrow \quad a - b = \pm 1$

$\therefore |b-a| = |-(a-b)| = |a-b| = |\pm 1| = 1$

2. (b) Mean

$$= \frac{101 + d(1+2+3+\ldots+100)}{101}$$

$$= 1 + \frac{d \times 100 \times 101}{101 \times 2} = 1 + 50d$$

$\because$ Mean deviation from the mean $= 255$ (given)

$$\Rightarrow \frac{1}{101}[|1-(1+50d)| + |(1+d) - (1+50d)| + |(1+2d) - (1+50d)| + \ldots + |(1+100d) - (1+50d)|] = 255$$

$\Rightarrow 2d(1+2+3+\ldots+50) = 101 \times 255$

$\Rightarrow \quad 2d \times \frac{50 \times 51}{2} = 101 \times 255$

$\Rightarrow \quad d = \frac{101 \times 255}{50 \times 51} = \frac{101}{10}$

$\Rightarrow \quad d = 10.1$

3. (b) Mean deviation is minimum, when it is considered about the item, equidistant from the beginning and the end i.e. the median.

In this case, median is $\left(\frac{101+1}{2}\right)$th observation, i.e. 51th observation (or item) i.e. x_{51}.

4. (b) Let $y = \frac{ax+b}{c} \Rightarrow y = \frac{a}{c}x + \frac{b}{c}$

$\Rightarrow y = Ax + B$, where $A = \frac{a}{c}$ and $B = \frac{b}{c}$

So, $\bar{y} = A\bar{x} + B$ and hence,

$$y - \bar{y} = Ax + B - (A\bar{x} + B) = A(x - \bar{x})$$

$\Rightarrow \quad (y-\bar{y})^2 = A^2(x-\bar{x})^2$

$\Rightarrow \quad \Sigma(y-\bar{y})^2 = A^2\Sigma(x-\bar{x})^2$

$\Rightarrow \quad n\sigma_y^2 = A^2(n\sigma_x^2)$

$\Rightarrow \quad \sigma_y = |A|\sigma_x$

$\Rightarrow \quad \sigma_y = \left|\frac{a}{c}\right|\sigma \quad (\because \sigma_x = \sigma)$

5. (b) Given, mean of (a, b, 8, 5 and 10) = 6

$\Rightarrow \frac{a+b+8+5+10}{5} = 6$

$\Rightarrow \quad a + b = 7 \quad$ ...(i)

Variance of a, b, 8, 5 and 10 is 6.80

$$\Rightarrow \frac{(a-6)^2 + (b-6)^2 + (8-6)^2 + (5-6)^2 + (10-6)^2}{5} = 6.80$$

$\Rightarrow a^2 - 12a + 36 + (1-a)^2 + 21 = 34$ [from Eq. (i)]

$\Rightarrow 2a^2 - 14a + 24 = 0$

$\Rightarrow \quad a^2 - 7a + 12 = 0$

$\Rightarrow a = 3$ or 4; $\therefore b = 4$ or 3

Hence, the possible values of a and b are $a = 3$ and $b = 4$ or $a = 4$ and $b = 3$

6. (a) Mean and standard deviation (σ) of the combined group are

$$M = \frac{63 \times 27.6 + 26 \times 19.2}{63 + 26} = 25.1$$

Thus, AM is decreased by $27.6 - 25.1 = 2.5$

$$\sigma^2 = \frac{63 \times (7.1)^2 + 26 \times (6.2)^2}{89} + \frac{63(25.1 - 27.6)^2 + 26(25.1 - 19.2)^2}{89}$$

$\Rightarrow \sigma = 7.8$ (approx)

7. (a) $\bar{x} = \frac{\Sigma x_i}{n}$ and $\sigma^2 = \frac{\Sigma x_i^2}{n} - (\bar{x})^2$

$$\text{New variance} = \frac{\Sigma(5x_i - 4)^2}{n} - \left(\frac{\Sigma(5x_i - 4)}{n}\right)^2$$

$$= \frac{\Sigma(25x_i^2 - 40x_i + 16)}{n} - (5\bar{x} - 4)^2$$

$$= \frac{25\,\Sigma x_i^2}{n} - 40\bar{x} + 16 - 25(\bar{x})^2 + 40\bar{x} - 16$$

$$= 25\left[\frac{\Sigma xi^2}{n} - (\bar{x})^2\right] = 25\sigma^2$$

8. (d) Given, $n = 5$

mean $= \bar{x} = 6$

$\Sigma x^2 = 765$

$$\sigma = \sqrt{\frac{\Sigma x^2}{n} - \bar{x}^2} = \sqrt{\frac{765}{5} - 6^2}$$

$$= \sqrt{153 - 36} = \sqrt{117} \approx 11$$

$$CV = \frac{\sigma}{\bar{x}} \times 100 = \frac{11}{6} \times 100$$

$$= \frac{1100}{6} \approx 180\%$$

9. (c) p : A number is a prime.

q : It is odd.

We have, $p \Rightarrow q$

The inverse of $p \Rightarrow q$ is $\sim p \Rightarrow \sim q$

i.e. if a number is not a prime, then it is not odd.

10. (b) Let p : Siwan is district of Bihar

and q : Siwan is in India.

$\sim p$: Siwan is not the district of Bihar

$\sim q$: Siwan is not in India.

Contrapositive of the statement $p \to q$ is

If $(\sim q)$, then $(\sim p)$

If Siwan is not in India, then Siwan is not the district of Bihar.

11. (d) Option (a) is incorrect because $p \wedge q$ is true only when both p and q are true.

Option (b) is incorrect because $p \to q$ is false only when p is true and q is false.

Option (c) is incorrect because pq is true only when either p and q both are true or both are false.

Option (d) is correct because $\sim (p \vee q)$ is the only when $(p \vee q)$ is false, i.e. p and q both are false.

12. (a) $\sim q \to \sim p$ is contrapositive of $p \to q$ and both convey the same meaning.

13. (a) A contradiction

p	q	$\sim p$	$\sim q$	$p \wedge \sim q$	$\sim p \vee q$	$(p \wedge \sim q) \wedge (\sim p \vee q)$
T	T	F	F	F	T	F
T	F	F	T	T	F	F
F	T	T	F	F	T	F
F	F	T	T	F	T	F

Clearly, $(p \wedge \sim q) \wedge (\sim p \vee q)$ is a contradiction.

14. (c) $p \to q$ is false only when p is true and q is false.

$p \to (\sim p \vee q)$ is false only when p is true and $(\sim p \vee q)$ is false.

i.e. $\sim p \vee q$ is false, if q is false because $\sim p$ is false.

15. (c)

p	q	$p \to q$	$\sim p$	$\sim p \vee q$	$(p \to q) \leftrightarrow (\sim p \vee q)$
T	T	T	F	T	T
T	F	F	F	F	T
F	T	T	T	T	T
F	F	T	T	T	T

16. (c) We consider following truth table.

p	q	$\sim p$	$\sim q$	$p \wedge q$	$p \vee q$	$[\sim (p \vee q)]$	$(p \wedge q) \wedge [\sim (p \vee q)]$
T	T	F	F	T	T	F	F
T	F	F	T	F	T	F	F
F	T	T	F	F	T	F	F
F	F	T	T	F	F	T	F

Clearly, last column of the above truth table contains only F.

Hence, $(p \wedge q) \wedge [\sim (p \vee q)]$ is a contradiction.

17. (b)

p	$\sim p$	$\sim(\sim p)$	$\sim(\sim p) \to p$	$p \to \sim(\sim p)$	$\sim(\sim p) \leftrightarrow p$
T	F	T	T	T	T
F	T	F	T	T	T

Since, last column of the above truth table contains only T.

Hence, $\sim(\sim p) \leftrightarrow p$ is a tautology.

18. (d) **Option (a)** $p \to (q \to p) \equiv p \to (\sim q \vee p) \equiv \sim p \vee (\sim q \vee p)$

$\equiv (\sim p \vee p) \vee - q \equiv t \vee \sim q \equiv t$

Option (b) $p \to (p \vee q) \equiv \sim p \vee (p \vee q) \equiv t \vee q \equiv t$

Option (c) $p \vee q \to (\sim p \wedge \sim q) \equiv \sim (p \vee q) \vee [\sim (p \vee q)] \equiv \sim (p \vee q)$

Option (d) $(p \vee \sim p) \to (q \wedge \sim q) \equiv t \to c \equiv (-t \vee c) \equiv c \vee c \equiv c$

19. (d)

p	q	$\sim q$	$p \wedge \sim q$	$\sim(p \wedge \sim q)$	$p \to \sim(p \wedge \sim q)$
T	T	F	F	T	T
T	F	T	T	F	F
F	T	F	F	T	T
F	F	T	F	T	T

Result is neither tautology nor contradiction.

20. (c) $[(p \wedge \sim q) \vee q] \vee (\sim p \wedge q)$

$= (p \vee q) \wedge (\sim q \vee q) \vee (\sim p \wedge q)$

$= (p \vee q) \wedge [t \vee (\sim p \wedge q)]$

$= (p \vee q) \wedge t = p \vee q$

21. (6.25) $w_i = lx_i + k$, $\bar{x}_i = 48$, $S(x_i) = 12$, $\bar{w}_i = 55$ and $S(w_i) = 15$

where, $S(x_i) =$ SD of x_i's

$S(w_i) =$ S.D. of w_i's

Then, $\bar{w}_i = l\bar{x}_i + k$

Now, mean of $w_i = l$ (mean of x_i) $+ k$

$\Rightarrow \quad 55 = l.48 + k \quad ...(i)$

Now, SD of $w_i =$ (SD of x_i) $|l|$

$\Rightarrow \quad 15 = 12|l| \Rightarrow |l| = \frac{15}{12}$

$\Rightarrow \quad l = \pm 1.25 \quad ...(ii)$

From Eq. (i), $55 = (\pm 1.25) \times 48 + k$

$\Rightarrow \quad k = 55 \mp (1.25 \times 48) = \mp 5$

Hence, $|l - k| = |1.25 - (\mp 5)| = 6.25$

22. (3) Given, $a - b < b < a < 2a + b$

$\therefore$ Median $= \frac{1}{2}(a+b)$

and range $= (2a+b) - (a-b) = a + 2b$

Thus, $\frac{1}{2}(a+b) = 15$, $a + 2b = 42$ (given)

$\Rightarrow \quad a + b = 30$, $a + 2b = 42$

$\Rightarrow \quad a = 18$, $b = 12$

Let $A = \frac{1}{2}(a+b) = 15$

$\therefore \sigma^2 = \frac{1}{2}[(18-15)^2 + (12-15)^2]$

$= \frac{1}{2}[(3)^2 + (-3)^2] = \frac{1}{2}[9+9] = 9$

$\therefore \sigma = 3$

23. (54.93) Corrected

$\Sigma x = 40 \times 200 - 50 + 40 = 7990$

$\therefore$Corrected mean $(\bar{x}) = \frac{7990}{200} = 39.95$

Incorrect $\Sigma x^2 = n[\sigma^2 + \bar{x}^2]$

$= 200\,[15^2 + 40^2] = 365000$

Corrected

$\Sigma x^2 = 365000 - 2500 + 1600 = 364100$

$\therefore$Corrected $\sigma = \sqrt{\frac{364100}{200} - (39.95)^2}$

$= \sqrt{(1820.5 - 1596)}$

$= \sqrt{224.5}$

$= 14.98$

Hence, sum $= 39.95 + 14.98 = 54.93$

24. (28.80) If $x_1, x_2, x_3, x_4, \ldots\ldots, x_n$ have standard deviation σ, then $x_1 + \alpha, x_2 + \alpha, x_3 + \alpha, x_4 + \alpha, \ldots\ldots, x_n + \alpha$ also have SD (σ). So, standard deviation of new wages = ₹ 28.80

25. (1.5) $\sum_{j=1}^{18}(x_j - 8) = 9 \Rightarrow \sum_{j=1}^{18} x_j = 153$

and $\sum_{j=1}^{18}(x_j - 8)^2 = 45$

$\Rightarrow \sum_{j=1}^{18}(x_j^2 - 16x_j + 64) = 45$

$\Rightarrow \sum_{j=1}^{18} x_j^2 = 45 - (64 \times 18) + 16\sum_{j=1}^{18} x_j$

$= 45 - 1152 + 2448 = 1341$

$\therefore$Standard deviation

$(\sigma) = \sqrt{\frac{\Sigma x_j^2}{n} - \left(\frac{\Sigma x_j}{n}\right)^2}$

$= \sqrt{\frac{1341}{18} - \left(\frac{153}{18}\right)^2}$

$= \sqrt{74.5 - 72.25} = 1.5$

26. (2) Suppose, the student attempts m questions correctly and $(30 - m)$ questions incorrectly. Then, his total score is $4m$.

$\therefore \quad \bar{x} = \frac{4m}{30} = \frac{2}{15}m$

and $30\sigma^2 = m\left(4 - \frac{2}{15}m\right)^2 + (30-m)\left(0 - \frac{2}{15}m\right)^2$

$= m\left(16 - \frac{16}{15}m + \frac{4m^2}{225}\right) + \frac{8}{15}m^2 - \frac{4}{225}m^3$

$\Rightarrow 30\sigma^2 = 16\,m - \frac{8}{15}m^2$

$= \frac{8}{15}(30m - m^2)$

$= \frac{8}{15}[15^2 - (15-m)^2]$

Thus, σ^2 is maximum, when $m = 15$ and maximum possible value of σ^2 is 4.

$\therefore$ Maximum possible value of σ is 2.

27. (14) Let x and y be the remaining two observations.

Then, mean = 8

$\Rightarrow \frac{2 + 4 + 10 + 12 + 14 + x + y}{7} = 8$

$\Rightarrow 42 + x + y = 56$

$\Rightarrow \quad x + y = 14 \quad ...(i)$

Variance = 16

$\Rightarrow \frac{1}{7}[2^2 + 4^2 + 10^2 + 12^2 + 14^2 + x^2 + y^2] - (\text{mean})^2 = 16$

$\Rightarrow \frac{1}{7}(4 + 16 + 100 + 144 + 196 + x^2 + y^2) - 64 = 16$

$\Rightarrow \quad 460 + x^2 + y^2 = 7 \times 80$

$\Rightarrow \quad x^2 + y^2 = 100 \quad ...(ii)$

Now, $(x+y)^2 + (x-y)^2 = 2(x^2 + y^2)$

$\Rightarrow \quad 196 + (x-y)^2 = 2 \times 100$

[using Eqs. (i) and (ii)]

$\Rightarrow (x-y)^2 = 4 \Rightarrow x - y = \pm 2$

If $x - y = 2$ and $x + y = 14$, then $x = 8$ and $y = 6$

If $x - y = -2$ and $x + y = 14$, then $x = 6$ and $y = 8$

So, the remaining two observations are 6 and 8.

Hence, sum $= 6 + 8 = 14$

28. (1) $\sigma_x^2 = \frac{\Sigma d_i^2}{n}$ (here, deviations are taken from the mean). Since, A and B both have 100 consecutive integers, therefore both have same standard deviation and hence the variance.

$\therefore \frac{V_A}{V_B} = 1$ (as Σd_i^2 is same in both the cases).

29. (8.25) The first 10 positive integers are 1, 2, 3, 4, 5, 6, 7, 8, 9 and 10. On multiplying each number by (-1), we get

$-1, -2, -3, -4, -5, -6, -7, -8, -9$ and -10

On adding 1 to each number, we have $0, -1, -2, -3, -4, -5, -6, -7, -8$ and -9

$\therefore \Sigma x_i = \frac{-9 \times 10}{2} = -45$

[using $1 + 2 + 3 + \ldots + n = \frac{n(n+1)}{2}$]

and $\Sigma x_i^2 = 0^2 + (-1)^2 + (-2)^2 + (-3)^2 + (-4)^2 + (-5)^2 + (-6)^2 + (-7)^2 + (-8)^2 + (-9)^2$

$= \frac{9 \times 10 \times 19}{6} = 285$

$\left(\text{using } 1^2 + 2^2 + 3^2 + \ldots + n^2 = \frac{n(n+1)(2n+1)}{6}\right)$

$\therefore \text{SD} = \sqrt{\frac{285}{10} - \left(-\frac{45}{10}\right)^2}$

$= \sqrt{\frac{285}{10} - \frac{2025}{100}}$

$= \sqrt{\frac{2850 - 2025}{100}}$

$= \sqrt{8.25}$

Hence, variance $= (\text{SD})^2$

$= (\sqrt{8.25})^2$

$= 8.25$

30. (16) We know that, for positive real numbers $x_1, x_2, x_3, \ldots\ldots, x_n$.

We have,

$$\frac{\Sigma x_i^2}{n} \ge \left(\frac{\Sigma x_i}{n}\right)^2 \Rightarrow \frac{400}{n} \ge \left(\frac{80}{n}\right)^2$$

$$\Rightarrow \frac{400}{n} \ge \frac{6400}{n^2} \Rightarrow \frac{1}{n} \ge \frac{16}{n^2}$$

$(\because n > 0 \text{ always})$

$$\therefore n \times \frac{1}{n} \ge n \times \frac{16}{n^2} \Rightarrow \frac{16}{n} \le 1$$

$$\Rightarrow n \ge 16$$

Hence, minimum possible value of $n = 16$.

Qualifier 15
(Vector Algebra)

1. (d) Let $\mathbf{a} = \hat{i} + \lambda\hat{j} + 3\hat{k}$

and $\mathbf{b} = 4\hat{i} + (4\lambda - 2)\hat{j} + 2\hat{k}$

$= 2[2\hat{i} + (2\lambda - 1)\hat{j} + \hat{k}]$

Since, doubling (the magnitude) does not change the direction cosines of a vector.

$\therefore$Before doubling (the vector on rotation) $= 2\hat{i} + (2\lambda - 1)\hat{j} + \hat{k} = \mathbf{c}$ (say)

As well as, the length of vector remains same, i.e. $|\mathbf{a}| = |\mathbf{c}|$

$$\Rightarrow |\mathbf{a}|^2 = |\mathbf{c}|^2$$

$$\Rightarrow 1 + \lambda^2 + 9 = 4 + (2\lambda - 1)^2 + 1$$

$$\Rightarrow 10 + \lambda^2 = 4 + 4\lambda^2 + 1 - 4\lambda + 1$$

$$\Rightarrow 3\lambda^2 - 4\lambda - 4 = 0$$

$$\Rightarrow (\lambda - 2)(3\lambda + 2) = 0$$

$$\Rightarrow \lambda = 2, -\frac{2}{3}$$

2. (c) Given, $\mathbf{OP} = \mathbf{a} = \hat{i} + 3\hat{j} - 2\hat{k}$

and $\mathbf{OQ} = \mathbf{b} = 3\hat{i} - \hat{j} - 2\hat{k}$

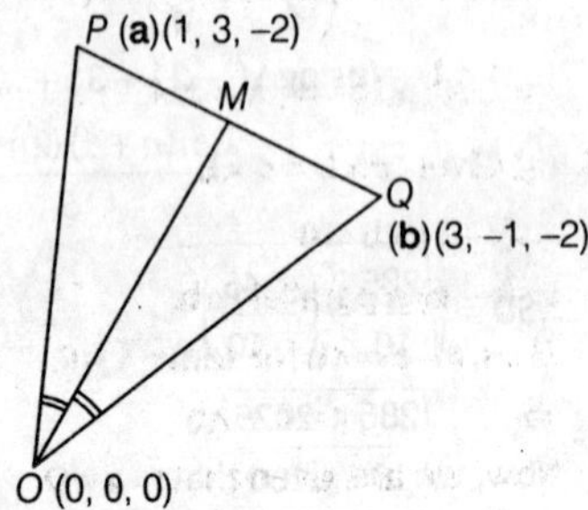

Since, OM is bisector of $\angle POQ$.

$$\therefore \frac{PM}{MQ} = \frac{OP}{OQ}$$

$$\Rightarrow \frac{PM}{MQ} = \frac{\sqrt{14}}{\sqrt{14}} = 1$$

$$\Rightarrow PM = MQ$$

$\therefore M$ is mid-point of PQ, then

$$M \equiv \left(\frac{1+3}{2}, \frac{3-1}{2}, \frac{-2-2}{2}\right) = (2, 1, -2)$$

Hence, $\mathbf{OM} = 2\hat{i} + \hat{j} - 2\hat{k}$.

3. (b) $\mathbf{OP} = \frac{5\hat{i}}{k+1} + \frac{(5k)\hat{j}}{k+1} = \frac{5\hat{i} + (5k)\hat{j}}{k+1}$

$$\mathbf{PO} = \mathbf{b} = \frac{-5\hat{i} - 5k\hat{j}}{k+1} = -\mathbf{OP}$$

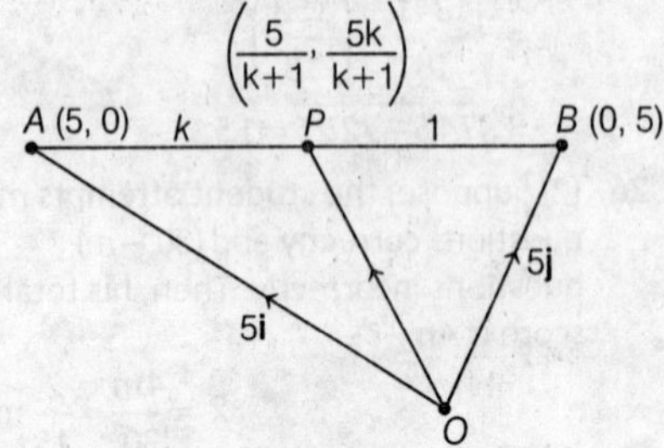

Given, $|\mathbf{b}| \le \sqrt{37} \Rightarrow \frac{25 + 25k^2}{(k+1)^2} \le 37$

$$\Rightarrow 25 + 25k^2 \le 37k^2 + 74k + 37$$

$$\Rightarrow 12k^2 + 74k + 12 \ge 0$$

$$\Rightarrow 6k^2 + 37k + 6 \ge 0$$

$$\Rightarrow 6k(k+6) + 1(k+6) \ge 0$$

$$\Rightarrow (k+6)(6k+1) \ge 0$$

$$\Rightarrow (k+6)\left(k + \frac{1}{6}\right) \ge 0$$

$$\Rightarrow (k - (-6))\left(k - \left(-\frac{1}{6}\right)\right) \ge 0$$

$$\Rightarrow K \in (-\infty, -6] \cup \left[-\frac{1}{6}, \infty\right)$$

4. (a) Given, $\alpha + \beta + \gamma = a\delta$ ...(i)

$\beta + \gamma + \delta = b\alpha$ ...(ii)

From Eq. (i),

$\alpha + \beta + \gamma + \delta = (a+1)\delta$ ...(iii)

From Eq. (ii),

$\alpha + \beta + \gamma + \delta = (b+1)\alpha$ ...(iv)

So, from Eqs. (iii) and (iv), we have

$(a+1)\delta = (b+1)\alpha$ ...(v)

Given, α is not parallel to δ.

Hence, $a + 1 = 0$ and $b + 1 = 0$ [From Eq. (v)]

From Eq. (iii), $\alpha + \beta + \gamma + \delta = 0$

5. (d) Given, $\mathbf{a} = \hat{i} + \hat{j} + \hat{k}$,

$\mathbf{b} = 4\hat{i} + 3\hat{j} + 4\hat{k}$ and $\mathbf{c} = \hat{i} + \alpha\hat{j} + \beta\hat{k}$

Also given $\mathbf{a}, \mathbf{b}, \mathbf{c}$ are linearly dependent.

So, linear combination

$1 \cdot (\hat{i} + \hat{j} + \hat{k}) + \lambda(4\hat{i} + 3\hat{j} + 4\hat{k}) + \mu$

$(\hat{i} + \alpha\hat{j} + \beta\hat{k}) = 0 \cdot \hat{i} + 0 \cdot \hat{j} + 0 \cdot \hat{k}$

where λ and μ are scalars.

$\Rightarrow (1 + 4\lambda + \mu)\hat{i} + (1 + 3\lambda + \alpha\mu)\hat{j}$

$+ (1 + 4\lambda + \beta\mu)\hat{k} = 0 \cdot \hat{i} + 0 \cdot \hat{j} + 0 \cdot \hat{k}$

Therefore,

$1 + 4\lambda + \mu = 0 \Rightarrow 4\lambda + \mu = -1$ ...(i)

$1 + 3\lambda + \alpha\mu = 0 \Rightarrow 3\lambda + \alpha\mu = -1$ ...(ii)

$1 + 4\lambda + \beta\mu = 0 \Rightarrow 4\lambda + \beta\mu = -1$ ...(iii)

Also, given $|\mathbf{c}| = \sqrt{3} \Rightarrow |\mathbf{c}|^2 = 3$

$\Rightarrow 1 + \alpha^2 + \beta^2 = 3 \Rightarrow \alpha^2 + \beta^2 = 2$ ...(iv)

From Eqs. (i) and (iii), we get

$$4\lambda + \mu = 4\lambda + \beta\mu \Rightarrow \beta = 1$$

From Eq. (iv); $\alpha^2 + (1)^2 = 2 \Rightarrow \alpha = \pm 1$

6. (b) Given, $A \equiv (-4, 0, 3)$ and $B \equiv (14, 2, -5)$

$\therefore \mathbf{OA} = -4\hat{i} + 3\hat{k}$, $\mathbf{OB} = 14\hat{i} + 2\hat{j} - 5\hat{k}$

$$\Rightarrow \mathbf{OA} = \frac{-4\hat{i} + 3\hat{k}}{5}, \mathbf{OB} = \frac{14\hat{i} + 2\hat{j} - 5\hat{k}}{15}$$

Any vector in the direction of angle bisectors of the form $\lambda(\hat{\mathbf{a}} + \hat{\mathbf{b}})$.

So, a vector in the direction of angle bisector of **OA** and **OB**

$$= \lambda\left(\frac{-4\hat{i} + 3\hat{k}}{5} + \frac{14\hat{i} + 2\hat{j} - 5\hat{k}}{15}\right)$$

$$= \frac{\lambda}{15}(2\hat{i} + 2\hat{j} + 4\hat{k}) = \frac{2\lambda}{15}(\hat{i} + \hat{j} + 2\hat{k})$$

Hence, option (b) is correct with $\lambda = \frac{15}{2}$.

7. (c) As we know that, the incident ray, reflected ray and normal lie in a plane and angle of incidence = angle of reflection.

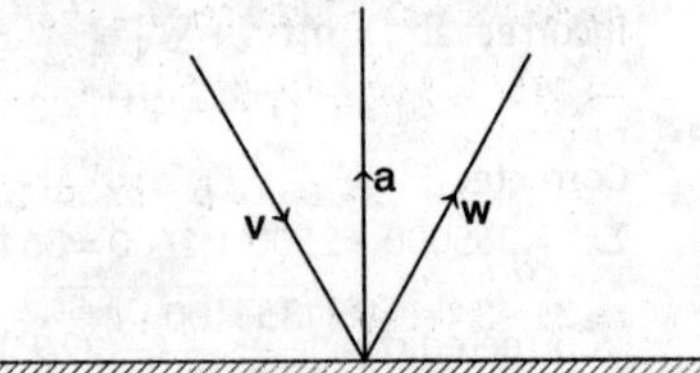

Fig. (a) According to question

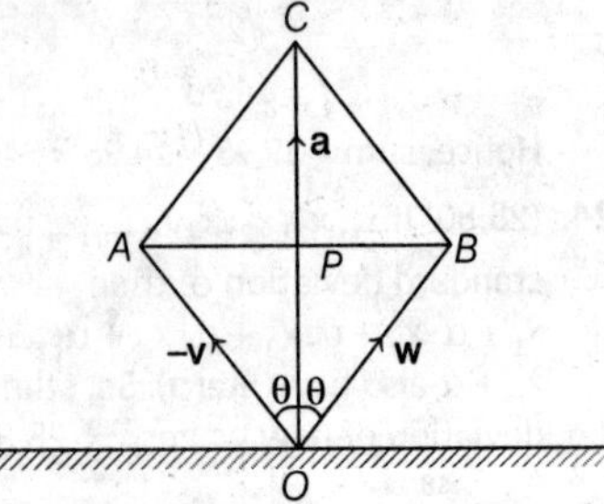

Fig. (b) Constructed/Construction in fig (a)

Thus, $\hat{\mathbf{a}}$ will be along the angle bisector of $\hat{\mathbf{w}}$ and $(-\hat{\mathbf{v}})$.

$$\therefore \hat{\mathbf{a}} = \frac{\hat{\mathbf{w}} - \hat{\mathbf{v}}}{|\hat{\mathbf{w}} - \hat{\mathbf{v}}|}$$

Now, $|\hat{\mathbf{w}} - \hat{\mathbf{v}}| = OC = 2 \cdot OP$

$= 2|\hat{\mathbf{w}}| \cos\theta = 2\cos\theta$

$$\therefore \hat{\mathbf{a}} = \frac{\hat{\mathbf{w}} - \hat{\mathbf{v}}}{2\cos\theta} \Rightarrow \hat{\mathbf{w}} = \hat{\mathbf{v}} + 2\cos\theta\hat{\mathbf{a}}$$

$\Rightarrow \hat{\mathbf{w}} = \hat{\mathbf{v}} - 2(-\cos\theta)\,\hat{\mathbf{a}}$

$\Rightarrow \hat{\mathbf{w}} = \hat{\mathbf{v}} - 2(\hat{\mathbf{a}} \cdot \hat{\mathbf{v}})\,\hat{\mathbf{a}}$

$$\left[\begin{array}{l} \because \hat{\mathbf{a}} \cdot \hat{\mathbf{v}} = |\mathbf{a}||\mathbf{v}|\cos(\pi - \theta) \\ \Rightarrow \hat{\mathbf{a}} \cdot \hat{\mathbf{v}} = |1 \times 1| \times (-\cos\theta) \\ \Rightarrow \hat{\mathbf{a}} \cdot \hat{\mathbf{v}} = -\cos\theta \end{array}\right]$$

8. (b) The required vector **c** is given by

$$\lambda\left(\frac{\mathbf{a}}{a} + \frac{\mathbf{b}}{b}\right)$$

Now, $\dfrac{\mathbf{a}}{a} = \dfrac{1}{9}(7\hat{\mathbf{i}} - 4\hat{\mathbf{j}} - 4\hat{\mathbf{k}})$

and $\dfrac{\mathbf{b}}{|\mathbf{b}|} = \dfrac{1}{3}(-2\hat{\mathbf{i}} - \hat{\mathbf{j}} + 2\hat{\mathbf{k}})$

$$\Rightarrow \quad \mathbf{c} = \lambda\left(\frac{1}{9}\hat{\mathbf{i}} - \frac{7}{9}\hat{\mathbf{j}} + \frac{2}{9}\hat{\mathbf{k}}\right)$$

$$\Rightarrow \quad |\mathbf{c}|^2 = \lambda^2 \times \frac{27}{81} \times 2$$

$(\because |\mathbf{c}| = 5\sqrt{6}$, given)

Therefore, $\lambda^2 = 225$ or $\lambda = \pm 15$

$$c = +\frac{5}{3}(\hat{\mathbf{i}} - 7\hat{\mathbf{j}} + 2\mathbf{k})$$

9. (a) Given, $|\mathbf{a}| = 2\,|\mathbf{b}| = 4\,|\mathbf{c}|$ ...(i)

Also, $2\mathbf{a} - 3\mathbf{b} + 6\mathbf{c} = 0$

$\Rightarrow 2\mathbf{a} - 3\mathbf{b} = -6\mathbf{c} \Rightarrow |2\mathbf{a} - 3\mathbf{b}|^2 = 36|\mathbf{c}|^2$

$\Rightarrow 4\mathbf{a}^2 + 9\mathbf{b}^2 - 12\mathbf{a} \cdot \mathbf{b} = 36\mathbf{c}^2$

$\Rightarrow 4a^2 + 9b^2 - 12ab\cos\theta = 36c^2$

$\Rightarrow 16b^2 + 9b^2 - 12 \cdot 2b^2 \cdot \cos\theta$

$= 36 \cdot \dfrac{1}{4} \cdot b^2$ [from Eq. (i)]

$\Rightarrow 25 - 24\cos\theta = 9 \Rightarrow \cos\theta = \dfrac{2}{3}$

10. (b) Component vector of projection of $\mathbf{a} = (6\hat{\mathbf{i}} - 3\hat{\mathbf{j}} - 6\hat{\mathbf{k}})$ on

$$\mathbf{b} = (\hat{\mathbf{i}} + \hat{\mathbf{j}} + \hat{\mathbf{k}}) = \frac{\mathbf{a} \cdot \mathbf{b}}{(\mathbf{b})^2}\mathbf{b}$$

$$= \frac{-3}{3}(\hat{\mathbf{i}} + \hat{\mathbf{j}} + \hat{\mathbf{k}}) = -(\hat{\mathbf{i}} + \hat{\mathbf{j}} + \hat{\mathbf{k}})$$

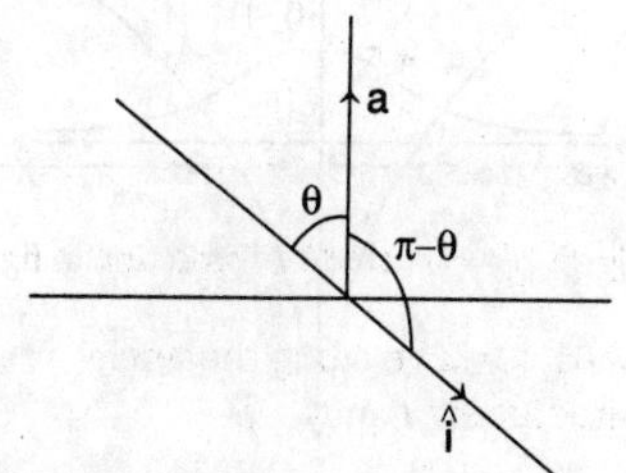

The perpendicular component

$= \mathbf{a} + (\hat{\mathbf{i}} + \hat{\mathbf{j}} + \hat{\mathbf{k}})$

$= (6\hat{\mathbf{i}} - 3\hat{\mathbf{j}} - 6\hat{\mathbf{k}}) + (\hat{\mathbf{i}} + \hat{\mathbf{j}} + \hat{\mathbf{k}})$

$= 7\hat{\mathbf{i}} - 2\hat{\mathbf{j}} - 5\mathbf{k}$

11. (d) Let $\mathbf{c} = \langle c_1, c_2, c_3 \rangle$, then

$|\mathbf{c}| = |\mathbf{a}| = |\mathbf{b}| = \sqrt{2} = \sqrt{c_1^2 + c_2^2 + c_3^2}$

It is given that the angles between the vectors are identical, and equal to θ (say). Then,

$$\cos\theta = \frac{\mathbf{a} \cdot \mathbf{b}}{|\mathbf{a}||\mathbf{b}|} = \frac{0 + 1 + 0}{\sqrt{2}\,\sqrt{2}} = \frac{1}{2}$$

$$\frac{\mathbf{a} \cdot \mathbf{c}}{|\mathbf{a}||\mathbf{c}|} = \frac{c_1 + c_2}{\sqrt{2}\,\sqrt{2}} = \frac{1}{2}$$

and $\dfrac{\mathbf{b}.\mathbf{c}}{|\mathbf{b}||\mathbf{c}|} = \dfrac{c_2 + c_3}{2} = \dfrac{1}{2}$

Hence, $c_1 + c_2 = 1$ and $c_2 + c_3 = 1$

i.e. $c_1 = 1 - c_2$ and $c_3 = 1 - c_2$.

$\Rightarrow 2 = c_1^2 + c_2^2 + c_3^2 = (1 - c_2)^2 + c_2^2 + (1 - c_2)^2 = 3c_2^2 + 2 - 4c_2$

Therefore, $c_2 = 0$ or $c_2 = \dfrac{4}{3}$.

If $c_2 = 0$, then $c_1 = 1$ and $c_3 = 1$ and if $c_2 = 4/3$, then $c_1 = -\dfrac{1}{3}$, $c_3 = -\dfrac{1}{3}$.

Hence the coordinates of c are

$(1, 0, 1)$ or $\left(-\dfrac{1}{3}, \dfrac{4}{3}, -\dfrac{1}{3}\right)$.

12. (c) Given, $\mathbf{a} = a_1\hat{\mathbf{i}} + a_2\hat{\mathbf{j}} + a_3\hat{\mathbf{k}}$,

$\mathbf{b} = b_1\hat{\mathbf{i}} + b_2\hat{\mathbf{j}} + b_3\hat{\mathbf{k}}$ and

$\mathbf{c} = c_1\hat{\mathbf{i}} + c_2\hat{\mathbf{j}} + c_3\hat{\mathbf{k}}$

Also given is a unit vector perpendicular to both **a** and **b**.

So, $|\mathbf{c}| = 1$

$\Rightarrow \quad c_1^2 + c_2^2 + c_3^2 = 1$

and $\mathbf{a} \cdot \mathbf{c} = 0$ and $\mathbf{b} \cdot \mathbf{c} = 0$

$\Rightarrow a_1c_1 + a_2c_2 + a_3c_3 = 0$

and $b_1c_1 + b_2c_2 + b_3c_3 = 0$

Now, angle between **a** and **b** is $\dfrac{\pi}{6}$.

$$\therefore \cos\frac{\pi}{6} = \frac{a_1b_1 + a_2b_2 + a_3b_3}{\sqrt{a_1^2 + a_2^2 + a_3^2}\,\sqrt{b_1^2 + b_2^2 + b_3^2}}$$

$$\Rightarrow \frac{\sqrt{3}}{2}(a_1^2 + a_2^2 + a_3^2)^{1/2}(b_1^2 + b_2^2 + b_3^2)^{1/2} = a_1b_1 + a_2b_2 + a_3b_3$$

Now,

$$\begin{vmatrix} a_1 & b_1 & c_1 \\ a_2 & b_2 & c_2 \\ a_3 & b_3 & c_3 \end{vmatrix}^2 = \begin{vmatrix} a_1 & b_1 & c_1 \\ a_2 & b_2 & c_2 \\ a_3 & b_3 & c_3 \end{vmatrix}\begin{vmatrix} a_1 & b_1 & c_1 \\ a_2 & b_2 & c_2 \\ a_3 & b_3 & c_3 \end{vmatrix}$$

$$= \begin{vmatrix} a_1^2 + a_2^2 + a_3^2 & a_1b_1 + a_2b_2 + a_3b_3 & a_1c_1 + a_2c_2 + a_3c_3 \\ a_1b_1 + a_2b_2 + a_3b_3 & b_1^2 + b_2^2 + b_3^2 & b_1c_1 + b_2c_2 + b_3c_3 \\ a_1c_1 + a_2c_2 + a_3c_3 & b_1c_1 + b_2c_2 + b_3c_3 & c_1^2 + c_2^2 + c_3^2 \end{vmatrix}$$

$$= \begin{vmatrix} a_1^2 + a_2^2 + a_3^2 & a_1b_1 + a_2b_2 + a_3b_3 & 0 \\ a_1b_1 + a_2b_2 + a_3b_3 & b_1^2 + b_2^2 + b_3^2 & 0 \\ 0 & 0 & 1 \end{vmatrix}$$

$$= (a_1^2 + a_2^2 + a_3^2)(b_1^2 + b_2^2 + b_3^2) - (a_1b_1 + a_2b_2 + a_3b_3)^2$$

$$= (a_1^2 + a_2^2 + a_3^2)(b_1^2 + b_2^2 + b_3^2) - \frac{3}{4}(a_1^2 + a_2^2 + a_3^2)(b_1^2 + b_2^2 + b_3^2)$$

$$= \frac{1}{4}(a_1^2 + a_2^2 + a_3^2)(b_1^2 + b_2^2 + b_3^2)$$

13. (c) Given, $|\mathbf{a}| = |\mathbf{c}| = 1$, $|\mathbf{b}| = 4$,

$\mathbf{b} - 2\mathbf{c} = \lambda\mathbf{a}$ ...(i)

and $|\mathbf{b} \times \mathbf{c}| = \sqrt{15}$.

$\Rightarrow |\mathbf{b}||\mathbf{c}|\sin\theta = \sqrt{15}$, where we assume θ is the angle between **b** and **c**.

$$\Rightarrow \quad \sin\theta = \frac{\sqrt{15}}{4}$$

$$\therefore \quad \cos\theta = \frac{1}{4}$$

From Eq. (i), $\quad \mathbf{b} - 2\mathbf{c} = \lambda\mathbf{a}$

On squarring, $\quad (\mathbf{b} - 2\mathbf{c})^2 = (\lambda\mathbf{a})^2$

$\Rightarrow \quad (\mathbf{b})^2 + 4(\mathbf{c})^2 - 4\mathbf{b} \cdot \mathbf{c} = \lambda^2(\mathbf{a})^2$

$\Rightarrow (4)^2 + 4(1)^2 - 4(|\mathbf{b}||\mathbf{c}|\cos\theta) = \lambda^2(1)^2$

$\Rightarrow 16 + 4 - 4\left(4 \times 1 \times \dfrac{1}{4}\right) = \lambda^2$

$\Rightarrow \quad \lambda^2 = 16 \Rightarrow \lambda = \pm 4$

14. (a) Given, $\mathbf{r} \times \mathbf{b} = \mathbf{c} \times \mathbf{b}$

$\Rightarrow (\mathbf{r} - \mathbf{c}) \times \mathbf{b} = 0$

$\Rightarrow (\mathbf{r} - \mathbf{c})$ is parallel to **b**.

Thus, $\mathbf{r} - \mathbf{c} = \lambda\mathbf{b}$ for some $\lambda \in R$.

$\Rightarrow \quad \mathbf{r} = \mathbf{c} + \lambda\mathbf{b}$ ...(i)

Now, we are given that $\mathbf{r} \cdot \mathbf{a} = 0$

$\Rightarrow \quad (\mathbf{c} + \lambda\mathbf{b}) \cdot \mathbf{a} = 0$

$\Rightarrow \quad \mathbf{a} \cdot \mathbf{c} + \lambda\mathbf{a} \cdot \mathbf{b} = 0$

$$\Rightarrow \lambda = -\frac{\mathbf{a} \cdot \mathbf{c}}{\mathbf{a} \cdot \mathbf{b}} = -\frac{8 + 7}{2 + 0 + 1} = -5$$

From Eq. (i),

$\mathbf{r} = \mathbf{c} + \lambda\mathbf{b} = \mathbf{c} - 5\mathbf{b} = (4\hat{\mathbf{i}} - 3\hat{\mathbf{j}} + 7\hat{\mathbf{k}}) - 5(\hat{\mathbf{i}} + \hat{\mathbf{j}} + \hat{\mathbf{k}}) = -\hat{\mathbf{i}} - 8\hat{\mathbf{j}} + 2\hat{\mathbf{k}}$

$\Rightarrow x\hat{i}+y\hat{j}+z\hat{k}=-\hat{i}-8\hat{j}+2\hat{k}$

$\therefore \quad x+y+z=-7$

$\Rightarrow \quad |x+y+z|=|-7|=7$

15. (d) Given, angle between and $=\cos^{-1}(1/4)=\theta$ (say)

$\therefore \quad \cos\theta=\frac{1}{4}$

and $|\ |=|\ |=1, |\ |=4$

Also given, $\times \ =2\ \times$

$\Rightarrow \quad =\lambda\ +2$

$\Rightarrow \frac{-2}{\lambda}= \Rightarrow \times\ -2\ \times\ =0$

$\Rightarrow \quad \times\ -\ \times 2\ =0$

$\Rightarrow \quad \times(\ -2\ )=0$

$\therefore$ is collinear to $(\ -2\ )$.

$\Rightarrow -2\ =\lambda \Rightarrow (\ -2\ )^2=\lambda^2|\ |^2$

$\Rightarrow |\ |^2+4|\ |^2-4|\ ||\ |\cos\theta=\lambda^2|\ |^2$

$\Rightarrow 16+4(1)^2-4\times4\times1\times\frac{1}{4}=\lambda^2$

$\Rightarrow \lambda^2=16 \Rightarrow \lambda=\pm 4$

16. (d) Given, **a**, **b**, **c** are three mutually **orthogonal unit** vectors.

So, $|\mathbf{a}|=|\mathbf{b}|=|\mathbf{c}|=1$

as well as $\mathbf{a}\cdot\mathbf{b}=\mathbf{b}\cdot\mathbf{c}=\mathbf{c}\cdot\mathbf{a}=0$

Now, $[\mathbf{a}+\mathbf{b}+\mathbf{c}\ \ \mathbf{a}+\mathbf{b}\ \ \mathbf{b}+\mathbf{c}]$

$=(\mathbf{a}+\mathbf{b}+\mathbf{c})\cdot\{(\mathbf{a}+\mathbf{b})\times(\mathbf{b}+\mathbf{c})\}$

$=(\mathbf{a}+\mathbf{b}+\mathbf{c})\cdot\{(\mathbf{a}\times\mathbf{b}+\mathbf{a}\times\mathbf{c}+\mathbf{b}\times\mathbf{c})\}$

$(\because \mathbf{b}\times\mathbf{b}=\mathbf{0})$

$=[\mathbf{a}\ \mathbf{b}\ \mathbf{c}]+[\mathbf{b}\ \mathbf{a}\ \mathbf{c}]+[\mathbf{c}\ \mathbf{a}\ \mathbf{b}]$

$=[\mathbf{a}\ \mathbf{b}\ \mathbf{c}]-[\mathbf{a}\ \mathbf{b}\ \mathbf{c}]+[\mathbf{a}\ \mathbf{b}\ \mathbf{c}]=[\mathbf{a}\ \mathbf{b}\ \mathbf{c}]$

Since, we know that,

$$[\mathbf{a}\ \mathbf{b}\ \mathbf{c}]^2=\begin{vmatrix}\mathbf{a}\cdot\mathbf{a} & \mathbf{a}\cdot\mathbf{b} & \mathbf{a}\cdot\mathbf{c}\\ \mathbf{b}\cdot\mathbf{a} & \mathbf{b}\cdot\mathbf{b} & \mathbf{b}\cdot\mathbf{c}\\ \mathbf{c}\cdot\mathbf{a} & \mathbf{c}\cdot\mathbf{b} & \mathbf{c}\cdot\mathbf{c}\end{vmatrix}=\begin{vmatrix}1&0&0\\0&1&0\\0&0&1\end{vmatrix}$$

$\Rightarrow [\mathbf{a}\ \mathbf{b}\ \mathbf{c}]^2=1(1-0)=1$

$\therefore \quad [\mathbf{a}\ \mathbf{b}\ \mathbf{c}]=\pm 1$

17. (a) Given, $\mathbf{p}=\mathbf{a}+\mathbf{b}-2\mathbf{c}$, $\mathbf{q}=3\mathbf{a}-2\mathbf{b}+\mathbf{c}$ and $\mathbf{r}=\mathbf{a}-4\mathbf{b}+2\mathbf{c}$

Also given, $V_1=[\mathbf{a}\ \mathbf{b}\ \mathbf{c}]$

and $\quad V_2=[\mathbf{p}\ \mathbf{q}\ \mathbf{r}]$

Hence,

$$V_2=[\mathbf{p}\ \mathbf{q}\ \mathbf{r}]=\begin{vmatrix}1&1&-2\\3&-2&1\\1&-4&2\end{vmatrix}[\mathbf{a}\ \mathbf{b}\ \mathbf{c}]$$

$\Rightarrow \quad V_2=\{1(-4+4)-1(6-1)-2(-12+2)\}[\mathbf{a}\ \mathbf{b}\ \mathbf{c}]$

$\Rightarrow \quad V_2=(0-5+20)[\mathbf{a}\ \mathbf{b}\ \mathbf{c}]$

$\Rightarrow \quad V_2=15[\mathbf{a}\ \mathbf{b}\ \mathbf{c}]$

Hence, $\frac{V_2}{V_1}=\frac{15[\mathbf{a}\ \mathbf{b}\ \mathbf{c}]}{1\cdot[\mathbf{a}\ \mathbf{b}\ \mathbf{c}]}=\frac{15}{1}=15:1$

18. (d) Given, $|\mathbf{u}|=\sqrt{3}, |\mathbf{v}|=1, |\mathbf{w}|=2$

$\mathbf{u}\times(\mathbf{u}\times\mathbf{w})+3\mathbf{v}=0$

$\Rightarrow \quad (\mathbf{u}\cdot\mathbf{w})\mathbf{u}-(\mathbf{u}\cdot\mathbf{u})\mathbf{w}=-3\mathbf{v}$

(using vector triple product)

$\Rightarrow (|\mathbf{u}||\mathbf{w}|\cos\theta)\mathbf{u}-(3)\mathbf{w}=-3\mathbf{v}$

(given angle between **u** and **w** $=\theta$)

$\Rightarrow (2\sqrt{3}\cos\theta)\mathbf{u}-3\mathbf{w}=-3\mathbf{v}$

Squaring on both sides, we get

$|\mathbf{u}|^2\cdot(2\sqrt{3}\cos\theta)^2+9|\mathbf{w}|^2$

$-12\sqrt{3}\cos\theta|\mathbf{u}||\mathbf{w}|\cos\theta=9|\mathbf{v}|^2$

$(\because \mathbf{a}^2=\mathbf{a}\cdot\mathbf{a}=(\mathbf{a})^2=|\mathbf{a}|^2)$

$\Rightarrow 3\times12\cos^2\theta+9\times4-72\cos^2\theta=9$

$\Rightarrow \quad 36\cos^2\theta=36-9$

$\Rightarrow \quad \cos^2\theta=\frac{27}{36}=\frac{3}{4}$

19. (b)

$|\ |=1, |\ |=5, |\ |=3$

$\Rightarrow \quad \times(\ \times\ )=$

$\Rightarrow |\ \times(\ \times\ )|=|\ |$

$\Rightarrow |\ ||\ \times\ |\sin 90^\circ=|\ |$

$\Rightarrow \quad |\ ||\ ||\ |\sin\theta=|\ |$

$\Rightarrow \quad 5\sin\theta=3$

$\Rightarrow \quad \sin\theta=\frac{3}{5}$

$\therefore \quad \tan\theta=\frac{3}{4}$

20. (a) Equation of line joining $6\mathbf{a}-4\mathbf{b}-5\mathbf{c}$ and $-4\mathbf{c}$ is

$\mathbf{r}=(6\mathbf{a}-4\mathbf{b}-5\mathbf{c})+\lambda(-6\mathbf{a}+4\mathbf{b}+\mathbf{c})$

$\Rightarrow \mathbf{r}=\mathbf{a}(6-6\lambda)+\mathbf{b}(-4+4\lambda)+\mathbf{c}(-5+\lambda)$ ...(i)

and equation of line joining $-\mathbf{a}-2\mathbf{b}-3\mathbf{c}$ and $\mathbf{a}+2\mathbf{b}-5\mathbf{c}$ is

$\mathbf{r}=(-\mathbf{a}-2\mathbf{b}-3\mathbf{c})+\mu(2\mathbf{a}+4\mathbf{b}-2\mathbf{c})$

$=\mathbf{a}(-1+2\mu)+\mathbf{b}(-2+4\mu)+\mathbf{c}(-3-2\mu)$ ... (ii)

On comparing Eqs. (i) and (ii), we get

$6-6\lambda=-1+2\mu, -4+4\lambda=-2+4\mu$ and $-5+\lambda=-3-2\mu$

After solving, we get $\lambda=1, \mu=\frac{1}{2}$

Hence, the point of intersection is $\mathbf{r}=-4\mathbf{c}$. [on putting $\lambda=1$ in Eq. (i)]

21. (0) Let $\mathbf{a}+2\mathbf{b}=x\mathbf{c}$ and $\mathbf{b}+3\mathbf{c}=y\mathbf{a}$.

Then, $\mathbf{a}+2\mathbf{b}+6\mathbf{c}=(x+6)\mathbf{c}$

and also, $\mathbf{a}+2\mathbf{b}+6\mathbf{c}=(1+2y)\mathbf{a}$

So, $(x+6)\mathbf{c}=(1+2y)\mathbf{a}$

$\because$ **a** and **c** are non-zero and non-collinear, then

$x+6=0$ and $1+2y=0$

i.e. $x=-6$ and $y=-\frac{1}{2}$.

In either case, we have

$\mathbf{a}+2\mathbf{b}+6\mathbf{c}=$

$\Rightarrow \quad |\mathbf{a}+2\mathbf{b}+6\mathbf{c}|=0$

22. (2) $\because |\mathbf{a}+\mathbf{b}|=|\mathbf{a}|+|\mathbf{b}|$

$\therefore \mathbf{a}||\mathbf{b}$

Given, $\mathbf{a}=\hat{i}+\lambda\hat{j}+\hat{k}$

and $\quad \mathbf{b}=\hat{i}+\hat{j}+\hat{k}$

So, $\lambda=1$ because $\mathbf{a}||\mathbf{b}$.

Now, $f(x)=\int_0^{x^2}\log_2(1+t^2)dt$

$\Rightarrow \quad f'(x)=\log_2(1+x^4)\cdot 2x+0$

$\Rightarrow \quad f'(\lambda)=2\cdot\lambda\cdot\log_2(1+\lambda^4)$

Hence, $f'(1)=2\times1\times\log_2(1+1)$

$=2\times\log_2 2$

$=2\times1$

$\Rightarrow \quad f'(\lambda)=f'(1)=2$

23. (0) Since, r_1 and r_2 are orthogonal.

$\therefore \quad r_1\cdot r_2=0$

$\Rightarrow \ln|a|(1+a^2)-a+a-1=0$

$\Rightarrow \ln|a|=\frac{1}{1+a^2}$

Now, we draw the corresponding graphs, i.e. for $y=\ln|a|$ and $y=\frac{1}{1+a^2}$.

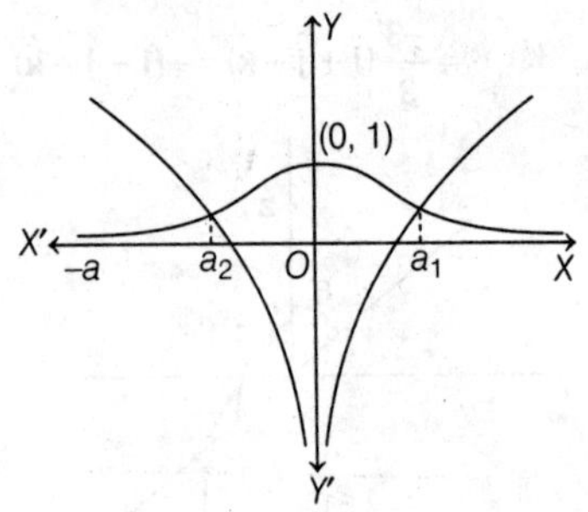

From the graph, it is clear that number of possible values of 'a' are two, i.e. a_1, a_2 and $a_1 + a_2 = 0$.

24. (17) $\mathbf{AB} = 2\hat{i} + 10\hat{j} + 11\hat{k}$

$\therefore\ |\mathbf{AB}| = \sqrt{2^2 + 10^2 + 11^2} = 15$ units

and $\mathbf{AD} = -\hat{i} + 2\hat{j} + 2\hat{k}$

$\therefore\ |\mathbf{AD}| = \sqrt{(-1)^2 + 2^2 + 2^2} = 3$ units

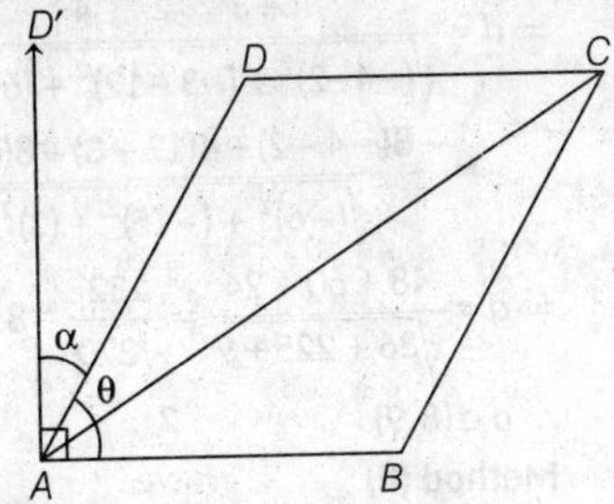

Let θ = angle between AB and AD.

$\therefore\ \cos\theta = \frac{}{|\ \ ||\ \ |}$

$= \frac{-2 + 20 + 22}{45} = \frac{40}{45} = \frac{8}{9}$

After rotation by α the angle is

$(\theta + \alpha) = 90° \Rightarrow \alpha = 90° - \theta$

$\Rightarrow \cos\alpha = \cos\left(\frac{\pi}{2} - \theta\right) = \sin\theta$

$= \frac{\sqrt{17}}{9} = \frac{\sqrt{\lambda}}{\lambda - 8}$

$\therefore\ \ \lambda = 17$

25. (300) Given, angle between and $= 120°$.

$\therefore\ \mathbf{a}\cdot\mathbf{b} = |\mathbf{a}||\mathbf{b}|\cos 120°$

$= 1\cdot 2\cdot\left(-\frac{1}{2}\right) = -1$

$(\because |\mathbf{a}| = 1 \text{ and } |\mathbf{b}| = 2, \text{ given})$

Now, $[(\mathbf{a} + 3\mathbf{b}) \times (3\mathbf{a} - \mathbf{b})]^2$

$= \{3\mathbf{a}\times\mathbf{a} - \mathbf{a}\times\mathbf{b} + 9\mathbf{b}\times\mathbf{a} - 3\mathbf{b}\times\mathbf{b}\}^2$

$= \{0 - \mathbf{a}\times\mathbf{b} - 9\mathbf{a}\times\mathbf{b} - 0\}^2$

$= \{-10(\mathbf{a}\times\mathbf{b})\}^2 = 100(\mathbf{a}\times\mathbf{b})^2$

$= 100\{\mathbf{a}^2\mathbf{b}^2 - (\mathbf{a}\cdot\mathbf{b})^2\} = 100(4-1)$

$= 100 \times 3 = 300$

26. (8) $|\mathbf{a}_1 \times \mathbf{a}_2| = |\mathbf{a}_1||\mathbf{a}_2|\sin\frac{2\pi}{n}$ ...(i)

$|\mathbf{a}_1 \cdot \mathbf{a}_2| = |\mathbf{a}_1||\mathbf{a}_2|\cos\frac{2\pi}{n}$ ...(ii)

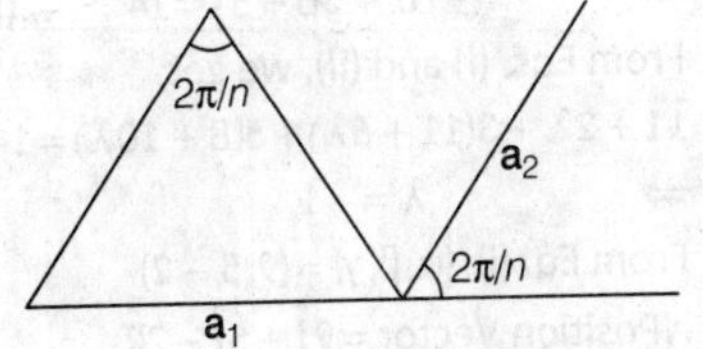

Given,

$|\mathbf{a}_1 \times \mathbf{a}_2 + \mathbf{a}_2 \times \mathbf{a}_3 + \mathbf{a}_3 \times \mathbf{a}_4 + \ldots + \mathbf{a}_n \times \mathbf{a}_1| =$

$|\mathbf{a}_1 \cdot \mathbf{a}_2 + \mathbf{a}_2 \cdot \mathbf{a}_3 + \mathbf{a}_3 \cdot \mathbf{a}_4 + \ldots + \mathbf{a}_n \cdot \mathbf{a}_1|$ ...(iii)

For regular polygon,

$|\mathbf{a}_1| = |\mathbf{a}_2| = |\mathbf{a}_3| = |\mathbf{a}_4| = \ldots = |\mathbf{a}_n|$ ...(iv)

When we are using Eqs. (i), (ii) and (iv), Eq. (iii) reduces to

$n\cdot\sin\frac{2\pi}{n} = n\cos\frac{2\pi}{n}$

$\Rightarrow \tan\left(\frac{2\pi}{n}\right) = 1 \Rightarrow \frac{2\pi}{n} = m\pi + \frac{\pi}{4}, m \in I$

$\Rightarrow\ \ n = \frac{8}{1 + 4m}$

The smallest and only possible value of n corresponds to $m = 0$, which is $n = 8$.

27. (4) Given, $|\mathbf{a}| = |\mathbf{b}| = |\mathbf{c}| = 2$

and $\mathbf{a}\cdot\mathbf{b} = \mathbf{b}\cdot\mathbf{c} = \mathbf{c}\cdot\mathbf{a} = 2$

$[\mathbf{a}\ \ \mathbf{b}\ \ \mathbf{c}]^2 = \begin{vmatrix} \mathbf{a}\cdot\mathbf{a} & \mathbf{a}\cdot\mathbf{b} & \mathbf{a}\cdot\mathbf{c} \\ \mathbf{b}\cdot\mathbf{a} & \mathbf{b}\cdot\mathbf{b} & \mathbf{b}\cdot\mathbf{c} \\ \mathbf{c}\cdot\mathbf{a} & \mathbf{c}\cdot\mathbf{b} & \mathbf{c}\cdot\mathbf{c} \end{vmatrix}$

$= \begin{vmatrix} 4 & 2 & 2 \\ 2 & 4 & 2 \\ 2 & 2 & 4 \end{vmatrix} = 32$

$\Rightarrow\ \ [\mathbf{a}\ \ \mathbf{b}\ \ \mathbf{c}] = 4\sqrt{2}$

$\Rightarrow\ [\mathbf{a}\ \ \mathbf{b}\ \ \mathbf{c}]\cos 45° = 4$

28. (1) Given, $\mathbf{a}\times\mathbf{b} + \mathbf{c} = \mathbf{b}\times\mathbf{c} + \mathbf{a}$

Taking dot with $\mathbf{a}$, we get

$\mathbf{a}\ (\mathbf{a}\times\mathbf{b}) + \mathbf{a}\cdot\mathbf{c} = \mathbf{a}\cdot(\mathbf{b}\times\mathbf{c}) + \mathbf{a}\cdot\mathbf{a}$

$\Rightarrow [\mathbf{a}\ \ \mathbf{a}\ \ \mathbf{b}] + \mathbf{a}\cdot\mathbf{c} = [\mathbf{a}\ \ \mathbf{b}\ \ \mathbf{c}] + 1$

$\Rightarrow 0 + \mathbf{a}\cdot\mathbf{c} = [\mathbf{a}\ \ \mathbf{b}\ \ \mathbf{c}] + 1$

$\Rightarrow \mathbf{a}\cdot\mathbf{c} = [\mathbf{a}\ \ \mathbf{b}\ \ \mathbf{c}] + 1$

Hence, $[\mathbf{a}\ \ \mathbf{b}\ \ \mathbf{c}] = -1$ $[\because \mathbf{a}\cdot\mathbf{c} = 0, \text{ given}]$

So, volume of parallelopiped $= |[\mathbf{a}\ \ \mathbf{b}\ \ \mathbf{c}]| = |-1| = 1$

29. (0) Given, $[\mathbf{a}\ \ \mathbf{b}\ \ \mathbf{c}] = 0$ and $|\mathbf{a}| = 1$, $|\mathbf{b}| = 1$ and $|\mathbf{c}| = 1$.

Now, $[2\mathbf{a} - \mathbf{b}\ \ \ 2\mathbf{b} - \mathbf{c}\ \ \ 2\mathbf{c} - \mathbf{a}]$

$= (2\mathbf{a} - \mathbf{b})\cdot\{(2\mathbf{b} - \mathbf{c})\times(2\mathbf{c} - \mathbf{a})\}$

$= (2\mathbf{a} - \mathbf{b})\cdot\{(4\mathbf{b}\times\mathbf{c}) - 2\mathbf{b}\times\mathbf{a} - 2\mathbf{c}\times\mathbf{c} + (\mathbf{c}\times\mathbf{a})\}$

$= (2\mathbf{a} - \mathbf{b})\cdot\{(4\mathbf{b}\times\mathbf{c}) + 2(\mathbf{a}\times\mathbf{b}) - 0 + (\mathbf{c}\times\mathbf{a})\}$

$= 8\mathbf{a}\cdot(\mathbf{b}\times\mathbf{c}) + 4\mathbf{a}\cdot(\mathbf{a}\times\mathbf{b}) + 2\mathbf{a}\cdot(\mathbf{c}\times\mathbf{a}) - 4\mathbf{b}\cdot(\mathbf{b}\times\mathbf{c}) - 2\mathbf{b}\cdot(\mathbf{a}\times\mathbf{b}) - \mathbf{b}\cdot(\mathbf{c}\times\mathbf{a})$

$= 8[\mathbf{a}\ \ \mathbf{b}\ \ \mathbf{c}] + 0 + 0 - 0 - 0 - [\mathbf{a}\ \ \mathbf{b}\ \ \mathbf{c}]$

$= 7[\mathbf{a}\ \ \mathbf{b}\ \ \mathbf{c}] = 7 \times 0 = 0$

$(\because [\mathbf{a}\ \ \mathbf{b}\ \ \mathbf{c}] = 0)$

30. (1.5) $\mathbf{a}\times\mathbf{b} = 2\hat{i} - 2\hat{j} + \hat{k}$

$\therefore |(\mathbf{a}\times\mathbf{b})\times\mathbf{c}| = |\mathbf{a}\times\mathbf{b}||\mathbf{c}|\sin 30°$

$= \sqrt{(2)^2 + (-2)^2 + (1)^2}\,.\,|\mathbf{c}|\,.\,\frac{1}{2} = \frac{3}{2}|\mathbf{c}|$

Given, $|\mathbf{c} - \mathbf{a}| = 2\sqrt{2} \Rightarrow (\mathbf{c} - \mathbf{a})^2 = 8$

$\Rightarrow (\ \ )^2 + (\mathbf{a})^2 - 2\mathbf{c}\cdot\mathbf{a} = 8$

$\Rightarrow\ \ |\mathbf{c}|^2 + 9 - 2|\mathbf{c}| = 8$

$[\because \mathbf{a}\cdot\mathbf{c} = |\mathbf{c}|, \text{ given}]$

$\Rightarrow\ \ (|\mathbf{c}| - 1)^2 = 0$

$\Rightarrow\ \ |\mathbf{c}| = 1$

Hence, $|(\mathbf{a}\times\mathbf{b})\times\mathbf{c}| = \frac{3}{2}\times 1 = \frac{3}{2} = 1.5$

Qualifier 16 (Three Dimensional Geometry)

1. (a) Let M be the mid-point of ST.

$\therefore M \equiv \left(\frac{2+0}{2}, \frac{1+1}{2}, \frac{0-1}{2}\right) \equiv \left(1, 1 - \frac{1}{2}\right)$

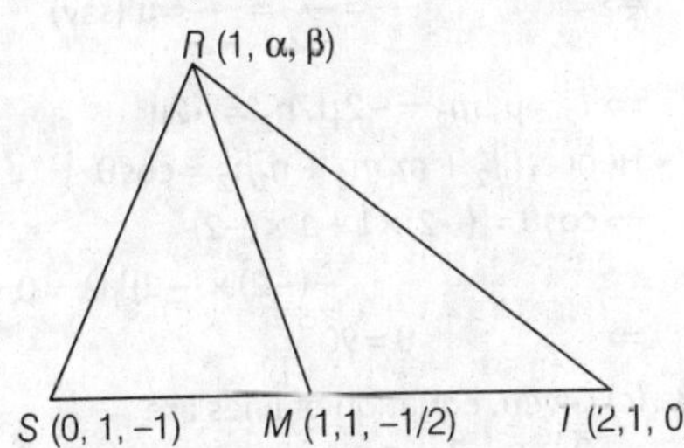

Direction ratios of median RM are

$\left(1 - 1, 1 - \alpha, -\frac{1}{2} - \beta\right)$

$\Rightarrow \left(0, 1 - \alpha, -\frac{1}{2} - \beta\right) \equiv (a, b, c)$ (say)

Given that the median through R is equally inclined to the coordinate axes, then direction cosines are equal.

So, $l = m = n \Rightarrow \frac{a}{\sqrt{a^2 + b^2 + c^2}}$

$= \frac{b}{\sqrt{a^2 + b^2 + c^2}} = \frac{c}{\sqrt{a^2 + b^2 + c^2}}$

$\Rightarrow a = b = c$

$\Rightarrow 0 = 1 - \alpha = -\frac{1}{2} - \beta \Rightarrow \alpha = 1$

and $\ \ \beta = -\frac{1}{2}$

Now, $[3312\beta^2 + 626\beta) + 271\alpha^7]$

$= \left[\left(3312 \times \frac{1}{4} - 626 \times \frac{1}{2}\right) + 271 \times 1\right]$

$= [(828 - 313) + 271] = 515 + 271 = 786$

2. (b) Given $2l+2m-n=0$ ...(i)

$$mn+nl+lm=0 \quad ...(ii)$$

From Eq. (i), $n=2l+2m$ put in Eq. (ii), we get

$$m(2l+2m)+l(2l+2m)+lm=0$$

$$\Rightarrow \quad 2l^2+5lm+2m^2=0$$

$$\Rightarrow \quad (l+2m)(2l+m)=0$$

Case (I) When $l+2m=0$

$$\Rightarrow \quad \frac{l}{-2}=\frac{m}{1}$$

$\therefore$ From Eq. (i), $n=l \Rightarrow \frac{l}{-2}=\frac{n}{-2}$

$$\Rightarrow \quad \frac{l}{-2}=\frac{m}{1}=\frac{n}{-2}=\lambda \text{ (say)}$$

$\therefore l_1=-2\lambda,\ m_1=\lambda,\ n_1=-2\lambda$

Case (II) When $2l+m=0$

$$\Rightarrow \quad \frac{l}{1}=\frac{m}{-2}$$

From Eq. (i), $\frac{n}{-2}=\frac{m}{-2}$

$$\Rightarrow \quad \frac{l}{1}=\frac{m}{-2}=\frac{n}{-2}=\mu \text{ (say)}$$

$\Rightarrow l_2=\mu,\ m_2=-2\mu,\ n_2=-2\mu$

Hence, $l_1l_2+m_1m_2+n_1n_2=\cos\theta$

$$\Rightarrow \cos\theta=[(-2)\times 1+1\times(-2)+(-2)\times(-2)]\mu\lambda=0$$

$$\Rightarrow \quad \theta=90^\circ$$

3. (c) Given, equation of lines are

$$\frac{x-2}{1}=\frac{y-3}{1}=\frac{z-4}{-k} \text{ and}$$

$$\frac{x-1}{k}=\frac{y-4}{2}=\frac{z-5}{1}$$

Since these lines are coplanar, then

$$\begin{vmatrix} 2-1 & 3-4 & 4-5 \\ 1 & 1 & -k \\ k & 2 & 1 \end{vmatrix}=0$$

$$\Rightarrow \begin{vmatrix} 1 & -1 & -1 \\ 1 & 1 & -k \\ k & 2 & 1 \end{vmatrix}=0$$

$$\Rightarrow 1(1+2k)+1(1+k^2)-1(2-k)=0$$

$$\Rightarrow \quad 1+2k+1+k^2-2+k=0$$

$$\Rightarrow \quad k^2+3k=0$$

$$\Rightarrow \quad k=0,-3$$

4. (a) Let DR's of L_3 is 2, 1, 1 ...(A)

and Let $L_1: \frac{x-1}{2}=\frac{y-2}{3}=\frac{z-3}{4}$ ...(i)

and $L_2: \frac{x-2}{1}=\frac{y+1}{2}=\frac{z+2}{3}$ ...(ii)

Now, coordinates of any point P on L_1 will be of the form

$P \equiv (2\lambda+1, 3\lambda+2, 4\lambda+3)$ for some λ.

Similarly, $Q=(\mu+2, 2\mu-1, 3\mu-2)$ for some μ.

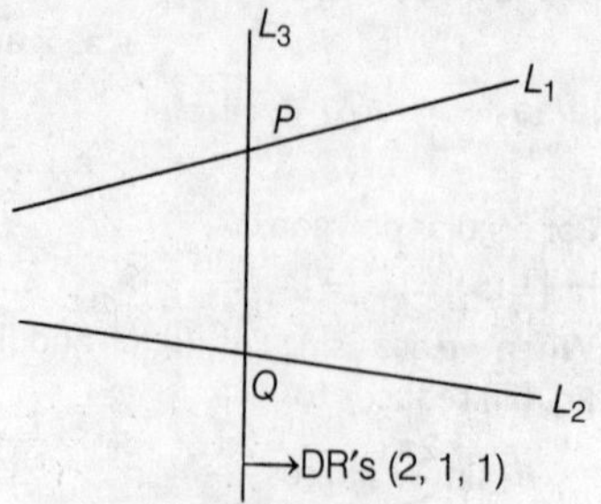

Now, direction ratios of

$PQ=2\lambda-\mu-1, 3\lambda-2\mu+3, 4\lambda-3\mu+5$ ...(B)

From Eqs. (A) and (B),

$$\underset{\text{(i)}}{\frac{2\lambda-\mu-1}{2}}=\underset{\text{(ii)}}{\frac{3\lambda-2\mu+3}{1}}=\underset{\text{(iii)}}{\frac{4\lambda-3\mu+5}{1}}$$

On solving Eqs. (i) and (ii), we get

$$4\lambda-3\mu+7=0 \quad ...(iv)$$

On solving Eqs. (ii) and (iii), we get

$$\lambda-\mu+2=0 \quad ...(v)$$

On solving Eqs. (iv) and (v), we get

$\lambda=-1$ and $\mu=1$

$\therefore P \equiv (-1,-1,-1)$ and $Q \equiv (3,1,1)$

$$\Rightarrow PQ=|PQ|$$

$$=\sqrt{(3+1)^2+(1+1)^2+(1+1)^2}$$

$$=\sqrt{16+4+4}\ \sqrt{24}=2\sqrt{6}$$

5. (c) Let $A=(1,-1,0)$

and $\frac{x-1}{2}=\frac{y+1}{-3}=z=t$ (say)

The coordinates of any point P on the given line are $(2t+1, -3t-1, t)$

$$AP=4\sqrt{14}$$

$$(2t)^2+(-3t)^2+(t)^2=(4\sqrt{14})^2$$

$$\Rightarrow \quad 14t^2=16\times 14 \Rightarrow t=\pm 4$$

So, the coordinates of the required point are $(9,-13,4)$ and $(-7,11,-4)$.

Now, distance between (0, 0, 0) and $(9,-13,4)=\sqrt{266}$

and distance between (0, 0, 0) and $(-7,11,-4)=\sqrt{186}$

$\because \sqrt{186}<\sqrt{266}$

$\therefore (-7,11,-4)$ is nearer to the origin.

6. (d) **Method I**

Given, equation of lines are

$$\frac{x-5}{3}=\frac{y-7}{-1}=\frac{z+2}{1} \quad ...(i)$$

$$\frac{x+3}{-3}=\frac{y-3}{2}=\frac{z-6}{4} \quad ...(ii)$$

Given, shortest distance between Eqs. (i) and (ii) $=d$

$$d=\frac{\begin{vmatrix} x_2-x_1 & y_2-y_1 & z_2-z_1 \\ l_1 & m_1 & n_1 \\ l_2 & m_2 & n_2 \end{vmatrix}}{\sqrt{(m_1n_2-m_2n_1)^2+(l_2n_1-l_1n_2)^2+(l_1m_2-l_2m_1)^2}}$$

$$\Rightarrow d=\frac{\begin{vmatrix} -8 & -4 & 8 \\ 3 & -1 & 1 \\ -3 & 2 & 4 \end{vmatrix}}{\sqrt{(-4-2)^2+(-3-12)^2+(6-3)^2}}$$

$$=\frac{-8(-4-2)+4(12+3)+8(6-3)}{\sqrt{(-6)^2+(-15)^2+(3)^2}}$$

$$\Rightarrow d=\frac{48+60+24}{\sqrt{36+225+9}}=\frac{132}{\sqrt{270}}\simeq 8.03$$

$\therefore d\in(8,9)$

Method (II)

$\mathbf{a}_1=5\hat{\mathbf{i}}+7\hat{\mathbf{j}}-2\hat{\mathbf{k}},\ \mathbf{a}_2=-3\hat{\mathbf{i}}+3\hat{\mathbf{j}}+6\hat{\mathbf{k}}$

$\mathbf{b}_1=3\hat{\mathbf{i}}-\hat{\mathbf{j}}+\hat{\mathbf{k}},\ \mathbf{b}_2=-3\hat{\mathbf{i}}+2\hat{\mathbf{j}}+4\hat{\mathbf{k}}$

Now, $\mathbf{a}_2-\mathbf{a}_1=-8\hat{\mathbf{i}}-4\hat{\mathbf{j}}+8\hat{\mathbf{k}}$

and $\mathbf{b}_1\times\mathbf{b}_2=-6\hat{\mathbf{i}}-15\hat{\mathbf{j}}+3\hat{\mathbf{k}}$

So, $d=\frac{|(\mathbf{a}_2-\mathbf{a}_1)\cdot(\mathbf{b}_1\times\mathbf{b}_2)|}{|\mathbf{b}_1\times\mathbf{b}_2|}=\frac{132}{\sqrt{270}}$

$\simeq 8.03$

Hence, $d\in(8,9)$

7. (c) Let image of $P(7,-1,2)$ w.r.t. the given line be $Q(\alpha,\beta,\gamma)$. Then,

mid-point of PQ is $\left(\frac{\alpha+7}{2},\frac{\beta-1}{2},\frac{\gamma+2}{2}\right)$ lies on the line.

$$\mathbf{r}=9\hat{\mathbf{i}}+5\hat{\mathbf{j}}+5\hat{\mathbf{k}}+\lambda(\hat{\mathbf{i}}+3\hat{\mathbf{j}}+5\hat{\mathbf{k}})$$

$$\therefore \frac{\alpha+7}{2}\hat{\mathbf{i}}+\frac{\beta-1}{2}\hat{\mathbf{j}}+\frac{\gamma+2}{2}\hat{\mathbf{k}}=9\hat{\mathbf{i}}+5\hat{\mathbf{j}}+5\hat{\mathbf{k}}+\lambda(\hat{\mathbf{i}}+3\hat{\mathbf{j}}+5\hat{\mathbf{k}})$$

On comparing, we get

$$\left.\begin{array}{l} \frac{\alpha+7}{2}=9+\lambda \Rightarrow \alpha=11+2\lambda \\ \frac{\beta-1}{2}=5+3\lambda \Rightarrow \beta=11+6\lambda \\ \frac{\gamma+2}{2}=5+5\lambda \Rightarrow \gamma=8+10\lambda \end{array}\right\} ...(i)$$

Also, PQ and given line are perpendicular.

So, $(\alpha-7)\cdot 1+(\beta+1)\cdot 3+(\gamma-2)\cdot 5=0$

$\Rightarrow \alpha-7+3\beta+3+5\gamma-10=0$

$$\Rightarrow \quad \alpha+3\beta+5\gamma=14 \quad ...(ii)$$

From Eqs. (i) and (ii), we get

$11+2\lambda+3(11+6\lambda)+5(8+10\lambda)=14$

$$\Rightarrow \quad \lambda=-1$$

From Eq. (i), $(\alpha,\beta,\gamma)=(9,5,-2)$

$\therefore$ Position Vector $=9\hat{\mathbf{i}}+5\hat{\mathbf{j}}-2\hat{\mathbf{k}}$

8. (c) We have, $z=0$ for the point where the line intersects the curve.

$\therefore \frac{x-2}{3}=\frac{y+1}{2}=\frac{0-1}{-1}$

$\Rightarrow \frac{x-2}{3}=1$ and $\frac{y+1}{2}=1$

$\Rightarrow \quad x=5$ and $y=1$

Putting these values in $xy=c^2$, we get

$5\times1=c^2 \Rightarrow c=\pm\sqrt{5}$

9. (c) Given planes are

$4x-3y+12z+13=0$ ...(i)

and $x+2y+2z=9$ ...(ii)

The equations of bisecting planes are

$$\frac{x+2y+2z-9}{\sqrt{1^2+2^2+2^2}}=\pm\frac{4x-3y+12z+13}{\sqrt{4^2+3^2+12^2}}$$

$\Rightarrow 13(x+2y+2z-9)$
$=\pm3(4x-3y+12z+13)$

$\Rightarrow 13x+26y+26z-117$
$=\pm(12x-9y+36z+39)$

$\Rightarrow x+35y-10z=156$
(Taking + ve sign) ...(iii)

and $25x+17y+62z=78$
(Taking − ve sign) ...(iv)

Let θ be the angle between the planes (ii) and (iv), then

$$\cos\theta=\left(\frac{1}{3}\right)\left(\frac{25}{\sqrt{4758}}\right)+\left(\frac{2}{3}\right)\left(\frac{17}{\sqrt{4758}}\right)+\left(\frac{2}{3}\right)\left(\frac{62}{\sqrt{4758}}\right)>\frac{1}{\sqrt{2}}$$
$=\cos45°$

$\Rightarrow \quad \theta<45°$

($\because \cos\theta$ is decreasing in $\left(0,\frac{\pi}{2}\right)$;
$\therefore$ Inequality gets reversed)

$\Rightarrow$ Plane (iii), i.e. $x+35y-10z=156$ is the bisector of obtuse angle between the planes.

10. (c)

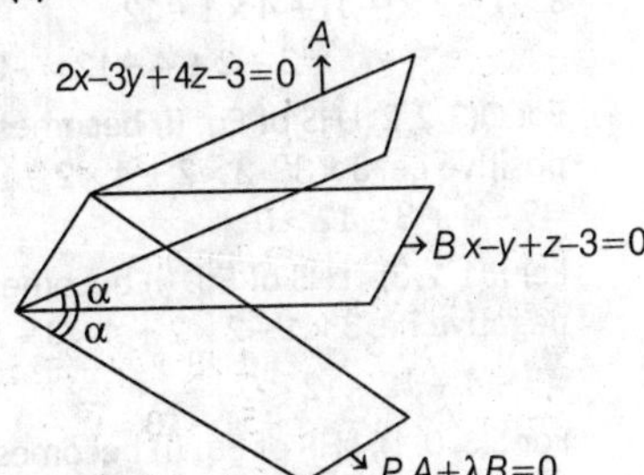

Given, equation of planes

$A: 2x-3y+4z-3=0$ ...(i)

$B: x-y+z-3=0$ ...(ii)

Let P be the reflection of plane A in plane B.

So, equation of P will be

$A+\lambda B=0$ ...(iii)

$\Rightarrow (2x-3y+4z-3)$
$+\lambda(x-y+z-3)=0$

$\Rightarrow (2+\lambda)x-(3+\lambda)y+(4+\lambda)z$
$-3(1+\lambda)=0$ ...(iv)

$\because$ Angle between A and B must be same as angle between B and P.

So,

$$\frac{|2\times1+(-3)(-1)+4\times(-1)|}{\sqrt{2^2+(-3)^2+(4)^2}\sqrt{(1)^2+(-1)^2+(1)^2}}$$
$$=\frac{|(2+\lambda)\times1+(3+\lambda)\times(1)+(4+\lambda)\times1|}{\sqrt{(2+\lambda)^2+(3+\lambda)^2+(4+\lambda)^2}\sqrt{(1)^2+(-1)^2+(1)^2}}$$

$\Rightarrow 81(3\lambda^2+18\lambda+29)=29(3\lambda+9)^2$

$\Rightarrow 9(3\lambda^2+18\lambda+29)=29(x^2+6\lambda+9)$

$\Rightarrow \quad 2\lambda^2+12\lambda=0$

$\Rightarrow \quad 2\lambda(\lambda+6)=0$

$\Rightarrow \quad \lambda=0,-6$

But $\lambda=0$ (not acceptable) because when we put $\lambda=0$ in Eq. (iii) or Eq. (iv), we get same equation of reflection plane and A.

So, we put $\lambda=-6$ in Eq. (iv), we get

The equation of image plane or reflected plane $-4x+3y-2z+15=0$

$\Rightarrow 4x-3y+2z-15=0$

11. (b) Let $\frac{x+2}{2}=\frac{y+1}{-1}=\frac{z}{3}=k$ (say) then

$(2k-2,-k-1,3k)$ is a point on the line.

Let the foot of the perpendicular from this point on the plane $x+y+z-3=0$ be (α,β,γ), then it is given by

$$\frac{\alpha-(2k-2)}{1}=\frac{\beta+(k+1)}{1}=\frac{\gamma-3k}{1}$$
$$=\frac{-[(2k-2)+(-k-1)+(3k)-3]}{3}$$
$$=\frac{6-4k}{3}$$

Thus, $\alpha=\frac{2k}{3},\beta=1-\frac{7k}{3},\gamma=2+\frac{5k}{3}$

Then, the line is given by

$$\frac{x}{\frac{2}{3}}=\frac{y-1}{-\frac{7}{3}}=\frac{z-2}{\frac{5}{3}}$$

i.e $\frac{x}{2}=\frac{y-1}{-7}=\frac{z-2}{5}$

12. (a) The equation of plane passing through three non-collinear points $P(x_1,y_1,z_1)$, $Q(x_2,y_2,z_2)$ and $R(x_3,y_3,z_3)$ is given by

$$\begin{vmatrix} x-x_1 & y-y_1 & z-z_1 \\ x_2-x_1 & y_2-y_1 & z_2-z_1 \\ x_3-x_1 & y_3-y_1 & z_3-z_1 \end{vmatrix}=0$$

$$\Rightarrow \begin{vmatrix} x-1 & y-0 & z-2 \\ -1-1 & 1-0 & 2-2 \\ 5-1 & 0-0 & 3-2 \end{vmatrix}=0$$

$$\Rightarrow \begin{vmatrix} x-1 & y & z-2 \\ -2 & 1 & 0 \\ 4 & 0 & 1 \end{vmatrix}=0$$

$\Rightarrow (x-1)(1-0)-y(-2-0)$
$+(z-2)(0-4)=0$

$\Rightarrow x-1+2y-4z+8=0$

$\Rightarrow \quad x+2y-4z+7=0$ ...(i)

Given plane $\frac{x}{2}+y-2z+7=0$ can be written as,

$x+2y-4z+14=0$ ...(ii)

Plane given by Eqs. (i) and (ii) are parallel.

$\therefore$ Required distance

$$=\frac{|14-7|}{\sqrt{1^2+2^2+(-4)^2}}=\frac{7}{\sqrt{21}}=\sqrt{\frac{7}{3}}$$

13. (d) Let the direction ratios of required line be a, b, c.

According to situation given in problem,

$a-b+2c=0$ ...(i)

$3a+b+c=0$ ...(ii)

(Since required line is parallel to the planes $x-y+2z=5$ and $3x+y+z=6$).

[**Note** If a line is parallel to any plane, then this line must be perpendicular to normal of that plane.]

Now, solving Eqs. (i) and (ii), we get

$$\frac{a}{\begin{vmatrix}-1 & 2\\ 1 & 1\end{vmatrix}}=\frac{b}{\begin{vmatrix}2 & 1\\ 1 & 3\end{vmatrix}}=\frac{c}{\begin{vmatrix}1 & -1\\ 3 & 1\end{vmatrix}}$$

$\Rightarrow \quad \frac{a}{-3}=\frac{b}{5}=\frac{c}{4}$

$\therefore$ Equation of required line

$$\frac{x-1}{-3}=\frac{y-2}{5}=\frac{z-3}{4}$$

14. (b) Let $P\equiv(2,1,-2)$

Given equation of line is

$$\frac{x-1}{2}=\frac{y+1}{1}=\frac{z-3}{-3} \quad ...(i)$$

Any point Q taken on Eq. (i) is of the form $(2t+1,t-1,-3t+3)$

$\therefore$ DR's of PQ is $(2t+1-2,$
$t-1-1,-3t+3+2)$

$\Rightarrow (2t-1,t-2,-3t+5)$

According to question, PQ is measured parallel to the given plane.

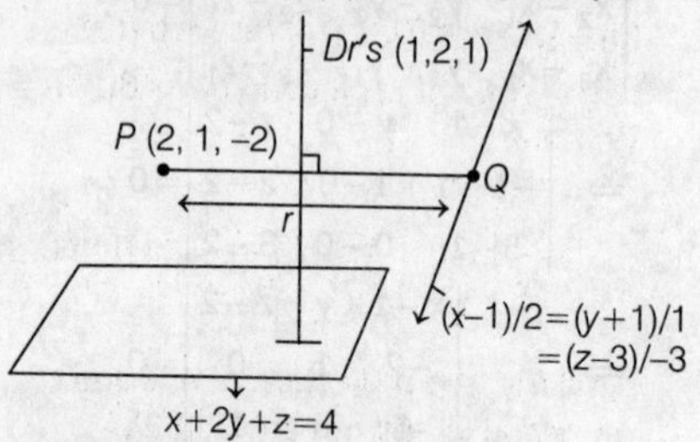

It means PQ is perpendicular to normal to the plane (as shown in figure).

So, $(2t-1)\times 1+(t-2)\times 2$
$+(-3t+5)\times 1=0$

$\Rightarrow 2t-1+2t-4-3t+5=0 \Rightarrow t=0$

$\therefore Q\equiv(2\times 0+1, 0-1, -3\times 0+3)$
$\equiv(1,-1,3)$

Hence,

$PQ=r=\sqrt{(2-1)^2+(1+1)^2+(-2-3)^2}$
$=\sqrt{1+4+25}=\sqrt{30}$

15. (d)

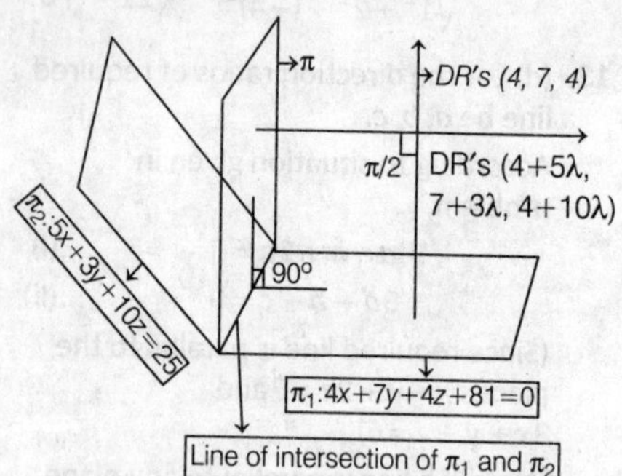

Given planes are

$\pi_1: 4x+7y+4z+81=0$ ...(i)

$\pi_2: 5x+3y+10z=25$ ...(ii)

Equation of plane (π) passing through line of intersection of Eqs. (i) and (ii) is given by

$(4x+7y+4z+81)$
$+\lambda(5x+3y+10z-25)=0$

$\Rightarrow (4+5\lambda)x+(7+3\lambda)y+(4+10\lambda)z$
$+81-25\lambda=0$ ...(iii)

According to question, plane (iii) is perpendicular to plane (i) (means angle between their corresponding normals $=\frac{\pi}{2}$).

So, $4(4+5\lambda)+7(7+3\lambda)$
$+4(4+10\lambda)=0$

$\Rightarrow \qquad \lambda=-1$

From Eq. (iii),

$-x+4y-6z+106=0$ ...(iv)

(putting $\lambda=-1$ in Eq. (iii))

Also, given distance of plane (iv) from $(0, 0, 0)=\sqrt{k}$

So, $\dfrac{|106|}{\sqrt{1+16+36}}=\sqrt{k}\Rightarrow k=212$

16. (a)

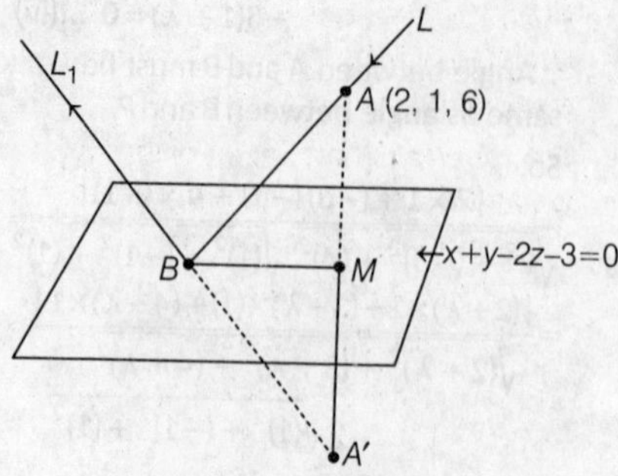

Given equation of plane is

$x+y-2z-3=0$ ...(i)

Its DR's $(1, 1, -2)$ ...(ii)

Also, given equation of line

$L: \dfrac{x-2}{3}=\dfrac{y-1}{4}=\dfrac{z-6}{5}$ ...(iii)

Now direction ratios (DR's) of $A'A$ are proportional to Eq. (ii), i.e $1, 1, -2$.

$\therefore$ Equation of AA' is

$\dfrac{x-2}{1}=\dfrac{y-1}{1}=\dfrac{z-6}{-2}=\lambda$ (say)

Then $A'\equiv(\lambda+2, \lambda+1, -2\lambda+6)$ for some λ.

Let M be the mid-point of AA'.

$\therefore M\equiv\left(\dfrac{\lambda+4}{2}, \dfrac{\lambda+2}{2}, \dfrac{-2\lambda+12}{2}\right)$

Since, M lies on Eq. (i).

$\therefore \dfrac{\lambda+4}{2}+\dfrac{\lambda+2}{2}-2\left(\dfrac{-2\lambda+12}{2}\right)$

$-3=0\Rightarrow \dfrac{\lambda+4+\lambda+2+4\lambda-24-6}{2}=0$

$\Rightarrow 6\lambda=24\Rightarrow\lambda=4$

$\therefore\ A'=(6, 5, -2)$

$\because B$ is a point on given line L.

$L: \dfrac{x-2}{3}=\dfrac{y-1}{4}=\dfrac{z-6}{5}=\mu$ (say)

$\Rightarrow B\equiv(3\mu+2, 4\mu+1, 5\mu+6)$

Since, B lies on the given plane (i).

So, $2+3\mu+4\mu+1-10\mu-12-3=0$

$\Rightarrow -3\mu-12=0\ \Rightarrow \mu=-4$

So, $B\equiv(-10, -15, -14)$

Now, DR's of reflected ray are same as that of $A'B$.

$\Rightarrow$ DR's of reflected ray are proportional to 16, 20, 12 i.e. 4, 5, 3.

Hence, equation of the reflected ray is

$\dfrac{x+10}{4}=\dfrac{y+15}{5}=\dfrac{z+14}{3}$

17. (d)

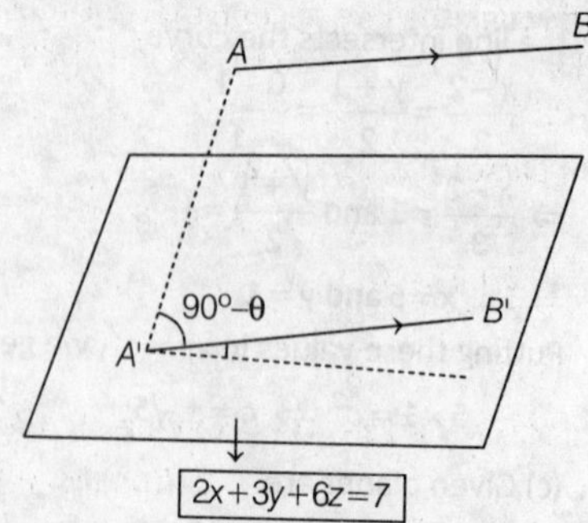

Let $A\equiv(1, -1, 0)$ and $B\equiv(-1, 0, 1)$

$\mathbf{AB}=-2\hat{\mathbf{i}}+\hat{\mathbf{j}}+\hat{\mathbf{k}}\Rightarrow|\mathbf{AB}|=\sqrt{6}$

Projection of $\mathbf{AB}$ in the plane $2x+3y+6z=7$ is

$|\mathbf{AB}|\cos\theta=|\mathbf{A'B'}|\cos\theta$

Direction ratios of normal to the given plane is 2, 3, 6.

$\cos(90^\circ-\theta)=\dfrac{2(-2)+3(1)+6(1)}{\sqrt{2^2+3^2+6^2}\sqrt{2^2+1^2+1^2}}$

$=\dfrac{5}{7\sqrt{6}}$

$\Rightarrow \quad \sin\theta=\dfrac{5}{7\sqrt{6}}$

$\Rightarrow \quad \cos\theta=\dfrac{\sqrt{(7\sqrt{6})^2-5^2}}{7\sqrt{6}}$

$\Rightarrow \quad \cos\theta=\dfrac{\sqrt{269}}{7\sqrt{6}}$

$\therefore$ Required projection

$=|\mathbf{AB}|\cos\theta=\sqrt{6}\times\dfrac{\sqrt{269}}{7\sqrt{6}}=\dfrac{\sqrt{269}}{7}$

18. (b) Equation of plane parallel to the plane $3x-2y+4z=7$ and passing through $(2, -1, 1)$ is

$3(x-2)-2(y+1)+4(z-1)=0$

$\Rightarrow \quad 3x-2y+4z-12=0$ ...(i)

For $P(1, -1, 1)$ LHS of Eq. (i) becomes negative i.e.

$3\times 1-2\times(-1)+4\times 1-12$
$=3+2+4-12=-3<0$

For $Q(3, 2, 2)$ LHS of Eq. (i) becomes positive i.e. $3\times 3-2\times 2+4\times 2-12$
$=9-4+8-12>0$

For $R(1, 2, 3)$, LHS of Eq. (i) becomes negative i.e. $3\times 1-2\times 2+4\times 3-12$
$=3-4+12-12<0$

For $S(3, 0, 1)$, LHS of Eq. (i) becomes positive i.e.

$3\times 3-2\times 0+4\times 1-12>0$

So, Q and S are on one side of the plane and P, R are on other sides.

Hence, the line segment QR intersects the plane.

19. (d) Equation of the plane passing through the intersection of P_1 and P_2 is
$(3x-y+2z-4)+\lambda(x+y+z-2)=0$ ...(i)

It passes through (2, 2, 1).

Hence, $6-2+2-4+\lambda(5-2)=0$

$\Rightarrow 2+3\lambda=0$

$\Rightarrow \lambda=-\frac{2}{3}$

$\therefore 3(3x-y+2z-4)-2(x+y+z-2)=0$ [from Eq. (i)]

$\Rightarrow 7x-5y+4z=8$

$\Rightarrow \frac{7x}{2}-\frac{5y}{2}+2z=4$

$\therefore (a+b+c)=\frac{7}{2}-\frac{5}{2}+4=5$

20. (a) **Method 1**

Substituting $z=0$ in equations of w_1 and w_2, we get

$\left.\begin{array}{l}x-2y=1\\x+2y=5\end{array}\right\}\Rightarrow$ Solving these two equations, we get $x=3, y=1$

$\therefore$ Point (3, 1, 0) lies on the planes w_1 and w_2.

Again substituting $z=1$ in equations of w_1 and w_2, we get

$\left.\begin{array}{l}x-2y=0\\x+2y=7\end{array}\right\}\Rightarrow$ on solving, $x=\frac{7}{2}, y=\frac{7}{4}$

$\therefore$ Point $\left(\frac{7}{2},\frac{7}{4},1\right)$ lies on the planes w_1 and w_2.

Now, equation of the line joining the point (3, 1, 0) and $\left(\frac{7}{2},\frac{7}{4},1\right)$ is

$$\frac{x-3}{\frac{7}{2}-3}=\frac{y-1}{\frac{7}{4}-1}=\frac{z-0}{1-0}$$

i.e. $\frac{x-3}{\frac{1}{2}}=\frac{y-1}{\frac{3}{4}}=\frac{z}{1}=\lambda$ (say)

Then a point say M, on the line of intersection of w_1 and w_2 is

$\left(3+\frac{\lambda}{2},1+\frac{3\lambda}{4},\lambda\right)$

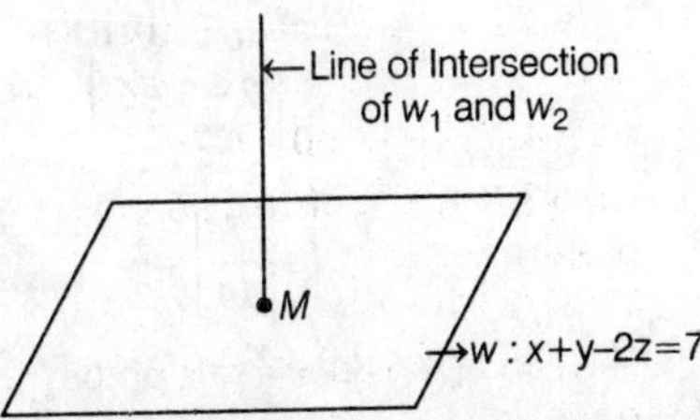

Now, point M lies on plane w.

$\therefore \left(3+\frac{\lambda}{2}\right)+\left(1+\frac{3\lambda}{4}\right)-2\lambda=7$

$\Rightarrow \lambda=-4$

$\therefore M\equiv(1,-2,-4)\equiv(\alpha,\beta,\gamma)$

i.e. $\alpha=1, \beta=-2, \gamma=-4$

Now, $\alpha+\beta=-1, \alpha-3\beta+\gamma=3, 2\beta=\gamma$ and $4\alpha+\gamma=0$

Method (2)

The required point lies on planes w_1, w_2 and w. So, the required point is the solution of the equations

$$x-2y+z=1$$
$$x+2y-2z=5$$
$$x+y-2z=7$$

Now, $\Delta=\begin{vmatrix}1&-2&1\\1&2&-2\\1&1&-2\end{vmatrix}=-3$

$\Delta_1=\begin{vmatrix}1&-2&1\\5&2&-2\\7&1&-2\end{vmatrix}=-3$

$\Delta_2=\begin{vmatrix}1&1&1\\1&5&-2\\1&7&-2\end{vmatrix}=6$

$\Delta_3=\begin{vmatrix}1&-2&1\\1&2&5\\1&1&7\end{vmatrix}=12$

By Cramer's rule, $x=\frac{\Delta_1}{\Delta}=1$,

$y=\frac{\Delta_2}{\Delta}=-2$

and $z=\frac{\Delta_3}{\Delta}=-4$

Hence, $(x,y,z)=(1,-2,-4)\equiv(\alpha,\beta,\gamma)$ and then check the options.

21. (18)Let the x, y and z components of the line segment vector be a, b, c respectively.

Then, $a^2+b^2+c^2=(63)^2$ ...(i)

Also, $\frac{a}{3}=\frac{b}{-2}=\frac{c}{6}=\lambda$ (say)

$\Rightarrow a=3\lambda, b=-2\lambda, c=6\lambda$

From Eq. (i), $9\lambda^2+4\lambda^2+36\lambda^2=(63)^2$

$\Rightarrow 49\lambda^2=(63)^2$

$\Rightarrow \lambda=\pm\frac{63}{7}$

$\Rightarrow \lambda=\pm 9$

$\because a=3\lambda<0$ as the line makes obtuse angle with X-axis.

($\because$ cos (obtuse angle) = – ve)

$\therefore \lambda=-9$ acceptable only

Hence, y-component $=-2\lambda=18$

22. (7) The coordinates of the projection of A, B, C on the yz-plane are $(0,2,3)$, $(0,-1,1)$ and $(0,2,-4)$ respectively.

$\therefore \Delta x=$ Area of projection of ΔABC on yz-plane.

$$=\frac{1}{2}\left\|\begin{matrix}2&3&1\\-1&1&1\\2&-4&1\end{matrix}\right\|=\frac{21}{2}\text{ sq units}$$

Similarly, the projection of A, B and C on zx and xy -planes are $(1,0,3)$, $(2,0,1)$, $(1,0,-4)$ and $(1,2,0)$, $(2,-1,0)$, $(1,2,0)$ respectively also.

Let Δy and Δz be the areas of the projection of the ΔABC on zx and xy-planes respectively.

Then, $\Delta y=\frac{1}{2}\left\|\begin{matrix}1&3&1\\2&1&1\\1&-4&1\end{matrix}\right\|=\frac{7}{2}$ sq units

and $\Delta z=\frac{1}{2}\left\|\begin{matrix}1&2&1\\2&-1&1\\1&2&1\end{matrix}\right\|=0$ sq unit

$\therefore$ The required area $=\sqrt{\Delta_x^2+\Delta_y^2+\Delta_z^2}$

$$=\sqrt{\left(\frac{21}{2}\right)^2+\left(\frac{7}{2}\right)^2+(0)^2}$$

$=\frac{7}{2}\sqrt{10}$ sq units

$\lambda=\frac{7}{2}\sqrt{10}$ sq units $\Rightarrow \frac{2\lambda}{\sqrt{10}}=7$

23. (2) $\frac{x-1}{2}=\frac{y-k}{3}=\frac{z-3}{4}=\lambda$ (say)

and $\frac{x-4}{5}=\frac{y-1}{k}=\frac{z-0}{1}=m$ (say)

A point on the first line is $P(2\lambda+1, 3\lambda+k, 4\lambda+3)$ and a point on the second line is $Q(5m+4, km+1, m)$.

The given two lines intersect if and only if,

$2\lambda+1=5m+4$ ...(i)

$3\lambda+k=km+1$ ...(ii)

and $4\lambda+3=m$ ...(iii)

From Eqs. (i) and (iii), we get

$2\lambda+1=5(4\lambda+3)+4$

$\Rightarrow 2\lambda+1=20\lambda+19$

$\Rightarrow \lambda=-1$

From Eq. (iii),

$m=4(-1)+3=-1$

Substituting the values of λ and m in Eq. (ii), we get

$-3+k=-k+1$

$\Rightarrow 2k=4$

$\Rightarrow k=2$

24. (149) L_1 and L_2 can be written as

$L_1 : \frac{x-1}{2} = \frac{y-1}{-1} = \frac{z-1}{3}$

and $L_2 : \frac{x-2}{3} = \frac{y+1}{6} = \frac{z-4}{0}$

DR's of $L_1 = 2, -1, 3$ and DR's of $L_2 = 3, 6, 0$

Given, θ = angle between L_1 and L_2

$$\Rightarrow \cos\theta = \frac{2\times3+(-1)\times6+3\times0}{\sqrt{14}\sqrt{45}}$$

$$= 0$$

$$= \cos\frac{\pi}{2}$$

$$\therefore \quad \theta = \frac{\pi}{2}$$

i.e. L_1 is perpendicular to L_2.

Let $I = \int_0^{\theta} \frac{1}{1+\tan x}\,dx$

$$\Rightarrow I = \int_0^{\pi/2} \frac{\cos x}{\cos x + \sin x}\,dx \quad \text{...(i)}$$

$$\Rightarrow I = \int_0^{\frac{\pi}{2}} \frac{\cos\left(\frac{\pi}{2}-x\right)}{\cos\left(\frac{\pi}{2}-x\right)+\sin\left(\frac{\pi}{2}-x\right)}\,dx$$

$$\Rightarrow I = \int_0^{\frac{\pi}{2}} \frac{\sin x}{\sin x + \cos x}\,dx \quad \text{...(ii)}$$

Adding Eqs. (i) and (ii), we get

$$2I = \int_0^{\frac{\pi}{2}} dx$$

$$\Rightarrow \quad 2I = \frac{\pi}{2}$$

$$\Rightarrow \quad I = \frac{\pi}{4} = k \text{ (given)}$$

$$\therefore \quad \frac{596k}{\pi} = \frac{596}{\pi}\times\frac{\pi}{4}$$

$$= 149$$

25. (3) Equation of plane which contains the

line $\frac{x-2}{3} = \frac{y-3}{1} = \frac{z-1}{2}$ is

$(x-2-3(y-3)) + \lambda(2(y-3)-(z-1)) = 0$

$\Rightarrow \quad x + (2\lambda-3)y - \lambda z + 7 - 5\lambda = 0$

If plane is parallel to

$$\frac{x-1}{1} = \frac{y-2}{2} = \frac{z-3}{3}$$

Then, $1 + (2\lambda-3)\cdot2 - 3\lambda = 0$

$\Rightarrow \quad \lambda = 5$

So, equation of plane which contains second line and parallel to first is $x + 7y - 5z - 18 = 0$.

Similarly, equation of plane which contains first line and parallel to second is $(x-1) + 7(y-2) - 5(z-3) = 0$

$\Rightarrow \quad x + 7y - 5z = 0$

Hence, equidistant plane is

$$\frac{(x+7y-5z-18)+(x+7y-5z)}{2} = 0$$

$$\Rightarrow \quad x + 7y - 5z - 9 = 0 \quad \text{...(i)}$$

$\therefore$ Sum of DR's of normal to Eq. (i) is

$$(1+7-5) = 3$$

26. (0) Let the DR's of the required plane be a, b, c.

$\Rightarrow -3a + 2b + c = 0$ and $a - 3b + 2c = 0$

On solving;

$$\frac{a}{4+3} = \frac{b}{1+6} = \frac{c}{9-2}$$

$$\Rightarrow \quad \frac{a}{7} = \frac{b}{7} = \frac{c}{7}$$

$$\Rightarrow \quad a = b = c$$

Equation of plane passing through $(0, 7, -7)$ and having DR's $(1, 1, 1)$ is $1(x-0) + 1(y-7) + 1(z+7) = 0$

$\Rightarrow x + y + z = 0$, if also contains point $(-1, p, -2)$.

$$\therefore \quad -1 + p - 2 = 0$$

$$\Rightarrow \quad p = 3$$

$\therefore$ Equation of the first line is

$$L_1 \equiv \frac{x+1}{-3} = \frac{y-3}{2} = \frac{z+2}{1} = \lambda \quad \text{(say)}$$

Now, general point on line L_1 is $(-3\lambda-1, 2\lambda+3, \lambda-2)$

and $L_2 \equiv \frac{x}{1} = \frac{y-7}{-3} = \frac{z+7}{2} = \mu$ (say)

So, general point on line L_2 is $(\mu, -3\mu+7, 2\mu-7)$

Now, solving for point of intersection of the lines L_1 and L_2.

We have,

$$-3\lambda - 1 = \mu, \Rightarrow 3\lambda + \mu + 1 = 0$$

$$\lambda - 2 = 2\mu - 7$$

$\Rightarrow \quad \lambda - 2\mu + 5 = 0$

and $\quad 2\lambda + 3 = -3\mu + 7$

$\Rightarrow 2\lambda + 3\mu - 4 = 0$

On solving above equations, we get

$$\lambda = -1 \text{ and } \mu = 2$$

$\therefore$ Point of intersection $= (2, 1, -3)$

Hence, sum of x, y and z coordinates $= 2 + 1 - 3 = 0$

27. (8) Let **CD** be $\mathbf{r}_1$.

$$\mathbf{r}_1 = (-a\hat{\mathbf{i}}) + \lambda(a\hat{\mathbf{i}} + a\hat{\mathbf{k}})$$

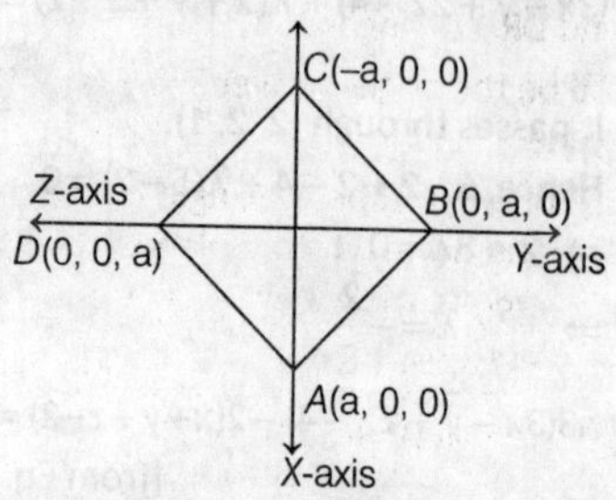

Similarly, $\mathbf{AB} = \mathbf{r}_2 = (a\hat{\mathbf{i}}) + \mu(-a\hat{\mathbf{i}} + a\hat{\mathbf{j}})$

So, shortest distance (SD)

$$= \frac{|2a\hat{\mathbf{i}}\cdot(a\hat{\mathbf{i}}+a\hat{\mathbf{k}})\times(-a\hat{\mathbf{i}}+a\hat{\mathbf{j}})|}{|(a\hat{\mathbf{i}}+a\hat{\mathbf{k}})\times(-a\hat{\mathbf{i}}+a\hat{\mathbf{j}})|}$$

$$= \frac{|2a^3\hat{\mathbf{i}}\cdot(-\hat{\mathbf{i}}-\hat{\mathbf{j}}+\hat{\mathbf{k}})|}{a^2|-\hat{\mathbf{i}}-\hat{\mathbf{j}}+\hat{\mathbf{k}}|}$$

$$= \frac{2a}{\sqrt{3}} \text{ units}$$

$$= \frac{\alpha\cdot a}{\sqrt{\beta}} \quad \text{(given)}$$

Hence, $\alpha + 2\beta = 2 + 2\times3 = 8$

28. (2) **Method I**

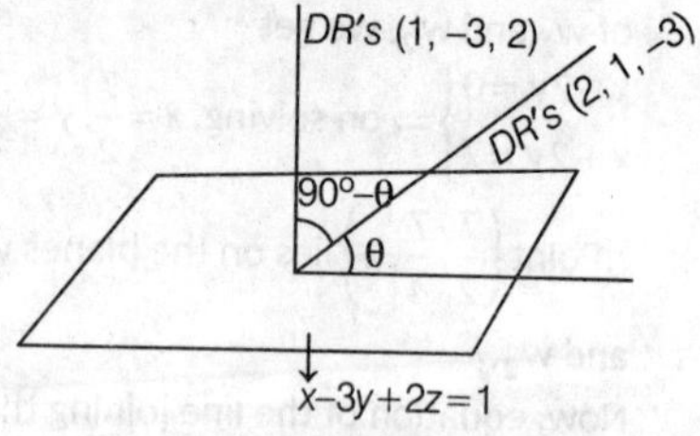

Given equation of plane is

$$x - 3y + 2z = 1$$

and the equation of line is

$$\frac{x-1}{2} = \frac{y-1}{1} = \frac{z-1}{-3}$$

Vector normal to the plane is $\mathbf{n} = \hat{\mathbf{i}} - 3\hat{\mathbf{j}} + 2\hat{\mathbf{k}}$ and vector along the line is $\mathbf{v} = 2\hat{\mathbf{i}} + \hat{\mathbf{j}} - 3\hat{\mathbf{k}}$

Now, $\cos(90°-\theta) = \sin\theta = \frac{\mathbf{n}\cdot\mathbf{v}}{|\mathbf{n}||\mathbf{v}|}$

$$= \left|\frac{2-3-6}{\sqrt{14}\sqrt{14}}\right|$$

$$= \left|\frac{7}{14}\right| = \frac{1}{2}$$

$$\therefore \quad \operatorname{cosec}\theta = 2$$

Method 2

DR's of normal to the plane is 1, −3, 2 and DR's of line is 2, 1, −3.

$\because \theta$ be the angle between line and plane.

$\therefore (90° - \theta)$ will be the angle between line and normal to the plane.

$\therefore \cos(90° - \theta)$

$$= \frac{|1 \times 2 + (-3) \times 1 + 2 \times -3|}{\sqrt{(1)^2 + (-3)^2 + (2)^2}\sqrt{(2)^2 + (1)^2 + (-3)^2}}$$

$$= \left|\frac{-7}{\sqrt{14}\sqrt{14}}\right| = \frac{7}{14} = \frac{1}{2}$$

$\therefore \operatorname{cosec} \theta = 2$

29. (5) Normal vector of the plane

$$\mathbf{n} = \begin{vmatrix} \hat{\mathbf{i}} & \hat{\mathbf{j}} & \hat{\mathbf{k}} \\ 3 & 0 & -1 \\ 1 & 2 & -1 \end{vmatrix}$$

$$\Rightarrow \mathbf{n} = 2\hat{\mathbf{i}} + 2\hat{\mathbf{j}} + 6\hat{\mathbf{k}} = 2(\hat{\mathbf{i}} + \hat{\mathbf{j}} + 3\hat{\mathbf{k}})$$

$\therefore$ Equation of plane

$$1(x + 1) + 1(y - 2) + 3(z - 0) = 0$$

$$\Rightarrow \qquad x + y + 3z = 1$$

Hence, $(a + b + c) = 1 + 1 + 3 = 5$

30. (1/2) Given equation of plane is

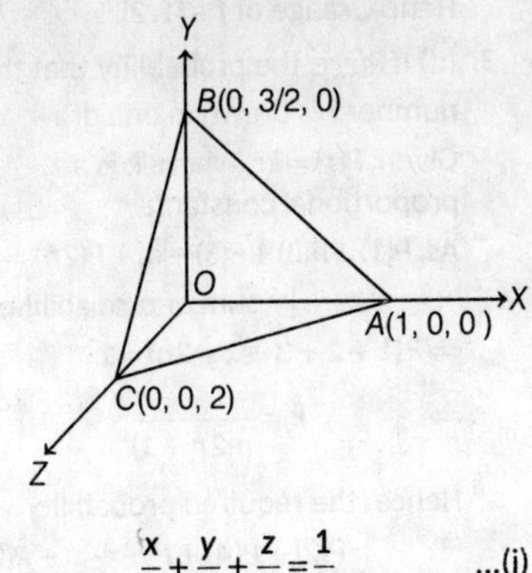

$$\frac{x}{2} + \frac{y}{3} + \frac{z}{4} = \frac{1}{2} \qquad \text{...(i)}$$

For x-intercept, put $y = z = 0$ in Eq. (i),

$$A \equiv (1, 0, 0)$$

For y-intercept, put $x = z = 0$ in Eq. (i)

$$B \equiv \left(0, \frac{3}{2}, 0\right)$$

For z-intercept, put $x = y = 0$ in Eq. (i),

$$C \equiv (0, 0, 2)$$

$\therefore$ Volume of tetrahedron (V)

$$= \frac{1}{6}[\mathbf{OA}\ \mathbf{OB}\ \mathbf{OC}]$$

$$= \frac{1}{6}\left[\hat{\mathbf{i}}\ \ \frac{3}{2}\hat{\mathbf{j}}\ \ 2\hat{\mathbf{k}}\right]$$

$$= \frac{1}{6}\left[\hat{\mathbf{i}} \cdot \left(\frac{3}{2}\hat{\mathbf{j}} \times 2\hat{\mathbf{k}}\right)\right]$$

$$= \frac{1}{6}[\hat{\mathbf{i}} \cdot (3\hat{\mathbf{i}})] = \frac{3}{6} = \frac{1}{2}$$

PART TESTS

Part Test 01

1. (c) Given, $2\cos^2\theta + \sin\theta \le 2$

$\Rightarrow \quad 2 - 2\sin^2\theta + \sin\theta \le 2$

$\Rightarrow \quad 2\sin^2\theta - \sin\theta \ge 0$

$\Rightarrow \quad \sin\theta(2\sin\theta - 1) \ge 0$

$\Rightarrow \sin\theta \ge 0$ and $2\sin\theta - 1 \ge 0$

or $\sin\theta \le 0$ and $2\sin\theta - 1 \le 0$

$\Rightarrow \sin\theta \ge 0$ and $\sin\theta \ge \frac{1}{2}$

or $\sin\theta \le 0$ and $\sin\theta \le \frac{1}{2}$

$\Rightarrow \frac{\pi}{6} \le \theta \le \frac{5\pi}{6}$ but $B = \left\{\theta : \frac{\pi}{2} \le \theta \le \frac{3\pi}{2}\right\}$

or $\sin\theta \le 0 \Rightarrow \pi \le \theta \le 2\pi$

But $\quad B = \left\{\theta : \frac{\pi}{2} \le \theta \le \frac{3\pi}{2}\right\}$

$\therefore \quad A \cap B = \left\{\theta : \frac{\pi}{2} \le \theta \le \frac{5\pi}{6}\right\} \quad$ ...(i)

$\therefore \quad A \cap B = \left\{\theta : \pi \le \theta \le \frac{3\pi}{2}\right\} \quad$ ...(ii)

From Eqs. (i) $\cup$ (ii), we get

$$A \cap B = \left\{\theta : \frac{\pi}{2} \le \theta \le \frac{5\pi}{6}\right\} \cup \left\{\theta : \pi \le \theta \le \frac{3\pi}{2}\right\}$$

2. (b) Given,

$$f(x) = \log_2\left(\frac{\sin x - \cos x + 3\sqrt{2}}{\sqrt{2}}\right)$$

$$= \log_2\left(\sin\left(x - \frac{\pi}{4}\right) + 3\right) = y \quad \text{(say)}$$

$\Rightarrow \quad 2^y = \sin\left(x - \frac{\pi}{4}\right) + 3$

$\Rightarrow 2^y - 3 = \sin\left(x - \frac{\pi}{4}\right)$

As we know that

$-1 \le \sin\left(x - \frac{\pi}{4}\right) \le 1$

$\Rightarrow \quad -1 \le 2^y - 3 \le 1$

$\Rightarrow \quad 2 \le 2^y \le 4$

$\Rightarrow \quad 2^1 \le 2^y \le 2^2$

$\Rightarrow \quad 1 \le y \le 2 \Rightarrow y \in [1, 2]$

Hence, range of $f \in [1, 2]$.

3. (d) If $P(r)$ is the probability that the number r is drawn in one draw.

Given, $P(r) = kr$, where k is a proportional constant.

As, $P(1) + P(2) + P(3) + \ldots + P(2n) = 1$

[$\because$ sum of probabilities $= 1$]

$\Rightarrow k(1 + 2 + 3 + .. + 2n) = 1$

$\Rightarrow \quad k = \frac{1}{n(2n+1)}$

Hence, the required probability

$= P(2) + P(4) + P(6) + \ldots + P(2n)$

$\Rightarrow 2k(1 + 2 + 3 + \ldots + n)$

$= \frac{2}{n(2n+1)} \cdot \frac{n(n+1)}{2} = \frac{n+1}{2n+1}$

4. (c) Since, α and β are the roots of the equations.

$\sin^2 x + a\sin x + b = 0 \quad$ ...(i)

and $\cos^2 x + c\cos x + d = 0 \quad$ ...(ii)

So, $\left.\begin{array}{l}\sin^2\alpha + a\sin\alpha + b = 0 \\ \text{and } \sin^2\beta + a\sin\beta + b = 0\end{array}\right\}$ [from Eq. (i)]

$\Rightarrow \quad \sin\alpha + \sin\beta = -a \quad$ ...(iii)

Similarly,

$\left.\begin{array}{l}\cos^2\alpha + c\cos\alpha + d = 0 \\ \cos^2\beta + c\cos\beta + d = 0\end{array}\right\}$ [from Eq. (ii)]

$\Rightarrow \quad \cos\alpha + \cos\beta = -c \quad$ ...(iv)

Now, from Eq. (iii), we get

$2\sin\left(\frac{\alpha+\beta}{2}\right) \cdot \cos\left(\frac{\alpha-\beta}{2}\right) = -a \quad$ ...(v)

and from Eq. (iv), we get

$2\cos\left(\frac{\alpha+\beta}{2}\right) \cdot \cos\left(\frac{\alpha-\beta}{2}\right) = -c \quad$ ...(vi)

Now, dividing Eq. (v) by Eq. (vi), we get

$\Rightarrow \tan\left(\frac{\alpha+\beta}{2}\right) = \frac{a}{c}$

$\therefore \quad \sin(\alpha+\beta) = \frac{2\tan\left(\frac{\alpha+\beta}{2}\right)}{1 + \tan^2\left(\frac{\alpha+\beta}{2}\right)}$

$= \frac{2ac}{a^2 + c^2}$

5. (a) Since, $\left(x^{\frac{2}{3}} + 4x^{\frac{1}{3}} + 4\right)^5$

$= \left(x^{\frac{1}{3}} + 2\right)^{10} \quad$ ...(i)

and $\left(\frac{1}{x^{\frac{1}{3}} - 1} + \frac{1}{x^{\frac{2}{3}} + x^{\frac{1}{3}} + 1}\right)^{-9}$

$= \left(\frac{x^{\frac{2}{3}} + 2x^{\frac{1}{3}}}{x - 1}\right)^{-9}$

$= \frac{(x-1)^9}{x^3\left(x^{\frac{1}{3}} + 2\right)^9} \quad$ ...(ii)

On multiplying Eqs. (i) and (ii), we get

$\left(x^{\frac{2}{3}} + 4x^{\frac{1}{3}} + 4\right)^5 \left(\frac{1}{x^{\frac{1}{3}} - 1} + \frac{1}{x^{\frac{2}{3}} + x^{\frac{1}{3}} + 1}\right)^{-9}$

$= \frac{\left(x^{\frac{1}{3}} + 2\right)(x-1)^9}{x^3}$

$(x^9 - \ldots ({}^9C_3)x^3 - ({}^9C_2)x^2 + 9x - 1)$

Hence, the constant term is $2\,({}^9C_3)$

$= 2 \times 84 = 168$

6. (d) Let ABC be a triangle such that $\angle A = 60°$ and $AC = b$, $AB = c$ [given]

Let $b = \sqrt{3} + 1$ and $c = \sqrt{3} - 1$

So, $\angle B + \angle C = 180° - \angle A = 120° \quad$ ...(i)

As we know, tangent law is

$$\frac{b-c}{b+c}\cot\left(\frac{A}{2}\right) = \tan\left(\frac{B-C}{2}\right)$$

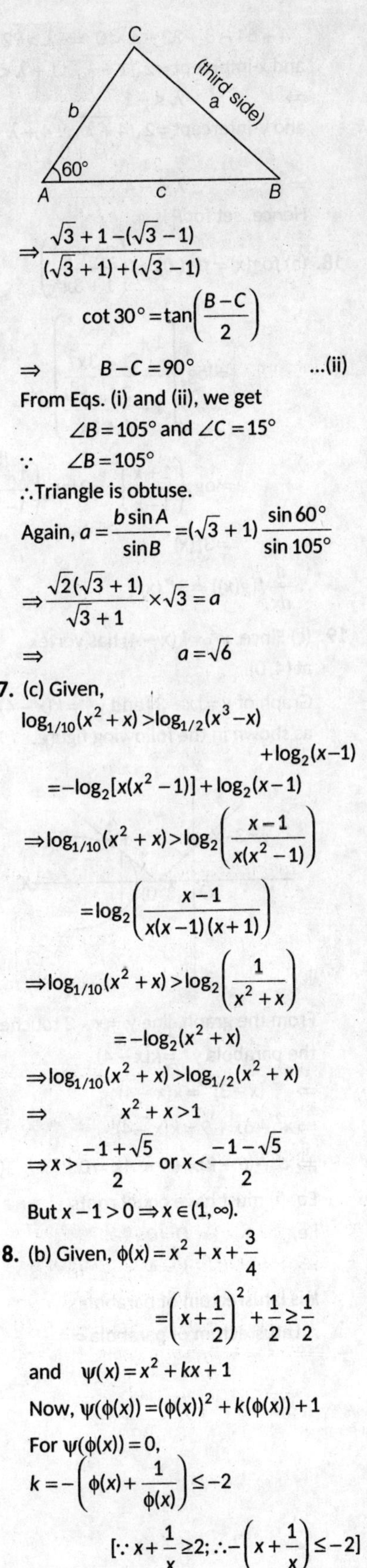

$$\Rightarrow \frac{\sqrt{3}+1-(\sqrt{3}-1)}{(\sqrt{3}+1)+(\sqrt{3}-1)}$$

$$\cot 30° = \tan\left(\frac{B-C}{2}\right)$$

$$\Rightarrow \quad B-C = 90° \quad \text{...(ii)}$$

From Eqs. (i) and (ii), we get

$$\angle B = 105° \text{ and } \angle C = 15°$$

$$\because \quad \angle B = 105°$$

$\therefore$ Triangle is obtuse.

Again, $a = \frac{b \sin A}{\sin B} = (\sqrt{3}+1)\frac{\sin 60°}{\sin 105°}$

$$\Rightarrow \frac{\sqrt{2}(\sqrt{3}+1)}{\sqrt{3}+1} \times \sqrt{3} = a$$

$$\Rightarrow \quad a = \sqrt{6}$$

7. (c) Given,

$$\log_{1/10}(x^2+x) > \log_{1/2}(x^3-x) + \log_2(x-1)$$

$$= -\log_2[x(x^2-1)] + \log_2(x-1)$$

$$\Rightarrow \log_{1/10}(x^2+x) > \log_2\left(\frac{x-1}{x(x^2-1)}\right)$$

$$= \log_2\left(\frac{x-1}{x(x-1)(x+1)}\right)$$

$$\Rightarrow \log_{1/10}(x^2+x) > \log_2\left(\frac{1}{x^2+x}\right)$$

$$= -\log_2(x^2+x)$$

$$\Rightarrow \log_{1/10}(x^2+x) > \log_{1/2}(x^2+x)$$

$$\Rightarrow \quad x^2+x > 1$$

$$\Rightarrow x > \frac{-1+\sqrt{5}}{2} \text{ or } x < \frac{-1-\sqrt{5}}{2}$$

But $x-1>0 \Rightarrow x \in (1, \infty)$.

8. (b) Given, $\phi(x) = x^2 + x + \frac{3}{4}$

$$= \left(x+\frac{1}{2}\right)^2 + \frac{1}{2} \geq \frac{1}{2}$$

and $\psi(x) = x^2 + kx + 1$

Now, $\psi(\phi(x)) = (\phi(x))^2 + k(\phi(x)) + 1$

For $\psi(\phi(x)) = 0$,

$$k = -\left(\phi(x) + \frac{1}{\phi(x)}\right) \leq -2$$

$$\left[\because x + \frac{1}{x} \geq 2; \therefore -\left(x+\frac{1}{x}\right) \leq -2\right]$$

$\therefore$ If $k > -2$, $\psi(\phi(x)) = 0$ has no solutions.

9. (a) Here, range $= (r) =$ largest value $-$ smallest value

$$= \max |x_i - x_j|, \text{ where } i \neq j$$

and $E^2 = \frac{1}{n-1}\sum_{i=1}^{n}(x_i - \bar{x})^2$

Now,

$$(x_i - \bar{x})^2 = \left[x_i - \frac{x_1 + x_2 + x_3 + \ldots + x_n}{n}\right]^2$$

$$= \frac{1}{n^2}[(x_i - x_1) + (x_i - x_2) + (x_i - x_3) + \ldots + (x_i - x_n)]^2$$

$$= \frac{1}{n^2}[(x_i - x_1) + (x_i - x_2) + (x_i - x_3) + \ldots + (x_i - x_{i-1}) + (x_i - x_{i+1}) \ldots + (x_i - x_n)]^2$$

$$\Rightarrow (x_i - \bar{x})^2 \leq \frac{1}{n^2}[(n-1)\cdot r]^2$$

$$[\because |x_i - x_j| \leq r]$$

$$\Rightarrow \frac{1}{n-1}\sum_{i=1}^{n}(x_i - \bar{x})^2 \leq \frac{1}{n^2(n-1)} \Sigma[(n-1)r]^2$$

[summing up and dividing by $(n-1)$ on both sides]

$$= \frac{1}{n^2} \times \frac{1}{n-1} \cdot n(n-1)^2 r^2$$

$$= \frac{n-1}{n} r^2 < \frac{n}{n-1} r^2 \quad \left[\because n > 1, n > \frac{1}{n}\right]$$

Hence, $E^2 < \frac{n}{n-1} r^2$ or $E < r\sqrt{\frac{n}{n-1}}$

10. (b) Given, equation of circle is

$$x^2 + y^2 = 4 \quad \text{...(i)}$$

So, $\quad x^2 \leq 4 \quad$ ...(ii)

and $\quad y^2 \leq 4 \quad$ ...(iii)

$$\tan^4 x + \cot^4 x + 1 = 3\sin^2 y$$

$$\Rightarrow (\tan^2 x - \cot^2 x)^2 + 3 = 3\sin^2 y$$

$$\because (\tan^2 x - \cot^2 x)^2 + 3 \geq 3$$

$$\therefore \quad 3\sin^2 y \geq 3$$

Hence, $\tan^2 x = \cot^2 x$ and $\sin^2 y = 1$

When $\tan^2 x = \cot^2 x$

$$\Rightarrow \quad \tan^4 x = 1 \Rightarrow \tan x = \pm 1$$

$$\Rightarrow \quad x = \pm\frac{\pi}{4}, \pm\frac{3\pi}{4}$$

But $x^2 \leq 4 \Rightarrow -2 \leq x \leq 2$

$$\Rightarrow \quad y = \pm\frac{\pi}{2} \text{ only}$$

$$\Rightarrow \quad x = \pm\frac{\pi}{4} \text{ only}$$

and $\sin^2 y = 1$

$$\Rightarrow \sin y = \pm 1$$

$$\Rightarrow y = \pm\frac{\pi}{2}, \pm\frac{3\pi}{2}, \ldots \text{ but } y^2 \leq 4$$

$$\Rightarrow \quad -2 \leq y \leq 2$$

Hence, total four solutions are possible.

11. (b) Given, expression can be written as

$$\frac{\sum_{r=1}^{r=n}[r(n-r+1)^2]}{\sum_{r=1}^{n} r^3} = \frac{\sum_{r=1}^{n} r((n+1)-r)^2}{\sum_{r=1}^{n} r^3}$$

$$= \frac{\sum_{r=1}^{n}[(n+1)^2 r - 2(n+1)r^2 + r^3]}{\sum_{r=1}^{n} r^3}$$

$$\because \lim_{n\to\infty} \frac{1\cdot n^2 + 2(n-1)^2 + \ldots + n\cdot 1^2}{1^3 + 2^3 + 3^3 + \ldots + n^3}$$

$$\Rightarrow \lim_{n\to\infty}\left[4\cdot\frac{(n+1)^2}{n^2(n+1)^2}\cdot\frac{n(n+1)}{2} - \frac{4\times 2(n+1)\cdot n\cdot(n+1)(2n+1)}{6\cdot n^2(n+1)^2} + \frac{\sum_{r=1}^{n} r^3}{\sum_{r=1}^{n} r^3}\right]$$

$$\therefore \lim_{n\to\infty}\left[\left(\frac{n+1}{n}\right)(2) - \frac{4}{3}\left(\frac{2n+1}{n}\right) + 1\right]$$

$$= 2(1) - \frac{8}{3} + 1 = 3 - \frac{8}{3} = \frac{1}{3}$$

12. (b) Let $b = ar$, $c = ar^2$

For ΔABC, $a + b > c \Rightarrow a + ar > ar^2$

$$\Rightarrow \quad r^2 - r - 1 < 0 \quad [\because a > 0]$$

$$\Rightarrow \quad \frac{1-\sqrt{5}}{2} < r < \frac{1+\sqrt{5}}{2}$$

Also, $b + c > a \Rightarrow a(r + r^2) > a$

$$\Rightarrow \quad r^2 + r - 1 > 0 \quad [\because a, b, c > 0]$$

$$\Rightarrow r \in \left(-\infty, \frac{-1-\sqrt{5}}{2}\right) \cup \left(\frac{-1+\sqrt{5}}{2}, \infty\right)$$

Finally, $a + c > b$

$$\Rightarrow a[1 + r^2] > ar \Rightarrow r^2 - r + > 0$$

which is true for all values of r.

In this case, 'r' can not be negative.

$$\therefore \quad r \in \left(\frac{\sqrt{5}-1}{2}, \frac{1+\sqrt{5}}{2}\right)$$

13. (c)

p	q	$\sim p$	$p \Rightarrow q$	$\sim p \wedge q$	$(p \Rightarrow q) \Leftrightarrow (\sim p \wedge q)$
T	T	F	T	F	F
T	F	F	F	F	T
F	T	T	T	T	T
F	F	T	T	F	F

Hence, the given statement is neither tautology nor contradiction.

14. (c) Total number of ways of choosing 6 pens out of 8 different brands

$$= {}^{8+6-1}C_6 = {}^{13}C_6$$

15. (b) The first pair of lines is

$$l^2x^2 - m^2y^2 - n(lx + my) = 0$$

i.e. $(lx - my)(lx + my) - n(lx + my) = 0$

$\Rightarrow \quad (lx + my)(lx - my - n) = 0$

$\Rightarrow \quad lx + my = 0 \quad$ ...(i)

and $\quad lx - my - n = 0 \quad$ ...(ii)

The second pair of lines is given by

$$l^2x^2 - m^2y^2 + n(lx - my) = 0$$

$\Rightarrow (lx - my)(lx + my) + n(lx - my) = 0$

$\Rightarrow \quad (lx - my)(lx + my + n) = 0$

$\Rightarrow \quad lx - my = 0 \quad$ ...(iii)

and $\quad lx + my + n = 0 \quad$ ...(iv)

Clearly, line (i) is parallel to lines (iii) and (ii) is parallel to line (iv).

Let d_1 = distance between line (i) $\times$ line (iii)

d_2 = distance between line (ii) $\times$ line (iv)

So, $d_1 = \dfrac{|-n-0|}{\sqrt{l^2 + (-m)^2}} = \dfrac{n}{\sqrt{l^2 + m^2}}$

and $d_2 = \dfrac{|0-n|}{\sqrt{l^2 + m^2}} = \dfrac{n}{\sqrt{l^2 + m^2}}$

Since, distances d_1 and d_2 between the two pairs of parallel lines are equal, so the quadrilateral formed by the given lines is a rhombus.

Hence, the area of this rhombus

$$= \left|\frac{(-n-0)(0-n)}{\begin{vmatrix} l & -m \\ l & m \end{vmatrix}}\right| = \frac{n^2}{2|l \cdot m|}$$

16. (c) For $0 < x < \dfrac{\pi}{2}, 0 < \sin^2 x < 1$

Now, $y = \exp[(\sin^2 x + \sin^4 x + \sin^6 x + \dots \infty)\log_e 2]$

$$= \exp\left[\left(\frac{\sin^2 x}{1 - \sin^2 x}\right) \cdot \ln 2\right]$$

$$\left[\because S_\infty = \frac{a}{1-r} \text{ for GP}\right]$$

$= \exp(\tan^2 x \log_e 2)$

$= \exp(\log_e 2)^{\tan^2 x})$

$= e^{(\log_e 2)^{\tan^2 x}}$

$\Rightarrow \quad y = 2^{\tan^2 x} \quad$ ...(i)

Since, y satisfies the equation

$$x^2 - 9x + 8 = 0$$

So, $\quad y^2 - 9y + 8 = 0$

$\Rightarrow \quad y = 1$ or $y = 8$

For $\quad y = 1$

$\Rightarrow \quad 2^{\tan^{2x}} = 1$

$\Rightarrow \quad \tan x = 0 \Rightarrow x = 0 \quad$ ...(ii)

but $0 < x < \dfrac{\pi}{2} \quad$ ...(iii)

From Eqs. (ii) $\cap$ (iii), we get

$$x \in \phi$$

$\therefore y = 1$ is not possible.

For $y = 8$

$\Rightarrow 2^{\tan^2} x = 8 = 2^3$

$\Rightarrow \tan x = \sqrt{3}$

$\Rightarrow \quad x = \dfrac{\pi}{3} \in \left(0, \dfrac{\pi}{2}\right)$

$\therefore \quad y = 8$ is possible.

Hence, $\dfrac{\sin x + \cos x}{\sin x - \cos x} = \dfrac{\tan x + 1}{\tan x - 1}$

[by dividing $\cos x$ in numerator and denominator]

$$= \frac{\sqrt{3}+1}{\sqrt{3}-1} = \frac{(\sqrt{3}+1)^2}{(\sqrt{3}-1)(\sqrt{3}+1)} = 2 + \sqrt{3}$$

17. (d) For $P(2, 8)$ lies in interior of the circle $x^2 + y^2 - 2x + 4y - \lambda = 0$ is

$$4 + 64 - 8 + 32 - \lambda < 0 \Rightarrow \lambda > 92$$

and x-intercept $= 2\sqrt{1+\lambda}, \therefore 1 + \lambda < 0$

$\Rightarrow \quad \lambda < -1$

and y-intercept $= 2\sqrt{4+\lambda}, \therefore 4 + \lambda < 0$

$\Rightarrow \quad \lambda < -4$

Hence, set for P is ϕ.

18. (a) $fog(x) = f(g(x)) = f\left(\dfrac{3x + x^3}{1 + 3x^2}\right)$

$$= \log_e \left(\frac{1 + \dfrac{3x + x^3}{1 + 3x^2}}{1 - \dfrac{3x + x^3}{1 + 3x^2}}\right)$$

$$= \log_e \left(\frac{1+x}{1-x}\right)^3 = 3 \log_e \left(\frac{1+x}{1-x}\right)$$

$$= 3f(x)$$

$\therefore \dfrac{d}{dx} f(g(x)) = 3f'(x)$

19. (c) Since, $y^2 = k(x - 4)$ has vertex at $(4, 0)$.

Graph of $y = |x - 3|$ and $y^2 = k(x - 4)$ is as shown in the following figure.

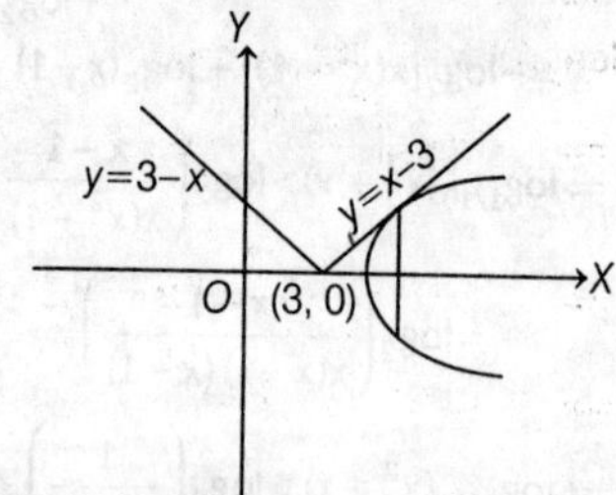

From the graph, line $y = x - 3$ touches the parabola $y^2 = k(x - 4)$.

$\Rightarrow \quad (x - 3)^2 = k(x - 4)$

$\Rightarrow x^2 - 6x + 9 = k(x - 4)$

$\Rightarrow x^2 - (6 + k)x + 9 + 4k = 0 \quad$ ...(i)

Eq. (i) must have equal roots

i.e. $\quad D = 0$

$\Rightarrow \quad k = 4$

k is latusrectum of parabola.

$\therefore$ Latusrectum of parabola $= 4$

20. (d) Given, $4x^2+5y^2=20$

$$\Rightarrow \frac{x^2}{5}+\frac{y^2}{4}=1$$

Now, equation of tangent with slope m is $y=mx\pm\sqrt{5m^2+4}$

This tangent passes through $P(x_1, y_1)$.

$$\therefore \quad y_1=mx_1\pm\sqrt{5m^2+4}$$

$$\Rightarrow (x_1^2-5)m^2-2x_1y_1m+y_1^2-4=0$$

$$\Rightarrow \quad m_1+m_2=\frac{2x_1y_1}{x_1^2-5} \quad ...(i)$$

and $$m_1m_2=\frac{y_1^2-4}{x_1^2-5} \quad ...(ii)$$

Given, $\cot\alpha+\cot\beta=2$

$$\Rightarrow \frac{1}{\tan\alpha}+\frac{1}{\tan\beta}=2 \Rightarrow \frac{1}{m_1}+\frac{1}{m_2}=2$$

$$\Rightarrow \frac{2x_1y_1}{x_1^2-5}=\frac{2(y_1^2-4)}{x_1^2-5}$$

[from Eq. (i) and (ii)]

$$\Rightarrow \quad y_1^2-4=x_1y_1$$

$\therefore$ Locus of $P(x_1, y_1)$ is $y^2-4=xy$

21. (7) We have,

$\log_{16}(\lambda+7)-\log_{16}\lambda=0.25$

$$\Rightarrow \quad \log_{16}\left(\frac{\lambda+7}{\lambda}\right)=0.25$$

$$\Rightarrow \quad \frac{\lambda+7}{\lambda}=(16)^{\frac{1}{4}}=2$$

$$\Rightarrow \quad \lambda=7$$

22. (13) Given, equations of circle is

$$x^2+y^2-8x+15=0$$

$$\Rightarrow \quad (x-4)^2+y^2=1$$

$\therefore$ Centre $(C)=(4, 0)$

Radius $=1$

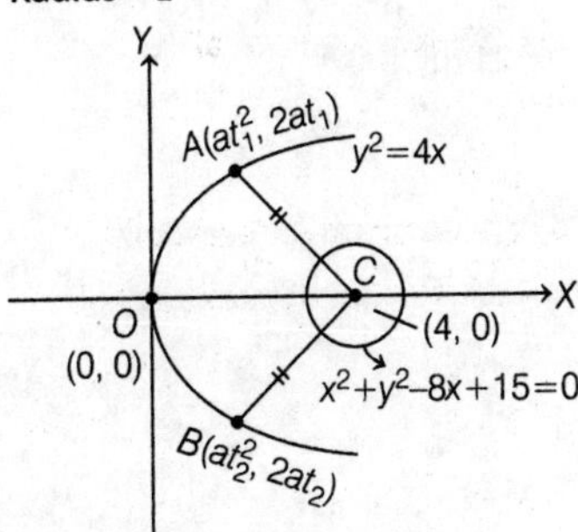

Also, given equation of parabola is $y^2=4x$

Now, equation of normal to $y^2=4x$ at $(t^2, 2t)$ is

$$y=-tx+t+t^3 \quad ...(i)$$

Now, the distance between the curves be minimum if Eq. (i) must pass through the centre of the circle.

So, $0=-4t+t+t^3$

$$\Rightarrow \quad t^3-3t=0$$

$$\Rightarrow \quad t=0, \pm\sqrt{3}$$

$\therefore A(at_1^2, 2at_1)=(3, 2\sqrt{3})$

and $\quad B=(3, -2\sqrt{3})$

Now, $\quad CA=CB=\sqrt{13}$

$\therefore$ Required square of the minimum distance $=13$

23. (1) Given, $f_k(\alpha)=\left(\cos\frac{\alpha}{k^2}+i\sin\frac{\alpha}{k^2}\right)$

$$\left(\cos\frac{2\alpha}{k^2}+i\sin\frac{2\alpha}{k^2}\right)\ldots\left(\cos\frac{\alpha}{k}+i\sin\frac{\alpha}{k}\right)$$

$$=e^{\frac{i\alpha}{k^2}}\cdot e^{\frac{i2\alpha}{k^2}}\ldots e^{\frac{i\alpha}{k}}$$

$$=e^{\frac{i\alpha}{k^2}(1+2+3+\ldots+k)}\left[\because e^{\frac{i\alpha}{k}}=e^{i\alpha k/k^2}\right]$$

$$=e^{\frac{i\alpha}{k^2}\left[\frac{k(k+1)}{2}\right]}=e^{\frac{i\alpha}{2}\left[\frac{k^2+k}{k^2}\right]}$$

$$=e^{\frac{i\alpha}{2}\left(1+\frac{1}{k}\right)}$$

$$\therefore \lim_{n\to\infty} f_n(\pi)=\lim_{n\to\infty} e^{\frac{i\pi}{2}\left(1+\frac{1}{n}\right)}=e^{\frac{i\pi}{2}}$$

$$=\cos\frac{\pi}{2}+i\sin\frac{\pi}{2}=i$$

Hence, $\left[\lim_{n\to\infty} f_n(\pi)\right]^4=(i)^4=1$

24. (7) Since, a, b, c are in AP.

Let $d=$ common difference of that AP.

So, $b-a=d$ and $c-b=d$

$\Rightarrow a=b-d$ and $c=b+d$

Given, $abc=4 \Rightarrow (b-d)(b+d)\cdot b=4$

$$\Rightarrow \quad b(b^2-d^2)=4 \quad ...(i)$$

$$\because \quad b^2-d^2\le b^2$$

$\therefore b(b^2-d^2)\le b^3 \Rightarrow 4\le b^3$

[from Eq. (i)]

$$\Rightarrow \quad b^3\ge 2^2 \Rightarrow b\ge 2^{\frac{2}{3}}.$$

So, minimum value of b is $2^{\frac{2}{3}}$

On comparing with $\alpha^{\frac{\beta}{\gamma}}$, we get

$$\alpha=2, \beta=2, \gamma=3$$

So, $\alpha+\beta+\gamma=2+2+3=7$

25. (1) Let

$$\gamma=\frac{z-1}{\cos\alpha+i\sin\alpha}+\frac{\cos\alpha+i\sin\alpha}{z-1}$$

$\because$ β is an imaginary part of γ.

$$\therefore \quad \beta=\frac{\gamma-\bar{\gamma}}{2i}$$

Given, $\beta=0 \Rightarrow \gamma-\bar{\gamma}=0$

$$\Rightarrow \frac{z-1}{\cos\alpha+i\sin\alpha}+\frac{\cos\alpha+i\sin\alpha}{z-1}-\frac{\bar{z}-1}{\cos\alpha-i\sin\alpha}-\frac{\cos\alpha-i\sin\alpha}{\bar{z}-1}=0$$

$$\Rightarrow \left(\frac{z-1}{\cos\alpha+i\sin\alpha}-\frac{\cos\alpha-i\sin\alpha}{\bar{z}-1}\right)+\left(\frac{\cos\alpha+i\sin\alpha}{z-1}-\frac{\bar{z}-1}{\cos\alpha-i\sin\alpha}\right)=0$$

$$\Rightarrow \frac{\{(z-1)(\bar{z}-1)-1\}\{\cos\alpha-i\sin\alpha\}}{(\bar{z}-1)}+\frac{\{(1-(z-1)(\bar{z}-1)\}(\cos\alpha+i\sin\alpha)}{z-1}=0$$

$$\Rightarrow \frac{(z-1)\{(z-1)(\bar{z}-1)-1\}}{(\bar{z}-1)\{(z-1)(\bar{z}-1)-1\}}=\frac{\cos\alpha+i\sin\alpha}{\cos\alpha-i\sin\alpha}$$

$$\Rightarrow |z-1||(z-1)(\bar{z}-1)-1|=|\bar{z}-1||(z-1)(\bar{z}-1)-1|$$

$$\Rightarrow (z-1)(\bar{z}-1)-1=0$$

$$\Rightarrow \quad x^2+y^2-2x=0$$

$$\Rightarrow (x^2-2x+1)+y^2=1$$

$$\Rightarrow \quad (x-1)^2+y^2=(1)^2$$

which represents equation of a circle whose radius $=1$

26. (0) Let $c_1: y=x^2+3kx+12$ is parabola which is concave upward.

$c_2: 4y^2-9=0$ represents a pair of straight lines.

$\because$ c_1 and c_2 meet exactly at three distinct points, line $y=-\frac{3}{2}$ must be tangent to parabola as shown in figure.

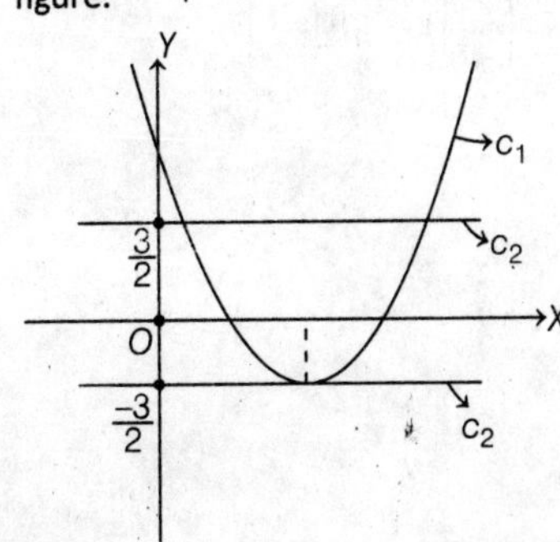

i.e. $\frac{-D}{4a}=-\frac{3}{2}$

$\Rightarrow \frac{9k^2-4\times 12}{4\times 1}=\frac{3}{2}$

$\Rightarrow 9k^2=54$

$\Rightarrow k^2=6$

$\Rightarrow k=\pm\sqrt{6}$

Hence, the sum of all values of

$k=\sqrt{6}+(-\sqrt{6})=0$

27. (28) We know that asymptotes of rectangular hyperbola are mutually perpendicular and thus other asymptote should be $4x+3y+\lambda=0$.

Intersection point of asymptotes is also the center of the hyperbola.

Hence, point of intersection of $3x-4y-6=0$ and $4x+3y+\lambda=0$ is $\left(\frac{18-4\lambda}{25}, \frac{-12\lambda-96}{100}\right)$ and it should lie on the line $x-y-1=0$.

So, $\frac{18-4\lambda}{25}-\frac{-12\lambda-96}{100}-1=0$

$\Rightarrow \lambda=17$

Hence, equation of other asymptote is $4x+3y+17=0$.

On comparing with $Ax+By+C=0$, we get

$A=4, B=3, C=17$

$\therefore 2A+B+C=28$

28. (0) Let $f(y)=y^2-my+1$

Since, 1 lies between the roots of the equation $y^2-my+1=0$

$\therefore m^2-4>0$ and $1-m+1<0$

[$\because$ discriminant >0 and $f(1)<0$]

$\Rightarrow (m<-2$ or $m>2)$ and $(m>2)$

Hence, $m>2$

[after taking common values]

Now, AM $\geq$ GM

$\Rightarrow \frac{|x|^2+16}{2}\geq 4|x| \Rightarrow 0$

$\leq \frac{4|x|}{|x|^2+16}\leq\frac{1}{2}$

$\Rightarrow 0<\left(\frac{4|x|}{|x|^2+16}\right)^m<1$

$\Rightarrow \left[\left(\frac{4|x|}{|x|^2+16}\right)^m\right]=0$

29. (7) The given lines are

$y-\sqrt{3}|x|=2$

i.e. $y-\sqrt{3}x=2, x\geq 0$ ...(i)

and $y+\sqrt{3}x=2, x\leq 0$ ...(ii)

Since, both the lines are symmetrical about the Y-axis and hence, Y-axis is the bisector of the angle between them.

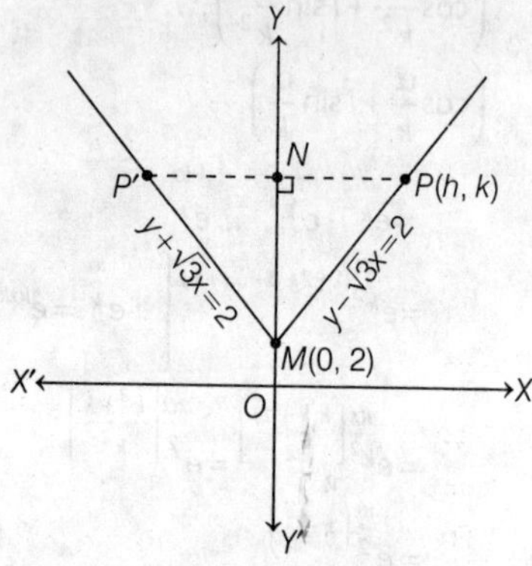

On solving Eqs. (i) and (ii), we get

$M\equiv(0,2)$

$\because$ Both the lines are symmetrical about the bisector of angle between them, so we can take point P on either of these lines. (here note that, the foot of perpendicular from P on the bisector of angle between the lines will be same)

Let $P(h,k)$ lies on $y-\sqrt{3}x=2$

$\therefore k-\sqrt{3}h=2 \Rightarrow k=\sqrt{3}h+2$

Also, $PM=5 \Rightarrow PM^2=25$

$\Rightarrow (h-0)^2+(k-2)^2=25$

$\Rightarrow h^2+k^2-4k+4=25$

$\Rightarrow h^2+(\sqrt{3}h+2)^2-4(\sqrt{3}h+2)=21$

$\Rightarrow 4h^2=25 \Rightarrow h=\frac{5}{2}$.

[here, (h,k) lies on $y-\sqrt{3}x=2, x\geq 0$ and h and $k>0$]

$\therefore k=\frac{5\sqrt{3}}{2}+2=\frac{4+5\sqrt{3}}{2}$

$\therefore P\equiv\left(\frac{5}{2}, \frac{4+5\sqrt{3}}{2}\right)$

$\therefore$ The foot of the perpendicular from P on Y-axis is

$N\left(0, \frac{4+5\sqrt{3}}{2}\right)$

On comparing, we get

$\alpha=0, \beta=4, \gamma=5, \delta=3, \lambda=2$

$\therefore \lambda\alpha+\beta\delta-\gamma=0+12-5=7$

30. (21) As $AB=9$ m, $BC=7$ m, $AC=8$ m are known, so using cosine formula for finding the $\angle C$.

$\therefore \cos C=\frac{a^2+b^2-c^2}{2ab}=\frac{2}{7}$

In ΔBEC, $BC=7$ m, $CE=4$ m, $\cos C=\frac{2}{7}$

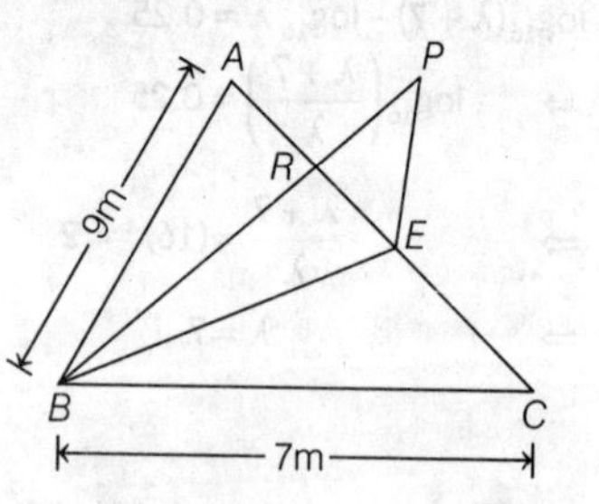

$\therefore BE^2=4^2+7^2-2\times 4\times 7\times\frac{7}{2}=49$

$\Rightarrow BE=7$ m

If h is the height of the lamp post EP at E, then $\frac{PE}{BE}=\frac{h}{7}=\tan(\tan^{-1}3)=3$

$h=21$ m

Part Test 02

1. (a) Each side of $S_1 = K$ units

$\therefore$ Each side of $S_2 = \sqrt{\left(\frac{K}{2}\right)^2 + \left(\frac{K}{2}\right)^2}$

$= \frac{K}{\sqrt{2}}$ units

Similarly,

each side of $S_3 = \sqrt{\left(\frac{K}{2\sqrt{2}}\right)^2 + \left(\frac{K}{2\sqrt{2}}\right)^2}$

$= \sqrt{\frac{2K^2}{8}} = \frac{K}{2}$ units

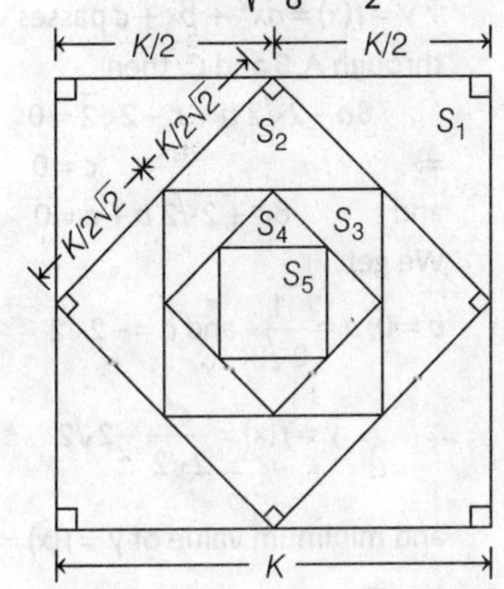

Each side of $S_4 = \sqrt{\left(\frac{K}{4}\right)^2 + \left(\frac{K}{4}\right)^2}$

$= \sqrt{\frac{2K^2}{16}} = \frac{K}{2\sqrt{2}}$ units and so on.

Now, $\lim_{n \to \infty} (P_1 + P_2 + P_3 + P_4 \dots + P_n)$

$= 4K + \frac{4K}{\sqrt{2}} + \frac{4K}{2} + \frac{4K}{2\sqrt{2}} + \dots + \infty$

This is sum of infinite GP with first term $4K$ and common ratio $\frac{1}{\sqrt{2}}$.

$\lim_{n \to \infty} (P_1 + P_2 + P_3 + P_4 \dots + P_n)$

$= \frac{4K}{1 - \frac{1}{\sqrt{2}}} = \frac{4K \times \sqrt{2}}{(\sqrt{2} - 1)} = \frac{4\sqrt{2}K}{(\sqrt{2} - 1)}$

Similarly,

$\lim_{n \to \infty} (A_1 + A_2 + A_3 + A_4 \dots + A_n)$

$= K^2 + \frac{K^2}{2} + \frac{K^2}{4} + \frac{K^2}{8} + \dots$

$= \frac{K^2}{1 - \frac{1}{2}} = 2K^2$

Now, $\lim_{n \to \infty} \left[\frac{A_1 + A_2 + A_3 + A_4 + \dots + A_n}{P_1 + P_2 + P_3 + P_4 + \dots + P_n}\right]$

$= \frac{2K^2}{\frac{4\sqrt{2}K}{\sqrt{2} - 1}} = \frac{2K^2}{1} \times \frac{\sqrt{2} - 1}{4\sqrt{2}K}$

$= \frac{(\sqrt{2} - 1)K}{2\sqrt{2}} \times \frac{(\sqrt{2} + 1)}{(\sqrt{2} + 1)}$

$= \frac{(2 - 1)K}{2\sqrt{2}(\sqrt{2} + 1)} = \frac{K}{2(2 + \sqrt{2})}$

2. (c) Given,

$4x^2 - 20\lambda x + 25\lambda^2 + 15\lambda - 66 = 0$

The roots of the given equation are real.

$\therefore (-20\lambda)^2 - 4 \times 4(25\lambda^2 + 15\lambda - 66) \ge 0$

$\Rightarrow \quad -15\lambda + 66 \ge 0$

$\Rightarrow \quad \lambda \le \frac{22}{5}$ ...(i)

$\because$ Each root exceeds $2 \cdot f(2) > 0$.

$\Rightarrow 16 - 40\lambda + 25\lambda^2 + 15\lambda - 66 > 0$

$\Rightarrow \quad 25\lambda^2 - 25\lambda - 50 > 0$

$\Rightarrow \quad \lambda^2 - \lambda - 2 > 0$

$\Rightarrow \quad (\lambda + 1)(\lambda - 2) > 0$

$\Rightarrow \quad \lambda < -1$

or $\quad \lambda > 2$ ...(ii)

Also sum of the roots is greater than 4.

$\Rightarrow \quad \frac{20\lambda}{4} > 4$

$\Rightarrow \quad 5\lambda > 4$

$\Rightarrow \quad \lambda > 4/5$ ...(iii)

From inequations (i), (ii) and (iii), we get

$$\lambda \in \left(2, \frac{22}{5}\right)$$

3. (d) Given, $\sqrt{3}\sin x + \sqrt{2\sqrt{3}}\cos x - \sin x$

$= -K^2 + 4K + 14$

$\Rightarrow (\sqrt{3} - 1)\sin x + \sqrt{2\sqrt{3}}\cos x$

$= -K^2 + 4K + 14$

$\Rightarrow |(\sqrt{3} - 1)\sin x + \sqrt{2\sqrt{3}}\cos x|$

$\le \sqrt{(\sqrt{3} - 1)^2 + (2\sqrt{3})} = 2$

$\Rightarrow \quad |-K^2 + 4K + 14| \le 2$

$\Rightarrow -2 \le -K^2 + 4K + 14 \le 2$

Case I When $K^2 - 4K - 16 \le 0$

$\Rightarrow \quad (K - 2)^2 - 20 \le 0$

$\Rightarrow \quad |K - 2| \le 2\sqrt{5}$

$\Rightarrow \quad K \in [2 - 2\sqrt{5}, 2 + 2\sqrt{5}]$ ...(i)

Case II $k^2 - 4K - 12 \ge 0$

$\Rightarrow \quad (K - 6)(K + 2) \ge 0$

$\Rightarrow \quad K \in (-\infty, -2] \cup [6, \infty)$ ...(ii)

From Eqs. (i) and (ii), we get

$K \in [2 - 2\sqrt{5}, -2] \cup [6, 2 + 2\sqrt{5}]$

Hence, integral values of K are -2 and 6 only.

4. (c) Since, centre of C lies right bisector of OA.

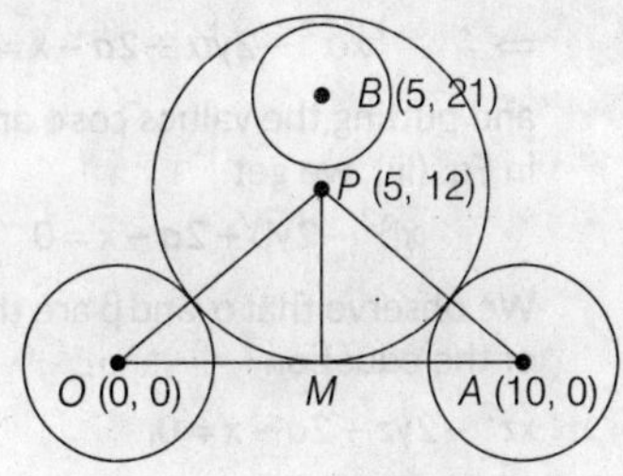

Hence, x-coordinate of $P = x = 5$.

$\left[\because M \equiv \left(\frac{10 + 0}{2}, \frac{0 + 0}{2}\right)\right]$

Now, let r = radius of circle C,

OP = radius of circle C_1 + radius of circle C

$\Rightarrow \quad 1 + r = \sqrt{OM^2 + PM^2}$

$\Rightarrow \quad 1 + r = \sqrt{25 + r^2}$

$\Rightarrow 1 + r^2 + 2r = 25 + r^2$

$\Rightarrow r = 12 = PM = y$-coordinate of P

$\therefore$ Centre of circle C is $P \equiv (5, 12)$.

Hence, the equation of circle C is

$(x - 5)^2 + (y - 12)^2 = (12)^2$

Circle C also touches the X-axis at $(5, 0)$.

Now, circles C_1, C_2 and C start rolling with constant speed in anticlockwise, then relative position of vertices of ΔOAB remain unchanged.

$PG = 5$

and $\quad P \equiv (5, 12)$

Centroid $G(x, y)$ is

$(x - 5)^2 + (y - 12)^2 = 25$

5. (b,c,d) Let $\tan(\theta/2) = \alpha$

and $\quad \tan(\phi/2) = \beta$

According to question,

$\alpha - \beta = 2b$ ...(i)

As we know that

$\cos\theta = \frac{1 - \tan^2(\theta/2)}{1 + \tan^2(\theta/2)} = \frac{1 - \alpha^2}{1 + \alpha^2}$

and $\sin\theta = \frac{2\tan(\theta/2)}{1 + \tan^2(\theta/2)} = \frac{2\alpha}{1 + \alpha^2}$

Similarly, $\cos\phi = \frac{1 - \beta^2}{1 + \beta^2}$

and $\sin\phi = \frac{2\beta}{1 + \beta^2}$

Given, $(x - a)\cos\theta + y\sin\theta = a$ ...(ii)

and $(x - a)\cos\phi + y\sin\phi = a$ ...(iii)

Putting the values of $\cos\theta$ and $\sin\theta$ in Eq. (ii), we get

$$(x-a)\left(\frac{1-\alpha^2}{1+\alpha^2}\right)+y\left(\frac{2\alpha}{1+\alpha^2}\right)=a$$

$\Rightarrow \quad x\alpha^2-2y\alpha+2a-x=0$

and putting the values $\cos\phi$ and $\sin\phi$ in Eq. (iii), we get

$$x\beta^2-2y\beta+2a-x=0$$

We observe that α and β are the roots of the equation

$xz^2-2yz+2a-x=0,$

so that $\alpha+\beta=2y/x$

and $\quad \alpha\beta=(2a-x)/x$

Now, from $(\alpha+\beta)^2=(\alpha-\beta)^2+4\alpha\beta$, we get

$$\left(\frac{2y}{x}\right)^2=(2b)^2+\frac{4(2a-x)}{x}$$

$\Rightarrow y^2=2ax-(1-b^2)x^2$

Also, from $\alpha+\beta=2y/x$ and $\alpha-\beta=2b$, we get

$\alpha=y/x+b$ and $\beta=y/x-b$

$\Rightarrow \quad \tan(\theta/2)=\frac{1}{x}(y+bx)$

and $\tan(\phi/2)=\frac{1}{x}(y-bx)$

6. (a,d) Given, $|z-3-4i|\le 10$

$\therefore |z|_{max}=15, |z|_{min}=0$

Now, $\alpha=\sin^{-1}(\sin|z|_{max})$

$\Rightarrow \quad \alpha=\sin^{-1}(\sin 15)\Rightarrow \alpha=5\pi-15$

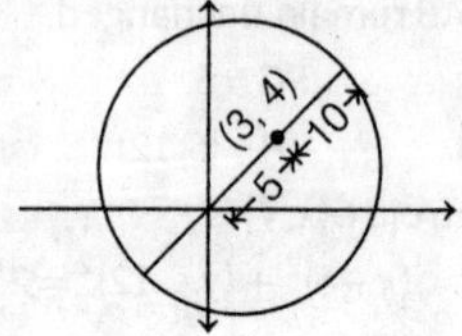

and $\beta=\cos^{-1}\left[\cos\left(-\frac{|z|_{max}+|z|_{min}}{3}\right)\right]$

$=\cos^{-1}\left[\cos\left(-\frac{15+0}{3}\right)\right]=\cos^{-1}(\cos(-5))$

$=\cos^{-1}(\cos 5)=2\pi-5$

$\therefore \quad \alpha-3\beta=-\pi$

and hence, $\sin^2\alpha+\cos^2 3\beta$

$=\sin^2 15+\cos^2 15=1$

7. (c, d) Let $f(1)=\cos\alpha$ and $g(1)=\sin\alpha$

Then, $f(2)=\cos(\alpha+g(1))$,

$g(2)=\sin(\alpha+g(1))$

Similarly,

$f(n+1)=\cos(\alpha+g(1)+g(2)+\ldots+g(n))$

$g(n+1)=\sin(\alpha+g(1)+g(2)+\ldots+g(n))$

Also, for all $x\in(0,\pi)$, $\sin x<\pi-x$,

$\sin x+x<\pi$

So, $\alpha+g(1)+g(2)+\ldots+g(n)<\pi$

$\Rightarrow \quad \alpha+g(1)+g(2)+\ldots+g(n+1)<\pi$

Hence, $h(n)$ is monotonically increasing but bounded.

So, $\lim_{n\to\infty} g(n)=0$

$\Rightarrow \quad \lim_{n\to\infty} f(n)=-1$

Therefore, $\lim_{n\to\infty}[f(n)+g(n)]=-1$

8. (b) Given,

$P(X)+P(Y)-2P(X\cap Y)=1-K \quad$ ...(i)

$P(Y)+P(Z)-2P(Y\cap Z)=1-2K \quad$ ...(ii)

$P(Z)+P(X)-2P(Z\cap X)=1-K \quad$ ...(iii)

and $\quad P(X\cap Y\cap Z)=K^2 \quad$ ...(iv)

Now, $P(X\cup Y\cup Z)$

$=P(X)+P(Y)+P(Z)-P(X\cap Y)-P(Y\cap Z)-P(Z\cap X)+P(X\cap Y\cap Z)$

$=\frac{1}{2}[P(X)+P(Y)-2P(X\cap Y)+P(Y)+P(Z)-2P(Y\cap Z)+P(Z)+P(X)-2P(Z\cap X)]+P(X\cap Y\cap Z)$

$=\frac{1}{2}[1-K+1-2K+1-K]+K^2$

[using Eqs. (i), (ii), (iii), and (iv)]

$=\frac{3}{2}-2K+K^2=(K-1)^2+\frac{1}{2}>\frac{1}{2}$

$[\because K\ne 1]$

9. (a,b,c,d)

Let $\log_{10}a=x, \log_{10}b=y$ and $\log_{10}c=z$

Then, the given system of equations reduces to

$x+y-xy=4-\log_{10}2000=\log_{10}5$ ...(i)

$y+z-yz=1-\log_{10}2=\log_{10}5 \quad$ ...(ii)

and $\quad z+x-zx=0 \quad$ ...(iii)

From Eqs. (i) and (ii), we get

$$x+y-xy=y+z-yz$$

$\Rightarrow (z-x)-y(z-x)=0$

$\Rightarrow \quad (z-x)(1-y)=0$

But $1-y\ne 0$

So, $\quad z-x=0\Rightarrow z=x$

From Eq. (iii), we get

$$2x-x^2=0\Rightarrow x=0,2$$

Then, $z=x\Rightarrow z=0,2$

and $y=\log_{10}5, 2-\log_{10}5$

$\therefore \log_{10}a=0,2$

$\Rightarrow \quad a=10^0, 10^2=1,100$

So, $a_1=1$ and $a_2=100$

and $\log_{10}b=\log_{10}5, 2-\log_{10}5$

$=\log_{10}5, \log_{10}20$

$\Rightarrow \quad b=5,20$

$\Rightarrow \quad b_1=5$ and $b_2=20$

and $\log_{10}c=0,2$

$\Rightarrow c=10^0, 10^2=1,100$

$\therefore c_1=1$ and $c_2=100$

Finally, $a_1+a_2=1+100=101$

$b_1+b_2=5+20=25$

$a_1a_2=1\times 100=100$

and $\quad c_1c_2=1\times 100=100$

10. (a, b) Given, $AC=4\sqrt{2}$ units

$\therefore AB=BC=\frac{AC}{\sqrt{2}}=4$ units

and $OB=\sqrt{(BC)^2-(OC)^2}$

$=\sqrt{(4)^2-(2\sqrt{2})^2}=2\sqrt{2}$ units

$\therefore A\equiv(-2\sqrt{2},0), B\equiv(0,-2\sqrt{2})$,

$C\equiv(2\sqrt{2},0)$

$\because y=f(x)=ax^2+bx+c$ passes through A, B and C, then

$8a-2\sqrt{2}b+c-2\sqrt{2}=0$

$\Rightarrow \quad c=0$

and $\quad 8a+2\sqrt{2}b+c=0$

We get,

$b=0, a=\frac{1}{2\sqrt{2}}$ and $c=-2\sqrt{2}$

$\therefore \quad y=f(x)=\frac{x^2}{2\sqrt{2}}-2\sqrt{2}$

and minimum value of $y=f(x)=\frac{x^2}{2\sqrt{2}}-2\sqrt{2}$ occurs at $x=0$

$\therefore \quad (y)_{min}=-2\sqrt{2}$

11. (3) Here, $A\equiv(a,0), B\equiv(0,a)$

Let $\frac{AS}{SB}=k;\ \therefore S\equiv\left(\frac{a}{K+1},\frac{ak}{K+1}\right)$

Now, equation of RS is

$$x-y=\frac{a}{k+1}-\frac{ak}{k+1}=\frac{a(1-k)}{k+1}$$

$$R\equiv\left(0,\frac{a(k-1)}{k+1}\right)$$

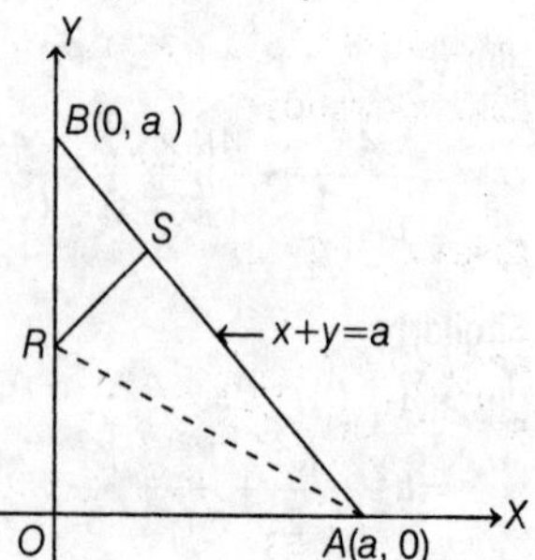

Now, area of

$$\Delta RSA=\frac{1}{2}\begin{vmatrix} a & 0 & 1\\ \frac{a}{k+1} & \frac{ak}{k+1} & 1\\ 0 & \frac{a(k-1)}{k+1} & 1\end{vmatrix}$$

$$=\frac{1}{2}a^2\begin{vmatrix}1 & 0 & 1\\ \frac{1}{k+1} & \frac{k}{k+1} & 1\\ 0 & \frac{k-1}{k+1} & 1\end{vmatrix}$$

$$=\frac{1}{2}a^2\left[\left(\frac{k}{k+1}-\frac{k-1}{k+1}\right)+1\left(\frac{1}{k+1}\cdot\frac{k-1}{k+1}-0\right)\right]$$

$$=\frac{a^2}{2}\left[\left(\frac{1}{k+1}+\frac{k-1}{(k+1)^2}\right)\right]$$

$$=\frac{a^2}{2}\times\frac{2k}{(k+1)^2}$$

$$=\frac{a^2k}{(k+1)^2}=\frac{3}{8}\times\text{area of }\Delta AOB$$ [given]

$\Rightarrow\ 3(k+1)^2=16k$

$\Rightarrow\quad k=\frac{1}{3}, k=3$

When $k=\frac{1}{3}$, then $R\equiv\left(0,-\frac{a}{2}\right)$

which lies outside of OB.

Hence, $k=3$

12. (4) Given, $f(x)=x^3+3x-9$ ...(i)

$\therefore\quad f'(x)=3x^2+3$ ...(ii)

Hence, $f'(x)>0$ in $[-5,3]$, then $f(x)$ is an increasing function on $[-5,3]$.

So, $f(x)$ will have greatest value at $x=3$.

Greatest value of $f(x)=f(x)|_{x=3}$

$=(3)^3+3\times3-9=27$

Let $a, ar, ar^2, ar^3,\ldots$ be a GP with common ratio $|r|<1$

[$\because$ given infinite GP]

Given, $S_\infty=27\Rightarrow\frac{a}{1-r}=27$ ...(iii)

and $f'(0)=a-ar$ [given]

$\Rightarrow\quad a(1-r)=f'(0)=3$

[from Eq. (i), $f'(0)=3$]

i.e. $a(1-r)=3$ ...(iv)

Divide Eq. (iv) by Eq. (iii), we get

$(1-r)^2=\frac{1}{9}$

$\Rightarrow\quad 1-r=\pm\frac{1}{3}$

$\Rightarrow\quad r=1\pm\frac{1}{3}=\frac{4}{3},\frac{2}{3}$

But $r\neq\frac{4}{3}$ because $|r|<1$

$\therefore\quad r=\frac{2}{3}$

Hence, $9\left[7r\sin^{-1}\left(\frac{1}{\sqrt{3r}}\right)\right]^{2\log_{\frac{7\pi}{6}} r}$

$$=9\left[7\times\frac{2}{3}\sin^{-1}\left(\frac{1}{\sqrt{3\times\frac{2}{3}}}\right)\right]^{2\log_{\frac{7\pi}{6}} 2/3}$$

$$=9\left(7\times\frac{2}{3}\times\frac{\pi}{4}\right)^{\log_{\frac{7\pi}{6}}(2/3)^2}$$

$$=9\left(\frac{7\pi}{6}\right)^{\log_{\frac{7\pi}{6}}4/9}=9\times\frac{4}{9}=4$$

13. (6) Let $x\cos\theta+y\sin\theta=6$ is any tangent to the circle $x^2+y^2=36$ which is a directrix to the parabola.

Now, if $P(\alpha,\beta)$ is focus of parabola, then

$$\sqrt{(\alpha-5)^2+\beta^2}=\frac{|5\cos\theta-6|}{\sqrt{\cos^2\theta+\sin^2\theta}}$$ and

$$\sqrt{(\alpha+5)^2+\beta^2}=\frac{|-5\cos\theta-6|}{\sqrt{\cos^2\theta+\sin^2\theta}}$$

$\Rightarrow\quad(5-\alpha)^2+\beta^2=(5\cos\theta-6)^2$ ...(i)

and $(5+\alpha)^2+\beta^2=(5\cos\theta+6)^2$ ...(ii)

Subtracting Eq. (i) from Eq. (ii), we get

$20\alpha=120\cos\theta$

$\Rightarrow\cos\theta=\frac{\alpha}{6}$ putting in Eq. (i), we get

$$(5-\alpha)^2+\beta^2=\left(\frac{5\alpha}{6}-6\right)^2$$

$$\Rightarrow\frac{\alpha^2}{36}+\frac{\beta^2}{11}=1$$

Hence, $k=6$

14. (3) Given, $\sum_{\mu=1}^{n}f(\lambda+\mu)=16(2^n-1)$ ...(i)

and $f(x+y)=f(x)\cdot f(y),\ \forall\ x,y\in N$ ...(ii)

and $\quad f(2)=2$ ...(iii)

On putting $x=y=1$ in Eq. (ii), we get

$f(1+1)=f(1)\cdot f(1)=2\times2$

$\Rightarrow\quad f(2)=2^2$ ...(iv)

Now, putting $x=1$, $y=2$ in Eq. (ii), we get,

$f(1+2)=f(1)\cdot f(2)=2\cdot2^2$

$\Rightarrow\quad f(3)=2^3$ [using Eq. (iv)]

Putting $x=y=2$ in Eq. (ii), we get

$f(2+2)=f(2)\cdot f(2)$

$\Rightarrow\ f(4)=2^2\cdot2^2=2^4$. [using Eq. (iv)]

and so on.

Similarly, $f(k)=2^k, k\in N$

$\therefore f(\lambda+\mu)=2^{\lambda+\mu}$, where $(\lambda+\mu)\in N$

From Eq. (i), we get

$$\sum_{\mu=1}^{n}2^{\lambda+\mu}=16(2^n-1)$$

$$\Rightarrow\quad 2^\lambda\sum_{\mu=1}^{n}2^\mu=16=(2^n-1)$$

$$\Rightarrow 2^\lambda(2^1+2^2+2^3+2^4+\ldots+2^n)=16(2^n-1)$$

$$\Rightarrow 2^\lambda\cdot\frac{2(2^n-1)}{(2-1)}=16(2^n-1)$$

$\Rightarrow\quad 2^{\lambda+1}=16=2^4$

$\Rightarrow\quad \lambda+1=4\Rightarrow\lambda=3$

15. (8) Given, $R_n=\sum_{r=0}^{n-3}{}^nC_r\cdot{}^nC_{r+3}$

$={}^nC_0\cdot{}^nC_3+{}^nC_1\cdot{}^nC_4+{}^nC_2\cdot{}^nC_5+\ldots+{}^nC_{n-3}\cdot{}^nC_n$ ...(i)

$\because(1+x)^n={}^nC_0+{}^nC_1x+{}^nC_2x^2+\ldots+{}^nC_nx^n$ ...(ii)

$\Rightarrow(x+1)^n={}^nC_0x^n+{}^nC_1x^{n-1}+{}^nC_2x^{n-2}+\ldots+{}^nC_n$ ...(iii)

Now, $R_n=$ Coefficient of x^{n+3} in $(1+x)^{2n}={}^{2n}C_{n+3}$

Also given, $5R_n=3R_{n+1}$

$$\Rightarrow 5\cdot\frac{(2n)!}{(n+3)!\,(n-3)!}=3\cdot\frac{(2n+2)!}{(n+4)!\,(n-2)!}$$

$\Rightarrow\quad 5(n^2+2n-8)=3(4n^2+6n+2)$

$\Rightarrow\quad 7n^2+8n+46=0$ ...(iv)

Let n_1 and n_2 be two roots of Eq. (v), then

$(1-n_1)(1-n_2)=1-(n_1+n_2)+n_1n_2$

$$=1-\left(\frac{-8}{7}\right)+\frac{46}{7}=\frac{61}{7}$$

$$\therefore[(1-n_1)(1-n_2)]=\left[\frac{61}{7}\right]=8$$

16. (2) From figure, $OB=\tan\alpha$

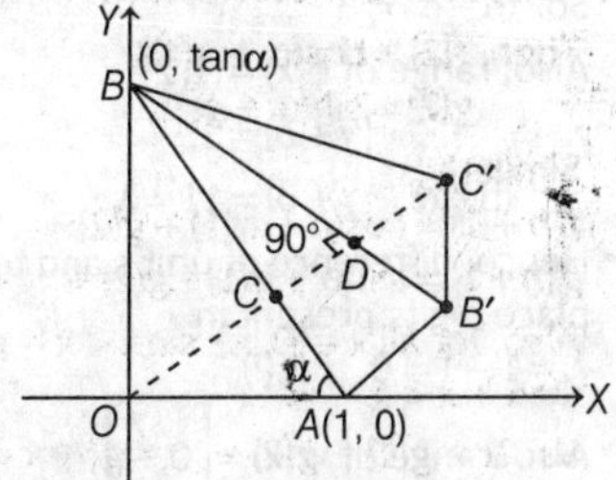

$\therefore$ Coordinates of point $C \equiv \left(\frac{1}{2}, \frac{\tan\alpha}{2}\right)$.

So, equation of the line OC is

$$y = x\tan\alpha \quad \text{...(i)}$$

$\Rightarrow \quad \angle COA = \alpha$

Now, $AB = \sqrt{1+\tan^2\alpha}$

$\Rightarrow \quad AB = \sec\alpha \quad$ ...(ii) $[\because \alpha > \pi/4]$

$\therefore \quad AC = BC = \frac{1}{2}\sec\alpha$

In ΔBDC, $\angle BCD = (180° - 2\alpha)$

$[\because \angle COA = \alpha]$

$\Rightarrow BD = BC\sin(180° - 2\alpha)$

$$= \frac{\sec\alpha}{2} \times \sin 2\alpha$$

$$= \frac{1}{2} \times \sec\alpha \times 2\sin\alpha \times \cos\alpha$$

$$= \sin\alpha$$

$\Rightarrow BD = B'D = \sin\alpha$

$[\because B'$ is a mirror image of B in line $OC]$

Clearly, ΔBDC and $\Delta BDC'$ are congruent.

$$BC' = BC = \frac{1}{2}\sec\alpha$$

and $\angle ABB' = \angle B'BC' \quad$ ...(iii)

Now, $\frac{\text{area of } \Delta ABB'}{\text{area of } \Delta BB'C'}$

$$= \frac{AB \times BB' \times \sin\angle ABB'}{BB' \times BC' \times \sin\angle B'BC'}$$

$[\because \angle ABB' = \angle B'BC']$

$$= \frac{AB}{BC'} = \frac{\sec\alpha}{\frac{1}{2}\sec\alpha} = 2$$

[using Eqs. (ii) and (iii)]

17. (0) For $\phi(x) = f(|x|)$

$-3 \le |x| \le 4$

$\Rightarrow \quad 0 \le |x| \le 4$

$\Rightarrow -4 \le x \le 4$

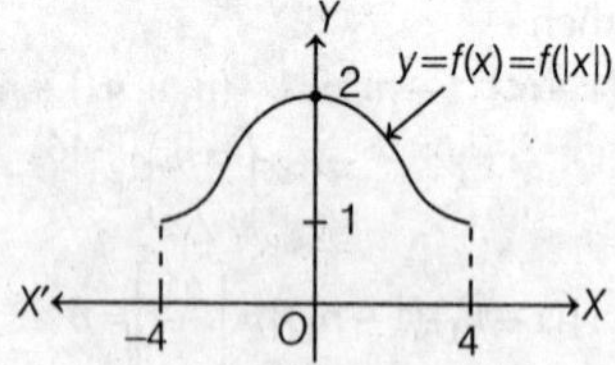

$\therefore$ Domain of $\phi(x) = [-4, 4]$

So, $(\beta - \alpha) = 8$

Also, range of $\phi(x) = [1, 2]$

$\therefore \quad (\gamma + \delta) = 3$

$\therefore \quad (\beta - \alpha + \gamma + \delta) = 11 = \lambda$

Hence, difference of unit's and ten's place digits present in

$\lambda = 1 - 1 = 0 \quad$ ...(i)

Also, range of $\psi(x) = \left[0, \frac{7}{2}\right]$

and number of solutions of $\psi(x) = \frac{1}{4}$ is $n = 4$.

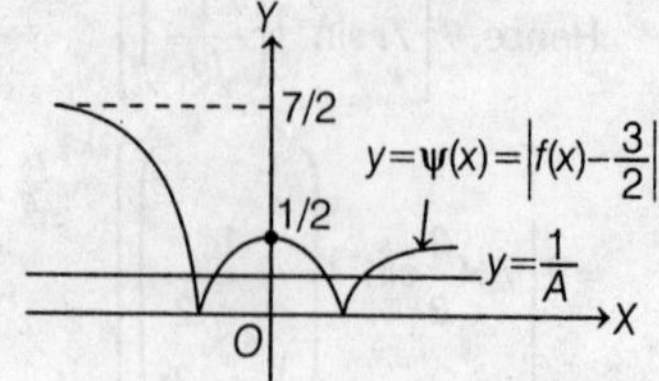

So, $n + p + 2q = 4 + 0 + 7 = 11 = \mu$

$\therefore$ Sum of digits in the value of

$$\mu = 1 + 1 = 2 \quad \text{...(ii)}$$

Therefore, $k = \frac{0}{2} = 0$

[from Eqs. (i) and (ii)]

Hence, $(2\sin k + \tan 2k)$

$$= 2 \times \sin 0° + \tan 0° = 0$$

18. (24)

Given, $\sum_{n=0}^{\infty} \frac{\sin(nx)}{3^n} = \frac{a + b\sqrt{b}}{c} \quad$ ...(i)

$\because \sin(nx) = \frac{e^{nix} - e^{-nix}}{2i}$

$\therefore \sum_{n=0}^{\infty} \frac{\sin(nx)}{3^n} = \frac{1}{2i} \sum_{n=0}^{\infty} \frac{e^{nix} - e^{-nix}}{3^n}$

$$= \frac{1}{2i}\left[\sum_{n=0}^{\infty}\left(\frac{e^{ix}}{3}\right)^n - \sum_{n=0}^{\infty}\left(\frac{e^{-ix}}{3}\right)^n\right]$$

$$= \frac{1}{2i}\left[\begin{array}{l}\left\{1 + \frac{e^{ix}}{3} + \left(\frac{e^{-ix}}{3}\right)^2 + \left(\frac{e^{ix}}{3}\right)^3 + \dots\right\} \\ -\left\{1 + \frac{e^{-ix}}{3} + \left(\frac{e^{-ix}}{3}\right)^2 + \dots\right\}\end{array}\right]$$

$$= \frac{1}{2i}\left[\frac{1}{1 - \frac{e^{ix}}{3}} - \frac{1}{1 - \frac{e^{-ix}}{3}}\right]$$

$$= \frac{1}{2i}\left[\frac{\left(1 - \frac{e^{-ix}}{3}\right) - \left(1 - \frac{e^{ix}}{3}\right)}{\left(1 - \frac{e^{ix}}{3}\right)\left(1 - \frac{e^{-ix}}{3}\right)}\right]$$

$$= \frac{1}{2i}\left[\frac{1}{3}(e^{ix} - e^{-ix})\right]\left[\frac{1}{1 - \frac{e^{-ix}}{3} - \frac{e^{ix}}{3} + \frac{2}{9}}\right]$$

$$= \frac{1}{2i}\left[\frac{1}{3}(2i\sin x)\frac{1}{\frac{10}{9} - \left(\frac{1}{3}2\cos x\right)}\right]$$

$$= \frac{2\sin x}{3} \times \frac{9}{(10 - 6\cos x)}$$

$$= \frac{6\sin x}{10 - 6\cos x} = \frac{3\sin x}{5 - 3\cos x}$$

$$= \frac{2}{5 - 3\sqrt{1 - (1/9)}} = \frac{1}{5 - 2\sqrt{2}}$$

$$= \frac{5 + 2\sqrt{2}}{(5 - 2\sqrt{2})(5 + 2\sqrt{2})}$$

$$= \frac{5 + 2\sqrt{2}}{17} = \frac{a + b\sqrt{b}}{c} \quad \text{[from Eq. (i)]}$$

On comparing, we get

$$a = 5, b = 2 \text{ and } c = 17$$

$\therefore \quad a + b + c = 5 + 2 + 17 = 24$

19. (588)

There are 9 letters

T, T, R, R, R, E, O, I, S

k = Number of four lettered words (no restriction)

$$= \text{Coefficient of } X^4 \text{ in } \left[4!\left(1 + \frac{x}{1!} + \frac{x^2}{2!}\right)\left(1 + \frac{x}{1!} + \frac{x^2}{2!} + \frac{x^3}{3!}\right)(1+x)^4\right]$$

$= 626$

m = Number of four lettered words (no vowels)

$$= \text{Coefficient of } x^4 \text{ in } \left[4!\left(1 + \frac{x}{1!} + \frac{x^2}{2!}\right)\left(1 + \frac{x}{1!} + \frac{x^2}{2!} + \frac{x^3}{3!}\right)(1+x)^4\right]$$

$= 38$

$\therefore$ Required ways (atleast one vowels)

$= 626 - 38 = 588$

20. (5)

Equation of hyperbola

$(x-1)(y-2) = 4$

$\Rightarrow \quad XY = 4$

If normal at $\left(ct, \frac{c}{t}\right)$ intersect curve again at $\left(ct', \frac{c}{t'}\right)$, then $t' = \frac{-1}{t^3}$

$$2t = 4 \Rightarrow t = 2$$

$\therefore \quad (X', Y') = \left(\frac{-1}{4}, -16\right)$

$(\alpha, \beta - 29) = \left(\frac{3}{4}, -14\right)$

$\Rightarrow \quad \alpha = \frac{3}{4}$ and $\beta = 15$

$\therefore \quad \frac{\beta}{4\alpha} = \frac{15 \times 4}{3 \times 4} = 5$

21. (27) $x^3 - k_1x^2 + k_2x - 8 = 0$ ...(i)

$\alpha\beta\gamma = 8$

[$\because \alpha, \beta$ and γ are roots of Eq. (i)]

$\because \{\sqrt{A}\} = 0 \Rightarrow \alpha, \beta$ and γ are even numbers.

$\Rightarrow A = 3^2 \cdot 2^2 \cdot 5^2$ and $f(x) = (x-2)^3$

$\therefore$ The number of divisors of $3^2 \cdot 2^2 \cdot 5^2$ is $(2+1)(2+1)(2+1)$

$= 3^3 = 27$

22. (a) (I) $f(1) + 2f(2) + 3f(3) + \ldots + nf(n) = n(n+1)f(n)$ [given] ...(i)

Replacing 'n' by '$n+1$', the equation become,

$f(1) + 2f(2) + 3f(3) + \ldots + nf(n) + (n+1)f(n+1)$

$= (n+1)(n+2)f(n+1)$ ...(ii)

Subtracting Eq. (i) from Eq. (ii), we get

$(n+1)f(n+1) = (n+1)(n+2)f(n+1) - n(n+1)f(n)$

$\Rightarrow \quad nf(n) = (n+1)f(n+1) \; [n \ge 2]$

From above equation, we can conclude that

$2f(2) = 3f(3) = 4f(4) = \ldots = nf(n)$

[where, $n \ge 2$]

Substituting the values of $2f(2), 3f(3)$, ... in terms of $nf(n)$ in Eq. (i), then we get

$f(1) + (n-1)n\,f(n) = n(n+1)f(n)$

$f(1) = 2nf(n)$

$\frac{1}{f(n)} = \frac{2n}{f(1)}$

$\frac{1}{f(n)} = \frac{2n}{1}$

Putting $n = 6$, we get

$\frac{1}{f(6)} = 12$

Hence, $I \to R$

(II) Let equation of ellipse be

$$\frac{x^2}{a^2} + \frac{y^2}{b^2} = 1$$

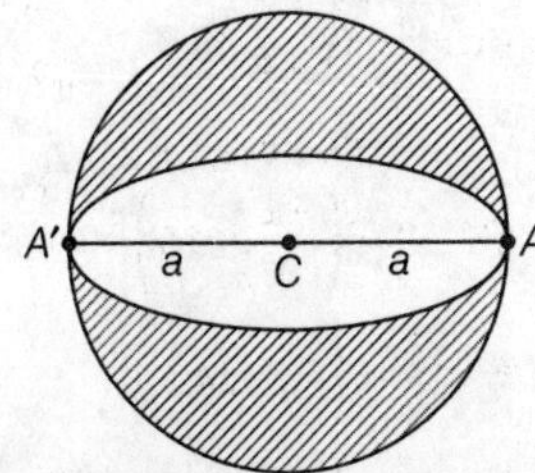

As we know that

Area of ellipse $= \pi ab = \pi a^2\sqrt{(1-e^2)}$

$= \pi a^2\sqrt{1 - \frac{8}{9}} = \frac{\pi a^2}{3}$

area of circle $= \pi a^2$

$\therefore$ The required probability

$$= \frac{\pi a^2 - \frac{\pi a^2}{3}}{\pi a^2} = \frac{2}{3}$$

Hence, II $\to$ P

(III) For $\phi(x)$ to be defined

(a) $16 - x > 0 \Rightarrow x < 16$

(b) $2x - 1 \ge 0 \Rightarrow x \ge \frac{1}{2}$

(c) $16 - x \ge 2x - 1 \Rightarrow x \le \frac{17}{3}$

(d) $20 - 3x > 0 \Rightarrow x < \frac{20}{3}$

(e) $4x - 5 \ge 0 \Rightarrow x \ge \frac{5}{4}$

(f) $20 - 3x \ge 4x - 5 \Rightarrow x \le \frac{25}{7}$

Combining all, we get $x \in \left[\frac{5}{4}, \frac{25}{7}\right)$

$\therefore x \in I$

$\therefore x = 2, 3$

At $x = 2$, $\phi(x) = {}^{14}C_3 + {}^{14}C_3$

$= 2\,{}^{14}C_3$

$= 728$

At $x = 3$, $\phi(x) = {}^{13}C_5 + {}^{11}C_7$

$= 1617$

$\therefore$ Maximum value of $\phi(x)$ i.e. $M = 1617$ and minimum value of $\phi(x)$ i.e. $m = 728$

Then, $(M + m) = (1617 + 728) = 2345$

According to the question,

$$\frac{(M+m)}{2345} = \frac{2345}{2345} = 1$$

Hence, III $\to$ T

(IV) It is given that

$f(x, y) = f(2x + 2y, 2y - 2x)$ ...(i)

Replacing 'x' by $(2x + 2y)$ and 'y' by $(2y - 2x)$, we get

$f(2x + 2y, 2y - 2x)$

$= f\{2(2x + 2y) + 2(2y - 2x), 2(2y - 2x) - 2(2x + 2y)\}$ ...(ii)

$= f(8y, -8x)$

From Eqs. (i) and (ii), we get

$f(x, y) = f(8y, 8x)$ ...(iii)

Again, replacing 'x' by $(8y)$ and 'y' by $(-8x)$, we get

$f(8y, -8x) = f(-64x, -64y)$ ...(iv)

From Eqs. (iii) and (iv), we get

$f(x, y) = f'(-64x, -64y)$ ...(v)

Again, replacing 'x' by $(-64x)$ and 'y' by$(-64y)$, we get

$f(-64x, -64y)$

$= f\{-64(-64x), -64(-64y)\}$

$= f(2^{12}x, 2^{12}y)$

From Eqs. (v) and (vi), we get

$f(x, y) = f(2^{12}x, 2^{12}y)$

$\Rightarrow f(x, 0) = f(2^{12}x, 0)$ [putting $y = 0$]

Replacing x by 2^x, then

$f(2^x, 0) = f(2^{x+12}, 0)$

$\Rightarrow \quad g(x) = g(x + 12)$

Hence, $g(x)$ is a periodic function with period 12.

Hence, IV $\to$ R

23. (d) (I) $\because \alpha$ and β are the roots of $x^2 + \lambda x + \mu = 0$

Then, $\alpha + \beta = -\lambda$ and $\alpha\beta = \mu$ ...(i)

Also, α and β are the roots of

$x^{14244} + \lambda^{7122}x^{7122} + \mu^{7122} = 1$

$\therefore \quad \alpha^{7122} + \beta^{7122} = \lambda^{7122}$

and $\quad \alpha^{7122}\beta^{7122} = \mu^{7122}$ ...(ii)

Now, $\frac{\alpha}{\beta}$ is a root of

$x^m + 1 + (x+1)^m = 0$

Then, $\left(\frac{\alpha}{\beta}\right)^m + 1 + \left(\frac{\alpha}{\beta} + \beta\right)^m = 0$

$\Rightarrow \quad \alpha^m + \beta^m + (\alpha + \beta)^m = 0$

$\Rightarrow \quad \alpha^m + \beta^m + (-\lambda)^m = 0$

[$\because \alpha + \beta = -\lambda$]

$\alpha^m + \beta^m = -(-\lambda)^m$ ...(iii)

From Eqs. (ii) and (iii), we get

$m = 7122$

$\Rightarrow \quad \frac{m}{7122} = 1$

Hence, I $\to$ T

(II) $(\sqrt{3})^{\sec^2\theta} = (\tan^2\theta + 1)^2 - 1$

$= (\sec^2\theta)^2 - 1$

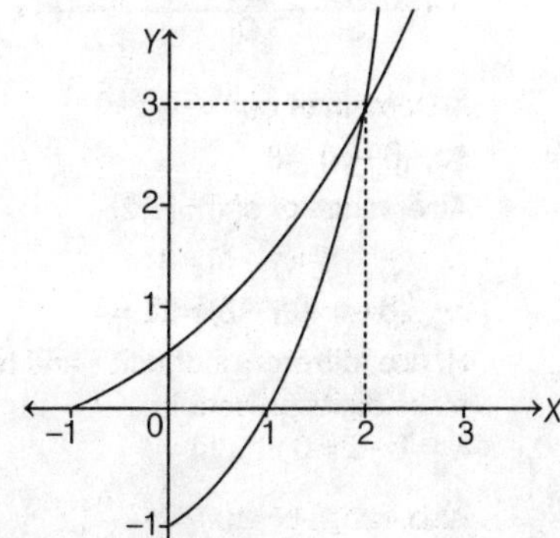

Put $\sec^2\theta = x$ $[\because x \ge 1]$

Then, $(\sqrt{3})^x = x^2 - 1$

Let $y = (\sqrt{3})^x = (x^2 - 1)$ $[x > 1]$

Now, graphs of $y = (\sqrt{3})^x$ and $y = x^2 - 1$ intersect at one point i.e. $x = 2$, then $y = 3$

$\therefore \quad \sec^2\theta = 2$

$\Rightarrow \quad \sec\theta = \pm\sqrt{2}$

$\Rightarrow \quad \theta = \pm 45° \in \left(-\frac{\pi}{2}, \frac{\pi}{2}\right)$

$\because \quad \sec\theta = -\sqrt{2}$ $\left[\text{not possible in} \left(-\frac{\pi}{2}, \frac{\pi}{2}\right)\right]$

As, $\sec\theta$ is positive in $\left(-\frac{\pi}{2}, \frac{\pi}{2}\right)$

$\therefore$ Two values of θ is possible in $\theta \in \left(\frac{\pi}{2}, \frac{\pi}{2}\right)$

Hence, II $\rightarrow$ R

(III) Given equation is

$e^{4x} + e^{3x} - 4e^{2x} + e^x + 1 = 0$

Let $e^x = y > 0$

So, $y^4 + y^3 - 4y^2 + y + 1 = 0$

$$\Rightarrow \left(y^2 + \frac{1}{y^2}\right) + \left(y + \frac{1}{y}\right) - 4 = 0$$

[on dividing by y^2]

$$\Rightarrow \left(y + \frac{1}{y}\right)^2 + \left(y + \frac{1}{y}\right) - 6 = 0$$

Again, let $y + \frac{1}{y} = t$, then $t^2 + t - 6 = 0$

$\Rightarrow t^2 + 3t - 2t - 6 = 0$

$\Rightarrow t(t + 3) - 2(t + 3) = 0$

$\Rightarrow (t - 2)(t + 3) = 0$

$\Rightarrow t = -3, 2$

$\therefore y + \frac{1}{y} = -3$ or 2

$\Rightarrow e^x + \frac{1}{e^x} = -3$ or 2

$\Rightarrow e^x + \frac{1}{e^x} = 2$

$\left[\text{as}, e^x + \frac{1}{e^x} \ne 3, \therefore e^x > 0\right]$

$\Rightarrow (e^x - 1)^2 = 0$

$\Rightarrow e^x = 1$

$\Rightarrow x = 0$

$\therefore$ Number of real roots of given equation is 1.

Hence, III $\rightarrow$ T

(IV)

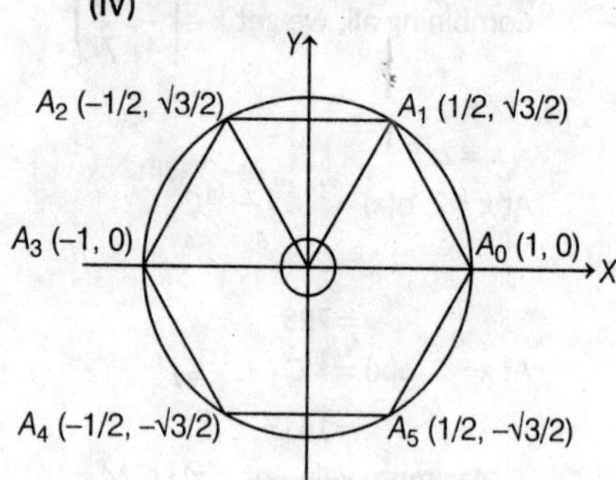

Let O be the centre of the circle of unit radius and the coordinates of A_0 be $(1, 0)$.

Since, each side of the regular hexagon makes an angle of $60°$ at the centre O.

$\therefore$ Coordinates of A_1 are $(r\cos 60°, r\sin 60°)$

$(\cos 60°, \sin 60°) = \left(\frac{1}{2}, \frac{\sqrt{3}}{2}\right)$

As, are $\cos(120°, \sin 120°)$

$= \left(-\frac{1}{2}, \frac{\sqrt{3}}{2}\right)$

A_3 are $(-1, 0)$

A_4 are $\left(-\frac{1}{2}, -\frac{\sqrt{3}}{2}\right)$

and A_5 are $\left(\frac{1}{2}, \frac{\sqrt{3}}{2}\right)$

$$\text{Now, } A_0A_1 = \sqrt{\left(1 - \frac{1}{2}\right)^2 + \left(\frac{\sqrt{3}}{2}\right)^2} = \sqrt{\frac{1}{4} + \frac{3}{4}} = 1$$

$$A_0A_2 = \sqrt{\left(1 + \frac{1}{2}\right)^2 + \left(\frac{\sqrt{3}}{2}\right)^2} = \sqrt{\frac{9}{4} + \frac{3}{4}} = \sqrt{3} = A_0A_4$$

$\therefore (A_0A_1)(A_0A_2)(A_0A_1) = 3$

Hence, IV $\rightarrow$ P

Part Test 03

1. (c) Given, $\phi(x) = \int_{x^2}^{x^3} \frac{1}{\ln t} dt$

$\therefore \phi'(x) = \frac{3x^2}{3\ln x} - \frac{2x}{2\ln x}$

[using Newton-Leibnitz theorem]

$\Rightarrow \phi'(x) = \frac{6x^2 - 6x}{6\ln x} = \frac{6x(x-1)}{6\ln x} = \frac{x(x-1)}{\ln x}$

For maxima or minima, put $\phi'(x) = 0$ then, we get

$x = 0, 1$

As $x > 0$

$\therefore x = 1$

Now, for $x < 1$, $\phi'(x)$

= negative · negative = positive

and for $x > 1$, $\phi'(x)$ = positive · positive = positive

$\therefore \phi'(x)$ does not change its sign in the immediate neighbourhood (*nbd*) of $x = 1$.

So, $x = 1$ is neither the point of maxima nor point of minima.

But $\phi'(x) > 0 \; \forall \; x < 1$ and $x > 1$

$\therefore \phi(x)$ is an increasing function, $\forall \; x \in R$.

2. (a) From the given determinant, we observe that $D(x)$ is a polynomial of degree at most 6 in x.

If $D(x) = a_0 + a_1x + a_2x^2 + a_3x^3 + \ldots + a_6x^6$, then

$D'(x) = a_1 + 2a_2x + 3a_3x^2 + \ldots + 6a_6x^5$.

$\Rightarrow a_1 = D'(0)$

$$\text{Now, } D'(x) = \begin{vmatrix} 1 & (x-1)^2 & x^3 \\ 1 & x^2 & (x+1)^3 \\ 1 & (x+1)^2 & (x+2)^3 \end{vmatrix} + \begin{vmatrix} x-2 & 2(x-1) & x^3 \\ x-1 & 2x & (x+1)^3 \\ x & 2(x+1) & (x+2)^3 \end{vmatrix} + \begin{vmatrix} x-2 & (x-1)^2 & 3x^2 \\ x-1 & x^2 & 3(x+1)^2 \\ x & (x+1)^2 & 3(x+2)^2 \end{vmatrix}$$

$$\Rightarrow D'(0) = \begin{vmatrix} 1 & 1 & 0 \\ 1 & 0 & 1 \\ 1 & 1 & 8 \end{vmatrix} + \begin{vmatrix} -2 & -2 & 0 \\ -1 & 0 & 1 \\ 0 & 2 & 8 \end{vmatrix} + \begin{vmatrix} -2 & 1 & 0 \\ -1 & 0 & 3 \\ 0 & 1 & 12 \end{vmatrix}$$

$= -8 - 12 + 18 = -2$

3. (b) Since, $f(x)$ and $g(x)$ are differentiable at $x = 0$.

So, $f(x)$ must be continuous at $x = 0$

$\therefore a \times e^0 = 0 + 0 + 2b$

$\Rightarrow a = 2b$

Now, $f'(x) = \begin{cases} a^2e^{ax}, & -\infty < x < 0 \\ 2x + 4, & 0 < x < \infty \end{cases}$

For $f(x)$ to be differentiable at $x = 0$, $f'(0^-) = a^2$ and $f'(0^+) = 4$ are equal

i.e. $a^2 = 4 \Rightarrow a = \pm 2$

When $a = 2$, then $b = 1$

When $a = -2$, then $b = -1$

$\therefore g(x) = \sin|x|$ or $g(x) = \sin|-x-4| = \sin|x+4|$

Since, $\sin|x|$ is non-differentiable at $x = 0$.

But given that $g(x)$ is differentiable at $x = 0$.

Hence, $g(x) = \sin|x+4|$, which is clearly non-differentiable at $x = -4$.

4. (d) Let $I = \int_e^{e^{7122}} \frac{1}{x}\left(1 + \frac{1-\ln x}{\ln x \cdot \ln\left(\frac{x}{\ln x}\right)}\right) dx$

Putting $\ln x = z$

$\Rightarrow \frac{1}{x} dx = dz$

x	e	e^{7122}
z	1	7122

$\therefore I = \int_1^{7122} \left(1 + \frac{1-z}{z(z - \ln z)}\right) dz$

$= \int_1^{7122} dz + \int_1^{7122} \frac{\frac{1}{z} - 1}{z - \ln z} dz$

$= [z]_1^{7122} - [\ln(z - \ln z)]_1^{7122}$

$= 7121 - [\ln(7122 - \ln(7122))]$

$[\because \ln(1) = 0]$

5. (a)

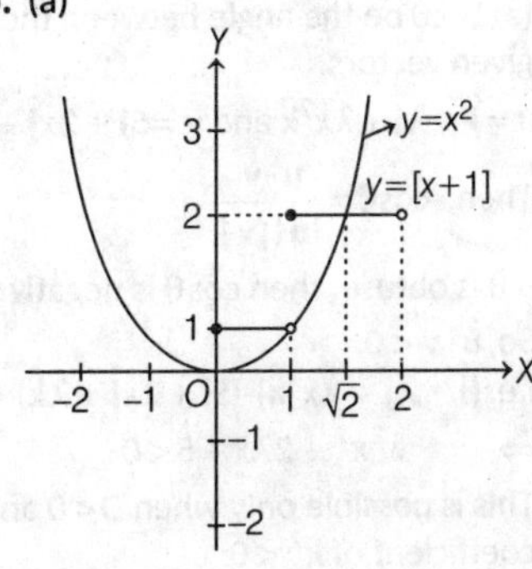

$\therefore$ Required area

$= \int_0^1 (1 - x^2)dx + \int_1^{\sqrt{2}} (2 - x^2)dx$

$= \left[x - \frac{x^3}{3}\right]_0^1 + \left[2x - \frac{x^3}{3}\right]_1^{\sqrt{2}}$

$= \frac{4\sqrt{2}}{3} - 1$

6. (b) $\sum_{k=0}^{7} A_k = \sum_{k=0}^{7} \begin{bmatrix} a_k & 0 \\ 0 & b_k \end{bmatrix}$

$= \begin{bmatrix} a & 0 \\ 0 & b \end{bmatrix}$

$\therefore a = \sum_{k=0}^{7} a_k = \sum_{k=0}^{7} k \cdot ({}^7C_k)$

and $b = \sum_{k=0}^{7} b_k = \sum_{k=0}^{7} (7-k) \cdot ({}^7C_k)$

$\Rightarrow a + b = 7 \cdot \sum_{k=0}^{7} {}^7C_k = 7(2^7)$

$= 7 \times 128 = 896$

$\therefore \frac{a+b}{7} = 128$

7. (c) Given,

$\sin^{-1}\lambda + \sin^{-1}\mu + \sin^{-1}\delta = \frac{3\pi}{2}$

$\Leftrightarrow \sin^{-1}\lambda = \frac{\pi}{2} = \sin^{-1}\mu = \sin^{-1}\delta$

$\Leftrightarrow \lambda = \mu = \delta = 1$

Now, $\phi(x + y) = \phi(x) \cdot \phi(y) \; \forall \; x, y \in R$. [given]

$\therefore \phi(2 + 2) = \phi(2) \cdot \phi(2) = \phi(2)^2 = (2)^2 = 4$

$[\because \phi(2) = 2 \text{ (given)}]$

$\therefore \phi(4) = 4$

Again,

$\phi(4 + 2) = \phi(4) \cdot \phi(2) = \phi(6) = 4 \times 2 = 8$

Now, given expression yield

$= 3 - \frac{3(1)}{3} = 3 - 1 = 2$

8. (a) Given, system is consistent

i.e. $\begin{vmatrix} 1 & 1 & -1 \\ 2 & -1 & -c \\ -b & 3b & c \end{vmatrix} = 0$

$\Rightarrow c + bc - 6b + b + 2c + 3bc = 0$

$\Rightarrow 3c + 4bc - 5b = 0 \Rightarrow c = \frac{5b}{3 + 4b}$

Given, $c < 1$

$\Rightarrow \frac{5b}{3 + 4b} < 1$

$\Rightarrow \frac{5b}{3+4b} - 1 < 0 \Rightarrow \frac{b-3}{3+4b} < 0$

$\Rightarrow b \in \left(-\frac{3}{4}, 3\right)$

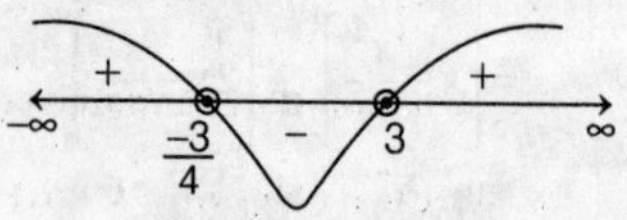

9. (d) As $\frac{f(5)-f(2)}{5-2} = \frac{15-0}{3} = 5$

$\therefore$ Average change is 5 and $f'(x) \le 5$

$\Rightarrow f'(x) = 5, \forall x \in [2,5]$

$\Rightarrow f(x) = 5x + c$

$\because \quad f(2) = 0 \Rightarrow 10 + c = 0 \Rightarrow c = -10$

$\therefore \quad f(3) = 15 - 10 = 5$

10. (d) Let $z_1 \in c - \{0\}$

$\therefore \frac{z_1 - z_2}{z_1 + z_2} = 0 = 0 + i0$, which is real.

(i) So, $z_1 R z_1 \Rightarrow R$ is reflexive

$\therefore$ Option (a) is correct.

(ii) Let $z_1 R z_2 \Rightarrow \frac{z_1 - z_2}{z_1 + z_2}$ is real

$\Rightarrow -\frac{z_1 - z_2}{z_1 + z_2}$ is real.

$\Rightarrow \frac{z_2 - z_1}{z_2 + z_1}$ is real.

$\therefore z_2 R z_1$

$\Rightarrow R$ is symmetric

Option (b) is also correct.

(iii) Let $z_1 R z_2$ and $z_2 R z_3$

$\therefore \frac{z_1 - z_2}{z_1 + z_2}$ and $\frac{z_1 - z_3}{z_2 + z_3}$ are real.

Let $z_1 = x_1 + iy_1, z_2 = x_2 + iy_2$

and $z_3 = x_3 + iy_3$

$\Rightarrow I_m\left(\frac{z_1 + z_2}{z_1 + z_2}\right) = 0 \Rightarrow \frac{x_1}{y_1} = \frac{x_2}{y_2}$ ...(i)

Similarly, $\frac{x_2}{y_2} = \frac{x_3}{y_3}$ ...(ii)

From Eqs. (i) and (ii), we get

$\frac{x_1}{y_1} = \frac{x_3}{y_3} \Rightarrow x_1 y_3 = x_3 y_1$

$\therefore \frac{z_1 - z_3}{z_1 + z_3}$ is real.

$\therefore z_1 R z_3 \Rightarrow R$ is transitive.

Option (c) is also correct.

Hence, finally R is an equivalence relation.

11. (b) Let a, b, c be the direction ratios of the line of intersection of the planes

$2x + y - 5z - 12 = 0$

and $4x - 3y + 7z = 0$

So, $\quad 2a + b - 5c = 0$ ...(i)

and $4a - 3b + 7c = 0$ ...(ii)

On solving Eqs. (i) and (ii), we get

$$\frac{a}{4} = \frac{b}{17} = \frac{c}{5}$$

Let a', b', c' be the direction ratios of the required line.

Since, this line lies in the plane $2x + y - 5z - 12 = 0$ and perpendicular to the line of intersection of the given two planes.

$2a' + b' - 5c' = 0$ ...(iii)

and $\quad 4a' + 17b' + 5c' = 0$ ...(iv)

On solving Eqs. (iii) and (iv), we get

$$\frac{a'}{3} = \frac{b'}{-1} = \frac{c'}{1}$$

$\Rightarrow$ Equation of the required line which passes through (2, 3 – 1) and having direction ratios (a', b', c') is

$$\frac{x-2}{3} = \frac{y-3}{-1} = \frac{z+1}{1}$$

12. (c) Given, $x^2 = 4y$ ...(i)

and P be a point on it.

In this case, PA must be normal to the given curve.

Now, $\frac{dy}{dx} = \frac{x}{2}$ [from Eq. (i)]

Thus, equation of normal at $P(\alpha, \beta)$ is

$y - \frac{\alpha^2}{4} = \frac{-2}{\alpha}(x - \alpha)$ ...(ii)

Since, Eq. (ii) passes through (0, 4).

So, $\left(4 - \frac{\alpha^2}{4}\right) = -\frac{2}{\alpha}(0 - \alpha) = 2$

$\Rightarrow \quad \alpha = \pm\sqrt{8}$

Now, we observe that Y-axis is also a normal to the curve passing through $A(4, 0)$ and corresponding $\alpha = 0$.

If $\alpha = 0$, then $P \equiv (0, 0)$

$\Rightarrow \quad PA = 4$

If $\alpha = \pm\sqrt{8}$, then $P \equiv (\pm\sqrt{8}, 2)$

$\Rightarrow \quad PA = \sqrt{8+4} = \sqrt{12}$

Hence, $P \equiv (\pm\sqrt{8}, 2)$

13. (a) Let θ be the angle between the given vectors.

$\mathbf{u} = \hat{\mathbf{i}} + \lambda\hat{\mathbf{j}} + \lambda x^2\hat{\mathbf{k}}$ and $\mathbf{v} = 5\hat{\mathbf{i}} + 2x\hat{\mathbf{j}} + \lambda\hat{\mathbf{k}}$

Then, $\cos\theta = \frac{\mathbf{u}\cdot\mathbf{v}}{|\mathbf{u}||\mathbf{v}|}$

If θ is obtuse, then $\cos\theta$ is negative.

So, $\mathbf{u}\cdot\mathbf{v} < 0$

i.e. $(\hat{\mathbf{i}} + \lambda\hat{\mathbf{j}} + \lambda x^2\hat{\mathbf{k}}) \cdot (5\hat{\mathbf{i}} + 2x\hat{\mathbf{j}} + \lambda\hat{\mathbf{k}}) < 0$

$\Rightarrow \quad \lambda^2 x^2 + 2\lambda x + 5 < 0$ ...(i)

This is possible only when $D < 0$ and coefficient of $x^2 < 0$

i.e. if $4\lambda^2 - 20\lambda^2 < 0$ and $\lambda^2 < 0$, which is not possible because $\lambda^2 \ge 0$

Hence, inequality (i) does not hold for any real values of λ.

$\therefore$ The set of values of λ for which **u** and **v** make an obtuse angle $= \phi$

14. (b) $f(x) = \int \frac{5x^8 + 7x^6}{(x^2 + 1 + 2x^7)^2} dx$

$= \int \frac{\frac{5}{x^8} + \frac{7}{x^8}}{\left(2 + \frac{1}{x^7} + \frac{1}{x^5}\right)} dx$

[taking x^{14} as common from numerator and denominator]

Put $2 + \frac{1}{x^7} + \frac{1}{x^5} = z$

$\Rightarrow \left(-\frac{7}{x^8} - \frac{5}{x^6}\right) dx = dz$

$\therefore \quad I = -\int \frac{dz}{z^2} = \frac{1}{z} + C$

$= \left(\frac{x^7}{2x^7 + x^2 + 1}\right) + C$

$\because f(0) = 0$ [given]

$\therefore \quad C = 0$

$\therefore f(x) = \left(\frac{x^7}{2x^7 + x^2 + 1}\right)$

Hence, $f(1) = \frac{1}{4}$

15. (c) $f(x) = \text{sgn}(x - x^4 + x^7 - x^8 - 1)$

For $x \in (0, 1)$; $x - 1 < 0$, $x^7 - x^4 < 0$

$\therefore \quad x - x^4 + x^7 - x^8 - 1 < 0$

For $x \in (1, \infty)$; $x < x^4$, $x^7 < x^8$

$\therefore \quad x - x^4 + x^7 - x^8 - 1 < 0$

Also for $x = 1$; $x - x^4 + x^7 - x^8 - 1 = -1$

Hence, $x - x^4 + x^7 - x^8 - 1 < 0 \ \forall \ x \in R^+$.

Thus, $\text{sgn}(x - x^4 + x^7 - x^8 - 1) = -1$, $\forall x \in R^+$

Therefore, $f(x)$ is many-one and into.

16. (d) Given, $f(x) = x^3 + 3x + 1$

$\therefore \quad f(1) = 5; \therefore g(5) = 1$

[$\because g$ is the inverse of f]

Now, $g''(x) = -\frac{f''(g(x))}{[f'(g(x))]^3}$

$\Rightarrow \quad g''(5) = -\frac{f''(g(5))}{[f'(g(5))]^3} = -\frac{f''(1)}{[f'(1)]^3}$

$\Rightarrow \quad f'(x) = 3x^2 + 3$ and $f''(x) = 6x$

Now, $\ f'(1) = 6$ and $f''(1) = 6$

Hence, $g''(5) = \frac{-6}{216} = \frac{-1}{36}$

17. (a) Let E_1 : Jockey B rides horse A.

E_2 : Jockey C rides horse A.

E : The horse A wins.

$\therefore \quad P(E_1)=\frac{2}{3}$

[$\because$ odds in favour of E_1 are 2 : 1]

and $P\left(\frac{E}{E_1}\right)=\frac{1}{6}$

Again $P(E_2)=1-P(E_1)=1-\frac{2}{3}=\frac{1}{3}$

and $P\left(\frac{E}{E_2}\right)=3P\left(\frac{E}{E_1}\right)=\frac{1}{2}$

Now, the required probability

$=P(E)=P(E_1\cap E)+P(E_2\cap E)$

$=P(E_1)\,P\left(\frac{E}{E_1}\right)+P(E_2)\,P\left(\frac{E}{E_2}\right)$

$=\frac{2}{3}\times\frac{1}{6}+\frac{1}{3}\times\frac{1}{2}=\frac{5}{18}$

Hence, the odds against winnings of A are 13 : 5.

18. (b) We have, $f(x)\frac{dy}{dx}=(f(x))^2+f(x)\cdot y+f'(x)\cdot y$

$\Rightarrow \quad \frac{dy}{dx}=f(x)+y+\frac{f'(x)}{f(x)}\cdot y$

$\Rightarrow \quad \frac{dy}{dx}-\left(1+\frac{f'(x)}{f(x)}\right)\cdot y=f(x)$

$\therefore \quad \text{IF}=e^{-\int\left(1+\frac{f'(x)}{f(x)}\right)dx}$

$=e^{-(x+\ln f(x))}$

$=\frac{e^{-x}}{f(x)}$

Hence, solution is

$y\times\frac{e^{-x}}{f(x)}=\int\frac{e^{-2}}{f(x)}\cdot f(x)dx$

$\Rightarrow \quad \frac{ye^{-x}}{f(x)}=-e^{-x}+C$

$\Rightarrow \quad y=-f(x)+Ce^x f(x)$

19. (a) $f(x)=(pq-q^2-2)x+\int_0^x(\sin^4\theta+\cos^4\theta)d\theta$

$\therefore f'(x)=(pq-q^2-2)+(\sin^4 x+\cos^4 x)$

Also, $f'(x)\le 0$ as $f(x)$ is a decreasing function.

$\Rightarrow (pq-q^2-2)+\sin^4 x+\cos^4 x\le 0$

$\Rightarrow (pq-q^2-2)+(1-2\sin^2 x\cdot\cos^2 x)\le 0$

$\Rightarrow (pq-q^2-2)+1-\frac{1}{2}\sin^2 2x\le 0$

$\Rightarrow 2(pq-q^2-1)\le\sin^2 2x$

$\Rightarrow (pq-q^2-1)\le 0$ as $\min(\sin^2 2x)=0$

$\Rightarrow 1\cdot q^2-pq+1\ge 0$ [here, $a=1>0$]

$\Rightarrow \quad D=p^2-4\le 0$

$\Rightarrow \quad |p|\le 2$

20. (d) We have, $C=K\tan\theta$

$\Rightarrow \quad \frac{dC}{d\theta}=K\cdot\sec^2\theta$

$\Rightarrow \quad \frac{dC}{d\theta}\cdot\delta\theta=K\cdot\sec^2\theta\,\delta\theta$

$\Rightarrow \quad \delta c=K\cdot\sec^2\theta\cdot\delta\theta$

$\left[\because \delta C=\frac{dC}{d\theta}\cdot\delta\theta\right]$

Now, $\frac{\delta C}{C}\times 100=\frac{K\sec^2\theta\cdot\delta\theta}{K\tan\theta}\times 100$

$=\frac{\sec^2\theta}{\tan\theta}\cdot\delta\theta\times 100$

$=2\times\frac{\pi}{4}\times\frac{\delta\theta}{\theta}\times 100$

$=\frac{\pi}{2}\times 0.7$

$=1.57\times 0.7$

$=1.10$

$\therefore$ Percentage of error in C is 1.1.

21. (1) $f(x)=\begin{cases}-\frac{x^2}{2}, & x\le 0\\ x^n\sin\frac{1}{x}, & x>0\end{cases}$

$f(x)$ is continuous at $x=0$.

$\therefore \quad f(0)=0$

$\text{LHL}=\lim_{x\to 0^-}f(x)=\lim_{x\to 0^-}\left(-\frac{x^2}{2}\right)=0$

$\text{RHL}=\lim_{x\to 0^+}f(x)=\lim_{x\to 0^+}x^n\sin\frac{1}{x}$

For continuity,

$\lim_{x\to 0^+}f(x)=\lim_{x\to 0^-}f(x)=f(0)$

$\Rightarrow \lim_{x\to 0^+}x^n\sin\frac{1}{x}=0$

$\Rightarrow \quad n>0 \quad$ ...(i)

Now, $f'(0^-)=\lim_{h\to 0^-}\frac{f(h+0)-f(0)}{2}$

$=\lim_{h\to 0^-}\frac{-\frac{h^2}{2}-0}{h}$

$=\lim_{h\to 0^-}-\frac{h}{2}=0$

$f'(0^+)=\lim_{h\to 0^+}\frac{f(h+0)-f(0)}{h}$

$=\lim_{h\to 0^+}\frac{h^n\sin\frac{1}{h}}{h}\ne 0$ (LHD)

because non-differentiable at $x=0$.

$\therefore \lim_{h\to 0^+}h^{n-1}\cdot\sin\left(\frac{1}{h}\right)\ne 0\Rightarrow n-1\le 0$

$\Rightarrow \quad n\le 1 \quad$ ...(ii)

From Eqs. (i) and (ii), we get

$n\in(0,1]$

Hence, number of integral value of $n=1$.

22. (1) Given, planes are

$x-cy-bz=0 \quad$ ...(i)

$cx-y+az=0 \quad$ ...(ii)

$bx+ay-z=0 \quad$ ...(iii)

Equation of plane passing through the line of intersection of planes (i) and (ii) may be taken as

$(x-cy-bz)+\lambda(cx-y+az)=0$

$\Rightarrow (1+\lambda c)x-y(c+x)+z(a\lambda-b)=0 \quad$ ...(iv)

If planes (iii) and (iv) are same, then

$\frac{1+\lambda c}{b}=\frac{-(c+\lambda)}{a}=\frac{a\lambda-b}{-1}$

$\Rightarrow \quad \lambda=-\frac{a+bc}{ac+b}=-\frac{ab+c}{1-a^2}$

$\Rightarrow a-a^3+bc-a^2bc$

$=a^2bc+ac^2+ab^2+bc$

$\Rightarrow a^2+b^2+c^2+2abc=1$

23. (2) $\because 3x^2h=1 \quad$ ...(i)

$\therefore \quad S=6x^2+8hx$

$S(x)=6x^2+8x\times\frac{1}{3x^2}$ [from Eq. (i)]

$S'(x)=12x-\frac{8}{3x^2}$

Now, $S'(x)=0\Rightarrow 36x^3=8\Rightarrow x^3=\frac{2}{9}$

Also, $S''(x)>0$

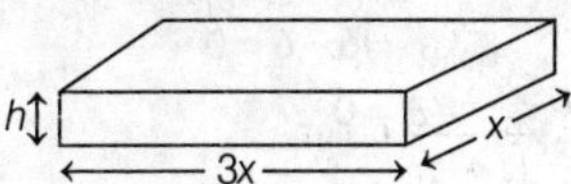

So, $x=\left(\frac{2}{9}\right)^{\frac{1}{3}}$ is point of minima.

Hence, $a^3=\frac{2}{9}$

$\Rightarrow \quad 9a^3=2$

24. (28) Let $x = z^2$

$$\therefore I_n = \int_0^1 2z(1+z^2+z^4+\ldots+z^{2n-2})(1+3z^2+5z^4+\ldots+(2n-3)z^{2n-4}+(2n-1)z^{2n-2})dz$$

$$= \int_0^1 2(z+z^3+z^5+..+z^{2n-1})(1+3z^2+5z^4+\ldots+(2n-3)z^{2n-4}+(2n-1)z^{2n-2})dz$$

Let $z+z^3+z^5+\ldots+z^{2n-1}=t$

$\Rightarrow [1+3z^2+5z^4+..+(2n-1)z^{2n-2}]dz = dt$

When $x=0, t=0$

and $z=1, t=n$

$$\therefore \quad I_n = 2\int_0^n t\,dt = 2\times\left(\frac{t^2}{2}\right)_0^n = n^2$$

$$\therefore \sqrt{I_{28}} = \sqrt{(28)^2} = 28$$

25. (9) Let the angle between **a** and **b** be α and that between $\mathbf{a}\times\mathbf{b}$ and **c** be β.

$\therefore |[\mathbf{a}\,\mathbf{b}\,\mathbf{c}]| = 6 \Rightarrow \sin\alpha\cdot\cos\beta = 1$

$\Rightarrow \sin\alpha = 1, \cos\beta = 1 \Rightarrow \alpha = 90°, \beta = 0°$

So, **a**, **b** and **c** are mutually perpendicular.

$\therefore |(\mathbf{a}\times\mathbf{c})\cdot\mathbf{d}|^2 + |(\mathbf{a}\times\mathbf{c})\times\mathbf{d}|^2$

$= |\mathbf{a}\times\mathbf{c}|^2|\mathbf{d}|^2 = |\mathbf{a}|^2|\mathbf{c}|^2|\mathbf{d}|^2 = 9$

26. (3) Given, $x+y+z=1$ ...(i)

$x+2y+4z=p$ ...(ii)

$x+4y+10z=p^2$ ...(iii)

$$\text{Now, } \Delta = \begin{vmatrix} 1 & 1 & 1 \\ 1 & 2 & 4 \\ 1 & 4 & 10 \end{vmatrix}$$

Applying $R_1 \to R_1 - R_2, R_2 \to R_2 - R_3$, we get

$$\Delta = \begin{vmatrix} 0 & -1 & -3 \\ 0 & -2 & -6 \\ 1 & 4 & 10 \end{vmatrix}$$

$= 0 + 1(0+6) - 3(0+2)$

$= 6 - 6 = 0$

$\because \quad \Delta = 0$

$\therefore$ Solution is not unique.)

The system will have infinite solution,

If, $\Delta_1 = 0, \Delta_2 = 0, \Delta_3 = 0$

$$\text{Now, } \Delta_1 = \begin{vmatrix} 1 & 1 & 1 \\ p & 2 & 4 \\ p^2 & 4 & 10 \end{vmatrix} = 0$$

Applying $C_3 \to C_3 - C_2$, we get

$$\Delta_1 = \begin{vmatrix} 1 & 1 & 0 \\ p & 2 & 2 \\ p^2 & 4 & 6 \end{vmatrix} = 0$$

$\Rightarrow 1(12-8) - 1(6p - 2p^2) = 0$

$\Rightarrow \quad p^2 - 3p + 2 = 0 \Rightarrow p = 1 \text{ or } 2$

So, sum $= 1 + 2 = 3$

27. (0.20)

Let A = The event of the selected number being composite.

E = The event of there being no remainder

$$P(A) = \frac{n(A)}{n(S)} = \frac{15}{25} = \frac{3}{5}$$

$$\therefore \quad P(\bar{A}) = \frac{2}{5}$$

$$\because \quad P\left(\frac{E}{A}\right) = \frac{4}{15}$$

$$\therefore \quad P\left(\frac{E}{\bar{A}}\right) = \frac{1}{10}$$

$$\text{Now, } P(E) = P(A)\cdot P\left(\frac{E}{A}\right) + P(\bar{A})\cdot P\left(\frac{E}{\bar{A}}\right)$$

$$= \frac{3}{5}\times\frac{4}{15} + \frac{2}{5}\times\frac{1}{10}$$

$$= \frac{4}{25} + \frac{1}{25}$$

$$= \frac{1}{5} = 0.20$$

28. (6) $\lim_{x\to 1^+} g(x)$

$$= \lim_{x\to 1^+}\left\{\lim_{m\to\infty}\frac{x^m f(x) + h(x) + 3}{2x^m + 4x + 1}\right\}$$

$$= \lim_{m\to\infty}\lim_{x\to 1^+}\left\{\frac{x^m f(x) + h(x) + 3}{2x^m + 4x + 1}\right\}$$

$$= \lim_{m\to\infty}\lim_{x\to 1^+}\left\{\frac{f(x) + \frac{h(x)+3}{x^m}}{2 + \frac{4x+1}{x^m}}\right\}$$

$$= \frac{f(1)}{2}$$

$\lim_{x\to 1^-} g(x)$

$$= \lim_{x\to 1^-}\left\{\lim_{x\to\infty}\frac{x^m f(x) + h(x) + 3}{2x^m + 4x + 1}\right\}$$

$$= \lim_{m\to\infty}\lim_{x\to 1^-}\left[\frac{x^m f(x) + h(x) + 3}{2x^m + 4x + 1}\right]$$

$$= \frac{h(1)+3}{5}$$

$\because g(x)$ is continuous at $x = 1$.

$$\therefore \quad \frac{f(1)}{2} = \frac{h(1)+3}{5}$$

$\Rightarrow \quad 5f(1) - 2h(1) = 6$

29. (5) Eccentricity of ellipse $= \frac{1}{2}$

$$\frac{de}{dt} = -0.1 \quad \text{[given]}$$

Eccentricity of auxiliary circle $= 0$

$$\Rightarrow \quad \int_{\frac{1}{2}}^{0} de = -0.1\int_0^T dt$$

T is time at which it will touch the auxiliary circle.

$\Rightarrow \quad -\frac{1}{2} = -0.1(T-0)$

$\Rightarrow \quad T = 5\text{ s}$

30. (8) $g(x) = \cos^{-1}x_1 + \sin^{-1}x_2 + \cos^{-1}x_3 + \sin^{-1}x_4 + \ldots + \cos^{-1}x_{2n-1} + \sin^{-1}x_{2n}$

$$= \frac{2n\pi}{2} - f(x)$$

$= n\pi - f(x)$

So, $g(x)$ will be maximum when $f(x)$ will be minimum.

$\therefore g(x)|_{\max} + f(x)|_{\min} = n\pi = 8\pi$ [given]

Hence, $n = 8$

Part Test 04

1. (a) We have, $t_n = \tan^{-1}\left(\frac{3}{9n^2+3n-1}\right)$

$$= \tan^{-1}\left(\frac{3}{1+(3n+2)(3n-1)}\right)$$

$$= \tan^{-1}\left(\frac{(3n+2)-(3n-1)}{1+(3n+2)(3n-1)}\right)$$

$$= \tan^{-1}(3n+2) - \tan^{-1}(3n-1)$$

$\therefore$ Sum of first 10 terms

$$= \sum_{r=1}^{10} a_r = \sum_{r=1}^{10} [\tan^{-1}(3r+2) - \tan^{-1}(3r-1)]$$

$$= (\tan^{-1}5 - \tan^{-1}2) + (\tan^{-1}8 - \tan^{-1}5) + \ldots + (\tan^{-1}32 - \tan^{-1}29)]$$

$$= \tan^{-1}32 - \tan^{-1}2 = \tan^{-1}\left(\frac{32-2}{1+2\times32}\right)$$

$$= \tan^{-1}\left(\frac{30}{65}\right) = \tan^{-1}\left(\frac{6}{13}\right)$$

According to question,

$$\tan^{-1}\left(\frac{6}{13}\right) = \cot^{-1}\left(\frac{\lambda}{\mu}\right)$$

$$\Rightarrow \cot^{-1}\left(\frac{13}{6}\right) = \cot^{-1}\left(\frac{\lambda}{\mu}\right)$$

$\therefore \quad \lambda = 13$ and $\mu = 6$

Hence, $2\lambda + \mu = 26 + 6 = 32$

2. (c) Given, $f(x) + f\left(x+\frac{1}{2}\right) = 1$ ...(i)

Replacing x by $\left(x+\frac{1}{2}\right)$, we get

$$f\left(x+\frac{1}{2}\right) + f(x+1) = 1 \quad \text{...(ii)}$$

Now, subtracting Eq. (i) from Eq. (ii), we get

$$f(x) = f(x+2) \quad \text{...(iii)}$$

Also, $g(x+1^2) = \int_x^{x+1^2} f(t)\cdot dt$

$$= \int_0^x f(t)\,dt + \int_x^{x+2^2} f(t)\cdot dt$$

$$\Rightarrow g(x+1^2) = \int_0^x f(t)\,dt + 1^2\cdot\int_0^1 f(t)\cdot dt$$

(by the help of Eq. (iii))

Similarly,

$$g(x+2^2) = \int_0^x f(t)\cdot dt + 2^2\cdot\int_0^1 f(t)\cdot dt \quad \text{...(iv)}$$

$$g(x+3^2) = -\int_0^x f(t)\cdot dt + 3^2\cdot\int_0^1 f(t)\cdot dt$$

$$g(x+k^2) = \int_0^x f(t)\cdot dt + k^2\cdot\int_0^1 f(t)\,dt$$

and $g(x+k) = \int_0^x f(t)\cdot dt + k\cdot\int_0^1 f(t)\cdot dt$ ...(v)

So, $\sum_{k=1}^{n}(g(x+k^2) - g(x+k))$

$$= \sum_{k=1}^{n}(k^2-k)\cdot\int_0^1 f(t)\,dt$$

$$= \sum_{k=1}^{n}(k^2-k)\cdot g(1),$$

[given $g(x) = \int_0^x f(t)\,dt$]

$$= \left(\frac{n(n+1)(2n+1)}{6} - \frac{n(n+1)}{2}\right)\times 1$$

$$= \frac{n(n-1)(n+1)}{3}$$

$$\therefore \sum_{n=2}^{\infty}\left[\frac{8}{\sum_{k=2}^{n}(g(x+k^2)-g(x+k))}\right]$$

$$= \sum_{n=2}^{\infty}\frac{8\times3}{n(n-1)(n+1)}$$

$$= 12\times\sum_{n=2}^{\infty}\left[\frac{(n+1)-(n-1)}{n(n-1)\cdot(n+1)}\right]$$

$$= 12\times\sum_{n=2}^{\infty}\left[\frac{1}{n(n-1)} - \frac{1}{n(n+1)}\right]$$

$$= 12\left[\left(\frac{1}{1\times2}-\frac{1}{2\times3}\right)+\left(\frac{1}{2\times3}-\frac{1}{3\times4}\right) + \ldots + \left(\frac{1}{n(n-1)}-\frac{1}{n(n+1)}\right)\right]$$

$$= 12\left(\frac{1}{2} - \frac{1}{n(n+1)}\right)_{n\to\infty} = 6$$

3. (a) Given, $|\mathbf{a}| = |\mathbf{b}| = |\mathbf{c}| = 1$ ...(i)

and $\mathbf{a}\cdot\mathbf{c} = \mathbf{b}\cdot\mathbf{c}$ ...(ii)

Now, $\mathbf{a}\times(\mathbf{b}\times\mathbf{c}) + \mathbf{b}\times(\mathbf{c}\times\mathbf{a})$

$$= (\mathbf{a}\cdot\mathbf{c})\mathbf{b} - (\mathbf{a}\cdot\mathbf{b})\mathbf{c} + (\mathbf{a}\cdot\mathbf{b})\mathbf{c} - (\mathbf{b}\cdot\mathbf{c})\mathbf{a}$$

$$= (\mathbf{a}\cdot\mathbf{c})\mathbf{b} - (\mathbf{b}\cdot\mathbf{c})\mathbf{a}$$

$$= (4+x^2)\mathbf{b} - (4x\cos^2\theta)\mathbf{a} \quad \text{(given)}$$

$$\Rightarrow \quad \mathbf{a}\cdot\mathbf{c} = 4 + x^2 \quad \text{...(iii)}$$

and $\quad \mathbf{b}\cdot\mathbf{c} = 4x\cos^2\theta$ ...(iv)

From Eqs. (iii) and (iv),

$$4 + x^2 = 4x\cos^2\theta$$

$$\Rightarrow \quad 4 + x^2 = 4x - 4x\sin^2\theta$$

$$(x-2)^2 = -4x\sin^2\theta \quad \text{...(v)}$$

$\because (x-2)^2 \geq 0, \forall x\in R$ and $0 \leq \sin^2\theta \leq 1$

$\therefore$ For Eq. (v) to be true;

$$(x-2)^2 = 0 = \sin\theta \quad [\because x>0, \therefore x\neq 0]$$

Given, $x = 2, \theta = 0°, \pi$

Hence, $x = 2$ and $\theta = 0°$ and π

4. (c) According to question,

$$p = q = \frac{1}{2}$$

Probability of getting tail odd number of times

$$= {}^nC_1pq^{n-1} + {}^nC_3p^3q^{n-3} + {}^nC_5p^5q^{n-5} + \ldots$$

$$= ({}^nC_1 + {}^nC_3 + {}^nC_5 + \ldots)\left(\frac{1}{2}\right)^n$$

$$= 2^{n-1}\times\left(\frac{1}{2}\right)^n = \frac{1}{2}$$

Probability of getting atleast one tail

$$= 1 - q^n = 1 - \frac{1}{2^n} > 0.99$$

On solving, we get

$$n \geq 7$$

5. (a,c)

Since, $f'(x) = \lim_{h\to0}\frac{f(x+h)-f(x)}{h}$

$$= \lim_{h\to0}\frac{f\left(x\left(1+\frac{h}{x}\right)\right)-f(x)}{h}$$

$$= \lim_{h\to0}\frac{f(x)\cdot f\left(1+\frac{h}{2}\right)-f(x)}{x}$$

$$= \lim_{h\to0}\frac{f\left(1+\frac{h}{x}\right)-1}{h}\times f(x)$$

[as $f(x\cdot y) = f(x)\cdot f(y)$]

$$\Rightarrow f'(x) = \frac{f(x)}{x}\cdot\left(\lim_{h\to0}\frac{f\left(1+\frac{h}{x}\right)-f(1)}{\frac{h}{x}}\right)$$

$$= \frac{f(x)}{x}\cdot f'(1)$$

$$\Rightarrow \frac{f'(x)}{f(x)} = \frac{f'(1)}{x}$$

Integrating both sides,

$$\ln(f(x)) = (\ln x)(f'(1)) + \ln c$$

As $\quad f(1) = 1$

$\Rightarrow \quad \ln c = 0$

$\therefore \quad f(x) = x^{f'(1)} = x^n$ (say)

Now, $f(1+x) = (1+x)^n$

$$= 1 + nx + \frac{n(n-1)}{2}x^2 = 1 + x(n+g(x))$$

$\therefore n = 1 \Rightarrow f(x) = x$

(a) $f(x) = x \in [0,1]$ if $x\in[0,1]$

(b) $\frac{f(x)}{x}$ is discontinuous at $x = 0$

(c) $\frac{1}{f(x)} = \frac{1}{x} \in (-\infty,\infty) - \{0\}$

which is unbounded.

(d) $\lim_{x\to0}(1+f(x))^{1/x} = \lim_{x\to0}(1-x)^{1/x}$

$$= e^{\lim_{x\to0}\frac{1}{x}\ln(1+x)} = e^1 = e$$

6. (a,d)

Let coordinates of A' are (x_2, y_2, z_2) be image of (2, 1, 6) about mirror $x + y - 2z = 3$, then

$$\frac{x_2 - 2}{1} = \frac{y_2 - 1}{1} = \frac{z_2 - 6}{-2}$$

$$= -2 \cdot \left[\frac{2 + 1 - 12 - 3}{1^2 + 1^2 + 2^2}\right] = 4$$

$\Rightarrow \quad A' = (6, 5, -2)$

Now, $\frac{x-2}{3} = \frac{y-1}{4} = \frac{z-6}{5} = \lambda$ (say)

$\Rightarrow x = 3\lambda + 2,\ y = 4\lambda + 1,\ z = 5\lambda + 6$ lies on plane, then B is point where line cuts plane.

Then, $B \equiv (-10, -15, -14)$.

the equation of reflected ray will be

$$\frac{x+10}{6+10} = \frac{y+15}{15+5} = \frac{z+14}{-2+14}$$

$$\Rightarrow \frac{x+10}{16} = \frac{y+15}{20} = \frac{z+14}{12}$$

i.e. $\frac{x+10}{4} = \frac{y+15}{5} = \frac{z+14}{3}$

7. (a,b,c)

Since, **r** is perpendicular to (**a** + **b** + **c**).

$\therefore \quad \mathbf{r} \cdot (\mathbf{a} + \mathbf{b} + \mathbf{c}) = 0$

$\Rightarrow \quad \mathbf{r} \cdot \mathbf{a} + \mathbf{r} \cdot \mathbf{b} + \mathbf{r} \cdot \mathbf{c} = 0$ ...(i)

Now, $\mathbf{r} \cdot \mathbf{a} = 0 + \cos y [\mathbf{a}\,\mathbf{b}\,\mathbf{c}] + 0$

$[\because \mathbf{a} \cdot (\mathbf{a} \times \mathbf{b}) = [\mathbf{a}\,\mathbf{a}\,\mathbf{b}] = 0 \text{ etc}]$

Similarly, $\mathbf{r} \cdot \mathbf{b} = 2[\mathbf{a}\,\mathbf{b}\,\mathbf{c}]$

and $\quad \mathbf{r} \cdot \mathbf{c} = \sin x\,[\mathbf{c}\,\mathbf{a}\,\mathbf{b}]$

From Eq. (i),

$[\mathbf{a}\,\mathbf{b}\,\mathbf{c}](\sin x + \cos y + 2) = 0$

As **a**, **b**, **c** are non-coplanar.

$\therefore \quad [\mathbf{a}\,\mathbf{b}\,\mathbf{c}] \neq 0$

$\therefore \quad \sin x + \cos y + 2 = 0$

$\Rightarrow \quad \sin x + \cos y = -2$

$\Rightarrow \quad \sin x = -1 = \cos y$

$[\because -1 \le \sin x \le 1, -1 \le \cos y \le 1]$

$\Rightarrow x = 2n\pi - \frac{\pi}{2};\ y = (2m+1)\pi$

where $m, n \in I$

$\Rightarrow \quad x = \frac{-\pi}{2}, \frac{-3\pi}{2}, \frac{3\pi}{2}, \frac{7\pi}{2}$ etc

and $y = -\pi, \pi, -3\pi, 3\pi, \ldots$

$\therefore x^2 + y^2$ can be $\frac{\pi^2}{4} + \pi^2 = \frac{5\pi^2}{4}$

or $\frac{\pi^2}{4} + 9\pi^2 = \frac{37\pi^2}{4}$

$x = \frac{3\pi}{2}, y = 4\pi$

$$\therefore \quad x^2 + y^2 = \left(\frac{3\pi}{2}\right)^2 + (4\pi)^2$$

$$= \frac{9\pi^2}{4} + 16\pi^2 = \frac{73\pi^2}{4}$$

8. (a,b,d)

Since, graph is symmetrical about (4, 0)

$\Rightarrow g(4 + x) = -g(4 - x)$

$\Rightarrow \quad g(x) = -g(8 - x)$ ...(i)

Now, let $g(x) = 2022$, then

$g(8 - x) = -g(x) = -2022$

$\therefore g^{-1}(2022) + g^{-1}(-2022) = 8$

Option (a) is true

$\int_{-2010}^{2018} g(x)\, dx$

$\because |-2010 - 4| = 2014$,

$|2018 - 4| = 2014$

$\therefore$ Option (b) is true.

also, $x^2 - g'(10)x - g'(10) = 0$

$\because g'(-100) > 0$ [given]

$g'(10) > 0 \Rightarrow D > 0$

$\therefore$ Option (c) is false

further, $g'(10) = g'(-2)$

$[\because g(x) = g'(8 - x)]$

$\therefore$ If $g'(10) = 20$, then $g'(-2) = 20$.

9. (b,c,d)

Let λ white and $(m - \lambda)$ black balls are transferred to B_2 and rest λ black and $m - \lambda$ white balls are transferred to B_3 with a probability $\frac{{}^mC_\lambda\, {}^mC_{m-\lambda}}{{}^{2m}C_m}$

Now, one ball is drawn from each box B_2 and B_3, then probability that they are of same colour is $\left(\frac{\lambda}{m}\right)\left(\frac{m-\lambda}{m}\right) \cdot 2$

So, total probability $P(m)$ is

$$P(m) = \sum_{k=0}^{m} \frac{{}^mC_r\, {}^mC_{m-\lambda}}{{}^{2m}C_m} \left(\frac{\lambda}{m}\right)\left(\frac{m-\lambda}{m}\right) \cdot 2$$

$$= \sum_{k=1}^{m-1} \frac{{}^{m-1}C_{\lambda-1}\, {}^{m-1}C_{m-1-\lambda}}{{}^{2m}C_m} \cdot 2$$

$$= \left(\sum_{k=1}^{m-1} \frac{{}^{m-1}C_{\lambda-1} \cdot {}^{m-1}C_\lambda}{{}^{2m}C_m}\right) \cdot 2$$

$$= \frac{2 \times \text{Coefficient of } x^{m-2} \text{ in } (1+x)^{2m-2}}{{}^{2m}C_m}$$

$$= \frac{2 \cdot {}^{2m-2}C_{m-2}}{{}^{2m}C_m} = \frac{m-1}{2m-1} > \frac{1000}{2017}$$

$\Rightarrow m > 59.82$

10. (a, b)

Let $\phi(x) = f(x) - g(x);\ x > 0$

$$= (x+1)\ln(1+x) - x - \frac{x^2}{2}$$

$\therefore$

$$\phi'(x) = (x+1) \times \frac{1}{x+1} + \ln(1+x) - 1 - x$$

$$= \ln(1+x) - x$$

and $\phi''(x) = \frac{1}{1+x} - 1 = \frac{-x}{1+x} < 0$,

$\forall x > 0$

$\Rightarrow \phi'(x)$ is decreasing function, $\forall x > 0$

and $\phi'(0) = 0$

$\Rightarrow \quad \phi'(x) < \phi'(0)$

$\Rightarrow \quad \phi'(x) < 0, \forall x \in (0, \infty)$

$\Rightarrow \phi'(x)$ is decreasing,

$\forall x > 0$ and $\phi(0) = 0$

$\Rightarrow \quad \phi(x) < \phi(0)$

$\Rightarrow \quad f(x) - g(x) < 0$

$\Rightarrow f(x) < g(x), \forall x > 0$

Again, let $\psi(x) = f(x) - h(x), x > 0$

$$= (x+1)\ln(1+x) - x - \frac{x^2}{2} + \frac{x^3}{3}$$

$$\Rightarrow \psi'(x) = (x+1) \times \frac{1}{x+1} + \ln(x+1)$$

$$-1 - x + x^2 = \ln(1+x) - x + x^2$$

$$\Rightarrow \quad \psi''(x) = \frac{1}{1+x} - 1 + 2x$$

$$= \frac{2x^2 + x}{x+1} > 0, \forall x > 0$$

$\therefore \psi'(x)$ is an increasing function, $\forall x > 0$ and $\psi'(0) = 0$

$\Rightarrow \quad \psi'(x) > \psi'(0) \Rightarrow \psi'(x) > 0$

$\Rightarrow \psi(x)$ is an increasing function $\forall x > 0$ and $\psi(0) = 0$

$\Rightarrow \quad \psi(x) > \psi(0) \Rightarrow \psi(x) > 0$

$\Rightarrow \quad f(x) > h(x), \forall x > 0$

11. (1)

Given, $x^2 \frac{dy}{dx} - xy = 1 + \cos\left(\frac{y}{x}\right)$

$$\Rightarrow \quad \frac{x(xdy - ydx)}{dx} = 1 + \cos(y/x)$$

$$\Rightarrow \quad \frac{\frac{(xdy - ydx)}{x^2}}{1 + \cos(y/x)} = \frac{dx}{x^3}$$

$$\Rightarrow \quad \int \frac{d(y/x)}{1 + \cos(y/x)} = \int \frac{dx}{x^3}$$

$$\Rightarrow \quad \frac{1}{2} \int \frac{d(y/x)}{\cos^2\left(\frac{y}{2x}\right)} = \int \frac{dx}{x^3}$$

$$\Rightarrow \quad \frac{1}{2} \frac{\tan\left(\frac{y}{2x}\right)}{\frac{1}{2}} = \frac{x^{-2}}{-2} + c$$

$$\Rightarrow \quad \tan\left(\frac{y}{2x}\right) = c - \frac{1}{2x^2}$$

On comparing, we get

$p = q = 2$

$$\therefore \quad \frac{p+q}{pq} = \frac{2+2}{2 \times 2} = \frac{4}{4} = 1$$

12. (8)

Given, $f(x)$ is fourth degree polynomial and $\lim_{x \to -1} \frac{f(x)}{(x+1)^3} = 1$

For limit to be exist,

$$f(-1) = f'(-1) = f''(-1) = 0$$

and $f'''(-1) = 6$ ...(i)

$\therefore \quad f(x) = A(x+1)^4 + (x+1)^3$ [with the help of Eq. (i)]

$$f'''(x) = 24A(x+1) + 6$$

Given, $f'''(0) = 0$

$\Rightarrow \quad 24A + 6 = 0$

$\Rightarrow \quad A = \frac{-1}{4}$

$\therefore f(x) = (x+1)^3 - \frac{1}{4}(x+1)^4$ ...(ii)

So, $f'(x) = 3(x+1)^2 - (x+1)^3$

$$f''(x) = 6(x+1) - 3(x+1)^2$$

Now, put $f'(x) = 0$

$\Rightarrow (x+1)^2(2-x) = 0$

$\Rightarrow \quad x = -1, 2$

Here, $f''(2) = -9 < 0$

$\therefore$ Maximum value is

$f(2) = 27 - \frac{81}{4} = \frac{27}{4}$

Also, $\quad f(0) = 1 - \frac{1}{4}$ [from Eq. (ii)]

$$= \frac{3}{4}$$

and $\quad f'(0) = 2$

$\therefore$ Subnormal at $x = 0$ is

$$f(0) \cdot f'(0) = \frac{3}{4} \times 2 = \frac{3}{2}$$

Hence, required value

$$= \frac{27}{4} + \frac{3}{2} = \frac{33}{4} = 8.25 \approx 8$$

13. (1)

$$|A| = \begin{bmatrix} \sec x & \cos x & \sec^2 x + \cot x \cdot \operatorname{cosec} x \\ \cos^2 x & \cos^2 x & \operatorname{cosec}^2 x \\ 1 & \cos^2 x & \cos^2 x \end{bmatrix}$$

Applying $R_1 \to R_2 - (\sec x) R_3$

$$|A| = \begin{bmatrix} 0 & 0 & \sec^2 x + \cot x \cdot \operatorname{cosec} x - \cos x \\ \cos^2 x & \cos^2 x & \operatorname{cosec}^2 x \\ 1 & \cos^2 x & \cos^2 x \end{bmatrix}$$

$$= (\sec^2 x + \cot x \cdot \operatorname{cosec} x - \cos x)$$
$$(\cos^4 x - \cos^2 x)$$

$$= (\sin^2 x + \cos^5 x) \neq 0 \text{ in } (0, \pi/2)$$

Hence, A^{-1} must exist

So, $|AA^T(A^{-1})^2| = 1$

14. (5)

$$\frac{dy}{dx} + \frac{y}{x-1} = xy^{1/3}$$

$$\Rightarrow \frac{2}{3y^{1/3}} \cdot \frac{dy}{dx} + \frac{2}{3} \cdot \frac{y^{2/3}}{(x-1)} = \frac{2x}{3}$$

$$\Rightarrow \frac{dz}{dx} + \frac{2}{3} \cdot \frac{z}{x-1} = \frac{2x}{3}$$

$$\left(\text{where, } z = y^{2/3}, \ \therefore \frac{dz}{dx} = \frac{2}{3y^{1/3}} \frac{dy}{dx}\right)$$

which upon solving, we get

$$z \cdot (x-1)^{2/3} = k_1(x-1)^{-2/3} + \frac{1}{4}(x-1)^2 + \frac{2}{5}(x-1)$$

So, $k_2 = 5$

15. (5)

Given, $\quad \alpha + \beta = 1$ ...(i)

$\quad 2\alpha^2 + 2\beta^2 = 1$ ...(ii)

On solving Eqs. (i) and (ii), we get

$$\alpha = \beta = \frac{1}{2}$$

$\therefore \quad q = \frac{\alpha}{\beta} = 1$ ...(iii)

Also given,

$f(2+x) + f(x) = 2, \forall x \in [0,2]$ ...(iv)

Now, $p = \int_0^4 f(x)\,dx - 4$

$$= \int_0^2 f(x)dx + \int_2^4 f(x)\,dx - 4$$

$$= \int_0^2 f(x)\,dx + \int_0^2 f(t+2)\,dt - 4$$

[let $x = t + 2$ for second integration]

$\Rightarrow \quad p = \int_0^2 f(x)\,dx + \int_0^2 \{2 - f(x)\}\,dx - 4$

$= \int_0^2 f(x)\,dx + 2 \cdot \int_0^2 dx - \int_0^2 f(x)\,dx - 4 = 0$

Then, $p = 0, q = 1$.

Let the roots of equation $ax^2 - bx + c = 0$ be α and β.

$\therefore f(x) = ax^2 - bx + c = a(x-\alpha)(x-\beta)$ ...(v)

Since, equation $f(x) = 0$ has both roots between 0 and 1.

$\therefore \quad f(0) \cdot f(1) > 0$ ...(vi)

But $f(0) \cdot f(1) = c(a - b + c) =$ an integer ...(vii)

$\therefore$ Least value of $f(0) \cdot f(1) = 1$ ...(viii)

Now, from Eq. (v),

$f(0) \cdot f(1) = a \cdot \alpha\beta \cdot a(1-\alpha)(1-\beta)$

$= a^2\alpha\beta(1-\alpha)(1-\beta)$ ...(ix)

As we know that

$\alpha(1-\alpha)$ has greatest value $\frac{1}{4}$ at

$$\alpha = \frac{1}{2}$$

and $\beta(1-\beta)$ has greatest value $\frac{1}{4}$ at

$$\beta = \frac{1}{2} \text{ but } \alpha \neq \beta$$

Hence, from Eq. (viii) greatest value of

$$f(0) \cdot f(1) < \frac{a^2}{16}$$ ...(x)

$\therefore$ From Eqs. (viii) and (x), we get

$$1 < \frac{a^2}{16} \Rightarrow a^2 - 16 > 0$$

$\Rightarrow \quad a < -4$ or $a > 4$

But $a \in N$

$\therefore$ Least value of $a = 5$

16. (11)

Let $T_1 = \tan^{-1}\frac{1}{3} = \tan^{-1}2 - \tan^{-1}1$

$T_2 = \tan^{-1}\frac{1}{7} = \tan^{-1}3 - \tan^{-1}2$

$T_3 = \tan^{-1}\frac{1}{13} = \tan^{-1}4 - \tan^{-1}3$

$\vdots \quad \vdots \quad \vdots$

$T_n = \tan^{-1}(n+1) - \tan^{-1}n$

Hence, $S_n = \tan^{-1}(n+1) - \tan^{-1}(1)$

$\Rightarrow \quad S_n = \tan^{-1}\left(\frac{n+1-1}{1+(n+1)\cdot 1}\right)$

$$= \frac{1}{2}\left(2\tan^{-1}\frac{n}{n+2}\right)$$

[using $2\tan^{-1}x = \cos^{-1}\frac{1-x^2}{1+x^2}, \forall x \geq 0$]

$$= \frac{1}{2}\cos^{-1}\left[\frac{1-\left(\frac{n}{n+2}\right)^2}{1+\left(\frac{n}{n+2}\right)^2}\right]$$

$$= \frac{1}{2}\cos^{-1}\left(\frac{2(n+1)}{n^2+2n+2}\right)$$

$$= \frac{1}{2}\cos^{-1}\left(\frac{24}{145}\right) \quad \text{[given]}$$

On comparing, we get

$$\frac{2(n+1)}{n^2+2n+2} = \frac{24}{145}$$

$\therefore \ 145(n+1) = \{(n+1)^2 + 1\} \times 12$

$\Rightarrow 12(n+1)^2 - 145(n+1) + 12 = 0$

$\Rightarrow 12(n+1)^2 - 144(n+1) - (n+1) + 12 = 0$

$\Rightarrow \{(n+1) - 12\}\{12(n+1) - 1\} = 0$

$\therefore \quad n+1=12, \frac{1}{12} \Rightarrow n=11, \frac{-11}{12}$

But $n \in N$

$\therefore \quad n \neq \frac{-11}{12}$, hence $n=11$

17. (0)

$$\int \frac{1}{f(x)}\,dx = \ln(g(x))^2 + c$$

On differentiating both sides, we get

$$\frac{1}{f(x)} = \frac{2}{f(x)} \cdot f'(x)$$

$\therefore \quad f'(x) = \frac{1}{2}$

$\Rightarrow \quad f(x) = \frac{x}{2} + c'$

$f(2) = 1 + c' = 2$

$\Rightarrow \quad c' = 1$

$\therefore \quad f(x) = \frac{x}{2} + 1$

$\text{sgn}\,(\ln(f(|x|))) = 1 - x^2$

$\therefore \quad f(|x|) > 1$

$\Rightarrow \quad \ln(f(|x|)) > 0, \forall\, x \in D_f$

From the graph it is clear that there is no solution.

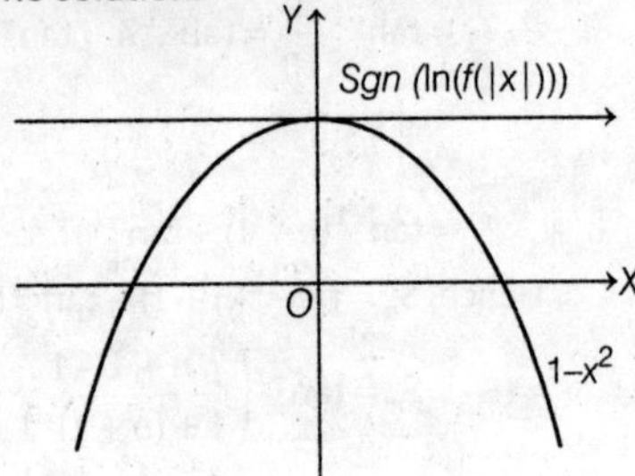

18. (143)

$$\begin{vmatrix} 2 & 1 & 1 \\ 1 & -1 & 1 \\ k & -1 & 3 \end{vmatrix} = 0$$

$\Rightarrow 2(-3+1) - 1(3-k) + 1(-1+k) = 0$

$\Rightarrow \quad -4-3+k-1+k = 0$

$\Rightarrow \quad 2k = 8 \Rightarrow k = 4$

Now, putting $z=0$ in the planes π_1 and π_2, we have

$$2x + y = 1 \text{ and } x - y = 2$$

After solving these, we get the coordinates of point $R \equiv (1, -1, 0)$

Again putting $x=0$ in the planes π_1 and π_2, we get

$$y + z = 1 \text{ and } -y + z = 2$$

On solving these, we get

$$S \equiv \left(0, \frac{1}{2}, \frac{3}{2}\right)$$

P

R (1, –1, 0) S (0, 1/2, 3/2)

O (0, 0, 0)

Now, equation of line RS is

$$\frac{x-1}{1} = \frac{y+1}{1/2} = \frac{z}{3/2} = \lambda \quad \text{(say)}$$

Let $P \equiv \left(-\lambda+1, \frac{\lambda}{2} - 1, \frac{3\lambda}{2}\right)$

$\because OR \perp PQ$

$\therefore -1(\lambda+1) + \frac{1}{2}\left(\frac{\lambda}{2} - 1\right) + \frac{9\lambda}{4} = 0$

$\Rightarrow \lambda = \frac{3}{7}$

$\therefore \quad P \equiv \left(\frac{4}{7}, -\frac{11}{14}, \frac{9}{14}\right)$

$\therefore \quad a = \frac{4}{7}, b = \frac{-11}{14}, c = \frac{9}{14}$

Hence, $\left(\frac{a}{2} - 180\,b + 2c\right)$

$$= \left(\frac{4}{14} + \frac{1980}{14} + \frac{18}{14}\right)$$

$$= \frac{2002}{14}$$

$$= 143$$

19. (65)

$$\lambda(x) = x + \int_0^1 t \cdot x\lambda(t)\,dt + \int_0^1 t^2 \lambda(t)\,dt$$

$$\Rightarrow \lambda(x) = x + x\int_0^1 t\lambda(t)\,dt + \int_0^1 t^2\lambda(t)\,dt$$

$\Rightarrow \lambda(x) = x + px + q$, where

$$p = \int_0^1 t\lambda(t)\,dt \text{ and}$$

$$q = \int_0^1 t^2 \cdot \lambda(t)\,dt$$

Now,

$$p = \int_0^1 t \cdot \lambda(t)\,dt = \int_0^1 t(t + pt + q)\,dt$$

$$= \left[\frac{t^3}{3} + \frac{pt^3}{3} + \frac{qt^2}{2}\right]_0^1$$

$$p = \frac{1}{3} + \frac{p}{3} + \frac{q}{2}$$

$\Rightarrow \quad \frac{2p}{3} - \frac{q}{2} = \frac{1}{3}$

$\Rightarrow \quad 4p - 3q = 2 \quad \text{...(i)}$

Also, $q = \int_0^1 t^2\lambda(t)\,dt$

$$= \int_0^1 t^2(t + pt + q)\,dt$$

$\Rightarrow \quad q = \frac{1}{4} + \frac{p}{4} + \frac{q}{3}$

$\Rightarrow \quad \frac{2}{3}q - \frac{p}{4} = \frac{1}{4} \Rightarrow 8q - 3p = 3 \quad \text{...(ii)}$

On solving Eqs. (i) and (ii), we get

$$p = \frac{25}{23} \text{ and } q = \frac{18}{23}$$

$$\therefore \lambda(x) = x + px + q = \frac{48}{23}x + \frac{18}{23}$$

Hence, $\int_0^1 \lambda(x)\,dx = \left[\frac{24}{23}x^2 + \frac{18}{23}x\right]_0^1$

$$= \frac{24}{23} + \frac{18}{23} = \frac{42}{23} = \frac{a}{b}$$

$\therefore \quad a + b = 65$

20. (21) Given system of linear equations

$$x + y + z = 4$$
$$2x + y + 3z = 6$$
$$x + 2y + mz = n$$

Now, $\Delta_1 = \begin{vmatrix} 1 & 1 & 1 \\ 2 & 1 & 3 \\ 1 & 2 & m \end{vmatrix}$

$$= 1(m-6) - 1(2m-3) + 1(4-1)$$
$$= m - 6 - 2m + 3 + 3 = m - 2m$$
$$= -m$$

$$\Delta_1 = \begin{vmatrix} 4 & 1 & 1 \\ 6 & 1 & 3 \\ n & 2 & m \end{vmatrix}$$

$$= 4(m-6) - 1(6m-3n) + 1(12-n)$$
$$= 4m - 24 - 6m + 3n + 12 - n$$
$$= -2(m-n+6)$$

$$\Delta_2 = \begin{vmatrix} 1 & 4 & 1 \\ 2 & 6 & 3 \\ 1 & n & m \end{vmatrix} = -2m - n + 6$$

$$\Delta_3 = \begin{vmatrix} 1 & 1 & 4 \\ 2 & 1 & 6 \\ 1 & 2 & n \end{vmatrix} = 6 - n$$

By cramer's rule,

$$x = \frac{\Delta_1}{\Delta} = \frac{-2(m-n+6)}{-m}$$
$$= \frac{2(m-n+6)}{m},$$
$$y = \frac{\Delta_2}{\Delta} = \frac{2m+n-6}{m}$$

and $z = \frac{\Delta_3}{\Delta} = \frac{n-6}{m}$

Now, for unique solution, $m \neq 0, n \in R$

$\therefore$ Total number of ordered pairs (m, n)

$$= 20 \times 21 = 420$$

i.e. $\quad P = 420$

For no solution, $m = 0, n \neq 6$

$\therefore$ Total number of ordered pairs of (m, n)

$$= 1 \times 20 = 20$$

i.e. $\quad Q = 20$

For infinite many solutions, $m = 0$, $n = 6$

$\therefore$ Total number of ordered pairs (m, n)

$$= 1 \times 1 = 1$$

i.e. $\quad R = 1$

Hence, $\frac{P}{QR} = \frac{420}{20 \times 1} = 21$

21. (25) $\prod_{r=1}^{9} I_{\left(\frac{r}{10}\right)} = I_{\frac{1}{10}} \cdot I_{\frac{2}{10}} \cdot I_{\frac{3}{10}} \ldots I_{\frac{9}{10}}$

$$= \left(I_{\frac{1}{10}} \cdot I_{\frac{9}{10}}\right)\left(I_{\frac{2}{10}} \cdot I_{\frac{8}{10}}\right)\left(I_{\frac{3}{10}} \cdot I_{\frac{7}{10}}\right)\left(I_{\frac{4}{10}} \cdot I_{\frac{6}{10}}\right)\left(I_{\frac{5}{10}}\right)$$

$$= \frac{\pi}{\sin\frac{\pi}{10}} \cdot \frac{\pi}{\sin\frac{2\pi}{10}} \cdot \frac{\pi}{\sin\frac{3\pi}{10}} \cdot \frac{\pi}{\sin\frac{4\pi}{10}} \cdot \sqrt{\frac{\pi}{\sin\frac{\pi}{2}}}$$

$$= \frac{\pi^{9/2}}{\left(\sin\frac{\pi}{10}\cos\frac{\pi}{10}\right)\left(\sin\frac{2\pi}{10} \cdot \cos\frac{2\pi}{10}\right)}$$

$$= \frac{4\pi^{9/2}}{\sin\frac{2\pi}{10} \cdot \sin\frac{4\pi}{10}}$$

$$= \frac{8\pi^{9/2}}{\cos\frac{2\pi}{10} \cdot \cos\frac{6\pi}{10}}$$

$$= \frac{16\pi^{9/2}}{\sqrt{5}} = 16\sqrt{\frac{\pi^9}{5}}$$

On comparing, we get

$$\lambda = 16 \text{ and } \mu = 9$$

$$\therefore \quad \lambda + \mu = 25$$

22. (b) (I) Let $I = \int \frac{e^{2x} - 1}{e^{2x} + 1} dx$

Dividing N^r and D^r by e^x, we get

$$I = \int \frac{e^x - e^{-x}}{e^x + e^{-x}} dx$$

Now, let $e^x + e^{-x} = t$

$\Rightarrow (e^x - e^{-x})dx = dt$

$$\therefore \quad I = \int \frac{dt}{t} = \log t + C$$

$$= \log(e^x + e^{-x}) + C$$

$$\Rightarrow \quad I = \log\left(e^x + \frac{1}{e^x}\right) + C$$

$$= \log\left(\frac{e^{2x} + 1}{e^x}\right) + C$$

$$\Rightarrow \quad I = \log(e^{2x} + 1) - \log e^x + C$$

$$\Rightarrow \quad I = \log(e^{2x} + 1) - x + C$$

Hence, I $\rightarrow$ R

(II) Let $I = \int \frac{dx}{(e^x + e^{-x})^2}$

$$\Rightarrow I = \int \frac{dx}{\left(\frac{e^{2x} + 1}{e^x}\right)^2} = \int \frac{e^{2x}}{(e^{2x} + 1)^2} dx$$

Let $e^{2x} + 1 = t \Rightarrow 2e^{2x}\, dx = dt$

$$\Rightarrow \quad e^{2x} dx = \frac{dt}{2}$$

$$\therefore \quad I = \frac{1}{2}\int \frac{dt}{t^2} = \frac{1}{2}\left(-\frac{1}{t}\right) + C$$

$$I = \frac{-1}{2(e^{2x} + 1)} + C$$

Hence, II $\rightarrow$ S

(III) Let $I = \int \frac{e^{-x}}{1 + e^x} dx$

$$\Rightarrow \quad I = \int \frac{e^{-x} \cdot e^{-x}}{e^{-x} + 1} dx$$

Now, let $e^{-x} + 1 = t \Rightarrow e^{-x} = (t - 1)$

and $e^{-x} dx = -dt$

$$\therefore \quad I = -\int \frac{(t-1)}{t} dt$$

$$= \int \left(\frac{1 - t}{t}\right) dt$$

$$= \int \frac{1}{t} dt - \int dt$$

$$\Rightarrow \quad I = \log t - t + C$$

$$\Rightarrow \quad I = \log(e^{-x} + 1) - (e^{-x} + 1) + C$$

$$\Rightarrow \quad I = \log\left(\frac{1 + e^x}{e^x}\right) - e^{-x} - 1 + C$$

$\Rightarrow$

$$I = \log(1 + e^x) - \log e^x - e^{-x} - 1 + C$$

$$\Rightarrow \quad I = \log(1 + e^x) - x - e^{-x} + C$$

Hence, III $\rightarrow$ Q

(IV) Let $I = \int \frac{1}{\sqrt{1 - e^{2x}}} dx$

Dividing N^r and D^r by e^x, we get

$$I = \int \frac{e^{-x}}{\sqrt{e^{-2x} - 1}} dx$$

Now, let $e^{-x} = t \Rightarrow -e^{-x} dx = dt$

$$\Rightarrow \quad e^{-x} dx = -dt$$

$$\therefore \quad I = -\int \frac{dt}{\sqrt{t^2 - 1}}$$

$$I = -\log[t + \sqrt{t^2 - 1}] + C$$

$$= -\log[e^{-x} + \sqrt{e^{-2x} - 1}] + C$$

$$= -\log\left[\frac{1}{e^x} + \frac{\sqrt{1 - e^{2x}}}{e^x}\right] + C$$

$$= -\log[1 + \sqrt{1 - e^{2x}}] + \log e^x + C$$

$$= x - \log[1 + \sqrt{1 - e^{2x}}] + C$$

Hence, IV $\rightarrow$ P

23. (a) (I) Since A is idempotent; we have

$$A^2 = A$$

$$A^3 = AA^2 = AA = A^2 = A$$

$$A^4 = AA^3 = AA = A^2 = A$$

and $A^n = A$

$$(I - A)^n = {}^nC_0 I - {}^nC_1 A + {}^nC_2 A^2 - {}^nC_3 A^3 + \ldots\ldots$$

$$= I + (-{}^nC_1 + {}^nC_2 - {}^nC_3 + \ldots) A$$

$$= I + [({}^nC_0 - {}^nC_1 + {}^nC_2 + \ldots) - {}^nC_0] A$$

$$= I - {}^nC_0 A$$

$$= I - A$$

Hence, I $\rightarrow$ S

(II) A is involuntary, hence

$$A^2 = I$$

$$A^3 = A^5 = \ldots = A$$

and $\quad A^2 = A^4 = A^6 = \ldots = I$

$$(I - A)^n = {}^nC_0 I - {}^nC_1 A + {}^nC_2 A^2 - {}^nC_3 A^3 + \ldots$$

$$= {}^nC_0 I - {}^nC_1 A + {}^nC_2 I - {}^nC_3 I + \ldots$$

$$= ({}^nC_0 + {}^nC_2 + {}^nC_4 + \ldots) I - ({}^nC_1 + {}^nC_3 + {}^nC_5 + \ldots) A$$

$$= 2^{n-1}(I - A)$$

$$\Rightarrow \quad [(I - A)^n] A^{-1} = 2^{n-1}(I - A) A^{-1}$$

$$= 2^{n-1}(A^{-1} - I)$$

Hence, II $\rightarrow$ P

(III) If A is nilpotent of index 2, then

$$A^2 = A^3 = A^4 = A^n = 0$$

$$(I - A)^n = {}^nC_0 I - {}^nC_1 A + {}^nC_2 A^2 - {}^nC_n A^3 + \ldots$$

$$= I - nA$$

Hence, III $\rightarrow$ Q

(IV) If A is orthogonal, then

$$AA^T = I$$

Pre-multiplying A^{-1} both sides, we get

$$A^{-1}AA^T = A^{-1}T$$

$$\Rightarrow \quad IA^T = A^{-1}$$

$$\Rightarrow \quad A^T = A^{-1}$$

$$\Rightarrow \quad (AT)^{-1} = (A^{-1})^{-1} = A$$

$$\therefore \quad (A^T)^{-1} = A$$

Hence, IV $\rightarrow$ A

KNOCKOUTS

Knockout 1

1. (b) Since we know that $|\tan x|$ and $e^{|x|}$ are not differentiable at $x = 0$ for $f(x)$ to be differentiable at $x = 0$, we must have $a = 0$, $b = 0$ and c can be any real number.

2. (c) Given parabola $y^2 = 4x$ ...(i)

Let $(t^2, 2t)$ be parametric point on given parabola.

$\therefore$ Equation of tangent at $(t^2, 2t)$

$$ty = x + t^2$$

$$\Rightarrow \quad x - ty + t^2 = 0 \quad \text{...(ii)}$$

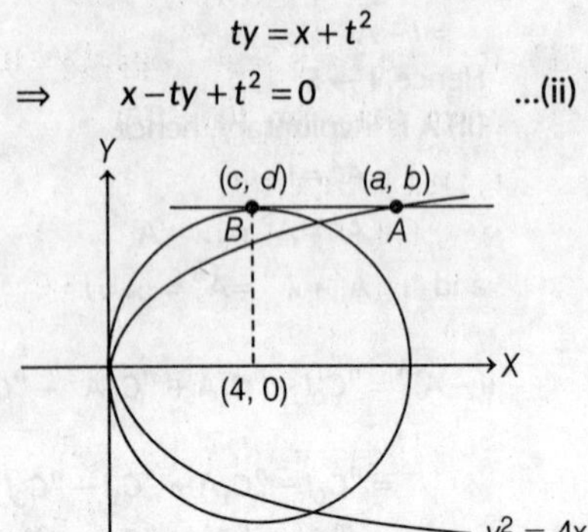

$\because$ Eq. (ii) is the tangent to circle $(x-4)^2 + y^2 = 16$ having centre (4, 0) and radius 4.

$\therefore$ Distance of tangent from (4, 0) = radius

$$\left|\frac{4 - t(0) + t^2}{\sqrt{1 + t^2}}\right| = 4$$

Let $t^2 = u$

$$4 + u = 4\sqrt{1 + u}$$

On squaring both side

$$16 + u^2 + 8u = 16 + 16u$$

$$\Rightarrow \quad u^2 - 8u = 0$$

$$\Rightarrow \quad u = 0, u = 8$$

$$\therefore \quad t = 0, t = 2\sqrt{2}$$

$\therefore$ Hence, $A = (a, b) = (t^2, 2t) = (8, 4\sqrt{2})$

$$\therefore \quad b = 4\sqrt{2}$$

$\because (c, d)$ is the foot of perpendicular drawn from (4, 0) to the tangent $x - 2\sqrt{2}y + 8 = 0$.

$$\therefore \frac{c-4}{1} = \frac{d-0}{-2\sqrt{2}} = \frac{-(4-0+8)}{1^2 + (2\sqrt{2})^2}$$

$$\therefore c - 4 = \frac{-12}{9} \Rightarrow c = \frac{8}{3}$$

$$\therefore b + c = \left(4\sqrt{2} + \frac{8}{3}\right)$$

3. (c) Equation of tangents is

$$y = mx \pm \sqrt{a^2m^2 + b^2}$$

$$\Rightarrow \quad y = \frac{-4}{3}x \pm \sqrt{18 \times \frac{16}{9} + 32}$$

$$\Rightarrow \quad y = \frac{-4}{3}x \pm 8$$

Hence, tangents are

$$y = -\frac{4}{3}x + 8 \text{ and } y = -\frac{4}{3}x - 8$$

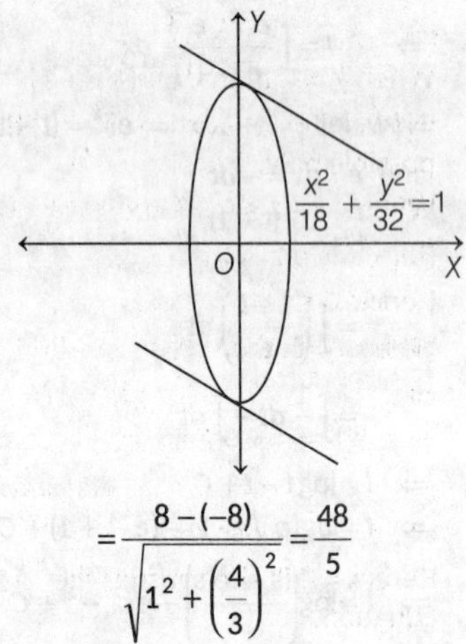

$$= \frac{8 - (-8)}{\sqrt{1^2 + \left(\frac{4}{3}\right)^2}} = \frac{48}{5}$$

4. (d) Given that, $|z - 2 + i| \le 2$ ...(i)

$$\because \quad |z - 2 + i| \ge ||z| - |2 - i||$$

$$\Rightarrow \quad |z - 2 + i| \ge ||z| - \sqrt{5}| \quad \text{...(ii)}$$

From Eqs. (i) and (ii), we have

$$||z| - \sqrt{5}| \le |z - 2 + i| \le 2$$

$$\Rightarrow \quad ||z| - \sqrt{5}| \le 2$$

$$\Rightarrow -2 \le |z| - \sqrt{5} \le 2$$

$$\Rightarrow \quad \sqrt{5} - 2 \le |z| \le \sqrt{5} + 2$$

5. (b) Given, equation of curves are

$$y = x^2 \quad \text{...(i)}$$

$$\text{and} \quad y = \frac{2}{1 + x^2} \quad \text{...(ii)}$$

For intersection point,

$$x^2 = \frac{2}{1 + x^2}$$

$$\Rightarrow \quad x^4 + x^2 - 2 = 0$$

$$\Rightarrow \quad (x^2 + 2)(x^2 - 1) = 0$$

$$\because \quad x^2 + 2 = 0$$

(not possible in R)

$$\therefore \quad x^2 - 1 = 0 \Rightarrow x = \pm 1$$

Hence, the required area

$$= 2\int_0^1 \left(\frac{2}{1 + x^2} - x^2\right) dx$$

$$= 2\left[2\tan^{-1} x - \frac{x^3}{3}\right]_0^1$$

$$= 2\left(\frac{\pi}{2} - \frac{1}{3}\right) = \pi - \frac{2}{3}$$

6. (c) **Case I**

When two points selecting from 7 non-collinear points and two points taken from 5 collinear points to form a quadrilateral then number of possible quadrilaterals $= {}^7C_2 \times {}^5C_2$.

Case II

When three points selecting from 7 non-collinear points and one point from 5 collinear points are taken to form a quadrilateral.

$\therefore$ Number of possible quadrilaterals $= {}^7C_3 \times {}^5C_1$.

Case III

All the four points are taken from a non-collinear points to form a quadrilateral.

Number of possible quadrilateral $= {}^7C_4$

Hence, total possible quadrilateral

$${}^7C_2 \times {}^5C_2 + {}^7C_3 \times {}^5C_1 + {}^7C_4$$

$$= 21 \times 10 + 35 \times 5 + 35 = 420$$

7. (d) The given equation can be written as

$$x = 7^{1/3} + 7^{2/3}$$

(cubing both sides)

$$\Rightarrow \quad x^3 = 7 + 49 + 3 \cdot 7 (7^{1/3} + 7^{2/3})$$

$$\Rightarrow \quad x^3 = 56 + 21 \cdot x$$

$$\Rightarrow \quad x^3 - 21x - 56 = 0$$

$\therefore$ Product of all the roots is

$$\frac{(-1)^3(-56)}{(1)} = 56$$

8. (a) Here, $D(0) = 0$

($\because R_1$ and R_2 are identical)

Hence, $\lim_{x\to 0} \frac{D(x)}{x}$ attains/takes form $\left(\frac{0}{0}\right)$

∴ Applying L-Hospital's rules,

$$\lim_{x\to 0} \frac{D(x)}{x} = \lim_{x\to 0} \frac{D'(x)}{1} = D'(0)$$

Given,

$$D(x) = \begin{vmatrix} g(x+K) & g(x+2K) & g(x+3K) \\ g(K) & g(2K) & g(3K) \\ g'(K) & g'(2K) & g'(3K) \end{vmatrix}$$

$\therefore D'(x)$

$$= \begin{vmatrix} g'(x+K) & g'(x+2K) & g'(x+3K) \\ g(K) & g(2K) & g(3K) \\ g'(K) & g'(2K) & g'(3K) \end{vmatrix} + \begin{vmatrix} g(x+K) & g(x+2K) & g(x+3K) \\ 0 & 0 & 0 \\ g'(K) & g'(2K) & g'(3K) \end{vmatrix} + \begin{vmatrix} g(x+K) & g(x+2K) & g(x+3K) \\ g(K) & g(2K) & g(3K) \\ 0 & 0 & 0 \end{vmatrix}$$

$$\therefore D'(x) = \begin{vmatrix} g'(x+K) & g'(x+2K) & g'(x+3K) \\ g(K) & g(2K) & g(3K) \\ g'(K) & g'(2K) & g'(3K) \end{vmatrix}$$

$\left(\because K \text{ is constant}; \therefore \frac{dK}{dx} = 0\right)$

$$\Rightarrow D'(0) = \begin{vmatrix} g'(K) & g'(2K) & g'(3K) \\ g(K) & g(2K) & g(3K) \\ g'(K) & g'(2K) & g'(3K) \end{vmatrix}$$

$\Rightarrow D'(0) = 0$ ($\because R_1$ and R_3 are identical)

$\therefore \quad \lim_{x\to 0} \frac{D(x)}{x} = D'(0) = 0$

9. (a) Since, $x - x + \sqrt{2} = \sqrt{2}$ which is an irrational number.

So, xRx for all $x \in R$.

Hence, R is reflexive.

R is not symmetric because $(\sqrt{2}, 1) \in R$ but $(1, \sqrt{2}) \notin R$.

Again R is not transitive, since $(\sqrt{2}, 1) \in R$ and $(1, 2\sqrt{2}) \in R$ but $(\sqrt{2}, 2\sqrt{2}) \notin R$.

Hence, R is reflexive.

10. (d) Clearly,

$$f(-x) = \begin{vmatrix} -x^3 & -\sin x & -\tan x \\ \cos x & x^8 & 1 \\ e^{x^2} & \sec x & 2 \end{vmatrix} = -f(x)$$

$\Rightarrow f(x)$ is odd function.

Hence, $\int_{-\pi/2}^{\pi/2} f(x)dx = 0$

11. (a) From the equation, we can write

$$\log_3(\sqrt{x} + |\sqrt{x}-1|)$$
$$= \frac{1}{2}\log_3[4(\sqrt{x} + |\sqrt{x}-1|) - 3]$$
$$\Rightarrow \log_3(\sqrt{x} + |\sqrt{x}-1|)^2 = \log_3[4(\sqrt{x} + |\sqrt{x}-1|) - 3]$$
$$\Rightarrow (\sqrt{x} + |\sqrt{x}-1|)^2 = 4(\sqrt{x} + |\sqrt{x}-1|) - 3$$
$$\Rightarrow \quad y^2 - 4y + 3 = 0,$$

where $y = \sqrt{x} + |\sqrt{x} - 1|$

$\Rightarrow \quad y = 1, 3$

When $y = 1$, then $\sqrt{x} + |\sqrt{x} - 1| = 1$

$\Rightarrow |\sqrt{x} - 1| = 1 - \sqrt{x} = -(\sqrt{x} - 1)$ this is possible only.

When $\sqrt{x} - 1 \le 0 \Rightarrow \sqrt{x} \le 1$ or $x \le 1$

But $\sqrt{x}$ is real if $x \ge 0$.

Hence, $0 \le x \le 1$

When $y = 3$, then $\sqrt{x} + |\sqrt{x} - 1| = 3$

$\Rightarrow \quad |\sqrt{x} - 1| = 3 - \sqrt{x}$

$\Rightarrow x + 1 - 2\sqrt{x} = 9 + x - 6\sqrt{x}$ (on squarring)

$\Rightarrow \quad \sqrt{x} = 2$ or $x = 4$

Here, $x = 4$ is also satisfies the equation.

Hence, the solutions are $0 \le x < 1, x = 4$

12. (b) $\sim(p \vee q) \vee (\sim p \wedge q) \equiv (\sim p \wedge \sim q)$

$$\vee(\sim p \wedge q)$$
$$\equiv (\sim p) \wedge (\sim q \vee q)$$
$$\equiv (\sim p) \wedge T \equiv \sim p$$

13. (d) We are given,

$$np = 4 \quad \text{...(i)}$$

and $npq = 2 \Rightarrow (4)q = 2$

$\Rightarrow \quad q = \frac{1}{2}$

$\therefore p = 1 - q = 1 - \frac{1}{2} \Rightarrow p = \frac{1}{2}$

Now, $n\left(\frac{1}{2}\right) = 4 \Rightarrow n = 8$ [From Eq. (i)]

$\therefore \quad p(X = 1) = {}^nC_1 pq^{n-1} = 8pq^7$

$$= 8\left(\frac{1}{2}\right)\left(\frac{1}{2}\right)^7$$
$$= 8 \times \frac{1}{2} \times \frac{1}{128} = \frac{1}{32}$$

14. (a) $\because \left(x^4 + 2 + \frac{1}{x^4}\right)^{10} = \left(x^2 + \frac{1}{x^2}\right)^{20}$

General term = $(r+1)$th term of $\left(x^2 + \frac{1}{x^2}\right)^{20}$ is

$$T_{r+1} = {}^{20}C_r \cdot (x^2)^{20-r} \cdot \left(\frac{1}{x^2}\right)^r$$
$$= {}^{20}C_r \cdot x^{40-4r}$$

For the coefficient of x^8,

Put $40 - 4r = 8 \Rightarrow r = 8$

and for the coefficient of x^{-24},

put $40 - 4r = -24$

$\Rightarrow \quad r = 16$

$\therefore \quad \alpha = {}^{20}C_8$ and $\beta = {}^{20}C_{16}$

$$\Rightarrow \quad \frac{\alpha}{\beta} = \frac{20!}{8!12!} \times \frac{16!4!}{20!}$$
$$= \frac{16 \times 15 \times 14 \times 13}{8 \times 7 \times 6 \times 5} = 26$$

15. (b) Since, $f(x)$ is continuous at $x = 0$.

$\therefore \lim_{x\to 0^-} f(x) = \lim_{x\to 0^+} f(x) = f(0)$

i.e. LHL = RHL= $f(0)$ ...(i)

Now, LHL at $x = 0$ i.e. $f(0^-)$

$$\lim_{x\to 0^-} f(x) = \lim_{x\to 0^-} (\cos x - \sin x)^{\operatorname{cosec} x}$$
$$= \lim_{h\to 0} (\cos h + \sin h)^{-\operatorname{cosec} h}$$
$$= \lim_{h\to 0} [1 + (\cos h + \sin h - 1)]$$

(i.e. 1^∞ form)

$$= e^{\lim_{h\to 0} \{\cos h + \sin h - 1\}\left(\frac{-1}{\sin h}\right)}$$
$$= e^{\lim_{h\to 0} \left\{-2\sin^2\frac{h}{2} + 2\sin\frac{h}{2}\cos\frac{h}{2}\right\}\left(\frac{-1}{2\sin\frac{h}{2}\cdot\cos\frac{h}{2}}\right)}$$
$$= e^{\lim_{h\to 0}\left(\frac{\sin\frac{h}{2} - \cos\frac{h}{2}}{\cos\frac{h}{2}}\right)} = e^{-1} = \frac{1}{e}$$

$\Rightarrow \quad \text{LHL} = \frac{1}{e}$ ...(i)

RHL at $x = 0 = \lim_{x\to 0^+} f(x)$

$$= \lim_{x\to 0^+} \frac{e^{1/x} + e^{2/x} + e^{3/x}}{ae^{2/x} + be^{3/x}}$$
$$= \lim_{h\to 0} \frac{e^{3/h}\left\{\frac{1}{e^{2/h}} + \frac{1}{e^{1/h}} + 1\right\}}{e^{3/h}\left\{\frac{a}{e^{1/h}} + b\right\}}$$

$\Rightarrow$ RHL $= \frac{1}{b}$ and $f(0) = a$

From Eq. (i), $a = e^{-1} = \frac{1}{b}$

$\Rightarrow \quad a = \frac{1}{e}$ and $b = e$

16. (c) $P(A' \cap B' | C) = \frac{P(A' \cap B' \cap C)}{P(C)}$

$$= \frac{P(C) - P(C \cap A) - P(C \cap B)}{P(C)}$$

$$= \frac{P(C) - P(C) \cdot P(A) - P(C) \cdot P(B)}{P(C)}$$

$$= 1 - P(A) - P(B)$$

$$= P(A') - P(B)$$

17. (a) $S_n = \sum_{k=1}^{n} \tan^{-1}\left(\frac{2K}{1 + (K^4 + K^2 + 1)}\right)$

$$= \sum_{k=1}^{n} \tan^{-1}\left(\frac{2K}{1 + (K^2 + K + 1)(K^2 - K + 1)}\right)$$

$$= \sum_{k=1}^{n} \tan^{-1}\left(\frac{(K^2 + K + 1) - (K^2 - K + 1)}{1 + (K^2 + K + 1)(K^2 - K + 1)}\right)$$

$$\Rightarrow S_n = \sum_{k=1}^{n} [\tan^{-1}(K^2 + K + 1) - \tan^{-1}(K^2 - K + 1)]$$

$$\Rightarrow S_n = [(\tan^{-1} 3 - \tan^{-1} 1) + (\tan^{-1} 7 - \tan^{-1} 3) + (\tan^{-1} 13 - \tan^{-1} 7) + \dots + \{\tan^{-1}(n^2 + n + 1) - \tan^{-1}(n^2 - n + 1)\}]$$

$$= \tan^{-1}(n^2 + n + 1) - \tan^{-1} 1$$

$$= \tan^{-1}\left(\frac{n^2 + n}{1 + n^2 + n + 1}\right)$$

$$\Rightarrow S_n = \tan^{-1}\left(\frac{n^2 + n}{n^2 + n + 2}\right)$$

$$\therefore \lim_{n \to \infty} S_n = \lim_{n \to \infty} \tan^{-1}\left(\frac{1 + \frac{1}{n}}{1 + \frac{1}{n} + \frac{2}{n^2}}\right) = \frac{\pi}{4}$$

18. (b) Given, $y(x) = f(e^x) e^{f(x)}$,

$f(0) = f(1) = 0, f'(1) = 2$

$\therefore y'(x) = f'(e^x) \cdot e^x \cdot e^{f(x)} + f(e^x) \cdot e^{f(x)} f'(x)$

$y'(0) = f'(1) \cdot 1 \cdot e^{f(0)} + f(1) \cdot e^{f(0)} \cdot f'(0)$

$= 2e^0 + 0 \cdot e^0 \cdot f'(0)$

$= 2 + 0$

$y'(0) = 2$

19. (c) For acute angle, $\mathbf{a} \cdot \mathbf{b} > 0$

i.e. $2x^2 - 3x + 1 > 0$

$\Rightarrow (2x - 1)(x - 1) > 0$

$\Rightarrow 2\left(x - \frac{1}{2}\right)(x - 1) > 0$

$\Rightarrow \left(x - \frac{1}{2}\right)(x - 1) > 0$

$\Rightarrow x \in \left(-\infty, \frac{1}{2}\right) \cup (1, \infty)$ ....(i)

$\because$ Axis of ordinate is Y-axis.

From question, $\mathbf{b} \cdot \hat{\mathbf{j}} < 0 \Rightarrow x < 0$

i.e. $x \in (-\infty, 0)$ ....(ii)

From Eqs. (i) and (ii), we get

$x \in (-\infty, 0)$ i.e. for all $x < 0$

20. (d) Equation of required plane is

$$\begin{vmatrix} x-1 & y-1 & z-1 \\ 1 & 2 & 3 \\ 1 & 3 & 5 \end{vmatrix} = 0$$

$\Rightarrow (x - 1) - 2(y - 1) + (z - 1) = 0$

$\Rightarrow x - 2y + z = 0$

21. Given, $f(x) = a \sin x + \frac{1}{4} \sin 4x$

On differentiating w.r.t. x, we get

$f'(x) = a \cos x + \frac{1}{4}(4 \cos 4x)$

$f'(x) = a \cos x + \cos 4x$

For maximum value of $f(x)$

$f'(x) = 0$

At $x = \frac{\pi}{4}$,

$f'\left(\frac{\pi}{4}\right) = 0$

$a \cos\left(\frac{\pi}{4}\right) + \cos 4\left(\frac{\pi}{4}\right) = 0$

$\frac{a}{\sqrt{2}} + (-1) = 0$

$a = \sqrt{2} \Rightarrow a^2 = 2$

22. $\overline{x} = \frac{1}{n} \sum_{i=1}^{n} x_i = 5$

and $\frac{1}{n} \sum x_i^2 - \overline{x}^2 = 0$

$\Rightarrow \frac{1}{n} \sum x_i^2 = \overline{x}^2 = 25$

$\Rightarrow 25n = 400$

$\Rightarrow n = 16$

$\Rightarrow a^2 = 2$

23. Method 1

As we know that latusrectum is the least focal chord.

$\therefore$ Length of latusrectum $= 32 = x$ (given)

$\because$ Divisors of 32 are 1, 2, 4, 8, 16, 32

$\therefore$ Number of divisiors $= 6$

Method 2

As we know that, length of focal chord having one extremily $(at^2, 2at)$ is given by $a\left(t + \frac{1}{t}\right)^2$

i.e. $PQ = a\left(t + \frac{1}{t}\right)^2$

$\because \left|t + \frac{1}{t}\right| \geq 2$ [using $AM \geq GM$]

$\Rightarrow \left|t + \frac{1}{t}\right|^2 \geq 4$

$\Rightarrow \left(t + \frac{1}{t}\right)^2 \geq 4$

$\Rightarrow a\left(t + \frac{1}{t}\right)^2 \geq 4a$ [here $a = 8 > 0$]

$\Rightarrow PQ \geq 32$

Hence, $\lambda = 32$

Therefore, number of divisiors of $\lambda = 6$.

24. The different possibilities of answering are as shown below

$A(6)$	$B(5)$	Number of ways
3	4	${}^6C_3 \times {}^5C_4 = 100$
4	3	${}^6C_4 \times {}^5C_3 = 150$
5	2	${}^6C_5 \times {}^5C_2 = 60$
6	1	${}^6C_6 \times {}^5C_1 = 5$
		Sum $= 100 + 150 + 60 + 5 = 315$

25. Applying $R_1 \rightarrow R_1 - R_3$,

$$\Delta = \begin{vmatrix} 0 & 3\cos\theta - \sin\theta & 0 \\ \sin\theta & 1 & 3\cos\theta \\ 1 & \sin\theta & 1 \end{vmatrix}$$

$$= (\sin\theta - 3\cos\theta)^2$$

$$\Rightarrow \Delta = 10\left(\frac{1}{\sqrt{10}} \sin\theta - \frac{3}{\sqrt{10}} \cos\theta\right)^2$$

$$= 10(\sin\theta \cdot \cos\alpha - \cos\theta \sin\alpha)^2$$

Where, $\cos\alpha \frac{1}{\sqrt{10}}$

and $\sin\alpha = \frac{3}{\sqrt{10}}$

$\therefore \Delta = 10 [\sin(\theta - \alpha)]$

$\Rightarrow \Delta \leq 10$

$\therefore (\Delta)_{max} = 10$

26. Solving $2x + 3y = 1$ and $x + 2y = 1$, we get

$A \equiv (-1, 1)$

Orthocentre $\equiv (0, 0)$

$\therefore$ Slope of altitude $AD = -1$ = Slope of AD

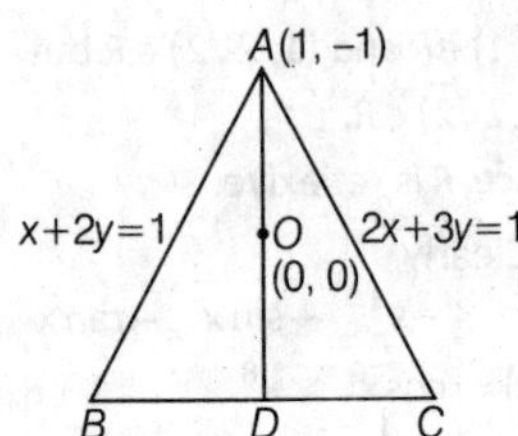

Now, equation of BC is $x - y = K$

On solving $x - y = K$ and $x + 2y = 1$, we get

$B \equiv \left(\frac{1+2K}{3}, \frac{1-K}{3}\right)$

Slope of $OB = \frac{1-K}{1+2K}$,

Slope of $AC = \frac{-2}{3}$

$\therefore \quad \frac{1-K}{1+2K} = \frac{3}{2}$

$\Rightarrow \quad K = \frac{-1}{8}$

Hence, equation of BC is $x - y + \frac{1}{8} = 0$

$\Rightarrow \quad -8x + 8y - 1 = 0$

On comparing, we get

$a = -8, b = 8$

$\therefore \quad \frac{b-a}{4} = \frac{8-(-8)}{4} = 4$

27. Let $x^2 = 4\cos^2\theta + \sin^2\theta$

Then, $(4 - x^2) = 3\sin^2\theta$

and $\quad (x^2 - 1) = 3\cos^2\theta$

$\therefore \quad f(x) = \sqrt{3}\,|\sin\theta| + \sqrt{3}\,|\cos\theta|$

$\Rightarrow f(x)_{min} = \sqrt{3}$

and $f(x)_{max} = \sqrt{3}\left(\frac{1}{\sqrt{2}} + \frac{1}{\sqrt{2}}\right) = \sqrt{6}$

Hence, range of $f(x)$ is $[\sqrt{3}, \sqrt{6}]$.

$\therefore$ Maximum value of $(f(x))^2$ is 6.

28. When a ball is dropped from the height of 48 m, the covered distance = 48 m.

The covered distance in first bounce

$= \frac{2}{3} \times 48$ m

The covered distance in second bounce

$= \frac{2}{3} \times \left(\frac{2}{3} \times 48\right)$ m

The covered distance in third bounce

$= \frac{2}{3} \times \left(\frac{2}{3}\right)^2 \times 48$ m

Thus, process is being infinitely.

$\therefore$ Total distance

$= 48 + 2$

$\left[\left(\frac{2}{3}\right)48 + \left(\frac{2}{3}\right)^2 \cdot 48 + \left(\frac{2}{3}\right)^3 48 + \ldots \infty\right]$

$= 48 + 2 \times 48 \times \frac{2}{3}\left[1 + \frac{2}{3} + \left(\frac{2}{3}\right)^2 + \ldots \infty\right]$

$= 48 + 64 \times \frac{1}{1 - \frac{2}{3}}$

$\left(\because S_\infty = \frac{a}{1-r}, \text{for GP}\right)$

$= 48 + 64 \times \frac{1}{\frac{1}{3}} = 48 + 64 \times 3$

$= 48 + 192 = 240$ m

29. The given differential equation is

$\frac{dy}{dx} = \frac{y}{x}\left(\log_e\left(\frac{y}{x}\right) + 1\right) \quad \ldots(i)$

Put $\ y = Vx \Rightarrow \frac{dy}{dx} = V + \frac{dV}{dx} \cdot x$

From Eq. (i),

$V + x\frac{dV}{dx} = V(\ln V + 1)$

$\Rightarrow \quad \frac{dV}{V \cdot \ln V} = \frac{dx}{x}$

On integrating,

$\ln(\ln V) = \ln x + \ln c$

$\Rightarrow \quad \ln\left(\frac{y}{x}\right) = cx$

$\Rightarrow \quad y = x \cdot e^{cx} \quad \ldots(ii)$

When $x = 1, y = 2$

From Eq. (ii), $2 = 1 \cdot e^{c \cdot 1} \Rightarrow e^c = 2$

$\therefore \quad y = x \cdot (e^c)^x = x(2)^x$

$\therefore \quad y(2) = 2 \cdot (2)^2 = 8$

30. Let P_1T_1 and P_2T_2 be two towers, M be the mid-point of P_1P_2.

From the right angled triangles T_1MP_1 and T_2MP_2

$\frac{P_1T_1}{MP_1} = \tan\left(\frac{\pi}{3}\right) = \sqrt{3} \quad \ldots(i)$

and $\quad \frac{P_2T_2}{MP_2} = \tan\left(\frac{\pi}{6}\right) = \frac{1}{\sqrt{3}} \quad \ldots(ii)$

From Eqs. (i) and (ii), we get

$\frac{P_1T_1}{MP_1} \times \frac{MP_2}{P_2T_2} = \frac{\sqrt{3}}{\frac{1}{\sqrt{3}}}$

$= \sqrt{3} \times \sqrt{3} = 3$

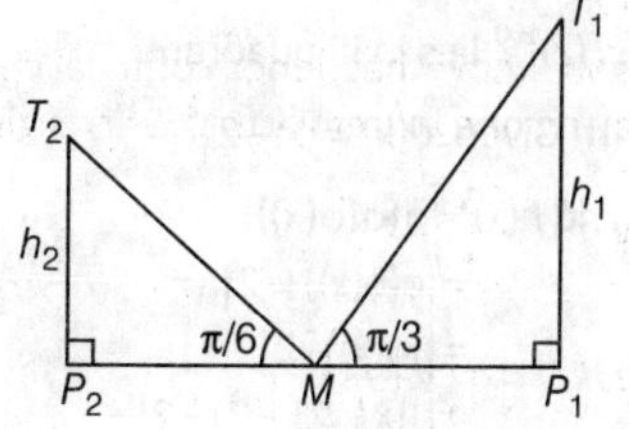

$\Rightarrow \quad \frac{P_1T_1}{P_2T_2} = 3 \quad (\because MP_1 = MP_2)$

$\Rightarrow \quad \frac{h_1}{h_2} = 3$

Knockout 2

1. (c) **Method I**

Given, $n(A) = 2$ and $n(B) = 4$

$\therefore$ Number of elements in set

$(A \times B) = n(A \times B)$

$= n(A) \times n(B)$

$= 2 \times 4 = 8$

$\therefore$ Total number of subsets of

$(A \times B) = 2^8 = 256$

Now, number of subsets having zero elements $= {}^8C_0 = 1$

and number of subsets having 1 elements each $= {}^8C_1 = 8$

and number of subsets having 2 elements each $= {}^8C_2$

$= \frac{8!}{2!\,6!} = \frac{8 \times 7 \times 6!}{2 \times 6!} = 28$

$\therefore$ Number of subsets having atleast 3 elements $= 256 - 1 - 8 - 28$

$= 256 - 37 = 219$

Method II

$\because \ n(A) = 2$ and $n(B) = 4$

$\therefore \ n(A \times B) = 8$

$\therefore$ Required number of subsets i.e. number of subsets having atleast 3 elements

$= {}^8C_3 + {}^8C_4 + {}^8C_5 + {}^8C_6 + {}^8C_7 + {}^8C_8$

$\{({}^8C_0 + {}^8C_1 + {}^8C_2) + {}^8C_3 + {}^8C_4 + \ldots\ldots + {}^8C_8\} - ({}^8C_0 + {}^8C_1 + {}^8C_2)$

$= 2^8 - {}^8C_0 - {}^8C_1 - {}^8C_2$

[$\because$ sum of binomial coefficients $= 2^n$ in the explansion of $(x + a)^n$. Here, $n = 8$]

$= 256 - 1 - 8 - 28$

$= 256 - 37 = 219$

2. (c) For the first player, distribute the cards in ${}^{52}C_{17}$ ways. Now, out of 35 cards left, 17 cards can be put for second player in ${}^{35}C_{17}$ ways.

Similarly, for third player put them in ${}^{18}C_{17}$ ways. One card for the last player can be put in ${}^1C_1$ way. Therefore, the required number of ways for the proper distribution

$= {}^{52}C_{17} \times {}^{35}C_{17} \times {}^{18}C_{17} \times {}^1C_1$

$= \frac{52!}{35!\,17!} \times \frac{35!}{18!\,17!} \times \frac{18!}{17!\,1!} \times 1!$

$= \frac{52!}{(17!)^3}$

3. (b) **Method 1**

Given, $z^2 + pz + q = 0$ ...(i)

$\Rightarrow \quad z = \dfrac{-p \pm \sqrt{p^2 - 4q}}{2 \times 1}$

$= \dfrac{-p \pm \sqrt{(-1)(4q - p^2)}}{2}$

$= \dfrac{-p \pm i\sqrt{4q - p^2}}{2}$

$\Rightarrow \quad z = \left(-\dfrac{1}{2}p\right) \pm i\left(\dfrac{\sqrt{4q - p^2}}{2}\right)$

Let z_1, z_2 be two roots of Eq. (i).

So, $z_1 = \left(-\dfrac{1}{2}p\right) + i\left(\dfrac{\sqrt{4q-p^2}}{2}\right)$

and $z_2 = \left(-\dfrac{1}{2}p\right) - i\left(\dfrac{\sqrt{4q-p^2}}{2}\right)$

Let $z_3 = 0$ [given]

Now, $|z_1| = \sqrt{\dfrac{p^2}{4} + \dfrac{4q - p^2}{4}}$

$= \sqrt{\dfrac{p^2 + 4q - p^2}{4}} = \sqrt{q}$

Similarly, $|z_2| = \sqrt{q}$

and $|z_1 - z_2| = \left|0 + 2i\left(\dfrac{\sqrt{4q-p^2}}{2}\right)\right|$

$= \sqrt{0^2 + 4\left(\dfrac{4q-p^2}{4}\right)}$

$= \sqrt{4q - p^2}$

Since, z_1, z_2 and z_3 form an equilateral triangle.

So, $|z_1| = |z_2| = |z_1 - z_2|$

$\Rightarrow \sqrt{q} = \sqrt{4q - p^2}$

$\Rightarrow \quad q = 4q - p^2$

$\Rightarrow p^2 = 3q$

Method 2

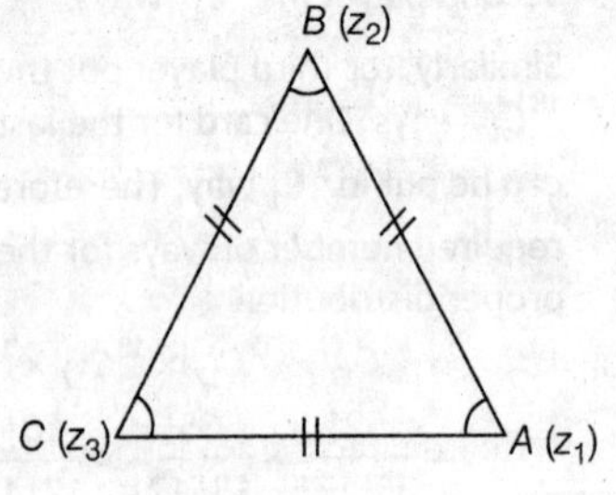

Given, $z^2 + pz + q = 0$ ...(i)

Let z_1, z_2 be the roots of Eq. (i), then sum of roots $= z_1 + z_2 = p$ ...(ii)

and product of roots $= z_1 z_2 = q$ ...(iii)

If z_1, z_2, z_3 are the vertices of an equilateral triangle.

Then, $z_1^2 + z_2^2 + z_3^2$

$= z_1 z_2 + z_2 z_3 + z_3 z_1$ [result]

If z_3 is origin then $z_1^2 + z_2^2 = z_1 z_2$

$\Rightarrow z_1^2 + z_2^2 + 2z_1 z_2 = z_1 z_2 + 2z_1 z_2$

[on adding $2z_1 z_2$ both sides]

$\Rightarrow (z_1 + z_2)^2 = 3z_1 z_2 \Rightarrow p^2 = 3q$

[from Eq. (ii) and Eq. (iii)]

4. (c) Given,

$z = \dfrac{1 + i\sqrt{3}}{\sqrt{3} + i} = \dfrac{i(\sqrt{3} - i)}{(\sqrt{3} + i)} \times \dfrac{(\sqrt{3} - i)}{(\sqrt{3} - i)}$

$= \dfrac{i[3 - 1 - 2\sqrt{3}i]}{(\sqrt{3})^2 - (i)^2} = \dfrac{i[2 - 2\sqrt{3}i]}{3 + 1}$

$= \dfrac{2[i - \sqrt{3}i^2]}{4} = \dfrac{i + \sqrt{3}}{2} = \dfrac{\sqrt{3}}{2} + \dfrac{i}{2}$

$\Rightarrow z = \cos\dfrac{\pi}{6} + i\sin\dfrac{\pi}{6}$

$\therefore \bar{z} = \cos\dfrac{\pi}{6} - i\sin\dfrac{\pi}{6} = \cos\left(-\dfrac{\pi}{6}\right) + i\sin\left(-\dfrac{\pi}{6}\right)$

$\Rightarrow$

$(\bar{z})^{100} = \left[\cos\left(-\dfrac{\pi}{6}\right) + i\sin\left(-\dfrac{\pi}{6}\right)\right]^{100}$

$= \cos\left\{100\left(-\dfrac{\pi}{6}\right)\right\} + i\sin\left\{100\left(-\dfrac{\pi}{6}\right)\right\}$

[using De-moivre's Theorem]

$= \cos\left(-\dfrac{50\pi}{3}\right) + i\sin\left(-\dfrac{50\pi}{3}\right)$

$= \cos\left(-16\pi - \dfrac{2\pi}{3}\right) + i\sin\left(-16\pi - \dfrac{2\pi}{3}\right)$

$= \cos\left(-\dfrac{2\pi}{3}\right) + i\sin\left(-\dfrac{2\pi}{3}\right)$

$\therefore (\bar{z})^{100}$ lies in III quadrant.

5. (d) Given, $\phi(x) = |x - 2|$

and $h(x) = \phi(\phi(\phi(x)))$

$= |\phi(\phi(x)) - 2|$

$= ||\phi(x) - 2| - 2|$

$= |||x - 2| - 2| - 2|$

Now, $h(x) = \dfrac{3}{2}$

$\Rightarrow \quad |||x - 2| - 2| - 2| = \dfrac{3}{2}$

$\Rightarrow \quad ||x - 2| - 2| = 2 \pm \dfrac{3}{2} = \dfrac{7}{2}, \dfrac{1}{2}$

$\Rightarrow \quad |x - 2| = 2 \pm \dfrac{7}{2}, 2 \pm \dfrac{1}{2}$

$= \dfrac{11}{2}, -\dfrac{3}{2}, \dfrac{3}{2}, \dfrac{5}{2}$

But $\quad |x - 2| \geq 0, \forall x \in R.$

$\therefore \quad |x - 2| = \dfrac{11}{2}, \dfrac{3}{2}, \dfrac{5}{2}$

$\Rightarrow \quad x = 2 \pm \dfrac{11}{2}, 2 \pm \dfrac{3}{2}, 2 \pm \dfrac{5}{2}$

$\Rightarrow \quad x = \dfrac{15}{2}, \dfrac{-7}{2}, \dfrac{7}{2}, \dfrac{1}{2}, \dfrac{9}{2}, -\dfrac{1}{2}$

Hence, total number of solutions of $h(x) = \dfrac{3}{2}$ is 6.

6. (c) Given, $A \equiv (1, 0, 3), B \equiv (-1, 3, 4), C \equiv (1, 2, 1), D \equiv (K, 2, 5)$

Let $\quad \mathbf{a} = \mathbf{OA} = \hat{\mathbf{i}} + 3\hat{\mathbf{k}}$

$\mathbf{b} = \mathbf{OB} = -\hat{\mathbf{i}} + 3\hat{\mathbf{j}} + 4\hat{\mathbf{k}}$

$\mathbf{c} = \mathbf{OC} = \hat{\mathbf{i}} + 2\hat{\mathbf{j}} + \hat{\mathbf{k}}$

$\mathbf{d} = \mathbf{OD} = K\hat{\mathbf{i}} + 2\hat{\mathbf{j}} + 5\hat{\mathbf{k}}$

Since, *A,B,C,D* are coplanar.

Then [**d b c**] + [**d c a**] + [**d a b**] = [**a b c**]

$\Rightarrow \begin{vmatrix} K & 2 & 5 \\ -1 & 3 & 4 \\ 1 & 2 & 1 \end{vmatrix} + \begin{vmatrix} K & 2 & 5 \\ 1 & 2 & 1 \\ 1 & 0 & 3 \end{vmatrix}$

$+ \begin{vmatrix} K & 2 & 5 \\ 1 & 0 & 3 \\ -1 & 3 & 4 \end{vmatrix} = \begin{vmatrix} 1 & 0 & 3 \\ -1 & 3 & 4 \\ 1 & 2 & 1 \end{vmatrix}$

$\Rightarrow -5K - 15 + 6K - 14 - 9K + 1 = -20$

$\Rightarrow \quad -8K - 28 = -20$

$\Rightarrow \quad K = -1$

Method (2)

From the given points, we have

$\mathbf{AB} = -2\hat{\mathbf{i}} + 3\hat{\mathbf{j}} + \hat{\mathbf{k}}$

$\mathbf{BC} = 2\hat{\mathbf{i}} - \hat{\mathbf{j}} - 3\hat{\mathbf{k}}$

and $\quad \mathbf{CD} = (K - 1)\hat{\mathbf{i}} + 0\hat{\mathbf{j}} + 4\hat{\mathbf{k}}$

Now, *A,B,C,D* are coplanar, then

[**AB BC CD**] = 0

$\Rightarrow \quad \begin{vmatrix} -2 & 3 & 1 \\ 2 & -1 & -3 \\ K-1 & 0 & 4 \end{vmatrix} = 0$

$\Rightarrow -2(-4 + 0) - 2(12 - 0) + (K - 1)(-9 + 1) = 0$

$\Rightarrow 8 - 24 - 8K + 8 = 0$

$\Rightarrow \quad 8K = -8$

$\Rightarrow \quad K = -1$

7. (a) Given, $\sin 3x < \sin x$

$\Rightarrow \quad \sin 3x - \sin x < 0$

$\Rightarrow \quad 2\sin x \cdot \cos 2x < 0$ ...(i)

where $x \neq 0, \pi, 2\pi$

Case I Let $x \in (0, \pi) \Rightarrow 2x \in (0, 2\pi)$

In this case, $\sin x > 0$ and $\cos 2x < 0$ [from Eq. (i)]

[$\because \sin x > 0$ for $x \in (0, \pi)$]

$\Rightarrow \quad \frac{\pi}{2} < 2x < \frac{3\pi}{2}$

$\left[\begin{array}{l}\text{when } \theta \in (0, 2\pi) \text{ then} \\ \because \cos\theta < 0 \\ \therefore \theta \in \left(\frac{\pi}{2}, \frac{3\pi}{2}\right)\end{array}\right]$

$\Rightarrow \quad \frac{\pi}{4} < x < \frac{3\pi}{4}$

Case II Let $x \in (\pi, 2\pi) \Rightarrow 2x \in (2\pi, 4\pi)$

In this case,

$\sin x < 0$

then $\cos 2x > 0$ [from Eq. (i)]

$\Rightarrow \quad 2\pi < 2x < \frac{5\pi}{2}$

$\left[\begin{array}{l}\text{when } \theta \in (2\pi, 4\pi) \text{ then} \\ \because \cos\theta > 0 \\ \therefore \theta \in \left(2\pi, \frac{5\pi}{2}\right) \cup \left(\frac{2\pi}{2}, 4\pi\right)\end{array}\right]$

or $\frac{7\pi}{2} < 2x < 4\pi$

$\Rightarrow \quad \pi < x < \frac{5\pi}{4}$

or $\frac{7\pi}{4} < x < 2\pi$

$\therefore$ Solution set

$\left(\frac{\pi}{4}, \frac{3\pi}{4}\right) \cup \left(\pi, \frac{5\pi}{4}\right) \cup \left(\frac{7\pi}{4}, 2\pi\right)$

Hence, $b - a + d - c + q - p = \pi$.

8. (b) The function $\ln|x-4|$ i.e. $\log|x-4|$ is not defined at $|x-4| = 0 \Rightarrow x = 4$

So, $x = 4$ is a point of discontinuity.

Also, for $f(x)$ to be defined

$\log|x-4| \neq 0 \Rightarrow |x-4| \neq 1 \Rightarrow x - 4 \neq \pm 1$

$\Rightarrow x \neq \pm 1 + 4 \Rightarrow x \neq 3, 5$

i.e. at $x = 3$ and $x = 5$, $f(x)$ is not defined.

So, $f(x)$ is also discontinuous at $x = 3, 5$ also,

Hence, $x = 3, 4, 5$ are three points of discontinuity.

9. (c) $P(A \cup B) = P(A) + P(B) - P(A \cap B)$

$\Rightarrow P(A \cap B) = P(A) + P(B) - P(A \cap B)$

[$\because P(A \cap B) = P(A \cup B)$]

$\Rightarrow \quad 2P(A \cap B) = P(A) + P(B)$

$\Rightarrow 2 \cdot P(A) \cdot \frac{P(A \cap B)}{P(A)} = P(A) + P(B)$

$\Rightarrow \quad 2P(A) \cdot P(B|A) = P(A) + P(B)$

10. (c) $\because$ General term in $(x + y + z)^{17}$ is

$$\frac{17!}{p!q!r!} x^p y^q z^r$$

where $p + q + r = 17$

if $p = 4, q = 10, r = 3$

So, coefficient of $x^4 y^{10} z^3$ is

$$\frac{17!}{4!10!3!}$$

11. (a) As the two ellipse intersect in four distinct points, $a > 1$.

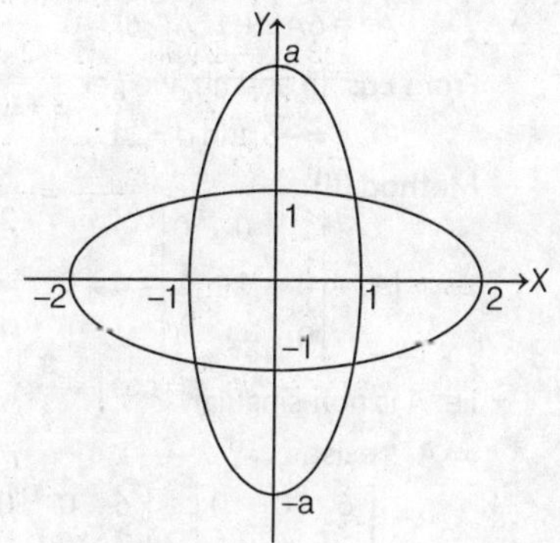

Thus, $b^2 - 5b + 7 > 1$

$\Rightarrow \quad (b-2)(b-3) > 0$

$\Rightarrow \quad b < 2$ or $b > 3$

Hence $b \notin (2, 3)$.

12. (c)

p	q	$\sim p \vee q$	$\sim p \wedge \sim q$	$\sim(p \vee q) \wedge (\sim p \wedge \sim q)$
T	T	T	F	F
T	F	F	F	F
F	T	T	F	F
F	F	T	T	T

Thus, the resulting statement is neither tautology nor contradiction.

13. (d) The best approach to solve this problem is graphical approach.

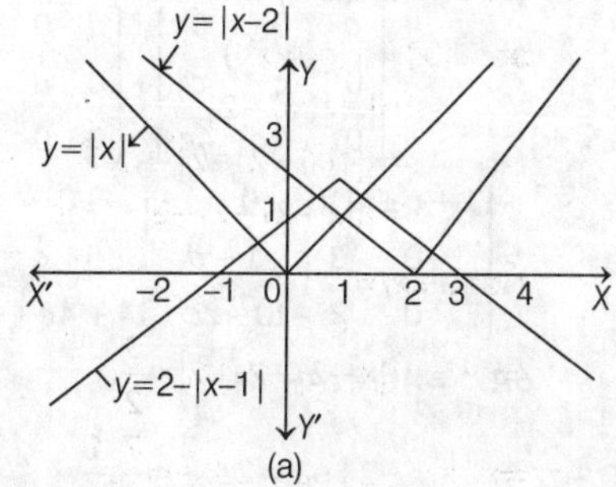

(a)

Fig. (a) graph of $y = |x|, |x-2|$ and $2 - |x-1|$

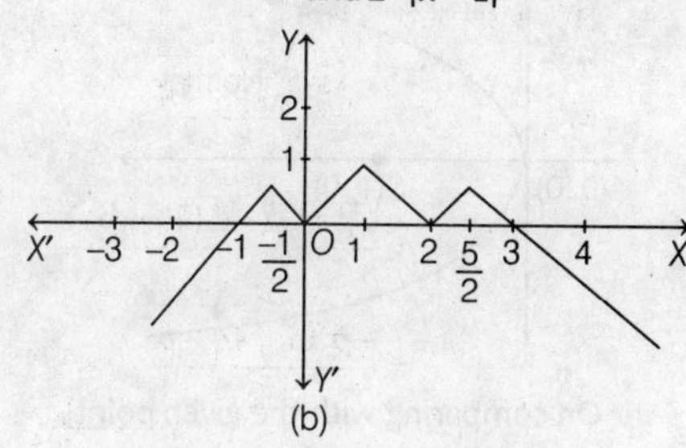

(b)

Fig. (b) graph of $y = f(x) = \min\{|x|, |x-2|, 2-|x-1|\}$

It is clear from figure (b) that $f(x)$ is continuous $\forall x \in R$ but non-differentiable at $x = -\frac{1}{2}, 0, 1, 2, \frac{5}{2}$.

$\therefore$ Sum of non-differentiable points

$$= -\frac{1}{2} + 0 + 1 + 2 + \frac{5}{2}$$

$$= \frac{-1 + 6 + 5}{2} = \frac{10}{2} = 5$$

14. (b) Mean of 501, 503, ..., 549

$$= \frac{501 + 503 + \ldots + 549}{25} = 525$$

Mean of 502, 504, ..., 550

$$= \frac{502 + 504 + \ldots + 550}{25} = 526$$

Variance (V_A)

$$= \frac{(501-525)^2 + (503-525)^2 + \ldots + (549-525)^2}{25}$$

$\Rightarrow$

$$V_A = \frac{(24)^2 + (22)^2 + \ldots + 0 + \ldots + (24)^2}{25} \quad \ldots(i)$$

Variance (V_B)

$$= \frac{(502-526)^2 + (504-526)^2 + \ldots + (550-526)^2}{25}$$

$\Rightarrow$

$$V_B = \frac{(24)^2 + (22)^2 + \ldots + 0 + \ldots + (24)^2}{25} \quad \ldots(ii)$$

From Eqs. (i) and (ii),

$$\frac{V_A}{V_B} = 1$$

15. (b) Let $P = (9, 6)$

According to parametric point

$P = (at^2, 2at)$

$\because \quad y^2 = 4x \Rightarrow a = 1$

$\therefore \quad P = (t^2, 2t)$

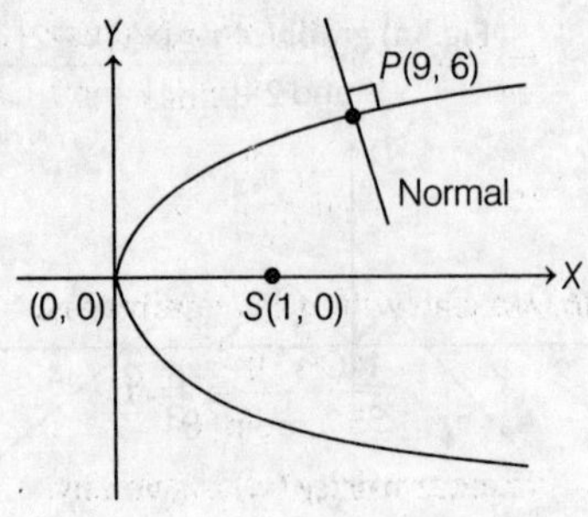

On comparing with the given point,

$$2t = 6 \Rightarrow t = 3$$

We know that slope of normal $= -t$

$$= -3$$

$\therefore$ Equation of L at $(9, 6)$ is

$$y - 6 = -3(x - 9)$$

$\Rightarrow \quad 3x + y - 33 = 0$

16. (c)

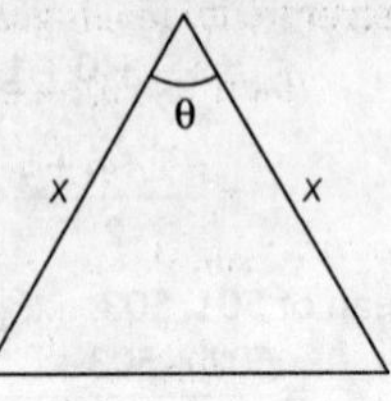

$$A = \frac{1}{2}x^2 \sin\theta$$

$$\Rightarrow \quad 2A = x^2 \sin\theta$$

$$\Rightarrow 2 \cdot \frac{dA}{dt} = x^2 \cos\theta \frac{d\theta}{dt} + 2x \cdot \frac{dx}{dt} \sin\theta$$

$$\Rightarrow 2 \cdot \frac{dA}{dt} = (144)\left(\frac{1}{\sqrt{2}}\right)\frac{\pi}{180} + \frac{1}{\sqrt{2}} \times 2 \times 12 \times \frac{1}{12}$$

$$= \frac{12\pi}{15\sqrt{2}} + \frac{2}{\sqrt{2}}$$

$$\therefore \quad \frac{dA}{dt} = \frac{2\pi}{5\sqrt{2}} + \frac{1}{\sqrt{2}} = \frac{\sqrt{2}\pi}{5} + \frac{\sqrt{2}}{2}$$

$$\Rightarrow \quad \frac{dA}{dt} = \sqrt{2}\left(\frac{\pi}{5} + \frac{1}{2}\right) = 2^{\frac{1}{2}}\left(\frac{1}{2} + \frac{\pi}{5}\right)$$

17. (d) $\frac{dV}{dt} + \frac{K}{m}V = -g$

$$\Rightarrow \quad \frac{dV}{dt} = -\frac{K}{m}\left(V + \frac{mg}{K}\right)$$

$$\Rightarrow \quad \frac{dV}{V + mg/K} = -\frac{K}{m}dt$$

$$\Rightarrow \quad \ln\left(V + \frac{mg}{K}\right) = -\frac{K}{m}t + \ln c$$

$$\Rightarrow \quad V + \frac{mg}{K} = c \cdot e^{-Kt/m}$$

$$V = c \cdot e^{-Kt/m} - \frac{mg}{K}$$

18. (a) **Method (I)**

$$6A^{-1} = A^2 + cA + dI$$

$$\Rightarrow \quad 6I = A^3 + cA^2 + dA$$

$$\Rightarrow \quad A^3 + cA^2 + dA - 6I = 0 \quad \text{...(i)}$$

$$\text{Now, } |A - \lambda I| = \begin{vmatrix} 1-\lambda & 0 & 0 \\ 0 & 1-\lambda & 1 \\ 0 & -2 & 4-\lambda \end{vmatrix}$$

$$= (1-\lambda)(\lambda^2 - 5\lambda + 4 + 2)$$

$$= -\lambda^3 + 6\lambda^2 - 11\lambda + 6$$

Putting $\quad |A - \lambda I| = 0$

$\Rightarrow -\lambda^3 + 6\lambda^2 - 11\lambda + 6 = 0$

$\Rightarrow \quad \lambda^3 - 6\lambda^2 + 11\lambda - 6 = 0$

Cayley Hamilton theorem gives

$$A^3 - 6A^2 + 11A - 6I = 0 \quad \text{...(ii)}$$

From Eqs. (i) and (ii), we get

$$c = -6 \text{ and } d = 11$$

Method (II)

$$|A| = \begin{vmatrix} 1 & 0 & 0 \\ 0 & 1 & 1 \\ 0 & -2 & 4 \end{vmatrix} = 6 \neq 0 \quad \text{...(i)}$$

i.e. A is non-singular.

$\Rightarrow A^{-1}$ exist.

$$\text{adj}A = \begin{bmatrix} 6 & 0 & 0 \\ 0 & 4 & 2 \\ 0 & -1 & 1 \end{bmatrix}' = \begin{bmatrix} 6 & 0 & 0 \\ 0 & 4 & -1 \\ 0 & 2 & 1 \end{bmatrix} \quad \text{...(ii)}$$

From Eqs. (i) and (ii), we get

$$A^{-1} = \frac{\text{adj}A}{|A|} = \frac{1}{6}\begin{bmatrix} 6 & 0 & 0 \\ 0 & 4 & -1 \\ 0 & 2 & 1 \end{bmatrix}$$

$$A^2 = \begin{bmatrix} 1 & 0 & 0 \\ 0 & 1 & 1 \\ 0 & -2 & 4 \end{bmatrix}\begin{bmatrix} 1 & 0 & 0 \\ 0 & 1 & 1 \\ 0 & -2 & 4 \end{bmatrix}$$

$$= \begin{bmatrix} 1 & 0 & 0 \\ 0 & -1 & 5 \\ 0 & -10 & 14 \end{bmatrix}$$

$$\text{Now, } A^2 + cA + dI = \begin{bmatrix} 1 & 0 & 0 \\ 0 & -1 & 5 \\ 0 & -10 & 14 \end{bmatrix} + \begin{bmatrix} c & 0 & 0 \\ 0 & c & c \\ 0 & -2c & 4c \end{bmatrix} + \begin{bmatrix} d & 0 & 0 \\ 0 & d & 0 \\ 0 & 0 & d \end{bmatrix}$$

$$= \begin{bmatrix} 1+c+d & 0 & 0 \\ 0 & c-1+d & 5+c \\ 0 & -10-2c & 14+4c+d \end{bmatrix}$$

$$6A^{-1} = A^2 + cA + dI$$

$$\Rightarrow \begin{bmatrix} 6 & 0 & 0 \\ 0 & 4 & -1 \\ 0 & 2 & 1 \end{bmatrix} = \begin{bmatrix} 1+c+d & 0 & 0 \\ 0 & c-1+d & 5+c \\ 0 & -10-2c & 14+4c+d \end{bmatrix}$$

$$\Rightarrow \quad 1 + c + d = 6, \; c - 1 + d = 4$$

$$5 + c = -1, \; -10 - 2c = 2$$

$$14 + 4c + d = 1$$

$$\Rightarrow \quad c = -6 \text{ and } d = 11$$

19. (b) In ΔO_1AB, we have

$$\tan 45° = \frac{40}{x} \Rightarrow x = 40 \text{ m}$$

In ΔAO_2B, we have,

$$\cot 30° = \frac{y}{40}$$

$$\Rightarrow \quad y = 40\cot 30° = 40\sqrt{3}$$

$\therefore$ Distance between the men $= x + y$

$$= 40 + 40\sqrt{3} = 109.28 \text{ m}$$

20. (d) We have, $\frac{a + 1 + a^2 + 1}{2} = 11,$

$$\frac{a - 1 + a^2 - 1}{2} = 9$$

$$\Rightarrow \quad a + a^2 - 20 = 0$$

$$\Rightarrow \quad a = -5 \text{ or } 4$$

and $\quad \frac{a^2 + 1 + a^3 + 1}{2} = 41$

$$\frac{a^2 - 1 + a^3 - 1}{2} = 39$$

$$\Rightarrow \quad a^2 + a^3 = 80,$$

which holds for $a = 4$.

So, the given points are A (5, 3), B(17, 15), C(65, 63) and coordinates of F are $\left(\frac{65+5}{2}, \frac{63+3}{2}\right) = (35, 33)$ and

$$(BF)^2 = (35 - 17)^2 + (33 - 15)^2$$

$$= (18)^2 + (18)^2 = 648 = 8 \times 9^2$$

$\therefore \quad K = 9$

21. Given, $2x + 3|y| + 5[z] = 0 \quad \text{...(i)}$

$$x + |y| - 2[z] = 4 \quad \text{...(ii)}$$

$$x + |y| + [z] = 1 \quad \text{...(iii)}$$

From Eqs. (ii) and (iii), we get

$$-3[z] = 3 \Rightarrow [z] = -1$$

Putting $[z]=-1]$ in Eqs. (i) and (ii), we get

$$2x+3|y|=5 \text{ and } x+|y|=2$$

On solving, we get

$$x=1, |y|=1$$

Since, $[z]=-1 \Rightarrow -1\le z<0$

$\Rightarrow \quad 0<z^2\le 1$, i.e. $0<\gamma^2\le 1$

$\Rightarrow 0+1+1+<1+1+\gamma^2\le 1+1+1$

$\Rightarrow \quad 2<\alpha^2+\beta^2+\gamma^2\le 3$

$[\because x=\alpha, y=\beta, z=\gamma]$

$\therefore$ Maximum value of $\alpha^2+\beta^2+\gamma^2=3$

22. Equation of the given plane can be written as

$$\frac{x}{20}+\frac{y}{15}+\frac{z}{-12}=1$$

which meets the coordinate axes in points

$A(20, 0, 0)$, $B(0, 15, 0)$, $C(0, 0, -12)$ and the coordinates of the origin are $(0, 0, 0)$.

$\therefore$ The volume of the tetrahedron $OABC$ is

$$\frac{1}{6}\left|\begin{vmatrix} 0 & 0 & 0 & 1\\ 20 & 0 & 0 & 1\\ 0 & 15 & 0 & 1\\ 0 & 0 & -12 & 1\end{vmatrix}\right|$$

$$=\left|\frac{1}{6}\times 20\times 15\times(-12)\right|-600$$

23. Area bounded by X-axis, the curve $y=f(x)$ and the ordinates $x=1, x=a$ is

$$\int_1^a f(x)dx=\sqrt{(1+a^2)}-\sqrt{2}$$

[given]

Differentiating both sides w.r.t. a, we get

$$f(a)=\frac{a}{\sqrt{1+a^2}}$$

Hence, $f(x)=\dfrac{x}{\sqrt{1+x^2}}$

So, $\quad f(0)=0$

24. $\Delta=\begin{vmatrix}\alpha & 1 & 1\\ 1 & \alpha & 1\\ 1 & 1 & \alpha\end{vmatrix}$

$$=\alpha(\alpha^2-1)-1(\alpha-1)+1(1-\alpha)$$

$$=\alpha^3-3\alpha+2=(\alpha+2)(\alpha-1)^2$$

$$\Delta_1=\begin{vmatrix}\alpha-1 & 1 & 1\\ \alpha-1 & \alpha & 1\\ \alpha-1 & 1 & \alpha\end{vmatrix}=(\alpha-1)\begin{vmatrix}1 & 1 & 1\\ 1 & \alpha & 1\\ 1 & 1 & \alpha\end{vmatrix}$$

$$=(\alpha-1)[1(\alpha^2-1)-1(\alpha-1)+1(1-\alpha)]$$

$$=(\alpha-1)(\alpha^2-2\alpha+1)=(\alpha-1)^3$$

For $\alpha=-2, \Delta=0$, but $\Delta_1\ne 0$

$\Rightarrow$ The given system of equations has no solution for

$$\alpha=-2=2K \qquad \text{(given)}$$

$\therefore \quad K=-1$

Hence, $K+9=-1+9=8$

25. Let $I=\displaystyle\int\frac{1}{\sin x+\sin 2x}dx$

$$=\int\frac{1}{\sin x(1+2\cos x)}dx$$

$$=\int\frac{1}{\sin^2 x(1+2\cos x)}\times\sin x\,dx$$

$$=\int\frac{1}{(1-\cos x)(1+\cos x)(1+2\cos x)}\times\sin x\,dx$$

Let $\cos x=z\Rightarrow \sin x\,dx=-dz$

$$\therefore \quad I=\int\frac{1}{(z-1)(z+1)(1+2z)}dz$$

Let $\dfrac{1}{(z-1)(z+1)(1+2z)}=\dfrac{A}{z-1}+\dfrac{B}{z+1}+\dfrac{C}{1+2z}$

$\Rightarrow 1=A(z+1)(2z+1)+B(z-1)(2z+1)+C(z^2-1)$

On comparing the coefficient, we get

$$\left.\begin{aligned}2A+2B+C&=0\\ 3A-B&=0\\ A-B-C&=1\end{aligned}\right\}$$

By solving, we get

$$A=\frac{1}{6}, B=\frac{1}{2}, C=-\frac{4}{3}$$

$$\therefore I=\frac{1}{6}\int\frac{1}{z-1}dz+\frac{1}{2}\int\frac{1}{z+1}dz-\frac{4}{3}\int\frac{1}{2z+1}dz$$

$$\Rightarrow I=\frac{1}{6}\ln|z-1|+\frac{1}{2}\ln|z+1|-\frac{2}{3}\ln|2z+1|+C$$

$\Rightarrow$

$$I=\frac{1}{6}\ln|\cos x-1|+\frac{1}{2}\ln|1+\cos x|-\frac{2}{3}\ln|2\cos x+1|+C$$

$$\Rightarrow I=\frac{1}{6}\ln\frac{|1+\cos x|^3|\cos x-1|}{|2\cos x+1|^4}+C$$

$$\Rightarrow f(x)=\frac{1}{6}\ln\frac{|1+\cos x|^3|\cos x-1|}{|2\cos x+1|^4}$$

$$\therefore \quad f\left(\frac{\pi}{2}\right)=0$$

26. We can write the hyperbola as

$$\frac{x^2}{5}-\frac{y^2}{5\sin^2\theta}=1$$

Its eccentricity (e_1) is given by

$$5\sin^2\theta=5(e_1^2-1)$$

$$\Rightarrow \quad e_1^2=1+\sin^2\theta$$

We can write the ellipse

$$x^2\text{cosec}^2\theta+y^2=5$$

as $\quad \dfrac{x^2}{5\sin^2\theta}+\dfrac{y^2}{5}=1$

Its eccentricity (e_2) is given by

$$5\sin^2\theta=5(1-e_2^2)$$

$$\Rightarrow \quad e_2^2=\cos^2\theta$$

Now, $7-7\sin^2\theta=1+\sin^2\theta$

$$\Rightarrow \quad \sin\theta=\frac{\sqrt{3}}{2}$$

$$\Rightarrow \quad \theta=\frac{\pi}{3}$$

$$\Rightarrow \quad \frac{\pi}{\theta}=3$$

27. Let $A=\tan^{-1}\left(\dfrac{x-1}{x-2}\right)\Rightarrow$

$$\tan A=\left(\frac{x-1}{x-2}\right)$$

and $B=\tan^{-1}\left(\dfrac{x+1}{x+2}\right)$

$$\Rightarrow \tan B=\left(\frac{x+1}{x+2}\right)$$

Given, $A+B=-\dfrac{3\pi}{4}$

$$\tan(A+B)=\tan\left(-\frac{3\pi}{4}\right)$$

$$\frac{\tan A+\tan B}{1-\tan A\tan B}=1$$

$$\frac{\left(\frac{x-1}{x-2}\right)+\left(\frac{x+1}{x+2}\right)}{1-\left(\frac{x-1}{x-2}\right)\left(\frac{x+1}{x+2}\right)}=1$$

On solving this, $x=\dfrac{1}{\sqrt{2}}$ or $x=-\dfrac{1}{\sqrt{2}}$

Given that

$$\tan^{-1}\left(\frac{x-1}{x-2}\right)+\tan^{-1}\left(\frac{x+1}{x+2}\right)=-\frac{3\pi}{4} \quad \text{... (i)}$$

On substituting $x=\frac{1}{\sqrt{2}}$ in Eq. (i)

$\tan^{-1}$ (+ ve values) + $\tan^{-1}$

(+ ve values) $=-\frac{3\pi}{4}$ which is not possible.

Similarly, $x=-\frac{1}{\sqrt{2}}$ will also not satisfy Eq. (i).

$\therefore$ Number of solution $=0$

28. Given $f(x)=x(x^2+mx+n)+2$

Then, $f'(x)=3x^2+2mx+n$

According to question,

$$f(1)=f(2)$$

$$\Rightarrow 1\cdot(1+m+n)+2 = 2\cdot(4+2m+n)+2$$

$$\Rightarrow \quad 3m+n+7=0 \quad \text{...(i)}$$

and $f'(x)$ at $x=\frac{4}{3}$ is equal to zero.

i.e. $3\times\frac{16}{9}+2m\times\frac{4}{3}+n=0$

$$\Rightarrow \quad 8m+3n+16=0 \quad \text{....(ii)}$$

On solving Eqs. (i) and (ii), we get

$$m=-5$$

and $\quad n=8$

$\therefore \quad m+n=-5+8=3$

29. Centre of the circle lies on the line through $(2,-2)$ and perpendicular to $x+y=0$, that is, on $(x-2)-(y+2)=0$

or $\quad x-y=4$

As centre lies on the on the X-axis, the centre of circle is $(4, 0)$ and its radius is

$\sqrt{(4-2)^2+(-2-0)^2}=2\sqrt{2}$

For maximum possible value of h, (h,k) will lie on Q.

$\therefore Q=(4+2\sqrt{2}, 0)$,

where $2\sqrt{2}$ is radius.

$\therefore h\le 4+2\sqrt{2}$

Thus, $h-2\sqrt{2}\le 4$.

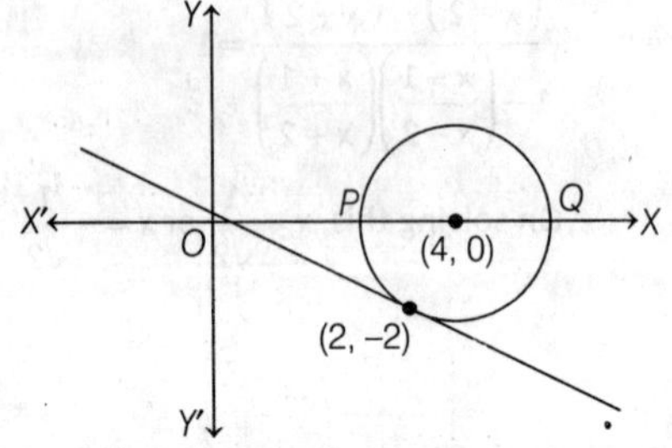

30. Since we know that

$$\log_{a^b} x=\frac{1}{b}\log_a x$$

Here, $\log_{5^1} x+\log_{5^{1/2}} x+\log_{5^{1/3}} x +\ldots+\log_{5^{1/10}} x=110$

$\log_5 x+2\log_5 x+3\log_5 x +\ldots+10\log_5 x=110$

$\log_5 x.(1+2+3+\ldots.+10)=110 \quad \text{...(i)}$

$\because \quad \Sigma n=\frac{n(n+1)}{2}$

$$\sum_{n=1}^{10} n=\frac{10(11)}{2}=55$$

From Eq. (i)

$$55\log_5 x=110$$

$\Rightarrow \quad \log_5 x=2$

$\Rightarrow \quad x=5^2$

$\Rightarrow \quad x=25$

Knockout 3

1. (c) $f(h(x))=\ln\frac{1+h(x)}{1-h(x)}$

$$=\ln\frac{1+\dfrac{x^3+3x}{3x^2+1}}{1-\dfrac{x^3+3x}{3x^2+1}}$$

$$=\ln\frac{(1+x)^3}{(1-x)^3}=\ln\left(\frac{1+x}{1-x}\right)^3$$

$$=3\ln\left(\frac{1+x}{1-x}\right)=3f(x)$$

2. (a) Let equation of circle passing through (p, q) be

$$x^2+y^2+2gx+2fy+c=0 \quad \text{... (i)}$$

$$\Rightarrow p^2+q^2+2pg+2qf+c=0 \quad \text{... (ii)}$$

Since Eq. (i) cuts $x^2+y^2=r^2$

Orthogonally,

$$(2g)\cdot 0+(2f)\cdot 0=c-r^2$$

$\Rightarrow \quad c=r^2$

On putting in Eq. (ii),

$$2pg+2qf+(p^2+q^2+r^2)=0$$

Locus of centre $(-g,-f)$ is

$$2px+2qy-(p^2+q^2+r^2)=0$$

3. (a) Given, $(x^2+x+1)^x<1$

$$\Rightarrow \quad (x^2+x+1)^x<(x^2+x+1)^0 \quad \text{...(i)}$$

Since, $x^2+x+1>0$, $\forall x\in R$ because $a>0$ and $D<0$.

But we do not know whether x^2+x+1 is greater than 1 or smaller than 1.

Therefore, the following two cases arises.

Case I When $x^2+x+1>1$

i.e. $x^2+x>0$ i.e. $x<-1$ or $x>1$ ...(A)

Form Eq. (i), $x<0$ ...(B)

Hence, $A\cap B\Rightarrow x<-1$ ... (S_1)

Case II When $0<x^2+x+1+<1$

$$\Rightarrow \begin{cases}x^2+x+1>0\\ x^2+x+1<1\end{cases} \Rightarrow \begin{cases}x\in R\\ -1<x<0\end{cases}$$

$\Rightarrow \quad -1<x<0$ ...(C)

From Eq. (i), $x>0$ ....(D)

Hence, $C\cap D\Rightarrow x\in\phi$ ...(S_2)

Therefore, final answer is $S_1\cup S_2$

i.e. $x<-1 \Rightarrow x\in(-\infty,-1)$

4. (b) $|z-i|=|z+1|$

$\Rightarrow z$ lies on the angle bisector of $A(-1, 0)$ and $B(0, 1)$.

i.e. z lies on $x+y=0$

It intersects the circle $|z|=1$ in two points, as shown in figure.

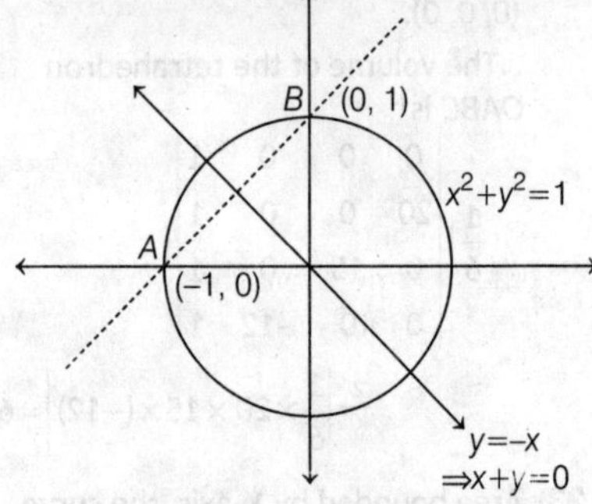

5. (d) Let T_r be the rth term of the given series. Then,

$$T_r=\frac{r}{1+r^2+r^4}, r=1, 2, 3, \ldots, n$$

$$=\frac{r}{(r^2+r+1)(r^2-r+1)}$$

$$=\frac{1}{2}\left[\frac{1}{r^2-r+1}-\frac{1}{r^2+r+1}\right]$$

$\therefore$Sum of the series is

$$\sum_{r=1}^{n} T_r=\frac{1}{2}\left[\sum_{r=1}^{n}\left(\frac{1}{r^2-r+1}-\frac{1}{r^2+r+1}\right)\right]$$

$$=\frac{1}{2}\left[\left(1-\frac{1}{3}\right)+\left(\frac{1}{3}-\frac{1}{7}\right)+\left(\frac{1}{7}-\frac{1}{13}\right) +\ldots+\left(\frac{1}{n^2-n+1}+\frac{1}{n^2+n+1}\right)\right]$$

$$=\frac{1}{2}\left[1-\frac{1}{n^2+n+1}\right]$$

$$=\frac{n^2+n}{2(n^2+n+1)}$$

6. (a) Dividing N^r and D^r by x^2, then the given integral can be written as

$$\int \frac{\left(1-\frac{1}{x^2}\right)dx}{\left[\left(x+\frac{1}{x}\right)^2+1\right]\tan^{-1}\left(x+\frac{1}{x}\right)}$$

$$=\int \frac{dt}{(t^2+1)\tan^{-1}t}$$

where $t = x+\frac{1}{x}$

Let $u=\tan^{-1}t \Rightarrow du=\frac{1}{1+t^2}dt$

So, $\int \frac{dt}{(t^2+1)\tan^{-1}t}=\int \frac{du}{u}=\ln|u|+C$

$$=\ln\left|\tan^{-1}\left(\frac{x^2+1}{x}\right)\right|+C$$

On comparing, $k=1$

7. (a) Children of Mr. A and Ms. B is $10-(x+x+1)=9-2x$

Let N is the number of fights between children of different parents.

= Total number of fights that can take place among children − (the number of fights among the children of the same parents)

$$= {}^{10}C_2-({}^{x}C_2+{}^{x+1}C_2+{}^{9-2x}C_2)$$

$$=\frac{10\times 9}{2}-\left[\frac{x(x-1)}{2}+\frac{(x+1)x}{2}+\frac{(9-2x)(8-2x)}{2}\right]$$

$$=45-\frac{1}{2}(x^2-x+x^2+x+72-34x+4x^2)$$

$$=9+17x-3x^2=-3\left[x^2-\frac{17}{3}x-3\right]$$

$$=-3\left[\left(x-\frac{17}{6}\right)^2-\frac{397}{36}\right]$$

$$=\frac{397}{12}-3\left(x-\frac{17}{6}\right)^2$$

For N to be maximum x must be $\frac{17}{6}$.

As x cannot be in fraction, we take $x=3$.

Thus, maximum value of $N=33$ and is attained when $x=3$.

8. (b) The given curves are $y=\ln(x+e)$

and $x=\ln\left(\frac{1}{y}\right)$

$\Rightarrow \frac{1}{y}=e^x$

$\Rightarrow y=e^{-x}$

From the Figure,

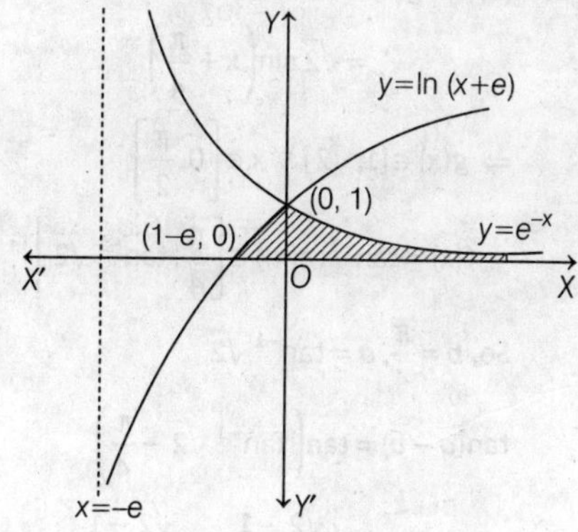

∴ Required area

$$=\int_{1-e}^{0}\log_e(x+e)dx+\int_0^{\infty}e^{-x}dx$$

$$=\int_{1-e}^{0}\log t\,dt+\int_0^{\infty}e^{-x}dx$$

[∵ putting $x+e=t$]

$$=[t\ln t-t]_1^e-[e^{-x}]_0^{\infty}$$

$$=1+1=2 \text{ sq units}$$

9. (c) For non-trivial solution,

$$\begin{vmatrix}\sin\theta & -\cos\theta & \lambda+1\\ \cos\theta & \sin\theta & -\lambda\\ \lambda & \lambda+1 & \cos\theta\end{vmatrix}=0$$

$\Rightarrow$

$$\sin^2\theta\cdot\cos\theta+\lambda^2\cos\theta+(\lambda+1)^2\cos\theta-\sin\theta\lambda(\lambda+1)+\cos^3\theta+\sin\theta\lambda(\lambda+1)=0$$

$\Rightarrow \quad 2\cos\theta(\lambda^2+\lambda+1)=0$

$\because \quad \lambda^2+\lambda+1\neq 0$ because $D<0$

i.e. $\quad \lambda^2+\lambda+1>0, \forall\lambda\in R$

$\therefore \quad 2\cos\theta=0$

$\Rightarrow \quad \cos\theta=0$

$\Rightarrow \quad \theta=(2n+1)\frac{\pi}{2}, \lambda\in R, n\in I$

10. (d) We have, $q\leftrightarrow(\sim p\vee\sim q)$

$\equiv q\leftrightarrow\sim(p\wedge q)$

$\equiv[q\to\sim(p\wedge q)]\wedge[\sim(p\wedge q)\to q]$

$\equiv[\sim q\vee\sim(p\wedge q)]\wedge[(p\wedge q)\vee q]$

$\equiv\sim[q\wedge(p\wedge q)]\wedge q$

$\equiv\sim(p\wedge q)\wedge q$

$\equiv(\sim p\vee\sim q)\wedge q$

$\equiv(\sim p\wedge q)\vee(\sim q\wedge q)\equiv(\sim p\wedge q)$

11. (a)

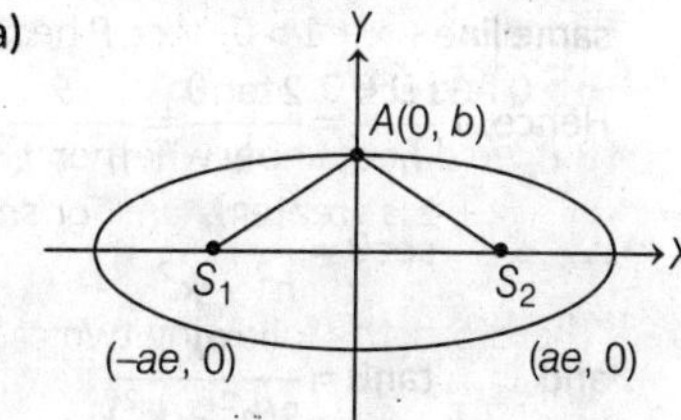

$$\frac{b-0}{0-ae}\times\frac{b-0}{0+ae}=-1$$

$\Rightarrow \quad b^2=a^2e^2$

$\Rightarrow a^2(1-e^2)=a^2e^2$

$\Rightarrow \quad e=\frac{1}{\sqrt{2}}$

12. (a) $|z|^2\omega-z|\omega|^2-z+\omega=0$ ...(i)

$\Rightarrow \omega(|z|^2+1)-z(|\omega|^2+1)=0$

$\Rightarrow \quad \frac{\omega}{z}=\frac{|\omega|^2+1}{|z|^2+1}$

$\Rightarrow \quad \frac{\omega}{z}$ is a real number

$\therefore \quad \frac{\omega}{z}=\frac{\overline{\omega}}{\overline{z}}\Rightarrow \overline{\omega}z=\overline{z}\omega$ ...(ii)

From Eq. (i),

$z\overline{z}\omega-z\omega\overline{\omega}-z+\omega=0$

$(\because z\overline{z}=|z|^2)$

$\Rightarrow z(z\overline{\omega}-1)-\omega(\overline{\omega}z-1)=0$ [using Eq. (ii)]

$\Rightarrow \quad (z-\omega)(z\overline{\omega}-1)=0$

$\Rightarrow \quad z=\omega$ or $z\overline{\omega}=1$

13. (b) As we know that,

$$\lim_{n\to\infty}x^{2n}=\begin{cases}0, & x^2<1\\ 1, & x^2=1\\ \infty, & x^2>1\end{cases}$$

$$=\begin{cases}0, & -1<x<1\\ 1, & x=\pm 1\\ \infty, & x<-1 \text{ or } x>1\end{cases}$$

$$\therefore h(x)=\lim_{n\to\infty}\frac{x^{2n}f(x)+g(x)}{x^{2n}+1}$$

$$=\begin{cases}\frac{0\cdot f(x)+g(x)}{0+1}, & -1<x<1\\ \frac{1\cdot f(x)+g(x)}{1+1}, & x=\pm1\\ \frac{f(x)+\frac{g(x)}{x^{2n}}}{1+\frac{1}{x^{2n}}}, & x<-1 \text{ or } x>1\end{cases}$$

$$h(x)=\begin{cases}g(x), & -1<x<1\\ \frac{f(x)+g(x)}{2}, & x=\pm1\\ f(x), & x<-1 \text{ or } x>1\end{cases}$$

Hence, $h(x)=f(x)$ when $x\in R-[-1,1]$.

14. (a) $\sigma^2=\left[\frac{\Sigma x_i^2}{n}-\left(\frac{\Sigma x_i}{n}\right)^2\right]$

$$=\left[\frac{\Sigma n^2}{n}-\left(\frac{\Sigma n}{n}\right)^2\right]$$

$\Rightarrow \sigma^2 = \frac{n^2-1}{12}$

So, standard deviation $= \sqrt{\frac{n^2-1}{12}}$

Mean $(\bar{x}) = \frac{\Sigma x_i}{n}$

$= \frac{n(n+1)}{2n}$

$= \frac{n+1}{2}$

Hence, coefficient of variance

$= \frac{\sigma}{\bar{x}} \times 100$

$= \sqrt{\frac{(n-1)}{3(n+1)}} \times 100$

15. (c) Let (h, k) be the coordinate of centroid of the given triangle with vertex $c(\alpha, \beta)$.

Then, $\quad h = \frac{\alpha+2+4}{3}$

and $\quad k = \frac{\beta+5-11}{3}$

i.e. $\alpha = 3h-6$ and $\beta = 3k+6$

Since $c(\alpha, \beta)$ lies on the line L.

Hence, $9(3h-6)+7(3k+6)+4=0$

$\Rightarrow \quad 3(9h+7k)-8=0$

$\therefore$ Locus of the centroid (h, k) is

$3(9x+7y)-8=0$

$\Rightarrow 27x-21y-8=0$ which is a line parallel to $9x+7y+4=0$

16. (b) The tree diagram with respective probabilities

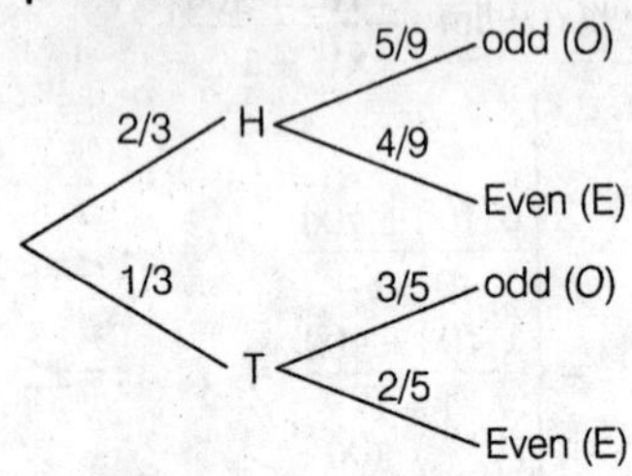

The probability of selecting an even number from the numbers 1 through 9 is $\frac{4}{9}$, since there are four even numbers out of the 9 numbers. Whereas the probability of selecting an even number from the numbers 1 through 5 is $\frac{2}{5}$, since there are two even numbers out of the 5 numbers.

Hence, $p = P(E) = \frac{2}{3} \times \frac{4}{9} + \frac{1}{3} \times \frac{2}{5}$

$= \frac{58}{135}$

17. (b) Let $g(x) = \sin x + \cos x$

$= \sqrt{2} \sin\left(x + \frac{\pi}{4}\right)$

$\Rightarrow g(x) \in [1, \sqrt{2}] \; \forall \; x \in \left[0, \frac{\pi}{2}\right]$

$f(x) = \tan^{-1}(g(x)) \in \left[\frac{\pi}{4}, \tan^{-1}\sqrt{2}\right]$

So, $b = \frac{\pi}{4}, a = \tan^{-1}\sqrt{2}$

$\tan(a-b) = \tan\left(\tan^{-1}\sqrt{2} - \frac{\pi}{4}\right)$

$= \frac{\sqrt{2}-1}{1+\sqrt{2}\times 1} = \frac{\sqrt{2}-1}{\sqrt{2}+1}$

$= \frac{1}{3+2\sqrt{2}} = (3-2\sqrt{2})$

18. (d) Equation of hyperbola and circle are

$$\frac{x^2}{9} - \frac{y^2}{4} = 1 \qquad \text{...(i)}$$

and $\quad x^2 + y^2 = 9 \qquad$ ...(ii)

Any point on hyperbola (i) is taken as $P(3\sec\theta, 2\tan\theta)$.

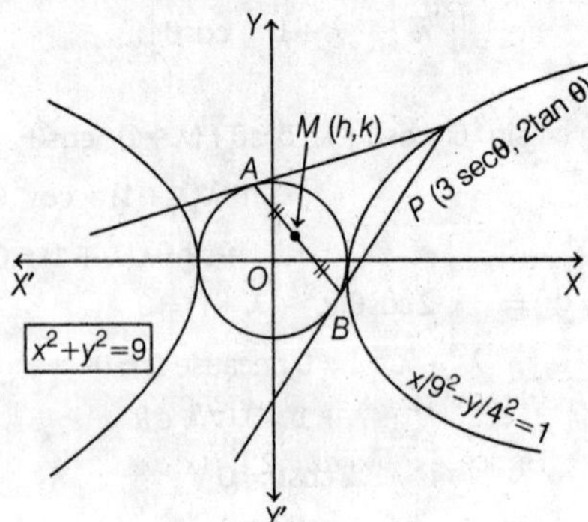

Now, equation of chord of contact of circle w.r.t. point P is $T = 0$

i.e. $(3\sec\theta)x + (2\tan\theta)y - 9 = 0$ ...(iii)

Also, the equation of chord AB of circle with mid-point $M(h, k)$ is

$T = S_1$

i.e. $\quad hx + ky - 9 = h^2 + k^2 - 9$

$\Rightarrow \quad hx + ky = h^2 + k^2$

$\Rightarrow \quad hx + ky - (h^2 + k^2) = 0 \qquad$ ...(iv)

Since, Eqs. (iii) and (iv) represent same line.

Hence, $\frac{3\sec\theta}{h} = \frac{2\tan\theta}{k} = \frac{9}{h^2+k^2}$

$\therefore \quad \sec\theta = \frac{3h}{h^2+k^2}$

and $\quad \tan\theta = \frac{9k}{2(h^2+k^2)}$

As we know that,

$\sec^2\theta - \tan^2\theta = 1$

$\Rightarrow \frac{9h^2}{(h^2+k^2)^2} - \frac{81k^2}{4(h^2+k^2)^2} = 1$

$\Rightarrow 9(4h^2 - 9k^2) = 4(h^2+k^2)^2$

Locus of $M(h, k)$ is $9(4x^2 - 9y^2)$

$= 4(x^2+y^2)^2$

19. (d) For $-1 < x < 0; [x] = -1$

$\therefore f(x) = \min\{x(-1), |-x-2|+2\} = -x$

$(\because -x < 1, |-x-2|+2 \ge 2)$

For $\quad 0 \le x < 1; [x] = 0$

$\therefore f(x) = \min\{0, |0-2|+2\} = 0$

For $\quad 1 \le x < 2; [x] = 1$

$\therefore \quad f(x) = \min\{x, -|x-2|+2\} = x$

$(\because 1 \le x < 2, |x-2|+2 \ge 2)$

For $2 \le x < 3; [x] = 2$

$\therefore f(x) = \min\{2x, |2x-2|+2\}$

$= \min\{2x, 2x-2+2\} = 2x$

Thus, $f(x) = \begin{cases} -x, & -1 < x < 0 \\ 0, & 0 \le x < 1 \\ x, & 1 \le x < 2 \\ 2x, & 2 \le x < 3 \end{cases}$

From above we observe that $f(x)$ is not continuous at $x = 1$ and $x = 2$ and $f(x)$ is not differentiable at $x = 0, 1$ and 2.

20. (d) Given, $\frac{dy}{dx} = (e^y - x)^{-1}$

$\Rightarrow \quad \frac{dx}{dy} = e^y - x$

$\Rightarrow \quad \frac{dx}{dy} + x = e^y$

So, Integrating factor (IF) $= e^{\int dy} = e^y$

$\therefore$ General solution is given by

$x \times (\text{IF}) = \int e^y \times (\text{IF})\, dy$

$x \cdot e^y = \frac{1}{2}e^{2y} + C$

$\Rightarrow \quad x = \frac{1}{2}e^y + Ce^{-y}$

Also, given $y(0) = 0$

$\Rightarrow \quad 0 = \frac{1}{2}e^0 + C \cdot e^{-0}$

$\Rightarrow \quad C = -\frac{1}{2}$

Thus, $\quad x = \frac{1}{2}e^y - \frac{1}{2}e^{-y}$

$\Rightarrow \quad e^{2y} - 2xe^y - 1 = 0$

$\Rightarrow \quad 2e^y = 2x \pm \sqrt{4x^2+4}$

Hence, $y = \ln(x + \sqrt{1+x^2})$

21. Two parabolas are equal, if the lengths of their latusrectum are equal.

Now, the length of latusrectum of $y^2 = ax$ is a. The equation of second parabola can be written as

$$\sqrt{(x-3)^2+(y+2)^2} = \left(\frac{3x-4y-2}{5}\right)$$

So, focus is $(3, -2)$ and the equation of the directrix is $3x - 4y - 2 = 0$

$\therefore$ Length of latusrectum

$= 2 \times$ (Distance between focus and directrix)

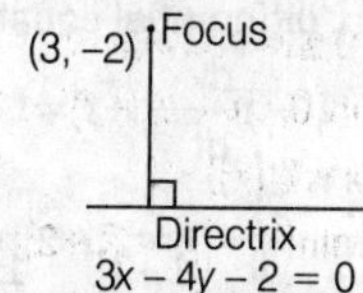

Thus, two parabolas are equal if $a = 6$.

22. $\because$ $2t, t, [t^2 - 14]$ are in GP.

$\therefore$ $t^2 = 2t[t^2 - 14]$

$\therefore$ $\frac{t}{2} = [t^2 - 14]$

$\therefore$ t must be an even integer.

Hence, $t = 4$

Now, required sequence is

1, 12, 24, 40, …

or, 1, 4(1 + 2), 4(1 + 2 + 3), 4(1 + 2 + 3 + 4),…

$\therefore$ 51th term

$= 4(1 + 2 + 3 + 4 + \ldots + 51)$

$= 4 \times \frac{51}{2}(1 + 51)$

$= 4 \times 51 \times 26 = 5304$

23. $(1 - 3x + 2x^2)^6 = \Sigma \frac{6!}{\alpha!\beta!\lambda!} \cdot 1^\alpha \cdot (-3x)^\beta \cdot (2x^2)^\gamma$

where α, β, γ are non- negative integers, such that $\alpha + \beta + \gamma = 6$ and $\beta + 2\gamma = 4$.

Possible values of α, β, γ are shown as

α	β	γ
2	4	0
3	2	1
4	0	2

$\therefore$ Coefficient of x^4 in $(1 - 3x + 2x^2)^6$ is

$\frac{6!}{\alpha!\beta!\gamma!} \cdot 1^\alpha \cdot (-3)^\beta \cdot (2)^\gamma$

$= \frac{6!}{2!4!0!} \cdot 1^2 \cdot (-3)^4 \cdot (2)^0$

$+ \frac{6!}{3!2!1!} \cdot 1^3 (-3)^2 \cdot (2)^1$

$+ \frac{6!}{4!0!2!} \cdot 1^4 \cdot (-3)^0 \cdot 2^2$

$= 1215 + 1080 + 60 = 2355$

24. Given, $\log_{0.04}(x-1) \geq \log_{0.2}(x-1)$ …(i)

$\Rightarrow$ $\log_{(0.2)^2}(x-1) \geq \log_{0.2}(x-1)$

$\Rightarrow$ $\frac{1}{2}\log_{0.2}(x-1) \geq \log_{0.2}(x-1)$

$\Rightarrow$ $\log_{0.2}(x-1) \geq 2\log_{0.2}(x-1)$

$\Rightarrow$ $\log_{0.2}(x-1) \geq \log_{0.2}(x-1)^2$

$\Rightarrow$ $(x-1) \leq (x-1)^2$

$\Rightarrow$ $(x-1)^2 - (x-1) \geq 0$

$\Rightarrow$ $(x-1)(x-1-1) \geq 0$

$\Rightarrow$ $(x-1)(x-2) \geq 0$

$\Rightarrow$ $x \leq 1$ or $x \geq 2$ …(ii)

For Eq. (i) to be defined;

$x > 1$ …(iii)

From Eqs. (ii) and (iii), we get

$x \geq 2$

$\therefore$ Minimum value of $x = 2$

25. $f(x) = \begin{cases} x^2, & x \leq -1 \\ 2 + [x] + [-x], & -1 < x < 1 \\ -x^2, & x \geq 1 \end{cases}$

$= \begin{cases} -x^2, & x \leq -1 \\ 1, & -1 < x < 0 \\ 2, & x = 0 \\ 1, & 0 < x < 1 \\ -x^2, & x \geq 1 \end{cases}$

Clearly, $f(x)$ is even function.

Hence, $\int_{-2}^{2} f(x)\,dx = 2\int_0^2 f(x)\,dx$

$= 2\left(\int_0^1 f(x)dx + \int_1^2 f(x)dx\right)$

$= 2\left([x]_0^1 - \left[\frac{x^3}{3}\right]_1^2\right) = \frac{-8}{3}$

$= -2.6666\ldots..$

$\therefore$ $\left[\int_{-2}^{2} f(x)\,dx\right] = -3$ where $[\cdot]$ denotes greatest integer factor.

Hence, $\left[\int_{-2}^{2} f(x)\,dx\right] + \frac{277}{25}$

$= -3 + 11.08$

$= 8.08$

26. Let $OT = h$ and $OA = b$

From right-angled ΔTAO and ΔFSO,

$\frac{h}{b} = \frac{OT}{OA} = \tan\theta$ …(i)

and $\frac{h+6}{b+2\sqrt{3}} = \tan\theta$ …(ii)

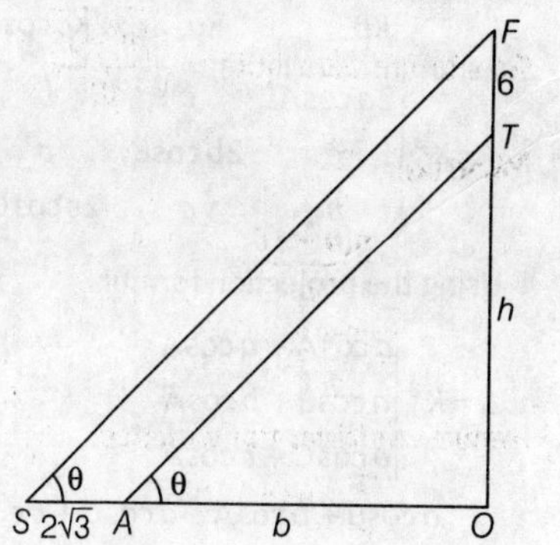

From Eqs. (i) and (ii), we have

$\frac{h}{b} = \frac{h+6}{b+2\sqrt{3}}$

$\Rightarrow$ $bh + 2\sqrt{3}h = bh + 6b$

$\Rightarrow$ $2\sqrt{3}h = 6b$

$\Rightarrow$ $\frac{h}{b} = \sqrt{3}$

$\therefore$ $\sqrt{3}\tan\theta = \sqrt{3} \cdot \frac{h}{b}$

$= \sqrt{3} \cdot \sqrt{3}$

$= 3$

27. Given, $|\mathbf{a}| = |\mathbf{b}| = |2\mathbf{c}| = 3$,

$\mathbf{a} \cdot (\mathbf{b} + \mathbf{c}) = \mathbf{a} \cdot \mathbf{b} + \mathbf{c} \cdot \mathbf{a} = 0$ …(i)

$\mathbf{b} \cdot (\mathbf{c} + \mathbf{a}) = \mathbf{b} \cdot \mathbf{c} + \mathbf{a} \cdot \mathbf{b} = 0$ …(ii)

$\mathbf{c} \cdot (\mathbf{a} + \mathbf{b}) = \mathbf{c} \cdot \mathbf{a} + \mathbf{b} \cdot \mathbf{c} = 0$ …(iii)

So, $2(\mathbf{a} \cdot \mathbf{b} + \mathbf{b} \cdot \mathbf{c} + \mathbf{c} \cdot \mathbf{a}) = 0$

[on adding Eqs. (i), (ii) and (iii)]

Now, $|\mathbf{a} + \mathbf{b} + \mathbf{c}|^2 = a^2 + b^2 + c^2 + 2(\mathbf{a} \cdot \mathbf{b} + \mathbf{b} \cdot \mathbf{c} + \mathbf{c} \cdot \mathbf{a})$

$= (9) + (9) + \left(\frac{9}{4}\right) + 0$

$= \frac{81}{4}$

$\therefore$ $|\mathbf{a} + \mathbf{b} + \mathbf{c}| = \frac{9}{2} = 4.5$

28. Given, determinant can be written as

$$\Delta = \begin{vmatrix} 2\sin A\cos A & \sin C & \sin B \\ \sin C & 2\sin B\cos B & \sin A \\ \sin B & \sin A & 2\sin C\cos C \end{vmatrix}$$

Using sine law of triangle, i.e.

$\sin A = Ka, \sin B = Kb$ and $\sin C = Kc$

$$\Delta = \begin{vmatrix} 2Ka\cos A & Kc & Kb \\ Kc & 2Kb\cos B & Ka \\ Kb & Ka & 2Kc\cos C \end{vmatrix}$$

$$= K^3 \begin{vmatrix} 2a\cos A & c & b \\ c & 2b\cos B & a \\ b & a & 2c\cos C \end{vmatrix}$$

Using the projection formula,

$$\Delta = K^3 \begin{vmatrix} a\cos A + a\cos A & a\cos B + b\cos A & a\cos C + c\cos A \\ a\cos B + b\cos A & b\cos B + b\cos B & b\cos C + c\cos B \\ a\cos C + c\cos A & b\cos C + c\cos B & c\cos C + c\cos C \end{vmatrix}$$

This can be written as

$$\Delta = K^3 \begin{vmatrix} \cos A & a & 0 \\ \cos B & b & 0 \\ \cos C & c & 0 \end{vmatrix} \times \begin{vmatrix} a & \cos A & 0 \\ b & \cos B & 0 \\ c & \cos C & 0 \end{vmatrix}$$

$= 0 \times 0 = 0$

29. Let $L_1: \dfrac{x-1}{1} = \dfrac{y-(-3)}{-\lambda} = \dfrac{z-1}{\lambda} = S$

and $L_2: \dfrac{x}{\left(\dfrac{1}{2}\right)} = \dfrac{y-1}{1} = \dfrac{z-2}{-1} = t$

i.e. $\dfrac{x-0}{1} = \dfrac{y-1}{2} = \dfrac{z-2}{-2} = t$

Lines L_1 and L_2 will be coplanar, if

$$\begin{vmatrix} x_1 - x_2 & y_1 - y_2 & z_1 - z_2 \\ l_1 & m_1 & n_1 \\ l_2 & m_2 & n_2 \end{vmatrix} = 0$$

i.e. $\begin{vmatrix} 1 & -4 & -1 \\ 1 & -\lambda & \lambda \\ 1 & 2 & -2 \end{vmatrix} = 0$

$\Rightarrow \quad -5\lambda - 10 = 0$

$\Rightarrow \quad \lambda = -2$

$\therefore \quad \lambda + 4 = -2 + 4 = 2$

30. The equation of given curve is $y = a^{1-n} \cdot x^n$.

Taking (log) both sides and differentiate w.r.t. x

$$\frac{1}{y} \cdot \frac{dy}{dx} = \frac{n}{x}$$

$\Rightarrow \quad \dfrac{dy}{dx} = \dfrac{ny}{x},$

Length of subnormal

$$= y \cdot \frac{dy}{dx} = \frac{ny^2}{x}$$

$$= na^{2-2n} \cdot x^{2n-1}$$

It's given that subnormal is of constant length.

So,

$$x^{2n-1} = x^0$$

$\Rightarrow \quad n = \dfrac{1}{2}$

$\Rightarrow \quad 6n = 6 \times \dfrac{1}{2} = (3)$

Knockout 4

1. (d) Given, $e^{||x|-2|+b} = 2$ ...(i)

$\Rightarrow \quad ||x|-2| + b = \ln 2$

$\Rightarrow \quad ||x|-2| = \ln 2 - b$

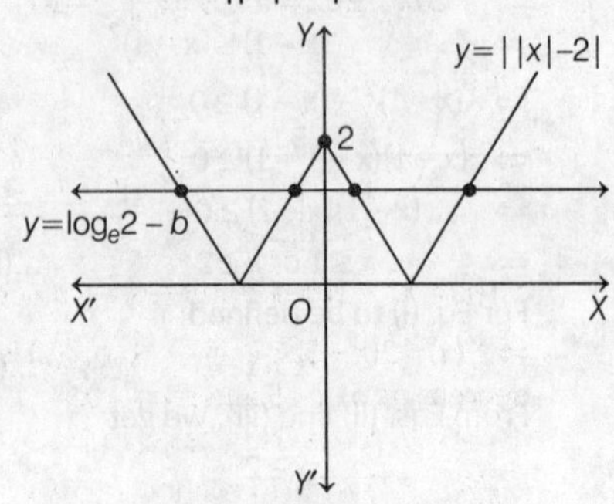

From graph, it is clear that the Eq. (i) has 4 real roots, if $0 < \ln 2 - b < 2$

$\Rightarrow \quad -\ln 2 < -b < 2 - \ln 2$

$\Rightarrow \quad \ln 2 - 2 < b < \ln 2$

2. (b) $\sum_{r=0}^{n} \sum_{s=0}^{n} (r^nC_r \cdot {}^nC_s + s \cdot {}^nC_r {}^nC_s)$

$$= \sum_{r=0}^{n} \sum_{s=0}^{n} r \cdot {}^nC_r \cdot {}^nC_s + \sum_{r=0}^{n} \sum_{s=0}^{n} s \cdot {}^nC_r \cdot {}^nC_s$$

$$= \sum_{r=0}^{n} r \cdot {}^nC_r \left(\sum_{s=0}^{n} {}^nC_s \right) + \sum_{s=0}^{n} s \cdot {}^nC_s \left(\sum_{r=0}^{n} {}^nC_r \right)$$

$$= \sum_{r=0}^{n} r \cdot {}^nC_r \cdot 2^n + \sum_{s=0}^{n} s \cdot {}^nC_s \cdot 2^n$$

$$= 2^n \left[\sum_{r=0}^{n} r({}^nC_r) \right] + 2^n \left[\sum_{s=0}^{n} s({}^nC_s) \right]$$

$$= 2^n \left[\sum_{r=0}^{n} r \cdot \left(\frac{n}{r}\right) {}^{n-1}C_{r-1} \right] + 2^n \left[\sum_{s=0}^{n} s \cdot \left(\frac{n}{s}\right) {}^{n-1}C_{s-1} \right]$$

$$= 2^n \cdot (n \cdot 2^{n-1}) + 2^n (n \cdot 2^{n-1})$$

$$= n(2^{2n-1}) + n(2^{2n-1}) = n \cdot 2^{2n}$$

3. (a) In case of function given in option (a), $f(x)$ is continuous on [0, 1] but not differentiable at $x = \dfrac{1}{2} \in (0,1)$ i.e.

$-1 \neq 0$

i.e. $\quad Lf'\left(\dfrac{1}{2}\right) \neq Rf'\left(\dfrac{1}{2}\right)$

Thus, the Lagrange's mean value theorem (LMVT) is not applicable.

The function given in option (b) is continuous on [0, 1] and differentiable on (0, 1) and hence the Lagrange's mean value theorem (LMVT) is applicable.

The function given in option (c), if $f(x) = x|x| = x \cdot x = x^2$ and in option (d), if $f(x) = |x| = x$ on [0, 1]. As both are polynomial function.

So, Lagrange's mean value theorem (LMVT) is applicable.

4. (c) Given, differential equation

$$(1+t)\frac{dy}{dt} - t \cdot y = 1$$

$\Rightarrow \quad \dfrac{dy}{dt} - \dfrac{t}{1+t} y = \dfrac{1}{1+t}$ ...(i)

This is linear differential equation and its integrating factor (IF)

$$= \exp\left(-\int \frac{t}{1+t} dt\right)$$

$$= e^{-t + \log_e(1+t)}$$

$$= e^{-t} \cdot (1+t)$$

Multiplying both the sides of Eq. (i) by $e^{-t}(1+t)$, we get

$$e^{-t}(1+t) \cdot \frac{dy}{dt} - t \cdot e^{-t} y = e^{-t}$$

$\Rightarrow \quad \dfrac{d}{dt}[e^{-t}(1+t)y] = e^{-t}$

$\Rightarrow \quad d[e^{-t}(1+t)y] = e^{-t} dt$

On integrating both sides, we get

$$e^{-t}(1+t)y = \int e^{-t} dt = -e^{-t} + C$$

$\Rightarrow \quad y = \dfrac{-1}{1+t} + \dfrac{Ce^t}{1+t}$ ...(ii)

Given, when $t = 0$, then $y = -1$

From Eq. (ii),

$$-1 = -1 + C$$

$\Rightarrow \quad C = 0$

Thus, $\quad y = \dfrac{-1}{1+t}$

$\therefore \quad y(1) = \dfrac{-1}{2}$

5. (a) At first, we have to accommodate those 5 animals in cages which cannot enter in 4 small cages, therefore number of ways are ${}^6P_5$.

Now, after accommodating 5 animals we left with 5 cages and 5 animals, therefore number of ways are 5!.

Hence, required number of ways

$$= {}^6P_5 \times 5! = \frac{6!}{1!} \times 5! = 86400$$

6. (b) Let the sides are

$a-d, a, a+d, (d>0)$

$\Rightarrow a^2+(a-d)^2=(a+d)^2$

$\Rightarrow \quad a=4d$

So sides are $3d, 4d, 5d$

$\because \quad \text{Area}=24\text{ cm}^2$

$\Rightarrow \frac{1}{2}\times 3d\times 4d=24 \Rightarrow d=2$

So, smallest side $=(a-d)=4d-d=3d$

$=6$ cm

7. (d) Given, $\omega=\alpha+i\beta$, where $\beta\neq 0$ and $z\neq 1$

and $\frac{\omega-\bar{\omega}z}{1-z}$ is purely real $=k$ (say)

$\Rightarrow \quad \omega-\bar{\omega}z=k-kz$

$\Rightarrow \quad (k-\bar{\omega})z=k-\omega$

$\Rightarrow \quad z=\frac{k-\omega}{k-\bar{\omega}}$

$\Rightarrow z=\frac{k-(\alpha+i\beta)}{k-(\alpha-i\beta)}=\frac{(k-\alpha)-i\beta}{(k-\alpha)+i\beta}$

$\because \quad \beta\neq 0$

$\therefore \quad |z|=1$ and $z\neq 1$

8. (a) Given that,

$|A|=|B|=1$ and $A(\text{adj }A+\text{adj }B)=B$

$\Rightarrow |A|I+A\cdot\text{adj }B=B$

$[\because A(\text{adj}A)=(\text{adj}A)\cdot A=|A|I_n]$

$\Rightarrow (I+A\cdot\text{adj}B)B=B^2 \quad [\because |A|=1]$

$\Rightarrow \quad B+A\cdot|B|\cdot I=B^2$

$\Rightarrow \quad A+B=B^2 \quad [\because |B|=1]$

$\therefore \quad |A+B|=|B^2|=|B|\cdot|B|=1\cdot 1=1$

9. (c) Let the equation of the side BC be $y=0$.

Then, the coordinates of B and C are $(-t,0)$ and $(-u,0)$, respectively, where $(1+t)x-ty+t(1+t)=0$ and $(1+u)x-uy+u(1+u)=0$, are equations of AB and AC respectively.

Now, equation of BE is

$$y=\frac{-u}{1+u}(x+t) \quad \text{...(i)}$$

and equation of CF is

$$y=\frac{-t}{1+t}(x+u) \quad \text{...(ii)}$$

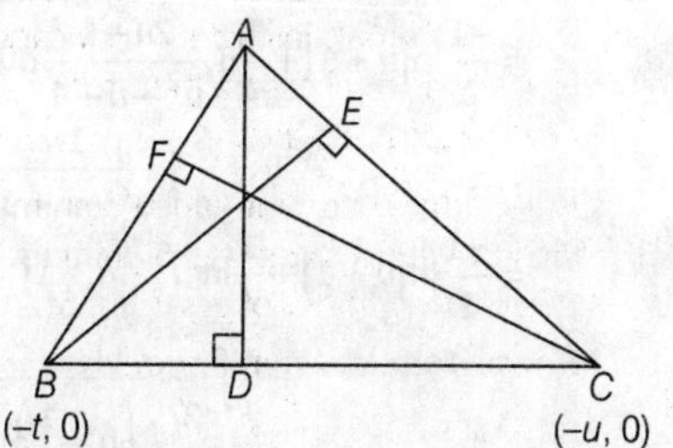

On solving Eqs. (i) and (ii), we get

$$x\left(\frac{u}{1+u}-\frac{t}{1+t}\right)=\frac{tu}{1+t}-\frac{tu}{1+u}$$

$\Rightarrow \quad x=tu$ and $y=-tu$.

So, that orthocentre is the point $(tu,-tu)$, which lies on the line $x+y=0$.

10. (d) Given, $f(5+x)=f(5-x)$

$\Rightarrow (5+x)^2+p(5+x)+q$

$=(5-x)^2+p(5-x)+q$

$\Rightarrow (5+x)^2-(5-x)^2+p(5+x-5+x)$

$=0\ \forall\ x$

$\Rightarrow \quad 20x+2px=0\ \forall x \Rightarrow p=-10$

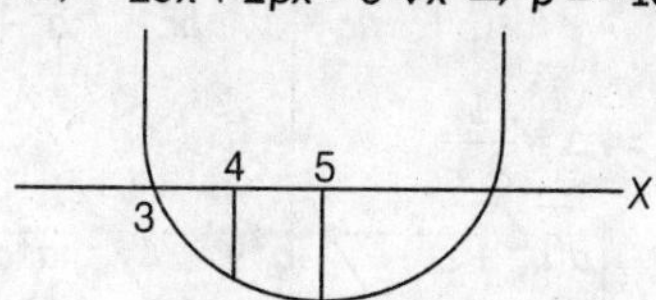

$\therefore f(x)=x^2-10x+q=(x-5)^2+q-25$

$\Rightarrow f'(x)=2(x-5)<0$, if $x<5$ i.e. $f(x)$ is decreasing in $x<5$ and $f'(x)>0$, if $x>5$ i.e. $f(x)$ is decreasing in $x<5$.

$\therefore f(3)>f(4)>f(5)$ (see above figure)

[If 'f' is decreasing and $a<b<c$, then $f(a)<f(b)<f(c)$]

11. (c) P lies in major segment, then P lies in the interior of the circle $x^2+y^2=16$ and O and P lie on the same side of $x+y=2$.

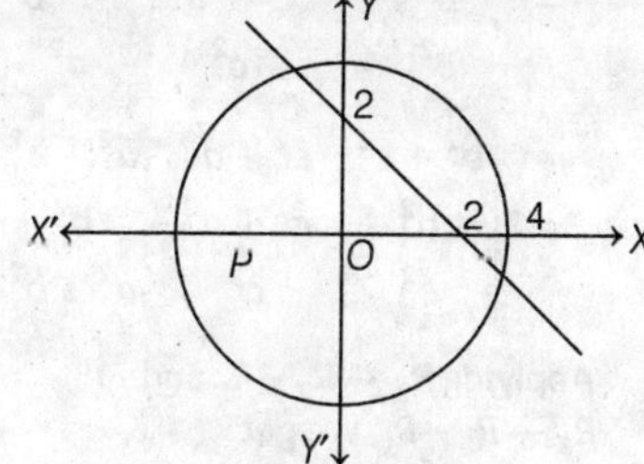

$\therefore (-5+r)^2+(-3+r)^2<16$

$\Rightarrow \quad 2r^2-16r+18<0$

$\Rightarrow \quad r^2-8r+9<0$

$\Rightarrow \quad (r-4)^2<7$

$\Rightarrow \quad \sqrt{(r-4)^2}<\sqrt{7}$

$\Rightarrow \quad |r-4|<\sqrt{7}$

$\Rightarrow \quad -\sqrt{7}<r-4<\sqrt{7}$

$\Rightarrow \quad 4-\sqrt{7}<r<4+\sqrt{7}$

Also, $[(-5+r)+(-3+r)-2]$

$[0+0-2]>0$

$\Rightarrow \quad 2r-10<0 \Rightarrow r<5$

Hence, $\quad 4-\sqrt{7}<r<5$

i.e. $\quad r\in(4-\sqrt{7},5) \quad$ ...(i)

Options (a), (b) and (d) are subsets of Eq. (i) but option (c) $(4-\sqrt{7},4+\sqrt{7})\not\in(4-\sqrt{7},5)$

12. (b) Let $A=$ Ball drawn from bag II is pink.

$E_1=$ Ball transferred from bag II to bag I is blue.

$E_2=$ Ball transferred from bag II to bag I is pink.

$$P(E_1)=\frac{6}{9}, P(E_2)=\frac{3}{9},$$

$$P(A/E_1)=\frac{5}{8}$$

and $\quad P(A/E_2)=\frac{6}{8}$

By Baye's Theorem,

$$P(E_1/A)=\frac{P(E_1)\cdot P(A/E_1)}{P(E_1)P(A/E_1)+P(E_2)\cdot P(A/E_2)}$$

$$=\frac{\frac{6}{9}\times\frac{5}{8}}{\frac{6}{9}\times\frac{5}{8}+\frac{3}{9}\times\frac{6}{8}}=\frac{5}{8}$$

13. (a) Here, $\sigma_1^2=4, \sigma_2^2=5, \bar{x}_1=2, \bar{x}_2=4$

and $\quad n_1=n_2=5$

$\therefore \quad \bar{x}=\frac{n_1\bar{x}_1+n_2\bar{x}_2}{n_1+n_2}=3$

$d_1=\bar{x}_1-\bar{x}=2-3=-1$

and $\quad d_2=\bar{x}_2-\bar{x}=4-3=1$

Let σ^2 be the combined variance, then

$$\sigma^2=\frac{n_1(\sigma_1^2+d_1^2)+n_2(\sigma_2^2+d_2^2)}{n_1+n_2}$$

$$=\frac{(4+1)+(5+1)}{2}=\frac{11}{2}$$

14. (d) The circle ABC is incircle of ΔPQR,.

$|PQ|=3, |QR|=5$ and $|PR|=4$

$\Rightarrow \Delta PQR$ is a right-angled triangle

$\therefore$ Area of $\Delta PQR(\Delta)=\frac{1}{2}\times 3\times 4=6$

and $\quad s=\frac{1}{2}(3+4+5)=6$

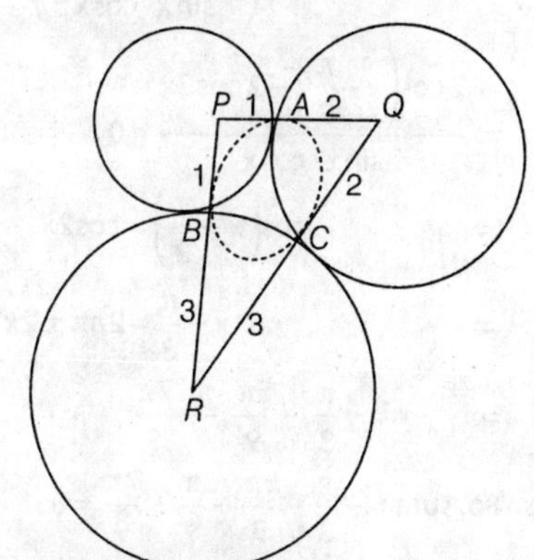

$\therefore$ Area of $\Delta PQR(\Delta)=r\cdot s$

$\Rightarrow \quad r=\frac{\Delta}{s}=\frac{6}{6}=1$

15. (b) Given, $f(x)=\int_0^x \sqrt{1-f^2(t)}\,dt+\frac{1}{2}$

$\Rightarrow \quad f'(x)=\sqrt{1-f^2(x)}$

$\Rightarrow \frac{f'(x)}{\sqrt{1-f^2(x)}}=1 \Rightarrow \sin^{-1}\{f(x)\}=x+C$

For $x=0$, $\sin^{-1}\left(\frac{1}{2}\right)=C$ and thus $C=\frac{\pi}{6}$

$\Rightarrow \quad f(x)=\sin\left(x+\frac{\pi}{6}\right)$

$\therefore \quad f(\pi)=\sin\left(\pi+\frac{\pi}{6}\right)=-\sin\frac{\pi}{6}$

$\Rightarrow \quad f(\pi)=\sin\left(-\frac{\pi}{6}\right)$

$\Rightarrow \quad \sin^{-1}\{f(\pi)\}=-\frac{\pi}{6}$

16. (c) Equation of (P_1) is $y^2-8x=0$ and Equation of (P_2) is $y^2+16x=0$

Tangent to $y^2-8x=0$, passes through $(-4,0)$

$\Rightarrow m_1(-4)+\frac{2}{m_1}=0 \Rightarrow \frac{1}{m_1^2}=2$

Now, tangent to $y^2+16x=0$ passes through $(2,0)$

$\Rightarrow \quad m_2\times 2-\frac{4}{m_2}=0$

$\Rightarrow \quad m_2^2=2$

So, $\frac{1}{m_1^2}+m_2^2=4$

17. (d) $\sqrt{3}\sec x+\operatorname{cosec} x+2(\tan x-\cot x)=0$

$\Rightarrow \frac{\sqrt{3}}{\cos x}+\frac{1}{\sin x}+2\left(\frac{\sin x}{\cos x}-\frac{\cos x}{\sin x}\right)=0$

$\Rightarrow \frac{\sqrt{3}\sin x+\cos x}{\sin x\cdot\cos x}+2\left(\frac{\sin^2 x-\cos^2 x}{\sin x\cdot\cos x}\right)=0$

$\Rightarrow \frac{2\cos\left(x-\frac{\pi}{3}\right)-2\cos 2x}{\sin x\cdot\cos x}=0$

$\Rightarrow \quad \cos\left(x-\frac{\pi}{3}\right)=\cos 2x$

$\Rightarrow \quad x-\frac{\pi}{3}=2n\pi\pm 2x$

$\Rightarrow \quad x=-\frac{\pi}{3},-\frac{5\pi}{9},\frac{\pi}{9},\frac{7\pi}{9}$

So, sum $=-\frac{\pi}{3}-\frac{5\pi}{9}+\frac{\pi}{9}+\frac{7\pi}{9}=0$

18. (b) The compound statement with 'and' is '396 is a multiple of 6 and 8'.

$\Rightarrow P$ is true and Q is false.

Thus, the statement 'P' and 'Q' is not valid $V_1=F$.

Now, the compound statement with 'or' is '396 is a multiple of 6 or 8'

$\Rightarrow P$ is true and Q is false.

So, the compound statement with 'or' is true. Thus, the statement 'P' or 'Q' is true.

$V_2=T$

$\therefore \quad V_1\wedge V_2=F\wedge T=F$

19. (d) Let $\Delta=\begin{vmatrix} b^2+c^2 & ab & ac \\ ab & c^2+a^2 & bc \\ ac & bc & a^2+b^2\end{vmatrix}$

$\Rightarrow \Delta=\frac{1}{abc}\begin{vmatrix} a(b^2+c^2) & a^2b & a^2c \\ ab^2 & b(c^2+a^2) & b^2c \\ ac^2 & bc^2 & c(a^2+b^2)\end{vmatrix}$

By taking a, b and c common from C_1, C_2 and C_3 respectively, we get;

$\Rightarrow \Delta=\frac{abc}{abc}\begin{vmatrix} b^2+c^2 & a^2 & a^2 \\ b^2 & c^2+a^2 & b^2 \\ c^2 & c^2 & a^2+b^2\end{vmatrix}$

Applying $R_1\to R_1+R_2+R_3$, we get

$\Delta=\begin{vmatrix} 2(b^2+c^2) & 2(c^2+a^2) & 2(a^2+b^2) \\ b^2 & c^2+a^2 & b^2 \\ c^2 & c^2 & a^2+b^2\end{vmatrix}$

$=2\begin{vmatrix} b^2+c^2 & c^2+a^2 & a^2+b^2 \\ b^2 & c^2+a^2 & b^2 \\ c^2 & c^2 & a^2+b^2\end{vmatrix}$

Applying $R_2\to R_2-R_1$ and $R_3\to R_3-R_1$, we get

$\Delta=2\begin{vmatrix} b^2+c^2 & c^2+a^2 & a^2+b^2 \\ -c^2 & 0 & -a^2 \\ -b^2 & -a^2 & 0\end{vmatrix}$

Applying $R_1\to R_1+R_2+R_3$, we get

$\Delta=2\begin{vmatrix} 0 & c^2 & b^2 \\ -c^2 & 0 & -a^2 \\ -b^2 & -a^2 & 0\end{vmatrix}$

$=2[-c^2(-a^2b^2)+b^2(c^2a^2)]$

$\Rightarrow \quad \Delta=4a^2b^2c^2$

Comparing with the given condition, we get

$k=4$

20. (d)

X	0	1	2	3
P(X)	a	b	0.3	$2b$

Let $P(X=0)=a$ and $P(X=1)=b$

Given, $P(X=3)=2P(X=1)=2b$

$P(X=2)=0.3$

$\Sigma P_i=1=a+b+0.3+2b$

$\Rightarrow a+3b=0.7$

$\Sigma P_iX_i=0+b+0.6+6b=1.3$

$[\because \Sigma P_iX_i=1.3]$

$7b=0.7\Rightarrow b=0.1$

$\because \quad a=0.7-3(0.1)$

$=0.7-0.3=0.4$

$\because \quad P(X=0)=0.4$

21. (3) $\mathbf{a}\cdot\mathbf{p}=\frac{\mathbf{a}\cdot(\mathbf{b}\times\mathbf{c})}{[\mathbf{a}\,\mathbf{b}\,\mathbf{c}]}=\frac{[\mathbf{a}\,\mathbf{b}\,\mathbf{c}]}{[\mathbf{a}\,\mathbf{b}\,\mathbf{c}]}=1$

$\mathbf{b}\cdot\mathbf{p}=\frac{\mathbf{b}\cdot(\mathbf{b}\times\mathbf{c})}{[\mathbf{a}\,\mathbf{b}\,\mathbf{c}]}=\frac{0}{[\mathbf{a}\,\mathbf{b}\,\mathbf{c}]}=0$

$\mathbf{b}\cdot\mathbf{q}=\frac{\mathbf{b}\cdot(\mathbf{c}\times\mathbf{a})}{[\mathbf{a}\,\mathbf{b}\,\mathbf{c}]}=\frac{(\mathbf{b}\times\mathbf{c})\cdot\mathbf{a}}{[\mathbf{a}\,\mathbf{b}\,\mathbf{c}]}$

$=\frac{\mathbf{a}\cdot(\mathbf{b}\times\mathbf{c})}{[\mathbf{a}\,\mathbf{b}\,\mathbf{c}]}=\frac{[\mathbf{a}\,\mathbf{b}\,\mathbf{c}]}{[\mathbf{a}\,\mathbf{b}\,\mathbf{c}]}$

$\mathbf{c}\cdot\mathbf{q}=\frac{\mathbf{c}\cdot(\mathbf{c}\times\mathbf{a})}{[\mathbf{a}\,\mathbf{b}\,\mathbf{c}]}=0$

$\mathbf{c}\cdot\mathbf{r}=\frac{\mathbf{c}\cdot(\mathbf{a}\times\mathbf{b})}{[\mathbf{a}\,\mathbf{b}\,\mathbf{c}]}=\frac{(\mathbf{a}\times\mathbf{b})\cdot\mathbf{c}}{[\mathbf{a}\,\mathbf{b}\,\mathbf{c}]}$

$=\frac{[\mathbf{a}\,\mathbf{b}\,\mathbf{c}]}{[\mathbf{a}\,\mathbf{b}\,\mathbf{c}]}=1$ and $\mathbf{a}\cdot\mathbf{r}=0$

$\therefore$ Given expression is equal to

$1+0+1+0+1+0=3$

22. (1) Let $I=\int\sqrt[3]{\tan x}\,dx$ ...(i)

Let $\tan x=t^3$

$\Rightarrow \quad \sec^2 x\,dx=3t^2dt$

$\Rightarrow (1+\tan^2 x)\,dx=3t^2dt$

$\Rightarrow \quad dx=\frac{3t^2}{1+t^6}dt$

$\Rightarrow \quad I=\int\frac{3t^3}{1+t^6}dt$

[from Eq. (i)]

Let $t^2=u\Rightarrow t\,dt=\frac{1}{2}du$

$I=\int\frac{3}{2}\left(\frac{u}{1+u^3}\right)du$

$=\frac{3}{2}\int\left[\frac{-1}{3}\cdot\frac{1}{u+1}+\frac{1}{3}\left(\frac{u+1}{u^2-u+1}\right)\right]du$

$=\frac{-1}{2}\ln|u+1|+\frac{1}{2}\int\frac{u+1}{u^2-u+1}du$

$=\frac{-1}{2}\ln|u+1|+\frac{1}{4}\int\frac{2u-1}{u^2-u+1}du+\frac{3}{4}\int\frac{1}{u^2-u+1}du$

$=\frac{-1}{2}\ln|u+1|+\frac{1}{4}\ln|u^2-u+1|+\frac{3}{4}\int\frac{1}{\frac{3}{4}+\left(u-\frac{1}{2}\right)^2}du$

$$=\frac{1}{2}\ln\left|\frac{\sqrt{u^2-u+1}}{u+1}\right|+\frac{3}{4}\times\frac{2}{\sqrt{3}}\tan^{-1}\left(\frac{u-\frac{1}{2}}{\frac{\sqrt{3}}{2}}\right)+C$$

$$=\frac{1}{2}\ln\left|\frac{\sqrt{u^2-u+1}}{u+1}\right|+\frac{\sqrt{3}}{2}\tan^{-1}\left(\frac{2u-1}{\sqrt{3}}\right)+C$$

Where, $u=(\tan x)^{2/3}$

$\Rightarrow \quad \lambda=\frac{1}{2}$ and $\mu=\frac{\sqrt{3}}{2}$

$\therefore \quad \lambda^2+\mu^2=1$

23. (2) An equation of tangent to the parabola $y^2=4x$ is

$$y=mx+\frac{1}{m}$$

It will passes through the point (1, 4), if

$$4=m+\frac{1}{m}$$

$\Rightarrow \quad m^2-4m+1=0$

Let m_1, m_2 be roots of this equation, then

$$\tan\theta=\left|\frac{m_1-m_2}{1+m_1m_2}\right|=\left|\frac{\sqrt{(m_1+m_2)^2-4m_1m_2}}{1+m_1m_2}\right|$$

$$=\frac{\sqrt{16-4}}{1+1}=\sqrt{3}$$

$\Rightarrow \quad \theta=\frac{\pi}{3}\Rightarrow 4\cos\theta=2$

24. (20) **Method 1**

Let *OA* be the breadth of the river and *OP* be the tree which makes an angle of 60° at a point *A* on the opposite bank.

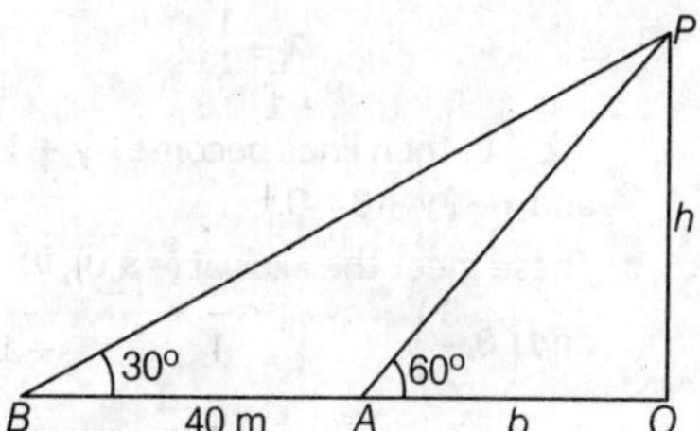

In ΔAOP and ΔBOP, we have,

$\cot 60°=\frac{b}{h}$ and $\cot 30°=\frac{b+40}{h}$

$\Rightarrow b=h\cot 60°$ and $b+40=h\cot 30°$

$\therefore \quad \frac{b}{b+40}=\frac{\cot 60°}{\cot 30°}$

$\Rightarrow \quad \frac{b}{b+40}=\frac{\frac{1}{\sqrt{3}}}{\sqrt{3}}$

$\Rightarrow \quad 3b=b+40$

$\Rightarrow \quad b=20$ m

Method 2

From the figure,

$$b=a\sin\alpha\cos\beta\,\mathrm{cosec}(\beta-\alpha)$$

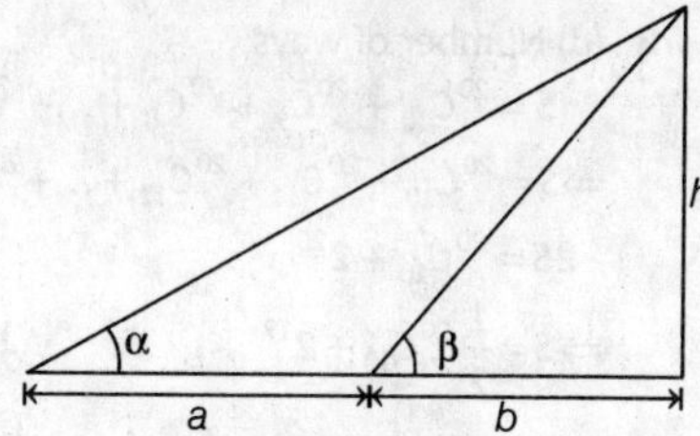

But we have,

$a=40$ m, $\alpha=30°$ and $\beta=60°$

$\therefore$

$$b=40\times\sin 30°\times\cos 60°\times\mathrm{cosec}\,30°$$

$$=40\times\frac{1}{2}\times\frac{1}{2}\times 2=20\text{ m}$$

25. (1) Given, curve is

$$x^{3/2}+y^{3/2}=2a^{3/2} \quad \text{...(i)}$$

$\therefore \quad \frac{3}{2}\sqrt{x}+\frac{3}{2}\sqrt{y}\frac{dy}{dx}=0$

$$\frac{dy}{dx}=-\frac{\sqrt{x}}{\sqrt{y}}$$

Since, tangent is equally inclined to the axes.

$\therefore \quad \frac{dy}{dx}=\pm 1$

$\Rightarrow \quad -\frac{\sqrt{x}}{\sqrt{y}}=\pm 1$

$\Rightarrow \quad \frac{-\sqrt{x}}{\sqrt{y}}=-1 \quad [\because \sqrt{x}>0, \sqrt{y}>0]$

$\Rightarrow \quad \sqrt{x}=\sqrt{y}$

Putting $\sqrt{y}=\sqrt{x}$ in Eq. (i), we get

$$2x^{3/2}=2a^{3/2}$$

$\Rightarrow \quad x^3=a^3$

$\therefore \quad x=a$

and so, $\quad y=a$

Hence, total number of tangents drawn is 1

26. (4) $\sin^{-1}(\sin 6x)=x$

$\Rightarrow \quad \sin 6x=\sin x$

$\Rightarrow \quad x=\frac{\pi}{7},\frac{3\pi}{7},\frac{5\pi}{7},\pi,0,\frac{2\pi}{5},\frac{4\pi}{5}$

But $\frac{5\pi}{7}, \pi$ and $\frac{4\pi}{5}$ are rejected as any value of *x* which is solution of given equation can't exceed $\frac{\pi}{2}$.

Hence, number of solutions is 4

27. (19) Using LMVT for some $c\in(1,6)$ such that

$$f'(c)=\frac{f(6)-f(1)}{5}$$

$$=\frac{f(6)+2}{5}\geq 4.2$$

$\Rightarrow \quad f(6)+2\geq 21$

$\Rightarrow \quad f(6)\geq 19$

Hence, smallest possible value of $f(6)$ is 19.

28. (5) An equation of normal to the hyperbola

$\frac{x^2}{4}-\frac{y^2}{1}=1$ at $(2\sec\theta, \tan\theta)$ is

$$2x\cos\theta+y\cot\theta=5 \quad \text{...(i)}$$

Its intercepts on the axes are $\frac{5}{2\cos\theta}$ and $\frac{5}{\cot\theta}$, respectively.

The intercepts are positive and equal

$0<\theta<\frac{\pi}{2}$ and $\frac{5}{2\cos\theta}=\frac{5}{\cot\theta}$

$\Rightarrow \quad \sin\theta=\frac{1}{2}\Rightarrow\theta=\frac{\pi}{6}$

From, Eq. (i), $2x\cos\frac{\pi}{6}+y\cot\frac{\pi}{6}=5$

$\Rightarrow \quad \sqrt{3}x+\sqrt{3}y=5$

$\Rightarrow \quad y=-x+\left(\frac{5}{\sqrt{3}}\right)$

This will touch the ellipse $\frac{x^2}{a^2}+\frac{y^2}{b^2}=1$,

if $\left(\frac{5}{\sqrt{3}}\right)^2=a^2m^2+b^2=a^2+b^2$

$\Rightarrow \quad \frac{3}{5}(a^2+b^2)=5$

29. (12) Equation of any plane passing through $(-2,-2,2)$ is

$$a(x+2)+b(y+2)+c(z-2)=0$$

Since, it contains the line joining the points (1, 1, 1) and (1, −1, 2), it contains these points as well.

So, that $\quad 3a+3b-c=0$

and $\quad 3a+b+0=0$

On solving, we get

$$\frac{a}{1}=\frac{b}{-3}=\frac{c}{-6}$$

and thus the equation of the plane is

$$x+2-3(y+2)-6(z-2)=0$$

$$\Rightarrow \quad x-3y-6z+8=0$$

$$\Rightarrow \quad \frac{x}{-8}+\frac{y}{8/3}+\frac{z}{8/6}=1$$

$\therefore$ The required sum $=8+\frac{8}{3}+\frac{8}{6}=12$

30. (6) We have,

$$f(x)=x^2+2bx+2c^2$$

$$=(x+b)^2+2c^2-b^2$$

$\Rightarrow$ Min $f(x)=2c^2-b^2$

Also, $g(x)=-x^2-2cx+b^2$

$$=b^2-\{x^2+2cx+c^2-c^2\}$$

$$=b^2+c^2-(x+c)^2$$

$\Rightarrow$ Max $g(x)=b^2+c^2$

Since, min $f(x)>$ max $g(x)$, we get

$$2c^2-b^2>b^2+c^2$$

$$\Rightarrow \quad c^2>2b^2 \Rightarrow |c|>|b|\sqrt{2}$$

So, $\quad k=\sqrt{2}$

Hence,

$$k^2+\sqrt{2}k+2=(\sqrt{2})^2+\sqrt{2}\times\sqrt{2}+2$$

$$=2+2+2=6$$

Knockout 5

1. (a) Given, $f(x)=\frac{x}{1+x}=1-\frac{1}{1+x}$

As, $\quad x\geq 0$

$$\Rightarrow \quad 1+x\geq 1 \Rightarrow 0<\frac{1}{1+x}\leq 1$$

Thus, $f(x)<1\ \forall x\in[0,\infty)$

In other words, $f(x)$ cannot be onto.

Also, $f'(x)=\frac{1}{(1+x)^2}>0\ \forall x\in[0,\infty)$

$\therefore f(x)$ is a strictly increasing function.

Thus, $f(x)$ is one-one.

Hence, $f(x)$ is one-one but not onto.

2. (c) Given, $y=\frac{3\sqrt{3}x-14}{5}$ ...(i)

In $\frac{x^2}{5}+\frac{y^2}{3}=1$, we get

$$\frac{1}{5}x^2+\frac{1}{3}\left(\frac{3\sqrt{3}x-14}{5}\right)^2=1$$

$$\Rightarrow 15x^2+27x^2-84\sqrt{3}x+121=0$$

$$\Rightarrow \quad 42x^2-84\sqrt{3}x+121=0$$

Let x_1, x_2 be the roots of the equation, then $x_1+x_2=2\sqrt{3}$

and $y_1+y_2=\frac{1}{5}[3\sqrt{3}(x_1+x_2)-28]$

[from Eq. (i)]

$$=\frac{1}{5}(3\sqrt{3}\times 2\sqrt{3}-28)=-2$$

Thus, the mid-point of the chord is

$$\left(\frac{x_1+x_2}{2},\frac{y_1+y_2}{2}\right)=\left(\frac{2\sqrt{3}}{2},\frac{-2}{2}\right)$$

$$=(\sqrt{3},-1)$$

$\therefore$ Equation of required line is

$$y=\left(\frac{-1-0}{\sqrt{3}-0}\right)x$$

$$\Rightarrow x+\sqrt{3}y=0$$

3. (d) Number of ways,

$$S={}^{20}C_{10}+{}^{20}C_9+{}^{20}C_8+\ldots+{}^{20}C_0$$

$$\Rightarrow S={}^{20}C_{10}+{}^{20}C_{11}+{}^{20}C_{12}+\ldots+{}^{20}C_{20}$$

$$2S={}^{20}C_{10}+2^{20}$$

$$\Rightarrow S=\frac{1}{2}\,{}^{20}C_{10}+2^{19}$$

4. (c) Let the equation $x^2-6x+a=0$ have roots α and β.

Also, let the equation $x^2-cx+6=0$ have roots α and γ.

Given that, $\frac{\beta}{\gamma}=\frac{4}{3} \Rightarrow \frac{\alpha\beta}{\alpha\gamma}=\frac{4}{3}$

$$\Rightarrow \quad \frac{a}{6}=\frac{4}{3}\Rightarrow a=8$$

So, first equation is $x^2-6x+8=0$, having roots $x=2,4$.

For $\alpha=2$ and $\beta=4$, $\gamma=\frac{3\beta}{4}=3$

For $\alpha=4$ and $\beta=2$, $\gamma=\frac{3\beta}{4}=\frac{3}{2}$ which is not an integer.

So, common root is $\alpha=2$

Hence, at $x=\alpha=2$, $x^2-3x+1<0$

5. (d) $xRx \Leftrightarrow 2x^2-3x(x)+x^2=0;\ \forall x\in N$

So, R is reflexive.

For $x=1$ and $y=2$

$$2x^2-3xy+xy^2=0$$

$$1R2=2(1)^2-3(1)(2)+(2)^2=0$$

but $2R1=2(2)^2-3(2)(1)+(1)^2=3\neq 0$

So, 2 is not related to 1.

So, R is not symmetric.

6. (b) Given that,

$$\frac{dy}{dx}+\frac{1}{x}\tan y=\frac{1}{x^2}\tan y\cdot\sin y$$

$$\Rightarrow \cot y\cdot\operatorname{cosec} y\frac{dy}{dx}+\frac{1}{x}\operatorname{cosec} y=\frac{1}{x^2}$$

Putting $\operatorname{cosec} y=t$, we get,

$\frac{dt}{dx}-\frac{t}{x}=\frac{-1}{x^2}$ which is linear differential equation.

$$\text{IF}=e^{\int -\frac{1}{x}dx}=e^{-\ln x}=\frac{1}{x}$$

Therefore, solution is

$$\frac{t}{x}=\int -\frac{1}{x^3}dx$$

$$\Rightarrow \quad \frac{t}{x}=\frac{1}{2x^2}+K$$

$$\Rightarrow \quad 2xt=1+2Kx^2$$

$\Rightarrow 2x=\sin y(1+cx^2)$, where $c=2K$

and $K=$ constant of integration

7. (b) If $\lambda\neq 0$, then $\lambda x-y+1=0$ and $x-2y+3=0$ meet the axes at $A\left(\frac{-1}{\lambda},0\right)$, $B(0,1)$, $C(-3,0)$ and $D\left(0,\frac{3}{2}\right)$.

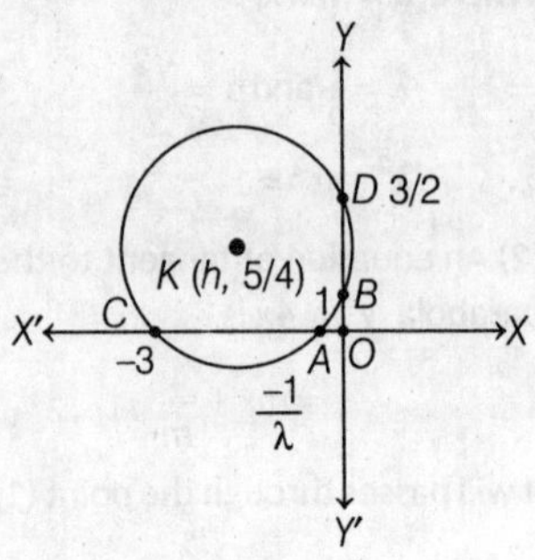

The centre of circle lies on the perpendicular bisector of BD,

i.e. on $y=\frac{5}{4}$

Let the centre of the circle be $K\left(h,\frac{5}{4}\right)$

Then, $\quad KC^2=KB^2$

$$\Rightarrow (h+3)^2+\left(\frac{5}{4}\right)^2=h^2+\left(\frac{1}{4}\right)^2$$

$$h=\frac{-7}{4}$$

As, $KA^2=KB^2$, we get;

$$\left(\frac{-1}{\lambda}+\frac{7}{4}\right)^2+\left(\frac{5}{4}\right)^2=\left(\frac{-7}{4}\right)^2+\left(\frac{1}{4}\right)^2$$

$$\Rightarrow \quad \left(\frac{1}{\lambda}-\frac{7}{4}\right)^2=\frac{49}{16}-\frac{24}{16}=\frac{25}{16}$$

$$\Rightarrow \quad \frac{1}{\lambda}=\frac{7}{4}\pm\frac{5}{4}=3,\frac{1}{2}$$

$$\Rightarrow \quad \lambda=\frac{1}{3},2$$

If $\lambda=0$, then lines become $-y+1=0$ and $x-2y+3=0$.

These meet the axes at $(-3,0)$, $(0,1)$ and $\left(0,\frac{3}{2}\right)$.

As, these three points are non-collinear, they lie on a circle.

Thus, $\lambda=0,\ 2,\ \frac{1}{3}$

Hence, $\lambda\neq\frac{-1}{3}$

8. (a)

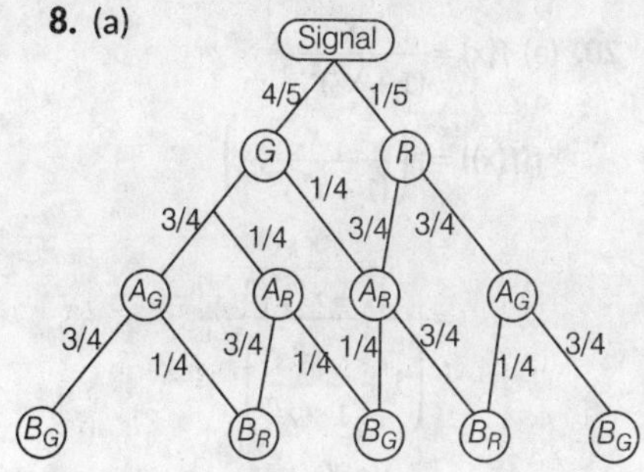

From the tree diagram.

$$P(B_G)=\frac{4}{5}\times\frac{3}{4}\times\frac{3}{4}+\frac{4}{5}\times\frac{1}{4}\times\frac{1}{4}+\frac{1}{5}\times\frac{3}{4}\times\frac{1}{4}+\frac{1}{5}\times\frac{1}{4}\times\frac{3}{4}=\frac{23}{40}$$

$$P(B_G\,|\,G)=\frac{3}{4}\times\frac{3}{4}+\frac{1}{4}\times\frac{1}{4}=\frac{10}{16}=\frac{5}{8}$$

$$\therefore P(B_G\cap G)=P(G)\cdot P(B_G\,|\,G)=\frac{4}{5}\times\frac{5}{8}=\frac{1}{2}$$

$\therefore$ Required probability $=P(G\,|\,B_G)$

$$=\frac{P(B_G\cap G)}{P(B_G)}=\frac{\frac{1}{2}}{\frac{23}{40}}=\frac{20}{23}$$

9. (d) Let $I=\int_{1/2}^{2} e^{\left|x-\frac{1}{x}\right|}dx$ ...(i)

Putting $x=\frac{1}{z}\Rightarrow dx=\frac{-1}{z^2}dz$

$$\therefore\quad I=-\int_{2}^{1/2} e^{\left|z-\frac{1}{z}\right|}\frac{dz}{z^2} \quad ...(ii)$$

Adding Eqs. (i) and (ii), we get;

$$2I=\int_{1/2}^{2} e^{\left|x-\frac{1}{x}\right|}\left(1+\frac{1}{x^2}\right)dx$$

$$\left[\because -\int_{2}^{1/2} e^{\left|z-\frac{1}{z}\right|}\cdot\frac{1}{z^2}dz=\int_{1/2}^{2} e^{\left|x-\frac{1}{x}\right|}\cdot\frac{dx}{x^2}\right]$$

[by the property of definite integration]

$$=\int_{1/2}^{1} e^{-\left(x-\frac{1}{x}\right)}\left(1+\frac{1}{x^2}\right)dx+\int_{1}^{2} e^{\left(x-\frac{1}{x}\right)}\left(1+\frac{1}{x^2}\right)dx$$

$$=\int_{-3/2}^{0} e^{-y}dy+\int_{0}^{3/2} e^{t}\cdot dt$$

[putting $x-\frac{1}{x}=y$ in first integral and $x-\frac{1}{x}=t$ in second integral]

$$\Rightarrow\quad 2I=2(e\sqrt{e}-1)$$

$$\Rightarrow\quad I=e\sqrt{e}-1$$

10. (b) Let $\angle APC=\beta$ and $AC=CB=x$

Given, $AP=n\cdot AB$

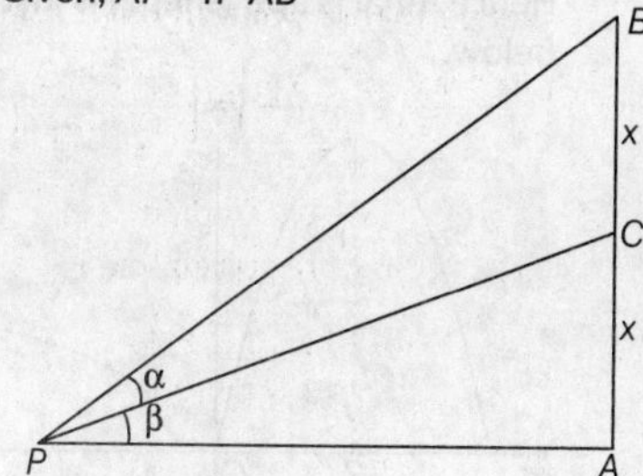

In ΔAPC, we have

$$\tan\beta=\frac{AC}{AP}=\frac{x}{2nx}=\frac{1}{2n} \quad ...(i)$$

In ΔAPB, we have

$$\tan(\alpha+\beta)=\frac{AB}{AP}=\frac{2x}{2nx}=\frac{1}{n} \quad ...(ii)$$

Now, $\tan\alpha=\tan\{(\alpha+\beta)-\beta\}$

$$\Rightarrow \tan\alpha=\frac{\tan(\alpha+\beta)-\tan\beta}{1+\tan(\alpha+\beta)\cdot\tan\beta}$$

$$=\frac{\frac{1}{n}-\frac{1}{2n}}{1+\frac{1}{2n^2}}$$

$$\Rightarrow \frac{n}{2n^2+1}=\tan\alpha$$

$$\Rightarrow\quad n=(2n^2+1)\tan\alpha$$

11. (c) $\begin{vmatrix} x & 1 & 1\\ 1 & y & 1\\ 1 & 1 & z\end{vmatrix}=x(yz-1)-1(z-1)+1(1-y)$

$$=xyz-(x+y+z)+2$$

$\because\quad AM\ge GM$

$$\Rightarrow\quad \frac{x+y+z}{3}\ge(xyz)^{1/3}$$

$$\Rightarrow\quad x+y+z\ge 3(xyz)^{1/3} \quad ...(i)$$

The value of determinant is non-negative.

$$\Rightarrow xyz-(x+y+z)+2\ge 0$$

$$\Rightarrow xyz+2\ge x+y+z\ge 3(xyz)^{1/3}$$

[from Eq. (i)]

$$\Rightarrow xyz-3(xyz)^{1/3}+2\ge 0 \quad ...(ii)$$

Let $(xyz)^{1/3}=u\Rightarrow xyz=u^3$

From Eq. (ii),

$$u^3-3u+2\ge 0$$

$$\Rightarrow (u+2)(u-1)^2\ge 0$$

$$\Rightarrow\quad u+2\ge 0\quad[\because (u-1)^2\ge 0\,\forall u]$$

$$\Rightarrow\quad u\ge -2$$

$$\Rightarrow\quad (xyz)^{1/3}\ge -2$$

$$\Rightarrow\quad xyz\ge -8$$

Hence, least value of xyz is -8.

12. (a) Given, $(1+x^2)^4(1+x^3)^7(1+x^4)^{12}$

Power of (x) from each factor altogether is 11

$$\Rightarrow\ 2x_1+3x_2+4x_3=11$$

Total possibilities for (x_1,x_2,x_3) are (0, 1, 2), (1, 3, 0), (2, 1, 1), (4, 1, 0)

$\therefore$ Required coefficients

$$=({}^4C_0\times{}^7C_1\times{}^{12}C_2)+({}^4C_1\times{}^7C_3\times{}^{12}C_0)+({}^4C_2\times{}^7C_1\times{}^{12}C_1)+({}^4C_4\times{}^7C_1\times 1)$$

$$=462+140+504+7=1113$$

13. (b) Let $y=\frac{ax+b}{c}$ i.e. $y=\left(\frac{a}{c}\right)x+\left(\frac{b}{c}\right)$

i.e. $y=Ax+B$, where $A=\frac{a}{c}$ and $B=\frac{b}{c}$

$$\therefore\quad \bar{y}=A\bar{x}+B$$

Now, $\quad y-\bar{y}=A(x-\bar{x})$

$$\Rightarrow\quad (y-\bar{y})^2=A^2(x-\bar{x})^2$$

$$\Rightarrow \Sigma(y-\bar{y})^2=A^2\Sigma(x-\bar{x})^2$$

$$\Rightarrow\quad n\cdot\sigma_y^2=A^2\cdot n\sigma_x^2$$

$$\Rightarrow\quad \sigma_y^2=A^2\sigma_x^2\Rightarrow \sigma_y=|A|\,\sigma_x$$

$$\Rightarrow\quad \sigma y=\left|\frac{a}{c}\right|\sigma_x=\left|\frac{a}{c}\right|\sigma$$

$[\sigma_x=\sigma$ given$]$

14. (a) Let $L=\lim_{n\to\infty}[\sqrt{n^2+n+1}-(\sqrt{n^2+n+1})]$

$$\because\quad n<\sqrt{n^2+n+1}<n+1$$

$$\therefore\quad (\sqrt{n^2+n+1})=n$$

So, $L=\lim_{n\to\infty}(\sqrt{n^2+n+1}-n)$

$$=\lim_{n\to\infty}\frac{(\sqrt{n^2+n+1}-n)(\sqrt{n^2+n+1}+n)}{(\sqrt{n^2+n+1}+n)}$$

$$=\lim_{n\to\infty}\frac{n^2+n+1-n^2}{n\sqrt{1+\frac{1}{n}+\frac{1}{n^2}}+n}$$

$$=\lim_{n\to\infty}\frac{n\left(1+\frac{1}{n}\right)}{n\left(\sqrt{1+\frac{1}{n}+\frac{1}{n^2}}+1\right)}=\frac{1+0}{1+1}=\frac{1}{2}$$

15. (a) Slope of tangent $=2$

The tangents will be

$$y=2x\pm\sqrt{9\times 4-4}$$

$$\Rightarrow\quad 2x-y=\pm 4\sqrt{2}$$

$$\Rightarrow\quad \frac{x}{2\sqrt{2}}-\frac{y}{4\sqrt{2}}=1$$

and $\quad \frac{x}{-2\sqrt{2}}+\frac{y}{4\sqrt{2}}=1$

So, points of contact are

$$\left(\frac{9}{2\sqrt{2}},\frac{1}{\sqrt{2}}\right)\text{ and }\left(\frac{-9}{2\sqrt{2}},-\frac{1}{\sqrt{2}}\right)$$

i.e. (a,b) and $(c,d)\Rightarrow|a+d|=\left(\frac{7}{2\sqrt{2}}\right)$

16. (d)

p	q	r	$p \wedge q$	$(p \wedge q) \to r$
T	T	T	T	T
T	T	F	T	F
T	F	T	F	T
T	F	F	F	T
F	T	T	F	T
F	T	F	F	T
F	F	T	F	T
F	F	F	F	T

Truth value of $(p \wedge q) \to r$ is F, if p and q both are T and r is F.

17. (c) $S_n = C_0 + 3C_1 + 5C_2 + 7C_3 + \ldots + (2n+1)C_n$

$$= (C_0 + C_1 + C_2 + C_3 + \ldots + C_n) + 2(C_1 + 2C_2 + 3C_3 + \ldots + nC_n)$$

$$= 2^n + 2\left[n + n(n-1) + \frac{n(n-1)(n-2)}{2} + \ldots + n\right]$$

$$= 2^n + 2n\left[1 + (n-1) + \frac{(n-1)(n-2)}{2} + \ldots + 1\right]$$

$$= 2^n + 2n(1+1)^{n-1}$$

$$= 2^n + n\cdot(2^n) = (n+1)\cdot 2^n$$

$\therefore\ S_9 = 10(2^9) = 5(2^{10}) = 2^{10}\cdot 3^0 \cdot 5^1$

On comparing, we get

$a = 10, b = 0$

and $c = 1$

Now, $abc = 0$, $a + c = 11$,

$a + b + c = 11$, $ab + bc + ca = 10$

18. (d) Given, $f(x) = \begin{cases} \sqrt{x}, & x \ge 1 \\ x^3, & 0 \le x \le 1 \\ \dfrac{x^3}{3} - 4x, & x < 0 \end{cases}$

Now, draw the graph of $f(x)$ and then discuss.

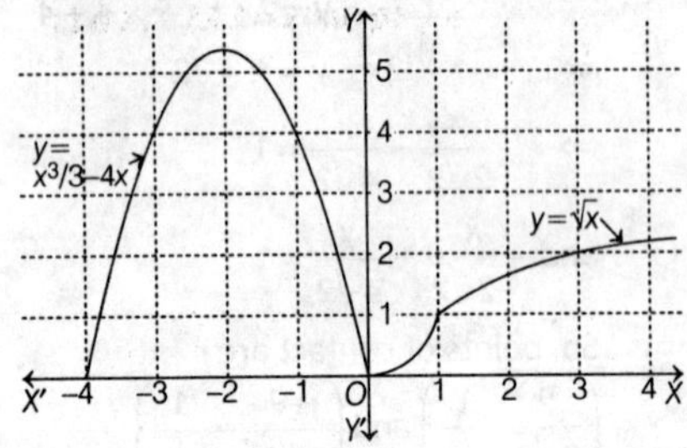

Fig. (a) Graph of $f(x)$

Hence, final graph (shape) is just like below.

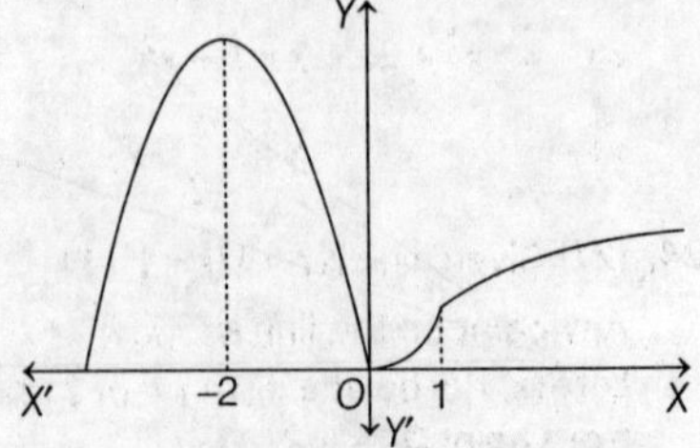

From graph; function is increasing in $(-\infty, -2) \cup (0, \infty)$ and decreasing in $(-2, 0)$ i.e. options (c) is incorrect.

$-\infty \quad + \quad -2 \quad - \quad 0 \quad + \quad \infty$

Sign scheme for $f'(x)$

That is, $f'(x)$ changes its sign twice as x varies from $-\infty$ to ∞. (option (d) is correct

$\therefore\ x = -2$ is local maxima point and $x = 0$ is local minima point.

i.e. the function attains extrema at $x_1 = -2$ and $x_2 = 0$.

So, $x_1 \cdot x_2 = 0$

$\Rightarrow$ option (b) is incorrect

Since, $f(x)$ has corner points at $x = 0$ and $x = 1$, then $f(x)$ is differentiable for all $x \in R - \{0, 1\}$ and it is continuous for all $x \in R$. i.e. option (a) is incorrect

19. (b) As $\omega^n = 1$, n must be a multiple of 3.

Let $n = 3m$

Then,

$$(\omega + x)^{3m} = \omega^{3m} + 3m\omega^{3m-1}x + \frac{1}{2}(3m)(3m-1)\omega^{3m-2}x^2 + \ldots$$

$$= 1 + 3m\overline{\omega}x + \frac{1}{2}(3m)(3m-1)\omega x^2 + \ldots$$

On comparing, we get

$$3mx = 12 \text{ and } \frac{1}{2}(3m)(3m-1)x^2 = 69$$

$$\Rightarrow \frac{3m-1}{3m} = \frac{69 \times 2}{12 \times 12} = \frac{23}{24}$$

$$m = 8$$

Thus, $n = 24$

and $x = \dfrac{1}{2}$

20. (a) $f(x) = \dfrac{x}{(1+x^n)^{1/n}}$

$$f(f(x)) = f\left(\frac{x}{(1+x^n)^{1/n}}\right)$$

$$= \frac{\dfrac{x}{(1+x^n)^{1/n}}}{\left(1 + \dfrac{x^n}{1+x^n}\right)^{1/n}}$$

$$= \frac{x}{(1+2x^n)^{1/n}}$$

$$f(f(f(x))) = f\left(\frac{x}{(1+2x^n)^{1/n}}\right)$$

$$= \frac{\dfrac{x}{(1+2x^n)^{1/n}}}{\left(1 + \dfrac{x^n}{1+2x^n}\right)^{1/n}}$$

$$= \frac{x}{(1+3x^n)^{1/n}}$$

and so on, leads to

$$\underbrace{(fofofo\ldots fof)}_{n\text{-times}}(x) = \frac{x}{(1+nx^n)^{1/n}} = g(x)$$

Now, $\displaystyle\int g(x)\cdot x^{n-2}dx = \int \frac{x^{n-1}}{(1+nx^n)^{1/n}}dx$

Let $1 + nx^n = z \Rightarrow n^2x^{n-1}dx = dz$

Then, $\displaystyle\int g(x)x^{n-2}dx = \frac{1}{n^2}\int \frac{1}{z^{1/n}}dz$

$$= \frac{1}{n^2}\left(\frac{z^{\frac{n-1}{n}}}{\frac{n-1}{n}}\right) + C$$

$$= \frac{1}{n(n-1)}(1+nx^n)^{1-\frac{1}{n}} + C$$

21. (0) Let coordinates of P be $\left(ct_1, \dfrac{c}{t_1}\right)$ and that of Q be $\left(ct_2, \dfrac{c}{t_2}\right)$,

where, $t_1t_2 > 0$

An equation of line PQ is

$$y - \frac{c}{t_1} = \frac{\dfrac{c}{t_2} - \dfrac{c}{t_1}}{ct_2 - ct_1}(x - ct_1)$$

$$\Rightarrow y - \frac{c}{t_1} = -\frac{1}{t_1t_2}(x - ct_1)$$

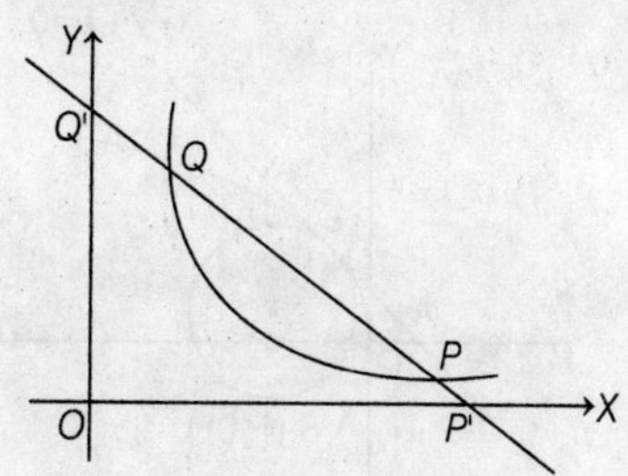

This line meets the X-axis at $P'(c(t_1+t_2),0)$ and Y-axis at $Q'\left(0, c\left(\frac{1}{t_1}+\frac{1}{t_2}\right)\right)$

Now, $PP' = c\sqrt{t_2^2+\left(\frac{1}{t_1}\right)^2}$

and $QQ' = c\sqrt{t_2^2+\left(\frac{1}{t_1}\right)^2}$

$\Rightarrow PP' - QQ' = 0$

22. (4) $f(2+x) = f(2-x)$

$\Rightarrow \quad f'(2+x) = -f'(2-x)$

When $x=0$, then $f'(2) = -f'(2) = 0$

When $x=-1$, then $f'(1) = -f'(3) = 0$

When $x = \frac{-3}{2}$, then

$f'\left(\frac{1}{2}\right) = -f'\left(\frac{7}{2}\right) = 0$

$\therefore f'\left(\frac{1}{2}\right) = f'(1) = f'(2)$

$= f'(3) = f'\left(\frac{7}{2}\right) = 0$

Using Rolle's theorem of $f'(x)$, minimum number of roots of $f''(x)=0$ is 4.

23. (3) $\because \cot^{-1}x = \sin^{-1}\left(\frac{1}{\sqrt{1+x^2}}\right)$

$\Rightarrow \sin(\cot^{-1}(1+x))$

$= \frac{1}{\sqrt{1+(1+x)^2}}$

$= \frac{1}{\sqrt{x^2+2x+2}}$

$\Rightarrow \quad \cos(\tan^{-1}x) = \frac{1}{\sqrt{1+x^2}}$ and

$\Rightarrow \sin(\cot^{-1}(1+x)) = \cos(\tan^{-1}x)$

$\Rightarrow \quad x^2+2x+2 = 1+x^2$

$\Rightarrow \quad x = -\frac{1}{2} \Rightarrow -6x = 3$

24. (27) Given, line is $\mathbf{r} = \lambda(\hat{\mathbf{i}}+\hat{\mathbf{j}}+\hat{\mathbf{k}})$

Any point on the line is $Q(\lambda,\lambda,\lambda)$

Let $P(x,y,z)$ be at a distance of 3 units from point Q

$\therefore \quad PQ^2 = 9$

$\Rightarrow (x-\lambda)^2+(y-\lambda)^2+(2-\lambda)^2 = 9$ ...(i)

Also, PQ is perpendicular to the given line.

$\therefore \quad \mathbf{QP}\cdot(\hat{\mathbf{i}}+\hat{\mathbf{j}}+\hat{\mathbf{k}}) = 0$

$\Rightarrow \quad x-\lambda+y-\lambda+z-\lambda = 0$

$\Rightarrow \quad \lambda = \frac{x+y+z}{3}$

Putting this value of λ in Eq. (i), we get locus of point P as

$x^2+y^2+z^2-xy-yz-zx = \frac{27}{2}$

So, $\quad k = \frac{27}{2}$

$\therefore \quad 2k = \frac{27}{2}\times 2 = 27$

25. (1) We know that

$|A| = \det(A) = a_{11}A_{11}+a_{12}A_{21}+a_{13}A_{31}$

(because adj A is given in question)

$= (1)(-2)+3(-1)+2(3\alpha) = 6\alpha-5$

and $|A|^2 = |\operatorname{adj}A| = -10+17\alpha-6\alpha^2$

$\Rightarrow (6\alpha-5)^2 = -6\alpha^2+17\alpha-10$

$\Rightarrow 42\alpha^2-77\alpha+35 = 0 \Rightarrow \alpha = 1, \frac{5}{6}$

But $\alpha \in N \quad \therefore \alpha = 1$

$\therefore |A| = 6\alpha-5 = 6-5 = 1$

26. (2) Given, $\frac{\pi}{2} < \left|3x-\frac{\pi}{2}\right| \le \pi$

$\Rightarrow \quad \frac{\pi}{2} < \left(3x-\frac{\pi}{2}\right) \le \pi$

or $\quad -\pi \le \left(3x-\frac{\pi}{2}\right) < \frac{-\pi}{2}$

$\Rightarrow \quad \pi < 3x \le \frac{3\pi}{2}$ or $\frac{-\pi}{6} \le x < 0$

$\Rightarrow \quad x \in \left[\frac{-\pi}{6}, 0\right) \cup \left(\frac{\pi}{3}, \frac{\pi}{2}\right]$

Now, $1+\cos x+\cos 2x+\sin x+\sin 2x + \sin 3x = 0$

$\Rightarrow 2\cos^2 x+\cos x+\sin 2x + 2\sin 2x\cdot\cos x = 0$

$\Rightarrow \cos x(2\cos x+1) + \sin 2x(2\cos x+1) = 0$

$\Rightarrow \quad (\cos x+\sin 2x)(2\cos x+1) = 0$

$\Rightarrow \cos x(1+2\sin x)(2\cos x+1) = 0$

$\Rightarrow \quad \cos x = 0$ or $\sin x = \frac{-1}{2}$

(as for given interval, $\cos x \ge 0$)

$\Rightarrow \quad x = \frac{\pi}{2}$ or $x = \frac{-\pi}{6}$

Hence, there are 2 solutions.

27. (1.25) Given, $y = x^2 \Rightarrow \frac{dy}{dx} = 2x$

$\therefore \quad \left(\frac{dy}{dx}\right)_{(1,1)} = 2$

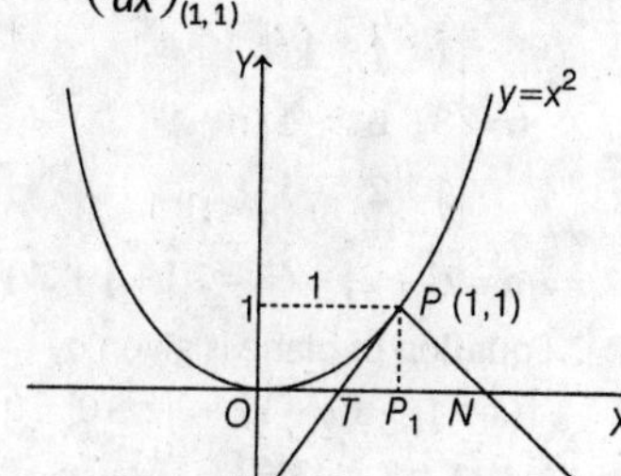

$\therefore$ Equation of tangent PT at $P(1,1)$ is

$(y-1) = 2(x-1)$ i.e. $y = 2x-1$

So, $\quad T \equiv \left(\frac{1}{2}, 0\right)$

Equation of normal PN at $P(1,1)$ is

$y-1 = -\frac{1}{2}(x-1)$ i.e. $2y = -x+3$

So, $N \equiv (3,0)$

Now, $P_1T = OP_1 - OT = 1-\frac{1}{2} = \frac{1}{2}$

and $P_1N = ON - OP_1 = 3-1 = 2$

$\therefore$ Required area $= (\Delta PP_1T + \Delta PP_1N)$

$= \frac{1}{2}\times PP_1\times P_1T + \frac{1}{2}\times PP_1\times P_1N$

$= \frac{1}{2}\times 1\times\frac{1}{2} + \frac{1}{2}\times 2\times 1$

$= \frac{5}{4}$ sq units $= 1.25$ sq units

28. (1) Given, system is homogeneous system having infinitely many solutions.

$\Rightarrow$ The given system has non-trivial solutions

$$\Rightarrow \begin{vmatrix} 2 & 4 & \lambda \\ 4 & \lambda & 2 \\ \lambda & 2 & 2 \end{vmatrix} = 0$$

$\Rightarrow 2(2\lambda - 4) - 4(8 - 2\lambda) + \lambda(8 - \lambda^2) = 0$

$\Rightarrow \lambda^3 + 4\lambda - 40 = 0$

Which is a cubic equation which has atleast one real root (i).

Let $f(\lambda) = \lambda^3 + 4\lambda - 40$

$\Rightarrow f'(\lambda) = 3\lambda^2 + 4 > 0 \Rightarrow f$ is increasing

$\Rightarrow f(\lambda) = 0$ has atmost one real root ...(ii)

From Eqs. (i) and (ii),

$f(\lambda) = 0$ has one real root.

29. (5) Normal vector of the plane

$$\mathbf{n} = \begin{vmatrix} \hat{i} & \hat{j} & \hat{k} \\ 3 & 0 & -1 \\ 1 & 2 & -1 \end{vmatrix}$$

$\Rightarrow \mathbf{n} = 2\hat{i} + 2\hat{j} + 6\hat{k} = 2(\hat{i} + \hat{j} + 3\hat{k})$

$\therefore$ Equation of plane is given by

$1(x+1) + 1(y-2) + 3(z-0) = 0$

$\Rightarrow P: x + y + 3z = 1$

Hence, $a + b + c = 1 + 1 + 3 = 5$

30. (6) **Concept** Foot of the perpendicular form the focus to any tangent of the parabola lies on the tangent at the vertex to the parabola

An equation of line through (1, 2) and perpendicular to $x - y = 0$ is

$(x-1) + (y-2) = 0 \Rightarrow x + y = 3$

Foot of perpendicular from (1, 2) to $x - y = 0$ is the point of intersection of $x - y = 0$ and $x + y = 3$. i.e. $A\left(\frac{3}{2}, \frac{3}{2}\right)$

Similarly, foot of perpendicular from (1, 2) to $x + y = 0$ is $B\left(\frac{-1}{2}, \frac{1}{2}\right)$.

Thus, equation of tangent at the vertex of the parabola is (an equation of AB) is

$$\frac{x - \frac{3}{2}}{\frac{-1}{2} - \frac{3}{2}} = \frac{y - \frac{3}{2}}{\frac{1}{2} - \frac{3}{2}} \Rightarrow x - 2y + \frac{3}{2} = 0$$

Now, l = length of latus rectum

$= 4$ (distance of tangent at vertex from the focus)

$$= 4\frac{\left|1 - 2(2) + \frac{3}{2}\right|}{\sqrt{1+4}} = \frac{6}{\sqrt{5}}$$

$\Rightarrow \sqrt{5}l = 6$

Knockout 6

1. (a) Given,

$$f(x) = \sqrt[6]{4^x + 8^{(2/3)(x-2)} - 52 - 2^{2(x-1)}}$$

$f(x)$ is defined, if

$4^x + 8^{(2/3)(x-2)} - 52 - 2^{2(x-1)} \geq 0$

$\Rightarrow \quad 2^{2x} + 2^{2(x-2)} - 2^{2(x-1)} \geq 52$

$\Rightarrow \quad 2^{2x}[1 + 2^{-4} - 2^{-2}] \geq 52$

$\Rightarrow \quad 2^{2x}\left(\frac{13}{16}\right) \geq 52$

$\Rightarrow \quad 2^{2x} \geq 64$

$\Rightarrow \quad 2x \geq 6$

$\Rightarrow \quad x \geq 3$

$\therefore \quad x \in [3, \infty)$

2. (c) Given, $(x-5)^{x^2-5x+6} = 1$ ...(i)

$\Rightarrow \quad x^2 - 5x + 6 = 0$

$\Rightarrow \quad (x-3)(x-2) = 0$

$x = 2, 3$ satisfies Eq. (i)

$x - 5 = 1 \Rightarrow x = 6$

Satisfies Eq. (i)

$x - 5 = -1$

$\Rightarrow \quad x = 4$

Also, satisfies the Eq. (i)

Hence, solutions are $x = 2, 3, 4, 6$.

So, product $= 2 \times 3 \times 4 \times 6 = 144$

3. (d) Let $I = \int \{x(1-x^2)\}^{1/3} \cdot x^{-4} dx$

$$= \int \frac{(x - x^3)^{1/3}}{x^4} dx$$

$$= \int \frac{x\left(\frac{1}{x^2} - 1\right)^{1/3}}{x^4} dx$$

$$= \int \left(\frac{1}{x^2} - 1\right)^{1/3} \cdot \frac{1}{x^3} dx$$

Put $\frac{1}{x^2} - 1 = z$

$\Rightarrow \quad \frac{1}{x^3} dx = -\frac{dz}{2}$

$$I = -\frac{1}{2}\int z^{1/3} dz = -\frac{1}{2} \cdot \frac{z^{4/3}}{\frac{4}{3}} + C_1$$

$$= \frac{-3}{8}\left(\frac{1}{x^2} - 1\right)^{4/3} + C_1$$

Comparing this to $A(x^B - 1)^C + K$, we get

$A = \frac{-3}{8}, B = -2, C = \frac{4}{3}$ and $K = C_1$

So, $\quad 8A + B + 3C + 1 = 0$

4. (b) Focus at $S(1, 0)$ and P is (1, 2).

Equation of circle touching the parabola at (1, 2) is

$(x-1)^2 + (y-2)^2 + \lambda(x - y + 1) = 0$

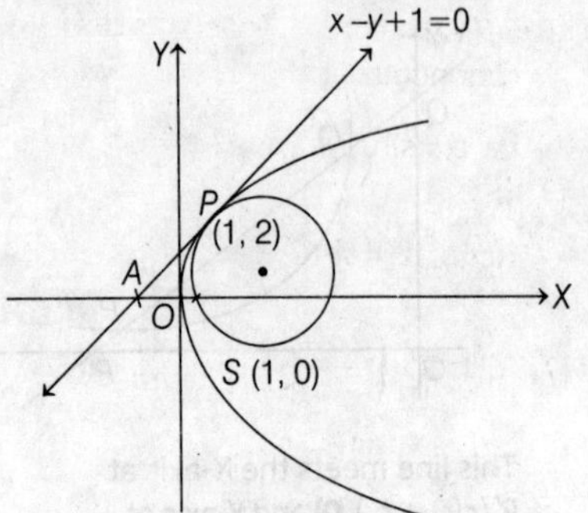

It passes through (1, 0).

$\therefore \quad 4 + 2\lambda = 0$

$\Rightarrow \quad \lambda = -2$

Hence, the required circle is

$(x-1)^2 + (y-2)^2 - 2(x - y + 1) = 0$

$\Rightarrow \quad x^2 + y^2 - 4x - 2y + 3 = 0$

$\therefore$ Its radius is $\sqrt{4 + 1 - 3} = \sqrt{2}$ units

5. (c) $y = 81^{\sin^2 x} + 81^{\cos^2 x} - 30$ ...(i)

Since Eq. (i) intersect X-axis, so $y = 0$

i.e. $\quad 81^{\sin^2 x} + 81^{\cos^2 x} - 30 = 0$

$\Rightarrow \quad 81^{\sin^2 x} + 81^{1 - \sin^2 x} - 30 = 0$

$\Rightarrow (81)^{2\sin^2 x} - 30 \cdot (81)^{\sin^2 x} + 81 = 0$

$\Rightarrow \quad (81^{\sin^2 x} - 3)(81^{\sin^2 x} - 27) = 0$

$\Rightarrow \quad \sin^2 x = \frac{1}{4}$ or $\sin^2 x = \frac{3}{4}$

$\Rightarrow \quad \sin x = \pm\frac{1}{2}$ or $\sin x = \pm\frac{\sqrt{3}}{2}$

$\Rightarrow \quad x = \pm\frac{\pi}{6}, \pm\frac{5\pi}{6}$

or $x = \pm\frac{\pi}{3}, \pm\frac{2\pi}{3}$ in $-\pi \leq x \leq \pi$

Hence, total number of points of intersection of curve (i) with X-axis is 8 in $-\pi \leq x \leq \pi$.

6. (a) LHL

$$= \lim_{x \to -2^-} f(x) = \lim_{x \to -2^-} \frac{a \cdot e^{\frac{1}{|x+2|}} - 1}{2 - e^{\frac{1}{|x+2|}}}$$

$$= \lim_{x \to -2^-} \frac{a - e^{-1/|x+2|}}{2 \cdot e^{-1/|x+2|} - 1} = -a$$

$$\text{LHL} = -a \quad \left[\because \frac{1}{|x+2|} \to \infty \text{ as } x \to -2^-\right]$$

$$\text{RHL} = \lim_{x \to -2^+} (x) = \lim_{x \to -2^+} \sin\left(\frac{x^4 - 16}{x^5 + 32}\right)$$

$$= \lim_{x \to -2^+} \sin\left[\frac{(x+2)(x-2)(x^2+4)}{(x+2)(x^4 - 2x^3 + 4x^2 - 8x + 16)}\right]$$

$$= \sin\left[\frac{(-4) \cdot 8}{16 + 16 + 16 + 16 + 16}\right] = \sin\left(\frac{-2}{5}\right)$$

value of function (VF)

$= f(-2) = b$ For $f(x)$ to be continuous at $x = -2$; LHL = RHL = VF

i.e. $b = \sin\left(\frac{-2}{5}\right)$ and $-a = b = \sin\left(\frac{-2}{5}\right)$

Hence, $a = \sin\left(\frac{2}{5}\right)$ and $b = \sin\left(\frac{-2}{5}\right)$

7. (d) $\log_{1/2}\left(\frac{2a-5}{a-3}\right) \geq 0$

$\Rightarrow \log_{1/2}\left(\frac{2a-5}{a-3}\right) \geq \log_{1/2} 1$

$\Rightarrow \frac{2a-5}{a-3} \leq 1 \Rightarrow \frac{2a-5}{a-3} - 1 \leq 0$

$-\infty$ + 2 − 3 + ∞

$\Rightarrow \frac{a-2}{a-3} \leq 0, a \in [2,3)$

So, the only integral value of 'a' is 2.

Let $I = \int_0^{\sqrt{2}-1} \frac{1}{1+x} dx$

$= [\ln(1+x)]_0^{\sqrt{2}-1} - \ln\sqrt{2}$

$\Rightarrow \frac{1}{r} = e^{\ln\sqrt{2}}$

$\Rightarrow r = \frac{1}{\sqrt{2}}$

So, sum of GP,

$S = a + ar + ar^2 + ar^3 + \ldots$

$= \frac{a}{1-r} = \frac{2}{1-\frac{1}{\sqrt{2}}} = \frac{2\sqrt{2}}{\sqrt{2}-1}$

8. (b) Given,

$1 + \log_5(x^2+1) \geq \log_5(ax^2 + 4x + a)$ ...(i)

For log to be defined, argument condition

$x^2 + 1 > 0, \forall x \in R$

and $ax^2 + 4x + a > 0, \forall x \in R$

$\Rightarrow 16 - 4a^2 < 0$ and $a > 0$

$(\because ax^2 + bx + c > 0, \forall x \in R,$ if $D < 0$ and $a > 0)$

$\Rightarrow (a < -2$ or $a > 2)$ and $a > 0$

$\Rightarrow a > 2$ ...(ii)

From Eq. (i),

$\log_5 5 + \log_5(x^2+1) \geq \log_5(ax^2 + 4x + a), \forall x \in R$

$\Rightarrow 5x^2 + 5 \geq ax^2 + 4x + a, \forall x \in R$

$\Rightarrow (a-5)x^2 + 4x + (a-5) \leq 0, \forall x \in R$

$\Rightarrow (4)^2 - 4(a-5)^2 \leq 0$ and $a - 5 < 0$

$(\because ax^2 + bxc + c \leq 0, \forall x \in R,$ if $D \leq 0$ and $a < 0)$

$\Rightarrow (4 - 2a + 10)(4 + 2a - 10) \leq 0$

and $a - 5 < 0$

$\Rightarrow (a \leq 3$ or $a \geq 7)$ and $a < 5$

$\Rightarrow a \leq 3$ ...(iii)

From Eqs. (ii) and (iii), we get

$2 < a \leq 3$

9. (c) By truth table;

p	q	$\sim p$	$p \Rightarrow q$	$\sim p \wedge q$	$(p \Rightarrow q) \Leftrightarrow (\sim p \wedge q)$
T	T	F	T	F	F
T	F	F	F	F	T
F	T	T	T	T	T
F	F	T	T	F	F

Hence, given statement is neither a tautology nor a contradiction.

10. (b) Equation of any line through the points of intersection of the given lines $2x + 3y - 6 = 0$ and $3x + 2y - 6 = 0$ is

$(2x + 3y - 6) + \lambda(3x + 2y - 6) = 0$

$\Rightarrow (2 + 3\lambda)x + (3 + 2\lambda)y - 6(\lambda + 1) = 0$

$\Rightarrow \frac{x}{\frac{6(\lambda+1)}{(2+3\lambda)}} + \frac{x}{\frac{6(\lambda+1)}{(3+2\lambda)}} = 1$

when $\lambda \neq -1$

and in this case, sum of reciprocals of the intercepts made by this line on the coordinate axis is equal to

$\frac{2 + 3\lambda + 3 + 2\lambda}{6(\lambda+1)} = \frac{5(\lambda+1)}{6(\lambda+1)} = \frac{5}{6}$

11. (d) Given, $z|z| - az + 1 = 0$

Putting $z = a + 2i$, we have

$(a + 2i)\sqrt{a^2+4} = a(a+2i) - 1$

$= a^2 - 1 + 2ai$

On comparing real and imaginary parts, we get

$a\sqrt{a^2+4} = a^2 - 1$

and $2\sqrt{a^2+4} = 2a$

$\Rightarrow \sqrt{a^2+4} = \frac{a^2-1}{a}, \frac{a^2-1}{a} = a$

$\Rightarrow a^2 = a^2 - 1$ which is an absurd.

Hence, no such complex number exists.

12. (d) Given standard deviation of numbers 2, 3, a and 11 is 3.5.

$\therefore (3.5)^2 = \frac{\Sigma x_i^2}{4} - (\bar{x})^2$

$\Rightarrow (3.5)^2 = \frac{4 + 9 + a^2 + 121}{4} - \left(\frac{2+3+a+11}{4}\right)^2$

On solving, we get

$3a^2 - 32a + 84 = 0$

13. (a) Let $\mathbf{x} = \lambda\mathbf{b} + \mu\mathbf{a}$

Since, $\mathbf{x} \perp \mathbf{b}$

So, $\mathbf{x} \cdot \mathbf{b} = 0$

$\Rightarrow (\lambda\mathbf{b} + \mu\mathbf{a}) \cdot \mathbf{b} = 0$

$\Rightarrow \lambda\mathbf{b}^2 + \mu\mathbf{a} \cdot \mathbf{b} = 0$

$\Rightarrow 5\lambda - \mu = 0$ ...(i)

$(\because \mathbf{b}^2 = |\mathbf{b}|^2 = 5$ and $\mathbf{a} \cdot \mathbf{b} = -1)$

Now, $\mathbf{x} \cdot \mathbf{a} = (\lambda\mathbf{b} + \mu\mathbf{a}) \cdot \mathbf{a}$

$= \lambda\mathbf{a} \cdot \mathbf{b} - \mu\mathbf{a}^2 = 7$

$\Rightarrow 3\mu - \lambda = 7$ ...(ii)

From Eqs. (i) and (ii), we get

$\lambda = \frac{1}{2}$ and $\mu = \frac{5}{2}$

$\therefore \mathbf{x} = \frac{1}{2}(2\hat{\mathbf{i}} + \hat{\mathbf{k}}) + \frac{5}{2}(-\hat{\mathbf{i}} + \hat{\mathbf{j}} + \hat{\mathbf{k}})$

$= \frac{-3}{2}\hat{\mathbf{i}} + \frac{5}{2}\hat{\mathbf{j}} + 3\hat{\mathbf{k}}$

14. (b)

	Number of terms	First term	Last term
First group	1	1	1^2
Second group	3	2	2^2
Third group	5	5	3^2
⋮	⋮	⋮	⋮
nth group	$(2n-1)$	$(n-1)^2 + 1$	n^2

Sum of the numbers in nth group

$= \frac{2n-1}{2}[(n-1)^2 + 1 + n^2]$

$= (n-1)^3 + n^3$

15. (a) Given, differential equation can be written as

$\frac{dy}{dx} + 2\sin\frac{y}{2} \cdot \cos\frac{y}{2} + x\left(2\cos^2\frac{y}{2}\right) = 0$

$\Rightarrow \frac{1}{2}\sec^2\frac{y}{2}\frac{dy}{dx} + \tan\frac{y}{2} + x = 0$

(dividing both sides by $2\cos^2\frac{y}{2}$)

Putting $\tan\frac{y}{2} = z$

$\Rightarrow \frac{1}{2}\sec^2\frac{y}{2}\frac{dy}{dx} = \frac{dz}{dx}$

So, $\frac{dz}{dx} + z = -x$, which is a linear differential equation. $= f(-2) = b$

$$IF = e^{\int 1 \cdot dx} = e^x$$

Its solution is $z \times e^x = -\int x \cdot e^x dx$

$\Rightarrow \tan\frac{y}{2} \cdot e^x = -(x-1) \cdot e^x + C$

$\Rightarrow \tan\frac{y}{2} = -(x-1) + Ce^{-x}$ ...(i)

Given, $y(0) = \frac{\pi}{2}$ i.e. putting, $x = 0$ and $y = \frac{\pi}{2}$ in Eq. (i).

$\Rightarrow 1 = 1 + C$

$\Rightarrow C = 0$

Hence, $\tan\left(\frac{y}{2}\right) = 1 - x$

So, $\tan\left[\frac{y(1/4)}{2}\right] = \left(1 - \frac{1}{4}\right)$

$= \frac{3}{4} = 0.75$

16. (b) Given, $3P(A) = 2P(B)$

$\Rightarrow \frac{P(A)}{2} = \frac{P(B)}{3}$

and $P(B) = 2P(C) \Rightarrow \frac{P(B)}{2} = \frac{P(C)}{1}$

Hence, $\frac{P(A)}{4} = \frac{P(B)}{6} = \frac{P(C)}{3} = K$ (say)

$\Rightarrow P(A) = 4K, P(B) = 6K$ and $P(C) = 3K$

Since, A, B, C are mutually exclusive and exhaustive.

$\therefore P(A \cup B \cup C) = P(A) + P(B) + P(C) = 1$

$\Rightarrow 1 = 4K + 6K + 3K$

$\Rightarrow 13K = 1$

$\Rightarrow K = \frac{1}{13}$

Hence, $P(A \cup B) = P(A) + P(B)$

$= \frac{10}{13}$

$\Rightarrow \frac{1}{P(A \cup B)} = \frac{13}{10}$

17. (a) As the system of equation has no solution

$$\frac{k+1}{k} = \frac{8}{k+3} = \frac{4k}{3k-1}$$

But $\frac{k+1}{k} = \frac{8}{k+3}$

$\Rightarrow k^2 + 4k + 3 = 8k$

$\Rightarrow (k-1)(k-3) = 0$

$\Rightarrow k = 1, 3$

For $k = 1$, $\frac{8}{k+3} = \frac{4k}{3k-1}$

and for $k = 3$, $\frac{8}{k+3} = \frac{8}{6}$

$\Rightarrow \frac{8}{k+3} = \frac{4}{3}$ and $\frac{4k}{3k-1} = \frac{3}{2}$

Hence, there is exactly one such value of k.

18. (d) $2 \cdot {}^mC_{r+1} = {}^mC_r + {}^mC_{r+2}$

$\Rightarrow 4 \cdot {}^mC_{r+1} = {}^{m+1}C_{r+1} + {}^{m+1}C_{r+2}$

$= {}^{m+2}C_{r+2}$

$\Rightarrow 4 \cdot \frac{m!}{r+1!(m-r-1)!} = \frac{m+2!}{r+2!m-r!}$

$\Rightarrow 4 = \frac{(m+2)(m+1)}{(r+2)(m-r)}$

$\Rightarrow 4r^2 + r(8-4m) + m^2 - 5m + 2 = 0$

$\Rightarrow r = \frac{(m-2) \pm \sqrt{m+2}}{2}$

$\Rightarrow m = 7$, gives $r = 4$ and $m = 14$ gives $r = 8$

So, the smallest value of m which satisfies the equation is 7.

19. (d) Taking $n!, (n+1)!$ and $(n+2)!$ common from R_1, R_2 and R_3, respectively.

$$\Delta_n = n!(n+1)!(n+2)! \begin{vmatrix} 1 & n+1 & (n+1)(n+2) \\ 1 & n+2 & (n+2)(n+3) \\ 1 & n+3 & (n+3)(n+4) \end{vmatrix}$$

Applying $R_2 \to R_2 - R_1$ and $R_3 \to R_3 - R_2$, we get

$$\Delta_n = n!(n+1)!(n+2)! \begin{vmatrix} 1 & n+1 & (n+1)(n+2) \\ 0 & 1 & 2(n+2) \\ 0 & 1 & 2(n+3) \end{vmatrix}$$

Expanding along C_1

$\Delta_n = 2n!(n+1)!(n+2)!$

$\Delta_{n+1} = 2(n+1)!(n+2)!(n+3)!$

Now, $\frac{\Delta_n}{\Delta_{n+1}} = \frac{1}{(n+1)(n+2)(n+3)}$

$\therefore \lim_{n\to\infty} \frac{(-n^3 + 2n^2 + 5n)}{(n+1)(n+2)(n+3)} = -1$

20. (a) Given, A and B both are idempotent matrices.

So, $A^2 = A$ and $B^2 = B$

Since, $(A+B)$ is also an idempotent matrix (given)

So, $(A+B)^2 = A + B$

Now, $A + B = (A+B)^2 = (A+B)(A+B)$

$= AA + BA + AB + BB$

$\Rightarrow A + B = A^2 + BA + AB + B^2$

$= A + BA + AB + B$

$\Rightarrow AB + BA = 0 =$ null matrix

21. (36) Given,

$|z_1| = 1$

$\Rightarrow |z_1|^2 = 1$

$\Rightarrow z_1\bar{z}_1 = 1 \Rightarrow z_1 = \frac{1}{\bar{z}_1}$

$\Rightarrow |z_2| = 2 \Rightarrow |z_2|^2 = 4$

$\Rightarrow z_2\bar{z}_2 = 4 \Rightarrow z_2 = \frac{4}{\bar{z}_2}$

$\Rightarrow |z_3| = 3 \Rightarrow |z_3|^2 = 9$

$\Rightarrow z_3\bar{z}_3 = 9 \Rightarrow z_3 = \frac{9}{\bar{z}_3}$

Now, $|z_2z_3 + 8z_3z_1 + 27z_1z_2|$

$= \left|z_1z_2z_3\left(\frac{1}{z_1} + \frac{8}{z_2} + \frac{27}{z_3}\right)\right|$

$= |z_1||z_2||z_3||\bar{z}_1 + 2\bar{z}_2 + 3\bar{z}_3|$

$= 1 \times 2 \times 3 \times 6 = 36$

$[\because \overline{z_1 + 2z_2 + 3z_3} = \bar{z}_1 + 2\bar{z}_2 + 3\bar{z}_3]$

22. (2) Given,

$$L = \lim_{x\to\infty} x^2 \cdot \sin\left(\log_e \sqrt{\cos\frac{\pi}{x}}\right)$$

$$\Rightarrow L = \lim_{x\to\infty} \frac{x^2 \cdot \sin\left(\log_e \sqrt{\cos\frac{\pi}{x}}\right)}{\left(\log_e \sqrt{\cos\frac{\pi}{x}}\right)} \cdot \left(\log_e \sqrt{\cos\frac{\pi}{x}}\right)$$

$$= \lim_{x\to\infty} x^2 \cdot \log_e \sqrt{\cos\frac{\pi}{x}} \quad \left(\because \lim_{y\to 0} \frac{\sin y}{y} = 1\right)$$

$$= \lim_{x\to\infty} \frac{x^2}{2} \cdot \log_e\left(\cos\frac{\pi}{x}\right)$$

$$= \lim_{x\to\infty} \frac{x^2}{2} \cdot \frac{\log_e\left[1 + \left(\cos\frac{\pi}{x} - 1\right)\right]}{\left(\cos\frac{\pi}{x} - 1\right)} \times \left(-2\sin^2\frac{\pi}{2x}\right)$$

$$= \lim_{x\to\infty} \frac{x^2}{2} \cdot \frac{\left(-2 \cdot \sin^2\frac{\pi}{2x}\right)}{\left(\frac{\pi}{2x}\right)^2} \cdot \left(\frac{\pi}{2x}\right)^2$$

$$\Rightarrow L = -\frac{\pi^2}{4}$$

Hence, $\frac{-8L}{\pi^2} = \left(\frac{-8}{\pi^2}\right)\left(\frac{-\pi^2}{4}\right) = 2$

23. (484) Given, equation of curves are

$$y = 4x - x^2 \quad \text{...(i)}$$

and $$y = x^2 - x \quad \text{...(ii)}$$

On solving Eqs. (i) and (ii), we get

$$4x - x^2 = x^2 - x$$

$$\Rightarrow \quad 2x^2 = 5x$$

$$\Rightarrow \quad x(2x-5) = 0 \Rightarrow x = 0, \frac{5}{2}$$

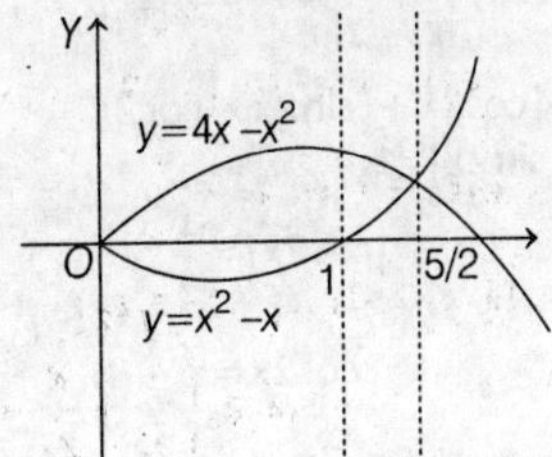

Now, $a = \int_0^{5/2} (4x - x^2)dx - \int_1^{5/2} (x^2 - x)\, dx$

$$= \left[\frac{4}{2}\cdot(x^2)_0^{5/2} - \frac{1}{3}(x^3)_0^{5/2}\right] - \left[\frac{1}{3}(x^3)_1^{5/2} - \frac{1}{2}(x^2)_1^{5/2}\right]$$

$$= \left(\frac{4}{2}\times\frac{25}{4} - \frac{1}{3}\times\frac{125}{8}\right) - \left[\frac{1}{3}\times\left(\frac{125}{8} - 1\right) - \frac{1}{2}\times\left(\frac{25}{4} - 1\right)\right]$$

$$= \frac{300-125}{24} - \left(\frac{1}{3}\times\frac{117}{8} - \frac{1}{2}\times\frac{21}{4}\right)$$

$$= \frac{175}{24} - \frac{54}{24} = \frac{121}{24}$$

$$b = \left|\int_0^1 (x^2 - x)\,dx\right| = \left|\frac{1}{3}(x^3)_0^1 - \frac{1}{2}(x^2)_0^1\right|$$

$$= \left|\frac{1}{3}\times(1) - \frac{1}{2}\times(1)\right| = \left|\frac{-1}{6}\right| = \frac{1}{6}$$

So, $a : b = \frac{121}{24} : \frac{1}{6} = 121 : 4$

Hence, $ab = 121 \times 4 = 484$

24. (9) Let the variable plane intersects the coordiante axes at $A(a,0,0)$, $B(0,b,0)$ and $C(0,0,c)$.

Then, the equation of the plane will be $\frac{x}{a} + \frac{y}{b} + \frac{z}{c} = 1$

Let $P(\alpha,\beta,\gamma)$ be the centroid of tetrahedron $OABC$, then

$$\alpha = \frac{a}{4}, \beta = \frac{b}{4}, \gamma = \frac{c}{4}$$

or, $a = 4\alpha, b = 4\beta, c = 4\gamma$

$\therefore$ Volume of tetrahedron

$$= \frac{1}{3}(\text{area of } \Delta OAB)\cdot OC$$

$$\Rightarrow \quad 64k^3 = \frac{1}{3}\left(\frac{1}{2}ab\right)\cdot c = \frac{abc}{6}$$

$$= \frac{(4\alpha)(4\beta)(4\gamma)}{6}$$

$$\Rightarrow \quad k^3 = \frac{\alpha\beta\gamma}{6}$$

$\therefore$ Required locus of $P(\alpha,\beta,\gamma)$ is $xyz = 6k^3$

On comparing with $xyz = \lambda k^{\mu}$, we get

$$\lambda = 6, \mu = 3$$

Hence, $\lambda + \mu = 6 + 3 = 9$

25. (60) 1(2) 3 (4) 5 (6) 7 (8) 9 positions

Four odd digits 3, 3, 5, 5 occupy four even positions is $\frac{4!}{2!2!} = 6$ ways

Rest five digits 2, 2, 8, 8, 8 can occupy rest positions is $\frac{5!}{2!3!} = 10$ ways

$\therefore$ Required number of numbers

$$= 6 \times 10 = 60$$

26. (0) As we know that, $[x+1] < (x+1)$

$$\Rightarrow \quad \frac{[x+1]}{e^x} < \frac{(x+1)}{e^x} \quad \text{...(i)}$$

Let $f(x) = \frac{x+1}{e^x} = (x+1)e^{-x}$

On differentiating both sides, we get

$f'(x) = -(x+1)e^{-x} + e^{-x} = -xe^{-x}$

$\Rightarrow f'(x) < 0$ for $x > 0$

i.e. $f(x)$ is decreasing function for $x > 0$

Also, $\frac{x+1}{e^x} = 1$ for $x = 0$ i.e. $f(0) = 1$

For $x > 0$

$$\Rightarrow \quad f(x) < f(0)$$

($\because f$ is decreasing function)

$$\Rightarrow \quad \frac{x+1}{e^x} < 1, \forall x > 0$$

Hence, $\frac{[x+1]}{e^x} < 1$ [from Eq. (i)]

$$\Rightarrow \quad \left[\frac{[x+1]}{e^x}\right] = 0$$

$$\therefore \quad \int_0^{\infty}\left[\frac{[x+1]}{e^x}\right]dx = \int_0^{\infty} 0\cdot dx = 0$$

27. (8) Equation of circle touching the line $y = x$ at $(2,2)$ is

$$(x-2)^2 + (y-2)^2 + a(x-y) = 0$$

$$\Rightarrow x^2 + y^2 - (4-\lambda)x - (4+\lambda)y + 8 = 0 \quad \text{...(i)}$$

Its centre $= \left(\frac{4-\lambda}{2}, \frac{4+\lambda}{2}\right)$ lies on Y-axis

$$\therefore \quad \frac{4-\lambda}{2} = 0$$

$$\Rightarrow \quad \lambda = 4$$

From Eq. (i),

$$x^2 + y^2 - 8y + 8 = 0$$

Its radius $= \sqrt{16-8} = \sqrt{8}$

Hence, $(\text{radius})^2 = 8$

28. (20) From ΔRTO,

$$\frac{h}{b} = \frac{OT}{OR} = \tan 60° = \sqrt{3}$$

$$\Rightarrow \quad h = \sqrt{3}b \quad \text{...(i)}$$

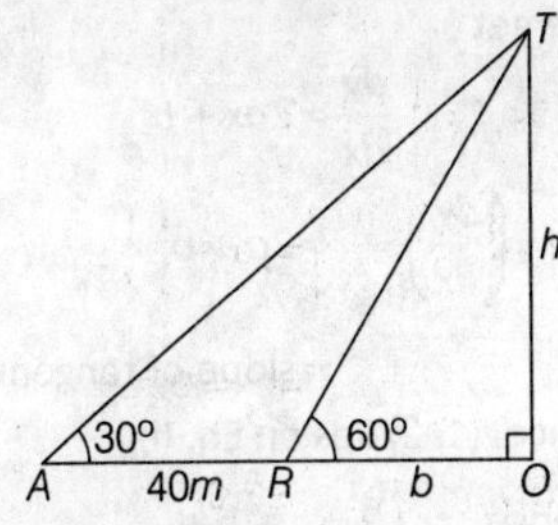

From ΔATO,

$$\frac{h}{b+40} = \frac{OT}{OA} = \tan 30° = \frac{1}{\sqrt{3}}$$

$$\Rightarrow \quad \sqrt{3}h = b + 40 \quad \text{...(ii)}$$

From Eq. (i) and (ii), we get

$$\sqrt{3}(\sqrt{3}b) = b + 40$$

$$\Rightarrow \quad b = 20$$

Hence, breadth of river is 20 m.

29. (8) Given, $x = \lambda(t) = t^5 - 5t^3 - 20t + 7$

and $y = u(t) = 4t^3 - 3t^2 - 18t + 3$

where $t \in [-2, 2]$

Now, $\frac{dx}{dt} = \lambda'(t) = 5t^4 - 15t^2 - 20$

$$= 5(t^2 - 4)(t^2 + 1)$$

and $\frac{dy}{dt} = \mu'(t) = 12t^2 - 6t - 18$

$$= 6(t+2)(2t-3)$$

$$\therefore \quad \frac{dy}{dx} = \frac{\frac{dy}{dt}}{\frac{dx}{dt}} = \frac{6(t+1)(2t-3)}{5(t^2-4)(t^2+1)}$$

$$= \frac{6(t+1)(2t-3)}{5(t-2)(t+2)(t^2+1)}$$

Sign scheme for $\frac{dy}{dx}$

$$-\infty \quad -2 \quad - \quad -1 \quad + \quad 3/2 \quad - \quad 2 \quad \infty$$

Here, $\frac{dy}{dx} > 0$ for $t \in \left(-1, \frac{3}{2}\right)$, where $y = f(x)$ increases.

and $\frac{dy}{dx} < 0$ for $t \in [-2,-1) \cup \left(\frac{3}{2}, 2\right]$, where $y = f(x)$ decreases.

Also, $t = -1$ is the point of minima and $t = \frac{3}{2}$ is the point of maxima.

Hence, $\alpha + 6\beta = (-1) + 6\left(\frac{3}{2}\right)$

$$= -1 + 9 = 8$$

30. (6) Given, $y = ax^2 + bx + \frac{7}{2}$ ...(i)

On differentiating Eq. (i) w.r.t. x, we get

$$\frac{dy}{dx} = 2ax + b$$

$$\Rightarrow \left(\frac{dy}{dx}\right)_{(1,2)} = 2a + b$$

$$= \text{slope of tangent} \quad ...(A)$$

Since, (1, 2) lies on Eq. (i).

Hence, $2 = a + b + \frac{7}{2}$

$$\Rightarrow a + b = \frac{-3}{2} \quad ...(B)$$

For $y = x^2 + 6x + 10$ ...(ii)

$$\frac{dy}{dx} = 2x + 6$$

$$\Rightarrow \left(\frac{dy}{dx}\right)_{(-2,2)} = 2$$

$\therefore$ Slope of normal $= -\frac{1}{2}$ ...(C)

From Eqs. (A) and (C),

$$2a + b = \frac{-1}{2} \quad ...(D)$$

On solving Eqs. (B) and (D), we get

$$a = 1, b = \frac{-5}{2}$$

Hence, $a - 2b = 6$

Knockout 7

1. (c) Given, $f(x) + f\left(1 - \frac{1}{x}\right) = 1 + x$ ...(i)

Replacing x by $1 - \frac{1}{x}$ in Eq. (i), we get

$$f\left(1 - \frac{1}{x}\right) + f(x) = 1 + 1 - \frac{1}{x} \quad ...(ii)$$

and replacing x by $\frac{1}{1-x}$ in Eq. (i), we get

$$f\left(\frac{1}{1-x}\right) + f(x) = 1 + \frac{1}{1-x} \quad ...(iii)$$

Now, adding Eqs. (i) and (ii) and the subtracting Eq. (iii), we get

$$2f(x) = 1 + x + 1 + \frac{1}{1-x} - 2 + \frac{1}{x}$$

$$= x + \frac{1}{1-x} + \frac{1}{x}$$

$$\Rightarrow 2f(x) = \frac{x^3 - x^2 - 1}{x(x-1)}$$

Now, given $g(x) = 2f(x) - x + 1$

$$= \frac{x^3 - x^2 - 1}{x(x-1)} - x + 1 = \frac{-2 + 2x^2 - 2x}{2x(x-1)}$$

$$\Rightarrow g(x) = \frac{x^2 - x - 1}{x(x-1)}$$

Now, for $y = \sqrt{g(x)}$, we must be

$$\frac{x^2 - x - 1}{x(x-1)} \geq 0$$

$$\Rightarrow \frac{\left(x - \frac{1-\sqrt{5}}{2}\right)\left(x - \frac{1+\sqrt{5}}{2}\right)}{x(x-1)} \geq 0$$

$$\Rightarrow x \in \left(-\infty, \frac{1-\sqrt{5}}{2}\right] \cup (0, 1) \cup \left[\frac{1+\sqrt{5}}{2}, \infty\right)$$

2. (a) $\cos 60° = \frac{b^2 + c^2 - a^2}{2bc}$

$$\Rightarrow \frac{1}{2} = \frac{b^2 + c^2 - a^2}{2bc}$$

$$\Rightarrow b^2 + c^2 - a^2 = bc$$

$$\Rightarrow b^2 + c^2 - bc = a^2$$

$$\Rightarrow b^2 + c^2 + 2bc = a^2 + 3bc$$

$$\Rightarrow (b + c)^2 = a^2 + 3bc$$

$$\Rightarrow 4a^2 = a^2 + 3bc$$

$[\because (b + c) = 2a$ given$]$

$$\Rightarrow 3a^2 = 3bc$$

$$\Rightarrow bc = a^2 \quad ...(i)$$

$$\because b + c = 2a \quad ...(ii)$$

$$\Rightarrow (b + c)^2 = 4a^2$$

$$\therefore (b - c)^2 = (b + c)^2 - 4bc$$

$$= 4a^2 - 4a^2$$

[from Eq. (i)]

$$\Rightarrow b - c = 0 \quad ...(iii)$$

From Eqs. (ii) and (iii), we get

$$2b = 2a \Rightarrow b = a$$

From Eq. (iii), we get

$$b = c = a$$

$\because$ Triangle is equilateral.

Now, $A = \frac{\sqrt{3}}{4}a^2 = \frac{1}{2}(3 + 4 + 5)a$

$$\Rightarrow a = \frac{24}{\sqrt{3}}$$

[i.e. circum radius]

$\because$ Radius of circum-circle of equilateral triangle

$$(R) = \frac{\text{Side of equilateral triangle}}{\sqrt{3}}$$

$$\Rightarrow R = \frac{a}{\sqrt{3}} = \frac{24/\sqrt{3}}{\sqrt{3}} = 8$$

3. (b) Let $z = e^{ix}, x \in [0, 2\pi)$, then $\bar{z} = e^{-ix}$

Given, $\left|\frac{z}{\bar{z}} + \frac{\bar{z}}{z}\right| = 1 \Rightarrow |z^2 + \bar{z}^2| = 1$

$\Rightarrow |\cos 2x + i\sin 2x + \cos 2x - i\sin 2x| = 1$

$$\Rightarrow |\cos 2x| = \frac{1}{2}$$

$$\Rightarrow \cos 2x = \pm\frac{1}{2}$$

$$\Rightarrow x = \frac{\pi}{6}, \frac{5\pi}{6}, \frac{7\pi}{6}, \frac{11\pi}{6} \left(\text{for } \cos x = \frac{1}{2}\right)$$

$$\Rightarrow x = \frac{\pi}{3}, \frac{2\pi}{3}, \frac{4\pi}{3}, \frac{5\pi}{3} \left(\text{for } \cos x = \frac{-1}{2}\right)$$

Hence, number of solutions = 8

4. (a) $y = K \cdot e^{Kx}$ cuts the Y-axis at $x = 0$

$$\frac{dy}{dx} = K^2 e^{Kx}$$

$$\therefore \left(\frac{dy}{dx}\right)_{x=0} = K^2$$

$\alpha = \tan^{-1}(K^2)$ this is angle made by X-axis,

Angle made by Y-axis

$$= \frac{\pi}{2} - \tan^{-1}(K^2) = \cot^{-1}(K^2)$$

5. (b) $\therefore$ Area of triangle $= \frac{1}{2} \times$ base $\times$ height

$$\Delta = \left(\frac{1}{2} \times \frac{1}{2} \times 2\right) + \left(\frac{1}{2} \times \frac{1}{4} \times 4\right) + \left(\frac{1}{2} \times \frac{1}{8} \times 6\right) + ... \infty$$

$$= \frac{1}{2}\left(\frac{1}{2} \times 2 + \frac{1}{2^2} \times 4 + \frac{1}{2^3} \times 6 + ... \infty\right)$$

$$= \frac{A}{2} \quad ...(i)$$

where, $A = \frac{1}{2} \times 2 + \frac{1}{2^2} \times 4 + \frac{1}{2^3} \times 6 + ... + \infty$ ... (ii)

which is an AGP, where first term = 2

Common difference = 2

Common ratio $= \frac{1}{2}$

Then, $\frac{A}{2} = 0 + \frac{1}{2^2} \times 2 + \frac{1}{2^3} \times 4 + \frac{1}{2^4} \times 6 + ... \infty$ ... (iii)

Subtracting Eqs. (ii) and (iii), we get

$$\frac{A}{2}=\frac{1}{2}\times 2+\frac{1}{2^2}\times 2+\frac{1}{2^3}\times 2+\ldots\infty$$

$$\Rightarrow \Delta=2\left(\frac{1}{2}+\frac{1}{2^2}+\frac{1}{2^3}+\ldots\infty\right)$$ [using Eq. (i)]

$$=2\times\frac{\frac{1}{2}}{1-\frac{1}{2}}$$

[∵ Sum of infinite term of GP, $S_\infty=\frac{a}{1-r}$]

$$=2\times 1=2$$

∴ $\Delta=2$ sq units

6. (c) t_{r+1} of $\left(\frac{3x^2}{2}-\frac{1}{3x}\right)^9={}^9C_r\left(\frac{3}{2}x^2\right)^r\left(\frac{-1}{3x}\right)^{9-r}$

$$={}^9C_r\left(\frac{3}{2}\right)^r\left(\frac{-1}{3}\right)^{9-r}\cdot x^{3r-9}$$

t_{r+1} is independent of x, if $3r-9=0$.

$\Rightarrow$ $r=3$

For $r=3$,

$${}^9C_r\left(\frac{3}{2}\right)^r\left(\frac{-1}{3}\right)^{9-r}={}^9C_3\left(\frac{3}{2}\right)^3\left(\frac{-1}{3}\right)^{9-3}=\frac{7}{18}$$

t_{r+1} contains $\frac{1}{x^3}$, if $3r-9=-3$

$\Rightarrow$ $r=2$

For $r=2$, ${}^9C_r\left(\frac{3}{2}\right)^r\left(\frac{-1}{3}\right)^{9-r}$

$$={}^9C_2\left(\frac{3}{2}\right)^2\left(\frac{-1}{3}\right)^7=\frac{-1}{27}$$

∴ Coefficient of the term independent of x in the given expression

$$=\frac{-2}{27}+\frac{7}{18}=\frac{-4+21}{54}=\frac{17}{54}$$

7. (d) RHL $=\lim_{x\to 0^+}f(x)=\lim_{x\to 0^+}\frac{\tan^2\{x\}}{(x^2-[x]^2)}$

$$=\lim_{x\to 0^+}\frac{\tan^2 x}{x^2}$$

[∵ $x\to 0^+$, then $[x]=0$ and $\{x\}=x$]

$$=\lim_{x\to 0^+}\left(\frac{\tan x}{x}\right)^2=1$$

LHL $=\lim_{x\to 0^-}f(x)=\lim_{x\to 0^-}\sqrt{\{x\}\cot\{x\}}$

[∵ $x\to 0^-$, then $[x]=-1$ and $\{x\}=x-[x]\Rightarrow\{x\}=x+1$, so $\{x\}=1$ when $x\to 0^-$]

$$=\sqrt{1\cdot\cot 1}=\sqrt{\cot 1}$$

Also,

$$\cot^{-1}\left[\lim_{x\to 0^-}f(x)\right]^2=\cot^{-1}(\cot 1)=1$$

and $\tan^{-1}\left[\lim_{x\to 0^+}f(x)\right]=\tan^{-1}1=\frac{\pi}{4}$

∵ LHL $\neq$ RHL

∴ $\lim_{x\to 0}f(x)$ does not exist.

8. (b) The straight lines l_1, l_2, l_3 are parallel and i.e. in the same plane

Total number of points $=m+n+k$

Total number of triangles formed with vertices $={}^{m+n+k}C_3$.

By joining three given points on the same line we don't obtain a triangle.

Therefore, the maximum number of triangles

$$={}^{m+n+k}C_3-{}^mC_3-{}^nC_3-{}^kC_3$$

9. (b) We have,

$$A=\begin{bmatrix}x & x\\ x & x\end{bmatrix}\Rightarrow A^2=\begin{bmatrix}2x^2 & 2x^2\\ 2x^2 & 2x^2\end{bmatrix}$$

and $A^3=\begin{bmatrix}2^2x^3 & 2^2x^3\\ 2^2x^3 & 2^2x^3\end{bmatrix}$ and so on

$$e^A=I+A+\frac{A^2}{2!}+\ldots$$

$$=\begin{bmatrix}1+x+\frac{2x^2}{2!}+\frac{2^2x^3}{3!}+\ldots & x+\frac{2x^2}{2!}+\frac{2^2x^3}{3!}+\ldots\\ x+\frac{2x^2}{2!}+\frac{2^2x^3}{3!}+\ldots & 1+x+\frac{2x^2}{2!}+\frac{2^2x^3}{3!}+\ldots\end{bmatrix}$$

$$=\begin{bmatrix}\frac{1}{2}\left(1+2x+\frac{(2x)^2}{2}+\ldots\right)+\frac{1}{2} & \frac{1}{2}\left(1+2x+\frac{(2x)^2}{2!}+\ldots\right)-\frac{1}{2}\\ \frac{1}{2}\left(1+2x+\frac{(2x)^2}{2!}+\ldots\right)-\frac{1}{2} & \frac{1}{2}\left(1+2x+\frac{(2x)^2}{2!}+\ldots\right)+\frac{1}{2}\end{bmatrix}$$

$$=\frac{1}{2}\begin{bmatrix}e^{2x}+1 & e^{2x}-1\\ e^{2x}-1 & e^{2x}+1\end{bmatrix}$$

$\Rightarrow f(x)=e^{2x}+1$ and $g(x)=e^{2x}-1$

Now, $\int\frac{f(x)}{\sqrt{g(x)}}dx=\int\frac{e^{2x}+1}{\sqrt{e^{2x}-1}}dx$

$$=\int\frac{e^{2x}}{\sqrt{e^{2x}-1}}dx+\int\frac{1}{\sqrt{e^{2x}-1}}dx$$

$$=\frac{1}{2}\int\frac{2\cdot e^{2x}}{\sqrt{e^{2x}-1}}dx+\int\frac{e^x}{e^x\sqrt{(e^x)^2-1}}dx$$

$$=\frac{1}{2}\cdot 2\sqrt{e^{2x}-1}+\int\frac{d(e^x)}{e^x\sqrt{(e^x)^2-1}}$$

$$=\sqrt{e^{2x}-1}+\sec^{-1}(e^x)+C$$

10. (a) Since, the rotation of axes does not affect the distance between the origin and the point, we have

$$4p^2+1=(p+1)^2+1$$

$\Rightarrow$ $p+1=\pm 2p$

$\Rightarrow$ $p=1$ or $p=\frac{-1}{3}$

11. (c) **Method (1)**

Given, $x+y=2$ ...(i)

$3x-4y=6$ ...(ii)

$x-y=0$ ...(iii)

Solving Eqs. (i), (ii) and (iii), we obtain vertices of triangle as (2, 0), (1, 1) and (–6, –6).

An equation of circle through (2, 0) and (1, 1) is

$$(x-2)(x-1)+(y-0)(y-1)+\lambda\begin{vmatrix}x & y & 1\\ 2 & 0 & 1\\ 1 & 1 & 1\end{vmatrix}=0$$

As it passes through (–6, –6), we get

$$(-6-2)(-6-1)+(-6-0)(-6-1)+\lambda\begin{vmatrix}-6 & -6 & 1\\ 2 & 0 & 1\\ 1 & 1 & 1\end{vmatrix}=0$$

$\Rightarrow$ $56+42+\lambda(14)=0$

$\Rightarrow$ $\lambda=-7$

Thus, equation of required circle is

$$(x^2-3x+2)+(y^2-y)-7[-x-y+2]=0$$

$$\Rightarrow x^2+y^2+4x+6y-12=0$$

Method (2)

Equation of any curve through intersection of three given lines is

$$(x+y-2)(3x-4y-6)+\alpha(3x-4y-6)(x-y)+\beta(x-y)(x+y-2)=0$$

It will represent a circle, if coefficient of x^2 – coefficient of $y^2=0$ and coefficient of $xy=0$.

i.e. $(3+3\alpha+\beta)-(-4+4\alpha-\beta)=0$

and $(-1)+\alpha(-7)+\beta(0)=0$

$\Rightarrow$ $7-\alpha+2\beta=0$ and $7\alpha=-1$

$\Rightarrow$ $\alpha=\frac{-1}{7}$ and $\beta=\frac{-25}{7}$

∴ Equation of required circle is

$$x^2(3+3\alpha+\beta)+y^2(-4+4\alpha-\beta)+x(-6-6-6\alpha-2\beta)+y(8-6+6\alpha+2\beta)+12=0$$

$$\Rightarrow -x^2-y^2-4x-6y+12=0$$

$$\Rightarrow x^2+y^2+4x+6y-12=0$$

12. (a) Let the number of red and blue balls be r and b, respectively.

Then, the probability of drawing two red balls is

$$p_1 = \frac{^rC_2}{^{r+b}C_2} = \frac{r(r-1)}{(r+b)(r+b-1)}$$

The probability of drawing two blue ball is

$$p_2 = \frac{^bC_2}{^{r+b}C_2} = \frac{b(b-1)}{(r+b)(r+b-1)}$$

The probability of drawing one red and one blue ball is

$$p_3 = \frac{^rC_1 \times {^bC_1}}{^{r+b}C_2} = \frac{2br}{(r+b)(r+b-1)}$$

By hypothesis, $p_1 = 5p_2$ and $p_3 = 6p_2$

$\Rightarrow r(r-1) = 5b(b-1)$ and

$2br = 6b(b-1)$

After solving these two equations, we get

$$r = 6,\ b = 3$$

13. (c) The given lines are $y + 2x = 3$ and $y + 2x = 5$ which are parallel.

Equation of any line through $P(2,3)$ is

$$\frac{x-2}{\cos\theta} = \frac{y-3}{\sin\theta} = r$$

Since, this line makes an intercept of 2 between the given lines

if $(2 + r\cos\theta, 3 + r\sin\theta)$ lies on $y + 2x = 3$,

then $(2 + (r+2)\cos\theta, 3 + (r+2)\sin\theta)$ lies on $y + 2x = 5$

$\Rightarrow 3 + r\sin\theta + 2(2 + r\cos\theta) = 3$ and

$3 + (r+2)\sin\theta + 2(2 + (r+2)\cos\theta) = 5$

Subtracting, we get

$$2\sin\theta + 4\cos\theta = 2$$

$\Rightarrow \quad \sin\theta + 2\cos\theta = 1$

$\Rightarrow \quad 4\cos^2\theta = (1 - \sin\theta)^2$

$\Rightarrow (1 - \sin\theta)[4 + 4\sin\theta - 1 + \sin\theta] = 0$

$\Rightarrow \quad \sin\theta = 1$ or $\sin\theta = \frac{-3}{5}$

Now, if $\sin\theta = \frac{-3}{5}$, $\cos\theta = \frac{4}{5}$ and the equation of the required line is

$$\frac{5(x-2)}{4} = \frac{5(y-3)}{-3} \Rightarrow 3x + 4y = 18$$

and if $\sin\theta = 1$, $\cos\theta = 0$ and the required line is $x - 2 = 0$.

14. (c) The numbers are $a, 2a, 3a \ldots, 50a$

The median of these numbers is

$$\frac{25a + 26a}{2} = 25.5a$$

$\therefore$ Mean deviation about median

$$= \frac{|a - 25.5a| + |2a - 25.5a| + \ldots + |-0.5a| + |0.5a| + \ldots + |50a - 25.5a|}{50}$$

$$= \frac{|a|}{25}(0.5 + 1.5 + 2.5 + \ldots + 24.5)$$

$$= \frac{|a|}{25} \times \frac{25}{2}(0.5 + 24.5) = \frac{25|a|}{2}$$

$\therefore \quad 50 = \frac{25|a|}{2} \Rightarrow |a| = 4$

15. (a) Since, $f(x)$ is differentiable in $[0, 4]$.

Using LMVT,

$$f'(b) = \frac{f(4) - f(0)}{4 - 0}, b \in (0, 4) \quad \ldots(i)$$

Now, $[f(4)]^2 - [f(0)]^2 = \frac{4[f(4) - f(0)]}{4}[f(4) + f(0)]$

$$= 4f'(b)[f(4) + f(0)] \quad \ldots(ii)$$

Also, from IMVT (Intermediate Mean value theorem);

$$\frac{f(4) + f(0)}{2} = f(a) \text{ for } a \in (0, 4)$$

Hence, from Eq. (ii),

$$[f(4)]^2 - [f(0)]^2 = 8f'(b)f(a)$$

16. (d)

$$\Delta = \begin{vmatrix} 1 + 2ax + a^2x^2 & 1 + 2ay + a^2y^2 & 1 + 2az + a^2z^2 \\ 1 + 2bx + b^2x^2 & 1 + 2by + b^2y^2 & 1 + 2bz + b^2z^2 \\ 1 + 2cx + c^2x^2 & 1 + 2cy + c^2y^2 & 1 + 2cz + c^2z^2 \end{vmatrix}$$

$$= \begin{vmatrix} 1 & 2a & a^2 \\ 1 & 2b & b^2 \\ 1 & 2c & c^2 \end{vmatrix} \begin{vmatrix} 1 & 1 & 1 \\ x & y & z \\ x^2 & y^2 & z^2 \end{vmatrix}$$

$$= 2(a-b)(b-c)(c-a)(x-y)(y-z)(z-x)$$

17. (c) $\because \ 2x + 2y = 4L$

$\Rightarrow \quad x + y = 2L \quad \ldots(i)$

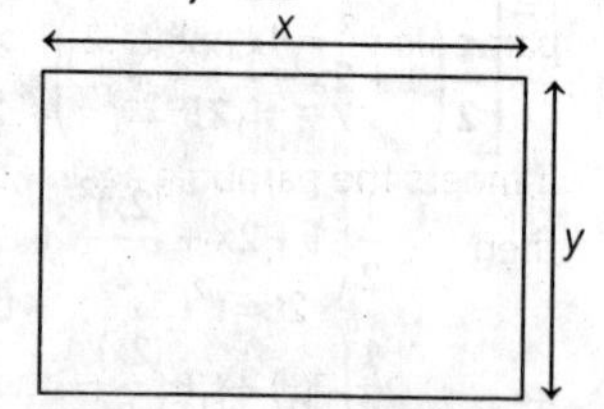

$\therefore$ The area of the rectangle $= xy$

$= x(2L - x)$ [from Eq. (i)]

But given, $\quad x(2L - x) \le \frac{L^2}{4}$

$\Rightarrow \quad x^2 - 2Lx + \frac{L^2}{4} \ge 0$

$\Rightarrow \quad (x - L)^2 - L^2 + \frac{L^2}{4} \ge 0$

$\Rightarrow (x - L)^2 - \left(\frac{L\sqrt{3}}{2}\right)^2 \ge 0$

$\Rightarrow \left(x - L + \frac{L\sqrt{3}}{2}\right)\left(x - L - \frac{L\sqrt{3}}{2}\right) \ge 0$

$\Rightarrow \left\{x - \left(\frac{2-\sqrt{3}}{2}\right)L\right\}\left\{x - \left(\frac{2+\sqrt{3}}{2}\right)L\right\} \ge 0$

$\therefore x \in \left[0, \left(\frac{2-\sqrt{3}}{2}\right)L\right] \cup \left[\left(\frac{2+\sqrt{3}}{2}\right)L, 2L\right]$

Now, x takes values in the interval $[0, 2L]$.

$\therefore$ Required probability

$$= \frac{\int_0^{\left(\frac{2-\sqrt{3}}{2}\right)} dx + \int_{\left(\frac{2+\sqrt{3}}{2}\right)}^{2L} dx}{\int_0^{2L} dx}$$

$$= \frac{\left(\frac{2-\sqrt{3}}{2}\right)L + 2L - \left(\frac{2+\sqrt{3}}{2}\right)L}{2L - 0}$$

$$= \frac{2L - \sqrt{3}L}{2L} = \frac{2 - \sqrt{3}}{2}$$

18. (b) Let θ be the angle which the line makes with X-axis, then

$$3\cos^2\theta = 1 \text{ or } \cos\theta = \pm\frac{1}{\sqrt{3}}$$

Thus, the direction cosines are equal.

Hence, the equation of the line is

$$\frac{x-2}{1} = \frac{y+3}{1} = \frac{z-5}{1} \quad \ldots(i)$$

P (1,–2, 3)

Q

(r+2, r–3, r+5)

$\frac{x-2}{1} = \frac{y+3}{1} = \frac{z-5}{1}$

Any point Q on this line has coordinates $(r+2, r-3, r+5)$.

If P is $(1, -2, 3)$, then direction ratios of PQ are $r+1, r-1, r+2$.

Choose Q such that PQ is perpendicular to the line (i).

So, $1 \times (r+1) + 1(r-1) + 1(r+2) = 0$

$\Rightarrow \quad r = \frac{-2}{3}$

Foot of the perpendicular is $\left(\frac{4}{3}, \frac{-11}{3}, \frac{13}{3}\right)$ and

$$PQ = \sqrt{\left(\frac{4}{3} - 1\right)^2 + \left(\frac{-11}{3} + 2\right)^2 + \left(3 - \frac{13}{3}\right)^2}$$

$$= \frac{1}{3}\sqrt{1 + 25 + 16} = \sqrt{\frac{14}{3}} \text{ units}$$

19. (a) $[(p \vee q) \wedge \sim p] \to q$

$\equiv [(p \wedge \sim p) \vee (q \wedge \sim p)] \to q$ (Distributive law)

$\equiv [F \vee (q \wedge \sim p)] \to q$ (Complement law)

$\equiv (q \wedge \sim p) \to q$ (Identity law)

$\equiv \sim (q \wedge \sim p) \vee q$ (Conditional law)

$\equiv [(\sim q \vee \sim (\sim p)] \vee q$ (Negation of conjunction)

$\equiv (\sim q \vee p) \vee q$ (commutative law)

$\equiv (p \vee \sim q) \vee q$ (Associative law)

$\equiv p \vee T$ (Complement law)

$\equiv T$ (Identity law)

Since, the truth value of the given statement pattern is T, therefore it is a tautology.

20. (b) Continuous in (0, 2) and differentiable in $(0, 1) \cup (1, 2)$.

Given, $f(x) = x^3 - x^2 + x + 1$

$\therefore \quad f(t) = t^3 - t^2 + t + 1$

$\Rightarrow \quad f'(t) = 3t^2 - 2t + 1$

Discriminant of $f'(t)$

$= (-2)^2 - 4 \times 3 \times 1 = -8 < 0$

and coefficient of $t^2 = 3 > 0$

Hence, $f'(t) > 0$ for all real t.

$\Rightarrow f(t)$ is strictly increasing.

Thus, $f(t)$ is maximum when t is maximum and $t_{max} = x \quad (\because 0 \le t \le x)$

$\therefore \max f(t) = f(x)$

$$\Rightarrow g(x) = \begin{cases} x^3 - x^2 + x + 1, & 0 \le x \le 1 \\ 3 - x, & 1 < x \le 2 \end{cases}$$

Now, it can be easily seen that $f(x)$ is continuous in (0, 2) and differentiable in (0, 2) except at $x = 1$ because at $x = 1$, LHD > 0, while RHD $= -1 < 0$

21. (2) Given, $f(x) = f(3x - 4y) + f(4y - 2x) - (3x - 4y)(4y - 2x)$

$\Rightarrow f((3x - 4y) + (4y - 2x)) = f(3x - 4y) + f(4y - 2x) - (3x - 4y)(4y - 2x)$

$\Rightarrow f(x + y) = f(x) + f(y) - xy \quad$ ...(i)

Now, $f'(2) = \lim_{h \to 0} \dfrac{f(2 + h) - f(2)}{h}$

$= \lim_{h \to 0} \dfrac{f(2) + f(h) - 2h - f(2)}{h}$ [using Eq. (i)]

$= \lim_{h \to 0} \dfrac{f(h) - 2h}{h}$

$= \lim_{h \to 0} \dfrac{f(h)}{h} - \lim_{h \to 0} \dfrac{2h}{h}$

$= 4 - 2 = 2$

22. (1) Given, $x + 8y + 7z = 0 \quad$ ...(i)

$9x + 2y + 3z = 0 \quad$ ...(ii)

$x + y + z = 0 \quad$ ...(iii)

From Eqs. (ii) and (iii), we get

$y = 6x$

Let $\quad x = K \Rightarrow y = 6K$

From Eq. (i), $K + 8(6K) + 7z = 0$

$\Rightarrow \quad z = -7K$

According to the given condition,

$a = K, b = 6K, c = -7K$

(a, b, c) lies on $x + 2y + z = 6$

$\Rightarrow \quad K + 2(6K) + (-7K) = 6 \Rightarrow K = 1$

$\therefore \quad a = 1, b = 6, c = -7$

Hence, $2a + b + c = 2 + 6 - 7 = 1$

23. (12) Given, $(\mathbf{c} - \mathbf{a}) \cdot (\mathbf{b} - \mathbf{c}) = 0$

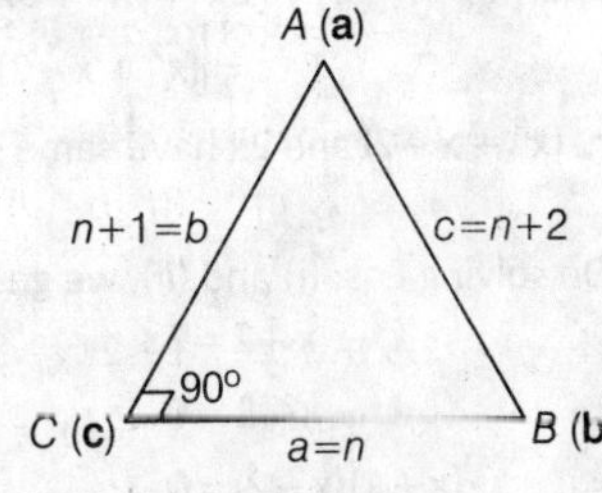

$\Rightarrow \quad \angle C = 90°$

$\therefore \quad a^2 + b^2 = c^2$

$\Rightarrow \quad (n + 2)^2 = n^2 + (n + 1)^2$

$\Rightarrow n^2 + 4 + 2n = n^2 + n^2 + 1 + 2n$

$\Rightarrow \quad n^2 = 3 \Rightarrow n = \pm 3$

But $n = -3$ (not acceptable)

$\therefore \quad n = 3$, then $a = 3$, $b = 4$, $c = 5$

Hence, $\quad \Delta = \dfrac{1}{2} \times 3 \times 4 = 6$

So, $|\mathbf{a} \times \mathbf{b} + \mathbf{b} \times \mathbf{c} + \mathbf{c} \times \mathbf{a}|$

$= 2\Delta = 2 \times 6 = 12$

24. (4) An equation of normal to the parabola $y^2 = 4x$ at $P(t_1^2, 2t_1)$ is

$y = -t_1 x + 2t_1 + t_1^3$

If meets the parabola again at $(t^2, 2t)$, then

$2t = t^2 t_1 + 2t_1 + t_1^3$

$\Rightarrow \quad 2(t - t_1) = t_1(t_1^2 - t^2)$

$\Rightarrow \quad 2 = -t_1(t + t_1)$

$\Rightarrow \quad t = -t_1 - \dfrac{2}{t_1}$

Similarly, if the normal at $Q(t_2^2, 2t_2)$ meets the parabola at $(t^2, 2t)$, then

$t = -t_2 - \dfrac{2}{t_2}$

If normals of P and Q meet at the same point on the parabola, then

$-t_1 - \dfrac{2}{t_1} = -t_2 - \dfrac{2}{t_2}$

$\Rightarrow \quad t_2 - t_1 = 2\left(\dfrac{1}{t_1} - \dfrac{1}{t_2}\right)$

$\Rightarrow \quad t_1 t_2 = 2$

As, $\quad t_1^2 + t_2^2 = a + 4 - a = 4$

$(y_1 + y_2)^2 = 4(t_1 + t_2)^2$

$= 4(t_1^2 + t_2^2 + 2t_1 t_2) = 32$

$\Rightarrow \quad |y_1 + y_2| = 4\sqrt{2}$

$\therefore \dfrac{1}{\sqrt{2}} |y_1 + y_2| = 4$

25. (1) We have,

$\cos y \left(\dfrac{dy}{dx} + e^{-x}\right) + \sin y \left(e^{-x} - \dfrac{dy}{dx}\right) = e^{e^{-x}}$

$\Rightarrow (\cos y - \sin y)\dfrac{dy}{dx} + (\cos y + \sin y)e^{-x} = e^{e^{-x}} \quad$ ...(i)

Let $\quad \cos y + \sin y = z$

$\Rightarrow \quad (\cos y - \sin y)\dfrac{dy}{dx} = \dfrac{dz}{dx}$

$\therefore$ Eq. (i) reduces to $\dfrac{dz}{dx} + e^{-x} \cdot z = e^{e^{-x}}$,

which is linear differential equation whose integrating factor (IF)

$= e^{\int e^{-x} dx} = e^{-e^{-x}}$

and solution is

$z \times (\text{IF}) = \int e^{e^{-x}} \times (\text{IF})\, dx$

$\Rightarrow \quad z \cdot e^{-e^{-x}} = \int e^{e^{-x}} e^{-e^{-x}} dx$

$\Rightarrow \quad z \cdot e^{-e^{-x}} = \int e^{(e^{-x} - e^{-x})} dx$

$\Rightarrow \quad \int e^{o} dx = \int dx = x + c$

$\Rightarrow \quad (\cos y + \sin y) e^{-e^{-x}} = x + c \quad$ ...(ii)

But Eq. (ii) passes through $\left(0, \dfrac{-\pi}{4}\right)$.

So, $\quad c = 0$

$\Rightarrow \quad (\cos y + \sin y) e^{-e^{-x}} = x \quad$ ...(iii)

Putting $(t, 0)$ i.e. $x = t$ and $y = 0$, in Eq. (iii), we get

$e^{-e^{-t}} = t$

$\Rightarrow \quad \dfrac{t}{e^{-e^{-t}}} = 1$

$\Rightarrow \quad t \cdot e^{e^{-t}} = 1$

$\Rightarrow \quad \left|t \cdot e^{e^{-t}}\right| = |1| = 1$

26. (0) For idempotent matrix,

$A^2 = A$

$\Rightarrow \quad A^{-1}A^2 = A^{-1}A$

($\because A$ is non-singular)

$\Rightarrow \quad A = I$

Thus, non-singular idempotent matrix is always a unit matrix.

$\therefore \quad l^2-3=1 \Rightarrow l=\pm 2$

$\Rightarrow \quad m^2-8=1 \Rightarrow m=\pm 3$

$\Rightarrow \quad n^2-15=1 \Rightarrow n=\pm 4$

and $\quad p=q=r=0$

Hence, the required sum $=0$

27. (14) $\int_0^x f(t)\,dt+\int_0^x t\cdot f(x-t)\,dt=e^{-x}-1$

$\Rightarrow \int_0^x f(t)\,dt+\int_0^x (x-t)f(t)\,dt=e^{-x}-1$

$\Rightarrow \int_0^x f(t)\,dt+x\int_0^x f(t)\,dt-\int_0^x t\cdot f(t)\,dt$
$=e^{-x}-1$

Differentiating w.r.t. x, we get

$f(x)+xf(x)+\int_0^x f(t)\,dt-xf(x)=-e^{-x}$ ...(i)

$\Rightarrow \quad f(x)+\int_0^x f(t)\,dt=-e^{-x}$

Again differentiating w.r.t. x, we get

$f'(x)+f(x)=e^{-x}$

$\Rightarrow e^x f'(x)+e^x f(x)=1$

$\Rightarrow \quad (e^x f(x))'=1$

$\Rightarrow \quad e^x f(x)=x+c$ [on integrating]

From Eq. (i), $f(0)=-1$

$\therefore \quad c=-1$

$\therefore \quad f(x)\cdot e^x=x-1$

Hence, $e^{15}f(15)=14$

28. (41) Since, $-2\le \sin x-\sqrt{3}\cos x\le 2$, we have

$$-2\le \frac{4m-6}{4-m}\le 2$$

$$\Rightarrow \quad -1\le \frac{2m-3}{4-m}\le 1$$

If $\frac{2m-3}{4-m}\le 1$, we have

$$\frac{(2m-3)-(4-m)}{4-m}\le 0$$

or $\quad \frac{3m-7}{m-4}\ge 0 \quad$ ...(i)

Also, $\quad -1\le \frac{2m-3}{4-m}$

$\Rightarrow \quad \frac{m+1}{m-4}\le 0 \quad$ ...(ii)

From Eqs. (i) and (ii), we get

$$m\in\left[-1,\frac{7}{3}\right]$$

Hence, possible integers are $-1,0,1,2$

Therefore, number of integral values of $m=4$

29. (2.33)

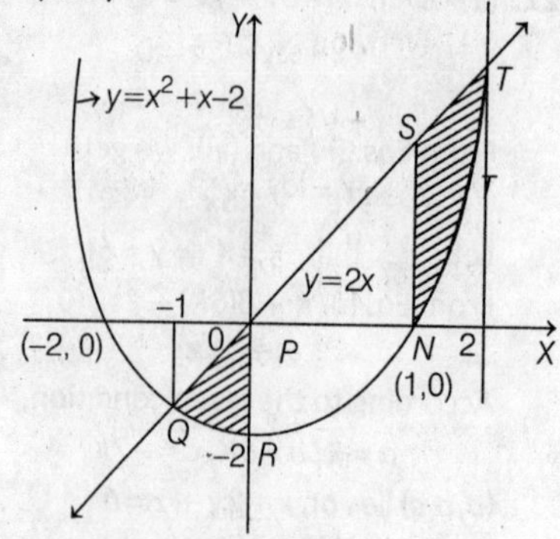

Given equation of curves are

$y=x^2+x-2$ ...(i)

and $\quad y=2x$ ...(ii)

and $|x^2+x-2|+|2x|=|x^2+3x-2|$
$=|(x^2+x-2)+2x|$

$\therefore$ (x^2+x-2) and $2x$ have same sign. ...(A)

On solving Eqs. (i) and (ii), we get

$x^2+x-2=2x$

$\Rightarrow \quad x^2-x-2=0$

$\Rightarrow \quad (x+1)(x-2)=0$

$\Rightarrow \quad x=-1,2$

From figure,

For $-1\le x<0$; $y=x^2+x-2<0$

and $\;y=2x<0$

For $0\le x<1$; $y=x^2+x-2<0$

and $y=2x\ge 0$

For $1\le x<2$; $y=x^2+x-2\ge 0$

and $y=2x>0$

Thus, $-1\le x<0$ and $1\le x<2$ are acceptable but $0\le x<1$ rejected because of statement (*A*).

$\therefore$Required area $=$ Shaded region

$=$ Area of $PQR+$ Area of SNT

$$=\int_{-1}^{0}[2x-(x^2+x-2)]\,dx+\int_1^2[2x-(x^2+x-2)]\,dx$$

$$=\left[\frac{x^2}{2}-\frac{x^3}{3}+2x\right]_{-1}^{0}+\left[\frac{x^2}{2}-\frac{x^3}{3}+2x\right]_{1}^{2}$$

$$=\frac{7}{6}+\left[\frac{10}{3}-\frac{13}{6}\right]=\frac{7}{6}+\frac{7}{6}=\frac{7}{3}=2.33$$

30. (8) Let equation of ellipse E be

$$\frac{x^2}{a^2}+\frac{y^2}{b^2}=1$$

As it passes through $(3,-1)$

Then $\quad \frac{9}{a^2}+\frac{1}{b^2}=1$

$\Rightarrow \quad 9b^2+a^2=a^2b^2$ ...(i)

As $y=-x+2\sqrt{5}$ is a tangent to E.

Then, $(2\sqrt{5})^2=a^2(-1)^2+b^2$

$\Rightarrow \quad a^2+b^2=20$ ...(ii)

From Eqs. (i) and (ii), we get

$a^2=18,10$

For $a^2=10$, then $b^2=10$ and hence E becomes a circle.

So, $a^2=10$ (Rejected)

Thus, $a^2=18$, then $b^2=2$

Now, $b^2=a^2(1-e^2)$

$\Rightarrow 18e^2=16\Rightarrow 9e^2=8$

Knockout 8

1. (a) Given, f is differentiable at $x=0$

So $\quad f'(0^-)=f'(0^+)=f'(0)$ ...(i)

$\therefore \lim\limits_{h\to 0}\frac{f(h)-f(-2h)}{h}$

$=\lim\limits_{h\to 0}\frac{f(h)-f(0)-[f(-2h)-f(0)]}{h}$

$=\lim\limits_{h\to 0}\frac{f(h)-f(0)}{h}+\lim\limits_{h\to 0}\frac{2[f(-2h)-f(0)]}{-2h}$

$=f'(0^+)+2f'(0^-)$

$=f'(0)+2f'(0)=3\cdot f'(0)$ [from Eq. (i)]

$=3\times 1=3$

2. (b) Given, $\tan A,\tan B$ and $\tan C$ are in AP.

$\therefore \quad 2\tan B=\tan A+\tan C$ ...(i)

Also, $\Sigma\tan A=\Pi\tan A$ ...(ii)

From Eqs. (i) and (ii), we get

$2\tan B+\tan B=\tan A\cdot\tan B\cdot\tan C$

$\Rightarrow \tan A\cdot\tan C=3$

$\Rightarrow \quad \tan C=\frac{3}{K}$

[$\because \tan A=K$, given]

and $\quad 2\tan B=K+\frac{3}{K}=\frac{K^2+3}{K}$

[from Eq. (i)]

$\Rightarrow \quad \tan B=\frac{K^2+3}{2K}$

$\because \quad \tan A=K\Rightarrow \sin A=\frac{K}{\sqrt{1+K^2}}$

$\Rightarrow \quad \tan B=\frac{K^2+3}{2K}$

$\Rightarrow \quad \sin B=\frac{K^2+3}{\sqrt{(K^2+1)(K^2+9)}}$

$\Rightarrow \quad \tan C=\frac{3}{K}$

$\Rightarrow \quad \sin C=\frac{3}{\sqrt{K^2+9}}$

Hence, $\frac{\sin A\cdot\sin C}{\sin B}=\frac{3K}{K^2+3}$

3. (b) Given, curves are $y=\sqrt{4-x^2}$ ...(i)

$$y \geq \sqrt{2}\sin\left(\frac{\pi x}{2\sqrt{2}}\right) \quad ...(ii)$$

Curves Eqs. (i) and (ii) intersect at $x=\sqrt{2}$.

Area of the left of Y-axis π sq units and area of the right Y-axis

$$=\int_0^{\sqrt{2}}\left[\sqrt{4-x^2}-\sqrt{2}\sin\left(\frac{\pi x}{2\sqrt{2}}\right)\right]dx$$

$$=\left[\frac{x\sqrt{4-x^2}}{2}+\frac{4}{2}\sin^{-1}\frac{x}{2}\right]_0^{\sqrt{2}}+\frac{4}{\pi}\left[\cos\left(\frac{\pi x}{2\sqrt{2}}\right)\right]_0^{\sqrt{2}}$$

$$=\left(1+2\cdot\frac{\pi}{4}\right)+\frac{4}{\pi}(0-1)$$

$$=1+\frac{\pi}{2}-\frac{4}{\pi}=\frac{2\pi+\pi^2-8}{2\pi}$$

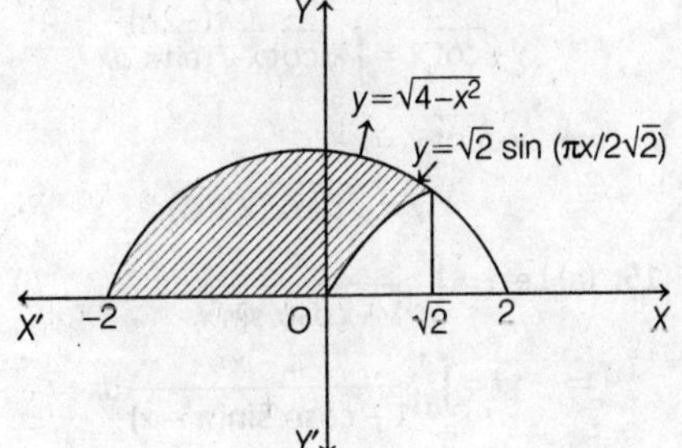

$\therefore$ Required ratio $=\dfrac{2\pi^2}{2\pi+\pi^2-8}$

4. (b) p, q, r are in AP

$\Rightarrow \quad 2q=p+r$ ... (i)

Given, condition : $p+1, q, r$ are in GP or $p, q, r+2$ are in GP

Therefore, $q^2=(p+1)r$ ... (ii)

or $\quad q^2=(r+2)p$ ... (iii)

From Eqs. (ii) and (iii),

$$(p+1)r=p(r+2)$$

$\Rightarrow \quad pr+r=pr+2p \Rightarrow r=2p$

From Eq. (ii), $q^2=(p+1)2p$

Also, from Eq. (i),

$$2q=p+2p=3p$$

$\Rightarrow \quad q=\frac{3}{2}p$

$\Rightarrow \frac{9}{4}p^2=(p+1)2p$

$\Rightarrow \quad \frac{9}{8}p=p+1$

$\Rightarrow \quad p=8, r=16$ and $q=12$

$\Rightarrow q-p=12-8=4$

5. (d) Given, $\log_{100}|x+y|=\frac{1}{2}$

$\Rightarrow \quad |x+y|=(100)^{1/2}=10$ ...(i)

and $\log_{10}y-\log_{10}|x|=\log_{100}4$

$\Rightarrow \log_{10}\left(\frac{y}{|x|}\right)=\log_{10^2}4=\frac{1}{2}\log_{10}4$

$=\log_{10}(4)^{1/2}=\log_{10}2$

$\Rightarrow \quad \frac{y}{|x|}=2 \Rightarrow y=2|x|$ ....(ii)

From Eqs. (i) and (ii),

$$|x+2|x||=10$$

If $x\geq 0$	If $x<0$
then $\|x+2x\|=10$	then $\|x-2x\|=10$
$\Rightarrow \|3x\|=10$	$\Rightarrow \|-x\|=10$
$\Rightarrow 3x=10$	$\Rightarrow -x=10$
$\Rightarrow x=\frac{10}{3}$	$\Rightarrow x=-10$
$\therefore y=\frac{20}{3}$	$\therefore y=20$

So, $(x,y)=\left(\frac{10}{3},\frac{20}{3}\right)$

or $(x,y)=(-10,20)$

6. (d) Given,

$$f(x)=\ln\left(\sqrt{\sqrt{x^2+1}+x}+\sqrt{\sqrt{x^2+1}-x}\right)$$

$$=\frac{1}{2}\ln\left[\sqrt{\sqrt{x^2+1}+x}+\sqrt{\sqrt{x^2+1}-x}\right]^2$$

$$=\frac{1}{2}\ln\left[\sqrt{x^2+1}+x+\sqrt{x^2+1}-x+2\sqrt{\sqrt{(x^2+1)^2}-x^2}\right]$$

$\Rightarrow \quad f(x)=\frac{1}{2}\ln\left[2\sqrt{x^2+1}+2\right]$

Also, $f(-x)=\frac{1}{2}\ln\left[2\sqrt{(-x)^2+1}+2\right]$

$$=\frac{1}{2}\ln\left[2\sqrt{x^2+1}+2\right]$$

Here, $f(x)-f(-x)=0$

So, $f(x)$ is an even function.

Hence, $f(x)$ is neither one-one nor onto.

7. (a) **Method (1)**

Given, $L_1: x+y-30=0$ ...(i)

$L_2: x-y+12=0$ ...(ii)

$L_3: x-3y-30=0$ ...(iii)

From figure, $O(0,0)$ and (a,a^2) lying on same side of each of the lines L_1, L_2 and L_3.

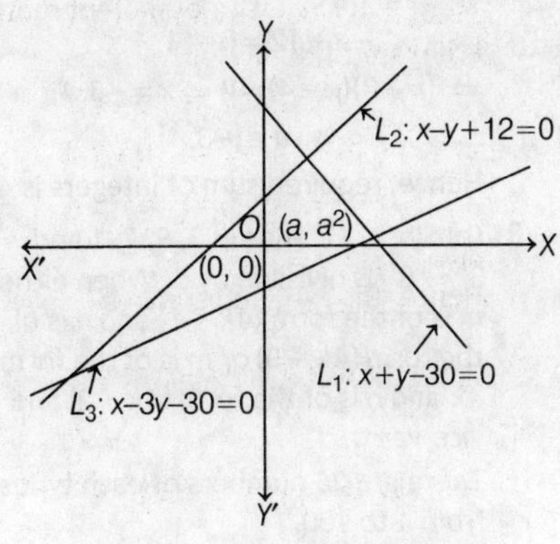

Now, putting $O(0, 0)$ in the LHS of L_1, then we get a negative number.

So, at (a,a^2), LHS of L_1 must be negative i.e. $a+a^2-30\leq 0$

(here equality hold because (a,a^2) may lie on the side of triangle)

$\Rightarrow \quad a^2+a-30\leq 0$

$\Rightarrow \quad (a+6)(a-5)\leq 0$

$\Rightarrow \quad a\in[-6,5]$ ...(iv)

Similar concept for line L_2 and L_3 apply

For $L_2: x-y+12=0$

At $\quad (a,a^2), a-a^2+12\geq 0$

$\Rightarrow \quad a^2-a-12\leq 0$

$\Rightarrow \quad (a+3)(a-4)\leq 0$

$\Rightarrow \quad a\in[-3,4]$ ...(v)

For $L_3: x-3y-30=0$

At $\quad (a,a^2), a-3a^2-30\leq 0$

$\Rightarrow \quad 3a^2-a+30\geq 0 \Rightarrow a\in R$ ...(vi)

(because coefficient of a^2 is positive and its discriminant is negative)

So, from Eqs. (iv), (v) and (vi), intersection value of a is $a\in[\ 3,4]$

i.e. integral values of $a=\{-3,-2,-1,0,1,2,3,4\}$

Hence, its sum $=-3-2-1+0+1+2+3+4=4$

Method (2)

Since, point (a,a^2) always lying on the parabola $y=x^2$.

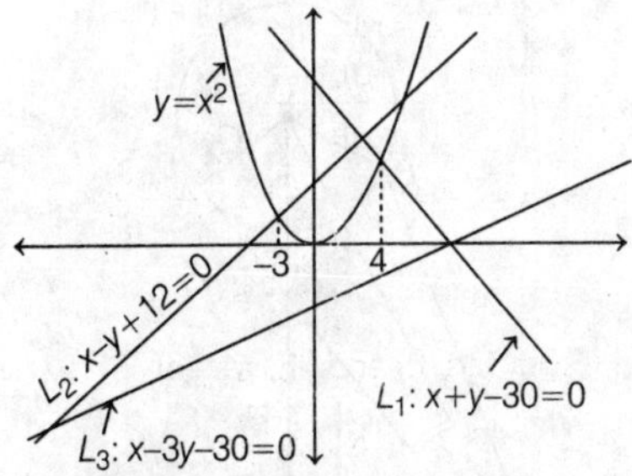

For point lying inside or on the triangle, solving equations $y=x^2$ and $y=x+12$, we get

$$x^2=x+12$$

$\Rightarrow \quad x^2 - x - 12 = 0$

$\Rightarrow (x+3)(x-4) = 0 \Rightarrow x = -3, 4$

$\therefore \quad a \in [-3, 4]$

Hence, required sum of integers is 4.

8. (b) Since, 3^m ends in 3, 9, 7, 1 and $3^m + 3^n$ is divisible by 5. When either m is of the form $(4k+1)$ and n is of the form $(4k+3)$ or m is of the form $4k$ and n is of the form $(4k+2)$ and *vice-versa*.

There are 25 numbers of each types from 1 to 100.

$\therefore$ Required probability

$$= \underset{\begin{pmatrix} m=4k \\ n=4k+2 \end{pmatrix}}{\frac{1}{4}\times\frac{1}{4}} + \underset{\begin{pmatrix} m=4k+2 \\ n=4k \end{pmatrix}}{\frac{1}{4}\times\frac{1}{4}} + \underset{\begin{pmatrix} m=4k+1 \\ n=4k+3 \end{pmatrix}}{\frac{1}{4}\times\frac{1}{4}} + \underset{\begin{pmatrix} m=4k+3 \\ n=4k+1 \end{pmatrix}}{\frac{1}{4}\times\frac{1}{4}}$$

$$= \frac{4}{16} = \frac{1}{4}$$

9. (c)

p	q	$\sim p$	$\sim q$	$(p \to q)$	$[(p \to q) \wedge \sim q]$	$[(p \to q) \wedge \sim q] \to (\sim p)$
T	T	F	F	T	F	T
T	F	F	T	F	F	T
F	T	T	F	T	F	T
F	F	T	T	T	T	T

All the entries in the last column of the above truth table is T.

So, $[(p \to q) \wedge \sim q] \to (\sim p)$ is tautology.

10. (b) Let C be the centre of the balloon and O be the position of the observer at the horizontal line OX.

Let OA and OB be the tangents to the balloon. It is given that $\angle AOB = \alpha$ and $\angle XOC = \beta$.

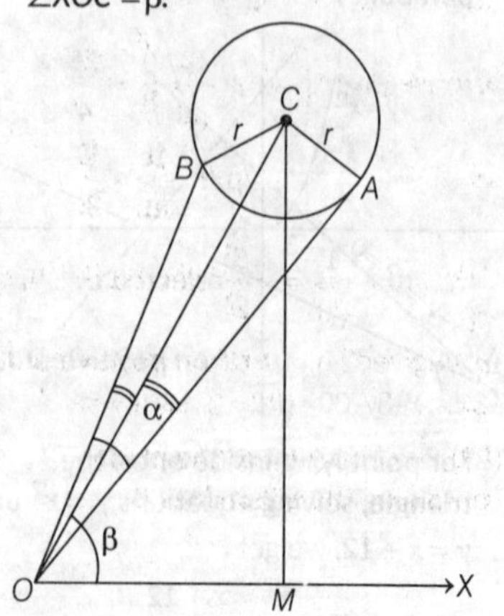

Let r be the radius of the balloon.

Then, $\quad CA = CB = r$

From figure, the right angled ΔOAC and ΔOBC are congruent.

$\therefore \quad \angle AOC = \angle BOC = \frac{\alpha}{2}$

In ΔAOC, we have

$$\sin\frac{\alpha}{2} = \frac{r}{OC}$$

$$\Rightarrow \quad OC = r\,\text{cosec}\frac{\alpha}{2} \quad \text{...(i)}$$

Let CM be perpendicular from C on OX.

In ΔOCM, we have

$$\sin\beta = \frac{CM}{OC}$$

$$\Rightarrow CM = OC \cdot \sin\beta = r\,\text{cosec}\frac{\alpha}{2}\sin\beta$$

[from Eq. (i)]

So, height of the centre of the balloon is $r\ \text{cosec}\frac{\alpha}{2}\sin\beta$.

11. (c) Number of different necklace

= number of ways by which we can put 5 identical balls in 3 different boxes

= {(5, 0, 0), (4, 1, 0), (3, 2, 0), (2, 2, 1), (3, 1, 1)}

= 5

12. (c) Since, $\sqrt{\frac{\Sigma x_i^2}{n}} \ge \frac{\Sigma x_i}{n}$

$$\therefore \quad \sqrt{\frac{400}{n}} \ge \frac{80}{n} \Rightarrow \frac{20}{\sqrt{n}} \ge \frac{80}{n}$$

$$\Rightarrow \quad \sqrt{n} \ge 4$$

[$\because n$ is positive, $\therefore \sqrt{n}$ = positive]

$$\Rightarrow \quad n \ge 16$$

$\therefore n = 18$ is possible value.

13. (d) As, $T_n = \cot^{-1}\left[\frac{(n+1)(n+2)x}{2} + \frac{2}{x}\right]$

$$= \cot^{-1}\left[\frac{(n+1)(n+2)x^2 + 4}{2x}\right]$$

$$= \tan^{-1}\left[\frac{2x}{4 + (n+1)(n+2)x^2}\right]$$

$$= \tan^{-1}\left[\frac{\left(\frac{n+2}{2}\right)x - \left(\frac{n+1}{2}\right)x}{1 + \left(\frac{n+2}{2}\right)\left(\frac{n+1}{2}\right)x^2}\right]$$

$$= \tan^{-1}\left[\left(\frac{n+2}{2}\right)x\right] - \tan^{-1}\left[\frac{(n+1)}{2}x\right]$$

$$\therefore S_n = \Sigma T_n = \tan^{-1}\left[\left(\frac{n+2}{2}\right)x\right] - \tan^{-1}(x)$$

$$\lim_{n\to\infty} S_n = \lim_{n\to\infty}\left[\tan^{-1}\left(\frac{n+2}{2}\right)x - \tan^{-1}x\right]$$

$$= \frac{\pi}{2} - \tan^{-1}x$$

$$\Rightarrow \quad 1 = \cot^{-1}x \quad \text{(given } \lim_{n\to\infty} S_n = 1\text{)}$$

$$\Rightarrow \quad x = \cot 1$$

14. (b) Given,

$$\sin 2x\left(\frac{dy}{dx} - \sqrt{\tan x}\right) - y = 0$$

$$\Rightarrow \quad \frac{dy}{dx} + \left(\frac{-1}{\sin 2x}\right)y = \sqrt{\tan x}$$

which is a linear differential equation.

$$\therefore \quad \text{IF} = e^{-\int \text{cosec}\,2x\,dx}$$

$$= e^{\frac{-1}{2}\log_e \tan x}$$

$$= \sqrt{\cot x}$$

Therefore, general solution is

$$y\sqrt{\cot x} = \int \sqrt{\cot x}\sqrt{\tan x}\,dx$$

$$\Rightarrow \quad y\sqrt{\cot x} = x + C$$

$$\Rightarrow \quad y = \sqrt{\tan x}(x + C)$$

15. (a) Let $I = \int_0^\pi \frac{x}{1 - \cos\alpha \sin x}dx \quad \text{...(i)}$

$$\Rightarrow \quad I = \int_0^\pi \frac{\pi - x}{1 - \cos\alpha \sin(\pi - x)}dx$$

$$\Rightarrow \quad I = \int_0^\pi \frac{\pi - x}{1 - \cos\alpha \sin x}dx \quad \text{...(ii)}$$

On adding Eqs. (i) and (ii), we get

$$2I = \int_0^\pi \frac{\pi}{1 - \cos\alpha \sin x}dx$$

$$= 2\pi \int_0^{\pi/2} \frac{dx}{1 - \cos\alpha \sin x}$$

$$\Rightarrow \quad I = \pi \int_0^1 \frac{2dt}{(1+t^2)\left(1 - \cos\alpha \frac{2t}{1+t^2}\right)}$$

$$\left[\begin{array}{l} \because \text{putting} \tan\frac{x}{2} = t \Rightarrow \frac{1}{2}\sec^2\frac{x}{2}dx = dt \\ \Rightarrow dx = \frac{2dt}{\sec^2\frac{x}{2}} = \frac{2dt}{1 + \tan^2\frac{x}{2}} = \frac{2dt}{1+t^2} \end{array}\right]$$

$$= 2\pi \int_0^1 \frac{dt}{t^2 + 1 - 2t\cos\alpha}$$

$$= 2\pi \int_0^1 \frac{dt}{(t - \cos\alpha)^2 + \sin^2\alpha}$$

$$= \frac{2\pi}{\sin\alpha}\tan^{-1}\left(\frac{t - \cos\alpha}{\sin\alpha}\right)\Bigg|_0^1$$

$$\left[\text{using} \int \frac{1}{x^2 + a^2}dx = \frac{1}{a}\tan^{-1}\frac{x}{a} + C\right]$$

$$=\frac{2\pi}{\sin\alpha}\left[\tan^{-1}\left(\frac{1-\cos\alpha}{\sin\alpha}\right)-\tan^{-1}\left(-\frac{\cos\alpha}{\sin\alpha}\right)\right]$$

$$=\frac{2\pi}{\sin\alpha}\left[\tan^{-1}\left(\frac{2\sin^2\alpha/2}{2\sin\alpha/2\cos\alpha/2}\right)-\tan^{-1}\left\{\tan\left(\frac{\pi}{2}-\alpha\right)\right\}\right]$$

$$\Rightarrow I=\frac{2\pi}{\sin\alpha}\left[\tan^{-1}\left(\tan\frac{\alpha}{2}\right)-\tan^{-1}\left(\tan\left(\frac{\pi}{2}-\alpha\right)\right)\right]$$

$$\Rightarrow I=\frac{2\pi}{\sin\alpha}\left[\frac{\alpha}{2}+\left(\frac{\pi}{2}-\alpha\right)\right]$$

$$=2\pi(\sin\alpha)^{-1}\times\frac{1}{2}[\pi-\alpha]$$

$$\Rightarrow I=\pi(\pi-\alpha)(\sin\alpha)^{-1}$$

16. (c) The maximum value of $\frac{f(\theta)}{\cos\theta+\sin\theta}$ is 1.

$$f(\theta)=\begin{vmatrix}\sin\theta & \cos\theta & \sin\theta\\ \cos\theta & \sin\theta & \cos\theta\\ 0 & 0 & \sin\theta-\cos\theta\end{vmatrix}$$

[applying $R_3\to R_3-R_2$]

$$\Rightarrow f(\theta)=(\sin\theta-\cos\theta)(\sin^2\theta-\cos^2\theta)$$

$$=(\sin\theta-\cos\theta)^2(\sin\theta+\cos\theta)$$

$$=(1-\sin2\theta)(\sin\theta+\cos\theta)$$

$\Rightarrow f(\theta)=0 \Rightarrow \sin2\theta=1$

or $\tan\theta=-1$

$$\Rightarrow \theta=\frac{\pi}{4},\frac{3\pi}{4}$$

Now,

$$\frac{f(\theta)}{1-\sin2\theta}=\frac{(1-\sin2\theta)(\sin\theta+\cos\theta)}{(1-\sin2\theta)}$$

$$=\sin\theta+\cos\theta$$

and the range of $\sin\theta+\cos\theta$ is $[-\sqrt{2},\sqrt{2}]$.

Also, $\frac{f(\theta)}{\cos\theta+\sin\theta}=1-\sin2\theta$ which has minimum value 0 and maximum value is 2.

17. (b) Centre of O lies on the line through the point $A(1,-1)$ and perpendicular to $2x+3y+1=0$ i.e. on $y+1=\frac{3}{2}(x-1)$

$$\Rightarrow \frac{x-1}{2}=\frac{y+1}{3}=\lambda \text{ (say)}$$

Let centre of O be $(2\lambda+1, 3\lambda-1)$

Then, equation of C is

$$[x-(2\lambda+1)]^2+[y-(3\lambda-1)]^2=(2\lambda)^2+(3\lambda)^2$$

$$\Rightarrow x^2+y^2-2(2\lambda+1)x-2(3\lambda-1)y-2\lambda+2=0 \quad ...(i)$$

Equation of circle C_1 is

$$(x-0)(x+2)+(y+1)(y-3)=0$$

$$\Rightarrow x^2+y^2+2x-2y-3=0 \quad ...(ii)$$

As, Eqs. (i) and (ii) cut orthogonally.

So, $-2(2\lambda+1)(1)-2(3\lambda-1)(-1)=-2\lambda+2-3$

$$\Rightarrow \lambda=\frac{3}{4}$$

Thus, required equation of circle is

$$x^2+y^2-5x-\left(\frac{5}{2}\right)y+\frac{1}{2}=0$$

18. (d) We have,

$$A_r={}^{10}C_r, B_r={}^{20}C_r \text{ and } C_r={}^{30}C_r$$

$$\therefore \sum_{r=1}^{10}A_r(B_{10}B_r-C_{10}A_r)$$

$$=B_{10}\sum_{r=1}^{10}A_rB_r-C_{10}\sum_{r=1}^{10}(A_r)^2$$

$$=B_{10}\left(\sum_{r=1}^{10}{}^{10}C_r\cdot{}^{20}C_r\right)-C_{10}\sum_{r=1}^{10}({}^{10}C_r)^2$$

$$=B_{10}\left(\sum_{r=0}^{10}{}^{10}C_r\cdot{}^{20}C_r-1\right)-C_{10}\times\left(\sum_{r=0}^{10}({}^{10}C_r)^2-1\right)$$

$$=B_{10}\times\{\text{coefficient of } x^{20} \text{ in } (1+x)^{10}(1+x)^{20}-1\}-C_{10}\times\{{}^{20}C_{10}-1\}$$

$$\left[\because (1+x)^n=\sum_{r=0}^{n}{}^nC_r\cdot x^r\right]$$

$$=B_{10}\times({}^{30}C_{20}-1)-C_{10}\times({}^{20}C_{10}-1)$$

$$=B_{10}\times({}^{30}C_{10}-1)-C_{10}({}^{20}C_{10}-1)$$

$$=B_{10}(C_{10}-1)-C_{10}(B_{10}-1)=C_{10}-B_{10}$$

19. (c) Given, $f(x)=\frac{1}{1-x}$

The point $x=1$ is a discontinuous point of the function $f(x)=\frac{1}{1-x}$.

If $x\neq1$, then $\lambda(x)=f(f(x))=\frac{x-1}{x}$

Hence, $x=0$ is a point of discontinuity of the function $\lambda(x)$.

If $x\neq0$ and $x\neq1$, then $fofof(x)=x$

Hence, $y=f^{3n}(x)=(f^3(x)^n)=x$ is continuous everywhere.

Therefore, 0 and 1 are the only points of discontinuity of y.

20. (c) Let $\mathbf{c}=x\hat{\mathbf{i}}+y\hat{\mathbf{j}}+z\hat{\mathbf{k}}$

$\because$ **a**,**b** and **c** are coplanar.

$$\text{So, }\begin{vmatrix}x & y & z\\ 1 & 1 & -1\\ 1 & -1 & 1\end{vmatrix}=0$$

$$\Rightarrow 0\cdot x-2y-2z=0 \Rightarrow y+z=0$$

Also, **c** is perpendicular to **a**

$$\therefore x+y-z=0$$

$$\text{Therefore, }\frac{x}{-2}=\frac{y}{1}=\frac{z}{-1}$$

and $x^2+y^2+z^2=1$

(**c** being a unit vector), we have

$$x=\frac{-2}{\sqrt{6}}, y=\frac{1}{\sqrt{6}} \text{ and } z=\frac{-1}{\sqrt{6}}$$

$$\text{Thus, }\mathbf{c}=\frac{1}{\sqrt{6}}(-2\hat{\mathbf{i}}+\hat{\mathbf{j}}-\hat{\mathbf{k}})$$

$$\text{and }\mathbf{d}=\frac{\mathbf{a}\times\mathbf{c}}{|\mathbf{a}\times\mathbf{c}|}=\frac{1}{\sqrt{6}}\cdot\frac{1}{|\mathbf{a}\times\mathbf{c}|}\begin{vmatrix}\hat{\mathbf{i}} & \hat{\mathbf{j}} & \hat{\mathbf{k}}\\ 1 & 1 & -1\\ -2 & 1 & -1\end{vmatrix}$$

$$=\frac{1}{\sqrt{6}}\frac{1}{|\mathbf{a}\times\mathbf{c}|}(0\hat{\mathbf{i}}+3\hat{\mathbf{j}}+3\hat{\mathbf{k}})$$

$$=\frac{1}{\sqrt{2}}(\hat{\mathbf{j}}+\hat{\mathbf{k}})\left[\because|\mathbf{a}\times\mathbf{c}|=\frac{1}{\sqrt{6}}\times3\sqrt{2}\right]$$

21. (4) We are given that

$$\frac{at_1^2}{at_2^2}=\mu^2 \Rightarrow t_1=\mu t_2$$

Then, $h=a\mu t_2^2$, $k=a(\mu t_2+t_2)$

Eliminating t_2, we get

$$k^2=a^2(\mu+1)^2t_2^2=a^2(\mu+1)^2\left(\frac{h}{a\mu}\right)=a\left(\sqrt{\mu}+\frac{1}{\sqrt{\mu}}\right)^2h$$

$$\text{We are given, }\left(\sqrt{\mu}+\frac{1}{\sqrt{\mu}}\right)^2=\frac{25}{4}$$

$$\Rightarrow \sqrt{\mu}+\frac{1}{\sqrt{\mu}}=\frac{5}{2}$$

$\left[\because \sqrt{\mu}+\frac{1}{\sqrt{\mu}}=-\frac{5}{2}\right.$ rejected because $\mu>1$ given i.e. $\sqrt{\mu}$ taken positive only$\left.\right]$

$$\Rightarrow \sqrt{\mu}=2 \Rightarrow \mu=4$$

22. (28) The equation of the plane containing the given lines is

$$\begin{vmatrix} x-1 & y-2 & z-3 \\ 2 & 3 & 4 \\ 3 & 4 & 5 \end{vmatrix} = 0$$

$$\Rightarrow \begin{vmatrix} x-1 & y-2 & z-3 \\ 2 & 3 & 4 \\ 1 & 1 & 1 \end{vmatrix} = 0$$

[applying $R_3 \to R_3 - R_2$]

$$\Rightarrow \begin{vmatrix} x-1 & y-x-1 & z-x-2 \\ 2 & 1 & 2 \\ 1 & 0 & 0 \end{vmatrix} = 0$$

Applying $C_2 \to C_2 - C_1$ and $C_3 \to C_3 - C_1$, we get

$\Rightarrow 2y - 2x - 2 - z + x + 2 = 0$

$\Rightarrow \quad x - 2y + z = 0$ ...(i)

This plane must be parallel to $Ax - 2y + z = d$ and so

$A = 1$ ...(ii)

The distance between the lines (i) and (ii) is

$$\frac{|d|}{\sqrt{1+4+1}} = \sqrt{6} \Rightarrow |d| = 6$$

Hence, $10A + 3|d| = 10 \times 1 + 3 \times 6 = 28$

23. (1) Let $I = \int \frac{1}{x + \sqrt{x^2 - x + 1}} dx$ ...(i)

Let $\quad x + \sqrt{x^2 - x + 1} = t$

$\Rightarrow \quad \sqrt{x^2 - x + 1} = t - x$

On squaring, we get

$x^2 - x + 1 = (t - x)^2 = t^2 + x^2 - 2tx$

$\Rightarrow \quad (2t - 1)x = t^2 - 1$

$\Rightarrow \quad x = \frac{t^2 - 1}{2t - 1}$

$\Rightarrow \quad dx = \frac{2t(t-1) - 2(t^2 - 1)}{(2t-1)^2} dt$

$\Rightarrow \quad dx = \frac{2t^2 - 2t + 2}{(2t-1)^2} dt$

From Eq. (i),

$$I = \int \frac{1}{t} \frac{2t^2 - 2t + 2}{(2t-1)^2} dt = 2\int \frac{t^2 - t + 1}{t(2t-1)^2} dt$$

By partial fractions,

$$I = 2\int \left[\frac{1}{t} - \frac{3}{2(2t-1)} + \frac{3}{2(2t-1)^2}\right] dt$$

$$\Rightarrow I = 2\log_e|t| - \frac{3}{2}\log_e|2t-1| - \frac{3}{2(2t-1)} + C,$$

where $t = x + \sqrt{x^2 - x + 1}$

On comparing, $m = 2$, $n = \frac{-3}{2}$ and $p = \frac{-3}{2}$.

Hence, $2m + n + p$

$$= 2 \times 2 + \left(-\frac{3}{2}\right) + \left(\frac{-3}{2}\right) = 4 - 3 = 1$$

24. (1) Given, $\begin{vmatrix} \sin x & \cos x & \cos x \\ \cos x & \sin x & \cos x \\ \cos x & \cos x & \sin x \end{vmatrix} = 0$

Applying $C_1 \to C_1 + C_2 + C_3$

$$\begin{vmatrix} \sin x + 2\cos x & \cos x & \cos x \\ \sin x + 2\cos x & \sin x & \cos x \\ \sin x + 2\cos x & \cos x & \sin x \end{vmatrix} = 0$$

$$\Rightarrow (\sin x + 2\cos x)\begin{vmatrix} 1 & \cos x & \cos x \\ 1 & \sin x & \cos x \\ 1 & \cos x & \sin x \end{vmatrix} = 0$$

Applying $R_2 \to R_2 - R_1$ and $R_3 \to R_3 - R_1$, we get $\Rightarrow (\sin x + 2\cos x)$

$$\begin{vmatrix} 1 & \cos x & \cos x \\ 0 & \sin x - \cos x & 0 \\ 0 & 0 & \sin x - \cos x \end{vmatrix} = 0$$

$\Rightarrow (\sin x + 2\cos x)(\sin x - \cos x)^2 = 0$

$\Rightarrow \quad \tan x = -2$ or $\tan x = 1$

Given, $\frac{-\pi}{4} \le x \le \frac{\pi}{4} \Rightarrow -1 \le \tan x \le 1$

$\therefore \quad \tan x = -2$ (rejected)

Hence, $\tan x = 1 \Rightarrow x = \frac{\pi}{4}$

Therefore, number of distinct real roots $= 1$

25. (6) As $\left(ae, \frac{b^2}{a}\right)$ and $\left(-ae, \frac{b^2}{a}\right)$ lie on the parabola $x^2 = 3(y+3)$, we get

$$a^2e^2 = 3\left(\frac{b^2}{a} + 3\right) = 3[a(e^2 - 1) + 3]$$

$[\because b^2 = a^2(e^2 - 1)]$

$\Rightarrow \quad (a - 3)(ae^2 + 3) = 0 \Rightarrow a = 3$

Hence, length of transverse axis $= 2a = 6$ units

26. (2) Since,

$$\lim_{x \to -2} \frac{\tan \pi x}{x + 2} = \lim_{x \to -2} \frac{\tan \pi(x+2)}{x+2}$$

$$= \lim_{t \to 0} \frac{\pi \tan t}{t} \quad [\text{put}, t = \pi(x+2)]$$

$$= \pi$$

and $$\lim_{x \to \infty}\left(1 + \frac{1}{x^2}\right)^x = \lim_{x \to \infty}\left(1 + \frac{1}{x^2}\right)^{x^2\left(\frac{1}{x}\right)}$$

$$= \lim_{x \to \infty}\left(1 + \frac{1}{x^2}\right)^{x^2 \cdot \lim_{x \to \infty} \frac{1}{x}} = e^0 = 1$$

Hence, $\lambda = \pi + 1 \approx 3.14 + 1 \approx 4.14$

$\therefore \quad \frac{[\lambda]}{2} = \frac{4}{2} = 2$

27. (6) Let $z = a + ib$, the given equation can be written as $z^2 = \bar{z}^3$ ...(i)

$\Rightarrow |z|^2 = |\bar{z}|^3 \Rightarrow |z|^2 = |z|^3$

$\Rightarrow \quad |z| = 0$ or $|z| = 1$

If $|z| = 0$, then $z = 0$

If $|z| = 1$, then $\bar{z} = \frac{1}{z}$ $\quad [\because z\bar{z} = |z|^2]$

From Eq. (i),

$$z^2 = \frac{1}{z^3} \Rightarrow z^5 = 1 \text{ which has 5 roots.}$$

Thus, there are 6 complex numbers satisfying the given equation.

28. (0) We have, $\frac{dy}{dx} = \frac{y}{x} - \cos^2\left(\frac{y}{x}\right)$

Putting $y = vx$, so that $\frac{dy}{dx} = v + x\frac{dv}{dx}$,

we get $v + x\frac{dv}{dx} = v - \cos^2 v$

$\Rightarrow \frac{dv}{\cos^2 v} = -\frac{dx}{x} \Rightarrow \sec^2 v\,dv = \frac{-1}{x}dx$

On integrating both sides, we get

$\tan v = -\ln x + \ln C$

$\Rightarrow \quad \tan\left(\frac{y}{x}\right) = -\ln x + \ln C$ ...(i)

Since, Eq. (i) passes through $\left(1, \frac{\pi}{4}\right)$.

So, $\quad 1 = \ln C \Rightarrow C = e$

From Eq. (i), $\tan\left(\frac{y}{x}\right) = -\ln x + \ln e$

$\Rightarrow \quad y = x\tan^{-1}\left(\ln\left(\frac{e}{x}\right)\right) = \phi(x)$ given

Hence, $\phi(e) = e \cdot \tan^{-1}\left(\ln\left(\frac{e}{e}\right)\right)$

$= e \cdot \tan^{-1}(0) = 0$

29. (2) $A = \begin{bmatrix} 0 & 1 & -1 \\ 4 & -3 & 4 \\ 3 & -3 & 4 \end{bmatrix}$

$$\Rightarrow A^2 = A \cdot A = \begin{bmatrix} 0 & 1 & -1 \\ 4 & -3 & 4 \\ 3 & -3 & 4 \end{bmatrix}$$

$$\begin{bmatrix} 0 & 1 & -1 \\ 4 & -3 & 4 \\ 3 & -3 & 4 \end{bmatrix} = \begin{bmatrix} 1 & 0 & 0 \\ 0 & 1 & 0 \\ 0 & 0 & 1 \end{bmatrix}$$

$\Rightarrow \quad A^2 = 1$

$\therefore \quad A^4 = A^6 = A^8 = \ldots = 1$

Now, $\quad A^x = I \Rightarrow x = 2, 4, 6, 8 \ldots$

$\therefore \Sigma(\cos^x\theta + \sin^x\theta) = (\cos^2\theta + \sin^2\theta)$
$+ (\cos^4\theta + \sin^4\theta) + (\cos^6\theta + \sin^6\theta)$
$+ (\cos^8\theta + \sin^8\theta) + \ldots$
$= (\cos^2\theta + \cos^4\theta + \cos^6\theta + \cos^8\theta + \ldots)$
$+ (\sin^2\theta + \sin^4\theta + \sin^6\theta + \sin^8\theta + \ldots)$

$$=\frac{\cos^2\theta}{1-\cos^2\theta}+\frac{\sin^2\theta}{1-\sin^2\theta}\quad\left[\because \text{ sum of infinite, } S_\infty \text{ GP}=\frac{a}{1-r}\right]$$

$=\cot^2\theta+\tan^2\theta$ which has minimum value $=2$ [using AM $\geq$ GM]

30. (4) Equation of any tangent to ellipse $\frac{x^2}{16}+\frac{y^2}{b^2}=1$ is $\frac{x}{4}\cos\theta+\frac{y}{b}\sin\theta-1=0$

We have, $p_1=\dfrac{\left|\frac{4e}{b}\sin\theta-1\right|}{\sqrt{\frac{\cos^2\theta}{16}+\frac{\sin^2\theta}{b^2}}}$

$$\Rightarrow p_1^2\left(\frac{\cos^2\theta}{16}+\frac{\sin^2\theta}{b^2}\right)=\left(\frac{4e}{b}\sin\theta-1\right)^2 \quad ...(i)$$

Similarly,

$$p_2^2\left(\frac{\cos^2\theta}{16}+\frac{\sin^2\theta}{b^2}\right)=\left(\frac{4e}{b}\sin\theta+1\right)^2 \quad ...(ii)$$

Adding Eqs. (i) and (ii), we get

$$(p_1^2+p_2^2)\left(\frac{\cos^2\theta}{16}+\frac{\sin^2\theta}{b^2}\right)=2\left(\frac{16e^2}{b^2}\sin^2\theta+1\right)$$

$$=2\left(\frac{16-b^2}{b^2}\sin^2\theta+1\right)\quad\left[\because b^2=a^2(1-e^2)\quad \therefore e^2=1-\frac{b^2}{a^2}=1-\frac{b^2}{16}\right]$$

$$=2\left(\frac{16\sin^2\theta-b^2\sin^2\theta+b^2}{b^2}\right)$$

$$=32\left(\frac{\sin^2\theta}{b^2}+\frac{\cos^2\theta}{16}\right)$$

$$\Rightarrow \frac{p_1^2+p_2^2}{8}=4$$

Knockout 9

1. (c) Given, $f(x)=x^3-\frac{3x^2}{2}+x+\frac{1}{4}$

$$=\frac{1}{4}(4x^3-6x^2+4x+1)$$

$$=\frac{1}{4}(4x^3-6x^2+4x-1+2)$$

$$=\frac{1}{4}[x^4-(1-x^4)]+\frac{2}{4}$$

$$\therefore \quad f(1-x)=\frac{1}{4}[(1-x)^4-x^4]+\frac{2}{4}$$

$$\therefore f(x)+f(1-x)=\frac{2}{4}+\frac{2}{4}=1 \quad ...(i)$$

Replacing x by $f(x)$, we have

$$f[f(x)]+f[1-f(x)]=1 \quad ...(ii)$$

Now, $I=\int_{1/4}^{3/4} f(f(x))dx \quad ...(iii)$

$$\Rightarrow \quad I=\int_{1/4}^{3/4} f(f(1-x))dx$$

$$\left[\because \int_a^b f(x)dx=\int_a^b f(a+b-x)\,dx\right]$$

$$=\int_{1/4}^{3/4} f(1-f(x))dx \quad ...(iv)$$

[from Eq. (i)]

Adding Eqs. (iii) and (iv), we get

$$2I=\int_{1/4}^{3/4}[f(f(x))+f(1-f(x))]\,dx=\int_{1/4}^{3/4}1\,dx$$

[from Eq. (ii)]

$$=[x]_{1/4}^{3/4}=\frac{1}{2}$$

$$\Rightarrow I=\frac{1}{4}$$

Hence, $(I)^{-3/2}=\left(\frac{1}{4}\right)^{-3/2}=4^{3/2}$

$$=(4^{1/2})^3=2^3=8$$

2. (b) Let $A=$ event that a sum of 5 occurs

$B=$ event that a sum of 7 occurs

$C=$ event that neither a sum of 5 nor a sum of 7 occurs.

Then, $\quad P(A)=\frac{4}{36}=\frac{1}{9}$

$$P(B)=\frac{6}{36}=\frac{1}{6}$$

$$P(C)=\frac{26}{36}=\frac{13}{18}$$

Thus, probability that A occurs before B is

$P[A \text{ or } (C\cap A) \text{ or } (C\cap C\cap A) \text{ or } ....]$

$=P(A)+P(C\cap A)+P(C\cap C\cap A)+......$

$=P(A)+P(C)\cdot P(A)+[P(C)]^2\cdot P(A)+......$

$$=\frac{1}{9}+\left(\frac{13}{18}\right)\times\left(\frac{1}{9}\right)+\left(\frac{13}{18}\right)^2\times\frac{1}{9}+.........$$

$$=\frac{1/9}{1-13/18}=\frac{2}{5}$$

3. (d) Vector perpendicular to the face *OAB* is

$$\mathbf{OA}\times\mathbf{OB}=(\hat{\mathbf{i}}+2\hat{\mathbf{j}}+\hat{\mathbf{k}})\times(2\hat{\mathbf{i}}+\hat{\mathbf{j}}+3\hat{\mathbf{k}})$$

$$=5\hat{\mathbf{i}}-\hat{\mathbf{j}}-3\hat{\mathbf{k}}$$

Vector perpendicular to the face *ABC* is $\mathbf{AB}\times\mathbf{AC}=(\hat{\mathbf{i}}-\hat{\mathbf{j}}+2\hat{\mathbf{k}})\times(-2\hat{\mathbf{i}}-\hat{\mathbf{j}}+\hat{\mathbf{k}})$

$$=\hat{\mathbf{i}}-5\hat{\mathbf{j}}-3\hat{\mathbf{k}}$$

Since, the angle between the face = angle between their normal

$$\therefore \quad \cos\theta=\frac{5+5+9}{\sqrt{35}\sqrt{35}}=\frac{19}{35}$$

$$\Rightarrow \quad \theta=\cos^{-1}\left(\frac{19}{35}\right)$$

4. (a) The distance between $(2, 2m)$ and $(5, 5m)$ is less than 5.

$$\Rightarrow \quad (5-2)^2+(5m-2m)^2<25$$

$$\Rightarrow \quad 9m^2<16$$

$$\Rightarrow \quad m^2<\frac{16}{9}\Rightarrow |m|<\frac{4}{3}$$

$$\Rightarrow \quad -\frac{4}{3}<m<\frac{4}{3}$$

5. (b) On circle w_1, take a point P and on circle w_2, take a point Q.

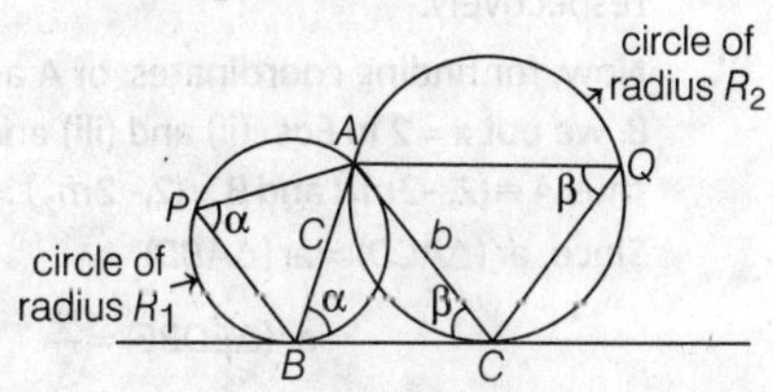

In ΔAPB, $\quad \frac{c}{\sin\alpha}=2R_1 \quad ...(i)$

In ΔAQC,

$$\frac{b}{\sin\beta}=2R_2 \quad ...(ii)$$

From Eqs. (i) and (ii), we get

$$\frac{bc}{\sin\alpha\cdot\sin\beta}=4R_1R_2 \quad ...(iii)$$

In ΔABC,

$$2R=\frac{c}{\sin\beta}=\frac{b}{\sin\alpha}$$

$$\Rightarrow \quad \frac{bc}{\sin\alpha\cdot\sin\beta}=4R^2 \quad ...(iv)$$

From Eqs. (iii) and (iv), we get

$$4R^2=4R_1R_2\Rightarrow R^2=R_1R_2$$

$\Rightarrow R_1, R, R_2$ form a GP.

6. (b) Area bounded by $y=\sqrt{2}\sin\left(\frac{\pi x}{4}\right)$ and *X*-axis between the lines $x=2$ and $x=4$ is

$$\Delta=\sqrt{2}\int_2^4 \sin\left(\frac{\pi x}{4}\right)dx$$

$$=\frac{-4\sqrt{2}}{\pi}\cdot\cos\left(\frac{\pi x}{4}\right)\Bigg|_2^4$$

$$\Rightarrow \quad \Delta=\frac{4\sqrt{2}}{\pi}\text{ sq units} \quad ...(i)$$

Consider two lines L_1 and L_2 with slopes m_1 and m_2 respectively.

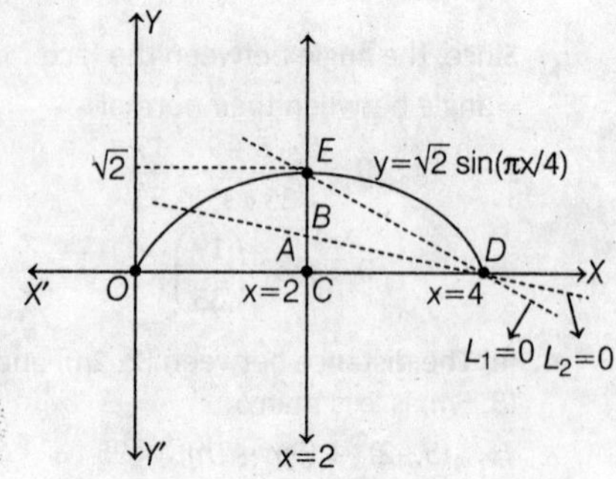

Then, equation of L_1 passing through (4, 0) is

$$y-0=m_1(x-4)$$

$$\Rightarrow \quad y-m_1(x-4)=0 \quad \text{...(ii)}$$

$$L_2: y-m_2(x-4)=0 \quad \text{...(iii)}$$

Similarly, let A and B be the points of intersection of L_1 and L_2 with $x=2$, respectively.

Now, for finding coordinates of A and B, we put $x=2$ in Eqs. (ii) and (iii) and thus $A\equiv(2,-2m_1)$ and $B\equiv(2,-2m_2)$.

Since, ar (ΔACD) = ar (ΔABD)

$$= \text{ar}(\Delta EDBE)=\frac{\Delta}{3}$$

(given)

Now, $\text{ar}(\Delta ACD)=\dfrac{\Delta}{3}$

$$\Rightarrow \quad \frac{4\sqrt{2}}{3\pi}=\frac{1}{2}\times 2\times(-2m_1)$$

$$\Rightarrow \quad m_1=\frac{-2\sqrt{2}}{3\pi}$$

Also, $\text{ar}(\Delta BCD)=\text{ar}(\Delta ACD)+\text{ar}(\Delta ABD)$

$$=\frac{\Delta}{3}+\frac{\Delta}{3}=\frac{2\Delta}{3}$$

$$\Rightarrow \quad \frac{8\sqrt{2}}{3\pi}=\frac{1}{2}\times 2\times(-2m_2)$$

$$\Rightarrow \quad m_2=\frac{-4\sqrt{2}}{3\pi}$$

$\therefore$ Required sum $=\dfrac{-2\sqrt{2}}{\pi}$

7. (a) Let $f(x)=A+Bx+cx^2+Dx^3+$ ....

$$\text{i.e.}\begin{vmatrix} x & (1+\sin x)^3 & \cos x \\ 1 & \ln(1+x) & 2 \\ x^2 & (1+x)^2 & 0 \end{vmatrix}$$

$$=A+Bx+Cx^2+Dx^3+\ldots\ldots$$

Differentiating both sides w.r.t. x, we get

$$\begin{vmatrix} 1 & (1+\sin x)^3 & \cos x \\ 0 & \ln(1+x) & 2 \\ 2x & (1+x)^2 & 0 \end{vmatrix}$$

$$+\begin{vmatrix} x & 3(1+\sin x)^2\cos x & \cos x \\ 1 & \dfrac{1}{1+x} & 2 \\ x^2 & 2(1+x) & 0 \end{vmatrix}$$

$$+\begin{vmatrix} x & (1+\sin x)^3 & -\sin x \\ 1 & \ln(1+x) & 0 \\ x^2 & (1+x)^2 & 0 \end{vmatrix}$$

$$=O+B+2Cx+3Dx^2+\ldots\ldots$$

Putting $x=0$, then, we get

$$B=\begin{vmatrix} 1 & 1 & 1 \\ 0 & 0 & 2 \\ 0 & 1 & 0 \end{vmatrix}+\begin{vmatrix} 0 & 3 & 1 \\ 1 & 1 & 2 \\ 0 & 2 & 0 \end{vmatrix}+\begin{vmatrix} 0 & 1 & 0 \\ 1 & 0 & 0 \\ 0 & 1 & 0 \end{vmatrix}$$

$$\Rightarrow B=(0-2)-(0-2)-0=0$$

$\therefore$ Coefficient of x in $f(x)=0$

8. (d) Let $p=\dfrac{1+\sqrt{2a}}{2}$, $q=\dfrac{1-\sqrt{2a}}{2}$

Now, equation of circle can be written as

$$2x^2+2y^2-2px-2qy=0$$

$$\Rightarrow \quad x^2+y^2-px-qy=0 \quad \text{...(i)}$$

As, M lies on $x+y=0$, then we may take coordinates of M as $(\alpha,-\alpha)$.

$\because$ M is the mid-point of AB.

$\because$ Coordinates of B are $(2\alpha-p,-2\alpha-q)$

As, B lies on the circle (1).

So, $(2\alpha-p)^2+(-2\alpha-q)^2-p(2\alpha-p)$

$$-q(-2\alpha-q)=0$$

$$\Rightarrow \quad 8\alpha^2+6\alpha(q-p)+2(p^2+q^2)=0$$

$$\Rightarrow \quad 4\alpha^2+3\alpha(q-p)+(p^2+q^2)=0$$

As, there are two distinct chords. Hence, value of α must be distinct i.e. discriminant >0.

$$\Rightarrow \quad 9(q-p)^2-16(p^2+q^2)>0$$

$$\Rightarrow \quad 9(-\sqrt{2}a)^2-8(1+2a^2)>0$$

$$\Rightarrow \quad 2a^2-8>0$$

$$\Rightarrow \quad a^2>4$$

$$\Rightarrow \quad |a|>2$$

$$\Rightarrow a\in(-\infty,-2)\cup(2,\infty)$$

9. (c) Given, $f(x)+f(-x)=0$

$\Rightarrow f(x)$ is an odd function.

Since, points $(-3,2)$ and $(5,4)$ lies on the curve.

So, $(3,-2)$ and $(-5,-4)$ will also lie on the curve because $f(x)$ is symmetrical about origin as $f(x)$ is an odd function.

For minimum number of roots, graph of continuous function $f(x)$ is as follows

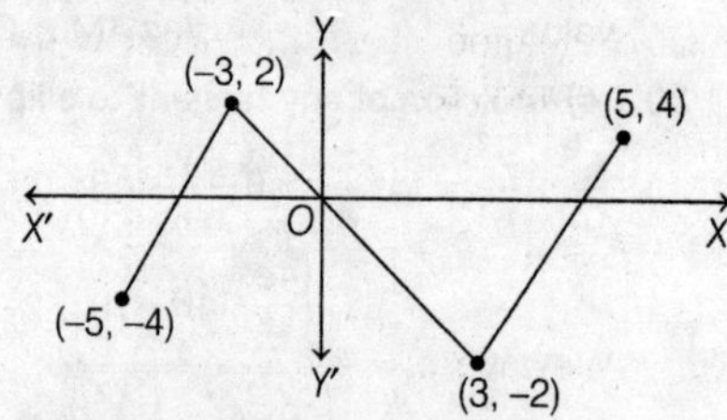

From the above graph of $f(x)$, it is clear that equation $f(x)=0$ has atleast three real roots.

10. (b) Let x_1,x_2,x_3,x_4 ...... x_{30} be actual weights of 30 fishes

and $y_1,y_2,y_3,y_4,\ldots\ldots y_{30}$ be the weights of fishes taken from misaligned increasing scale.

Then, $y_i=x_i+2, i=1,2,3,4,\ldots\ldots\ldots\ldots,30$

$$\Rightarrow \quad \overline{Y}=\overline{X}+2 \text{ and } \sigma_y=\sigma_x$$

[$\because$ standard deviation is independent of change of origin]

$$\Rightarrow \quad 30=\overline{X}+2 \text{ and } \sigma_y=2$$

$$\Rightarrow \quad \overline{X}=28 \text{ and } \sigma_y=2$$

11. (a) Let $\theta=$ semi-vertical angle of the cone.

Then, $\tan\theta=\dfrac{R}{H}$,

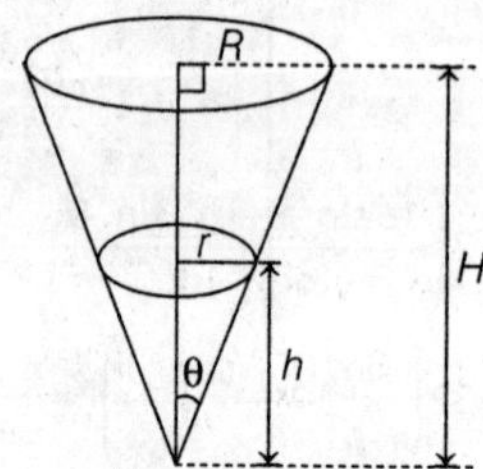

Let the radius and height of the water cone at time t be r and h respectively.

Then, $\tan\theta=\dfrac{r}{h}$

If V is the volume of the water and S is the surface area of the cone in contact with air at time t, then

$$V=\frac{1}{3}\pi r^2 h=\frac{1}{3}\pi r^3\cot\theta$$

and $S=\pi r^2$

we are given, $\dfrac{dV}{dt}\propto S$

$$\Rightarrow \quad \frac{dV}{dt}=-kS \quad [\because V \text{ is decreasing}]$$

$$\Rightarrow \quad \frac{1}{3}\pi(3r^2)\cot\theta.\frac{dr}{dt}=-k(\pi r^2)$$

Integrating, we get

$r=(-k\tan\theta)t+C$

When $t=0, r=R$

$\therefore \quad C=R$

Thus, $r=(-k\tan\theta)t+R$

when the cone is empty, $r=0$. If T is the time taken for the cone to be empty, then

$$0=(-k\tan\theta)T+R$$

$$\Rightarrow \quad T=\frac{R}{k\tan\theta}=\frac{R}{k(R/H)}$$

$$\Rightarrow \quad T=\frac{H}{k}$$

12. (c) In ΔABP,

$$\cot\phi=\frac{d}{150}$$

$$\Rightarrow d=150\cot\phi=60\text{m} \quad \left[\because \tan\phi=\frac{5}{2}\right]$$

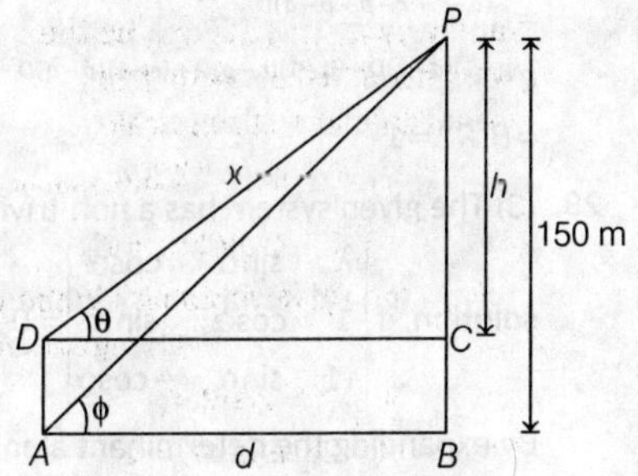

In ΔDCP,

$$\tan\theta=\frac{h}{d}$$

$$\Rightarrow \quad h=60\ \tan\theta=80\text{ m}$$

$$\left[\because \tan\theta=\frac{4}{3}, \text{given}\right]$$

In ΔPCD,

$$x=\sqrt{(80)^2+(60)^2}=100\text{ m}$$

13. (c) $\displaystyle\int\frac{1}{1+x^4}dx=\frac{1}{2}\int\frac{1+x^2+1-x^2}{1+x^4}dx$

$$=\frac{1}{2}\int\frac{1+\frac{1}{x^2}}{x^2+\frac{1}{x^2}}dx-\frac{1}{2}\int\frac{1-\frac{1}{x^2}}{x^2+\frac{1}{x^2}}dx$$

$$=\frac{1}{2}\int\frac{d\left(x-\frac{1}{x}\right)}{\left(x-\frac{1}{x}\right)^2+2}-\frac{1}{2}\int\frac{d\left(x+\frac{1}{x}\right)}{\left(x+\frac{1}{x}\right)^2-2}$$

$$=\frac{1}{2}\cdot\frac{1}{\sqrt{2}}\tan^{-1}\left(\frac{x-\frac{1}{x}}{\sqrt{2}}\right)$$

$$-\frac{1}{2}\cdot\frac{1}{2\sqrt{2}}\ln\left|\frac{x+\frac{1}{x}-\sqrt{2}}{x+\frac{1}{x}+\sqrt{2}}\right|+C$$

$$=\frac{1}{2\sqrt{2}}\tan^{-1}\left(\frac{x^2-1}{x\sqrt{2}}\right)-\frac{1}{4\sqrt{2}}\ln\left|\frac{x^2-\sqrt{2}x+1}{x^2+\sqrt{2}x+1}\right|+C$$

Hence,

$$f(x)=\frac{x^2-1}{\sqrt{2}x}, g(x)=\frac{x^2-\sqrt{2}x+1}{x^2+\sqrt{2}x+1}$$

$$m=2\sqrt{2}, n=4\sqrt{2} \Rightarrow n=2m$$

Also, $f(2)=\dfrac{3}{2\sqrt{2}}$ and $g(\sqrt{2})=\dfrac{1}{5}$ and

$(m+n)$ is an irrational number .

14. (d) LHL $=\displaystyle\lim_{x\to-1^-}\frac{1}{\sqrt{|x|-\{-x\}}}$

$$=\lim_{x\to-1^-}\frac{1}{\sqrt{-x-(x+2)}}$$

$$=\lim_{x\to-1^-}\frac{1}{\sqrt{-2x-2}}=\infty$$

$$\text{RHL}=\lim_{x\to-1^+}\frac{1}{\sqrt{|x|-\{-x\}}}$$

$$=\lim_{x\to-1^+}\frac{1}{\sqrt{-x-(x+1)}}$$

$$=\lim_{x\to-1^+}\frac{1}{\sqrt{-2x-1}}=1$$

LHL $\neq$ RHL

$\Rightarrow$ Limit does not exist

15. (d) Let $A\equiv(p\to q)\wedge(q\to p)$ and $B\equiv(\sim p)\vee q$

1	2	3	4	5	6	7	8	9
p	q	$\sim p$	$p\to q$	$q\to p$	$p\leftrightarrow q$	$q\leftrightarrow p$	A	B
T	T	F	T	T	T	T	T	T
T	F	F	F	T	F	F	F	F
F	T	T	T	F	F	F	F	T
F	F	T	T	T	T	T	T	T

Columns 6 and 8 are identical

$(p\leftrightarrow q)\equiv(p\to q)\wedge(q\to p)$

Columns 4 and 9 are identical

$(p\to q)\equiv(\sim p)\vee q$

Columns 6 and 7 are identical

$(p\leftrightarrow q)\equiv(q\leftrightarrow p)$

16. (a) Let $A=(x_1,y_1)$ and $B=(x_2,y_2)$

$\because \quad \mathbf{OA}\cdot\hat{\mathbf{i}}=-1\Rightarrow x_1=-1$

$\therefore \quad y_1=2^{x_1+2}=2^{-1+2}=2$

So, $A=(-1,2)$ and hence,

$\mathbf{OA}=\mathbf{a}=-\hat{\mathbf{i}}+2\hat{\mathbf{j}}$ and $\mathbf{B}\cdot\hat{\mathbf{i}}=2$ (given)

$\Rightarrow \quad x_2=2$

$\therefore \quad y_2=2^{x_2+2}=2^{2+2}=16$

So, $B=(2,16)$ and hence

$\mathbf{OB}=\mathbf{b}=2\hat{\mathbf{i}}+16\hat{\mathbf{j}}$

Now, $\mathbf{c}=2\mathbf{a}+\mathbf{b}$

$$=2(-\hat{\mathbf{i}}+2\hat{\mathbf{j}})+(2\hat{\mathbf{i}}+16\hat{\mathbf{j}})$$

$$=0\cdot\hat{\mathbf{i}}+20\hat{\mathbf{j}}$$

$$\therefore \cos\theta=\frac{\mathbf{a}\cdot\mathbf{c}}{|\mathbf{a}||\mathbf{c}|}=\frac{40}{\sqrt{5}\sqrt{400}}$$

$$=\frac{40}{\sqrt{5}\times20}=\frac{2}{\sqrt{5}}$$

$$\therefore \sin^2\theta=1-\cos^2\theta=1-\frac{4}{5}=\frac{1}{5}$$

$$\Rightarrow \sin\theta=\pm\frac{1}{\sqrt{5}}$$

But $0<\theta<\dfrac{\pi}{2}$, then $\sin\theta>0$

$$\therefore \quad \sin\theta=\frac{1}{\sqrt{5}}$$

Now, $\tan\theta=\dfrac{\sin\theta}{\cos\theta}$

$$\left[\because \theta\in\left(0,\frac{\pi}{2}\right), \text{then}\tan\theta>0\right]$$

$$=\frac{\frac{1}{\sqrt{5}}}{\frac{2}{\sqrt{5}}}=\frac{1}{2}$$

$$\Rightarrow \quad \theta=\tan^{-1}(1/2)=\tan^{-1}(0.5)$$

17. (c)

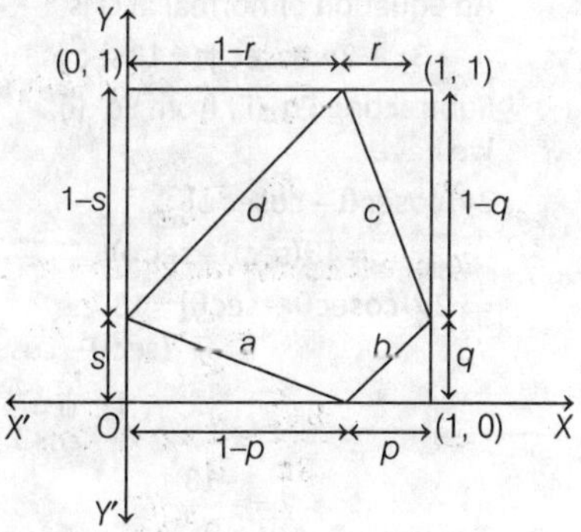

Form figure,

$$a^2=p^2+(1-s)^2$$

$$b^2=(1-p)^2+q^2$$

$$c^2=(1-q)^2+r^2$$

$$d^2=(1-r)^2+s^2$$

$$\therefore a^2+b^2+c^2+d^2$$

$$=[p^2+(1-p^2)]+[q^2+(1-q)^2]+[r^2+(1-r)^2]+[s^2+(1-s)^2],$$

where $p,q,r,s\in[0,1]$.

Now, consider the function,

$$y=x^2+(1-x)^2,\ 0\le x\le1$$

$$\Rightarrow y=2x^2-2x+1$$

$$=2\left(x-\frac{1}{2}\right)^2+\frac{1}{2}$$

Hence, minimum value of y is $\frac{1}{2}$, when $x=\frac{1}{2}$ and maximum value of y is 1, when $x=1$ (because $x \in [0,1]$)

Therefore,

minimum value of $[p^2+(1-p)^2]=\frac{1}{2}$

and maximum value $=1$

minimum value of $[q^2+(1-q)^2]=\frac{1}{2}$

and maximum value $=1$

minimum value of $[r^2+(1-r)^2]=\frac{1}{2}$

and maximum value $=1$

minimum value of $[s^2+(1-s)^2]=\frac{1}{2}$

and maximum value $=1$

Hence, minimum value of

$$a^2+b^2+c^2+d^2=\frac{1}{2}+\frac{1}{2}+\frac{1}{2}+\frac{1}{2}=2$$

and maximum value of

$$a^2+b^2+c^2+d^2=1+1+1+1=4$$

$\therefore$ Range $=[2,4]$

18. (b) An equation of normal at P is $3x \cos\theta + 2y\cot\theta = 9+4$.

$$\Rightarrow \quad 3x+2y\operatorname{cosec}\theta = 13\sec\theta \quad \text{...(i)}$$

An equation of normal at Q is

$$3x+2y\operatorname{cosec}\phi = 13\sec\phi \quad \text{...(ii)}$$

Subtracting Eq. (ii) from Eq .(i), we have

$$2y[\operatorname{cosec}\theta-\operatorname{cosec}\phi] = 13(\sec\theta-\sec\phi)$$

$$\Rightarrow 2y[\operatorname{cosec}\theta-\sec\theta]=13(\sec\theta-\operatorname{cosec}\theta) \quad \left[\because \phi=\frac{\pi}{2}-\theta\right]$$

$$\Rightarrow \quad y=\frac{-13}{2}$$

19. (d) Given points are

$A=(2,3,4)$ and $B=(5,6,7)$

Now, BC = projection of **AB** on $2\hat{i}+\hat{j}+\hat{k}$

$$=\frac{3\cdot 2+3\cdot 1+3\cdot 1}{\sqrt{6}}=2\sqrt{6}$$

$\left[\because \text{direction cosine's of } BC \text{ are } \frac{2}{\sqrt{6}},\frac{1}{\sqrt{6}},\frac{1}{\sqrt{6}}\right]$

Now in ΔABC

$$AC^2=AB^2-BC^2=(3\sqrt{3})^2-(2\sqrt{6})^2 = 27-24=3$$

$\therefore AC=\sqrt{3}=\lambda$

Hence, $\lambda^8=(\sqrt{3})^8=81$

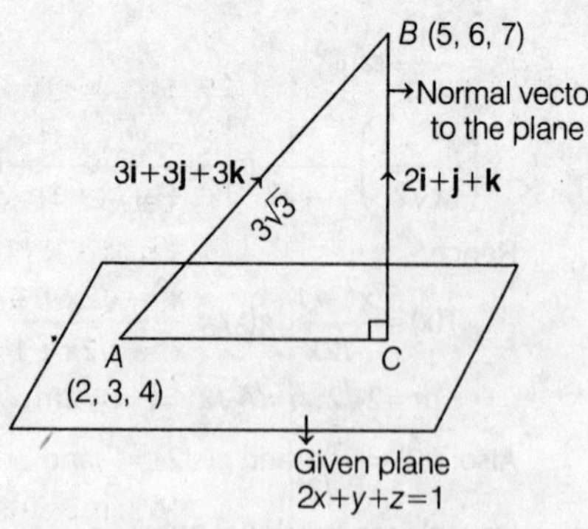

20. (a) $y=x$ touches $y=x^2+bx+c$ at $(1,1)$

$$\therefore \quad 1=1+b+c \Rightarrow b+c=0 \quad \text{...(i)}$$

and $\frac{dy}{dx}=2x+b|_{(1,1)}=2+b=1$

[$\because$ slope of $y=x$ is (i)] ...(ii)

On solving Eqs. (i) and (ii), we get

$$b=-1,\ c=1$$

21. (0) Focus of $y^2=36x$ is $(9, 0)$

Let the other end point of the focal chord be $B(t_1^2, 6t_1)$, then equation of AB is

$$y-6t=\frac{6t_1-6t}{t_1^2-t^2}(x-t^2)$$

$$\Rightarrow \quad y-6t=\frac{6(t_1-t)}{(t_1-t)(t_1+t)}(x-t^2)$$

$$\Rightarrow 6(x-t^2)=(t_1+t)(y-6t)$$

It will pass through (9,0) , if

$$6(9-t^2)=(t_1+t)(0-6t)$$

$$\Rightarrow \quad t_1=\frac{-9}{t} \quad \text{...(i)}$$

Now, length of AB is given by

$$AB^2=(t_1^2-t^2)^2+(6t_1-6t)^2$$

$$=[(t_1-t)^2(t_1+t)^2]+[6(t_1-t)]^2$$

$$=(t_1-t)^2[(t_1+t)^2+36]$$

$$=\left(\frac{9}{t}+t\right)^2\left[\left(t-\frac{9}{t}\right)^2+36\right] \quad \text{[using Eq. (i)]}$$

$$=\left(\frac{9}{t}+t\right)^2\left(t+\frac{9}{t}\right)^2=\left(t+\frac{9}{t}\right)^4$$

$$\Rightarrow AB=\left(t+\frac{9}{t}\right)^2=100 \quad \text{(given)}$$

$$\Rightarrow \quad t+\frac{9}{t}=\pm 10$$

$$\Rightarrow \quad t=1,-1$$

$\therefore$ Sum of values of

$$t=1+(-1)=0$$

22. (1) **For AP**

Let first term $=A$

common difference $=D$

For GP

First term $=B$

common ratio $=R$

Then,

$a=A+(p-1)D$ and $a=BR^{p-1}$

$b=A+(q-1)D$ and $b=BR^{q-1}$

$c=A+(r-1)D$ and $c=BR^{r-1}$

$$\therefore \quad a-b=(p-q)D$$
$$b-c=(q-r)D$$
$$c-a=(r-p)D$$

Now,

$$a^{b-c}\cdot b^{c-a}\cdot c^{a-b}=[BR^{p-1}]^{(q-r)D}\times[BR^{q-1}]^{(r-p)D}\times[BR^{r-1}]^{(p-q)D}$$

$$=B^{(q-r+r-p+p-q)D}$$

$$R^{(p-1)(q-r)D+(q-1)(r-p)D+(r-1)(p-q)D}$$

$$=B^0R^0=1$$

23. (3) The given system has a non-trivial solution, if $\begin{vmatrix}\lambda & \sin\alpha & \cos\alpha\\ 1 & \cos\alpha & \sin\alpha\\ -1 & \sin\alpha & -\cos\alpha\end{vmatrix}=0$

By expanding the determinant along 1st column, we get

$$\lambda=\sin 2\alpha+\cos 2\alpha$$

As we know that

$$-\sqrt{2}\le \sin 2\alpha+\cos 2\alpha\le\sqrt{2}$$

$$\Rightarrow -\sqrt{2}\le\lambda\le\sqrt{2}$$

Hence, integral values of λ are $-1,0,1$.

$\therefore$ Total number of integral values of $\lambda=3$

24. (210) $\frac{x+1}{x^{2/3}-x^{1/3}+1}-\frac{x-1}{x-x^{1/2}}$

$$=\frac{(x^{1/3})^3+(1)^3}{x^{2/3}-x^{1/3}+1}-\frac{x-1}{x^{1/2}(x^{1/2}-1)}$$

$$=\frac{(x^{1/3}+1)(x^{2/3}-x^{1/3}+1)}{(x^{2/3}-x^{1/3}+1)}-\frac{(x^{1/2}+1)(x^{1/2}-1)}{x^{1/2}(x^{1/2}-1)}$$

$$=x^{1/3}+1-1-x^{-1/2}$$

$$=x^{1/3}-x^{-1/2}$$

$$\therefore\left(\frac{x+1}{x^{2/3}-x^{1/3}+1}-\frac{x-1}{x-x^{1/2}}\right)^{10}=(x^{1/3}-x^{-1/2})^{10}$$

Let T_{r+1} be the general term in $(x^{1/3}-x^{-1/2})^{10}$.

Then, $T_{r+1}={}^{10}C_r(x^{1/3})^{10-r}(-1)^r(x^{-1/2})^r$

For this term to be independent of x, we must have

$$\frac{10-r}{3}-\frac{r}{2}=0$$

$\Rightarrow 20-2r-3r=0 \Rightarrow r=4$

Hence, required coefficient $= {}^{10}C_4(-1)^4 = 210$

25. (0) Given trigonometric equations, is

$$2^{\tan(x-\pi/4)}-2(0.25)^{\frac{\sin^2(x-\pi/4)}{\cos 2x}}+1=0 \quad \text{... (i)}$$

Since, $\frac{\sin^2(x-\pi/4)}{\cos 2x}=\frac{\frac{1}{2}(\sin x-\cos x)^2}{\cos^2 x-\sin^2 x}$

$$=\frac{-\frac{1}{2}(\sin x-\cos x)}{(\sin x+\cos x)}=-\frac{1}{2}\tan\left(x-\frac{\pi}{4}\right)$$

So, Eq. (i) reduces to

$$2^{\tan(x-\pi/4)}-2(0.25)^{-\frac{1}{2}\tan(x-\pi/4)}+1=0$$

$\Rightarrow \quad 2^{\tan(x-\pi/4)}-2.2^{\tan(x-\pi/4)}+1=0$

$\Rightarrow \quad -2^{\tan(x-\pi/4)}+1=0$

$\Rightarrow \quad 2^{\tan(x-\pi/4)}=2^{\circ} \Rightarrow \tan\left(x-\frac{\pi}{4}\right)=0$

$\Rightarrow x=\frac{\pi}{4}$, which is not possible as

$\cos 2x=0$ for this value of x, which does not define the original equation.

Hence, number of roots $=0$.

26. (78) The number of ways can be given as follows

2 bowlers and 9 other players : ${}^4C_2 \times {}^9C_9$

3 bowlers and 8 other players : ${}^4C_3 \times {}^9C_8$

4 bowlers and 7 other players : ${}^4C_4 \times {}^9C_7$

Hence, required number of ways is $6\times1+4\times9+1\times36=78$.

27. (1) $\prod_{r=0}^{3} cis\left(\frac{6K\pi+\pi}{4}\right)=cis\left(\frac{\pi}{4}+\frac{7\pi}{4}+\frac{13\pi}{4}+\frac{19\pi}{4}\right)=cis(10\pi)=1$

28. (48) Let population $= x$ at time t yr

Given, $\frac{dx}{dt}\propto x \Rightarrow \frac{dx}{dt}=kdt$

Integrating, $\ln x = kt+\ln C$

$\Rightarrow \quad \frac{x}{C}=e^{kt} \Rightarrow x=Ce^{kt}$

If initially i.e. when time $t=0$, $x=x_0$, then $x_0=Ce^0=C$

Given, $x=2x_0$, when $t=30$

Then, $2x_0=x_0e^{30k} \Rightarrow 2=e^{30k}$

$\therefore \quad \ln 2=30k \quad \text{...(i)}$

To find t, when t triples, $x=3x_0$

Thus, $3x_0=x_0e^{kt} \Rightarrow 3=e^{kt}$

$\therefore \quad \ln 3=kt \quad \text{...(ii)}$

On dividing Eq. (ii) by Eq. (i), we get

$$\frac{t}{30}=\frac{\ln 3}{\ln 2}$$

$\Rightarrow t=30\times\frac{\ln 3}{\ln 2}=30\times1.5849=48$ yr (approx)

29. (4) Coordinates of any point on the ellipse $\frac{x^2}{49}+\frac{y^2}{25}=1$ are of the form $(7\cos\theta, 5\sin\theta)$, $0\le\theta<2\pi$.

Let $x=7\cos\theta$, $y=5\sin\theta$, where x and y are integers.

As $-1\le\sin\theta\le1 \Rightarrow -5\le5\sin\theta\le5$

$\Rightarrow \quad 5\sin\theta=-5,-4,-3,-2,-1,0,1,2,3,4,5$ (integer values)

Now, $5\sin\theta=-5 \Rightarrow \sin\theta=-1$

$\Rightarrow \quad \theta=\frac{3\pi}{2}$ and $7\cos\theta=7\cos\left(\frac{3\pi}{2}\right)=0$

When, $5\sin\theta=\pm4 \Rightarrow \cos\theta=\pm\frac{3}{5}$

$\Rightarrow 7\cos\theta=\pm\frac{21}{5}$, which are not integer.

Similarly, $5\sin\theta=\pm3,\pm2,\pm1$, then $7\cos\theta$ is not an integer.

when, $5\sin\theta=0, \theta=0,\pi \Rightarrow 7\cos\theta=7,-7$

When, $5\sin\theta=5$, then $7\cos\theta=0$

Thus, lattice points on the ellipse are $(0,-5),(7,0),(0,5)$ and $(-7,0)$.

30. (8) $L=\lim_{x\to0}\frac{(1+x^2)^{1/3}-(1-2x)^{1/4}}{x+x^2}$

$$=\lim_{x\to0}\frac{\left(1+\frac{1}{3}x^2+\dots\right)-\left(1-\frac{x}{2}+\dots\right)}{x(1+x)}$$

$\Rightarrow \quad L=\lim_{x\to0}\frac{\frac{1}{2}+\frac{x}{3}+\dots}{1+x}=\frac{1}{2}$

$\therefore \quad 16L=16\times\frac{1}{2}=8$

Knockout 10

1. (a) Given, $f\left(\frac{5x-3y}{2}\right)=\frac{5f(x)-3f(y)}{2}$

$\Rightarrow f\left(\frac{5x-3y}{5-3}\right)=\frac{5f(x)-3f(y)}{5-3}$

which satisfies section formula for abscissa on LHS and ordinate on RHS. Hence, $f(x)$ must be the linear function (as only straight line satisfies such section formula)

So, $\quad f(x)=ax+b$

But $f(0)=3$ or $a\times0+b=3 \Rightarrow b=3$ and $f'(0)=2$ or $a=2$

Thus, $\quad f(x)=2x+3$

$\therefore$ Period of $\sin(f(x))=$ Period of $\sin(2x+3)=\frac{2\pi}{|2|}=\pi$

2. (c)

p	q	r	$\sim p$	$\sim q$	$p\vee\sim q$	$\sim p\wedge q$	$(p\vee\sim q)\vee(\sim p\wedge q)$	$[(p\vee\sim q)\vee(\sim p\wedge q)]\wedge r$
T	T	T	F	F	T	F	T	T
T	T	F	F	F	T	F	T	F
T	F	T	F	T	T	F	T	T
T	F	F	F	T	T	F	T	F
F	T	T	T	F	F	T	T	T
F	T	F	T	F	F	T	T	F
F	F	T	T	T	T	F	T	T
F	F	F	T	T	T	F	T	F

From above, we observe that the entries in the last column are a combination of T and F.

And we know that, a compound statement which is neither a tautology nor a contradiction is called a contigency.

So, the given statement is a contigency.

3. (d) Let $C(h,k)$ be the centre and r is the radius of the given circle.

Since, it touches $y=x$ at P, then we have

$$\frac{k-h}{\sqrt{2}}=\pm r \quad \text{...(i)}$$

As it makes an intercept $6\sqrt{2}$ on the line $x+y=0$ i.e. $y=-x$, we have

$$SQ=6\sqrt{2}, RS=3\sqrt{2} \text{ and } CS=r$$

$$\therefore \quad CR^2=r^2-18$$

$$\Rightarrow \left(\frac{k+h}{\sqrt{2}}\right)^2=r^2-18$$

$$\Rightarrow \frac{(k+h)^2}{2}=\frac{(k-h)^2}{2}-18$$

[from Eq. (i)]

$$\Rightarrow \frac{1}{4}(4kh)+18=0$$

$$\Rightarrow 2kh+18=0$$

$$\Rightarrow kh=-9 \quad \text{...(ii)}$$

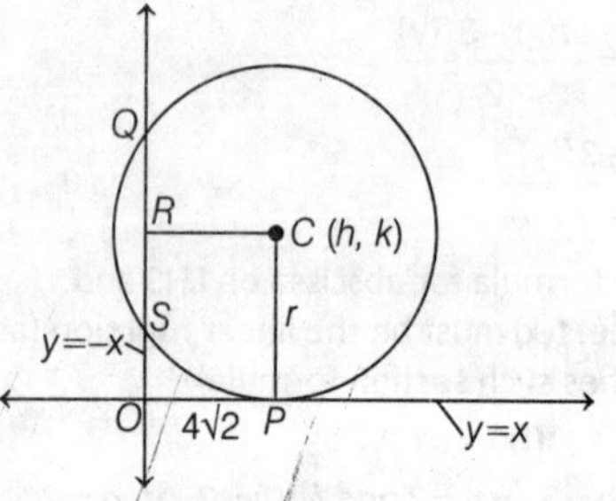

Also, $CR=\frac{|k+h|}{\sqrt{2}}=OP=4\sqrt{2}$

$$\Rightarrow |k+h|=(4\sqrt{2})(\sqrt{2})=8$$

$$\Rightarrow k+h=\pm 8 \quad \text{...(iii)}$$

and then $r^2=\frac{(k+h)^2}{2}+18=50$

Also, since the given circle contains the point $(-10,2)$ in its interior.

So, $\quad (h+10)^2+(k-2)^2<50 \quad$ ...(iv)

From Eqs. (ii) and (iii), we get

$$(h,k)=(-9,1) \text{ or } (9,-1)$$

Since, $(h,k)=(-9,1)$ only, satisfies Eq. (iv), then the required equation of the circle is $(x+9)^2+(y-1)^2=50$

$$\Rightarrow x^2+y^2+18x-2y+32=0$$

4. (b) Given equation can be written as

$$\sin^{-1}\left[\cos\left(\frac{2x^2+10|x|+4}{x^2+5|x|+3}\right)\right]$$

$$=\cot\left[\cot^{-1}\left(\frac{2-18|x|}{9|x|}\right)\right]+\frac{\pi}{2}$$

$$\Rightarrow \frac{\pi}{2}-\cos^{-1}$$

$$\left[\cos\left(\frac{2(x^2+5|x|+3)-2}{x^2+5|x|+3}\right)\right]$$

$$=\cot\left[\cot^{-1}\left(\frac{2}{9|x|}-2\right)\right]+\frac{\pi}{2}$$

$$-2+\frac{2}{x^2+5|x|+3}=\frac{2}{9|x|}-2$$

$$\Rightarrow x^2-4|x|+3=0$$

$$\Rightarrow (|x|-1)(|x|-3)=0$$

$$\Rightarrow |x|=1,3$$

$$\Rightarrow x=\pm 1, \pm 3$$

$$\therefore \quad \text{Product}=9$$

5. (c) Equation of the tangent at $(3\sqrt{3}\cos\theta, \sin\theta)$ is

$$\frac{x}{3\sqrt{3}}\cos\theta+y\sin\theta=1$$

It intercepts on coordinate axes are $3\sqrt{3}\sec\theta$ and $\operatorname{cosec}\theta$.

If S denotes their sum, then

$$S=3\sqrt{3}\sec\theta+\operatorname{cosec}\theta$$

$$\Rightarrow \frac{dS}{d\theta}=3\sqrt{3}\sec\theta\tan\theta-\operatorname{cosec}\theta\cot\theta$$

For minimum value of S, put

$$\frac{dS}{d\theta}=0$$

$$\Rightarrow \frac{3\sqrt{3}\sin\theta}{\cos^2\theta}-\frac{\cos\theta}{\sin^2\theta}=0$$

$$\Rightarrow \tan^3\theta=3\sqrt{3}$$

$$\Rightarrow \tan\theta=\sqrt{3}=\tan\left(\frac{\pi}{3}\right)$$

$$\Rightarrow \theta=\frac{\pi}{3}$$

Also, $\frac{d^2S}{d\theta^2}=3\sqrt{3}\sec\theta\tan^2\theta$

$$+3\sqrt{3}\sec^3\theta$$

$$+\operatorname{cosec}^2\theta\cot\theta+\operatorname{cosec}^3\theta$$

$$\Rightarrow \left.\frac{d^2S}{d\theta^2}\right|_{\theta=\pi/3}=+ve$$

Hence, S is least when

$$\theta=\frac{\pi}{3}.$$

6. (a) Equation of plane passing through (2, 1, 0), (5, 0, 1) and (4, 1, 1) is

$$\begin{vmatrix} x-2 & y-1 & z-0 \\ 5-2 & 0-1 & 1-0 \\ 4-2 & 1-1 & 1-0 \end{vmatrix}=0$$

$$\Rightarrow \begin{vmatrix} x-2 & y-1 & z \\ 3 & -1 & 1 \\ 2 & 0 & 1 \end{vmatrix}=0$$

$$\Rightarrow (x-2)(-1-0)-(y-1)(3-2)$$
$$+z(0+2)=0$$

$$\Rightarrow x+y-2z=3 \quad \text{...(i)}$$

Direction rations of normal to Eq. (i) are (1, 1, –2).

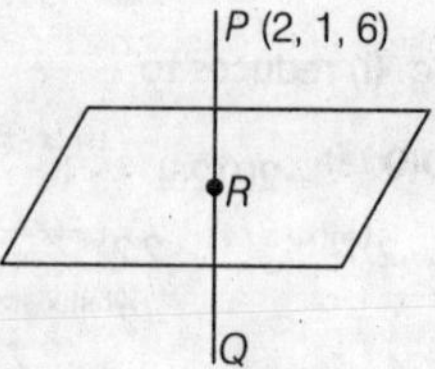

An equation of PQ is

$$\frac{x-2}{1}=\frac{y-1}{1}=\frac{z-6}{-2}=r \quad \text{(say)}$$

$$\Rightarrow \quad x=r+2, y=r+1$$

and $\quad z=-2r+6$

Let coordinates of Q be $(r+2, r+1, -2r+6)$

Let R be the mid-point of PQ, then coordinates of R are

$$\left(\frac{r}{2}+2, \frac{r}{2}+1, -r+6\right).$$

It will lie on Eq. (i), if

$$\frac{r}{2}+2+\frac{r}{2}+1+2r-12=3$$

$$\Rightarrow \quad 3r=12 \Rightarrow r=4$$

$\therefore$ Coordinates of Q are (6, 5, –2).

7. (b) $D^*(x)=\lim_{h\to 0}\frac{f^2(x+h)-f^2(x)}{h}$

$$=\lim_{h\to 0}\left[\left(\frac{f(x+h)-f(x)}{h}\right)(f(x+h)+f(x))\right]$$

$$=\lim_{h\to 0}\frac{f(x+h)-f(x)}{h}(f(x+0)+f(x))$$

$$=2f(x)\cdot f'(x)$$

$$\therefore D^*(x\log_e x)=2x\log_e x(1+\log_e x)$$

$$\Rightarrow \left.D^* f(x)\right|_{x=e}$$

$$=2\times e\times\log_e e(1+\log_e e)$$

$$=4e$$

8. (d) An equation of tangent to the ellipse

$$\frac{x^2}{25}+\frac{y^2}{4}=1 \text{ is}$$

$$y = mx + \sqrt{25m^2 + 4} \quad \text{...(i)}$$

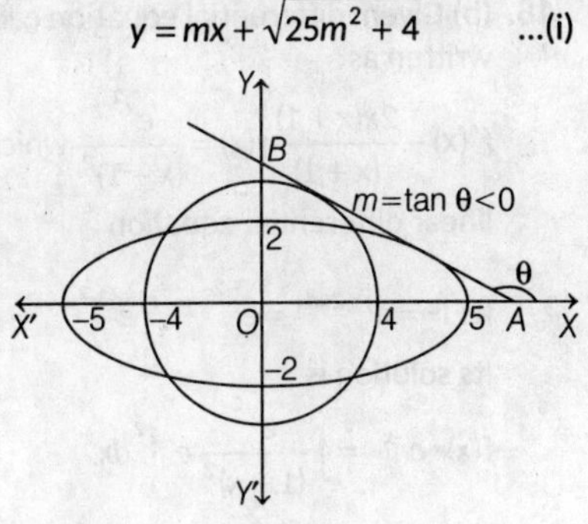

As this tangent has to lie in the first quadrant.

$\therefore \quad m < 0$

The line (i) will touch the circle $x^2 + y^2 = 16$, if perpendicular distance from $O(0, 0)$ to Eq. (i) is equal to 4.

i.e. if $\left|\dfrac{m \times 0 - 0 + \sqrt{25m^2 + 4}}{\sqrt{m^2 + 1}}\right| = 4$

$\Rightarrow \quad 25m^2 + 4 = 16(m^2 + 1)$

$\Rightarrow \quad 9m^2 = 12 \Rightarrow m^2 = \dfrac{4}{3}$

$\Rightarrow \quad m = \pm\sqrt{\dfrac{4}{3}}$ but $m < 0$

$\therefore \quad m = -\dfrac{2}{\sqrt{3}}$

From Eq. (i),

$$y = \frac{-2}{\sqrt{3}}x + \sqrt{25\left(\frac{4}{3}\right) + 4}$$

$\Rightarrow \quad 2x + \sqrt{3}y = 4\sqrt{7} \quad \text{...(ii)}$

Line (ii) meets the coordinate axes in $A(2\sqrt{7}, 0)$ and $B\left(0, \dfrac{4\sqrt{7}}{\sqrt{3}}\right)$.

So, $AB^2 = 4(7) + 16\left(\dfrac{7}{3}\right) = (4)(7)\left(\dfrac{7}{3}\right)$

$\Rightarrow AB = \dfrac{14}{\sqrt{3}}$ units.

9. (b) Let E_i be the event when integer $(2i)$ is chosen, where $i = 1, 2, 3, 4 \dots, n$

Let A be the event that an even number is chosen.

Then, $A = E_1 \cup E_2 \cup E_3 \cup \dots \cup E_n$

All E_i's are mutually exclusive.

$\Rightarrow P(A) = P(E_1) + P(E_2) + P(E_3) + \dots + P(E_n) \quad \text{...(i)}$

Given, $\quad P(E_i) \propto \log 2i$

$\Rightarrow \quad P(E_i) = \lambda \log 2i,$

where, λ = Proportional constant.

From Eq. (i),

$$P(A) = \lambda\log 2 + \lambda\log 4 + \lambda\log 6 + \dots + \lambda\log 2n$$

$$= \lambda\log(2\cdot4\cdot6 \dots 2n)$$

$$= \lambda\log(2^n(1\cdot2\cdot3\dots n))$$

$[\because 2\cdot4\cdot6\dots2n = (2\times1)\cdot(2\times2)\cdot(2\times3)\dots(2\times n)]$

$$= \lambda(n\log 2 + \log n!)$$

Let B be the event that integer 2 is chosen.

$$\therefore P(B/A) = \frac{P(A\cap B)}{P(A)} = \frac{P(E_1)}{P(A)}$$

$$= \frac{\lambda\log 2}{\lambda(n\log 2 + \log n!)}$$

$$= \frac{\log 2}{n\log 2 + \log n!}$$

10. (b) Let $I = \displaystyle\int_5^{41} \frac{dx}{[f^{-1}(x)]^5 + 5[f^{-1}(x)]}$

Put $f^{-1}(x) = z \Rightarrow x = f(z)$

$\Rightarrow \quad dx = f'(z)\,dz$

Now, $f(x) = x^5 + 5x - 1$

$\Rightarrow \quad f(1) = 5 \Rightarrow f^{-1}(5) = 1$

and $\quad f(2) = (2)^5 + 5\times2 - 1 = 41$

$\Rightarrow f^{-1}(41) = 2$

$$\therefore \; I = \int_1^2 \frac{f'(z)dz}{z^5 + 5z} = \int_1^2 \frac{5z^4 + 5}{z^5 + 5z}dz$$

$[\because f(x) = x^5 + 5x - 1$

$\therefore f(z) = z^5 + 5z - 1$

$\Rightarrow f'(z) = 5z^4 + 5]$

$$= \log_e(z^5 + 5z)\Big|_1^2$$

$$= \log_e 42 - \log_e 6 = \log_e 7$$

11. (c) Given, $e^{|\sin x|} + e^{-|\sin x|} + 4\lambda = 0 \quad \text{...(i)}$

Let $u = e^{|\sin x|} \Rightarrow u \in [1, e]$

$(\because |\sin x| \in [0,1] \; \therefore u \in [e^0, e^1])$

From Eq. (i), $u + \dfrac{1}{u} + 4\lambda = 0$

$\Rightarrow \quad u + \dfrac{1}{u} = -4\lambda \quad \text{...(ii)}$

Let, $f(u) = u + \dfrac{1}{u}$

$\Rightarrow f'(u) = 1 - \dfrac{1}{u^2} = \dfrac{u^2 - 1}{u^2} \geq 0, \forall u \in [1, e]$

$\therefore f(u)$ is increasing function for $u \in [1, e]$.

Now, $1 \leq u \leq e$

$\Rightarrow \quad f(1) \leq f(u) \leq f(e)$

[inequality remains unchanged because f is increasing function]

$\Rightarrow \quad 1 + \dfrac{1}{1} \leq f(u) \leq e + \dfrac{1}{e}$

$\Rightarrow \quad 2 \leq -4\lambda \leq \dfrac{e^2 + 1}{e} \quad$ [from Eq. (ii)]

$\Rightarrow \quad \dfrac{-1}{2} \geq \lambda \geq \dfrac{e^2 + 1}{-4e}$

$\Rightarrow \quad \dfrac{-(e^2 + 1)}{4e} \leq \lambda \leq \dfrac{-1}{2}$

$\Rightarrow \quad \lambda \in \left[\dfrac{-1 - e^2}{4e}, \dfrac{-1}{2}\right]$

12. (b) Let $I = \displaystyle\int \frac{(\sqrt{x})^5}{(\sqrt{x})^7 + x^6}dx$

$$= \int \frac{\dfrac{(\sqrt{x})^5}{(\sqrt{x})^5}}{\dfrac{(\sqrt{x})^7}{(\sqrt{x})^5} + \dfrac{(\sqrt{x})^{12}}{(\sqrt{x})^5}}dx$$

$$= \int \frac{dx}{(\sqrt{x})^2 + (\sqrt{x})^7}$$

$$= \int \frac{dx}{(\sqrt{x})^7\left[1 + \dfrac{1}{(\sqrt{x})^5}\right]}$$

Putting $\dfrac{1}{(\sqrt{x})^5} = z$

$\Rightarrow \quad dz = \dfrac{-5}{2(\sqrt{x})^7}dx$

So, $I = \displaystyle\int \frac{-2dz}{5(1 + z)} = \frac{-2}{5}\ln|1 + z| + C$

$$= \frac{2}{5}\ln\left|\frac{1}{1 + z}\right| + C$$

$$= \frac{2}{5}\ln\left|\frac{1}{1 + \dfrac{1}{(\sqrt{x})^5}}\right| + C$$

$$= \frac{2}{5}\ln\left|\frac{(\sqrt{x})^5}{(\sqrt{x})^5 + 1}\right| + C$$

On comparing, $a = \dfrac{2}{5}$ and $k = \dfrac{5}{2}$

13. (a) We have,

$$\bar{x} = \frac{0\cdot{}^{10}C_0 + 1\cdot{}^{10}C_1 + 2\cdot{}^{10}C_2 + \dots + 10\cdot{}^{10}C_{10}}{{}^{10}C_0 + {}^{10}C_1 + {}^{10}C_2 + \dots + {}^{10}C_{10}}$$

$$= \frac{\sum_{r=0}^{10} r\cdot{}^{10}C_r}{\sum_{r=0}^{10}{}^{10}C_r} = \frac{10\cdot\sum_{r=1}^{10}{}^{9}C_{r-1}}{2^{10}}$$

$$= \frac{10}{2^{10}}({}^9C_0 + {}^9C_1 + {}^9C_2 + \dots + {}^9C_9)$$

$$= \frac{10}{2^{10}} \times 2^9 = 5$$

Now, $\dfrac{1}{N}\Sigma f_i x_i^2 = \dfrac{1}{2^{10}}\displaystyle\sum_{r=0}^{10} r^2\cdot{}^{10}C_r$

$$=\frac{1}{2^{10}}\sum_{r=0}^{10}(r^2-r+r)\ ^{10}C_r$$

$$=\frac{1}{2^{10}}\left[\sum_{r=0}^{10}r(r-1)\ ^{10}C_r+\sum_{r=0}^{10}r\cdot {}^{10}C_r\right]$$

$$=\frac{1}{2^{10}}$$

$$[90\cdot({}^8C_0+{}^8C_1+{}^8C_2+\ldots {}^8C_8)+10({}^9C_0+{}^9C_1+\ldots+{}^9C_9)]$$

$$=\frac{1}{2^{10}}(90\times 2^8+10\times 2^9)$$

$$=\frac{10\times 2^8}{2^{10}}(9+2)=\frac{55}{2}$$

$$\text{Var}(X)=\frac{1}{N}\Sigma f_i x_i^2-(\bar{x})^2=\frac{55}{2}-(5)^2=\frac{5}{2}$$

14. (d) $\because x=4t^2-1\Rightarrow\frac{x+1}{4}=t^2$

and $y=8t-2\Rightarrow\frac{y+2}{8}=t$

$$\Rightarrow\quad\frac{x+1}{4}=\left(\frac{y+2}{8}\right)^2$$

$$\Rightarrow(y+2)^2=\frac{64}{4}(x+1)$$

$$\Rightarrow(y+2)^2=16(x+1)$$

Which is of the for $Y^2=4AX$

where $Y=y+2$,

$4A=16\Rightarrow A=4$

$X=x+1$

$\therefore$ Equation of latus rectum

$X=A$

$x+1=4\Rightarrow x-3=0$

15. (c) Since, coefficient of x^2+ax+1 are symmetrical.

So, roots will be $\alpha,\frac{1}{\alpha}$

($\because$ coefficient of x^2 = constant term)

Now, $\lim_{x\to 1/\alpha}\frac{\sin(x^2+ax+1)}{(\alpha x-1)}$

$$=\lim_{x\to 1/\alpha}\frac{\sin\left[\left(x-\frac{1}{\alpha}\right)(x-\alpha)\right]}{\left(x-\frac{1}{\alpha}\right)(x-\alpha)}\cdot\frac{\left(x-\frac{1}{\alpha}\right)(x-\alpha)}{(\alpha x-1)}$$

$$=\lim_{x\to 1/\alpha}\frac{(x-\alpha)}{\alpha}=\frac{\frac{1}{\alpha}-\alpha}{\alpha}=\frac{1-\alpha^2}{\alpha^2}$$

16. (a) **Method (1)**

Since, $|z_2|=6$ represents a circle with radius $=6$ units.

Now, $|z_1+z_2|=|z_2-(-z_1)|$

$\Rightarrow|z_2+z_1|=|z_2-(-24-7i)|$

represents distance between point on the circle $|z_2|=6$ and the point $C(-24-7i)$

$|z_1+z_2|$ will be greatest and least at points B and A which are the end points of the diameter of the circle through C.

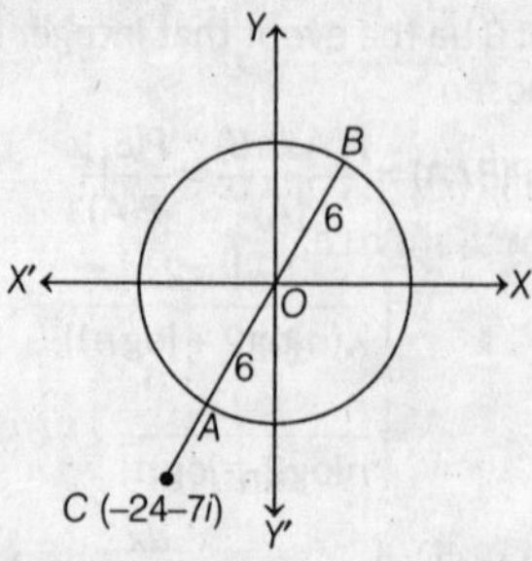

$$\because\quad OC=\sqrt{(-24)^2+(-7)^2}=25$$

$$\therefore\quad CA=OC-OA=25-6=19$$

(least value)

and $CB=OC+OB=25+6=31$

(greatest value)

Method (2)

$\because|z_2|=6\Rightarrow z_2=6\cdot e^{i\theta}$, where $\theta\in R$

$\therefore$

$$|z_1+z_2|^2=|24+7i+6(\cos\theta+i\sin\theta)|^2$$

$$=(24+6\cos\theta)^2+(7+6\sin\theta)^2$$

$$=576+36\cos^2\theta+288\cos\theta+49+36\sin^2\theta+84\sin\theta$$

$$=625+36+12(24\cos\theta+7\sin\theta)$$

$$=661+12(25)\sin(\theta+\alpha)$$

($\because$ put $7=r\cos\alpha$ and $24=r\sin\alpha$)

$$=661+300\sin(\theta+\alpha)$$

Thus, greatest possible value of $|z_1+z_2|^2$ is $661+300=961$ and the least possible value of $|z_1+z_2|^2$ is 361.

Hence, greatest and least possible values of $|z_1+z_2|$ are 31 and 19.

17. (d) Slope of LF_1 is $\tan 30°$

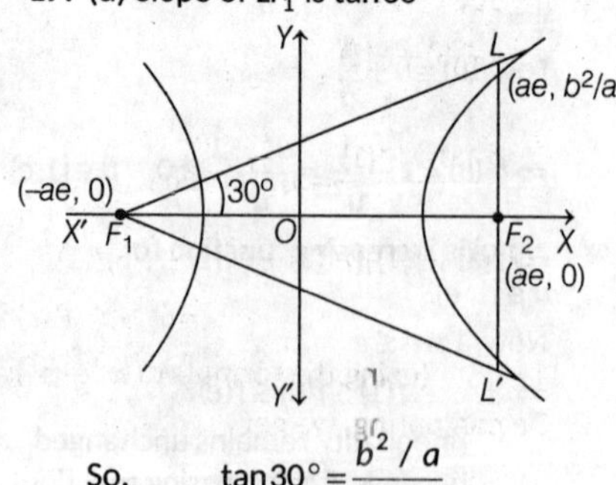

So, $\tan 30°=\frac{b^2/a}{2ae}$

$$\Rightarrow\quad\frac{1}{\sqrt{3}}=\frac{a^2(e^2-1)}{2a^2e}=\frac{e^2-1}{2e}$$

$$\Rightarrow\quad e=\sqrt{3}$$

18. (b) Given, differential equation can be written as

$f'(x)-\frac{2x(x+1)}{(x+1)}f(x)=\frac{e^{x^2}}{(x+1)^2}$ which is linear differential equation

Its IF $=e^{\int-2x dx}=e^{-2\cdot\frac{x^2}{2}}=e^{-x^2}$

Its solution is

$$f(x)\cdot e^{-x^2}=\int\frac{e^{x^2}}{(1+x)^2}e^{-x^2}dx$$

$$=\int\frac{1}{(1+x)^2}dx=\frac{-1}{1+x}+C$$

Given, $f(0)=5$ i.e. at $x=0$, $f(0)=5$.

$\therefore C=6$ and hence,

$$f(x)=\left(\frac{-1}{1+x}+6\right)e^{x^2}=\left(\frac{6x+5}{x+1}\right)e^{x^2}$$

19. (c) We have, $\mathbf{r}\times\mathbf{a}=\mathbf{b}\times\mathbf{a}$

$\Rightarrow\quad(\mathbf{r}\cdot\mathbf{b})\times\mathbf{a}=0$

$\Rightarrow\quad\mathbf{r}-\mathbf{b}$ is parallel to $\mathbf{a}$

$\Rightarrow\quad\mathbf{r}=\mathbf{b}+\lambda\mathbf{a}$ ...(i)

Now, $\quad\mathbf{r}\cdot\mathbf{c}=0$

$\Rightarrow\quad(\mathbf{b}+\lambda\mathbf{a})\cdot\mathbf{c}=0$

$\Rightarrow\quad\mathbf{b}\cdot\mathbf{c}+\lambda(\mathbf{a}\cdot\mathbf{c})=0\Rightarrow\lambda=-\frac{\mathbf{b}\cdot\mathbf{c}}{\mathbf{a}\cdot\mathbf{c}}$

On putting the value of λ in Eq. (i), we get

$$\mathbf{r}=\mathbf{b}-\frac{(\mathbf{b}\cdot\mathbf{c})}{(\mathbf{a}\cdot\mathbf{c})}\mathbf{a}$$

20. (d) Applying $m-n$ theorem (or cotangent theorem), we get

$$(c+c)\cot(\theta-30°)=c\cot 15°-c\cot 30°$$

$$\Rightarrow 2c\cot(\theta-30°)=c\left(\frac{\cos 15°}{\sin 15°}-\frac{\cos 30°}{\sin 30°}\right)$$

$$\Rightarrow\cot(\theta-30°)=\frac{\cos 15°\sin 30°-\cos 30°\sin 15°}{2\sin 15°\sin 30°}$$

$$\Rightarrow\quad\cot(\theta-30°)=\frac{\sin(30°-15°)}{2\sin 15°\times\frac{1}{2}}$$

$$\Rightarrow\quad\cot(\theta-30°)=1\Rightarrow\theta-30°=45°$$

$$\Rightarrow\quad\theta=75°$$

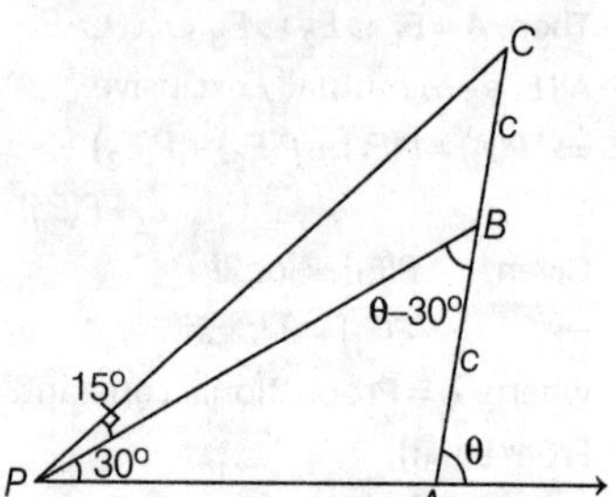

Section II

21. (12) Given,

$$f(x)=\begin{cases}-2x+\log_{1/2}(\lambda^2-6\lambda+8) & , -2\le x<-1\\ x^3+3x^2+4x+1 & , -1\le x\le 3\end{cases}$$

Also,

$f'(x)=3x^2+6x+4>0, \forall x\in[-1,3]$

So, $f(x)$ is increasing on $[-1, 3]$.

and $f'(x)=-2\times1+0$

$=-2<0, \forall x\in[-2,-1)$

So, $f(x)$ is decreasing on $(-2,-1)$.

$\therefore$ If $f(x)$ has smallest values at $x=-1$, then we must have

$\lim_{h\to0} f(-1-h)\ge f(-1)$

$\Rightarrow \lim_{h\to0}[-2(-1-h)+\log_{1/2}(\lambda^2-6\lambda+8)]$

$\ge(-1)^3+3(-1)^2+4(-1)+1$

$\Rightarrow\ 2+\log_{1/2}(\lambda^2-6\lambda+8)\ge-1$

$\Rightarrow\ \log_{1/2}(\lambda^2-6\lambda+8)\ge-3$

$\Rightarrow\ \log_2(\lambda^2-6\lambda+8)\le3$

$\Rightarrow\ \lambda^2-6\lambda+8\le8$

$\Rightarrow\ \lambda^2-6\lambda\le0$

$\Rightarrow\ \lambda(\lambda-6)\le0$

$\Rightarrow\ 0\le\lambda\le6$ ...(i)

But in order to define $\log_{1/2}(\lambda^2-6\lambda+8)$ we must have,

$\lambda^2-6\lambda+8>0$

$\Rightarrow\ (\lambda-2)(\lambda-4)>0$

$\Rightarrow\ \lambda<2$ or $\lambda>4$ ...(ii)

From Eqs. (i) and (ii), we get

$\lambda\in[0,2)\cup(4,6]$

$\Rightarrow$ Possible integer(s) in the range of λ are 0, 1, 5, 6.

Hence, the sum of all possible positive integer (s) in the range of $\lambda=1+5+6=12$

22. (1) Given, $C_n=\int_{1/n+1}^{1/n}\frac{\tan^{-1}(nx)}{\sin^{-1}(nx)}dx$

Putting, $nx=z$

$\Rightarrow\ dx=\frac{1}{n}dz$

x	$\frac{1}{n+1}$	$\frac{1}{n}$
z	$\frac{n}{n+1}$	1

$\therefore\ C_n=\frac{1}{n}\int_{n/n+1}^{1}\frac{\tan^{-1}(z)}{\sin^{-1}(z)}dz$

Now, $L=2$

$\lim_{n\to\infty} n^2\cdot C_n=\lim_{n\to\infty} n\cdot\int_{n/n+1}^{1}\frac{\tan^{-1}(z)}{\sin^{-1}(z)}dz$

(form $0\times\infty$)

$$L=2\cdot\lim_{n\to\infty}\frac{\int_{n/n+1}^{1}\frac{\tan^{-1}(z)}{\sin^{-1}(z)}dz}{\frac{1}{z}}\quad\left(\text{form}\frac{0}{0}\right)$$

Applying Leibnitz rule and L' Hospital's rule,

$$L=2\cdot\lim_{n\to\infty}\frac{\left[0-\frac{\tan^{-1}\left(\frac{n}{n+1}\right)}{\sin^{-1}\left(\frac{n}{n+1}\right)}\left(\frac{1}{(n+1)^2}\right)\right]}{\frac{-1}{n^2}}$$

$=\frac{\pi}{4}\times\frac{2}{\pi}\times2=1$

23. (31) **Case I** If all are different, then the number of ways $={}^6C_3=20$

Case II If three each of two colours, then combination is

3 0 → 2!

2 1 → 2!

$=2!+2!=4$ ways

Case III If two each of three colours, then combination is

2 1 0 → 3!

1 1 1 → 1!

$=3!+1!=7$ ways

$\therefore$ Required number of ways

$=20+4+7=31$ ways

24. (12) Let $F(x)=f^3(x)$

And $F(x)$ is continuous and differentiable function in [1, 3] using Lagrange's mean value theorem, we get

$\frac{F(3)-F(1)}{3-1}=F'(c)$

$\therefore\ \frac{f^3(3)-f^3(1)}{2}=3f^2(c)\cdot f'(c)$

$\Rightarrow[f(3)-f(1)][f^2(3)+f^2(1)+f(3)f(1)]$

$=6f^2(c)\cdot f'(c)$

(using the formula of a^3-b^3)

On comparing, we get

$k=6$

$\therefore\ 2k=12$

25. (10) 7th term in $\left[\sqrt[6]{3}\sqrt{2}+\frac{1}{\sqrt[3]{3}}\right]^n$

$={}^nC_6(2^{1/2}3^{1/6})^{n-6}\left[\frac{1}{3^{1/3}}\right]^6$

7th term from the end in $\left[\sqrt[6]{3}\sqrt{2}+\frac{1}{\sqrt[3]{3}}\right]^n$

$={}^nC_6\cdot\left(\frac{1}{3^{1/3}}\right)^{n-6}(3^{1/6}2^{1/2})^6$

According to the question,

$$\frac{{}^nC_6(2^{1/2}3^{1/6})^{n-6}\left(\frac{1}{3^{1/3}}\right)^6}{{}^nC_6\left(\frac{1}{3^{1/3}}\right)^{n-6}(3^{1/6}2^{1/2})^6}=\frac{1}{6}$$

$$\Rightarrow\ \frac{2^{\frac{n-6}{2}}\cdot3^{\frac{n-6}{6}}}{3^{\frac{6-n}{3}}\cdot2^3\cdot3^1}\times\frac{1}{3^2}=\frac{1}{6}$$

$$\Rightarrow\frac{2^{\frac{n-6}{2}}}{3^{\frac{6-n}{3}}}\times\frac{1}{3^{-\left(\frac{n-6}{3}\right)}}\times\frac{1}{2^3\times3^3}=\frac{1}{6}$$

$\Rightarrow\ 2^{\frac{n-6}{2}}\cdot3^{\frac{n-6}{2}}=2^2\times3^2$

$\Rightarrow\ \frac{n-6}{2}=2$

$\Rightarrow\ n=10$

26. (11) Given, curves are

$y=ex\ln x$ ...(i)

and $y=\frac{\ln x}{ex}$ ...(ii)

Points of intersection of Eqs. (i) and (ii) are $P\left(\frac{1}{e},-1\right)$ and $Q(1,0)$.

For curve (i),

$y<0$ for $0<x<1$

and $y\ge0$ for $x\ge1$

Obviously $y\to0$ when $x\to0$

For curve (ii), $y<0$ for $0<x<1$

and $y\ge0$ for $x\ge1$

Obviously $y\to0$ when $x\to\infty$

Thus, the shape of the two curves are as shown in the figrue below

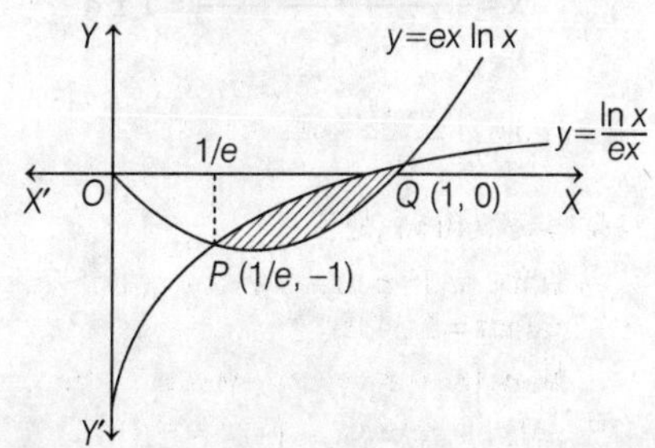

$\therefore$ Required area

$$= \left|\int_{1/e}^{1} ex\ln x dx\right| - \left|\int_{1/e}^{1} \frac{\ln x}{ex} dx\right|$$

$$= \left|\left[\frac{1}{4}ex^2(2\ln x - 1)\right]_{1/e}^{1}\right| - \left|\left[\frac{1}{2e}(\ln x)^2\right]_{1/e}^{1}\right|$$

$$= \left|\frac{1}{4e}(3-e^2)\right| - \left|-\frac{1}{2e}\right|$$

$$= \frac{e^2-3}{4e} - \frac{1}{2e} = \frac{e^2-5}{4e} \text{ sq units}$$

On comparing, we get

$$\alpha = 2, \beta = -5 \text{ and } \gamma = 4$$

Hence, $\alpha - \beta + \gamma = 2 + 5 + 4 = 11$

27. (1) For no solution or infinitely many solutions.

$$\begin{vmatrix} \alpha & -1 & -1 \\ 1 & -\alpha & -1 \\ 1 & -1 & -\alpha \end{vmatrix} = 0$$

$\Rightarrow \alpha(\alpha^2 - 1) - 1(\alpha - 1) + 1(1 - \alpha) = 0$

$\Rightarrow \alpha(\alpha^2 - 1) - 2\alpha + 2 = 0$

$\Rightarrow \alpha(\alpha - 1)(\alpha + 1) - 2(\alpha - 1) = 0$

$\Rightarrow (\alpha - 1)(\alpha^2 + \alpha - 2) = 0$

$\Rightarrow (\alpha - 1)(\alpha + 2)(\alpha - 1) = 0$

$\Rightarrow (\alpha - 1)^2(\alpha + 2) = 0$

$\Rightarrow \alpha = 1, 1, -2$

But for $\alpha = 1$ there are infinite solutions, when $\alpha = -2$, we have

$$-2x - y - z = -3$$
$$x + 2y - z = -3$$
$$x - y + 2z = -3$$

On adding, we get $0 = -9$ which is not true. Hence, there is no solution

So, $\alpha = k = -2$

Hence, $[\pi + k] = [\pi + (-2)] = 1$

28. (8) Let $f_1(x) = x^2 - 2x - (a^2 - 1) = 0$ ...(i)

$f_2(x) = x^2 - 2(a+1)x + a(a-1) = 0$ ...(ii)

From Eq. (i),

$$x = \frac{2 \pm \sqrt{4 + 4(a^2 - 1)}}{2} = 1 \pm a$$

Now, roots of Eq. (i) lie between roots of Eq. (ii). Hence, graph of function $f_1(x)$ and $f_2(x)$ are as follows

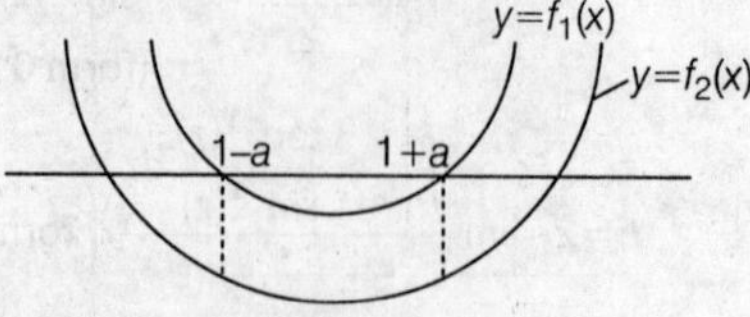

From the graph, we have

$f_2(1-a) < 0$ and $f_2(1+a) < 0$

$\Rightarrow (1-a)^2 - 2(a+1)(1-a) + a(a-1) < 0$

and $(1+a)^2 - 2(a+1)(a+1) + a(a-1) < 0$

$\Rightarrow (1-a)[(1-a) - 2a - 2 - a] < 0$

and $-(a+1)^2 + a(a-1) < 0$

$\Rightarrow (1-a)(-4a-1) < 0$

and $-a^2 - 2a - 1 + a^2 - a < 0$

$\Rightarrow (a-1)(4a+1) < 0$

and $3a + 1 > 0$

$\Rightarrow \frac{-1}{4} < a < 1$ and $a > \frac{-1}{3}$

$\Rightarrow a \in \left(\frac{-1}{4}, 1\right)$

On comparing, we get

$$\lambda = \frac{-1}{4} \text{ and } \mu = 1$$

So, $7\mu - 4\lambda = 7 \times 1 - 4\left(\frac{-1}{4}\right)$

$= 7 + 1 = 8$

29. (2) Given, $f(x) = \begin{vmatrix} \cos x & x & 1 \\ 2\sin x & x^2 & 2x \\ \tan x & x & 1 \end{vmatrix}$

On differentiating both sides w.r.t. x, we get

$f'(x) =$

$$\begin{vmatrix} -\sin x & x & 1 \\ 2\cos x & x^2 & 2x \\ \sec^2 x & x & 1 \end{vmatrix} + \begin{vmatrix} \cos x & 1 & 1 \\ 2\sin x & 2x & 2x \\ \tan x & 1 & 1 \end{vmatrix} + \begin{vmatrix} \cos x & x & 0 \\ 2\sin x & x^2 & 2 \\ \tan x & x & 0 \end{vmatrix}$$

$$\Rightarrow \frac{f'(x)}{x} = \begin{vmatrix} -\sin x & 1 & 1 \\ 2\cos x & x & 2x \\ \sec^2 x & 1 & 1 \end{vmatrix} + \begin{vmatrix} \cos x & 1 & 0 \\ 2\sin x & x & 2 \\ \tan x & 1 & 0 \end{vmatrix}$$

[$\because$ the second determinant is zero because $C_2 = C_3$]

$$\Rightarrow \lim_{x \to 0} \frac{f'(x)}{x} = \begin{vmatrix} 0 & 1 & 1 \\ 2 & 0 & 0 \\ 1 & 1 & 1 \end{vmatrix} + \begin{vmatrix} 1 & 1 & 0 \\ 0 & 0 & 2 \\ 0 & 1 & 0 \end{vmatrix}$$

$= 0 - 2 = 2$

Hence, absolute value of

$$\lim_{x \to 0} \frac{f'(x)}{x} = |-2| = 2$$

30. (3) Given,

$$|2\sin x - \sqrt{3}|^{(2\cos^2 x - 3\cos x + 1)} = 1$$

Case I $2\cos^2 x - 3\cos x + 1 = 0$

$\Rightarrow \cos x = \frac{1}{2}, 1$

$\Rightarrow x = 0, \frac{\pi}{3} \in [0, \pi]$

But at $x = \frac{\pi}{3}$; LHS $= 0^0$

$\therefore x = \frac{\pi}{3}$ (rejected),

Hence, $x = 0$ is a solution.

Case II $2\sin x - \sqrt{3} = 1, -1$

$\therefore \sin x = \frac{\sqrt{3}+1}{2}, \frac{\sqrt{3}-1}{2}$

But $\sin x = \frac{\sqrt{3}+1}{2}$

(rejected because $-1 \le \sin x \le 1$)

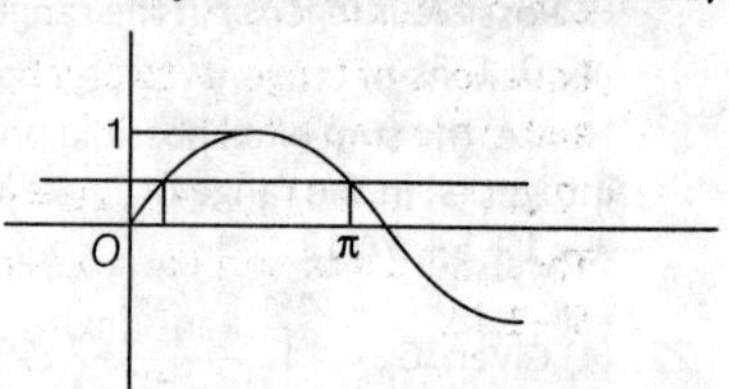

So, $\sin x = \frac{\sqrt{3}-1}{2} \Rightarrow \sin x \simeq 0.366$

$\therefore x$ has 2 values in $[0, \pi]$.

Hence, total number of solutions $= 2 + 1 = 3$

Knockout 11

Paper 1

1. (0.25) Firstly, we obtain the coordinates of P and Q.

For this, we solve the equations

$$x^2+y^2=9 \quad \text{...(i)}$$

$$y^2=8x \quad \text{...(ii)}$$

From Eq. (i), $y^2=9-x^2$ put in Eq. (ii), we get $9-x^2=8x$

$\Rightarrow \quad x^2+8x-9=0 \Rightarrow (x+9)(x-1)=0$

$\Rightarrow \quad x=1 \quad [\because x+9>9]$

(or we see that when $x=-9$, then from Eq. (i), $y=$ imaginary number]

$\therefore \quad y^2=8$

$\Rightarrow \quad y=\pm 2\sqrt{2}$

Thus, coordinates of P are $(1, 2\sqrt{2})$ and that of Q are $(1, -2\sqrt{2})$.

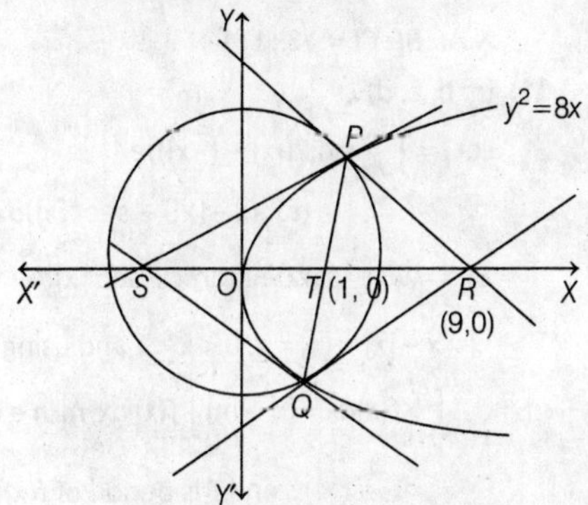

Equations of tangents to the circle at P and Q are respectively,

$x+2\sqrt{2}y=9$ and $x-2\sqrt{2}y=9$

On solving these, we obtain coordinates of R as $(9, 0)$.

Equations of tangents to parabola at P and Q are respectively,

$2\sqrt{2}y=4(x+1)$ and $-2\sqrt{2}y=4(x+1)$

These lines intersect each other at $S(-1, 0)$.

Let $\Delta_1=$ Area of $\Delta PQS=\frac{1}{2}(PQ)(ST)$

$$=\frac{1}{2}(2)(4\sqrt{2})=4\sqrt{2} \text{ sq units}$$

and $\quad \Delta_2=$ Area of ΔPQR

$$=\frac{1}{2}(PQ)(TR)=\frac{1}{2}(4\sqrt{2})(8)$$

$$=16\sqrt{2} \text{ sq units}$$

$\therefore \Delta_1:\Delta_2=4\sqrt{2}:16\sqrt{2}=1:4$

2. (13) $6=\underbrace{0(2)+6(1)}_{(1+1+1+1+1+1)}=\underbrace{1(2)+4(1)}_{(2+1+1+1+1)}$

$$=\underbrace{2(2)+2(1)}_{(2+2+1+1)}=\underbrace{3(2)+0(1)}_{(2+2+2)}$$

Number of 2's	Number of 1's	Number of permutations
0	6	1
1	4	$\frac{5!}{4!}=5$
2	2	$\frac{4!}{2!2!}=6$
3	0	$\frac{3!}{3!}=1$
		Total = 13

$\therefore \quad f(6)=13$

3. (0.67) Since, given that $P(v_i)\propto i$

$\Rightarrow \quad P(v_i)=Ci$ (where C is constant)

But $\Sigma P(v_i)=1$

$\Rightarrow \quad \Sigma Ci=1 \Rightarrow C\Sigma i=1$

$\Rightarrow \quad C\left[\frac{n(n+1)}{2}\right]=1$

$\Rightarrow \quad C=\frac{2}{n(n+1)}$

$\Rightarrow \quad P(v_i)=\frac{2i}{n(n+1)}$

Now, by total probability theorem, we get

$$P(w)=\sum_{i=1}^{n} P(v_i)P\left(\frac{w}{v_i}\right)$$

$$=\sum_{i=1}^{n}\frac{2i}{n(n+1)}\times\frac{i}{n+1}$$

$$=\frac{2}{n(n+1)^2}\sum_{i=1}^{n} i^2$$

$$=\frac{2}{n(n+1)^2}\left[\frac{n(n+1)(2n+1)}{6}\right]$$

$$=\frac{(2n+1)}{(3n+3)}$$

$$\therefore \lim_{n\to\infty}P(w)=\lim_{n\to\infty}\frac{2n+1}{3n+3}$$

$$=\lim_{n\to\infty}\frac{2+\frac{1}{n}}{3+\frac{3}{n}}=\frac{2}{3}=0.67$$

4. (0) We have,

$$6\int f(x)\cdot g(x)\,dx=x^6+3x^4+3x^2+C$$

On differentiating both sides, we get

$$6f(x)\cdot g(x)=6x^5+12x^3+6x$$

$\Rightarrow \quad f(x)\cdot g(x)=x^5+2x^3+x \quad \text{...(i)}$

and $\quad 2\int\frac{g(x)\,dx}{f(x)}=x^2+C$

$\Rightarrow \quad \frac{g(x)}{f(x)}=x \quad \text{...(ii)}$

Multiplying Eqs. (i) and (ii), we get

$$\{g(x)\}^2=x^6+2x^4+x^2$$

$\Rightarrow \quad \{g(x)\}^2=(x^3+x)^2$

$\Rightarrow \quad g(x)=x^3+x$

So, $f(x)=x^2+1$

$$\lim_{x\to 0}\frac{\log\{f(x)\}}{g(x)}=\lim_{x\to 0}\frac{\log(x^2+1)}{x+x^3}$$

$$=\lim_{x\to 0}\frac{\log(1+x^2)}{x^2}\cdot\frac{x^2}{x+x^3}$$

$$=0$$

5. (1) Given, system of linear equations

$$x+2y+3z=\alpha$$

$$4x+5y+6z=\beta$$

$$7x+8y+9z=\gamma-1$$

So, $\Delta=\begin{vmatrix}1 & 2 & 3\\ 4 & 5 & 6\\ 7 & 8 & 9\end{vmatrix}=0$

Thus, the given system of equations will be consistent, if $\alpha=\beta=\gamma-1=0$

So, $\alpha=0, \beta=0, \gamma=1$ i.e. the system of equations will be converted to homogeneous system.

Thus, $|M|=\begin{vmatrix}0 & 2 & 1\\ 0 & 1 & 0\\ -1 & 0 & 1\end{vmatrix}=1$

[putting $\alpha=0, \beta=0, \gamma=1$]

6. (105) $T_{n+1}={}^{110}C_n(2^{1/2})^{110-n}(3^{1/11})^n$

$$={}^{110}C_n 2^{55-\frac{n}{2}}\cdot 3^{\frac{n}{11}}$$

If T_{n+1} is rational, then $\frac{n}{2}$ and $\frac{n}{11}$ are integers.

So, n is multiple of 22, which is LCM of (2, 11).

$\because \quad 0\le n\le 110$

$\Rightarrow \quad n=0, 22, 44, 66, 88, 110.$

So, the numbers of rational terms is 6

Hence, number of irrational terms

= (total number of terms)

− (total number of rational terms)

$=111-6=105$

7. (4) Let $R=\sin x$

Given equation can be written as

$3\lambda R-(\lambda^3+R^3)=1$

$\Rightarrow 3\lambda R-(\lambda+R)^3+3\lambda R(\lambda+R)=1$

$\Rightarrow 3\lambda R(1+\lambda+R)=1+(\lambda+R)^3$

$\Rightarrow (1+\lambda+R)(1+(\lambda+R)^2-(\lambda+R))$

$$\lambda+R+1=0$$

or $\;1+(\lambda+R)^2-(\lambda+R)=3\lambda R$

$$R=-(\lambda+1)$$

or $\lambda^2+R^2-\lambda R-\lambda-R+1=0$

Case 1. $R=-(\lambda+1)$ will have a solution, if

$-1\le-(\lambda+1)\le1\Rightarrow-1\le\lambda+1\le1$

$-2\le\lambda\le0\Rightarrow\lambda=-2,-1,0$

Case 2. $R^2-R(\lambda+1)+\lambda^2-\lambda+1=0$

$$R=\frac{(\lambda+1)\pm\sqrt{-3(\lambda-1)^2}}{2}$$

which is possible only when $\lambda=1$, then $R=1$

$\Rightarrow x=(4n+1)\frac{\pi}{2}$

Hence, the number of integer value of λ is 4.

8. (0.80) Given, equation is $|x-1|=2[x]-3\{x\}$

(i) If $x\ge1$, then $x-1=2[x]-3\{x\}$

$\Rightarrow\quad [x]+\{x\}-1=2[x]-3\{x\}$

$4\{x\}<1+[x]$

$\therefore\quad 0\le1+[x]<4$

$\therefore\quad -1\le[x]<3$

$\therefore$ Possible value of $[x]$ are 1 and 2

If $[x]=1$, then $\{x\}=\frac{1}{2}\therefore x=\frac{3}{2}$

If $[x]=2$, then $\{x\}=\frac{3}{4}\therefore x=\frac{11}{4}$

(ii) $x<1$, then the equation becomes

$1-x=2[x]-3\{x\}$

$\Rightarrow 1-[x]-\{x\}=2[x]-3\{x\}$

$\Rightarrow\quad 2\{x\}=3[x]-1$

$\therefore 0\le3[x]-1<2$ i.e., $1\le3[x]<3$

i.e., $\frac{1}{3}\le[x]<1$ which is not possible.

$\therefore x=\frac{3}{2},\frac{11}{4}$ are the only solution.

So, $\sum x_i=\frac{3}{2}+\frac{11}{4}=1.5+2.75=4.25$

$\Rightarrow[\sum x_i]=4$

Hence, $\frac{[\sum x_i]}{5}=\frac{4}{5}=0.80$

9. (a, b, c)

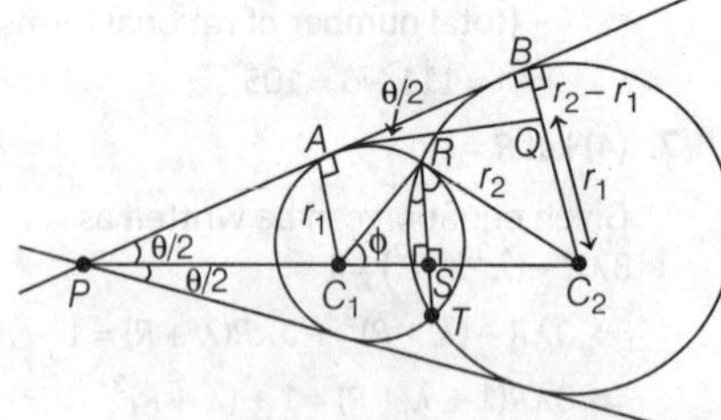

Let $2d=$ Length of the common chord

$\therefore\quad RS=ST=d$

Also, $\angle BPC_2=\angle BAQ=\frac{\theta}{2}$ (say)

Let $\angle RC_1S=\phi$, then $\angle RC_2S=\phi$

In right angled ΔRSC_1,

$$\sin\phi=\frac{d}{r_1}\qquad\text{...(i)}$$

In right angled ΔRSC_2,

$$\cos\phi=\frac{d}{r_2}\qquad\text{...(ii)}$$

On squaring and adding Eqs. (i) and (ii),

$$\frac{d_1^2}{r_1^2}+\frac{d_2^2}{r_2^2}=1\Rightarrow d=\frac{r_1r_2}{\sqrt{r_1^2+r_2^2}}$$

$$\Rightarrow\quad 2d=\frac{2r_1r_2}{\sqrt{r_1^2+r_2^2}}=\frac{24}{5}\quad\text{[given]}$$

Given, $r_1=3$

$$\therefore\quad 2d=\frac{6r_2}{\sqrt{9+r_2^2}}=\frac{24}{5}\Rightarrow r_2=4\text{ units}$$

In right angled ΔABQ,

$$\sin\frac{\theta}{2}=\frac{BQ}{AQ}=\frac{BC_2-QC_2}{C_1C_2}=\frac{r_2-r_1}{C_1C_2}\qquad\text{...(iii)}$$

In ΔC_1RC_2

$(C_1C_2)^2=r_1^2+r_2^2\qquad[\because H^2=P^2+B^2]$

$\Rightarrow C_1C_2=\sqrt{3^2+4^2}=5\quad[\because C_1C_2>0]$

From Eq. (iii), $\sin\frac{\theta}{2}=\frac{4-3}{5}=\frac{1}{5}$

$\therefore\quad\cos\frac{\theta}{2}=\frac{\sqrt{24}}{5}$

So, $\sin\theta=2\sin\frac{\theta}{2}\cdot\cos\frac{\theta}{2}$

$=2\times\frac{1}{5}\times\frac{\sqrt{24}}{5}=\frac{4\sqrt6}{25}$

$\Rightarrow\theta=\sin^{-1}\left(\frac{4\sqrt6}{25}\right)=$ Angle between the direct common tangents.

Also, $AB=\sqrt{(C_1C_2)^2-(r_1-r_2)^2}$

$=\sqrt{25-1}=\sqrt{24}=2\sqrt6$ units

10. (a, b, c)

Given, $AF=AD=4$ and $CF=CE=2$

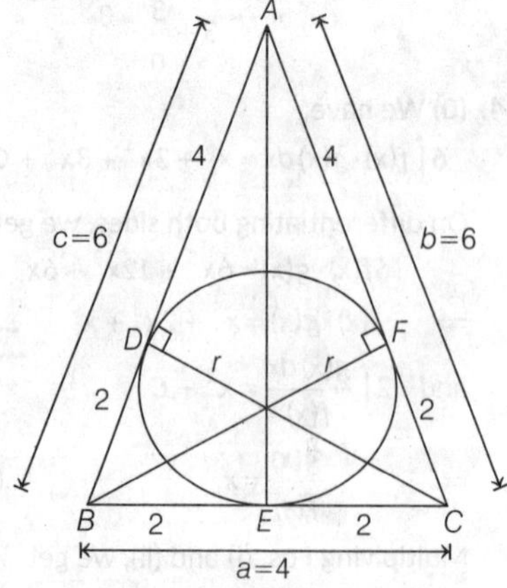

$\therefore\quad AC=AF+FC=4+2=6=AB$

$[\because AB=AC,\text{ given}]$

Now, $BD=AB-AD=6-4=2$

$\therefore\quad BD=BE=2$

and $BC=BE+EC=2+2=4$

Now, $s=\frac{a+b+c}{2}=\frac{4+6+6}{2}=8$

$\Delta=\sqrt{s(s-a)(s-b)(s-c)}$

$=\sqrt{8(4)(2)(2)}$

$=\sqrt{128}=8\sqrt2$

$\therefore\quad r=\frac{\Delta}{s}=\sqrt2$

and $R=\frac{abc}{4\Delta}=\frac{6\cdot6\cdot4}{4\cdot8\sqrt2}=\frac{9}{2\sqrt2}=\frac{9\sqrt2}{4}$

$\Delta R=36\ne a^2$

$AI=\sqrt{IF^2+AF^2}=\sqrt{2+16}=3\sqrt2$

$BI=\sqrt{BE^2+IE^2}=\sqrt{4+2}=\sqrt6$

$CI=\sqrt{CF^2+IF^2}=\sqrt{4+2}=\sqrt6$

$\therefore AI:BI:CI=\sqrt3:1:1$

11. (a, b, c, d)

Let $I=\int_{-39}^{59}\sin(2(\{x\}+\{-x\}))e^{\{x\}}$ $(\tan(x-[x])+\sec^2\{x\})dx$

$\Rightarrow I=98\int_0^1(\sin2)e^x(\tan x+\sec^2x)dx$

$[\because x-[x]=\{x\}=x,\ 0<x<1$ and using $\int_{mT}^{nT}f(x)dx=(n-m)\int_0^Tf(x)\,dx,\ m,n\in I$ and T is period of $f(x)]$

$=98(\sin2)[e^x\tan x]_0^1$

$[\because\int e^x(f(x)+f'(x))\,dx=e^xf(x)+C]$

$=98\times2(\sin1)(\cos1)(e)\cdot(\tan1)$

$=196\cdot e\cdot\sin^21$

On comparing, we get

$p=196$ and $q=1$

Hence, $p-q=195=$ An odd number

$\Rightarrow\quad p+6q=196+6\times1=202$

$=$ A palindrome number

$\Rightarrow p-168q=196-168=28$

$=$ A perfect number

$\Rightarrow\sqrt p-\sqrt q=\sqrt{196}-\sqrt1$

$=14-1=13$

$=$ A fibonacci number.

Extra Points

Some definitions related to number theory and is useful for question number 13 options.

1. **Palindrome Number** A palindrome number is the number that remains the same, when its digits get reversed e.g. 2882, 2002, 8888, 202 etc.

2. **Fibonacci Numbers**

In mathematics, the fibonacci numbers commonly denoted by F_n form a sequence, called the fibonacci sequence, such that each number is the sum of the two preceding ones, starting from 0 and 1. i.e. $F_0 = 0$ and $F_1 = 1$

For $n > 1$, the sequence starts 0, 1, 1, 2, 3, 5, 8, 13, 21, 34, 55, 89, 144, ...

12. (a, c, d)

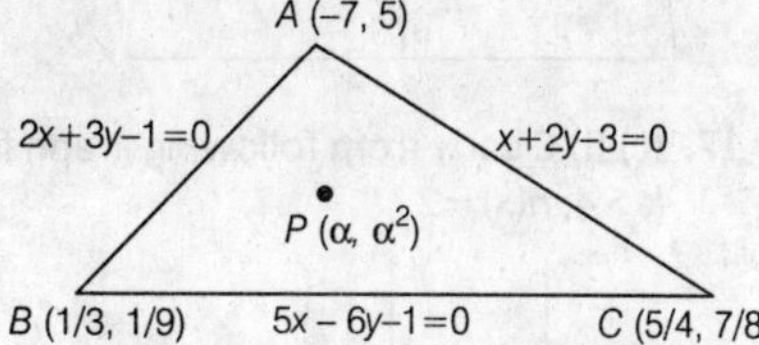

Solving equations of the lines two at a time, we get the vertices of the given triangle as, $A(-7, 5)$, $B\left(\frac{1}{3}, \frac{1}{9}\right)$ and $C\left(\frac{5}{4}, \frac{7}{8}\right)$.

Let $P(\alpha, \alpha^2)$ be a point inside the ΔABC.

Since, A and P lie on the same side of the line $5x - 6y - 1 = 0$, both $\{5(-7) - 6(5) - 1\}$ and $(5\alpha - 6\alpha^2 - 1)$ must have the same sign.

$5\alpha - 6\alpha^2 - 1 < 0$ or $6\alpha^2 - 5\alpha + 1 > 0$

$\Rightarrow (3\alpha - 1)(2\alpha - 1) > 0$

$\Rightarrow \quad \alpha < \frac{1}{3}$ or $\alpha > \frac{1}{2}$ ...(i)

Again, since B and P lie on the same side of the line $x + 2y - 3 = 0$

i.e. $\left\{\left(\frac{1}{3}\right) + \left(\frac{2}{9}\right) - 3\right\}$ and $\alpha + 2\alpha^2 - 3$ have the same sign.

$\Rightarrow \quad 2\alpha^2 + \alpha - 3 < 0$

$\Rightarrow (2\alpha + 3)(\alpha - 1) < 0$

$\Rightarrow \quad -\frac{3}{2} < \alpha < 1$ ...(ii)

Lastly, since C and P lie on the same side of the line $2x + 3y - 1 = 0$

i.e. $\{2 \times (5/4) + 3 \times (7/8) - 1\}$ and $(2\alpha + 3\alpha^2 - 1)$ have the same sign.

$\Rightarrow \quad 3\alpha^2 + 2\alpha - 1 > 0$

$\Rightarrow \quad (3\alpha - 1)(\alpha + 1) > 0$

$\Rightarrow \quad \alpha < -1$ or $\alpha > \frac{1}{3}$ ...(iii)

Now, Eqs. (i), (ii) and (iii) hold simultaneously, if

$-\frac{3}{2} < \alpha < -1$ or $\frac{1}{2} < \alpha < 1$

13. (a, b, c, d)

Let $R_{n+1} - 2R_n + R_{n-1}$

$$= \int_0^{\pi/2} \frac{\sin^2(n+1)x}{\sin^2 x} dx - 2\int_0^{\pi/2} \frac{\sin^2 nx}{\sin^2 x} dx + \int_0^{\pi/2} \frac{\sin^2(n-1)x}{\sin^2 x} dx$$

$$= \int_0^{\pi/2} \frac{\{\sin^2(n+1)x - \sin^2 nx\} - \{\sin^2 nx - \sin^2(n-1)x\}}{\sin^2 x} dx$$

$$= \int_0^{\pi/2} \frac{\sin(2n+1)x \cdot \sin x - \sin(2n-1)x \cdot \sin x}{\sin^2 x} dx$$

$$= \int_0^{\pi/2} \frac{2\cos 2nx \cdot \sin x}{\sin x} dx$$

$$= 2\int_0^{\pi/2} \cos 2nx\, dx = 2\left[\frac{\sin 2nx}{2n}\right]_0^{\pi/2}$$

$$= \frac{1}{n}(\sin n\pi - \sin 0) = 0 - 0 [\because \sin n\pi = 0]$$

$= 0$

$\therefore R_{n+1} - 2R_n + R_{n-1} = 0$

$\Rightarrow \quad R_{n-1} + R_{n+1} = 2R_n$

i.e. R_{n-1}, R_n, R_{n+1} form an AP.

Now, $R_1 = \int_0^{\pi/2} 1\, dx = \frac{\pi}{2}$

and $R_2 = \int_0^{\pi/2} \frac{\sin^2 2x}{\sin^2 x} dx$

$$= 4\int_0^{\pi/2} \cos^2 x\, dx = \pi$$

$\therefore$ Common difference of AP

$$= R_2 - R_1 = \frac{\pi}{2}$$

So, $R_n - R_{n-1} = \frac{\pi}{2}, \forall\, n = 1, 2, 3$

$\therefore R_n = R_1 + (n-1)d$

$$= \frac{\pi}{2} + (n-1) \cdot \frac{\pi}{2} = \frac{n\pi}{2}$$

14. (a, b, c)

We have,

$\mathbf{a} \times \mathbf{b} = \mathbf{b} \times \mathbf{c} = p\mathbf{a} + q\mathbf{b} + r\mathbf{c}$ ...(i)

Taking dot product with , we get

$[\mathbf{a\,b\,c}] = p\mathbf{a} \cdot \mathbf{a} + q\mathbf{a} \cdot \mathbf{b} + r\mathbf{a} \cdot \mathbf{c}$

$[\because [\mathbf{a\,a\,b}] = 0]$

$\Rightarrow [\mathbf{a\,b\,c}] = p + q\cos\theta + r\cos\theta$ ...(ii)

$[\because \mathbf{a} \cdot \mathbf{a} = 1$ and $|\mathbf{a}| = |\mathbf{b}| = |\mathbf{c}| = 1]$

Similarly, taking dot product with **b** and **c**, we get

$0 = p\cos\theta + q + r\cos\theta$ ...(iii)

and $[\mathbf{a\,b\,c}] = p\cos\theta + q\cos\theta + r$ ...(iv)

From Eqs. (ii) and (iv), we get

$p = r$

Adding Eqs. (ii), (iii) and (iv), we get

$2[\mathbf{a\,b\,c}] = (2\cos\theta + 1)(p + q + r)$

$\Rightarrow \frac{2[\mathbf{a\,b\,c}]}{2\cos\theta + 1} = p + q + r$ ...(v)

On multiplying Eq. (v) by $\cos\theta$ and subtracting from Eq. (ii), we get

$[\mathbf{a\,b\,c}] - \frac{2\cos\theta[\mathbf{a\,b\,c}]}{2\cos\theta + 1} = p(1 - \cos\theta)$

$\Rightarrow \frac{[\mathbf{a\,b\,c}]}{(2\cos\theta + 1)(1 - \cos\theta)} = p$

Similarly, $q = \frac{-2[\mathbf{a\,b\,c}]\cos\theta}{(2\cos\theta + 1)(1 - \cos\theta)}$

Now, $[\mathbf{a\,b\,c}]^2 = \begin{vmatrix} \mathbf{a}\cdot\mathbf{a} & \mathbf{a}\cdot\mathbf{b} & \mathbf{a}\cdot\mathbf{c} \\ \mathbf{b}\cdot\mathbf{a} & \mathbf{b}\cdot\mathbf{b} & \mathbf{b}\cdot\mathbf{c} \\ \mathbf{c}\cdot\mathbf{a} & \mathbf{c}\cdot\mathbf{b} & \mathbf{c}\cdot\mathbf{c} \end{vmatrix}$

$$= \begin{vmatrix} 1 & \cos\theta & \cos\theta \\ \cos\theta & 1 & \cos\theta \\ \cos\theta & \cos\theta & 1 \end{vmatrix}$$

$$= (1 + 2\cos\theta)\begin{vmatrix} 1 & 1 & 1 \\ \cos\theta & 1 & 1 \\ \cos\theta & \cos\theta & 1 \end{vmatrix}$$

$$= (1 + 2\cos\theta)\begin{vmatrix} 1 & 0 & 0 \\ \cos\theta & 1 - \cos\theta & 0 \\ \cos\theta & 0 & 1 - \cos\theta \end{vmatrix}$$

$= (1 + 2\cos\theta)(1 - \cos\theta)^2$

$\Rightarrow [\mathbf{a\ b\ c}] = (\sqrt{1 + 2\cos\theta})(1 - \cos\theta)$

$[\because \theta$ is acute, $0 < \cos\theta < 1]$

Hence, $p = r = \frac{1}{\sqrt{1 + 2\cos\theta}}$

and $q = \frac{-2\cos\theta}{\sqrt{1 + 2\cos\theta}}$

Also, $r = \frac{1}{\sqrt{1 + 2\cos\theta}} = \frac{\sqrt{\sec\theta}}{\sqrt{2 + \sec\theta}}$

15. (d) (I) $f'(x) = \frac{g'(x)}{\sqrt{1 + [g(x)]^3}}$ and

$g'(x) = [1 + \sin(\cos^2 x)] \cdot (-\sin x)$

So, $f'(x) = \frac{[1 + \sin(\cos^2 x)](-\sin x)}{\sqrt{1 + [g(x)]^3}}$

$\therefore f'(\pi/2) = \frac{(1 + 0)(-1)}{\sqrt{1 + [g(\pi/2)]^3}} = \frac{-1}{\sqrt{1 + 0}}$

$(\because g(\pi/2) = 0)$

$\therefore f'(\pi/2) = -1$

(II) On differentiating both sides w.r.t. x, we get

$f(x) = 2 \cdot f(x) \cdot f'(x)$

$\Rightarrow \quad f'(x) = \frac{1}{2}$

On integrating both sides, we get

$$f(x) = \frac{x}{2} + C$$

But $f(0) = 0$

$$\therefore \quad f(x) = \frac{x}{2} \Rightarrow f(6) = 3$$

(III) Area bounded by the curve $y = -x^2 + x + 2$, $x = a$, $x = b$ and X-axis is maximum when $a = -1$ and $b = 2$.

($-1, 2$ are roots of $-x^2 + x + 2 = 0$)

So, $a + b = -1 + 2 = 1$

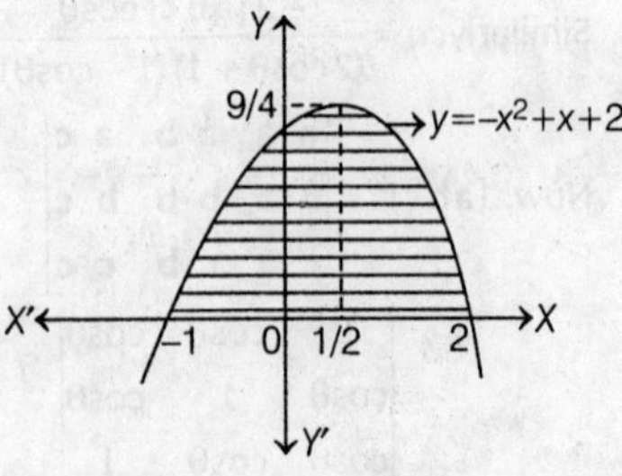

(IV) $4 \lim\limits_{n \to \infty} \frac{a_n}{b_n} = 4 \left[\lim\limits_{n \to \infty} \frac{\int_{1/n+1}^{1/n} \tan^{-1}(nx)\, dx}{\int_{1/n+1}^{1/n} \sin^{-1}(nx)\, dx} \right]$

Putting $nx = z$

$\Rightarrow \quad n dx = dz$

$\Rightarrow \quad dx = \frac{1}{n} dz$

x	$1/n+1$	$1/n$
z	$\frac{n}{n+1}$	1

$$\therefore 4 \lim_{n \to \infty} \frac{\frac{1}{n}\int_{n/n+1}^{1} \tan^{-1}(z)\, dz}{\frac{1}{n}\int_{n/n+1}^{1} \sin^{-1}(z)\, dz} \left(\text{Form } \frac{0}{0}\right)$$

$$\Rightarrow 4 \left[\lim_{n \to \infty} \frac{0 - \tan^{-1}\left(\frac{n}{n+1}\right)}{0 - \sin^{-1}\left(\frac{n}{n+1}\right)} \right]^{n/n+1}$$

(using L' Hospital Rule).

$$\Rightarrow \quad 4 \left[\frac{\tan^{-1}(1)}{\sin^{-1}(1)} \right]$$

$$\Rightarrow \quad 4 \left[\frac{\pi/4}{\pi/2} \right] = 4 \times \frac{1}{2} = 2$$

16. (a) (I) The slope of the line is 1 or -1.

Let the equation of the line be $x + y = |a|$

The centre of the circle is (0, 0) and radius is $2\sqrt{2}$ units. The line will intersect the circle, if

$$\frac{|a|}{\sqrt{2}} < 2\sqrt{2} \Rightarrow |a| < \sqrt{4 \times 4}$$

$\therefore \quad |a| < 4$

(II) The equation of the circle is $S = x^2 + y^2 - 8x - 12y + p = 0$

The point (2, 5) lies inside the circle

If $S_1 < 0$

$\Rightarrow (2)^2 + (5)^2 - (8 \times 2) - (12 \times 5) + p < 0$

$\Rightarrow \quad 4 + 25 - 16 - 60 + p < 0$

$\Rightarrow \quad p - 47 < 0$

$\therefore \quad p < 47$

Again the circle neither touches nor cuts any of the axes

If $16 - p < 0$ and $36 - p < 0$

$\Rightarrow \quad p > 16$ and $p > 36$

$\Rightarrow \quad p > 36$

$\therefore \quad p \in (36, 47)$

$\Rightarrow |p| \in (36, 47)$

$\therefore \sqrt{|p|} \in (6, \sqrt{47})$

(III) According to the question,

$(y - 2)^2 = 0$ ...(i)

and $\left(x - \frac{4}{5}\right)(x - 5) = 0$ ...(ii)

Adding Eqs. (i) and (ii), we get the equation of circle

$$\left(x - \frac{4}{5}\right)(x - 5) + (y - 2)^2 = 0$$

$$\Rightarrow x^2 - \frac{4x}{5} - 5x + 4 + y^2 + 4 - 4y = 0$$

$$\Rightarrow x^2 + y^2 - \frac{29}{5}x - 4y + 8 = 0$$

which is of the form $x^2 + y^2 + 2gx + 2fy + c = 0$

Here, $g = \frac{-29}{10}$, $f = -2$ and $c = 8$

$\therefore$ Radius of the above circle is

$$r = \sqrt{g^2 + f^2 - c} = \sqrt{\left(\frac{-29}{10}\right)^2 + (-2)^2 - 8}$$

$$= \sqrt{\frac{841}{100} + 4 - 8} = \sqrt{\frac{841 - 400}{100}}$$

$$\Rightarrow r = \sqrt{\frac{441}{100}} = \frac{21}{10}$$

(IV) As the given,

$y = \sqrt{25 - x^2}$ represents the semi-circle lying above X-axis, whose centre lies at (0, 0) and radius = 5 units

We have,

$$a + 1 > 0$$

$\Rightarrow \quad a > -1$ ...(i)

and $\quad a^2 + (a+1)^2 < 25$

$\Rightarrow \quad 2a^2 + 2a + 1 - 25 < 0$

$\Rightarrow \quad a^2 + a - 12 < 0$

$\Rightarrow \quad (a + 4)(a - 3) < 0$

$\therefore \quad a \in (-4, 3)$ ...(ii)

Thus the required values of a is Eq. (i) $\cap$ Eq. (ii) i.e., $a \in (-1, 3)$

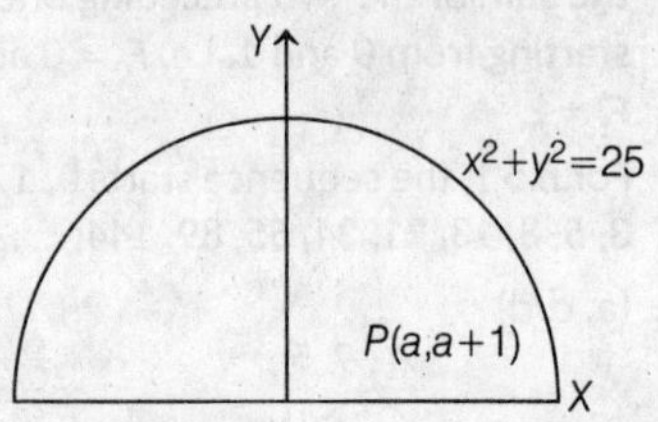

17. (c) (I) Clearly from following graph for $k > 4$, $n(x) = 2$

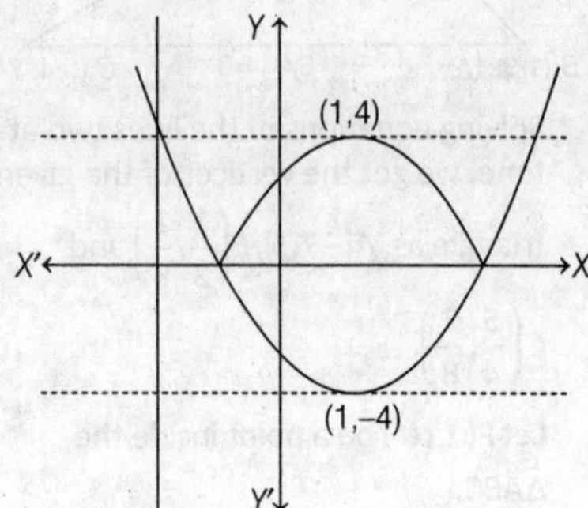

(II) $f(x) = \frac{1}{1-x}$, $x \neq 1$

$$\text{Now, } f(f(x)) = \frac{1}{1 - \left(\frac{1}{(1-x)}\right)}$$

$$= \frac{1-x}{1-x-1} = \frac{1-x}{-x}$$

$$\therefore \ f(f(x)) = \frac{x-1}{x}, x \neq 0$$

$$\text{Again, } f(f(f(x))) = \frac{\frac{1}{1-x} - 1}{\frac{1}{1-x}}$$

$$= \frac{1 - 1 + x}{1-x} \times \frac{(1-x)}{1}$$

$\therefore \ f(f(f(x))) = x$

Hence, $f(f(f(x)))$ is not defined at $x = 0, 1$ only.

(III) $\frac{1}{p}, \frac{1}{h_1}, \frac{1}{h_2}, \ldots \frac{1}{h_{2010}}, \frac{1}{q}$ are in AP

Let $n = 2010$

$$(n+1)\, d = \frac{1}{q} - \frac{1}{p}$$

$$\left[\begin{array}{l} \because a_{n+2} = a_1 + (n+1)\, d \\ \Rightarrow \frac{1}{q} = \frac{1}{p} + (n+2-1) \end{array} \right]$$

$$\Rightarrow \quad d = \frac{p-q}{pq} \times \frac{1}{(n+1)}$$

(after simplification)

$$\therefore \quad d = \frac{p-q}{pq(n+1)}$$

Now, $\frac{1}{h_1} = \frac{1}{p} + d \qquad \{\because a_2 = a_1 + d\}$

$$= \frac{1}{p} + \frac{p-q}{pq(n+1)}$$

$$= \frac{nq+q+p-q}{(n+1)pq} = \frac{nq+p}{(n+1)pq}$$

$$\Rightarrow \frac{1}{h_n} = \frac{1}{q} - d = \frac{1}{q} - \frac{p-q}{pq(n+1)}$$

$$= \frac{pn+p-p+q}{(n+1)pq} = \frac{pn+q}{(n+1)pq}$$

$\therefore$

$$h_1 - h_n = (n+1)pq\left(\frac{1}{p+nq} - \frac{1}{np+q}\right)$$

$$= \frac{(n^2-1)pq(p-q)}{(p+nq)(np+q)}$$

$$\Rightarrow h_1 - h_n = \frac{(n^2-1)ac(a-c)}{ac(n^2+1)+n(a^2+c^2)} \quad \text{...(i)}$$

[put $p = a, q = c$]

Now,

$n^2(1-pq) - n(p^2+q^2) - (1+ac) = 0$

Put in Eq. (i), we get

$h_1 - h_n = pq(p-q)$

Hence, $\frac{h_1 - h_n}{pq(p-q)} = 1$

Put $n = 2010$, $\frac{h_1 - h_{2010}}{pq(p-q)} = 1$

(IV) We have, $f(x) = \begin{cases} x, & x \le 0 \\ x^2, & 0 < x \le 1 \\ 1, & x > 1 \end{cases}$

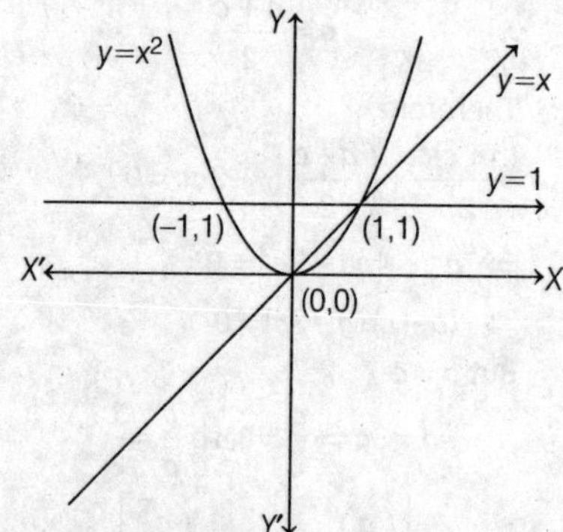

$\therefore f(x=2) = 1$

Because for $x > 1$

$\therefore \qquad f(x) = 1$

18. (b) (I) If the mid-point of the given points is (h, k), then

$$h = t$$

and $\qquad k = \sqrt{1-t^2}$

$\Rightarrow \qquad h^2 + k^2 = 1$

$\therefore$ The locus of middle point is the circle $x^2 + y^2 = 1$

Clearly, the line $x + y = 1$ intercepts a chord of length $\sqrt{2}$ units from the circle.

(II)

$$\angle AOM = \frac{\pi}{2a}, \angle CON = \frac{\pi}{a}$$

$$M = \sqrt{3} + 1$$

$$\Rightarrow 2\cos\left(\frac{\pi}{2a}\right) + 2\cos\left(\frac{\pi}{a}\right) = \sqrt{3} + 1$$

$$\Rightarrow 2\cos\theta + 2\cos 2\theta = \sqrt{3} + 1 \qquad \left\{\because \theta = \frac{\pi}{2a}\right\}$$

$$\Rightarrow 4\cos^2\theta + 2\cos\theta - 3 = 0$$

$$\cos\theta = \frac{\sqrt{3}}{2} \text{ or } \frac{-\sqrt{3}+1}{2}$$

$$\therefore \quad \theta = \frac{\pi}{6} \text{ or } \frac{\pi}{2a} = \frac{\pi}{6}$$

$$\Rightarrow \quad a = 3$$

(III) The equation of the required circle will be given by,

$(2x - y + 1)(x - 2y + 3) + \lambda xy = 0$

$\Rightarrow 2x^2 + 2y^2 + (\lambda - 4)xy + 7x - 5y + 3 = 0$

It represents a circle, if $\lambda = 4$ and the coordinates of the centre are $\left(\frac{-7}{4}, \frac{5}{4}\right)$

$$\therefore a = \left|\frac{5}{4} - \left(\frac{-7}{4}\right)\right| = \frac{12}{4} = 3$$

$$\Rightarrow \quad a = 3$$

(IV) Let the radius of the first circle at an instant 'S' be 'r'

$$\therefore \quad \frac{dr}{dS} = 0.3$$

The initial radius is 1 and after S s. It is r_1, then

$$\int_1^{r_1} 1\, dr = \int_0^S 0.3\, dS$$

$$\Rightarrow \quad r_1 = 0.3S + 1$$

Similarly for second circle $r_2 = 0.4S + 2$

The distance between their centres $C_1(1, 2)$ and $C_2(7, 10)$ is $C_1C_2 = 10$

The circles touch after 'S' s, if

$$r_1 + r_2 = C_1C_2$$

$\Rightarrow \; 0.3S + 1 + 0.4S + 2 = 10$

$\Rightarrow \; 0.7S = 10 - 3 = 7$

$$\Rightarrow \quad S = \frac{7}{0.7} = 10 \text{ s}$$

or $\qquad r_2 - r_1 = C_1C_2$

$\Rightarrow \; (0.4S + 2) - (0.3S + 1) = 10$

$\Rightarrow \qquad 0.1S + 1 = 10$

$$\therefore \quad S = \frac{9}{0.1} = 90 \text{ s}$$

$$\therefore \quad a = S = \frac{10}{60} \text{ min}$$

or $\qquad \frac{90}{60}$ min

$$\therefore \quad a = \frac{1}{6} \text{ or } \frac{3}{2} \text{ min}$$

Paper 2

1. (1) Given, function

$$f(x) = \frac{2x^3}{3} - (x\log_e|x| - x) - kx + 10$$

$f(x)$ is strictly increasing for $x \in R - \{0\}$

$\therefore f'(x) = 2x^2 - \log_e|x| - k \ge 0 \quad \forall x \in R - \{0\}$

$\Rightarrow k \le 2x^2 - \log_e|x| \; \forall x \in R - \{0\}$

$\Rightarrow k \le$ Minimum value of $2x^2 - \log_e|x|$

Now, let $g(x) = 2x^2 - \log_e|x|$

$$\therefore \quad g'(x) = 4x - \frac{1}{x}$$

When $g'(x) = 0$, then $x = \pm\frac{1}{2}$

Also, $g''(x) = 4 + \frac{1}{x^2}$

So, both $x = \frac{1}{2}$ and $x = -\frac{1}{2}$ are points of minima.

It can be verified that $x = \pm\frac{1}{2}$ are points of global minima.

So, $k \le g\left(\frac{1}{2}\right)$ or $g\left(-\frac{1}{2}\right)$

$$\Rightarrow k \le 2 \times \frac{1}{4} - \ln\frac{1}{2} \Rightarrow k \le \frac{1}{2} + \ln 2$$

$[\because \ln 2 \simeq 0.6931]$

Hence, maximum integral value of k is 1.

2. (4) Given, $xy_1 - 4y - x^2\sqrt{y} = 0$

$$\Rightarrow \frac{xy_1}{\sqrt{y}} - 4\sqrt{y} = x^2$$

Putting $\sqrt{y} = z \Rightarrow \frac{1}{2\sqrt{y}}\frac{dy}{dx} = \frac{dz}{dx}$

So, $2x\frac{dz}{dx} - 4z = x^2 \Rightarrow \frac{dz}{dx} - \frac{2}{x}z = \frac{x}{2}$

which is linear differential equation.

$\therefore$ IF $= e^{\int -\frac{2}{x}dx} \Rightarrow$ IF $= e^{-2\ln x} = \frac{1}{x^2}$

Hence, its solution will be

$$z \times \frac{1}{x^2} = \int \frac{x}{2} \times \frac{1}{x^2}\,dx$$

$$\Rightarrow \sqrt{y} \times \frac{1}{x^2} = \int \frac{1}{2x}\,dx$$

$$\Rightarrow \frac{\sqrt{y}}{x^2} = \frac{1}{2}\ln x + C \quad ...(i)$$

Given, $y(1) = (\ln 4)^2$

$$\therefore \frac{\sqrt{(\ln 4)^2}}{1} = \frac{1}{2}\ln 1 + C \Rightarrow C = \ln 4$$

From Eq. (i), $\frac{\sqrt{y}}{x^2} = \frac{1}{2}\ln x + \ln 4$

$$\Rightarrow y = x^4\left(\frac{1}{2}\ln x + \ln 4\right)^2$$

Now, $y(2) = 16\left(\frac{1}{2}\ln 2 + 2\ln 2\right)^2$

$$= 16\left(\frac{5}{2}\ln 2\right)^2$$

$$= (10\ln 2)^2 = 4(5\ln 2)^2$$

$$\Rightarrow y(2) = 4(\ln 32)^2$$

So, $\frac{16(\log_e 32)^2}{y(2)} = \frac{16(\log_e 32)^2}{4(\log_e 32)^2} = 4$

3. (5) Given, $E = a^2\cot 9° + b^2\cot 27° + c^2\cot 63° + d^2\cot 81°$

$$= (a^2\cot 9° + d^2\tan 9°) + (b^2\cot 27° + c^2\tan 27°)$$

Also, given $a + b + c + d = 5$ ...(i)

Let $a + d = k_1$ and $b + c = k_2$

From Eq. (i), $k_1 + k_2 = 5$

Let $E_1 = a^2\cot 9° + d^2\tan 9°$

$\Rightarrow E_1 = a^2\cot 9° + (k_1 - a)^2\tan 9°$ ...(ii) $[\because a + d = k_1]$

$\Rightarrow E_1 = a^2(\cot 9° + \tan 9°) - 2ak_1\tan 9° + k_1^2\tan 9°$

which is quadratic in 'a' whose minimum value is obtained at

$$x = \frac{-B}{2A}$$

i.e. $a = \frac{2k_1\tan 9°}{2(\cot 9° + \tan 9°)} = k_1\sin^2 9°$

Let $E_2 = b^2\cot 27° + c^2\tan 27°$

$\Rightarrow E_2 = b^2\cot 27° + (k_2 - b)^2\tan 27°$ ...(iii) $[\because b + c = k_2]$

$\Rightarrow E_2 = b^2(\cot 27° + \tan 27°) - 2bk_2\tan 27° + k_2^2\tan 27°$

and hence E_2 minimum obtained at

$$b = \frac{-B}{2A}$$

i.e. $b = \frac{2k_2\tan 27°}{2(\cot 27° + \tan 27°)} = k_2\sin^2 27°$

From Eq. (ii),

$(E_1)_{\min} = k_1^2\sin^4 9°\cdot\cot 9° + (k_1\cos^2 9°)^2\tan 9°$ $[\because a = k_1\sin^2 9°]$

$= k_1^2\sin 9°\cdot\cos 9°(\sin^2 9° + \cos^2 9°)$

$= k_1^2\sin 9°\cos 9°$

Similarly, from Eq. (ii),

$(E_2)_{\min} = k_2^2\sin 27°\cos 27°$

$\therefore (E)_{\min} = (E_1)_{\min} + (E_2)_{\min}$

$k_1^2\sin 9°\cos 9° + k_2^2\sin 27°\cos 27°$

$= \frac{1}{2}[k_1^2\sin 18° + (5 - k_1)^2\sin 54°]$ $[\because k_1 + k_2 = 5]$

$= \frac{1}{2}[k_1^2(\sin 18° + \cos 36°) - 10k_1\cos 36° + 25\cos 36°]$ $[\because \sin 54° = \cos 36°]$

$\therefore E_{\min} = \frac{-D}{4A}$ (for quadratic in k_1)

$$= \frac{25}{2}\left[\frac{\cos 36°\cdot\sin 18°}{\sin 18° + \cos 36°}\right] = \frac{25}{4\sqrt{5}}$$

$\left[\because \sin 18° = \frac{-1+\sqrt{5}}{4} \text{ and } \cos 36° = \frac{1+\sqrt{5}}{4}\right]$

$$= \frac{5\sqrt{5}}{4} = \frac{\sqrt{125}}{4} = \frac{\sqrt{x}}{y}$$

Hence, $x = 125$ and $y = 4$

So, $x - 30y = 125 - 30 \times 4 = 5$

4. (8) Volume $(V) = \frac{1}{3}A_1h_1 \Rightarrow h_1 = \frac{3V}{A_1}$

$h_2 = \frac{3V}{A_2}$, $h_3 = \frac{3V}{A_3}$ and $h_4 = \frac{3V}{A_4}$

$\therefore (A_1 + A_2 + A_3 + A_4)(h_1 + h_2 + h_3 + h_4)$

$= (A_1 + A_2 + A_3 + A_4)\left(\frac{3V}{A_1} + \frac{3V}{A_2} + \frac{3V}{A_3} + \frac{3V}{A_4}\right)$

$= 3V(A_1 + A_2 + A_3 + A_4)\left(\frac{1}{A_1} + \frac{1}{A_2} + \frac{1}{A_3} + \frac{1}{A_4}\right)$

Now, using AM-HM inequality in A_1, A_2, A_3 and A_4, we get

$$\frac{A_1 + A_2 + A_3 + A_4}{4} \ge \frac{4}{\frac{1}{A_1} + \frac{1}{A_2} + \frac{1}{A_3} + \frac{1}{A_4}}$$

$$\Rightarrow (A_1 + A_2 + A_3 + A_4)\left(\frac{1}{A_1} + \frac{1}{A_2} + \frac{1}{A_3} + \frac{1}{A_4}\right) \ge 16$$

Hence, the minimum value of

$(A_1 + A_2 + A_3 + A_4)(h_1 + h_2 + h_3 + h_4)$

$= 3V(16)$

$= 48V = 48 \times \frac{1}{6} = 8$

5. (2) We have,

$$(\alpha + \beta)^2 = \left(\frac{1}{\alpha} + \frac{1}{\beta}\right)(\alpha^2 + \beta^2)$$

$$\Rightarrow (\alpha + \beta)^2 = \left(\frac{1}{\alpha} + \frac{1}{\beta}\right)[(\alpha + \beta)^2 - 2\alpha\beta]$$

Substituting $\alpha + \beta = \frac{-b}{a}$ and $\alpha\beta = \frac{c}{a}$,

we have

$$\frac{b^2}{a^2} = \frac{-b}{c}\left(\frac{b^2}{a^2} - \frac{2c}{a}\right)$$

$\Rightarrow cb^2 + b(b^2 - 2ac) = 0$

$\Rightarrow b[bc + b^2 - 2ac] = 0$

$\because b \ne 0$

[$\because a, b$ and c are all different, given in question i.e. $a \ne b \ne c \ne 0$]

$\therefore bc + b^2 - 2ac = 0$

$\because a, b$ and c are in AP.

$\therefore b = \frac{a+c}{2}$

Therefore,

$$\frac{(a+c)c}{2} + \left(\frac{a+c}{2}\right)^2 - 2ac = 0$$

$\Rightarrow a^2 - 4ac + 3c^2 = 0$

$\Rightarrow (a - c)(a - 3c) = 0$

But $a \ne c$

$\therefore a = 3c \Rightarrow \frac{a}{c} = 3$, so $\frac{c}{a} = \frac{1}{3}$

Hence, $\left[\left(\frac{a}{c}\right)^4 + 79\log_3\left(\frac{c}{a}\right)\right]$

$= [(3)^4 + 79\log_3 3^{-1} - 1]$

$= 81 + 79(-1) \times 1$

$= 81 - 79 = 2$

6. (9) Given, $\sin^2 x - \sin x + \cos x = 1$

$\Rightarrow \quad \cos x - \sin x = \cos^2 x$

$\Rightarrow (\cos x)(1-\cos x) = \sin x$

$\Rightarrow 1 - \cos x = \tan x \Rightarrow 2\sin^2 \frac{x}{2} = \frac{\sin x}{\cos x}$

$\Rightarrow 2\sin^2 \frac{x}{2} = \frac{2\sin\frac{x}{2}.\cos\frac{2x}{2}}{\cos x}$

$\Rightarrow 2\sin^2 \frac{x}{2}\cos x - 2\sin\frac{x}{2}\cos\frac{x}{2} = 0$

$\Rightarrow 2\sin\frac{x}{2}\left[\sin\frac{x}{2}\cos x - \cos\frac{x}{2}\right] = 0$

$\Rightarrow \frac{x}{2} = n\pi$ or $\sin\frac{x}{2}.\cos x - \cos\frac{x}{2} = 0 \Rightarrow \frac{x}{2} = n\pi$ ...(i)

or $\quad \cos x = \cot\frac{x}{2}$

$\Rightarrow \frac{1-\tan^2\frac{x}{2}}{1+\tan^2\frac{x}{2}} = \frac{1}{\tan\frac{x}{2}} \Rightarrow \tan\frac{x}{2} - \tan^3\frac{x}{2} = 1 + \tan^2\frac{x}{2}$ ...(ii)

Let $\tan\frac{x}{2} = t$, then Eq. (ii) becomes,

$t - t^3 = 1 + t^2 \Rightarrow t^3 + t^2 - t + 1 = 0$

Let $f(t) = t^3 + t^2 - t + 1$

$\Rightarrow f'(t) = 3t^2 + 2t - 1 = (3t-1)(t+1)$

Now, $f'(t) = 0 \Rightarrow t = -1$ or $t = \frac{1}{3}$

Graph of $y = f(t)$ will be as shown below figure (i)

Clearly, $f(t) = 0$ has only one root

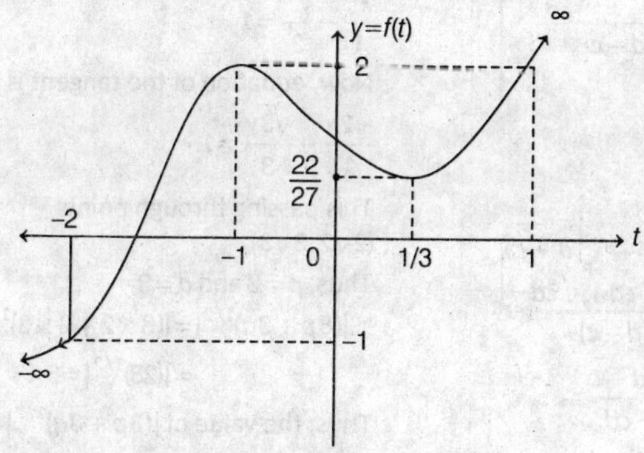

$t = t_0$ (say) in $t \in [-2, -1]$

i.e. $\tan\frac{x}{2} = t_0 \in [-2, -1]$

$\because \quad x \in [-4\pi, 4\pi]$

i.e. $\quad \frac{x}{2} \in [-2\pi, 2\pi]$

$\therefore \quad \tan\frac{x}{2} = t_0 \in [-2, -1]$

will be attained 4 times i.e. when

$\frac{x}{2} \in \left(-\frac{3\pi}{2}, -\pi\right) \cup \left(-\frac{\pi}{2}, 0\right) \cup \left(\frac{\pi}{2}, \pi\right) \cup \left(\frac{3\pi}{2}, 2\pi\right)$

and it is clear from figure (ii), as shown below

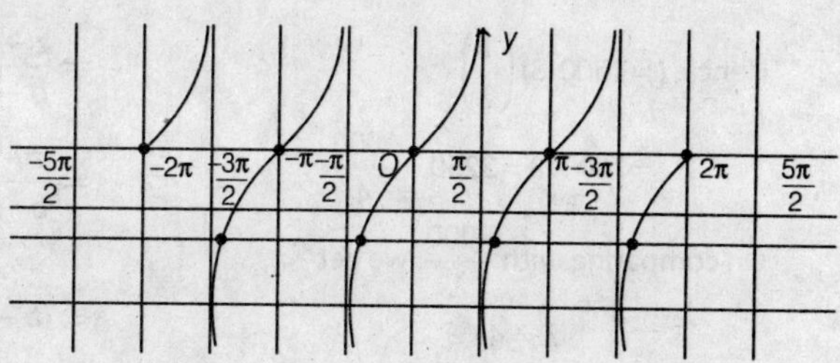

From Eq. (i), $\frac{x}{2} = n\pi \Rightarrow x = 2n\pi, n \in z$

$\therefore$ For $x \in [-4\pi, 4\pi]$, x will attain the values $x = -4\pi, -2\pi, 0, 2\pi$ and 4π.

Hence, total $(4+5)$ i.e. 9 solutions.

7. (5) Given, equation is

$\cos^3 3x + \cos^3 5x = (2\cos x \cos 4x)^3 = (\cos 5x + \cos 3x)^2$

$\Rightarrow 3\cos 3x \cos 5x(\cos 5x + \cos 3x) = 0$

$[\because (a+b)^3 - (a^3 + b^3) = 3ab(a+b)]$

$\Rightarrow 6\cos 3x \cos 5x \cos x \cos 4x = 0$

$\Rightarrow \cos x = 0$ or $\cos 3x = 0$ or $\cos 4x = 0$ or $\cos 5x = 0$

For $100 < x < 200$, $\cos x = 0$ has no solution

$\cos 3x = 0 \Rightarrow 3x = 450 \rightarrow x = 150$

$\cos 4x = 0 \Rightarrow 4x = 450, 630 \Rightarrow x = \frac{450}{4}, \frac{630}{4}$

$\cos 5x = 0 \Rightarrow 5x = 630, 710, 890 \Rightarrow x = 126, 142, 178$

$\therefore$ Sum of all values of x

i.e. $k = 150 + \frac{450}{4} + \frac{630}{4} + 126 + 142 + 178 \Rightarrow k = 906$

Sum of digits of $k = 15$

$\therefore \frac{1}{3} \times$ sum of digit of $k = \frac{1}{3} \times 15 = 5$

8. (8) We have, $F(x) + F\left(x + \frac{1}{2}\right) = 3$ ...(i)

Replace x by $\left(x + \frac{1}{2}\right)$ in Eq. (i), we get

$$F\left(x + \frac{1}{2}\right) + F(x+1) = 3 \quad \text{...(ii)}$$

$\therefore$ From Eqs. (i) and (ii), we get

$$F(x) = F(x+1)$$

$\Rightarrow F(x)$ is periodic function

Now, consider $I = \int_0^{1500} F(x)\,dx$

$$= 1500\left|\int_0^{1/2} F(x)\,dx + \int_{1/2}^{1} F(x)\,dx\right|$$

Put $x = y + \frac{1}{2}$ in second integral, we get

$$I = 1500\left|\int_0^{1/2} F(x)\,dx + \int_0^{1/2} F\left(y + \frac{1}{2}\right)dy\right|$$

$$= 1500\int_0^{1/2}\left(F(x) + F\left(x + \frac{1}{2}\right)\right)dx = 1500\int_0^{1/2} 3\,dx$$

[using Eq. (i)]

Hence, $I = 1500(3)\left(\frac{1}{2}\right)$

$$= 750 \times 3 = 2250 = \frac{9000}{4}$$

On comparing with $\frac{9000}{\lambda}$, we get

$$\lambda = 4$$

So, $2\lambda = 2 \times 4 = 8$

9. (a,b,d) $f(x)$ may be written in the form, $f(x) = \sum_{k=1}^{n} \frac{1}{2^{k-1}} \cos(a_k + x)$

$$\Rightarrow f(x) = \sum_{k=1}^{n} \frac{1}{2^{k-1}} (\cos a_k \cdot \cos x - \sin a_k \cdot \sin x)$$

$$\Rightarrow f(x) = \left(\sum_{k=1}^{n} \frac{1}{2^{k-1}} \cos a_k\right) \cos x - \left(\sum_{k=1}^{n} \frac{1}{2^{k-1}} \sin a_k\right) \sin x$$

$\Rightarrow f(x) = A\cos x - B\sin x$, where

$$A = \sum_{k=1}^{n} \frac{1}{2^{k-1}} \cos a_k$$

and $B = \sum_{k=1}^{n} \frac{1}{2^{k-1}} \sin a_k$

Now, A and B both cannot be zero.

$\because \quad f(x_1) = f(x_2) = 0$

i.e. $A\cos x_1 - B\sin x_1 = 0$

$$\Rightarrow \quad \tan x_1 = \frac{A}{B} \quad \text{...(i)}$$

and $A\cos x_2 - B\sin x_2 = 0$

$$\Rightarrow \quad \tan x_2 = \frac{A}{B} \quad \text{...(ii)}$$

From Eqs. (i) and (ii), we get

$\tan x_2 = \tan x_1$

$\Rightarrow x_2 = k\pi + x_1, k \in I$

$\Rightarrow x_2 - x_1 = k\pi, k \in I$

So, (a), (b) and (d) are correct.

10. (b) Since, a, b, c and d lie on the circle $|z| = r$, we have

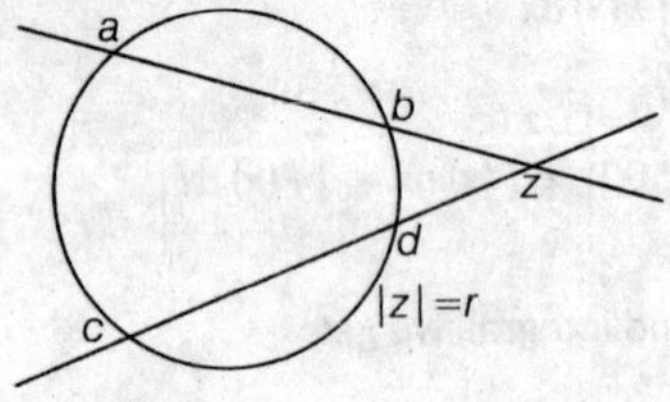

$$|a| = |b| = |c| = |d| = r$$

$$\Rightarrow \quad a\bar{a} = b\bar{b} = c\bar{c} = d\bar{d} = r^2 \quad \text{...(i)}$$

$$[\because z\bar{z} = |z|^2]$$

Now, a, b and z are collinear, then $z - b = \lambda(b - a)$

$$\Rightarrow \frac{z-b}{b-a} = \lambda \Rightarrow \frac{z-b}{b-a} = \text{purely real}$$

$$\Rightarrow \frac{z-b}{b-a} = \overline{\left(\frac{z-b}{b-a}\right)} = \frac{\overline{z-b}}{\overline{b-a}} = \frac{\bar{z}-\bar{b}}{\bar{b}-\bar{a}}$$

$$[\because \text{if } z \text{ is purely real, then } z = \bar{z}]$$

$$\Rightarrow (\bar{b}-\bar{a})z - (b-a)\bar{z} + \bar{a}b - a\bar{b} = 0$$

$$\Rightarrow \quad \bar{z} = \frac{(\bar{b}-\bar{a})z + \bar{a}b - a\bar{b}}{b-a} \quad \text{...(ii)}$$

Similarly, c, d and z are collinear, then

$$\bar{z} = \frac{(\bar{d}-\bar{c})z + \bar{c}d - c\bar{d}}{d-c} \quad \text{...(iii)}$$

From Eqs. (ii) and (iii), we get

$$\frac{(\bar{b}-\bar{a})z + \bar{a}b - a\bar{b}}{b-a} = \frac{(\bar{d}-\bar{c})z + \bar{c}d - c\bar{d}}{d-c} \quad \text{...(iv)}$$

Using Eq. (i) in Eq. (iv), we obtain

$$\frac{\left(\frac{r^2}{b} - \frac{r^2}{a}\right)z + \frac{r^2 b}{a} - \frac{r^2 a}{b}}{b-a} = \frac{\left(\frac{r^2}{d} - \frac{r^2}{c}\right)z + \frac{r^2 d}{c} - \frac{r^2 c}{d}}{d-c}$$

$$\Rightarrow r^2\left[\frac{\frac{(a-b)z}{ab} + \frac{b^2-a^2}{ab}}{b-a}\right] = r^2\left[\frac{\frac{(c-d)z}{cd} + \frac{d^2-c^2}{cd}}{d-c}\right]$$

$$\Rightarrow \frac{(b-a)\left[\frac{(-z)}{ab} + \frac{b+a}{ab}\right]}{(b-a)} = \frac{(d-c)\left[\frac{-z}{cd} + \frac{d+c}{cd}\right]}{(d-c)}$$

$$\Rightarrow z\left(\frac{1}{ab} - \frac{1}{cd}\right) = \frac{b+a}{ab} - \frac{d+c}{cd}$$

$$= \frac{1}{a} + \frac{1}{b} - \frac{1}{c} - \frac{1}{d}$$

$$= a^{-1} + b^{-1} - c^{-1} - d^{-1}$$

$$\Rightarrow z = \frac{a^{-1} + b^{-1} - c^{-1} - d^{-1}}{a^{-1}b^{-1} - c^{-1}d^{-1}}$$

11. (b,c,d) Let $(1, 1, 1), (1, -1, 1) (-1, 1, 1)$ and $(-1, -1, 1)$ be vector and rest of them a, b, c and d. Now, let we find the number of ways of selecting coplanar vector.

Since, those vectors are said to be coplanar, if their scalar triple product is zero i.e. if **a**, **b**, **c** are coplanar.

$$\Rightarrow \quad [\mathbf{a}, \mathbf{b}, \mathbf{c}] = (\mathbf{a} \times \mathbf{b}) \cdot \mathbf{c} = 0$$

Here, we observed that out of any 3 coplanar vectors, two will be collinear (anti-parallel).

Now, number of ways of selecting anti-parallel pair = 4.

Since, we have four pair namely $(a, -a), (b, -b), (c, -c)$ and $(d, -d)$ and number of ways selecting third vector $= 6$

Thus, total number of coplanar vectors $= 4 \times 6 = 24$

Hence, the number of non-coplanar selections $= {}^8C_3 - 24 = 32 = 2^5$

Thus, $P = 5$

12. (a,b,c) Let the equation of the hyperbola is

$\frac{x^2}{a^2} - \frac{y^2}{b^2} = 1$ and its foci $(\pm 2, 0)$

$$\therefore \quad a^2e^2 = 4b^2 = a^2(e^2 - 1)$$

$$\Rightarrow a^2 + b^2 = 4 \quad \text{... (i)}$$

Since, hyperbola also passes through the point $(\sqrt{2}, \sqrt{3})$.

$$\text{Thus, } \frac{2}{a^2} - \frac{3}{b^2} = 1 \quad \text{... (ii)}$$

Now solving Eqs. (i) and (ii), we get

$$a^2 = 1 \text{ and } b^2 = 3$$

Thus, the equation of hyperbola is

$$\frac{x^2}{1} - \frac{y^2}{3} = 1$$

Now, equation of the tangent is

$$\frac{\sqrt{2}x}{1} - \frac{\sqrt{3}y}{3} = 1.$$

This passing through points $(2\sqrt{2}, 3\sqrt{3})$.

Thus, $p = 2$ and $q = 3$

$$\therefore |(8p + 3q)^{1/2}| = |(8 \times 2 + 3 \times 3)^{1/2}|$$

$$= |(25)^{1/2}| = 5$$

Thus, the value of $|(8p + 3q)^{1/2}|$ is 5.

$$\therefore \quad p^2 + q^2 = (2)^2 + (3)^2 = 4 + 9 = 13$$

$$pq = 2 \times 3 = 6$$

13. (a, b, c, d)

$$f(x) = x^{1/3}(x - 1)$$

or

$$\frac{df(x)}{dx} = \frac{4}{3}x^{1/3} - \frac{1}{3} \cdot \frac{1}{x^{2/3}}$$

$$= \frac{1}{3x^{2/3}}(4x - 1)$$

Thus, $f'(x)$ changes sign from '–ve' to '+ve', at $x = \frac{1}{4}$, which is point of minima.

Also, $f'(x)$ does not exist at $x=0$ as $f(x)$ has vertical tangent at $x=0$

$$f''(x)=\frac{4}{9}\cdot\frac{1}{x^{2/3}}+\frac{1}{3}\cdot\frac{2}{3}\cdot\frac{1}{x^{5/3}}$$

$$=\frac{2}{9x^{2/3}}\left(2+\frac{1}{x}\right)=\frac{2}{9x^{2/3}}\left(\frac{2x+1}{x}\right)$$

Thus, $f''(x)=0$ at $x=-\frac{1}{2}$, which is the point of inflection.

At $x=0$, $f''(x)$ does not exist but $f''(x)$ changes sign.

Hence, $x=0$ is also the point of inflection.

From the above information, the graph of $y=f(x)$ is as shown below

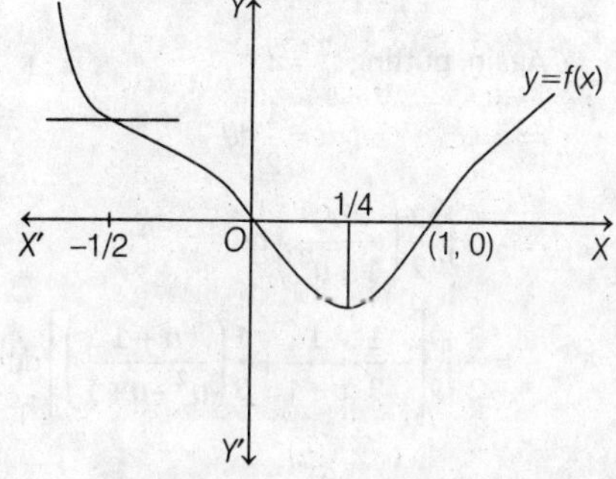

Also, minimum value of $f(x)$ is at $x=\frac{1}{4}$, which is $(-3\times 2^{-8/3})$

Hence, range is $[-3\times 2^{-8/3},\infty)$

14. (a, b, c)

$$\sum_{r=0}^{100}{}^{100}C_r\sin rx=\text{Im}\left(\sum_{r=0}^{100}{}^{100}C_r\cdot e^{irx}\right),$$

where Im = Imaginary part.

$$=\text{Im}\left[\sum_{r=0}^{100}{}^{100}C_r\cdot(e^{ix})^r\right]$$

$$=\text{Im}[(1+e^{ix})^{100}]$$

$$=\text{Im}(1+\cos x+i\sin x)^{100}$$

$$=\text{Im}\left(2\cos^2\frac{x}{2}+2i\sin\frac{x}{2}\times\cos\frac{x}{2}\right)^{100}$$

$$=\text{Im}\left(2\cos\frac{x}{2}\left(\cos\frac{x}{2}+i\sin\frac{x}{2}\right)\right)^{100}$$

$$=2^{100}\cdot\cos^{100}\frac{x}{2}\cdot\sin(50x)$$

$$\sum_{r=0}^{50}{}^{50}C_r\cdot a^r\times b^{50-r}\times\cos[rB-(50-r)A]$$

$$=\text{Re}\left(\sum_{r=0}^{50}{}^{50}C_r a^r\times b^{50-r}\times e^{i[rB-(50-r)A]}\right)$$

$$=\text{Re}\left[\sum_{r=0}^{50}{}^{50}C_r(a\times e^{iB})^r\times(b\times e^{-iA})^{50-r}\right]$$

$$=\text{Re}(ae^{iB}+be^{-iA})^{50}$$

$$=\text{Re}$$

$$(a\cos B+i\,a\sin B+b\cos A-ia\sin A)^{50}$$

$$=\text{Re}(a\cos B+b\cos A)^{50}$$

$$\left[\because a\sin B=b\sin A\text{ because }\frac{a}{\sin A}=\frac{b}{\sin B}\right]$$

$$=c^{50}\quad[\because a=b\cos C+c\cos B,\ b=c\cos A+a\cos C\text{ and }c=a\cos B+b\cos A]$$

$$=(a+b+c-a-b)^{50}$$

$$=(25-a-b)^{50}$$

$$\frac{\sum_{r=0}^{50}{}^{50}C_r\cdot\sin^2 rx}{\sum_{r=0}^{50}{}^{50}C_r\cdot\cos^2 rx}$$

$$=\frac{\sum_{r=0}^{50}{}^{50}C_{50-r}\sin 2(50-r)x}{\sum_{r=0}^{50}{}^{50}C_{50-r}\cos 2(50-r)x}$$

$$=\frac{\sum_{r=0}^{50}{}^{50}C_r[\sin 2rx+\sin 2(50-r)x]}{\sum_{r=0}^{50}{}^{50}C_r[\cos(2rx)+\cos 2(50-r)x]}$$

$$=\frac{\sum_{r=0}^{50}{}^{50}C_r\cdot 2\sin(50x)\cdot\cos(2r-50)x}{\sum_{r=0}^{50}{}^{50}C_r\cdot 2\cos(50x)\cdot\cos(2r-50)x}$$

$$=\tan(50x)$$

$$\Rightarrow f(\pi/8)=\tan\left(50\times\frac{\pi}{8}\right)$$

$$-\tan\left(\frac{25\pi}{4}\right)$$

$$=\tan\left(6\pi+\frac{\pi}{4}\right)=1$$

15. (a) Circle (C_2) centred at Q has variable radius r. We need to express the area A of ΔQSR in terms of r.

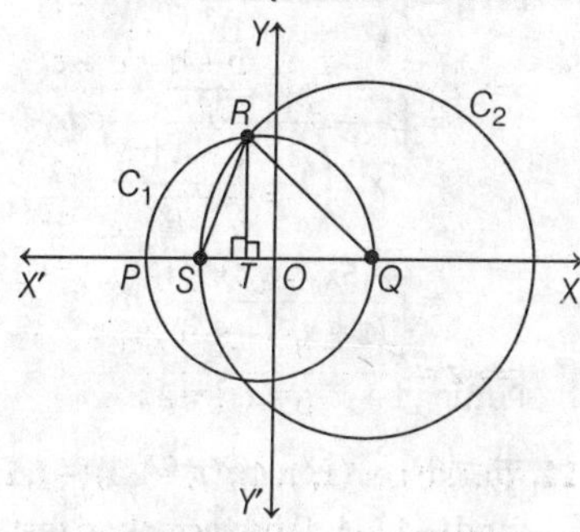

Observe ΔQSR carefully in the diagram. QR and QS are known (both are equal to r).

We need to find RT (the height) in terms of r. We can do this by finding the coordinates of R.

Let $\quad C_1: x^2+y^2=1 \quad$ ...(i)

and C_2: Circle centred at Q.

From Eq. (i),

Centre $=(0,0)$ and radius $=1$

$\therefore\quad Q\equiv(1,0)$

So, equation of C_2 is given by

$$C_2:(x-1)^2+y^2=r^2 \quad\text{...(ii)}$$

Now, we have to solve Eqs. (i) and (ii), to get the coordinates of R.

Subtracting Eq. (ii) from Eq. (i),

$$x^2-(x-1)^2=1-r^2$$

$$\Rightarrow x^2-x^2+2x-1=1-r^2$$

$$\Rightarrow\quad 2x=2-r^2$$

$$\Rightarrow\quad x=1-\frac{r^2}{2}$$

From Eq. (i),

$$y^2=1-x^2=1-\left(1-\frac{r^2}{2}\right)^2$$

$$=1-\left(1+\frac{r^4}{4}-r^2\right)=r^2-\frac{r^4}{4}$$

$$\Rightarrow y=\pm\sqrt{r^2\left(1-\frac{r^2}{4}\right)}\Rightarrow$$

$$y=|r|\sqrt{\frac{4-r^2}{4}}$$

[$\because R$ lies above the X-axis, $\therefore y$-coordinate of $R>0$]

$$\Rightarrow y=r\frac{\sqrt{4-r^2}}{2}$$

[$\because r$ is radius $>0\ \therefore |r|=r$]

$$\text{Hence, } R\equiv\left(1-\frac{r^2}{2},\frac{r\sqrt{4-r^2}}{2}\right)$$

$$\therefore\quad RT=\frac{r\sqrt{4-r^2}}{2}$$

Now, area

$$=A=\frac{1}{2}\times QS\times RT=\frac{1}{4}r^2\sqrt{4-r^2}$$

For maximum area, $\frac{dA}{dr}=0$

and $\frac{d^2A}{dr^2}<0$

$$\text{Now, }\frac{dA}{dr}=\frac{1}{4}\left[2r\sqrt{4-r^2}-\frac{r^3}{\sqrt{4-r^2}}\right]$$

$$=\frac{8r-3r^3}{4\sqrt{4-r^2}}$$

$\frac{dA}{dr}=0$, if $8r-3r^3=0$

$\Rightarrow \quad r=\sqrt{\frac{8}{3}}$

and verify that $\left.\frac{d^2A}{dr^2}\right|_{r=\sqrt{8/3}}<0$

$\therefore r = \sqrt{\frac{8}{3}}$ is a local maximum for A and

$A_{max}=\left.\frac{1}{4}r^2\sqrt{4-r^2}\right|_{r=r}=\frac{4\sqrt{3}}{9}$

16. (d) We have,

$1\cdot2\cdot3+2\cdot3\cdot4+3\cdot4\cdot5+.....+$ upto n terms $=\sum_{K=1}^{n}k(k+1)(k+2)$

$=\sum_{k=1}^{n}[(k+1)-1][(k+1)+1](k+1)$

$=\sum_{k=1}^{n}[(k+1)^2-1](k+1)$

$=\sum_{k=1}^{n}(k+1)^3-\sum_{k=1}^{n}(k+1)$

$=\sum_{k=2}^{n+1}k^3-\sum_{k=2}^{n+1}k=\sum_{r=1}^{n+1}r^3-\sum_{r=1}^{n+1}r \quad [\because 1^3=1]$

$=\frac{1}{4}(n+1)^2(n+2)^2-\frac{1}{2}(n+1)(n+2)$

$=\frac{1}{4}(n+1)(n+2)[(n+1)(n+2)-2]$

$=\frac{1}{4}(n+1)(n+2)(n^2+3n)$

$=\frac{1}{4}n(n+1)(n+2)(n+3)$

Also, $1\cdot2+2\cdot3+3\cdot4+....+n(n+1)$

$=\sum_{k=1}^{n}k(k+1)=\sum_{k=1}^{n}k^2+\sum_{k=1}^{n}k$

$=\frac{1}{6}n(n+1)(2n+1)+\frac{1}{2}n(n+1)$

$=\frac{1}{6}n(n+1)(2n+1+3)$

$=\frac{1}{3}n(n+1)(n+2)$

Thus, $\lim_{n\to\infty}\frac{1\cdot2\cdot3+2\cdot3\cdot4+3\cdot4\cdot5+....\text{upto } n \text{ terms}}{n(1\cdot2+2\cdot3+3\cdot4+....\text{upto } n \text{ terms})}$

$=\lim_{n\to\infty}\frac{\frac{1}{4}n(n+1)(n+2)(n+3)}{\frac{1}{3}n(n+1)(n+2)\times n}$

$=\lim_{n\to\infty}\frac{3}{4}\left(1+\frac{3}{n}\right)=\frac{3}{4}(1+0)=\frac{3}{4}$

17. (b) The direction ratios of OP are α,β and γ.

So, the equation of the plane through $P(\alpha,\beta,\gamma)$ and at right angle to OP is

$\alpha(x-\alpha)+\beta(y-\beta)+\gamma(z-\gamma)=0$

$\Rightarrow \alpha x+\beta y+\gamma z=\alpha^2+\beta^2+\gamma^2$

$=OP^2=p^2 \quad ...(i)$

$\Rightarrow \frac{x}{p^2/\alpha}+\frac{y}{p^2/\beta}+\frac{z}{p^2/\gamma}=1,$

which meets the coordinate axes at $A\left(\frac{p^2}{\alpha},0,0\right), B\left(0,\frac{p^2}{\beta},0\right)$ and $C\left(0,0,\frac{p^2}{\gamma}\right)$

Let A_{XY}, A_{YZ} and A_{ZX} represent the areas of the projections of the area of the ΔABC on the XY, YZ and ZX-planes, respectively.

Then, $A_{XY}=$ area of the ΔOAB

$=\frac{1}{2}\begin{vmatrix}p^2/\alpha & 0 & 0\\ 0 & p^2/\beta & 0\\ 0 & 0 & 1\end{vmatrix}$

$=\frac{1}{2}\frac{p^4}{\alpha\beta}$

Similarly, $A_{YZ}=\frac{1}{2}\frac{p^4}{\beta\gamma}$ and $A_{ZX}=\frac{1}{2}\frac{p^4}{\gamma\alpha}$

$\therefore \Delta^2=A_{XY}^2+A_{YZ}^2+A_{ZX}^2$

$\Rightarrow \Delta=\sqrt{\frac{1}{4}\frac{p^8}{\alpha^2\beta^2}+\frac{1}{4}\frac{p^8}{\beta^2\gamma^2}+\frac{1}{4}\frac{p^8}{\gamma^2\alpha^2}}$

$=\frac{p^4}{2\alpha\beta\gamma}\sqrt{\alpha^2+\beta^2+\gamma^2}$

$\Rightarrow \Delta=\frac{p^5}{2\alpha\beta\gamma} \quad$ [from Eq. (i)]

18. (d) k_1 and k_2 are two non-consecutive prime numbers.

Let $I_1=\int\frac{5x^9+4x^{10}}{(x^5+x+1)^3}dx$

$=\int\frac{5x^9+4x^{10}}{x^{15}\left(1+\frac{1}{x^4}+\frac{1}{x^5}\right)^3}dx$

$=\int\frac{5x^{-6}+4x^{-5}}{(1+x^{-4}+x^{-5})^3}dx$

Putting $1+x^{-4}+x^{-5}=z$

$\Rightarrow -(4x^{-5}+5x^{-6})\,dx=dz$

$\therefore \quad I_1=-\int\frac{1}{z^3}dz=\frac{1}{2z^2}+C$

$=\frac{1}{2(1+x^{-4}+x^{-5})^2}+C$

$\Rightarrow I_1=\frac{x^{10}}{2(x^5+x+1)^2}+C$

On comparing, we get

$\alpha=10, \beta=5, \gamma=1, k=2$ and $\lambda=2$

Now, $\alpha-\beta\lambda=10-(5\times2)=0$

Let $I_2=\int_{\alpha-\beta\lambda}^{\frac{k\pi}{8}}\sqrt[3]{\tan x}\,dx$

$=\int_0^{\pi/4}\sqrt[3]{\tan x}\,dx$

Putting $\tan x=t^3$

$\Rightarrow \sec^2 x\,dx=3t^2dt \Rightarrow dx=\frac{3t^2}{1+t^6}dt$

$\therefore I_2=\int_0^1\frac{3t^3}{1+t^6}dt$

Again, putting $t^2=u$

$\Rightarrow \quad t\,dt=\frac{1}{2}du$

$\therefore I_2=\int_0^1\frac{3}{2}\left(\frac{u}{1+u^3}\right)du$

$=\frac{3}{2}\int_0^1\left[-\frac{1}{3}\cdot\frac{1}{u+1}+\frac{1}{3}\left(\frac{u+1}{u^2-u+1}\right)\right]du$

$=\left[-\frac{1}{2}\ln|u+1|\right]_0^1+\frac{1}{2}\int_0^1\frac{u+1}{u^2-u+1}du$

$=\left[-\frac{1}{2}\ln|u+1|\right]_0^1+\frac{1}{4}\int_0^1\frac{2u-1}{u^2-u+1}du+\frac{3}{4}\int_0^1\frac{1}{1+u^2-u}du$

$=\left[-\frac{1}{2}\ln|u+1|+\frac{1}{4}\ln|u^2-u+1|\right]_0^1+\frac{3}{4}\int_0^1\frac{1}{\frac{3}{4}+\left(u-\frac{1}{2}\right)^2}du$

$=\left[\frac{1}{2}\ln\left|\frac{\sqrt{u^2-u+1}}{u+1}\right|+\frac{3}{4}\times\frac{2}{\sqrt{3}}\tan^{-1}\left(\frac{u-\frac{1}{2}}{\sqrt{3}/2}\right)\right]_0^1$

$=\left[\frac{1}{2}\ln\left|\frac{\sqrt{u^2-u+1}}{u+1}\right|+\frac{\sqrt{3}}{2}\tan^{-1}\left(\frac{2u-1}{\sqrt{3}}\right)\right]_0^1$

$=\left(\frac{1}{2}\ln\frac{1}{2}+\frac{\sqrt{3}}{2}\times\frac{\pi}{6}\right)-\left[0+\frac{\sqrt{3}}{2}\times\left(-\frac{\pi}{6}\right)\right]$

$=-\frac{1}{2}\ln2+\frac{\sqrt{3}\pi}{12}+\frac{\sqrt{3}\pi}{12}=\frac{1}{2}\left(\frac{\pi}{\sqrt{3}}-\ln2\right)$

On comparing, we get
$k_1 = 2, k_2 = 3$ and $k_3 = 2$
Hence, $k = k_1 = k_3 = \lambda = 2$ = The oddest prime → Option (a) is correct.
$4\gamma + k_3 = 2k_2 = 6$ = A perfect number → Option (b) is correct.
$[(\alpha + \beta + 4\gamma + k + \lambda) - (k_1 + k_2 + k_3)]$
$= (23 - 7) = 16$ = A perfect square number → Option (c) is correct.
$k_1 = 2$ and $k_2 = 3$ are two consecutive prime numbers.
Hence, option (d) is correct.

Extra Points

Some definitions related to number theory and is useful for question number 4 options

1. **Oddest Prime**
2 is the smallest prime number and the only even prime number. For this reason it is sometimes called 'the oddest prime'.
i.e. all prime numbers with the exception of 2 are odd. This makes 2 the oddest prime number.

2. **Perfect Number**
In number theory, a perfect number is a positive integer that is equal to the sum of its positive divisors, excluding the number itself (i.e. proper divisors).
In alternative way : The sum of divisors of a number, excluding the number itself, is called its aliquot sum.
So, a perfect number is one that is equal to its aliquot sum.
e.g. 6 has divisors 1, 2 and 3 (excluding itself) and $1 + 2 + 3 = 6$. So, 6 is a perfect number. Also, 6 is the smallest perfect number.
Other perfect numbers are 28, 496, 8128 and so on.

3. **Consecutive Prime Number**
2 and 3 are only consecutive prime numbers as 2 is the only even prime number and after that each consecutive pair contains one even and another odd number.

Knockout 12

Paper 1

1. (–1) Given, $\begin{vmatrix} 2 & 1 & 2 \\ 1+\alpha & \alpha & \beta \\ 4-\beta & 3-\beta & \alpha+1 \end{vmatrix} = 0$

Applying $C_1 \to C_1 - C_2$, we have

$$\begin{vmatrix} 1 & 1 & 2 \\ 1 & \alpha & \beta \\ 1 & 3-\beta & \alpha+1 \end{vmatrix} = 0$$

Applying $C_2 \to C_2 - C_1$ and $C_3 \to C_3 - 2C_1$, we get

$$\begin{vmatrix} 1 & 0 & 0 \\ 1 & \alpha-1 & \beta-2 \\ 1 & 2-\beta & \alpha-1 \end{vmatrix} = 0$$

$\Rightarrow \quad (\alpha - 1)^2 + (\beta - 2)^2 = 0$ [expanding along R_1]

$\Rightarrow \quad \alpha = 1$ and $\beta = 2$

$\because$ α, β, γ are in GP.

$\therefore \quad \beta^2 = \alpha\gamma$

$\Rightarrow \quad 4 = 1 \times \gamma \Rightarrow \gamma = 4$

So, $\Sigma\alpha = 1 + 2 + 4 = 7$,
$\Sigma\alpha\beta = 2 + 8 + 4 = 14$
and $\Sigma\alpha\beta\gamma = 1 \times 2 \times 4 = 8$

∴ The cubic equation is
$$x^3 - 7x^2 + 14x - 8 = 0$$
Hence, $a = -7, b = 14, c = -8$
$a + b + c = -7 + 14 - 8 = -1$

2. (–1) Given, $f(x + y) = 2^x f(y) + 4^y f(x)$ ...(i)

and $\quad f'(0) = \ln 2$

On interchanging x and y, we get
$$f(x + y) = 2^y f(x) + 4^x f(y) \quad ...(ii)$$
From Eqs. (i) and (ii), we get
$$2^y f(x) + 4^x f(y) = 2^x f(y) + 4^y f(x)$$
$\Rightarrow \quad (4^y - 2^y) f(x) = (4^x - 2^x) f(y)$

$\Rightarrow \quad \dfrac{f(x)}{4^x - 2^x} = \dfrac{f(y)}{4^y - 2^y} = K$ (say)

$\Rightarrow \quad f(x) = (4^x - 2^x) \cdot K$

$\Rightarrow \quad f'(x) = K \cdot (4^x \ln 4 - 2^x \ln 2)$

$\because \quad f'(0) = \ln 2$ [given]

$\therefore \quad \ln 2 = K(\ln 4 - \ln 2) = K \ln 2$

$\Rightarrow \quad K = 1$

Hence, $f(x) = 4^x - 2^x$

Now, $f(x) = (2^x)^2 - 2^x = \left(2^x - \dfrac{1}{2}\right)^2 - \dfrac{1}{4}$

Thus, $f(x)$ has least value $= \dfrac{-1}{4}$ at

$2^x - \dfrac{1}{2} = 0$ i.e. at $x = -1$

3. (1) Given,
$1 + 2|z|^2 = |z^2 + 1|^2 + 2|z + 1|^2$

$\Rightarrow 1 + 2z\bar{z} = (z^2 + 1)(\bar{z}^2 + 1) + 2(z + 1)(\bar{z} + 1)$

$\Rightarrow (z\bar{z})^2 + 2(z + \bar{z}) + z^2 + \bar{z}^2 + 2 = 0$

$\Rightarrow \quad (z\bar{z} - 1)^2 + (z + \bar{z} + 1)^2 = 0$

$\Rightarrow \quad z\bar{z} = 1$ and $(z + \bar{z} + 1)^2 = 0$

$\Rightarrow \quad \bar{z} = \dfrac{1}{z}$ and $z + \dfrac{1}{z} + 1 = 0$

$\Rightarrow \quad z^2 + z = -1$

$\Rightarrow \quad |z^2 + z| = 1 \Rightarrow |z(z + 1)| = 1$

4. (28) $\because$ AM ≥ GM

So, $\quad \dfrac{\alpha + \beta}{2} \geq \sqrt{\alpha\beta}$

$\Rightarrow \quad \gamma\left(\dfrac{\alpha + \beta}{2}\right) \geq \gamma\sqrt{\alpha\beta}$ ...(i)

Similarly, $\alpha\left(\dfrac{\beta + \gamma}{2}\right) \geq \alpha\sqrt{\beta\gamma}$ ...(ii)

and $\quad \beta\left(\dfrac{\alpha + \gamma}{2}\right) \geq \beta\sqrt{\alpha\gamma}$ ...(iii)

Now, adding Eqs. (i), (ii) and (iii), we get
$\alpha\beta + \beta\gamma + \gamma\alpha \geq \alpha\sqrt{\beta\gamma} + \beta\sqrt{\alpha\gamma} + \gamma\sqrt{\alpha\beta}$ ...(iv)

From Eq. (iv), $\alpha\beta + \beta\gamma + \gamma\alpha \geq 1$ ...(v)

Also, we have,
$(\alpha + \beta + \gamma)^2 = \alpha^2 + \beta^2 + \gamma^2 + 2(\alpha\beta + \beta\gamma + \gamma\alpha)$
$\geq 3(\alpha\beta + \beta\gamma + \gamma\alpha)$
$(\because \alpha^2 + \beta^2 + \gamma^2 \geq \alpha\beta + \beta\gamma + \gamma\alpha)$

$\Rightarrow (\alpha + \beta + \gamma)^2 \geq 3$ [from Eq. (v)]

∴ Minimum/least value of
$\alpha + \beta + \gamma = \sqrt{3}$

Hence, $\lambda = 3$

So, $3\lambda^2 + 1 = 3 \times 9 + 1 = 28$

5. (766) The required number are 1, 2, 11, 12, 21, 22, ... 122222222

Let us calculate how many numbers are these.

There are 2-one-digit such numbers.

There are 2^2 two-digit such numbers and so on.

There are 2^8 eight-digit such numbers.

All the nine-digit numbers beginning with 1 and written by means of 1 and 2 are smaller than $2 \cdot 10^8$.

Thus, there are 2^8, such nine-digit number.

Hence, the required number of natural number is

$2 + 2^2 + ... + 2^8 + 2^8 = \dfrac{2(2^8 - 1)}{2 - 1} + 2^8$
$= 2^9 - 2 + 2^8 = 766$

6. (5) Let
$$I = \int_{\sqrt{\ln 2}}^{\sqrt{\ln 3}} \frac{x \sin x^2}{\sin x^2 + \sin(\ln 6 - x^2)} dx$$

Putting $x^2 = z$

$\Rightarrow 2x\,dx = dz$

When $x = \sqrt{\ln 2}$, then $z = \ln 2$

When $x = \sqrt{\ln 3}$, then $z = \ln 3$

Thus, $I = \dfrac{1}{2}\displaystyle\int_{\ln 2}^{\ln 3} \frac{\sin z}{\sin z + \sin(\ln 6 - z)} dz$ ...(i)

$$\Rightarrow I=\frac{1}{2}\int_{\ln 2}^{\ln 3}\frac{\sin(\ln 2+\ln 3-z)}{\sin(\ln 2+\ln 3-z)+\sin z}\,dz$$

$$\therefore\ I=\frac{1}{2}\int_{\ln 2}^{\ln 3}\frac{\sin(\ln 6-z)}{\sin(\ln 6-z)+\sin z}\,dz \quad \text{...(ii)}$$

Adding Eqs. (i) and (ii), we get

$$2I=\frac{1}{2}\int_{\ln 2}^{\ln 3}1\,dz=\frac{1}{2}[\ln 3-\ln 2]$$

$$\Rightarrow I=\frac{1}{4}\ln\left(\frac{3}{2}\right)$$

This compare with $\frac{\lambda}{\mu}\ln\left(\frac{b}{a}\right)$, we get

$$\lambda=1, \mu=4, b=3 \text{ and } a=2$$

$$\text{Thus, } \left|\frac{\sqrt{9\lambda^2+\mu^2}}{b-a}\right|=\left|\frac{\sqrt{9(1)^2+(4)^2}}{3-2}\right|$$

$$=|\pm 5|=5$$

7. (11)

$$\cot^{-1}\left(\frac{1+2^{2n+1}}{2^n}\right)=\tan^{-1}\left(\frac{2^n}{1+2^{2n+1}}\right)$$

$$=\tan^{-1}\left(\frac{2^{n+1}-2^n}{1+2^n\cdot 2^{n+1}}\right)$$

$$=\tan^{-1}(2^{n+1})-\tan^{-1}(2^n)$$

$\therefore$Sum

$$=\tan^{-1}(2^1)-\tan^{-1}(2^0)+\tan^{-1}(2^2)-\tan^{-1}(2^1)+\tan^{-1}(2^3)-\tan^{-1}(2^2)+\ldots\tan^{-1}(2^{11})-\tan^{-1}(2^{10})$$

$$=\tan^{-1}(2^{11})-\tan^{-1}(2^1)=\cot^{-1}(a/b)$$

$$\Rightarrow \tan^{-1}\left(\frac{2^{11}-1}{1+2^{11}}\right)=\tan^{-1}\left(\frac{b}{a}\right)$$

$$\Rightarrow b=2^{11}-1 \text{ and } a=2^{11}+1$$

$$\therefore\ \log_2\left(\frac{a+b}{a-b}\right)=\log_2(2\cdot 2^{11}/2)=11$$

8. (72) Given, $a_1e_1=a_2e_2$ ...(i)

$$PF_1^2+PF_2^2=4a_1^2e_1^2 \quad \text{...(ii)}$$

[using Pythagoras theorem]

$$PF_1+PF_2=2a_1 \quad \text{...(iii)}$$

$$PF_1-PF_2=2a_2 \quad \text{... (iv)}$$

On squarring and adding Eqs. (iii) and (iv),

$$2(PF_1^2+PF_2^2)=4(a_1^2+a_2^2) \quad \text{...(v)}$$

From Eqs. (ii) and (v), we get

$$2(a_1^2+a_2^2)=4a_1^2e_1^2$$

$$\Rightarrow \quad a_1^2+a_2^2=2(a_1^2e_1^2)$$

$$\therefore\ 1+\left(\frac{a_2}{a_1}\right)^2=2e_1^2$$

$$\Rightarrow 1+\left(\frac{e_1}{e_2}\right)^2=2e_1^2$$

$$\therefore\quad \frac{1}{e_1^2}+\frac{1}{e_2^2}=2$$

Let $\frac{1}{e_1}=\sqrt{2}\cos\theta$ and $\frac{1}{e_2}=\sqrt{2}\sin\theta$

$$A=121e_1^2+e_2^2=121\left(\frac{1}{\sqrt{2}}\sec\theta\right)^2+\left(\frac{1}{\sqrt{2}}\operatorname{cosec}\theta\right)^2$$

$$\therefore A=121\left(\frac{1}{2}\sec^2\theta\right)+\left(\frac{1}{2}\operatorname{cosec}^2\theta\right)$$

$$=\frac{1}{2}[121\sec^2\theta+\operatorname{cosec}^2\theta]$$

$$=\frac{1}{2}[121(1+\tan^2\theta)+1+\cot^2\theta]$$

$$\Rightarrow A=\frac{1}{2}[122+121\tan^2\theta+\cot^2\theta]$$

$$=61+\frac{121\tan^2\theta+\cot^2\theta}{2}$$

$$=61+(\geq 11)\geq 72$$

$$\left[\text{using AM}\geq\text{GM } \frac{121\tan^2\theta+\cot^2\theta}{2}\geq\sqrt{121\tan^2\theta\cdot\cot^2\theta}\right]$$

$$\therefore\quad A_{\min}=72$$

9. (a,b,c,d)

$$\text{Given, } L=\lim_{x\to\infty}x^2\sin\left(\log_e\sqrt{\cos\frac{\pi}{x}}\right)$$

[form $0\times\infty$]

$$=\lim_{x\to\infty}\frac{x^2\sin\left(\ln\sqrt{\cos\frac{\pi}{x}}\right)}{\left(\ln\sqrt{\cos\frac{\pi}{x}}\right)}\times\left(\ln\sqrt{\cos\frac{\pi}{x}}\right)$$

$$=\lim_{x\to\infty}x^2\left(\ln\sqrt{\cos\frac{\pi}{x}}\right)$$

$$=\lim_{x\to\infty}\frac{x^2}{2}\ln\left(\cos\frac{\pi}{x}\right)$$

$$=\lim_{x\to\infty}\frac{x^2}{2}\frac{\ln\left[1+\left(\cos\frac{\pi}{x}-1\right)\right]}{\left(\cos\frac{\pi}{x}-1\right)}\left(-2\sin^2\frac{\pi}{2x}\right)$$

$$=\lim_{x\to\infty}\frac{x^2}{2}\frac{\left(-2\sin^2\frac{\pi}{2x}\right)}{\left(\frac{\pi}{2x}\right)^2}\left(\frac{\pi}{2x}\right)^2$$

$$\Rightarrow \quad L=-\frac{\pi^2}{4}$$

$$\text{So, } \frac{-16L}{\pi^2}=\left(\frac{-16}{\pi^2}\right)\times\left(\frac{-\pi^2}{4}\right)=4$$

$$\therefore\quad R=\log_{(4140)\sqrt{4}}\sqrt[5]{4}$$

$$=\log_{(4)^{1/4140}}(4)^{1/5}$$

$$=\frac{4140}{5}\log_4 4=828\times 1$$

$$\Rightarrow \quad R=828$$

We know that

$828=2\times2\times3\times3\times23=2^2\times3^2\times23$

So, its prime factors are 2, 3, 23 and hence this is not a prime number but composite number as well as this is palindrome number.

10. (b,d) Given, equation of hypotenuse of an isosceles right angled triangle is

$$\frac{x+6}{5}=\frac{y+10}{3}=\frac{z+14}{8} \quad \text{...(i)}$$

and its opposite vertex is $P(7,2,4)$

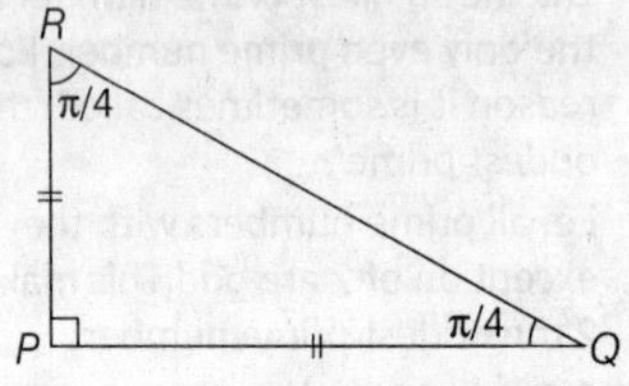

Now, any point taken on Eq. (i) is of the form $Q(5\lambda-6, 3\lambda-10, 8\lambda-14)$.

Direction ratios of line PQ are $<5\lambda-13, 3\lambda-12, 8\lambda-18>$

Direction ratios of line QR are $<5,3,8>$

Since, angle between PQ and QR is $\frac{\pi}{4}$

$$\therefore \cos\frac{\pi}{4}=\frac{(5\lambda-13)5+(3\lambda-12)3+(8\lambda-18)8}{\sqrt{5^2+3^2+8^2}\cdot\sqrt{(5\lambda-13)^2+(3\lambda-12)^2+(8\lambda-18)^2}}$$

On squaring and solving, we get $\lambda=3,2$

Hence, equation of lines are

$$\frac{x-7}{2}=\frac{y-2}{-3}=\frac{z-4}{6}$$

$$\text{and} \quad \frac{x-7}{3}=\frac{y-2}{6}=\frac{z-4}{2}$$

11. (b,c,d) Given, $P(Q)=\frac{1}{2}$ and $P(R)=\frac{2}{3}$

As we know,

$$P(Q\cup R)\geq\max\{P(Q),P(R)\}$$

$$\text{i.e.} \quad P(Q\cup R)\geq\frac{2}{3} \quad \text{... (i)}$$

$[\because P(Q)<P(R)]$

and $P(Q\cap R)\leq\min\{P(Q),P(R)\}$

$$\text{i.e.} \quad P(Q\cap R)\leq\frac{1}{2} \quad \text{...(ii)}$$

But $P(Q\cap R)=P(Q)+P(R)-P(Q\cup R)$

$\Rightarrow \quad P(Q \cap R) \geq P(Q) + P(R) - 1$

[$\because$ maximum value of $P(Q \cup R) = 1$]

$\Rightarrow \quad P(Q \cap R) \geq \frac{1}{2} + \frac{2}{3} - 1$

$\Rightarrow \quad P(Q \cap R) \geq \frac{1}{6}$ ...(iii)

From Eqs. (ii) and (iii),

$\frac{1}{6} \leq P(Q \cap R) \leq \frac{1}{2}$ ...(iv)

Now, $P(Q \cap R') = P(Q) - P(Q \cap R)$

$\Rightarrow \quad P(Q \cap R') \leq \frac{1}{2} - \frac{1}{6}$

$\Rightarrow \quad P(Q \cap R') \leq \frac{1}{3}$ ...(v)

Also, $P(Q' \cap R) = P(R) - P(Q \cap R)$

$\therefore \quad \frac{1}{6} \leq P(Q \cap R) \leq \frac{1}{2}$

$\Rightarrow \frac{2}{3} - \frac{1}{6} \geq P(R) - P(Q \cap R) \geq \frac{2}{3} - \frac{1}{2}$

$\Rightarrow \quad \frac{1}{6} \leq P(Q' \cap R) \leq \frac{1}{2}$ ...(vi)

12. (a, b, d)

Given, $A = \cos\frac{9\pi}{13} \cdot \cos\frac{3\pi}{13} + \cos\frac{3\pi}{13} \cdot \cos\frac{\pi}{13} + \cos\frac{9\pi}{13} \cdot \cos\frac{\pi}{13}$

$\therefore 2A = 2 \cdot \cos\frac{9\pi}{13} \cdot \cos\frac{3\pi}{13} + 2 \cdot \cos\frac{3\pi}{13} \cdot \cos\frac{\pi}{13} + 2 \cdot \cos\frac{9\pi}{13} \cdot \cos\frac{\pi}{13}$

$= \cos\frac{12\pi}{13} + \cos\frac{6\pi}{13} + \cos\frac{4\pi}{13} + \cos\frac{2\pi}{13} + \cos\frac{10\pi}{13} + \cos\frac{8\pi}{13}$

$= \sum_{k=1}^{6} \cos\frac{2k\pi}{13}$

Also, $\cos\left(\frac{2\pi}{13}\right) = \cos\left(2\pi - \frac{2\pi}{13}\right) = \cos\left(\frac{24\pi}{13}\right)$

and $\cos\left(\frac{4\pi}{13}\right) = \cos\left(2\pi - \frac{4\pi}{13}\right) = \cos\left(\frac{22\pi}{13}\right)$

$\cos\left(\frac{6\pi}{13}\right) = \cos\left(2\pi - \frac{6\pi}{13}\right) = \cos\left(\frac{20\pi}{13}\right)$

and so on

$2\sum_{k=1}^{6} \cos\left(\frac{2k\pi}{13}\right) = \sum_{k=1}^{12} \cos\left(\frac{2k\pi}{13}\right)$

$= \frac{\sin\left(\frac{12\pi}{13}\right)}{\sin\left(\frac{\pi}{13}\right)} \cdot \cos\left(\frac{\frac{2\pi}{13} + \frac{24\pi}{13}}{2}\right)$

$\Rightarrow \quad 2 \cdot \sum_{k=1}^{6} \cos\left(\frac{2k\pi}{13}\right) = -1$

$\Rightarrow \quad \sum_{k=1}^{6} \cos\left(\frac{2k\pi}{13}\right) = -\frac{1}{2}$

13. (c) The set $P = \{1, 2, 3, \ldots, 20\}$ is to be partitioned into the four equal sets of equal size i.e. each having 5-5 members.

Thus, the number of ways in which it can be done

$= {}^{20}C_5 \times {}^{15}C_5 \times {}^{10}C_5 \times {}^{5}C_5$

$= \frac{20!}{15! \times 5!} \times \frac{15!}{10! \times 5!} \times \frac{10!}{5! \times 5!} \times \frac{5!}{5!}$

$= \frac{20!}{15! \times 5!} \times \frac{15!}{10! \times 5!} \times \frac{10!}{5! \times 5!} \times 1$

$= \frac{20! \times 15! \times 10!}{15! \times 10! \times (5!)^4} = \frac{20!}{(5!)^4}$

Hence, the number of ways it can be done is $\frac{20!}{(5!)^4}$.

14. (d) Here,

$p = \{\omega^n\} = \left\{\left(\cos\frac{\pi}{6} + i\sin\frac{\pi}{6}\right)^n\right\}$

$= \left\{\cos\frac{n\pi}{6} + i\sin\frac{2\pi}{6}\right\}$

where $n = 1, 2, 3 \ldots$

$H_1 = \left\{Z \in \not\subset ; R \subset (Z) > \frac{1}{2}\right\}$

Since, $p \cap H_1$ represents those points for which $\cos\frac{n\pi}{6}$ is positive.

Hence, it belongs to I or IV quadrant.

$\Rightarrow \; Z_1 \in p \cap H_1$

$= \cos\frac{\pi}{6} + i\sin\frac{\pi}{6}$

or $\cos\frac{11\pi}{6} + i\sin\frac{11\pi}{16}$

$\therefore \quad z_1 = \frac{\sqrt{3}}{2} + \frac{i}{2}$ or $\frac{\sqrt{3}}{2} - \frac{i}{2}$

$\therefore$ Simplify, $Z_2 \in p \cap H_2$ i.e. those points for which $\cos\frac{n\pi}{6} < 0$.

$\Rightarrow Z_2 = \cos\pi + i\sin\pi, \cos\frac{5\pi}{6} + i\sin\frac{5\pi}{6}$

and $\quad \cos\frac{7\pi}{6} + i\sin\frac{7\pi}{6}$

$\Rightarrow Z_2 = -1, \frac{-\sqrt{3}}{2} + \frac{i}{2}, -\frac{\sqrt{3}}{2} - \frac{i}{2}$

So, $\angle Z_1 O Z_2 = \frac{2\pi}{3}, \frac{5\pi}{6}$

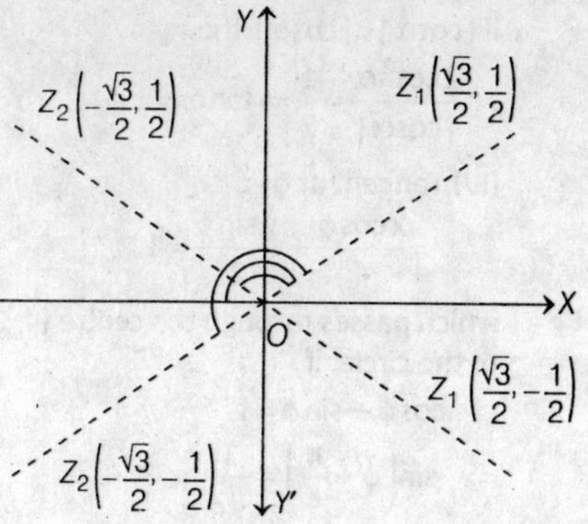

15. (b) (I) Tangent at $(3\sqrt{3}\cos\phi, \sin\phi)$ is

$\frac{x}{3\sqrt{3}}\cos\phi + y\sin\phi = 1$

Sum of the intercept on the axes

$= 3\sqrt{3}\sec\phi + \operatorname{cosec}\phi = f(\phi)$ (say)

Then,

$f'(\phi) = 3\sqrt{3}\sec\phi\tan\phi - \operatorname{cosec}\phi\cot\phi$

$= \frac{(\sqrt{3}\sin\phi)^3 - (\cos\phi)^3}{\sin^2\phi\cos^2\phi}$

$\therefore f'(\phi) = 0$

$\Rightarrow \tan\phi = \frac{1}{\sqrt{3}} \Rightarrow \phi = \frac{\pi}{6}$

Due to symmetry $\phi = \frac{5\pi}{6}, \frac{7\pi}{6}, \frac{11\pi}{6}$

(II) If $T(h, k)$ be the point of intersection of tangents at P and Q, then equation of PQ is $hx + 2ky = 6$, which is a tangent to $x^2 + 4y^2 = 4$, if

$\left(\frac{3}{k}\right)^2 = 4\left(\frac{h}{2k}\right)^2 + 1$

$\Rightarrow \quad \frac{9}{k^2} = 4 \times \frac{h^2}{4k^2} + 1$

$\Rightarrow \quad \frac{9}{k^2} = \frac{h^2 + k^2}{k^2}$

$\Rightarrow h^2 + k^2 = 9$

Thus (h, k) lies on the circle $x^2 + y^2 = 9$,

which is the director circle of $x^2 + 2y^2 = 6$.

(III) The ellipse is $\frac{x^2}{\cot^2\alpha} + \frac{y^2}{\cos^2\alpha} = 1$

If $|\cot\alpha| > |\cos\alpha|$, then

$$\frac{2\cos^2\alpha}{|\cot\alpha|}=\frac{1}{2}$$

$$\Rightarrow \quad \sin 2\alpha=\pm\frac{1}{2}$$

$$\alpha=\frac{\pi}{12},\frac{5\pi}{12},\frac{7\pi}{12},\frac{11\pi}{12}$$

If $|\cot\alpha|<|\cos\alpha|$, then

$$\frac{2\cot^2\alpha}{|\cos\alpha|}=\frac{1}{2}\Rightarrow \tan\alpha=\pm 4$$

(IV) Tangent at ϕ is,

$$\frac{x\cos\phi}{4}+\frac{y\sin\phi}{2}=1,$$

which passes through the centre (4, 2) of the circle, if

$$\cos\phi+\sin\phi=1$$

$$\Rightarrow \quad \sin\left(\phi+\frac{\pi}{4}\right)=\frac{1}{\sqrt{2}}$$

$$\therefore \ \phi=0 \text{ or } \frac{\pi}{2}$$

16. (c) (I) $A_1=\int_0^{\pi/2} 1\,dx=\frac{\pi}{2}, A_2=\pi$

Also, $a_{n+2}+a_n-2a_{n+1}$

$$=\int_0^{\pi/2}\frac{2\cos(2n+2)x-\cos(2n+4)-\cos(2nx)}{1-\cos 2x}dx$$

$$=\int_0^{\pi/2}\frac{2\cos(2n+2)x-2\cos(2n+4)x\cos(2x)}{1-\cos 2x}dx$$

$$=\int_0^{\pi/2}2\cos(2n+2)x\,dx$$

$$=\frac{2}{2n+2}\sin(2n+2)x\Big|_0^{\pi/2}=0$$

$\therefore a_1, a_2, a_3 \ldots$ are in AP

(II) $I_{n+1}+I_{n+3}$

$$=\int_0^{\pi/4}\tan^{n+1}x\sec^2 x\,dx$$

$$=\frac{1}{n+2}\tan^{n+2}x\Big|_0^{\pi/4}=\frac{1}{n+2}$$

$\therefore a_n=n+2$

$\therefore a_1, a_2, a_3, \ldots$ are in AP

(III)

$$I_n-I_{n-1}=\int_0^{\pi/2}\frac{\sin^2(nx)-\sin^2(n-1)x}{\sin x}dx$$

$$=\int_0^{\frac{\pi}{2}}\frac{\sin(2n-1)x\sin x}{\sin x}dx$$

$$=\frac{-1}{2n-1}\cos(2n-1)x\Big|_0^{\pi/2}=\frac{1}{2n-1}$$

$a_1, a_2, a_3\ldots$ are in HP $\forall\, n\geq 0$

(IV) $b_n=\int_0^{\pi/2}\frac{1-\cos 2nx}{1-\cos 2x}dx$

$$=\frac{n\pi}{2}\ \ a_n=\frac{\pi}{2}\ \forall n$$

$\therefore a_1, a_2, a_3 \ldots$ are in AP, GP and HP

Also, $a_1, a_2, a_3 \ldots$ is a constant sequence.

17. (a) (I) The centre of circle is $C\left(\frac{a}{2},\frac{b}{2}\right)$.

If the chord is bisected at $P(h, 0)$, then

slope of CP is $m=\dfrac{\frac{b}{2}-0}{\frac{a}{2}-h}$

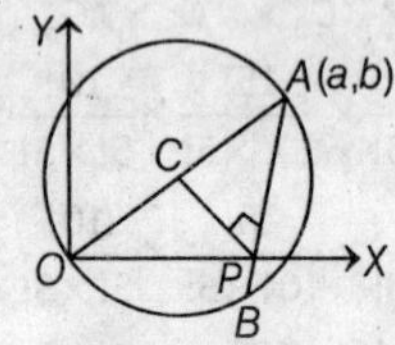

Slope of the chord is $\frac{-1}{m}$. The equation of the chord bisected at P is

$$y-0=-\left\{-\frac{\frac{a}{2}-h}{\frac{b}{2}}\right\}(x-h)$$

$$\Rightarrow \quad y\cdot\frac{b}{2}=\left(h-\frac{a}{2}\right)(x-h)$$

It passes through $A(a, b)$, so

$$h^2-\frac{3a}{2}h+\frac{b^2}{2}+\frac{a^2}{2}=0$$

For two distinct chords

$$\left(\frac{-3a}{2}\right)^2-4\left(\frac{a^2+b^2}{2}\right)>0$$

$$\Rightarrow \quad a^2>8b^2$$

Now, the discriminant at $at^2-8bt+2a=0$ is

$$D=64b^2-8a^2=8(8b^2-a^2)<0$$

(II) Homogenising the equation of the circle $x^2+y^2=b^2$ with equation of the chord

$$x\cos\theta+y\sin\theta-a=0$$

$$\Rightarrow \frac{x\cos\theta+y\sin\theta}{a}=1, \text{ we get}$$

$$(a^2-b^2\cos^2\theta)x^2+(a^2-b^2\sin^2\theta)y^2-2b^2\cos\theta\sin\theta\,xy=0$$

It represents a pair of perpendicular line, if

$$a^2-b^2\cos^2\theta+a^2-b^2\sin^2\theta=0$$

or $\quad 2a^2-b^2=0$

Now, the discriminant of $at^2+\sqrt{2}bt+a=0$ is

$$D=(\sqrt{2}b)^2-4a^2=2(b^2-2a^2)=0$$

(III) Any point of $x^2+y^2=a^2$ is $A(a\cos\theta, a\sin\theta)$. The chord of contact of tangents drawn from A to $x^2+y^2=b^2$ is

$$(a\cos\theta)x+(a\sin\theta)y=b^2$$

$$\Rightarrow x\cos\theta+y\sin\theta=\frac{b^2}{a}$$

It touches the circle $x^2+y^2=c^2$,

if $\frac{b^2}{a}=c\Rightarrow b^2=ac$

$\therefore b$ is geometric mean of a and c

$$\Rightarrow \ b<\frac{a+c}{2}$$

Now, the discriminant of the equation $bt^2+(a+c)t+b=0$ is

$$D=(a+c)^2-4b^2>0$$

(IV) The equation of chord of $x^2+y^2=25$ bisected at (a, b) is $ax+ay=a^2+b^2$. It is same line as $x+2y-10=0$

$$\Rightarrow \ \frac{a}{1}=\frac{b}{2}=\frac{a^2+b^2}{10}$$

$$\Rightarrow \ a=0, b=0 \text{ or } a=2, b=4$$

$\therefore a=2, b=4$, so equation $t^2+bt+a=0$

$\Rightarrow t^2+4t+2=0$ has the roots

$$t=\frac{-4\pm\sqrt{16-8}}{2}=-2\pm\sqrt{2}$$

18. (b) $f(0)>0$ and tangent at $\left(\frac{5}{2},P\right)$ to $f(x)$ is parallel to X-axis.

So both roots should be positive

$$f'(x)=0 \text{ at } x=\frac{5}{2}\Rightarrow a=(-5)$$

So, quadratic equation is

$$x^2-5x+b=0$$

Possible cases are $(x-1)(x-4)=0$ and $(x-2)(x-3)=0\Rightarrow b=4$ or 6

So, $a+b$ can be (-1) or 1

Vertex may be $\left(\frac{5}{2},\frac{-1}{4}\right)$ or $\left(\frac{5}{2},\frac{-9}{4}\right)$

So, P may be $\frac{-1}{4}$ or $\frac{-9}{4}$

$$[P]=-1 \text{ or } -3$$

$\therefore g(x)=(x-1)(x-2)$ or $(x-3)$

So, $g(|x|)$ is non-differentiable at one point and $|g(|x|)|$ is non-differentiable at 3 or 5 points.

Paper 2

1. (9) Given $A^2 = I, B = \begin{bmatrix} 1 & \sqrt{2} \\ 0 & 1 \end{bmatrix}$

and $C = ABA$

$\therefore C^2 = (ABA)^2 = (ABA)(ABA)$

$= AB(AA)BA = AB^2A$

$C^3 = (ABA)^3 = (AB^2A)(ABA)$

$= AB^2(AA)BA = AB^3A$

$C^4 = (ABA)^4 = (AB^3A)(ABA)$

$= AB^3(AA)BA = AB^4A$

Continuing in this manner, we get

$C^{1989} = AB^{1989}A$

Now,

$$B^2 = \begin{bmatrix} 1 & \sqrt{2} \\ 0 & 1 \end{bmatrix}\begin{bmatrix} 1 & \sqrt{2} \\ 0 & 1 \end{bmatrix} = \begin{bmatrix} 1 & 2\sqrt{2} \\ 0 & 1 \end{bmatrix}$$

$$B^3 = \begin{bmatrix} 1 & 2\sqrt{2} \\ 0 & 1 \end{bmatrix}\begin{bmatrix} 1 & \sqrt{2} \\ 0 & 1 \end{bmatrix} = \begin{bmatrix} 1 & 3\sqrt{2} \\ 0 & 1 \end{bmatrix}$$

$$B^4 = \begin{bmatrix} 1 & 3\sqrt{2} \\ 0 & 1 \end{bmatrix}\begin{bmatrix} 1 & \sqrt{2} \\ 0 & 1 \end{bmatrix} = \begin{bmatrix} 1 & 4\sqrt{2} \\ 0 & 1 \end{bmatrix}$$

Continuing in this manner, we get

$$B^{1989} = \begin{bmatrix} 1 & 1989\sqrt{2} \\ 0 & 1 \end{bmatrix}$$

$$\therefore \quad C^{1989} = A\begin{bmatrix} 1 & 1989\sqrt{2} \\ 0 & 1 \end{bmatrix}A$$

Comparing this to

$C^{1989} = A\begin{bmatrix} \alpha & \beta\sqrt{\gamma} \\ 0 & \delta \end{bmatrix}A$, we get

$\alpha = 1, \beta = 1989, \gamma = 2$ and $\delta = 1$

Hence, $|(\alpha + \delta) - (\beta + \gamma)| = |2 - 1991|$

$= |-1989| = 1989]$

$\Rightarrow 221k = 1989 \Rightarrow k = 9$

2. (2) Given, $(a+b+c)(a+b-c)$

$(b+c-a)(c+a-b)$

$$= \frac{8a^2b^2c^2}{a^2+b^2+c^2}$$

$$= \frac{16(a^2b^2c^2)}{2(a^2+b^2+c^2)}$$

$$\Rightarrow \frac{(a+b+c)}{2} \cdot \frac{(a+b-c)}{2} \frac{(b+c-a)}{2} \cdot \frac{(c+a-b)}{2}$$

$$= \frac{a^2b^2c^2}{2(a^2+b^2+c^2)}$$

$$\Rightarrow \left(\frac{a+b+c}{2}\right)\left(\frac{a+b+c}{2} - c\right)\left(\frac{a+b+c}{2} - a\right)\left(\frac{a+b+c}{2} - b\right)$$

$$= \frac{a^2b^2c^2}{2(a^2+b^2+c^2)}$$

$$\Rightarrow s(s-c)(s-a)(s-b) = \frac{a^2b^2c^2}{2(a^2+b^2+c^2)}$$

$$\left(\because s = \frac{a+b+c}{2}\right)$$

$$\Rightarrow \quad \Delta^2 = \frac{a^2b^2c^2}{2(a^2+b^2+c^2)}$$

$$(\because \Delta = \sqrt{s(s-a)(s-b)(s-c)})$$

$$\Rightarrow \quad a^2+b^2+c^2 = \frac{a^2b^2c^2}{2\Delta^2} \quad \text{...(i)}$$

As we know that,

$$\Delta = \frac{1}{2}bc\sin A = \frac{abc}{4R}$$

$$\left(\because \frac{a}{\sin A} = \frac{b}{\sin B} = \frac{c}{\sin C} = 2R\right)$$

From Eq. (i),

$$a^2+b^2+c^2 = \frac{a^2b^2c^2}{2\cdot\left(\frac{abc}{4R}\right)^2} = 8R^2$$

$$\Rightarrow 4R^2(\sin^2 A + \sin^2 B + \sin^2 C) = 8R^2$$

$$\left(\because \frac{a}{\sin A} = \frac{b}{\sin B} = \frac{c}{\sin C} = 2R\right)$$

$$\Rightarrow \sin^2 A + \sin^2 B + \sin^2 C = 2 \quad \text{...(ii)}$$

As we know,

$\cos^2 A + \cos^2 B + \cos^2 C$

$= 1 - 2\cos A \cdot \cos B \cdot \cos C$

$\Rightarrow 3 - (\sin^2 A + \sin^2 B + \sin^2 C)$

$= 1 - 2\cos A \cdot \cos B \cdot \cos C$

$\Rightarrow \sin^2 A + \sin^2 B + \sin^2 C$

$= 2 + 2\cos A \cdot \cos B \cdot \cos C$

Hence, from Eq. (ii),

$2 + 2\cos A \cdot \cos B \cdot \cos C = 2$

$\Rightarrow \quad \cos A \cdot \cos B \cdot \cos C = 0$

$$\therefore \quad \frac{(\sin^2 A + \sin^2 B + \sin^2 C)^2 + 2(\cos A \cdot \cos B \cdot \cos C)}{2^2 - 2} = 2$$

3. (5) Given, $\alpha^2 + \sqrt{\beta^2 - 2\beta} = 2\alpha - 1$

$\Rightarrow \alpha^2 - 2\alpha + 1 = -\sqrt{\beta^2 - 2\beta}$

$\Rightarrow \quad (\alpha - 1)^2 = -\sqrt{\beta^2 - 2\beta} \quad \text{...(i)}$

Since, $(\alpha - 1)^2 \ge 0$ and $-\sqrt{\beta^2 - 2\beta} \le 0$

So, Eq. (i) is possible only when

$(\alpha - 1)^2 = 0$ and $-\sqrt{\beta^2 - 2\beta} = 0$

$\Rightarrow \quad \alpha = 1$ and $\beta = 0, 2$

But β is positive real solution.

$\therefore \quad \beta = 0 \quad$ [rejected]

Hence, $\alpha = 1, \beta = 2$

Thus, $x^2 - bx + c = (x-1)(x-2)$

$= x^2 - 3x + 2$

$\Rightarrow \quad b = 3$ and $c = 2$

$\therefore \quad b + c = 3 + 2 = 5$

Hence, $(b+c)_{\min} = 5$

4. (1) We have,

$\mathbf{a} \times (\mathbf{b} \times \mathbf{c}) + (\mathbf{a} \cdot \mathbf{b})\mathbf{b} = (4 - 2\beta - \sin\alpha)\mathbf{b}$

$+ (\beta^2 - 1)\mathbf{c}$ ...(i)

and $\quad (\mathbf{c} \cdot \mathbf{c})\mathbf{a} = \mathbf{c} \quad$ ...(ii)

where **b** and **c** are non-collinear vectors and α, β are scalars.

From Eq. (ii),

$(\mathbf{c} \cdot \mathbf{c})\mathbf{a} \cdot \mathbf{c} = \mathbf{c} \cdot \mathbf{c} \Rightarrow \mathbf{a} \cdot \mathbf{c} = 1 \quad$ ...(iii)

From Eq. (i), $(\mathbf{a} \cdot \mathbf{c})\mathbf{b} - (\mathbf{a} \cdot \mathbf{b})\mathbf{c} + (\mathbf{a} \cdot \mathbf{b})\mathbf{b}$

$= (4 - 2\beta - \sin\alpha)\mathbf{b} + (\beta^2 - 1)\mathbf{c}$

$\Rightarrow [1 + (\mathbf{a} \cdot \mathbf{b})]\mathbf{b} - (\mathbf{a} \cdot \mathbf{b})\mathbf{c}$

$= (4 - 2\beta - \sin\alpha)\mathbf{b} + (\beta^2 - 1)\mathbf{c}$

[from Eq. (iii)]

$\Rightarrow 1 + \mathbf{a} \cdot \mathbf{b} = 4 - 2\beta - \sin\alpha$

and $\mathbf{a} \cdot \mathbf{b} = -(\beta^2 - 1) = (1 - \beta^2) \quad$ ...(iv)

$\therefore \quad \sin\alpha = 1 + (1 - \beta)^2 \quad$ [from Eq. (iv)]

This equation exist or true only, if

$(1 - \beta)^2 = 0$ because $-1 \le \sin\alpha \le 1$

So, $\beta = 1$ and $\sin\alpha = 1 \Rightarrow \alpha = \frac{\pi}{2}$

i.e. $\quad \alpha = 2n\pi + \frac{\pi}{2}, \beta = 1$

$\therefore \quad \beta^2 = 1$

5. (8) Equation of any line passing through (h, k) is

$y - k = m(x - h) \quad$ ...(i)

Line (i) meets Y-axis at $P(0, k - mh)$ and X-axis at $(h - k/m, 0)$.

So, the area of ΔOPQ is

$$A = \frac{1}{2m}(k - mh)(hm - k)$$

$$= hk - \frac{1}{2}mh^2 - \frac{1}{2m}k^2$$

Now, $\frac{dA}{dm} = -\frac{-1}{2}h^2 + \frac{1}{2m^2}k^2$

Putting $\frac{dA}{dm} = 0 \Rightarrow \frac{-1}{2}h^2 + \frac{k^2}{2m^2} = 0$

$\Rightarrow \quad m^2 = \frac{k^2}{h^2} \Rightarrow m = \pm\frac{k}{h}$

Also, $\frac{d^2A}{dm^2} = \frac{-1}{m^3}k^2 > 0$ when $m = \frac{-k}{h}$

[because $h, k > 0$]

Hence, the minimum value of A is at $m = \frac{-k}{h}$ and this will be equal to

$$h \cdot k + \frac{1}{2}\frac{k}{h} \cdot h^2 + \frac{h}{2k} \cdot k^2 = 2kh$$

If $h = k = 2$, then $A_{\min} = 2(2)(2) = 8$

6. (5) We have,

$$(x+3)^{n-1}+(x+3)^{n-2}(x+2)$$
$$+(x+3)^{n-3}(x+2)^2+\ldots+(x+2)^{n-1}$$
$$=\frac{(x+3)^n-(x+2)^n}{(x+3)-(x+2)}$$
$$\left[\because \frac{x^n-a^n}{x-a}=x^{n-1}+x^{n-2}\cdot a + x^{n-3}\cdot a^2+\ldots+a^{n-1}\right]$$
$$=(x+3)^n-(x+2)^n$$

Therefore, coefficient of x^r in the given expression is equal to the coefficient of x^r in $[(x+3)^n-(x+2)^n]$, which is given by

$$^nC_r 3^{n-r}-{}^nC_r\cdot 2^{n-r}={}^nC_r(3^{n-r}-2^{n-r})$$
$$\Rightarrow \quad p=3, q=2$$
$$\Rightarrow \quad p+q=5$$

7. (1) Given, $\left|\frac{x}{x-1}\right|+|x|=\frac{x}{|x-1|}$

Case I When $x>1$

$$\Rightarrow \quad \frac{x}{x-1}+x=\frac{x}{x-1}$$
$$\Rightarrow \quad x+x(x-1)=x$$
$$\Rightarrow \quad x=0,1$$

So, no solution exist.

Case II When $0\le x<1$

$$\frac{x}{1-x}+x=\frac{x}{1-x}$$
$$\Rightarrow \quad x+x(1-x)=x\Rightarrow x=0,1$$

So, $x=0$ is the only solution.

Case III When $x<0$,

$$\frac{-x}{1-x}-x=\frac{x}{1-x}$$
$$\Rightarrow \quad \frac{-2x}{1-x}-x=0$$
$$\Rightarrow \quad x\left[\frac{-3+x}{1-x}\right]=0\Rightarrow x=0, x=3$$

So, no solution exist.

Hence, only one solution exist i.e. $x=0$

Thus, the above equation has one solution.

8. (2) Given, $\frac{dy}{dx}=\frac{x^2+y^2}{2xy}$ ...(i)

This is homogeneous differential equation.

Putting $y=vx$,

$$\Rightarrow \quad \frac{dy}{dx}=v+x\cdot\frac{dv}{dx}$$

From Eq. (i),

$$\Rightarrow v+x\frac{dv}{dx}=\frac{x^2+v^2x^2}{2x(vx)}=\frac{1+v^2}{2v}$$
$$\Rightarrow \quad x\frac{dv}{dx}=\frac{1+v^2}{2v}-v=\frac{1-v^2}{2v}$$
$$\Rightarrow \quad \frac{2v\cdot dv}{1-v^2}=\frac{dx}{x}$$
$$\Rightarrow \quad -\ln(1-v^2)=\ln x - C$$
$$\Rightarrow \quad \ln[(1-v^2)x]=C$$
$$\Rightarrow \quad (1-v^2)x=e^C$$
$$\Rightarrow \quad (1-v^2)x=k_1,\text{ where } k_1=e^C$$

When $x=2, y=1$ and hence $v=\frac{1}{2}$

So, $k_1=\frac{3}{2}$

Hence, the equation of the curve is

$$x^2-y^2=\frac{3x}{2}\Rightarrow\left(x-\frac{3}{4}\right)^2-y^2=\frac{9}{16}$$

which is a rectangular hyperbola with eccentricity $\sqrt{2}$ (because eccentricity of a rectangular hyperbola $=\sqrt{2}$)

Therefore, $k=2$ (by the question)

$$\therefore \sin\left(\frac{\pi}{k}\right)+2\cos^2\left(\frac{\pi}{2k}\right)$$
$$=\sin\left(\frac{\pi}{2}\right)+2\cos^2\left(\frac{\pi}{4}\right)$$
$$=1+2\times\frac{1}{2}=1+1=2$$

9. (a, b, d)

The required point of intersection of three planes

$$x-2y+z-1=0 \quad \text{...(i)}$$
$$x+2y-2z-5=0 \quad \text{...(ii)}$$
$$x+y-2z-7=0 \quad \text{....(iii)}$$

From Eq. (i), $x=1+2y-z$

From Eq. (ii),

$$(1+2y-z)+2y-2z-5=0$$
$$\Rightarrow \quad 4y-3z=4 \quad \text{...(iv)}$$

From Eq. (iii),

$$(1+2y-z)+y-2z-7=0$$
$$\Rightarrow \quad 3y-3z=6 \quad \text{...(v)}$$

Subtracting Eq. (v) from Eq. (iv), we get

$$y=-2$$

From Eq. (iv), $-8-3z=4\Rightarrow z=-4$

From Eq. (i), $x+4-4-1=0\Rightarrow x=1$

$\therefore$ Point $(\alpha,\beta,\gamma)\equiv(1,-2,-4)$

Now, $\alpha^2+\beta^2+\gamma^2=1+4+16=21$

and $\alpha\beta+\beta\gamma+\gamma\alpha=-2+8-4=2$

and $\alpha-\beta+\gamma+1=1+2-4+1=0$

10. (b) Given that PQ is a focal chord, so if P is $(at^2, 2at)$.

Then, coordinate of Q is $\left(\frac{a}{t^2},-\frac{2a}{t}\right)$

and R and S coordinate are given by $(ar^2, 2ar)$ and $(as^2, 2as)$.

Also, given that, $QR \parallel PK$.

Then, $m_{QR}=m_{PK}$ [$\because$ slope are equal]

$$\Rightarrow \quad \frac{2ar+\frac{2a}{t}}{ar^2-\frac{a}{t^2}}=\frac{2at-0}{at^2-2a}$$
$$\Rightarrow \quad \frac{2a\left(r+\frac{1}{t}\right)}{a\left(r+\frac{1}{t}\right)\left(r-\frac{1}{t}\right)}=\frac{2at}{a(t^2-2)}$$
$$\Rightarrow rt-1=t^2-2\Rightarrow rt=t^2-1$$
$$\Rightarrow \quad r=\frac{t^2-1}{t}$$

11. (a, b, c, d)

Let

$$I=\int\left(\frac{\ln a^{a^{x/2}}}{3\cdot a^{5x/2}\cdot b^{3x}}+\frac{\ln b^{b^x}}{2a^{2x}\cdot b^{4x}}\right)\cdot x\,dx$$
$$=\int\left(\frac{a^{x/2}\cdot\ln a}{3\cdot a^{5x/2}\cdot b^{3x}}+\frac{b^x\ln b}{2\cdot a^{2x}\cdot b^{4x}}\right)\cdot x\,dx$$
$$=\int\left(\frac{\ln a}{3\cdot a^{2x}\cdot b^{3x}}+\frac{\ln b}{2a^{2x}\cdot b^{3x}}\right)x\,dx$$
$$=\int\frac{1}{a^{2x}\cdot b^{3x}}\left(\frac{\ln a^x}{3}+\frac{\ln b^x}{2}\right)dx$$
$$=\int\frac{1}{a^{2x}\cdot b^{3x}}\left(\frac{2\ln a^x+3\ln b^x}{6}\right)dx$$
$$=\int\frac{\ln a^{2x}\cdot b^{3x}}{6a^{2x}\cdot b^{3x}}dx$$

Let $a^{2x}b^{3x}=z\Rightarrow(a^2b^3)^x=z$

$$\Rightarrow \quad a^{2x}\cdot b^{3x}\cdot\ln(a^2b^3)dx=dz$$
$$\therefore I=\frac{1}{6(\ln a^2b^3)}\int\frac{\ln(z)}{z^2}dz$$
$$=\frac{1}{6(\ln a^2b^3)}\left(\frac{-\ln z}{z}-\int\frac{-1}{z^2}dz\right)+K$$

[using IBP]

$$=\frac{1}{6(\ln a^2b^3)}\left(-\frac{\ln z}{z}-\frac{1}{z}\right)+K$$
$$=\frac{-1}{6(\ln a^2b^3)}\left(\frac{\ln ez}{z}\right)+K$$
$$=\frac{-1}{6\ln a^2b^3}\left(\frac{\ln(a^{2x}\cdot b^{3x}\cdot e)}{a^{2x}\cdot b^{3x}}\right)+K$$
$$\Rightarrow I=\frac{1}{6\cdot\ln a^2b^3}\times\frac{1}{a^{2x}\cdot b^{3x}}\cdot\ln\left(\frac{1}{e\cdot a^{2x}\cdot b^{3x}}\right)+K$$

On comparing this to

$$I=\frac{1}{\lambda\cdot\ln(a^{\alpha}\cdot b^{\beta})}\times\frac{1}{a^{2x}\times b^{3x}}$$

$$\times\ln\left(\frac{1}{\mu\cdot a^{2x}b^{3x}}\right)+K, \text{ we get}$$

$$\lambda=6,\alpha=2,\beta=3,\mu=e$$

Now, $\ln\alpha+\ln\beta=\ln2+\ln3$

$$=\ln(2\times3)=\ln6=\ln\lambda$$

and

$$\ln\lambda-(\ln\alpha+\ln\beta)=\ln6-(\ln2+\ln3)$$

$$=\ln6-\ln6=0=\ln\mu-1$$

and $e^{\alpha\beta}=e^{2\times3}=e^6=\mu^{\lambda}$

and $\sin\left[\frac{\pi}{149}\{\ln(e^{\lambda})-\beta\cdot\ln(\mu^{\alpha})\}\right]$

$$=\sin\left[\frac{\pi}{149}\{\ln(e^6)-3\times\ln(e)^2\}\right]$$

$$=\sin\left[\frac{\pi}{149}(6-3\times2)\right]=\sin\left[\frac{\pi}{149}\times0\right]$$

$$=\sin0=0$$

12. (a, b, c)

$$P(A\cup B\cup C)=P(A\cup B)+P(C)$$
$$-P\{(A\cup B)\cap C\}\le P(A\cup B)+P(C)$$
$$\le P(A)+P(B)+P(C)$$
$$[\because P(A\cup B)\le P(A)+P(B)]$$

Now, P (exactly one of A,B,C occurs)

$$=P(A\cap\bar{B}\cap\bar{C})+(\bar{A}\cap\bar{B}\cap C)+P(\bar{A}\cap B\cap\bar{C})$$
$$=P(A\cap\overline{BUC})+P(\overline{AUB}\cap C)+P(B\cap\overline{AUC})$$
$$=P(A)-P\{A\cap(B\cup C)\cup(A\cap C)\}+P(C)-P\{(C\cap A)\cup(C\cap B)\}+P(B)-P\{(B\cap A)\cup(B\cap C)\}$$
$$=P(A)+P(B)+P(C)-2P(A\cap B)-2P(B\cap C)-2P(C\cap A)+3P(A\cap B\cap C)$$
$$=[P(A)+P(B)+P(C)-P(A\cap B)-P(B\cap C)-P(C\cap A)]-[P(A\cap B)+P(B\cap C)+P(C\cap A)-3P(A\cap B\cap C)]$$
$$=P(A)+P(B)+P(C)-P(A\cap B)-P(B\cap C)-P(C\cap A)-P$$

(exactly two of A,B,C occur)

$$\le P(A)+P(B)+P(C)-P(A\cap B)-P(B\cap C)-P(C\cap A)$$

Now, P (exactly two of A,B,C occur)

$$=P(A\cap B\cap\bar{C})+P(A\cap\bar{B}\cap C)+P(\bar{A}\cap B\cap C)$$
$$=P(A\cap B)-P(A\cap B\cap C)+P(A\cap C)-P(A\cap B\cap C)+P(B\cap C)-P(A\cap B\cap C)$$
$$=P(A\cap B)+P(B\cap C)+P(C\cap A)-3P(A\cap B\cap C)$$
$$\le P(A\cap B)+P(B\cap C)+P(C\cap A)$$

13. (c, d) Given equation of ellipse

$$E_1:\frac{x^2}{9}+\frac{y^2}{4}=1 \quad \text{...(i)}$$

Now, let a vertex of rectangle of largest area with sides parallel to the axes, inscribed in E_1 be $(3\cos\theta, 2\sin\theta)$.

So, area of rectangle

$$R_1=2(3\cos\theta)\times2(2\sin\theta)=12\sin(2\theta)$$

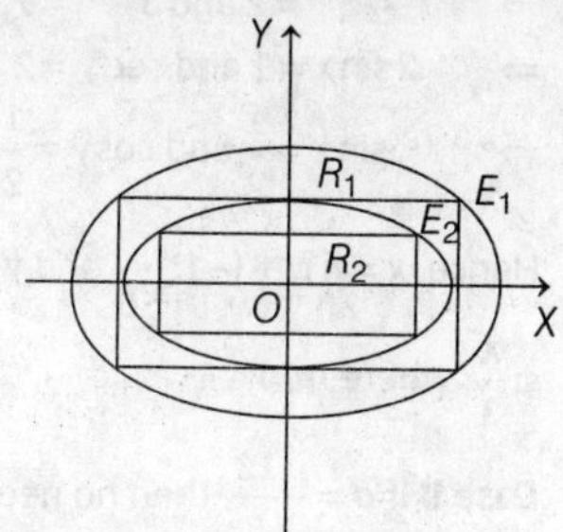

The area of R_1 will be maximum, if $\theta=\frac{\pi}{4}$ and maximum area is 12 sq units and length of sides of rectangle R_1 are $2a\cos\theta=\sqrt{2}\,a=3\sqrt{2}$ = length of major axis of ellipse E_2 and $2b\sin\theta=\sqrt{2}\,b=2\sqrt{2}$ = length of minor axis of ellipse E_2.

So, $E_2:\frac{x^2}{\left(\frac{a}{\sqrt{2}}\right)^2}+\frac{y^2}{\left(\frac{b}{\sqrt{2}}\right)^2}=1$ and

maximum area of rectangle

$$R_2=2\left(\frac{a}{\sqrt{2}}\right)\left(\frac{b}{\sqrt{2}}\right) \text{ and so on.}$$

So, $E_n=\frac{x^2}{\left(\frac{a}{(\sqrt{2})^{n-1}}\right)^2}+\frac{y^2}{\left(\frac{b}{(\sqrt{2})^{n-1}}\right)^2}=1,$

and maximum area of rectangle

$$R_n=2\left(\frac{a}{(\sqrt{2})^{n-1}}\right)\left(\frac{b}{(\sqrt{2})^{n-1}}\right)$$

From option (a),

Since, eccentricity of ellipse

$$E_n=e_n'=\sqrt{1-\frac{(b_n)^2}{(a_n)^2}}$$

$$=\sqrt{1-\frac{\left(\frac{b}{(\sqrt{2})^{n-1}}\right)^2}{\left(\frac{a}{(\sqrt{2})^{n-1}}\right)^2}}$$

$$=\sqrt{1-\frac{b^2}{a^2}}=\sqrt{1-\frac{4}{9}}=\frac{\sqrt{5}}{3}$$

is independent of 'n', so eccentricity of E_{18} and E_{19} are equal.

From option (b),

Distance between focus and centre of

$$E_9=e\cdot a_9=\frac{a}{(\sqrt{2})^8}(e)$$

$$=\frac{3}{2^4}\times\frac{\sqrt{5}}{3}=\frac{\sqrt{5}}{16}\text{ unit}$$

From option (c),

$$\because\sum_{n=1}^{N}(\text{area of } R_n)<(\text{area of } R_1)+(\text{area of } R_2)+\dots\infty$$

$$<2ab+2\frac{ab}{2}+2\frac{ab}{2^2}+\dots$$

$$<2ab\left(1+\frac{1}{2}+\frac{1}{2^2}+\dots\right)$$

$$<12\left(\frac{1}{1-1/2}\right)$$

$$\Rightarrow\sum_{n=1}^{N}(\text{area of } R_n)<24, \text{ for each}$$

positive integer N.

From option (d),

$\therefore$ Length of latusrectum

$$E_9=\frac{2b_9^2}{a_9}=\frac{2b^2}{a(\sqrt{2})^8}$$

$$=\frac{2\times4}{3\times16}=\frac{1}{6}\text{ units}$$

14. (a, b, d) Consider a non-right angled ΔPQR.

Now, by sine rule

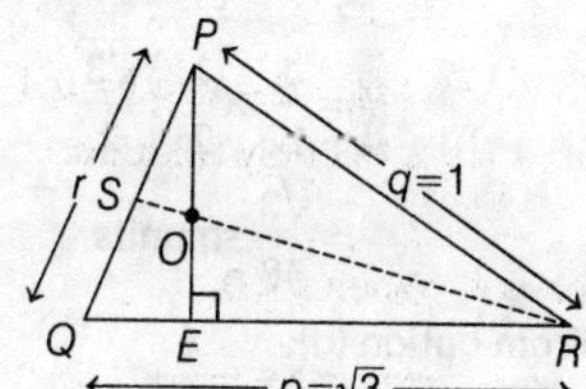

$$\frac{p}{\sin P}=\frac{q}{\sin Q}=\frac{r}{\sin R}=2\times\text{circumradius}$$

$$\Rightarrow\frac{\sqrt{3}}{\sin P}=\frac{1}{\sin Q}=\frac{r}{\sin R}=2\times1$$

[circumradius = 1 unit]

$$\Rightarrow\sin P=\frac{\sqrt{3}}{2}\text{ and }\sin Q=\frac{1}{2}$$

$$\Rightarrow P=120^\circ\text{ and }Q=30^\circ$$

[$\because$ ΔPQR is non-right angled triangle]

So, $R=30^\circ$

$\Rightarrow r=1$, so ΔPQR is an isosceles triangle. And, since RS and PE are the median of ΔPQR, so 'O' is centroid of the ΔPQR.

Now,
From option (a),
From Apollonius theorem,

$$2(PE^2+QE^2)=PQ^2+PR^2$$

$$\Rightarrow 2\left(PE^2+\frac{3}{4}\right)=1+1$$

$$\Rightarrow PE^2=1-\frac{3}{4}\Rightarrow PE^2=\frac{1}{4}$$

$$\Rightarrow PE=\frac{1}{2}\text{ units}$$

and $OE=\frac{1}{3}PE=\frac{1}{6}$ units

[$\because$ O divides PE is 2 : 1]

From option (b),
Again from Apollonius theorem,

$$2(PS^2+RS^2)=PR^2+QR^2$$

$$\Rightarrow 2\left(\frac{1}{4}+RS^2\right)=1+3$$

$$\Rightarrow RS^2=2-\frac{1}{4}$$

$$\Rightarrow RS^2=\frac{7}{4}$$

$$\Rightarrow RS=\frac{\sqrt{7}}{2}\text{ units}$$

From option (c),
Area of

$$\Delta SOE=\frac{1}{2}(OE)(ST)$$

$$=\frac{1}{2}\times\frac{1}{6}[(PS)\sin 60°]$$

$$=\frac{1}{12}\times\frac{1}{2}\times\frac{\sqrt{3}}{2}$$

$$=\frac{\sqrt{3}}{48}\text{ sq units}$$

From option (d),
$\because$ Inradius of ΔPQR

$$=\frac{\Delta}{s}=\frac{\frac{1}{2}pq\sin R}{\frac{1}{2}(p+q+r)}$$

$$=\frac{\frac{1}{2}(\sqrt{3})(1)\frac{1}{2}}{\frac{1}{2}(\sqrt{3}+1+1)}$$

$$=\frac{\sqrt{3}}{2}(2-\sqrt{3})\text{ units}$$

15. (a) $x=n\pi+(-1)^n\frac{\pi}{6}, y=2m\pi\pm\frac{\pi}{3}$,

where $m,n\in I$

$$4^{\sin x}+3^{\sec y}=11 \quad \text{...(i)}$$

$$5(16)^{\sin x}-2(3)^{\sec y}=2 \quad \text{...(ii)}$$

Let $4^{\sin x}=a, 3^{\sec y}=b$

From Eq. (i) $\Rightarrow a+b=11$ ... (iii)

From Eq. (ii) $\Rightarrow 5a^2-2b=2$

$\Rightarrow 5a^2-2(11-a)=2$ [from Eq. (iii)]

$\Rightarrow 5a^2+2a-24=0$

$$\Rightarrow a=\frac{-2\pm\sqrt{484}}{10}\Rightarrow a=2,\frac{-12}{5}$$

Case I If $a=2$, then $b=9$ [from Eq. (iii)]

$\Rightarrow 4^{\sin x}=2$ and $3^{\sec y}=9$

$\Rightarrow 2\sin x=1$ and $\sec y=2$

$\Rightarrow \sin x=\frac{1}{2}$ and $\cos y=\frac{1}{2}$

Hence, $x=n\pi+(-1)^n\frac{\pi}{6}$ and $y=2m\pi$ $\pm\frac{\pi}{3}$, where $m,n\in I$.

Case II If $a=-\frac{12}{5}$, then no need to find the value of b, because

$$a=-\frac{12}{5}$$

$\Rightarrow (4)^{\sin x}=-\frac{12}{5}$, which is not possible as $4^{\sin x}>0, \forall x\in R$

So, the case $a=-\frac{12}{5}$ and $b=\frac{67}{5}$ i.e. case (II) is not possible.

Therefore, $x=n\pi+(-1)^n\frac{\pi}{6}$ and $y=2m\pi\pm\frac{\pi}{3}$,

where $m,n\in I$, is the solution for Eqs. (i) and (ii).

16. (c) Let $y=f(x)=\frac{x-1}{a+1-x^2}$

$\Rightarrow (a+1-x^2)y=x-1$

$\Rightarrow yx^2+x-[(a+1)y+1]=0$

As, x is real. So, $D\geq 0$

i.e. $1+4y[(a+1)y+1]=0$

$\Rightarrow 4ay^2+4y^2+4y+1\geq 0$

$$\Rightarrow 4ay^2+(2y+1)^2\geq 0 \quad \text{...(i)}$$

We want this relation not to hold for all $y\in\left[-1,\frac{-1}{3}\right]$

If $a\geq 0$, then Eq. (i) holds for all $y\in R$ because sum of non-negative terms are always non-negative.

Hence, a must be negative (according to question).

Let us consider the equation,

$$(2y+1)^2=-4ay^2$$

$$\Rightarrow (2y+1)=\pm 2\sqrt{-a}y$$

$$\Rightarrow 1=-2(1\pm\sqrt{-a})y$$

$$\Rightarrow y=\frac{-1}{2(1\pm\sqrt{-a})}$$

i.e. $y=\frac{-1}{2(1+\sqrt{-a})}, y=-\frac{1}{2(1-\sqrt{-a})}$

Now, $y=\frac{-1}{2(1+\sqrt{-a})}>-\frac{1}{3}$

$$\Rightarrow \frac{1}{1+\sqrt{-a}}<\frac{2}{3}\Rightarrow 1+\sqrt{-a}>\frac{3}{2}$$

$$\Rightarrow \sqrt{-a}>\frac{1}{2}\Rightarrow -a>\frac{1}{4}$$

$$\Rightarrow a<-\frac{1}{4}$$

and $\frac{-1}{2(1-\sqrt{-a})}<-1$

$$\Rightarrow \frac{1}{1-\sqrt{-a}}>2$$

$$\Rightarrow 1-\sqrt{-a}<\frac{1}{2}$$

$$\Rightarrow -\sqrt{-a}<-\frac{1}{2}$$

$$\Rightarrow \sqrt{-a}>\frac{1}{2}$$

$$\Rightarrow -a>\frac{1}{4}\Rightarrow a<-\frac{1}{4}$$

Thus, $a\in\left(-\infty,\frac{-1}{4}\right)$.

17. (b) Since, $P^2=(P)P=PQP=PQ=P$

[$\because PQ=P$ and $QP=Q$]

and

$Q^2=(Q)Q=(QP)Q=Q(PQ)=QP=Q$

$\therefore \quad P=P^2=P^3=P^4$ .....

and $Q=Q^2=Q^3=Q^4=$ ....

Now, $(P^{1192}+Q^{1490})^{2889}=(P+Q)^{2889}$

$(P+Q)^2=P^2+Q^2+PQ+QP=2(P+Q)$

and

$(P+Q)^3=2(P+Q)(P+Q)=2^2(P+Q)$

Hence, $(P+Q)^{2889}=2^{2888}(P+Q)$

18. (c) Given,

$$I=\int_{e^{\pi/6}}^{e^{\pi/2}}\frac{\sin(\ln(\sin(\ln x)))\cdot\cos(\ln x)}{x\sin(\ln x)}dx$$

Putting $\ln(\sin(\ln x))=z$

$$\Rightarrow \frac{1}{\sin(\ln x)}.\cos(\ln x).\frac{1}{x}dx=dz$$

x	$e^{\pi/6}$	$e^{\pi/2}$
z	$-\ln 2$	0

$$\therefore I=\int_{-\ln 2}^{0}\sin z\,dz$$

$$=[-\cos z]_{-\ln 2}^{0}=\cos(\ln 2)-1$$

$$\therefore \cos^{-1}(I+1)=\ln 2$$

Knockout 13

Paper 1

1. (0.5) Given,

$$f'(x)=\begin{vmatrix} 2ax & 2ax-1 & 2ax+b+1 \\ b & b+1 & -1 \\ 2(ax+b) & 2ax+2b+1 & 2ax+b \end{vmatrix}$$

Applying $C_1 \to C_1 - C_3, C_2 \to C_2 - C_3$, we get

$$f'(x)=\begin{vmatrix} -(b+1) & -(b+2) & 2ax+b+1 \\ (b+1) & (b+2) & -1 \\ b & b+1 & 2ax+b \end{vmatrix}$$

Applying $R_1 \to R_1 + R_2, R_3 \to R_3 - R_2$, we get

$$f'(x)=\begin{vmatrix} 0 & 0 & 2ax+b \\ b+1 & b+2 & -1 \\ -1 & -1 & 2ax+b+1 \end{vmatrix}$$

$$\Rightarrow \quad f'(x)=2ax+b$$

$$\Rightarrow \quad f(x)=ax^2+bx+c$$

$$f(0)=2 \Rightarrow c=2$$

$$f(1)=1$$

$$\Rightarrow a+b+2=1 \Rightarrow a+b=-1$$

$$f'\left(\frac{5}{2}\right)=0 \Rightarrow 5a+b=0$$

$$\therefore \quad a=\frac{1}{4} \text{ and } b=-\frac{5}{4}$$

Hence, $f(x)=\frac{1}{4}x^2-\frac{5}{4}x+2$

$$\therefore \quad f(2)=\frac{1}{2}=0.5$$

2. (192)

$$I=\int_0^{\pi/4}(\pi x-4x^2)\ln(1+\tan x)\,dx \quad \text{...(i)}$$

$$I=\int_0^{\pi/4}(\pi x-4x^2)[\ln(2) - \ln(1+\tan x)]\,dx \quad \text{...(ii)}$$

$$\left[\text{using} \int_0^a f(x)\,dx=\int_0^a f(a-x)\,dx\right]$$

Adding Eqs. (i) and (ii), we get

$$2I=\ln 2\int_0^{\pi/4}(\pi x-4x^2)\,dx$$

$$I=\frac{\ln 2}{2}\left[\frac{\pi x^2}{2}-\frac{4}{3}x^3\right]_0^{\pi/4}$$

$$I=\frac{\ln 2}{2}\left[\frac{\pi^3}{32}-\frac{\pi^3}{48}\right]=\frac{\pi^3}{192}\ln 2$$

Hence, $k=192$

3. (8) Given, $f'(1)=\tan\frac{\pi}{6}, f'(2)=\tan\frac{\pi}{3}$,

$$f'(3)=\tan\frac{\pi}{4}.$$

Now, $\int_2^3 f'(x)f''(x)\,dx+\int_1^3 f''(x)\,dx$

$$=\left[\frac{(f'(x))^2}{2}\right]_2^3+(f'(x))_1^3$$

$$=\frac{\{(f'(3)\}^2-\{f'(2)\}^2}{2}+\{f'(3)-f'(1)\}$$

$$=\frac{(1)^2-(\sqrt{3})^2}{2}+\left(1-\frac{1}{\sqrt{3}}\right)$$

$$=\frac{1-3}{2}+\left(1-\frac{1}{\sqrt{3}}\right)$$

$$=-1+1-\frac{1}{\sqrt{3}}$$

$$=-\frac{1}{\sqrt{3}}$$

Thus, $p=-1$ and $q=3$, then

$$(p+q)^3=(-1+3)^3$$

$$=(2)^3=8$$

4. (8) Slope of $AC=\tan 120°=-\sqrt{3}$

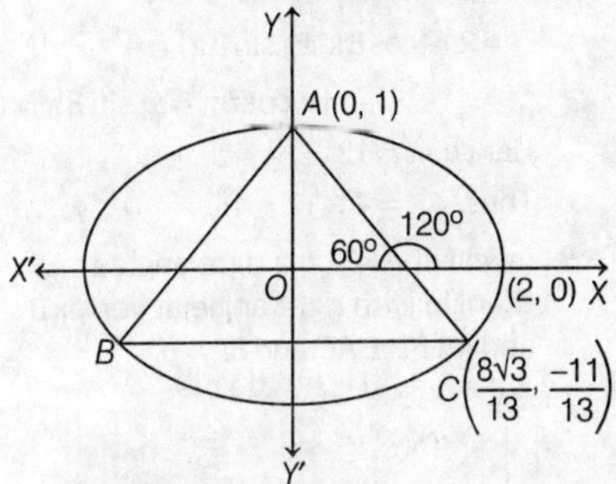

$\therefore$ Equation of AC is

$$\sqrt{3}x+y=1 \quad \text{...(i)}$$

Given, equation of ellipse is

$$\frac{x^2}{4}+\frac{y^2}{1}=1 \quad \text{...(ii)}$$

On solving Eqs. (i) and (ii), we have

$$\frac{x^2}{4}+(1-\sqrt{3}x)^2=1$$

$$\Rightarrow \quad \frac{x^2}{4}+3x^2-2\sqrt{3}x=0$$

$$\Rightarrow \quad x=\frac{8\sqrt{3}}{13}, y=1-\frac{24}{13}=\frac{-11}{13}$$

[$\because x=0$ and $y=1$ already, given]

$$\therefore AC=K=\frac{\sqrt{64\times 3+576}}{13}$$

[using distance formula]

$$\Rightarrow K=\frac{16\sqrt{3}}{13}$$

Hence, $\frac{13K}{\sqrt{12}}=\frac{16\sqrt{3}}{13}\times\frac{13}{\sqrt{12}}=8$

5. (50)

$$AB=\begin{bmatrix} 2 & 0 & 7 \\ 0 & 1 & 0 \\ 1 & -2 & 1 \end{bmatrix}\begin{bmatrix} -x & 14x & 7x \\ 0 & 1 & 0 \\ x & -4x & -2x \end{bmatrix}$$

$$\Rightarrow \quad AB=\begin{bmatrix} 5x & 0 & 0 \\ 0 & 1 & 0 \\ 0 & (10x-2) & 5x \end{bmatrix}$$

Since, $(AB)^2=I$

So, $\begin{bmatrix} 5x & 0 & 0 \\ 0 & 1 & 0 \\ 0 & 10x-2 & 5x \end{bmatrix}\begin{bmatrix} 5x & 0 & 0 \\ 0 & 1 & 0 \\ 0 & 10x-2 & 5x \end{bmatrix}=\begin{bmatrix} 1 & 0 & 0 \\ 0 & 1 & 0 \\ 0 & 0 & 1 \end{bmatrix}$

$$\Rightarrow \begin{bmatrix} 25x^2 & 0 & 0 \\ 0 & 1 & 0 \\ 0 & (60x-12) & 25x^2 \end{bmatrix}=\begin{bmatrix} 1 & 0 & 0 \\ 0 & 1 & 0 \\ 0 & 0 & 1 \end{bmatrix}$$

On comparing both sides, we get

$$25x^2=1 \text{ and } 60x-12=0$$

$$\Rightarrow \quad x=\pm\frac{1}{5} \text{ and } x=\frac{1}{5}$$

Since, $AB \neq I$. So, $x=\frac{1}{5}$ rejected,

we get $x=-\frac{1}{5}$

So, $AB=\begin{bmatrix} -1 & 0 & 0 \\ 0 & 1 & 0 \\ 0 & -4 & -1 \end{bmatrix} \Rightarrow tr(AB)=-1$

Now, $(AB)^2=\begin{bmatrix} 1 & 0 & 0 \\ 0 & 1 & 0 \\ 0 & 0 & 1 \end{bmatrix}$

$$\Rightarrow tr\{(AB^2)\}=3$$

and $(AB)^3=\begin{bmatrix} -1 & 0 & 0 \\ 0 & 1 & 0 \\ 0 & -4 & -1 \end{bmatrix}$

$$\Rightarrow tr\{(AB)^3\}=-1$$

Hence, observe that

$$tr((AB)+(AB)^2+...+(AB)^{50})$$

$$=tr(AB)+tr(AB)^2+tr(AB)^3+...+tr(AB)^{50}$$

$$=\underbrace{(-1)+3}+\underbrace{(-1)+3}+....+\underbrace{(-1)+3}$$

$$=50$$

6. (8) Let us consider

$$P(x)=a(x-2)^4+b(x-2)^3+c(x-2)^2+d(x-2)+e$$

Given, $P(2) = -1$

$\Rightarrow a\times 0 + b\times 0 + c\times 0 + d\times 0 + e = -1$

$\Rightarrow e = -1$

and $P'(2) = 0 \Rightarrow d = 0$

and $P''(2) = 2 \Rightarrow 2c = 2 \Rightarrow c = 1$

Also, $P'''(2) = -12$

$\Rightarrow 6b = -12 \Rightarrow b = -2$

and $P''''(2) = 24$

$\Rightarrow 24a = 24 \Rightarrow a = 1$

Thus, $P''(x) = 12(x-2)^2 - 12(x-2) + 2$

$\therefore P''(1) = 12 - 12(-1) + 2 = 26$

Hence, sum of digits in the value of $P''(1) = 2 + 6 = 8$.

7. (2860) Since, V_n denotes the sum of the first n terms of an arithmetic progression (AP) whose first terms is n and the common difference is $(2n-1)$ is

$$\frac{n}{2}[2(n) + (n-1)(2n-1)]$$

$$V_n = \frac{n}{2}[2n + 2n^2 - 3n + 1]$$

$$= \frac{n}{2}[2n^2 - n + 1] = n^3 - \frac{n^2}{2} + \frac{n}{2}$$

Now, $\sum_{n=1}^{n} V_n = \sum_{n=1}^{n}\left(n^3 - \frac{n^2}{2} + \frac{n}{2}\right)$

$$= (1^3 + 2^3 + \dots + n^3) - \frac{1}{2}(1^2 + 2^2 + \dots + n^2) + \frac{1}{2}(1 + 2 + \dots + n)$$

$$= \left[\frac{n(n+1)}{2}\right]^2 - \frac{1}{2}\left[\frac{n(n+1)(2n+1)}{6}\right] + \frac{1}{2}\left[\frac{n(n+1)}{2}\right]$$

$$= \frac{n(n+1)}{12}[3n(n+1) - 2n - 1 + 3]$$

$$= \frac{n(n+1)(3n^2 + n + 2)}{12}$$

Thus, put $n = 10$.

Then, $V_1 + V_2 + \dots + V_{10}$

$$= \frac{10(10+1)(3\times 10^2 + 10 + 2)}{12}$$

$$= \frac{110\times 312}{12}$$

$$= 110\times 26$$

$$= 2860$$

8. (48) We have, $\alpha^2 - 6\alpha + 12 = 0$

$\therefore \quad 6(\alpha - 2) = \alpha^2 \quad$ ...(i)

and $\quad \beta^2 - 6\beta + 12 = 0$

$\therefore \quad \beta(\beta - 6) + 12 = 0$

$\Rightarrow \quad \beta - 6 = \frac{-12}{\beta} \quad$ ...(ii)

So, $(\alpha-2)^{24} - \frac{(\beta-6)^8}{\alpha^8} + 1$

$$= (\alpha-2)^{24} - \frac{12^8}{\alpha^8\beta^8} + 1 \text{ [from Eq. (ii)]}$$

$$= (\alpha-2)^{24} - \frac{12^8}{12^8} + 1$$

[$\because \alpha, \beta$ are roots of $x^2 - 6x + 12 = 0$

$\therefore \alpha\beta = \frac{12}{1} = 12 \therefore (\alpha\beta)^8 = (12)^8$]

$$= (\alpha-2)^{24} = (3 \pm \sqrt{3}i - 2)^{24}$$

[$\because \alpha^2 - 6\alpha + 12 = 0 \therefore \alpha = 3 \pm \sqrt{3}i$]

$$= (1 \pm \sqrt{3}i)^{24}$$

$$= \left[2(\cos\frac{\pi}{3} \pm i\sin\frac{\pi}{3})\right]^{24}$$

$$= 2^{24}(\cos 8\pi \pm i\sin 8\pi) = 4^{12}$$

[$\because \cos 8\pi = 1, \sin 8\pi = 0$]

Hence, $\lambda = 12$

Thus, $4\lambda = 4\times 12 = 48$

9. (a, c) Let ABC be a right angled triangle with right angle at vertex B and let $BL \perp AC$ and $BL = p$.

A, B, C, L, c, a, p, 4p=b

So, $AC = 4p = b$

Now, area of $\Delta ABC = \frac{1}{2}ac = \frac{1}{2}(4p)(p)$

$\Rightarrow \quad ac = 4p^2 \quad$ ...(i)

Now, $(a-c)^2 = a^2 + c^2 - 2ac$

$$= b^2 - 2(4p^2)$$

[using Eq. (i) and $a^2 + c^2 = b^2$]

$$= (4p)^2 - 8p^2 \quad [\because b = 4p]$$

$$= 16p^2 - 8p^2 = 8p^2$$

and $(a+c)^2 = a^2 + c^2 + 2ac$

$$= b^2 + 2(4p^2)$$

$$= 16p^2 + 8p^2 = 24p^2$$

So, $\left(\frac{a-c}{a+c}\right)^2 = \frac{8p^2}{24p^2} = \frac{1}{3}$

$\Rightarrow \quad \frac{a-c}{a+c} = \pm\frac{1}{\sqrt{3}} \quad$ ...(ii)

By Napier's analogy,

$$\tan\left(\frac{A-C}{2}\right) = \frac{a-c}{a+c}\cot\frac{B}{2}$$

$$= \frac{a-c}{a+c}\cot 45°$$

[$\because \angle B = 90°$]

$$\Rightarrow \tan\left(\frac{A-C}{2}\right) = \frac{a-c}{a+c} = \pm\frac{1}{\sqrt{3}}$$

$\Rightarrow \tan\left(\frac{A-C}{2}\right) = \frac{1}{\sqrt{3}}$ for $A > C$

and $\tan\left(\frac{A-C}{2}\right) = \frac{-1}{\sqrt{3}}$ for $A < C$

$\Rightarrow \quad \frac{A-C}{2} = 30°$ for $A > C$

and $\quad \frac{A-C}{2} = -30°$ for $A < C$

$\Rightarrow A - C = 60°$ for $A > C$

and $A - C = -60°$

i.e. $C - A = 60°$

for $A < C$

Also, $\angle A + \angle C = 90°$, as $\angle B = 90°$

Hence, $\angle A = 75°, \angle B = 90°, \angle C = 15°$ for $A > C$ or $\angle A = 15°, \angle B = 90°, \angle C = 75°$ for $A < C$

10. (a, b, d)

Let $P = \lim_{x\to\frac{\pi}{2}} \frac{\sin(x\cos x)}{\cos(x\sin x)}$

$$= \lim_{x\to\frac{\pi}{2}} \frac{(\cos(x\cos x))(\cos x - x\sin x)}{(-\sin(x\sin x))(\sin x + x\cos x)}$$

[applying L-Hospital rule]

$$= \frac{(1)\left(-\frac{\pi}{2}\right)}{(-1)(1)} = \frac{\pi}{2}$$

Now, as given that

$$\tan^{-1}(x+2) + \cot^{-1}(\sqrt{4x+20}) = \frac{\pi}{2}$$

$\Rightarrow \quad (x+2) = \sqrt{4x+20}$

$\Rightarrow \quad (x+2)^2 = (4x+20)$

$\Rightarrow \quad x^2 = 16$

$\Rightarrow \quad x = \pm 4$

But $x = -4$ not possible solution of above equation, so only possible solution is 4.

Since, a satisfied the above equation, So, $a = 4$.

How, $\lim_{x\to 0} \frac{\sqrt[4]{1+x} - \frac{(1+x)^{1/x}}{e} - bx}{5x + kx^2 + x^3} = 0$

$$\Rightarrow \lim_{x\to 0}\frac{\sqrt[4]{1+x}-\frac{1}{e}((1+x)^{1/x})-bx}{x(x^2+kx+5)}=0$$

$\Rightarrow$

$$\lim_{x\to 0}\frac{\left(1+\frac{x}{4}\right)-\frac{1}{e}\left(e\left(1-\frac{x}{2}\right)\right)-bx}{5x}=0$$

$\forall k \in R$

$$\Rightarrow \left(\frac{1}{4}+\frac{1}{2}-b\right)=0 \Rightarrow b=\frac{3}{4}$$

Thus, $a=4,\ b=\frac{3}{4},\ k\in R$

So, $ab=3 \quad \left[\because a=4, b=\frac{3}{4}\right]$

11. (a, b, d)

$$I_n=\int_{-\pi}^{\pi}\frac{\sin(nx)}{(1+\pi^x)\sin x}dx$$

$$=\int_0^{\pi}\left[\frac{\sin nx}{(1+\pi^x)\sin x}+\frac{\sin nx}{(1+\pi^{-x})\sin x}\right]dx$$

$$\left[\because \int_{-a}^{a} f(x)dx=\int_0^{a}[f(x)+f(-x)]dx\right]$$

$$=\int_0^{\pi}\frac{\sin nx}{\sin x}\left(\frac{1}{1+\pi^x}+\frac{\pi^x}{1+\pi^x}\right)dx$$

$$\therefore I_n=\int_0^{\pi}\frac{\sin(nx)}{\sin x}dx$$

$$\Rightarrow I_{n+2}-I_n=\int_0^{\pi}\frac{\sin(n+2)x-\sin(nx)}{\sin x}dx$$

$$=2\int_0^{\pi}\cos(n+1)x\,dx=2\left[\frac{\sin(n+1)x}{n+1}\right]_0^{\pi}$$

$\Rightarrow \quad I_{n+2}-I_n=0$

$\Rightarrow \quad I_{n+2}=I_n$

$\Rightarrow I_n=I_{n-2}=I_{n-4}=\ldots\ldots=I_4=I_2,$

if n is even

and $I_n=I_{n-2}=I_{n-4}=\ldots\ldots\ldots I_3=I_1,$

if n is odd.

Since, $I_1=\int_0^{\pi}1\,dx=\pi-0=\pi$

and $\quad I_2=\int_0^{\pi}\frac{\sin 2x}{\sin x}dx$

$$=2\int_0^{\pi}\cos x\,dx=2[\sin x]_0^{\pi}=0$$

$\Rightarrow \quad I_n=0$, if n is even.

$\quad = \pi$, if n is odd.

$$\Rightarrow \sum_{m=1}^{10}I_{2m}=0 \text{ and } \sum_{m=1}^{10}I_{2m+1}=10\pi$$

12. (a, c, d)

The binomial coefficient of 2nd, 3rd and 4th terms in the expansion are ${}^mC_1$, ${}^mC_2$ and ${}^mC_3$, which are given in AP.

Hence, $2\,{}^mC_2={}^mC_1+{}^mC_3$

$$\Rightarrow \frac{2m(m-1)}{2!}=m+\frac{m(m-1)(m-2)}{3!}$$

$$\Rightarrow m(m^2-9m+14)=0$$

$$\Rightarrow \quad m(m-2)(m-7)=0$$

$$\Rightarrow \quad m=0,2,7$$

But $m\neq 0$ of 2 as 6th term is given equal to 21.

$\therefore \quad m=7$

Now, 6th term in the expansion, when $m=7$ is

$${}^7C_5[\sqrt{\{2^{\log(10-3^x)}\}}]^{7-5}\times[\sqrt[5]{\{2^{(x-2)\log 3}\}}]^5 = 21 \text{ [given]}$$

$$\Rightarrow \frac{7\times 6}{2!}2^{\log(10-3^x)}\times 2^{(x-2)\log 3}=21$$

$$\Rightarrow \quad 2^{\log(10-3^x)+(x-2)\log 3}=1=2^0$$

$$\Rightarrow \log(10-3^x)+(x-2)\log 3=0$$

$$\Rightarrow \quad \log[(10-3^x)(3)^{(x-2)}]=0$$

$$\Rightarrow \quad (10-3^x)\times 3^x\times 3^{-2}=1$$

$$\Rightarrow \quad 10\times 3^x-(3^x)^2=9$$

$$\Rightarrow \quad (3^x)^2-10\times 3^x+9=0$$

$$\Rightarrow \quad (3^x-1)(3^x-9)=0$$

$$\Rightarrow \quad 3^x-1=0 \text{ or } 3^x-9=0$$

$$\Rightarrow \quad 3^x=1 \text{ or } 3^x=9$$

$$\Rightarrow \quad x=0 \text{ or } x=2$$

$\therefore$ Product of all possible values of

$$x=0\times 2=0$$

Now, when $x=2$

$$\left[\sqrt{\{2^{\log(10-3^x)}\}}+\sqrt[5]{\{2^{(x-2)\log 3}\}}\right]^m$$

$$=[1+1]^7$$

$$=128$$

When $x=0$

$$\left[\sqrt{\{2^{\log(10-3^0)}\}}+\sqrt[5]{\{2^{(0-2)\log 3}\}}\right]^7$$

$$=\left[\sqrt{2^{\log 9}}+\sqrt[5]{2^{-2\log 3}}\right]^7$$

$$=\left[(2)^{\frac{\log 9}{2}}+\frac{1}{(2)^{\frac{\log 9}{5}}}\right]^7>2^7$$

Hence, the minimum value is 128.

13. (a, b, c)

Let $k=3$

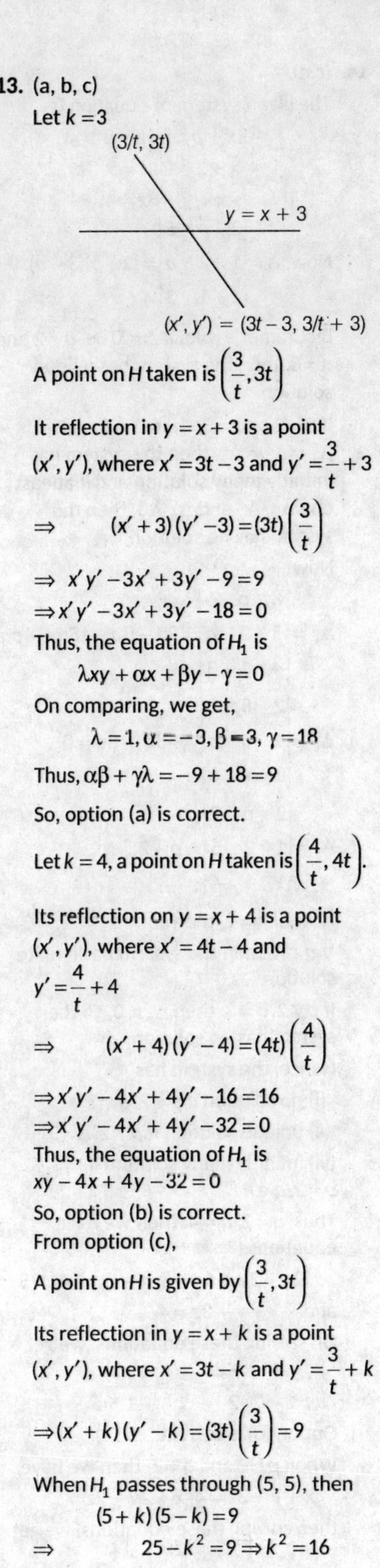

A point on H taken is $\left(\frac{3}{t},3t\right)$

It reflection in $y=x+3$ is a point (x', y'), where $x'=3t-3$ and $y'=\frac{3}{t}+3$

$$\Rightarrow \quad (x'+3)(y'-3)=(3t)\left(\frac{3}{t}\right)$$

$$\Rightarrow x'y'-3x'+3y'-9=9$$

$$\Rightarrow x'y'-3x'+3y'-18=0$$

Thus, the equation of H_1 is

$$\lambda xy+\alpha x+\beta y-\gamma=0$$

On comparing, we get,

$$\lambda=1, \alpha=-3, \beta=3, \gamma=18$$

Thus, $\alpha\beta+\gamma\lambda=-9+18=9$

So, option (a) is correct.

Let $k=4$, a point on H taken is $\left(\frac{4}{t},4t\right)$.

Its reflection on $y=x+4$ is a point (x', y'), where $x'=4t-4$ and

$y'=\frac{4}{t}+4$

$$\Rightarrow \quad (x'+4)(y'-4)=(4t)\left(\frac{4}{t}\right)$$

$$\Rightarrow x'y'-4x'+4y'-16=16$$

$$\Rightarrow x'y'-4x'+4y'-32=0$$

Thus, the equation of H_1 is

$xy-4x+4y-32=0$

So, option (b) is correct.

From option (c),

A point on H is given by $\left(\frac{3}{t},3t\right)$

Its reflection in $y=x+k$ is a point (x', y'), where $x'=3t-k$ and $y'=\frac{3}{t}+k$

$$\Rightarrow (x'+k)(y'-k)=(3t)\left(\frac{3}{t}\right)=9$$

When H_1 passes through (5, 5), then

$$(5+k)(5-k)=9$$

$$\Rightarrow \quad 25-k^2=9 \Rightarrow k^2=16$$

$$\Rightarrow \quad k=\pm 4$$

Since, $k>0$ given, thus $k=4$

14. (c,d)

The given system of equation is

$$2x+py+6z=8$$
$$x+2y+qz=5$$
$$x+y+3z=4$$

Now, $\Delta=\begin{vmatrix}2 & p & 6\\1 & 2 & q\\1 & 1 & 3\end{vmatrix}=(2-p)(3-q)$

By Cramer's rule, if $\Delta\neq 0$ i.e. $p\neq 2$ and $q\neq 3$, then the system has unique solution.

If $p=2$ or $q=3$, then $\Delta=0$ and if $\Delta_x=\Delta_y=\Delta_z$, then the system has infinitly many solution and if atleast one Δ_x, Δ_y and $\Delta_z\neq 0$, then the system has no solution

Now,

$$\Delta_x=\begin{vmatrix}8 & p & 6\\5 & 2 & q\\4 & 1 & 3\end{vmatrix}=30-8q-15p+4pq$$

$$\Delta_y=\begin{vmatrix}2 & 8 & 6\\1 & 5 & q\\1 & 4 & 3\end{vmatrix}=-8q+8q=0$$

$$\Delta_z=\begin{vmatrix}2 & p & 8\\1 & 2 & 5\\1 & 1 & 4\end{vmatrix}=p-2$$

Now, if $p=2$, then $\Delta_x=\Delta_y=\Delta_z=0$ $\forall\, q\in R$, then the system has infinite solution.

If $p\neq 2, q=3$, then $\Delta_z\neq 0$, so the system has no solution.

Hence, the system has

(i) no solution if $p\neq 2, q=3$

(ii) unique solution if $p\neq 2, q\neq 3$

(iii) infinitly many solution if $p=2, q\in R$

Thus, $p=2$, $q=4$, then we have equations

$$2x+2y+6z=8,\ x+2y+4z=5$$

and $x+y+3z=4$

On solving these equations, we get

$$\frac{x-1}{2}=\frac{y}{1}=\frac{1-z}{1}$$

Option (d) is correct.

When $p=2$ and $q=2$, then we have

$x+y+3z=4,\ x+2y+2z=5,$

then solving these equations, we get

$$\frac{x-7}{-4}=\frac{y}{1}=\frac{z+1}{1}$$

So, option (c) is correct.

15. (a) (I) $0<\dfrac{3}{x^2+1}\leq 3$

$\Rightarrow \dfrac{3}{x^2+1}=2\Rightarrow x=\dfrac{1}{\sqrt{2}}$ and $\dfrac{3}{x^2+1}=1$

$\Rightarrow \quad x=\sqrt{2}$

$$I=\int_0^{1/\sqrt{2}}2dx+\int_{\frac{1}{\sqrt{2}}}^{\sqrt{2}}1\cdot dx+\int_{\sqrt{2}}^{\infty}0dx$$

$$=\sqrt{2}+\sqrt{2}-\frac{1}{\sqrt{2}}$$

$\Rightarrow 2\sqrt{2}-\dfrac{1}{\sqrt{2}}=\dfrac{3}{\sqrt{2}}$

(II) $\displaystyle\int_{-10}^{10}\frac{3^x}{3^{[x]}}dx\Rightarrow 20\int_0^1 3^{x-[x]}\,dx$

$\Rightarrow 20\displaystyle\int_0^1 3^x\,dx$

$\Rightarrow 20\left[\dfrac{3^x}{\ln 3}\right]_0^1=\dfrac{40}{\ln 3}$

(III) $\displaystyle\int_{-1}^{1}[x[1+\sin\pi x]+1]dx$

$$=\int_{-1}^{0}[x[1+\sin\pi x]+1]\,dx$$
$$+\int_0^1[x[1+\sin\pi x]+1]\,dx$$

Now, $-1<x<0\Rightarrow[1+\sin\pi x]=0$

and $0<x<1\Rightarrow[1+\sin\pi x]=1$

$\Rightarrow [x[1+\sin\pi x]+1]=1$, so,

$\displaystyle\int_{-1}^{1}[x[1+\sin\pi x]+1]\,dx=2$

(IV) The L.H.S of given inequality is equal to

$$\left[a^2\left(\frac{\sin 3x}{12}+\frac{3}{4}\sin x\right)-a\cos x-20\sin x\right]_0^{\pi/2}$$

$\Rightarrow a^2\left(\dfrac{-1}{12}+\dfrac{3}{4}\right)-a(0-1)-20$

$\Rightarrow \dfrac{2a^2}{3}+a-20$

Thus the given inequality is

$\dfrac{2a^2}{3}+a-20\leq\dfrac{-a^2}{3}$ i.e.,

$a^2+a-20\leq 0$

$\Rightarrow -5\leq a\leq 4$

Since 'a' positive integer, so $a=1,2,3,4$

16. (b) (I) $y=|\cos^{-1}(\sin x)|-|\sin^{-1}(\cos x)|$

$$=\left|\cos^{-1}\cos\left(\frac{\pi}{2}-x\right)\right|-\left|\sin^{-1}\sin\left(\frac{\pi}{2}+x\right)\right|$$

$$=\left|\frac{5\pi}{2}-x\right|-\left|x-\frac{3\pi}{2}\right|=4\pi-2x$$

$\therefore$ Required area

$$=\int_{3\pi/2}^{2\pi}(4\pi-2x)\,dx=\frac{\pi^2}{4}\text{ sq units}$$

$\therefore\ k=1$

(II) The given circle is $(x+1)^2+(y+2)^2=9$ has radius 3.

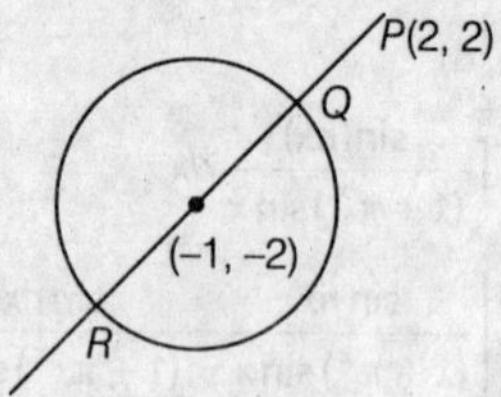

The point on the circle which are nearest and farthest to the point $P(2,2)$ are Q and R, respectively. Thus circle centered at Q having radius PQ will be smallest required circle while circle centred at R having radius PR will be the largest required circle.

$\therefore$ Difference between radii

$$=|PQ-PR|=6$$

(III) $I=\displaystyle\int_0^1 xf''(2x)\,dx=\left(\frac{xf'(2x)}{2}\right)_0^1-\int_0^1\frac{f'(2x)}{2}dx$

$$=\frac{1}{2}(f'(2))-\left(\frac{f(2x)}{4}\right)_0^1$$

$$=\frac{5}{2}-\frac{1}{4}(f(2)-f(0))$$

$$=\frac{5}{2}-\frac{3}{4}+\frac{1}{4}=2$$

(IV) Let $f^{-1}(-4)=x\Rightarrow f(x)=-4$

$\Rightarrow\ x^3+4x^2+6x+4=0$

$\Rightarrow(x+2)(x^2+2x+2)=0\Rightarrow x=-2$

17. (a) (I) As, $a, b, c>0$, so $f(x)$ can take minimum value 0 at

$$x=\frac{1}{a}=\frac{1}{b}=\frac{1}{c}=\frac{1}{2}$$

So, $a=b=c=2$

So, $a^{16}+b^{17}+c^{16}$

$=2^{16}(1+2+1)=2^{18}$

(II) $\left|x+\dfrac{\sqrt[3]{k}}{x}\right|=16$

Now, $k \leq 0$ will given solutions as, for that LHS $\in [0, \infty)$

For $k > 0$, $16 = \left| x + \frac{\sqrt[3]{k}}{x} \right| \geq 2 \times k^{1/6}$

$\Rightarrow k \leq 2^{18}$

(III) Every alternate place must be occupied with 1 and the rest by 2, 3, 5 or 7

So, the required number $= 2 \times 4^8 = 2^{17}$

(IV) ${}^{20}C_1 + {}^{20}C_3 + {}^{20}C_5 + \ldots + {}^{20}C_{19}$

$$= \frac{(1+x)^{20} - (1-x)^{20}}{2} = 2^{19} \text{ (at } x = 1)$$

As, ${}^{20}C_1 = {}^{20}C_{19}$, ${}^{20}C_3 = {}^{20}C_{17}, \ldots$

$${}^{20}C_1 + {}^{20}C_3 + {}^{20}C_5 + {}^{20}C_7 + {}^{20}C_9 = \frac{1}{2}(2^{19}) = 2^{18}$$

18. (d) (I) $\Rightarrow {}^{(n+2)}C_4 + {}^{(n+2)}C_3 = {}^{(n+3)}C_4$

$$\Rightarrow {}^{(n+3)}C_4 > {}^{(n+3)}C_3 \Rightarrow \frac{{}^{(n+3)}C_4}{{}^{(n+3)}C_3} > 1$$

$\Rightarrow n > 4$ or $n \geq 5$

(II) $(3053)^{456} - (2417)^{333}$

$$= (339 \times 9 + 2)^{456} - (269 \times 9 - 4)^{333}$$

remainder of given number is same as remainder of $4^{333} + 2^{456}$ and

$$2^{456} + 4^{333} = (64)^{76} + (64)^{111}$$
$$= (1 + 63)^{76} + (1 + 63)^{111}$$
$$= (1 + 9 \times 7)^{76} + (1 + 9 \times 7)^{111}$$

Hence, the remainder is 2.

(III) We know that $n!$ terminates In 0 for $n \geq 5$ and 3^{4n} terminates in 1 $(\because 3^4 = 81)$

Therefore, $3^{100} = (3^4)^{45}$ terminates in 1.

Also, $3^3 = 27$ terminates in 7.

Hence, $183! + 3^{183}$ terminates in 7

i.e., the digit in the unit place is 7.

(IV) We are given

${}^mC_0 + {}^mC_1 + {}^mC_2 = 46$

$\Rightarrow 2m + m(m-1) = 90$

$\Rightarrow m^2 + m - 90 = 0$

$\Rightarrow \quad m = 9$ as $m > 0$

Now, $(r+1)$th term of $\left(x^2 + \frac{1}{x}\right)^9$ is

$${}^9C_r (x^2)^{9-r} \left(\frac{1}{x}\right)^r = {}^9C_r x^{18-3r}$$

For this to be independent of x,

Put $18 - 3r = 0 \Rightarrow r = 6$

Paper 2

1. (7) Area of curvilinear trapezoid

$$OABCO = \int_0^x f(x)\, dx$$

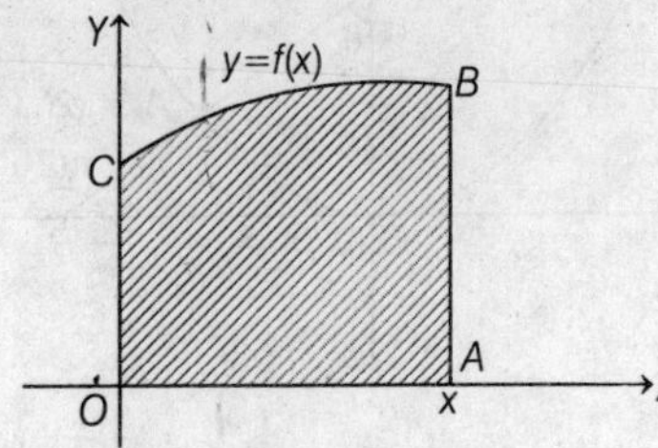

According to problem,

$$\int_0^x f(x)\, dx \propto [f(x)]^{n+1}$$

$$\Rightarrow \int_0^x f(x)\, dx = K[f(x)]^{n+1} \quad \ldots(i)$$

where K is proportional constant. Differentiating Eq. (i) both sides w.r.t. x, we get

$$f(x) = K(n+1)(f(x))^n \cdot f'(x)$$

$$\Rightarrow \quad [f(x)]^{n-1} f'(x) = \frac{1}{K(n+1)}$$

On integrating both sides w.r.t x, we get

$$\frac{[f(x)]^n}{n} = \frac{x}{K(n+1)} + C$$

Putting $x = 0$ in above, we get

$$\frac{[f(0)]^n}{n} = \frac{0}{K(n+1)} + C \Rightarrow 0 = 0 + C$$

$[\because f(0) = 0$, given$]$

$\Rightarrow \quad C = 0$

Hence, $\dfrac{[f(x)]^n}{n} = \dfrac{x}{K(n+1)}$

$$\Rightarrow \quad [f(x)]^n = \frac{nx}{K(n+1)} \quad \ldots(ii)$$

Given, $f(1) = 1$ in question

$$\therefore \quad [f(1)]^n = \frac{n \times 1}{K(n+1)}$$

$$\Rightarrow \quad 1 = \frac{n}{K(n+1)} \quad \ldots(iii)$$

From Eq. (ii),

$$[f(x)]^n = 1 \times x$$
$$\Rightarrow \quad f(x) = x^{1/n}$$
$$\Rightarrow \quad f(5/2) = (5/2)^{1/n}$$

Hence, $[f(5/2)]^n = \left[\left(\frac{5}{2}\right)^{\frac{1}{n}}\right]^n = \frac{5}{2}$

$\therefore \quad p + q = 5 + 2 = 7$

2. (1) According to the question, perimeter of rectangle $= 4L$

$\Rightarrow \quad 2x + 2y = 4L$

$\Rightarrow \quad x + y = 2L \quad \ldots(i)$

The area of the rectangle

$= xy = x(2L - x)$ [from Eq. (i)]

But given, $x(2L - x) \leq \dfrac{L^2}{4}$

$$\Rightarrow \quad x^2 - 2Lx + \frac{L^2}{4} \geq 0$$

$$\Rightarrow \quad (x - L)^2 - L^2 + \frac{L^2}{4} \geq 0$$

$$\Rightarrow (x - L)^2 - \left(\frac{L\sqrt{3}}{2}\right)^2 \geq 0$$

$$\Rightarrow \left(x - L + \frac{L\sqrt{3}}{2}\right)\left(x - L - \frac{L\sqrt{3}}{2}\right) \geq 0$$

$$\Rightarrow \left\{x - \left(\frac{2-\sqrt{3}}{2}\right)L\right\} \left\{x - \left(\frac{2+\sqrt{3}}{2}\right)L\right\} \geq 0$$

$\Rightarrow$

$$x \in \left(-\infty, \left(\frac{2-\sqrt{3}}{2}\right)L\right) \cup \left(\left(\frac{2+\sqrt{3}}{2}\right)L, \infty\right)$$

But x takes values in the interval $[0, 2L]$.

Hence,

$$x \in \left[0, \left(\frac{2-\sqrt{3}}{2}\right)L\right] \cup \left[\left(\frac{2+\sqrt{3}}{2}\right)L, 2L\right]$$

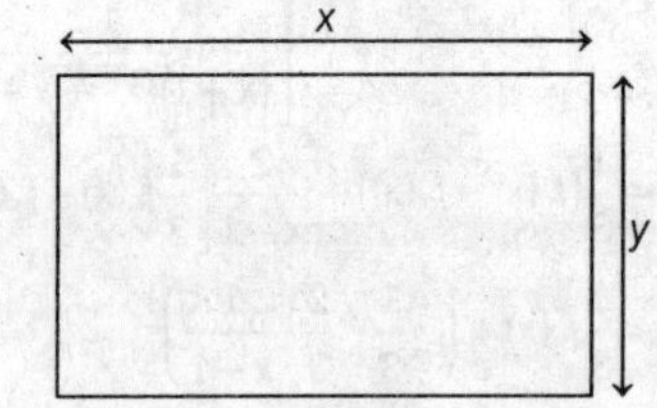

$\therefore$ Required probability

$$= \frac{\int_0^{\left(\frac{2-\sqrt{3}}{2}\right)L} dx + \int_{\left(\frac{2+\sqrt{3}}{2}\right)L}^{2L} dx}{\int_0^{2L} dx}$$

$$= \frac{\left(\frac{2-\sqrt{3}}{2}\right)L + 2L - \left(\frac{2+\sqrt{3}}{2}\right)L}{2L - 0}$$

$$= \frac{2L - \sqrt{3}L}{2L} = \frac{2-\sqrt{3}}{2} = 1 - \frac{\sqrt{3}}{2}$$

$\therefore p = 3$ and $q = 2$

Now, $\dfrac{p^2 + q^2}{13} = \dfrac{9+4}{13} = \dfrac{13}{13} = 1$

3. (4) Let $a^2 = p^2 + 2$

and $b^2 = p^2 + 4$.

Let 'e' be the eccentricity of the ellipse.

Foci of the ellipse are $F_1(0, -be)$, $F_2(0, be)$.

Its directrices are $y = -\frac{b}{e}$

and $y = \frac{b}{e}$

Suppose coordinates of P are $(a\cos\theta, b\sin\theta)$, we have

$PF_1 = $ ex Distance of P from $y = -\frac{b}{e}$

$$= e\left|-\frac{b}{e} - eb\sin\theta\right|$$

$$= |b + be\sin\theta|$$

and $PF_2 = |b - eb\sin\theta|$

Now, $PF_1 \cdot PF_2 = b^2 - b^2e^2\sin^2\theta \le b^2$

$$= p^2 + 4$$

$\therefore\ PF_1 \cdot PF_2 - p^2 \le 4$

Hence, the maximum possible value of

$PF_1 \cdot PF_2 - p^2$ is 4.

4. (2) $\frac{(x+1)}{(x-1)^2(x^2+x+1)}$

$$= \frac{(x-1)+2}{(x-1)^2(x^2+x+1)}$$

$$= \frac{1}{(x-1)(x^2+x+1)} + \frac{2}{x-1}\left[\frac{1}{(x-1)(x^2+x+1)}\right]$$

$$= \frac{1}{3}[f_1(x) - f_2(x)] + \frac{2}{x-1}\left[\frac{1}{3}f_1(x) - f_2(x)\right]$$

$$= \frac{1}{3}f_1(x) + \left(-\frac{1}{3} - \frac{2}{3}\cdot\frac{1}{x-1}\right)f_2(x) + \frac{2}{3}\cdot\frac{1}{(x-1)^2}$$

$\therefore\ a = \frac{1}{3}, b = -\frac{1}{3}, c = -\frac{2}{3}, d = \frac{2}{3}$

Thus, $\begin{vmatrix} a & b \\ c & d \end{vmatrix} = \begin{vmatrix} \frac{1}{3} & -\frac{1}{3} \\ -\frac{2}{3} & \frac{2}{3} \end{vmatrix} = 0$

$\therefore\ \begin{vmatrix} a & b \\ c & d \end{vmatrix} + 9|a+ib|^2 = 0 + 9\left|\frac{1}{3} - i\frac{1}{3}\right|^2$

$$= \frac{9}{9}(1+1) = 2$$

Thus, the value of

$\begin{vmatrix} a & b \\ c & d \end{vmatrix} + 9(a+ib)^2 = 2$.

5. (4) The given parabola is

$$y = \frac{x^2}{4} \Rightarrow x^2 = 4y \quad \text{...(i)}$$

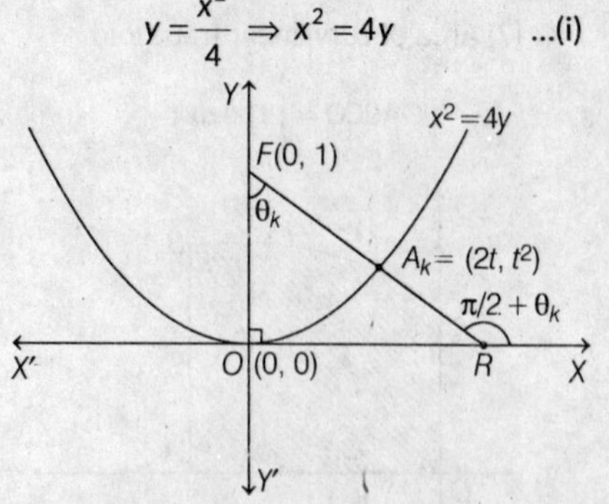

Let $A_k = (2t, t^2)$, a point on the parabola and $\angle OFA_k = \theta_k$

$\because\ \angle FOR = \frac{\pi}{2}$

$\therefore \angle ORF = \frac{\pi}{2} - \theta_k$, so, $\angle XRF = \frac{\pi}{2} + \theta_k$

Now, slope of

$$FA_k = \frac{t^2-1}{2t-0} = \tan\left(\frac{\pi}{2} + \theta_k\right) = -\cot\theta_k$$

$$\Rightarrow \tan\theta_k = \frac{2t}{1-t^2} = \tan(2\phi) \text{ (say)},$$

where $t = \tan\phi$.

$$\Rightarrow \tan\theta_k = \tan(2\phi) \Rightarrow \phi = \frac{\theta_k}{n} = \frac{k\pi}{4n}$$

$$\left[\text{since } \angle OFA_k = \theta_k = \frac{k\pi}{2n}\right]$$

Also, $FA_k = \sqrt{(t^2-1)^2 + (2t^2)^2}$

$$= \sqrt{t^4 - 2t^2 + 1 + 4t^2}$$

$$= \sqrt{t^4 + 2t^2 + 1}$$

$$= \sqrt{(t^2+1)^2} = |t^2+1|$$

Since, $t^2 \ge 0$

$\Rightarrow 1 + t^2 \ge 1$

$\Rightarrow\ FA_k = t^2 + 1$

So, $FA_k = 1 + \tan^2\phi$

$$= \sec^2\phi = \sec^2\left(\frac{k\pi}{4n}\right)$$

Now, $\lim_{n\to\infty}\frac{1}{n}\sum_{k=1}^{n} FA_k$

$$= \lim_{n\to\infty}\frac{1}{n}\sum_{k=1}^{n}\sec^2\left(\frac{\pi}{4}\left(\frac{k}{n}\right)\right)$$

$$= \int_0^1 \sec^2\left(\frac{\pi x}{4}\right)dx$$

$$= \frac{4}{\pi}\left[\tan\left(\frac{\pi x}{4}\right)\right]_0^1 = \frac{4}{\pi}$$

On comparing with $\frac{\lambda}{\pi}$, we get

$$\lambda = 4$$

6. (6) Since, a, b, c are in GP

So, a, ar, ar^2 are in GP,

where r is common ratio.

Given, $a^2 + b^2 + c^2 = t^2$

$\Rightarrow a^2 + (ar)^2 + (ar^2)^2 = t^2$

$\Rightarrow\ a^2 + a^2r^2 + a^2r^4 = t^2 \quad \text{...(i)}$

and $a + b + c = \alpha t$

$\Rightarrow\ a + ar + ar^2 = \alpha t$

$\Rightarrow\ (a + ar + ar^2)^2 = \alpha^2 t^2 \quad \text{...(ii)}$

Now, Eq. (i) divide by Eq. (ii),

$$\frac{a^2 + a^2r^2 + a^2r^4}{(a+ar+ar^2)^2} = \frac{t^2}{\alpha^2t^2} = \frac{1}{\alpha^2}$$

$$\Rightarrow \alpha^2 = \frac{(r^2+r+1)^2}{(r^4+r^2+1)}$$

$$= \frac{(r^2+r+1)(r^2+r+1)}{(r^2+r+1)(r^2-r+1)}$$

$$\Rightarrow \alpha^2 = \frac{r^2+r+1}{r^2-r+1}$$

Let $\alpha^2 = y \Rightarrow y = \frac{r^2+r+1}{r^2-r+1}$

$\Rightarrow (y-1)r^2 - r(y+1) + (y-1) = 0$

For real 'r', we get

$(y+1)^2 - 4(y-1)^2 \ge 0 \Rightarrow \frac{1}{3} \le y \le 3$

$[\because r \ne 1, 0, -1]$

But $y \ne \left(\frac{1}{3}, 3, 1\right)$ so, $\frac{1}{3} < y < 3$ and $y \ne 1$

$\Rightarrow a^2 \in \left(\frac{1}{3}, 3\right) - \{1\}$

So, $p = 3, q = 3$

and given, $s = \frac{1}{r} + r$

$\Rightarrow\ s \in (-\infty, -2) \cup (2, \infty)$

$\Rightarrow\ r = -2$ and $s = 2$

Thus, $p + q + r + s = 3 + 3 - 2 + 2 = 6$

7. (4) Since, $\alpha, \beta \in [-\pi, \pi]$

$\Rightarrow (\alpha - \beta)$ and $(\alpha + \beta) \in [-2\pi, 2\pi]$

Given, $\cos(\alpha - \beta) = 1$

and $\cos(\alpha + \beta) = \frac{1}{e}$

$\Rightarrow\ \alpha - \beta = 0, 2\pi, -2\pi$

Hence, $\alpha = \beta$ or $\alpha = \pi$, $\beta = -\pi$, $\alpha = -\pi$, $\beta = \pi$

For $\alpha = \beta$, $\cos 2\alpha = \frac{1}{e}$

$\Rightarrow\ 2\cos^2\alpha = \frac{1}{e} + 1$

$\Rightarrow\ \cos^2\alpha = \frac{e+1}{2} = k \quad \text{(say)}$

where $k < 1$

$\Rightarrow \quad \cos\alpha = \pm\sqrt{k}, \alpha \in [-\pi, \pi]$

and $\sqrt{k} < 1$

and $-\sqrt{k} > -1$

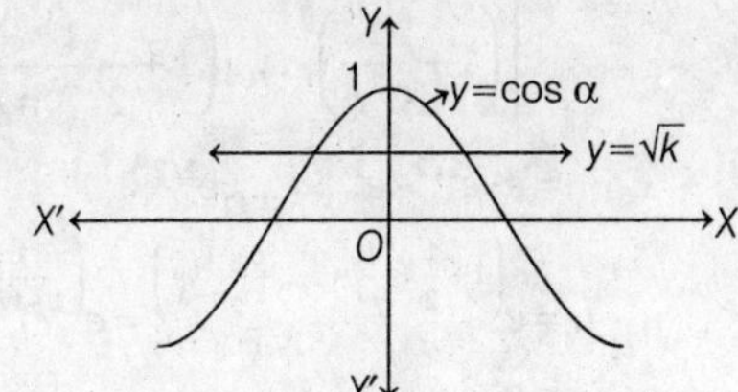

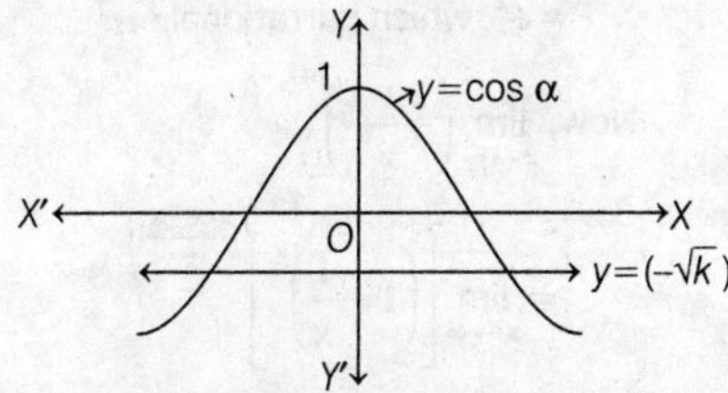

Hence, there will be 4 solution.

8. (1) Given, $P(A^C) = 0.3, P(B) = 0.4$

and $P(A \cap B^C) = 0.5$

Since, $P(A^C) = 0.3$

$\Rightarrow \quad P(A) = 1 - P(A^C) = 1 - 0.3 = 0.7$

and $P(B) = 0.4$

$\Rightarrow P(B^C) = 1 - P(B) = 1 - 0.4 = 0.6$

Consider, $P(A \cap B^C) = P(A) - P(A \cap B)$

$\Rightarrow \quad 0.5 = 0.7 - P(A \cap B)$

$\Rightarrow \quad P(A \cap B) = 0.2$

Now, $P\left[\dfrac{B}{(A \cup B^C)}\right] = \dfrac{P[B \cap (A \cup B^C)]}{P(A \cup B^C)}$

$= \dfrac{P[(B \cap A) \cup (B \cap B^C)]}{P(A) + P(B^C) - P(A \cap B^C)}$

$= \dfrac{P(B \cap A)}{P(A) + P(B^C) - P(A \cap B^C)}$

$= \dfrac{0.2}{0.7 + 0.6 - 0.5} = \dfrac{0.2}{0.8} = \dfrac{1}{4}$

Thus, $4 \times [P(B/(A \cup B^C))] = 4 \times \dfrac{1}{4} = 1$

9. (b, c, d) Let $\mathbf{a} = a_1\hat{\mathbf{i}} + a_2\hat{\mathbf{j}} + a_3\hat{\mathbf{k}}$

and $\mathbf{b} = b_1\hat{\mathbf{i}} + b_2\hat{\mathbf{j}} + b_3\hat{\mathbf{k}}$.

Taking cross product with **a** on both sides of $\mathbf{a} + \mathbf{b} = \hat{\mathbf{i}} - 3\hat{\mathbf{j}} - 4\hat{\mathbf{k}}$, we get,

$\mathbf{a} \times (\mathbf{a} + \mathbf{b}) = \mathbf{a} \times \mathbf{b} = \mathbf{a} \times (\hat{\mathbf{i}} - 3\hat{\mathbf{j}} - 4\hat{\mathbf{k}})$

$$= \begin{vmatrix} \hat{\mathbf{i}} & \hat{\mathbf{j}} & \hat{\mathbf{k}} \\ a_1 & a_2 & a_3 \\ 1 & -3 & -4 \end{vmatrix}$$

$\Rightarrow 2\hat{\mathbf{i}} + 2\hat{\mathbf{j}} - \hat{\mathbf{k}} = (-4a_2 + 3a_3)\hat{\mathbf{i}} + (a_3 + 4a_1)\hat{\mathbf{j}} + (-3a_1 - a_2)\hat{\mathbf{k}}$

Hence, $-4a_2 + 3a_3 = 2$ ...(i)

$a_3 + 4a_1 = 2$ ...(ii)

$-3a_1 - a_2 = -1$ ...(iii)

Now, solving Eqs. (i), (ii) and (iii) to obtain the value of a_1, a_2 and a_3.

Let $a_3 = \lambda$, where λ being any real number.

From Eq. (i), $-4a_2 + 3\lambda = 2$

$\Rightarrow \quad a_2 = \dfrac{3\lambda - 2}{4}$

From Eq. (ii), $\lambda + 4a_1 = 2$

$\Rightarrow \quad a_1 = \dfrac{2 - \lambda}{4}$

Also, $b_1 = 1 - a_1 = 1 - \dfrac{2-\lambda}{4} = \dfrac{2+\lambda}{4}$

$b_2 = -3 - a_2 = -3 - \dfrac{3\lambda - 2}{4} = \dfrac{-10 - 3\lambda}{4}$

$b_3 = -4 - a_3 = -4 - \lambda$

Hence, $\mathbf{a} = \left(\dfrac{2-\lambda}{4}\right)\hat{\mathbf{i}} + \left(\dfrac{3\lambda - 2}{4}\right)\hat{\mathbf{j}} + \lambda\hat{\mathbf{k}}$,

$\mathbf{b} = \left(\dfrac{2+\lambda}{4}\right)\hat{\mathbf{i}} - \left(\dfrac{10 + 3\lambda}{4}\right)\hat{\mathbf{j}} - (4 + \lambda)\hat{\mathbf{k}}$.

10. (a) From the figure,

$AD = AB\cos\theta = 2R\cos\theta$

$AE = AD\cos\theta = 2R\cos^2\theta$

[since, $AD = 2R\cos\theta$]

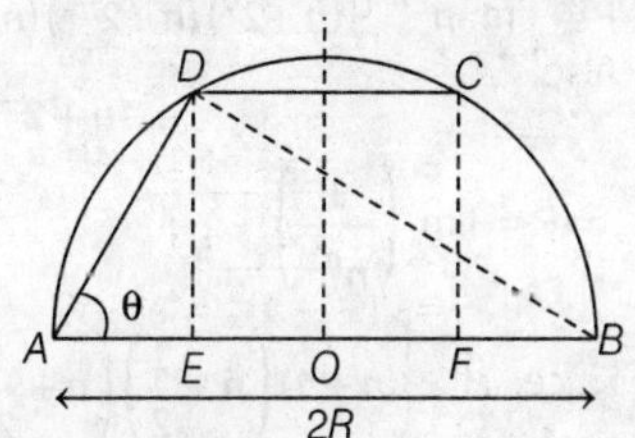

Now, $EF = AB - 2AE = 2R - 4R^2\cos^2\theta$

Since, $EF = CD$.

So, $CD = 2R - 4R^2\cos^2\theta$

$DE = 2R\sin\theta\cos\theta$

Thus, area of trapezium is

$(A) = \dfrac{1}{2}(AB + CD) \times DE$

$= \dfrac{1}{2}(2R + 2R - 4R\cos^2\theta) \times 2R\cos\theta\sin\theta$

$\therefore A = 4R^2\sin^3\theta \cdot \cos\theta$

$\Rightarrow \dfrac{dA}{d\theta} = 12R^2\sin^2\theta \cdot \cos^2\theta - 4R^2\sin^4\theta$

$= 4R^2\sin^2\theta(3\cos^2\theta - \sin^2\theta)$

For maximum area, $\dfrac{dA}{d\theta} = 0$

$\Rightarrow 4R^2\sin^2\theta(3\cos^2\theta - \sin^2\theta) = 0$

$\Rightarrow \tan^2\theta = 3$

$\Rightarrow \quad \tan\theta = \sqrt{3}$ [since, θ is acute]

$\Rightarrow \quad \theta = \dfrac{\pi}{3}$

So, $A_{max} = 4R^2 \cdot \left(\sin\dfrac{\pi}{3}\right)^3 \cdot \cos\dfrac{\pi}{3}$

$= 4R^2 \cdot \left(\dfrac{\sqrt{3}}{2}\right)^3 \cdot \dfrac{1}{2} = \dfrac{3\sqrt{3}}{4}R^2$

$\therefore \quad A_{max} = \dfrac{3\sqrt{3}}{4}R^2$

11. (a, b, c)

Direction ratios of *PQ* are proportional to $4\cos t, 4\sin t, -4$.

$\therefore$ Equation of *PQ* is

$\dfrac{x - 4\cos t}{4\cos t} = \dfrac{y - 4\sin t}{4\sin t} = \dfrac{z-3}{-4} = \lambda$ (say)

A point *R* on *PQ* is

$\{4(\lambda+1)\cos t, 4(\lambda+1)\sin t, 3 - 4\lambda\}$

Since, *R* is the point of intersection of line *PQ* and plane $z = 0$.

So, $3 - 4\lambda = 0 \Rightarrow \lambda = \dfrac{3}{4}$

$\therefore R = (7\cos t, 7\sin t, 0)$

So, option (a) is correct.

Direction ratios of *PQ*

= Direction ratios of normal to *w*.

$\Rightarrow$ Direction ratios of normal are proportional to $4\cos t, 4\sin t, -4$.

$\therefore$ Equation of plane *w* is

$4\cos t(x - 7\cos t) + 4\sin t(y - 7\sin t) - 4(z - 0) = 0$

$\Rightarrow x\cos t + y\sin t - 7(\cos^2 t + \sin^2 t) - z = 0$

$\Rightarrow x\cos t + y\sin t - z = 7$

So, option (b) is correct.

$\therefore$ Direction ratios of *OA* are (10, 10, 40).

$$\cos\theta = \dfrac{|10\cos t + 10\sin t - 40|}{\sqrt{10^2 + 10^2 + 40^2}\sqrt{\cos^2 t + \sin^2 t + 1}}$$

$= \dfrac{|\cos t + \sin t - 4|}{(3\sqrt{2})(\sqrt{2})}$

$= \dfrac{1}{6}\left(4 - \sqrt{2}\left(\dfrac{1}{\sqrt{2}}\sin t + \dfrac{1}{\sqrt{2}}\cos t\right)\right)$

[$\because \cos t + \sin t < 4$,

$\therefore |\cos t + \sin t - 4| = -(\cos t + \sin t - 4)$

$= 4 - \sin t - \cos t$]

$= \dfrac{1}{6}\left(4 - \sqrt{2}\sin\left(t + \dfrac{\pi}{4}\right)\right)$,

So, option (c) is correct.

where $0 \le t < 2\pi \Rightarrow \dfrac{\pi}{4} \le t + \dfrac{\pi}{4} < \dfrac{9\pi}{4}$

For $\sin\left(t+\frac{\pi}{4}\right)=-1$, which occurs at

$$t+\frac{\pi}{4}=\frac{3\pi}{2}\Rightarrow t=\frac{5\pi}{4}$$

$\cos\theta$ takes its maximum value

$$\Rightarrow \sin\left(t+\frac{\pi}{4}\right)=-1$$

$$\Rightarrow \quad \cos\theta=\frac{4+\sqrt{2}}{6}=\frac{2\sqrt{2}+1}{3\sqrt{2}}$$

From this, we observe that option (d) is incorrect.

12. (a, b, c)

Using AM $\geq$ GM for $s-a, s-b, s-c, s-d$, we have,

$$\frac{s-a+s-b+s-c+s-d}{4}\geq\sqrt{A}$$

$$[\because A=\sqrt{(s-a)(s-b)(s-c)(s-d)}]$$

$$\Rightarrow \frac{4s-2s}{4}\geq 1\Rightarrow 2s\geq 4$$

$$[\because 2s=a+b+c+d]$$

If the length of diagonals are d_1 and d_2, then the area of quadrilateral is given

by area $=\frac{1}{2}d_1d_2\sin\theta$, where θ is angle between diagonals.

$$\Rightarrow \quad d_1d_2=\frac{2}{\sin\theta} \quad [\because A=1]$$

$$\Rightarrow \quad d_1d_2\geq 2$$

Also, $\quad d_1+d_2\geq 2\sqrt{d_1d_2}$

[using AM $\geq$ GM]

i.e. $d_1+d_2\geq 2\sqrt{d_1d_2}\geq 2\sqrt{2}$

When the perimeter is minimum,

$$s-a=s-b=s-c=s-d$$

$$\Rightarrow \quad a=b=c=d$$

Hence, $ABCD$ is a square.

[$\because$ cyclic quadrilateral]

13. (a, b, c, d)

Given, $z_3=(1-\lambda)z_1+\lambda z_2$

$$\Rightarrow \quad z_3=\frac{(1-\lambda)z_1+\lambda z_2}{(1-\lambda)+\lambda}$$

$A(z_1)$, $B(z_2)$, $C(z_3)$

$D(z_1')$, $E(z_2')$, $F(z_3')$

Hence, z_3 divides the line joining $A(z_1)$ and $B(z_2)$ in the ratio $\lambda:(1-\lambda)$. That means, the given points are collinear. Also, z_3 divides the line joining z_1 and z_2 internally, if $\frac{\lambda}{1-\lambda}>0$ i.e. $0<\lambda<1$.

Similarly, z_3' divides the line joining z_1' and z_2' externally, if $\frac{\mu}{1-\mu}<0$ i.e. $\mu<0$ or $\mu>1$. When λ,μ are complex numbers, where $\lambda=\mu$, we have

$$z_3=(1-\lambda)z_1+\lambda z_2\Rightarrow\frac{z_3-z_1}{z_2-z_1}=\lambda$$

and hence $z_3'=(1-\lambda)z_1'+\lambda z_2'$

$$\Rightarrow \quad \frac{z_3'-z_1'}{z_2'-z_1'}=\lambda \qquad (\because \lambda=\mu)$$

On comparing the values of λ, we get;

$$\frac{z_3-z_1}{z_2-z_1}=\frac{z_3'-z_1'}{z_2'-z_1'}\Rightarrow\left|\frac{z_3-z_1}{z_2-z_1}\right|=\left|\frac{z_3'-z_1'}{z_2'-z_1'}\right|$$

and $\arg\left(\frac{z_3-z_1}{z_2-z_1}\right)=\arg\left(\frac{z_3'-z_1'}{z_2'-z_1'}\right)$

$$\Rightarrow \frac{AC}{AB}=\frac{DF}{DE} \text{ and } \angle BAC=\angle EDF$$

Hence, ΔABC and ΔDEF are similar.

14. (a, d) Given,

$$P=\lim_{n\to\infty}n^{-n^2}\{(n+2^0)(n+2^{-1})(n+2^{-2})\ldots\ldots(n+2^{-n+1})\}^n$$

$$\Rightarrow P=\lim_{n\to\infty}\left(\frac{1}{n^{n^2}}\right)\left\{(n+1)\left(n+\frac{1}{2}\right)\left(n+\frac{1}{2^2}\right)\ldots\ldots\left(n+\frac{1}{2^{n-1}}\right)\right\}^n$$

$$\Rightarrow P=\lim_{n\to\infty}\left[\frac{(n+1)\left(n+\frac{1}{2}\right)\left(n+\frac{1}{2^2}\right)\ldots\ldots\left(n+\frac{1}{2^{n-1}}\right)}{n^n}\right]^n$$

$$\Rightarrow P=\lim_{n\to\infty}\left[\left(\frac{n+1}{n}\right)\left(\frac{n+1/2}{n}\right)\left(\frac{n+1/2^2}{n}\right)\ldots\ldots\left(\frac{n+\frac{1}{2^{n-1}}}{n}\right)\right]^n$$

$$\Rightarrow P=\lim_{n\to\infty}\left[\left(1+\frac{1}{n}\right)^n\left(1+\frac{1}{2n}\right)^n\left(1+\frac{1}{2^2n}\right)^n\ldots\ldots\left(1+\frac{1}{2^{n-1}n}\right)^n\right]$$

$$=e\cdot e^{1/2}\cdot e^{1/2^2}\ldots\ldots e^{1/2^{n-1}}$$

$$=e^{\left(1+\frac{1}{2}+\frac{1}{2^2}+\ldots\ldots+\frac{1}{2^{n-1}}\right)}=e^{\left(\frac{1}{1-1/2}\right)}$$

$$=e^2$$

$\therefore P=e^2$, which is irrational.

Now, $\lim_{x\to\infty}\left(\frac{1+x}{x}\right)^{\ln x-x}$

$$=\lim_{x\to\infty}\left[\left(1+\frac{1}{x}\right)^x\right]^{\left(\frac{\ln x-x}{x}\right)}$$

$$=e^{\lim_{x\to\infty}\left(\frac{\ln x-x}{x}\right)}$$

$$=e^{\lim_{x\to\infty}\left(\frac{\ln x}{x}-1\right)}$$

$$=e^{-1}=\frac{1}{e}$$

Thus, $P>\lim_{x\to\infty}\left(\frac{1+x}{x}\right)^{\ln x-x}$.

15. (d) We have,

$$\Delta_1=\frac{1}{2}\begin{vmatrix}0 & 0 & 1\\ a\tan\alpha & b\cot\alpha & 1\\ a\sin\alpha & b\cos\alpha & 1\end{vmatrix}$$

$$=\frac{1}{2}ab|\sin\alpha-\cos\alpha| \qquad \ldots(i)$$

and

$$\Delta_2=\frac{1}{2}\begin{vmatrix}a & b & 1\\ a\sec^2\alpha & b\operatorname{cosec}^2\alpha & 1\\ a+a\sin^2\alpha & b+b\cos^2\alpha & 1\end{vmatrix}$$

Applying $C_1\to C_1-aC_3$ and $C_2\to C_2-bC_3$, we get

$$\Delta_2=\frac{1}{2}ab\begin{vmatrix}0 & 0 & 1\\ \tan^2\alpha & \cot^2\alpha & 1\\ \sin^2\alpha & \cos^2\alpha & 1\end{vmatrix}$$

$$=\frac{1}{2}ab(\sin^2\alpha-\cos^2\alpha) \qquad \ldots(ii)$$

and $$\Delta_3=\frac{1}{2}\begin{vmatrix}0 & 0 & 1\\ a\tan\alpha & -b\cot\alpha & 1\\ a\sin\alpha & b\cos\alpha & 1\end{vmatrix}$$

$$=\frac{1}{2}ab|\sin\alpha+\cos\alpha| \qquad \ldots(iii)$$

So that $\Delta_1\Delta_3=\frac{1}{2}ab\,\Delta_2$

Now, Δ_1,Δ_2 and Δ_3 are in GP, if $\Delta_1\Delta_3=\Delta_2^2$

$\Rightarrow \quad \frac{1}{2}ab\Delta_2 = \Delta_2^2 \Rightarrow \Delta_2 = \frac{1}{2}ab$

$\Rightarrow \quad \frac{1}{2}ab(\sin^2\alpha - \cos^2\alpha) = \frac{1}{2}ab$ [from Eq. (ii)]

$\Rightarrow \sin^2\alpha - \cos^2\alpha = 1$

$\Rightarrow \quad -\cos^2\alpha = \cos^2\alpha$

$\Rightarrow \quad \cos\alpha = 0$

$\Rightarrow \quad \alpha = (2m+1)\frac{\pi}{2}, m \in I$

But for this value of α, the vertices of the given triangle are not defined.

Hence, Δ_1, Δ_2 and Δ_3 cannot be in GP for any value of α. Thus, total number of required values of $\alpha = 0$.

16. (b) Given, $\lim_{x\to 0}\left(\frac{a^x+b^x}{2}\right)^{\frac{2}{x}}$

$$\lim_{x\to 0}\left(1+\frac{a^x+b^x-2}{2}\right)^{\frac{2}{a^x+b^x-2}\lim_{x\to 0}\left(\frac{a^x-1+b^x-1}{x}\right)}$$

$= e^{\log_e ab} = ab = 6$ (given)

Total number of possible ways in which a, b can take values is $6 \times 6 = 36$.

Total possible ways are (1,6) (6,1) (2,3), (3,2).

$\therefore$ Total number of possible ways are 4.

Hence, the required probability

$$= \frac{4}{36} = \frac{1}{9}$$

17. (c) Given, $f(x) = (x+2)^2 - 4$

For $\quad x \ge -2, f(x) \ge -4$

Let $\quad y = f(x) - (x+2)^2 - 4$

$\Rightarrow y + 4 = (x+2)^2$

$\Rightarrow \quad x = -2 + \sqrt{y+4}, \forall y \ge -4$

$\Rightarrow f^{-1}(x) = -2 + \sqrt{x+4}, \forall x \ge -4$

Now, $\quad f(x) = f^{-1}(x)$

$\Rightarrow \quad (x+2)^2 - 4 = \sqrt{x+4} - 2$

$\Rightarrow (x+4-2)^2 - 4 = \sqrt{x+4} - 2$

$\Rightarrow$

$(x+4)^2 + 4 - 4(x+4) - 4 = \sqrt{x+4} - 2$

$\Rightarrow (x+4)^2 - 4(x+4) - \sqrt{x+4} + 2 = 0$ ...(i)

Let $\sqrt{x+4} = t$, then Eq. (i) becomes,

$$t^4 - 4t^2 - t + 2 = 0$$

$\Rightarrow t^2(t-2)(t+2) - (t-2) = 0$

$\Rightarrow \quad (t-2)[t^2(t+2) - 1] = 0$

$\Rightarrow \quad (t-2)[t^3 + 2t^2 - 1] = 0$

$\Rightarrow (t-2)(t+1)(t^2+t-1) = 0$

$\Rightarrow t = -1, 2, \frac{1}{2}(\sqrt{5}-1), -\frac{1}{2}(\sqrt{5}+1)$

$\Rightarrow \sqrt{x+4} = 2, \frac{1}{2}(\sqrt{5}-1), -1, -\frac{1}{2}(\sqrt{5}+1)$

$\because \quad \sqrt{x+4} \ge 0$

$\Rightarrow \quad \sqrt{x+4} = 2$

$\Rightarrow \quad x + 4 = 4$

$\Rightarrow \quad x = 0$

and $\quad \sqrt{x+4} = \frac{1}{2}(\sqrt{5}-1)$

$\Rightarrow \quad x + 4 = \frac{6-2\sqrt{5}}{4}$

$\Rightarrow x = \frac{6-2\sqrt{5}}{4} - 4 = \frac{6-2\sqrt{5}-16}{4}$

$\Rightarrow x = \frac{-10-2\sqrt{5}}{4} = -\frac{1}{2}(5+\sqrt{5})$

(rejected because $x \ge -2$)

Hence, $S = \{0\}$

18. (a) Given, equation is

$$(2a - x)y^2 = x^3 \quad \text{...(i)}$$

Differentiating Eq. (i) w.r.t. x, we get

$$(2a-x)\cdot 2y\frac{dy}{dx} - y^2 = 3x^2$$

$\Rightarrow 2\cdot(2a-x)y\cdot\frac{dy}{dx} = 3x^2 + y^2$ ...(ii)

Eliminating a with the help of Eqs. (i) and (ii), we get

$$y(3x^2+y^2)\frac{dx}{dy} = 2x^3$$

$\left[\because 2a - x = \frac{x^3}{y^2} \text{ from Eq. (i)}\right]$

Replacing $\frac{dy}{dx}$ by $-\frac{dx}{dy}$, we have

$2x^3 + y(3x^2+y^2)\frac{dy}{dx} = 0$

$\Rightarrow \quad \frac{dy}{dx} = \frac{-2x^3}{(3x^2+y^2)\cdot y}$ ...(iii)

which is a homogeneous equation.

Now, putting $y = vx$,

$\Rightarrow \quad \frac{dy}{dx} = v + x\frac{dv}{dx}$

From Eq. (iii),

$v + x\frac{dv}{dx} = \frac{-2}{(3+v^2)\cdot v}$

$\Rightarrow x\frac{dv}{dx} = -\left[\frac{2+3v^2+v^4}{(3+v^2)v}\right]$

$\Rightarrow \quad \frac{dx}{x} = -\frac{(3+v^2)v}{(1+v^2)(2+v^2)}dv$

$= -\left[\frac{2v}{1+v^2} - \frac{v}{2+v^2}\right]dv$

$\Rightarrow \log_e x^2 = -\log_e\frac{(1+v^2)^2}{2+v^2} + \log_e C$

[after integrating and solving]

$\Rightarrow \log_e x^2 + \log_e\left[\frac{\left(1+\frac{y^2}{x^2}\right)^2}{\left(2+\frac{y^2}{x^2}\right)}\right] = \log_e C$

$\Rightarrow \quad \frac{x^2(1+y^2/x^2)^2}{2+y^2/x^2} = C$

$\Rightarrow \quad (x^2+y^2)^2 = C(y^2+2x^2)$

Knockout 14

Paper 1

1. (b) To check option (a)

$$\sqrt{f(x)}\log_{\sec^2(8.5)}\left(\frac{25-x^2}{16}\right)>0$$

$$\Rightarrow \frac{25-x^2}{16}>1 \quad ...(i)$$

[$\because \sqrt{f(x)}$ gives always non-negative values and $\sec^2(8.5)>1$]

$$\Rightarrow 25-x^2>16 \Rightarrow x^2<9 \Rightarrow |x|<3$$

$$\Rightarrow x\in(-3,3) \quad ...(ii)$$

Also, $f(x)$ must be greater than or equal to zero i.e. $f(x)\geq 0$

$$\Rightarrow \log_{\frac{25-x^2}{16}}\left(\frac{24-2x-x^2}{14}\right)\geq 0$$

From Eq. (i), $\frac{25-x^2}{16}>1$

So, $\frac{24-2x-x^2}{14}\geq 1 \Rightarrow x^2+2x-10\leq 0$

$$\Rightarrow x\in(-1-\sqrt{11},-1+\sqrt{11}) \quad ...(iii)$$

From Eqs. (ii) and (iii), we get

$x\in(-3,-1+\sqrt{11})\rightarrow$ Incorrect option.

To check option (b)

Given, $0<\frac{25-x^2}{16}<1$

$$\Rightarrow 0<25-x^2<16$$

$$\Rightarrow x\in(-5,-3)\cup(3,5) \quad ...(iv)$$

Now,

$$f(x)>1 \Rightarrow \log_{\frac{25-x^2}{16}}\left(\frac{24-2x-x^2}{14}\right)>1$$

$$\Rightarrow \frac{24-2x-x^2}{14}<\frac{25-x^2}{16}$$

$$\Rightarrow x^2+16x-17>0$$

$$\Rightarrow x\in(-\infty,-17)\cup(1,\infty) \quad ...(v)$$

From Eqs. (iv) and (v), we get

$x\in(3,5)\rightarrow$ Correct option.

To check option (c)

Given, $\frac{25-x^2}{16}>1 \Rightarrow x^2-9<0$

$$\Rightarrow x\in(-3,3) \quad ...(vi)$$

Now, $f(x)>1$

$$\Rightarrow \frac{24-2x-x^2}{14}>\frac{25-x^2}{16}$$

$$\Rightarrow x^2+16x-17<0$$

$$\Rightarrow x\in(-17,1) \quad ...(vii)$$

From Eqs. (vi) and (viii), we get

$x\in(-3,1)\rightarrow$ Incorrect option.

2. (d) Since, the particle is in equilibrium.

So, $\mathbf{F}_1+\mathbf{F}_2+\mathbf{F}_3+\mathbf{F}_4=0$

$$\Rightarrow -10\mathbf{k}+u\left(\frac{4}{13}\hat{\mathbf{i}}-\frac{12}{13}\hat{\mathbf{j}}+\frac{3}{13}\hat{\mathbf{k}}\right)+v\left(-\frac{4}{13}\hat{\mathbf{i}}-\frac{12}{13}\hat{\mathbf{j}}+\frac{3}{13}\hat{\mathbf{k}}\right)+w(\cos\theta\hat{\mathbf{i}}+\sin\theta\hat{\mathbf{j}})=0$$

$$\Rightarrow \left(\frac{4}{13}u-\frac{4}{13}v+w\cos\theta\right)\hat{\mathbf{i}}+\left(-\frac{12}{13}u-\frac{12}{13}v+w\sin\theta\right)\hat{\mathbf{j}}+\left(-10+\frac{3}{13}u+\frac{3}{13}v\right)\hat{\mathbf{k}}=0$$

Since, $\hat{\mathbf{i}},\hat{\mathbf{j}}$ and $\hat{\mathbf{k}}$ are linearly independent.

So, $\frac{4}{13}u-\frac{4}{13}v+w\cos\theta=0 \quad ...(i)$

$$-\frac{12}{13}u-\frac{12}{13}v+w\sin\theta=0 \quad ...(ii)$$

$$-10+\frac{3}{13}(u+v)=0 \quad ...(iii)$$

From Eq. (iii),

$$u+v=\frac{130}{3} \quad ...(iv)$$

Substituting this value in Eq. (ii), we get

$$-\frac{12}{13}\times\frac{130}{3}+w\sin\theta=0$$

$$\Rightarrow w=40 \quad \theta \quad ...(v)$$

From Eq. (i),

$$u-v=-\frac{13}{4}w\cos\theta=-130\cos\theta\cdot \quad \theta$$

[from Eq. (v)]

$$\Rightarrow u-v=-130\cot\theta \quad ...(vi)$$

On solving Eqs. (iv) and (vi), we get

$u=65\left(\frac{1}{3}-\cot\theta\right)$ and

$v=65\left(\frac{1}{3}+\cot\theta\right)$

3. (c) Given, equation of circle is

$$x^2+y^2=\frac{a^2}{2} \quad ...(i)$$

and that of parabola is $y^2=4ax$ ...(ii)

Now, equation of any tangent to the parabola $y^2=4ax$ (having slope m) is

$$y=mx+\frac{a}{m} \quad ...(iii)$$

Eq. (iii) touches the circle (i), if

$$\left(\frac{a}{m}\right)^2=\frac{a^2}{2}(m^2+1)$$

$$\Rightarrow 2=m^4+m^2$$

$$\Rightarrow m^4+m^2-2=0$$

$$\Rightarrow (m^2+2)(m^2-1)=0$$

$$\because m^2+2>0 \quad \text{(always)}$$

$$\therefore m^2-1=0 \Rightarrow m=\pm 1$$

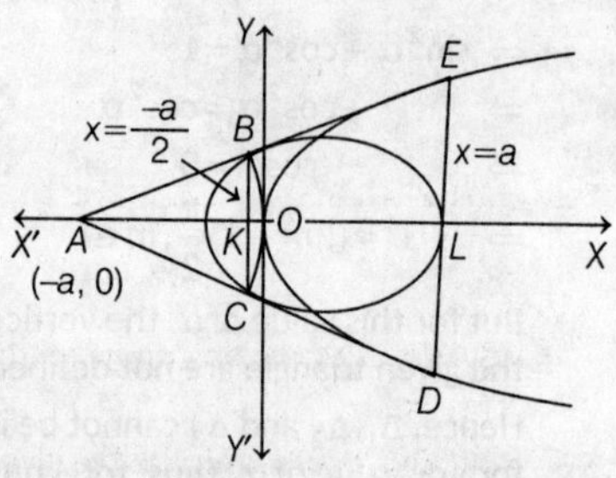

Thus, the two common tangents are $y=x+a$ and $y=-x-a$ [from Eq. (iii)]

These two common tangents intersect at $A(-a,0)$.

Now, the chord of contact of $A(-a,0)$ for the circle $x^2+y^2=\frac{a^2}{2}$ is

$$(-a)x+0\cdot y=\frac{a^2}{2}\Rightarrow x=-\frac{a}{2}=OK \quad ...(iv)$$

and chord of contact of $A(-a,0)$ for the parabola $y^2=4ax$ is

$$0\cdot y=2a(x-a)$$

$$\Rightarrow x=a=OL \quad ...(v)$$

In right angled ΔBKO,

$$BK=\sqrt{OB^2-OK^2}$$

$\therefore$ Length of $BC=2BK=2\sqrt{OB^2-OK^2}$

$$=2\sqrt{\frac{a^2}{2}-\frac{a^2}{4}}$$

[from Eq. (iv) and $BO=$ radius]

$$\Rightarrow BC=2\sqrt{\frac{a^2}{4}}=a \quad ...(vi)$$

and $KL=KO+OL=\frac{a}{2}+a$

$$\Rightarrow KL=\frac{3a}{2} \quad ...(vii)$$

Again, we see that,

$DE=$ Length of latusrectum of Eq. (ii)

$$\Rightarrow DE=4a \quad ...(viii)$$

Hence, area of trapezium

$$BCDE=\frac{1}{2}(BC+DE)(KL)$$

$$=\frac{1}{2}(a+4a)\left(\frac{3a}{2}\right)$$

[using Eqs. (vi), (vii) and (viii)]

$$=\frac{15a^2}{4}\text{ sq units}$$

4. (a)

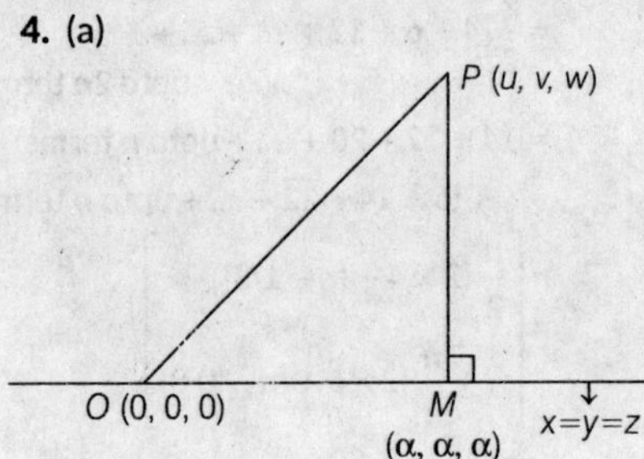

Let $M(\alpha,\alpha,\alpha)$ be any point on the line $x=y=z$.
Also, $O(0, 0, 0)$ lies on line the given line.
Now, $(PM)^2=(OP)^2-(OM)^2$

$$=u^2+v^2+w^2-3\alpha^2 \quad \text{...(i)}$$

Also, PM is perpendicular to the line

$$x=y=z$$

So, $(u-\alpha)+(v-\alpha)+(w-\alpha)=0$

$$\Rightarrow \quad u+v+w=3\alpha \quad \text{...(ii)}$$

Let $d=$ Distance between $P(u, v, w)$ and the given plane $=\dfrac{|u+v+w-1|}{\sqrt{1^2+1^2+1^2}}$

$$\Rightarrow \quad d^2=\frac{(u+v+w-1)^2}{3} \quad \text{...(iii)}$$

According to the question,

$$PM=2d$$

$$\Rightarrow \quad PM^2=4d^2$$

$$\Rightarrow u^2+v^2+w^2-3\alpha^2$$

$$=\frac{4}{3}[(u+v+w)-1]^2$$

[using Eqs. (i) and (iii)]

$$\Rightarrow 3(u^2+v^2+w^2)-(u+v+w)^2$$

$$=4[(u+v+w)^2-2(u+v+w)+1]$$

[using Eq. (ii) and $u^2+v^2+w^2=(u+v+w)^2$ if $uv+vw+wu=0$]

$$\Rightarrow 2(u^2+v^2+w^2)$$

$$-8(u+v+w)+4=0$$

$$\Rightarrow u^2+v^2+w^2-4(u+v+w)=-2$$

Solution (Q.Nos. 5-6)

5. (3) Given, $A=\begin{bmatrix}1&0&0\\1&0&1\\0&1&0\end{bmatrix}$ ...(i)

$$A^{50}U_1=\begin{bmatrix}1\\25\\25\end{bmatrix} \quad \text{...(ii)}$$

$$A^{50}U_2=\begin{bmatrix}0\\1\\0\end{bmatrix} \quad \text{...(iii)}$$

$$A^{50}U_3=\begin{bmatrix}0\\0\\1\end{bmatrix} \quad \text{...(iv)}$$

and $\quad A^n=A^{n-2}+A^2-I\ \forall\ n\ge 3$

$$\Rightarrow A^n-A^{n-2}=A^2-I$$

$$\therefore \ A^{50}=A^{48}+A^2-I$$

Similarly, $A^{48}=A^{46}+A^2-I$

$$A^{46}=A^{44}+A^2-I$$

$$\vdots \quad \vdots \quad \vdots \quad \vdots$$

$$A^4=A^2+A^2-I$$

$$A^{50}=25A^2-24I$$

Here,

$$A^2=A\cdot A=\begin{bmatrix}1&0&0\\1&0&1\\0&1&0\end{bmatrix}\begin{bmatrix}1&0&0\\1&0&1\\0&1&0\end{bmatrix}$$

$$=\begin{bmatrix}1&0&0\\1&1&0\\1&0&1\end{bmatrix}$$

$$\Rightarrow A^{50}=\begin{bmatrix}25&0&0\\25&25&0\\25&0&25\end{bmatrix}-24\begin{bmatrix}1&0&0\\0&1&0\\0&0&1\end{bmatrix}$$

$$=\begin{bmatrix}1&0&0\\25&1&0\\25&0&1\end{bmatrix}$$

$$\therefore tr(A^{50})=1+1+1=3$$

6. (1) From Eq. (ii),

$$\begin{bmatrix}1&0&0\\25&1&0\\25&0&1\end{bmatrix}\begin{bmatrix}x\\y\\z\end{bmatrix}=\begin{bmatrix}1\\25\\25\end{bmatrix}$$

$$\Rightarrow \quad U_1=\begin{bmatrix}1\\0\\0\end{bmatrix}$$

Similarly applying for Eqs. (iii) and (iv), we get

$$U_2=\begin{bmatrix}0\\1\\0\end{bmatrix} \text{ and } U_3=\begin{bmatrix}0\\0\\1\end{bmatrix}$$

$$\therefore \quad U=\begin{bmatrix}1&0&0\\0&1&0\\0&0&1\end{bmatrix}\Rightarrow |U|=1$$

Solution (Q.Nos. 7-8)

7. (2) Integrating $\dfrac{d^2y}{dx^2}=6x-4$, we get

$$\frac{dy}{dx}=3x^2-4x+C_1 \quad \text{...(i)}$$

When $x=1$, $\dfrac{dy}{dx}=0$ and hence $C_1=1$

From Eq. (i),

$$\frac{dy}{dx}=3x^2-4x+1 \quad \text{...(ii)}$$

Integrating, we get

$$y=x^3-2x^2+x+C_2 \quad \text{...(iii)}$$

When $x=1$, $y=5$, then $C_2=5$

From Eq. (iii)

$$y=x^3-2x^2+x+5 \quad \text{...(iv)}$$

From Eq. (ii), we get the critical points $x=\dfrac{1}{3}$ and $x=1$.

Hence, number of critical points $=2$

8. (7) Now, at critical points $\dfrac{d^2y}{dx^2}$ is negative at $x=\dfrac{1}{3}$.

Therefore, at $x=\dfrac{1}{3}$, y has a local maximum at $x=1$, $\dfrac{d^2y}{dx^2}$ is positive.

Therefore, at $x=1$, y has a local minimum.

Also, $f(1)=5$

$$f\left(\frac{1}{3}\right)=\frac{139}{27}$$

$$f(0)=5 \text{ and } f(2)=7$$

Hence, the global maximum value $=7$ (as well as global minimum value $=5$)

Sol. (Q.Nos. 9-10)

Given, $n\ge 2$ be an integer.

Since, 'n' distinct point on a circle and join each pair of points by a line segment.

Thus, the total number of line segment joining every pair of points $={}^nC_2$

And, clearly the number of line segment obtained by joining every pair of adjacent points $=n$

So, the number of green lines $=n$

and the number of blue lines $={}^nC_2-n$

Given, that the number of green and blue lines segment are equal.

So, ${}^nC_2-n=n\Rightarrow {}^nC_2=2n$

$$\Rightarrow \quad \frac{n!}{2!\,n-2!}=2n$$

$$\Rightarrow \frac{n(n-1)\,n-2!}{2.\dfrac{n-2!}{5}}=2n\Rightarrow n=5$$

9. (10) $\quad\therefore$

$${}^nC_2={}^5C_2=\frac{5!}{2!3!}=\frac{5\times 4}{2}=\frac{20}{2}=10$$

10. (5) Number of green and blue lines are n and $({}^nC_2 - n)$ i.e. 5 and 5.

So, the total number of blue line is $({}^nC_2 - n)$ i.e. $({}^5C_2 - 5) = 5$.

11. (a), (c)

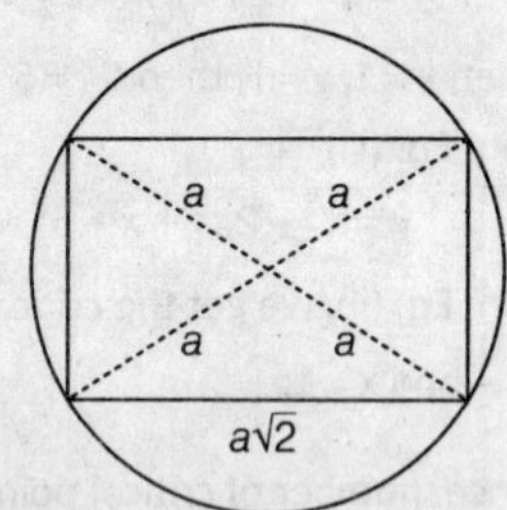

Let a be the radius of the circle.

$\therefore$ Area of the inscribed square

$$=(a\sqrt{2})^2 = 2a^2$$

$$\therefore \quad p_1 = \frac{2a^2}{\pi a^2} = \frac{2}{\pi}$$

and $$p_2 = \frac{\pi a^2 - 2a^2}{\pi a^2} = \frac{\pi - 2}{\pi}$$

$$\therefore \; p_1 - p_2 = \frac{2}{\pi} - \left(\frac{\pi - 2}{\pi}\right) = \frac{4}{\pi} - 1 > 0$$

$\Rightarrow p_1 > p_2 \rightarrow$ option (a) is correct.

Also, $(p_1 - p_2)(p_1 + p_2) = \left(\frac{4-\pi}{\pi}\right)(1)$

But $3 < \pi < 4 \Rightarrow$

$(p_1^2 - p_2^2) = \left(\frac{4-\pi}{\pi}\right) < \frac{1}{3}$

Hence, $(p_1^2 - p_2^2) < \frac{1}{3}$

Option (c) is correct.

12. (a), (b), (c)

Let $D(\alpha, \beta)$ be an interior point of a circle $x^2 + y^2 = a^2$.

Then, $\alpha^2 + \beta^2 < a^2$ ...(i)

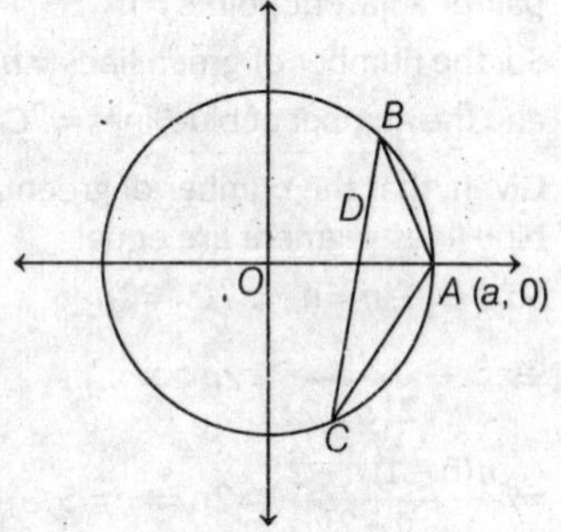

Now, the equation of BC is

$$\frac{x-\alpha}{\cos\theta} = \frac{y-\beta}{\sin\theta}$$

Let $DB = r$. Then, the coordinates of B are $(\alpha + r\cos\theta, \beta + r\sin\theta)$.

It lies on $x^2 + y^2 = a^2$

Therefore,

$$(\alpha + r\cos\theta)^2 + (\beta + r\sin\theta)^2 = a^2$$

$$\Rightarrow \; r^2 + 2r(\alpha\cos\theta + \beta\sin\theta) + \alpha^2 + \beta^2 - a^2 = 0 \quad \text{...(ii)}$$

This is quadratic in r, which gives the values of r, one each for points B and C.

Let $DB = r_1$ and $DC = r_2$

Then, r_1 and r_2 are the roots of Eq. (ii).

Therefore,

$$r_1 + r_2 = -2(\alpha\cos\theta + \beta\sin\theta) \quad \text{...(iii)}$$

Also, $r_1 r_2 = \alpha^2 + \beta^2 - a^2$

The HM of r_1 and r_2 is

$$\frac{2r_1r_2}{r_1 + r_2} = \frac{2(\alpha^2 + \beta^2 - a^2)}{-2(\alpha\cos\theta + \beta\sin\theta)} = -\frac{(\alpha^2 + \beta^2 - a^2)}{(\alpha\cos\theta + \beta\sin\theta)}$$

Now, let $G(x_1, y_1)$ be the centroid of ΔABC. Then,

$$3x_1 = a + r_1\cos\theta + r_2\cos\theta$$

and $$3y_1 = r_1\sin\theta + r_2\sin\theta$$

Eliminating θ, we get the required equation of locus as

$$(3x - a)^2 + (3y)^2 = (r_1 + r_2)^2$$

$$\Rightarrow \left(x - \frac{a}{3}\right)^2 + (y)^2 = \left(\frac{r_1 + r_2}{3}\right)^2$$

Now, radius of circle is

$$\left|\frac{r_1 + r_2}{3}\right| = \left|\frac{-2(\alpha\cos\theta + \beta\sin\theta)}{3}\right| \le \frac{2}{3}$$

$$\sqrt{\alpha^2 + \beta^2} < \frac{2a}{3}$$

13. (a, c, d)

Given, $P_n = \sum_{k=1}^{4n} (-1)^{\frac{k(k+1)}{2}} \cdot \frac{k^2}{2}$

$$= \frac{1}{2}\sum_{k=1}^{4n} (-1)^{\frac{k(k+1)}{2}} \cdot k^2$$

$$= \frac{1}{2}[-1^2 - 2^2 + 3^2 + 4^2 - 5^2 - 6^2 + 7^2 + 8^2 - 9^2 - 10^2 + \ldots]$$

$$= \frac{1}{2}[(3^2 - 1^2) + (4^2 - 2^2) + (7^2 - 5^2) + (8^2 - 6^2) + \ldots]$$

$$= \frac{1}{2}[2 \cdot 4 + 2 \cdot 6 + 2 \cdot 12 + 2 \cdot 14 + \ldots \text{ upto } 2n \text{ terms}]$$

$$= \frac{2}{2}[4 + 6 + 12 + 14 + \ldots + \text{ upto } 2n \text{ terms}]$$

$$= [(4 + 12 + 20 + \ldots + \text{upto } n \text{ terms}) + (6 + 14 + 22 + \ldots + \text{upto } n \text{ terms})$$

$$= \left[\frac{n}{2}\{2 \times 4 + (n-1)8\} + \frac{n}{2}\{2 \times 6 + (n-1)\,8\}\right]$$

$$= \frac{n}{2}[8 + (n-1)\,8 + 12 + (n-1)8]$$

$$= \frac{n}{2}[4 + 16n] = \frac{4n}{2}(4n+1)$$

$$= 2n(4n+1)$$

Take $n = 4$, then option (a) is true.

Take $n = 8$, then option (c) true.

Take $n = 9$, option (d) true.

14. (a), (b), (d)

Let $|\alpha| = r > 1$

and $\alpha = r\cos\theta$, then

$$z = x + iy \quad \text{...(i)}$$

Given, $z = \alpha + \frac{1}{\alpha} = r\cos\theta$

$$\theta + \frac{\cos(-\theta)}{r} = \left(r\cos\theta + \frac{1}{r}\cos\theta\right) + i\left(r\sin\theta - \frac{1}{r}\sin\theta\right)$$

$$\Rightarrow \quad x = \left(r + \frac{1}{r}\right)\cos\theta$$

and $y = \left(r - \frac{1}{r}\right)\sin\theta$ [from Eq. (i)]

Eliminating θ gives,

$$\frac{x^2}{\left(r+\frac{1}{r}\right)^2} + \frac{y^2}{\left(r-\frac{1}{r}\right)^2} = 1,$$ which is an ellipse.

$$a = r + \frac{1}{r} \text{ and } b = r - \frac{1}{r}$$

$\because \quad r = |\alpha| > 1$

$\therefore \quad r + \frac{1}{r} > r - \frac{1}{r}$

$\Rightarrow \quad a > b$

$$\therefore \quad e = \sqrt{1 - \frac{b^2}{a^2}} = \frac{2}{r + \frac{1}{r}} = \frac{2|\alpha|}{1 + |\alpha|^2}$$

$\therefore$ Distance between foci

$$= 2ae = 2\left(r + \frac{1}{r}\right) \times \frac{2}{\left(r + \frac{1}{r}\right)}$$

$$= 4 \text{ units}$$

$\therefore$ Distance between directrices

$$=\frac{2a}{e}=\frac{2\left(r+\frac{1}{r}\right)^2}{2}$$

$$=\left(|\alpha|+\frac{1}{|\alpha|}\right)^2$$

$\therefore$ Length of the latusrectum is

$$\frac{2b^2}{a}$$

$$=\frac{2\left(r-\frac{1}{r}\right)^2}{\left(r+\frac{1}{r}\right)}=\frac{2(r^2-1)}{r(r^2+1)}$$

$$=\frac{2(|\alpha|^2-1)^2}{|\alpha|(|\alpha|+1)}$$

15. (a), (c), (d)

Given, $\angle A=45^\circ, \angle B=30^\circ, \angle C=105^\circ$ and $\Delta=1$

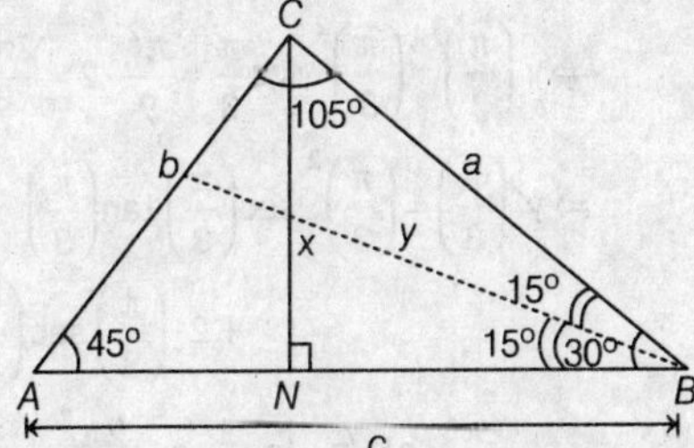

Now, $\Delta=\frac{1}{2}ac\sin B$

$\Rightarrow \quad 2=ac\sin 30^\circ \Rightarrow ac=4$

$\Rightarrow (2R\sin A)(2R\sin C)=4$

$$\left(\because \frac{a}{\sin A}=\frac{b}{\sin B}=\frac{c}{\sin C}=2R\right)$$

$$\Rightarrow R^2\times\frac{1}{\sqrt{2}}\times\frac{\sqrt{3}+1}{2\sqrt{2}}=1$$

$$\left(\because \sin 105^\circ=\cos 15^\circ=\frac{\sqrt{3}+1}{2\sqrt{2}}\right)$$

$$\Rightarrow \quad R^2=\frac{4}{\sqrt{3}+1}$$

$$\Rightarrow \quad R^2=2(\sqrt{3}-1)$$

Now, $\Delta=\frac{abc}{4R}$

$\because \Delta=1$ and $ac=4$

$\because 1=\frac{4b}{4R}\Rightarrow R=b$ which is smallest side.

(OR you may use $\frac{b}{\sin B}=2R$

$\Rightarrow \frac{b}{\sin 30^\circ}=2R\Rightarrow 2b=2R$

$\Rightarrow b=R$)

Also, $CN=b\sin 45^\circ=\frac{b}{\sqrt{2}}=\frac{R}{\sqrt{2}}$

$\Rightarrow \quad R=\sqrt{2}\,CN\Rightarrow R^2=2(CN)^2=2x^2$

Now, length of angle bisector from vertex $B=y=\frac{2ac}{a+c}\cos 15^\circ$

$$\Rightarrow y=\frac{2\times 4}{a+c}\times\frac{\sqrt{3}+1}{2\sqrt{2}}=\frac{4(\sqrt{3}+1)}{\sqrt{2}(a+c)} \quad \text{...(i)}$$

But $\frac{a+c}{2}>\sqrt{ac}$ (using AM > GM because $a\neq c$ and $a, c>0$)

$\Rightarrow \quad a+c>2\sqrt{ac}$

$\Rightarrow \quad a+c>2\times 2$

$\Rightarrow \quad a+c>4$

From Eq. (i),

$$y<\frac{4(\sqrt{3}+1)}{\sqrt{2}\times 4}$$

i.e. $$y<\frac{\sqrt{3}+1}{\sqrt{2}}$$

(when $a+c$ is minimum, then y will be maximum)

$$\Rightarrow \quad y<\frac{\sqrt{2}(\sqrt{3}+1)}{\sqrt{2}\times\sqrt{2}}$$

$$\Rightarrow \quad y<\frac{\sqrt{6}+\sqrt{2}}{2}$$

Hence, length of angle bisector from the vertex B cannot exceed $\frac{\sqrt{6}+\sqrt{2}}{2}$.

16. (a), (d)

To check option (a)

$$\text{Let } I_1=\int_0^{\pi}\frac{dx}{1+(\sin x)^{\cos x}} \quad \text{...(i)}$$

$$\therefore I_1=\int_0^{\pi}\frac{dx}{1+(\sin x)^{(-\cos x)}} \quad \text{...(ii)}$$

$$\left[\text{using } \int_a^b f(x)\,dx=\int_a^b f(a+b-x)dx \text{ or, } \int_0^a f(x)\,dx=\int_0^a f(a-x)\,dx\right]$$

On adding Eqs. (i) and (ii), we get

$$2I_1=\int_0^{\pi}1\cdot dx \Rightarrow I_1=\frac{\pi}{2}$$

To check option (c)

$$\text{Let } I_2=\int_0^{\pi/2}\frac{dx}{1+\tan^5 x} \quad \text{...(iii)}$$

$$\therefore I_2=\int_0^{\pi/2}\frac{dx}{1+\cot^5 x}=\int_0^{\pi/2}\frac{\tan^5 x}{1+\tan^5 x}dx \quad \text{...(iv)}$$

On adding Eqs. (iii) and (iv), we get

$$2I_2=\int_0^{\pi/2}1\cdot dx$$

$$\Rightarrow I_2=\frac{\pi}{4}$$

To check option (b)

$$\text{Let } I_3=\int_0^{\infty}\frac{x^2+1}{x^4-x^2+1}dx$$

$$=\int_0^{\infty}\frac{1+\frac{1}{x^2}}{x^2+\frac{1}{x^2}-1}dx$$

Putting $x-\frac{1}{x}=z$

$$\Rightarrow \quad \left(1+\frac{1}{x^2}\right)dx=dz$$

$$\text{So, } I_3=\int_{-\infty}^{\infty}\frac{dz}{z^2+1}=(\tan^{-1}z)_{-\infty}^{\infty}=\pi$$

To check option (d)

$$\text{Let } I_4=\int_0^{\pi/2}\frac{\ln(\sec x)}{\ln 2}dx$$

$$=-\frac{1}{\ln 2}\int_0^{\pi/2}\ln(\cos x)dx$$

$$=-\frac{1}{\ln 2}\left(-\frac{\pi}{2}\ln 2\right)$$

$$=\frac{\pi}{2}$$

17. (3954) Using the formula for the sum of a geometric progression. We find

$$(1+x)^{1000}+x(1+x)^{999}+x^2(1+x)^{998}+\dots+x^{1000}$$

$$=\frac{(1+x)^{1000}\left[1-\left(\frac{x}{1+x}\right)^{1001}\right]}{\left[1-\left(\frac{x}{1+x}\right)\right]}$$

$$=\frac{(1+x)^{1000}-\frac{x^{1001}}{1+x}}{\frac{x+1-x}{1+x}}$$

$$=(1+x)^{1001}-x^{1001}$$

Hence, the coefficient of $x^{50}={}^{1001}C_{50}$

$$=\frac{(1001)!}{(50)!\,(951)!}$$

On comparing, we get

$\lambda=1001, \mu=50$ and $v=951$

$\therefore \lambda+2\mu+3v=1001+100+2853$

$=3954$

18. (7) $f(x)=\dfrac{\sqrt{1-f^2(x)}}{f'(x)}$

(applying L' Hospital rule)

$\Rightarrow \quad f'(x)\cdot f(x)=\sqrt{1-f^2(x)}$

$\Rightarrow \int \dfrac{f(x)\cdot f'(x)}{\sqrt{1-f^2(x)}}dx=\int 1\cdot dx$

$\Rightarrow \quad -\sqrt{1-f^2(x)}=x+c \quad$ ...(i)

As, $f\left(\dfrac{1}{2}\right)=\dfrac{\sqrt{3}}{2} \quad [\therefore c=-1]$

From Eq. (i), $-\sqrt{1-f^2(x)}=x-1$

$\therefore \quad f\left(\dfrac{1}{4}\right)=\dfrac{\sqrt{7}}{4}$

Hence, $16(f(1/4))^2=16\times\dfrac{(\sqrt{7})^2}{16}=7$

19. (7) Let $y=\sqrt{9-a^2+2ax-x^2}$

and $\quad y=\sqrt{16-x^2}$

$\Rightarrow y^2+(x-a)^2=9$

and $\quad y^2+x^2=16$

Graph of both functions are semi-circle above the X-axis.

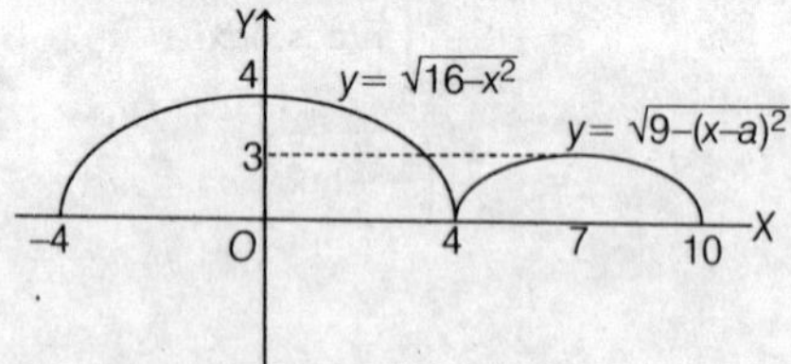

From the above figure, if $a>7$, no solution exist.

$\therefore \quad a\le 7 \Rightarrow [a]=7$

Hence, maximum value of 'a' is 7.

Paper 2

1. (a), (b), (c), (d)

$f(\theta)=||(\sin\theta-3\cos\theta)+2\cos\theta|+\cos\theta|$

$=||\sin\theta-\cos\theta|+\cos\theta|$

$=|\sin\theta-\cos\theta+\cos\theta|=|\sin\theta|=\sin\theta$

Now,

$\int_{\pi/2}^{\pi} f(\theta)\,d\theta=\int_{\pi/2}^{\pi}\sin\theta\,d\theta=-[\cos\theta]_{\pi/2}^{\pi}$

$=-[-1-0]=1$

$\because \quad f(\theta)=\sin\theta$

$\therefore \quad f'(\theta)=\cos\theta$

$\Rightarrow f'\left(\dfrac{5\pi}{6}\right)=-\dfrac{\sqrt{3}}{2}$

Also, let $I=\int_{\pi/2}^{\pi} f^2(\theta)d\theta=\int_{\pi/2}^{\pi}\sin^2\theta\,d\theta$ ...(i)

$\Rightarrow I=\int_{\pi/2}^{\pi}\left[\sin\left(\pi+\dfrac{\pi}{2}-\theta\right)\right]^2 d\theta$

$=\int_{\pi/2}^{\pi}\cos^2\theta\,d\theta \quad$ ...(ii)

On adding Eqs. (i) and (ii), we get

$2I=\int_{\pi/2}^{\pi}1\cdot d\theta=\dfrac{\pi}{2}\Rightarrow I=\dfrac{\pi}{4}$

Further, $f'\left(\dfrac{2\pi}{3}\right)=\cos\left(\dfrac{2\pi}{3}\right)=-\dfrac{1}{2}$

2. (a) From the given matrix, we observe

that $AA^T=3I\Rightarrow A^{-1}=\dfrac{A^T}{3}$ and

$|A|=-3\sqrt{3}$

$|\text{adj}(\text{adj }A)|=|A|^{(3-1)^2}=|A|^4$

So, $\dfrac{|A^{-1}+A^T|}{|\text{adj}(\text{adj }A)|}=\dfrac{\left|\dfrac{A^T}{3}+A^T\right|}{|A|^4}$

$=\dfrac{\left|\dfrac{4A^T}{3}\right|}{|A|^4}=\left(\dfrac{4}{3}\right)^3\dfrac{|A^T|}{|A|^4} \quad (\because |A|=|A^T|)$

$=\dfrac{64}{27\times|A|^3}=\dfrac{64}{27\times(-3\sqrt{3})^3}$

$=-\dfrac{64}{3^7\sqrt{3}}=-\dfrac{2^6\sqrt{3}}{3^8}$

3. (a), (c) Plane P_1 contains the line $\mathbf{r}=\hat{\mathbf{i}}+\hat{\mathbf{j}}+\hat{\mathbf{k}}+\lambda(\hat{\mathbf{i}}-\hat{\mathbf{j}}-\hat{\mathbf{k}})$, hence contains the point $\hat{\mathbf{i}}+\hat{\mathbf{j}}+\hat{\mathbf{k}}$ and is normal to vectors $(\hat{\mathbf{i}}+\hat{\mathbf{j}})$.

Hence, equation of plane is

$[\mathbf{r}-(\hat{\mathbf{i}}+\hat{\mathbf{j}}+\hat{\mathbf{k}})]\cdot(\hat{\mathbf{i}}+\hat{\mathbf{j}})=0$

$\Rightarrow \quad x+y=2$

Plane P_2 contains the line

$\mathbf{r}=\hat{\mathbf{i}}+\hat{\mathbf{j}}+\hat{\mathbf{k}}+\lambda(\hat{\mathbf{i}}-\hat{\mathbf{j}}-\hat{\mathbf{k}})$ and point $\hat{}$.

Hence, equation of plane is

$$\begin{vmatrix} x-0 & y-1 & z-0\\ 1-0 & 1-1 & 1-0\\ 1 & -1 & -1\end{vmatrix}=0$$

$\Rightarrow \quad x+2y-z=2$

If θ is the acute angle between P_1 and P_2, then

$\cos\theta=\dfrac{\mathbf{n}_1\cdot\mathbf{n}_2}{|\mathbf{n}_1||\mathbf{n}_2|}=\left|\dfrac{(\hat{\mathbf{i}}+\hat{\mathbf{j}})\cdot(\hat{\mathbf{i}}+2\hat{\mathbf{j}}-\hat{\mathbf{k}})}{\sqrt{2}\sqrt{6}}\right|$

$=\dfrac{3}{\sqrt{2}\sqrt{6}}=\dfrac{\sqrt{3}}{2}$

$\Rightarrow \theta=\cos^{-1}\left(\dfrac{\sqrt{3}}{2}\right)=\dfrac{\pi}{6}=\cot^{-1}(\sqrt{3})$

As L is contained in $P_2 \Rightarrow \theta=0°$

4. (a, c) Given, $y'-y\tan x=2x\sec x$ ...(i)

This Eq. (i) compare with

$\dfrac{dy}{dx}+P(x)y=Q(x)$

Where, $P(x)=-\tan x$, $Q(x)=2x\sec x$

$\therefore$ IF $=e^{\int P(x)dx}=e^{\int(-\tan x)dx}=\cos x$

Thus, Eq. (i) reduce to

$y\cdot\cos x=\int(2x\cdot\sec x)\cdot\cos x\,dx$

$+C=x^2+C$

Since, $y(0)=0$, then $C=0$

$\Rightarrow y\cdot\cos x=x^2$

$\Rightarrow y(x)=x^2\cdot\sec x\ \forall\ x\in R$

Thus, as $x\to\infty$, $y(x)\to\infty$, so $y(x)$ is not bounded $\forall\ x\in R$.

Now, $y'(x)=x^2\sec x\tan x+2x\sec x$

$y\left(\dfrac{\pi}{4}\right)=\left(\dfrac{\pi}{4}\right)^2\sec\dfrac{\pi}{4}=\dfrac{\pi^2}{16}.\sqrt{2}=\dfrac{\pi^2}{8\sqrt{2}}$

$\Rightarrow y\left(\dfrac{\pi}{4}\right)=\dfrac{\pi^2\sqrt{2}}{16}$

$\Rightarrow y\left(\dfrac{\pi}{3}\right)=\left(\dfrac{\pi}{3}\right)^2\sec\dfrac{\pi}{3}=\dfrac{\pi^2}{9}\cdot 2=\dfrac{2\pi^2}{9}$

$\Rightarrow y'\left(\dfrac{\pi}{3}\right)=\left(\dfrac{\pi}{3}\right)^2\sec\left(\dfrac{\pi}{3}\right)\tan\left(\dfrac{\pi}{3}\right)$

$+2\cdot\left(\dfrac{\pi}{3}\right)\sec\left(\dfrac{\pi}{3}\right)$

$=\dfrac{\pi^2}{9}\cdot 2\cdot\sqrt{3}+2\cdot\dfrac{\pi}{3}\cdot 2=\dfrac{2\pi^2}{3\sqrt{3}}+\dfrac{4\pi}{3}$

$\therefore y'\left(\dfrac{\pi}{3}\right)=\dfrac{4\pi}{3}+\dfrac{2\pi^2}{3\sqrt{3}}$

5. (a), (d) Given,

$(1-\tan^2\theta)\sec^2\theta+2\tan^2\theta=0$,

$\theta\in\left(-\dfrac{\pi}{2},\dfrac{\pi}{2}\right)$ has $\theta_1,\theta_2,\theta_3,\ldots,\theta_n$ are solution.

$\Rightarrow(1-\tan^2\theta)(1+\tan^2\theta)+2\tan^2\theta=0$

$\Rightarrow \quad 1-\tan^4\theta+2\tan^2\theta=0$

$\Rightarrow \quad \tan^4\theta-2\tan^2\theta-1=0$

$\Rightarrow \quad \tan^2\theta=\dfrac{2\pm\sqrt{8}}{2}$

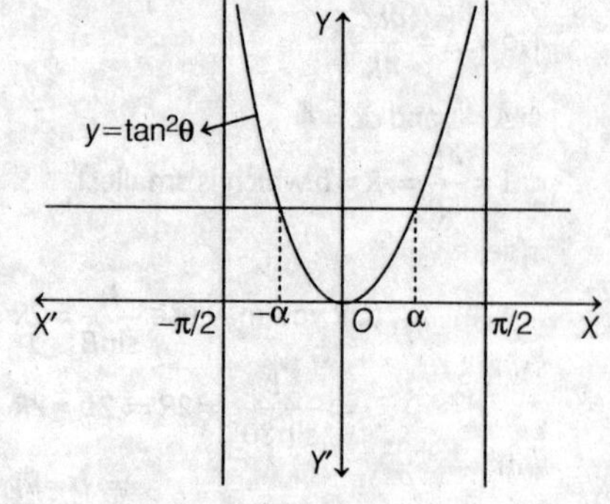

$\Rightarrow \tan^2\theta = 1 \pm \sqrt{2}$

$\Rightarrow \tan^2\theta = 1 + \sqrt{2}$ $\quad (\because 1 - \sqrt{2} < 0)$

$\Rightarrow \theta = \alpha, -\alpha$ are two real solutions.

$\Rightarrow \theta_1 = \alpha$ and $\theta_2 = -\alpha$ only two solutions.

Thus, $n = 2$ and $\theta_1 + \theta_2 = 0$

6. (b,c,d) Let the number of blue marbles is a and number of green marbles is b.

$$\therefore \quad \frac{ab}{a + {}^bC_2} = \frac{1}{2}$$

$$\Rightarrow \quad (a + b)(a + b - 1) = 4ab$$

$$\Rightarrow b^2 - (2a + 1)b + a^2 - a = 0$$

But $b \in R$

$\Rightarrow D = (2a + 1)^2 - 4(a^2 - a) = 8a + 1$

$\therefore 8a + 1$ must be a perfect square.

Hence, possible values of a are 3, 6, 10.

Sol. (Q.Nos. 7-8)

7. (2) Given that,

$$\sqrt{1 - x^2}\frac{dy}{dx} - \frac{xy}{\sqrt{1 - x^2}} = x^4 + 2x$$

$$\Rightarrow \frac{dy}{dx} - \frac{x}{1 - x^2}y = \frac{x^4 + 2x}{\sqrt{1 - x^2}}$$

These equation comparing with $\frac{dy}{dx} + P(x)y = Q(x)$, where $P(x) = \frac{-x}{1 - x^2}$

and $Q(x) = \frac{x^4 + 2x}{\sqrt{1 - x^2}}$

Now,

IF

$$= e^{\int \frac{-x}{1 - x^2}dx} = e^{\frac{1}{2}\log|1 - x^2|} = \sqrt{1 - x^2}$$

Thus, the solution is

$$y.\sqrt{1 - x^2} = \int \frac{x^4 + 2x}{\sqrt{1 - x^2}}.\sqrt{1 - x^2}\, dx$$

$$= \int (x^4 + 2x)\, dx = \frac{x^5}{5} + x^2 + C$$

Since, $y(0) = 0 \Rightarrow C = 0$

$$\therefore \ y(x) = \frac{x^5 + 5x^2}{5\sqrt{1 - x^2}}$$

At $x = \frac{1}{2}$, then

$$y\left(\frac{1}{2}\right) = \frac{\left(\frac{1}{2}\right)^5 + 5\left(\frac{1}{2}\right)^2}{5\sqrt{1 - \left(\frac{1}{2}\right)^2}} = \frac{41}{80\sqrt{3}}$$

Thus, $y\left(\frac{1}{2}\right) = \frac{41}{80\sqrt{3}}$, this compare with $\frac{\mu}{\lambda\sqrt{3}}$, then

$\mu = 41$ and $\lambda = 80$

$$\text{Thus, } \frac{\lambda}{\mu - 1} = \frac{80}{(41 - 1)} = \frac{80}{40} = 2$$

8. (4) Now, $\int_{-1/2}^{1/2} f(x)\, dx = \int_{-1/2}^{1/2} \frac{\frac{x^5}{5} + x^2}{\sqrt{1 - x^2}}dx$

$$= \int_{-1/2}^{1/2} \frac{x^5}{5\sqrt{1 - x^2}}dx + \int_{-1/2}^{1/2} \frac{x^2 dx}{\sqrt{1 - x^2}} \quad \text{... (i)}$$

We know that, 'x^5' is odd function and 'x^2' is even function

Thus, first part of (i) is zero

$$\text{Here, } \int_{-1/2}^{1/2} f(x)\, dx + \int_{-1/2}^{1/2} \frac{x^2 dx}{\sqrt{1 - x^2}}$$

$$= 2\int_0^{1/2} \frac{x^2}{\sqrt{1 - x^2}}dx$$

Let $x = \sin\theta \Rightarrow dx = \cos\theta\, d\theta = 2$

$$\int_0^{\pi/6} \frac{\sin^2\theta \cdot \cos\theta}{\cos\theta}d\theta$$

$$= \int_0^{\pi/6} (1 - \cos 2\theta)d\theta = \left(\frac{\pi}{6} - \frac{\sqrt{3}}{4}\right)$$

Now, $\int_{-1/2}^{1/2} f(x)dx = \left(\frac{\pi}{6} - \frac{\sqrt{3}}{4}\right)$, this is compare with $\left(\frac{\pi}{k} - \frac{\sqrt{a}}{b}\right)$

Thus, $a = 3$, $b = 4$ and $k = 6$

$$\Rightarrow \frac{b^2 + 2(a + 1)}{k} = \frac{4^2 + 2(3 + 1)}{6}$$

$$= \frac{16 + 8}{6} = \frac{24}{6} = 4$$

Sol. (Q.Nos. 9-10)

9. (3) Given, $f(x) = x^2 + ax + 3$

and $F(x) = \lim_{n \to \infty} \frac{f(x) + x^{2n}g(x)}{1 + x^{2n}}$

$$= \begin{cases} f(x), & 0 \le x^2 < 1 \\ \frac{f(x) + g(x)}{2}, & x^2 = 1 \\ g(x), & x^2 > 1 \end{cases}$$

$$= \begin{cases} g(x) & x < -1 \\ \frac{f(-1) + g(-1)}{2}, & x = -1 \\ f(x), & -1 < x < 1 \\ \frac{f(1) + g(1)}{2}, & x = 1 \\ g(x), & x > 1 \end{cases}$$

If $F(x)$ is continuous $\forall\ x \in R$, $F(x)$ must be made continuous at $x = \pm 1$.

For continuity at $x = -1$,

$f(-1) = g(-1) \Rightarrow 1 - a + 3 = b - 1$

$$\Rightarrow \quad a + b = 5 \quad \text{...(i)}$$

For continuity at $x = 1$,

$f(1) = g(1) \Rightarrow 1 + a + 3 = 1 + b$

$$\Rightarrow \quad a - b = -3 \quad \text{... (ii)}$$

Hence, $a - b + 6 = 3$

10. (8) On solving Eqs. (i) and (ii), we get

$a = 1$ and $b = 4$

So, $[a + b + \pi] = [1 + 4 + \pi] = 8$

$$\left(\begin{array}{l} \because 3 < \pi < 4 \\ \Rightarrow 3 + 5 < 5 + \pi < 4 + 5 \\ \Rightarrow 8 < 5 + \pi < 9 \end{array}\right)$$

Sol. (Q.Nos. 11-12)

11. (6720) **Vowels** O O I I E

Consonants M M S S R C N

Selection and arrangement of 2 vowels can be done in following ways

(i) Both alike; selected in 2 ways and can be arranged in 2 ways.

(ii) Both different; selected in ${}^3C_2 = 3$ ways and can be arranged in 6 ways.

Total = 8 ways

Selection and arrangement of 3 consonants can be done in following ways

(i) 2 alike + 1 different;

Selected in ${}^2C_1 \cdot {}^4C_1 = 8$ ways and arranged in $8 \times \frac{3!}{2!} = 24$ ways.

(ii) All 3 different;

Selected in ${}^5C_3 = 10$ ways and arranged in $10 \cdot 3! = 60$ ways

Total = 84 ways

Two places to fix vowels can be selected in ${}^5C_2$ ways.

Hence, number of words

$$= {}^5C_3 \cdot 8 \cdot 84 = 6720$$

12. (2880)

MM	II	OO	II

Other letters |E||R|C|N| can be arranged in 4! ways and 4 gaps out of 5 can be selected in ${}^5C_4$ ways and can be arranged in 4! ways.

$\therefore$ Total ways $= 4!\, {}^5C_4 \cdot 4!$

$= 576 \times 5 = 2880$

13. (b) Let $I(a) = \int_0^1 \frac{x^a - 1}{\ln x}dx$ $\quad$...(i)

Differentiating Eq. (i) w.r.t. 'a' keeping x as constant.

$$\frac{dI(a)}{da}=\int_0^1 \frac{d}{da}\left(\frac{x^a-1}{\ln x}\right)dx$$

$$=\int_0^1 \frac{x^a \ln x}{\ln x}dx=\int_0^1 x^a\,dx$$

$$\left(\because \frac{da^x}{dx}=a^x\cdot \ln a, \text{in usual similarly}, \frac{dx^a}{da}=x^a\cdot \ln x, \text{in this case}\right)$$

$$=\left[\frac{x^{a+1}}{a+1}\right]_0^1=\frac{1}{a+1}$$

Integrating both sides w.r.t. 'a', we get

$$I(a)=\ln(a+1)+c$$

For $a=0$, $I(0)=\ln 1+c$

$\Rightarrow\ 0=0+c \Rightarrow c=0$

$\therefore\ I=\ln(a+1)$

14. (a) Let $I(a)=\int_0^{\pi/2}\ln\left(\frac{1+a\sin x}{1-a\sin x}\right)\frac{dx}{\sin x}$

$$\Rightarrow \frac{dI}{da}=\int_0^{\pi/2}\frac{2\sin x}{1-a^2\sin^2 x}\times\frac{dx}{\sin x}$$

$$=\int_0^{\pi/2}\frac{2\sec^2 x\,dx}{1+\tan^2 x-a^2\tan^2 x}$$

(dividing by $\cos^2 x$ in numerator and denominator)

$$=\int_0^{\pi/2}\frac{2\sec^2 x\,dx}{1+(1-a^2)\tan^2 x}$$

$$=\int_0^{\infty}\frac{2dt}{1+(1-a^2)t^2} \quad (\text{putting } \tan x=t)$$

$$=\frac{2}{\sqrt{1-a^2}}[\tan^{-1}(t\sqrt{1-a^2})]_0^{\infty}$$

$$\Rightarrow \frac{dI}{da}=\frac{\pi}{\sqrt{1-a^2}}$$

Sol. (Q.Nos. 15-16)

15. (c) **16.** (d)

Given, that the three lines are

$$2x+3y-1=0 \quad \text{...(i)}$$
$$x+2y-3=0 \quad \text{...(ii)}$$
$$5x-6y-1=0 \quad \text{...(iii)}$$

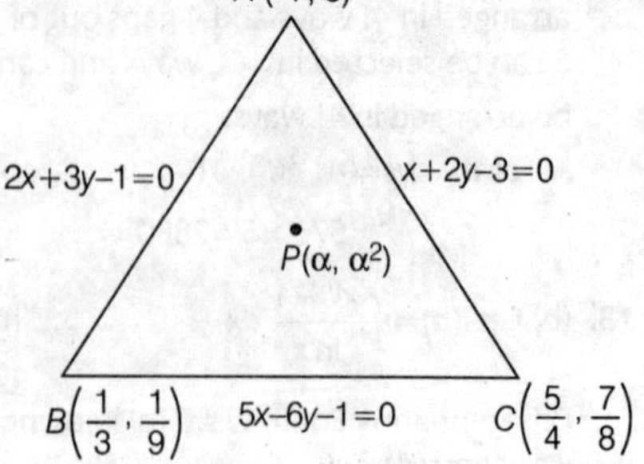

Solving Eqs. (i) and (ii), we get one vertex $A(-7,5)$.

Similarly, solving others equations, we get, vertices $B\left(\frac{1}{3},\frac{1}{9}\right)$ and $C\left(\frac{5}{4},\frac{7}{8}\right)$

Let $P(\alpha,\alpha^2)$ be a point inside the ΔABC. Since, $A(-7,5)$ and $P(\alpha,\alpha^2)$ both the point lie on the same side of the line $5x-6y-1=0$, so that $(5\cdot(-7)-6\cdot(5)-1)$ and $(5\cdot\alpha-6\cdot\alpha^2-1)$ both the point must have same sign.

So, $5\alpha-6\alpha^2-1<0$

$\Rightarrow 5\alpha-6\alpha^2-1>0$

$\Rightarrow (3\alpha-1)(2\alpha-1)>0$

$$\Rightarrow \quad \alpha<\frac{1}{3} \text{ or } \alpha>\frac{1}{2} \quad \text{... (i)}$$

Again, since, B and P both the point lie on the same side of the line $x+2y-3=0$. i.e. $\left\{\left(\frac{1}{3}\right)+\left(\frac{2}{9}\right)-3\right\}$ and $\{2\alpha^2+\alpha-3\}$ have the same sign.

$\Rightarrow 2\alpha^2+\alpha-3<0$

$\Rightarrow (2\alpha+3)(\alpha-1)<0$

$$\Rightarrow -\frac{3}{2}<\alpha<1 \quad \text{... (ii)}$$

Again also, since, $C\left(\frac{5}{4},\frac{7}{8}\right)$ and $P(\alpha,\alpha^2)$ lie on the same side of the line $2x+3y-1=0$.

i.e. $\left\{2\times\left(\frac{5}{4}\right)+3\left(\frac{7}{8}\right)-1\right\}$ and $(2\alpha+3\alpha^2-1)$ have the same sign

$\Rightarrow (3\alpha^2+2\alpha-1)>0$

$\Rightarrow (3\alpha-1)(\alpha+1)>0$

$$\Rightarrow \quad \alpha<-1 \text{ or } \alpha>\frac{1}{3} \quad \text{... (iii)}$$

Now, from Eqs. (i), (ii) and (iii), we get

$$-\frac{3}{2}<\alpha<-1 \text{ or } \frac{1}{2}<\alpha<1$$

Thus, option (c) is correct.

Since, $A(-7,5)$, $B\left(\frac{1}{3},\frac{1}{9}\right)$ and $C\left(\frac{5}{4},\frac{7}{8}\right)$ are three vertex of ΔABC.

So, Let, $(x_1,y_1)=(-7,5)$, $(x_2,y_2)=\left(\frac{1}{3},\frac{1}{9}\right)$ and $(x_3,y_3)=\left(\frac{5}{4},\frac{7}{8}\right)$

$\therefore$ Area of ΔABC

$$=\left|\frac{1}{2}\left[x_1(y_2-y_3)+x_2(y_3-y_1)+x_3(y_1-y_2)\right]\right|$$

$$=\left|\frac{1}{2}\left[(-7)\left(\frac{1}{9}-\frac{7}{8}\right)+\left(\frac{1}{3}\right)\left(\frac{7}{8}-5\right)+\frac{5}{4}\left(\frac{45-1}{9}\right)\right]\right|$$

$$=\left|\frac{1}{2}(-7)\left(\frac{8-63}{72}\right)+\frac{1}{3}\left(\frac{7-40}{8}\right)+\frac{5}{4}\left(\frac{45-1}{9}\right)\right|$$

$$=\left|\frac{1}{2}\left[\frac{385}{72}+\frac{-33}{24}+\frac{220}{36}\right]\right|$$

$$=\left|\frac{1}{2}\left[\frac{385-33\times3+220\times2}{72}\right]\right|$$

$$=\left|\frac{1}{2}\left[\frac{726}{72}\right]\right|=\left|\frac{726}{144}\right|=\frac{121}{24} \text{ sq units}$$

17. (3) Given, $\omega=e^{\frac{i\pi}{3}}$ and $x=a+b+c$,

$$y=a+b\omega+c\omega^2$$

and $\quad z=a+b\omega^2+c\omega$

Now, $|x|^2=x\bar{x}=(a+b+c)\overline{(a+b+c)}$

$=(a+b+c)(\bar{a}+\bar{b}+\bar{c})$

$=a\bar{a}+b\bar{b}+c\bar{c}+a\bar{b}+a\bar{c}+b\bar{a}+b\bar{c}+c\bar{a}+c\bar{b}$

$=|a|^2+|b|^2+|c|^2+a\bar{b}+b\bar{a}+a\bar{c}+b\bar{c}+c\bar{a}+c\bar{b}$ ... (i)

$|y|^2=(a+b\omega+c\omega^2)\overline{(a+b\omega+c\omega^2)}$

$=(a+b\omega+c\omega^2)(\bar{a}+\bar{b}\omega^2+\bar{c}\omega)$

$=|a|^2+|b|^2+|c|^2+a\bar{b}\omega^2+a\bar{c}\omega^2+b\bar{a}\omega+b\bar{c}\omega^2+c\bar{a}\omega^2+c\bar{b}\omega$ ... (ii)

and

$|z|^2=(a+b\omega^2+c\omega)\overline{(a+b\omega^2+c\omega)}$

$=(a+b\omega^2+c\omega)(\bar{a}+\bar{b}\omega+\bar{c}\omega^2)$

$=|a|^2+|b|^2+|c|^2+a\bar{b}\omega+a\bar{c}\omega^2+b\bar{a}\omega^2+b\bar{c}\omega+c\bar{a}\omega+c\bar{b}\omega^2$ ... (iii)

Now, adding Eqs. (i), (ii) and (iii), we get

$|x|^2+|y|^2+|z|^2=3|a|^2+3|b|^2+3|c|^2+a\bar{b}(1+\omega+\omega^2)+a\bar{c}(1+\omega+\omega^2)+b\bar{a}(1+\omega+\omega^2)+b\bar{c}(1+\omega+\omega^2)+c\bar{a}(1+\omega+\omega^2)+c\bar{b}(1+\omega+\omega^2)$ ... (iv)

Since, $\omega^3=1\Rightarrow 1+\omega+\omega^2=0$

So, from Eq. (iv), we get

$|x|^2+|y|^2+|z|^2=3|a|^2+3|b|^2+3|c|^2$

$$\Rightarrow \frac{|x|^2+|y|^2+|z|^2}{|a|^2+|b|^2+|c|^2}=3$$

18. (257) Since, $(1+x)^n = \sum_{r=0}^{n} C_r x^r$

$\therefore \quad x(1+x)^n = \sum_{r=0}^{n} C_r x^{r+1}$

On differentiating both sides w.r.t., we get

$(1+x)^{n-1}(1+x+nx) = \sum_{r=0}^{n}(r+1)C_r x^r$

Again multiplying both sides by x, we get

$(1+x)^{n-1}(x+x^2+nx^2)$

$= \sum_{r=0}^{n}(r+1)C_r \cdot x^{r+1}$

Again, differentiating both sides w.r.t. x, we get

$(1+x)^{n-2}[(1+x)(1+2x+2nx) + (n-1)(x+x^2+nx^2)]$

$= \sum_{r=0}^{n}(r+1)^2 C_r x^r$

Putting $x=1$ both sides, then we have

$\sum_{r=0}^{n}(r+1)^2 C_r = 2^{n-2}(n^2+5n+4)$

$\therefore \quad f(n) = n^2+5n+4$

Then, $f(x) = x^2+5x+4 = (x+1)(x+4)$

$\therefore \quad \alpha = -1$ and $\beta = -4$

Hence, $\alpha^4+\beta^4 = (-1)^4+(-4)^4$

$= 1+256 = 257$

19. (2) Let $\tan^{-1}x = A$, $\tan^{-1}y = B$ and $\tan^{-1}z = c$

Also, $\tan^{-1}x+\tan^{-1}y+\tan^{-1}z = \frac{\pi}{4}$

and $\quad x+y+z=1 \quad$ (given)

$\therefore \quad \tan(A+B+C)=1$

$\Rightarrow \quad \frac{x+y+z-xyz}{1-xy-yz-zx} = 1$

$\Rightarrow x+y+z-xyz = 1-xy-yz-zx$

$\Rightarrow \quad 1-xyz = 1-xy-yz-zx$

$\Rightarrow \quad xyz = xy+yz+zx$

$\Rightarrow xyz-xy-yz-zx+x+y+z=1$

(as $x+y+z-1=0$)

$\Rightarrow (x-1)(y-1)(z-1)=0$

If $x=1$, then $y+z=0$

as $\quad x+y+z-1=0$

$\therefore x^3+y^3+z^3-3 = (1)^3+y^3-y^3-3$

$= 1-3 = -2$

$\Rightarrow |x^3+y^3+z^3-3| = |-2| = 2$

Knockout 15

Paper-1

1. (d) Let us consider the diagonal AC and an adjacent parallel line PQ. Length of the line $PQ = RS$

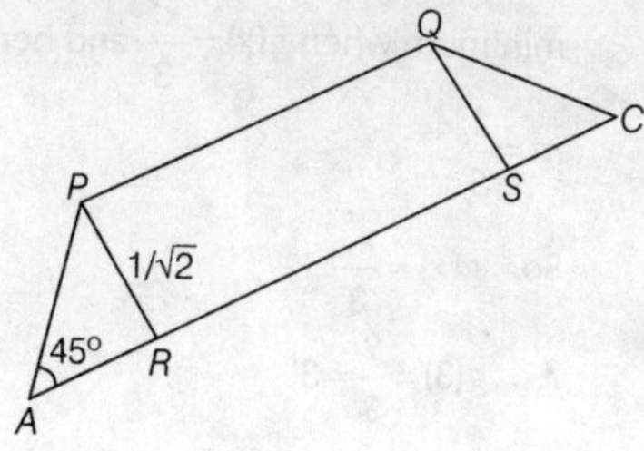

$AC-(AR+SC) = AC-2AR$

$[\because AR = SC]$

$= AC-2PR$

$[\because \angle PAR = 45°; \therefore AR = PR]$

$= n\sqrt{2} - 2.\frac{1}{\sqrt{2}} = n\sqrt{2}-\sqrt{2}$

$-(n-1)\sqrt{2}$ cm

Length of line adjacent to PQ, other than AC, will be

$((n-1)-1)\sqrt{2} = (n-2)\sqrt{2}$ cm

Therefore, sum of the lengths of all possible line segments and the diagonal $= 2\times[n\sqrt{2}+(n-1)\sqrt{2} + (n-2)\sqrt{2}+\ldots+2]$

$\underbrace{-n\sqrt{2}}$ $\quad, n \in N$

(because there is only one diagonal)

$= 2\times\sqrt{2}[n+(n-1) + (n-2)+\ldots+1] - n\sqrt{2}$

$= 2\sqrt{2}\times\frac{n(n+1)}{2} - n\sqrt{2}$

$= n\sqrt{2}\,[n+1-1]$

$= n^2(\sqrt{2})$ cm

2. (c) Given, $y = \int_0^x f(t)\sin\{k(x-t)\}dt$

$\Rightarrow \quad y = \text{Im}\int_0^x f(t)\cdot e^{ik(x-t)}dt$

$[\because e^{ik(x-t)} = \cos\{k(x-t)\} + i\sin\{k(x-t)\}]$

$\therefore \text{Im}(e^{ik(x-t)} = \sin\{k(x-t)\}]$

$\Rightarrow \quad y = \text{Im}\left\{e^{ikx}\int_0^x f(t)\cdot e^{-ikt}\,dt\right\} \quad$ ...(i)

$\therefore \frac{dy}{dx} = \text{Im}\{e^{ikx}\cdot f(x)e^{-ikx} + \int_0^x f(t)e^{-ikt}dt \times ik\cdot e^{ikx}\}$

$= 0+\text{Im}\left\{ik\cdot e^{ikx}\int_0^x f(t)e^{-ikt}dt\right\}$

Now, $\frac{d^2y}{dx^2} = \text{Im}$

$\left\{\begin{matrix} ik(e^{ikx}\cdot f(x)\cdot e^{-ikx} \\ +\int_0^x f(t)\cdot e^{-ikt}dt\times ike^{ikx}\end{matrix}\right\}$

$= kf(x)-k^2y$

[using Eq. (i) and $i^2 = -1$]

$\therefore \quad \frac{d^2y}{dx^2}+k^2y = k\cdot f(x)$

3. (c) Given, $\alpha(x^2-x)-\beta(x^2+1) + (x^2+x+2) = 0 \;\forall\, x \in R$

$\Rightarrow (\alpha-\beta+1)x^2-(\alpha-1)x-(\beta-\alpha) = 0 \;\forall\, x \in R \quad$ ...(i)

This is identity of x,

Thus, $\alpha-\beta+1=0, \alpha-1=0$ and $\beta-2=0$

Then, solving above equations, we get

$\alpha = 1$ and $\beta = 2$

Also, given that, $\frac{3x}{a}-\frac{4y}{b}+\frac{6}{c} = 0$ ... (ii)

and $\quad \frac{1}{a}-\frac{2}{b}+\frac{1}{c} = 0$ ... (iii)

Comparing Eqs. (ii) and (iii), we get

$\frac{3x}{1} = \frac{4y}{2} = \frac{6}{1}$

$\Rightarrow \quad x=2$ and $y=3$

Thus, $(p, q) = (2, 3)$

$\therefore$ Centriod $\left(\frac{h+3}{3}, \frac{k+5}{3}\right)$ of ΔABC lies on the line $3x-6y+2=0$

So, $3\left(\frac{h+3}{3}\right) - 6\left(\frac{k+5}{3}\right)+2=0$

$\Rightarrow \quad (h+3)-2(k+5)+2=0$

$\Rightarrow \quad h-2k=5$

Thus, locus of $C(h,k)$ is

$x-2y=5$

4. (b) Given, α and β are the roots of $x^2-x+p=0$ and r, δ are the roots of $x^2-4x+9=0$

So, $\alpha+\beta=1$, $\alpha\beta=p$, $\gamma+\delta=4$ and $\gamma\delta=q$

Also, α, β, γ and δ are in GP

So, $\quad \frac{\beta}{\alpha} = \frac{\delta}{r} \Rightarrow \frac{\beta+\alpha}{\beta-\alpha} = \frac{\delta+\gamma}{\delta-\gamma}$

[using componendo and dividendo]

$$\Rightarrow \frac{(\beta+\alpha)^2}{(\beta+\alpha)^2-4\alpha\beta}=\frac{(\delta+\gamma)^2}{(\delta+\gamma)^2-4\delta\gamma}$$

$$\Rightarrow \frac{1}{1-4p}+\frac{16}{16-4q}=\frac{4}{4-q}$$

$$\Rightarrow \quad 4-q=4-16p \Rightarrow q=16p$$

Now, $\qquad p\geq 2 \qquad$ ...(i)

$\therefore \qquad q\geq 32 \qquad$ ...(ii)

For the given equation $ax^2+bx+c=0$ to have real roots,

$$D\geq 0 \Rightarrow b^2-4ac\geq 0$$

$$\Rightarrow 4ac\leq b^2 \Rightarrow ac\leq \frac{b^2}{4}$$

For total number of possible pairs (a, c), see the table given in next page

$\frac{b^2}{4}$	Possible values of (ac) such that $ac\leq\frac{b^2}{4}$	Number of possible pairs (a, c)	Value of ac	Possible pairs (a, c)
			1	(1, 1)
1	1	1	2	(1, 2), (2, 1)
2.25	1, 2	3	3	(1, 3), (3, 1)
4	1, 2, 3, 4	8	4	(1, 4), (4, 1), (2, 2)
6.25	1, 2, 3, 4, 5, 6	12	5	(1, 5), (5, 1)
			6	(2, 3), (3, 2)
		Total = 24		

Hence, number of quadratic equation with real roots,

$$r=24 \qquad \text{...(iii)}$$

Now, from Eqs. (i), (ii) and (iii), the minimum value of pqr

$$=2\times 32\times 24=1536$$

Sol. (Q.Nos. 5-6)

5. (3) $f(x)=\begin{vmatrix}5 & 7 & 3\\ 2 & 9g^2(x) & 2x^2\\ x & 3g(x)-x^2 & 1\end{vmatrix}$

$$-\begin{vmatrix}4 & 5 & 2\\ 2 & 9g^2(x) & 2x^2\\ x & 3g(x)-x^2 & 1\end{vmatrix}+\begin{vmatrix}0 & -2 & -1\\ 2 & 9g^2(x) & 2x^2\\ x & 3g(x)-x^2 & 1\end{vmatrix}$$

$$\Rightarrow f(x)=\begin{vmatrix}1 & 0 & 0\\ 2 & 9g^2(x) & 2x^2\\ x & 3g(x)-x^2 & 1\end{vmatrix}$$

$$\Rightarrow f(x)=9g^2(x)-6x^2g(x)+2x^4$$

$$m=\int_0^1[\{3g(x)-x^2\}^2+x^4]\,dx$$

$$=\int_0^1\{3g(x)-x^2\}^2\,dx+\frac{1}{5} \text{ is}$$

minimum when $g(x)=\frac{x^2}{3}$ and hence

$$m=\frac{1}{5}$$

So, $\quad g(x)=\frac{x^2}{3}$

$\therefore \quad g(3)=\frac{9}{3}=3$

6. (0) $\phi(x)=\int_0^x\left(\int_0^t\frac{y^2}{3}dy-(e^t-e^{-t})\right)dt$

$$=\int_0^x\left\{\frac{t^3}{9}-e^t+e^{-t}\right\}dt$$

$$\Rightarrow \qquad \phi'(x)=\frac{x^3}{9}-e^x+e^{-x}$$

(using Newton-Leibnitz Rule)

$$\Rightarrow \qquad \phi''(x)=\frac{x^2}{3}-e^x-e^{-x}$$

According to the question, putting $\phi''(x)=0$, we get

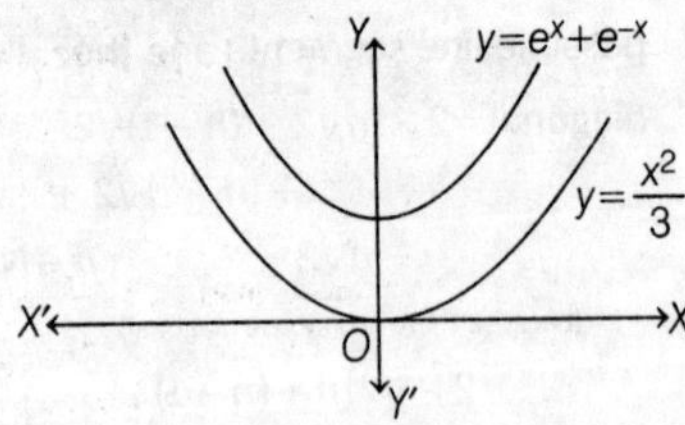

$$\frac{x^2}{3}=e^x+e^{-x}$$

$\Rightarrow$ No solution

Hence, number of point of inflection is 0.

Sol. (Q.Nos. 7-8)

7. (1.5) Obviously, $\angle P=90^\circ$ and

$\angle POR=\frac{x}{2}$ and $OP=1$

In ΔOPR, $\tan\frac{x}{2}=\frac{PR}{1}$

$$\Rightarrow PR=\tan\left(\frac{x}{2}\right)=RQ$$

[$\because$ length of tangents from a point outside the circle are equal]

and $\angle PRQ=\pi-x$

$\therefore \qquad T(x)=\frac{1}{2}\cdot RP\cdot RQ\sin(\pi-x)$

$$\left[\because \Delta=\frac{1}{2}ab\sin C\right]$$

$$=\frac{1}{2}\tan^2\left(\frac{x}{2}\right)\sin x$$

$$=\frac{1}{2}(\sec^2(x/2)-1)\cdot\sin x$$

$$=\tan\left(\frac{x}{2}\right)-\frac{\sin x}{2}$$

and $\quad S(x)=$ Area of sector OPQ $-$ Area of ΔOPQ

$$=\frac{1}{2}(1)^2\cdot x-\frac{1}{2}(1)^2\sin x=\frac{x-\sin x}{2}$$

Now, $\lim\limits_{x\to 0}\frac{T(x)}{S(x)}=\lim\limits_{x\to 0}\frac{\tan\left(\frac{x}{2}\right)-\frac{\sin x}{2}}{\left(\frac{x-\sin x}{2}\right)}$

$$=\lim_{x\to 0}\frac{\tan^2\left(\frac{x}{2}\right)\cdot\sin x}{(x-\sin x)}$$

$$=\lim_{x\to 0}\frac{\left[\frac{\tan\left(\frac{x}{2}\right)}{(x/2)}\right]^2\left(\frac{\sin x}{x}\right)}{\left(\frac{x-\sin x}{x^3}\right)}\times\frac{1}{4}$$

$$=\frac{(1)^2\cdot 1}{4\times\frac{1}{6}}=\frac{3}{2}=1.5$$

$$\left(\because \lim_{x\to 0}\frac{x-\sin x}{x^3}=\frac{1}{6} \text{ by using } L\text{-Hospital rule}\right)$$

8. (11) Also, $\frac{x}{2}-S(x)=T(x)$

$$\Rightarrow \frac{x}{2}-\left(\frac{x-\sin x}{2}\right)=\tan\left(\frac{x}{2}\right)-\frac{\sin x}{2}$$

$$\Rightarrow \sin x=\tan\left(\frac{x}{2}\right)$$

$$\Rightarrow \frac{2\tan\left(\frac{x}{2}\right)}{1+\tan^2\left(\frac{x}{2}\right)}=\tan\left(\frac{x}{2}\right)$$

$$\Rightarrow 2=1+\tan^2\left(\frac{x}{2}\right) \qquad \left[\because \tan\frac{x}{2}\neq 0\right]$$

$$\Rightarrow \tan^2\left(\frac{x}{2}\right)=1\Rightarrow\tan\left(\frac{x}{2}\right)=1$$

$$\Rightarrow \qquad \frac{x}{2}=\frac{\pi}{4}\Rightarrow x=\frac{\pi}{2}$$

So, $\alpha=\frac{\pi}{2}$

Hence,

$$[\alpha]+10=\left[\frac{\pi}{2}\right]+10=1+10=11$$

$$\left[\because 3<\pi<4\Rightarrow\frac{3}{2}<\frac{\pi}{2}<\frac{4}{2}\right]$$

Sol. (Q.Nos. 9-10)

9. (0.5) Given that, the equation $\sqrt{3}\, a\cos x + 2b\sin x = c$ has two distinct roots α and β, such that

$$\sqrt{3}\, a\cos\alpha + 2b\sin\alpha = c$$

$$\Rightarrow \sqrt{3}\cos\alpha + \frac{+2b}{a}\sin\alpha = \frac{c}{a} \quad \text{... (i)}$$

and $\sqrt{3}a\cos\beta + 2b\sin\beta = c$

$$\Rightarrow \sqrt{3}\cos\beta + \frac{2b}{a}\sin\beta = \frac{c}{a} \quad \text{...(ii)}$$

Now, substracting Eq. (ii) from Eq. (i), we get

$$\sqrt{3}(\cos\alpha - \cos\beta) + \frac{2b}{a}(\sin\alpha - \sin\beta) = 0$$

$$\Rightarrow \sqrt{3}\left[-2\sin\left(\frac{\alpha+\beta}{2}\right)\cdot\sin\left(\frac{\alpha-\beta}{2}\right)\right] + \frac{2b}{a}\left[2\cos\left(\frac{\alpha+\beta}{2}\right)\sin\left(\frac{\alpha-\beta}{2}\right)\right] = 0$$

$$\Rightarrow -\sqrt{3}\left[2\cdot\sin\left(\frac{\pi}{6}\right)\cdot\sin\left(\frac{\alpha-\beta}{2}\right)\right] + \frac{2b}{a}\left[2\cos\left(\frac{\pi}{6}\right)\cdot\sin\left(\frac{\alpha-\beta}{2}\right)\right] = 0$$

$$\left[\text{since, } \alpha+\beta = \frac{\pi}{3} \text{ given}\right]$$

$$= -\sqrt{3}\left[2\cdot\frac{1}{2}\cdot\sin\left(\frac{\alpha-\beta}{2}\right)\right] + \frac{2b}{a}\left[2\cdot\frac{\sqrt{3}}{2}\cdot\sin\left(\frac{\alpha-\beta}{2}\right)\right] = 0$$

$$\Rightarrow \sin\left(\frac{\alpha-\beta}{2}\right)\left[\frac{2b\sqrt{3}}{a} - \sqrt{3}\right] = 0 \quad \text{...(iii)}$$

Now, if $\sin\left(\frac{\alpha-\beta}{2}\right) = 0$, then $\alpha = \beta$, but this is impossible case. So, from Eq. (iii) we clearly see that

$$\left(\frac{2b\sqrt{3}}{a} - \sqrt{3}\right) = 0 \Rightarrow 2b = a \Rightarrow \frac{b}{a} = \frac{1}{2} = 0.5$$

Thus, the value of $\frac{b}{a}$ is 0.5.

10. (5) Now, $\left(\frac{a}{2b}\right)^2 + \cos^3\left(\frac{\alpha+\beta}{2}\right)$

$$= (1)^2 + \cos^3\left(\frac{\pi}{6}\right) \quad \left[\text{since, } \alpha+\beta = \frac{\pi}{3}\right]$$

$$= 1^2 + \left(\frac{\sqrt{3}}{2}\right)^3 = 1 + \frac{3\sqrt{3}}{8}$$

This compare with $q + \frac{3\sqrt{p}}{8}$, then

$$p = 3 \text{ and } q = 1$$

$$\Rightarrow \sqrt{p^2 + 16q^2} = \sqrt{3^2 + 16(1)^2}$$

$$= \sqrt{9+16} = \sqrt{25} = 5$$

11. (a), (b)

Given, $|a| = |b| = |c| = 1$, $\angle POQ = \theta$ and $|z_1| = 1$

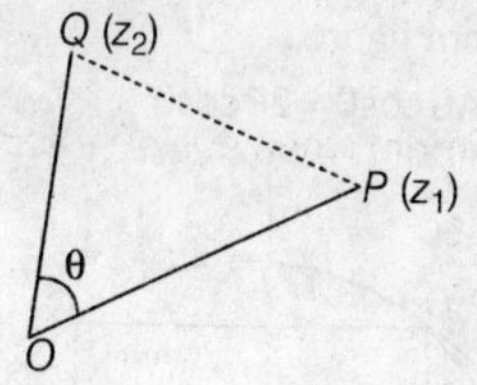

Also given z_1, z_2 are the roots of the equation $az^2 + bz + c = 0$. Then,

$$|z_1 z_2| = \left|\frac{c}{a}\right| = 1 \quad \text{...(i)}$$

and $$|z_1 + z_2| = \left|\frac{-b}{a}\right| = 1 \quad \text{...(ii)}$$

From Eq. (i), $|z_1||z_1| = 1 \Rightarrow |z_2| = 1$

$$(\because |z_1| = 1) \quad \text{...(iii)}$$

Now, $(z_1 + z_2)\overline{(z_1 + z_2)} = |z_1 + z_2|^2$

$$\Rightarrow (z_1 + z_2)(\bar{z}_1 + \bar{z}_2) = (1)^2$$

[from Eq. (ii)]

$$\Rightarrow z_1\bar{z}_1 + z_2\bar{z}_2 + z_1\bar{z}_2 + z_2\bar{z}_1 = 1$$

$$\Rightarrow |z_1|^2 + |z_2|^2 + z_1\bar{z}_2 + \bar{z}_1 z_2 = 1$$

$$\Rightarrow 2 + z_1\bar{z}_2 + \bar{z}_1 z_2 = 1 \quad [\because |z_1| = |z_2| = 1]$$

$$\Rightarrow 2 + \frac{z_2}{z_1} + \frac{z_1}{z_2} = 1$$

$$\left[\because \bar{z}_1 = \frac{1}{z_1} \text{ and } \bar{z}_2 = \frac{1}{z_2} \text{ with } |z_1| = |z_2| = 1\right]$$

$$\Rightarrow \frac{(z_1 + z_2)^2}{z_1 z_2} = 1 \Rightarrow (z_1 + z_2)^2 = z_1 z_2$$

$$\Rightarrow \frac{b^2}{a^2} = \frac{c}{a} \Rightarrow b^2 = ac$$

Now, $z_2 = z_1 e^{i\theta}$

$$\Rightarrow z_2 + z_1 = z_1 + z_1 e^{i\theta} = z_1(1 + e^{i\theta})$$

$$\Rightarrow |z_1 + z_2| = |z_1||1 + e^{i\theta}|$$

$$= (1) \times |1 + \cos\theta + i\sin\theta|$$

$$\Rightarrow |z_1 + z_2| = \left|2\cos^2\frac{\theta}{2} + i\left(2\sin\frac{\theta}{2}\cos\frac{\theta}{2}\right)\right|$$

$$\Rightarrow 2\cos\frac{\theta}{2}\left|\cos\frac{\theta}{2} + i\sin\frac{\theta}{2}\right| = 1$$

$$(\because |z_1 + z_2| = 1)$$

$$\Rightarrow 2\cos\frac{\theta}{2} = 1 \Rightarrow \cos\frac{\theta}{2} = \frac{1}{2} \Rightarrow \frac{\theta}{2} = \frac{\pi}{3}$$

$$\Rightarrow \theta = \frac{2\pi}{3}$$

Now, $PQ = |z_2 - z_1| = |z_1 e^{i\theta} - z_1|$

$$= |z_1||e^{i\theta} - 1|$$

$$= (1)|\cos\theta + i\sin\theta - 1|$$

$$= \left|1 - 2\sin^2\frac{\theta}{2} + i\left(2\sin\frac{\theta}{2}\cdot\cos\frac{\theta}{2}\right) - 1\right|$$

$$= \left|2\sin\frac{\theta}{2}\right|\left|-\sin\frac{\theta}{2} + i\cos\frac{\theta}{2}\right|$$

$$= \left|2\sin\frac{\theta}{2}\right|\sqrt{\sin^2\frac{\theta}{2} + \cos^2\frac{\theta}{2}}$$

$$\Rightarrow PQ = |z_2 - z_1| = \left|2\sin\frac{\theta}{2}\right| = \left|2\sin\left(\frac{\frac{2\pi}{3}}{2}\right)\right|$$

$$= \left|2\sin\frac{\pi}{3}\right|$$

$$\Rightarrow PQ = |z_2 - z_1| = \sqrt{3}$$

12. (a) Given that,

Equation of the hyperbola is

$$\frac{x^2}{4} - \frac{y^2}{5} = 1$$

Meets X-axis and Y-axis at A and B respectively. We know that the whose extremity latusrectum of the hyperbola

$$\frac{x^2}{4} - \frac{y^2}{5} = 1 \text{ is } P\left(ae, \frac{b^2}{a}\right)$$

where,

$$e = \sqrt{1 + \frac{b^2}{a^2}} = \sqrt{1 + \frac{5}{4}} = \sqrt{\frac{9}{4}} = \frac{3}{2}$$

Given that $a = 2$ and $b = \sqrt{5}$

Thus, $P \equiv \left(2\cdot\frac{3}{2}, \frac{(\sqrt{5})^2}{2}\right) = \left(3, \frac{5}{2}\right)$

Now, tangent equation of the hyperbola $\frac{x^2}{4} - \frac{y^2}{5} = 1$ is

$$\frac{xx_1}{4} - \frac{yy_1}{5} = 1.$$

Since, tangent at an extremity of latusrectum is $\frac{3x}{4} - \frac{5/2y}{5} = 1$

$$\Rightarrow \frac{3x}{4} - \frac{y}{2} = 1$$

Since, tangent of hyperbola meet X-axis and Y-axis at A and B, respectively.

Thus, the coordinates of A is $\left(\frac{4}{3}, 0\right)$ and coordinate of B is $(6, -2)$ and co-ordinate of $O(0, 0)$.

So, $(OA)^2 - (OB)^2 = \left(\frac{4}{3}\right)^2 - (2)^2$

$$= \frac{16}{9} - 4 = \frac{16 - 36}{9}$$

$$= -\frac{20}{9}$$

13. (d) The required line passing through the point $P(2, 1, 1)$ in the plane $2x + y - 5z = 0$ and is having greatest slope, so it must be perpendicular to the line of intersection of the planes

$$2x + y - 5z = 0 \quad \text{...(i)}$$

and $$4x - 3y + 7z = 0 \quad \text{...(ii)}$$

Let the direction ratios of the line of intersection of Eqs. (i) and (ii) are a, b, c

$\Rightarrow \quad 2a + b - 5c = 0 \quad$ ...(iii)

and $\quad 4a - 3b + 7c = 0 \quad$ ...(iv)

(as direction ratios of straight line (a, b, c) is perpendicular to direction ratios of normal to both the planes)

On solving Eqs. (iii) and (iv), we get

$$\frac{a}{4} = \frac{b}{17} = \frac{c}{5}$$

Now, let the direction ratio of required line be proportional to l, m, n, then its equation be

$$\frac{x-2}{l} = \frac{y-1}{m} = \frac{z-1}{n}$$

where, $2l + m - 5n = 0 \quad$ ...(v)

and $4l + 17m + 5n = 0 \quad$ ...(vi)

On solving Eqs. (v) and (vi), we get

$$\frac{l}{3} = \frac{m}{-1} = \frac{n}{1}$$

Thus, the required line is

$$\frac{x-2}{3} = \frac{y-1}{-1} = \frac{z-1}{1}.$$

14. (a), (b), (c), (d)

To check option (a),

Fixing 246 in the first 3 places, we can fill the remaining 6 places in 6^6 ways.

Hence, probability $= \dfrac{6^6}{6^9} = \dfrac{1}{6^3}$

To check option (b),

Same as option (a), fix number 135 in the end and fill the remaining 6 places in 6^6 ways.

$\therefore \quad P = \dfrac{6^6}{6^9} = \dfrac{1}{6^3}$

To check option (c),

Fix 246 and 135 at respective places. Now, fill the remaining 3 places in 6^3 ways.

$\therefore \quad P = \dfrac{6^3}{6^9} = \dfrac{1}{6^6}$

To check option (d),

Begin with 246 or end with 135

$$P(E \cup F) = P(E) + P(F) - P(E \cap F)$$
$$= \frac{1}{6^3} + \frac{1}{6^3} - \frac{1}{6^6} = \frac{431}{6^6}$$

15. (a) From figure,

$AD = AB\cos\theta = 2R\cos\theta$

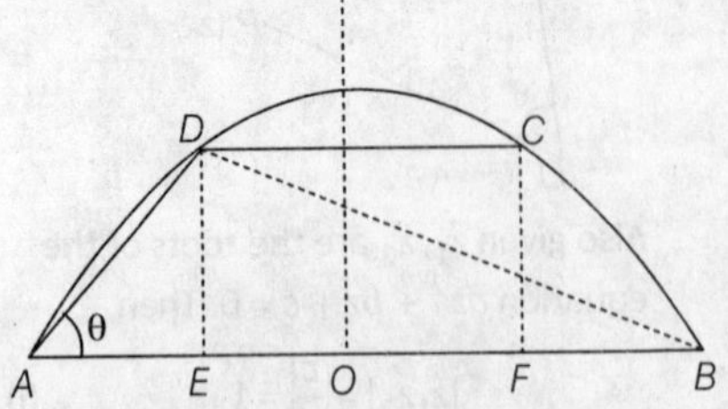

$AE = AD\cos\theta = 2R\cos^2\theta$

or $EF = AB - 2AE = 2R - 4R\cos^2\theta$

$DE = AD\sin\theta = 2R\sin\theta \cdot \cos\theta$

Thus, area of trapezium,

$$S = \frac{1}{2}(AB + CD) \times DE$$

$$\Rightarrow S = \frac{1}{2}(2R + 2R - 4R\cos^2\theta) \times 2R\sin\theta \cdot \cos\theta$$

$$\Rightarrow S = 4R^2\sin^3\theta \cdot \cos\theta$$

$$\therefore \frac{dS}{d\theta} = 12R^2\sin^2\theta \cdot \cos^2\theta - 4R^2\sin^4\theta$$
$$= 4R^2\sin^2\theta(3\cos^2\theta - \sin^2\theta)$$

For maximum area, $\dfrac{dS}{d\theta} = 0$

$\Rightarrow \tan^2\theta = 3 \Rightarrow \tan\theta = \sqrt{3} \quad (\because \theta$ is acute)

$\therefore \quad S_{\max} = \dfrac{3\sqrt{3}}{4}R^2$

16. (a), (c)

$$\mathbf{a} \times (\mathbf{b} \times \mathbf{c}) + (\mathbf{a} \cdot \mathbf{b})\mathbf{b} = (4 - 2x - \sin y)\mathbf{b} + (x^2 - 1)\mathbf{c}$$

or $(\mathbf{a} \cdot \mathbf{c})\mathbf{b} - (\mathbf{a} \cdot \mathbf{b})\mathbf{c} + (\mathbf{a} \cdot \mathbf{b})\mathbf{b}$
$= (4 - 2x - \sin y)\mathbf{b} + (x^2 - 1)\mathbf{c} \quad$ ...(i)

Also, given $(\mathbf{c} \cdot \mathbf{c})\mathbf{a} = \mathbf{c}$. Therefore, $(\mathbf{c} \cdot \mathbf{c})(\mathbf{a} \cdot \mathbf{c}) = (\mathbf{c} \cdot \mathbf{c})$ or $\mathbf{a} \cdot \mathbf{c} = 1$

From Eq. (i),

$1 + \mathbf{a} \cdot \mathbf{b} = 4 - 2x - \sin y \quad$ ...(ii)

and $\quad x^2 - 1 = -(\mathbf{a} \cdot \mathbf{b}) \quad$ ...(iii)

From Eqs. (ii) and (iii), we get

$$1 = 4 - 2x - \sin y + x^2 - 1$$

$\Rightarrow \sin y = x^2 - 2x + 2 = (x-1)^2 + 1$

But $\sin y \le 1$

$\Rightarrow \quad x = 1, \sin y = 1$

$\Rightarrow \quad y = (4n+1)\dfrac{\pi}{2}, n \in I$

17. (5) Let $(4\cos\theta + 4, 3\sin\theta + 3)$ be any point on the ellipse

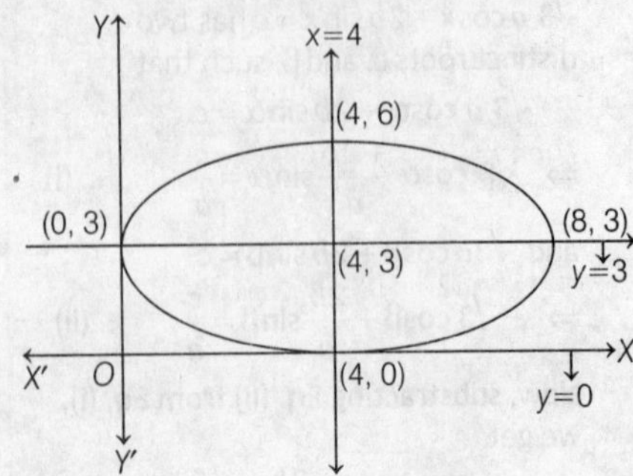

$$\frac{(x-4)^2}{16} + \frac{(y-3)^2}{9} = 1$$

Image of $(4\cos\theta + 4, 3\sin\theta + 3)$ about the line $x - y - 2 = 0$ is (h, k) then

$$\frac{h - 4\cos\theta - 4}{1} = \frac{k - 3\sin\theta - 3}{-1}$$
$$= -\frac{2(4\cos\theta - 3\sin\theta - 1)}{2}$$

$\Rightarrow h = 3\sin\theta + 5$ and $k = 4\cos\theta + 2$

Locus of (h, k) is

$$\left(\frac{x-5}{3}\right)^2 + \left(\frac{y-2}{4}\right)^2 = 1$$

$\Rightarrow \quad 16x^2 + 9y^2 - 160x - 36y + 292 = 0$

$\Rightarrow \quad k_1 + k_2 = 25$

Hence, $\dfrac{k_1 + k_2}{5} = \dfrac{25}{5} = 5$

18. (91) Number of ways of selecting n coupons consisting of C or A $= 2^n$

($\because$ the word CAT cannot be written. if atleast one letter is not selected).

Now, number of ways of selecting n coupons bearing only A $= 1^n$.

$\therefore$ Total number of ways

$$= 2^n + 2^n + 2^n - 1^n - 1^n - 1^n$$
$$= 3(2^n - 1)$$

Given, $3(2^n - 1) = 189$

$\Rightarrow \quad 2^n - 1 = 63$

$\Rightarrow \quad 2^n = 64$

$\Rightarrow \quad n = 6$

Then, $\Sigma n^2 = \dfrac{n(n+1)(2n+1)}{6}$

$$= \frac{6 \cdot 7 \cdot 13}{6}$$
$$= 91$$

19. (0)

We have, $J=\int_{-5}^{-4}(3-x^2)\tan(3-x^2)dx$

Put $x+5=t$, then

$$J=\int_0^1\{3-(t-5)^2\}\tan\{3-(t-5)^2\}\,dt$$

$$\Rightarrow J=\int_0^1(-22+10t-t^2)\tan(-22+10t-t^2)\,dt \quad \text{...(i)}$$

Now,

$$K=\int_{-2}^{-1}(6-6x+x^2)\tan(6x-x^2-6)\,dx$$

Put $(x+2)=z$, then

$$K=\int_0^1\{6-6(z-2)+(z-2)^2\}\tan\{6(z-2)-(z-2)^2-6\}\,dz$$

$$\Rightarrow k=\int_0^1(22-10z+z^2)\tan(-22+10z-z^2)\,dz \quad \text{...(ii)}$$

From Eqs. (i) and (ii), we get

$$J+K=0$$

Paper 2

1. (a), (d)

Given, p,q,r,s are in AP.

Let $d=$ common difference of an AP.

So, $p=$ first term $=p$

$q=$ second term $=p+d$

$r=$ third term $=p+2d$

and $s=$ fourth term $=p+3d$

Now,

$$F(x)=\begin{vmatrix}p+\sin x & p+\sin x+d & p-(p+2d)+\sin x\\ p+\sin x+d & p+\sin x+2d & -1+\sin x\\ p+\sin x+2d & p+\sin x+3d & (p+3d)-(p+d)+\sin x\end{vmatrix}$$

Applying $R_1\to R_1-R_2, R_2\to R_2-R_3$, we get

$$F(x)=\begin{vmatrix}-d & -d & -2d+1\\ -d & -d & -(2d+1)\\ p+2d+\sin x & p+3d+\sin x & 2d+\sin x\end{vmatrix}$$

Applying $R_1\to R_1-R_2$, we get

$$F(x)=2\begin{vmatrix}-d & -d\\ p+2d+\sin x & p+3d+\sin x\end{vmatrix}$$

$$=-2d\begin{vmatrix}1 & 1\\ p+2d+\sin x & p+3d+\sin x\end{vmatrix}$$

$$\Rightarrow \quad F(x)=-2d^2$$

Given, $\int_0^2 F(x)dx=-4$

$$\Rightarrow \int_0^2(-2d^2)\,dx=-4\Rightarrow \int_0^2 d^2dx=2$$

$$\Rightarrow \quad 2d^2=2$$

$$\Rightarrow \quad d^2=1\Rightarrow d=\pm 1$$

2. (a), (c), (d)

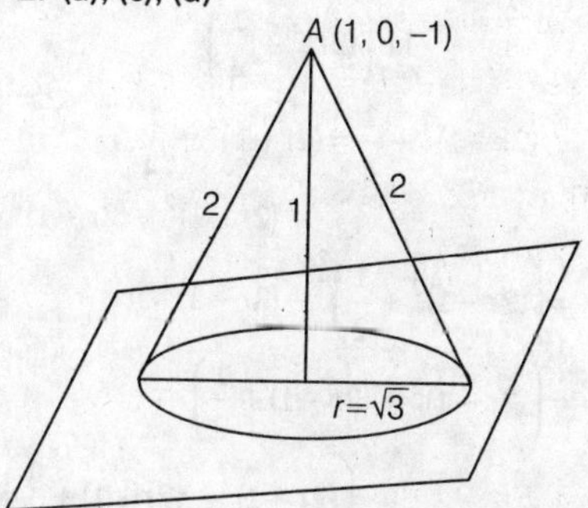

The rod sweeps out the figure which is a cone. The distance of point $A(1,0,-1)$ from the plane is $\frac{|1-2+4|}{\sqrt{9}}=1$ unit

The slant height l of the cone is 2 units.

Then, the radius of the base of the cone is $\sqrt{l^2-1}=\sqrt{4-1}=\sqrt{3}$

Hence, the volume of the cone is $\frac{\pi}{3}(\sqrt{3})^2\cdot 1=\pi$ cubic units. Area of the circle on the plane which the rod traces is 3π. Also, the centre of the circle is $Q(x,y,z)$. Then,

$$\frac{x-1}{1}=\frac{y-0}{-2}=\frac{z+1}{2}=\frac{-(1-0-2+4)}{(1)^2+(-2)^2+(2)^2}$$

$$\Rightarrow Q(x,y,z)=\left(\frac{2}{3},\frac{2}{3},\frac{-5}{3}\right)$$

3. (a), (c)

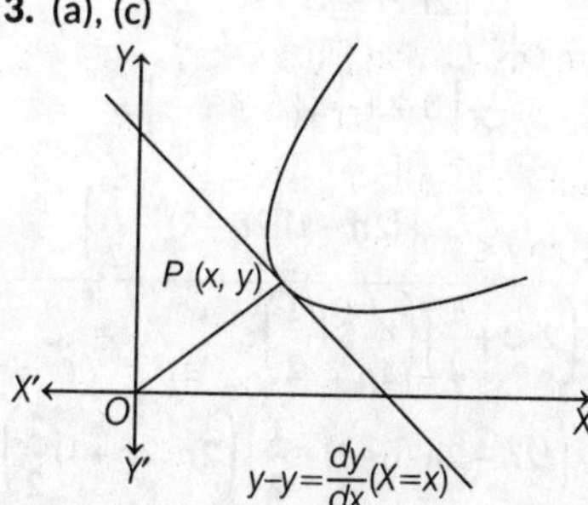

Equation of tangent is

$$X\frac{dy}{dx}-Y-x\frac{dy}{dx}+y=0$$

Perpendicular distance from origin $(0,0)=x$ (given)

$$\Rightarrow \left|\frac{0-0-x\frac{dy}{dx}+y}{\sqrt{\left(\frac{dy}{dx}\right)^2+1}}\right|=x$$

$$\Rightarrow \left|\frac{x\frac{dy}{dx}-y}{\sqrt{\left(\frac{dy}{dx}\right)^2+1}}\right|=x$$

$$\Rightarrow \left(x\frac{dy}{dx}-y\right)^2=x^2\left(1+\left(\frac{dy}{dx}\right)^2\right)$$

$$\Rightarrow x^2\left(\frac{dy}{dx}\right)^2+y^2-2xy\frac{dy}{dx}=x^2+x^2\left(\frac{dy}{dx}\right)^2$$

$$\Rightarrow \quad \frac{y^2-x^2}{2xy}=\frac{dy}{dz} \quad \text{...(i)}$$

which is homogeneous differential equation

Put $y=vx\Rightarrow v+x\frac{dv}{dx}=\frac{v^2-1}{2v}$ [from Eq. (i)]

$$\Rightarrow \int\frac{2v}{v^2+1}dv=-\int\frac{dx}{x}$$

$$\Rightarrow \quad \ln(v^2+1)=-\ln x+\ln C$$

$$\Rightarrow v^2+1=\frac{C}{x}\Rightarrow\frac{y^2+x^2}{x^2}=\frac{C}{x}$$

$$\Rightarrow \quad y^2+x^2=Cx$$

It passes through (1, 1). Then, $C=2$

So, equation of curve is

$$x^2+y^2-2x=0 \quad \text{...(ii)}$$

For intercept of curve on X-axis, put $y=0$ in Eq. (ii), we get

$x^2+0-2x=0\Rightarrow x=0,2$ and

y-intercept is $0+y^2-0=0\Rightarrow y=0$

Hence, length of x-intercept $=2$

4. (b), (c) Given, $\mathbf{A}\cdot\mathbf{a}=1$

and $\mathbf{A}+\mathbf{B}=\mathbf{a}\Rightarrow\mathbf{A}\cdot\mathbf{a}+\mathbf{B}\cdot\mathbf{a}=\mathbf{a}\cdot\mathbf{a}$

$$\Rightarrow \quad 1+\mathbf{B}\cdot\mathbf{a}=a^2$$

$$\Rightarrow \quad \mathbf{B}.\mathbf{a}=a^2-1 \quad \text{...(i)}$$

Also, given $\mathbf{A}\times\mathbf{B}=\mathbf{b}$

$$\Rightarrow \quad \mathbf{a}\times(\mathbf{A}\times\mathbf{B})=\mathbf{a}\times\mathbf{b}$$

$$\Rightarrow(\mathbf{a}\cdot\mathbf{B})\mathbf{A}-(\mathbf{a}\cdot\mathbf{A})\mathbf{B}=\mathbf{a}\times\mathbf{b}$$

$$\Rightarrow(a^2-1)\mathbf{A}-\mathbf{B}=\mathbf{a}\times\mathbf{b} \quad \text{...(ii)}$$

[using Eq. (i)]

and $\mathbf{A}+\mathbf{B}=\mathbf{a} \Rightarrow \mathbf{B}=\mathbf{a}-\mathbf{A}$ ...(iii)

From Eqs. (ii) and (iii), we get

$$\mathbf{A}=\frac{(\mathbf{a}\times\mathbf{b})+\mathbf{a}}{a^2}$$

$$\mathbf{B}=\mathbf{a}-\left\{\frac{(\mathbf{a}\times\mathbf{b})+\mathbf{a}}{a^2}\right\}$$

$$=\frac{(\mathbf{b}\times\mathbf{a})+\mathbf{a}(a^2-1)}{a^2}$$

5. (a)

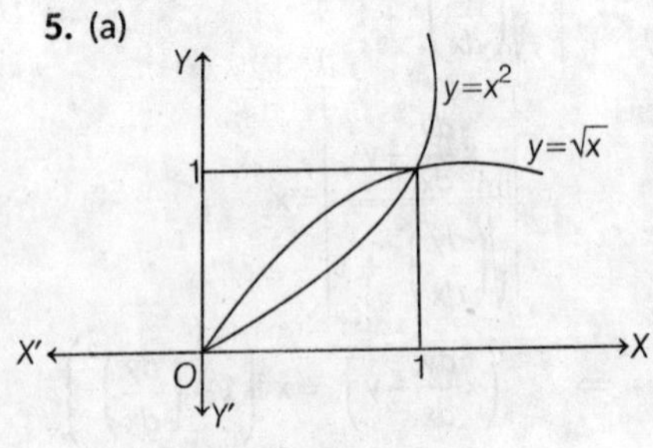

$$P(A)=\frac{\int_0^1\sqrt{x}\,dx}{\int_0^1 dx}=\frac{2}{3}$$

$$P(B)=\frac{\int_0^1\sqrt{y}\,dy}{\int_0^1 dy}=\frac{2}{3}$$

$$\therefore (P\cap B)=\frac{\int_0^1\sqrt{x}\,dx-\int_0^1 x^2 dx}{\int_0^1 dx}$$

$$=\frac{2}{3}-\frac{1}{3}=\frac{1}{3}$$

6. (a) We have,

$$(\alpha+\beta)^2=\left(\frac{1}{\alpha}+\frac{1}{\beta}\right)(\alpha^2+\beta^2)$$

$$\Rightarrow (\alpha+\beta)^2=\left(\frac{1}{\alpha}+\frac{1}{\beta}\right)((\alpha+\beta)^2-2\alpha\beta)$$

Substituting $\alpha+\beta=-\frac{b}{a}$ and $\alpha\beta=\frac{c}{a}$

$$\Rightarrow \left(-\frac{b}{a}\right)^2=\left(-\frac{b}{c}\right)\left(\frac{b^2}{a^2}-\frac{2c}{a}\right)$$

$$\Rightarrow \frac{b^2}{a^2}=-\left(\frac{b}{c}\right)\left(\frac{b^2}{a^2}-\frac{2c}{a}\right)$$

$$\Rightarrow cb^2+b(b^2-2ac)=0$$

$$\Rightarrow b[bc+b^2-2ac]=0$$

Since, $b\neq 0$, (since a, b, c are different and non-zero given that)

$$\Rightarrow bc+b^2-2ac=0$$

Since, a, b, c are in AP, then $b=\frac{a+c}{2}$

Therefore,

$$\frac{(a+c)c}{2}+\left(\frac{(a+c)}{2}\right)^2-2ac=0$$

$$\Rightarrow \quad a^2-4ac+3c^2=0$$

$$\Rightarrow \quad (a-c)(a-3c)=0$$

But $a\neq c$, $a=3c \Rightarrow \frac{a}{c}=3$

$$\Rightarrow \quad \frac{c}{a}=\frac{1}{3}$$

Thus, $\left|\left(\frac{a}{c}\right)^4+79\log_3\left(\frac{c}{a}\right)\right|+5$

$$=|81+79\log_3 3^{-1}|+5$$

$$=|81+79(-1)|+5$$

$$=|2|+5=2+5=7$$

Sol. (Q.Nos. 7-8)

7. (2)

8. (5.5) $P=\dfrac{\prod_{r=1}^{n}\left((2r-1)^4+\frac{1}{4}\right)}{\prod_{r=1}^{n}\left((2r)^4+\frac{1}{4}\right)}$

$$\because (2r-1)^4+\frac{1}{4}=(2r-1)^4+\frac{1}{4}+(2r-1)^2-(2r-1)^2$$

$$=\left((2r-1)^2+\frac{1}{2}\right)^2-(2r-1)^2$$

$$=\left((2r-1)^2+(2r-1)+\frac{1}{2}\right)\left((2r-1)^2-(2r-1)+\frac{1}{2}\right)$$

$$\Rightarrow (2r-1)^4+\frac{1}{4}=\left((2r-1)\,2r+\frac{1}{2}\right)\left((2r-1)(2r-2)+\frac{1}{2}\right) \quad ...(i)$$

Now,

$$(2r)^4+\frac{1}{4}=(2r)^4+\frac{1}{4}+(2r)^2-(2r)^2$$

$$=\left((2r)^2+\frac{1}{2}\right)^2-(2r)^2$$

$$=\left((2r)^2+2r+\frac{1}{2}\right)\left((2r)^2-2r+\frac{1}{2}\right)$$

$$\Rightarrow (2r)^4+\frac{1}{4}=\left(2r(2r+1)+\frac{1}{2}\right)\left(2r(2r-1)+\frac{1}{2}\right) \quad ...(ii)$$

From Eqs. (i) and (ii), we get

$$P=\frac{\prod_{i=1}^{n}\left((2r-1)(2r-2)+\frac{1}{2}\right)}{\prod_{i=1}^{n}\left(2r(2r+1)+\frac{1}{2}\right)}$$

$$P=\frac{\frac{1}{2}\cdot\left(3\cdot 2+\frac{1}{2}\right)\left(5\cdot 4+\frac{1}{2}\right)\ldots\left((2n-1)(2n-2)+\frac{1}{2}\right)}{\left(2\cdot 3+\frac{1}{2}\right)\left(4\cdot 5+\frac{1}{2}\right)\ldots\left((2n-2)(2n-1)+\frac{1}{2}\right)\left(2n(2n+1)\frac{1}{2}\right)}$$

$$\Rightarrow P=\frac{1}{2\left(2n(2n+1)+\frac{1}{2}\right)} \quad ...(iii)$$

As $\lim_{n\to\infty} n^\alpha P$ exists.

$$\Rightarrow \lim_{n\to\infty} n^\alpha\frac{1}{\left(2(2n(2n+1)+\frac{1}{2}\right)} \text{ exists}$$

$$\Rightarrow \quad \alpha=2 \text{ and } \lim_{n\to\infty} n^\alpha P=\frac{1}{8}$$

So, $44\left(\lim_{n\to\infty} n\,\alpha\,P\right)=\frac{44}{8}=5.5$

Sol. (Q.Nos. 9-10)

9. (137)

Number of lines formed by joining the points

$$={}^{18}C_2-({}^3C_2+{}^4C_2+{}^5C_2)+3=137$$

10. (948)

Number of quadrilaterals

$$={}^4C_2\times{}^5C_2+{}^3C_2\times{}^5C_2+{}^3C_2\times{}^4C_2$$
$$+{}^3C_1\times{}^4C_2+{}^5C_1+{}^3C_1\times{}^4C_1\times{}^5C_2$$
$$+{}^3C_2\times{}^4C_1\times{}^5C_1=378$$

Number of pentagons

$$={}^3C_1\times{}^4C_2\times{}^5C_2+{}^3C_2\times{}^4C_1\times{}^5C_2$$
$$+{}^3C_2\times{}^4C_2\times{}^5C_1=390$$

Number of hexagons

$$={}^3C_2\cdot{}^4C_2\cdot{}^5C_2=3\times 6\times 10=180$$

$\therefore$ Total number of n-gons

$$=378+390+180=948$$

Sol. (Q.Nos. 11-12)

11. (40)

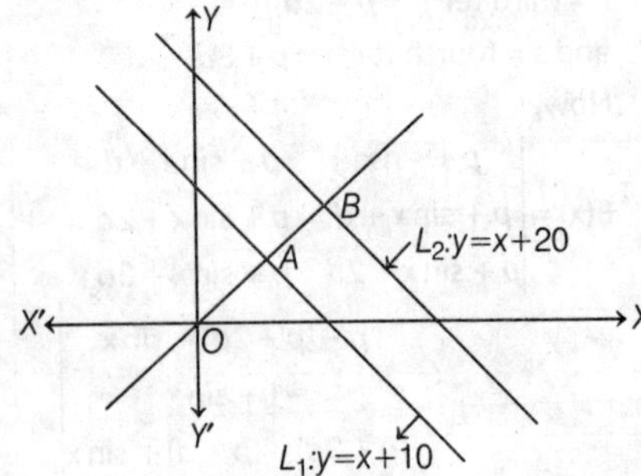

Let the parametric equation of the line drawn be

$$\frac{x}{\cos\theta}=\frac{y}{\sin\theta}=r$$

$$\Rightarrow \quad x=r\cos\theta,\ y=r\sin\theta$$

Putting it in L_1, we get

$$r\sin\theta=r\cos\theta+10$$

$$\Rightarrow \quad \frac{1}{OA}=\frac{\sin\theta-\cos\theta}{10} \quad ...(i)$$

Similarly, putting the general point of drawn line in the equation of L_2, we get

$$\frac{1}{OB}=\frac{\sin\theta-\cos\theta}{20} \quad ...(ii)$$

Let $P(h,k)$ and $OP=r$, then $r\cos\theta=h$, $r\sin\theta=k$, we have

$$\frac{2}{r}=\frac{\sin\theta-\cos\theta}{10}+\frac{\sin\theta-\cos\theta}{20}$$

$$\left(\because \text{ given } \frac{2}{OP}=\frac{1}{OA}+\frac{1}{OB}\right)$$

$\Rightarrow 40=3r\sin\theta-3r\cos\theta \Rightarrow 3y-3x=40$

On comparing it with $\alpha x+\beta y=\gamma$, we get $\alpha=-3,\beta=3$ and $\gamma=40$

So, $\alpha+\beta+\gamma=40$

12. (200)

Given, $OP^2=OA\times OB$

$$\Rightarrow r^2=\frac{10\times 20}{(\sin\theta-\cos\theta)^2}$$

[from Eqs. (i) and (ii)]

$\Rightarrow (r\sin\theta-r\cos\theta)^2=200$

Hence, the locus is $(y-x)^2=200$

Sol. (Q.Nos. 13-14)

13. (16)

14. (1)

Given that, X and Y denote the total points scored by teams T_1 and T_2, respectively. Also, given probability of $T_1\text{(win)}=\frac{1}{2}$, probability of T_1 (draw) $=\frac{1}{6}$ and probability of T_1 (lose) $=\frac{1}{3}$

Now, draw a table for T_1,

T_1	1st match	2nd match	X	Y
	W	W	6	0
	W	D	4	1
	W	L	3	3
	D	W	4	1
	D	D	2	2
	D	L	1	4
	L	W	3	3
	L	D	1	4
	L	L	0	6

Now, for find $P(X>Y)$ take the only three cases from above table are WW, WD, DW

Thus, $P(X>Y)=WW+WD+DW$

$$=\frac{1}{2}\times\frac{1}{2}+\frac{1}{2}\times\frac{1}{6}+\frac{1}{6}\times\frac{1}{2}$$

$$=\frac{1}{4}+\frac{1}{12}+\frac{1}{12}=\frac{3+1+1}{12}=\frac{5}{12}$$

Again,

Similarly, to find probability $(X=Y)$ take only three events are WL, LW and DD

$$\text{Thus, } P(X=Y)=\frac{1}{2}\times\frac{1}{3}+\frac{1}{3}\times\frac{1}{2}+\frac{1}{6}\times\frac{1}{6}$$

$$=\frac{1}{6}+\frac{1}{6}+\frac{1}{36}=\frac{13}{36}$$

$$\text{Hence, } P(X>Y)=\frac{5}{12}=\frac{a}{b+1}$$

Thus, $a=5$ and $b=11 \Rightarrow a+b=16$

and $P(X=Y)=\frac{13}{36}=\frac{c}{d}$

$\Rightarrow c=13$ and $d=36$

$$\Rightarrow\left(\frac{d-c}{23}\right)^2=\left(\frac{36-13}{23}\right)^2=(1)^2=1$$

Sol. (Q.Nos. 15-16)

15. (d) $\operatorname{cosec}^{-1}(\sqrt{5})+\operatorname{cosec}^{-1}(\sqrt{65})+\operatorname{cosec}^{-1}(\sqrt{325})+\ldots\infty$

$$=\cot^{-1}(2)+\cot^{-1}(8)+\cot^{-1}(18)+\ldots\infty$$

$$=\lim_{n\to\infty}\sum_{r=1}^{n}\cot^{-1}(2r^2)$$

$$=\lim_{n\to\infty}\sum_{r=1}^{n}\tan^{-1}\left(\frac{2}{4r^2}\right)$$

$$=\lim_{n\to\infty}\sum_{r=1}^{n}\tan^{-1}\left(\frac{2}{1+4r^2-1}\right)$$

$$=\lim_{n\to\infty}\sum_{r=1}^{n}\tan^{-1}\left[\frac{(2r+1)-(2r-1)}{1+(2r+1)(2r-1)}\right]$$

$$=\lim_{n\to\infty}\sum_{r=1}^{n}[\tan^{-1}(2r+1)-\tan^{-1}(2r-1)]$$

$$=\lim_{n\to\infty}[\tan^{-1}(2n+1)-\tan^{-1}(1)]$$

$$=\tan^{-1}\infty-\tan^{-1}1$$

$$=\frac{\pi}{2}-\frac{\pi}{4}=\frac{\pi}{4}$$

16. (c) $\lim_{n\to\infty}\sum_{r=1}^{n}\cot^{-1}\left(2^{r+1}+\frac{1}{2^r}\right)$

$$=\lim_{n\to\infty}\sum_{r=1}^{n}\tan^{-1}\left(\frac{2^r}{1+2^r\cdot 2^{r+1}}\right)$$

$$=\lim_{n\to\infty}\sum_{r=1}^{n}\tan^{-1}\left(\frac{2^{r+1}-2^r}{1+2^r\cdot 2^{r+1}}\right)$$

$$=\lim_{n\to\infty}\sum_{r=1}^{n}(\tan^{-1}2^{r+1}-\tan^{-1}2^r)$$

$$=\lim_{n\to\infty}(\tan^{-1}2^{n+1}-\tan^{-1}2)$$

$$=\tan^{-1}\infty-\tan^{-1}2$$

$$=\frac{\pi}{2}-\tan^{-1}2=\cot^{-1}2$$

17. (1) Given, $f(x)+f(y)=f\left(\frac{x+y}{1-xy}\right)$ ...(i)

Putting $x=y=0$ in Eq. (i), we get

$$f(0)=0$$

Putting $y=-x$, we get

$$f(x)+f(-x)=f(0)=0$$

$$\Rightarrow \quad f(-x)=-f(x) \quad ...(ii)$$

Also, $\lim_{x\to 0}\frac{f(x)}{x}=2$ (given)

$$\text{Now, } f'(x)=\lim_{h\to 0}\frac{f(x+h)-f(x)}{h}$$

$$=\lim_{h\to 0}\frac{f(x+h)+f(-x)}{h} \quad \text{[from Eq. (ii)]}$$

$$\Rightarrow f'(x)=\lim_{h\to 0}\frac{f\left[\frac{x+h-x}{1-(x+h)(-x)}\right]}{h}$$

[from Eq. (i)]

$$\Rightarrow f'(x)=\lim_{h\to 0}\left[\frac{f\left(\frac{h}{1+x(x+h)}\right)}{h}\right]$$

$$\Rightarrow f'(x)=\lim_{h\to 0}\frac{f\left(\frac{h}{1+xh+x^2}\right)}{\left(\frac{h}{1+xh+x^2}\right)}\times\left(\frac{1}{1+xh+x^2}\right)$$

$$\Rightarrow f'(x)=\lim_{h\to 0}\frac{f\left(\frac{h}{1+xh+x^2}\right)}{\left(\frac{h}{1+xh+x^2}\right)}\times\lim_{h\to 0}\frac{1}{1+xh+x^2}$$

$$\Rightarrow f'(x)=2\times\frac{1}{1+x^2}$$

$$\left[\text{using } \lim_{x\to 0}\frac{f(x)}{x}=2\right]$$

$$\Rightarrow f'(x)=\frac{2}{1+x^2}$$

Integrating both sides, we get

$$f(x)=2\tan^{-1}x+C$$

$\because \quad f(0)=0$

$\therefore \quad C=0$

Thus, $f(x)=2\tan^{-1}x$

$$\text{Hence, } f\left(\frac{1}{\sqrt{3}}\right)=2\tan^{-1}(1/\sqrt{3})$$

$$=2\times\frac{\pi}{6}=\frac{\pi}{3}$$

$$\simeq 1.0466$$

$\therefore \quad [f(1/\sqrt{3})]=1$

18. (29) Let $S = {}^{20}C_2 + 2\cdot{}^{20}C_3 + 3\cdot{}^{20}C_4 + \ldots + 19\cdot{}^{20}C_{20}$ ...(i)

add ${}^{20}C_0 + {}^{20}C_1 + \ldots + {}^{20}C_{20} (= 2^{20})$

On both sides of Eq. (i),

$$S + 2^{20} = {}^{20}C_2 + 2\cdot{}^{20}C_3 + 3\cdot{}^{20}C_4 + \ldots + 19\cdot{}^{20}C_{20} + {}^{20}C_0 + {}^{20}C_1 + {}^{20}C_2 + {}^{20}C_3 + {}^{20}C_4 + \ldots + {}^{20}C_{20}$$

$$\Rightarrow S + 2^{20} = 1 + {}^{20}C_1 + 2\cdot{}^{20}C_2 + 3\cdot{}^{20}C_3 + 4\cdot{}^{20}C_4 + \ldots + 20\cdot{}^{20}C_{20} \quad \ldots\text{(ii)}$$

Now, $(1+x)^n = C_0 + C_1x + C_2x^2 + C_3x^3 + \ldots + C_nx^n$

On differentiating it w.r.t. x, we get

$$n(1+x)^{n-1} = C_1 + 2C_2x + 3C_3x^2 + \ldots + {}^nC_nx^{n-1}$$

Put $x = 1$ and $n = 20$ in above, we get

$$20\cdot 2^{19} = {}^{20}C_1 + 2\cdot{}^{20}C_2 + 3\,{}^{20}C_3 + \ldots + 20\cdot{}^{20}C_{20}$$

From Eq. (ii), $S + 2^{20} = 1 + 20\cdot 2^{19}$

$$\Rightarrow \quad S = 1 + 20\cdot 2^{19} - 2^{20}$$

$$= 1 + 10\cdot 2^{20} - 2^{20} = 1 + 9\cdot 2^{20}$$

On comparing this by $1 + p\cdot 2^q$, we get

$$p = 9, q = 20$$

Hence, $(p+q)_{\text{least}} = 9 + 20 = 29$

19. (2) The situation described in the question is depicted in the sequence of figures below, as the pole is being moved from one corridor to the other.

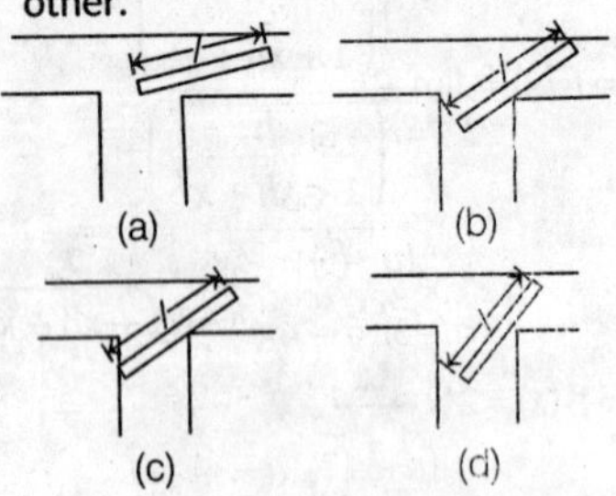

(a) (b) (c) (d)

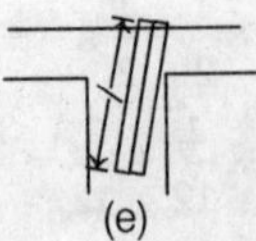

(e)

Let the width of the second corridor be W. convirus. Yourself that if W is below a particular value (if the second corridor is too narrow), the pole will never be able to be moved into the second corridor. Now, consider the cases when W has a value such that the pole is just able to move into the second corridor. This situation is depicted in the figure above. Observe (and visualise in your mind) carefully that an instant will come when the ends of the pole touch the walls of both the corridors and the pole touches the corner (turning). This is depicted in the figure above [part (c)] and reproduced below in more detail.

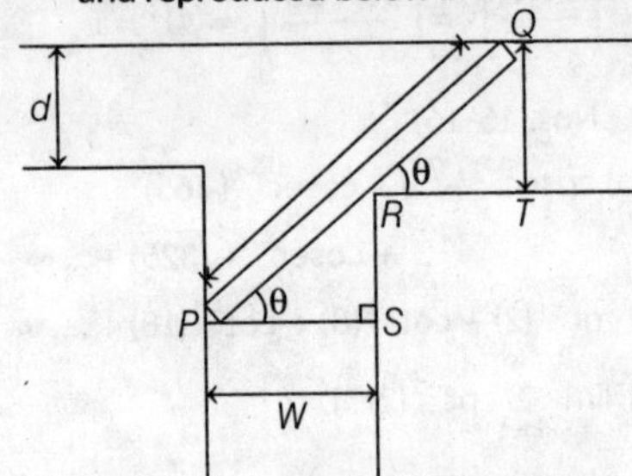

(P and Q deonte the end points of the pole)

For the entire movement of the rod from one corridor to the other (while all the time touching the point R), the instant depicted above will be the one when the horizontal component of PR, i.e. PS, will be maximum. Before and after this instant, PS will have a lower value. Therefore, the width W must be atleast greater than the maximum value of PS, only then will the pole pass,

$$W_{\min} = PS_{\max}$$

Therefore, our target is to find $PS_{\max}$.

From the geometry of the figure, we can write

$$d\operatorname{cosec}\theta + (PS)\sec\theta = l$$

$$\Rightarrow \quad PS = \frac{l - d\operatorname{cosec}\theta}{\sec\theta} = l\cos\theta - d\cot\theta$$

For PS to be maximum, $\dfrac{d(PS)}{d\theta} = 0$ and $\dfrac{d^2(PS)}{d\theta^2} < 0$.

Now, $\dfrac{d(PS)}{d\theta} = -l\sin\theta + d\operatorname{cosec}^2\theta$

This is zero when $l\sin\theta = d\operatorname{cosec}^2\theta$

$$\Rightarrow \quad \sin\theta = \left(\frac{d}{l}\right)^{1/3}$$

and hence verify that,

$$\left.\frac{d^2(PS)}{d\theta^2}\right|_{\theta = \sin^{-1}\left(\frac{d}{l}\right)^{1/3}} < 0$$

$\therefore \sin\theta = \left(\dfrac{d}{l}\right)^{1/3}$ is a point of maximum for PS.

$$\therefore \; PS_{\max} = l\cos\theta - d\cot\theta\Big|_{\theta = \sin^{-1}(d/l)^{1/3}}$$

$$= (l^{2/3} - d^{2/3})^{3/2}$$

Hence, $W_{\min} = (l^{2/3} - d^{2/3})^{3/2}$

On comparing this by $W_{\min} = (l^\alpha - d^\beta)^\gamma$, we get

$$\alpha = \frac{2}{3}, \beta = \frac{2}{3} \text{ and } \gamma = \frac{3}{2}$$

$$\text{So, } (\alpha + \beta)\times\gamma = \left(\frac{2}{3} + \frac{2}{3}\right)\times\frac{3}{2}$$

$$= \frac{4}{3}\times\frac{3}{2} = 2$$

REAL NUTS

24 June 2022, Shift-I

1. (d) Given that,

$$A = \{z \in C : 1 \le |z-(1+i)| \le 2\}$$

and $B = \{z \in A : |z-(1-i)| = 1\}$.

Here, 'A' represents all those points lying inside the region of circle having radius greater than or equal to 1 or less than or equal to 2 and B represents all these points lying inside the circle having radius 1.

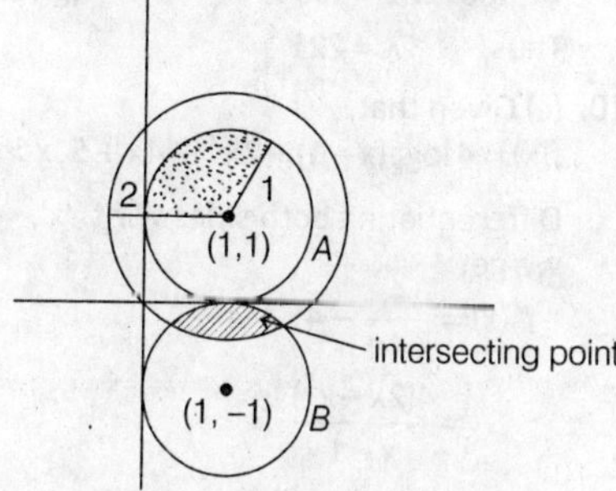

Clearly, from the above diagram, the set B has infinite point in it.

So, B is an infinite set.

2. (d) Given that

$$3^{2022} = (3^2)^{1011} = (9)^{1011} = (10-1)^{1011}$$

Now, applying binomial theorem

$$3^{2022} = {}^{1011}C_0(10)^{1011} - {}^{1011}C_1(10)^{1010} + \ldots + {}^{1011}C_{1010}(10)^1 - {}^{1011}C_{1011}$$

$$\Rightarrow 3^{2022} = 10\,\{{}^{1011}C_0(10)^{1010} - {}^{1011}C_1(10)^{1009} + \ldots + {}^{1011}C_{1010}\} - 1$$

$\Rightarrow 3^{2022} = 10k - 1$, where $k \in z$

$\Rightarrow 3^{2022} = 10k + 5 - 5 - 1$

[adding and subtracting by '5']

$\Rightarrow 3^{2022} = (10k - 5) + (5 - 1)$

$\Rightarrow 3^{2022} = 5(2k - 1) + 4$

$\Rightarrow 3^{2022} = 5\lambda + 4;\ \lambda \in z$

Now, 3^{2022} i.e. $5\lambda + 4$ is divided by '5, then the remainder is 4

Thus, the remainder is 4.

3. (a) We know that, surface area of a balloon of spherical shape is

$$'S' = 4\pi r^2,$$

where 'r' is a radius.

Now, $S = 4\pi r^2$

Differentiating both side w.r.t. 't', we get

$$\frac{dS}{dt} = 8\pi r\frac{dr}{dt}$$

Given that, surface area of a balloon increases at a constant rate.

So, $\dfrac{dS}{dt}$ = constant (k say),

Thus, $k = 8\pi\left(r\dfrac{dr}{dt}\right) \Rightarrow r\dfrac{dr}{dt} = \lambda,$

where $\lambda = \dfrac{k}{8\pi}$ = constant (say)

$\Rightarrow \quad rdr = \lambda dt$

Now, integrating on both sides, we get

$$\frac{r^2}{2} = \lambda t + C$$

At, $\quad r = 3, t = 0$, then $C = \dfrac{9}{2}$

Thus, $\dfrac{r^2}{2} = \lambda t + \dfrac{9}{2}$

Now, given when $t = 5$, then $r = 7$

Thus, $\dfrac{(7)^2}{2} = \lambda \cdot 5 + \dfrac{9}{2}$

$\Rightarrow \quad \dfrac{49}{2} - \dfrac{9}{2} = \lambda \cdot 5$

$\Rightarrow \quad \dfrac{40}{2} = 5\lambda \Rightarrow \lambda = 4$

Hence, $\dfrac{r^2}{2} = 4t + \dfrac{9}{2}$

Now, at $t = 9$;

$$\frac{r^2}{2} = 4 \times 9 + \frac{9}{2}$$

$\Rightarrow \quad r^2 = 72 + 9 = 81 \Rightarrow r = 9$

Hence, its radius after 9 s is 9 units.

4. (c) Given that, Bag 'A' contains 2 white, 1 black and 3 red balls and Bag 'B' contains 3 black, 2 red and 'n' white balls.

A
2W 1B 3R

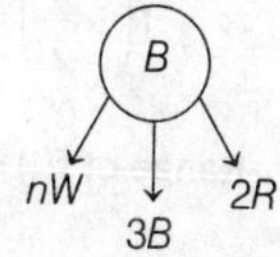

Thus, $P(1B \text{ and } 1R) = P(A) \cdot P\left(\dfrac{1R1B}{A}\right) + P(B) \cdot P\left(\dfrac{1R1B}{B}\right) \quad \ldots(i)$

$\therefore \quad P(A) = \dfrac{1}{2}$ and $P(B) = \dfrac{1}{2}$

$$P\left(\frac{1R1B}{A}\right) = \frac{{}^3C_1 \cdot {}^1C_1}{{}^6C_2}$$

and $P\left(\dfrac{1R1B}{B}\right) = \dfrac{{}^3C_1 \cdot {}^2C_1}{{}^{n+5}C_2}$

From Eq. (i), we get

$$p\,(1R \text{ and } 1B) = \frac{1}{2}\cdot\frac{{}^3C_1 \cdot {}^1C_1}{{}^6C_2} + \frac{1}{2}\cdot\frac{{}^3C_1 \cdot {}^2C_1}{{}^{n+5}C_2}$$

$$\therefore P\left(\frac{1R \text{ and } 1B}{A}\right) = \frac{\frac{1}{2}\cdot\frac{{}^3C_1 \cdot {}^1C_1}{{}^6C_2}}{\frac{1}{2}\cdot\frac{{}^3C_1 \cdot {}^1C_1}{{}^6C_2} + \frac{1}{2}\cdot\frac{{}^3C_1 \cdot {}^2C_1}{{}^{n+5}C_2}}$$

Given that, $\quad P\left(\dfrac{1R \text{ and } 1B}{A}\right) = \dfrac{6}{11}$

$$\Rightarrow \frac{\frac{1}{2}\cdot\frac{{}^3C_1 \cdot {}^1C_1}{{}^6C_2}}{\frac{1}{2}\cdot\frac{{}^3C_1 \cdot {}^1C_1}{{}^6C_2} + \frac{1}{2}\cdot\frac{{}^3C_1 \cdot {}^2C_1}{{}^{n+5}C_2}} = \frac{6}{11}$$

$$\Rightarrow \frac{\frac{1}{2}\cdot\frac{3}{15}}{\frac{1}{2}\cdot\frac{3}{15} + \frac{1}{2}\cdot\frac{6 \cdot 2}{(n+5)(n+4)}} = \frac{6}{11}$$

$$\Rightarrow \frac{\frac{1}{10}}{\frac{1}{10} + \frac{6}{(n+5)(n+4)}} = \frac{6}{11}$$

$$\Rightarrow \frac{6}{10} + \frac{36}{(n+5)(n+4)} = \frac{11}{10}$$

$$\Rightarrow \frac{36}{(n+5)(n+4)} = \frac{5}{10} = \frac{1}{2}$$

$\Rightarrow \quad (n+5)(n+4) - 72 = 0$

$\Rightarrow \quad n^2 + 9n - 52 = 0$

$\Rightarrow \quad (n+13)(n-4) = 0$

$\Rightarrow \quad n = -13$ or $n = 4$

$n = -13$ not possible case.

So, the only possibility case is $n = 4$.

5. (a) Given that, circle is

$$x^2 + y^2 + Ax + By + C = 0 \quad \ldots(i)$$

Parabola is $y = x^2 \quad \ldots(ii)$

Since, Eqs. (i) and (ii) touching at (2, 4).

$\therefore$ (2, 4) lies on Eq. (i),

$\Rightarrow \quad 2A + 4B + C + 20 = 0$

$\Rightarrow \quad 2A + 4B + C = -20 \quad \ldots(iii)$

Now, differentiating Eq. (i) w.r.t. 'x', we get

$$2x + 2y\frac{dy}{dx} + A + B\frac{dy}{dx} = 0 \quad \ldots(iv)$$

Also differentiating Eq. (ii) w.r.t. 'x', we get

$$\frac{dy}{dx}=2x \Rightarrow \left(\frac{dy}{dx}\right)_{(2,4)}=4$$

Now, from Eq. (iv), we get

$$4+32+A+4B=0 \qquad \left[\text{put } \left.\frac{dy}{dx}\right|_{(2,4)}=4\right]$$

$$\Rightarrow \quad A+4B=-36 \qquad \text{...(v)}$$

Now, subtracting Eq. (v) from Eq. (iii), we get

$$(2A+4B+C)-(A+4B)=(-20)-(-36)$$

$$\Rightarrow \quad A+C=16$$

Thus, $A+C$ is equal to 16.

6. (b) The given system of equation is

$$x+y+z=\alpha$$
$$\alpha x+2\alpha y+3z=-1$$
$$x+3\alpha y+5z=4$$

is inconsistent if $\Delta=0$

where, $\Delta=\begin{vmatrix}1 & 1 & 1\\ \alpha & 2\alpha & 3\\ 1 & 3\alpha & 5\end{vmatrix}=0$

$$=1(10\alpha-9\alpha)-1(5\alpha-3)+1(3\alpha^2-2\alpha)$$

$$=3\alpha^2-6\alpha+3=0$$

$$\Rightarrow \quad (\alpha-1)^2=0$$

Hence, the value of 'α' is 1.

7. (b) Given that, the equation is

$$3x^2+\lambda x-1=0$$

and also given that α and β are roots of the above equation.

According to question,

$$\frac{1}{\alpha^2}+\frac{1}{\beta^2}=15 \qquad \text{... (i)}$$

Since, α and β are roots of $3x^2+\lambda x-1=0$.

Thus, $\alpha+\beta=-\frac{\lambda}{3}$ and $\alpha\beta=-\frac{1}{3}$

Hence from Eq. (i), $\frac{\alpha^2+\beta^2}{\alpha^2\beta^2}=15$

$$\Rightarrow \quad \frac{(\alpha+\beta)^2-2\alpha\beta}{\alpha^2\beta^2}=15$$

$$\Rightarrow \quad \frac{\frac{\lambda^2}{9}+\frac{2}{3}}{\frac{1}{9}}=15$$

$$\Rightarrow \quad \frac{\lambda^2}{9}+\frac{2}{3}=\frac{15}{9}=\frac{5}{3}$$

$$\Rightarrow \quad \frac{\lambda^2}{9}=1 \Rightarrow \lambda^2=9$$

Now, $\alpha^3+\beta^3=(\alpha+\beta)(\alpha^2+\beta^2-\alpha\beta)$

$$=(\alpha+\beta)[(\alpha+\beta)^2-3\alpha\beta]$$

$$=\left(-\frac{\lambda}{3}\right)\left\{\left(-\frac{\lambda}{3}\right)^2-3\left(-\frac{1}{3}\right)\right\}$$

$$=\left(-\frac{\lambda}{3}\right)\left\{\frac{\lambda^2}{9}+1\right\}$$

$$=-\frac{\lambda}{3}\left(\frac{9}{9}+1\right) \qquad [\text{since}, \lambda^2=9]$$

$$=-\frac{\lambda}{3}\cdot 2=-\frac{2\lambda}{3}$$

Thus, $6(\alpha^3+\beta^3)^2=6\left\{-\frac{2\lambda}{3}\right\}^2$

$$=6\times\frac{4\lambda^2}{9}$$

$$=\frac{24\lambda^2}{9}$$

$$=\frac{24\times 9}{9} \qquad [\because \lambda^2=9]$$

$$=24$$

8. (a) Given that,

$$(\tan^{-1}x)^3+(\cot^{-1}x)^3=k\pi^3$$

Let $\quad \tan^{-1}x=t\in\left(-\frac{\pi}{2},\frac{\pi}{2}\right)$

$$\cot^{-1}x=\frac{\pi}{2}-t$$

Thus, $\quad f(t)=t^3+\left(\frac{\pi}{2}-t\right)^3$

$$\Rightarrow \quad f'(t)=3t^2-3\left(\frac{\pi}{2}-t\right)^2$$

[Differentiating on both sides]

$$f'(t)=0 \text{ at } t=\frac{\pi}{4}$$

So, $\quad f(t)|_{\min}=\frac{\pi^3}{64}+\frac{\pi^3}{64}=\frac{\pi^3}{32}$

Thus, maxima will be occur around $t=-\frac{\pi}{2}$.

$$\therefore \quad f\left(-\frac{\pi}{2}\right)=-\frac{\pi^3}{8}+\pi^3=\frac{7}{8}\pi^3$$

Range of $f(t)=\left[\frac{\pi^3}{32},\frac{7\pi^3}{8}\right)$

Thus, $\quad k\pi^3\in\left[\frac{\pi^3}{32},\frac{7\pi^3}{8}\right)$

$$\Rightarrow \quad k\in\left[\frac{1}{32},\frac{7}{8}\right)$$

9. (b) Let $S=\{\sqrt{n}, 1\le n\le 50 \text{ and } n \text{ is odd}\}$

$$=\{1,\sqrt{3},\sqrt{5},\sqrt{7},\sqrt{9},\ldots,\sqrt{49}\}$$

Also given,

$$A=\begin{bmatrix}1 & 0 & a\\ -1 & 1 & 0\\ -a & 0 & 1\end{bmatrix}$$

$$\Rightarrow \quad |A|=1+a^2$$

$$\Rightarrow |\det \operatorname{adj} A|=|A|^{3-1}=|A|^2=(a^2+1)^2$$

$$\therefore \sum_{a\in S}\det(\operatorname{adj}A)=\sum_{a\in S}(a^2+1)^2$$

$$=(1+1)^2+(3+1)^2+(5+1)^2+\ldots+(49+1)^2$$

$$=2^2(1^2+2^2+3^2+\ldots+25^2)$$

$$=4.\frac{25\cdot(25+1)(2\cdot 25+1)}{6}$$

$$\Rightarrow 100\cdot 221=100\lambda \qquad \text{(given)}$$

Thus, $\quad \lambda=221$

10. (c) Given that,

$f(x)=4\log_e(x-1)-2x^2+4x+5, x>1$

Differentiating both sides w.r.t. 'x', we get

$$f'(x)=\frac{4}{x-1}-4x+4$$

$$=\frac{4(2x-x^2)}{x-1}$$

$$=\frac{-4x(x-2)}{x-1} \qquad \text{... (i)}$$

Since, if $1<x<2$ then $f'(x)>0$, thus the function increasing but if $x\ge 2$, then $f'(x)<0$, thus the function decreasing.

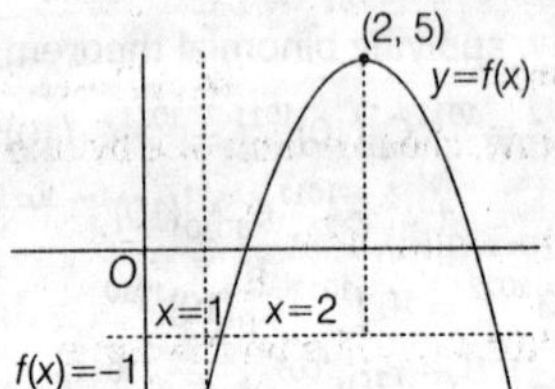

So that f is increasing in (1, 2) and decreasing in $(2,\infty)$.

From Eq. (i), $f(x)$ has maxima occurs at $x=2$

$$f(2)=4\times 0-2\times 2^2+4\times 2+5=5$$

Clearly $f(x)=-1$ has exactly two solutions.

Now differentiating Eq. (i) w.r.t. 'x', we get

$$f''(x)=\frac{4(x-1)(-2x+2)-4(2x-x^2)}{(x-1)^2}$$

Now, $f'(e)=\frac{4(2e-e^2)}{(e-1)}<0$

and $f''(2)=-8<0$

From above,

$$\therefore \quad f'(e)-f''(2)>0$$

Thus, $f'(e)-f''(2)<0$ is not correct.

11. (d) The given curve is

$$y = x^3 + 3x^2 + 5 \quad \text{... (i)}$$

Now, the slope is $\left(\frac{dy}{dx}\right) = 3x^2 + 6x$

$$\therefore \quad \left(\frac{dy}{dx}\right)_{(x_1, y_1)} = 3x_1^2 + 6x_1$$

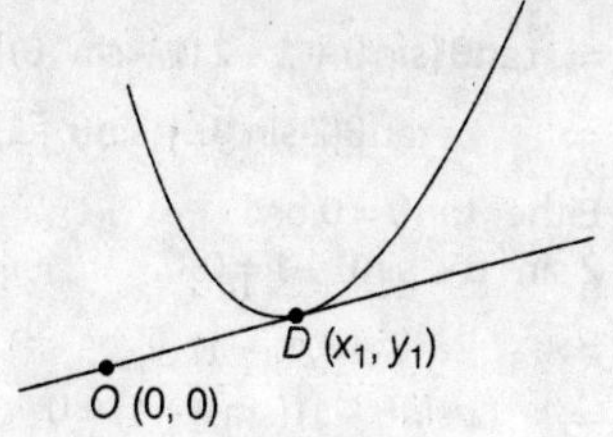

Now, equation of the line *OD* is

$$(y - y_1) = \frac{y_1 - 0}{x_1 - 0}(x - x_1)$$

According to question,

$$m \text{ tangent} = m_{OD}$$

$$\Rightarrow \quad 3x_1^2 + 6x_1 = \frac{y_1 - 0}{x_1 \;\; 0}$$

$$\Rightarrow \quad y_1 = 3x_1^3 + 6x_1^2 \quad \text{... (ii)}$$

Since, (x_1, y_1) point lie on the given curve (i).

Thus, $y_1 = x_1^3 + 3x_1^2 + 5 \quad$ ... (iii)

Now using Eqs. (ii) and (iii), we get

$$x_1^3 + 3x_1^2 + 5 = 3x_1^3 + 6x_1^2$$

$$\Rightarrow \quad 2x_1^3 + 3x_1^2 - 5 = 0$$

$$\Rightarrow (x_1 - 1)(2x_1^2 + 5x_1 + 5) = 0$$

So, $\quad (x_1, y_1) = (1, 9)$

Now, check option one by one

Option (a), $1^2 + \frac{9^2}{81} = 2 = 2$

Thus, (x_1, y_1) lie on the curve

$$x^2 + \frac{y^2}{81} = 2$$

Option (b), $\frac{9^2}{9} - 1^2 = 9 - 1 = 8 = 8$

Thus, (x_1, y_1) lie on the curve $\frac{y^2}{9} - x^2 = 8$.

Option (c), (x_1, y_1) also lie on the curve $y = 4x^2 + 5$.

Option (d),

$$\text{LHS} = \frac{1}{3} - 9^2 = \frac{1}{3} - 81$$

$$= \frac{-242}{3} \neq 2$$

$$\neq \text{RHS}$$

$\therefore (x_1, y_1)$ does not lie on the curve $\frac{x}{3} - y^2 = 2$.

12. (*) The given function is,

$$f(x) = |2x^2 + 3x - 2| + \sin x \cos x, x \in [0, 1]$$

$$= |(2x - 1)(x + 2)| + \frac{\sin 2x}{2}, x \in [0, 1]$$

$$\therefore \quad f(x) = \begin{cases} -(2x^2 + 3x - 2) + \frac{\sin 2x}{2}, 0 \le x \le \frac{1}{2} \\ (2x^2 + 3x - 2) + \frac{\sin 2x}{2}, x > \frac{1}{2} \end{cases}$$

For, $0 \le x \le \frac{1}{2}$, then

$$f(x) = -(2x^2 + 3x - 2) + \frac{\sin 2x}{2}$$

$$\Rightarrow f'(x) = (-4x - 3) + \cos 2x$$

Clearly, $f'(x) < 0$ if $0 \le x \le \frac{1}{2}$

Thus, $f(x)$ is decreasing on $\left[0, \frac{1}{2}\right]$.

For $x \ge \frac{1}{2}$, then

$$f(x) = (2x^2 + 3x - 2) + \frac{\sin 2x}{2}$$

$$\Rightarrow \quad f'(x) = (4x + 3) + \cos 2x$$

Clearly, $f'(x) > 0$ if $x > \frac{1}{2}$

So, clearly from above, minima occurs at $x = \frac{1}{2}$.

$$f(x)|_{\min} = \left|2\left(\frac{1}{2}\right)^2 + \frac{3}{2} - 2\right| + \sin\left(\frac{1}{2}\right) . \cos\left(\frac{1}{2}\right)$$

$$= \frac{1}{2}\sin(1)$$

And maxima is possible at $x = 0$ or $x = 1$.

Now checking for $x = 0$ and $x = 1$, we can see it attains its value at $x = 1$.

$$f(x)|_{\max} = |2 + 3 - 2| + \frac{\sin 2}{2} = 3 + \frac{1}{2}\sin 2$$

$\therefore$Sum of absolute maxima and absolute minimum value

$$= 3 + \frac{1}{2}(\sin(1) + \sin(2))$$

$$= 3 + \frac{1}{2}(\sin(1) + 2\sin(1) \cdot \cos(1))$$

13. (b) Given that, $\{a_i\}_{i=1}^n$, where '*n*' is an even integer is an arithmetic progression with common difference 1 and $\sum_{i=1}^{n} a_i = 192$,

$$\sum_{i=1}^{n/2} a_{2i} = 120$$

Thus, $\underbrace{a_1 + a_2 + ... + a_n}_{n\text{-terms}} = 192$

$$\Rightarrow \quad \frac{n}{2}[a_1 + a_n] = 192$$

$$\Rightarrow \quad a_1 + a_n = \frac{384}{n} \quad \text{... (i)}$$

and $\quad \sum_{i=1}^{n/2} a_{2i} = 120$

$$\Rightarrow \quad \underbrace{a_2 + a_4 + ... + a_n}_{n\text{-terms}} = 120$$

$$\Rightarrow \quad \frac{n}{4}(a_2 + a_n) = 120$$

Since, $\{a_i\}_{i=1}^n$ is an AP with common difference 1.

So $a_n = a_1 + n - 1, n = 1, 2, 3, ..., n$

$$\Rightarrow \quad \frac{n}{4}\{a_1 + 1 + a_n\} = 120$$

$$\Rightarrow \quad a_1 + a_n + 1 = \frac{480}{n} \quad \text{... (ii)}$$

Putting the value of $(a_1 + a_n)$ in the Eq. (ii), we get

$$\frac{384}{n} + 1 = \frac{480}{n}$$

$$\Rightarrow \quad \frac{480}{n} - \frac{384}{n} = 1$$

$$\Rightarrow \quad \frac{96}{n} = 1$$

$$\Rightarrow \quad n = 96$$

14. (a) The given differential equation is

$$\frac{dx}{dy} = \frac{2x}{y} + y^2(y + 1)e^y, x(1) = 0$$

$$\Rightarrow \quad \frac{dx}{dy} - \frac{2x}{y} = y^2(y + 1)e^y$$

This is the form of linear differential equation thus,

$$\text{IF} = e^{\int \frac{-2}{y} dy} = e^{-2\ln y} = \frac{1}{y^2}$$

Thus, the solution is

$$x \cdot \frac{1}{y^2} = \int y^2(y + 1) \cdot e^y \cdot \frac{1}{y^2} dy$$

$$= \int (y + 1)e^y dy$$

$$\Rightarrow \quad \frac{x}{y^2} = ye^y + C$$

$\because \quad x(1) = 0$

So, $\quad 0 = 1(e^1) + C$

$$\Rightarrow \quad C = -e$$

Now, $\quad \frac{x}{y^2} = (ye^y - e)$

At $y = e$,

$$x = e^2(ee^e - e) = e^3(e^e - 1)$$

15. (d) The given equation of hyperbola

$$a^2x^2 - y^2 = b^2$$

i.e. $$\frac{x^2}{\left(\frac{b^2}{a^2}\right)} - \frac{y^2}{b^2} = 1 \quad \text{... (i)}$$

Tangent to Eq. (i) is

$$y = mx \pm \sqrt{\frac{b^2m^2}{a^2} - b^2} \quad \text{... (ii)}$$

Given that $\lambda x - 2y = \mu$ be a tangent to the hyperbola.

So, $$y = \frac{\lambda x}{2} - \frac{\mu}{2} \quad \text{... (iii)}$$

Now comparing Eqs. (ii) and (iii), we get

$$m = \frac{\lambda}{2}, \frac{b^2m^2}{a^2} - b^2 = \frac{\mu^2}{4}$$

Substituting $m = \frac{\lambda}{2}$ in

$\frac{b^2m^2}{a^2} - b^2 = \frac{\mu^2}{4}$, we get

$$\frac{b^2}{a^2} \times \frac{\lambda^2}{4} - b^2 = \frac{\mu^2}{4}$$

$$\Rightarrow \quad \frac{\lambda^2}{a^2} - \frac{\mu^2}{b^2} = 4$$

$$\Rightarrow \quad \left(\frac{\lambda}{a}\right)^2 - \left(\frac{\mu}{b}\right)^2 = 4$$

16. (c) Given, $\hat{\mathbf{b}} = \mathbf{c} + 2(\mathbf{c} \times \hat{\mathbf{a}}) \quad$ ...(i)

Taking dot product on both sides with $\mathbf{c}$, we get

$$\hat{\mathbf{b}} \cdot \mathbf{c} = (\mathbf{c} + 2(\mathbf{c} \times \hat{\mathbf{a}})) \cdot \mathbf{c} = |\mathbf{c}|^2 + 2(\mathbf{c} \times \hat{\mathbf{a}}) \cdot \mathbf{c}$$

$$= |\mathbf{c}|^2 + 2(\mathbf{c} \times \hat{\mathbf{a}}) \cdot \mathbf{c}$$

$$= |\mathbf{c}|^2 + 0 \quad [\because [\mathbf{c}\ \hat{\mathbf{a}}\ \mathbf{c}] = 0]$$

$$\Rightarrow \hat{\mathbf{b}} \cdot \mathbf{c} = |\mathbf{c}|^2 \quad \text{... (ii)}$$

From Eq. (i), we get

$$\hat{\mathbf{b}} - \mathbf{c} = 2(\mathbf{c} \times \hat{\mathbf{a}})$$

$$\Rightarrow |\hat{\mathbf{b}}|^2 + |\mathbf{c}|^2 - 2 \cdot \hat{\mathbf{b}} \cdot \mathbf{c} = 4|\mathbf{c}|^2 |\hat{\mathbf{a}}|^2 \sin^2 \frac{\pi}{12}$$

$$\Rightarrow 1 + |\mathbf{c}|^2 - 2|\mathbf{c}|^2 = 4|\mathbf{c}|^2 \cdot \left(\frac{\sqrt{3}-1}{2\sqrt{2}}\right)^2$$

where, $\hat{\mathbf{a}}$ and $\hat{\mathbf{b}}$ are unit vector and

$$\sin\frac{\pi}{12} = \sin 15°$$

$$= \sin(45° - 30°)$$

$$= \frac{\sqrt{3}}{2.\sqrt{2}} - \frac{1}{2\sqrt{2}} = \frac{\sqrt{3}-1}{2\sqrt{2}}$$

$$\Rightarrow \quad 1 - |\mathbf{c}|^2 = 4|\mathbf{c}|^2 \cdot \frac{(\sqrt{3}-1)^2}{8}$$

$$= 4|\mathbf{c}|^2 \cdot \frac{(4 - 2\sqrt{3})}{8}$$

$$= |\mathbf{c}|^2 (2 - \sqrt{3})$$

$$\Rightarrow \quad 1 = |\mathbf{c}|^2 (3 - \sqrt{3})$$

$$\Rightarrow \quad 36|\mathbf{c}|^2 = \frac{36}{3-\sqrt{3}} = \frac{36(3+\sqrt{3})}{6}$$

$$\Rightarrow \quad |6\mathbf{c}|^2 = 6(3 + \sqrt{3})$$

17. (a) We know that,

$P(X = n)$ for a binomial distribution is ${}^nC_r p^r (1-p)^{n-r}$ or ${}^nC_r\, p^r q^{n-r}$,

where $p + q = 1$

Given, $n = 33$ such that,

$$3P(X = 0) = P(X = 1)$$

$$\Rightarrow 3 \cdot {}^nC_0 \cdot p^0 (1-p)^n = {}^nC_1 p^1 (1-p)^{n-1}$$

$$\Rightarrow 3 \times {}^{33}C_0 \times p^0 \times (1-p)^{33}$$

$$= {}^{33}C_1 p^1 (1-p)^{32}$$

$$\Rightarrow \frac{3}{33} = \frac{p}{(1-p)}$$

$$\Rightarrow \quad p = \frac{1}{12} \text{ and } 1 - p = \frac{11}{12}$$

or $\quad q = \frac{11}{12} \quad [\because q = 1 - p]$

Now,

$$\frac{P(X=15)}{P(X=18)} - \frac{P(X=16)}{P(X=17)}$$

$$= \frac{{}^{33}C_{15}\, p^{15} q^{18}}{{}^{33}C_{18}\, p^{18} q^{15}} - \frac{{}^{33}C_{16}\, p^{16} q^{17}}{{}^{33}C_{17}\, p^{17} q^{16}}$$

$$= \left(\frac{q}{p}\right)^3 - \left(\frac{q}{p}\right) = 11^3 - 11 = 1320$$

18. (d) The given function is

$$f(x) = \frac{\cos^{-1}\left(\frac{x^2 - 5x + 6}{x^2 - 9}\right)}{\log_e(x^2 - 3x + 2)}$$

Clearly, $-1 \le \frac{x^2 - 5x + 6}{x^2 - 9} \le 1$

and $x^2 - 3x + 2 > 0$ and $\neq 1$

$$\Rightarrow \quad \frac{(x-3)(2x+1)}{x^2 - 9} \ge 0 \text{ and } \frac{5(x-3)}{x^2 - 9} \ge 0$$

$$\Rightarrow \quad \frac{(2x+1)}{(x+3)} \ge 0 \text{ and } \frac{5}{(x+3)} \ge 0$$

Solution of this inequality is

$$x \in \left[-\frac{1}{2}, \infty\right) - \{-3\} \quad \text{... (i)}$$

For $x^2 - 3x + 2 > 0$ and $\neq 1$

Then, $\quad x \in (-\infty, 1) \cup (2, \infty)$

$$-\left\{\frac{3+\sqrt{5}}{2}, \frac{3-\sqrt{5}}{2}\right\} \text{... (ii)}$$

Taking Eqs. (i) $\cap$ (ii), we get

$$x \in \left[-\frac{1}{2}, 1\right) \cup (2, \infty) - \left\{\frac{3+\sqrt{5}}{2}, \frac{3-\sqrt{5}}{2}\right\}$$

19. (b) $\because \sin\theta \tan\theta + \tan\theta = \sin 2\theta$

$$\Rightarrow \quad \tan\theta(\sin\theta + 1) - \sin 2\theta = 0$$

$$\Rightarrow \quad \tan\theta(\sin\theta + 1 - 2\cos^2\theta) = 0$$

$$\Rightarrow \tan\theta[\sin\theta + 1 - 2(1 - \sin^2\theta)] = 0$$

$$\Rightarrow \quad \tan\theta(2\sin^2\theta + \sin\theta - 1) = 0$$

Either $\tan\theta = 0$ or

$2\sin^2\theta + \sin\theta - 1 = 0$

$$\Rightarrow \quad \theta = 0, \pi, -\pi$$

$$\Rightarrow \quad (2\sin\theta - 1)(\sin\theta + 1) = 0$$

$$\Rightarrow \quad \sin\theta = \frac{1}{2} \text{ and } \sin\theta = -1$$

$$\sin\theta = -1 \Rightarrow \theta = \frac{-\pi}{2},$$

which is not possible thus the possible values of 'θ' are $0, \pi, -\pi, \frac{5\pi}{6}$ and $\frac{\pi}{6}$.

Thus, $n(S) = 5$

$$T = \sum_{\theta \in S} \cos 2\theta = \cos 0 + \cos 2\pi$$

$$+ \cos(-2\pi) + \cos\left(\frac{5\pi}{3}\right) + \cos\left(\frac{\pi}{3}\right)$$

$$= 1 + 1 + 1 + \frac{1}{2} + \frac{1}{2} = 1 + 1 + 1 + 1$$

$\therefore T = 4$

Thus, $T + n(S) = 4 + 5 = 9$

20. (b) **Case I** When Δ same as '∨'

Then, $(p \,\Delta \sim q) \vee [(\sim p) \,\Delta q]$ becomes $(p \vee (\sim q)) \vee ((\sim p) \,\Delta q)$ always true.

Hence, $(p \vee q) \Rightarrow (p \vee \sim q) \vee ((\sim p) \vee q)$ is a tautology.

Case II When Δ same as '∧'

Then $(p \wedge q) \Rightarrow (p \wedge \sim q) \vee (\sim p \wedge q)$ becomes $p \wedge q$ is true, then $(p \wedge \sim q) \vee (\sim p \wedge q)$ is false.

So, the above expression is not a tautology.

Case III When Δ same as

$\Rightarrow$ Then $(p \Rightarrow \sim q) \vee (\sim p \Rightarrow q)$ is same as $(\sim p \vee \sim q) \vee (p \vee q)$ which is always true.

Thus, the expression

$(p \Rightarrow q) \Rightarrow (p \Rightarrow \sim q) \vee (\sim p \Rightarrow q)$ is a tautology.

Case IV When Δ same as ⇔

Then,

$(p \Leftrightarrow q) \Rightarrow (p \Leftrightarrow \sim q) \vee (\sim p \Leftrightarrow q)$

Clearly, $p \Leftrightarrow q$ is true when p and q have same truth values where $p \Leftrightarrow \sim q$ and $\sim p \Leftrightarrow q$ both are false.

Hence, the expression

$(p \Leftrightarrow q) \Rightarrow (p \Leftrightarrow \sim q) \vee (\sim p \Leftrightarrow q)$ is not a tautology.

Thus, '2' number of choices are available such that

$(p \Delta q) \Rightarrow (p \Delta \sim q) \vee ((\sim p) \Delta q)$ is a tautology.

21. (31) Given $3f(c) + 2f(a) + f(d) = f(b)$

Value of f (c)	Value of f (a)	Number of functions
0	1	7
	2	5
	3	3
	4	2
1	0	6
	2	2
	3	1
2	0	3
	1	1
3	0	1

Thus, total number of functions is 31.

22. (40) Let the student marks 'x' correct answers and 'y' incorrect. So, $3x - 2y = 5$ and $x + y \le 5$ where $x, y \in W$.

Thus, only possible solution is $(x, y) = (3, 2)$.

The student can mark correct answer by only one choice but for incorrect answers there are two choices.

So, total number of ways a student appearing in the examination gets 5 marks is

$${}^5C_3(1)^3 \cdot (2)^2 = \frac{5!}{3! \times 2!} \times 1 \times 4$$

$$= \frac{5 \times 4 \times 3!}{3! \times 2} \times 4 = 40$$

23. (8) Given that $A\left(\frac{3}{\sqrt{a}}, \sqrt{a}\right)$, $a > 0$ be a fixed point in the xy-plane, the image of A in Y-axis is $B\left(-\frac{3}{\sqrt{a}}, \sqrt{a}\right)$ and the image of B in X-axis is $C\left(\frac{-3}{\sqrt{a}}, -\sqrt{a}\right)$ and also given $D(3\cos\theta, a\sin\theta)$ in the fourth quadrant.

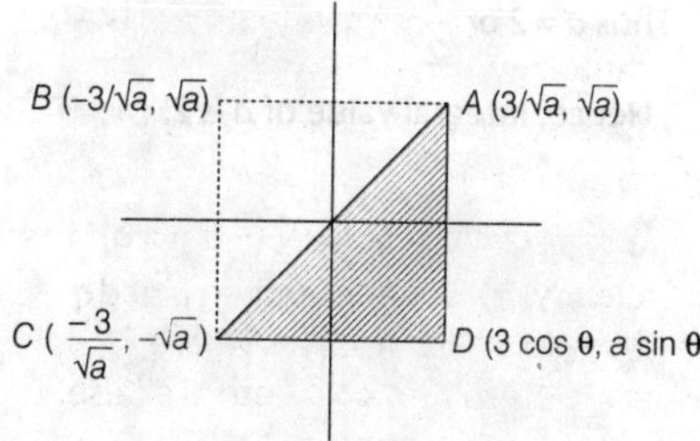

Thus, Area of

$$\Delta ACD = \frac{1}{2}\begin{vmatrix} \frac{3}{\sqrt{a}} & \sqrt{a} & 1 \\ -\frac{3}{\sqrt{a}} & -\sqrt{a} & 1 \\ 3\cos\theta & a\sin\theta & 1 \end{vmatrix}$$

Applying $R_1 \to R_1 + R_2$,

$$\Delta = \frac{1}{2}\begin{vmatrix} 0 & 0 & 2 \\ -\frac{3}{\sqrt{a}} & -\sqrt{a} & 1 \\ 3\cos\theta & a\sin\theta & 1 \end{vmatrix}$$

$$\Rightarrow \quad \Delta = \left|\frac{1}{2} 2\{-3\sqrt{a}\sin\theta + 3\sqrt{a}\cos\theta\}\right|$$

$$\Rightarrow \quad \Delta = |3\sqrt{a}(-\sin\theta + \cos\theta)|$$

$$\Rightarrow \quad \Delta = 3\sqrt{a}\,|-\sin\theta + \cos\theta|$$

$$\therefore \Delta_{max} = 3\sqrt{a} \cdot \sqrt{2} = 12 \text{ (given)}$$

$$\Rightarrow \sqrt{a} = 2\sqrt{2}$$

$$\Rightarrow \quad a = (2\sqrt{2})^2$$

$$= 8$$

24. (84) Given that,

A line having direction ratios $1, -4, 2$ intersect the lines

$$\frac{x-7}{3} = \frac{y-1}{-1} = \frac{z+2}{1}$$

and $\frac{x}{2} = \frac{y-7}{3} = \frac{z}{1}$ at the points A and B respectively.

Thus, $\frac{x-7}{3} = \frac{y-1}{-1} = \frac{z+2}{1} = \lambda$ (say)

$$\Rightarrow \quad A \equiv (3\lambda + 7, 1 - \lambda, \lambda - 2)$$

and $\frac{x}{2} = \frac{y-7}{3} = \frac{z}{1} = \mu$ (say)

$$\Rightarrow \quad B \equiv (2\mu, 3\mu + 7, \mu)$$

Thus, direction ratio of AB is

$$3\lambda - 2\mu + 7, -(\lambda + 3\mu + 6), \lambda - \mu - 2$$

Clearly,

$$\frac{3\lambda - 2\mu + 7}{1} = -\frac{(\lambda + 3\mu + 6)}{-4} = \frac{\lambda - \mu - 2}{2}$$

Taking above equation, we get

$$\lambda - \mu = -2 \quad \text{... (i)}$$

and $\quad \lambda - 5\mu = 10 \quad$ ... (ii)

Thus, solving Eqs. (i) and (ii), we get

$$\lambda = -5, \mu = -3$$

Hence, $A = (-8, 6, -7)$

and $\quad B = (-6, -2, -3)$

$$AB = \sqrt{(-8+6)^2 + (6+2)^2 + (-7+3)^2}$$

$$= \sqrt{4 + 64 + 16}$$

$$= \sqrt{84}$$

$$\therefore \quad (AB)^2 = 84$$

Thus, required answer is 84.

25. (7) The given function is

$$f(x) = \begin{cases} |2x^2 - 3x - 7| \text{ if } x \le -1 \\ [4x^2 - 1] \text{ if } -1 < x < 1 \\ ||x+1| + |x-2| \text{ if } x \ge 1 \end{cases}$$

Since, clearly $f(-1) = 2$ and $f(1) = 3$

For $x \in (-1, 1), (4x^2 - 1) \in [-1, 3)$

Hence, $f(x)$ will be discontinuous at $x = 1$ and also whenever $4x^2 - 1 = 0, 1$ or 2.

$$\Rightarrow 4x^2 - 1 = 0 \Rightarrow x = \pm\frac{1}{2}$$

and $\quad 4x^2 = 2 \Rightarrow x = \pm\frac{1}{\sqrt{2}}$

and $\quad 4x^2 = 3 \Rightarrow x = \pm\frac{\sqrt{3}}{2}$

Thus, all discontinuous points of $f(x)$ are $1, \pm\frac{1}{2}, \pm\frac{1}{\sqrt{2}}, \pm\frac{\sqrt{3}}{2}$

26. (1) Given,

$$f(\theta) = \sin\theta + \int_{-\pi/2}^{\pi/2} (\sin\theta + t\cos\theta) f(t)\, dt$$

$$= \sin\theta\left(1 + \int_{-\pi/2}^{\pi/2} f(t)\, dt\right) + \cos\theta\left(\int_{-\pi/2}^{\pi/2} tf(t)\, dt\right)$$

Clearly, $f(\theta) = a\sin\theta + b\cos\theta$

where $a = 1 + \int_{-\pi/2}^{\pi/2} f(t)\, dt$

$$= 1 + \int_{\pi/2}^{\pi/2} (a\sin t + b\cos t)\, dt$$

$$= 1 - a\cos\theta \Big|_{-\pi/2}^{\pi/2} + b\sin t\Big|_{-\pi/2}^{\pi/2}$$

$$\therefore \quad a = 1 + 2b \quad \text{... (i)}$$

and $\quad b = \int_{-\pi/2}^{\pi/2} t f(t)\, dt$

$$= \int_{-\pi/2}^{\pi/2} (at\sin t + bt\cos t)\, dt$$

$$b = 2a \quad \text{... (ii)}$$

Now solving Eqs. (i) and (ii), we get

$$a = -\frac{1}{3} \text{ and } b = -\frac{2}{3}$$

$$\therefore \quad f(\theta) = -\frac{1}{3}(\sin\theta + 2\cos\theta)$$

$$\Rightarrow \left|\int_0^{\pi/2} f(\theta)\, d\theta\right|$$

$$= \frac{1}{3}\left|\int_0^{\pi/2} (\sin\theta + 2\cos\theta)\, d\theta\right|$$

$$= \frac{1}{3}(1 + 2 \times 1) = 1$$

27. (34) Given, $\max_{0\le x\le 2}\left\{\frac{9-x^2}{5-x}\right\}=\alpha$

and $\min_{0\le x\le 2}\left\{\frac{9-x^2}{5-x}\right\}=\beta$

Let $f(x)=\frac{9-x^2}{5-x}$

$\Rightarrow f'(x)=\frac{(x-1)(x-9)}{(x-5)^2}$

Clearly, if $0\le x<1$, then $f'(x)>0$ but if $1<x\le 2$, then $f'(x)<0$.

Thus, maximum value occurs at $x=1$ in $[0,2]$.

Thus, $\alpha=f(1)=2$

Similarly, $f(x)$ gets minimum value at $x=0$ or $x=2$

Thus, $\beta=\min\{f(0),f(2)\}=\left\{\frac{9}{5},\frac{5}{3}\right\}=\frac{5}{3}$

Thus, $\alpha=2$ and $\beta=\frac{5}{3}$

Now, $\int_{\beta-8/3}^{2\alpha-1}\max\left\{\frac{9-x^2}{5-x},x\right\}dx$

$=\int_{-1}^{3}\max\left\{\frac{x^2-9}{x-5},x\right\}dx$

$=\int_{-1}^{9/5}\frac{x^2-9}{x-5}dx+\int_{9/5}^{3}x\,dx$

$=\int_{-1}^{9/5}\left(x+5+\frac{16}{x-5}\right)dx+\left(\frac{x^2}{2}\right)_{9/5}^{3}$

$=\frac{28}{25}+14+16\,ln_e\left(\frac{8}{15}\right)+\frac{72}{25}$

$=4+14+16\log_e\left(\frac{8}{15}\right)$

$=18+16\log_e\left(\frac{8}{15}\right)$

$\therefore\ \alpha_1=18$ and $\alpha_2=16$

$\therefore\ \alpha_1+\alpha_2=18+16=34$

Hence, the required answer is 34.

28. (2929) The given ellipse is $25x^2+4y^2=1$

Since, (α,β) lies on the given ellipse,

$$25\alpha^2+4\beta^2=1 \quad \text{... (i)}$$

Tangent to the parabola $y^2=4x$ is $y=mx+\frac{1}{m}$ passing through (α,β).

So, $\alpha m^2-\beta m+1=0$ has roots m_1 and $4m_1$.

$m_1+4m_1=\frac{\beta}{\alpha}$

and $m_1\cdot 4m_1=\frac{1}{\alpha}$

$\Rightarrow\quad 4\beta^2=25\alpha \quad$ ... (ii)

$\Rightarrow\quad 25(\alpha^2+\alpha)=1 \quad$ ... (iii)

Now, $(10\alpha+5)^2+(16\beta^2+50)^2$

$=25(2\alpha+1)^2+2500(2\alpha+1)^2$

$=2525(4\alpha^2+4\alpha+1)$

$=2525\left(\frac{4}{25}+1\right)\quad\left[\because \alpha^2+\alpha=\frac{1}{25}\right]$

$=101(29)=2929$

29. (19) The given curve are

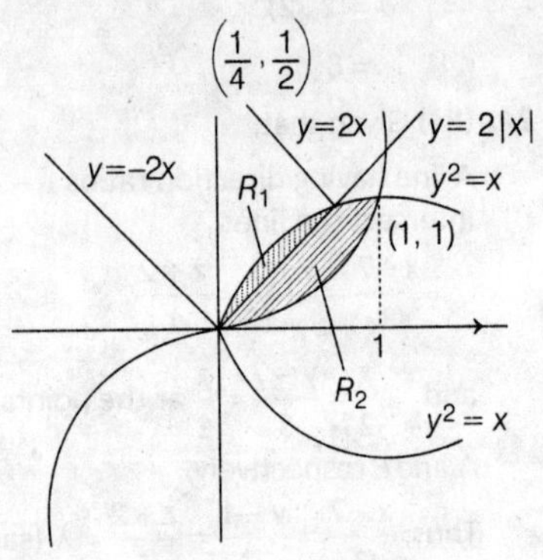

$c_1: y=x^3$,

$c_2: y^2=x$

and $c_3: y=2|x|$

and given that $\max\{R_1,R_2\}=R_2$

Thus, c_1 and c_2 intersect at (1,1) and c_2 and c_3 intersect at $\left(\frac{1}{4},\frac{1}{2}\right)$.

Clearly, $R_1=\left|\int_0^{1/4}(\sqrt{x}-2x)\,dx\right|$

$=\left|\left(\frac{2}{3}x^{3/2}\right)_0^{1/4}-(x^2)_0^{1/4}\right|$

$=\left|\frac{2}{3}\cdot\left(\frac{1}{8}\right)-\frac{1}{16}\right|$

$=\left|\frac{2}{24}-\frac{1}{16}\right|=\frac{1}{48}$

and $R_1+R_2=\int_0^1(\sqrt{x}-x^3)\,dx$

$=\frac{2}{3}-\frac{1}{4}$

$=\frac{5}{12}$

So, $\frac{R_2+R_1}{R_1}=\frac{\frac{5}{12}}{\frac{1}{48}}=20$

$\Rightarrow\quad \frac{R_2}{R_1}+1=20$

$\Rightarrow\quad \frac{R_2}{R_1}=19$

30. (2) Given that

$\mathbf{r}=(-\hat{i}+3\hat{k})+\lambda(\hat{i}-a\hat{j})$

and $\mathbf{r}=(-\hat{j}+2\hat{k})+\mu(\hat{i}-\hat{j}+\hat{k})$

So, let $\mathbf{b}_1=\hat{i}-a\hat{j}$ and $\mathbf{b}_2=\hat{i}-\hat{j}+\hat{k}$

$\mathbf{b}_1\times\mathbf{b}_2=\begin{vmatrix}\hat{i}&\hat{j}&\hat{k}\\1&-a&0\\1&-1&1\end{vmatrix}$

$=-a\hat{i}-\hat{j}+(a-1)\hat{k}$

Let $\mathbf{a}_1=-\hat{i}+3\hat{k}$ and $\mathbf{a}_2=-\hat{j}+2\hat{k}$

$\therefore\ \mathbf{a}_1-\mathbf{a}_2=(-\hat{i}+3\hat{k})-(-\hat{j}+2\hat{k})$

$=-\hat{i}+\hat{j}+\hat{k}$

Thus shortest distance

$=\left|\frac{(\mathbf{a}_1-\mathbf{a}_2)\cdot(\mathbf{b}_1\times\mathbf{b}_2)}{|\mathbf{b}_1\times\mathbf{b}_2|}\right|$

$\Rightarrow\sqrt{\frac{2}{3}}=$

$\left|\frac{(-\hat{i}+\hat{j}+\hat{k})\cdot(-a\hat{i}-\hat{j}+(a-1)\hat{k})}{\sqrt{a^2+1+(a-1)^2}}\right|$

$\Rightarrow\sqrt{\frac{2}{3}}=\frac{2(a-1)}{\sqrt{a^2+1+(a-1)^2}}$

$\Rightarrow\ 6(a^2-2a+1)=2a^2-2a+2$

$\Rightarrow\ 4a^2-10a+4=0$

$\Rightarrow\ 2a^2-5a+2=0$

$\Rightarrow\ (a-2)(2a-1)=0$

Thus $a=2$ or $\frac{1}{2}$

Hence, integral value of a is 2.

26 June 2022, Shift-II

1. (d) $f(x) = x - 1$

$$g(x) = \frac{x^2}{x^2 - 1}$$

$$fog(x) = f(g(x))$$

$$= \frac{x^2}{x^2 - 1} - 1$$

$$= \frac{x^2 - x^2 + 1}{x^2 - 1} = \frac{1}{x^2 - 1}$$

$fog(x) = \frac{1}{x^2 - 1}$ is an even function,

$x \neq \pm 1$

$\Rightarrow$ It is many one function.

$$y = \frac{1}{x^2 - 1}$$

$$x^2 = \frac{1}{y} + 1$$

$$\Rightarrow \quad x^2 = \frac{y + 1}{y}$$

$$\frac{y + 1}{y} \geq 0$$

sign of y sign of y

$+ \quad - \quad +$

-1 sign of y 0

$y \in (-\infty, -1] \cup (0, \infty)$

Range $\neq$ codomain $\Rightarrow fog(x)$ is into function.

2. (c) $\alpha x + y + z = 5$

$x + 2y + 3z = 4$

$x + 3y + 5z = \beta$

For infinitely many solutions,

$$\Delta = \Delta_1 = \Delta_2 = \Delta_3 = 0$$

$$\Delta = \begin{vmatrix} \alpha & 1 & 1 \\ 1 & 2 & 3 \\ 1 & 3 & 5 \end{vmatrix}$$

$$= \alpha(1) - (5 - 3) + (3 - 2)$$

$$= \alpha - 2 + 1 = \alpha - 1$$

$\therefore \quad \Delta = 0$

$\Rightarrow \quad \alpha - 1 = 0$

$\alpha = 1$

$$\Delta_1 = \begin{vmatrix} 5 & 1 & 1 \\ 4 & 2 & 3 \\ \beta & 3 & 5 \end{vmatrix} = 0$$

$\Rightarrow 5(10 - 9) - 4(5 - 3) + \beta(3 - 2) = 0$

$\Rightarrow \quad 5 - 8 + \beta = 0$

$\Rightarrow \quad -3 + \beta = 0$

$\Rightarrow \quad \beta = 3$

$\therefore \quad (\alpha, \beta) = (1, 3)$

3. (c) $A = \sum_{n=1}^{\infty} \frac{1}{(3 + (-1)^n)^n}$

$$= \frac{1}{2} + \frac{1}{4^2} + \frac{1}{2^3} + \frac{1}{4^4} + \ldots\ldots$$

$$= \left(\frac{1}{2} + \frac{1}{2^3} + \ldots\right) + \left(\frac{1}{4^2} + \frac{1}{4^4} + \ldots\right)$$

$$= \frac{\frac{1}{2}}{1 - \frac{1}{4}} + \frac{\frac{1}{16}}{1 - \frac{1}{16}}$$

$$= \frac{2}{3} + \frac{1}{15} = \frac{11}{15}$$

$$B = \sum_{n=1}^{\infty} \frac{(-1)^n}{(3 + (-1)^n)^n}$$

$$= \frac{-1}{2} + \frac{1}{4^2} - \frac{1}{2^3} + \frac{1}{4^4} - \ldots\ldots$$

$$= -\left(\frac{1}{2} + \frac{1}{2^3} + \ldots\right) + \left(\frac{1}{4^2} + \frac{1}{4^4} + \ldots\right)$$

$$= \frac{-\frac{1}{2}}{1 - \frac{1}{4}} + \frac{\frac{1}{16}}{1 - \frac{1}{16}}$$

$$= \frac{-2}{3} + \frac{1}{15} = \frac{-9}{15}$$

$$\therefore \frac{A}{B} = \frac{11}{15} \times \frac{15}{-9} = \frac{-11}{9}$$

4. (c) $\lim_{x \to 0} \frac{\cos(\sin x) - \cos x}{x^4}$

$$= \lim_{x \to 0} \frac{2 \sin\left(\frac{\sin x + x}{2}\right) \cdot \sin\left(\frac{x - \sin x}{2}\right)}{x^4} \quad \left[\frac{0}{0} \text{ form}\right]$$

$$= \lim_{x \to 0} \frac{2 \sin\left(\frac{\sin x + x}{2}\right)}{\left(\frac{\sin x + x}{2}\right)} \cdot \frac{\sin\left(\frac{x - \sin x}{2}\right)}{\left(\frac{x - \sin x}{2}\right)} \times \left(\frac{x + \sin x}{2}\right) \times \left(\frac{x - \sin x}{2}\right) \frac{1}{x^4}$$

$$= \lim_{x \to 0} 2 \left[\frac{\sin\left(\frac{\sin x + x}{2}\right)}{\left(\frac{\sin x + x}{2}\right)}\right] \left[\frac{\sin\left(\frac{x - \sin x}{2}\right)}{\left(\frac{x - \sin x}{2}\right)}\right] \left(\frac{x^2 - \sin^2 x}{4}\right) \cdot \frac{1}{x^4}$$

We know, $\lim_{t \to 0} \frac{\sin t}{t} = 1$

Now, $\lim_{x \to 0} 2 \left(\frac{x^2 - \sin^2 x}{4x^4}\right) \quad \left[\frac{0}{0} \text{ form}\right]$

Using L' Hospital's rule

$$\lim_{x \to 0} 2 \left(\frac{2x - 2 \sin x \cos x}{16x^3}\right)$$

$$= \lim_{x \to 0} \frac{2x - \sin 2x}{8x^3} \quad \left[\frac{0}{0} \text{ form}\right]$$

Using L' Hospital's rule,

$$\lim_{x \to 0} \frac{2 - 2 \cos 2x}{24x^2} \quad \left[\frac{0}{0} \text{ form}\right]$$

$$= \lim_{x \to 0} \left(\frac{4 \sin 2x}{48x}\right)$$

$$= \frac{1}{6} \lim_{x \to 0} \cdot \frac{\sin 2x}{2x} \quad \left[\lim_{t \to 0} \frac{\sin t}{t} = 1\right]$$

$$\therefore \quad = \frac{1}{6}$$

5. (b) Given, $f(x) = \min\{1, 1 + x \sin x\}$, $0 \leq x \leq 2\pi$

Number of non-differentiable points $= 1 (m)$

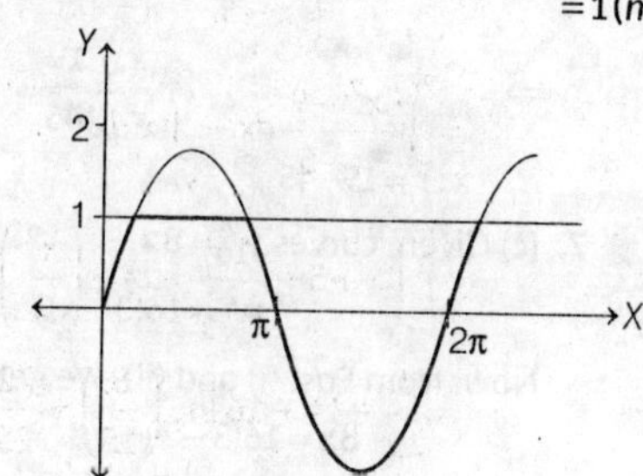

Number of non-continuous point $= 0 (n)$

$\therefore \quad (m, n) = (1, 0)$

6. (b) Dimensions of cuboid : $2x, 4x, 5x$

Radius of hemisphere r.

Let sum of surface area,

$$S = S_1 + S_2$$

$S_1 =$ Surface area of cuboid $= 3\pi r^2$

$S_2 =$ Surface area of hemisphere

$$= [2(2x)(4x) + (4x)(5x) + (2x)(5x)]$$

$$= (8x^2 + 20x^2 + 10x^2) \times 2$$

$$= 38x^2 \times 2 = 76x^2$$

$\therefore \quad S = 3\pi r^2 + 76x^2 = k$ (constant)

$$\frac{dS}{dx} = 0$$

$$\Rightarrow \quad 6\pi r\frac{dr}{dx}+152x=0$$

$$\Rightarrow \quad \frac{dr}{dx}=\frac{152x}{6\pi r} \quad \text{...(i)}$$

$V_1=$ Volume of cuboid

$=(2x)(4x)(5x)=40x^3$

$V_2=$ Volume of hemisphere $=\frac{2}{3}\pi r^3$

Total volume $=V_1+V_2=40x^3+\frac{2}{3}\pi r^3$

For maximum volume $\frac{dV}{dx}=0$

$$\frac{2}{3}\pi 3r^2\frac{dr}{dx}+120x^2=0$$

$$\Rightarrow \quad 2\pi r^2\frac{dr}{dx}+120x^2=0$$

$$\Rightarrow \quad 2\pi r^2\left(\frac{-76x}{3\pi r}\right)+120x^2=0$$

$$\Rightarrow \quad 8x\left[\frac{-19r}{3}+15x\right]=0$$

$$\Rightarrow \quad 8x=0$$

$$\Rightarrow \quad x=0$$

or $\quad \frac{-19r}{3}+15x=0$

$$\Rightarrow \quad 15x=\frac{19}{3}r$$

$$\Rightarrow \quad \frac{x}{r}=\frac{19}{45}$$

$\therefore \quad x:r=19:45$

7. (c) Given, curves $y^2=8x$ ...(i)

$y^2=16(3-x)$ ...(ii)

Now, from Eqs. (i) and (ii), we get

$$8x=16(3-x)$$

$$\Rightarrow \quad 8x=48-16x$$

$$\Rightarrow \quad 24x=48$$

$$\Rightarrow \quad x=2$$

$$\Rightarrow \quad y^2=8(2)$$

and $\quad y^2=16$

$$\Rightarrow \quad y=\pm 4$$

Common points of both the graphs

(2, 4), (2, –4)

Y, X, $y^2=8x$, (2, 4), (0, 0), (3, 0), (2, –4), $y^2=16(3-x)$

$$\text{Required area}=\left[\int_{-4}^{4}\left[\left(3-\frac{y^2}{16}\right)-\frac{y^2}{8}\right]dy\right]$$

$$=2\int_0^4\left[\left(3-\frac{y^2}{16}\right)-\frac{y^2}{8}\right]dy$$

$$=2\left[3y-\frac{y^3}{48}-\frac{y^3}{24}\right]_0^4$$

$$=2\left[12-\frac{64}{48}-\frac{64}{24}\right]=16$$

8. (a) Let $I=\int\frac{1}{x}\sqrt{\frac{1-x}{1+x}}dx$

Now, put $x=\cos 2\theta$

$$\Rightarrow \quad dx=-2\sin 2\theta d\theta$$

$$\therefore \quad I=\int\frac{1}{\cos 2\theta}\sqrt{\frac{1-\cos 2\theta}{1+\cos 2\theta}}(-2\sin 2\theta)d\theta$$

$$=-2\int\frac{\tan\theta}{\cos 2\theta}(2\sin\theta\cdot\cos\theta)d\theta$$

$$=-2\int\frac{(1-\cos 2\theta)}{\cos 2\theta}d\theta$$

$$=-2\int\sec 2\theta\, d\theta+2\int d\theta$$

$$=\frac{-2}{2}\ln|\sec 2\theta+\tan 2\theta|+2\theta+c$$

$$=\ln|\sec 2\theta-\tan 2\theta|+2\theta+c$$

$$=\ln\left|\frac{1-\sin 2\theta}{\cos 2\theta}\right|+\cos^{-1}x+c$$

$[2\theta=\cos^{-1}x]$

$$=\ln\left|\frac{1-\sqrt{1-x^2}}{x}\right|+\cos^{-1}x+c$$

$$\Rightarrow \quad g(x)=\ln\left|\frac{1-\sqrt{1-x^2}}{x}\right|+\cos^{-1}x$$

Now,

$$g\left(\frac{1}{2}\right)=\ln\left|\frac{1-\sqrt{1-\frac{1}{4}}}{\frac{1}{2}}\right|+\cos^{-1}\left(\frac{1}{2}\right)$$

$$g\left(\frac{1}{2}\right)=\ln|2-\sqrt{3}|+\frac{\pi}{3}$$

$$g\left(\frac{1}{2}\right)=\ln\left|\frac{(2-\sqrt{3})(\sqrt{3}+1)}{\sqrt{3}+1}\right|+\frac{\pi}{3}$$

$$g\left(\frac{1}{2}\right)=\ln\left|\frac{2\sqrt{3}+2-3-\sqrt{3})}{\sqrt{3}+1}\right|+\frac{\pi}{3}$$

$$g\left(\frac{1}{2}\right)=\ln\left|\frac{\sqrt{3}-1}{\sqrt{3}+1}\right|+\frac{\pi}{3}$$

9. (d) $x\frac{dy}{dx}+2y=xe^x$

Given, $y(1)=0$ and $\frac{dy}{dx}+\frac{2y}{x}=e^x$

$$\text{IF}=e^{\int\frac{2}{x}dx}=e^{2\ln x}=e^{\ln x^2}=x^2$$

Solution is $yx^2=\int e^x(x^2)dx+c$ ...(i)

$$\int e^x f(x)dx=e^x[f(x)-f'(x)+f''(x)$$

$$-f'''(x)+\ldots+(-1)^n f^n(x)]+c$$

$$\therefore \int e^x(x^2)dx=e^x[x^2-2x+2] \quad \text{...(ii)}$$

Put Eq. (ii) in Eq. (i),

$$yx^2=e^x[x^2-2x+2]+c$$

$$\Rightarrow \quad 0=e[1-2+2]+c$$

$$\Rightarrow \quad 0=e+c$$

$$\Rightarrow \quad c=-e$$

Thus, $\quad yx^2=e^x[x^2-2x+2]-e$

$$\Rightarrow \quad y=\frac{e^x}{x^2}[x^2-2x+2]-\frac{e}{x^2}$$

So, $z(x)=x^2\frac{e^x}{x^2}[x^2-2x+2]-\frac{ex^2}{x^2}-e^x$

$$=e^x[x^2-2x+2]-e-e^x$$

$$=e^x[x^2-2x+1]-e$$

$$z'(x)=e^x(x^2-2x+1)+e^x(2x-2)$$

$$=e^x x^2-2xe^x+e^x+2xe^x-e^x 2$$

$$=e^x x^2-e^x$$

$$z'(x)=e^x(x^2-1)$$

$$\Rightarrow z'(x)=0 \Rightarrow e^x(x^2-1)=0$$

$\therefore \quad e^x>0, \forall x\in R$

$\therefore \quad x^2-1=0$

$$(x-1)(x+1)=0$$

$$\Rightarrow \quad x=1,-1$$

$$z''(x)=e^x(2x)+(x^2-1)e^x$$

$$=e^x(x^2+2x-1)$$

$$z''(-1)=(e^{-1})(1-2-1)$$

$$=\frac{1}{e}(1-3)=\frac{-2}{e}<0$$

$\therefore$ Maxima at $x=-1$

Thus, $z(-1)=e^{-1}(1+2+1)-e$

$$=\frac{4}{e}-e$$

10. (c) Given,

$$\frac{dy}{dx}+e^x(x^2-2)y=(x^2-2x)(x^2-2)e^{2x};$$

$y(0)=0$

$$\text{IF}=e^{\int(x^2-2)e^x dx}$$

$$=e^{[\int x^2e^x dx-\int 2e^x dx]}$$

$$=e^{x^2e^x-2\int xe^x dx-2e^x}$$

$$=e^{x^2e^x-2[xe^x-e^x]-2e^x}$$

$$=e^{(x^2-2x)e^x}$$

∴ Solution is

$$ye^{(x^2-2x)e^x} = \int e^{(x^2-2x)e^x} \times (x^2-2x)(x^2-2)e^{2x}dx$$

Let $(x^2-2x)e^x = t$

$$e^x(x^2-2x)dx + e^x(2x-2)dx = dt$$

$$\Rightarrow \quad e^x(x^2-2x+2x-2)dx = dt$$

$$\Rightarrow \quad e^x(x^2-2)dx = dt$$

$$\Rightarrow \quad ye^{(x^2-2x)e^x} = \int e^t \cdot t dt$$

$$\Rightarrow \quad ye^{(x^2-2x)e^x} = e^t t - e^t + c$$

$$\Rightarrow \quad ye^{(x^2-2x)e^x} = e^t(t-1) + c$$

$$\Rightarrow \quad ye^{(x^2-2x)e^x} = e^{(x^2-2x)e^x}[(x^2-2x)e^x - 1] + c$$

$$y(0) = 0$$

$$\therefore \quad 0 = e^0[0-1] + c$$

$$0 = (-1) + c$$

$$\Rightarrow \quad c = 1$$

Thus, $ye^{(x^2-2x)e^x} = e^{(x^2-2x)e^x}[(x^2-2x)e^x - 1] + 1$

To find $y(2)$

$$ye^{(4-4)e^2} = e^{(4-4)e^2}[(4-4)e^2 - 1] + 1$$

$$\Rightarrow \quad ye^0 = e^0[-1] + 1$$

$$\Rightarrow \quad y = -1 + 1$$

$$\Rightarrow \quad y = 0$$

11. (b) Curves $\frac{x^2}{16} + \frac{y^2}{9} = 1$; $x^2 + y^2 = 12$

To find $= 12m^2$

Let the slope of common tangent be m.

Equation of tangent to $x^2 + y^2 = 12$

$$y = mx \pm \sqrt{12 + 12m^2}$$

Equation of tangent to ellipse

$$\frac{x^2}{16} + \frac{y^2}{9} = 1$$

$$y = mx \pm \sqrt{16m^2 + 9}$$

Both equations are identical,

$$mx \pm \sqrt{12 + 12m^2} = mx \pm \sqrt{16m^2 + 9}$$

$$\Rightarrow \quad 12 + 12m^2 = 16m^2 + 9$$

$$3 = 4m^2$$

$$\Rightarrow \quad m^2 = \frac{3}{4}$$

$$\therefore \quad 12m^2 = 12 \times \frac{3}{4} = 9$$

12. (c)

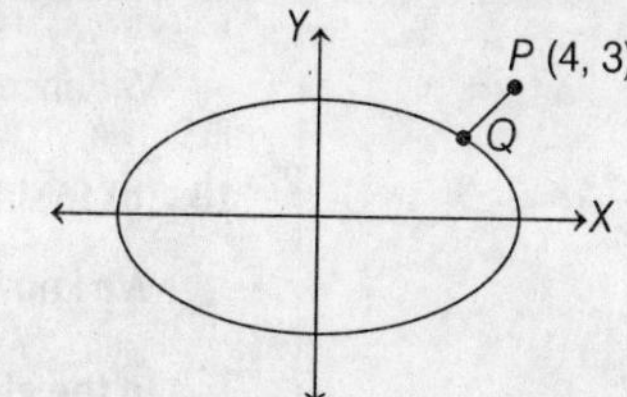

Equation of ellipse is

$$x^2 + 2y^2 = 4$$

$$\frac{x^2}{4} + \frac{y^2}{2} = 1$$

Let the point $Q(2\cos\theta, \sqrt{2}\sin\theta)$.

Let the mid-point of PQ be $R = (h, k)$

$\Rightarrow 2h = 4 + 2\cos\theta$ and $2k = 3 + \sqrt{2}\sin\theta$

$$\Rightarrow \quad (h-2)^2 + \left(\frac{2k-3}{\sqrt{2}}\right)^2 = 1$$

$$\Rightarrow \quad \frac{(x-2)^2}{1} + \frac{4\left(y-\frac{3}{2}\right)^2}{2} = 1$$

$$\therefore \text{ Locus is } \frac{(x-2)^2}{1} + \frac{\left(y-\frac{3}{2}\right)^2}{\frac{1}{2}} = 1$$

$$\Rightarrow \quad e^2 = 1 - \frac{1}{2} = \frac{1}{2}$$

$$\Rightarrow \quad e = \frac{1}{\sqrt{2}}$$

13. (c) Given $\frac{x^2}{a^2} - \frac{y^2}{9} = 1$; point $(8, 3\sqrt{3})$

$$\frac{64}{a^2} - \frac{9\times 3}{9} = 1$$

$$\Rightarrow \quad \frac{64}{a^2} - 3 = 1$$

$$\Rightarrow \quad \frac{64}{a^2} = 4$$

$$\Rightarrow \quad a^2 = 16$$

∴ Equation of normal at point $(8, 3\sqrt{3})$

$$(y - y_1) = \frac{-y_1a^2}{x_1b^2}(x - x_1)$$

$$\Rightarrow \quad (y - 3\sqrt{3}) = \frac{-3\sqrt{3}}{8} \times \frac{16}{9}(x-8)$$

$$y - 3\sqrt{3} = \frac{-2}{\sqrt{3}}(x-8)$$

Verify $(-1, 9\sqrt{3})$ in the equation of tangent

$$y - 3\sqrt{3} = -\frac{2}{\sqrt{3}}(-1-8)$$

$$\Rightarrow \quad y - 3\sqrt{3} = \frac{2}{\sqrt{3}}(9)$$

$$\Rightarrow \quad y - 3\sqrt{3} = 2(3\sqrt{3})$$

$$\Rightarrow \quad y = 6\sqrt{3} + 3\sqrt{3}$$

$$\Rightarrow \quad y = 9\sqrt{3}$$

Thus, $(-1, 9\sqrt{3})$ is the required point.

14. (c) Given, plane $2x + y - 5z = 0$

$$3x - y + 4z = 7$$

Both the planes are perpendicular to each other.

Let the equation of the plane formed be

$$2x + y - 5z + \lambda(3x - y + 4z - 7) = 0$$

$$\Rightarrow 2x + y - 5z + 3\lambda x - \lambda y + 4\lambda z - 7\lambda = 0$$

$$\Rightarrow (2+3\lambda)x + (1-\lambda)y + (-5+4\lambda)z - 7\lambda = 0 \quad \text{...(i)}$$

This plane is perpendicular to $2x + y - 5z = 0$

Then, $\quad a_1a_2 + b_1b_2 + c_1c_2 = 0$

$$2(2+3\lambda) + (1-\lambda) - 5(-5+4\lambda) = 0$$

$$\Rightarrow \quad 4 + 6\lambda + 1 - \lambda + 25 - 20\lambda = 0$$

$$\Rightarrow \quad -15\lambda + 30 = 0$$

$$\Rightarrow \quad -15\lambda = -30$$

$$\lambda = 2$$

Substitute $\lambda = 2$ in the Eq. (i),

$$(2+6)x + (1-2)y + (-5+8)z = 14$$

$$\Rightarrow \quad 8x - y + 3z = 14 \quad \text{...(ii)}$$

Put (1, 0, 2) in the given Eq. (ii).

LHS $= 8 - 0 + 6$

$= 14$

$=$ RHS

15. (b) $\mathbf{r} = (\hat{i} - \hat{j} + \hat{k}) + \lambda(3\hat{j} - \hat{k}) \quad$ ...(i)

$\mathbf{r} = (\alpha\hat{i} - \hat{j}) + \mu(2\hat{i} - 3\hat{k}) \quad$ ...(ii)

Given Eqs. (i) and (ii) are coplanar.

From Eq. (i), $x_1 = 1, y_1 = -1, z_1 = 1$

$a_1 = 0, b_1 = 3, c_1 = -1$

From Eq. (II), $x_2 = \alpha, y_2 = -1, z_2 = 0$

$a_2 = 2, b_2 = 0, c_2 = -3$

For coplanarity,

$$\begin{vmatrix} a_1 & b_1 & c_1 \\ a_2 & b_2 & c_2 \\ x_1 - x_2 & y_1 - y_2 & z_1 - z_2 \end{vmatrix} = 0$$

$$\Rightarrow \quad \begin{vmatrix} 0 & 3 & -1 \\ 2 & 0 & -3 \\ 1-\alpha & 0 & 1 \end{vmatrix} = 0$$

$$\Rightarrow \quad (1-\alpha)(-9) + (0-6) = 0$$

$$\Rightarrow \quad (\alpha - 1)9 - 6 = 0$$

$$\Rightarrow \quad 9\alpha - 9 - 6 = 0$$

$$\Rightarrow \quad 9\alpha = 15$$

$$\Rightarrow \quad \alpha = \frac{5}{3}$$

$$\text{Now, } \mathbf{n} = \begin{vmatrix} \hat{\mathbf{i}} & \hat{\mathbf{j}} & \hat{\mathbf{k}} \\ a_1 & b_1 & c_1 \\ a_2 & b_2 & c_2 \end{vmatrix} = \begin{vmatrix} \hat{\mathbf{i}} & \hat{\mathbf{j}} & \hat{\mathbf{k}} \\ 0 & 3 & -1 \\ 2 & 0 & -3 \end{vmatrix}$$

$$= -9\hat{\mathbf{i}} - 2\hat{\mathbf{j}} - 6\hat{\mathbf{k}} = (-9, -2, -6)$$

Equation of plane

$$-9(x - x_1) - 2(y - y_1) - 6(z - z_1) = 0$$

$$\Rightarrow \quad 9(x-1) + 2(y+1) + 6(z-1) = 0$$

$$\Rightarrow \quad 9x + 2y + 6z - 13 = 0$$

Perpendicular distance from $(\alpha, 0, 0)$,

$$\left|\frac{9 \cdot \frac{5}{3} + 0 + 0 - 13}{\sqrt{81 + 36 + 4}}\right| = \frac{2}{\sqrt{121}} = \frac{2}{11}$$

16. (d) Let $\mathbf{v} = \lambda \mathbf{a} + \mu \mathbf{b}$

$$\mathbf{v} = \lambda(1, 1, 2) + \mu(2, -3, 1)$$

$$\mathbf{v} = (\lambda + 2\mu, \lambda - 3\mu, 2\lambda + \mu)$$

$$\mathbf{v} \cdot \hat{\mathbf{j}} = 7$$

$$\mathbf{v} \cdot \frac{\mathbf{c}}{|\mathbf{c}|} = \frac{2}{\sqrt{3}}$$

$$\Rightarrow \quad \lambda - 3\mu = 7 \quad \text{...(i)}$$

$$\Rightarrow \quad \mathbf{v} \cdot \frac{\mathbf{c}}{\sqrt{3}} = \frac{2}{\sqrt{3}}$$

$$\mathbf{v} \cdot \mathbf{c} = 2$$

$$\Rightarrow (\lambda + 2\mu, \lambda - 3\mu, 2\lambda + \mu) \cdot (1, -1, 1) = 2$$

$$\Rightarrow \quad \lambda + 2\mu - \lambda + 3\mu + 2\lambda + \mu = 2$$

$$\Rightarrow \quad 2\lambda + 6\mu = 2$$

$$\Rightarrow \quad \lambda + 3\mu = 1 \quad \text{...(ii)}$$

and $\lambda - 3\mu = 7$ [from Eq. (i)]

$$\therefore \quad 2\lambda = 8 \Rightarrow \lambda = 4$$

and $\mu = -1$

Thus, $\mathbf{v} = (2, 7, 7)$

Hence, $\mathbf{v} \cdot (\hat{\mathbf{i}} + \hat{\mathbf{k}}) = (2, 7, 7) \cdot (1, 0, 1) = 2 + 7 = 9$

17. (c) (Mean) $= 15$

Standard deviation $= 2$

Number of observation $= 50$

Sum of correct and incorrect observation $= 70$

$(\text{Mean})_c = 16$, Variance $= ?$

$$(\text{Mean})_{\text{incorrect}} = \frac{\Sigma x_i}{50} = 15$$

$$\Rightarrow (\Sigma x_i)_{\text{incorrect}} = 750$$

$$(\text{Mean})_c = \frac{\Sigma x_i}{50} = 16 \Rightarrow (\Sigma x_i)_c = 800$$

$$\therefore (\Sigma x_i)_c - (\Sigma x_i)_{\text{incorrect}} = 800 - 750 = 50$$

If wrong observation was x corrected one is $x + 50$

$$\Rightarrow \quad x + (x + 50) = 70 \Rightarrow 2x = 20 \Rightarrow x = 10$$

Thus, correct observation $= 60$

$$\text{Variance} = \frac{\Sigma x_i^2}{50} - (15)^2 = 2^2 \Rightarrow \frac{\Sigma x_i^2}{50} = 229$$

$$\Rightarrow \quad (\Sigma x_i^2)_{\text{incorrect}} = 11450$$

Now, $(\Sigma x_i^2)_c = 11450 - (10)^2 + (60)^2 = 14950$

$$\text{Variance of correct set} = \frac{14950}{50} - (16)^2 = 299 - 256 = 43$$

18. (b) $16 \sin 20° \sin 40° \sin 80°$

We know that $\sin\theta \sin(60 - \theta) \sin(60 + \theta) = \frac{1}{4} \sin 3\theta$

In the given question, let $\theta = 20°$

$$\therefore 16 \sin 20° \sin(60° - 20°) \sin(60° + 20°) = 16 \times \frac{1}{4} \sin 60°$$

$$= \frac{4\sqrt{3}}{2} = 2\sqrt{3}$$

19. (c) $\cos^{-1}\left\{\frac{3}{10} \cos\left(\tan^{-1}\frac{4}{3}\right) + \frac{2}{5} \sin\left(\tan^{-1}\frac{4}{3}\right)\right\}$

Let $\tan^{-1}\left(\frac{4}{3}\right) = \theta \Rightarrow \tan\theta = \frac{4}{3}$

[Right triangle with sides 3 (base), 4 (perpendicular), 5 (hypotenuse), angle θ]

$$\therefore \quad \cos\theta = \frac{3}{5} \text{ and } \sin\theta = \frac{4}{5}$$

$$\text{So, } \cos^{-1}\left\{\frac{3}{10} \cos\left(\tan^{-1}\frac{4}{3}\right) + \frac{2}{5} \sin\left(\tan^{-1}\frac{4}{3}\right)\right\}$$

$$= \cos^{-1}\left\{\frac{3}{10} \cos\theta + \frac{2}{5} \sin\theta\right\} = \cos^{-1}\left\{\frac{3}{10} \times \frac{3}{5} + \frac{2}{5} \times \frac{4}{5}\right\}$$

$$= \cos^{-1}\left\{\frac{9}{50} + \frac{8}{25}\right\} = \cos^{-1}\left\{\frac{1}{2}\right\} = \frac{\pi}{3}$$

20. (c) Given that $r \vee (\sim p) \Rightarrow (p \wedge q) \vee r$ is a tautology.

Now take option (a) : $p = r$

$p = r$	q	$\sim p$	$r \vee (\sim p)$	$(p \wedge q)$	$(p \wedge q) \vee r$	$r \vee (\sim p) \Rightarrow (p \wedge q) \vee r$
T	T	F	T	T	T	T
T	F	F	T	F	T	T
F	T	T	T	F	F	F
F	F	T	T	F	F	F

Now take option (b).

$r = q$

p	$q = r$	$\sim p$	$r \vee (\sim p)$	$(p \wedge q)$	$(p \wedge q) \vee r$	$r \vee (\sim p) \Rightarrow (p \wedge q) \vee r$
T	T	F	T	T	T	T
T	F	F	T	F	F	F
F	T	T	T	F	T	T
F	F	T	T	F	F	F

Take option (c) : $r = \sim p$

p	q	$\sim p = r$	$r \vee (\sim p)$	$(p \wedge q)$	$(p \wedge q) \vee r$	$r \vee (\sim p) \Rightarrow (p \wedge q) \vee r$
T	T	F	F	T	T	T
T	F	F	F	F	F	T
F	T	T	T	F	T	T
F	F	T	T	F	T	T

$r = \sim p$ is correct option.

21. (248) Given,

$f(x+y)=2^x f(y)+4^y f(x), \forall x, y \in R$

$f(2)=3$

To calculate : $14\dfrac{f'(4)}{f'(2)}$

$f(x+y)=2^x f(y)+4^y f(x)$

Put $y=2$

$f(x+2)=2^x 3+4^2 f(x)$

$f(x+2)=2^x\cdot 3+16f(x)$

$f'(x+2)=16f'(x)+3\cdot 2^x \ln 2$

Put $x=2$, $f'(4)=16f'(2)+12\ln 2$ ...(i)

$f(y+2)=4f(y)+4^y\cdot 3$

$f'(y+2)=4f'(y)+3\cdot 4^y \ln 4$

Put $y=2$, $f'(4)=4f'(2)+96\ln 2$ ...(ii)

Solving Eqs. (i) and (ii), we get

$16f'(2)+12\ln 2=4f'(2)+96\ln 2$

$\Rightarrow \quad 12f'(2)=84\ln 2$

$\Rightarrow \quad f'(2)=7\ln 2$ ...(iii)

Put Eq. (iii) in Eq. (i), we get

$f'(4)=16(7\ln 2)+12\ln 2$

$\Rightarrow \quad f'(4)=112\ln 2+12\ln 2$

$\Rightarrow \quad f'(4)=124\ln 2$

$\therefore \quad 14\left(\dfrac{f'(4)}{f'(2)}\right)=\dfrac{14\times 124\ln 2}{7\ln 2}=248$

22. (4) Given, $p+q=3, p^4+q^4=369$

To find $=\left(\dfrac{1}{p}+\dfrac{1}{q}\right)^{-2}$

$p^4+q^4=369$

$\Rightarrow \quad (p^2+q^2)^2-2(pq)^2=369$

$\Rightarrow \quad ((p+q)^2-2pq)^2-2(pq)^2=369$

$\Rightarrow \quad (9-2pq)^2-2(pq)^2=369$

$\Rightarrow 81+4(pq)^2-36pq-2(pq)^2=369$

$\Rightarrow \quad 2(pq)^2-36pq=288$

$\Rightarrow \quad (pq)^2-18pq=144$

$\Rightarrow \quad (pq)^2-18pq-144=0$

$\Rightarrow \quad (pq)^2-24pq+6pq-144=0$

$\Rightarrow \quad pq(pq-24)+6(pq-24)=0$

$\Rightarrow \quad (pq-24)(pq+6)=0$

$\Rightarrow \quad pq=24$ or $pq=-6$

$pq=24$ (not possible)

If $pq=-6$

$\left(\dfrac{1}{p}+\dfrac{1}{q}\right)^{-2}=\dfrac{(pq)^2}{(p+q)^2}$

$=\dfrac{(-6)^2}{(3)^2}=4$

23. (2) Given, $z^2+z+1=0$

$\Rightarrow \quad z=\omega, \omega^2$

$=\left|\sum_{n=1}^{15}\left(z^n+(-1)^n\dfrac{1}{z^n}\right)^2\right|$

$=\left|\sum_{n=1}^{15}\left(z^{2n}+\dfrac{1}{z^{2n}}+2(-1)^n\right)\right|$

$=\left|\dfrac{\omega^2(1-\omega^{30})}{1-\omega^2}+\dfrac{\dfrac{1}{\omega^2}\left(1-\dfrac{1}{\omega^{30}}\right)}{1-\dfrac{1}{\omega^2}}+2(-1)\right|$

$=\left|\dfrac{\omega^2(1-1)}{1-\omega^2}+\dfrac{\dfrac{1}{\omega^2}(1-1)}{1-\dfrac{1}{\omega^2}}-2\right|$

$=|0+0-2|=2$

24. (100) Given,

$X=\begin{bmatrix}0&1&0\\0&0&1\\0&0&0\end{bmatrix}, Y=\alpha I+\beta X+\gamma X^2$

$Z=\alpha^2 I-\alpha\beta X+(\beta^2-\alpha\gamma)X^2$

$Y^{-1}=\begin{bmatrix}\frac{1}{5}&\frac{-2}{5}&\frac{1}{5}\\0&\frac{1}{5}&\frac{-2}{5}\\0&0&\frac{1}{5}\end{bmatrix}$

To find $(\alpha-\beta+\gamma)^2$

From given value of X

$X^2=\begin{bmatrix}0&0&1\\0&0&0\\0&0&0\end{bmatrix}$

Let $\quad Y=\begin{bmatrix}\alpha&\beta&\gamma\\0&\alpha&\beta\\0&0&\alpha\end{bmatrix}$

Then, $Z=\alpha^2 I-\alpha\beta X+(\beta^2-\alpha\gamma)X^2$

$=\alpha^2\begin{bmatrix}1&0&0\\0&1&0\\0&0&1\end{bmatrix}-\alpha\beta\begin{bmatrix}0&1&0\\0&0&1\\0&0&0\end{bmatrix}+(\beta^2+\alpha\gamma)\begin{bmatrix}0&0&1\\0&0&0\\0&0&0\end{bmatrix}$

$=\begin{bmatrix}\alpha^2&-\alpha\beta&\beta^2-\alpha\gamma\\0&\alpha^2&-\alpha\beta\\0&0&\alpha^2\end{bmatrix}$

Let $Y\cdot Y^{-1}=I$

$\begin{bmatrix}\alpha&\beta&\gamma\\0&\alpha&\beta\\0&0&\alpha\end{bmatrix}\begin{bmatrix}\frac{1}{5}&\frac{-2}{5}&\frac{1}{5}\\0&\frac{1}{5}&\frac{-2}{5}\\0&0&\frac{1}{5}\end{bmatrix}=\begin{bmatrix}1&0&0\\0&1&0\\0&0&1\end{bmatrix}$

$\dfrac{\alpha}{5}=1 \Rightarrow \alpha=5$

$\therefore \quad -\dfrac{2}{5}\alpha+\dfrac{\beta}{5}=0$

$\Rightarrow \quad \dfrac{\beta}{5}=\dfrac{2}{5}\alpha$

$\beta=5\times 2=10$

and $\quad \dfrac{\alpha}{5}-\dfrac{2}{5}\beta+\dfrac{\gamma}{5}=0$

$\Rightarrow \quad \dfrac{5}{5}-\dfrac{2}{5}\times 10+\dfrac{\gamma}{5}=0$

$\Rightarrow \quad 1-4+\dfrac{\gamma}{5}=0$

$\Rightarrow \quad \gamma=15$

$\therefore \quad (\alpha-\beta+\gamma)^2=(5-10+15)^2$

$=100$

25. (150) Total 3 digit number = 900

Required number (a number whose GCD with 369 is 2

= 3-digit even number −3-digit number that are multiples of 4 - 3-digit number that are multiples of 6 + 3-digit number that are multiples of 12.

3-digit even number $=\dfrac{900}{2}=450$

3- digit number divisible by 4,

100, 104, 108, ..., 996

$\therefore \quad 996=100+(n-1)4$

$\Rightarrow \quad \dfrac{896}{4}=n-1$

$\Rightarrow \quad n=225$

3-digit number divisible by 6,

102, 108, 114, ..., 996

$\therefore \quad 996=102+(n-1)6$

$\dfrac{894}{6}=n-1$

$\Rightarrow \quad n=150$

3-digit number divisible by 12

108, 120, ...996

$\therefore \quad 996=108+(n-1)12$

$\dfrac{888}{12}=n-1$

$n=75$

Thus, required number

$=450-225-150+75=150$

26. (102) $^{40}C_0 + {}^{41}C_1 + {}^{42}C_2 + ... + {}^{60}C_{20} = \frac{m}{n} \times {}^{60}C_{20}$

We know, $^{n}C_{r-1} + {}^{n}C_r = {}^{n+1}C_r$

Also $^{40}C_0 = {}^{41}C_0$

So, $^{40}C_0 + {}^{41}C_1 + {}^{42}C_2 + ... + {}^{60}C_{20}$

$= {}^{42}C_1 + {}^{42}C_2 + {}^{43}C_3 + ... + {}^{60}C_{20}$

$= {}^{43}C_2 + {}^{43}C_3 + ... + {}^{60}C_2$

$= {}^{60}C_{19} + {}^{60}C_{20}$

$= {}^{61}C_{20}$

$\therefore \quad {}^{61}C_{20} = \frac{m}{n} {}^{60}C_{20}$

$$\frac{61!}{20!(61-20)!} = \frac{m}{n} \frac{60!}{20!(60-20)!}$$

$$\Rightarrow \frac{61!}{20!41!} = \frac{m}{n} \frac{60!}{20!40!}$$

$$\Rightarrow \frac{61 \times 60!}{41 \times 40!} = \frac{m}{n} \frac{60!}{40!}$$

$$\Rightarrow \frac{61}{41} = \frac{m}{n}$$

$\therefore \quad m + n = 61 + 41 = 102$

27. (40) a_1, a_2, a_3, a_4, a_5, ..., GP.

Given, $a_2 + a_4 = 2a_3 + 1$ ...(i)

$3a_2 + a_3 = 2a_4$ ...(ii)

To find $a_2 + a_4 + 2a_5$

In GP $a_n = ar^{n-1}$

So, the Eqs. (i) and (ii) can be written as,

$a_1r + a_1r^3 = 2a_1r^2 + 1$ ...(iii)

and $3a_1r + a_1r^2 = 2a_1r^3$

$3 + r = 2r^2$

$\Rightarrow 2r^2 - r - 3 = 0$

$\Rightarrow 2r^2 - 3r + 2r - 3 = 0$

$\Rightarrow r(2r-3) + (2r-3) = 0$

$\Rightarrow (2r-3)(r+1) = 0$

$\Rightarrow r = \frac{3}{2}, r = -1$

Put $r = \frac{3}{2}$ in Eq. (iii),

$$a_1\frac{3}{2} + a_1\left(\frac{3}{2}\right)^3 = 2a_1\left(\frac{3}{2}\right)^2 + 1$$

$$\Rightarrow \frac{3}{2}a_1 + \frac{27}{8}a_1 = \frac{9}{2}a_1 + 1$$

$$\Rightarrow \frac{3}{2}a_1 + \frac{27a_1}{8} - \frac{9}{2}a_1 = 1$$

$$\Rightarrow \frac{3}{8}a_1 = 1$$

$$\Rightarrow a_1 = \frac{8}{3}$$

$\therefore a_2 + a_4 + 2a_5 = a_1r + a_1r^3 + 2a_1r^4$

$$= \left(\frac{8}{3}\right)\left(\frac{3}{2}\right) + \left(\frac{8}{3}\right)\left(\frac{3}{2}\right)^3 + 2\left(\frac{8}{3}\right)\left(\frac{3}{2}\right)^4$$

$$= 4 + 9 + 27 = 40$$

28. (3) $\frac{24}{\pi}\int_0^{\sqrt{2}} \frac{(2-x^2)}{(2+x^2)(\sqrt{4+x^4})} dx$

$$= \frac{24}{\pi}\int_0^{\sqrt{2}} \sqrt{2} \frac{\left(\frac{2}{x^2} - 1\right)}{\left(\frac{2}{x} + x\right)\sqrt{\left(\frac{2}{x} + x\right)^2 - 4}} dx$$

Let $\frac{2}{x} + x = t \Rightarrow \left(\frac{-2}{x^2} + 1\right) dx = dt$

At $x = 0, t = \infty$

and at $x = \sqrt{2}, t = 2\sqrt{2}$

$$I = \frac{-24}{\pi}\int_\infty^{2\sqrt{2}} \frac{dt}{t\sqrt{t^2-4}}$$

$$= \frac{-12}{\pi}\int_\infty^{2\sqrt{2}} \frac{2tdt}{t^2\sqrt{t^2-4}}$$

Let $t^2 - 4 = z^2 \Rightarrow 2tdt = 2zdz$

or $tdt = zdz$

At $t \to \infty$, $z \to \infty$

and at $t = 2\sqrt{2}$, $z = 2$

$$I = \frac{-12}{\pi}\int_\infty^2 \frac{2zdz}{z(z^2+4)}$$

$$I = \frac{-24}{\pi}\int_\infty^2 \frac{dz}{z^2+4}$$

$$= \frac{-24}{\pi}\frac{1}{2}\left(\tan^{-1}\frac{z}{2}\right)_\infty^2$$

$$= \frac{-24}{\pi}\left(\frac{\pi}{8} - \frac{\pi}{4}\right) = 3$$

29. (12) Equation of hyperbola $\frac{x^2}{16} - \frac{y^2}{4} = 1$

$L_1 : y = mx \pm \sqrt{16m^2 - 4}$ ...(i)

$L_2 : y = \frac{-1}{m}x$

$\Rightarrow \quad m = \frac{-x}{y}$ ...(ii)

Using Eq. (ii) in Eq. (i)

$$y = -\left(\frac{x}{y}\right)x \pm \sqrt{16\left(\frac{-x}{y}\right)^2 - 4}$$

$$\Rightarrow y = \frac{-x^2}{y} \pm \frac{\sqrt{16x^2 - 4y^2}}{y}$$

$\Rightarrow (y^2 + x^2)^2 = 16x^2 - 4y^2$ ...(iii)

Given, equation

$(x^2 + y^2)^2 = \alpha x^2 + \beta y^2$ ...(iv)

Comparing Eqs. (iii) and (iv),

$\alpha = 16, \beta = -4$

$\therefore \quad \alpha + \beta = 16 - 4 = 12$

30. (33) Total possibilities to make a 6-digit number using only 1 and 8

$\overline{2}\ \overline{2}\ \overline{2}\ \overline{2}\ \overline{2}\ \overline{2}$

Every position has 2 possibility either 1 or 8

$\therefore 2^6$

Number divisible by 21 :

1. for divisibility by 3

(sum of digits must be divisible by 3)

(a) Number of 1's = Number of 8

(b) Every digit is 1

(c) Every digit is 8.

2. for divisiblity by 7.

|2 (last digit) − remaining number| $= 7k$

$k \in z$

(a) all are 1 s ⇒ 1 no

(b) all are 8s ⇒ 1 no

(c) 31's and 38s $\Rightarrow \frac{6!}{3!3!}$

Total number divisible by 21

= number divisible by 3 and 7

$$= \frac{6!}{3!3!} + 2$$

$$= \left(\frac{6 \times 5 \times 4 \times 3!}{3! \times 3 \times 2}\right) + 2$$

$= 22$

$\therefore$ Probability $= \frac{22}{2^6} = p$

$$96p = 96 \times \frac{22}{2^6}$$

$$= 96 \times \frac{22}{2 \times 2 \times 2 \times 2 \times 2 \times 2}$$

$= 33$

29 June 2022, Shift-I

1. (c) All entries of a 2×2 matrix belongs to first 10 primes.

$\therefore$Total number of outcomes

$$= 10 \times 10 \times 10 \times 10 = 10^4$$

Now, let A is singular, then $|A| = 0$

Determinant of matrix will be zero when

(i) All entries are same.

or (ii) diagonal elements are same i.e. only two prime numbers are used in the matrix.

Number of favourable singular matrix

$$= 10 + 10 \times 9 \times (2!) = 190$$

$\therefore$Required probability $= \frac{190}{10^4} = \frac{19}{10^3}$

2. (a) $x\frac{dy}{dx} - y = \sqrt{y^2 + 16x^2}$

$$\frac{dy}{dx} = \frac{y + \sqrt{y^2 + 16x^2}}{x}$$

Let $\quad y = vx$

$$\Rightarrow \frac{dy}{dx} = v + x\frac{dv}{dx}$$

$$\therefore\ v + x\frac{dv}{dx} = \frac{vx + \sqrt{v^2x^2 + 16x^2}}{x}$$

$$\Rightarrow v + x\frac{dv}{dx} = v + \sqrt{v^2 + 16}$$

$$\Rightarrow \int \frac{dv}{\sqrt{v^2 + 16}} = \int \frac{dx}{x}$$

$$\Rightarrow \ln|v + \sqrt{v^2 + 16}| = \ln x + \ln c$$

$$\Rightarrow \frac{y}{x} + \frac{\sqrt{y^2 + 16x^2}}{x} = xc$$

$$\Rightarrow y + \sqrt{y^2 + 16x^2} = cx^2 \quad \ldots \text{(i)}$$

$\because \quad y(1) = 3$

$\therefore \quad 3 + \sqrt{9 + 16} = c$

$\Rightarrow \quad 3 + 5 = c \Rightarrow c = 8$

$y + \sqrt{y^2 + 16x^2} = 8x^2$ [from Eq. (i)]

Put $x = 2$,

$$\sqrt{y^2 + 64} = 32 - y$$

$\Rightarrow \quad y^2 + 64 = (32)^2 + y^2 - 64y$

$\Rightarrow \quad 64(1 + y) = 32 \times 32$

$\Rightarrow \quad y = 16 - 1 = 15$

$\quad y(2) = 15$

3. (c) The image or reflection (x, y, z) of a point (x_1, y_1, z_1) in a plane $ax + by + cz + d = 0$ is given by

$$\frac{x - x_1}{a} = \frac{y - y_1}{b} = \frac{z - z_1}{c}$$

$$= \frac{-2(ax_1 + by_1 + cz_1 + d)}{a^2 + b^2 + c^2}$$

$$\Rightarrow \frac{a-2}{3} = \frac{b-4}{-1} = \frac{c-7}{4}$$

$$= \frac{-2(6 - 4 + 28 - 2)}{9 + 1 + 16} = -\frac{28}{13}$$

$\therefore \quad a = 2 - \frac{84}{13} \Rightarrow a = -\frac{58}{13}$

$\quad b = 4 + \frac{28}{13} \Rightarrow b = \frac{80}{13}$

$\quad c = 7 - \frac{112}{13} \Rightarrow c = \frac{-21}{13}$

$$\therefore\ 2a + b + 2c = \frac{-116 + 80 - 42}{13}$$

$$= \frac{-78}{13} = -6$$

4. (c) $f(x) = \begin{cases} \max\{t^2 - 3t\}; & x \le 2 \\ t \le x & \\ x^2 + 2x - 6; & 2 < x < 3 \\ [x - 3] + 9; & 3 \le x \le 5 \\ 2x + 1; & x > 5 \end{cases}$

$$f(x) = \begin{cases} x^3 - 3x; & x \le -1 \\ 2; & -1 < x < 2 \\ x^2 + 2x - 6; & 2 < x < 3 \\ 9; & 3 \le x < 4 \\ 10; & 4 \le x < 5 \\ 11; & x = 5 \\ 2x + 1; & x > 5 \end{cases}$$

Using the simplified form of the function, we find that $f(x)$ is not differentiable at $x = 2, 3, 4, 5$ when we check the continuity and differentiability.

$\therefore \quad m = 4$

$$I = \int_{-2}^{2} f(x)\,dx = \int_{-2}^{-1} (x^3 - 3x)\,dx + \int_{-1}^{2} 2\,dx$$

$$= \frac{3}{4} + 6 = \frac{27}{4}$$

Hence, the ordered pair (m, I) is equal to $\left(4, \frac{27}{4}\right)$.

5. (a) $\mathbf{a} = \alpha\hat{\mathbf{i}} + 3\hat{\mathbf{j}} - \hat{\mathbf{k}}, \mathbf{b} = 3\hat{\mathbf{i}} - \beta\hat{\mathbf{j}} + 4\hat{\mathbf{k}}$ and $\mathbf{c} = \hat{\mathbf{i}} + 2\hat{\mathbf{j}} - 2\hat{\mathbf{k}}$

$$\frac{\mathbf{a} \cdot \mathbf{c}}{\mathbf{c}} = \frac{10}{3}$$

$$\Rightarrow \frac{\alpha + 6 + 2}{\sqrt{1 + 4 + 4}} = \frac{10}{3}$$

$$\Rightarrow \alpha = 2$$

$$\mathbf{b} \times \mathbf{c} = -6\hat{\mathbf{i}} + 10\mathbf{j} + 7\hat{\mathbf{k}}$$

$$\Rightarrow \begin{vmatrix} \hat{\mathbf{i}} & \hat{\mathbf{j}} & \hat{\mathbf{k}} \\ 3 & -\beta & 4 \\ 1 & 2 & -2 \end{vmatrix} = -6\hat{\mathbf{i}} + 10\hat{\mathbf{j}} + 7\hat{\mathbf{k}}$$

$$\Rightarrow (2\beta - 8)\hat{\mathbf{i}} - (-6 - 4)\hat{\mathbf{j}} + (6 + \beta)\hat{\mathbf{k}} = -6\hat{\mathbf{i}} + 10\mathbf{j} + 7\hat{\mathbf{k}}$$

$\therefore \quad 2\beta - 8 = -6 \Rightarrow \beta = 1$

Therefore, $\alpha + \beta = 3$.

6. (c) Given, $y^2 = 8x$ and $y = \sqrt{2}x$

Lines for triangle,

$y = \sqrt{2}x, x = 1, y = 2\sqrt{2}$

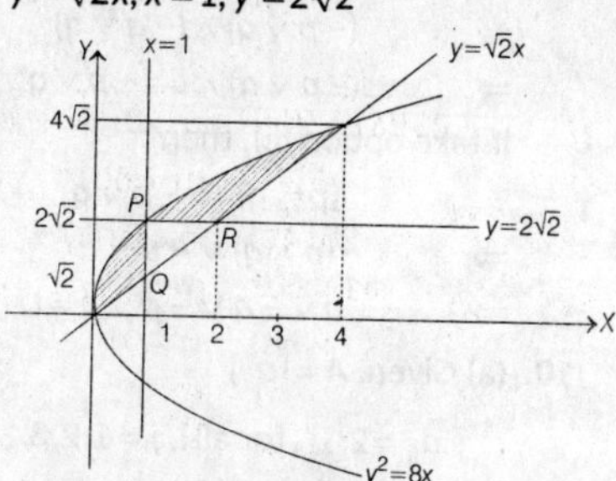

Required area

$$= \int_0^4 (y_{\text{curve}} - y_{\text{line}})\,dx - \text{Area of } \Delta PQR$$

$$= \int_0^4 (\sqrt{8x} - \sqrt{2}x)\,dx - \frac{1}{2} \times \sqrt{2} \times 1$$

$$= 2\sqrt{2}\left(\frac{16}{3} - \frac{0}{3}\right) - \sqrt{2}\left(\frac{16}{2} - \frac{0}{2}\right) - \frac{\sqrt{2}}{2}$$

$$= \frac{32\sqrt{2}}{3} - 8\sqrt{2} - \frac{\sqrt{2}}{2}$$

$$= \frac{64\sqrt{2} - 48\sqrt{2} - 3\sqrt{2}}{6} = \frac{13\sqrt{2}}{6}$$

7. (b) System of linear equations,

$$2x + y - z = 7,\ x - 3y + 2z = 1$$

$$x + 4y + \delta z = k, \text{ where } \delta, k \in R$$

For infinitely many solutions, $\Delta = 0$

$$\begin{vmatrix} 2 & 1 & -1 \\ 1 & -3 & 2 \\ 1 & 4 & \delta \end{vmatrix} = 0$$

$\Rightarrow -1(4 + 3) - 2(8 - 1) + \delta(-6 - 1) = 0$

$\Rightarrow \quad -7 - 14 - 7\delta = 0$

$\Rightarrow \quad \delta = -3$

and $\begin{vmatrix} 2 & 1 & 7 \\ 1 & -3 & 1 \\ 1 & 4 & k \end{vmatrix} = 0$

$\Rightarrow 7(4 + 3) - 1(8 - 1) + k(-6 - 1) = 0$

$\Rightarrow \ 49 - 7 - 7k = 0$

$\Rightarrow \quad k = 6$

$\quad \delta + k = -3 + 6 = 3$

8. (a) $x^2+(2i-1)=0 \Rightarrow x^2=1-2i$

$\because \alpha$ and β are the roots of the given equation.

$\therefore \quad \alpha^2=1-2i, \beta^2=1-2i$

Here, $\alpha^2=\beta^2 \Rightarrow \alpha^8=\beta^8$

Therefore,

$|\alpha^8+\beta^8|=|2\alpha^8|=2|\alpha^8|=2|\alpha^2|^4$

$=2|1-2i|^4=2(\sqrt{5})^4=50$

9. (c) $(p \wedge q) \Delta [(p \vee q) \Rightarrow q]$ is a tautology, where $\Delta \in \{\wedge, \vee \Rightarrow, \Leftrightarrow\}$

$p \vee q \Rightarrow q$

$\Rightarrow \quad \sim(p \vee q) \vee q$

$\Rightarrow \quad (\sim p \wedge \sim q) \vee q$

$\Rightarrow \quad (\sim p \vee q) \wedge (\sim q \vee q)$

$\Rightarrow \quad (\sim p \vee q) \wedge t = \sim p \vee q$

If take option (c), then

$(p \wedge q) \Rightarrow \sim p \vee q$

$\Rightarrow \quad \sim(p \wedge q) \vee \sim p \vee q$

$\Rightarrow \quad \sim p \vee \sim q \vee \sim p \vee q = t$

10. (a) Given, $A=[a_{ij}]$

$a_{ij}=2^{j-i}$, for all $i, j=1,2,3.$

$$A=\begin{bmatrix}1 & 2 & 2^2\\ 2^{-1} & 1 & 2\\ 2^{-2} & 2^{-1} & 1\end{bmatrix}=\begin{bmatrix}1 & 2 & 4\\ 1/2 & 1 & 2\\ 1/4 & 1/2 & 1\end{bmatrix}$$

$$A^2=\begin{bmatrix}1 & 2 & 4\\ 1/2 & 1 & 2\\ 1/4 & 1/2 & 1\end{bmatrix}\begin{bmatrix}1 & 2 & 4\\ 1/2 & 1 & 2\\ 1/4 & 1/2 & 1\end{bmatrix}$$

$$=\begin{bmatrix}3 & 6 & 12\\ 3/2 & 3 & 6\\ 3/4 & 3/2 & 3\end{bmatrix}=3A$$

$\therefore A^3=A^2 \cdot A=(3A)A=3A^2$

$=3(3A)=3^2A$

$\therefore A^2+A^3+A^4+\dots\dots A^{10}$

$=3A+3^2A+3^3A+\dots+3^9A$

$$=3\left[\frac{3^9-1}{3-1}\right]A=\left(\frac{3^{10}-3}{2}\right)A$$

11. (d) $A=A_1 \cup A_2 \cup A_3 \cup \dots\dots \cup A_k$

where $A_i \cap A_j = \phi$ for $i \neq j, 1 \leq i, j \leq k\}$

$R=\{(x,y); y \in A_i$ if and only if $x \in A_i, 1 \leq i \leq k\}$

Let $A=\{1,2,3\}$

Then, $R=\{(1,1)(1,2),(1,3)(2,1),(2,2),(2,3),(3,1),(3,2),(3,3)\}$

(i) R is reflexive. $[\because (a,a) \in R]$

(ii) R is symmetric. $[\because (a,b) \in R \Rightarrow (b,a) \in R]$

(iii) R is transitive. $[\because (a,b) \in R \cap (b,c) \in R \Rightarrow (a,c) \in R]$

$\therefore R$ is an equivalence relation.

12. (b) $a_0=a_1=0$

and $a_{n+2}=2a_{n+1}-a_n+1$

$a_2=2a_1-a_0+1=0-0+1=1$

$a_3=2a_2-a_1+1=2-0+1=3$

$a_4=2a_3-a_2+1=6-1+1=6$

On the basis of first four terms, a general term can be given as

$$a_n=\frac{n(n-1)}{2}$$

Let $\quad S=\sum_{n=2}^{\infty}\frac{n(n-1)}{2(7^n)}$

$$S=\frac{1}{7^2}+\frac{3}{7^3}+\frac{6}{7^4}+\frac{10}{7^5}+\frac{15}{7^6}+\dots \quad \text{...(i)}$$

$$\frac{S}{7}=\frac{1}{7^3}+\frac{3}{7^4}+\frac{6}{7^5}+\frac{10}{7^6}+\frac{15}{7^7}+\dots \quad \text{...(ii)}$$

On subtracting Eq. (ii) from Eq. (i), we get

$$\frac{6S}{7}=\frac{1}{7^2}+\frac{2}{7^3}+\frac{3}{7^4}+\frac{4}{7^5}+\dots \quad \text{...(iii)}$$

$$\frac{6S}{7^2}=\frac{1}{7^3}+\frac{2}{7^4}+\frac{3}{7^5}+\frac{4}{7^6}+\dots \quad \text{...(iv)}$$

On subtracting Eq. (iv) from Eq. (iii), we get

$$\frac{6S}{7}\cdot\frac{6}{7}=\frac{1}{7^2}+\frac{1}{7^3}+\frac{1}{7^4}+\dots$$

$$\Rightarrow \frac{6\times 6}{7\times 7}S=\frac{\frac{1}{7^2}}{1-\left(\frac{1}{7}\right)}$$

$$\Rightarrow \frac{6\times 6}{7\times 7}S=\frac{1}{7\times 6} \Rightarrow S=\frac{7}{216}$$

13. (c) A and A' lie on the line $y=2$

And point B is $(2,3)$.

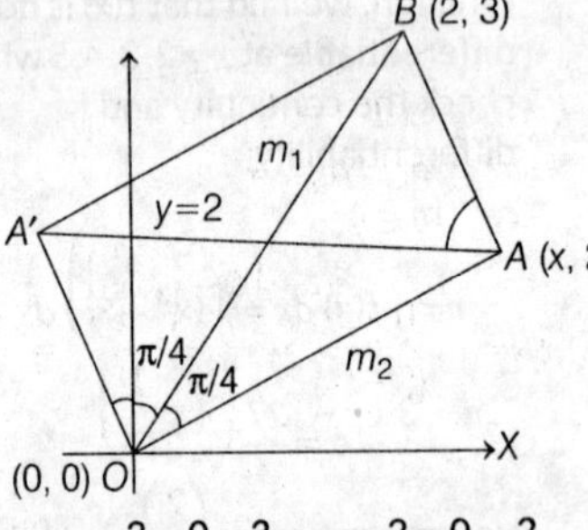

$$m_1=\frac{3-0}{2-0}=\frac{3}{2}, m_2=\frac{2-0}{x-0}=\frac{2}{x}$$

$$\tan\theta=\left|\frac{m_1-m_2}{1+m_1m_2}\right|$$

$$\Rightarrow \quad \tan\frac{\pi}{4}=\left|\frac{\frac{3}{2}-\frac{2}{x}}{1+\frac{3}{2}\cdot\frac{2}{x}}\right| \Rightarrow 1=\left|\frac{3x-4}{2x+6}\right|$$

$\Rightarrow \pm(2x+6)=3x-4$

It gives $x=-\frac{2}{5}, 10$

$x_1=-\frac{2}{5}$ and $x_2=10$

$$\therefore \quad AA'=\sqrt{\left(10+\frac{2}{5}\right)^2+(2-2)^2}$$

$$=10+\frac{2}{5}=\frac{52}{5}$$

14. (b) Let the length of one piece be x, then the length of other piece will be $22-x$.

Let first piece of length x is formed into a square and let it's side length be y.

Then, $\quad x=4y \Rightarrow y=\frac{x}{4} \quad$ ... (i)

From the second piece of length $(22-x)$ we make an equilateral triangle, then

Side of equilateral triangle $=\frac{22-x}{3}$

Combined area, $A=y^2+\frac{\sqrt{3}}{4}(\text{side})^2$

$$A=\left(\frac{x}{4}\right)^2+\frac{\sqrt{3}}{4}\left(\frac{22-x}{3}\right)^2$$

Differentiating w.r.t. x, we get

$$\frac{dA}{dx}=2\left(\frac{x}{4}\right)\left(\frac{1}{4}\right)+\frac{\sqrt{3}}{4}\cdot 2\left(\frac{22-x}{3}\right)\left(\frac{-1}{3}\right)$$

$$=\frac{x}{8}-\frac{\sqrt{3}}{18}(22-x)$$

For maximum or minimum value, we put $\frac{dA}{dx}=0$

$$\frac{x}{8}-\frac{\sqrt{3}}{18}(22-x)=0$$

$$\Rightarrow \quad \frac{x}{8}-\frac{11\sqrt{3}}{9}+\frac{\sqrt{3}}{18}x=0$$

$$\Rightarrow \quad x\left(\frac{1}{8}+\frac{1}{6\sqrt{3}}\right)=\frac{11\sqrt{3}}{9}$$

$$\Rightarrow \quad x\left(\frac{3\sqrt{3}+4}{24\sqrt{3}}\right)=\frac{11\sqrt{3}}{9}$$

$$\Rightarrow x=\frac{11\times 24\times 3}{9(3\sqrt{3}+4)}=\frac{11\times 8}{3\sqrt{3}+4}=\frac{88\sqrt{3}}{9+4\sqrt{3}}$$

$\therefore$ Side of equilateral triangle

$$=\frac{22-\frac{88\sqrt{3}}{(9+4\sqrt{3})}}{3}=\frac{198+88\sqrt{3}-88\sqrt{3}}{3(9+4\sqrt{3})}$$

$$=\frac{198}{3(9+4\sqrt{3})}=\frac{66}{9+4\sqrt{3}}$$

15. (d) Let $y=\cos^{-1}\left(\frac{2\sin^{-1}\left(\frac{1}{4x^2-1}\right)}{\pi}\right)$

$$-1 \le \frac{2\sin^{-1}\left(\frac{1}{4x^2-1}\right)}{\pi} \le 1$$

$$\Rightarrow -\frac{\pi}{2} \le \sin^{-1}\left(\frac{1}{4x^2-1}\right) \le \frac{\pi}{2}$$

$$\Rightarrow -1 \le \frac{1}{4x^2-1} \le 1$$

$$*1: -1 \le \frac{1}{4x^2-1}$$

$$\Rightarrow 0 \le \frac{x^2}{(2x+1)(2x-1)}$$

$\Rightarrow$ (number line: $-1/2$, 0, $1/2$)

$$*2: \frac{1}{4x^2-1} \le 1$$

$$\Rightarrow \frac{2-4x^2}{(2x+1)(2x-1)} \le 0$$

$$\Rightarrow \frac{(\sqrt{2}x-1)(\sqrt{2}x+1)}{(2x+1)(2x-1)} \ge 0$$

(number line: $-1/\sqrt{2}$, $-1/2$, $1/2$, $1/\sqrt{2}$)

Domain $(*1) \cap (*2)$

$$\Rightarrow \text{“}\left(-\infty, -\frac{1}{2}\right) \cup \left(\frac{1}{2}, \infty\right) \cup \{0\}\text{”}$$

$$\cap \text{“}\left(-\infty, -\frac{1}{2}\right] \cup \left(-\frac{1}{2}, \frac{1}{2}\right) \cup \left[\frac{1}{\sqrt{2}}, \infty\right)\text{”}$$

$$\Rightarrow \left(-\infty, -\frac{1}{\sqrt{2}}\right] \cup \{0\} \cup \left[\frac{1}{\sqrt{2}}, \infty\right)$$

16. (d) Given,

Constant term in the expansion of $\left(3x^3 - 2x^2 + \frac{5}{x^5}\right)^{10}$ is $2^k \cdot l$, where l is an odd integer.

General term, $T_{r+1} = \frac{10!}{r_1!\,r_2!\,r_3!}$

$$(3x^3)^{r_1}(-2x^2)^{r_2}\left(\frac{5}{x^5}\right)^{r_3}$$

$$= \frac{10!}{r_1!\,r_2!\,r_3!}(3)^{r_1}(-2)^{r_2}(5)^{r_3}(x)^{3r_1+2r_2-5r_3}$$

For constant term,

$$3r_1 + 2r_2 - 5r_3 = 0 \quad \text{... (i)}$$

and $\quad r_1 + r_2 + r_3 = 10 \quad$ ... (ii)

Now, Eq. (i) − Eq (ii) × 2, we get

$$r_1 - (5+2)r_3 = -20$$

$$\Rightarrow r_1 + 20 = 7r_3$$

$$\Rightarrow r_1 = 1, r_3 = 3 \text{ and } r_2 = 6$$

$\therefore$ Constant term

$$= \frac{10!}{(1)!\,(6)!\,(3)!}(3)^1(-2)^6(5)^3$$

$$= \frac{10 \cdot 9 \cdot 8 \cdot 7}{3 \cdot 2} \times 3 \times 2^6 \times 5^3$$

$$= 2^9 \times 3^2 \times 5^4 \times 7^1 = 2^k \times l$$

Hence, $k = 9$

17. (d) Let $I = \int_0^2 \cos\left(\pi\left(x - \left[\frac{x}{2}\right]\right)\right)dx + \int_2^4 \cos\left(\pi\left(x - \left[\frac{x}{2}\right]\right)\right)dx + \int_4^5 \cos\left(\pi\left(x - \left[\frac{x}{2}\right]\right)\right)dx$

$$= \int_0^2 \cos(\pi x - 0)\,dx + \int_2^4 \cos(\pi x - \pi)\,dx + \int_4^5 \cos(\pi x - 2\pi)\,dx$$

$$= \int_0^2 \cos(\pi x)\,dx - \int_2^4 \cos(\pi x)\,dx + \int_4^5 \cos(\pi x)\,dx$$

$$= \left[\frac{\sin \pi x}{\pi}\right]_0^2 - \left[\frac{\sin \pi x}{\pi}\right]_2^4 + \left[\frac{\sin \pi x}{\pi}\right]_4^5$$

$$= [0-0] - [0-0] + [0-0] = 0$$

18. (b) Given, that PQ is a focal chord of the parabola $y^2 = 4x$ which subtends an angle of $\frac{\pi}{2}$ at the point (3, 0).

(Figure: parabola with $P(t^2, 2t)$, $S(1, 0)$, $R(3, 0)$, $90°$, $Q\ (1/t^2, -2/t)$)

$$m_{PR} \cdot m_{RQ} = -1$$

$$\Rightarrow \frac{(0-2t)}{(3-t^2)} \times \frac{\left(0 - \left(-\frac{2}{t}\right)\right)}{\left(3 - \frac{1}{t^2}\right)} = -1$$

$$\Rightarrow \frac{2t\left(\frac{2}{t}\right)}{\frac{(3-t^2)(3t^2-1)}{t^2}} = 1$$

$$\Rightarrow \frac{4t^2}{9t^2 - 3 - 3t^4 + t^2} = 1$$

$$\Rightarrow 4t^2 = 10t^2 - 3 - 3t^4$$

$$\Rightarrow 3t^4 - 6t^2 + 3 = 0$$

$$\Rightarrow (t^2)^2 - 2(t)^2(1) + (1)^2 = 0$$

$$\Rightarrow (t^2-1)^2 = 0 \Rightarrow t = 1$$

$\Rightarrow P$ and Q must be end points of latusrectum.

$$P(1, 2) \text{ and } Q(1, -2)$$

$$\therefore \frac{2b^2}{a} = 4 \text{ and } ae = 1$$

$$\because b^2 = a^2(1-e^2)$$

$$\Rightarrow 2a = a^2 - 1$$

$$\Rightarrow a^2 - 2a - 1 = 0 \Rightarrow a = 1 + \sqrt{2}$$

Now, $e^2 = 1 - \frac{b^2}{a^2}$

$$\Rightarrow e^2 = 1 - \frac{2a}{a^2} = 1 - \frac{2}{a} = \frac{a-2}{a} = \frac{\sqrt{2}-1}{\sqrt{2}+1}$$

$$\Rightarrow \frac{1}{e^2} = \frac{\sqrt{2}+1}{\sqrt{2}-1} = \frac{\sqrt{2}+1}{\sqrt{2}-1} \times \frac{\sqrt{2}+1}{\sqrt{2}+1}$$

$$= 3 + 2\sqrt{2}$$

$$\Rightarrow \frac{1}{e^2} = 3 + 2\sqrt{2}$$

19. (c) $C_1 : x^2 + y^2 = 2$

$$C_2 : (x-3)^2 + (y-2)^2 = 5$$

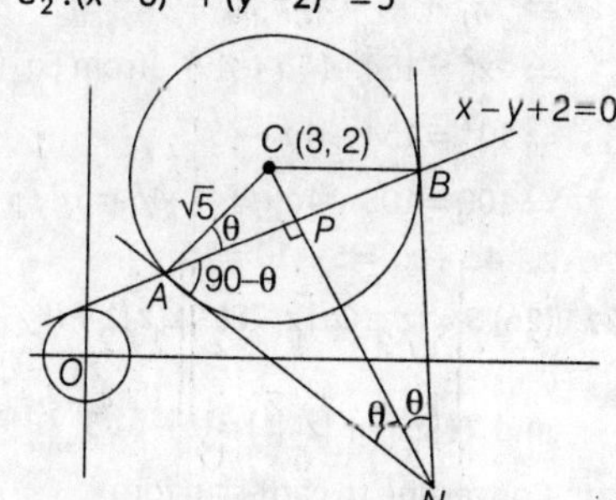

Line $AB : x - y + 2 = 0$

$$CP = \left|\frac{3-2+2}{\sqrt{(1)^2+(-1)^2}}\right| = \frac{3}{\sqrt{2}}$$

$$AP = \sqrt{(CA)^2 - (CP)^2} = \sqrt{5 - \frac{9}{2}} = \frac{1}{\sqrt{2}}$$

$$\tan\theta = \frac{CP}{AP} = \frac{\frac{3}{\sqrt{2}}}{\frac{1}{\sqrt{2}}} = 3$$

$$\therefore \sin\theta = \frac{3}{\sqrt{1+9}} = \frac{3}{\sqrt{10}} = \frac{AP}{AN}$$

$$\therefore AN = \frac{\sqrt{10}}{3} \times \frac{1}{\sqrt{2}} = \frac{\sqrt{5}}{3} = BN$$

Area of $\Delta ANB = \frac{1}{2} \times AB \times PN$

$$= \frac{1}{2} \times 2\,AP \times PN = \frac{1}{\sqrt{2}} \times [AN(\cos\theta)]$$

$$= \frac{1}{\sqrt{2}} \times \frac{\sqrt{5}}{3} \times \sqrt{1 - \frac{9}{10}}$$

$$= \frac{1}{\sqrt{2}} \times \frac{\sqrt{5}}{3} \times \frac{1}{\sqrt{10}} = \frac{1}{6}$$

20. (b) Given, $\bar{x} = \frac{\Sigma x_i}{5} = \frac{24}{5}$ ...(i)

and $\sigma^2 = \frac{\Sigma x_1^2}{5} - (\bar{x})^2 = \frac{194}{25}$ ... (ii)

$\therefore \quad \Sigma x_i = 24$ [from Eq. (i)]

$\Rightarrow x_1 + x_2 + x_3 + x_4 + x_5 = 24$ ...(iii)

And $\frac{\Sigma x_i^2}{5} - \left(\frac{24}{5}\right)^2 = \frac{194}{25}$ [from Eq. (ii)]

$\Rightarrow \quad \Sigma x_i^2 = \frac{194}{5} + \frac{576}{5}$

$\Rightarrow \quad \Sigma x_i^2 = \frac{770}{5} \Rightarrow \Sigma x_i^2 = 154$

$\Rightarrow x_1^2 + x_2^2 + x_3^2 + x_4^2 + x_5^2 = 154$ ...(iv)

$\because \quad \frac{x_1 + x_2 + x_3 + x_4}{4} = \frac{7}{2}$

$\therefore \quad x_1 + x_2 + x_3 + x_4 = 14$

$\Rightarrow \quad x_5 = 10$ [from Eq. (iii)]

and $\frac{x_1^2 + x_2^2 + x_3^2 + x_4^2}{4} - \left(\frac{7}{2}\right)^2 = a$

$\Rightarrow x_1^2 + x_2^2 + x_3^2 + x_4^2 = 4a + 49$

$\Rightarrow x_5^2 = 154 - (4a + 49)$ [from Eq. (iv)]

$\Rightarrow 10^2 = 154 - 4a - 49$

$\Rightarrow 100 = 105 - 4a \Rightarrow 4a = 5$

$\therefore 4a + x_5 = 5 + 10 = 15$

21. (26) $S = \{z \in C : |z - 2| \le 1, z(1+i) + \bar{z}(1-i) \le 2\}$

and $5(|z_1|^2 + |z_2|^2) = \alpha + \beta\sqrt{5}$

Converting to cartesian form

$|z - 2| \le 1 \equiv (x-2)^2 + (y-0)^2 \le 1$

$\Rightarrow$ Circle centred at (2, 0) and radius = 1

$z(1+i) + \bar{z}(1-i) \le 2$

$\Rightarrow (x+iy)(1+i) + (x-iy)(1-i) \le 2$

$\Rightarrow x + ix + iy - y + x - ix - iy - y \le 2$

$\Rightarrow \quad 2x - 2y \le 2$

$\Rightarrow \quad x - y \le 1 \Rightarrow y \ge x - 1$

$\Rightarrow$ Region above line $y = x - 1$.

The required common region.

$4i \equiv (0, 4), B \equiv (1, 0)$ and $C \equiv (2, 1)$

$PB = \sqrt{17}, PC = \sqrt{13}$

$\therefore$ Maximum is PB and minimum is PA.

Line $PA : y - 0 = \frac{0-4}{2-0}(x-2)$

$\Rightarrow \quad y = -2(x-2)$

On solving $y = -2(x-2)$

and $(x-2)^2 + y^2 = 1$

$(x-2)^2 + 4(x-2)^2 = 1$

$\Rightarrow (x-2)^2 = \frac{1}{5} \Rightarrow x = 2 \pm \frac{1}{\sqrt{5}}$

$\therefore \quad A \equiv \left(2 - \frac{1}{\sqrt{5}}, \frac{2}{\sqrt{5}}\right)$

Minimum : $z_1 = \left(2 - \frac{1}{\sqrt{5}}\right) + \frac{2i}{\sqrt{5}}$

Maximum : $z_2 = 1 + 0i$

$|z_1|^2 = \frac{25 - 4\sqrt{5}}{5} = 5 - \frac{4}{\sqrt{5}}$ and $|z_2|^2 = 1$

$\therefore 5(|z_1|^2 + |z_2|^2) = 5\left[5 - \frac{4}{\sqrt{5}} + 1\right]$

$= 30 - 4\sqrt{5} = \alpha + \beta\sqrt{5}$

$\therefore \quad \alpha + \beta = 30 - 4 = 26$

22. (2) $\frac{dy}{dx} + \frac{\sqrt{2}y}{2\cos^4 x - \cos 2x} = xe^{\tan^{-1}}(\sqrt{2}\cot 2x)$

$$\text{IF} = e^{\sqrt{2}\int \frac{dx}{2\cos^4 x - \cos 2x}}$$

$$= e^{\sqrt{2}\int \frac{dx}{2(\cos^2 x)^2 - (2\cos^2 x - 1)}}$$

$$= e^{\sqrt{2}\int \frac{dx}{2\cos^2 x\,(\cos^2 x - 1) + 1}}$$

$$= e^{\sqrt{2}\int \frac{dx}{-2\cos^2 x \sin^2 x + 1}}$$

$$= e^{\sqrt{2}\int \frac{dx}{\cos^4 x + \sin^4 x}}$$

$[\because \cos^4 x + \sin^4 x = (\cos^2 x + \sin^2 x)^2 - 2\cos^2 x \cdot \sin^2 x = 1 - 2\cos^2 x \sin^2 x]$

$$\therefore \text{IF} = e^{\sqrt{2}\int \frac{\text{cosec}^4 x\, dx}{1 + \cot^4 x}} = e^{\sqrt{2}\int -\frac{(t^2+1)}{1+t^4} dt}$$

[assuming $\cot x = t$]

$$= e^{\sqrt{2}\int \frac{\left(1 + \frac{1}{t^2}\right)}{t^2 + \frac{1}{t^2}}. dt} = e^{-\sqrt{2}\int \frac{\left(1 + \frac{1}{t^2}\right)}{\left(t - \frac{1}{t}\right)^2 + 2} dt}$$

$$= e^{\frac{-\sqrt{2}}{\sqrt{2}}\tan^{-1}\left(\frac{t - \frac{1}{t}}{\sqrt{2}}\right)} = e^{-\tan^{-1}\left(\frac{\cot^2 x - 1}{\sqrt{2}\cot x}\right)}$$

$$= e^{-\tan^{-1}\left(\frac{\sqrt{2}(\cot^2 x - 1}{2\cot x}\right)}$$

$$= e^{-\tan^{-1}(\sqrt{2}\cot 2x)}$$

$$y \cdot e^{-\tan^{-1}(\sqrt{2}\cot 2x)} = \int x\, dx$$

$$\Rightarrow \quad y \cdot e^{-\tan^{-1}(\sqrt{2}\cot 2x)} = \frac{x^2}{2} + c$$

At $\quad x = \frac{\pi}{4}, y = \frac{\pi^2}{32}$

$\therefore \quad \frac{\pi^2}{32}.e^{-0} = \frac{\pi^2}{32} + c \Rightarrow c = 0$

$\therefore \quad y = \frac{x^2}{2}.e^{\tan^{-1}}(\sqrt{2}\cot 2x)$

At $x = \frac{\pi}{3}, y = \frac{\pi^2}{18} e^{\tan^{-1}\left(\sqrt{2} \times \left(\frac{-1}{\sqrt{3}}\right)\right)}$

$\therefore \quad y\left(\frac{\pi}{3}\right) = \frac{\pi^2}{18} e^{-\tan^{-1}\left(\sqrt{\frac{2}{3}}\right)}$

Therefore, $\alpha = \sqrt{\frac{2}{3}} \Rightarrow 3\alpha^2 = 2$

23. (26) Points $P \equiv (1, 2, -1)$ and $Q \equiv (2, -1, 3)$

Plane : $-x + y + z = 1$ ... (i)

Let foot of the perpendicular of points P and Q be F_1 and F_2, respectively.

Line $PF_1 : \frac{x-1}{-1} = \frac{y-2}{1} = \frac{z+1}{1} = \lambda$

$F_1 \equiv (1 - \lambda, 2 + \lambda, -1 + \lambda)$

$-(1 - \lambda) + (2 + \lambda) + (-1 + \lambda) = 1$

[from Eq. (i)]

$\Rightarrow -1 + \lambda + 2 + \lambda - 1 + \lambda = 1 \Rightarrow \lambda = 1/3$

$F_1 \equiv \left(\frac{2}{3}, \frac{7}{3}, -\frac{2}{3}\right)$

Similarly, $F_2 \equiv \left(\frac{5}{3}, -\frac{2}{3}, \frac{10}{3}\right)$

$$\therefore F_1F_2 = \sqrt{\left(\frac{5}{3} - \frac{2}{3}\right)^2 + \left(-\frac{2}{3} - \frac{7}{3}\right)^2 + \left(\frac{10}{3} + \frac{2}{3}\right)^2}$$

$= \sqrt{(1)^2 + (-3)^2 + (4)^2}$

$= \sqrt{1 + 9 + 16} = \sqrt{26} = d$

$\Rightarrow d^2 = 26$

24. (32) $S = \{\theta \in [-4\pi, 4\pi] : 3\cos^2 2\theta + 6\cos 2\theta - 10\cos^2\theta + 5 = 0\}$

$3\cos^2 2\theta + 6\cos 2\theta - 10\cos^2\theta + 5 = 0$

$\Rightarrow 3\cos^2 2\theta + 6\cos 2\theta - 5(2\cos^2\theta - 1) = 0$

$\Rightarrow \quad 3\cos^2 2\theta + 6\cos 2\theta - 5\cos 2\theta = 0$

$\Rightarrow \quad 3\cos^2 2\theta + \cos 2\theta = 0$

$\Rightarrow \quad \cos 2\theta\,[3\cos 2\theta + 1] = 0$

$\cos 2\theta = 0$ or $\cos 2\theta = \frac{-1}{3}$

$2\theta = (2n+1).\frac{\pi}{2}$

$\therefore \theta = \pm\frac{\pi}{4}, \pm\frac{3\pi}{4}, \dots \pm\frac{15\pi}{4}$

$[\because \theta \in [-4\pi, 4\pi]]$

Similarly, $\cos 2\theta = \frac{-1}{3}$ gives 16 solution.

$\therefore$ The number of elements in the set S are $(16+16)=32$

25. (1) $2\theta - \cos^2\theta + \sqrt{2} = 0$

$\Rightarrow \quad 2\theta + \sqrt{2} = \cos^2\theta$

$\Rightarrow \quad y = 2\theta + \sqrt{2}$ and $y = \cos^2\theta$

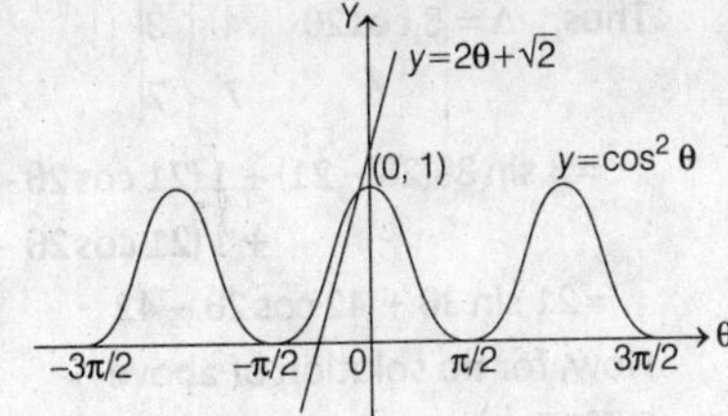

We can see that, $y = \cos^2\theta$ and $y = 2\theta + \sqrt{2}$ intersect at one point.

$\therefore$ Number of solutions is 1.

26. (29) $50\tan\left(3\tan^{-1}\left(\frac{1}{2}\right) + 2\cos^{-1}\left(\frac{1}{\sqrt{5}}\right)\right) + 4\sqrt{2}\tan\left(\frac{1}{2}\tan^{-1}(2\sqrt{2})\right)$

$= 50\tan\left(3\tan^{-1}\left(\frac{1}{2}\right) + 2\tan^{-1}\left(\frac{2}{1}\right)\right) + 4\sqrt{2}\tan\left(\frac{1}{2}\tan^{-1}2\sqrt{2}\right)$

$= 50\tan\left(\tan^{-1}\left(\frac{1}{2}\right) + 2\left(\tan^{-1}\frac{1}{2} + \tan^{-1}2\right)\right) + 4\sqrt{2}\tan(\theta)$ ... (i)

Let $\theta = \frac{1}{2}\tan^{-1}2\sqrt{2}$ in Eq. (i) where θ is in I-quadrant

$\Rightarrow \quad \tan 2\theta = 2\sqrt{2} \Rightarrow \frac{2\tan\theta}{1-\tan^2\theta} = 2\sqrt{2}$

$\Rightarrow \quad \tan\theta = \sqrt{2}(1-\tan^2\theta)$

$\Rightarrow \quad \sqrt{2}\tan^2\theta + \tan\theta - \sqrt{2} = 0$

$\Rightarrow \sqrt{2}\tan^2\theta + 2\tan\theta - \tan\theta - \sqrt{2} = 0$

$\Rightarrow \sqrt{2}\tan\theta(\tan\theta + \sqrt{2}) - 1(\tan\theta + \sqrt{2}) = 0$

$\Rightarrow \quad (\tan\theta + \sqrt{2})(\sqrt{2}\tan\theta - 1) = 0$

$\Rightarrow \quad \tan\theta = \frac{1}{\sqrt{2}}$

Therefore, the expression in Eq. (i) is

$50\tan\left(\tan^{-1}\frac{1}{2} + 2(\cot^{-1}2 + \tan^{-1}2)\right) + 4\sqrt{2}\tan(\theta)$

$= 50\tan\left(\tan^{-1}\frac{1}{2} + 2.\frac{\pi}{2}\right) + 4\sqrt{2}\times\frac{1}{\sqrt{2}}$

$= 50\tan\left(\pi + \tan^{-1}\frac{1}{2}\right) + 4$

$= 50\tan\left(\tan^{-1}\frac{1}{2}\right) + 4$

$= 50\times\frac{1}{2} + 4 = 25 + 4 = 29$

27. (3395) $f(x) = (c+1)x^2 + (1-c^2)x + 2k$ ... (i)

and $f(x+y) = f(x) + f(y) - x\cdot y$ ... (ii)

$f'(x) = \lim_{y\to 0}\frac{f(x+y)-f(x)}{y}$

$= \lim_{y\to 0}\frac{f(x)+f(y)-xy-f(x)}{y}$

$= \lim_{y\to 0}\frac{f(y)-xy}{y} = \lim_{y\to 0}\frac{f(y)}{y} - x$

$= \lim_{y\to 0}\frac{f(y+0)-f(0)}{y} - x$

$= f'(0) - x$

$f'(x) = f'(0) - x$

$\Rightarrow f(x) = f'(0)\cdot x - \frac{x^2}{2} + \lambda$ ... (iii)

From Eq. (ii), we have

$f(0+y) = f(0) + f(y) - 0 \Rightarrow f(0) = 0$

Putting $x = 0$ into Eq. (iii), we get

$0 = 0 - 0 + \lambda \Rightarrow \lambda = 0$

$\therefore \quad f(x) = (1-c^2)\cdot x - \frac{x^2}{2}$

$[\because f'(0) = 1 - c^2]$ ... (iv)

On comparing Eqs. (i) and (iv), we get

$c + 1 = -\frac{1}{2} \Rightarrow c = -\frac{3}{2}$

$\therefore \quad f(x) = -\frac{1}{2}x^2 - \frac{5}{4}x$

$|2[f(1) + f(2) + f(3) + \ldots + f(20)]|$

$= \left|2\sum_{x=1}^{20} f(x)\right| = \sum_{x=1}^{20} x^2 + \frac{5}{2}\sum_{x=1}^{20} x$

$= \frac{20(20+1)(2\times 20+1)}{6} + \frac{5}{2}\times\frac{20(20+1)}{2}$

$= 10\times 7\times 41 + 210\times\frac{5}{2}$

$= 2870 + 525 = 3395$

28. (88) $H: \frac{x^2}{a^2} - \frac{y^2}{b^2} = 1$

$e = \frac{\sqrt{11}}{2} \Rightarrow e^2 = \frac{11}{4} \Rightarrow 1 + \frac{b^2}{a^2} = \frac{11}{4}$

$\Rightarrow \quad b^2 = \frac{7}{4}a^2 \Rightarrow b^2 = \left(\frac{\sqrt{7}}{2}a\right)^2$

$\therefore \quad \frac{x^2}{a^2} - \frac{y^2}{\left(\frac{\sqrt{7}}{2}a\right)^2} = 1$

Length of transverse axis $= 2a$

Length of conjugate axis

$= 2\left(\frac{\sqrt{7}}{2}a\right) = \sqrt{7}a$

Sum of length of transverse axis and conjugate axis.

$2a + \sqrt{7}a = 4(2\sqrt{2} + \sqrt{14})$

$\Rightarrow \quad a(2+\sqrt{7}) = 4\sqrt{2}(2+\sqrt{7})$

$\Rightarrow \quad a = 4\sqrt{2}$

$\Rightarrow b^2 = \left(\frac{\sqrt{7}}{2}\times 4\sqrt{2}\right)^2 = (2\sqrt{14})^2$

$= 4\times 14 = 56$

$\therefore \; a^2 + b^2 = 32 + 56 = 88$

29. (28) $P_1: \mathbf{r}\cdot(2\hat{\mathbf{i}} + \hat{\mathbf{j}} - 3\hat{\mathbf{k}}) = 4$

$P_1: 2x + y - 3z = 4$

$P_2: \begin{vmatrix} x-2 & y+3 & z-2 \\ 2-2 & -2+3 & -3-2 \\ 1-2 & -4+3 & 2-2 \end{vmatrix} = 0$

$\Rightarrow \begin{vmatrix} x-2 & y+3 & z-2 \\ 0 & 1 & -5 \\ -1 & -1 & 0 \end{vmatrix} = 0$

$\Rightarrow \; (x-2)[0-5] - 1[-5(y+3) - 1(z-2)] = 0$

$\Rightarrow -5(x-2) + 5(y+3) + 1(z-2) = 0$

$\Rightarrow \quad -5x + 10 + 5y + 15 + z - 2 = 0$

$\Rightarrow \quad -5x + 5y + z + 23 = 0$

We have, $P_1: 2x + y - 3z = 4$

and $\quad P_2: -5x + 5y + z = -23$

For DR's of line of intersection,

$\frac{x}{\begin{vmatrix} 1 & -3 \\ 5 & 1 \end{vmatrix}} = \frac{y}{\begin{vmatrix} -3 & 2 \\ 1 & -5 \end{vmatrix}} = \frac{z}{\begin{vmatrix} 2 & 1 \\ -5 & 5 \end{vmatrix}}$

$\Rightarrow \quad \frac{x}{1+15} = \frac{y}{15-2} = \frac{z}{10+5}$

$\Rightarrow \quad \frac{x}{16} = \frac{y}{13} = \frac{z}{15} = \lambda$ (say)

$\Rightarrow x = 16\lambda, y = 13\lambda$ and $z = 15\lambda$

$\therefore \quad \alpha = 13$ and $\beta = 15$

$\therefore \alpha + \beta = 13 + 15 = 28$

30. (18915) $b_i \in \{1, 2, 3, \ldots, 100\}$

Let P = Set when b_1, b_2, b_3 are consecutive

$n(P) = 97 + 97 + 97 + \ldots$ (98 times)

$= 97\times 98$

Similarly, Q = Set when b_2, b_3, b_4 are consecutive

$n(Q) = 97\times 98$

$n(P\cap Q) = 97$

$n(P\cup Q) = n(P) + n(Q) - n(P\cap Q)$

$= 97\times 98 + 97\times 98 - 97$

$= 97(98 + 98 - 1)$

$= 97(195) = 18915$

Hence, the number of required permutations is 18915.

25 July 2022, Shift-I

1. (b) Given, $f:\{1,2,3,4\} \rightarrow \{1,2,3,4,5,6\}$ such that $f(1)+f(2)=f(3)$

Now, explanation goes to table form,

$f(1)$	$f(2)$	$f(3)$	$f(4)$
1	1	2	$f(4)$ has no restriction so only possible 6-ways
1	2	3	
2	1	3	
1	3	4	
3	1	4	
2	2	4	
1	4	5	
4	1	5	
2	3	5	
3	2	5	
1	5	6	
5	1	6	
2	4	6	
4	2	6	
3	3	6	

Total number of possible case

$=15\times$ [every time 6-ways of $f(4)$]

$=15\times 6=90$

2. (b) Given that, the equation is

$$x^4+x^3+x^2+x+1=0$$

and α, β, γ and δ are roots of the above equation.

Since, $x^4+x^3+x^2+x+1=0$

$$\Rightarrow \frac{x^5-1}{x-1}=0\ (x\neq 1)$$

$[\because (x-1)(x^4+x^3+x^2+x+1)=x^5-1]$

So, the roots of the above equation $\frac{x^5-1}{x-1}=0\ (x\neq 1)$ are

$$e^{2\pi i/5}, e^{4\pi i/5}, e^{6\pi i/5}, e^{8\pi i/5},$$

i.e. α, β, γ and δ.

We know that, property of nth root of unity

$$1^P+\alpha^P+(\alpha^2)^P+(\alpha^3)^P+\ldots\ldots+(\alpha^{n-1})^P$$

$$=\begin{cases}0, & p \text{ is not a multiple of } n\\ n, & p \text{ is a multiple of } n\end{cases}$$

Thus, from the above property, we get

$$1^{2021}+\alpha^{2021}+\beta^{2021}+\gamma^{2021}+\delta^{2021}=0$$

$$\Rightarrow 1+\alpha^{2021}+\beta^{2021}+\gamma^{2021}+\delta^{2021}=0$$

$$\Rightarrow \alpha^{2021}+\beta^{2021}+\gamma^{2021}+\delta^{2021}=-1$$

3. (*) Given, $S_n=\left\{z\in C, |z-3+2i|=\frac{n}{4}\right\}$ represents a circle with centre $C_1(3,-2)$ and radius $r_1=\frac{n}{4}$.

Also, $T_n=\left\{z\in C, |z-2+3i|=\frac{1}{n}\right\}$ also represent a circle with centre $C_2(2,-3)$ and radius $r_2=\frac{1}{n}$

Case I Since, $S_n\cap T_n=\phi$ (given)

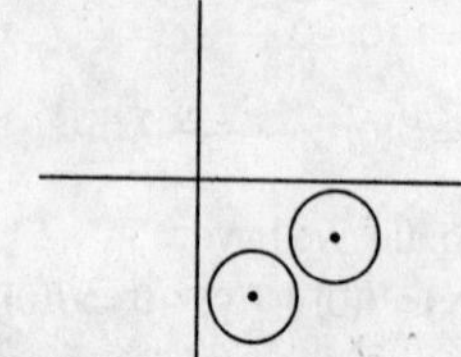

Thus, $C_1C_2>r_1+r_2$

$$\Rightarrow \sqrt{(3-2)^2+(-2+3)^2}>\frac{n}{4}+\frac{1}{n}$$

$$\Rightarrow \sqrt{2}>\frac{n^2+4}{4n}$$

$$\Rightarrow 4\sqrt{2}n>n^2+4$$

$$\Rightarrow n^2-4\sqrt{2}n+4<0$$

$$\Rightarrow n=\frac{4\sqrt{2}\pm\sqrt{32-16}}{2}=\frac{4\sqrt{2}\pm 4}{2}$$

$$=2\sqrt{2}\pm 2$$

$+\quad -\quad +$

$2\sqrt{2}-2(\approx 0)$ $\quad 2\sqrt{2}+2(\approx 4)$

Between these two numbers, there are four natural numbers 1, 2,3 and 4.

Thus, we get '4' value of n.

Case II

Since, $S_n\cap T_n=\phi$

$$\Rightarrow C_1C_2<|r_1-r_2|$$

$$\Rightarrow \sqrt{2}<\left|\frac{n}{4}-\frac{1}{n}\right|$$

$$\Rightarrow \sqrt{2}<\left|\frac{n^2-4}{4n}\right|$$

$$\Rightarrow 4\sqrt{2}<\frac{|n^2-4|}{n}\quad [\because 4\sqrt{2}\approx 5.6]$$

Clearly, the above relation hold for $n\geq 7$.

Thus, here n may take infinite values ≥ 7.

4. (b) Given, system of equation is

$$\left.\begin{aligned}3(\sin 3\theta)x-y+z&=2\\ 3(\cos 2\theta)x+4y+3z&=3\\ 6x+7y+7z&=9\end{aligned}\right\}\quad \ldots\text{(i)}$$

Thus, $\Delta=\begin{vmatrix}3\sin 3\theta & -1 & 1\\ 3\cos 2\theta & 4 & 3\\ 6 & 7 & 7\end{vmatrix}$

$$=3\sin 3\theta(28-21)+1(21\cos 2\theta-18)+1(21\cos 2\theta-24)$$

$$=21\sin 3\theta+42\cos 2\theta-42$$

Now, for no solution of above system (i).

Then, $\Delta=0$

$\Rightarrow 21\sin 3\theta+42\cos 2\theta-42=0$

$\Rightarrow \sin 3\theta+2\cos 2\theta-2=0$

$\Rightarrow \sin 3\theta=2(2\sin^2\theta)$

$[\because \cos 2\theta=1-2\sin^2\theta]$

$\Rightarrow 3\sin\theta-4\sin^3\theta=4\sin^2\theta$

$[\because \sin 3\theta=3\sin\theta-4\sin^3\theta]$

$\Rightarrow \sin\theta(3-4\sin^2\theta-4\sin\theta)=0$

$\therefore \sin\theta=0$ or $\sin\theta=\frac{1}{2}$ and $-\frac{3}{2}$

But given $\theta\in(0,4\pi)$ thus, $\sin\theta\neq -\frac{3}{2}$

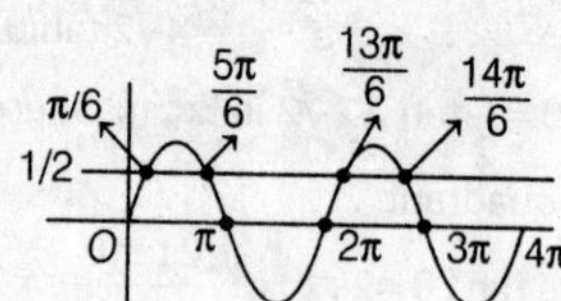

$$\therefore \theta=\pi, 2\pi, 3\pi, \frac{\pi}{6}, \frac{5\pi}{6}, \frac{13\pi}{6}, \frac{17\pi}{6}.$$

Thus, '7' value of $\theta\in(0,4\pi)$.

5. (c) $\lim_{n\to\infty}\left(\sqrt{n^2-n-1}+n\alpha+\beta\right)=0$

Let $n=\frac{1}{t}$ as $n\to\infty \Rightarrow t\to 0$

$$\Rightarrow \lim_{t\to 0}\left[\sqrt{\frac{1}{t^2}-\frac{1}{t}-1}+\frac{\alpha}{t}\right]=-\beta$$

$$\Rightarrow \lim_{t\to 0}\left(\frac{\sqrt{1-t-t^2}}{t}+\frac{\alpha}{t}\right)=-\beta$$

$$\Rightarrow \lim_{t\to 0}\left(\frac{\sqrt{1-t-t^2}+\alpha}{t}\right)=-\beta$$

Since, $\beta\neq 0$, thus clearly from above $\alpha=-1$ otherwise the above explanation invalid.

Now,

$$\lim_{t\to 0}\left(\frac{\sqrt{1-t-t^2}-1}{t}\right)=-\beta$$

Apply L-Hospital rule for $\frac{0}{0}$ form,

$$\lim_{t\to 0}\left(\frac{1-t-t^2-1}{t(\sqrt{1-t-t^2}+1)}\right)=-\beta$$

$$\Rightarrow \quad \lim_{t\to 0}\frac{-t(1+t^2)}{t(\sqrt{1-t-t^2}+1)}=-\beta$$

$$\Rightarrow \quad -\frac{1}{2}=-\beta$$

$$\Rightarrow \quad \beta=\frac{1}{2}$$

Thus, $8(\alpha+\beta)=8\left(-1+\frac{1}{2}\right)$

$$=8\left(-\frac{1}{2}\right)=-4$$

6. (b) Given, $f(x)=(x^2-2x+7)\cdot e^{(4x^3-12x^2-180x+31)}$

Let $f_1(x)=(x^2-2x+7)>0,\ \forall x\in R$

$f_1'(x)=2x-2=0 \Rightarrow x=1$

$$\underset{-3}{|}\quad - \quad \underset{0}{|}\quad \underset{1}{|}\quad +$$

Thus, $f(x)$ is decreasing in $[-3,0]$.

Also, let $f_2(x)=e^{4x^3-12x^2-180x+31}$

$$\Rightarrow \quad f_2'(x)=e^{4x^3-12x^2-180x+31}\cdot(12x^2-24x-180)$$

$$=12(x^2-2x-15)\cdot e^{4x^3-12x^2-180x+31}$$

$$=12(x+3)(x-5)\,e^{4x^3-12x^2-180x+31}$$

Thus, $\underset{-3}{+\ |}\ -\ \underset{0}{|}\ -\ \underset{5}{|}\ +$

$\therefore$ Clearly, $f_2(x)$ is also deceasing in $[-3,0]$ and also positive, $\forall x\in R$.

$\therefore$ Absolute maximum value of $f(x)$ occurs at $x=-3$

Given that, absolute maximum value of the above function in $[-3,0]$ is $f(\alpha)$.

Thus, $\alpha=-3$.

7. (a) Given,

$$f(x)=y=ax^3+bx^2+cx+5 \qquad \text{...(i)}$$

$$\Rightarrow \quad \frac{dy}{dx}=3ax^2+2bx+c \qquad \text{...(ii)}$$

Touches X-axis at $P(-2,0)$

$$\Rightarrow \quad \left.\frac{dy}{dx}\right|_{x=-2}=0$$

$$\Rightarrow 3a(-2)^2+2b(-2)+c=0$$

$$\Rightarrow \quad 12a-4b+c=0 \qquad \text{... (iii)}$$

and also $y|_{x=-2}=0$

$$\Rightarrow -8a+4b-2c+5=0 \qquad \text{... (iv)}$$

and $y=f(x)$ cut Y-axis at point Q, where y' is equal to 3.

Then, $\quad c=3 \qquad$ ... (v)

From Eqs. (iii), (iv) and (v), we get

$$a=-\frac{1}{2},\ b=-\frac{3}{4},\ c=3$$

Thus, $f(x)=-\frac{x^3}{2}-\frac{3}{4}x^2+3x+5$

$$\Rightarrow \quad f'(x)=-\frac{3}{2}x^2-\frac{3}{2}x+3$$

$$=-\frac{3}{2}(x^2+x-2)$$

$$=\frac{-3}{2}(x+2)(x-1)$$

Now, $f'(x)=0 \Rightarrow x=-2$ and 1

By first derivative test, $x=1$ is the point of Local maximum.

Hence, the local maximum value of $f(x)$ at $x=1$ is

$$f(1)=-\frac{1}{2}-\frac{3}{4}+3+5$$

$$=\frac{-2-3+12+20}{4}=\frac{27}{4}$$

8. (b) Given that,

$A=\{(x,y);x^2\le y\le \min\{x+2, 4-3x\}\}$

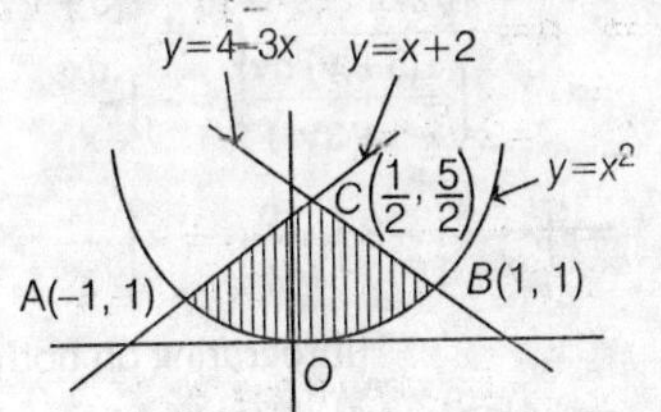

Thus, the point of intersection of $y=x^2$ and $y=4-3x$ is $B(1,1)$ and the point of intersection of $y=x+2$ and $y=x^2$ is $A(-1,1)$ and also the point of intersection of $y=x+2$ and $y=4-3x$ is $C\left(\frac{1}{2},\frac{5}{2}\right)$.

So, the required region $ACBA$ is

$$\int_{-1}^{1/2}(x+2-x^2)\,dx+\int_{1/2}^{1}(4-3x-x^2)\,dx$$

$$=\left[\frac{x^2}{2}+2x-\frac{x^3}{3}\right]_{-1}^{1/2}+\left[4x-\frac{3x^2}{2}-\frac{x^3}{3}\right]_{1/2}^{1}$$

$$=\left[\frac{1}{2}\left(\frac{1}{4}\right)+2\left(\frac{1}{2}\right)-\frac{1}{3}\left(\frac{1}{2}\right)^3\right]-\left[\frac{(-1)^2}{2}+2(-1)-\frac{(-1)^3}{3}\right]$$

$$+\left[4(1)-\frac{3}{2}(1)^2-\frac{(1)^3}{3}\right]-\left[4\left(\frac{1}{2}\right)-\frac{3\left(\frac{1}{2}\right)^2}{2}-\frac{\left(\frac{1}{2}\right)^3}{3}\right]$$

$$=\left(\frac{1}{8}+1-\frac{1}{24}\right)-\left(\frac{1}{2}-2+\frac{1}{3}\right)+\left(4-\frac{3}{2}-\frac{1}{3}\right)-\left(2-\frac{3}{8}-\frac{1}{24}\right)$$

$$=\frac{17}{6}$$

9. (a) Given, f is a real valued function defined on the interval $[-10,10]$ by

$$f(x)=\begin{cases}x-[x], \text{if } [x] \text{ is odd}\\ 1+[x]-x, \text{if } [x] \text{ is even}\end{cases}$$

The graph of $f(x)$ is

Clearly, $f(x)$ is an even function and also period is 2.

Thus, $\frac{\pi^2}{10}\int_{-10}^{10}f(x)\cos\pi x\,dx$

$$=\frac{\pi^2}{10}.20\int_0^1 f(x)\cos\pi x\,dx$$

$$f(x)=\begin{cases}-1-x, x\in[2,-1)\\ x+1, x\in[-1,0)\\ 1-x, x\in[0,1)\\ x-1, x\in[1,2)\\ 3-x, x\in[2,3)\\ x-3, x\in[3,4)\end{cases}$$

$$=\frac{\pi^2}{10}.20\int_0^1(1-x)\cos\pi x\,dx$$

$$=2\pi^2\left\{\left[(1-x)\frac{\sin\pi x}{\pi}\right]_0^1-\left[\frac{\cos\pi x}{\pi^2}\right]_0^1\right\}$$

$$=2\pi^2\left\{\frac{2}{\pi^2}\right\}=4$$

10. (b) Let $\frac{dy}{dx}$ is the slope of the tangent to a curve $C: y=y(x)$ at any point (x,y).

Given that, $\frac{dy}{dx}=\frac{2e^{2x}-6e^{-x}+9}{2+9e^{-2x}}$

$$\Rightarrow \quad \frac{dy}{dx}=e^{2x}-\frac{6e^{-x}}{2+9e^{-2x}}$$

$$\Rightarrow \int dy=\int e^{2x}\,dx-\int\frac{6e^{-x}}{2+9e^{-2x}}dx$$

$$\Rightarrow \quad y=\frac{e^{2x}}{2}-3\int\frac{e^{-x}}{1+\left(\frac{3e^{-x}}{\sqrt{2}}\right)^2}dx$$

On putting $e^{-x}=t$,

$$-e^{-x}\,dx=dt$$

$$\Rightarrow y(x)=\frac{e^{2x}}{2}-3\int\frac{-dt}{1+\left(\frac{3t}{\sqrt{2}}\right)^2}$$

$$=\frac{e^{2x}}{2}+\frac{3(\sqrt{2})}{3}\tan^{-1}\frac{3t}{\sqrt{2}}+C$$

$$\therefore\ y(x)=\frac{e^{2x}}{2}+\sqrt{2}\tan^{-1}\left(\frac{3e^{-x}}{\sqrt{2}}\right)+C$$

It is given that, the curve passes through $\left(0,\frac{1}{2}+\frac{\pi}{2\sqrt{2}}\right)$

$$\Rightarrow \frac{1}{2}+\frac{\pi}{2\sqrt{2}}=\frac{1}{2}+\sqrt{2}\tan^{-1}\left(\frac{3}{\sqrt{2}}\right)+C$$

$$\Rightarrow \quad C=\frac{\pi}{2\sqrt{2}}-\sqrt{2}\tan^{-1}\left(\frac{3}{\sqrt{2}}\right)$$

$$\text{Thus, } y(x)=\frac{e^{2x}}{2}+\sqrt{2}\tan^{-1}\left(\frac{3e^{-x}}{\sqrt{2}}\right)+\frac{\pi}{2\sqrt{2}}-\sqrt{2}\tan^{-1}\left(\frac{3}{\sqrt{2}}\right)$$

Now, $\left(\alpha,\frac{e^{2\alpha}}{2}\right)$ satisfies the curve, then

$$\frac{1}{2}e^{2\alpha}=\frac{e^{2\alpha}}{2}+\sqrt{2}\tan^{-1}\left(\frac{3e^{-\alpha}}{\sqrt{2}}\right)+\frac{\pi}{2\sqrt{2}}-\sqrt{2}\tan^{-1}\left(\frac{3}{\sqrt{2}}\right)$$

$$\Rightarrow \tan^{-1}\left(\frac{3}{\sqrt{2}}\right)-\tan^{-1}\left(\frac{3e^{-\alpha}}{\sqrt{2}}\right)=\frac{\pi}{2\sqrt{2}}\cdot\left(\frac{1}{\sqrt{2}}\right)=\frac{\pi}{4}$$

$$=\tan^{-1}\frac{\frac{3}{\sqrt{2}}-\frac{3e^{-\alpha}}{\sqrt{2}}}{1+\frac{3}{\sqrt{2}}\cdot\left(\frac{3e^{-\alpha}}{\sqrt{2}}\right)}=\frac{\pi}{4}$$

$$\left[\because \tan^{-1}x-\tan^{-1}y=\tan^{-1}\frac{x-y}{1+xy}\right]$$

$$\Rightarrow \frac{\frac{3}{\sqrt{2}}-\frac{3e^{-\alpha}}{\sqrt{2}}}{1+\frac{9}{2}e^{-\alpha}}=\tan\frac{\pi}{4}=1$$

$$\Rightarrow \frac{3}{\sqrt{2}}e^{\alpha}-\frac{3}{\sqrt{2}}=e^{\alpha}+\frac{9}{2}$$

$$\Rightarrow \quad e^{\alpha}=\frac{\frac{9}{2}+\frac{3}{\sqrt{2}}}{\frac{3}{\sqrt{2}}-1}=\frac{3}{\sqrt{2}}\left(\frac{3+\sqrt{2}}{3-\sqrt{2}}\right)$$

$$\therefore\quad e^{\alpha}=\frac{3}{\sqrt{2}}\left(\frac{3+\sqrt{2}}{3-\sqrt{2}}\right)$$

11. (a) Given,

$$(x-y^2)\,dx+y\,(5x+y^2)\,dy=0$$

$$\Rightarrow \quad y\frac{dy}{dx}=\frac{y^2-x}{5x+y^2}$$

$$\text{Let } y^2=z\Rightarrow 2y\frac{dy}{dx}=\frac{dz}{dx}$$

$$\Rightarrow y\frac{dy}{dx}=\frac{1}{2}\frac{dz}{dx}\ \Rightarrow\ \frac{1}{2}\frac{dz}{dx}=\frac{z-x}{5x+z}$$

Now, substitute $z=vx\Rightarrow\frac{dz}{dx}=v+x\frac{dv}{dx}$

$$\Rightarrow \quad \frac{1}{2}\left\{v+x\frac{dv}{dx}\right\}=\frac{v-1}{5+v}$$

$$\Rightarrow \quad v+x\frac{dv}{dx}=\frac{2v-2}{5+v}$$

$$\Rightarrow \quad x\left(\frac{dv}{dx}\right)=\frac{2v-2}{5+v}-v$$

$$=\frac{2v-2-5v-v^2}{5+v}$$

$$\Rightarrow \quad x\frac{dv}{dx}=\frac{-3v-2-v^2}{5+v}$$

$$\Rightarrow \quad \int\frac{(5+v)\,dv)}{v^2+3v+2}=-\int\frac{dx}{x}$$

$$\Rightarrow \int\frac{4dv}{v+1}-3\int\frac{dv}{v+2}=-\int\frac{dx}{x}$$

[integrating on both sides]

$$\Rightarrow \quad 4\log|v+1|-3\log|v+2|=-\log|x|+\log C$$

$$\Rightarrow \log|(v+1)^4|-\log|(v+2)^3|=\log\frac{C}{x}$$

$$\Rightarrow \quad \log\left|\frac{(v+1)^4}{(v+2)^3}\right|=\log\frac{C}{x}$$

$$\Rightarrow \left|\frac{\left(\frac{y^2}{x}+1\right)^4}{\left(\frac{y^2}{x}+2\right)^3}\right|=\frac{C}{x}\quad\left[\because v=\frac{z}{x}=\frac{y^2}{x}\right]$$

$$\Rightarrow \quad |(y^2+x)^4|=C\,|(y^2+2x)^3|$$

12. (c)

A(4, 3)

$\frac{\sqrt{29}}{3}$

$x-y=2$

B $\left(4-\frac{\sqrt{29}}{3}\cos\theta,\ 3-\frac{\sqrt{29}}{3}\sin\theta\right)$

θ

Let 'θ' be the inclination makes on given line passes through the point $A(4,3)$.

So, let the coordinate of B is $\left(4-\frac{\sqrt{29}}{3}\cos\theta, 3-\frac{\sqrt{29}}{3}\sin\theta\right)$ which also satisfies the line $x-y-2=0$ because B is the intersecting point shown in above figure.

Thus,

$$\left(4-\frac{\sqrt{29}}{3}\cos\theta\right)-\left(3-\frac{\sqrt{29}}{3}\sin\theta\right)-2=0$$

$$\Rightarrow 4-\frac{\sqrt{29}}{3}\cos\theta-3+\frac{\sqrt{29}}{3}\sin\theta-2=0$$

$$\Rightarrow \quad (\sin\theta-\cos\theta)\frac{\sqrt{29}}{3}=1$$

$$\Rightarrow \quad (\sin\theta-\cos\theta)=\frac{3}{\sqrt{29}}$$

Now, squaring on both sides, we get

$$\sin^2\theta+\cos^2\theta-2\sin\theta\cos\theta=\frac{9}{29}$$

$$\Rightarrow \quad 1-\sin 2\theta=\frac{9}{29}$$

$$\Rightarrow \quad \sin 2\theta=1-\frac{9}{29}=\frac{20}{29}$$

$$\Rightarrow \quad \frac{2\tan\theta}{1+\tan^2\theta}=\frac{20}{29}$$

$$\Rightarrow \quad \frac{\tan\theta}{1+\tan^2\theta}=\frac{10}{29}$$

Thus, we get a quadratic equation in $\tan\theta$, then $\tan\theta=\frac{5}{2}$ only (because given slope 'θ' is greater than 1).

Hence, $\sin\theta=\frac{5}{\sqrt{29}}$, $\cos\theta=\frac{2}{\sqrt{29}}$

$\sqrt{5^2+2^2}=\sqrt{29}$

5

2

θ

Thus, the point B is

$$\left(4-\frac{\sqrt{29}}{3}\cos\theta, 3-\frac{\sqrt{29}}{3}\sin\theta\right)$$

$$=\left(4-\frac{\sqrt{29}}{3}\left(\frac{2}{\sqrt{29}}\right), 3-\frac{\sqrt{29}}{3}\left(\frac{5}{\sqrt{29}}\right)\right)$$

$$=\left(4-\frac{2}{3}, 3-\frac{5}{3}\right)=\left(\frac{10}{3},\frac{4}{3}\right)$$

which is also satisfied the line $x+2y=6$ and remaining options are also false.

13. (c) Since, the locus of the centre $(\alpha, \beta), \beta > 0$ of the circle which touches the circle $x^2 + (y-1)^2 = 1$ externally and also touches the the X-axis be L.

Thus, $\alpha^2 + (\beta - 1)^2 = (|\beta| + 1)^2$

$\Rightarrow \alpha^2 + \beta^2 - 2\beta + 1 = \beta^2 + 1 + 2|\beta|$

$\Rightarrow \quad \alpha^2 = 4\beta$ as $\beta > 0$

Thus, the Locus 'L' is $x^2 = 4y, y > 0$

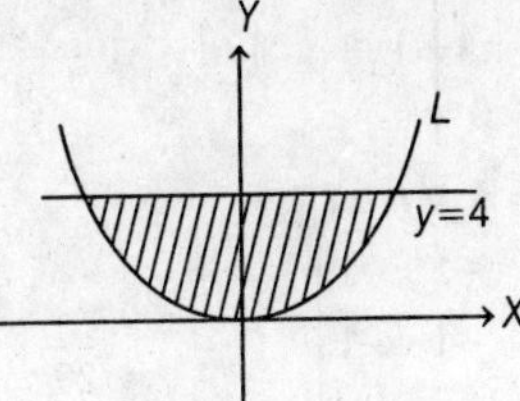

Hence, the area bounded by 'L' and the line $y = 4$ is

$$= 2\int_0^4 2\sqrt{y}\, dy = 4\left[\frac{2}{3}y^{\frac{3}{2}}\right]_0^4 = \frac{64}{3} \text{ sq units}$$

14. (c) Given, 'P' is the plane containing the straight line

$$\frac{x-3}{9} = \frac{y+4}{-1} = \frac{z-7}{-5}$$

Let (a, b, c) be the direction ratios of the plane containing lines

$$\frac{x}{2} = \frac{y}{3} = \frac{z}{5} \text{ and } \frac{x}{3} = \frac{y}{7} = \frac{z}{8}$$

$\therefore \quad 2a + 3b + 5c = 0 \quad$ ... (i)

and $\quad 3a + 7b + 8c = 0 \quad$ ... (ii)

From Eqs. (i) and (ii), we get

$$\frac{a}{24-35} = \frac{b}{15-16} = \frac{c}{14-9} = k$$

$$\Rightarrow \frac{a}{-11} = \frac{b}{-1} = \frac{c}{5} = k$$

$$\Rightarrow \frac{a}{11} = \frac{b}{1} = \frac{c}{-5} = k$$

Thus, $\quad a = 11k, b = k, c = -5k$

$\therefore$ Direction ratios of the plane are $(11, 1, -5)$.

Let direction ratio of the plane P be (a_1, b_1, c_1).

Then, $\quad 11a_1 + b_1 - 5c_1 = 0 \quad$ ... (iii)

and $\quad 9a_1 - b_1 - 5c_1 = 0 \quad$ ... (iv)

From Eqs. (iii) and (iv), we get

$$\frac{a_1}{-5-5} = \frac{b_1}{-45+55} = \frac{c_1}{-11-9} = k$$

$$\Rightarrow \frac{a_1}{-10} = \frac{b_1}{10} = \frac{c_1}{-20} = k$$

$$\Rightarrow \frac{a_1}{1} = \frac{b_1}{-1} = \frac{c_1}{2} = k$$

Thus $a_1 = k, b_1 = -k, c_1 = 2k$

$\therefore$ Direction ratios of the plane P are $(1, -1, 2)$.

Thus, equation of plane P is

$1(x-3) - 1(y+4) + 2(z-7) = 0$

$\Rightarrow \quad x - y + 2z - 21 = 0$

Now, given that, 'd' is the distance of P from the point $(2, -5, 11)$.

$$\text{Then, } d = \frac{|2+5+22-21|}{\sqrt{(1)^2 + (-1)^2 + (2)^2}}$$

$$= \frac{|2+5+1|}{\sqrt{6}} = \frac{8}{\sqrt{6}}$$

$$\Rightarrow d^2 = \frac{8^2}{6} = \frac{64}{6} = \frac{32}{3}$$

15. (c) Given, ABC is a triangle such that $\mathbf{BC} = \mathbf{a}$,

$\mathbf{CA} = \mathbf{b}, \mathbf{AB} = \mathbf{c}, |\mathbf{a}| = 6\sqrt{2}, |\mathbf{b}| = 2\sqrt{3}$ and $\mathbf{b} \cdot \mathbf{c} = 12$

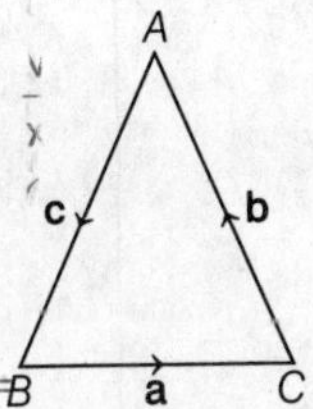

Since, $\quad \mathbf{a} + \mathbf{b} + \mathbf{c} = 0 \quad$ ... (i)

$\Rightarrow \quad \mathbf{a} + \mathbf{c} = -\mathbf{b}$

$\Rightarrow \quad (\mathbf{a} + \mathbf{c}) \times \mathbf{b} = -\mathbf{b} \times \mathbf{b}$

$\Rightarrow \quad (\mathbf{a} \times \mathbf{b}) + \mathbf{c} \times \mathbf{b} = 0 \quad$ ... (ii)

Now, from statement I

$|(\mathbf{a} \times \mathbf{b}) + (\mathbf{c} \times \mathbf{b})| - |\mathbf{c}| = 6(2\sqrt{2} - 1)$

$\Rightarrow \quad |0| - |\mathbf{c}| = (12\sqrt{2} - 6)$

$\Rightarrow \quad |\mathbf{c}| = 6 - 12\sqrt{2} < 0$

(which is impossible)

Hence, statement I is not correct.

For statement II, from Eq. (i), we get

$\mathbf{b} + \mathbf{c} = -\mathbf{a}$

$\Rightarrow \quad \mathbf{b} \cdot (\mathbf{b} + \mathbf{c}) = -\mathbf{b} \cdot \mathbf{a}$

$\Rightarrow \quad \mathbf{b} \cdot \mathbf{b} + \mathbf{b} \cdot \mathbf{c} = -\mathbf{a} \cdot \mathbf{b}$

$\Rightarrow \quad |\mathbf{b}|^2 + \mathbf{b} \cdot \mathbf{c} = -\mathbf{a} \cdot \mathbf{b}$

$\Rightarrow 12 + 12 = -|\mathbf{a}||\mathbf{b}| \cos(\pi - \angle ACB)$

$\Rightarrow \quad 24 = -6\sqrt{2} \cdot 2\sqrt{3}\,[-\cos(\angle ACB)]$

$$\Rightarrow \cos(\angle ACB) = \frac{24}{12\sqrt{6}} = \frac{2}{\sqrt{6}} = \sqrt{\frac{2}{3}}$$

$$\Rightarrow \angle ACB = \cos^{-1}\left(\sqrt{\frac{2}{3}}\right)$$

Hence, statement II is correct.

16. (c) Given that, the sum and product of mean and variance of a binomial distribution are 24 and 128, respectively.

Let n be the number of trials.

p be the probability of success and q be the probability of failure.

Thus, mean $= np$ and variance $= npq$ $\quad [\because q = 1 - p]$

Here, $\quad np + npq = 24 \quad$ ...(i)

and $\quad np \cdot npq = 128 \quad$ ... (ii)

Let $\alpha = np$ and $\beta = npq$.

Thus, $\alpha + \beta = 24$ and $\alpha\beta = 128$

$\therefore \quad x^2 - (\alpha + \beta)x + \alpha\beta = 0$

$\Rightarrow \quad x^2 - (24)x + 128 = 0$

$\Rightarrow \quad (x-8)(x-16) = 0$

$\Rightarrow \quad x = 8, 16$

$\because \alpha = np$ and $\beta = npq, np > npq$

So, $np = 16, npq = 8$

Thus, $q = \frac{1}{2}$ so, $p = 1 - q = 1 - \frac{1}{2} = \frac{1}{2}$

and $n = \frac{16}{1/2} = 32$

Thus, required probability is

$$p(X = 1 \text{ or } 2) = p(X=1) + p(X=2)$$

$$= {}^{32}C_1\left(\frac{1}{2}\right)^1\left(\frac{1}{2}\right)^{31} + {}^{32}C_2\left(\frac{1}{2}\right)^2 \cdot \left(\frac{1}{2}\right)^{30}$$

$$= {}^{32}C_1\left(\frac{1}{2}\right)^{32} + {}^{32}C_2\left(\frac{1}{2}\right)^{32}$$

$$= ({}^{32}C_1 + {}^{32}C_2)\left(\frac{1}{2}\right)^{32}$$

$$= \left(32 + \frac{32 \times 31}{2}\right) \cdot \frac{1}{2^{32}} = \frac{32 \cdot 33}{2} \cdot \frac{1}{2^{32}}$$

$$= 33\left(\frac{1}{2^{32} \cdot 2^{-4}}\right) = \frac{33}{2^{28}}$$

17. (a) If the numbers appeared on the two throws of a fair six faced die are α and β.

Thus, $\alpha, \beta \in \{1, 2, 3, \ldots, 6\}$.

Total possible choice of α and $\beta = 6 \times 6 = 36$

Now, $x^2 + \alpha x + \beta > 0, \forall x \in R$ hold, we should have $\alpha^2 - 4\beta < 0$. i.e. $\alpha^2 < 4\beta$

If $\alpha = 1, \beta$ can be 1, 2, 3, 4, 5, 6, i.e. 6 choices

It $\alpha = 2, \beta$ can be 2, 3, 4, 5, 6 i.e. 5 choices

If $\alpha = 3, \beta$ can be 3, 4, 5, 6 i.e. 4 choices

If $\alpha = 4, \beta$ can be 5, 6 i.e. 2 choices

If $\alpha = 6$, no choices

Hence, total favourable outcomes

$$= 6 + 5 + 4 + 2 + 0 = 17$$

Hence, required probability

$$= \frac{\text{Total favourable outcomes}}{\text{Total possible choice}} = \frac{17}{36}$$

18. (c)

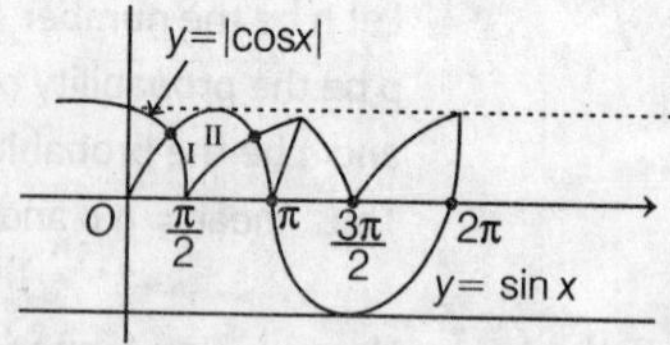

The number of solution of the equation $|\cos x| = \sin x$ $\forall\, x \in [-4\pi, 4\pi]$ will be equal to 4 times the number of solutions of the same equation $|\cos x| = \sin x$ for $x \in [0, 2\pi]$.

Clearly, from the above diagram, two solution of the equation $|\cos x| = \sin x$ in $[0, 2\pi]$.

Thus, total '8' solutions in $[-4\pi, 4\pi]$.

19. (a)

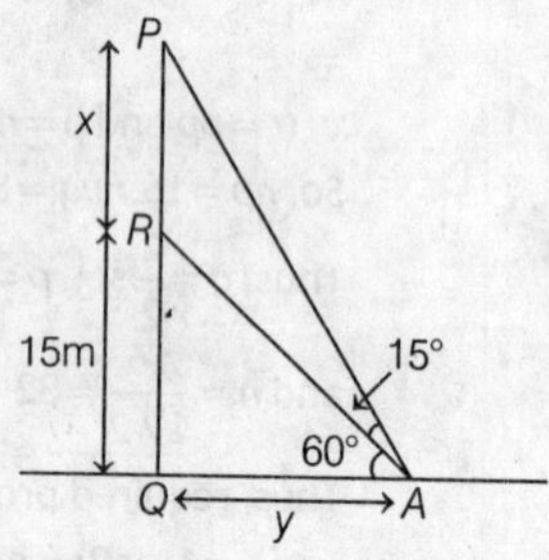

Given, $\angle RAQ = 60°$ and $\angle PAR = 15°$ and $RQ = 15$ m

Let $PR = x$ m and $QA = y$ m

Now, ΔPQA,

$$\frac{x+15}{y} = \tan 75° \quad \text{...(i)}$$

and ΔRQA,

$$\frac{15}{y} = \tan 60° \quad \text{... (ii)}$$

From Eqs. (i) and (ii), we get

$$\frac{x+15}{15} = \frac{\tan 75°}{\tan 60°} = \frac{\tan(45° + 30°)}{\tan 60°} = \frac{\dfrac{\tan 45° + \tan 30°}{1 - \tan 45° \tan 30°}}{\tan 60°}$$

$$\Rightarrow \frac{x+15}{15} = \frac{(1+\sqrt{3})}{(-1+\sqrt{3})\sqrt{3}}$$

$$\Rightarrow \frac{x+15}{15} = \frac{(1+\sqrt{3})(1+\sqrt{3})}{\sqrt{3}(-1+\sqrt{3})(1+\sqrt{3})} = \frac{4+2\sqrt{3}}{\sqrt{3}(-1+3)} = \frac{(2+\sqrt{3})}{\sqrt{3}} = \frac{(2+\sqrt{3})\sqrt{3}}{3}$$

$$\Rightarrow \frac{x+15}{15} = \frac{2\sqrt{3}+3}{3}$$

$$\Rightarrow x = 10\sqrt{3} \text{ m}$$

Thus, height of the tower $= (15 + 10\sqrt{3})\text{m} = 5(2\sqrt{3}+3)\text{m}$

20. (d) Truth table

p	q	$\sim p$	$\sim q$	$(\sim p) \vee q$	$q \to ((\sim p) \vee q)$
T	T	F	F	T	T
T	F	F	T	F	T
F	T	T	F	T	T
F	F	T	T	T	T

21. (17) Given, $A = \begin{bmatrix} 2 & -1 & -1 \\ 1 & 0 & -1 \\ 1 & -1 & 0 \end{bmatrix}$

Clearly, $A^2 = A \Rightarrow A^n = A, \forall\, n \geq 2$

and $B = A - I = \begin{bmatrix} 1 & -1 & -1 \\ 1 & -1 & -1 \\ 1 & -1 & -1 \end{bmatrix}$

$\Rightarrow$ $B^2 = -B \Rightarrow B^3 = B, \forall\, n = 3, 5, 7, 9, 11, \ldots$

and $\omega^n = 1$ iff n is a multiple of 3, i.e. 3, 6, 9, 12, ...

Thus, $A^n + (\omega B)^n = A + B$ hold only for

$$n = 3, 6, 9, 12, \ldots, 99.$$

Thus, last term $= 99 = 3 + (n-1)\cdot 6$

$\Rightarrow$ $96 = (n-1)6$

$\Rightarrow$ $n - 1 = 16 \Rightarrow n = 17$

The required number of elements in the set is 17.

22. (1492) The letters of the word 'MANKIND' are written in all possible order and arranged in serial order as in an english dictionary.

Represent serial order in dictionary	⑤ M	① A	⑥ N	④ K	③ I	⑥ N	② D
	$\frac{4}{2!}$	0	$\frac{3}{2!}$	2	1	1	0
	×	×	×	×	×	×	×
	6!	5!	4!	3!	2!	1!	0!
Outcomes	1440	0	36	12	2	1	

Thus, the serial number of the word MANKIND is $(1440 + 0 + 36 + 12 + 2 + 1) + 1 = 1491 + 1 = 1492$

23. (6006) The given expression is $\left(t^2 x^{1/5} + \frac{(1-x)^{1/10}}{t}\right)^{15}$ $x \geq 0$

the above expression for term independent on t, then power of t is equal to zero.

Thus, general term of the above expression

$$= {}^{15}C_r\, (t^2 x^{1/5})^{15-r} \left(\frac{(1-x)^{1/10}}{t}\right)^r$$

For term independent on t,

$$2(15 - r) - r = 0$$

$\Rightarrow$ $r = 10$

Thus, 11th term of above expression is independent of t.

$\therefore$ $t_{11} = {}^{15}C_{10}\, x(1-x)$

Now, maximum value of $x(1-x)$ occur at $x=\frac{1}{2}$

i.e. $[x(1-x)]_{max}=\frac{1}{2}\left(1-\frac{1}{2}\right)=\frac{1}{4}$

Since, the maximum value of the term independent of t in the expression is 'k' (given).

Thus, $k={}^{15}C_{10}\times\frac{1}{4}=\frac{15!}{10!\cdot 5!}\cdot\frac{1}{4}$

$$\Rightarrow\quad 8k=\frac{2(15)!}{10!5!}=\frac{2\cdot 15\cdot 14\cdot 13\cdot 12\cdot 11\cdot 10!}{10!5!}=6006$$

24. (38) Since, p, r are the roots of the equation $x^2-8ax+2a=0$

So, let $\frac{1}{p},\frac{1}{r}$ are the roots of the equation $2ax^2-8ax+1=0$

Similarly, $\frac{1}{q}$ and $\frac{1}{s}$ are also the roots of the equation $6bx^2+12bx+1=0$

Since, $\frac{1}{p},\frac{1}{q},\frac{1}{r},\frac{1}{s}$ are in AP.

So, let $\frac{1}{p}=a-3d$,

$\frac{1}{q}=(a-d)$,

$\frac{1}{r}=a+d$

and $\frac{1}{s}=a+3d$

Thus, $\frac{1}{p}+\frac{1}{r}=2a-2d$

and $\frac{1}{q}+\frac{1}{s}=2a+2d$

$\therefore\ 2a-2d=4$ and $2a+2d=-2$

Thus, $a=\frac{1}{2}, d=-\frac{3}{2}$

Now, product of roots

$\frac{1}{p}\cdot\frac{1}{r}=\frac{1}{2a}\Rightarrow -5=\frac{1}{2a}$

$\Rightarrow\quad a=-\frac{1}{10}$ and $\frac{1}{q}\cdot\frac{1}{s}=\frac{1}{6b}$

$\Rightarrow -8=\frac{1}{6b}\Rightarrow b=-\frac{1}{48}$

$$\therefore\quad a^{-1}-b^{-1}=-10-(-48)=-10+48=38$$

25. (27560) Let $a_1=1, b_1=1, a_n=a_{n-1}+2$ and $b_n=a_n+b_{n-1}$ for every natural number $n\geq 2$.

$$a_1=1, b_1=1$$

$$\Rightarrow\quad a_n=a_{n-1}+2\,(n\geq 2)$$

$$a_2=a_1+2=1+2=3$$

$$a_3=a_2+2=3+2=5$$

$$a_4=a_3+2=5+2=7$$

$$\vdots$$

$$a_{15}=a_{14}+2=29$$

$$\therefore\quad a_n=(2n-1), n\geq 2$$

and $b_n=a_n+b_{n-1}$

$$b_2=a_2+b_1=3+1=4=2^2$$

$$b_3=a_3+b_2=5+4=9=3^2$$

$$\vdots$$

$$b_{15}=225=(15)^2$$

$$\therefore\quad b_n=n^2$$

Now, $\sum_{n=1}^{15}a_n b_n=\sum_{n=1}^{15}(2n-1)n^2$

$$=\sum_{n=1}^{15}(2n^3-n^2)=2\sum_{n=1}^{15}n^3-\sum_{n=1}^{15}n^2$$

$$=2\left\{\frac{15\times 16}{2}\right\}^2-\left\{\frac{15\times 16\times 31}{6}\right\}=27560$$

26. (3) Given,

$$f(x)=\begin{cases}|4x^2-8x+5|, & 8x^2-6x+1\geq 0\\ [4x^2-8x+5], & 8x^2-6x+1<0\end{cases}$$

$$=\begin{cases}4x^2-8x+5, & x\in\left(-\infty,\frac{1}{4}\right]\cup\left[\frac{1}{2},\infty\right)\\ [4x^2-8x+5], & x\in\left(\frac{1}{4},\frac{1}{2}\right)\end{cases}$$

$$=\begin{cases}4x^2-8x+5, & x\in\left(-\infty,\frac{1}{4}\right]\cup\left[\frac{1}{2},\infty\right)\\ 3, & x\in\left(\frac{1}{4},\frac{2-\sqrt{2}}{2}\right)\\ 2, & x\in\left(\frac{2-\sqrt{2}}{2},\frac{1}{2}\right)\end{cases}$$

Thus, the above function is non-differentiable at $x=\frac{1}{4},\frac{1}{2},\frac{2-\sqrt{2}}{2}$.

Hence, the number of points are 3.

27. (5) $\lim_{n\to\infty}\frac{(n+1)^{k-1}}{n^{k+1}}[(nk+1)+(nk+2)\ldots..+(nk+n)]$

$$=33\lim_{n\to\infty}\frac{1}{n^{k+1}}[1^k+2^k+3^k+\ldots+n^k]$$

$$\Rightarrow\lim_{n\to\infty}\left(1+\frac{1}{n}\right)^{k-1}\frac{1}{n^2}\cdot n\sum_{r=1}^{n}\left(k+\frac{r}{n}\right)$$

$$=33\lim_{n\to\infty}\frac{1}{n}\sum_{k=1}^{n}\left(\frac{r}{n}\right)^k$$

$$\Rightarrow\quad\int_0^1(k+x)\,dx=33\int_0^1 x^k dx$$

$$\Rightarrow\quad\left(kx+\frac{x^2}{2}\right)_0^1=33\left(\frac{x^{k+1}}{k+1}\right)_0^1$$

$$\Rightarrow\quad\left(k+\frac{1}{2}\right)=33\left(\frac{1}{k+1}\right)$$

$$\Rightarrow\quad\frac{(2k+1)}{2}=\frac{33}{k+1}$$

$$\Rightarrow\quad(k+1)(2k+1)=66$$

$$\Rightarrow\quad 2k^2+3k+1-66=0$$

$$\Rightarrow\quad 2k^2+3k-65=0$$

$$\Rightarrow 2k^2-10k+13k-65=0$$

$$\Rightarrow\quad(2k+13)(k-5)=0$$

$$\Rightarrow\quad k-5=0$$

$$\Rightarrow\quad k=5$$

$[\because k=-13/2$ neglect$]$

Hence, the integral value of k is 5.

28. (2) The equation of circle is $x^2+y^2-2x+2fy+1=0$

and whose centre is $(1,-f)$

and diameters are $2px-y=1$ ... (i)

and $2x+py=4p$ ... (ii)

Solving Eqs. (i) and (ii), we get

$$x=\frac{5p}{2p^2+2}\text{ and }y=\frac{4p^2-1}{1+p^2}$$

Since, $x=1$, thus $2p^2+2=5p$

$$\Rightarrow\quad 2p^2-5p+2=0$$

$$\Rightarrow\quad p=\frac{1}{2}\text{ and }p=2$$

For $p=\frac{1}{2}\Rightarrow y=\frac{4\left(\frac{1}{2}\right)^2-1}{1+\left(\frac{1}{2}\right)^2}=0$

and $p=2\Rightarrow y=\frac{4(2)^2-1}{1+(2)^2}=3$

Thus, centres are $(1,0)$ and $(1,3)$.

Now, the tangent of the hyperbola $\frac{x^2}{1}-\frac{y^2}{3}=1$ is

$$y=mx\pm\sqrt{m^2-3} \quad \text{... (ii)}$$

Since (1, 0) not satisfied the above equation so substitute (1, 3) in above Eq. (ii), we get

$$3=m\pm\sqrt{m^2-3}$$

$$\Rightarrow (3-m)^2=(\pm\sqrt{m^2-3})^2$$

$$\Rightarrow 9-6m+m^2=m^2-3$$

$$\Rightarrow 6m=12$$

$$\Rightarrow m=2$$

29. (10) The given equation of parabola is $75x^2=64(y-3)$

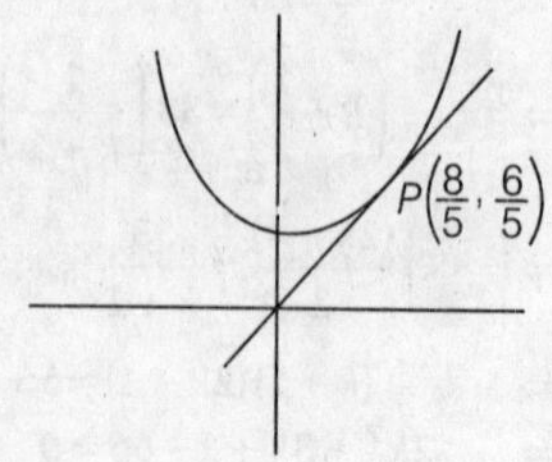

Now, equation of tangent to the parabola at $P\left(\frac{8}{5},\frac{6}{5}\right)$ is

$$75\left(x\left(\frac{8}{5}\right)\right)=64\left(5\left(\frac{y+\frac{6}{5}}{2}\right)-3\right)$$

$$\Rightarrow 120x=160\left(y+\frac{6}{5}\right)-192$$

$$\Rightarrow 120x=160y$$

$$\Rightarrow 3x=4y$$

Let equation of circle touching the given parabola at $P\left(\frac{8}{5},\frac{6}{5}\right)$ is

$$\left(x-\frac{8}{5}\right)^2+\left(y-\frac{6}{5}\right)^2+\lambda(3x-4y)=0$$

If this circle touches Y-axis, then

$$\frac{64}{25}+\left(y-\frac{6}{5}\right)^2+\lambda(-4y)=0 \quad [\text{put } x=0]$$

$$\Rightarrow y^2-\left(4\lambda+\frac{12}{5}\right)y+4=0$$

Now, discriminant $D=0$ (for equal roots)

$$\therefore \left(4\lambda+\frac{12}{5}\right)^2-4\cdot4\cdot1=0$$

$$\Rightarrow \left(2\lambda+\frac{6}{5}\right)^2=4$$

$$\Rightarrow (10\lambda+6)^2=100$$

$$\Rightarrow 100\lambda^2+120\lambda-64=0$$

$$\Rightarrow \lambda=\frac{2}{5} \text{ or } -\frac{8}{5}.$$

Now, putting the value of $\lambda=\frac{2}{5}$ in the equation

$$\left(x-\frac{8}{5}\right)^2+\left(y-\frac{6}{5}\right)^2+\left(\frac{2}{5}\right)(3x-4y)=0$$

$$\Rightarrow \left(x-\frac{8}{5}\right)^2+\left(y-\frac{6}{5}\right)^2+\frac{6}{5}x-\frac{8}{5}y=0$$

Thus, radius is $\sqrt{\left(\frac{3}{5}\right)^2+\left(-\frac{4}{5}\right)^2-0}$ (say)

$$r_1=\sqrt{\frac{16}{25}+\frac{9}{25}}=\sqrt{\frac{25}{25}}=1$$

$$\therefore r_1=1$$

Similarly, put $\lambda=-\frac{8}{5}$ in same equation, we get

$$\left(x-\frac{8}{5}\right)^2+\left(y-\frac{6}{5}\right)^2+\left(-\frac{24}{5}\right)x+\left(\frac{32}{5}\right)y=0$$

$$\Rightarrow \left(x-\frac{8}{5}\right)^2+\left(y-\frac{6}{5}\right)^2-\frac{24}{5}x+\frac{32}{5}y=0$$

$$\therefore r_2=\sqrt{\left(-\frac{12}{5}\right)^2+\left(\frac{16}{5}\right)^2}$$

$$=\sqrt{\frac{144+256}{25}}$$

$$=\sqrt{\frac{400}{25}}=\sqrt{16}=4$$

Thus, $r_1=1$ and $r_2=4$

than $2r_1=2, 2r_2=8$ (diameter)

Thus, sum of diameter are $2+8=10$

30. (*)

The given lines are

$$\frac{x-2}{0}=\frac{y-1}{1}=\frac{z}{1}$$

and $$\frac{x-3}{2}=\frac{y-5}{2}=\frac{z-1}{1}$$

So, let $\mathbf{b}_1=\hat{\mathbf{j}}+\hat{\mathbf{k}}$ and $\mathbf{b}_2=2\hat{\mathbf{i}}+2\hat{\mathbf{j}}+\hat{\mathbf{k}}$

Now, line of shortest distance will be along $\mathbf{b}_1\times\mathbf{b}_2$

$$\Rightarrow \mathbf{b}_1\times\mathbf{b}_2=\begin{vmatrix}\hat{\mathbf{i}} & \hat{\mathbf{j}} & \hat{\mathbf{k}}\\ 0 & 1 & 1\\ 2 & 2 & 1\end{vmatrix}$$

$$=-\hat{\mathbf{i}}+2\hat{\mathbf{j}}-2\hat{\mathbf{k}}$$

and $$\hat{\mathbf{n}}=a\hat{\mathbf{i}}-\hat{\mathbf{j}}-\hat{\mathbf{k}}$$

Thus, angle between $\mathbf{b}_1\times\mathbf{b}_2$ and plane P is

$$\sin\theta=\left|\frac{-a-2+2}{\sqrt{(-1)^2+(2)^2+(-2)^2}\sqrt{a^2+2}}\right|$$

$$=\left|\frac{-a}{3\sqrt{a^2+2}}\right|$$

Since, $\theta=\cos^{-1}\left(\sqrt{\frac{2}{27}}\right)$

$$\Rightarrow \cos\theta=\sqrt{\frac{2}{27}}$$

$$\Rightarrow \sin\theta=\sqrt{1-\cos^2\theta}$$

$$=\sqrt{1-\frac{2}{27}}$$

$$\Rightarrow \sin\theta=\frac{5}{\sqrt{27}}$$

$$\Rightarrow \frac{5}{\sqrt{27}}=\frac{|a|}{3\sqrt{a^2+2}}$$

$$\Rightarrow \frac{|a|}{\sqrt{a^2+2}}=\frac{5}{\sqrt{3}}$$

$$\Rightarrow \frac{a^2}{a^2+2}=\frac{25}{3}$$

$$\Rightarrow 3a^2=25a^2+50$$

$$\Rightarrow a^2=-\frac{50}{22}=-\frac{25}{11}$$

(This is impossible).

27 July 2022, Shift-II

1. (c) $f(x) = \sin^{-1}[2x^2 - 3] + \log_2[\log_{1/2}(x^2 - 5x + 5)]$

$[2x^2 - 3] \in [-1, 1]$

$\therefore \quad 2x^2 - 3 \in [-1, 2)$

$\Rightarrow \quad x^2 \in \left[1, \frac{5}{2}\right) \quad \text{...(i)}$

$\Rightarrow \quad x \in \left(-\sqrt{\frac{5}{2}}, -1\right] \cup \left[1, \sqrt{\frac{5}{2}}\right)$

$\log_{1/2}(x^2 - 5x + 5) > 0$

$\Rightarrow x^2 - 5x + 5 < 1$ and $x^2 - 5x + 5 > 0$

$\Rightarrow x^2 - 5x + 4 < 0$ and $x^2 - 5x + 5 > 0$

$\Rightarrow x \in (1, 4)$ and

$x \in \left(-\infty, \frac{5-\sqrt{5}}{2}\right) \cup \left(\frac{5+\sqrt{5}}{2}, \infty\right)$

$\Rightarrow \quad x \in \left(1, \frac{5-\sqrt{5}}{2}\right) \quad \text{...(ii)}$

$\therefore$ Domain of $f(x)$ is intersection of Eqs. (i) and (ii).

$\therefore$ Domain of $f(x)$ is $x \in \left(1, \frac{5-\sqrt{5}}{2}\right)$.

2. (c) $\alpha \in (\pi, 2\pi)$ and $\beta \in (\pi, 2\pi)$

$\frac{1 - i\sin\alpha}{1 + 2I\sin\alpha} = \frac{(1 - i\sin\alpha)(1 - 2i\sin\alpha)}{1 + 4\sin^2\alpha}$

is purely imaginary.

$\therefore \quad 1 - 2\sin^2\alpha = 0$

$\Rightarrow \quad \sin\alpha = \pm\frac{1}{\sqrt{2}}$

$\therefore \quad \alpha = \frac{5\pi}{4}$ or $\frac{7\pi}{4}$

$\frac{1 + i\cos\beta}{1 - 2i\cos\beta} = \frac{(1 + i\cos\beta)(1 + 2i\cos\beta)}{1 + 4\cos^2\beta}$

is purely real.

$\therefore \quad 2\cos\beta + \cos\beta = 0$

$\Rightarrow \quad \cos\beta = 0$

$\therefore \quad \beta = \frac{3\pi}{2}$

$\therefore \quad (\alpha, \beta) = \left(\frac{5\pi}{4}, \frac{3\pi}{2}\right)$ or $\left(\frac{7\pi}{4}, \frac{3\pi}{2}\right)$

$z_{\alpha\beta} = \left(\sin\frac{5\pi}{2} + i\cos 3\pi\right)$

or $\left(\sin\frac{7\pi}{2} + i\cos 3\pi\right)$

$\therefore \quad z_{\alpha\beta} = (1 - i)$ or $(-1 - i)$

$\therefore \quad \sum_{(\alpha,\beta)\in S}\left(iz_{\alpha\beta} + \frac{1}{i\bar{z}_{\alpha\beta}}\right)$

$= i + 1 + \frac{1}{i - 1} + 1 - i - \frac{1}{i + 1}$

$= 2 + \frac{-i - 1 - 1 + i}{2} = 1$

3. (b) Given, $x^2 - (5 + 3^{\sqrt{\log_3 5}} - 5^{\sqrt{\log_5 3}})x + 3(3^{(\log_3 5)^{1/3}} - 5^{(\log_3 5)^{2/3}} - 1) = 0$

Here, $3^{\sqrt{\log_3 5}} - 5^{\sqrt{\log_5 3}}$

$= 3^{\sqrt{\log_3 5}} - [3^{\log_3 5}]^{\sqrt{\log_5 3}}$

$\Rightarrow \quad 3^{\sqrt{\log_3 5}} - 3^{\sqrt{\log_3 5}} = 0$

and $\quad 3^{(\log_3 5)^{1/3}} - 5^{(\log_5 3)^{2/3}}$

$= 3^{(\log_3 5)^{1/3}} - [3^{(\log_3 5)}]^{(\log_5 3)^{2/3}}$

$= 3^{(\log_3 5)^{1/3}} - 3^{(\log_3 5)^{1/3}} = 0$

$\therefore$ Equation is $x^2 - 5x - 3 = 0$ roots are α and β.

Now, roots of new equation are $\alpha + \frac{1}{\beta}$, $\beta + \frac{1}{\alpha}$.

$\therefore$ New equation is

$x^2 - \left(\alpha + \frac{1}{\beta} + \beta + \frac{1}{\alpha}\right)x + \left(\alpha\beta + 1 + 1 + \frac{1}{\alpha\beta}\right) = 0$

$\Rightarrow \quad x^2 - \left(5 - \frac{5}{3}\right)x + \left(-3 + 2 - \frac{1}{3}\right) = 0$

$\Rightarrow \quad x^2 - \frac{10}{3}x - \frac{4}{3} = 0$

$\Rightarrow \quad 3x^2 - 10x - 4 = 0$

4. (b) $A = \begin{bmatrix} 4 & -2 \\ \alpha & \beta \end{bmatrix}$ satisfies

$A^2 + 4A + 18I = 0$

Characteristic equation of A is

$A^2 - (T_r(A))A + |A|I = 0$

Comparing this with given equation, we get $|A| = 18$

5. (b) $f(x) = \frac{\sqrt[7]{p(729 + x)} - 3}{\sqrt[3]{729 + qx} - 9}$

$\lim_{x\to 0} f(x)$ is finite and equal to $f(0)$.

$\therefore \quad \sqrt[7]{p(729)} - 3 = 0 \Rightarrow p = 3$

Now, $\lim_{x\to 0} f(x) = \lim_{x\to 0} \frac{\sqrt[7]{3(729 + x)} - 3}{\sqrt[3]{729 + qx} - 9}$

$= \lim_{x\to 0} \frac{1}{3} \times \frac{\left(1 + \frac{x}{3^6}\right)^{1/7} - 1}{\left(1 + \frac{qx}{9^3}\right)^{\frac{1}{3}} - 1}$

$\frac{1}{3} \times \frac{\frac{1}{7} \times \frac{1}{3^6}}{\frac{1}{3} \times \frac{q}{9^3}} = \frac{1}{7q} = f(0)$

$\Rightarrow \quad 7qf(0) = 1$

$\Rightarrow \quad 63qf(0) = 9 = p^2 \quad [\because p = 3]$

$63qf(0) - p^2 = 0$

6. (d) $f(x) = 2 + |x| - |x - 1| + |x + 1|, x \in R$

$\therefore \quad f(x) = -x, x \le -1$

$x + 2, -1 < x \le 0$

$3x + 2, 0 < x \le 1$

$x + 4, 1 < x$

$f'\left(\frac{-3}{2}\right) + f'\left(\frac{-1}{2}\right) + f'\left(\frac{1}{2}\right) + f'\left(\frac{3}{2}\right)$

$= -1 + 1 + 3 + 1 = 4$

$\int_{-2}^{2} f(x)dx = \int_{-2}^{-1}(-x)dx + \int_{-1}^{0}(x + 2)dx + \int_{0}^{1}(3x + 2)dx + \int_{1}^{2}(x + 4)dx$

$= \frac{3}{2} - \frac{1}{2} + 2 + \frac{3}{2} + 2 + \frac{3}{2} + 4$

$= 12$

Statement I is wrong and Statement II is correct.

7. (a) nth term of the AP is a_n

Now,

$S_{21} = \frac{21}{2}[a_1 + a_{21}] = 21 \times \left(\frac{a_1 + a_{21}}{2}\right)$

$[\because a_1 = 10ar, a_{21} = 10ar + 200ar^2,$

$= 21 \times a_{11}$

$\because a_{11} = 10ar + 100ar^2,$

$\because a_n = a_1 + (n - 1)d]$

8. (d) We have, $y \le 4x^2$

$y \ge \frac{x^2}{9}$ and $y \le 4$

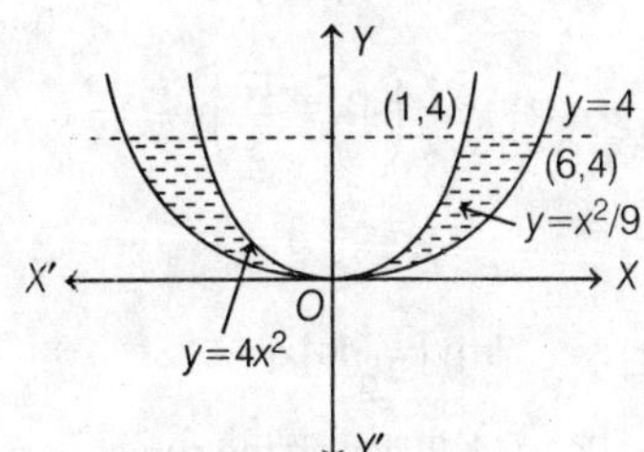

Area of shaded region

$$=2\int_0^4\left(3\sqrt{y}-\frac{\sqrt{y}}{2}\right)dy$$

$$=2\left[2y^{3/2}-\frac{1}{3}y^{3/2}\right]_0^4$$

$$=\frac{10}{3}[y^{3/2}]_0^4$$

$$=\frac{80}{3}$$

9. (b) $I=\int_0^2|2x^2-3x|dx+\int_0^2\left[x-\frac{1}{2}\right]dx$

$$=\int_0^{3/2}(-2x^2+3x)dx+\int_{3/2}^2(2x^2-3x)dx$$

$$+\int_0^{1/2}(-1)dx+\int_{1/2}^{3/2}(0)dx+\int_{3/2}^2 dx$$

$$=\left(\frac{-2x^3}{3}+\frac{3x^2}{2}\right)_0^{3/2}+\left(\frac{2x^3}{3}-\frac{3x^2}{2}\right)_{3/2}^2$$

$$+(-x)_0^{1/2}+(x)_{3/2}^2$$

$$=-2\times\frac{27}{8\times3}+3\times\frac{9}{4\times2}+2\times\frac{8}{3}$$

$$-3\times2-2\times\frac{27}{8\times3}+3\times\frac{9}{4\times2}-\frac{1}{2}+\frac{1}{2}$$

$$=\frac{-9}{4}+\frac{27}{8}+\frac{16}{3}-6-\frac{9}{4}+\frac{27}{8}$$

$$=\frac{19}{12}$$

10. (c) Here, $A_1=2A_2$

and $A_1+A_2=xy-8$

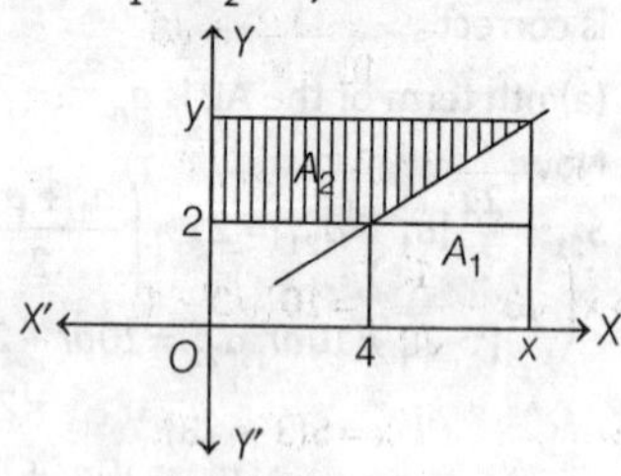

$\therefore\quad \frac{3A_1}{2}=xy-8$

$\therefore\ \frac{3}{2}\int_4^x f(x)dx=xy-8$

$\therefore\quad \frac{3}{2}f(x)=xy'+y$

$\therefore\quad xy'-\frac{y}{2}=0$

$\Rightarrow\quad \frac{y'}{y}=\frac{1}{2x}$

$\therefore\quad \ln|y|=\frac{1}{2}\ln|x|+C$

Point (4, 2) lies on the curve $y=f(x)$

$\ln 2=\ln 2+C\ \Rightarrow\ C=0$

$\because$ Curve is $y^2=x$ as it is first quadrant.

Now, normal is perpendicular to $2x-12y=15$

$\therefore$Tangent is parallel to $2x-12y=15$

$$y'=\frac{1}{6}=\frac{1}{2y}$$

$\Rightarrow\quad y=3$

$\Rightarrow\quad x=9$

Normal is $(y-3)=(-6)(x-9)$ which is $6x+y=57$

$\Rightarrow(10,-4)$does not lie on this normal.

11. (d) $AB\to 2x+y=0$

$AC\to x-y=3$

$BC\to x+py=39$

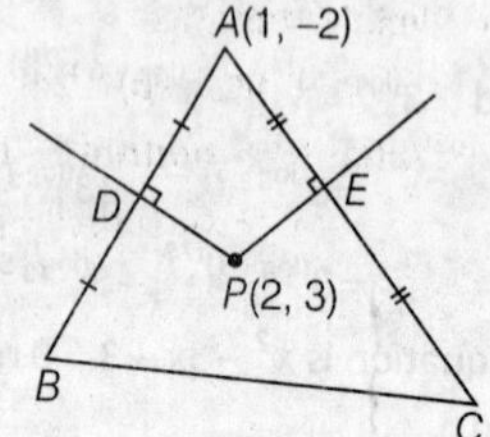

Point of intersection of AB, AC is vertex $A=(1,-2)$

Let PD be perpendicular bisector of AB.

Slope of AB is -2

$\therefore$Slope of $PD=\frac{1}{2}$

$\therefore$Equation of PD is $x-2y=-4$

$\therefore$Point D is $\left(\frac{-4}{5},\frac{8}{5}\right)$.

$\therefore$Point B is $\left(\frac{-13}{5},\frac{26}{5}\right)$.

Similarly, equation of PE is $x+y=5$

Point E is (4, 1).

$\therefore$Point C is (7, 4).

$\therefore AC=\sqrt{(1-7)^2+(-2-4)^2}=6\sqrt{2}$

Also C satisfies BC.

$\therefore\quad 7+4p=39$

$\Rightarrow\quad p=8$

$\Rightarrow\quad (AC)^2=72=8\times9=9p$

$(AC)^2+p^2=72+64=136$

$$\text{Area of }\Delta ABC=\left|\frac{1}{2}\begin{vmatrix}1 & -2 & 1\\ \frac{-13}{5} & \frac{26}{5} & 1\\ 7 & 4 & 1\end{vmatrix}\right|$$

$$=\left|\frac{1}{2}\left[1\left(\frac{26}{5}-4\right)+2\left(\frac{-13}{5}-7\right)+1\left(\frac{-52}{5}-\frac{182}{5}\right)\right]\right|$$

$$=\left|\frac{1}{2}\left[\frac{6}{5}-\frac{96}{5}-\frac{234}{5}\right]\right|$$

$$=\frac{1}{2}\left|\frac{-324}{5}\right|=32.4$$

12. (a) Centre of C_1 is (2, 0)

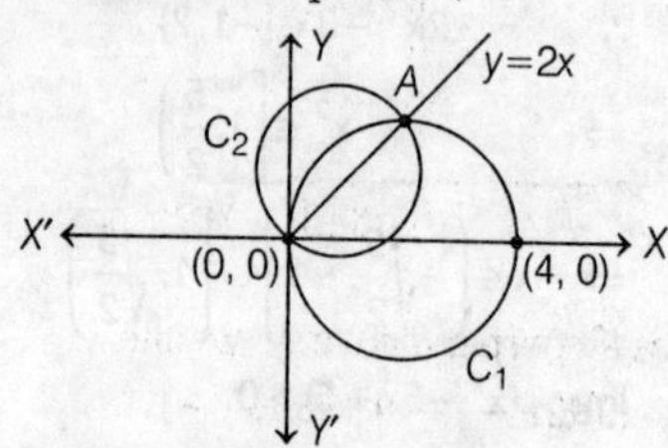

Equation of C_1 is $(x-2)^2+y^2=4$

$x^2+y^2-4x=0$ ...(i)

To find A, on putting $y=2x$

$x^2+4x^2-4x=0$

$\Rightarrow\quad 5x^2-4x=0$

$\Rightarrow\quad x=0$ or $x=\frac{4}{5}$

$\Rightarrow\quad A=\left(\frac{4}{5},\frac{8}{5}\right)$

Equation of C_2 is

$(x)\left(x-\frac{4}{5}\right)+(y)\left(y-\frac{8}{5}\right)=0$

$\Rightarrow\quad x^2+y^2-\frac{4x}{5}-\frac{8y}{5}=0$

Equation of tangent at $A\left(\frac{4}{5},\frac{8}{5}\right)$ is $T=0$

$\Rightarrow\quad \frac{4}{5}x+\frac{8}{5}y-\frac{2}{5}\left(x+\frac{4}{5}\right)-\frac{4}{5}\left(y+\frac{8}{5}\right)=0$

$\Rightarrow\quad \frac{2x}{5}+\frac{4y}{5}-\frac{8}{5}=0$

$\Rightarrow\quad x+2y-4=0$

$P\equiv(4,0), Q\equiv(0,2)$

$$\therefore\quad \frac{QA}{AP}=\frac{\sqrt{\frac{16}{25}+\frac{4}{25}}}{\sqrt{\frac{256}{25}+\frac{64}{25}}}=\frac{\sqrt{20}}{\sqrt{320}}=\frac{1}{4}$$

13. (c) Given, equation of tangent at vertex is $x+y-a=0$

Focus is (a, a).

$\therefore$ Latusrectum $=4\left|\frac{a+a-a}{\sqrt{2}}\right|=16$

$\Rightarrow\quad \left|\frac{a}{\sqrt{2}}\right|=4$

$\Rightarrow\quad \frac{a^2}{2}=16$

$\Rightarrow\quad a^2=32\Rightarrow|a|=4\sqrt{2}$

14. (b) Let R be $(2k-1, 3k+3, -k+1)$.

Direction ratios of PR are $<2k-1-a, 3k-1, -k-1>$

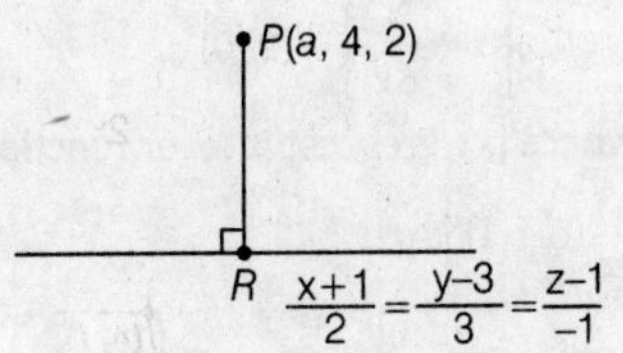

as PR perpendicular given line

$$(2)(2k-1-a)+(3)(3k-1)+(-1)(-k-1)=0$$

$\Rightarrow \quad 14k-4-2a=0$

$\Rightarrow \quad a=7k-2$

$$PR=\sqrt{(2k-1-a)^2+(3k-1)^2+(-k-1)^2}=2\sqrt{6}$$

$\Rightarrow 25k^2-10k+1+9k^2-6k+1+k^2+2k+1=24$

$\Rightarrow \quad 35k^2-14k-21=0$

$\Rightarrow \quad 5k^2-2k-3=0$

$\Rightarrow \quad k=1$ or $k=\frac{-3}{5}$

$\Rightarrow \quad a=5$ or $a=\frac{-31}{5}$

$\Rightarrow \quad a=5$

$P\equiv(5,4,2), R\equiv(1,6,0)$

$Q\equiv(-3,8,-2)$

$\therefore \quad a+\sum_{i=1}^{3}\alpha_i=5-3+8-2$

$=8$

15. (b) Planes are $ax+by-3=0$ and $ax+by+cz=0$

Line of intersection is parallel to $\mathbf{n}_1$ and $\mathbf{n}_2$.

$$\text{Now, } \mathbf{n}_1\times\mathbf{n}_2=\begin{vmatrix}\hat{\mathbf{i}} & \hat{\mathbf{j}} & \hat{\mathbf{k}}\\ a & b & 0\\ a & b & c\end{vmatrix}$$

$$=(bc)\hat{\mathbf{i}}-(ac)\hat{\mathbf{j}}$$

$\therefore$Direction cosines of line of intersection can be

$$\left(\frac{bc}{\sqrt{b^2c^2+a^2c^2}}, \frac{-ac}{\sqrt{b^2c^2+a^2c^2}}, 0\right)$$

or $\left(\frac{-bc}{\sqrt{b^2c^2+a^2c^2}}, \frac{ac}{\sqrt{b^2c^2+a^2c^2}}, 0\right)$

This line makes 30° with plane $y-z+2=0$

$\therefore$It makes 60° with normal $(0, 1, -1)$.

$$\therefore \cos 60° = \frac{-ac}{(\sqrt{2})\sqrt{b^2c^2+a^2c^2}}$$

$$\text{or } \cos 60° = \frac{ac}{(\sqrt{2})\sqrt{b^2c^2+a^2c^2}}$$

$\Rightarrow \quad \frac{1}{4}=\frac{a^2c^2}{(2)(b^2c^2+a^2c^2)}$

$\Rightarrow \quad a^2=b^2$

Direction cosines of line of intersection are $\left(+\frac{1}{\sqrt{2}}, \frac{-1}{\sqrt{2}}, 0\right)$.

16. (b) Mean $=np$

Variance $=np(1-p)$

Given, Mean + Variance

$=np+np(1-p)=24$

Mean × Variance $=(np)(np(1-p))=128$

$\Rightarrow \quad np=16, \ (np)(1-p)=8$

$\Rightarrow \quad 1-p=\frac{1}{2}$

$\Rightarrow \quad p=\frac{1}{2}$

$\Rightarrow \quad n=32$

$$P(X>n-3)=P(X=n-2)+P(X=n-1)+P(X=n)$$

$$={}^{32}C_{30}\left(\frac{1}{2}\right)^{32}+{}^{32}C_{31}\left(\frac{1}{2}\right)^{32}+{}^{32}C_{32}\left(\frac{1}{2}\right)^{32}$$

$$=\frac{16\times31+32+1}{2^{32}}=\frac{529}{2^{32}}$$

$k=529, n=32$

17. (d) Let $P(1)=k$

$\Rightarrow P$ (a prime number) $=\frac{2k}{3}$

and P (a composite number) $=\frac{k}{3}$

$\therefore P(1)=k, P(2)=P(3)=P(5)=\frac{2k}{3}$,

$P(4)=P(6)=\frac{k}{3}$

$$k+3\left(\frac{2k}{3}\right)+2\left(\frac{k}{3}\right)=1$$

$\Rightarrow \quad k+2k+\frac{2k}{3}=1$

$\Rightarrow \quad k=\frac{3}{11}$

$\therefore \ P(1)=\frac{3}{11}$,

$P(2)=P(3)=P(5)=\frac{2}{11}$,

$P(4)=P(6)=\frac{1}{11}$

p (number obtained is perfect square)

$=P(1)+P(4)=\frac{4}{11}$

A die is tossed twice.

$\therefore \quad n=2, p=\frac{4}{11}$

$\therefore$ Mean $=np=\frac{8}{11}$

18. (a) Given, $AB=d$, $\text{ar}(\square PBRQ)=\alpha$.

$PQ=10$

$\angle PAQ=45°$

$\Rightarrow \quad AQ=10$

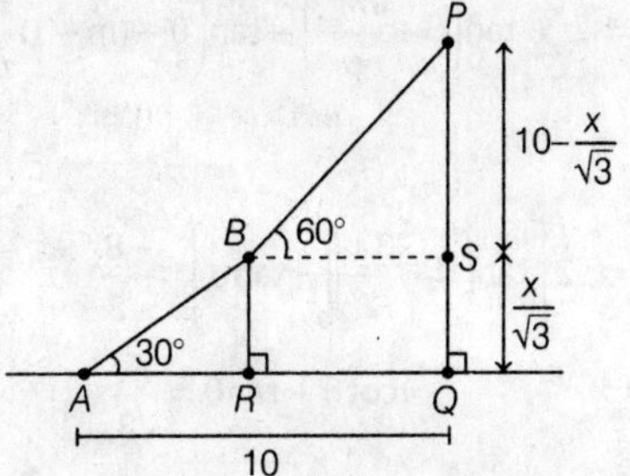

Let $\quad AR=x$

$\Rightarrow \quad BR=\frac{x}{\sqrt{3}}$

$\Rightarrow \quad RQ=10-x$

$\therefore$ Now, $\frac{PS}{BS}=\tan 60°$

$$=\frac{10-\frac{x}{\sqrt{3}}}{10-x}=\sqrt{3}$$

$\Rightarrow 10-\frac{x}{\sqrt{3}}=10\sqrt{3}-x\sqrt{3}$

$\Rightarrow x\left(\sqrt{3}-\frac{1}{\sqrt{3}}\right)=10(\sqrt{3}-1)$

$\Rightarrow \quad x=5(3-\sqrt{3})$

$\therefore \quad BR=5(\sqrt{3}-1)$

$$d=\sqrt{[5(\sqrt{3}-1)]^2+[5(3-\sqrt{3})]^2}$$

$\Rightarrow \quad d=5\sqrt{4-2\sqrt{3}+12-6\sqrt{3}}$

$=10(\sqrt{3}-1)$

Now, $\text{ar}(\square PBRQ)$

$$=\alpha=\frac{1}{2}\left(\frac{x}{\sqrt{3}}+10\right)(10-x)$$

$\Rightarrow \alpha=\frac{1}{2}(5\sqrt{3}-5+10)(10-15+5\sqrt{3})$

$=\frac{1}{2}(5)(\sqrt{3}+1)(5)(\sqrt{3}-1)$

$=25$

19. (c) Given,

$$\sum_{m=1}^{9} \frac{1}{\cos\left(\theta+(m-1)\frac{\pi}{6}\right)\cos\left(\theta+\frac{m\pi}{6}\right)} = \frac{-8}{\sqrt{3}}$$

$$\Rightarrow 2\sum_{m=1}^{9} \frac{\sin\left(\left(\theta+\frac{m\pi}{6}\right)-\left(\theta+(m-1)\frac{\pi}{6}\right)\right)}{\cos\left(\theta+(m-1)\frac{\pi}{6}\right)\cdot\cos\left(\theta+\frac{m\pi}{6}\right)} = \frac{-8}{\sqrt{3}}$$

$$\Rightarrow 2\sum_{m=1}^{9} \tan\left(\theta+\frac{m\pi}{6}\right)-\tan\left(\theta+(m-1)\frac{\pi}{6}\right) = \frac{-8}{\sqrt{3}}$$

$$\Rightarrow 2\left[\tan\left(\theta+\frac{3\pi}{2}\right)-\tan\theta\right] = \frac{-8}{\sqrt{3}}$$

$$\Rightarrow \cot\theta+\tan\theta = \frac{4}{\sqrt{3}}$$

$$\Rightarrow \tan\theta = \sqrt{3} \text{ or } \frac{1}{\sqrt{3}}$$

$$\Rightarrow \theta = \frac{\pi}{6} \text{ or } \frac{\pi}{3} \text{ as } \theta \in \left(0, \frac{\pi}{2}\right)$$

$$S = \left\{\frac{\pi}{6}, \frac{\pi}{3}\right\}, \sum_{\theta \in S} \theta = \frac{\pi}{6}+\frac{\pi}{3} = \frac{\pi}{2}$$

20. (d) $(P \wedge (\sim R)) \rightarrow ((\sim R) \wedge Q)$

$(\sim (P \wedge (\sim R))) \vee ((\sim R) \wedge Q)$

$((\sim P) \vee R) \vee ((\sim R) \wedge Q)$

$(\sim P) \vee ((R \vee (\sim R)) \wedge (R \vee Q))$

$(\sim P) \vee (T \wedge (R \vee Q))$

$(\sim P) \vee (R \vee Q)$ is false

$\Rightarrow$ $(\sim P)$ is false, R is false, Q is false

$\Rightarrow$ P is T, R is F, Q is F

$P \vee Q \rightarrow \sim R$ is T

$(R \vee Q) \rightarrow \sim P$ is T

$\sim (P \vee Q) \rightarrow \sim R$ is T

$\sim (R \vee Q) \rightarrow \sim P$ is F

21. (42)

$$A = \begin{bmatrix} \alpha & \beta & \gamma \\ \alpha^2 & \beta^2 & \gamma^2 \\ \beta+\gamma & \alpha+\gamma & \alpha+\beta \end{bmatrix}$$

$$A = \begin{bmatrix} \alpha & \beta & \gamma \\ \alpha^2 & \beta^2 & \gamma^2 \\ \beta+\gamma+\alpha & \alpha+\gamma+\beta & \alpha+\beta+\gamma \end{bmatrix}$$

take $R_3 \rightarrow R_3 + R_1$

$$A = \begin{bmatrix} \alpha & \beta & \gamma \\ \alpha^2 & \beta^2 & \gamma^2 \\ 1 & 1 & 1 \end{bmatrix}(\alpha+\beta+\gamma)$$

$$A = (\alpha+\beta+\gamma)\begin{bmatrix} 1 & 1 & 1 \\ \alpha & \beta & \gamma \\ \alpha^2 & \beta^2 & \gamma^2 \end{bmatrix}$$

$$|A| = (\alpha+\beta+\gamma)(\alpha-\beta)(\beta-\gamma)(\gamma-\alpha)$$

Now, $\dfrac{\det(\text{adj (adj (adj (adj A))))}}{(\alpha-\beta)^{16}(\beta-\gamma)^{16}(\gamma-\alpha)^{16}}$

$$= \frac{|A|^{16}}{(\alpha-\beta)^{16}(\beta-\gamma)^{16}(\gamma-\alpha)^{16}}$$

$\therefore\ (\alpha+\beta+\gamma)^{16} = 2^{32} \times 3^{16}$

$\therefore\ \alpha+\beta+\gamma = 2^2 \times 3$ [as $\alpha, \beta, \gamma \in N$]

$\alpha+\beta+\gamma = 12$

Total triplets $= {}^{12-1}C_{3-1}$

$= {}^{11}C_2$

$= 55$

If $\alpha = \beta = \gamma$, then only one case

$\Rightarrow$ $\alpha = 4, \beta = 4$ and $\gamma = 4$

If only two of them are equal.

Consider $\alpha = \beta = \gamma$, then

$2\alpha + \gamma = 12$

Triplets $\Rightarrow$ (1, 1, 10) (2, 2, 8) (3, 3, 6) (5, 5, 2)

When only two of them are equal total triplets $= 3 \times 4 = 12$

Total triplets where α, β and γ are distinct is

$55 - 1 - 12 = 42$

22. (1440)

$A = \{x \in N: x^2 - 10x + 9 \le 0\}$

$x^2 - 10x + 9 \le 0$

$\Rightarrow$ $x \in [1, 9]$

$A = \{1, 2, 3, 4, 5, 6, 7, 8, 9\}$

$B = \{n^2 : n \in N\}$

$f: A \rightarrow B, f(x) \le (x-3)^2 + 1$

$x = 1 \Rightarrow f(1) \le 5 \Rightarrow f(1) = 1$ or 4

$x = 2 \Rightarrow f(2) \le 2 \Rightarrow f(2) = 1$

$x = 3 \Rightarrow f(3) \le 1 \Rightarrow f(3) = 1$

$x = 4 \Rightarrow f(4) \le 2 \Rightarrow f(4) = 1$

$x = 5 \Rightarrow f(5) \le 5 \Rightarrow f(5) = 1$ or 4

$x = 6 \Rightarrow f(6) \le 10 \Rightarrow f(6) = 1$ or 4 or 9

$x = 7 \Rightarrow f(7) \le 17 \Rightarrow f(7) = 1$ or 4 or 9 or 16

$x = 8 \Rightarrow f(8) \le 26 \Rightarrow f(8) = 1$ or 4 or 9 or 16 or 25

$x = 9 \Rightarrow f(9) \le 37 \Rightarrow f(9) = 1$ or 4 or 9 or 16 or 25 or 36

Total function

$= 2 \times 1 \times 1 \times 1 \times 2 \times 3 \times 4 \times 5 \times 6 = 1440$

23. (24) If T_{r+1} is the greatest term

Then, $\left[\dfrac{n+1}{1+\dfrac{3}{6x}}\right] = 8,$

where $[x]$ greatest integer function

$\left[\dfrac{3}{4}(n+1)\right] = 8.$

$\therefore \dfrac{3}{4}(n+1) \in [8, 9), \Rightarrow n \in \left[\dfrac{29}{3}, 11\right)$

$\therefore$ Least value of $n = n_0 = 10$

Now, binomial expansion is $(3+6x)^{10}$

$$\frac{\text{Coefficient of } x^6}{\text{Coefficient of } x^3} = \frac{{}^{10}C_6 \times 3^4 \times 6^6}{{}^{10}C_3 \times 3^7 \times 6^3} = 14 = k$$

$\therefore$ $k + n_0 = 14 + 10 = 24$

24. (120) Here, $T_n = \dfrac{\sum_{r=1}^{n}(2r)^3 - \sum_{r=1}^{n}(2r-1)^3}{(n)(4n+3)}$

$$\therefore T_n = \frac{\sum_{r=1}^{n}(8r^3 - 8r^3 + 12r^2 - 6r + 1)}{(n)(4n+3)}$$

$$\therefore T_n = \frac{12 \times \dfrac{(n)(n+1)(2n+1)}{6} - 6 \times \dfrac{(n)(n+1)}{2} + n}{(n)(4n+3)}$$

$$= \frac{2(2n^3 + 3n^2 + n) - 3(n^2 + n) + n}{(n)(4n+3)}$$

$$= \frac{4n^3 + 3n^2}{(n)(4n+3)} = n$$

$$\sum_{n=1}^{15} T_n = \frac{15 \times 16}{2} = 120$$

25. (5)

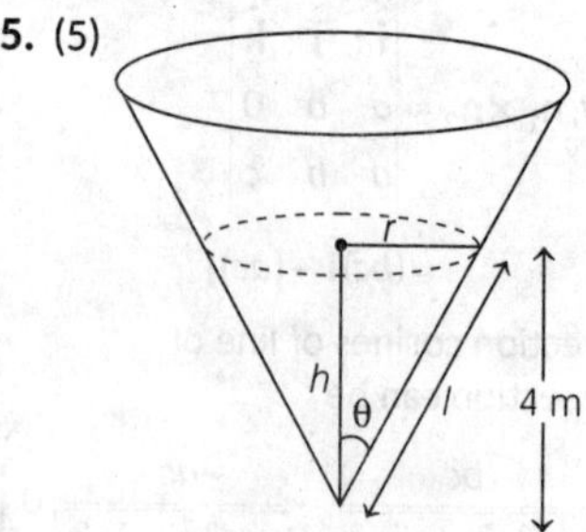

We have, $\tan\theta = \dfrac{3}{4} \Rightarrow \dfrac{r}{h} = \dfrac{3}{4}$

$\therefore$ $h = \dfrac{4r}{3}$

$\Rightarrow$ $l = \sqrt{r^2 + \dfrac{16r^2}{9}} = \dfrac{5r}{3}$

Volume of water $= V = \frac{1}{3}\pi r^2 h = \frac{4\pi(r)^3}{9}$

$$\frac{dV}{dt} = \frac{4\pi r^2}{3} \cdot \frac{dr}{dt} = 6$$

$$\therefore \quad \frac{dr}{dt} = \frac{9}{2\pi r^2}$$

Now, curved surface area $= S = \pi rl$

$$\therefore \quad S = \frac{5\pi r^2}{3}$$

$$\therefore \quad \frac{dS}{dt} = \frac{10\pi r}{3}\frac{dr}{dt} = \frac{10\pi r}{3} \times \frac{9}{2\pi r^2} = \frac{15}{r}$$

Now, $h = 4$

$\therefore \quad r = 3$

$$\frac{dS}{dt} = 5\text{m}^2/\text{h}$$

26. (16) Given,

$C\,(x^2 + y^2 - 3) + (x^2 - y^2 - 1)^5 = 0$

Point (α, α) lies on C and $\alpha > 0$

$$\therefore \quad 2\alpha^2 - 3 - 1 = 0$$

$$\Rightarrow \quad \alpha = \sqrt{2}$$

On differentiating w.r.t. x, we get

$C: (x^2 + y^2 - 3) + (x^2 - y^2 - 1)^5 = 0$

$\Rightarrow 2x + 2yy' + 5(x^2 - y^2 - 1)^4 (2x - 2yy') = 0$

On putting $x = \alpha, y = \alpha, \alpha = \sqrt{2}$,

$$\sqrt{2} + \sqrt{2}y' + 5(\sqrt{2} - \sqrt{2}y') = 0$$

$$\Rightarrow \quad 6\sqrt{2} = 4\sqrt{2}y'$$

$$\Rightarrow \quad y' = \frac{3}{2}$$

Again differentiating C,

$$2 + 2((y')^2 + yy'') + 20(x^2 - y^2 - 1)^3 (2x - 2yy') + 5(x^2 - y^2 - 1)^4 (2 - 2((y')^2 + yy'')) = 0$$

On putting $x = y = \sqrt{2}, y' = \frac{3}{2}$,

$$2 + \frac{9}{2} + 2\sqrt{2}y'' - 40 + 10 - \frac{45}{2} - 10\sqrt{2}y'' = 0$$

$$\Rightarrow \quad y'' = \frac{-23}{4\sqrt{2}}$$

$\therefore 3y' - y^3y''$ at $(\sqrt{2}, \sqrt{2})$

$$3 \times \frac{3}{2} - 2\sqrt{2} \times \left(\frac{-23}{4\sqrt{2}}\right) = 16$$

27. (385) Given,

$f(x) = \min\{[x-1], [x-2], \ldots\ldots, [x-10]\}$

$\Rightarrow f(x) = [x - 10] = [x] - 10$

$$I = \int_0^{10} f(x)dx + \int_0^{10} |f(x)|\,dx + \int_0^{10} (f(x))^2\,dx$$

$$\therefore \quad I = \int_0^{10} (f(x))^2\,dx \text{ as for } x \in (0, 10)$$

$|f(x)| = -f(x)$

$$\therefore \quad I = \int_0^1 (-10)^2\,dx + \int_1^2 (-9)^2 dx + \int_2^3 (-8)^2\,dx \ldots\ldots + \int_9^{10} (-1)^2\,dx$$

[as $f(x) < 0$]

$$\therefore \quad I = (10)^2 + 9^2 + 8^2 + \ldots\ldots + 1^2 = \frac{10 \times 11 \times 21}{6} = 385$$

28. (12) $f(x) = \frac{2}{\sqrt{3}} \int_0^{\sqrt{3}} f\left(\frac{\lambda^2 x}{3}\right) d\lambda, x > 0$

On putting $\frac{\lambda^2 x}{3} = t, \lambda = \frac{\sqrt{3}\sqrt{t}}{\sqrt{x}}$

$$\Rightarrow \quad d\lambda = \frac{\sqrt{3}}{2\sqrt{x}\sqrt{t}}\,dt$$

$$f(x) = \frac{2}{\sqrt{3}} \times \frac{\sqrt{3}}{2\sqrt{x}} \int_0^x \frac{f(t)}{\sqrt{t}}\,dt$$

$$f'(x) - \sqrt{x} f(x) = \int_0^x \frac{f(t)}{\sqrt{t}}\,dt$$

$$\Rightarrow \sqrt{x} \cdot f'(x) + \frac{f(x)}{2\sqrt{x}} = \frac{f(x)}{\sqrt{x}}$$

$$\Rightarrow \quad \sqrt{x} f'(x) = \frac{f(x)}{2\sqrt{x}}$$

$$\Rightarrow \quad \frac{dy}{y} = \frac{dx}{2x} \quad [\because y = f(x)]$$

$$\therefore \ln|y| = \frac{1}{2}\ln x + C$$

Now, $f(1) = \sqrt{3}$

$\therefore \quad \ln\sqrt{3} = C$

$\therefore \quad \ln|y| = \ln(\sqrt{3x})$

$\Rightarrow \quad y = \sqrt{3x}$,

this curve passes through $(\alpha, 6)$

$\therefore \quad 6 = \sqrt{3\alpha}$

$\Rightarrow \quad \alpha = 12$

29. (20) Given, $C_1 : \frac{x^2}{4} + \frac{y^2}{9} = 1$

and $\quad C_2 : \frac{x^2}{42} - \frac{y^2}{143} = 1$

Tangent to C_1 is $y = mx \pm \sqrt{4m^2 + 9}$

Tangent to C_2 is

$$y = mx \pm \sqrt{42m^2 - 143}$$

For common tangent,

$$4m^2 + 9 = 42m^2 - 143$$

$$\Rightarrow \quad 152 = 38m^2$$

$$\Rightarrow \quad m = \pm 2$$

If tangent does not pass through 4th quadrant, then $m > 0$ and y-intercept is positive.

$\therefore$Tangent is $y = 2x + 5$

This tangent touches C_1 at $(x_1\ y_1)$.

$\therefore$Tangent is $\frac{x_1 x}{4} + \frac{yy_1}{9} = 1$

Comparing, we get $\frac{x_1/4}{2} = \frac{1}{-5}$

$$\Rightarrow \quad x_1 = \frac{-8}{5}$$

Also point of contact with C_2 is (x_2, y_2).

Tangent is $\frac{xx_2}{42} - \frac{yy_2}{143} = 1$

$$\therefore \quad \frac{x_2/42}{2} = \frac{1}{-5}$$

$$\Rightarrow \quad x_2 = \frac{-84}{5}$$

$$\therefore \quad |2x_1 + x_2| = \frac{100}{5} = 20$$

30. (*) We have, $\mathbf{a} \times \mathbf{b} = 4\mathbf{c}, \mathbf{b} \times \mathbf{c} = 9\mathbf{a}, \mathbf{c} \times \mathbf{a} = \alpha\mathbf{b}$

$$\alpha > 0$$

Now, $\quad \mathbf{b} \times \frac{(\mathbf{a} \times \mathbf{b})}{4} = 9\mathbf{a}$

$\Rightarrow ((\mathbf{b} \cdot \mathbf{b})\mathbf{a} - (\mathbf{b} \cdot \mathbf{a})\mathbf{b} = 36\mathbf{a}$

Here, $\mathbf{a} \cdot \mathbf{b} = \mathbf{b} \cdot \mathbf{c} = \mathbf{a} \cdot \mathbf{c} = 0$

$\therefore \quad |\mathbf{b}|^2 = 36$

$\Rightarrow \quad |\mathbf{b}| = 6$

Similarly, $\quad \mathbf{a} \times \frac{(\mathbf{c} \times \mathbf{a})}{\alpha} = 4\mathbf{c}$

$\Rightarrow \quad (\mathbf{a} \cdot \mathbf{a})\mathbf{c} - (\mathbf{a} \cdot \mathbf{c})\mathbf{a} = 4\alpha\mathbf{c}$

$\Rightarrow \quad |\mathbf{a}|^2 = 4\alpha$

$\Rightarrow \quad |\mathbf{a}| = 2\sqrt{\alpha}$

Also, $\quad \mathbf{c} \times \frac{(\mathbf{b} \times \mathbf{c})}{9} = \alpha\mathbf{b}$

$\Rightarrow (\mathbf{c} \cdot \mathbf{c})\mathbf{b} - (\mathbf{c} \cdot \mathbf{b})\,\mathbf{c} = 9\alpha\mathbf{b}$

$\Rightarrow \quad |\mathbf{c}|^2 = 9\alpha$

$\Rightarrow \quad |\mathbf{c}| = 3\sqrt{\alpha}$

Now, $|\mathbf{a}| + |\mathbf{b}| + |\mathbf{c}| = \frac{1}{36}$

$\therefore \ 2\sqrt{\alpha} + 6 + 3\sqrt{\alpha} = \frac{1}{36}$

$$\therefore \quad 5\sqrt{\alpha} = \frac{-215}{36}$$

$$\Rightarrow \quad \sqrt{\alpha} = \frac{-43}{36}$$

$\therefore$Given, data is wrong. $[\because \alpha > 0$ given$]$

Solutions *(Real Nuts)*

Paper 1

1. (2.36) Let $I=\frac{3}{2}\cos^{-1}\sqrt{\frac{2}{2+\pi^2}}+\frac{1}{4}\sin^{-1}\frac{2\sqrt{2}\pi}{2+\pi^2}+\tan^{-1}\frac{\sqrt{2}}{\pi}$

$$=\frac{3}{2}\cos^{-1}\sqrt{\frac{1}{1+\frac{\pi^2}{2}}}+\frac{1}{4}\sin^{-1}\left(\frac{\frac{\sqrt{2}\pi}{2}}{1+\frac{\pi^2}{2}}\right)+\tan^{-1}\frac{\sqrt{2}}{\pi}$$

Let $\frac{\pi}{\sqrt{2}}=\tan\theta \Rightarrow \pi=\sqrt{2}\tan\theta$

Thus, $\theta\in\left(\frac{\pi}{4},\frac{\pi}{2}\right)$

$$=\frac{3}{2}\cos^{-1}\sqrt{\frac{1}{1+\tan^2\theta}}+\frac{1}{4}\sin^{-1}\left(\frac{2\tan\theta}{1+\tan^2\theta}\right)+\tan^{-1}(\cot\theta)$$

$$=\frac{3}{2}\cos^{-1}(\cos\theta)+\frac{1}{4}\sin^{-1}(\sin 2\theta)+\tan^{-1}(\cot\theta)$$

$$=\frac{3\theta}{2}+\frac{1}{4}\sin^{-1}(\sin 2\theta)+\frac{\pi}{2}-\cot^{-1}(\cot\theta)$$

Since, $\theta\in\left(\frac{\pi}{4},\frac{\pi}{2}\right) \Rightarrow 2\theta\in\left(\frac{\pi}{2},\pi\right)$.

and we also know that,

$$\sin^{-1}(\sin\theta)=\begin{cases}\theta, & -\frac{\pi}{2}\le\theta\le\frac{\pi}{2}\\ \pi-\theta, & \frac{\pi}{2}\le\theta\le\frac{3\pi}{2}\end{cases}$$

$$=\frac{3\theta}{2}+\frac{1}{4}(\pi-2\theta)+\frac{\pi}{2}-\theta$$

$$=\frac{3\theta}{2}+\frac{\pi}{4}-\frac{\theta}{2}+\frac{\pi}{2}-\theta$$

$$=\frac{\pi}{4}+\frac{\pi}{2}=\frac{3\pi}{4}=2.356\approx 2.36$$

2. (0.50) Given that, $f(x)=\sin\left(\frac{\pi x}{12}\right)$ and

$$g(x)=\frac{2\log_e(\sqrt{x}-\sqrt{\alpha})}{\log_e(e^{\sqrt{x}}-e^{\sqrt{\alpha}})}$$

Now, $\lim_{x\to\alpha^+} g(x)$

$$=\lim_{x\to\alpha^+}\frac{2\log_e(\sqrt{x}-\sqrt{\alpha})}{\log_e(e^{\sqrt{x}}-e^{\sqrt{\alpha}})} \quad \left[\frac{0}{0}\text{ form}\right]$$

$$=\lim_{x\to\alpha^+}\frac{\frac{2}{\sqrt{x}-\sqrt{\alpha}}\left(\frac{1}{2\sqrt{x}}\right)}{\frac{1}{e^{\sqrt{x}}-e^{\sqrt{\alpha}}}\left(\frac{1}{2\sqrt{x}}\times e^{\sqrt{x}}\right)}$$

[using L' Hospital rule]

$$=\lim_{x\to\alpha^+}\frac{e^{\sqrt{x}}-e^{\sqrt{\alpha}}}{\sqrt{x}-\sqrt{\alpha}}\cdot\frac{1}{e^{\sqrt{x}}}\cdot 2$$

$$=2\lim_{x\to\alpha^+}\frac{e^{\sqrt{x}}\cdot\frac{1}{2\sqrt{x}}}{\frac{1}{2\sqrt{x}}}\cdot\frac{1}{e^{\sqrt{x}}} \quad \left[\frac{0}{0}\text{ form}\right]$$

$$=2\cdot 1=2$$

Thus, $\lim_{x\to\alpha^+} g(x)=2$

$$\therefore \lim_{x\to\alpha^+} f[g(x)]=f\left(\lim_{x\to\alpha^+} g(x)\right)=f(2)$$

$$=\sin\left(\frac{2\pi}{12}\right)=\sin\left(\frac{\pi}{6}\right)$$

$$=\frac{1}{2}=0.50$$

Hence, the required answer is 0.50.

3. (0.80) Let $n(F)$ represent the number of persons had symptom of fever.

and $n(C)$ represent the number of persons had symptom of cough.

and $n(B)$ represent the number of persons had symptom of breathing problem.

So, let $n(F)=190, n(B)=220, n(C)=220$

Also, $n(F\cup C)=330, n(C\cup B)=350,$ $n(F\cup B)=340$

and $n(F\cap C\cap B)=30$

(all are given in data)

So, $n(F\cap C)=n(F)+n(C)-n(F\cup C)$

$=190+220-330=80$

Similarly, $n(F\cap B)=70$

and $n(B\cap C)=90$

Now, by Venn diagram,

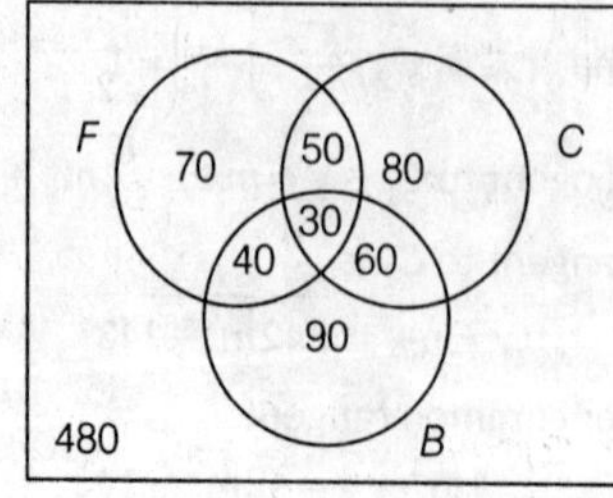

Thus, the number of persons having atmost one symptom

$=70+80+90+480=720$

Thus, required probability

$$=\frac{720}{900}=\frac{8}{10}=0.80$$

4. (0.50) Given, z is a complex number with non-zero imaginary part.

Let $\omega=\frac{4z^2+3z+2}{4z^2-3z+2}$

$$=1+\frac{6z}{4z^2-3z+2}$$

$$=1+\frac{6}{4z-3+\frac{2}{z}}$$

$$=1+\frac{6}{2\left(2z+\frac{1}{z}\right)-3}$$

Since, $\omega=\frac{4z^2+3z+2}{4z^2-3z+2}$ is a real number.

$\therefore 2z+\frac{1}{z}$ is a real number.

$$\Rightarrow 2z+\frac{1}{z}=2\bar{z}+\frac{1}{\bar{z}}$$

[$\because$ If α is real, then $\bar{z}=\alpha$]

$$\Rightarrow \quad 2(z-\bar{z})+\frac{1}{z}-\frac{1}{\bar{z}}=0$$

$$\Rightarrow \quad 2(z-\bar{z})+\frac{\bar{z}-z}{z\bar{z}}=0$$

$$\Rightarrow \quad 2(z-\bar{z})+\frac{\bar{z}-z}{|z|^2}=0 \; [\because |z|^2=z\bar{z}]$$

$$\Rightarrow \quad (z-\bar{z})\left(2-\frac{1}{|z|^2}\right)=0$$

Since, $z\ne\bar{z}$ (given)

So, $|z|^2=\frac{1}{2}\Rightarrow |z|^2=0.50$

5. (4) Given, $\bar{z}-z^2=i(\bar{z}+z^2)$

$$\Rightarrow \quad \bar{z}(1-i)=z^2(1+i)$$

$$\Rightarrow \quad |\bar{z}||1-i|=|z|^2|1+i|$$

[taking mod on both sides]

$$\Rightarrow \quad |\bar{z}|\sqrt{2}=|z|^2\sqrt{2}$$

$$\Rightarrow \quad |z|=|z|^2 \quad [\because |z|=|\bar{z}|]$$

$$\Rightarrow \quad |z|(|z|-1)=0 \Rightarrow |z|=0$$

or $\quad |z|=1$

Since, $|z|=0 \Rightarrow z=0$, which satisfied the given equation.

Again $|z|=1$, then from given equation,

$$\bar{z} - z^2 = i(\bar{z} + z^2)$$

$$\Rightarrow \quad |z|^2\left(\frac{1-i}{1+i}\right) = z^3$$

$$\Rightarrow \quad \frac{(1-i)(1-i)}{2} = z^3 \quad [\because |z|=1]$$

$\Rightarrow z^3 = -i$, since this is cubic equation.

So, it has three distinct roots.

So, total number of the distinct roots of given equation is $(1+3)=4$

6. (18900)

Since, $l_1, l_2, l_3, \ldots, l_{100}$ are consecutive terms of an arithmetic progression with common difference d_1 and also given, $w_1, w_2, \ldots, w_{100}$ are consecutive terms of another arithmetic progression with common difference d_2 with $d_1 d_2 = 10$.

Now, $A_{51} - A_{50} = 1000$ (given)

$\Rightarrow l_{51}w_{51} - l_{50}w_{50} = 1000$ (given, l_i be the length, w_i be the width and area is A_i)

$$\Rightarrow (a+50d_1)(b+50d_2) - (a+49d_1)(b+49d_2) = 1000$$

$$\Rightarrow ab + 50d_1 b + 50d_2 a + 2500 d_1 d_2 - ab - 49bd_1 - 49ad_2 - 2401\, d_1 d_2 = 1000$$

$$\Rightarrow \quad bd_1 + ad_2 + 99 d_1 d_2 = 1000$$

Since, $d_1 d_2 = 10$.

So, $bd_1 + ad_2 = 1000 - 990 = 10$ ...(i)

Now, $A_{100} - A_{90}$

$$l_{100}w_{100} - l_{90}w_{90} = (a+99d_1)(b+99d_2) - (a+89d_1)(b+89d_2)$$

$$= ab + 99d_1 b + 99 d_2 a + 99^2 d_1 d_2 - ab - 89bd_1 - 89ad_2 - 89^2 d_1 d_2$$

$$= 10(bd_1 + ad_2) + (99^2 - 89^2)\, d_1 d_2$$

$$= 10\cdot(10) + 1880\cdot d_1 d_2 \quad \text{[by Eq. (i)]}$$

$$= 100 + (1880)\cdot(10)$$

$$= 100 + 18800 = 18900$$

7. (569)

Counting integer starting from 2

***Case* I** If zero on 2nd place

i.e. $2\ 0\ 2\ \underset{5}{\uparrow} \rightarrow$ 5 cases

on $2\ 0\ \underset{4}{\uparrow}\ \underset{6}{\uparrow} \rightarrow$ 24 cases

***Case* II** If non-zero number on 2nd place.

i.e. $2\ \underset{5}{\uparrow}\ \underset{6}{\uparrow}\ \underset{6}{\uparrow}$ = 180 cases

Counting integer starting from 3.

i.e. $3\ \underset{6}{\uparrow}\ \underset{6}{\uparrow}\ \underset{6}{\uparrow}$ = 216 cases

Counting integer starting from 4.

***Case* I** If 0, 2, or 3 on 2nd place, then

i.e. $4\ \underset{3}{\uparrow}\ \underset{6}{\uparrow}\ \underset{6}{\uparrow}$ = 108 cases

***Case* II** If 4 on 2nd place, then

i.e. $4\ 4\ \underset{6}{\uparrow}\ \underset{6}{\uparrow}$ = 36 cases

$\therefore$ Thus, total number of 4-digit integers in the closed interval [2022, 4482] formed by using the above digit is

$$5 + 24 + 180 + 216 + 108 + 36 = 569$$

Thus, the required number is 569.

8. (0.84) Let A be the origin B on X-axis, C on Y-axis are shown below the figure.

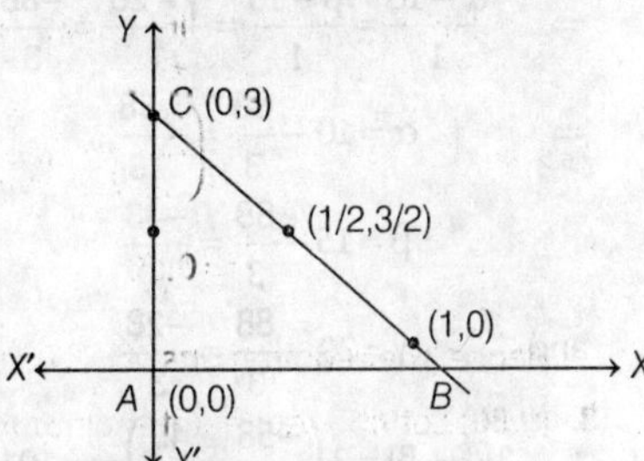

$\therefore$ Equation of circumcircle is

$$\left(x-\frac{1}{2}\right)^2 + \left(y-\frac{3}{2}\right)^2 = \left(\frac{1}{2}\right)^2 + \left(\frac{3}{2}\right)^2$$

$$= \frac{1}{4} + \frac{9}{4} = \frac{5}{2}$$

$$\therefore \quad \left(x-\frac{1}{2}\right)^2 + \left(y-\frac{3}{2}\right)^2 = \frac{5}{2} \quad \text{...(i)}$$

Required circle touches AB and AC have radius r.

Thus, equation be

$$(x-r)^2 + (y-r)^2 = r^2 \quad \text{...(ii)}$$

If circle in Eq. (ii) touches circumcircle internally, we have

$$d_{C_1C_2} = |r_1 - r_2|$$

$$\Rightarrow \left(\frac{1}{2}-r\right)^2 + \left(\frac{3}{2}-r\right)^2 = \left(\left|\sqrt{\frac{5}{2}} - r\right|\right)^2$$

$$\Rightarrow \quad \frac{1}{4} + r^2 - r + \frac{9}{4} + r^2 - 3r = \frac{5}{2} + r^2 - \sqrt{10}\,r$$

$$\Rightarrow 2r^2 - 4r + \frac{5}{2} = \frac{5}{2} + r^2 - \sqrt{10}r$$

$$\Rightarrow \quad r^2 - 4r + \sqrt{10}r = 0$$

$$\Rightarrow \quad r^2 - (4-\sqrt{10})r = 0$$

$$\Rightarrow \quad r\{r - (4-\sqrt{10})\} = 0$$

$\therefore \ r = 0$ (meaningless)

or $r = 4 - \sqrt{10} = 0.837 \cong 0.84$

Thus, the value of r is 0.84.

9. (c, d) Let $I = \int_1^e \frac{(\ln x)^{1/2}}{x[a-(\ln x)^{3/2}]^2}\,dx$

Let $a - (\ln x)^{3/2} = z$

$$\Rightarrow \quad -\frac{3}{2}(\ln x)^{1/2}\cdot\frac{1}{x}\,dx = dz$$

$$\Rightarrow \quad \frac{(\ln x)^{1/2}\,dx}{x} = -\frac{2}{3}\,dz$$

x	1	e
z	a	$a-1$

$$\therefore \ I = \int_a^{a-1} \frac{\left(-\frac{2}{3}\right)dz}{z^2}$$

$$= -\frac{2}{3}\left(\frac{z^{-2+1}}{-2+1}\right)_a^{a-1} = \frac{-2}{3}\left[\frac{z^{-1}}{-1}\right]_a^{a-1}$$

$$= \frac{2}{3}\left(\frac{1}{a-1} - \frac{1}{a}\right)$$

$$= \frac{2}{3}\left(\frac{a-a+1}{a^2-a}\right) = \frac{2}{3}\,\frac{1}{a(a-1)}$$

Given, $I = 1$

$$\Rightarrow \quad \frac{2}{3}\,\frac{1}{a(a-1)} = 1$$

$$\Rightarrow \quad 3a^2 - 3a - 2 = 0$$

$$\Rightarrow \quad a = \frac{3 \pm \sqrt{9 - 4\cdot(3)\cdot(-2)}}{6}$$

$$= \frac{3 \pm \sqrt{9+24}}{6}$$

$$\Rightarrow \quad a = \frac{3 \pm \sqrt{33}}{6}$$

Thus, options (c) and (d) are correct.

10. (b, c) Since, $a_1, a_2, a_3, \ldots$, is an arithmetic progression with $a_1 = 7$ and a common difference is 8.

Thus, $\quad a_n = 7 + (n-1)8$

and $\quad T_1 = 3$ (given)

and $\quad T_{n+1} = T_n + a_n$

$\therefore \quad T_n = T_{n-1} + a_{n-1}$

$\quad \vdots$

$\quad T_2 = T_1 + a_1$

$$\therefore T_{n+1} = (T_{n-1} + a_{n-1}) + a_n$$

$$= (T_{n-2} + a_{n-2}) + a_{n-1} + a_n$$

$$\vdots$$

$$T_{n+1} = T_1 + a_1 + a_2 + \ldots + a_{n-1} + a_n$$

$$= T_1 + \frac{n}{2}[2\,(7) + (n-1)\cdot 8]$$

$$= T_1 + n(4n+3)$$

$$\therefore T_{n+1} = 3 + n(4n+3) \quad \text{...(i)}$$

For $n = 19, T_{20} = 3 + 19(79) = 1504$

and $n = 29,\ T_{30} = 3 + 29(119) = 3454$

Thus, option (c) is true.

$$\text{Now, } \sum_{k=1}^{20} T_k = 3 + \sum_{k=2}^{20} T_k$$

$$= 3 + \sum_{k=1}^{19} (3 + 4n^2 + 3n)$$

$$= 3 + 3(19) + \frac{3(19)(20)}{2} + \frac{4(19)(20)(39)}{6}$$

$$= 3 + 57 + 570 + 9880$$

$$= 10510$$

Thus, option (b) is also true.

Similarly,

$$\sum_{k=1}^{30} T_k = 3 + \sum_{k=1}^{29} (4n^2 + 3n + 3)$$

$$= 35615$$

11. (a, b) Equation of pair of given planes is

$P : (10x + 15y + 12z - 60)$
$(-2x + 5y + 4z - 20) = 0$

We will be find a general point of each line and we will solve it with P. If we get more than one value of variable λ, then the line can be edge of given tetrahedron.

For option (a),

The point is $(1, 1, 5\lambda + 1)$

So, $(60\lambda - 23)(20\lambda - 17) = 0$

$$\Rightarrow \quad \lambda = \frac{23}{60}, \lambda = \frac{17}{20}$$

So, it can be edges of tetrahedron.

For option (b),

The point is $(-5\lambda + 6, 2\lambda, 3\lambda)$

So, $(16\lambda)(32\lambda - 32) = 0$

$$\Rightarrow \quad \lambda = 0, \lambda = 1$$

So, it can be edges of tetrahedron.

For option (c),

The point is $(-2\lambda, 5\lambda + 4, 4\lambda)$

So, $(103\lambda)(45\lambda) = 0$

$\Rightarrow \lambda = 0$ and $\lambda = 0$

So, it cannot be the edges of tetrahedron.

For option (d),

The point is $(\lambda, -2\lambda + 4, 3\lambda)$

$$\Rightarrow \quad (16\lambda)(0) = 0$$

So, it cannot be edge of tetrahedron.

12. (a, b, c)

Let equation of plane is

$$\mathbf{r} = -(t+p)\,\hat{\mathbf{i}} + t\hat{\mathbf{j}} + (1+p)\hat{\mathbf{k}}$$

$$\mathbf{r} = \hat{\mathbf{k}} + t(-\hat{\mathbf{i}} + \hat{\mathbf{j}}) + p(-\hat{\mathbf{i}} + \hat{\mathbf{k}})$$

So, equation of plane in standard form is,

$$[\mathbf{r} - \hat{\mathbf{k}}, -\hat{\mathbf{i}} + \hat{\mathbf{j}}, -\hat{\mathbf{i}} + \hat{\mathbf{k}}] = 0$$

$$\therefore \quad x + y + z = 1 \quad \text{...(i)}$$

Given that, the position vectors of Q and S are $10\hat{\mathbf{i}} + 15\hat{\mathbf{j}} + 20\hat{\mathbf{k}}$ and $\alpha\hat{\mathbf{i}} + \beta\hat{\mathbf{j}} + \gamma\hat{\mathbf{k}}$, respectively.

Thus, coordinate of $Q \equiv (10, 15, 20)$ and coordinate of $S \equiv (\alpha, \beta, \gamma)$.

$$\therefore \quad \frac{\alpha - 10}{1} = \frac{\beta - 15}{1} = \frac{\gamma - 20}{1} = \frac{-2(10 + 15 + 20 - 1)}{3}$$

$$\Rightarrow \quad \frac{\alpha - 10}{1} = \frac{\beta - 15}{1} = \frac{\gamma - 20}{1} = \frac{-88}{3}$$

$$\Rightarrow \quad \alpha = 10 - \frac{88}{3} = -\frac{58}{3},$$

$$\beta = 15 - \frac{88}{3} = \frac{-43}{3}$$

$$\text{and} \quad \gamma = 20 - \frac{88}{3} = \frac{-28}{3}$$

$$\therefore \quad 3(\alpha + \beta) = 3\left(\frac{-58}{3} - \frac{43}{3}\right) = -101$$

$$\text{and } 3\,(\beta + \gamma) = 3\left(-\frac{43}{3} - \frac{28}{3}\right) = -71$$

$$3\,(\gamma + \alpha) = 3\left(-\frac{28}{3} - \frac{58}{3}\right) = -86$$

$$\text{and } 3\,(\alpha + \beta + \gamma) = 3\left(-\frac{58}{3} - \frac{43}{3} - \frac{28}{3}\right)$$

$$= 3\left(-\frac{129}{3}\right) = -129$$

Thus, option (a), (b), (c) are correct.

13. (b, c, d) Given, equation of parabola is $y^2 = 4x$ and S be the focus of the parabola.

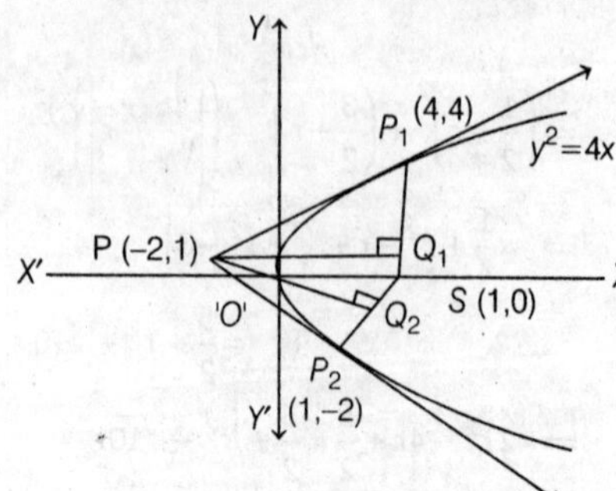

Let $P_1(t^2, 2t)$, then tangent at P_1 is

$$ty = x + t^2$$

Since, it passes through the point $(-2, 1)$.

$$\text{Thus,} \quad t^2 - t - 2 = 0$$

$$\Rightarrow \quad t = 2, -1$$

$\therefore P_1 \equiv (4, 4), P_2 \equiv (1, -2)$ and $S \equiv (1, 0)$

Thus, $\quad SP_1 : 4x - 3y - 4 = 0$

and $\quad SP_2 : x - 1 = 0$

$$\text{and for } Q_1 : \frac{x_1 + 2}{4} = \frac{y_1 - 1}{-3} = \frac{-(-8 - 3 - 4)}{25} = \frac{3}{5}$$

$$\Rightarrow \quad x_1 = \frac{2}{5} \text{ and } y_1 = -\frac{4}{5}.$$

$$\therefore \quad Q_1 = \left(\frac{2}{5}, \frac{-4}{5}\right)$$

and similarly, $Q_2 = (1, 1)$

$$\text{So,} \quad SQ_1 = \sqrt{\left(1 - \frac{2}{5}\right)^2 + \left(\frac{4}{5}\right)^2} = 1$$

$$\text{and } Q_1Q_2 = \sqrt{\frac{9}{25} + \frac{81}{25}} = \sqrt{\frac{90}{25}} = \frac{3\sqrt{10}}{5}$$

$$\text{and } PQ_1 = \sqrt{\frac{144}{25} + \frac{81}{25}} = \sqrt{\frac{225}{25}} = \sqrt{9} = 3$$

$$\therefore \quad SQ_2 = \sqrt{(1-1)^2 + (0-1)^2} = 1$$

Hence, option (b), (c), (d) are correct.

14. (a, c) Given that,

$$f(\theta) = \frac{1}{2}\begin{vmatrix} 1 & \sin\theta & 1 \\ -\sin\theta & 1 & \sin\theta \\ -1 & -\sin\theta & 1 \end{vmatrix} + \begin{vmatrix} \sin\pi & \cos\left(\theta + \frac{\pi}{4}\right) & \tan\left(\theta - \frac{\pi}{4}\right) \\ \sin\left(\theta - \frac{\pi}{4}\right) & -\cos\frac{\pi}{2} & \log_e\left(\frac{4}{\pi}\right) \\ \cot\left(\theta + \frac{\pi}{4}\right) & \log_e\left(\frac{\pi}{4}\right) & \tan\pi \end{vmatrix}$$

$$\text{Here,} \quad \cos\left(\theta + \frac{\pi}{4}\right) = -\sin\left(\theta - \frac{\pi}{4}\right),$$

$$\tan\left(\theta - \frac{\pi}{4}\right) = -\cot\left(\theta - \frac{\pi}{4}\right),$$

$$\log_e\left(\frac{4}{\pi}\right) = -\log_e\left(\frac{\pi}{4}\right)$$

$$\text{and} \quad \sin\pi = -\cos\frac{\pi}{2} = \tan\pi = 0$$

So, the second part is skew-symmetric matrix of odd order.

So, its determinant is zero.

$$\text{Thus, } f(\theta) = \frac{1}{2}\{(1 + \sin^2\theta) - \sin\theta\,(0) + 1\,(1 + \sin^2\theta)\}$$

$$\Rightarrow \quad f(\theta) = 1 + \sin^2\theta$$

Given, $g(\theta)=\sqrt{f(\theta)-1}+\sqrt{f\left(\frac{\pi}{2}-\theta\right)-1}$

$$=\sqrt{1+\sin^2\theta-1}+\sqrt{1+\cos^2\theta-1}$$

$\Rightarrow g(\theta)=|\sin\theta|+|\cos\theta|$

Thus, clearly, maximum and minimum value of $g(\theta)$ is $\sqrt{2}$ and 1, respectively.

Since, given $p(x)$ be a quadratic polynomial whose roots are maximum and minimum value of the function $g(\theta)$, then

$$p(x)=a(x-\sqrt{2})(x-1),$$

where $a\in R-\{0\}$

But given $p(2)=2-\sqrt{2}$, then $a=1$

$\therefore \quad p(x)=(x-\sqrt{2})(x-1)$

Now,

$$p\left(\frac{3+\sqrt{2}}{4}\right)=\left(\frac{3-3\sqrt{2}}{4}\right)\left(\frac{\sqrt{2}-1}{4}\right)<0$$

and

$$p\left(\frac{1+3\sqrt{2}}{2}\right)=\left(\frac{1-\sqrt{2}}{4}\right)\left(\frac{3\sqrt{2}-3}{4}\right)<0$$

and

$$p\left(\frac{5\sqrt{2}-1}{4}\right)=\left(\frac{\sqrt{2}-1}{4}\right)\left(\frac{5\sqrt{2}-5}{4}\right)>0$$

and

$$p\left(\frac{5-\sqrt{2}}{4}\right)=\left(\frac{5-5\sqrt{2}}{4}\right)\left(\frac{1-\sqrt{2}}{4}\right)>0$$

Thus, options (a) and (c) are correct.

15. (b)

For (I)

$$\left\{x\in\left[\frac{-2\pi}{3},\frac{2\pi}{3}\right],\cos x+\sin x=1\right\}$$

Since, $\cos x+\sin x=1$

$\Rightarrow \frac{1}{\sqrt{2}}\cos x+\frac{1}{\sqrt{2}}\sin x=\frac{1}{\sqrt{2}}$

$\Rightarrow \cos\frac{\pi}{4}\cdot\sin x+\sin\frac{\pi}{4}\cdot\cos x=\frac{1}{\sqrt{2}}$

$\Rightarrow \sin\left(x+\frac{\pi}{4}\right)=\frac{1}{\sqrt{2}}$

$\Rightarrow x+\frac{\pi}{4}=n\pi+(-1)^n\frac{\pi}{4}$

$\Rightarrow x=n\pi+(-1)^n\frac{\pi}{4}-\frac{\pi}{4}$

Since, $x\in\left[\frac{-2\pi}{3},\frac{2\pi}{3}\right]$, So, only 2 values of x in the set.

Thus, x has 2 elements. (I) $\rightarrow$ (P)

For (II) $\left\{x\in\left[\frac{-5\pi}{18},\frac{5\pi}{18}\right],\sqrt{3}\tan 3x=1\right\}$

Since, $\sqrt{3}\tan 3x=1$

$\Rightarrow \tan 3x=\frac{1}{\sqrt{3}}$

$\Rightarrow \tan 3x=\tan\left\{n\pi+\frac{\pi}{6}\right\}$

$\Rightarrow 3x=n\pi+\frac{\pi}{6}$

$\Rightarrow x=\frac{n\pi}{3}+\frac{\pi}{18}$

Since, $x\in\left[\frac{-5\pi}{18},\frac{5\pi}{18}\right]$.

So, only 2 values of x in the set.

Thus, x has 2 elements.

(II) $\rightarrow$ (P)

For (III) $\left\{x\in\left[\frac{-6\pi}{5},\frac{6\pi}{5}\right],2\cos 2x=\sqrt{3}\right\}$

Since, $2\cos 2x=\sqrt{3}$

$\Rightarrow \cos 2x=\frac{\sqrt{3}}{2}\Rightarrow 2x=2n\pi\pm\frac{\pi}{6}$

$\Rightarrow x=n\pi\pm\frac{\pi}{12}$

Thus, x has 6 elements.

(III) $\rightarrow$ (T)

For (IV)

$$\left\{x\in\left[-\frac{7\pi}{4},\frac{7\pi}{4}\right],\sin x-\cos x=1\right\}$$

Since, $\sin x-\cos x=1$

$\Rightarrow \frac{1}{\sqrt{2}}\sin x-\frac{1}{\sqrt{2}}\cos x=\frac{1}{\sqrt{2}}$

$\Rightarrow \sin\left(x-\frac{\pi}{4}\right)=\frac{1}{\sqrt{2}}$

$\Rightarrow x-\frac{\pi}{4}=n\pi+(-1)^n\frac{\pi}{4}$

$\Rightarrow x=n\pi+(-1)^n\frac{\pi}{4}+\frac{\pi}{4}$

Thus, since, $x\in\left[-\frac{7\pi}{4},\frac{7\pi}{4}\right]$.

So, x has '4' elements.

$\therefore$ (IV) $\rightarrow$ (R)

Hence, option (b) is correct.

16. (a) Since,

$P(X_i>Y_i)+P(X_i<Y_i)+P(X_i=Y_i)=1$

and $P(X_i>Y_i)=P(X_i<Y_i)=P$

For $i=2$,

$$P(X_2=Y_2)=2P(x>y)\cdot P(x<y)+(P(x=y))^2$$

$$=2\cdot\frac{^6C_2}{^{36}C_1}\times\frac{^6C_2}{^{36}C_1}+\left(\frac{^6C_1}{^{36}C_1}\right)^2$$

$$=\frac{25}{72}+\frac{1}{36}=\frac{27}{72}=\frac{3}{8}$$

and $P(X_2>Y_2)=\frac{1}{2}\left(1-\frac{3}{8}\right)=\frac{5}{16}$

$\therefore P(X_2\geq Y_2)=\frac{5}{16}+\frac{3}{8}=\frac{11}{16}$

$\therefore$ (I) $\rightarrow$ (Q), (II) $\rightarrow$ (R)

For $i=3$,

$P(X_3=Y_3)=6P(x>y)\cdot P(x<y)$

$P(x=y)+[P(x=y)]^3$

$$=6\cdot\frac{^6C_2}{36}\cdot\frac{^6C_2}{36}\cdot\frac{^6C_1}{36}+\left(\frac{^6C_1}{36}\right)^2$$

$$=6\cdot\frac{15}{36}\cdot\frac{15}{36}\cdot\frac{15}{36}+\frac{225}{1296}$$

$$=\frac{231}{1296}$$

$$=\frac{77}{432}$$

$\therefore$ (III) $\rightarrow$ T

and $P(X_3>Y_3)=\frac{1}{2}\left(1-\frac{77}{432}\right)$

$$=\frac{1}{2}\cdot\left(\frac{432-77}{432}\right)=\frac{355}{864}$$

(IV) $\rightarrow$ S

17. (b) Let p, q and r be non-zero real number that are, respectively the 10th, 100th, 1000th terms of an Harmonic progression.

So, $p=\frac{1}{a+9d}, q=\frac{1}{a+99d}$,

$$r=\frac{1}{a+999d}$$

Given, system of linear equations is,

$$x+y+z=1 \quad \text{...(i)}$$

$$10x+100y+1000z=0 \quad \text{...(ii)}$$

$$qrx+pry+pqz=0 \quad \text{...(iii)}$$

Now, Eq. (iii) can be written as,

$$\frac{x}{p}+\frac{y}{q}+\frac{z}{r}=0 \quad [\because p,q,r\neq 0]$$

Putting the values of p, q and r., we get

$$(a+9d)x+(a+99d)y+(a+999d)z=0$$

Now,

$$\Delta=\begin{vmatrix}1 & 1 & 1\\ 10 & 100 & 1000\\ a+9d & a+99d & a+999d\end{vmatrix}=0$$

$$\Delta_x=\begin{vmatrix}1 & 1 & 1\\ 0 & 100 & 1000\\ 0 & a+99d & a+999d\end{vmatrix}$$

$$=900(d-a)$$

$$\Delta_y=\begin{vmatrix}1 & 1 & 1\\ 10 & 0 & 1000\\ a+9d & 0 & a+999d\end{vmatrix}$$

$$=990(a-d)$$

$$\Delta_z=\begin{vmatrix}1 & 1 & 1\\ 10 & 100 & 0\\ a+9d & a+99d & 0\end{vmatrix}=90(d-a)$$

Now, for (I),

If $\frac{q}{r}=10 \Rightarrow a=d$

So, $\Delta=\Delta_x=\Delta_y=\Delta_z=0$

So, Eqs. (i) and (ii) represents non-parallel lines and Eqs. (ii) and (iii) represents same plane.

$\Rightarrow$ Infinitely many solutions.

(I) $\rightarrow$ (P), (Q), (R), (T)

For (II),

If $\frac{p}{r}\neq 100 \Rightarrow a\neq d$

So, $\Delta=0, \Delta_x=\Delta_y=\Delta_z\neq 0$

This case, get no solution.

(II) $\rightarrow$ (S)

For (III), $\frac{p}{q}\neq 10 \Rightarrow a\neq d$

$\therefore$ Also this case no solution.

(III) $\rightarrow$ (S)

For (IV),

If $\frac{p}{q}=10 \Rightarrow a=d$

So, infinity many solutions.

(IV) $\rightarrow$ (P), (Q), (R), (T)

Now, only one combination given the above four option in this question.

(IV) $\rightarrow$ (R)

So, (I) $\rightarrow$ (Q), (II) $\rightarrow$ (S), (III) $\rightarrow$ (S).

18. (c) Given, equation of the ellipse is $\frac{x^2}{4}+\frac{y^2}{3}=1$ and $H(\alpha, 0)$, $0<\alpha<2$ be a point.

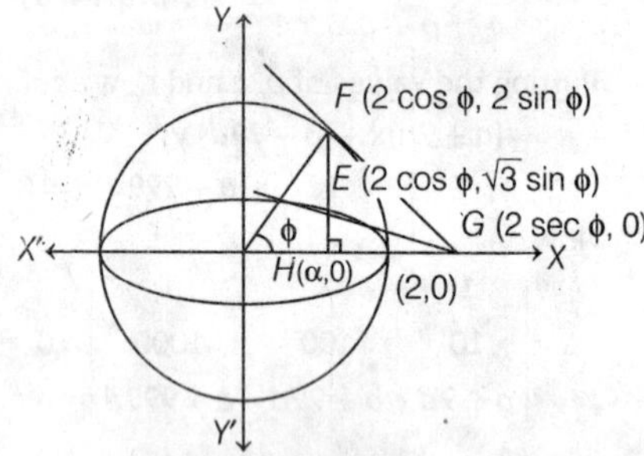

Clearly, $\alpha=2\cos\phi$

Now, tangent $E(2\cos\phi, \sqrt{3}\sin\phi)$ to ellipse $\frac{x^2}{4}+\frac{y^2}{3}=1$

i.e. $\frac{x\cos\phi}{2}+\frac{y\sin\phi}{\sqrt{3}}=1$ intersect X-axis at $G(2\sec\phi, 0)$.

Thus, area of ΔFGH is

$$=\frac{1}{2}(2\sec\phi-2\cos\phi)\cdot 2\sin\phi$$

$$=2\sin^2\phi\cdot\tan\phi$$

$$\Delta=(1-\cos 2\phi)\cdot\tan\phi$$

For condition (I),

If $\phi=\frac{\pi}{4}$, then

$$\Delta=\left(1-\cos\frac{\pi}{2}\right)\cdot\tan\frac{\pi}{4}=1$$

$\therefore$ (I) $\rightarrow$ (Q)

For condition (II),

If $\phi=\frac{\pi}{3}$, then

$$\Delta=2\cdot\left(\frac{\sqrt{3}}{2}\right)^2\cdot\sqrt{3}=\frac{3\sqrt{3}}{2}$$

$\therefore$ (II) $\rightarrow$ (T)

For condition (III),

If $\phi=\frac{\pi}{6}$, then

$$\Delta=2\cdot\left(\frac{1}{2}\right)^2\cdot\frac{1}{\sqrt{3}}=\frac{1}{2\sqrt{3}}$$

$\therefore$ (III) $\rightarrow$ (S)

For condition (IV),

If $\phi=\frac{\pi}{12}$, then

$$\Delta=\left(1-\frac{\sqrt{3}}{2}\right)\cdot(2-\sqrt{3})=\frac{(2-\sqrt{3})^2}{2}$$

$$=\frac{(\sqrt{3}-1)^4}{8}$$

$\therefore$ (IV) $\rightarrow$ (P)

Hence, (I) $\rightarrow$ (Q), (II) $\rightarrow$ (T), (III) $\rightarrow$ (S), (IV) $\rightarrow$ (P)

Hence, option (c) is correct.

Paper 2

1. (1) We have, $-\frac{\pi}{4}<\beta<0<\alpha<\frac{\pi}{4}$

$$\sin(\alpha+\beta)=\frac{1}{3}\Rightarrow\cos(\alpha+\beta)=\frac{2\sqrt{2}}{3}$$

and $\cos(\alpha-\beta)=\frac{2}{3}\Rightarrow\sin(\alpha-\beta)=\frac{\sqrt{5}}{3}$

Now, $\frac{\sin\alpha}{\cos\beta}+\frac{\cos\beta}{\sin\alpha}+\frac{\cos\alpha}{\sin\beta}+\frac{\sin\beta}{\cos\alpha}$

$$=\frac{\sin^2\alpha+\cos^2\beta}{\sin\alpha\cos\beta}+\frac{\cos^2\alpha+\sin^2\beta}{\cos\alpha\sin\beta}$$

$$=\frac{\sin^2\alpha+\cos^2\beta}{\sin\alpha\cos\beta}+\frac{1-\sin^2\alpha+1-\cos^2\beta}{\cos\alpha\sin\beta}$$

$$=(\sin^2\alpha+\cos^2\beta)\left(\frac{\sin\beta\cos\alpha-\sin\alpha\cos\beta}{\sin\alpha\cos\alpha\sin\beta\cos\beta}\right)+\frac{2}{\sin\beta\cos\alpha}$$

$$=\frac{4(\sin^2\alpha+\cos^2\beta)\sin(\beta-\alpha)}{[\sin(\alpha+\beta)+\sin(\alpha-\beta)][\sin(\alpha+\beta)-\sin(\alpha-\beta)]}+\frac{4}{[\sin(\alpha+\beta)-\sin(\alpha-\beta)]}$$

$$[\because \sin^2\alpha+\cos^2\beta=1+\sin^2\alpha-\sin^2\beta=1+\sin(\alpha+\beta)\sin(\alpha-\beta)=1+\frac{\sqrt{5}}{9}]$$

$$=\frac{-4\left(1+\frac{\sqrt{5}}{9}\right)\left(\frac{\sqrt{5}}{3}\right)}{\left(\frac{1+\sqrt{5}}{3}\right)\left(\frac{1-\sqrt{5}}{3}\right)}+\frac{4}{\left[\frac{1-\sqrt{5}}{3}\right]}$$

$$=(9+\sqrt{5})\frac{\sqrt{5}}{3}+\frac{12}{1-\sqrt{5}}$$

$$=3\sqrt{5}+\frac{5}{3}+\frac{12}{-4}(1+\sqrt{5})$$

$$=3\sqrt{5}+\frac{5}{3}-3-3\sqrt{5}=-\frac{4}{3}$$

$$\therefore\left(\frac{\sin\alpha}{\cos\beta}+\frac{\cos\beta}{\sin\alpha}+\frac{\cos\alpha}{\sin\beta}+\frac{\sin\beta}{\cos\alpha}\right)^2=\frac{16}{9}$$

and its greatest integer $=\left[\frac{16}{9}\right]=1$

2. (8) $x\,dy-(y^2-4y)\,dx=0, x>0, y(1)=2$

$$\int\frac{dy}{y(y-4)}=\int\frac{dx}{x}$$

$$\Rightarrow\quad\frac{1}{4}\int\frac{y-(y-4)}{y(y-4)}dy=\int\frac{1}{x}dx$$

$$\Rightarrow\quad\int\left(\frac{1}{y-4}-\frac{1}{y}\right)dy=4\int\frac{1}{x}dx$$

$$\Rightarrow\quad\ln|y-4|-\ln|y|=4\ln x+\ln c$$

$$\ln\left|\frac{y-4}{y}\right|=\ln(x^4c)\Rightarrow|y-4|=|y|x^4c$$

Given, $x=1, y=2$

$$2=2c\Rightarrow c=1$$

Curve $|y-4|=x^4|y|$

$$\Rightarrow\quad y-4=\pm y\cdot x^4$$

***Case*-I**

$$y-4=yx^4$$

$$\Rightarrow\quad y=\frac{4}{1-x^4}$$

$$\therefore\quad y(1)=\frac{4}{1-1}=\text{Not defined}$$

This case will be rejected.

***Case*-II**

$$y-4=-yx^4\Rightarrow y=\frac{4}{1+x^4}$$

Now, $y(1)=\dfrac{4}{1+1}=2$

$10y(\sqrt{2})=10\times\dfrac{4}{1+4}=8$

3. (5) $\int_1^2 \log_2(x^3+1)\,dx + \int_1^{\log_2 9}(2^x-1)^{1/3}\,dx$

Let $f(x)=y=\log_2(x^3+1)$

$\Rightarrow\ x^3+1=2^y$

$\Rightarrow\ x=(2^y-1)^{1/3}$

$\Rightarrow\ f^{-1}(x)=(2^x-1)^{1/3}$

By using,

$\int_a^b f(x)\,dx+\int_{f(a)}^{f(b)} f^{-1}(x)\,dx=bf(b)-af(a)$

So, $\int_1^2 \log_2(x^3+1)\,dx + \int_1^{\log_2 9}(2^x-1)^{1/3}\,dx$

$=2\log_2 9-1\times 1$

$=4\log_2 3-1$

$\therefore\ [4\log_2 3-1]=5$

4. (1) Given, $x^{[16(\log_5 x)^3-68\log_5 x]}=5^{-16}$

Take $\log_5$ both sides,

$[16(\log_5 x)^3-68(\log_5 x)]\log_5 x=-16$

Let $\log_5 x=t$

$(16t^3-68t)\,t=-16$

$\Rightarrow\ 4t^4-17t^2+4=0$

$\Rightarrow\ (4t^2-1)(t^2-4)=0$

$t=\pm\dfrac{1}{2},\pm 2$

$\log_5 x=\dfrac{1}{2},\dfrac{-1}{2},2,-2$

$x=\sqrt{5},\dfrac{1}{\sqrt{5}},25,\dfrac{1}{25}$

Let x_1,x_2,x_3,x_4 are $\sqrt{5},\dfrac{1}{\sqrt{5}},25,\dfrac{1}{25}$, respectively.

So, product $x_1,x_2,x_3,x_4=1$

5. (5) We have,

$$\beta=\lim_{x\to 0}\frac{e^{x^3}-(1-x^3)^{\frac{1}{3}}+[(1-x^2)^{1/2}-1]\sin x}{x\sin^2 x}$$

$$\beta=\lim_{x\to 0}\left[\frac{1}{x^3}e^{x^3}-\frac{1}{x^3}(1-x^3)^{1/3}+\frac{1}{x^2}\{(1-x^2)^{1/2}-1\}\frac{\sin x}{x}\right]\Big/\frac{\sin^2 x}{x^2}$$

$$\Rightarrow\beta=\lim_{x\to 0}\left[\frac{1}{x^3}\left\{1+\frac{x^3}{1!}+\frac{x^6}{2!}+\frac{x^9}{3!}+\ldots\right\}-\frac{1}{x^3}\left\{1-\frac{1}{3}x^3+\frac{\frac{1}{3}\left(\frac{1}{3}-1\right)}{2}(-x^3)^2+\cdots\right\}+\frac{1}{x^2}\left\{\left(1-\frac{1}{2}x^2+\frac{\frac{1}{2}\left(\frac{1}{2}-1\right)}{2}(-x^2)^2\right)-1\right\}\frac{\sin x}{x}\right]\Big/\left(\frac{\sin x}{x}\right)^2$$

$$\Rightarrow\ \beta=\lim_{x\to 0}\left[\left(\frac{1}{x^3}+1+\frac{x^3}{2!}\right)-\left(\frac{1}{x^3}-\frac{1}{3}-\frac{1}{9}x^3+\cdots\right)+\left(\frac{-1}{2}-\frac{1}{8}x^2\right)\frac{\sin x}{x}\right]\Big/\left(\frac{\sin x}{x}\right)^2$$

$\Rightarrow\beta=1+\dfrac{1}{3}-\dfrac{1}{2}=\dfrac{5}{6}$

$\therefore 6\beta=5$

6. (3) We have, $A=\begin{bmatrix}\beta & 0 & 1\\ 2 & 1 & -2\\ 3 & 1 & -2\end{bmatrix}$

$A^7-(\beta-1)A^6-\beta A^5$ is a singular matrix

i.e. $|A^7-(\beta-1)A^6-\beta A^5|=0$

$|A^5(A^2-(\beta-1)A-\beta I)|=0$

$|A|^5\,|(A^2-\beta A)+(A-\beta I)|=0$

$|A|^5\,|A(A-\beta I)+I(A-\beta I)|=0$

$|A|^5\,|(A+I)(A-\beta I)|=0$

$|A|^5\,|A+I|\,|A-\beta I|=0$

Now, $|A|=0+0-1=-1$

$|A+I|=\begin{vmatrix}\beta+1 & 0 & 1\\ 2 & 2 & -2\\ 3 & 1 & -1\end{vmatrix}$

$=0+0+1(-4)=-4$

$A-\beta I=\begin{bmatrix}\beta & 0 & 1\\ 2 & 1 & -2\\ 3 & 1 & -2\end{bmatrix}-\begin{bmatrix}\beta & 0 & 0\\ 0 & \beta & 0\\ 0 & 0 & \beta\end{bmatrix}$

$=\begin{bmatrix}0 & 0 & 1\\ 2 & 1-\beta & -2\\ 3 & 1 & -2-\beta\end{bmatrix}$

$|A-\beta I|=2-3(1-\beta)=3\beta-1$

Now, $|A|\neq 0, |A+I|\neq 0$. So, $|A-\beta I|$ have to be zero.

$|A-\beta I|=0$

$3\beta-1=0\Rightarrow\beta=\dfrac{1}{3}$

$9\beta=3$

7. (7) Hyperbola : $\dfrac{x^2}{100}-\dfrac{y^2}{64}=1$

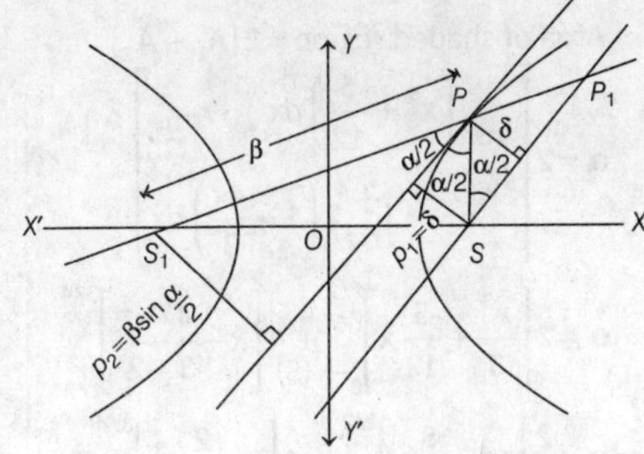

$a=10, b=8, e=\sqrt{1+\dfrac{64}{100}}=\dfrac{\sqrt{41}}{5}$

Product of perpendiculars on any tangent from focii S and S_1 = (semi-minor axis)^2

$p_1\cdot p_2=b^2$

$\delta\times\beta\sin\dfrac{\alpha}{2}=64$

$\dfrac{\beta\delta\sin\frac{\alpha}{2}}{9}=\dfrac{64}{9}$

$\left[\dfrac{\beta\delta}{9}\sin\dfrac{\alpha}{2}\right]=\left[\dfrac{64}{9}\right]=7$

8. (6) We have, $f,g:R\to R$

$f(x)=x^2+\dfrac{5}{12}$

and $g(x)=\begin{cases}2\left(1-\dfrac{4|x|}{3}\right), & |x|\le\dfrac{3}{4}\\ 0, & |x|>\dfrac{3}{4}\end{cases}$

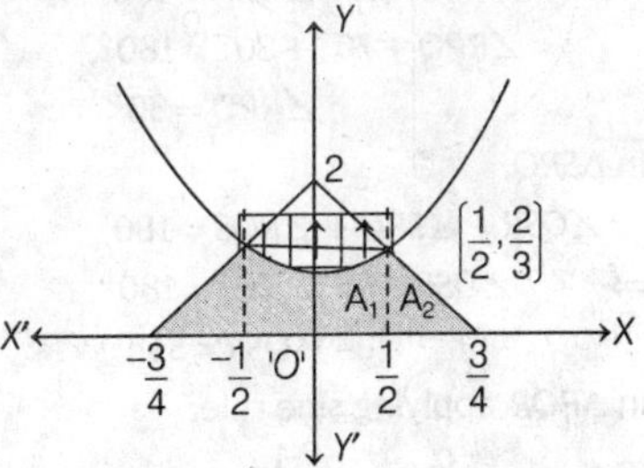

Finding intersection of f and g

$x^2+\dfrac{5}{12}=2\left(1-\dfrac{4x}{3}\right)$

$\Rightarrow\ x^2+\dfrac{5}{12}=\dfrac{6-8x}{3}$

$\Rightarrow\ 12x^2+5=24-32x$

$\Rightarrow\ 12x^2+32x-19=0$

$\Rightarrow\ (6x+19)(2x-1)=0 \Rightarrow x=\frac{1}{2},$

and $x=\frac{-19}{6}<-\frac{3}{4}$ rejected

The shaded region is symmetric about Y-axis

Area of shaded region $=2[A_1+A_2]$

$$\alpha=2\left[\int_0^{1/2}\left(x^2+\frac{5}{12}\right)dx+\int_{1/2}^{3/4}2\left(1-\frac{4x}{3}\right)dx\right]$$

$$\alpha=2\left[\frac{x^3}{3}+\frac{5}{12}x\right]_0^{1/2}+4\left[x-\frac{4}{3}\cdot\frac{x^2}{2}\right]_{1/2}^{3/4}$$

$$\alpha=\frac{2}{3}\left[x^3+\frac{5}{4}x\right]_0^{1/2}+4\left[x-\frac{2}{3}x^2\right]_{1/2}^{3/4}$$

$$\alpha=\frac{2}{3}\left[\frac{1}{8}+\frac{5}{8}-0-0\right]+4\left[\left(\frac{3}{4}-\frac{3}{8}\right)-\left(\frac{1}{2}-\frac{1}{6}\right)\right]$$

$$\alpha=\frac{1}{2}+4\left[\frac{3}{8}-\frac{1}{3}\right]=\frac{1}{2}+\frac{1}{6}=\frac{2}{3}$$

$$9\alpha=\frac{2}{3}\times 9=6$$

9. (a, b) In ΔPQR,

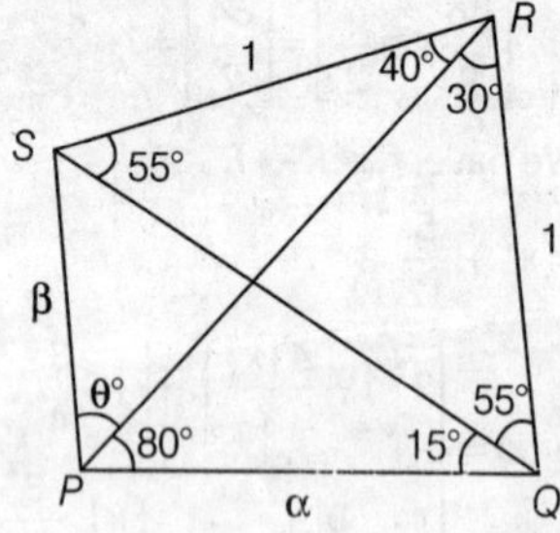

$$\angle RPQ+\angle PQR+\angle QRP=180^\circ$$
$$\angle RPQ+70^\circ+30^\circ=180^\circ$$
$$\angle RPQ=80^\circ$$

In ΔSRQ,

$$\angle QSR+\angle SRQ+\angle RQS=180^\circ$$
$$\Rightarrow\ \angle QSR+55^\circ+70^\circ=180^\circ$$
$$\therefore\ \angle QSR=55^\circ$$

In ΔPQR, applying sine rule,

$$\frac{\alpha}{\sin 30^\circ}=\frac{1}{\sin 80^\circ}$$

$$\Rightarrow\ \alpha=\frac{\sin 30^\circ}{\sin 80^\circ}=\frac{1}{2\sin 80^\circ}$$

In ΔPRS,

$$\frac{1}{\sin\theta}=\frac{\beta}{\sin 40^\circ}\Rightarrow\beta=\frac{\sin 40^\circ}{\sin\theta}$$

$$4\alpha\beta\sin\theta=4\frac{1}{2\sin 80^\circ}\times\sin 40^\circ$$

$$=\frac{2\sin 40^\circ}{2\sin 40^\circ\cos 40^\circ}=\sec 40^\circ$$

So, $\sec 30^\circ<\sec 40^\circ<\sec 45^\circ$

$$\frac{2}{\sqrt{3}}<\sec 40^\circ<\sqrt{2}$$

Hence, options (a) and (b) are true.

10. (a, b, c)

$$\alpha=\sum_{k=1}^{\infty}\sin^{2k}\left(\frac{\pi}{6}\right)=\sum_{k=1}^{\infty}\left(\sin^2\frac{\pi}{6}\right)^k$$

$$=\sum_{k=1}^{\infty}\left(\frac{1}{4}\right)^k$$

$$\alpha=\frac{1}{4}+\left(\frac{1}{4}\right)^2+\left(\frac{1}{4}\right)^3+\ldots\infty\text{ terms}$$

$$\alpha=\frac{\frac{1}{4}}{1-\frac{1}{4}}=\frac{\frac{1}{4}}{\frac{3}{4}}=\frac{1}{3}$$

$g:[0,1]\to R$

$g(x)=2^{\alpha x}+2^{\alpha(1-x)}$

$$g(x)=2^{\frac{x}{3}}+2^{\frac{1}{3}(1-x)}=2^{\frac{x}{3}}+2^{\frac{1}{3}}\cdot 2^{\frac{-x}{3}}$$

$$g'(x)=\left(\frac{1}{3}2^{\frac{x}{3}}-\frac{1}{3}2^{\frac{1}{3}}\cdot 2^{-\frac{x}{3}}\right)\log 2$$

$g'(x)=0$

$$\frac{1}{3}2^{x/3}=\frac{1}{3}2^{1/3}\,2^{-x/3}$$

$$2^{2x/3}=2^{1/3}\Rightarrow\frac{2x}{3}=\frac{1}{3}\Rightarrow x=\frac{1}{2}$$

So, $x=\frac{1}{2}$ is critical point.

Also, $g(0)=1+2^{1/3}, g(1)=1+2^{1/3}$

$$g\left(\frac{1}{2}\right)=2^{1/6}+2^{1/6}=2\cdot 2^{1/6}=2^{7/6}$$

So, graph of $g(x)$ in [0, 1].

$(0,1+2^{1/3})$ $(1,1+2^{1/3})$ $\left(\frac{1}{2},2^{7/6}\right)$ 0 $\frac{1}{2}$ 1

So, maximum value of function in [0, 1] is $1+2^{1/3}$.

Minimum value of function in [0, 1] is $2^{7/6}$.

$g(x)$ attains its maximum value at 0 and 1.

11. (a) Let $z=x+iy$

$$(\bar{z})^2+\frac{1}{z^2}=a+ib, a, b\in I$$

$$\Rightarrow(\bar{z})^2+\frac{(\bar{z})^2}{z^2\,\bar{z}^2}=a+ib, a, b\in I$$

$$\Rightarrow\bar{z}^2\left(1+\frac{1}{|z|^4}\right)=a+ib$$

$[|z|^4\to$ real number$]$

$$\{x^2-y^2-i(2xy)\}\left(1+\frac{1}{|z|^4}\right)=a+ib$$

On comparing,

$$(x^2-y^2)\left(1+\frac{1}{|z|^4}\right)=a \quad \ldots(i)$$

and $$-2xy\left(1+\frac{1}{|z|^4}\right)=b \quad \ldots(ii)$$

On squaring and adding Eqs. (i) and (ii), we get

$$(x^4+y^4-2x^2y^2+4x^2y^2)\left(1+\frac{1}{|z|^4}\right)^2=a^2+b^2$$

$$(x^2+y^2)^2\left(1+\frac{1}{|z|^4}\right)^2=a^2+b^2$$

$$|z|^4\left(1+\frac{1}{|z|^4}\right)^2=a^2+b^2$$

$$\left(|z|^2+\frac{1}{|z|^2}\right)^2=a^2+b^2$$

$$|z|^4+\frac{1}{|z|^4}+2=a^2+b^2$$

For option (a),

$$|z|=\left(\frac{43+3\sqrt{205}}{2}\right)^{1/4}$$

$$\Rightarrow|z|^4=\left(\frac{43+3\sqrt{205}}{2}\right)$$

$$\frac{1}{|z|^4}=\frac{2}{43+3\sqrt{205}}=\frac{(43-3\sqrt{205})}{2}$$

$$|z|^4+\frac{1}{|z|^4}+2=45$$

$$a^2+b^2=45$$

Only possible if $a=\pm 3, b=\pm 6$ or $a=\pm 6, b=\pm 3$

Option (a) is correct.

For option (b),

$$|z|^4=\frac{7+\sqrt{33}}{4},$$

$$\frac{1}{|z|^4}=\frac{4}{7+\sqrt{33}}=\frac{7-\sqrt{33}}{4}$$

$$|z|^4 + \frac{1}{|z|^4} + 2 = \frac{7}{2} + 2 = \frac{11}{2}$$

$$\Rightarrow \quad a^2 + b^2 = \frac{11}{2}$$

Sum of two integers can not be $\frac{11}{2}$, so wrong option.

For option (c),

$$|z|^4 = \frac{9+\sqrt{65}}{4}, \frac{1}{|z|^4} = \frac{9-\sqrt{65}}{4}$$

$$|z|^4 + \frac{1}{|z|^4} + 2 = \frac{9}{2} + 2 = \frac{13}{2}$$

$$a^2 + b^2 = \frac{13}{2}$$

Sum of two integers can not be $\frac{13}{2}$. So wrong option.

For option (d),

$$|z|^4 = \frac{7+\sqrt{13}}{6}, \frac{1}{|z|^4} = \frac{7-\sqrt{13}}{6}$$

$$|z|^4 + \frac{1}{|z|^4} + 2 = \frac{7}{3} + 2 = \frac{13}{3} = a^2 + b^2$$

Sum of two integers can not be $\frac{13}{2}$ so wrong option.

12. (c, d)

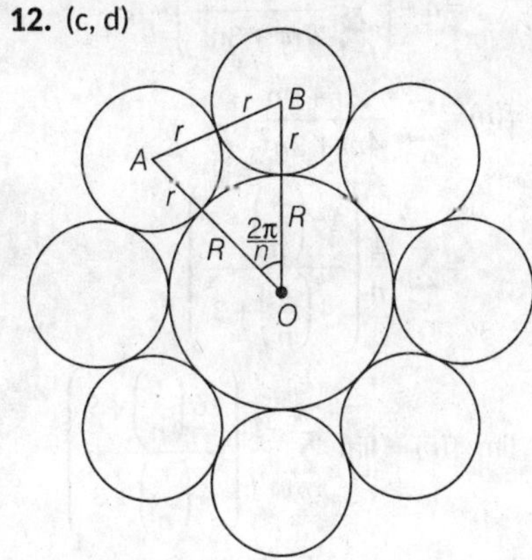

In ΔAOB,

$$\cos\frac{2\pi}{n} = \frac{(R+r)^2 + (R+r)^2 - (2r)^2}{2(R+r)(R+r)}$$

$$\Rightarrow 2(R+r)^2 \cos\frac{2\pi}{n} = 2(R+r)^2 - 4r^2$$

$$\Rightarrow 2(R+r)^2\left(\cos\frac{2\pi}{n} - 1\right) = -4r^2$$

$$\Rightarrow \quad 2r^2 = \left(1 - \cos\frac{2\pi}{n}\right)(R+r)^2$$

$$\Rightarrow \quad 2r^2 = 2\sin^2\frac{\pi}{n}(R+r)^2$$

$$\therefore r = (R+r)\sin\frac{\pi}{n} \Rightarrow R + r = r\operatorname{cosec}\frac{\pi}{n}$$

$$R = r\left(\operatorname{cosec}\frac{\pi}{n} - 1\right)$$

For option (a),

If $n = 4, R = r\left(\operatorname{cosec}\frac{\pi}{4} - 1\right) = r(\sqrt{2} - 1)$

Option (a) is wrong.

For option (b),

If $n = 5$,

$$R = r\left(\operatorname{cosec}\frac{\pi}{5} - 1\right) = r(1.7 - 1) = 0.7r$$

$R < r$

Option (b) is wrong.

For option (c), $n = 8$,

$$R = r\left(\operatorname{cosec}\frac{\pi}{8} - 1\right) = r(2.63 - 1)$$

$$R = 1.63r$$

$$\Rightarrow \quad (\sqrt{2}-1)r = 0.414r$$

$$(\sqrt{2}-1)r < R$$

Option (c) is correct.

For option (d), $n = 12$

$$R = r\left(\operatorname{cosec}\frac{\pi}{12} - 1\right) = r\left(\frac{1}{\sin 15^\circ} - 1\right)$$

$$R = r\left(\frac{1+\frac{x}{\varepsilon}}{\frac{\sqrt{3}-1}{2}} - 1\right) = \sqrt{3}r$$

$\sqrt{2}(\sqrt{3}+1)r > R$. (True)

So, option (d) is correct.

13. (b, c, d)

Given, $\mathbf{a} = 3\hat{\mathbf{i}} + \hat{\mathbf{j}} - \hat{\mathbf{k}}$

$$\mathbf{b} = \hat{\mathbf{i}} + b_2\hat{\mathbf{j}} + b_3\hat{\mathbf{k}}, b_2, b_3 \in R$$

$$\mathbf{c} = c_1\hat{\mathbf{i}} + c_2\hat{\mathbf{j}} + c_3\hat{\mathbf{k}}, c_1, c_2, c_3 \in R$$

$$b_2, b_3 > 0, \mathbf{a}\cdot\mathbf{b} = 0$$

$$3 + b_2 - b_3 = 0$$

$$b_3 - b_2 = 3$$

$$\begin{bmatrix} 0 & -c_3 & c_2 \\ c_3 & 0 & -c_1 \\ -c_2 & c_1 & 0 \end{bmatrix}\begin{bmatrix} 1 \\ b_2 \\ b_3 \end{bmatrix} = \begin{bmatrix} 3 - c_1 \\ 1 - c_2 \\ -1 - c_3 \end{bmatrix}$$

$$\begin{bmatrix} -b_2c_3 + b_3c_2 \\ c_3 - c_1b_3 \\ -c_2 + c_1b_2 \end{bmatrix} = \begin{bmatrix} 3 - c_1 \\ 1 - c_2 \\ -1 - c_3 \end{bmatrix}$$

On comparing,

$$b_3c_2 - b_2c_3 = 3 - c_1 \quad \text{...(i)}$$

$$c_3 - c_1b_3 = 1 - c_2 \quad \text{...(ii)}$$

$$c_1b_2 - c_2 = -1 - c_3 \quad \text{...(iii)}$$

Eq. (i) $\times\hat{\mathbf{i}}$ + Eq. (ii) $\times\hat{\mathbf{j}}$ + Eq. (iii) $\times\hat{\mathbf{k}}$

$$(b_3c_2 - b_2c_3)\hat{\mathbf{i}} + (c_3 - c_1b_3)\hat{\mathbf{j}} + (c_1b_2 - c_2)\hat{\mathbf{k}}$$

$$= (3\hat{\mathbf{i}} + \hat{\mathbf{j}} - \hat{\mathbf{k}}) - (c_1\hat{\mathbf{i}} + c_2\hat{\mathbf{j}} + c_3\hat{\mathbf{k}})$$

$$\mathbf{c}\times\mathbf{b} = \mathbf{a} - \mathbf{c}$$

$$(\mathbf{c}\times\mathbf{b})\cdot\mathbf{b} = \mathbf{a}\cdot\mathbf{b} - \mathbf{c}\cdot\mathbf{b}$$

$$0 = 0 - \mathbf{c}\cdot\mathbf{b} \qquad [\text{Given, } \mathbf{a}\cdot\mathbf{b} = 0]$$

$$\mathbf{c}\cdot\mathbf{b} = 0$$

Option (b) is correct.

Similarly, $\mathbf{c}\times\mathbf{b} = \mathbf{a} - \mathbf{c}$

$$(\mathbf{c}\times\mathbf{b})\cdot\mathbf{c} = \mathbf{a}\cdot\mathbf{c} - \mathbf{c}\cdot\mathbf{c}$$

$$0 = \mathbf{a}\cdot\mathbf{c} - |\mathbf{c}|^2$$

$$\mathbf{a}\cdot\mathbf{c} = |\mathbf{c}|^2$$

$$|\mathbf{a}||\mathbf{c}|\cos\theta = |\mathbf{c}|^2$$

$$|\mathbf{a}| = \frac{|\mathbf{c}|}{\cos\theta} \neq 0$$

Option (a) is wrong.

$$|\mathbf{c}| = |\mathbf{a}|\cos\theta = \sqrt{9+1+1}\cos\theta$$

$$|\mathbf{c}| = \sqrt{11}\cos\theta$$

$$|\mathbf{c}| \le \sqrt{11}$$

So, option (d) is correct.

Now, $\quad |\mathbf{b}| = \sqrt{1 + b_2^2 + b_3^2}$

Using, $\quad \mathbf{a}\cdot\mathbf{b} = 0$

$$b_3 - b_2 = 3$$

$$b_3^2 + b_2^2 - 2b_2b_3 = 9$$

$$1 + b_3^2 + b_2^2 = 10 + 2b_2b_3$$

$$|\mathbf{b}| = \sqrt{10 + 2b_2b_3} \quad [\text{Given, } b_2b_3 > 0]$$

$$|\mathbf{b}| > \sqrt{10}$$

So, option (c) is correct.

14. (c) Given, $\frac{dy}{dx} + 12y = \cos\left(\frac{\pi x}{12}\right)$

$$P = 12, Q = \cos\left(\frac{\pi x}{12}\right)$$

$$\text{IF} = e^{\int P\,dx} = e^{\int 12\,dx} = e^{12x}$$

$$\therefore \quad y \times \text{IF} = \int Q\cdot\text{IF}\,dx + C$$

$$y\cdot e^{12x} = \int e^{12x}\cos\left(\frac{\pi x}{12}\right)dx + C$$

Using $\int e^{ax}\cos bx\,dx = \frac{e^{ax}}{a^2+b^2}$ $(a\cos bx + b\sin bx) + C$

Now, $a = 12, b = \frac{\pi}{12}$

$$y\cdot e^{12x} = \frac{e^{12x}}{12^2 + \left(\frac{\pi}{12}\right)^2}\left(12\cos\frac{\pi x}{12} + \frac{\pi}{12}\sin\frac{\pi x}{12}\right) + C$$

$$y(0) = 0 \qquad [\text{given}]$$

$$0 = \frac{1}{12^2 + \frac{\pi^2}{12^2}}(12) + C$$

$$\Rightarrow C = \frac{-12}{12^2 + \frac{\pi^2}{12^2}}$$

Now, $y \cdot e^{12x} = \frac{e^{12x}}{12^2 + \left(\frac{\pi}{12}\right)^2}\left(12 \cos\frac{\pi x}{12} + \frac{\pi}{12}\sin\frac{\pi x}{12}\right) - \frac{12}{12^2 + \frac{\pi^2}{12^2}}$

$$y = \frac{1}{12^2 + \frac{\pi^2}{12^2}}\left(12 \cos\frac{\pi x}{12} + \frac{\pi}{12}\sin\frac{\pi x}{12} - 12e^{-12x}\right)$$

$$\frac{dy}{dx} = \frac{1}{12^2 + \frac{\pi^2}{12^2}}\left[-\pi \sin\left(\frac{\pi x}{12}\right) + \frac{\pi^2}{12^2}\cos\left(\frac{\pi x}{12}\right) + 12^2 e^{-12x}\right]$$

$$-\pi \sin\left(\frac{\pi x}{12}\right) + \frac{\pi^2}{12^2}\cos\left(\frac{\pi x}{12}\right) \in \left[-\sqrt{\pi^2 + \frac{\pi^4}{12^4}}, \sqrt{\pi^2 + \frac{\pi^4}{12^4}}\right]$$

Now, for $\forall x \le 0, \frac{dy}{dx} > 0$

and for $x > 0, \frac{dy}{dx}$ may be negative or positive.

So, $f(x)$ is neither increasing nor decreasing.

Now, $12 \cos\left(\frac{\pi x}{12}\right) + \frac{\pi}{12}\sin\left(\frac{\pi x}{12}\right)$ can be written as $\sin\left(\frac{\pi x}{12} + \alpha\right)$ where α is some angle and $y = \beta$ will cut $y = f(x)$ at infinite many points.

So, correct option is (c).

15. (a)

Box I	Box II	Box III	Box IV
3 R 2 B	3 R 2 B	3 R 2 B	3 R 2 B

All 20 balls are different.

We have to select at least one ball of each colour and two balls more from all four boxes.

***Case* I** One ball of each colour from each box and 2 balls from any one bag only. [3R1B or 2R2B]

$({}^3C_1 \times {}^2C_1) \times ({}^3C_1 \times {}^2C_1)({}^3C_1 \times {}^2C_1) \times {}^4C_1 \times [{}^3C_3 \times {}^2C_1 + {}^3C_2 \times {}^2C_2]$

$\underset{3R}{\downarrow}\ \underset{1B}{\downarrow}$ or $\underset{2R}{\downarrow}\ \underset{2RB}{\downarrow}$

$= 216 \times 4 \times 5 = 4320$

***Case* II** One ball of each colour from 2 boxes and 3 balls from other 2 boxes [$2R\ 1B$ or $1R\ 2B$]

$= {}^4C_2\,[(2R1B)^2(1R1B)^2 + (1R2B)^2(1R1B)^2 + 2(2R1B)(1R2B)(1R1B)]$

$= {}^4C_2\,[({}^3C_2 \times {}^2C_1)^2({}^3C_1 \times {}^2C_1)^2 + ({}^3C_1 \times {}^2C_2)({}^3C_1 \times {}^1C_1)^2 + 2({}^3C_2 \times {}^2C_1)({}^3C_1 \times {}^2C_2)({}^3C_1 \times {}^2C_1)^2]$

$= {}^4C_2\,[1296 + (36 \times 9) + (2 \times 6 \times 3 \times 36)]$

$= {}^4C_2 \times [1296 + 324 + 1296] = 17496$

Total ways $= 4320 + 17496 = 21816$

16. (a) $M = \begin{bmatrix} \frac{5}{2} & \frac{3}{2} \\ -\frac{3}{2} & -\frac{1}{2} \end{bmatrix} = \begin{bmatrix} 1+\frac{3}{2} & 0+\frac{3}{2} \\ 0-\frac{3}{2} & 1-\frac{3}{2} \end{bmatrix}$

$$M = \begin{bmatrix} 1 & 0 \\ 0 & 1 \end{bmatrix} + \begin{bmatrix} \frac{3}{2} & \frac{3}{2} \\ \frac{3}{2} & \frac{-3}{2} \end{bmatrix}$$

$$= \begin{bmatrix} 1 & 0 \\ 0 & 1 \end{bmatrix} + \frac{3}{2}\begin{bmatrix} 1 & 1 \\ -1 & -1 \end{bmatrix}$$

$$I = \begin{bmatrix} 1 & 0 \\ 0 & 1 \end{bmatrix},$$

Let $A = \begin{bmatrix} 1 & 1 \\ -1 & -1 \end{bmatrix}$

$$M = I + \frac{3}{2}A$$

$$M^2 = \left[I + \frac{3}{2}A\right]^2 = I^2 + \frac{9}{4}A^2 + 2 \cdot \frac{3}{2}A \cdot I$$

$$M^2 = I + \frac{9}{4}A^2 + 3A$$

$$A^2 = \begin{bmatrix} 1 & 1 \\ -1 & -1 \end{bmatrix}\begin{bmatrix} 1 & 1 \\ -1 & -1 \end{bmatrix} = \begin{bmatrix} 0 & 0 \\ 0 & 0 \end{bmatrix}$$

So, $M^2 = I + 3A$

$$M^4 = I^2 + 9A^2 + 6A = I + 6A$$

Similarly, $M^{2022} = I + 3033A = \begin{bmatrix} 1 & 0 \\ 0 & 1 \end{bmatrix} + \begin{bmatrix} 3033 & 3033 \\ -3033 & -3033 \end{bmatrix}$

$$= \begin{bmatrix} 3034 & 3033 \\ -3033 & -3032 \end{bmatrix}$$

17. (c)

Box I	Box II	Box III	Box IV
8 R 3 B 5 G	24 R 9 B 15 G	1 B 12 G 3 Y	10 G 16 O 6 W

Event A One of the chosen ball is White.

Event B At least one of the chosen balls is Green.

$$P(B) = \frac{{}^8C_1}{{}^{16}C_1} \times \frac{{}^{15}C_1}{{}^{48}C_1} + \frac{{}^3C_1}{{}^{16}C_1} \times \frac{{}^{12}C_1}{{}^{16}C_1} + \frac{{}^5C_1}{{}^{16}C_1} \times 1$$

$$P(A \cap B) = \frac{{}^{10}C_1}{{}^{32}C_1} \times \frac{6}{{}^{32}C_1} = \frac{5}{16} \times \frac{3}{16}$$

$$P\left(\frac{A}{B}\right) = \frac{P(A \cap B)}{P(B)}$$

$$= \frac{\frac{5}{16} \times \frac{3}{16}}{\frac{8}{16} \times \frac{15}{48} + \frac{3}{16} \times \frac{12}{16} + \frac{5}{16}}$$

$$= \frac{15}{40 + 36 + 80} = \frac{15}{156} = \frac{5}{52}$$

18. (b) Given,

$$f(n) = n + \frac{16 + 5n - 3n^2}{4n + 3n^2} + \frac{32 + n - 3n^2}{8n + 3n^2} + \frac{48 - 3n - 3n^2}{12n + 3n^2} + \ldots + \frac{25n - 7n^2}{4n^2 + 3n^2}$$

$$f(n) = n + \sum_{r=1}^{n} \frac{16r + (9 - 4r)n - 3n^2}{4n(r) + 3n^2}$$

$$f(n) = n + \sum_{r=1}^{n} \frac{(16r + 9n) - (4rn + 3n^2)}{4nr + 3n^2}$$

$$f(n) = n + \sum_{r=1}^{n}\left(\frac{16r + 9n}{4nr + 3n^2} - 1\right)$$

$$= n + \left(\sum_{r=1}^{n} \frac{16r + 9n}{4nr + 3n^2}\right) - n$$

$$f(n) = \sum_{r=1}^{n} \frac{16r + 9n}{4nr + 3n^2}$$

$$= \sum_{r=1}^{n} \frac{1}{n}\left(\frac{16\left(\frac{r}{n}\right) + 9}{4\left(\frac{r}{n}\right) + 3}\right)$$

$$\lim_{n \to \infty} f(n) = \lim_{n \to \infty} \sum_{r=1}^{n} \frac{1}{n}\left(\frac{16\left(\frac{r}{n}\right) + 9}{4\left(\frac{r}{n}\right) + 3}\right)$$

$$\lim_{n \to \infty} f(n) = \int_0^1 \frac{16x + 9}{4x + 3}\,dx$$

$$= 4\int_0^1 \frac{4x + \frac{9}{4} + 3 - 3}{4x + 3}\,dx$$

$$\lim_{n \to \infty} f(n) = 4\left[\int_0^1 \frac{(4x + 3) - \frac{3}{4}}{4x + 3}\,dx\right]$$

$$= \int_0^1 4\,dx - 3\int_0^1 \frac{1}{4x + 3}\,dx$$

$$= [4x]_0^1 - 3 \times \frac{1}{4}[\ln(4x + 3)]_0^1$$

$$= 4 - \frac{3}{4}[\ln 7 - \ln 3] = 4 - \frac{3}{4}\ln\left(\frac{7}{3}\right)$$